MW01259001

*In Sacred Loneliness*

# In Sacred Loneliness

## The Plural Wives of Joseph Smith

### TODD COMPTON

SIGNATURE BOOKS • SALT LAKE CITY

*To my parents*
*who gave me ideals of faith and honesty*

JACKET DESIGN BY RON STUCKI

© 1997 Signature Books. All rights reserved. Signature Books
is a registered trademark of Signature Books Publishing, LLC.
∞ Printed on acid-free paper. Printed in the United States.

2023 2022 2021 2020 2019    15 14 13 12 11 10

*Library of Congress Cataloging-in-Publication Data*
Compton, Todd
    In sacred loneliness : the plural wives of Joseph Smith /
by Todd Compton
        p.    cm.
    Includes bibliographical references.
    ISBN 10: 1-56085-085-X
    ISBN 13: 978-1-56085-085-4
    1. Mormon women—Biography.    2. Wives—United
States—Biography.    3. Smith, Joseph, 1805-1844.    I. Title.
BX8693.C65    1996
289.3'092'2—dc20
[B]
                                            96-19033
                                              CIP

# CONTENTS.

v

# CONTENTS

# CONTENTS

# CONTENTS

# INTRODUCTION.

This book had its genesis in a research fellowship I received from the Huntington Library in 1992. My interest, among other things, was Eliza R. Snow's pioneer diaries, housed in the Huntington's impressive document collection. As a leading woman of early Mormonism—a poet, female activist, secret polygamous wife to Latter-day Saint (LDS) church founder Joseph Smith, and later a wife of Brigham Young—Snow seemed significant enough to warrant further attention, even though much had already been written about her. Particularly interesting to me were her oblique allusions to other plural wives, sometimes referred to by given name, sometimes by maiden or married surname only. To identify these women, I knew I would have to consult reliable lists of the marriages of Brigham Young, Heber C. Kimball, and Joseph Smith. Jeffery Johnson had published a good list of Brigham Young's wives, and Stanley Kimball had provided a full list of Heber's. Nevertheless, for Smith himself, I could find no definitive listing of his plural marriage partners.

Andrew Jenson's century-old list of twenty-seven of Smith's plural wives provided a core of basic data. In the 1950s Stanley S. Ivins compiled an unpublished list of eighty-four women, but many of these were only sealings to Joseph after his death. The first fully annotated, footnoted inventory of Smith's plural wives was the appendix of Fawn Brodie's *No Man Knows My History*, published in 1945, with minor updating in the 1971 edition. Although Brodie was a pioneer in documenting Smith's polygamy, fifty years of secondary publications and classification of primary documents have dated her book, and, moreover, scholars have faulted her for relying on antagonistic sources that have since proven unreliable.

Eventually I concluded that a full, complete, up-to-date list of Joseph Smith's wives would be a valuable addition to Mormon studies, and my project on Eliza Snow metamorphosed into an investigation of all of the wives of Joseph Smith, with Snow being one among many. Since early polygamy was secret and not officially documented, there are still many uncertainties in even a conservative, carefully documented description of Smith's extended family. Nevertheless, this book furthers research on these women, provides an update to Brodie, and attempts a more balanced evaluation than her book offered.

## Viewing Joseph Smith's Wives Holistically

Since the evidence on many of these women is ambiguous and problematic, I divided my list into two categories: women who were certainly or very probably married to Joseph Smith during his lifetime and whose marriages are supported by affidavits, reliable testimony, or multiple pieces of evidence; and "possible" wives whose marriages to Smith are supported by limited and inconclusive evidence. In addition, there are women whose marriages to Smith are poorly documented (supported by weak evidence, often sensationalized, contradictory attestations, lacking multiple confirmations) and might be called improbable candidates. There is also a category of posthumous marriages in which women were married (i.e., sealed) to Joseph after his death without evidence of a marriage relationship during his life.

Having arrived at a group of "certain" wives, while other studies have analyzed the marriages of these women in some detail, I try to view them holistically, from birth to death, devoting a full chapter to each woman. A study of their whole lives, apart from the intrinsic value of looking at important early Mormon women carefully, also shows the impact of their connection to Smith in their later lives. Most of them, because of their marriages to the Mormon prophet, became "proxy wives" to Mormon apostles and other leading Mormons, especially to Brigham Young and Heber Kimball—sealed to Smith for eternity, with the apostle standing in as Smith's proxy in the flesh, to "raise seed" to Smith in this life—and thus the proxy husband was married to the woman only for time. This arrangement had significant advantages for the women (high status and visibility in Mormon society) and certain drawbacks. As Young and Kimball were among the most married of Mormons, many of Joseph Smith's widows experienced the difficult trial of living in very large polygamous families.

These women were extraordinary in many ways. Many were authentically heroic, living lives of loss, hardship, and tragedy. Most were pioneers, sometimes throughout their lives, moving from New England to Ohio, then to Missouri, to different parts of Missouri, to Nauvoo, to Winter Quarters, and on to Utah. Houses were built, then abandoned, with nearly every move. When they reached the Salt Lake Valley, and may have been anticipating a well-deserved rest, Brigham Young often sent them to settle outlying colonies in southern Utah, Idaho, Nevada, Colorado, California, and Arizona, where they endured desert conditions and were sometimes menaced by hostile Native Americans and outlaws. Eliza Partridge Lyman participated in virtually all of these migrations, helping to settle the almost inaccessible badlands of San Juan County in southeastern Utah. Another of Joseph's wives, Agnes Coolbrith, traveled from Boston to Ohio, Missouri, Illinois, and through Utah to California.

While my study may be revisionist in some ways, it is also unabashedly celebratory. As it praises thirty-three women, it nevertheless looks at them and other early Mormons seriously and we see Mormon history from a new perspective—not from the viewpoint of male church leaders but from the viewpoint of women. This book tries to celebrate early Mormons in a responsible, balanced way—all of its characters, female and male, Relief Society president and prophet, had weaknesses as well as strengths. Those who would portray Mormon history as carried on by superhuman men and women, without flaws, would turn them into inhuman automatons, which in fact betrays a deep disrespect for the real humanity of our foremothers and forefathers.

## Recovering Clues to Forgotten Lives

All historians are subject to the limitations of the evidence available, and this book is no exception. But it is surprising that these key women have been comparatively forgotten, especially considering the reverence Mormons hold for their founding prophet, and considering how important polygamy was to Smith. In fact, one occasionally meets Mormons who have no idea that Joseph Smith had plural wives at all; twentieth-century Mormons are undoubtedly uncomfortable with the details of nineteenth-century polygamy. In any event, many of these women are poorly documented, and it was difficult to reconstruct their lives. For some, even their death dates are unknown. Others, such as Sarah Bapson and Olive Andrews, have seemingly dropped out of history almost entirely.

When a woman is poorly documented, I have resorted to various strategies to trace the outline of her life. The first sources I have turned to are naturally the writings of the women themselves—diaries, autobiographies, letters—all of which, despite their obvious value, have limitations. Diaries lack hindsight and historical perspective. Eliza R. Snow's Nauvoo diary, for instance, never overtly mentions her marriage to Joseph Smith. On the other hand, autobiographies idealize and often lack precision in dating. Letters preserve only half of a conversation.

The writings of close relatives often have great value. The autobiography of Louisa Beaman's sister, Mary Beaman Noble, sheds considerable light on her sister's childhood, while Oliver Huntington's journal is an important source for studying his sisters Zina and Presendia. Later family histories are another important source of information for these women. These are nearly always idealized, second- and third-hand in nature, and generally too short. Also, generations of oral retellings invariably lose or change details. Nevertheless, family history often preserves valuable anecdotes and explanations for events that historians have misunderstood due to the fragmentary nature of the historical record.

Hints about a woman's life are also found in the bare bones of genealogy. If the woman's brothers and sisters die in Utah, it tells us that she probably had a support group in Mormonism throughout her life. The birth and death dates of children allow an imaginative reconstruction of the main patterns of a woman's life: joyful celebrations at her children's marriages and harrowing ordeals when a child dies.

History has too often neglected women in favor of their husbands, especially in a male-dominated social structure like Mormonism. Still, one finds information about women embedded in their husbands' stories. For instance, much has been written about Orson Hyde, including a biography and other book-length studies, but his first wife, Marinda Johnson, has had almost nothing written about her. Yet if one traces Orson's career, it is possible to follow her movements through his. When a husband is excommunicated, one imagines the wife's dismay. When he goes on a long mission, one visualizes the wife at home, struggling to keep herself and her family afloat. So the feminist biographer often must use men to unearth the buried lives of spouses and relatives.

When documents actually written by the woman or her siblings or children or close friends exist, I have let them speak for themselves when possible, using fairly long quotations. This brings the woman vividly to life, giving a flavor of the way she talked, thought, felt, and believed, evoking humor and humanity that overidealized or academic history sometimes ignores. Furthermore, there are problematic issues in the study of Mormon polygamy that must be examined closely, and the most effective way of doing this is to show the evidence when possible. Often, when one is treating an important issue, each relevant source needs careful interpretation, so I leave nineteenth-century texts unedited as much as possible. Original misspellings and grammatical idiosyncrasies are intact, with additions in brackets. No punctuation has been added beyond capitalizing the beginning of a quote. An uncertain reading is put within S brackets: { }. Since some readers will find these unpunctuated texts difficult, the end of a sentence or thought has been marked by an extra space between words.

### The Supernatural

The supernatural—revelations; prophecy fulfilled; miraculous healings and glossolalia; visitations from dead relatives, from angels, from demonic spirits, and from the Three Nephites—comprise a major element of nineteenth-century Mormon writings. While the traditional historical-critical method might simply judge these to be nonfactual and ignore them, I include supernatural elements in this book without offering positive or negative judgment so as to reproduce the world view of nineteenth-century Latter-day Saints. It would be naive to try to understand these women in their socio-cultural milieu without exploring and respecting their own ideology. For instance, Helen Mar Whitney's belief in the presence of demonic spirits by her bedside is the necessary backdrop for understanding her sickbed conversion to polygamy. Belief in Joseph Smith as a seer who knew the future and past in detail, a major theme in Mary Elizabeth Lightner's autobiography, provides insight into why she and other women agreed to become his polyandrous wives. This is the methodology used by Richard Bushman in his *Joseph Smith and the Beginnings of Mormonism*: "My method has been to relate events as the participants themselves experienced them, using their own words where possible. Insofar as the revelations were a reality to them, I have treated them as real in this narrative. General readers will surely be left with questions about the meaning of these experiences, but at least they will have an understanding of how early Mormons perceived the world."

## In Sacred Loneliness

Anti-Mormon polemicists saw polygamy as pure evil. Mormon men were viewed as insidious enslavers of women; polygamous women were seen as helpless, mindless victims. A representative period novel was entitled, *Elder Northfield's Home; or, Sacrificed on the Mormon Altar: A Story of the Blighting Curse of Polygamy*. After sweeping aside such melodramatic propaganda, one finds that in actuality Mormon polygamists, both female and male, were generally sincere, intensely religious, often intelligent and able, and men and women of good will. Nevertheless, my central thesis is that Mormon polygamy was characterized by a tragic ambiguity. On the one hand, it was more than secular, monogamous marriage—it was the new and everlasting covenant, having eternal significance, a restoration from the prophetic, patriarchal milieu of Abraham which gave the participant infinite dominion in the next life. On the other hand, day-to-day practical polygamous living, for many women, was less than monogamous marriage—it was a social system that simply did not work in nineteenth-century America. Polygamous wives often experienced what was essentially acute neglect. Despite the husband's sincere efforts, he could only give a specific wife a fraction of his time and means. Plural wife Annie Clark Tanner described herself as raising her ten children "alone." When one of her boys caused trouble, her "frank admission" to a neighbor was: "Well I am alone." The ambiguous nature of Mormon polygamy, for women, is summed up in a paragraph from Tanner's moving autobiography: "As a girl I had been proud that my father and mother had obeyed the highest principle in the Church ... I was aware now that my mother's early married life must have been humiliating and joyless on many occasions because of her position as a second wife."

Some feminist scholars have suggested that there were positive sides to the man's frequent absence in a polygamous wife's life; she became more independent, self-supporting, and closely tied to sister-wives, developing, as Annie Clark Tanner, noted, "an independence that women in monogamy never know." Ironically, Tanner's husband resented her independence and self-reliance. These advantages of polygamy, while real, are clearly consequences of the less-than-ideal absence of a marriage partner. Annie Tanner, in her discussion of the independence of women, also emphasized their isolation and insecurity. She often envied monogamous neighbors.

This is not to deny that there are examples of polygamous families that approached the supposed ideal. But special conditions (especially limited plurality) probably accounted for these successes. The more women a man married, the greater the danger for serious problems in the family, for the husband's time and resources became more and more divided. By an almost cruel irony, the greater the number of women married, the greater the man's exaltation, according to nineteenth-century Mormon theology.

Not surprisingly, therefore, polygamous wives, even those married to prominent, well-to-do men, were often not supported adequately financially. Annie Clark Tanner wrote: "We returned from Provo after a single school year there. All of us were conscious now that we would have to make our own way, if possible, independent of help from Mr. Tanner." In 1913 Annie's husband told her that she should "look to [her] stalwart sons for support." Clearly, monogamous men also struggled financially at times, but polygamy exacerbated financial problems.

As the polygamous husbands were generally church leaders, demands on their time further reduced their ability to be with their families. Polygamous husbands generally had favorite wives, which limited even more their time with other wives. As a result, some women left their polygamous husbands, but if they remained in the family, they compensated by developing especially close ties with sister wives, siblings, and children. Annie Clark Tanner wrote, "A woman in polygamy is compelled by her lone position to make a confidant of her children." Plural wife Olive Andelin Potter wrote, "I have worshiped my children all my life, as I have had no husband to love so all my love has been for them."

Polygamous marriage, by modern monogamous standards, often does not seem like marriage at all. Sometimes polygamous wives consciously steeled themselves to limit affection for their husbands, as a strategy for emotional survival during absences. Vilate Kimball advised a plural wife that "she must lay aside wholly all interest or thought in what her husband was doing while he was away from her" and be "pleased to see him when he came in as she was pleased to see any friend." Annie Clark Tanner wrote, of her husband, "When he came to my house, he was more like a guest."

Thus the title of this book, *In Sacred Loneliness*. Often plural wives who experienced loneliness also reported feelings of depression, despair, anxiety, helplessness, abandonment, anger, psychosomatic symptoms, and low self-esteem. Certainly polygamous marriage was accepted by nineteenth-century Mormons as thoroughly sacred—it almost defined what was most holy to them—but its practical result, for the woman, was solitude.

## Acknowledgements

My debts in writing this book are many. The descendants of the women I have written about have been generous in their help and encouragement, and this book is much richer because of their assistance. It has been greatly improved by the editorial and research assistance of the following: Ron Priddis, Gary Bergera, Richard Van Wagoner, Michael Marquardt, Linda King Newell, Maureen Ursenbach Beecher, D. Michael Quinn, Martha Sonntag Bradley, Lavina Fielding Anderson, Bob Fillerup, B. Carmon Hardy, Edward Leo Lyman, Newell Bringhurst, Elbert Peck, Tim Rathbone, Sue Bergin, Charles Hatch, William Russell, Ron Romig, John Sillito, Valeen Tippetts Avery, Lorie Winder Stromberg, Julia Monson, Jan Eyring, Irene Bates, E. Gary Smith, Elizabeth Shaw Smith, Richard Cracroft, James Kimball, Clark Layton, Lyman Platt, Mike, Dave, Richard, Donnae Tidwell, Robert M. Dudnik, Joseph Fasbinder, Perry Porter, Gene Wolfe (who advised me to always shoot the sheriff in the first paragraph), the Hauges (Tamara, Britanny, and Jacob, whose home I invaded while researching this book), Terry and Byron Harward, Tina Compton, and Tim and Virginia Compton. Any flaws in the book are, of course, my own. In a project this extensive, some errors are inevitable—I welcome information leading to corrections.

I would like to thank especially the Huntington Library, in San Marino, California, whose research grant and superb collection of Mormon manuscripts allowed this project to begin. The archivists at the historical department of the LDS church in Salt Lake City were unfailingly helpful and professional when I researched there; Linda Haslam even supplied cold medicine when I arrived at the archives one winter day when I should have stayed in bed. I am also grateful for the help of archivists at the Marriott Library on the University of Utah campus in Salt Lake City; the Merrill Library at Utah State University in Logan, Utah; the Utah State Historical Society in Salt Lake City; the Harold B. Lee Library at Brigham Young University in Provo, Utah; the Library and Archives of the Reorganized Church of Jesus Christ of Latter Day Saints in Independence, Missouri; the Howell Library at Weber State University; the Chicago Historical Society; the Illinois State Historical Archives in Springfield; and the Bancroft Library in Berkeley, California. Finally, I would like to thank the board and staff of Signature Books, who had faith in my project from the beginning.

# A Trajectory of Plurality:
## An Overview of Joseph Smith's Wives

*33!*

I have identified thirty-three well-documented wives of Joseph Smith, which some may regard as an overly conservative numbering (see chart). Historians Fawn Brodie, D. Michael Quinn, and George D. Smith list forty-eight, forty-six, and forty-three, respectively. Yet in problematic areas it may be advisable to err on the side of caution. Unless further evidence surfaces, I regard the "possible" wives as subjects for additional research rather than as women whose marriages to Joseph Smith can be conclusively demonstrated.

What criteria can be used to evaluate whether a woman's marriage to Joseph Smith (during his lifetime) can be reliably documented? In 1869 Joseph F. Smith, countering Reorganized Latter Day Saint Church (RLDS) denials of Joseph Smith's polygamy, had Joseph Smith's living widows sign affidavits documenting their marriages to him. An affidavit is very good evidence. A woman mentioning in a journal or autobiography that she married the prophet is also good evidence, as is a close family member's or friend's testimony or affidavit or reminiscence, especially if he or she supplies convincing detail, anecdotal or documentary.

Even without an affidavit or holographic evidence for a woman, multiple pieces of evidence can make a convincing case for her marriage. The contours of a woman's life support or weaken the likelihood that she married the Mormon leader. For instance, while two or three uncertain pieces of evidence suggest that Vienna Jacques may have married Smith, the rest of her life does not make her look like his plural wife. (Some assume she married him in Kirtland, Ohio, but then immediately left him and moved to Missouri, where she married another man. Nor did she have a proxy marriage to Smith in the Nauvoo temple.) If a woman lived in Smith's home, this is possible supporting evidence for a wedding but not conclusive by itself.

Certain lists have proved to be reliable. Though John C. Bennett was unscrupulous in many ways, he was a Nauvoo insider, and his 1842 list of Smith's wives has been adequately substantiated. Assistant Church Historian Andrew Jenson's 1887 list of twenty-seven wives, based on interviews and affidavits, is also a basic resource. Small lists, from sources both sympathetic and hostile to polygamy, have been authenticated.

The eight "Possible Wives" listed in the chart are supported by limited, problematic, or contradictory evidence, sometimes only one attestation in a late source. For instance, Hannah Dubois Dibble's marriage is supported only by two pieces of evidence in late sources. Hannah did live in the Smith home briefly, but Joseph officiated when she married Philo Dibble. Later she married Philo, not Joseph, for eternity in the Nauvoo temple.

For another example, Orson Whitney, son and nephew of two of Joseph's wives, referred to Mary Houston as a "[wife] of the Prophet." Mary certainly married Smith for eternity after his death and was sealed to Heber Kimball for time in a Nauvoo temple proxy marriage, and Whitney possibly assumed that this proved she married him while he was alive. But there is no evidence for a non-proxy marriage to Smith during his lifetime.

This leads us to my final category, "Early Posthumous Proxy Marriages"—sealings to Smith after his death. It is true that most of his wives recommemorated their marriages to him by proxy after his passing. But not all of the women sealed to him after his death had a previous marital relationship with him. For instance, Cordelia Morley stated in a memoir that she had never married Smith while he was living. Other early posthumous-only marriages to Smith include Augusta Adams Cobb Young (1848) and Amanda Barnes Smith (1852). Mary Ann Frost Stearns Pratt seems to have married Parley P. Pratt for eternity during Smith's lifetime, so her later sealing to Smith is also probably posthumous-only.

Thus I arrive at a list of thirty-three well-documented wives of Smith. Such a limited, but solid list allows a reliable overview that offers great insight into the women themselves, into Joseph Smith, and into pre-Utah polygamy. Antagonistic, often sensationalizing sources list other women as wives of Joseph Smith; he also proposed to at least five more women who turned him down.

### The Timing of Joseph Smith's Marriages

As we trace the trajectory of Smith's marriages, we see that he apparently experimented with plural marriage in the 1830s in Ohio and Missouri. Detailed records are not extant, but the evidence, when weighed carefully, suggests that these were probably authentic plural marriages. In 1841 Smith cautiously added three wives. But in 1842 he married eleven wives in the first eight months of the year. New marriages then stopped for five months—a significant gap—perhaps caused by the John Bennett exposé in which Smith's former right-hand man published a series of lurid articles chronicling Joseph's alleged misdeeds, including polygamy.

However, during the first half of 1843, Joseph married fourteen more wives, including five in May. After July his marriages stopped abruptly, with only two exceptions in September and November. He took no wives during the last eight months of his life—a striking fact, especially when contrasted with the number of women he married during the previous two years.

This puzzle has a number of possible solutions. Nauvoo stake president William Marks suggested in 1853 that Smith came to have doubts about polygamy before his death:

> When the doctrine of polygamy was introduced into the church as a principle of exaltation, I took a decided stand against it; which stand rendered me quite unpopular with many of the leading ones of the church ... Joseph, however, became convinced before his death that he had done wrong; for about three weeks before his death, I met him one morning in the street, and he said to me, "Brother Marks ... We are a ruined people." I asked, how so? he said: "This doctrine of polygamy, or Spiritual-wife system, that has been taught and practiced among us, will prove our destruction and overthrow. I have been deceived," said he, "in reference to its practice; it is wrong; it is a curse to mankind, and we shall have to leave the United States soon, unless it can be put down and its practice stopped in the church."

Smith then reportedly told Marks to excommunicate all polygamists. This testimony seems to reflect a slight RLDS partisan coloring; furthermore, Marks was not in the inner polygamy circle in Nauvoo. However, the eight-month cessation of plural marriages before Joseph's death might support Marks's story.

Another possibility is that the discontinuation of marriages resulted from tensions between Smith and his first wife, Emma, who threatened to leave him during this period. Such a scandal would have been disastrous for him and the church. He was also under pressure from his counselor in the First Presidency, William Law, a confirmed opponent of polygamy. Whether Smith came to believe polygamy was wrong or was merely pausing for tactical reasons, as he had during the Bennett scandal, is uncertain. But the eight-month cessation of marriages at the end of his life is a notable phenomenon.

The twenty-five or so wives whom Joseph married in early 1842 and 1843 bear impressive testimony to the fact that plural marriage was not simply a footnote to his life or theology, particularly since he was well aware of the threat of exposure. When he taught the principle of plural marriage to Sarah Kimball, wife of Hiram Kimball (such teaching usually presaging a proposal), "He said that in teaching this he realized that he jeopardized his life." Furthermore, some of his marriages were polyandrous, which incurred the danger of jealous husbands.

| NAME AT TIME OF MARRIAGE | MARRIAGE DATE | STATUS | AGE |
|---|---|---|---|
| 1. Fanny Alger | [early 1833} | sg | [16] |
| 2. Lucinda Pendleton (Morgan Harris) | [1838?} | md | 37? |
| 3. Louisa Beaman | 5 April 1841 | sg | 26 |
| 4. Zina Diantha Huntington (Jacobs) | 27 Oct. 1841 | md | 20 |
| 5. Presendia Lathrop Huntington (Buell) | 11 Dec. 1841 | md | 31 |
| 6. Agnes Moulton Coolbrith (Smith) | 6 Jan. 1842 | wd | 33 |
| 7. Sylvia Sessions (Lyon) | 8 Feb. 1842 | md | 23 |
| 8. Mary Elizabeth Rollins (Lightner) | late Feb. 1842 | md | 23 |
| 9. Patty Bartlett (Sessions) | 9 March 1842 | md | 47 |
| 10. Marinda Nancy Johnson (Hyde) | Apr. 1842 | md | 27 |
| 11. Elizabeth Davis (Goldsmith Brackenbury Durfee) | < June 1842 | md | 50-51? |
| 12. Sarah Kingsley (Howe Cleveland) | < 29 June 1842 | md | [53-54] |
| 13. Delcena Johnson (Sherman) | <July 1842 | wd | [37-38]? |
| 14. Eliza Roxcy Snow | 29 June 1842 | sg | 38 |

# Plural Wives

Fanny separated from JS and married Solomon Custer, non-LDS.

Lucinda remained with polyandrous first husband, George Harris, LDS; married by proxy in Nauvoo temple to JS {Harris}; later divorced Harris.

Louisa was married by proxy to JS {BY}

Zina remained with polyandrous first husband, Henry B. Jacobs, LDS; polyandrous proxy marriage to JS {BY} but remained with Jacobs; eventually left Jacobs and became BY's connubial wife.

Presendia remained with polyandrous first husband, Norman Buell, disaffected LDS; polyandrous proxy marriage to JS {HCK} but stayed with Buell; eventually left Buell and became HCK's connubial wife.

Agnes was married by proxy to Don Carlos Smith {G. A. Smith}. Don Carlos was JS's deceased brother and Agnes's first husband. She then married William Pickett, erratic LDS, in a technically polyandrous union; eventually separated from Pickett.

Sylvia remained with polyandrous first husband, Windsor Lyon, LDS; polyandrous proxy marriage to JS {HCK}; remained with Lyon until his death; married Ezekiel Clark, non-LDS; divorced Clark; moved to Utah (to be with HCK?).

Mary remained with polyandrous first husband, Adam Lightner, non-LDS; polyandrous proxy marriage to JS {BY}, but stayed with Lightner till his death.

Patty remained with polyandrous first husband, David Sessions, LDS, till his death; married John Parry for time.

Marinda remained with polyandrous first husband, Orson Hyde, LDS apostle, and was married eternally to him in the Nauvoo temple; later eternal proxy marriage to JS; eventually divorced Hyde.

Elizabeth apparently remained with polyandrous first husband, Jabez Durfee, LDS, after JS's death; separated from Durfee; proxy marriage to JS {Cornelius Lott}; separated from Lott.

Sarah remained with polyandrous first husband, John Cleveland, non-LDS; polyandrous proxy marriage to JS {John Smith}; stayed with Cleveland to her death.

Delcena was married by proxy to Lyman Sherman {Almon Babbitt}.

Eliza was married by proxy to JS {Brigham Young}.

*More* ☛

5

| NAME AT TIME OF MARRIAGE | MARRIAGE DATE | STATUS | AGE |
|---|---|---|---|
| 15. Sarah Ann Whitney | 27 July 1842 | sg | 17 |
| 16. Martha McBride (Knight) | Aug. 1842 | wd | 37 |
| 17. Ruth Vose (Sayers) | Feb. 1843 | md | 33 |
| 18. Flora Ann Woodworth | spring 1843 | sg | 16 |
| 19. Emily Dow Partridge | 4 March 1843 | sg | 19 |
| 20. Eliza Maria Partridge | 8 March 1843 | sg | 22 |
| 21. Almera Woodward Johnson | 2-22 April 1843 | sg | 30 |
| 22. Lucy Walker | 1 May 1843 | sg | 17 |
| 23. Sarah Lawrence | May 1843 | sg | 17 |
| 24. Maria Lawrence | May 1843 | sg | 19 |
| 25. Helen Mar Kimball | May 1843 | sg | 14 |
| 26. Hannah Ells | < mid-1843 | sg | 29-30 |
| 27. Elvira Annie Cowles (Holmes) | 1 June 1843 | md | 29 |
| 28. Rhoda Richards | 12 June 1843 | sg | 58 |
| 29. Desdemona Fullmer | July 1843 | sg | 32-33 |
| 30. Olive G. Frost | summer 1843 | sg | 27-28? |
| 31. Melissa Lott | 20 Sept. 1843 | sg | 19 |
| 32. Nancy M. Winchester | [1842-43?] | sg | [14?] |
| 33. Fanny Young (Carr Murray) | 2 Nov. 1843 | wd | 56 |

# Plural Wives (continued)

Sarah separated from Joseph Kingsbury, her "pretend" polyandrous husband; proxy marriage to JS {HCK}.

Martha married by proxy to JS {HCK}; separated from HCK?

Ruth remained with polyandrous first husband, Edward Sayers, non-LDS, till his death.

Flora married [Carlos] Gove, non-LDS.

Emily married by proxy to JS {BY}.

Eliza married by proxy to JS {Amasa Lyman}. Later divorced Lyman.

Almera married Reuben Barton (proxy marriage?).

Lucy married by proxy to JS {HCK}.

Sarah married by proxy to JS {HCK}; divorced HCK; married Joseph Mount.

Maria married by proxy to JS {BY}? Separated from BY? Proxy marriage to JS {Almon Babbitt}.

Helen married by proxy to JS {Horace Whitney}.

Hannah never remarried. Died [1845].

Elvira remained with polyandrous first husband, Jonathan Holmes, LDS; proxy marriage to JS {Holmes}.

Rhoda married by proxy to JS {BY}; separated from BY or never cohabited.

Desdemona married by proxy to JS {Ezra Taft Benson}; separated from Benson; married Harrison McLane but later separated.

Olive married by proxy to JS {BY}.

Melissa married by proxy to JS {John Bernhisel}; separated from Bernhisel; married Ira Willis.

Nancy married by proxy to JS {HCK}; divorced HCK; married Amos Arnold.

Fanny never remarried.

*More* ☞

# Possible Wives

| NAME AT TIME OF MARRIAGE | MARRIAGE DATE | STATUS | AGE |
|---|---|---|---|
| 1. Vienna Jacques | 1832-33/41-43? | sg/ md? | 43-44? 54-57? |
| 2. Hannah Ann Dubois (Smith) | 11 Feb 1841? | wd? | 32-33? |
| 3. Sarah Bapson | < June 1842? | sg? | 48-51? |
| 4. Mrs. G***** | June 1842? | md/ wd? | ? |
| 5. Sarah Scott (Mulholland) | 1841-43? | wd | 24-27? |
| 6. Mary Houston | 1841-43? | sg | 23-26? |
| 7. Mrs. Tailor | 1841-43? | md/ wd? | ? |
| 8. Mary Heron (Snider) | 1842/3? | md | 38-39? |

---

## EARLY POSTHUMOUS MARRIAGES TO JOSEPH SMITH

*The following women were sealed to Joseph Smith after his death (see proxy marriage below). There is no evidence that these women married him during his lifetime. Morley, in fact, stated that she had not married Joseph before his death:*

| | |
|---|---|
| Olive Andrews | January 15, 1846, Brigham Young proxy |
| Jane Tibbetts | January 17, 1846, Elam Luddington proxy |
| Phebe Watrous (Woodworth) | January 17, 1846, Lucien Woodworth proxy |
| Aphia Sanborn (Dow Yale) | January 27, 1846, Gad Yale proxy |
| Cordelia Morley | January 27, 1846, Frederick Cox proxy |
| Mary Ann Frost (Stearns Pratt) | February 6, 1846, Parley P. Pratt proxy |
| Sally Ann Fuller | January 29, 1847, Samuel Gully proxy |
| Lydia Kenyon (Carter) | possibly sealed in late 1844, HCK proxy |

---

### KEY TO ABBREVIATIONS

| | |
|---|---|
| < | earlier than |
| ? | unknown |
| [ ] | unverified |
| { } | "proxy" |
| sg | single at time of marriage to Smith |
| wd | widowed at time of marriage to Smith |

LATER LIFE

Vienna married Daniel Shearer in 1838; separated by 22 Jan. 1846.

Hannah married Philo Dibble 11 Feb. 1841; sealed to Dibble for eternity in Nauvoo temple 15 Jan. 1846.

?

?

Sarah married by proxy to James Mulholland {HCK}, 3 Feb. 1846.

Mary married by proxy to JS {HCK}, 3 Feb. 1846.

?

Mary continued with polyandrous first husband, John Snider.

ABBREVIATIONS, CONTINUED

md . . . . . . . married to another man at time of marriage to Smith, creating polyandry, as the woman continued to cohabit with the "first husband"
BY . . . . . . . Brigham Young
HCK . . . . . . Heber C. Kimball
JS . . . . . . . . Joseph Smith

TERMS

POLYGAMY ("many-marriage"): A man or woman has two or more marriage partners. Plural marriage is the preferred Mormon term. Anthropologically, polygamy is divided into two subcategories: polygyny and polyandry.

POLYGYNY (i.e., "many-woman"): A man is married to two or more women simultaneously.

POLYANDRY (i.e., "many-man"): A woman has multiple husbands.

PROXY: When one is sealed for eternity to a deceased person, with a living partner standing in for the deceased, the living surrogate is known as a proxy. In early Mormon history the woman was also sealed (for time, not eternity) to the living proxy. Children from the "time" marriage were sealed eternally to the deceased husband, not to the biological father. On this chart the living proxy's name is given within S brackets.

Thus the doctrine of plural marriage was of central importance to Smith for religious, doctrinal, ecclesiastical, and emotional reasons. William Clayton, his scribe and companion in Nauvoo, wrote that the Mormon prophet spoke of little else in private in the last year of his life. As he developed the principle of sealing ordinances that connected families for eternity, this doctrine was inextricably bound up with plural marriage. Later nineteenth-century Mormons taught that a monogamist could not gain complete salvation, a belief that was clearly based on Smith's teachings.

## The Number of Joseph Smith's Wives

Though thirty-three is less than forty-eight, it is still a remarkably large polygamous family. One may wonder why Smith married so many women when two or three wives would have complied with the reported divine command to enter polygamy. However, the church president apparently believed that complete salvation (in Mormon terminology, exaltation, including the concept of deification) depended on the extent of a man's family *sealed to him in this life*. Benjamin Johnson, a brother of Smith's plural wife Almera, wrote:

> The First Command was to "Multiply" and the Prophet taught us that Dominion & powr in the great Future would be Comensurate with the no [number] of "Wives Childin & Friends" that we inheret here and that our great mission to earth was to Organize a Neculi [nucleus] of Heaven to take with us. To the increace of which there would be no end —

The emphasis on increase echoes the Abrahamic promise, in which God promised Abraham that his posterity would be as plentiful as the dust of the earth, the stars in the sky, and the sands of the seashore (Gen. 13:16; 16:10; 17:6; 18:18; 22:17). Early Mormons taught that the doctrine of plural marriage was revealed to Smith "while he was engaged in the work of translation of the Scriptures," and historian Danel Bachman concludes that it was specifically the translation of Genesis, the Abraham passages, that caused Joseph to pray about polygamy in February 1831 and receive his first revelations on the topic. The example of Abraham and the Abrahamic promise are prominently mentioned in the LDS church's Doctrine and Covenants (D&C 132), the officially canonized revelation on polygamy and exaltation.

The idea that one had to be sealed to one's family nucleus *in this life* probably depended on another biblical passage, Matthew 22:30, in which Jesus states that "in the resurrection they neither marry nor are given in marriage." Smith apparently interpreted this to mean that one had to create one's "extended family," one's kingdom, by marriage while on earth. Orson Pratt, in a discourse given in 1859, taught this explicitly.

Thus the Mormon practice of polygamy, influenced strongly by these two scriptures, is an example of the early American biblical primitivism that shaped Joseph Smith and early Mormonism. The Old Testament, with its prophets and temples and polygamy, is a central thread running through Joseph's life and is clearly a primary source for his sense of prophetic mission and for his doctrine.

The importance of the size of one's eternal family, and the necessity of building it up on this earth, is shown by the custom of adoption practiced in the late Nauvoo period by Brigham Young and other Mormon leaders who would have grown men sealed to them as "sons." These "sons" even signed their names with their new "father's" last name. In the late Nauvoo period, Mormon leaders reportedly competed to add new members, "sons," to their adoptive families.

In Helen Mar Kimball's marriage to the prophet, Smith and her father Heber Kimball desired the marriage so that Heber's family would be linked eternally to Smith, thus assuring their salvation. D. Michael Quinn, with his interest in prosopography, emphasizes the fact that Smith's marriages linked him with important men in the church, giving them reciprocal earthly and eschatological advantages. When Jedediah Grant preached on plural marriage, he spoke of Smith "adding to his family": "When the family organization was revealed from heaven—the patriarchal order of God, and Joseph began, on the right and the left, to add to his family, what a quaking there was in Israel."

Thus in Smith's Nauvoo ideology, a fullness of salvation depended on the *quantity* of family members sealed to a person in this life. This puts the number of women Joseph married into an understandable context. This doctrine also makes it clear that, though Joseph's marriages undoubtedly had a sexual dimension, theological concepts also drove his polygamy, as well as the related purpose of gaining the highest possible exaltation by linking elite families to him for both earthly and eternal reasons.

## The Ages of Joseph Smith's Wives

In the group of Smith's well-documented wives, eleven (33 percent) were 14 to 20 years old when they married him. Nine wives (27 percent) were twenty-one to thirty years old. Eight wives (24 percent) were in Smith's own peer group, ages thirty-one to forty. In the group aged forty-one to fifty, there is a substantial drop off: two wives, or 6 percent, and three (9 percent) in the group fifty-one to sixty.

The teenage representation is the largest, though the twenty-year and thirty-year groups are comparable, which contradicts the Mormon folk-wisdom that sees the beginnings of polygamy as an attempt to care for older, unattached women. These data suggest that sexual attraction was an important part of the motivation for Smith's polygamy. In fact, the command to multiply and replenish the earth was part of the polygamy theology, so non-sexual marriage was generally not in the polygamous program, as Smith taught it.

One may ask why the Mormon leader married any older women at all. Two reasons can be offered. First, two of these women, Fanny Young Murray and Rhoda Richards, were sisters of favored apostles, so the marriages were dynastic. Interestingly, Joseph's youngest wife, Helen Mar Kimball, was the daughter of another loyal apostle, Heber C. Kimball, so that marriage may also be considered dynastic, not motivated solely by sexual interest. Second, older women served as teachers and messengers to introduce and convert younger women to the practice in Nauvoo. Elizabeth Durfee and Patty Sessions belong in this category. Eliza R. Snow acted in this capacity in Utah. For Mormon feminists unsympathetic to patriarchal polygamy, this will be one of the most troubling aspects of Mormon polygamy: women co-opting other, younger females into the order.

## Sexuality in Joseph Smith's Plural Marriages

Joseph Smith's first wife, Emma, allegedly told the wife of Apostle George A. Smith, Lucy, that Joseph Smith's plural wives were "celestial" only, that he had no earthly marital relations with them. "They were only sealed for eternity they were not to live with him and have children." Lucy later wrote that when she told this to her husband:

> He related to me the circumstance of his calling on Joseph late one evening and he was just taking a wash and Joseph told him that one of his wives had just been confined and Emma was the Midwife and he had been assisting her. He [George A. Smith] told me [Lucy Smith] this to prove to me that the women were married for time [as well as for eternity], as Emma had told me that Joseph never taught any such thing.

Because Reorganized Latter Day Saints claimed that Joseph Smith was not really married polygamously in the full (i.e., sexual) sense of the term, Utah Mormons (including Smith's wives) affirmed repeatedly that he had physical sexual relations with them—despite the Victorian conventions in nineteenth-century American culture which ordinarily would have prevented any mention of sexuality.

For instance, Mary Elizabeth Rollins Lightner stated that she knew of children born to Smith's plural wives: "I know he had six wives and I have known some of them from childhood up. I know he had three children. They told me. I think two are living today but they are not known as his children as they go by other names." Melissa Lott Willes testified that she had been Smith's wife "in very deed." Emily Partridge Young said she "roomed" with Joseph the night following her marriage to him, and said that she had "carnal intercourse" with him.

Other early witnesses also affirmed this. Benjamin Johnson wrote: "On the 15th of May ... the Prophet again Came and at my hosue [house] ocupied the Same Room & Bed with my Sister that the month previous he had ocupied with the Daughter of the Later Bishop Partridge as his wife." According to Joseph Bates Noble, Smith told him he had spent a night with Louisa Beaman.

When Angus Cannon, a Salt Lake City stake president, visited Joseph Smith III in 1905, the RLDS president asked rhetorically if these women were his father's wives, then "how was it that there was no issue from them." Cannon replied:

> All I knew was that which Lucy Walker herself contends. They were so nervous and lived in such constant fear that they could not conceive. He made light of my reply. He said, "I am informed that Eliza Snow was a virgin at the time of her death." I in turn said, "Brother Heber C. Kimball, I am informed, asked her the question if she was not a virgin although married to Joseph Smith and afterwards to Brigham Young, when she replied in a private gathering, 'I thought you knew Joseph Smith better than that.'"

Cannon then mentioned that Sylvia Sessions Lyon, a plural wife of Smith, had had a child by him, Josephine Lyon Fisher. Josephine left an affidavit stating that her mother, Sylvia, when on her deathbed, told her that she (Josephine) was the daughter of Joseph Smith. In addition, posterity (i.e., sexuality) was an important theological element in Smith's Abrahamic-promise justification for polygamy.

Since there is a great deal of evidence that Joseph Smith had sexual relations with his wives, one wonders why he did not have more polygamous children. However, some of his children apparently grew up under other names, as Mary Lightner suggested. Furthermore, he may not have had numerous posterity because he was not able to visit his wives regularly, both because he was often hiding from the law and because Emma, his first wife, watched him carefully. In addition, polygamy was illegal. On top of these pressures, he soon had many wives, which made it more difficult to visit all of them frequently and regularly. Since polygamists generally had favorite wives, Smith probably neglected some of his. Finally, some of his wives were married to other men in polyandrous relationships, so such wives would probably have had children by their "first husbands," with whom they were cohabiting regularly, not by Joseph. All of these factors would have combined to limit the number of his children. However, it is clear that some of his plural wives did have children by him, if we can rely on the statements of George A. Smith, Josephine Fisher, and Elizabeth Lightner.

Despite this evidence, some have argued that Joseph did not have marital relations with his wives, using the following arguments: First, some conclude that Helen Mar Kimball, who married Smith when she was fourteen, did not have marital relations with him. This is possible, as there are cases of Mormons in Utah marrying young girls and refraining from sexuality until they were older. But the evidence for Helen Mar is entirely ambiguous, in my view.

Some, like Emma Smith, conclude that Joseph's marriages were for eternity only, not for time (thus without earthly sexuality). But many of Joseph's wives affirmed that they were married to him for eternity *and* time, with sexuality included. Eliza Snow, in her autobiography, wrote that "I was sealed to the Prophet Joseph Smith, for time and eternity, in accordance with the <u>Celestial Law of Marriage</u> which God has revealed." Furthermore, there are no known instances of marriages for "eternity only" in the nineteenth century.

Some have pointed out that Mary Elizabeth Rollins Lightner said in 1905, "I ... was sealed to Joseph for Eternity." Thus, they argue, Smith had no relations with her, a polyandrous wife, as he was married to her for eternity only. However, Lightner apparently was merely emphasizing eternity in this statement; she testified in three different places that she was also sealed to Smith for time. For example, in a 1902 statement she said, "Brigham Young Sealed me to him [Smith], for time & all eternity."

Zina Huntington Young also had a polyandrous relationship with Smith and her first husband, Henry Jacobs. Some point out that she gave an interview in which she referred to her marriage to Smith as "eternal," not for "time." However, in the same interview she emphasized that she was married to the Mormon leader for time, as well:

> [Zina:] ... he [Joseph Smith] married me ... When Brigham Young returned from England, he repeated the ceremony for time and eternity. ... I was sealed to Joseph Smith for eternity.
> [Question:] Mrs. Young, you claim, I believe, that you were not married to him "for time?"
> [Zina:] "For eternity." I was married to Mr. Jacobs, but the marriage was unhappy and we parted ...
> [Q:] Is it a fact then, Mrs. Young, that Joseph was not married to you only in the sense of being sealed "for eternity?"
> [Zina:] As his wife for time and eternity.
> [Q:] Mrs. Young, you have answered that question in two ways; for time, and for time and eternity.
> [Zina:] I meant for eternity.

Some interpreters place great weight on these statements, as showing that Zina's marriage was "spiritual" only. But the interview is so contradictory on this issue, as the elderly Zina sounds defensive and confused while answering an RLDS judge's harsh questions, that it cannot be used as solid evidence. One even wonders if early Mormons did not use the term "marriage for eternity" to encompass "time and eternity," as Mormons do today.

In conclusion, though it is possible that Joseph had some marriages in which there were no sexual relations, there is no explicit or convincing evidence for this (except, perhaps, in the cases of the older wives, judging from later Mormon polygamy). And in a significant number of marriages, there is evidence for sexual relations.

### Marital Status at the Time of Marriage: Polyandry

Eighteen of Joseph's wives (55 percent) were single when he married them and had never been married previously. Another four (12 percent) were widows. One, Agnes Coolbrith Smith, was the widow of his younger brother, Don Carlos, making this a strict Levirate marriage. However, the remaining eleven women (33 percent) were married to other husbands and cohabiting with them when Smith married them. Another woman, Sarah Ann Whitney, married Smith, then married another man soon after in a civil, "pretend" marriage. I use the term polyandry—which means one woman being married to two men simultaneously—to describe this marital triangulation.

Polyandry is one of the major problems found in Smith's polygamy and many questions surround it. Why did he at first primarily prefer polyandrous marriages? Did the husbands know about the marriages, and, if so, how did they feel about them? Did they allow the marriages to Joseph willingly or reluctantly? Did such marriages include sexuality, and what was the doctrinal rationale for them?

In the past, polyandry has often been ignored or glossed over, but if these women merit serious attention, the topic cannot be overlooked. Joseph F. Smith, seventh president of the LDS church, and Andrew Jenson, Assistant Church Historian, documented these women's polyandrous marriages to Joseph Smith, including affidavits with dates of the ceremonies. Their civil marriages and dates of childbirths are also easily corroborated. Joseph F. Smith and Andrew Jenson have forced the issue for the serious historian, and the only option is to try to come to as complete and balanced an understanding of the phenomenon as possible.

A common misconception concerning Joseph Smith's polyandry is that he participated in only one or two such unusual unions. In fact, fully one-third of his plural wives, eleven of them, were married civilly to other men when he married them. If one superimposes a chronological perspective, one sees that of Smith's first twelve wives, nine were polyandrous. So in this early period polyandry was the norm, not the anomaly. His later marriages were largely to single women, with two exceptions in

1843. Polyandry might be easier to understand if one viewed these marriages to Smith as a sort of *de facto* divorce with the first husband. However, none of these women divorced their "first husbands" while Smith was alive and all of them continued to live with their civil spouses while married to Smith.

Some have suggested that the first husbands in these marriages were generally disaffected from Mormonism or were non-Mormon and that Smith married the women to offer them salvation. In such cases, the women would have wanted to be married to Smith as a righteous husband who could bring them exaltation. If so, one would have expected the women to leave the unworthy men.

The totality of the evidence, however, does not support this theory. In the eleven certain polyandrous marriages, only three of the husbands were non-Mormon (Lightner, Sayers, and Cleveland) and only one was disaffected (Buell). All other husbands were in good standing in the church at the time Joseph married their wives. Many were prominent church leaders and close friends of Smith. George W. Harris was a high councilor in Missouri and Nauvoo, a position equivalent to that of a twentieth-century general authority. Henry Jacobs was a devoted friend of Joseph and a faithful missionary. Orson Hyde was an apostle on his mission to Palestine when Smith married his wife. Jonathan Holmes was one of Smith's bodyguards and served as a pallbearer after Smith's death. Windsor Lyon was a member in good standing when Smith united with Sylvia Lyon, and he loaned the prophet money after the marriage. David Sessions was a devout Latter-day Saint.

These data suggest that Joseph may have married these women, often, not because they were married to non-members but because they were married to faithful Latter-day Saints who were his devoted friends. This again suggests that the men knew about the marriages and permitted them.

Another theory is that Joseph married polyandrously when the marriage was unhappy. If this were true, it would have been easy for the woman to divorce her husband, then marry Smith. But none of these women did so; some of them stayed with their "first husbands" until death. In the case of Zina Huntington Jacobs and Henry Jacobs—often used as an example of Smith marrying a woman whose marriage was unhappy—the Mormon leader married her just seven months after she married Jacobs, and then she stayed with Jacobs for years after Smith's death. Then the separation was forced when Brigham Young (who had married Zina polyandrously in the Nauvoo temple) sent Jacobs on a mission to England and began living with Zina himself.

Having rejected the theories that Smith married polyandrously when the marriages involved non-member husbands or were unhappy, we turn to statements in the historical record that do supply a convincing rationale for polyandry. First, Smith regarded marriages performed without Mormon priesthood authority as invalid (see D&C 132:7), just as he regarded baptisms performed without Mormon priesthood authority as invalid. Thus all couples in Nauvoo who accepted Mormonism were suddenly unmarried, granted Joseph's absolutist, exclusivist claims to divine authority. John D. Lee wrote:

> About the same time the doctrine of "sealing" for an eternal state was introduced, and the Saints were given to understand that their marriage relations with each other were not valid. That those who had solemnized the rites of matrimony had no authority of God to do so. That the true priesthood was taken from the earth with the death of the Apostles ... They were married to each other only by their own covenants, and that if their marriage relations had not been productive of blessings and peace, and they felt it oppressive to remain together, they were at liberty to make their own choice, as much as if they had not been married. That it was a sin for people to live together, and raise or beget children in alienation from each other. There should be an affinity between each other, not a lustful one, as that can never cement that love and affection that should exist between a man and his wife.

This is a radical, almost utopian rejection of civil, secular, sectarian, non-Mormon marriage. Civil marriage was even a "sin," unless a higher "affinity" "cemented" spouses together.

Another relevant doctrinal statement comes from an 1861 speech by Brigham Young:

> The Second Way in which a wife can be seperated from her husband, while he continues to be faithful to his God and his preisthood, I have not revealed, except to a few persons in this Church; and a few have received it from Joseph the prophet as well as myself. If a woman can find a man holding the keys of the preisthood with higher power and authority than her husband, and he is disposed to take her he can do so, otherwise she has got to remain where she is ... there is no need for a bill of divorcement ... To recapitulate. First if a man forfiets his covenants with a wife, or wives, becoming unfaithful to his God, and his preisthood, that wife or wives are free from him without a bill of divorcement. Second. If a woman claimes protection at the hands of a man, possessing more power in the preisthood and higher keys, if he is disposed to rescue her and has obtained the consent of her husband to make her his wife he can do so without a bill of divorcement.

This allows for two options: (1) if a man apostatized, his wife could leave him without a formal divorce; (2) if a woman desired to be married to a man with greater priesthood authority than her current husband, and if both men agreed, she could be sealed to the second man without formal divorce. In some ways this principle can be applied directly to Smith's polyandrous marriages, for clearly he was regarded as having more priesthood authority than any other living man. The emphasis on the desire of the woman is notable. In nineteenth-century Utah there are well-documented cases in which married women asked to be joined to a prominent church leader. In Nauvoo, however, such cases would not be frequent, as polygamy was secret. In Young's statement the husband is granted his own volition, which would be consistent with the suggestion made above that the first husbands in Smith's polyandrous marriages may have known about the marriages and permitted them.

Jedediah Grant's 1854 statement already referred to can now be quoted more fully:

> When the family organization was revealed from heaven—the patriarchal order of God, and Joseph began, on the right and the left, to add to his family, what a quaking there was in Israel. Says one brother to another, "Joseph says all covenants [previous marriages] are done away, and none are binding but the new covenants [marriage by priesthood sealing power]; now suppose Joseph should come and say he wanted your wife, what would you say to that?" "I would tell him to go to hell." This was the spirit of many in the early days of this Church [i.e., unwillingness to consecrate everything to Smith as the mouthpiece of God] ... What would a man of God say, who felt aright, when Joseph asked him for his money? [he would give it all willingly] Or if he came and said, "I want your wife?" "O yes," he would say, "here she is, there are plenty more." ... Did the Prophet Joseph want every man's wife he asked for? He did not ... the grand object in view was to try the people of God, to see what was in them. If such a man of God should come to me and say, "I want your gold and silver, or your wives," I should say, "Here they are, I wish I had more to give you, take all I have got." A man who has got the Spirit of God, and the light of eternity in him, has no trouble about such matters.

This remarkable sympathetic testimony to Smith's polyandrous marriages touches on many areas of interest. First, Grant sees the practice in terms of extended "family organization." Polyandry would obviously be useful in linking families to Smith. "Joseph says all covenants are done away, and none are binding but the new covenants." Here we have the doctrine that previous marriages are of no effect, "illegal," in Orson Pratt's words. Grant disapproves of those who were asked to give up their wives and refused. The proper response, according to Grant, would have been instant, unquestioning consecration of all "possessions" to the prophet. He states that Smith did not want *every* wife he asked for, which implies that he wanted some of them. The emphasis here is on Smith's testing his followers, as when Smith demanded Vilate Kimball from Heber Kimball. Yet the fact that at least eleven women were married to Joseph polyandrously, including the wife of prominent apostle Orson Hyde, shows that in many cases Joseph was not simply asking for wives as a test of loyalty; sometimes the test included giving up the wife.

Another doctrine that apparently served as underpinning for Smith's polyandry was his doctrine of a pre-existence, which holds that our spirits lived with God before birth and were given assignments there relating to what we would do here. According to Mary Elizabeth Lightner, who was married to Adam Lightner when Joseph proposed to her, "Joseph Said I was his, before I came here. he said all the Devils in Hell should never get me from him." Elsewhere she wrote that Smith told her he had been commanded to marry her, "or Suffer condemnation − for I [Mary] was created for him before the foundation of the Earth was laid." Apparently, if Smith had a spiritual intuition that he was linked to a woman, he asserted that she had been sealed to him in the pre-existence, even though she was legally married to another man. But, as we have seen, he taught that civil marriages performed without the priesthood sealing power were not valid, even at times sinful. Therefore, the link in the pre-existence would take immediate priority over a marriage performed by invalid, secular or "sectarian," authority in this life. John D. Lee wrote that a spiritual "affinity" took precedence over secular ceremonies. Perhaps Joseph Smith also felt, as the Brigham Young statement suggests, that men with higher priesthood had a greater aptitude for spiritual affinity.

According to an early, though antagonistic, eyewitness source, William Hall, the doctrine of "kindred spirits" was found in Nauvoo polyandry. According to this report, Smith taught that "all real marriages were made in heaven before the birth of the parties," which coincides neatly with Lightner. There is at least one early "friendly" reference to the "kindred spirit" doctrine. In an 1845 patriarchal blessing, William Smith said, "But the fullness of her salvation cannot be made perfect until her companion is with her and those who are of his Kingdom, for the kindred spirits are gathered up and are united in the Celestial Kingdom of one."

Thus heavenly marriage in the pre-existence required earthly polyandry here. Certain spirits were "kindred," matched in heaven, were born into this life, and, because of unauthorized marriages performed without priesthood sealing power, became linked "illegally" to the wrong partners. But when the kindred spirits recognized each other, the "illegal" marriages became of no effect from a religious, eternal perspective and the "kindred" partners were free to marry each other through the priesthood sealing power for eternity as well as for time.

19

Apparently, however, Joseph would allow the wife to continue living with her first husband after such a marriage. There were no divorces as a result of his polyandrous marriages. But the first husband probably recognized that he and the wife were married only until death, while Smith was married to her for eternity as well as for time. When eternal sealings were repeated in the Nauvoo temple in late 1845 and early 1846, two "first husbands," George W. Harris and Jonathan Holmes, stood proxy for the prophet as their wives were sealed to him for eternity. Another "first husband," Henry Jacobs, stood as witness when his wife, Zina, was sealed eternally to Smith (with Brigham Young, not Jacobs, standing proxy in this case), then witnessed his wife's sealing to Young for time. After which, Henry and Zina with their son Zebulon began the pioneer trek to the west together. Zina bore a second son to Jacobs, Henry Chariton, halfway across Iowa.

This kind of marriage was not viewed as eternal polyandry. A man could be sealed to many women for eternity, but a woman could be sealed to only one man for eternity. The distinction between civil and spiritual marriage produced what might be called practical polyandry— i.e., on earth there were clearly two co-existent marriages, but they were of different types. By Joseph Smith's authoritarian perspective, there was only one marriage that was "real," performed by priesthood authority—the eternal bond.

Neither of these concepts—the divine illegality of civil, sectarian marriage, and the idea of higher, spiritual "affinity" between male and female spirits (even though they may happen to be married civilly to other people)—was original to Joseph Smith, though he developed them in his idiosyncratic way. An 1868 study by William Hepworth Dixon, *Spiritual Wives*, traces the roots of "spiritual affinity" to Protestant Europe, in particular to the Swede Emanuel Swedenborg. In Joseph Smith's milieu, we find Rev. Erasmus Stone experiencing a vision of men and women in the sky looking at each other with yearning and pain; this meant, said Stone, that "in the present stage of being, men and women are nearly always wrongly paired in marriage." The people in the vision sought their spiritual mates with whom they had true "affinity," a crucial word in this tradition. Stone proceeded to find a spiritual affinity with a married woman, Eliza Porter. When true affinity is found, such love would not be limited to this life but would be eternal, and so we have a comparand to the Mormon doctrine of eternal marriage. Swedenborg also taught that spirits were matched in a pre-existent life: "Two souls which grew up together before life are bound to find each other again on earth," which foreshadows the doctrine Joseph taught Mary Elizabeth Lightner when he proposed to her.

Stone's story, like Joseph Smith's, was the product of the Burned-over District in New York, where a Protestant revival atmosphere served as a seeding ground for a great deal of religious and marital experimentation. The "Spiritual Wives" polyandrous doctrine, so foreign to twentieth-century Mormons, was part of Joseph Smith's *Zeitgeist*. Though the system was clearly subject to the danger of extremist abuse, it was developed by sincerely religious men: "The advocates of Spiritual wifehood are, and have been, for the most part ministers of the gospel, men of thought and learning," wrote Dixon.

Some historians have proposed the interpretation that Joseph either had no marital relations with his "polyandrous" wives, if the husband was faithful to the church, or that the "first husband" had no marital relations with the woman. Such a theoretical relationship has been called "pseudo-polyandry." However, the Josephine Lyon Fisher affidavit argues against this. According to Josephine, her mother Sylvia, one of Smith's polyandrous wives, "told me that I was the daughter of the Prophet Joseph Smith," she having been sealed to the Prophet at the time that her husband Mr. Lyon was out of fellowship with the Church."

Another piece of evidence used to show that polyandrous wives were married only for eternity, not for time, is the interview with Zina Huntington Jacobs, which, as we have seen, is unsatisfactory for taking either side of the argument. In the same way, Mary Elizabeth Lightner's statement that she was married to Smith for eternity (as a polyandrous wife) has been used to show that she was not married to him for time; but she elsewhere specifically and repeatedly stated that she was married to him for time and eternity. Patty Sessions, another polyandrous wife, wrote in a genealogical record that she had been married to Joseph Smith "for Eternity," but to clarify, wrote above the line, "time and all eternity." Therefore there is no good evidence that Joseph Smith did not have sexual relations with any wife, previously single or polyandrous. On the other hand, there is evidence that he did have relations with at least some of these women, including one polyandrous wife, Sylvia Sessions Lyon, who bore the only polygamous offspring of Smith for whom we have affidavit evidence.

Finally, one wonders why these "first husbands" apparently acquiesced to their wives' marriages to Smith. One possibility would be that they were promised spiritual rewards as a result of the marriages, as was the case with the families of three "single" plural wives. When Fanny Alger married Joseph, her family was proud of the sealing, according to Ann Eliza Webb. In the same way, when Sarah Whitney was sealed to the prophet, he rebaptized her parents and gave special blessings to her father, Newel Whitney. Heber C. Kimball greatly desired that his daughter

Helen should be married to the prophet so that there would be an eternal connection between the two families; Joseph himself told Helen that her marriage to him would ensure her family's salvation.

If this held true for the polyandrous families as well, including the husbands, it would explain some of the psychological dynamics of these unusual marriages. The husbands may have been promised that Smith's marriage to their wives would contribute to their own higher exaltation after this life. "Buckeye's Lament," an attack on Smith published shortly before his death, supports this interpretation: "But if you yield willingly,/ Your daughters and your wives,/ In *spiritual marriage* to our POPE,/ He'll bless you all your lives;/ He'll seal you up, be damned you can't, No matter what you do—If that you only *stick* to him,/ He swears HE'LL *take you through*." The phrase "your daughters and your wives" clearly suggests that Joseph offered salvation to "first husbands" as well as to the fathers of his brides.

It should also be borne in mind that the men and women involved in Nauvoo polygamy and polyandry did not understand it thoroughly. It was new doctrine, preached only in great secrecy, and though Smith taught polygamy to his inner circle, practical experience often differed from didactic religious doctrine. So a husband giving his wife to Joseph may not have understood fully what the marriage would entail. Helen Mar Kimball, a non-polyandrous wife, found her marriage to mean much more, on an earthly plane, than she had expected; possibly the husbands and wives in polyandrous triangles had the same experience. In Nauvoo-period theological terminology, there was some ambiguity in the terms "sealing" and "marriage," and it is possible that some men and women did not grasp that "sealing" also meant "marriage" and therefore sexual relations. It is unfortunate that we do not have a full, frank memoir from even one of the polyandrous "first husbands," although two polyandrous wives, Mary Elizabeth Lightner and Zina Huntington Jacobs, left autobiographies.

Whatever the uncertainties in documenting this aspect of Latter-day Saint practice, there is a clearly discernible outline of ideology in the historical record that explains the development and rationale for the practice of Smith's polyandry. "Gentile" (i.e., non-Mormon) marriages were "illegal," of no eternal value or even earthly validity; marriages authorized by the Mormon priesthood and prophets took precedence. Sometimes these sacred marriages were felt to fulfill pre-mortal linkings and so justified a sacred marriage superimposed over a secular one. Mormonism's intensely hierarchical nature allowed a man with the highest earthly authority—a Joseph Smith or Brigham Young—to request the wives of men holding lesser Mormon priesthood, or no priesthood. The authority of the prophet would allow him to promise higher exaltation to those involved in the triangle, both the wife and her first husband.

But with polyandry, as with the better-known polygyny, despite the elaborate doctrinal justifications, despite the reverence for a modern prophet and the unquestioning devotion to a restored biblical religion, the emotional challenges of this new marriage system must have been tremendous. In the cases of most of the polyandrous wives, the human dimensions of polyandry are not recorded; it is not even openly acknowledged. However, the wives and husbands must have felt conflicted. Puritanical New England morality and attachment to the first husband or wife undoubtedly warred with devotion to Joseph Smith, viewed as an infallible oracle of God, and to a church and community that was believed to be a restoration of primitive Christianity. Only in the marriage of Zina and Henry Jacobs, enigmatic as their relationship was, do we even have hints of the human price that Smith's polyandrous system demanded. The other polyandrous husbands and wives probably paid the same high price.

# Mormonism's First Plural Wife?

## *Fanny Alger (Smith Custer)*

In November 1836 a local judge in Wayne County, Indiana, performed a marriage of considerable significance for historians of Mormon polygamy. The clerk recorded: "Dublin November 16th, 1836 This day married by me Levi Eastridge a Justice of the Peace for Wayne County and State of Indiana Mr Solomon Custer and Miss Fanny Alger both of this town." This marriage was noteworthy because Fanny Alger was one of Joseph Smith's earliest plural wives, probably his first, but here she abandoned that sacred union for a secular marriage with a non-Mormon, leaving polygamy to embrace monogamy.

The details of Alger's courtship with and marriage to Custer are unknown, adding another puzzle to her mostly under-documented life. Yet she is important. First, she is the earliest plural wife of Smith for whom we have comparatively reliable documentation. Second, her marriage to him in Kirtland, Ohio, established a pattern that was repeated in Nauvoo, Illinois: Smith secretly marries a teenage servant or family friend living in his home, and his first wife Emma forces the young woman from the *Wow.* premises when she discovers the relationship. Third, Alger's marriage to the prophet set another pattern—that of strengthening a bond with a male friend, in this case Levi Hancock, while weakening the bond with another friend, in this case Oliver Cowdery.

We have no specific date for Alger's marriage to Smith. We have no date for her death. We know very little about her as a person except the comment of Benjamin Johnson, an early Mormon and a close friend of Smith, that she was "varry nice & comly," a young woman to whom "every one Seemed <u>partial</u> for the ameability of her character."

However, a neglected text, Mosiah Hancock's holographic autobiography, gives a valuable account of Fanny's marriage to Smith and offers a brief insight into the dynamics of her acceptance of patriarchal matrimony. The text has significance for several reasons. First, it has not been clear whether Alger's relationship was a true marriage or merely a liaison.

The Hancock text, if accepted, confirms that there was an actual, if non-traditional, wedding ceremony. It also documents a pattern that became important in later plural marriages: Smith first approaches a potential wife through one of her male relatives, thus creating a bond between Smith and the relative. The Hancock narrative is also a good example of the anthropologically interesting phenomenon known as "exchange of women." Finally, Alger's marriage reveals the extent to which women were involved in negotiating and deciding plural marriages, as the consultation with her mother and Fanny herself will show. She also exercised choice in her later marriage to Custer, which involved her rejection of Joseph Smith, plural marriage, and possibly Mormonism.

## I. The Algers

Fanny Alger was born to Samuel Alger and Clarissa Hancock Alger on September 20, 1816, in Rehoboth, Bristol, Massachusetts, just east of Providence, Rhode Island. Samuel, a thirty-year-old Massachusetts carpenter, had built a home for Heber C. Kimball's father in New York in 1810. Clarissa, twenty-six, also from Massachusetts, was a sister of Levi Hancock, who would become a stalwart Mormon, be ordained one of the presidents of the seventy in 1835, and serve as the chaplain of the Mormon Battalion. Fanny was the fourth of eleven siblings. The Algers' first five children, all born in Rehoboth, were: Eli Ward (1809), Samuel (1811), Saphony (1813), Fanny herself (1816), and Amy Saphony (1818). Samuel and Saphony died young.

The Algers moved to Lebanon Township, Ashtabula, Ohio, in the northeastern corner of the state, where John, Alva, and Samuel H. were born in 1820, 1822, and 1826. They then drifted west to the Cleveland and Kirtland area, where Thomas and Clarissa were born in Mayfield, Cuyahoga County, ten miles southwest of Kirtland, in 1828 and 1830.

That same year, in November, when Fanny was nearly fourteen, her father converted to Mormonism in Mayfield. Clarissa was evidently baptized about the same time by Parley Pratt. Thus Samuel and Clarissa were among Mormonism's early converts. It is not known when other family members were converted, except for John, Fanny's younger brother, who was baptized by her maternal uncle, Solomon Hancock, in Mayfield in March 1832.

## II. Beginnings of LDS Plurality

Approximately a year later, in early 1833, Joseph Smith, Jr., was joined to Fanny Alger in perhaps the first plural marriage in Mormon history. A number of sources, both contemporary and recollected, provide evidence that polygamy was developed and practiced in the New York and Kirtland period.

The Book of Mormon, which was translated from 1827 to 1829, deals with polygamy in Jacob 2:23-35 and has been misinterpreted as a blanket denunciation of all plural marriage. However, it condemns only unauthorized plurality, allowing for the possibility of polygamy when commanded by God: "For if I will, saith the Lord of Hosts, raise up seed unto me, I will command my people: otherwise, they shall hearken unto these things." This early statement supplies an important rationale for multiple wives: to "raise up seed" to God.

Joseph Bates Noble, who later married Smith to Louisa Beaman in the first plural marriage in Nauvoo, said that the "doctrine of celestial marriage was revealed to him [Smith] while he was engaged on the work of translation of the Scriptures," meaning Smith's "inspired revision" of the Bible. Historian Danel Bachman suggests that this occurred in February 1831. Reading about the patriarchs, especially given Smith's interest in Abraham, was a likely reason for him to begin thinking about plural marriage, a valid Christian primitivist doctrine. Perhaps it was inevitable that the Semitic custom be "restored" in a church that believed it was restoring all important ancient biblical revelation and practice. The importance polygamy was given in Mormonism is surprising, however. Smith and other nineteenth-century Mormons taught that plural marriage was necessary for complete salvation, while such a theological connection is never made in the Old Testament.

Apostle Lyman Johnson, who was the brother of one of Smith's plural wives, Marinda Johnson Hyde, told Apostle Orson Pratt that "Joseph had made known to him as early as 1831 that plural marriage was a correct principle" but "the time had not yet come to teach and practice it." Smith was living in the Johnson household while making his revision of the Old Testament, so Lyman's testimony is valuable. *flie Unto Kolob*

W. W. Phelps, in 1861, recorded that Smith received a revelation in Missouri on July 17, 1831, that directed Mormon men to intermarry with "Lamanite" (Native American) women. When Phelps later asked how the group in question, mostly married men, could take other wives, Smith immediately answered, "In the same manner that Abraham took Hagar and Keturah; that Jacob took Rachel, Bilhah, and Zilpah; by revelation—the saints of the Lord are always directed by revelations." A December 1831 letter by anti-Mormon Ezra Booth supports Phelps: "It had been made known by revelation" that God wanted "a matrimonial alliance with the natives" and that God would bless them "abundantly" if they obeyed. They would also "gain a residence" in Indian lands, despite the Indian agent's opposition. "It has been made known to one who has left his wife in the State of New York that he is entirely free from his wife, and is at pleasure to take him a wife from among the Lamanites."

Benjamin Johnson wrote: "In 1835 at Kirtland I learned from my Sisters Husband Lyman R. Shirman, who was close to the Prophet and Recieved it from him. That the ancient order of plural marriage was again to be practiced by the Church." In Nauvoo, when he helped arrange Smith's marriage to his sister Almera, Johnson was told by the prophet that the revelation on marriage had come to him in Kirtland.

Finally, in August 1835 Phelps and Oliver Cowdery, apparently, prepared an "Article on Marriage" in which they denied that the Latter-day Saint church had been practicing polygamy—a typical Mormon response to public accusations: "Inasmuch as this Church of Christ has been reproached with the crime of fornication, and polygamy, we declare that we believe that one man should have one wife, and one woman but one husband, except in case of death, when either is at liberty to marry again." This passage is certain evidence that Mormons were already beginning to be accused of the practice. Since Smith had developed a doctrine of restoration of Old Testament plural marriage by 1831, perhaps as early as 1829, a marriage to Fanny Alger in late 1832 or early 1833 would have occurred in a consistent historical context.

Fawn Brodie's 1946 biography of Smith presents his and Alger's relationship as an affair, not a marriage, and other scholars have accepted this interpretation. This position follows the earliest contemporary reference to the Smith-Alger relationship, an 1838 letter written by Oliver Cowdery at a time when he was estranged from Smith. He wrote, with vehement hyperbole, 'A dirty, nasty, filthy affair of his and Fanny Alger's was talked over in which I strictly declared that I had never deviated from the truth."

Nineteenth-century Mormons, however, regarded the Smith-Alger relationship as a marriage. Benjamin Johnson reports in his 1903 letter that church leader Heber C. Kimball once introduced an Alger family member as the brother of Smith's first plural wife. Johnson affirmed: "Without doubt in my mind Fanny Alger was at Kirtland the Prophets first plural wife." In 1890 Andrew Jenson listed her second on his tally of Smith's wives. He listed Louisa Beaman first, probably because her marriage date was solidly documented. Brodie felt that these references superimposed a later understanding of polygamy onto a sexual liaison. However, she does not mention that former Kirtland resident Chauncey Webb and his daughter Ann Eliza Webb Young, who were unsympathetic ex-Mormons, referred to the relationship as a "sealing." Ann Eliza reports that Alger's parents were proud of their connection to the prophet, which would hardly have been the case if the relationship had been merely a furtive affair.

### III. Mosiah Hancock's Autobiography

The fullest description of the Joseph Smith-Fanny Alger marriage is in the Mosiah Hancock autobiography. Mosiah, born on April 9, 1834, did not have first-hand knowledge of the marriage. But while writing his auto-biography, apparently in 1896, he reported the story as told to him by his father, Levi Hancock. Fanny was Levi's niece and Mosiah's first cousin.

The text is a late reminiscence, so the question of reliability is impor-tant. Mosiah Hancock, who lived to be seventy-three, placed his autobiog-raphy in the LDS church historical department in 1896. He tells the Fanny Alger stories as a continuation of his father's autobiography, which breaks off virtually in mid-sentence. Thus, on the negative side, the document is late and one step removed from its source. However, on the positive side, it approaches the atmosphere of an oral history, with Mosiah reporting his father's words. And because of the secrecy surrounding early polyg-amy, autobiographical accounts are often more useful than contemporary diaries. For example, Eliza R. Snow's diary contains only an oblique refer-ence to her wedding to Smith on June 29, 1842, but in her autobiography she dates the marriage and explains her inner conversion to polygamy. Zina Huntington's Nauvoo diary never mentions her marriage to Smith, though her autobiography tells the story of their union.

Furthermore, Mosiah's autobiography has the credibility of access. Levi was close to the Alger family, was in Kirtland in 1832 and 1833, and was a friend of Joseph Smith. If Mosiah Hancock is trustworthy, he heard the story directly from the man who performed the wedding of Fanny and Joseph. Mosiah explains his motive as simply to "bear testimony":

> Concerning the doctrine of celestial marriage the Prophet told my father in the days of Kirtland, that it was the will of the Lord for His servants who were faithful to step forth in that order ... My father made some things known to me concerning those days, and the part he took with the Prophet in trying to assist him to start the principle with a few chosen friends in those days. My father had required of me to bear testimony of these things at a proper time.

Mosiah's first-hand reminiscences are admittedly subject to the strengths and weaknesses generally found in Mormon and other autobiog-raphies: inaccuracies in dates, misremembered events, an easy willing-ness to accept the miraculous, and a tendency to overidealize oneself or a hero such as Joseph Smith. Nevertheless, I accept it as generally reliable, providing accurate information about his own life, his family's life, and Mormonism in Kirtland, Nauvoo, and Salt Lake City.

The validity of Mosiah's narrative can be corroborated from other sources, as can be seen in the story of the first performance of his father Levi's song, "The Independence of the United States." Mosiah writes, "We went up to Farwest to spend the fourth of July and early on the morning of the fourth Brother Joseph came along and said 'Brother Levi Can you make us a song to day and call it the Independence of the United States?['] Yes said Father and by ten o clock he had it ready and He and Uncle Solomon stood on the corner Stone of the Temple and sung Solomon the air [melody] Father the Bass." Mosiah was only four when this event occurred, so one can reasonably doubt that it is based exclusively on his memory. The details probably constituted a family story, a cherished memory of the prophet Joseph Smith, which is corroborated in the *History of the Church*. This states that on July 4, 1838, the cornerstones of the temple at Far West were laid; Sidney Rigdon delivered an oration, there was a Hosanna shout, then "a song, composed for the occasion by Levi W. Hancock, was sung by Solomon Hancock." Portions of sources for the *History of the Church* were published before the history first began to appear in 1902, but Hancock's account adds convincing anecdotal details not found elsewhere, such as Smith asking Levi to write the song, Levi singing the bass to Solomon's lead, and the two men standing and singing on a cornerstone.

In another example from Missouri, Hancock writes that when mobocracy was reigning, "Soon Joseph Holbrook was brought to our house cut to pieces and in a low state my Mother nursed him untill he was taken away." Other sources, including Holbrook's own autobiography, confirm that he was wounded in the Battle of Crooked River. He writes: "I was wounded in my left elbow with a sword after cutting through five thicknesses of cloth. [It] so fractured the bone that after the doctor had placed back the bones, it was very lame for some four months and so stiff that I could not feed myself with that hand." Nancy Tracy confirms that Holbrook underwent a long convalescence: "The brethren that were in the battle of Crooked River had all left for parts unknown except my husband and Brother Holbrook. Brother Holbrook had been wounded in the fight, but he played he was a sick woman in bed so nicely that he was not detected although the house was searched well."

Some details in Mosiah Hancock's narrative are supported by his father's autobiography. Mosiah had access to this document, but his own record is far from a simple mirroring of its events. He wrote: "Clarissa Reed [Mosiah's future mother] being in poor health Father takes her to his folks in Rome [Ohio, about twenty miles east of Kirtland] – The reason of mother's poor health was this She worked hard at the Prophets." This event is written on the page after his father's account of the Smith-Alger marriage, and it is corroborated by Levi's autobiography: "About this time Joseph Called on me to go to Rome with a hired girl by the name of Clarrisa Reed who had been living with him I went and returned with her in two weeks." Levi does not give a reason for the trip beyond Smith's request, but Mosiah does.

Later in his narrative Mosiah tells how his father was sent as the spiritual leader of the Mormon Battalion, which is widely documented. The Hancock family remained in Winter Quarters, Nebraska, living near a Sister Sprague. "The two Mothers [Clarissa and Sister Sprague] and Grandmother Reed put their wits together and conclude to send Ellen Sprague and I to the Indian Mill on Big Musquitio Creek to see if our Mothers could get employment to teach the halfbreed children." These geographical details are supported by the autobiography of Esaias Edwards, who wrote that he settled in Winter Quarters "on the Putawatomie lands near the Missouri River ... My location was on what was called Little Murketoe Creek, about 1 1/2 miles from the Indian Mill." "Murketoe" is a slight degeneration of "Musketoe," but "Indian Mill" is exact. Edwards confirms the Native American population in the area.

Another example of Mosiah's reliability is a convincing account of his parents' divorce in Utah, an event that Mosiah found painful: "Brother Brigham asked her wat [sic] charge She could bring against Brother Levi Nothing She said only she was deprived of his company."

One can also assess the accuracy of Mosiah's Fanny Alger narrative on its own terms. If it is implausible and unparalleled in every detail, one could be justified in rejecting it. However, it closely parallels Smith's practices in Nauvoo, yet has unique elements that do not appear to be derivative. Thus it has internal credibility. In brief, though one should regard this narrative with the same caution that any historical document deserves, there is no reason to reject it wholesale. At the very least, it deserves serious consideration.

### IV. "Successful in My Mission"

According to Mosiah Hancock, Joseph Smith introduced his father Levi to polygamy in spring 1832:

> As early as Spring of 1832 Bro Joseph said "Brother Levi, the Lord has revealed to me that it is his will that righteous men shall take Righteous women even a plurality of Wives that a Righteous race may be sent forth uppon the Earth preparatory to the ushering in of the Millenial Reign of our Redeemer – For the Lord has such a high respect for the nobles of his kingdom that he is not willing for them to come through the Loins of a Careles People – Therefore; it behoves those who embrace that Principle to pay strict atention to even the Least requirement of our Heavenly Father."

Levi, twenty-nine years old at the time, soon afterwards became en-

gaged to Temperance Jane Miller and left on a mission. But he soon felt
guilty that he had not reported the engagement to Smith. "When My Father had started on his first mission to preach this Gospel He felt that
perhaps he had done wrong in not telling the Prophet that he had made
arrangements to marry Temperance Jane Miller of New Lyme — When
Father returned from his mission he spoke to the Prophet concerning
the matter The Prophet said. 'Never mind Brother Levi about that for the
Lord has one prepared for you that will be a Blessing to you forever' —."
Levi apparently broke off the engagement to Temperance, which, with
his feeling that Smith should be consulted about the engagement, shows
the extent of his deference to Smith's prophetic counsel.

Meanwhile, seventeen-year-old Clarissa Reed, who had been a hired
girl in Smith's home, "told the Prophet She loved brother Levi Hancock
The Prophet had the highest respect for her feelings She had thought
that perhaps she might be one of the Prophet's wives as herself and Sister Emma were on the best of terms. My Father [Levi] and Mother
[Clarissa,] understanding each other[,] were inspired by the spirit of the
Lord to respect His word, through the Prophet."

The statement that the couple understood each other apparently indicates their mutual affection. Still they felt that they should first receive
Smith's approval for their marriage:

> Therefore Brother Joseph said ["]Brother Levi I want to make a bargain
> with you — If you will get Fanny Alger for me for a wife you may have
> Clarissa Reed. I love Fanny" "I will" Said Father. "Go brother Levi and
> the Lord will prosper you" Said Joseph — Father goes to the Father Sa-
> muel Alger — his Father's Brother in Law and [said] "Samuel[,] the
> Prophet Joseph loves your Daughter Fanny and wishes her for a wife
> what say you" — Uncle Sam Says — "Go and talk to the Old woman about
> it twill be as She says" Father goes to his Sister and said "Clarissy,
> Brother Joseph the Prophet of the most high God loves Fanny and
> wishes her for a wife what say you" Said She "go and talk to Fanny it will
> be all right with me" — Father goes to Fanny and said "Fanny Brother
> Joseph the Prophet loves you and wishes you for a wife will you be his
> wife?" "I will Levi" Said She — Father takes Fanny to Joseph and said
> "Brother Joseph I have been successful in my mission" — Father gave her
> to Joseph repeating the Ceremony as Joseph repeated to him.

There is much to comment on in this extraordinary passage. Very
prominent is the theme of exchange of women, which anthropologists
have noted in many cultures. The polygamous marriage proposal is indi-
rect, a remarkable combination of the romantic and the non-romantic. "I
love Fanny," Smith tells Hancock, yet he does not profess his love to
Fanny face to face. He uses an intermediary, a male relative, to propose

32

to her. Despite the indirection, this is entirely consistent with Smith's later method of approaching prospective plural wives in Nauvoo. For instance, his final proposal to Zina Huntington came through a male family member, her brother Dimick. Smith also proposed to Almera Johnson through her brother Benjamin. According to Knight family traditions, Smith himself brought a proposal from Hyrum Smith to Martha McBride Knight, Joseph's plural wife at the time, asking for the hand of her daughter, Almira, for Hyrum.

Samuel Alger, Levi's brother-in-law and Fanny's father, was the logical person to speak with in a patriarchal culture. But, surprisingly, instead of giving permission flatly, he deferred to his wife, Clarissa Hancock Alger, Levi's sister. Clarissa told Levi to ask Fanny herself and Fanny agreed to marry Smith. She was not forced into the marriage.

Having obtained his niece for Joseph, Levi escorted her to the prophet, and a marriage ceremony took place. Mosiah's narrative, if accepted, thus negates interpretations of a liaison. Joseph Smith dictated the marriage vows to Levi, who repeated them to the couple. An exact parallel occurred in Nauvoo when Louisa Beaman married Smith, a rite performed by Joseph Bates Noble, a brother-in-law of Louisa: "The Prophet gave the form of the ceremony, Elder Noble repeating the words after him."

Levi Hancock received his reward. Smith sanctioned his marriage to Clarissa Reed, which took place on March 29, 1833. Mosiah's narrative suggests that the Smith-Alger marriage occurred first, so Joseph probably married Fanny in February or March 1833, when she was sixteen and he was twenty-seven.

Again, Nauvoo plural marriages would show a similar pattern of "rewards" for those who helped solemnize Smith's marriages. Joseph Bates Noble and Brigham Young were granted plural wives, and others, such as Cornelius Lott and Newel Whitney, were sealed to their existing spouses in eternal marriage. Such relationships also provided powerful stimuli to keep the secret. Noble, by taking a plural wife after marrying Smith to his sister-in-law, became part of polygamy's inner circle, committed to its goals but vulnerable to its consequences if discovered. In addition, the promise of salvation, which was often linked to plural marriage, was further motivation. It is significant that the Alger parents felt it a spiritual honor to have their daughter married to Smith, just as the parents of Sarah Ann Whitney and Helen Mar Kimball did. Fanny Alger's marriage created a dynastic link not only between Smith and Hancock but between Smith and Fanny's parents. Smith may also have felt that a woman would probably have been less likely to refuse a polygamous proposal if it came through a close relative rather than from the polygamous suitor himself.

## V. Fanny and Emma

Another view of the Smith-Alger marriage is given by Ann Eliza Webb Young, the woman who divorced Brigham Young then wrote an exposé of polygamy. Though she was antagonistic when she wrote this account, and it was written comparatively late, her parents were eyewitnesses to the later part of the Alger-Smith story and it seems to be written without excessive rancor: "Mrs. Smith had an adopted daughter, a very pretty, pleasing young girl, about seventeen years old. She was extremely fond of her; no own mother could be more devoted, and their affection for each other was a constant object of remark, so absorbing and genuine did it seem." Fanny was probably living with the Smiths as a hired girl or live-in maid, a common occurrence in America at the time. She would have turned eighteen in September 1834, and Joseph would have been twenty-eight.

Ann Eliza continues: "Consequently it was with a shocked surprise that the people heard that sister Emma had turned Fanny out of the house in the night. ... it was felt that she [Emma] certainly must have had some very good reason for her action. By degrees it became whispered about that Joseph's love for his adopted daughter was by no means a paternal affection, and his wife, discovering the fact, at once took measures to place the girl beyond his reach." This same pattern was repeated when the Partridge sisters, hired girls in Joseph's home in Nauvoo, secretly married him and then were expelled by Emma; the latter also reportedly drove Eliza Snow suddenly from her house.

According to Ann Eliza Young, there was a fierce argument between Emma and Joseph, and he sent for Oliver Cowdery to help resolve the dispute. Young portrays Cowdery himself as a practicing polygamist (which is probably incorrect) and therefore he and Joseph were worried that a public scandal would expose plural marriage: "The worthy couple—the Prophet and his scribe—were sorely perplexed what to do with the girl, since Emma refused decidedly to allow her to remain in her house; but after some consultation, my mother offered to take her until she could be sent to her relatives," who were presumably still living in Mayfield.

Ann Eliza continues: "Although her parents were living, they considered it the highest honor to have their daughter adopted into the prophet's family, and her mother has always claimed that she [Fanny] was sealed to Joseph at that time." The use of the term "sealed" is somewhat anachronistic but confirms that the parents accepted the relationship as a marriage.

Ann Eliza's father, Chauncey Webb, gives another account of how Emma discovered the marriage: "He [Joseph Smith] was sealed there [in

Kirtland] secretly to Fanny Alger. Emma was furious, and drove the girl, who was unable to conceal the consequences of her celestial relation with the prophet, out of her house." Again an unsympathetic voice refers to the relationship as a marriage, a sealing. In addition, Webb acknowledges that this was a fully sexual union. Since there is no record of Fanny having a child, either Webb was mistaken (though this seems unlikely, if Fanny lived in his home after leaving the Smith home), the child was miscarried or died young, or it was raised under another name. Without further documentation, there is no way of knowing.

In an 1872 letter to Joseph Smith III, William McLellin wrote: "Again I told her [Emma] I heard that one night she missed Joseph and Fanny Alger. She went to the barn and saw him and Fanny in the barn together alone. She looked through a crack and saw the transaction!! She told me this story too was verily true." As this account contradicts Webb's and later statements on polygamy by Emma, it is possible that McLellin, or Emma, "bent" the truth in this case. I see Webb's statement as more primary and consistent than McLellin's. But whether Emma saw her husband in the barn or discovered evidence of Fanny's pregnancy, her reaction was the same.

Benjamin Johnson, a third major witness to the Fanny Alger marriage, reports that she was "A verry nice & Comly young woman about my own age ... and it was whisperd eaven then [1835] that Joseph Loved her." He also tells a story of Joseph and Fanny being "spied upon," though Emma does not appear in his version:

> and then [after the rumors] there was Some trouble with Oliver Cowdery. and whisper Said it was Relating to a girl then living in his [Smith's] Family And I was afterwords told by Warren Parish that he himself & Oliver Cowdery did know that Joseph had Fanny Alger as a wife for They ware Spied upon & found togather — And I Can now See that as at Nauvoo — So at Kirtland That the Suspicion or Knowledge of the Prophets Plural Relation was one of the Causes of Apostacy & disruption at Kirtland altho at the time there was little Said publickly upon the Subject.

As noted, Joseph apparently married Fanny in February or March 1833. From this point on, dates become fluid, the next firm event being the Alger family's departure from Kirtland in September 1836, three and a half years later. If one hypothesizes that Fanny became pregnant, the discovery could have occurred at almost any point, possibly within a few weeks, if she were ill, or as much as four or even five months later. We know that Joseph asked Oliver Cowdery to help calm Emma; whatever his success, she would not allow Fanny back in the house. The Webbs accommodated Fanny for a few weeks, presumably until she could move back to her parents in Mayfield, while Joseph's only mention of people leaving his home was on October 17, 1835, when he "called my family together aranged my domestick concerns and dismissed my boarders."

Historian Richard Van Wagoner presents the following attractive scenario, which suggests an August 1835 departure date for Fanny. He has Cowdery recommending that Joseph leave Kirtland for a time after the flareup with Emma. Smith took a trip to Michigan with Frederick Williams in August, and on the 17th the "Article on Marriage," which denied polygamy, was presented to and accepted by the church in Smith's absence. Clearly the statement represented an effort to counteract scandal and perhaps to defuse rumors of Fanny Alger's marriage, possible pregnancy, and expulsion. Smith returned to Kirtland on August 23.

### VI. In the Kirtland Temple

Mosiah Hancock reports a final episode involving Fanny Alger, Smith, and his father:

> As time progressed the Apostates thought they had a good hold on Joseph because of Fanny and some of the smart? ones Confined her in an upper room of the Temple determined that the Prophet should be settled, according to their notions. Brother Joseph came to Father and said "Brother Levi what can be done?" — There being a wagon and a dry goods Box close by and Joseph being strong and Father active Father soon gained the window Sill and Fanny was soon on the ground Father mounts his horse with Fanny behind him and altho dark they were in New Lyme fortyfive miles distant — And when the worthies? sent Fannys dinner the next day they were astonished not to be able to find her — Father by that time had returned and his animal was in the Stable.

Although Mosiah doubtless heard this dashing story from his father, it is more problematic than his account of the marriage. Still it can be roughly tested by related events. The Algers, with Fanny, left Kirtland for Missouri in September 1836. The second floor of the Kirtland temple had been completed at least by July 1835, when the roof was covered. The building was dedicated on March 27, 1836, and thereafter was used as a meeting-house and school. So, if this event occurred, it must have happened between the summer of 1835 and September 1836.

Probably the best context for the story is an ecclesiastical meeting in which leading church members opposed to Smith, possibly Cowdery and Warren Parrish, intended to have Alger testify about her relationship with him. She would have been brought in from Mayfield and asked to wait in the temple where the meeting would occur. Smith would not have wanted her to testify, but he did not want to appear to be preventing her either, so he asked for Levi's help in removing her from the temple. Benjamin Winchester mentions a scandal involving Smith, his involvement with a woman or women, and Smith proclaiming in the temple that since he had been called to establish God's kingdom on earth the members of the church had no right to question what he did. As a result, a number of people left Mormonism in the summer of 1836, as Winchester dates it.

As Mormons prepared to leave Kirtland, Smith still continued to take an interest in Alger, for in 1836 he asked Levi Hancock to take her to Missouri with his family. Hancock wrote: "about this time I received a letter from Solomon he said he ... was going to Misouri I saw Joseph Smith he told me to take fanny Alger and go ... we started the latter part of August for his [Solomon Hancock's] fatherinLaw and got there about the first of Sept 1836." Despite Smith's instructions, Fanny apparently decided to go to Missouri with her own family, not with Hancock. Benjamin Johnson, though he misdated the Alger family's departure, wrote, "Soon after the Prophet['s] flight in the winter of [18]37 x 8 The Alger Family left for the west and Stoping in Indiana for a time." The Samuel Alger obituary places the family's departure from Kirtland a year earlier, in September 1836, but it notes that they stayed in Wayne County, Indiana, for a year because of bad roads, which explains the discrepancy. They started for Missouri again the following September. Fanny, however, according to Johnson, "Soon Married to one of the Citizens ther [Indiana] & altho she never left the State She did not turn from the Church nor from her friendship for the Prophet while She lived."

The 1836 departure date for the Algers is verified by the marriage certificate discussed above. One can only speculate on Fanny's motives for marrying a non-Mormon, after a courtship that could have only been a matter of weeks. Perhaps she felt that Smith had abandoned her after Emma ejected her from the household. It is also possible that she simply fell in love with Solomon, who, unlike Smith, was her own age—nineteen.

In any event, the Alger family left Fanny and Solomon in Indiana and traveled to Randolph County, Missouri, in September 1837, moving to Illinois with the rest of the Mormons in February 1839. There the Algers lived in Quincy for eight months before moving to Bear Creek (Lima), where they then lived for a number of years.

Meanwhile Cowdery and Smith became increasingly estranged in 1837 and early 1838. Smith's relationship with Alger seems to have been a major issue in their conflict, which strengthens the hypothesis that Cowdery never practiced polygamy. Cowdery played a prominent role in trying to resolve the conflict involving Joseph, Fanny, and Emma; according to Johnson, he was a shocked eyewitness with Parrish of Smith's sexual relations with Fanny. In the summer of 1837 Apostle David Patten asked Cowdery: "if he Joseph Smith jr had confessed to his wife that he was guilty of adultery with a certain girl, when Cowdery cocked up his eye very knowingly, and hesitated to answer the question, saying he did not know as he was bound to answer the question yet conveyed the idea that it was true." Patten testified that he then asked Cowdery directly if: "a certain story was true respecting J. Smith's committing adultery with a certain girl, when he turned on his heel and insinuated as though he was guilty; he then went on and gave a history of some circumstances respecting the adultery scrape stating that no doubt it was true. Also said that Joseph told him, he had confessed to Emma." Though Oliver had assisted in counteracting the Smith-Alger crisis by helping to introduce the Article on Marriage, the circumstantial evidence is strong that Cowdery's respect for Joseph diminished after that point. This reaction would be understandable if Cowdery knew nothing of polygamy until he was confronted with a double offense: Joseph's behavior with Fanny and his possible mishandling of the domestic crisis with Emma. In contrast, Levi Hancock, involved at the beginning of the marriage, would have had a different perception of it.

If Cowdery allowed his statements and insinuations to circulate, Smith's anger becomes understandable—especially if he viewed his relationship with Alger as a marriage sanctioned by God. A confrontation apparently took place on November 6, 1837, in Far West. Apostle Thomas Marsh, in an affidavit-letter dated February 15, 1838, wrote: "I heard Oliver Cowdery say to Joseph Smith, Jr., while at George W. Harris' house, in Far West, that he (Joseph) never confessed to him, (Oliver) that he was guilty of the crime alledged to him [adultery]. And O. Cowdery gave me to understand that Joseph Smith Jr. never acknowledged to him, that he [Smith] ever confessed to any one, that he [Smith] was guilty of the above crime [adultery]." However, Harris, in Cowdery's excommunication trial, apparently refers to this same occasion, when "a conversation took place between Joseph Smith jr & Oliver Cowdery, when he [Cowdery] seemed to insinuate that Joseph Smith jr was guilty of adultery." But, says Harris, when Cowdery was asked if Smith had ever "acknowledged to him [Cowdery] that he was guilty of such a thing," Cowdery answered "No."

We see Cowdery's perspective in a January 21, 1838, letter to his brother, Warren, in which he vehemently denied that he had ever lied or admitted lying about Fanny Alger. He describes a meeting with Smith before witnesses (possibly the meeting at Far West), in which "in every instance I did not fail to affirm that what I had said was strictly true. A dirty, nasty, filthy affair of his and Fanny Alger's was talked over in which I strictly declared that I never deviated from the truth." The meeting ended with Smith wanting "to drop every past thing, in which [there] had been a difficulty or difference – he called witnesses to the fact, gave me his hand in their presence, and I might have supposed of an honest man, calculated to say nothing of former matters."

The tone of Cowdery's letter shows that the reconciliation did not last. He was tried for his membership on April 12, 1838, at Far West, and six of nine charges brought against him were sustained; he was excommunicated. One of the charges was: "For seeking to destroy the character of President Joseph Smith, Jun., by falsely insinuating that he was guilty of adultry." Certainly other factors were important in the excommunication, but the issue of adultery was crucial. Cowdery criticized the church for "endeavoring to make it a rule of faith for said church to uphold a certain man or men right or wrong."

Cowdery had been the scribe of the Book of Mormon, one of the three witnesses to its divinity, and a recipient with Smith of the Aaronic and Melchizedek priesthoods in reported angelic manifestations, so his excommunication was indeed a severe loss to the church. According to Benjamin Johnson, "as at Nauvoo – So at Kirtland That the Suspician or Knowledge of the Prophets Plural Relation was one of the Causes of Apostacy & disruption at Kirtland." Johnson links Jared Carter and Warren Parrish with Cowdery in this context as men who "ware not justifide of the Lord Either in there Criticisms upon the doings of the Prophet or in there becoming a 'Law unto themselves' Through which they lost the Light of there callings & ware left in Darkness." Parrish, formerly Smith's secretary, led a splinter group so influential that it gained partial control of the Kirtland temple and helped force church leaders out of the city. Jared Carter, a high councilor, was tried before a church court on September 16, 1835, for "rebelling against the advice and counsel" of the First Presidency and "erring in judgment." Apparently he wanted another wife (polygamous), and had built a house for her, but Smith would not allow it. Unlike the other two, Carter confessed and was forgiven.

*Polygamy finally did lead to Smith's death.*

The parallels in Nauvoo are clear. In 1843 and 1844 the dissent over polygamy intensified until it became a major contributor to the events that led to the deaths of Joseph and Hyrum Smith. William Law, of the First Presidency, and Austin Cowles, a counselor in the powerful Nauvoo Stake, both left the church to publish the *Nauvoo Expositor*, dedicated in part to publicizing Smith's extramonogamous activities. Smith's infallibility was an important issue, and polygamy was seen as evidence against it. Even in this aspect, the marriage of Smith and Alger was a troubling precursor to the future. *Yes. Fascinating*

## VII. Grocer's Wife

The rest of Fanny Alger's life can be reconstructed only in barest outline. According to her husband's obituary, the couple had nine children, although the names of only five appear in census records. In approximately 1840, when she was twenty-three, her first child by Solomon, Mary A. Custer, was born in Indiana, probably in Dublin, followed by Lewis A. Custer in approximately 1844.

It is possible that Fanny lived in Illinois at some point. When the Lima branch of the LDS church was organized on October 23, 1842, the Alger family is listed, and "Fanny Custer" is included. This may only have been a visit, as Solomon is not listed and Benjamin Johnson maintains that Fanny never stopped living in Indiana.

Joseph Smith died on June 27, 1844, and Benjamin Johnson writes that after his death, Fanny was questioned by one of her brothers about her relationship with the dead prophet. She replied, "That is all a matter of my – own. and I have nothing to Comunicate." After this sphinx-like statement, Fanny disappears entirely from the Latter-day Saint historical record. The rest of the Alger family moved to Nauvoo in the fall of 1845, and in May 1846 left Nauvoo for the west. Fanny would be separated from them now by the great wilderness. Her mother and father died in 1870 and 1874 in southern Utah.

More children joined the Custer family. Sophrona Allis was born in approximately 1848, Benjamin Franklin in approximately 1849, and finally Lafayette in approximately 1854, when Fanny was thirty-seven. At that time Mary was fourteen, Lewis ten, Sophrona six, and Benjamin five.

In the 1850 census, Solomon Custer, age thirty-two, is described as a "Laborer." Fanny's name and birthday are not precise—she is "Francis Custer," age thirty-one. Actually, she would have been thirty-three. At the time of the 1860 census, the Custers were still in Dublin. Solomon, age forty-three, was now a "Grocer," with real estate valued at $600 and a personal estate valued at $500. Living with him were "Fanny," forty-two years old; Lewis, sixteen; Allis, twelve; [Benjamin] Franklin, ten; Lafayette, six; and Sarah Seamon, sixteen, whose job is "House Work." Mary Custer had left home, perhaps married, and Fanny may have been a grandmother by this time. Another source describes Solomon as a "Baker" in 1859 and a "Merchant" in 1865. An anecdote by one of Fanny's grandchildren shows what kind of merchant Solomon was: "Like other grocerymen, Solomon had loafers around the stove. In those days people browned their coffee from green coffee beans. The beans came in large bags, which were used as seats by the loafers. Grandpa spied one of the loafers stealing coffee beans from a small hole torn in the bag, and when the culprit denied the act Grandpa bounched a chair off his noggin. That broke up the coffee stealing."

In 1870 the Custer family was not listed in the Indiana census, for unknown reasons. In 1880 they were still in Dublin, and all their children had left home, though a grandchild lived with them. Solomon was sixty-three; "Custer, Fanny W" was the same age; and the granddaughter ("G.D."), "Vickers, Ethel," born in Indiana, was five years old.

Solomon died of "typhoid pneumonia" on March 27, 1885. "His wife and three children, out of nine, survive him," according to his obituary. Fanny had buried six of her nine children. The only clue to the family's religion is that Solomon's "Funeral discourse [was] by Rev. Guthrie at the Universalist church, which was crowded to its utmost ... Being a Mason, his funeral rites were conducted by members from the lodges of Milton, Cambridge City and Dublin." There is no 1890 census, and Fanny cannot be found in the 1900 census. Either she had moved or died. She lived at least to the age of sixty-eight.

Thus for more than forty years the prophet's first polygamous wife lived as a non-Mormon, raising a family of five with a secular, patriotic husband who named his sons after Franklin and Lafayette. Despite her important role in initiating the era of Mormon polygamy, in the latter part of her life she lived the quiet, uneventful, stationary existence of a monogamous mother and grandmother.

## VIII. Exchange of Women

Though the Mosiah Hancock account (if accepted) elevates the Smith-Alger relationship from the status of a casual sexual liaison and affirms Smith's early absorption with a new order of marriage, it nevertheless raises problems of its own. Perhaps most troublesome from a modern perspective is its "exchange of women" theme. Smith offers Clarissa Reed to Levi Hancock in exchange for Fanny, Levi's niece, commissioning Levi to obtain Fanny for him. Levi considers this assignment a "mission," brings Fanny to Joseph, and is "given" Clarissa.

Feminist historian Gerda Lerner, referring to anthropologist Claude Levi-Strauss, writes that the "exchange of women," which is common in tribal societies, was "the leading cause of female subordination" in human history, and she makes theoretical reconstructions from prehistory. Women are indoctrinated from childhood to accept such arranged marriages as necessary for the benefit of their family and tribe. Levi-Strauss writes: "The total relationship of exchange which constitutes marriage is not established between a man and a woman ... but between two groups of men, and the woman figures only as one of the objects in the exchange, not as one of the partners." Even if the daughter is allowed to accept or reject the proposed marriage, she is not allowed to suggest her own possible husband. In many cultures the woman is not allowed to reject the husband her father has arranged for her.

Within this theme, the Hancock/Alger story offers some striking points of comparison and contrast. Smith and Hancock both act as "fathers"—Smith for Clarissa and Hancock for Fanny. Levi arranges the marriage with Fanny's family, and the women are exchanged. Joseph's and Levi's mutual success strengthens the bond between them. It is a good example of what Lerner calls the "commodification" of women.

Yet this story is not a simple patriarchal exchange of treaty "commodities." Levi and Clarissa feel mutual affection, and Joseph's "bestowal" of Clarissa on Levi is in accordance with her own wish. Furthermore, and most interestingly, when Levi approaches his brother-in-law, Samuel, Samuel defers to his wife, who in turn refers Levi to Fanny. The dual transaction thus hinges on Fanny's choice.

This still leaves unanswered the question of why Fanny agreed to the marriage. Mosiah says that Joseph "loved" her. One wonders how such a relation developed. Had he and she spent time alone together? Did Fanny in fact reciprocate Smith's feelings and choose him freely, or did she accept his proposal because, like Zina Huntington in Nauvoo, she regarded him as a prophet and feared to disobey divine revelation?

Historical documents also give no evidence as to what might have happened if Fanny had rejected the proposal. Would Joseph, Levi, Samuel, and Clarissa have pressured her to accept the marriage, as Helen Mar Kimball and Lucy Walker were pressured in Nauvoo? Would Joseph have forbidden Levi's and Clarissa's marriage if the uncle had not brought his niece back? Though Fanny accepted Smith's proposal in 1833, in 1836 she rejected him, the physical community of Mormonism, the geographical Zion that was a central tenet of the nineteenth-century faith, even though the choice involved separation from her family. One can only ask questions: Had she had become disillusioned with Smith's doctrine or practice of polygamy? If she had been in love with Joseph, was she now? How did the experience of being expelled from the Smith home, and possibly of being considered an unwed mother, affect her emotionally? She made a choice, even though her motives remain obscure and social structures worked against her complete freedom. Modern Latter-day Saints who are uncomfortable with polygamy may debate whether Fanny's choice was right or wrong.

## 2.

# Wife of Two Martyrs

## *Lucinda Pendleton (Morgan Harris Smith)*

In mid-June 1844 a non-Mormon journalist, B. W. Richmond, checked into the Nauvoo House, Joseph Smith's hotel, to write a story on the perpetually odd and controversial Mormons. He found he had arrived at a particularly stormy time, as Smith had been arrested and jailed by non-Mormons and would soon stand trial for treason. The Mormons were out-raged, while outsiders wanted blood. In his first few days at Nauvoo, Rich-mond stumbled upon a striking human-interest story: living in Nauvoo, as a Mormon, was Lucinda Pendleton Morgan Harris, the widow of William Morgan, the anti-masonic martyr, the man who had been kidnapped and apparently murdered just before he was to print an exposé on Masonry. Lucinda had become famous as Morgan's bereaved young widow left with two small children. Richmond called on Lucinda and asked about her late husband. She showed him a book which had Morgan's likeness in it—if the mob attacked Nauvoo, she said, she would take the book with her, no matter the cost.

A few days later there was another important martyrdom in American history: Joseph Smith was killed by a lynch mob in nearby Carthage, Illi-nois, along with his older brother Hyrum, and Richmond was present when the bodies were brought back to Nauvoo. He reported that widows Emma Smith and Mary Fielding Smith grieved over their dead husbands. But he was startled when he also noticed "a lady standing at the head of Joseph Smith's body, her face covered, and her whole frame convulsed with weeping." It was Lucinda Harris, grieving again, as she had years ear-lier when Morgan died. What Richmond could not have known was that Lucinda was once again grieving over a murdered husband.

"Lucinda Harris" is the third woman on Andrew Jenson's list of Joseph Smith's plural wives, though Jenson gives no date for the marriage and his source is not specified. In addition to this sympathetic attestation, the antagonistic Sarah Pratt reported that while in Nauvoo Lucinda had admitted a long-standing relationship with Smith. It is well-documented

43

that he stayed with the Harrises in 1838, and the Pratt reference concurs with this date. These data, along with an early Nauvoo temple proxy sealing to Smith and other corroborating details lead to the conclusion that Lucinda in fact married Smith, possibly in 1838. It is certain that it would have been a polyandrous arrangement, as she married George Washington Harris in 1830 and continued to live with him until approximately 1853. Harris was a typical "first husband": far from faithless, he was an active, prominent Mormon, a high councilor in Missouri, Illinois, and Nebraska.

Thus Lucinda lived an extraordinary life, having been married to two prominent figures in nineteenth-century American history: Joseph Smith, founding prophet of Mormonism, and William Morgan, forerunner to the anti-Masonic political movement. After experiencing traumatic bereavement twice, she eventually left her second husband, Harris, and little is known of her later life.

## I. William Morgan

Lucinda was born on September 27, 1801, in Washington County, Virginia, to Joseph Pendleton and Betsey Riley. Joseph was a planter and reportedly a Methodist clergyman of some sort. One writer described Lucinda as the Pendletons' oldest daughter. She had at least three sisters, for whom she did vicarious baptisms for the dead in Nauvoo: Eleanor, Elizabeth, and King Axley, and she may have had other siblings, as well. A description of her from the Nauvoo period, when she was forty-two, portrayed her as "a short person, with light hair and very bright blue eyes, and a pleasing countenance." If she was attractive in 1844, she might have been beautiful in early womanhood.

Lucinda enters history at the time of her marriage to Captain William Morgan on October 7, 1819. A Rev. Thomas Colby performed the ceremony in Washington County, Virginia, and according to one source, her father opposed the marriage. This was possibly because Morgan, who was a native of Virginia, was forty-five years old in 1845, while Lucinda was eighteen. William worked as a Richmond stone mason and a trader, stood five feet eight inches, and had a short nose and double chin. Because of his historical importance as an "anti-Masonic martyr," his personal life was subsequently vilified and defended. Masons allege that his business dealings were suspect and that he was an alcoholic, while anti-Masons assert that he drank no more than anyone else.

In the fall of 1821 the Morgans moved to Canada, where William was associated in some way with a brewery near Toronto. When it burned down, however, he and Lucinda moved to New York, where he "clerked" in Niagara County. By 1823 he was a stone mason in Rochester, then in Le Roy, twenty miles to the southwest and some twenty miles northwest of Palmyra, which is where the Joseph Smith family was residing. On August 23, 1824, Lucinda had her first child, Lucinda Wesley, at Rochester.

A half year later Morgan's involvement with Masonry begins to be documented. In May 1825 he received a York Rite degree and was initiated as a Royal Arch Mason in Western Star Chapter 33 at LeRoy. He and Lucinda and their little daughter eventually moved to Batavia, Genesee County, New York, midway between Rochester and Buffalo. According to Masonic sources, which must be viewed with caution, everywhere he went he accumulated debts and drank heavily.

Sometime in the year following his initiation at LeRoy, William signed a petition calling for another chapter of Masons to be established in Batavia. But one of the fraternity drew a line through his name, either because he had a reputation for drinking or for some unknown offense. Morgan was infuriated, and in March 1826 a printer named Miller and a Mr. Dyer drew up a partnership with him to print an exposé of Masonic ritual. As all Masons take an oath when initiated never to reveal the ritual on pain of death, this was a dangerous project.

Morgan continued to attend Masonic meetings for a short time, however, and on April 9 he is mentioned as a committee member in the minutes of a Batavia Masonic lodge. On July 4, as a storm of opposition gathered around her husband, Lucinda bore a second child, Thomas Jefferson Morgan, at Batavia.

News of the proposed exposé leaked out, and Morgan certainly stopped attending Masonic events; he also began to be legally harassed by angry Masons. On July 25 he was arrested, though he obtained bail. At the time, the family was boarding with a Mr. Stewart in the middle of Batavia, but Morgan worked elsewhere. He completed his manuscript, *Illustrations of Masonry by One of the Fraternity Who has Devoted Thirty Years to the Subject*, and gave it to the printers on August 14. He was arrested again four days later but was bailed out by Miller within two days. Though Morgan is the protagonist in conventional tellings of this story, one can imagine the toll these events would have taken on Lucinda.

At this point, the second important man in Lucinda's life enters the drama, George Washington Harris, a silversmith whose shop was situated beneath the Morgans' apartment. Soon after September 1 Harris met the family for the first time and became friendly with them. Like William, Harris was a member of the Batavia Masonic Lodge. On September 8 Samuel Greene, a Mason friendly to Morgan, heard some Masons plotting against Morgan and Miller, and though he did not want to approach them directly, he gave a message to Harris, who delivered it. Morgan and Miller began to carry weapons as a precaution. On September 10, when the book's proofs were produced, the printing press was set on fire, though the flame was extinguished before the building was destroyed.

Finally, on a Sunday night, a new era in Lucinda's life began. In a later court deposition she testified that at about sunset William left their apartment to go to work in the village, where the printing was taking place. One imagines the routine departure, with kisses for wife and children and a promise to be home for breakfast. Perhaps she watched him walk down a lane into the darkening twilight. It was the last time she would ever see him.

## II. "In Great Distress and in Tears"

William was arrested in the town of Batavia on September 11. At first he was charged with theft but was released for lack of evidence. He was then jailed for a small debt ($2.69) owed to an innkeeper. The next day he was freed from jail and must have felt a brief moment of euphoria as he emerged into the open street, but at that moment a band of men seized him and forced him into a carriage. He was never seen publicly again.

When Lucinda heard of the kidnapping, she must have felt panic and terror. On Tuesday morning she contacted a Sheriff William R. Thompson, who was apparently involved in the kidnapping plot. The young wife, now twenty-five, with a two-year-old child and one-month-old baby, asked whether Morgan could be ransomed if she gave up his manuscripts. Thompson stated that that would be "very likely" and suggested that she go to Canandaigua and give up the papers there. She agreed. There were negotiations to determine who would go with her, and she suggested a Mr. Gibbs, but Thompson pointed out that he was not a Mason and suggested a Nathan Follett instead. Follett was approached but refused to go unless he and a George Ketchem could see the Morgan papers first. Lucinda was reluctant but finally complied.

She traveled to Canandaigua, twenty miles southeast of Rochester, with Ketchum, a virtual stranger. Arriving there Wednesday at noon, she hired rooms at a tavern, while Ketchum took the papers and went out. When he returned, he said that the Masons did not trust him (probably a lie, as he was a Mason himself) and suggested that William probably had been taken to Pennsylvania for a debt he owed there. According to Lucinda's deposition, he then asked her when she would return home. She "expressed anxiety to return speedily, on account of having left her child of two years old, and having with her a baby of two months old. Then Ketchum went out, as he said, to take a passage in the stage, and returned after candle-light. This deponent was then walking the room in great distress and in tears."

Ketchum seemed to pity Lucinda and told her that Morgan would not be killed. Rather, he said, he would be detained until the Masons obtained the rest of the papers. "She asked him what papers were [held] back. He said there were some sheets of the Mark Master's degree [held] back; and they wanted also to see the printed sheets that Miller had printed on the three degrees."

Ketchum gave her two dollars for passage home and offered her $25 out of his own pocket and $100 from the lodge "if she could get what Miller had now." But according to her deposition, "Deponent told him she would not try to get the papers that Miller had, and would take no money, and would not let him have the papers she delivered to him, but on condition he would try and find out where Mr. Morgan was, and let her see him."

Ketchum swore he would do all he could to find Morgan. He left for Rochester, taking the large bundle of papers, and Lucy returned to Batavia. Her deposition ends:

> The deponent further says she has no knowledge of the place where her husband now is, or what is his situation, and feels the most anxious fears for his life; that she was born in Virginia, and is a stranger without intimate friends or relations in this county, and is left with two infant children without any money, except what is left of that given to her by said Ketchum, and has no property, or any means of supporting herself and children, her constitution being very feeble, and her health being bad most of the time.

On the way home an innkeeper, Ganson, a Mason, told Lucinda that she might not see Morgan for a year, or she might never see him again, but that she and her children would be well taken care of. After arriving home a Thomas McCully called to offer her Masonic aid. Again she refused. Greene meanwhile had heard threats against Miller and contacted Harris, who warned the printer. Both Miller and Harris locked themselves in their offices.

According to the anti-Masonic version of events, Morgan was brought to Canandaigua for a mock trial, then was taken secretly to Fort Niagara to be given to Canadian Masons. When the Canadians would not receive him, he was bound with weights and thrown into the river below the falls on September 19. If this is indeed what happened, Lucinda became a widow and a single mother on that date.

In the wake of Morgan's kidnapping and alleged murder, an anti-Masonic furor swept over New York and Lucinda gained some renown as the young widow of the martyr. In December Morgan's exposé was published, and in January 1827 the trials of Morgan's kidnappers began. They plead guilty but were given light sentences in a Mason-packed law court.

On October 7, 1828, events took a new twist when a decomposed body drifted ashore at Oak Orchard Creek on Lake Ontario. It was moved to Carlton, New York, thirty miles west of Rochester, where there were two inquests. Lucinda examined the body and declared it to be her husband. "I am fully convinced in my own mind that this is the body of William Morgan," she testified. It was buried in Batavia "with great (Antimasonic) pomp and ceremony." The funeral must have been an ordeal for Lucinda but probably brought her a welcome sense of finality.

However, two weeks later a Mrs. Timothy Munroe of Canada gave testimony in Orleans County, New York, and claimed that the body was her own drowned husband. She gave a detailed description of her husband's clothes, and a third coroner's jury was convinced by her identification. The body was reinterred under the name of Monroe and Lucinda was plunged once again into uncertainty.

In the years following Morgan's death, anti-Masonic groups helped care for Lucinda. In March 1830 she received a donation of $50 from a Frederick A. Sumner, "presented to me by Mr. George W. Harris, of this village, last week." The next chapter in her life is adumbrated by this presentation.

### III. George Washington Harris

Clearly, George Washington Harris stayed close to the widow Morgan, for on November 30, some four years after William's disappearance, Lucinda married him. He had by this time withdrawn from Masonry. The *Wayne Sentinel*, on December 3, reported in its marriage department: "In Batavia, on Tuesday last by the Hon. Simeon Cummings, Mr. GEORGE W. HARRIS, To Mrs. LUCINDA MORGAN, widow of the late Capt. William Morgan." At the time of the marriage Lucinda was twenty-nine and George was fifty. Presumably Harris's silversmith shop was prospering and Lucinda received a measure of security through this new marriage.

At some point between 1830 and 1834 the Harrises moved to Terre Haute, Indiana, where another major shift took place in her life. In late August 1834 Orson Pratt left Jackson County, Missouri, on a mission eastward and later wrote, "At Terre Haute I preached a few times, and baptized George W. Harris and his wife; about the last of November I ... continued my journey eastward." So the baptism took place in October or early November. After their conversion, George and Lucinda soon gathered to Zion in Missouri. By August 5, 1835, they had left Terre Haute, and by September 1836 George owned property in Far West.

George must have been an impressive, somewhat charismatic individual, for in the following years he became a prominent figure in Missouri Mormonism. By late February and early March 1838 he was a member of the Far West High Council, an office comparable to an apostle in to-day's LDS church.

## IV. Joseph Smith

Throughout most of the 1830s Mormonism was split between two gathering places, Ohio and Missouri. But as growing dissent and legal harassment dogged Joseph Smith in Kirtland, he made preparations to move permanently to Missouri in early 1838. The Saints in Zion organized to give their prophet a proper welcome. On February 24 George W. Harris, Edward Partridge, and Isaac Morley were appointed to meet Smith and Sidney Rigdon with wagons and financial aid, and when Joseph and Emma arrived at Far West on March 14, Smith wrote: "We were immediately received under the hospitable roof of George W. Harris who treated us with all kindness possible. here we refreshed ourselves with much sattisfaction after our long and tedious journey." They stayed with the Harrises for some two months, then moved to their own house.

There is no firm date for Smith's marriage to Lucinda, but these two months are a good possibility. He often married women while he was living in the same house with them, and the Sarah Pratt statement correlates with the year 1838, as well. Smith was thirty-two at the time and Lucinda was thirty-six, so he was the first of her husbands who was not an older man. George Harris may have given permission for the marriage, since he was a close friend of Smith and a church leader. He later stood proxy for Smith in the Nauvoo temple as his wife was sealed to the dead prophet for eternity. Despite the prophet's connection to Lucinda, she would not stop living with George, as was customary in Smith's polyandrous marriages.

Harris continued to be an important figure in Missouri. On May 12 he was assigned to a committee to give Smith and Rigdon remuneration for services in the printing office. When trouble with non-Mormons mounted, Harris reportedly was a member of the Mormon defensive paramilitary group, the Danites, and took part in the Mormon attack on Gallatin on October 18. At some point Lucinda's father, Joseph Pendleton, apparently became a Latter-day Saint and moved to Far West; on September 2 he was given a patriarchal blessing by Joseph Smith, Sr., as were Lucinda, George, and Lucinda's children.

An incident that probably took place in November offers a rare direct glimpse of Lucinda in Missouri. The mob militia had surrounded Far West and was threatening to open cannon fire on the Mormons. An uneasy stalemate ensued. Two of the militia entered the town and James Henry Rollins, brother of Mary Rollins Lightner, found the men talking to "Mrs. George Harris and my aunt Elizabeth Gilbert" in front of John M. Burk's tavern. Rollins rebuked the women for "talking to such men." Whatever the nature of their conversation, it may indicate some courage on the women's part.

George Harris can be documented through the period when the Mormon presence in Missouri dwindled. In early December 1838 he was one of the signers of a memorial sent to the Missouri legislature listing grievances. On January 16 the next year, he attended the last recorded high council meeting in Far West and two weeks later signed the covenant pledging to help the poor in their departure from the state. Finally, at some point, the Harrises themselves left Missouri with the rest of the Mormons and moved to Illinois.

## V. "Dined at Sister Agness with Joseph"

As Lucinda and George make their appearance in the Illinois historical record, we find immediate evidence of a close bond between them and Joseph Smith. In a letter dated May 24, 1839, Smith wrote that he had selected a lot for them "just across the street from my own," near that of Sarah Cleveland's, a woman who would also become one of his plural wives. Presumably the Harrises came to Nauvoo soon after this, in June or July.

George continued to have high status in Nauvoo. On October 6 he was chosen to serve on the Nauvoo High Council and he appears in all the minutes except when he was on a proselyting mission. By this time he was fifty-nine; Lucinda was thirty-eight.

Lucinda now appears as a minor character in a romantic vignette involving her daughter Lucinda Wesley and Benjamin Johnson. When Johnson and the sixteen-year-old Lucinda began to spend time together, Smith, a close friend of Johnson, noticed the bond. Johnson writes, "The Prophet, seeing our partiality for each other told me to make her my wife, seeming to enjoin it upon me." Once again we see Smith's willingness to arrange marriages among his followers. Johnson willingly obeyed, and he and Lucinda "pledged their vows" to each other in an informal engagement. However, the bane of Mormon romance, the mission field, intervened. Johnson left Nauvoo to preach the gospel, and in his absence the older Lucinda advised her daughter to marry another man. She agreed and sent Johnson a Dear John letter. On May 9, 1840, she married David Smith, of whom Johnson in later life still had a very low opinion. However, if one views the marriage through the eyes of the mother, one can imagine her joy on seeing her only daughter married to a young man she approved of.

The Nauvoo High Council minutes indicate that George borrowed money from Joseph Smith in 1839 or early 1840. In mid-July 1840 George was sent on a mission to travel eastward collecting funds and materials for church publications. He left soon after July 25, labored for a year in the eastern states, especially New York, then returned home in September 1841. Though one can only speculate, this period of his absence may have been a time when Joseph and Lucinda enjoyed a special closeness. In 1841 Lucinda did baptisms for her dead relatives, including William Morgan. On September 22 George resumed his seat on the high council. A month later he was elected alderman.

On January 17, 1842, Willard Richards wrote, "Dined at Sister Agness with Joseph & Sister Harris." "Sister Agness" is Agnes Coolbrith Smith, widow of Smith's brother Don Carlos and probably also a plural wife of Joseph by this time. So Smith was dining with two of his plural wives and with Richards, a polygamy insider.

In 1842 Harris continued to fill high ecclesiastical and civic callings, and on September 9 he was referred to as "President City Council at Nauvoo." In the same year the Female Relief Society of Nauvoo received its genesis, but it is a striking fact that Lucinda's name never shows up in the society's minutes. Perhaps the explanation for this anomaly lies in the fact that Emma Smith was president of the society, and there may have been tension between Lucinda and Emma at this time.

In 1843 and 1844 George is referred to as "Acting Associate Justice" and occasionally as president pro tem of the city council. He thus played a small but telling part in the events that led to Joseph's martyrdom. After the dissenting *Nauvoo Expositor* was published, George presided over a city council meeting on June 10, 1844, in which the council debated what action to take in response to the paper. After a great deal of testimony relating to the alleged wrongdoings of the *Expositor* staff, "Alderman Harris spoke from the chair, and expressed his feelings that the press ou[gh]t to be demolished." The council quickly agreed, passing a resolution that brought about the press's destruction. Harris undoubtedly acted under Smith's direction, so once again we find the phenomenon of a "first husband" acting as an unmistakable Smith loyalist.

Smith was arrested by outsiders for complicity in the *Expositor*'s destruction and was killed on June 27. Lucinda was once again widowed, though, strangely enough, she was still married to her legal husband. Only now, in the newspaper story by Richmond, does one appreciate the intensity of her love for the prophet, as she wept over his body with her "whole frame convulsed."

### VI. Proxy Marriage

After Smith's death, Harris remained a high councilor, president of the city council, and won re-election as an alderman in 1845. On July 22 Hosea Stout, Nauvoo police chief, began to write about George in his journal, the two men being obvious political cronies.

As the Mormons prepared to leave Illinois in late 1845, they worked feverishly to finish the temple and perform the all-important rituals that could only be solemnized there. On December 12 George and Lucinda received the endowment together in the temple and nine days later attended a prayer meeting there. Church leaders danced in the temple on January 5 of the new year, though Harris was not inclined to participate. William Clayton wrote, "His great gravity and superior wisdom forbade him to do so, and he thought that as he had not yet danced in his life, he would not begin at the present time."

Finally the strangeness of the polyandrous triangle with Smith was posthumously commemorated. On January 22, 1846, Lucinda was sealed to Joseph "for eternity" and to George for time in a proxy marriage. The complete entry from the Nauvoo temple record is quoted here to give the reader a sense of what the ritual was like:

N° 64   Jan 22 '46

Lucinda Pendleton [born] Sept. 27, 1801 {Kinghurstworks}, Washington Co. Vermont [Virginia], was Sealed to Jos. Smith (deceased born Dec. 23d 1805 Sharron Windsor Co Vert.) for time & all Eternity. George Washington Harris acting proxy for (Pres. J. Smith Jun. deceased) G. W. Harris & Lucinda Smith were then Sealed Husband & wife for time By Pres B. Young. In presance of Orson Pratt & {F. D.} Richards & A Lyman at 28 min past 6 a.m. ___   J. D. Lee clerk

This sealing seems to show George's awareness of his wife's connection to Joseph, and it certainly indicates his willingness to deliver up Lucinda to Joseph in the next life.

## VII. "Harris Has Gone to the Spirit World"

This is the last specific reference to Lucinda Morgan Harris in the Mormon historical record, though there are more references to her husband. It is certain that she had left George by 1853; an 1850 census shows him living alone, so the couple may have separated between January 1846 and 1850.

Lucinda probably accompanied George when he went west with the rest of the Latter-day Saints in February 1846. Hosea Stout appointed George commissary of his company and, on April 10, spiritual leader for his group of ten. By June 1 the Harrises were probably at Mt. Pisgah, Iowa, as Stout was there. Two days later they pushed ahead of Stout, reaching Council Bluffs a few days before July 5. Harris met Stout the next day and advised the policeman to enlist in the Mormon Battalion, though he did not do so.

At Council Bluffs George resumed his elite status; he was made a bishop on July 17 and four days later was given a seat on the high council. On September 5 he became a member of a committee to find a place for a ferry. On the 26th, for an unknown reason, he was replaced on the high council, but in a few weeks he was reseated.

At a meeting of the high council on January 14, 1847, Harris, with others, accepted a new revelation by Brigham Young (D&C 136) as word of the Lord, and the minutes record that "George W. Harris was so well satisfied that he wanted all to say Amen at once." He was, as always, the thoroughgoing loyalist. In late September he figured in the odd case of Daniel Russell, whom George declared "unqualified to sit in council as he had lost his privy members & was an eunech." Then Harris curiously confessed on Russell's behalf (one usually confesses for oneself), and "it was decidedly the best confession I ever heard," wrote Stout!

In 1848 George, a senior high councilor, was often consulted by Stout, and he sat as president of the high council on April 13, 1849, when Oliver Cowdery was received back into church, which was probably the last high water mark of George's elite status in the church. Most Mormons had gone west, and the Iowa Stake, of which Harris was a high councilor, was dwindling, while high councilors had become much less powerful than apostles.

The 1850 census shows Harris living alone; perhaps, if the 1853 divorce date is correct, Lucinda was merely away on a visit. In February of the next year George was taking the *Frontier Guardian*, published at Kanesville. In 1852, when Brigham Young directed all Iowa Saints to come to Utah, Harris's loyalism finally failed; he did not travel west to Utah, apparently because he felt that Jackson County, Missouri, would soon be redeemed, and he did not want to make the long trip across the plains twice. Young said in an 1860 sermon:

> There are a great many, who profess to be still in the faith, neglecting to gather and waiting for the time when Zion [Jackson County] will be redeemed. George W. Harris, whom many of you remember, was going to wait in Kanesville until we returned. Br. George A. Smith told him that the nearest way to the centre stake of Zion was through Great Salt Lake City. Harris has gone to the spirit world, and where his circuit will be I neither know nor care, though I am well convinced that br. Geo. A. Smith was right.

This sermon breathes a typical nineteenth-century Mormon distrust for Latter-day Saints not living with the main body of the church. Zion was now Utah in the truly far west.

### VIII. Sister of Charity

By 1853 Lucinda certainly had left Harris. In an 1856 legal document published in a local newspaper, George's lawyer wrote:

To Mrs. Lucinda Harris:

*Madam,*—You are hereby notified that there will be on file, in the clerk's office of the District Court of Pottawatomie county, Iowa, the petition of George W. Harris, claiming of you a divorce from the bonds of matrimony now existing between you and the said Geo. W. Harris, and charging you therein with willfully deserting him, and without reasonable cause absenting yourself for more than the space of three years.

George died in Council Bluffs, Iowa, the next year.

Lucinda's later life is shrouded in mystery; only a few scattered details are known, and since she apparently did not travel west to Utah and left no descendants who remained Mormon, Latter-day Saint history has no further mention of her. But Masons and anti-Masons were interested in William Morgan's widow, so it is a Masonic writer, Morris, who now picks up her story: "Mrs. Harris afterward joined the (Catholic) Sisters of Charity, and at the breaking out of the civil war, was acting in that capacity in the hospitals at Memphis Tennessee; there I lose sight of her." One reads Morris's paragraph on Lucinda Harris with a slight sense of shock. Lucinda, after her many years in Mormonism and her close relationship with the founding prophet, is last seen as a Catholic. The date and place of her death are not known.

Thus Lucinda married the key figures in two important antebellum American movements—William Morgan, whose exposé and disappearance triggered the anti-Masonry crusade and political party, and Joseph Smith, founding prophet of Mormonism. One might think of her as the archetypal Burned-over District woman. Her third husband, with whom she was married longer than she was to either of the others, was an important Mormon leader for decades. Yet her life was shadowed by disaster, as her first husband, Morgan, and her favorite husband, Smith, were killed violently, and she came to love her third husband so little that she left him. She seems to have lived the rest of her life as a single woman—a Catholic sister.

Lucinda is the only plural wife of Joseph Smith to turn eastward after Nauvoo and end up in the mainstream of American history, the Civil War. Despite a life filled with grief and loss, it is somehow comforting to have our last glimpse of her in the hospitals of the South, tending wounded, dying soldiers.

# 3.

# "Not Much Else but Sorrow and Affliction"

## *Louisa Beaman (Smith Young)*

On January 13, 1851, a large group of Mormons—119 men, 310 women, and eighteen children, with wagons and livestock—trudged slowly into Parowan Valley in southern Utah after a month-long, wintry journey from Salt Lake City, itself only two and a half years old. This company comprised the so-called Iron Mission, sent south by Brigham Young on a mining venture. It was led by an apostle, the massive, 300-plus-pound George A. Smith, a cousin of the martyred prophet Joseph. Wending toward red cliffs and mountains northeastward, they camped on Center Creek near a canyon, and the new settlement was begun. In the following days everyone worked hard to build a fort, mark out lots, construct cabins, irrigate, and sow seed. On February 9, a sabbath, the colonists gathered for an important address by George A., who christened the settlement with a surprising name: "Louisa." John D. Lee, the Iron Mission scribe, explained: "It was in honor of the first Woman who listened to the light & voice of Revelation — & yielded obedience to the Seal of the covenant, but since has taken her Exit to the world of Sperits, & for this Noble act, her Name is held in honorable rememberance in the History of the Saints." George A. organized the settlement ecclesiastically, dividing the main branch into four wards, called First, Second, Third, and Fourth, but the branch itself would be called Louisa, the settlement (modern Parowan) Fort Louisa. In a territory soon to be full of settlements named after men—Heber City, Brigham City, St. George, Fort Johnson, Woodruff, Grantsville—this was the only one named after a woman, even if the name would survive only a short time.

Who was the woman who inspired such a tribute from the stolidly patriarchal Mormon pioneers? Louisa Beaman was the first widely recognized plural wife of Joseph Smith, and as such she gained a semi-heroic status in Mormon folk tradition. The pattern of her marriage to Smith was not extraordinary. She was single at the time they exchanged vows. As was often the case with Joseph's wives, she came from a family that had known him for many years, and who were among his trusted and loyal followers. The marriage ceremony itself is well-documented but her marriage experience is not.

Although we know comparatively little about Louisa, there is no doubt that she was extraordinary. It is well documented that she was beloved by her sisters in the gospel (and presumably by her brothers, also). That she had a personality of great warmth is made clear by the two extant letters she wrote, and by references to her in the journals of her sister wives. A proxy plural wife of Brigham Young, she became close to the two most prominent nineteenth-century Utah Mormon women, Eliza R. Snow and Zina Huntington Young, and thus became an important figure in the Nauvoo and early Utah feminine hierarchy. She was also a close friend of Marinda Johnson Hyde, to whom the two extant letters were written.

Louisa was also heroized by a life of suffering. Most of Joseph Smith's wives had difficult lives, but Louisa stands out even among them. The mother of five children by Brigham Young, including two sets of twins, she lost them all and then died of breast cancer in early middle age—thus becoming the *mater dolorosa* of early Mormon polygamy.

## I. The Beamans

Louisa was born on February 7, 1815, to Alvah Beaman, a farmer, and Sarah ("Sally") Burtts in Livonia, Livingston, New York, some twenty-five miles southwest of Palmyra. She was the seventh of eight siblings, of whom the first five (Isaac, Betsey, Alvah, Sarah, and Margaret, born 1797-1808) apparently never converted to Mormonism. Her two closest siblings, however, have strong Mormon histories: Mary Adeline, born in 1810, would marry Mormon stalwart Joseph Bates Noble, who officiated when Joseph Smith married Louisa; and Artemisia, born in 1819, would marry Erastus Snow, later an apostle and colonizer of St. George, Utah.

A reminiscence by Mary Adeline gives an idea of the agrarian environment in which Louisa was raised. The Beaman farm was large, and Alvah was wealthy; he specialized in raising sheep, cattle, and flax. As Mary grew up she worked in the dairy, wove cloth, went to school in winter, and did farm work full time in the summer. She first attended a boarding school at age fourteen; later, when she was eighteen, she attended a "select school" for six months and a "grammar school" for six weeks. After this she and her classmates received a recommend stating that "we were well qualified for teaching any school." So Mary began to teach. Louisa's experiences were probably similar, though there is no record of her ever teaching.

## II. "A Grate Rodsman"

According to Joseph Bates Noble, Alvah Beaman was widely respected for his successful farming and honesty, though this did not prevent him from searching for treasure through magic, a relatively common pastime in early nineteenth-century New York. This interest probably drew him to the Smiths, for by the 1820s Joseph Smith, Jr., had become known in New York as a scryer, one who locates treasure by seeing visions in seerstones. Martin Harris remembers "old Mr. Beman" digging for treasure with the Smiths, and Joseph Knight, another early Mormon, described a Mr. "Beeman" as "a grate Rodsman," who used a divining rod to find treasure. Mary Adeline remembers that the Beaman family would visit the Smiths frequently during the 1820s.

As Joseph Smith made the transition from folk magic seership to Christian-primitivist seership in the late 1820s, Alvah Beaman at first could not make a similar transition. He evidently interpreted the Book of Mormon gold plates as a magical treasure and felt that he, as a partner, should have a percentage of the profit. According to Knight, on one occasion Alvah and Samuel Lawrence, a treasure-digging companion, visited Smith, and "Beeman took out his Rods and hild them up and they pointed Down[n] to the harth whare they [the plates] were hid. 'There,' says Beeman, 'it is under that harth.'" However, the Smiths were able to keep Alvah and Lawrence from obtaining the plates.

At some point Alvah was converted to the religious meaning of the gold plates and became one of the earliest disciples of Mormonism. According to Mary Beaman, he once handled the plates with a cloth over them and on one occasion helped Smith conceal them. Louisa would have been approximately twelve at this time, 1827; Joseph Smith twenty-one.

In 1829 Alvah sold his farm and moved to Avon, New York, also in Livingston County. Soon after that, probably in 1830, he purchased the first Book of Mormon that was seen in the area. As Mormonism began to grow, missionaries frequently traveled through Avon, and Alvah welcomed them in his home. Among them were Joseph Young and Brigham Young, whose powerful, sincere preaching made a deep impression on Mary Adeline. Though she did not know it, sixteen-year-old Louisa was meeting her future second husband at this time.

In the spring of 1834 Joseph Smith, Jr., with friends, stayed for a few days in the Beaman home in Avon. "His society I prized, his conversation was meat and drink to me," writes Mary Beaman. The teenaged Louisa probably felt the same way. During this visit Smith, Sidney Rigdon, future apostles Luke and Lyman Johnson, and about fourteen missionaries held a conference at the Beaman household. Mary remembers preparing meals for the visiting authorities, and "many very interesting interviews" she had with them. Parley P. Pratt was also traveling with Smith, and his account of the visit reveals that Louisa was a good singer: "Among those whose hospitality we shared in that vicinity was old father Beeman and his amiable and interesting family. He was a good singer, and so were his three daughters; we were much edified and comforted in their society, and were deeply interested in hearing the old gentleman and brother Joseph converse on their early acquaintance and history."

### III. "The Widow Beeman and Her Two Daughters"

On September 11, 1834, Mary Beaman married Joseph Bates Noble, leaving only Louisa and Artemisia at home with their parents. A week later Joseph Bates and Mary departed for Kirtland, Ohio. Alvah visited Kirtland on November 10 and Joseph Smith advised him to move there, so he, with his wife and two daughters, apparently did so in 1835. Already on January 11, 1836, Alvah was in Kirtland attending a solemn assembly, and four days later he was called to be President of the Elders at Kirtland. His succinct and humble acceptance speech is preserved: "Brethren you know that you are young and I am old and ignorant and kneed much instructions, but I wish to do the will of the Lord." He was sixty at the time.

There is no specific documentation for Louisa in Kirtland, though she lived there from 1836 to 1838, when she was twenty-one and twenty-two. One imagines her meeting Eliza Snow, Zina Huntington, and Marinda Hyde, her future sister-wives, for the first time.

The Beaman family received a blow on November 20, 1837, when Alvah died at age sixty-two. After the funeral the household of three women set their sights on the new Mormon gathering place in Missouri. The first specific reference to Louisa in the historical record is found in the Heber C. Kimball diary on July 1, 1838, when he lists her in a company of Mormons making the pilgrimage to "Zion," Missouri—"the Widow Beeman and her two daughters, Artemisia and Louisa." Also part of this company were Marinda Johnson Hyde, later one of Louisa's closest friends, and Erastus Snow, who would marry Artemisia within the year.

The company traveled to Wellsville (on the Ohio River) by wagon, then took a steamboat to St. Louis, arriving "nearly all sick from the intense heat of the weather." They then took a steamboat on the Missouri River to Richmond, in west Missouri, and from there traveled by land to Far West.

We know nothing specific about Louisa's stay in Missouri. She probably experienced the terror and misery of the persecutions in 1838. However, we do know that she and her family stayed at Far West longer than the main body of Mormons. On April 2, 1839, Heber C. Kimball, still in Far West, wrote to his wife, "Mother Beman Se[n]ds hur love to you and also Louisa and Sister [Artemisia] Snow and Sister [Mary] nobles and bats [Joseph Bates Noble]." Shortly thereafter Louisa came to Nauvoo.

## IV. "The Lord Heard Her Supplication"

Her first two years in Nauvoo are undocumented. Probably she underwent attacks of fever and chills, and survived. But her mother was not so fortunate, for she died in Nauvoo on September 29, 1840, perhaps a victim of malaria. Louisa, now twenty-five, moved in with Mary Adeline and Joseph Bates Noble.

Hitherto an obscure young Mormon woman quietly moving in the ebb and flow of early Mormon gatherings and hegiras, Louisa, now for a brief moment, occupied center stage in Mormon history. In the fall of 1840, according to Joseph Bates Noble, Joseph Smith, who had known Noble in Kirtland, taught him "the principle of celestial or plural marriage, or a plurality of wives," saying that an angel had given him a revelation on the subject and that "the angel of the Lord had commanded him (Smith) to move forward in the said order of marriage." Smith then asked Noble to officiate in marrying Louisa to himself. The prophet said, "In revealing this to you, I have placed my life in your hands, therefore do not in an evil hour betray me to my enemies."

If Louisa's case is similar to Almera Johnson's, Noble may have introduced the doctrine to her before Smith did. Whoever taught her the principle, she had to be converted to it, according to Brigham Young family tradition: "Sister Louisa asked the Lord in fervent prayer for a testimony concerning the principle. The Lord heard her supplication and granted her request, and after being convinced that the principle had emanated from God, she accepted it, and was married to the Prophet Joseph Smith."

By most accounts, the ceremony took place on April 5, 1841; she was twenty-six, Joseph thirty-five. Erastus Snow, Louisa's brother-in-law, said that she married the Mormon prophet "in a grove Near Main Street in the City of Nauvoo, The Prophet Joseph dictating the ceremony and Br Nobles repeating it after him." Louisa was disguised as a man during the ceremony. Nauvoo polygamy was so secretive that it almost had a cloak-and-dagger atmosphere—perhaps its very secrecy, giving participants a sense of being in the center of the innermost church, helped infuse it with its sense of sacrality.

In court testimony given in 1892, Noble reported that after the marriage he said to Smith, "'Blow out the lights and get into bed, and you will be safer there,' and he took my advice." Noble, under cross-examination, clarified that he did not actually see the couple get into bed, but "he [Smith] told me he did." There is no good reason to doubt that Louisa's marriage to Smith included sexuality. Noble further testified under oath,

"Question: where did they [Joseph and Louisa] sleep together? Answer: Right straight across the river at my house they slept together."

Very little is known about Louisa's experience as a plural wife in Nauvoo. Joseph Smith visited her on occasion; according to John C. Bennett, Smith once visited her at the house of Delcena Johnson Sherman, another of his plural wives. The connection between Louisa and Delcena is attested by another source, Benjamin Johnson, who, on arriving at Nauvoo in June 1842, visited Delcena, his sister, and found her living with Louisa. "And I Saw from apearances that they ware in his [Joseph Smith's] Care and that he provided for there Comfort." This statement is significant in suggesting that Smith sometimes provided for his wives financially, though such support would have been secret.

Louisa served as a witness in at least one other plural marriage, when Almera Johnson, Delcena's sister, married Smith in April 1843. Louisa helped prepare Almera for the marriage and then witnessed the ceremony at Delcena's house, which raises the discomforting theme of women preparing other women to enter polygamy, acting as spokespersons for the polygamous suitor.

It is interesting that virtually all of the above references connect Louisa with Delcena. Undoubtedly her marriage to Joseph Smith caused her to develop bonds of sororal affection with the other wives he married in 1842 and 1843. On February 25, 1843, Louisa, with Mary Adeline Noble, Marinda Hyde Smith, and Patty Sessions Smith, had a social gathering at the home of Sylvia Lyon Smith—a meeting of four of Smith's wives. As Louisa was sharing her husband with a demanding first wife and at least seventeen other women by this time, the support group of Joseph's wives, starting with Delcena, probably had become an important part of her life.

A few months later, in May, Smith rebaptized Louisa and at least one other plural wife for reasons that may have been linked to his marriage to Emily and Eliza Partridge. During this era rebaptism was a common way of demonstrating one's recommitment to previous covenants. Smith's journal for May 11, the same day he married the Partridge sisters for the second time, reads, "6 A.M. Baptized [blank space, probably Eliza] Snow, Louisa Beman, Sarah Alley, &c." Eliza and Louisa became close friends, as is evident from Snow's pioneer diary. Apart from these polygamy-related details, the only other thing we know about Louisa before Smith's death is that she joined the Nauvoo Female Relief Society on March 24, 1842, and contributed $.50 to it. On June 16, 1843, the Relief Society record reads, "Miss Beman will make clothes." So she was apparently sewing to help support herself.

When Smith was killed on June 27, 1844, Louisa was suddenly widowed. She turned to her sister-wives for support. For instance, she spent part of July 4 with Zina Huntington Jacobs, another of Smith's widows and a future sister wife of Brigham Young. They undoubtedly mourned their lost husband together. Zina would become Louisa's closest friend.

## V. "Grate Is the Work of the Lord"

Some three months later, on September 19, Brigham Young wrote in his journal, "Staed at home all day my wife is quite sick I Saw Sister Louisa B. Smith H.C. Kimball & Silva L. Smith &c. &c. grate is the work of the Lord in these Last days." "Saw" is apparently a code word for "sealed and wedded"—Young married Louisa, who became his eighth plural wife, and Kimball married Sylvia Sessions Lyon Smith. The rationale for these "proxy" marriages was Levirate, raising seed to the dead prophet in the brotherhood of the gospel. The fact that Young saw these marriages as a religious duty explains Louisa's quick remarriage.

Soon afterwards she was brought further into the inner circle of Nauvoo ritual practice. She received her endowment on January 26, 1845, and joined the Holy Order, or Quorum of the Anointed, also known as "the Priesthood," an elite group that met frequently to perform Joseph Smith's endowment rituals and pray together. Later that year, on December 25, her endowment was repeated in the Nauvoo temple in the same session with Emily Partridge Smith Young and Lucy Walker Smith Kimball. The proxy marriage was repeated on January 14, 1846, in the temple; she was sealed to Smith for eternity with Young standing proxy, then was sealed to Young for time.

She then left Nauvoo with the main body of the Mormons, beginning her long journey to Utah and a new chapter in her life. She would exchange the urban comfort of Nauvoo for life as an overland traveler, as a resident of Winter Quarters, and as a settler of primitive early Utah. The secret, experimental polygamy of Nauvoo would be replaced by the practical, open polygamy of a large frontier family—by the time Young left Nauvoo he had married some forty-one women. Most importantly, Louisa exchanged the childless years of her early life for the joys and sorrows of motherhood.

## VI. "Loiza Beman Came to See Me"

Throughout the rest of 1846 and the remainder of Louisa's life, there are frequent references to her in the diaries of Zina Huntington Young, Eliza Snow, and Patty Sessions, perhaps the most elite group of women in Mormonism. On February 18, at Sugar Creek, just across the Mississippi River, Eliza recorded a visit from "Loisa B.," Clara Decker Young, and Sarah Lawrence Smith Kimball. Four days later Patty noted in her diary that she visited "Loisa Beman and Eliza Snow." By March 8 Louisa's company was traveling across Iowa. ("Call'd on Loisa  Emily &c," writes Eliza.) A reference in Sessions's diary on April 15 reveals that Louisa was between Mt. Pisgah and Winter Quarters: "Loiza Beman came to see me I read my letters to her and she read one to me."

Sometime in the early months of 1846, according to Brigham Young family tradition, Louisa bore a pair of twins to Brigham named Joseph and Hyrum. They are mysteriously underdocumented but evidently died young. One can only imagine their birth, and Louisa's grief at their death. She quickly became pregnant again as she slowly made her way to Winter Quarters. Eliza Snow reached the Missouri River on August 28, and Louisa probably arrived about the same time. Snow wrote on November 26, "Loisa & Clarissa visit me <with kindnesses>." Louisa was approximately eight months pregnant.

The diaries allow a few glimpses into Louisa's social life in Winter Quarters. One reference in Snow's journal on December 30 shows that Louisa would sometimes accompany Brigham Young on social visits to friends and relatives. Louisa, Brigham, Eliza, and Brigham's first wife, Mary Ann, spent the afternoon at a Brother Pierce's home—probably Robert Pierce, the father of two of Brigham's wives—after which Pierce walked Louisa and Eliza home.

This was a time of frequent blessing, tongue-speaking meetings, which were dominated by women. On the first day of 1847 Louisa (very large with child), Eliza, Zina Young, and Patty celebrated with a blessing meeting filled with glossolalia and prophecy. As a close friend of Eliza and Zina, Louisa experienced these charismatic moments of prophetic power throughout her stay at Winter Quarters. The next day the inseparable Louisa, Eliza, and Patty met at Stephen Winchester's house.

On January 8 Louisa's baby arrived. Patty Sessions wrote, "Put Loiza[,] Adaline & Melissa all to bed in 6 hours and a half." The following day, Eliza Snow noted, "Loisa had a fine son born yest." A week later, on a "cold & blustering" day, close friends of Louisa and Brigham, including Eliza, Heber C. Kimball, and Willard Richards, gathered at Brigham's house, where Kimball blessed the new child, giving him the name Moroni, the last prophet of the Book of Mormon and the angel who Mormons believe appeared to Joseph Smith in 1823. At Brigham's suggestion, Eliza then stayed with Louisa a week.

The Winter Quarters experience, divided between death, sickness and cold on the one hand, and the warmth of close friends and charismatic meetings on the other, continued. On February 3 Louisa and Eliza attended a party of about a hundred at Brigham's where they sang, prayed, feasted, danced, and heard speeches by Brigham and Heber. Eliza slept at Louisa's home after the party. Three days later Louisa and

Eliza, with Clarissa Young, visited the Pierces again. An entry in Patty Sessions's diary on February 19 reveals that Louisa was apparently living with Marinda Hyde in February. Patty wrote, "visited with sister Hyde at Loizas she is making me a dress." All three were former wives of Smith.

Louisa appears in the diaries of Eliza and Patty throughout the months of March and May. Toward June the frequency and intensity of the blessing meetings increased, probably because the sisters were looking toward the trek west and inevitable partings. Although Louisa was not a prominent leader in these devotionals, she was an important participant, and on May 29 she apparently hosted a blessing meeting herself. Patty wrote, "Went to a meeting to Eliza [sic] Beamans with many of the sisters." Louisa, Eliza Snow, Zina Young, Emily (and possibly Eliza) Partridge all spoke in tongues on June 2. The next day Louisa, Eliza, Zina, and Emily laid their hands on Patty Sessions's head and gave her a prophetic blessing. After another blessing meeting during a rainstorm on June 9, Eliza "went home with Loisa & Z. [Zina] in the mud rejoicing." The next day Louisa, with others, spoke in tongues, and a day later she hosted a session in which "the gift" was bestowed—"we had a glorious time," wrote Eliza.

One day later Eliza Snow's company left Winter Quarters; Patty Sessions had already set out for Utah on June 5. Louisa's chroniclers were no longer near her, so little is known specifically about her during the winter of late 1847. However, one important event is recorded, which must have had a devastating impact on Louisa: Moroni died on August 10, after seven months of life, a victim of "teething and canker," evidently a malignant sore in the baby's mouth that became infected. Louisa, now thirty-two, endured for the third time the harrowing ordeal of tending a child as it died.

### VII. "I Desire to Bear My Afflictions with Patience"

Two and a half months later, on October 31, Brigham Young arrived back at Winter Quarters after his first journey to Salt Lake, then departed again for the distant valley on or around May 26, 1848, accompanied by Louisa, approximately six or seven months pregnant with twins. The first months of her journey must have been extremely uncomfortable. On July 23 the burden of pregnancy ended. John D. Lee wrote, "About 2 P.M. Louisa B. Young was delivered of 2 fine Boys which verry much del[i]ghted Pres. B.Y., the Father of the children, who with his co. roled on 3 ms." The twins were named Alvah and Alma.

Louisa's company straggled into Salt Lake Valley between September 20 and 24, and she and her twins moved into the Old Fort that stood in the middle of the great valley, at that time uncultivated and barren. But as others heaved sighs of relief at having safely reached their destination, Louisa was faced with a crisis on her second day in Utah. She tells the story in an April 1849 letter to Marinda Hyde: "I am led to think at times their is not much else but sorrow and affliction in this world for me, the next day after I arrived in the valley my babes were both taken sick with the bowell complaint the canker set in and on the 11. of Oct I was called upon to give up the oldest one and his little spirett took its flight to join with his brothers and father in Heaven."

So Louisa buried her fourth son. But after Alvah's death, Alma improved: "My anxiety was all turned towards the other that was living, the next day after this one was ... burried[,] the other commenced to get better. he got so that he seamed well and grew flashly [fleshy] as fast as I ever saw a child."

One imagines how desperately she longed for at least one child to live. But her ill-starred fate continued:

And I even deared [dared] to hope that I should raise him but I know [no] sooner hoped then [than] my hopes were all blasted one day all in a moment as it were he was taken down again with the same complaint, and all I could do both buy [by] faith and works, did not seame to do any good and on the 16. of Nov. he breathed his last and I was again left alone. you that have been mothers can better and losst children can better immagine my feelings then [than] I can disscribe them I had fondley hoped I should raise them they looked verry much alike indeed, there eyes were jest of a colour, I called them Alvah and Alma but they are gone, and I must be reconsiled to the will of God; and I desire ever to acknowledge his hand in all things I look forward to the time when I shall again behold them and claspe them to my bosome, will not my joy be full, I feel as though it would; I desire to bear all of my afflictions with patience, realising that my Heavenly father knows better what is for my good then [than] myself, and I feel to submit all things in to his hands and say his will be done and not mine.

The "bowell complaint" was probably bacterial dysentery, which caused diarrhea, fever, and dehydration. The psychic and physical toll on Louisa as her final child slowly expired must have been fearful. Nevertheless, she would have turned more closely to her network of sisters in the brave new world of patriarchal marriage practiced openly for the first time in the desolate expanses of the West. In the early Utah period Louisa appears frequently in Zina Huntington Young's journal, which shows her associating closely with her sister-wives and, on occasion, with Brigham. On December 15, a month after Alma's death, Zina wrote, "Spent the evening with Louisa, Clary & Susan Snively. Louisa is making me a black dress." So Louisa continued to work as a dressmaker, a typical womanly trade in early Utah. She was living in the Old Fort on December 23, when Zina wrote, "Spent the day with the Girls in the fort in Loises room."

According to Zina, on the day after Christmas "Louisa and I walked up to see Lucy, Emiline & Margret." Lucy Decker, Emmeline Free, and Margaret Pierce were all wives of Brigham. The next day Zina and Louisa ate supper with Emmeline Free Young and stayed the night at Lucy Decker's. And on the following day Louisa and Zina rode home with Brigham and Porter Rockwell on a sleigh. Louisa perhaps was making tallow to help support herself, for on January 6, 1849, Zina wrote, "Louisa brought me some tallow." A week later, on January 14, Patty Sessions accompanied Zina to visit Louisa, and Louisa went to Sunday meetings with Zina, the latter staying at Louisa's room for the night.

A complex web of friendships and affinities is evident in references such as these. Women eat together, sleep over together, and tend to each other's needs. There are occasional moments with the husband, though these are generally shared with other sister-wives. Feminist historian Carroll Smith-Rosenberg has written insightfully on the intense bonding felt by women in nineteenth-century Victorian America. Mormon polygamy, which by definition required an absentee husband much of the time, would only serve to heighten that bonding between women.

### VIII. "O How Precious Is a Sisters Kindness"

Louisa's April 8, 1849, letter to Marinda Hyde at Kanesville, part of which has already been quoted, introduces us to the next chapter in her tragic life. Apparently she had noticed the first symptoms of breast cancer—perhaps a growing lump in a breast or in her arm pit—back in Winter Quarters, two years earlier. Now the symptoms were returning or intensifying. This letter is nevertheless warm and good-natured. As so little remains that was written by Louisa, it may be appropriate to quote an extended passage:

Dear Sisters Marinda. Martha. and Mary Ann. I imbrace the preasant oppertunity of answering your letter bearing date Oct. 11 which was kindly received by me, I was truely thankful to get your letter and hear that you were all alive and well for I consider that as great a blessing as we can have. with out we can not injoy any thing, my health is quite good at preasant their is times when I am trouble[d] with that affliction that I was troubled [with] while at your house.

Here the cancer is mentioned briefly, and the description of the deaths of Alvah and Alma follows. Then she writes:

I prosume [presume] you would like to hear how we are prospering their has been a good many deaths since we arrived here it has been mostly amoung children; babes that have had the hooping cough, verry few grown persons have died, we do not begin to have the sikness to contend with we have had heretofore the winter has been rather severe, this winter has been much harder then [than] last winter but it would not have seamed hard had we have been prepared for it. As it regards provishion it is geting rather scarse some families are out of bread at the presant time it will be nothing strange if we should see rather heard [hard] times before harvest

This is a typical description of that early harsh winter in Utah. Nevertheless, she writes:

The Valley is a pleasant place I like it much it will seame more so when we get well to living, Mr Young has been quite sik for a few days he is a little better to day I am living about a half a mile from him at the preasant when we get settled for the summer he will live near us I am now living in the house with Clarrissa, Susan, Zina, Margaret, and Emeline

It is not certain what "the house" means. The women mentioned are probably Clarissa Decker, Susan Snively, Margaret Pierce, and Emmeline Free, all wives of Brigham Young. Louisa continues:

We often speak of you and wish you were here but [we] must wait patently untill you come, I could wish it might be this year but I heardly exspect it, I can not tell you how much I want to see you all, but my mind often wanders back to the hours I have spent in your house and of the kindness I have received from you all, and when I think of it I feel greatful to you and to my Heavenly father and I feel to pray that the choicest of heavens blessing[s] may rest upon you, I hope you have the society of sister Powers still; I want to see her much I felt thankful that you had been friends to her for I think her worthy of your friendship, sister P mentioned in her letter she drank a cup of tea occasionly for me I am quite glad she does for it is verry seldom that I get the chance to drink a cup for myself, tea and, coffee, and shugar is verry scarse with us know [now], their are many thing[s] I would like to write but pen and paper would fail  the bearer of this letter can tell more than I can write  br. Thomson will call at your house and he will tell you how things are a going on here, he has lived at Mr Young['s] ever since we left winter Quarters

Louisa then turns to another tragedy, the death of Daniel Browett, Martha's brother, at the hands of Indians. The closing of Louisa's letter once again gives a rich sense of the interconnectedness of many sister-wives in a large family.

I must soon close  give my love to all of the children and kiss them for me  tell Laura, Emily, and Frank [Marinda's children] to not forget me, my warmest respects to br Hyde, br Luke and wife  br Bently and wife, Mother Browett, Charls and Elsa [relatives of the Hyde family] and all that inquires after me, I will here mention that Lucy S. and Emily P. have each of them a young daughter, Manerva White a son, Artimesia a daughter sister Noble[s] health is verry [blank] this spring, Eliza Snow[s] health is rather poor this spring, Clarra {P.} has just come and wished to be kindly remembered to you allso the girls I am living with, I want you to write every oppertunity. May the Lord bless you is my prayr from your sincere friend (exscuse my poor writing and mistakes which are many!) Louisa

In this endearing, affecting letter, Louisa comes vividly to life. She captures the difficulty and privations of early pioneer Utah—the scarcity of food, the cramped living quarters, the exceptionally cold winter of 1849. Nevertheless, one also senses the warmth that the early Utah Saints shared.

Zina's diary continues to give prosaic, valuable references to Louisa's ongoing activities. On April 10 Zina records a Young family supper that included Louisa and Brigham. Three days later Brigham visited Eliza Snow, accompanied by "Loisa, Margaret & Clara." With Zina and nine other women, Louisa visited the graves of her children on April 15. Then, wrote Zina, "Louisa & I called at Sister Rockwoods. We had a blessing in the gifts." Louisa was a close friend of two of the most inveterate tongue-speakers in Mormonism, Eliza Snow and Zina Young. When the latter was sick, Louisa made her "a good cup of tea." "O how precious is a sisters kindness," her sister-wife journalized.

### IX. "Remember Me in My Affliction"

Zina would have many opportunities to care for Louisa in turn, for her cancer became progressively worse. In another letter to Marinda, Louisa wrote that she began to treat the sick breast in early May 1849. Still, on May 16, Eliza Partridge Smith Lyman wrote, "Visited at Wm Walker's with sisters Emily and Louisa Young and Sarah Ann and Lucy Kimball also Presnts Young and Kimball." This is one of many informal meetings attended by a group of Joseph Smith's widows and by Brigham and Heber.

Zina gave Louisa an emetic on May 18, probably lobelia, a purgative used in Thomsonian herbal medicine. A week later Louisa's face was swollen with erysipelas, skin eruptions accompanied by constitutional symptoms. On May 27 and June 4 she received more emetics. According to Zina, Louisa and four other sister wives "moved up" from one unspecified location to new quarters on June 11.

We have seen that Louisa spoke in tongues on occasion and once laid hands on Patty Sessions's head with other sisters. A June 19 entry in Zina's journal shows Louisa exercising priestly gifts once more: "Sister Washbern sent for Louisa[,] Sister Twist and my self to come and wash and annoint her daughter Mary Ann. She was taken very sick Sunday. Brigham Young sent his Carrage to carry us down. The Lord blest the administratin & she was better. Sister Eliza Snow came home with us. I was in Loises.

Brigham Young came in and we had quite a chat." That Young (the president and prophet of the church) would send a carriage to take three women to administer to another is a striking contrast to modern-day Mormon practice, in which only men are allowed to perform administrations for health.

Louisa made the sick Zina some ginger tea on June 28. On July 14 Louisa wrote another letter to Marinda Hyde at Winter Quarters, beginning with an account of her breast condition:

> Dear Sister Hyde. I imbrace the preasant oppertunity with pleasure, of communicateing a few lines to you to inform you how we are a prospering, my health is quite poor this summer I commenced the first of May to docter my breast, at times. it is quite painful which makes me feel verry miserable indeed; most of the time I can do a little  we are a trying to draw it to a head it get[s] along slow, how often I wish your brother Luke was here I think I should have more confidence in him than I have in those that are here, I was greatly in hopes I should hear that he; together with your family were a comeing on this season but I heare you are not, so I am disappointed, but hope if it is for the beast [best], you will come on next season.

These methods of treating her cancer were completely ineffectual. For the rest of her life, the pain would increase steadily. She then gives more details on the privations of early Salt Lake:

> Times has been rather heard [hard] here for some time since, their has been some families out of bread for a long time, but I feel as though I had no reason to complain  I have not set down to but one meal with out bread, and that went first rate yes. I feel as though we had been blesst  they are a thrashing wheet now and we shall have better times; their is not much sikness in the place at preasant.

Life in the Young family is described: "The girls are all usaly well I live in a family at preasant numbering 27. Mr Young['s] health is quite good at preasant, Sister Young['s] health is better than it was last winter, their was a number of us visiting together at br Kimball['s] not long since  we injoyed ourselves much." After mentioning some mutual friends, Louisa described the incursion of gentiles into Salt Lake: "We have had a great pleanty of the emigreants to visit us of late it seamed quite like old times to have the gentiles in our midest again, but I hope we shall not be troubled with them long, they have been a blessing to us in one respect they have been a and are; a {bearing} many good thing[s] with the saint[s] that they realy stood in great kneed of."

Louisa's final salutation is moving, as we think of her imminent death:

> Pleas give my respects to br Hyde ... give my best love to Martha and Mary Ann. I want to see them much  allso to the children kiss them for

me, and tell them not to forget me give much love, to Sister Powers if their [there] tell her I want to see her verry much indeed. I greatly hope she is on her way to this place, br Egan has not arrived yet I shall exspect to hear from you all when he does come, I wrote to you and sister Powers buy the last mail which you probably have recieved ere this, remember me in my affliction and pray for me. I give way for sister Eliz. from your sincere friend, Louisa.

And in the margin: "My respects to all that inquire after me, the girls that you are acquainted with all send their love [to] you Marth and Mary Ann."

Two days later Zina gave Louisa another emetic. On August 8 Patty Sessions visited; on September 21 Brigham had dinner with Louisa, Zina, and two others wives. Nevertheless, despite these moments of sociability and normalcy, Louisa's condition worsened inexorably. On December 10 Patty Sessions, the archetypal pioneer nurse, wrote in her journal, "As I came home I caled and see Louizas breast." Of course, Patty had no idea how to treat breast cancer; even today it is often incurable after it has developed.

Louisa celebrated her last birthday on February 7, 1850. Zina wrote, "Sister Louisa Beman viseted me. It was her birth day. She was 3__. Sistir Snow Gray Presendia & Caroline Clary Chase ... It was the last time Louisa was ever out of her room." One imagines the final bedridden months, the excruciating pain, the transformation of Louisa's body and face as the sickness ravaged her. Zina, Eliza, Patty, and a rotation of Brigham's wives must have waited at Louisa's bedside until she finally lapsed into a coma. The release came on May 15, and Louisa was able to join her five sons and first husband beyond the mortal veil. On May 18 Eliza Partridge Smith Lyman wrote in her journal, "Attended the funeral of Louisa Beman Young who died of cancer in the breast."

## X. Sisters

As we assess the significance of Louisa Beaman's life, we recognize that she was the important first plural wife in Nauvoo. Her marriage with Joseph Smith was esoteric, highly secret, sacred; though it reportedly had a sexual dimension, it produced no known children. Her marriage to Smith's successor, on the other hand, introduces us to practical polygamy—plurality practiced openly, with wives bearing children, living together and accompanying the husband to social events in small groups. Though Louisa's married life with Brigham was short, we still see in it an important phenomenon: the occasional visits with the husband, and the perpetual companionship of sister-wives. In both Nauvoo and Utah polygamy, there is rich evidence for close relationships between sister-wives who even helped initiate young women into the enlarged family. If interfeminine relationships were important in Victorian

America, in this respect Mormon women were more Victorian than
the Victorians proper.

# 4.

# Nauvoo Polyandry

## *Zina Diantha Huntington (Jacobs Smith Young)*

On February 2, 1846, in an inner room in the Nauvoo temple, Zina Huntington Jacobs stood by the side of Brigham Young, presiding apostle and de facto president of the Mormon church. Near Young was Heber C. Kimball, his first counselor. Somewhat apart stood Henry B. Jacobs, whom Zina had married in a civil ceremony in March 1841. She was now seven months pregnant with their second child, who would be named Henry Chariton Jacobs. That Henry Bailey was inside the temple shows that he was considered a faithful, worthy Latter-day Saint.

Zina and Brigham turned toward each other and Kimball sealed (married) Zina to Joseph Smith for eternity; Brigham stood proxy for the dead prophet, answering in his stead when the ceremony required a response. Henry, with Zina's father, William Huntington, and John D. Lee, stood as witnesses for the ritual, while Franklin D. Richards clerked. Then, as was customary in temple proxy marriages, Zina and Brigham turned to each other and were sealed to each other for time. Once again Henry stood as witness.

The two ordinances completed, one imagines the participants standing awkwardly in the sealing room. Perhaps the seven Mormons coalesced into two groups—Brigham, Kimball, Lee, and Richards conversing in hushed tones, while Zina, Henry, and William Huntington left the room together. Zina and Henry had much to do before they and their son, Zebulon, would leave Nauvoo for the West one week later in the main body of the Mormon migration.

One suspects that none of the four participants in these ceremonies understood their full significance. Henry and Zina probably felt that they would continue living together as man and wife, as they had during Joseph Smith's life. Young had married some women by proxy with whom he never lived, such as Mary Elizabeth Rollins Lightner and Rhoda Richards. But Brigham would eventually decide that Zina must become his wife fully, and the story of Zina Huntington would run its enigmatic course.

Zina is one of the best documented of Joseph Smith's plural wives; she kept a diary intermittently throughout her life and wrote a number of autobiographical sketches. Her siblings, children, and father have also left valuable journals and reminiscences. Furthermore, as a sister-wife, constant companion, and counselor of Eliza R. Snow, and as a General Relief Society president herself, she has begun to receive considerable scholarly attention. On the other hand, she was a polyandrous plural wife of both Joseph Smith and Brigham Young. It is well documented that she married Henry Jacobs in March 1841 and continued to live with him until May 1846, bearing him two children: Zebulon Jacobs (b. January 1842) and Henry Chariton Jacobs (b. March 1846). It is also well documented that Zina married Joseph Smith in October 1841 and Brigham Young in February 1846. While "official" Mormon biographies have Zina marrying Smith and Young after she left Henry, her marriages are so well documented that one is forced to reject this sequence and confront the issue of Nauvoo polyandry. Her biography sheds a great deal of light on Smith's and Young's polyandry, but these relationships were still so complex that Zina's marriage history often remains puzzling, despite the comparative wealth of evidence that illuminates it.

Zina was an extraordinary woman. She became the most important woman leader in nineteenth-century Utah, after Eliza R. Snow, and while Eliza was known for her impressive but somewhat forbidding intellect, Zina was known for her warmth. She was loved throughout her life for her service, compassion, and kindness.

## I. The Huntingtons

Zina Diantha Huntington was born on January 31, 1821, in Watertown, Jefferson County, New York, one hundred miles northeast of Palmyra, to William Huntington and Zina Baker. William, thirty-five, a native of New Hampshire, was a well-to-do farmer. Zina Baker, thirty-four, a devoutly religious woman, was also born in New Hampshire. They had married in November 1805 in Meridan, New Hampshire, but soon thereafter moved to Watertown, where they acquired a large farm and began clearing land and building a home and farm buildings.

Zina had seven older siblings, of whom two died before she was born. Chauncey Dyer and Nancy, twins, were born in 1806, but Nancy died a year later. Dimick Baker, who would become a faithful companion of Joseph Smith, a Danite in Missouri, a Mormon Battalion stalwart, and an Indian translator in Utah, was born in 1808. Presendia Lathrop, who would also marry Joseph Smith, was born in 1810. An unnamed boy died as an infant in 1813. Adaline Elizabeth and William Dresser joined the Huntingtons in 1815 and 1818. Zina's two younger siblings, Oliver Boardman and John Dickenson, were born in 1823 and 1827. Oliver, one of the fine diarists of early Mormonism, would be especially close to Zina throughout her life. She received her first experience of familial loss at the age of five when eleven-year-old Adaline died on November 26, 1826.

## II. On the Huntington Farm

Zina grew up in a large story-and-a-half stone farmhouse with a dairy behind it and two hundred acres of farm surrounding it. In later life she vividly remembered that outside the house "a profusion of lilac blossoms scented the air." The farmhouse had a kitchen with "typical old fire-place with its iron crane, upon which the kettles were hung, and a brick oven, built at the side for baking purposes." In addition to growing regular farm crops, the family harvested fruits from nearby orchards and made sugar and syrup from maples. Many farm animals had to be cared for. Zina Baker and her daughters spun and wove wool and flax, fashioning clothes, bedding, and table linen.

Zina recalls that as a girl she had delicate health, could do no heavy work, and attended school only at intervals. Still, her childhood was apparently peaceful, even idyllic. She later wrote:

> In my earliest reading of history Columbus & Wm Wallace I used to muse while watching the consuming bark log in our old fashion fireplaces why I could not have been born in a day when something was going on in the nations of the Earth not that I wished to see distress but some enterprise [beyond] the sabbath meeting schools. my relitives ware mostly close by, was all I ever anticipated to see.

Little did she realize what an adventurous life she would lead.

Her spiritual environment was Christianity at the time of the Second Great Awakening. The Huntingtons were strict Presbyterians who read the Bible daily before family prayers. "I was taught early by precept & example to call on our heavenly Father in prayer," she later wrote. Letters written by Zina Baker to her mother have been preserved, and they are steeped in religion. She seems almost fanatical as she dwells constantly on Christian moralizing themes rather than on news of the family. However, the Huntingtons were not strictly puritanical and loved music; they performed together in a family orchestra, William playing the bass viol, Zina Baker the cello, William Jr. the cornet, and Dimick the drum.

The Huntington family began to extend in 1827 when Presendia married Norman Buell. In 1830 Dimick united with Fanny Allen, and the following year Chauncey wedded Clarissa Bull.

### III. Baptism of Fire

In 1831 when Zina was ten, there was a local conflict between Presbyterians and Congregationalists on the method of selecting clergy and William decided to consult his Bible for the answer. Zina remembered her father "sitting quietly perusing the Bible, determined to find the right way, his firm lips closed with the determination to succeed if success was possible." After much study and pondering, he declared "that none of the churches were right according to the way he read the Bible, for none of them had the organization peculiar to the primitive church. There were no prophets, no apostles, no spiritual gifts as were possessed by the ancient saints. Nothing could shake him from his belief."

So William, like many Mormon converts, was almost pre-converted to the biblical primitivism that was one of Mormonism's most attractive features. When William heard of Joseph Smith, a prophet who had found a new, golden Bible, Zina wrote, "The very word 'prophet' caught my father's ear and arrested his attention. He was anxious at once to go to this so-called 'prophet' and test the strength of his claim." William's farm duties prevented his immediate departure, but a neighbor, Joseph Wakefield, was also interested in the new prophet and went to meet Smith. When he returned to Watertown, "he brought the glad news of a prophet a gain on the earth." He also brought a Book of Mormon. Zina was away from home attending school, but she heard about Wakefield's reports. When she returned home, she wrote, "I saw the Book of Mormon, that strange, new book, lying on the window sill of our sitting-room. I went up to the window, picked it up, and the sweet influence of the Holy Spirit accompanied it to such an extent that I pressed it to my bosom in a rapture of delight, murmuring as I did so, 'This is the truth, truth, truth!'" The mere idea of new scripture was intoxicating to her.

William and Zina Baker read the Book of Mormon two or three times, then, in April 1835, joined the Latter-day Saint church. Oliver remembers that the Huntington house subsequently became "a rendesvouse for all the Mormon preachers in that part of the country." In late July Hyrum Smith and David Whitmer stayed several days with the Huntingtons, and David encouraged Zina to join the church. However, she wanted to be baptized with Fanny, Dimick's wife. On the morning of the missionaries' expected departure, as Smith prayed, Zina remembers, "I had presented to me a heavenly vision of a man going down into the water and baptizing someone. So when this message came I felt it was a testimony that the time had come for me to receive baptism." Soon thereafter the news came that Fanny and Dimick desired immediate baptism as well, so Hyrum and David stayed a few days. On August 1, at the age of fourteen, Zina was baptized by Hyrum Smith.

Soon after this, when she was alone one day in the woods, she had an overpowering spiritual experience. "The gifts of the gospel were manifest the first time I ever sang in tongs after ~~being~~ baptised into the church of Jesus Christ of Latterday Saints around me was as light as the blaze of a candle I was surrounded [it was] a heavenly influence and no unpleasent sensation from that day the gift has remained with me." However, the gift of tongues rested upon her with such "overwhelming force" that she became "alarmed" and "checked its utterance." As a result, the gift left her, and she felt that she had offended the Holy Spirit. Burdened by guilt, Zina eventually told her mother of the loss while they were spinning together one day. Zina Baker told her daughter to pray earnestly for the return of the gift.

So Zina walked down to a favorite spring in a meadow, where she knelt and told God "if He could forgive my transgression, and give me back the lost gift, I would promise never to check it again, no matter where or when I felt its promptings." The gift returned, and Zina kept her vow; she would participate in glossolalia and interpreting tongue speech throughout the rest of her life. She and Eliza Snow, with Elizabeth Whitney, would be the most enthusiastic tongue-speakers in the early church. Thus women practiced a prophetic mode in early Mormonism; the "interpretation" of tongues was often apocalyptic and oracular. Emmeline Wells would later write that Zina gave "the interpretation of hymns, psalms and sacred songs in the most musical and happy manner, without thought or hesitation. There is something divinely beautiful in thus rendering, by the gift of inspiration, words uttered in an unknown tongue."

One of Zina Baker Huntington's experiences provides another example of how these early Mormons believed in the restoration of New Testament gifts. One night she was called to sit up all night with the body of a neighbor. Pondering "power, faith and the possibility of the dead being brought back to life now as well as in the days of the apostles," she felt that she had the faith to call the neighbor back from the dead. When she laid her hands on him, "The dead man obeyed, and opened his eyes full wide and gazed into hers." This was too much for Zina Baker, and she rushed from the room; the corpse lapsed back into lifelessness. She later explained to her children that the man was not meant to take up his mortal life again, but God had allowed his momentary revival "to show her that 'these signs do follow them that believe.'"

All of these early revelatory experiences of Zina Diantha provide background to help understand her later intense commitment to Mormonism, even when it demanded such an extraordinary social innovation as patriarchal polygamy. The early Mormons were not just Bible readers, they were living the Bible.

## IV. Kirtland, Ohio

At some point, Joseph Smith, Sr., visited the Huntington farm and counseled William to sell his property as soon as possible and gather with the Saints in Kirtland. William and his family obediently disposed of their beloved farm, then left Watertown on October 1, 1836, and were launched on their Mormon adventure. A steamboat ride on Lake Erie brought them to Ohio ten days later. Oliver remembers walking the twelve miles to Kirtland and the joy that came over their company when they saw the Kirtland temple in the distance. He likened the modern Mormon experience to the Old Testament model. "The Lords House! Solemnly exclaimed every one, as we were trudging along in a confused flock. It makes me think of tribes going up to Jerusalem to worship, anciently."

In Kirtland, William paid $3,000 for a good home and forty acres of land, and the Huntingtons put down new roots. Zina remembers seeing Joseph Smith for the first time: "He was 6 feet light auburn hair [and a heavy nose] blue eyes the [eye]ball[s] ful & round rather long-favoured when he was filled with the spiret of revilation or insperation—to talk to the saints his countenance would look clear & bright." Smith, for early Mormons, was more than a person; he was a religious ideal in physical form. The Huntingtons also began to meet a new set of friends who would remain with them throughout their lives; most importantly, Zina met Eliza R. Snow, with whom she would later provide leadership in the church for many years.

Zina became a member of the Kirtland Temple Choir, and the spiritual high point of her Kirtland experience undoubtedly involved meetings in the Kirtland temple. In that building, she wrote, she once heard angels singing: "One corner of the house seemed filled with music to [too] sweet for earth." Her parents were known for their generosity to the poor, and Zina Baker would often take "little Zina" with her on her expeditions to distribute goods to the needy.

For a time Kirtland was another idyllic moment in Zina's life. But soon misfortune overwhelmed the family. William invested much of his money in the Kirtland "anti-bank" and gave much of it to the poor. In the fall of 1837 he lost his land. "So when the bank went broke we were broken and as poor as the best of the Mormons; well, we expected to become poor but not quite so quick," wrote Oliver wryly. William was forced to work day labor, and the Huntingtons often had little to eat. But also in the fall, despite financial losses, William became a high counselor, the equivalent of a modern LDS general authority.

## V. Missouri

Soon the Huntingtons, with the rest of the Mormons, prepared to leave Kirtland for Missouri, and departed on May 21, 1838, when Zina was seventeen. They traveled in a small company that included Eliza Snow's family. All of the Huntingtons' possessions were packed into two double-loaded wagons. While the Mormon trek to Salt Lake City is better known than the earlier journey to Missouri, this was also a long, difficult hegira. Zina wrote, "Our Pilgramage to Farwest was like the journey of the Children of Israel in the wilderness; every thing was uncertain but one, and it was but by the hand and power of God that we ever got to our place of destination." They traveled a thousand miles in eight weeks and three days. Zina fondly remembered "a pleasent company  the ~~roling~~ prarie with its sea of flowers, its waving green was lovely  much more enjoyable than when a wind would strike us in the night with ~~lightn[ing]~~ the eliments all at war the rain in torrents & we had to sit and hold the covers on our wagons or be left without  I need not mention our condition in the morning."

The Huntingtons arrived at Far West on July 18 and met Dimick and Fanny, who had already gathered to the new Zion. Soon they moved on to Adam-ondi-Ahman, where William built a crude house and operated a grist mill. However, their stay in Missouri would be short-lived, for they had unfortunately arrived at a time when anti-Mormon tensions had reached a boiling point, and battles, mobbings, and quasi-military persecutions ensued. Both Dimick and Oliver Huntington served as Danites, and Dimick distinguished himself as a captain of the Danite guard. The family was forced to return to Far West, and before long they left Missouri entirely. "The history of these days are partially writen," Zina wrote, "but ... the sufferings can not be told." She, with her parents and two younger brothers, left Far West on April 18, 1839.

## VI. The Real Chill Fever

A week later they arrived at Quincy, Illinois, and stayed with Dimick two or three weeks. He was living in a log cabin at Judge Cleveland's farm, while Joseph Smith, who by this time had become an intimate friend of Dimick, was staying at the Cleveland house. If Zina, now eighteen, had not known Smith well previously, at Quincy she would have had the opportunity to associate with him on a daily basis. On May 16 the Huntingtons moved to Commerce (early Nauvoo) and stayed in a rented house.

However, a new disaster stunned the family on June 24 and delivered an especially heavy blow to Zina: her mother became seriously ill with "a congestive chill." As she lay sick, Zina Diantha and Oliver "came down with the real chill fever," as Oliver wrote. The ague, malaria, took a fearful toll on the new settlers in the early days of Nauvoo, built, as it was, on a swamp. Soon William and John were also suffering alternating fevers and chills. As Zina Baker neared death, she turned to Zina Diantha and said, "Zina my time has come to die. You will live many years; but O, how lonesome father will be. I am not afraid to die. All I dread is the mortal suffering. I shall come forth triumphant when the Savior comes with the just to meet the saints on the earth." On July 8, just before dawn, she passed away. Young Zina was extraordinarily close to her mother and the death must have caused her overwhelming grief. But she and Oliver were so sick that they could not even attend the funeral.

The Huntingtons endured months of the fever. Oliver wrote that he was so ill he was barely conscious—"In fact from that time until the next winter is but a mere cipher in my memory." Zina remembers Joseph Smith's adopted daughter, Julia, helping to tend them, and Smith himself making them tea. Some three weeks later Joseph Smith told William that the family would all die if they stayed where they were and offered to take them into his own home. The Huntingtons accepted, so the prophet hooked up his team and brought them home with him. Only Oliver was sent to another household.

Thus, as was the case with many of Joseph Smith's plural wives, Zina lived in his house before her marriage to him. Ironically, while living there, she met the man who would become her first husband, Henry Bailey Jacobs, a handsome, articulate twenty-three-year-old who played the violin. When Zina had recovered her health, she and Henry began to spend time together. A Mormon since 1832, he had survived the hardships of Kirtland and Missouri; was ordained a seventy, which was a missionary calling, on January 19, 1839, and had apparently gone on his first, short mission in May. This resumé of his early life offers the portrait of a staunch, committed Latter-day Saint, and Henry would serve many missions after his marriage. Oliver Huntington, who served two missions with him, portrays Henry as a dedicated, eloquent preacher, though a man with human imperfections.

It was perhaps during this stay in Joseph Smith's house that Zina learned an important, peculiar doctrine from the American prophet. She was grieving for her mother and asked Joseph if she would know her as her mother in the next life. "Certainly you will," he answered. "More than that, you will meet and become acquainted with your eternal Mother, the wife of your Father in Heaven." "And have I then a Mother in Heaven?" exclaimed the astonished teenager. "You assuredly have. How could a Father claim His title unless there were also a Mother to share that parenthood?" the Mormon leader replied. Eliza R. Snow learned of this doctrine soon afterward and wrote what became the Mormon hymn "Oh My Father," in which she addressed the Heavenly Father and Mother in prayer.

By August 20 the Huntingtons' health had improved somewhat, so they moved into a new house that Dimick built for them near his own on the bank of the Mississippi. Though they were still weak, they turned to the events of daily life. William rented new land and began farming again; he was soon chosen to be a member of the Nauvoo high council. Meanwhile, "Zina kept house for us, and a good Mother she was to us all," wrote Oliver.

In the summer of 1840, according to family tradition, the spirit of Zina Baker returned to the world of the living to deliver a message to Zina, though she came to Dimick's wife, Fanny. Oliver writes, "She left a short message for Zina and a word for each [child]." However, Fanny was terrified, and her mother-in-law departed suddenly. This would not be the last time that a Huntington woman would transcend the bounds of death.

Father Huntington married Lydia Partridge in August; she was the widow of Edward Partridge and mother of two future plural wives of Joseph Smith, Eliza and Emily Partridge. William, with Oliver and John, moved into the Partridge home, but as space was limited (Lydia had four daughters and one son), Zina went to live with Dimick. She and Henry Jacobs continued courting.

### VII. Henry and Joseph

Apparently in the midst of Henry Jacobs's suit, Joseph Smith taught Zina the principle of plural marriage and then proposed to her. One can only imagine the shock this must have caused her. The "cult of true womanhood" in nineteenth-century America required that a woman live by the ideals of purity, piety, domesticity, and submissiveness; and Smith's new doctrine offended against domesticity (the sanctity of the home), piety (typical American religious mores), and purity (the belief that sexuality should be reserved for monogamous Christian marriage). So it is not surprising that despite her religious reverence for the Mormon leader, she either flatly rejected his proposal or put him off. Furthermore, she was probably in love with Jacobs, not Smith, and may have revered Joseph's wife Emma, whom she probably realized would be unsympathetic to an extramonogamous union.

Nevertheless, Zina accepted Joseph as a prophet whose words were infallible revelations direct from God. Her older brother, Dimick, Smith's close associate, probably also encouraged her to marry the Mormon leader, so it is remarkable that while she was an impressionable nineteen-year-old, she would refuse his suit. Still, she felt conflicted and remembers praying: "O dear Heaven, grant me wisdom! Help me to know the way. O

Lord, my god, let thy will be done and with thine arm around about to guide, shield and direct. Illuminate our minds with inteligence as you do bless the earth with light and warmth."

Smith was always persistent in his marriage proposals, and rejections usually moved him to further effort, so he continued to press his suit with Zina at the same time that she was courting Henry. And Smith usually expressed his polygamous proposals in terms of prophetic commandments. In addition to the religious dilemmas she faced, Zina was also choosing between two men, both of whom she cared for in different ways. In early 1841 Zina made her choice: she would marry Henry Jacobs, her romantic soulmate. The engagement was announced. By making this decision, she probably felt that she had put an end to Smith's suit and to the specter of polygamy in her life. It is not known whether Henry knew that Smith had also proposed to Zina, but it is known that he was a close friend and disciple of Smith. According to family tradition, as the day of marriage approached, Henry and/or Zina asked Smith to perform the marriage, and he agreed. On March 7 Henry and Zina, with their friends and family, arrived at the place designated for the marriage, but Smith did not appear, so they turned to John C. Bennett, Nauvoo's mayor, to officiate. Zina must have felt a great sense of relief and finality as she and Henry exchanged vows and began their married life in Nauvoo.

However, Zina learned soon afterwards, undoubtedly to her complete astonishment, that Smith had not given up. Again according to family tradition, she and Henry saw Smith soon after the marriage and "asked why he had not come ... he told them the Lord had made it known to him she was to be his celestial wife." Once again Zina was plunged into a quandary. Smith told them that God had commanded him to marry her. However, he apparently also told them they could continue to live together as husband and wife. According to family tradition, Henry accepted this, but Zina continued to struggle. If polygyny offended against the American cult of true womanhood, polyandry offended even more. Nevertheless, if polygyny and polyandry offended against domesticity, piety, and purity, submissiveness required her to obey. Disobeying Smith would also be an offense against Mormon piety. So polygamy divided the cult of true womanhood against itself. If a woman interpreted Smith's polygyny and polyandry as sacred, she would become entirely devoted to the new system. It is well documented that American women of this period were intensely pious, much more so than their male counterparts.

Zina remained conflicted until a day in October, apparently, when Joseph sent Dimick to her with a message: an angel with a drawn sword had stood over Smith and told him that if he did not establish polygamy, he would lose "his position and his life." Zina, faced with the responsibility for his position as prophet, and even perhaps his life, finally acquiesced. The usual date for the marriage is October 27, and throughout her life Zina commemorated her marriage to Smith on this date. Dimick officiated at the ceremony and Fanny acted as witness. This marriage may be considered dynastic, to a certain extent, as it linked Smith to Dimick and also to high counselor William Huntington (if William knew about it).

Zina later wrote of her decision to enter polygamy:

When I heard that God had revealed the law of celestial marriag that we would have the privilige of associating in family relationships in <sup>the</sup> worlds to come I searched the scripture & buy [by] humble prayer to my Heavenly Father I obtained a testimony for myself that God had required that order to be established in this church. I mad[e] a greater sacrifise than to give my life for I never anticipated a gain [again] to be looked uppon as an honerable woman by those I dearly loved [but] could I compremise concience lay aside the sure testimony of the spiret of God for the Glory of this world after having been baptized by one having authority and covenanting to be obedient at the waters edge to live the life of a saint[?] ...

Zina's choice, as she explains it, was a choice to honor her conscience. She did not merely bow to Smith's pressure; she obtained her own testimony of polygamy by scriptural study (Smith usually pointed to Old Testament patriarchs when preaching polygamy) and by personal revelation. Apparently, Henry knew of the marriage and accepted it. He believed that "whatever the Prophet did was right, without making the wisdom of God's authorities bend to the reasoning of any man."

This wedding, soon after the marriage to Jacobs, does not harmonize with Zina's later explanation for her relationship with Joseph: "I was married to Mr. Jacobs, but the marriage was unhappy and we parted." This suggests the following sequence: wedding to Jacobs; unhappy marriage; parting; marriage to Joseph Smith. But, as one can see, Henry and Zina had not been married long when Smith proposed to her polyandrously, so they would have had little opportunity for an unhappy marriage by that time. In addition, Zina and Henry stayed married, cohabiting, throughout Smith's life. Thus Zina's explanation for her marriage to Smith may be a "revision" of history to gloss over her simultaneous marriage to both men. It is certain that the marriage was not unhappy enough to cause the couple to stop living together during Smith's lifetime, or for years after his death.

Almost nothing further is known about Zina's marriage to Joseph Smith. The problems and enigmas of all of Smith's marriages apply here.

Nothing specific is known about sexuality in their marriage, though judging from Smith's other marriages, sexuality was probably included. We do know that Zina and Henry continued living as husband and wife, though Henry was often absent on missions. Zina's emotional reaction to the marriage was one of awe: "It was something too sacred to be talked about; it was more to me than life or death. I never breathed it for years."

## VIII. Life in Nauvoo

When Zina married Joseph Smith, she was some seven months pregnant, and her first son, Zebulon Jacobs, was born on January 2, 1842. Zebulon remembered that Henry and Zina lived in a log house with dirt floor and crude straw bed in Nauvoo. "Their table a dry goods box. untill one could be build with hammer and nails from the box while an ordinary milk pan would have held all their table furnishings and be crouded." When Henry bought a coat that was much too big for him, Zina cut it up and made a new coat which fit him perfectly. "The next Sunday father had his new coat and proud as a lord." Henry, like Zina, was given to speaking in tongues, and in an 1852 letter he reminded Zina how they would share this gift in Nauvoo: "When I was at home with you and the children ... we could say our prayers together and speak together in tongues and bless each other in the name of the Lord." So a young couple would share the apostolic gifts in Mormon Nauvoo.

About a week after Zebulon's birth, on January 17, Henry served a short mission to nearby Chicago; Joseph Smith personally sent him on this errand. A year later, in early 1843, Henry served a two- or three-month mission with John D. Lee, who remembers that Jacobs would brag about Zina and "almost worshiped her."

After a short stay in Nauvoo, at the end of May, Henry, with brother-in-law Oliver Huntington and John Gleason, set out on a mission to western New York, where both Henry and Oliver had friends and relatives. Oliver kept a mission journal in which he wrote with sincere admiration about Henry's preaching. While Henry was absent, Zina is sketchily documented, as is typical of missionary wives. We do know that on March 24 she was accepted into the Female Relief Society of Nauvoo.

Henry and Oliver arrived home on October 11. Half a year later, on April 15, 1844, Henry was assigned a mission to Tennessee to campaign for Joseph Smith's U.S. presidential aspirations. By May 4 he had left Nauvoo; he returned on June 16. While he was still gone, Zina started writing a journal, which she kept sporadically throughout the rest of her life. It reveals an extraordinarily pious woman, for she often breaks into prayer; she is hard-working, often tired, many times sick. Above all, the diary reveals a woman of great charm—intelligent and perceptive, yet possessing a childlike innocence. She is a sensitive, gifted writer, and a disastrous speller.

The first entry ("June 5, 6, 7, 8, 9") is just as puzzling as is much of Zina's life: "Went with Henres uncles family uppon the hill. From this day I understand the Kinsmans degree of freemasonry. My husband, being a Master Mason, attended meeting. Hiram Smith spoke exceeding well also red a revelation. I went to see Sister Gleson, and Sister Abigal Thorn in the past wek." Since there is no Kinsman's degree of masonry, this must be a code word for an esoteric meeting, and her "husband" must have been Joseph Smith (whom she elsewhere referred to as a Master Mason), as Henry was still in Tennessee. We can probably gather from this passage that Zina attended ritual meetings with Smith on occasion.

Her journal then turns to events leading up to Smith's death on June 27. The day after the martyrdom, Zina took Zebulon to see the bodies of Joseph and Hyrum, her celestial husband (and Zebulon's father by sealing) and brother-in-law. An important chapter in her life had ended.

## IX. Brigham Young

One would think that Zina's marital situation had simplified, at least for this life. She and Henry, who had never stopped living together as husband and wife, probably expected to continue doing so now without a third member of a marriage triangle. Zina and her children would be Joseph Smith's in the eternities but she would remain Henry's throughout the rest of this life. In actuality, her situation was not that straightforward, for her marriage to Smith had started a chain of events that would not allow simplification even in this life. How and why the next complication occurred is not completely clear, though a few pieces of evidence allow a tentative reconstruction.

First, there is a family tradition that Brigham Young, Heber C. Kimball, and the rest of the Quorum of Twelve Apostles approached the widows of Joseph Smith and offered themselves as husbands. Smith reportedly had asked the apostles to do this if he should die. Thus Young and Kimball, in approaching Smith's wives, were not simply adding numerous wives to their own polygamous families as quickly as possible; they may have been acting out of a sense of responsibility to their fallen leader.

It is certain that many of Smith's widows did marry members of the Twelve. Brigham married between seven and nine of them; Kimball married approximately eleven. George A. Smith married one, as did Amasa Lyman. Prominent church leaders and Nauvoo insiders such as Ezra Taft Benson, Almon Babbitt, Cornelius Lott, John L. Smith, and John Bernhisel married others.

It is not known how Brigham's and Heber's offers of marriage were phrased. In the family traditions there is some emphasis on the choice of the widow. However, the preponderance of Joseph Smith's widows marrying Young and Kimball, the two most powerful men in Mormonism, is striking. One also wonders how these two approached the polyandrous wives of Smith who were still living with their "first husbands." Some of Smith's polyandrous wives remained married to their first husbands for time, though they were eventually sealed to Smith for eternity in the Nauvoo temple. For instance, Lucinda Pendleton remained married to George W. Harris and was sealed to him for time; Patty Sessions remained married to David Sessions; Marinda Hyde remained married to Orson Hyde and was sealed to him for eternity, an anomaly; Elvira Cowles stayed with Jonathan Holmes and was sealed to him for time. Others of the polyandrous wives were sealed to church leaders for time, then remained living with their "first husbands." In this group are Sarah Cleveland, who had a non-church-member first husband; Sylvia Sessions Lyon, who had an excommunicant first husband; Mary Lightner, who had a non-member first husband; and Zina's own sister, Presendia, who was married to a disaffected Mormon. Church leaders felt that a proxy marriage to Smith in the Nauvoo temple was necessary, and this always entailed a sealing for time to the man standing proxy; therefore, a non-member could not perform the proxy marriage. Accordingly, to be sealed to Joseph Smith in the temple, one had to be sealed to someone other than the non-member first husband for time. All of this is complicated but does have a general outline of discernible logic.

However, in Zina's case, the logic breaks down. Her "first husband" was a faithful church member in good standing, an active seventy, the veteran of numerous missions. He would be capable of standing proxy for Joseph Smith in the temple, as is evidenced by the fact that he did perform rituals in the Nauvoo temple. However, for reasons that are not completely clear, Brigham Young pressed his suit with Zina. According to family traditions, "President Young told Zina D. if she would marry him she would be in a higher glory." However, Zina was already sealed to Joseph Smith, so it is not clear how being sealed to Brigham for time would improve her chances for eternal salvation. In any event, Brigham approached her after Smith's death and she apparently married him for time in September 1844. Nevertheless, she remained married and cohabiting with Jacobs, which would be consistent with Smith's practice of polyandry.

How Zina and Henry reacted to this new marriage is not documented, but they probably responded obediently as faithful Latter-day Saints who believed that Brigham, president of the Quorum of the Twelve, was a church leader who could not err. If, as seems likely,

Henry knew about the marriage, he and Zina probably expected to continue living with each other throughout the rest of their lives.

Zina's journal from this period records only everyday happenings: visits with friends, visits with family, accounts of church meetings, sicknesses, moves. There are occasional interactions with Brigham. On September 20 Zina wrote, "Moving. I called at B Young. He was not in." Henry had bought a piece of land from Zina's brother William, and the Jacobses moved in with him until Henry could build a house on the lot. They spent Christmas in Lima, with the family gathering at Presendia's house.

Henry's faithfulness was underscored when he was ordained one of the presidents of Seventy on January 19, 1845. "HBJ the youngest of the Pres[idents]," as Zina noted, apparently with the normal pride of a wife. Two days later he left on another local mission. Zina writes, again like a wife, "Wilt thou Preserve me in his absence, O Lord, and my little son." On January 30, sponsored by Brigham and without Henry, she received her endowment and was admitted into the Holy Order, that inner circle of elite Mormons who met frequently in ritual prayer meetings. "Went to prayer meting. Had a good meeting," she wrote in her journal. The next night she dreamed of Joseph.

Henry returned on February 6. "He has ben prospered on his mission, had good success," Zina wrote, again with apparent pride. On the 11th he left on another local mission, from which he returned on March 1. Zina and Henry celebrated their fourth wedding anniversary six days later. Zina wrote, "4 years ago to day since we ware Marr[i]ed. O God let thy hand be over us still to prosper us." She and Henry continued to attend seventies meetings together and Henry worked on the new house again.

Throughout April, Zina's health was poor and Henry, with Oliver and "Father" Huntington, administered to her on April 3. On the 25th the Jacobses moved into a small log house owned by Jonathan Holmes, "first husband" of another wife of Joseph Smith, Elvira Cowles Holmes. Zina noted Henry's birthday on May 5, as she did for her closest family members, especially her parents.

Four days later Zina's diary includes a cryptic entry:

Never to be forgotten at 11 oclock, O then what shall I say. At or after 4 I went to sleep. O Lord have mercy uppon my Sole. Teache me the ways of eternal life ... Comfort us, yes, Henry in his trouble, for he has not repined a word. Accept of our thanks for life, forgive the weakness of my heart, and let me do nothing but what shall be to thy honour and Glory and my soles salvation.

Something had happened that profoundly troubled both Henry and Zina. Zina feels sympathy for Henry and prays for him. Though this event might have given him cause to be rebellious, he had not "repined" a word. She herself had "weakness" of heart. One can only speculate on what this event may have been, significant though it probably was. A month later, on June 11, Henry received some counsel from Brigham Young: "Henry went to see Pres. B. Young to be councel[ed] upon his and [his] families situation. O God be merciful to us, I ask in the Name of Jesus, thy Sone," Zina wrote.

Five days later Zina visited Eliza R. Snow Smith Young, who was sick; on the same day she went to a funeral with Patty Sessions Smith. The support group of sister-widows of Joseph Smith was now in operation. Her diary continues with family and friendly visits, sicknesses, meetings, and speaker reports. On September 17 Henry served with Stephen Markham in defending Nauvoo. Four days later Zina's Nauvoo journal ends with the following words: "All things move in order in the City."

## X. At the Chariton River

As persecution against the Mormons mounted and they prepared to leave for the "wilderness," and as the temple was simultaneously completed, Henry and Zina received their temple endowments together on January 3, 1846. A month later, on February 2, Zina, now twenty-five and seven months pregnant, married Joseph Smith "for eternity" and Brigham Young for "time," with Henry standing witness.

Zina, who was very pregnant, and Henry now had to face the long journey to the West. As Zebulon put it, "We staid there [Nauvoo] till the spring of 46, when we had a polite invitation from our Parrental government, in the shape of musket and saber with a good supply of bayonets to make it plainer understood to mozey on or in other words pick up and leave." As the Mormons did so often, Zina viewed the move in Old Testament terms: "On the 9th feb clear and cold we left our house all we possessed in a wagon left many things standing in our house unsold for most of our neighbours ware as our selves on the wing. the bells were ringing the temple was on fire and we leaving our homes for the wilderness trusting in God like abraham the fire was soon subdewed."

Zebulon remembers his father putting all the family's possessions into a wagon; Zeb was "ancious to get in and take a ride." When the family arrived at the top of a hill overlooking the Mississippi, Henry stopped for a moment. Before them the Mississippi was frozen over and teams were scattered up and down in every direction going over to the Iowa side of the river. They looked back at their beloved Nauvoo one last time, then, writes Zebulon, "we went down the hill onto the ice and over into Iowa."

After camping in Sugar Creek for a time, Zina and Henry started moving west on March 2, traveling in George A. Smith's company. In March the wanderers endured almost constant rain, which turned roads into mud and made rivers nearly impassable. It was an enormously uncomfortable and unhealthy migration and was doubly so for a pregnant woman. On March 16 Patty Sessions and Eliza Snow visited Zina, perhaps to wash and anoint her for her upcoming childbirth, a customary ritual among nineteenth-century Latter-day Saint women.

Early in the morning of March 22, as Zina ate her breakfast in the rain, George A. Smith encouraged her to travel as far as possible that day: "Go on sister Zina ride as long as you can it shal be wel with you do not stop the camp if possible." So Zina, perhaps in labor by now, traveled four miles before she called a halt to the march at the Chariton River. As Zina and Henry had become separated from the other Huntingtons, "Mother Lyman," a longtime family friend, was the only woman with Zina, and she probably acted as midwife. Zebulon remembers that Henry bundled him up, took him outside the wagon, where it was raining, deposited him underneath a scrub oak, and told him "to keep quiet or I would fall and crack my head." When Zebulon complained of this treatment, Henry told him to wait a few minutes and he would see something worth seeing. After a while Henry came out and summoned his eldest son into the wagon. "Father took the damp shawl off me then leaned me towards the head of mother's bed, 'What do you see over there?', 'Mama', 'What else?' At that moment I heard a baby sqeak. Catching sight of a little red squirming face, father was kept busy holding me. Mother said 'you have got a little brother, Henry Chariton Jacobs.'"

Zina's family then made a dangerous crossing of the rain-swollen Chariton. A rope was attached to Zina's wagon, and about fifty men holding onto it lowered it carefully down the bank of the river. As if that were not enough after a childbirth, Zina and company then traveled four more miles. One can only imagine that bumpy, stop-and-start ride, and the resulting physical pain for a woman who had just given birth, the rain soaking through the canvas above Zina's head, and her concern for the well-being of her two children. Many of Joseph Smith's widows endured similar childbirths as they traveled to Utah, making a sudden transition from urban easterners to frontierswomen on the Iowa trek.

Zina remembers that it was so cold that night that in the morning the cattle's feet had to be chopped out of the frozen mud. Mother Lyman prepared coffee and a biscuit for Zina and the journey continued. After the day's march, as Henry took care of the team, Zina was alone in the wagon, "my eldest son with me ... 4 years old and my darling babe so beautiful and good as dear ones are generally to there Mothers." Despite the bitter cold, the children remained healthy.

## XI. "I Dream of You Often"

Zina's other husband, Brigham, was, during this time, concerned with the herculean task of guiding the Saints across Iowa. He reached the way station, Mt. Pisgah, on May 18, and the Huntingtons arrived there at least by May 21, for on that date William Huntington was appointed to take charge of the camp.

The following day the next crucial event affecting Zina's and Henry's marriage took place. Though Henry was halfway across Iowa, driving a covered wagon for his wife and two sons, one of them newborn, through danger and privation, at this difficult time, of all times, he was suddenly sent away on a mission. In all his previous missions he had stayed in America, usually in Illinois, but now he was sent overseas to England. It is documented that Henry was sent by the de facto First Presidency, Brigham Young and the Quorum of the Twelve. In addition, Henry was extremely ill. Zebulon remembers that at Mt. Pisgah "my Father started on a mission to Europe he was that low in health that he had to be carried in a blanket to the waggon to start he went in full faith and done a good work." Once again, whatever Henry's faults, one has to be impressed by his faithfulness and obedience to the gospel and to its latter-day leaders.

On June 2 Brigham left Mt. Pisgah, where Zina would stay with her father. Henry's first mission letter is dated June 25 and was written at Nauvoo. It does not seem to be the letter of someone who considers himself estranged or divorced from his wife. Henry addressed his "Dear companion": "I dream of you often," he wrote, "and desire to see you very much." He tells of an apocalyptic dream he had and about his concern for his family's welfare: "O Zina ... it makes my Heart bleede to think you have nothing to Live upon  take all I have and dispose of it to the best advantage before you starve ... I do desire to see you and my Little Boys very much  my anxiety for my family are greate ... the team is a waiting I send you a silk Handkerchief and Likeness  wright to me as quick as you get this."

Jacobs met Oliver Huntington at Cambria, New York, at Oliver's in-laws, the Neals, on July 11. While staying there, Oliver matter of factly, without comment, noted that Jacobs had proposed to a woman. "While Sister Elsy was there, she & Bro. Jacobs got deep in love & promised to marry when he came back from his Mission & go west with him. But on his return she had changed her mind." This comes as something of a shock, after reading Henry's affectionate letter to Zina. However, it is explainable if we accept that Brigham Young advised Jacobs to take a polygamous wife on his mission to gain an eternal companion. Otherwise, Oliver, Zina's brother, presumably would have been outraged. One even wonders if this anecdote could be a "revision" of history by Oliver, written to justify Zina's marriage to Brigham. It is a retrospective entry rather than a contemporary record.

On August 19 Henry wrote Zina from Brooklyn, New York. She carefully saved all of his mission letters. He addressed her as "Dear and respected companion" and referred to "my sweete Litle family which I left behind in the wilderness  my feelings Are greate for them, not knowing how they fair or whether they have enough to eate." He professed a deep, even eternal love for his wife. "Zina I have not forgotten you my Love is as ever the same and much more abundantly And hope that it will cont[in]ue to grow stronger an[d] stronger to all Eternity worlds without End." Notable in this letter is a tone of mystification as to the way events have occurred on earth. In the eternities, though, "there will be shiftings in time and revisions"; "and all be mad[e] right in the End.' He admonished Zina to take good care of their livestock, then added a polite note to Brigham Young: "give my best respects to Brother Brigham an[d] family." He ended the letter, "I remane as ever your affectionate Husband in truth Henry B. Jacobs." Though Zina was married to another husband and Henry may have become engaged to a second wife (according to Oliver), his affection for Zina and his sons was apparently still sincere.

Henry and Oliver set sail for England on August 22, arriving there on October 1. Oliver's journal tells that sometimes he felt close to Jacobs, as a close friend in a far away strange land. At other times Zina's brother noted Henry's faults: his occasional financial pettiness and his habit of taking all the speaking time in meetings, leaving Oliver no time to preach. However, whether these were typical missionary difficulties or show serious character failings in Jacobs is not certain. Henry was made president of the Preston Conference, which shows that he was viewed as a church leader of some stature in the mission field.

## XII. Winter Quarters

Back at Mt. Pisgah, Zina lived peacefully with her father and two sons. However, a wave of sickness and death overwhelmed the settlement, and the inhabitants could not build coffins quickly enough for the corpses, Zina writes. On August 1 William Huntington became very sick; eighteen days later he died. "Sad was my heart," wrote Zina. "I alone of his own children [was there] I Mourned for them all."

Zina lived with her two children in a one-room log cabin at the time, but she had taken seven homeless Saints into the house with her, in a characteristic act of generosity. All were sick toward the end of September. Just as the death of Zina's mother had plunged her into black grief, so undoubtedly did the death of her father: "In the night time the falling leaves upon the roof as I went from one to the other [of her sick housemates] to wate uppon them reminded me of the fallen dear ones that ware worn out and gone, the grave yard was so near that I could hear the wolves howling as they viseted the place so sacred to us but all alike to them in there night rambles."

Though her stepmother, Lydia Partridge, and much of the Partridge family were still in Pisgah, two of Zina's brothers and one sister were ahead at Winter Quarters. Probably missing them, Zina left Pisgah on October 1, when Charles Decker, a young brother-in-law of Brigham, was passing through with a load of flour and agreed to take Zina and sons to Winter Quarters. The little family slept on barrel heads at night, "being careful to get the hip bone into the top of one barel, my babe had a chill evry day on the road and was teething, and I [had] the toothake," Zina wrote. And so she traveled across half of Iowa; she rarely had an easy journey.

At Winter Quarters the next development in Zina's marriage history took place: she began to live openly as Brigham's wife. She later wrote, "Those days of trial and grief [at Mt. Pisgah] were succeeded by my journey to Winter quarters, where in due time I arrived, and was welcomed by President Young into his family." This method of practicing polyandry contrasted sharply with Joseph Smith's. Smith had never required any of his polyandrous wives to leave their first husbands and never lived openly with any of his polyandrous wives. Another problematic aspect of Zina's relationship to Young was that they apparently did not write Henry and tell him of the development.

Accommodations at Winter Quarters were primitive. At first Zina lived with five or six in a tent, then crude log cabins were erected. Nevertheless, Winter Quarters, where so many of her friends lived, probably brought her out of her grief. She participated in the spiritual feasts of the women's blessing meetings, and there were, she writes, "now and then a dance to cheer us  good meetings friendly visets kind associations in this our new life  knowing we ware here because God had commanded the sun shone in the midst of all these temparary inconveniances."

In characterizing life in her new polygamous household, Zina emphasized Brigham's kindness:

> Some of the Girls it was the first time they had ever left there parents, but the Pres was so kind to us all, nothing but God could have taught him and others how to be so kindly to there large Familes  this order [polygamy] not being on the Earth for 1800 years  with all our traditions like garments woven around us  some could act uppon principal with better justice than others  not all are capaciaten [capacitated] alike in any respect in this life.

Nevertheless, the privations and sicknesses of the pioneer life, caused by inadequate food and no vegetables, fell heavily on Winter Quarters. Many died around Zina, and she was sick for three months with "chills & fever," as was the baby—this would have been a miserable, nerve-racking episode in her life. But Zebulon remembers Winter Quarters as a kind of Tom Sawyer interlude of adventure and escapades. Once, when he refused to obey his mother, this mild-mannered woman wore out three willows on him. After this, Zebulon writes, "Candidly, I was feeling a little mellow inside and out." Zina asked him what he had to say. "Putting my armes around her ... [I said] I promis [to obey]. poor mother could hardly stand."

Henry wrote Zina again on January 14, 1847, a typical affectionate letter: "Kiss my little ones and tell them about their father and send me word about Zebulon." On Valentine's Day Henry sent Zina another letter. After mentioning apocalyptic calamities coming to the world (a favorite topic of contemplation for him, as for many early Mormons), he apparently referred to her marriage to Brigham. Whatever happens, he wrote, his affection for her would never change. "Whether in Life, or in death, whether in time or Eternity, Zina my mind never will Change from Worlds Without End, no never the same affection is there and never can be moved." Painful as the revelations of the prophets Joseph and Brigham may be, he wrote, "I do not murmur nor complain at the Handlings of god no veryly no ... I do not Blame Eny person or persons no may the Lord our Father Bless Brother Brigham and all purtains unto him forever tell him for me I have no feelings against him nor never had, all is right according to the Law of the Celestial kingdom of our God Joseph."

Nevertheless, there was an emotional price to be paid for this self-sacrifice. "But I feel alone & no one to speak to to call my own I feell Like a Lamb without a Mother." He ended the letter with words of encouragement: "Zina be comforted be of good cheer ... I know your mind has ben troubled about menny things but fear not all things will work together for good for them that Love God ... Bless my Dear Little Sons Zebulon and Henry C with an Holy kiss for me in the name of the Lord for I do Love my little Lambs. O the felings I have for them and you they cannot be told."

In mid-April Brigham started west with the "pioneers," the first company to reach Utah. Back at Winter Quarters, on June 3, Zina took part in a typical blessing meeting, with at least five plural wives of Joseph Smith participating. Patty Sessions wrote: "E Beaman E Partrige Zina Jacobs came here laid their hands upon my hcad blcscd me, and so did E R Snow thank the Lord."

The final episode in Henry's marriage to Zina was approaching. Zina now knew that she was going to live as Brigham's earthly wife, not as Henry's, but Henry apparently did not understand this fully. On June 20 she wrote a letter to Oliver's wife in New York, Mary Neal Huntington, which has been lost, but in it she apparently told Mary that she was living with Brigham Young and was no longer married to Henry. In July Henry and Oliver left England, arriving in New York on August 12. Henry visited relatives in New York, then stayed with the Neals and Oliver in Cambria. While he was there, Mary read Zina's letter aloud to Oliver and Henry. The two men were stunned, and Henry was left feeling depressed and resigned.

Oliver immediately sat down and dashed off a letter to Zina, which she preserved. He wrote: "I got the letter you wrote to Mary dated June 20th day before yesterday. All is well. Henry is here and heard the letter. He sayes all is right, he dont care. He stands alone as yet. I have had all-moste as much trial about you as he has. I have had to hear feel and suffer everything he has—If you only knew my troubles you'd pitty me ... Henry will tell you all my mind." Before this Henry may have seen Zina's marriage to Brigham as ritual only; she would continue to live with him. Now he probably realized that she had in effect divorced him completely. However one might understand Zina preferring Brigham to Henry, one has to sympathize with Henry, considering how the divorce was effected—while he was far away, and after the polyandrous "second" husband himself had sent him on a mission.

The next chapter in Henry's story is curious. W. W. Phelps was in New York, and though he was ostensibly obtaining a printing press for Utah, "His business as much as anything was to get as many Women hung onto him as he could," wrote Oliver. Jacobs and Phelps decided to travel to Winter Quarters together, along with Phelps's prospective wives. On the way back, in St. Louis, Jacobs married Phelps to three of these women. At some point on this trip, according to Oliver, Henry himself married a woman named Aseneth Babcock.

Phelps, and presumably Jacobs, arrived in Winter Quarters on November 12, only to meet with official disapproval. On November 30 a church council was held to consider the case against Phelps and Jacobs, and Phelps was "cut off" (excommunicated) for marrying wives without authorization. Henry was "silenced" for his part in marrying the women to Phelps—his license for preaching taken from him, effectively stripping him of his priesthood, a form of disfellowshipment. However, his own new marriage was evidently permitted. Wilford Woodruff wrote, "Wm W. Phelps was cut off from the church for Breaking the laws of God. It was decided in Council that if a man lost his wife He was at liberty to marry again whare He pleased and was Justifyed." The latter sentence seems to justify Henry's marriage to Aseneth. Since New York, at least, he had known that he had lost his first wife.

## XIII. "Miles From Any Whare"

In spring 1848 Zina prepared to cross the plains with a large group of Saints. Brigham asked Oliver Huntington to drive her wagon, and he agreed, a typical case of sibling taking the husband's place in polygamy. In mid-May Zina, Oliver, Presendia, and William Huntington had a joyful family reunion at Winter Quarters. Zina, though her face was swollen with an ulcerated tooth, set out for Utah with the "Big Company," including some 426 wagons in two companies led by Young and Heber Kimball, on May 26. She traveled in Brother Perkins's hundred and Brother Free's ten. She wrote, "We had prayers evry night a strict guard kept for fear of the Indeins, many ware the peculier incidents that occured on our journey a cross the planes, toils and heardships cooking with buffalow-chips, stampedes occasionly laying a loved one by the way side, evry sabath we had meetings much good instruction was imparted to the saints ... many pleasent chats while walking." Oliver mentions the prairie dogs, the buffaloes, the new vistas such as Chimney Rock and the strange building-like bluffs, then the Rocky Mountains. Always there is the human dimension: "Eleven o'clock—all is well and Gate's is quarreling with his wife like hell," wrote Oliver on July 9.

Henry and Aseneth Jacobs came west in the same general migration, in Brigham's company, and in Perkins's hundred; Henry led his own ten, which shows his stature as a minor leader. Possibly he was in the John D. Lee fifty, for he appears in Lee's journal on June 5. This is the only moment when we see Jacobs in a rebellious mood, for Captain Perkins complained that Henry would not obey him, and that Jacobs used "unpleasant & disagreeable Language ... & said that no man must use Tyrany about him or he would tell him of it. Even Brigham Young shant Tyranise over him." Perkins told Lee that Jacobs "wished to dictate [to] him in all moves & in fact to take the entire control of the 50." Zebulon traveled part of the time with Henry, part with Zina.

When Zina and Oliver were forty miles from Salt Lake City, Dimick and his two sons came out to meet them. Zebulon remembers that as they reached the mouth of Emigration Canyon on September 20, they saw the valley for the first time, a desolate expanse with the Great Salt Lake glistening far to the west:

> As we looked over here and there my mother placed her arm around me (we were setting on the seat at the front end of the wagon) while tears were trickleing down her dust covered cheeks, there my son is our home, the place God has prepared for his people. pointing to the dark streaks of the adobie fort, when we get there we shall take a rest. The prospect was not flattering to look at. Sage brush to the fringe of Cotton-woods and brush lining the banks of City Creek, then more sage, some

willows and beyond the fort ... was willows, cane flags and rushes, but it was *HOME* and *REST* to the weary.

Zina, now twenty-seven, wrote that she saw "the body of one log house outside the old fort as it was called the only sign of civilization, there is no words to discribe our feelings this our future home to live razc families & die  as we used to say soon  miles from any whare." After this first view Zina, her two sons, and siblings made the descent into the valley.

## XIV. "BY & 17 Women Took Supper at Our House"

The early years in Salt Lake were difficult for the Latter-day Saint pioneers. Food was scarce, housing inadequate, winters bitterly cold and snowy, and all had to work hard. Zina lived in her wagon box for a while, then Dimick provided her and Presendia with a two-room house in the fort, where Zina taught school and hosted men's priesthood quorum meetings at night.

Toward the end of September, Zina began her journal again. Among its most interesting aspects is its portrait of life in Brigham Young's polygamous family. Her relations with Young were friendly and warm, but lacked the day-to-day intimacy of a monogamous marriage. Much-married men like Brigham and Heber, almost by necessity, seemed to make social calls on their individual wives. Zina wrote on October 26, "BY called and gave me an invitation to come up to his house tomorrow." On the next day "I attended a very agreeable viset at his house." A polygamous husband could not share a wife's daily tasks, so often Zina's brothers helped her. "I white washed the room. Oliver assisted me. Took up the floor &c," Zina wrote one day.

Zina did occasionally spend time alone with Young. On January 12, 1849, her journal reflects a quiet, pleasant evening with the church president. "In the evening BY came to my house and accompanied me over to Br. Mc Mullens and Spaldings. We had a nice supper and enjoyed it well. On our walk home we had a few words concerning Josephs kingdom." Another outing with Brigham ended with a family meeting: "BY took me in the Carage. Very agreeable ride accompanied by Pres HCK. T. Johnson drove the carage to A[l]bert Smiths." A double wedding was solemnized there. "Evry thing quiet and nice. An excelent supper ... Returned home just before the sun set in good sperets." The next sentences are possible only in Mormonism: "This day there was a family meeting. BY & 17 women took supper at our house. All first rate."

Zina invariably described Brigham as very kind, a man who provided for her as best he could. However, she leaned on Dimick and other relatives for financial support and worked hard to earn money herself. In the spring of 1849 she wrote: "I have toiled through the winter ... 33 dollars have I pade for wood this winter. I earned it my self. My school bill amounted to 75 dollars and 86 cts."

There are no overt criticisms of the church president, but a careful reading of Zina's diary reveals occasional difficulties. Once, after an interview with Brigham before a move, Zina collapsed into lonely tears:

As I sat in my wagon with a hart tender as if berieved of a dear friend meditating I was aroused by a knock on the wagon. BY came to inform me a room was finished &c, &c, &c. O did I not seek a lone retreat beside a murmering [rill] ... the water rolled over a fall of about 3 feet whare the sound of my voice would not be herd there. I wept yes wept bitterness of Soul ya [yea] sorrow and tears that wore [were] rung from a heavy hart. Sadness for a while took her seat in my hart and reigned Predominet for a short time. I could exclaim O Lord have mercy on me. Yes I did say it with all my heart & I believe he will hear me in his own time and answer me. About 4 PM I moved into the room.

A rare muted hint of criticism is found a few years later: "In the evening I went over to see the President about the relief society I met him in the new room  he greeted me with more kindness than he has for years." Despite Zina's loyalty to Brigham, she evidently was not a favorite wife, as was, for instance, Emmeline Free, who bore him ten children. Nevertheless, Zina's evaluations of Brigham are generally favorable. Evidently he treated his stepsons Zebulon and Chariton well. Zina wrote, in an autobiographical sketch,

No man could be more careful of women while bearing there children thoughtful & kind as far as means could be obtained than was Brigham Young  think of us here in this wilderness world creating from the elements the sustinance of life, cheerful and kind to all  I do not know how many Orphans he has reared to maturity, my two step sons of his I do not remember of his ever even speaking sharp to them  in clothes &c they shared with his own.

In addition, Zina viewed Brigham as a religious leader, a prophet. An entry on December 26 shows her fondness for his religious philosophizing: "BY spent the evening with us very a greebly. Red in the book of covenants the vision &c. It was truly comforting. Spake of woman and the situation &c. It should have ben writen wombman. O Lord when will thou unvail thy self." Mormons viewed their leaders as close to divine. Zina wrote on January 17, 1858, "Attended meting all day Eldr Talor spoke beautiful  the Pres [Brigham] addressed us like a Father and a God o how heavenly  strengthen me O Lord my God & I humbly pray to do thy will in all things."

Zina's relations with her "sister-wives" were generally friendly and close, though there were inevitable tensions with some wives. She had many "sisters"—all of Joseph Smith's wives, all of Brigham's wives, and she had close ties with Heber Kimball's wives also, as Presendia and many of Smith's widows were married to Kimball. The blessing meetings with Eliza Snow and Patty Sessions continued. Louisa Beaman was also a close friend; Zina sorrowed with her as she lost five children and then died of breast cancer in 1850.

A few passages from Zina's diary show the texture of a life lived in what outsiders called the Mormon seraglio. On Christmas Day, 1849, Zina spent the day "with the Girls in the fort in Loises [Louisa Beaman's] room. Had a beautiful supper but no {bred} therefore it was rather Lonely. In the evening Father Chace, Oliver B H[untington] & Brother Pierce came in & sung some songs & hims and conversed uppon the things pertaining to salvation. A very agreeable evening. Oliver came home withe me." Zina delighted in the humor of Laura Pitkin Kimball, who stayed with her for six weeks: "The pleasent time we spent together will never be forgotten Sister Laury used to some times say here I in pleasure sit this is my throne ye Queens come bow to it she was truly a pleasent companyon & the good spiret was with us."

The women comforted each other in moments of trial. After Presendia endured a difficult childbirth, Zina stayed the night with her. "She is some better. Ellen Sanders & I set up and conversed uppon the things of the kingdom and on experience until after three in the morning. She has ben tried since the death of her babe but now feels a renewing of her light & strength."

A June 19, 1849, entry shows the different dimensions of Zina's life: wife of Brigham, sister to many wives, priestess, doctor:

> We had a picking bee. All the family ware together and took supper in the ketchen. Sister Washbern sent for Louisa[,] Sister Twist and my self to come and wash and annoint her daughter Mary Ann. She was taken very sick Sunday. BY sent his Carrage to carry us down. The Lord blest the administratin & she was better. Sister Eliza Snow came home with us. I was in Loises. BY came in and we had quite a chat ————————.

Today's Mormon is startled by a prophet of the church sending a carriage to take women to perform rituals for other women. Apparently the long line is Zina's shorthand for a moment of conflict.

Days of hard work were punctuated by evening parties, such as one at John Higbee's, to which Brigham took his first wife, Mary Ann, along with Eliza Snow and Zina, while Heber Kimball took his first wife, Vilate, and three other wives, Cristeen Golden, Presendia Huntington, and Laura Pitkin. "Some chose [choice] jokes pased, [among] Eliza BY & HCK in regard to speret. We had a beautiful supper, good musick &c. All things passed agreeable," wrote Zina. On January 24, 1850, she penned an especially vivid party description:

A very large company gethered. All the familys of the brethren gone to foreign nations and the twelve. Musick and dansing all night. Dinner and supper at the presidents house. 16 eat in the Luces room. Amacy Limans family stoped all night with me. A noble looking company indeed to see them dansing. The room filled with noblest of Adams race. George A. Smith [who weighed over three hundred pounds] danced. All seemed to enjoy themselves extremely well. While the elements raged without Peace was enjoyed with in.

These parties often included sacred dancing and singing in tongues: "Musick dansing rejoicing prayer preaching & I sung a song of Zion & Br Huvy dansed the time. Wm H. and Wm Hide ... went to Presendes & there we had the interpretation."

In the spring of 1850 Zina apparently moved from the fort to a lot and lived in her wagon again for a time. On April 16, she began to live in a house that might have been crude and primitive, for this is when she broke down in tears. Then she moved to Brigham's Log Row in December and lived with Harriet Cook for a time. Harriet was one of Brigham's problematic wives, and an exchange between her and Zina, which is preserved in a family memoir, shows the ambiguous position of the "proxy wife" in Mormon society. Susa Young Gates, a daughter of Brigham, wrote, "On one occasion she [Harriet] said to Aunt Zina, loving kind Aunt Zina: 'You are nothing but a proxy wife. Brigham doesn't love you and neither does anybody else.'" Zina replied, "I love you Sister Harriet and you can't help yourself." Though Zina was secure enough not to be hurt by this taunt, the fact that Harriet would use the term "proxy wife" to try to diminish her shows that she saw such women as occupying a lower status in the family. One wonders if Brigham saw himself as providing for someone else's widows throughout his life, despite the fact that such women as Zina and Emily Partridge bore his children.

Though Harriet resented Zina, when this irascible woman much later became obsessed with the idea that somebody was practicing witchcraft against her, she asked Zina and Susa's mother (Lucy Bigelow Young) "to come to her in the Lion House and wash and anoint her rebuking the evil spirit which was tormenting her." So Zina acted as priestess in pioneer Utah. But it was her compassionate, forgiving nature that gave her this spiritual stature in Harriet's eyes.

## XV. Zina Presendia Young

In early March 1850 Zina, eight months pregnant, recorded in her journal, "My health quite poor & the 13th Chariton was taken with the measles." Soon after this she wrote, "No one will know the hours of paneful loneliness that I saw by day & by night." Once again, despite Brigham's kindness, he was not there with Zina in a moment of difficulty and loneliness. Polygamy, almost by definition, implied an absentee husband, despite the husband's good will and spiritual prestige. Chariton nearly died from the measles, but survived. Then, on April 3, Zina, who was now twenty-nine, bore a daughter, Zina Presendia, at Old Log Row, which doubtless left her overjoyed.

Toward the end of June, Zina and other plural wives of Brigham Young met to remember Joseph Smith's martyrdom. By the end of the year Zina had moved out of Log Row to take up residence in a small adobe house. She and her three children would live there for approximately three years.

## XVI. "Cat in a Strange Garret"

Henry's story continues by fits and starts of documentation. On October 15, 1848, Aseneth bore a child, George Theodore Jacobs, in the Salt Lake Valley, though it died a few months later. In a year Henry was living in California, at White Rock Springs, "on the road from Mormon Tavern to Sacramento." On May 24, 1850, apostles Amasa Lyman and Charles Rich "put up with H. Jacobs" while on their apostolic "gold Mission," according to Lyman's journal; a month later the Lyman party "lodged with br. H. Jacobs." It is not known why Henry went to California. Utah Mormons sometimes viewed church members in the coastal state as apostates by definition, but is not impossible that Henry went there with official permission, for Brigham authorized some "missions" to California. It is clear from Jacobs's next letter to Zina that he retained his testimony of Mormonism. In addition, Amasa Lyman referred to him as "br. H. Jacobs."

However, not long after this, on January 26, 1851, Brigham Young met with local authorities at Weber, north of Salt Lake City, and had Henry Jacobs disfellowshipped from the church for reasons that are not adequately known. Henry commented on this in his last extant letter to Zina, a document of remarkable historical significance, dated September 2, 1852, and written with Henry's characteristic eloquence and passion: "Dear Zina and beloved Children  it is with feelings of no small importence I will asure you that I take the Liberty of addressing you at this time  I do not know how to begin  I have writen So meny Letters to you and Children from first to last and got no Letters, that I feel allmost discourage[d]  I never have received but one from you cince I left the Lake." One wonders why Zina did not reply. Possibly Henry's letters were unwelcome because he was trying to convince her to return to him. He himself suspected that his letters had been intercepted. Some local color from California follows:

> I enjoy a portion of good health at this time  the Cholery is here  sevrel have dide  times ar very hard, large Emigration this season  Sto[c]k is high flour is worth 15 ctz per lb  every thing is on the rise here  Enough of this Wm Gheen is dead <sup>withfeever</sup>  Wm Hibbard is dead he was shot for Steeling horses  they Cut of[f] his head and preserved it  sevral of our friends have left this tenement of Clay and gon to there Long homes, there to wait the Sumons of the most high  I yet Live but I know not how Long  Death is certain and life is uncertain ... I feel like a Cat in a strange garret among the filth and Rags of the upper Story of California.

Jacobs now affirms his own religious faith, though he admits his imperfections:

> my mind is as ever the same and [I] change not  my faith in the gospel is the same ... Joseph is our Prophet stil the grate High Preist Ordained of God and sent forth to give us light  though I do not come up to my privelege as I aught  I am blest with meny improprieties of California being with wild men in one sence and [in] another they are not  but what can we expect from men in darkness whos eyes are blind and will not see the truth  I do not gambl nor get drunk  know [no] man living ever saw me drunk yet and I hope never will  though there is one thing I feel bad in  that is I do sware some times  I no [know] it is rong  it does not come from the heart but from the lips  for I know better and am sorry for it and will do better  O Zina do not tell my dear little sweete Children of it, I would hate to have <sup>them</sup> no of there fathers imperfections.

Henry, though thoroughly divorced from Zina, now turns to words of longing:

> O how happy I should be if I only could see you and the little Children bone of my bone and flesh of my flesh  I mean all I would like to see the litle babe; I Zina wish you to prospere  I wish you new what I have to bar [bear]  my feelings ar indiscribeable  I am unhappy  ther is now [no] peace for poor me  my pleasure is you  my Comfort has vanished  the glory of day has flead like the fog before a plesant morning  my youthful days are yet in my mind  yes never to be bloted out  I have had meny a good Dream about you and the litle ones  I have imagin[ed] myself at home with you and the Little Boys upon my kneese a singing and playing with them ~~wht~~ what a comfort what a Joyajoy to think upon those days that are gone by  O Heaven Bless me even poor me  shall I shall I ever see them again
>
>     I think of ~~of~~ you often very often  Zina ar you happy  do you enjoy your life as pleasent as you did with me when I was at home with you and the Children  when we could say our prayers together and speak together in toungs and Bless each other in the name of the Lord  O I think of those

happy days that ar past  when I sleep the sleep of death then I will not for get you and my little lambs  I love my affections I love my Children. O Zina can I ever will I ever get you again answer the question please  If you are at Liberty to answer the question write me soon as you get this my troubles her [here] ar greate greatere then I can bar [bear].

He then gives his perspective on the church action taken against him:

I have heard that I was Cut off from the Church  for what was I [cut off?] Oh how I do feel about it  never did I do eny thing worthy of being cut off  allways have I defended this cause  it Belongs to God the Father  I live in the city of Sacremento  kiss all the Chilldren for me  I would send something to them but it may be like the rest of my letters never get ther I have not forg$^{aton}$ my prom$^{is}$ to my dear children.

Henry certainly still has a deep belief in Mormonism, and he seems to have no idea why he was disfellowshipped. According to family tradition, he was disciplined because "he proceeded to try to win Zina back. Because of his persistence, he was excommunicated from the church by the High Council." The letter quoted above perhaps gives some support for this; even though both Zina and he had been married to other people for years, and each had had a child with the new spouse, Henry was still in love with her. The letter virtually begs for a reunion.

One can read the letter sympathetically or unsympathetically. In the sympathetic reading, Brigham (who already had a number of other wives), using his ecclesiastical position and privilege and specious religious argumentation and pressure, had maneuvered Henry away from his wife—whom Henry loved passionately and who perhaps still loved him—and had Henry marry another woman as a replacement. But Henry, who had lived with Zina for some time and had two children by her, had difficulty separating himself emotionally from her or from his two sons. Brigham sent him to England to effect the separation, leaving Zina husbandless with a newborn baby halfway across Iowa. In Utah, Brigham excommunicated him, despite the fact that he had been, as he said, a faithful defender of the faith since youth, and had given up his wife to the prophet Joseph, surely one of the ultimate tests of loyalty (though he had given her up only partially, and Smith never demanded the complete divorce that Brigham Young did). Then Young intercepted Jacobs's letters to Zina.

In the unsympathetic reading, Zina may have been sincerely incompatible with Henry (who perhaps was verbose and unreliable) and chose Brigham instead. Henry was the divorced husband who kept pressing himself on the ex-wife when his attentions were unwelcome, so she stopped answering his letters. Though obviously in a difficult situation, as is any man who still loves the woman who has rejected him, he was unable to accept his situation and constructively start his life again. His efforts to regain Zina were addressed to a woman who was married to someone else, and Brigham felt it necessary to have him excommunicated. One remembers the statement in the Lee journal in which Jacobs said he would not endure tyranny, even from Brigham Young. By the unsympathetic reading, then, this letter is less a sincere cry of pain than a self-pitying document by a weak man who could not deal with the painful reality of his divorce.

Both sides could be argued at greater length, and both no doubt have some truth to them; the story of Zina, Henry, Joseph, and Brigham probably will never be completely understood. Women did leave Henry repeatedly, even without the intervention of Brigham. By November 1852 Aseneth had left him. On an account sheet, Henry wrote, "Aseneth is Sick weary we are a part the ole woman is the cause of it no more at present HB Jacobs." But as one reads Zina's diary, one finds that, just as she noted the birthdays of close family members whom she loved dearly, she kept entering Henry's birthday in her diary years after she had married Brigham. In 1854 she wrote, "This is Henry B Jacobs bir{thday} he is 38 O Lord ... " It is interesting that Zina's descendants tend toward the sympathetic view of Jacobs.

## XVII. Touring with Brigham

Brigham Young would tour Utah periodically, and in May 1855 Zina accompanied him and other church leaders and their wives to Cedar City. She kept a full diary of the expedition, giving an interesting view of pioneer Utah and some insight into her marriage to Brigham. She keenly enjoyed the beauty of the Utah countryside. Outside of Nephi she traveled through "the most romantic kanjon that I ever saw such grandure in nature such a variety of colour." She appreciated the hospitality the company received at every stop. At Nephi a Sister Haywood gave them "a splended dinner & she supplied us butter cream cakes & pies for camping out in the afternoon."

Zina was always the supportive wife. On May 13 she "mended the Pres pants." They reached Fillmore on the 24th, in the morning, and after "Br Ray [was] ordained a pres over Filmore and a high priest I combed the Pres[ident's] head then went to meeting."

On May 25, as the party traveled northward, Zina was moved to descriptive poetry: "Winds high soon after we started the clouds darkened winds & rain but o what a lovely prarie pleasent hills flowers dales smooth fields and thousands of achors of pasterage, took supper at sister Hay wood's & how it rained." On the 27th the group arrived back in Salt Lake City.

Zina had one of the classic plural wife experiences on February 6, 1856: going to a party with a relative only to find her husband there with another wife or wives. Her diary entry also documents another of the trials of plurality: "Susan [Banler] spent most of the day with me  her husband took her sister Electa to wife last night  a day of trial for her  Allen Huntington took me to the Battallion ball  the Presidency ware there  an excelent time  good spirets  took Zina  at home at 1." On September 31 Zina moved to the Lion House, which Brigham had built for his wives as an experiment in communal living, and she occupied "the 5th room on the third floor on the west side, a lovely room." There she continued to raise Zina and Chariton; Zebulon was living with another family to learn the hatmaking trade.

Blessing meetings continued in the Lion House. One of these included Brigham: "I attended a blessing meeting in Sister Youngs Library ... John blest ... Joseph  Phineas & Brigham Young  the spiret especially attended the Pres to remark never did I hear better." The dormitory setting allowed frequent informal meetings with other plural wives. On January 4, 1858, Zina wrote: "Sister Eliza & Sister Rhody spent the evening with me." Living close to Eliza in the Lion House would allow that friendship to cement even closer than it had before. In March 1859 Zina wrote, "Ever to be rembered a happy day  I spent with Sister E R Snow it is my Fathers birth day."

In 1857 Zina went on another First Presidency expedition, this time a five-week trip north as far as the Salmon River in Oregon. In the second half of 1858, during the Utah War, she traveled south to Provo. When she returned, Brigham asked her to raise four children of a sister-wife, Clarissa Ross, who had died. Zina agreed, and her household of four suddenly doubled. Her new foster children were Maria Young (later Dougall), Willard Young, Phebe Young (later Beatie), and Mary Young (later Croxall). "The duty in this instance proved to be a perfect pleasure and the children became to me as though they were indeed my own," she wrote.

### XVIII. Man of Sorrow

When Henry Jacobs returned to Utah in late 1859, he must have met with his sons and Zina. He was in Utah by October 28 when he attended the hanging of a murderer, Thomas H. Ferguson. According to the *Deseret News*, "The condemned man [after speaking] then requested to have some one pray, when Mr. Henry Jacobs ascended the scaffold, kneeled with him and offered a brief prayer." Perhaps the displaced excommunicant, three-times-divorced Jacobs felt some kinship with this outcast. However, Jacobs was rebaptized soon after coming to Utah.

Before long Henry was married again. He may have met an old missionary companion, Jesse Haven, at the execution, for Haven mentions the event in his diary. On August 22 Haven divorced a plural wife of two years, the twenty-two-year-old Sarah Taylor, though he was evidently still in love with her, and the separation caused him great pain.

Henry married "Sally" Taylor on March 1, 1860, with Brigham's brother, John Young, officiating. In a letter to his former brother-in-law, Haven described Henry: "He is a man about 40, Sarah is his fourth wife though he is not now living with his former three. He truely has been a man of sorrow." Unless Haven's count of wives is imprecise, Aseneth had left Henry permanently, and he had married and separated from another woman. In this letter Haven wrote resignedly of Sally, "She is now gone and for the time being is the wife of another man. It is all right I will leave it in the hands of the Lord."

On March 25 Jacobs and Haven attended a party for the Fourteenth Quorum of Seventies and Henry told him that he and Sally planned to move to Springville. The next news Haven heard of Henry and Sally, however, filled him with anguish: they had departed for California, though Sally had been reluctant to do so. Haven immediately dashed off a letter to his former mother-in-law expressing his outrage. He wrote accusingly that Henry had always planned to return to California, though Jesse "tried to persuade him to stay with the Saints and redeem himself." However, in Utah Henry heard that people were gossiping about him, and he "said to me [Haven] that he would not live with such a people but would leave them." "O that you could have persuaded her to have stoped with you and with the Saints; and if Henry wished to go among the Gentiles and associate with the wicked and partake of their sins, let him go and receive their reward, but Sarah would have been justified by every good Saint if she had tarried with the people of God."

Haven went on to accuse his old companion of hypocrisy and apostasy. Of course, this was an embittered ex-husband speaking—one who held a typical nineteenth-century Mormon view of the automatic depravity of living in California. Henry gave health reasons for the departure; his poor health is well documented in his mission records. Henry, this "man of sorrows," undoubtedly also felt a chill of rejection in Utah, despite his rebaptism.

## XIX. Public Persona, Private Life

In the 1860s and 1870s Zina became prominent in various church and civic positions. Though she had always moved among elite Mormon women, she now became even more visible, holding organizational positions in the health sphere, in the silk industry, and in the development of women's and children's organizations in Mormonism.

She always tended the sick. For example, in 1850 she wrote, "Lucia

Presendia [a child of William Huntington] was very sick in the night. Came near dying with the croop. It seemed the Lord truly sent me." Her ministrations combined frontier medicine, folk remedies, and ritual blessing and healing. Patty Sessions records one administration: "Zina Young was here [when Patty was extremely sick] she washed and anointed me  she said I should get up in the morning well  the Elders laid hands on me." One of Zina's more notorious folk remedies treated "caked breasts, strains, lame backs, and rheumatism": "Good sized live Toads 4  put in boiling water—cook very soft  take them out boil the water down to 1/2 pint and add 1 lb fresh butter simmer  add 2 oz. tincture arnica."

Zina's ministrations were most prized for her kindness and compassion. The following testimonial is found in a famous anti-Mormon book by her sister-wife Ann Eliza Webb Young: "Her [Zina's] generous nature and strict sense of justice would not allow her to neglect anyone under her care, no matter how distasteful the person might be to her. She ... always gave her patient the tenderest, most watchful, and motherly care." Zina became the Young family midwife. In the early 1850s she took a formal medical course in obstetrics at Brigham Young's request and later led a school of obstetrics in Salt Lake City. She also established a school for nursing in the old Social Hall and lectured on health topics. After the Deseret Hospital was established, she was chosen as president in 1880, an office she held until 1892. On May 13, 1891, Zina's diary reflects this aspect of her life: "At 11,30, went to the hospital board meeting  Pres Hiram Clawson present  the board was wel represented & a good spiret with us, about 500 $ in debt, thousands of dollars been given to the poor  Yet we are blest & may the way be opened before us."

Zina was also an important figure in the silk industry, which was one of Brigham Young's pet projects. Though she was repulsed by the sight of silk worms, she accepted the call to manage Brigham's cocoonery for one year in 1869. "She fed and took care of millions of worms ... although there were months that her dreams were nightmare remembrances of her daily horror," wrote Susa Young Gates. On June 15, 1876, when the Utah Silk Association was organized, Zina was chosen president. In October 1879 she became the first woman to speak in the traditionally all-male general conference sessions; her subject, in part, was sericulture.

The Relief Society that began in Nauvoo had been discontinued there because of Emma Smith's opposition to polygamy. However, in early Utah local Relief Societies began to emerge and Eliza R. Snow became the informal leader of these groups. Zina, a close friend and sister-wife, served as her companion and informal counselor for many years.

In 1866 Brigham assigned Eliza Snow to formally organize Relief Societies again, and Zina undoubtedly helped her.

Behind the public woman was the private Zina. By the late 1860s and 1870s her children had grown to adulthood and were marrying; a large part of her private life would be involved in their careers and families. She was an affectionate mother who remained close to her children. Zebulon traveled to the Missouri River in 1861, 1862, and 1863 to help emigrants cross the plains. Three years later, on March 17, 1866, Zina had the pleasure of watching him marry; he and his wife, Frances Wood Carrington, would have five children, beginning with Zebulon Henry Jacobs, Zina's first grandchild, born on December 26, 1866. Soon after his marriage, Zebulon was called to Sanpete County for duty in the Black Hawk Indian war as a sergeant of cavalry. Then in 1867 and 1868 he filled a proselyting mission to England. After returning home, he worked as a conductor for the Utah Central Railway Company until 1887, then became a guard in the Utah State Penitentiary.

Henry Chariton, like Zebulon, served a mission in England from 1867 to 1870. He married Susan Stringham on April 23, 1871, a marriage which would produce seven children. Chariton had a varied career, working as a farmer in Sevier County until 1877, then with the Utah and Nevada Railway Company until 1884; then with the Utah Lime and Cement Company as a kiln manager. He was a rancher for a year in Bear River, buying and selling land; then worked for Boyle Furniture before returning to farming in 1894, this time in west Weber—interrupted by a colonizing mission to Idaho and Canada. In 1892 his first wife died suddenly, and he married Emma Rigby the next year, with whom he had a second family of eight children. In the church he served as a high councilor, bishop, and patriarch before his death in 1915.

Zina Presendia Young was described in 1869 in a *New York World* interview as "quite tall, and slim in proportion, somewhat pretty, and apparently about twenty years of age." A popular actress in Brigham Young's theater, in 1868, when she was eighteen, she became the second wife of forty-year-old Thomas Williams, one of Young's scribes. "He was much older than I," she wrote, "it never occurred to me to fall in love with him." She bore him two sons before he died in 1873. She subsequently became a faculty member at Brigham Young Academy, then married Charles Ora Card in 1884, again as a polygamous wife. However, polygamists were being prosecuted at this time, so Charles and Zina joined the "polygamy underground" and eventually resettled in Canada where they were among the early settlers of Cardston in southern Alberta.

As Huntington women were extraordinarily close to each other, this geographical distancing of mother and daughter was a severe trial for Zina

Diantha. She made frequent trips to Canada, and Zina Card visited Utah whenever possible. In 1876 Zina wrote to Chariton and Zina Card, "Now to Zina if she is with you I think she must be by this time, home is so lonly but I make the best of it I can do not come home until you get a good ready let it be just as long as you think it best." She had moved into a house by herself on January 1, 1870. Despite her friends, siblings, sons, and grandchildren living nearby, she was afflicted by moods of great loneliness when Zina Card and her children were far away. Of course, she had no husband in her daily life. One suspects that Brigham continued to be somewhat distant, as he was extremely busy with other wives, children, and church business. Zina Card bore Charles Ora three more children, including a Zina, fourth in the chain of Zinas. Zina Card became the female leader of the Canadian Mormon community and worked actively in the local Relief Society and Primary organizations throughout her life.

Zina Diantha's third marriage came to an end on August 29, 1877, when Brigham Young died in Salt Lake City. A year and a half later Dimick, Zina's older brother who had always migrated ahead of her and smoothed the way for her travels, also died. But before he departed, he visited the "spirit world" where departed spirits dwell and "saw some that he recognized and nearest to him was Mother—that all appeared to be busy & happy—that them that kept the faith & had the priesthood had power over all evil spirits." Zina Baker was never far from her children.

## XX. "He Burst into Tears"

Henry Jacobs settled in Livermore, California, near Oakland, and became a successful poultry farmer. In 1877 Zebulon was vacationing with a son in California and visited him. Zeb wrote:

> Found father a little better ... he had heard last night I was in the neighbourhood, and wanted to see me. I was glad to see the old man still alive, and he was pleased to see me. he burst into tears as he threw his arms around my neck and thanked God he had seen me again in the flesh. it made my heart ack[e] to [illegible] of the disease. Sarah is not so well today. her excitement yesterday was to much for her. seeing father, stretched out as he was his limbs stifened nails turning black, eyes set she thought he was gone.

Sometime before May 1880 Zebulon and Chariton brought Henry to Utah; there is no mention of Sally Taylor coming with him. However, Oliver Huntington called on Sally when he visited California in 1899, so relations between the two families were friendly. Henry reportedly lived in a bedroom of Zina's house and was cared for until his death by a hired woman. Zina may not have been living there, as she often rented out the house and lived with her daughter and sons.

Henry died of Bright's disease, a kidney complaint, on August 1, 1886, at the age of sixty-nine. He was buried in the Salt Lake City graveyard in his ceremonial temple clothes, a sign of full fellowship in the Mormon church.

## XXI. Widow of a Master Mason

Zina continued to act as Eliza Snow's de facto counselor in Relief Society work. In 1877 and 1879 they traveled south to St. George, often camping out overnight in the winter weather. In Utah's Dixie they did temple work and organized Relief Societies and Primaries (for children). Earlier in 1879 Zina attended the National Suffrage Association Convention in Washington, D.C.; from July to September she and Susa Young (Gates) visited Hawaii.

When Eliza Snow was formally called by John Taylor as general president of all Relief Societies on June 19, 1880, she selected as her counselors Zina Young and Elizabeth Whitney, her two comrades in tongue-speaking at Winter Quarters. Zina, now fifty-nine, would become increasingly well known throughout the rest of her life. In the seven years before Eliza died, they traveled together to many settlements in Utah, organized Relief Societies, Primaries, Young Women's Mutual Improvement Associations, and spoke frequently. A typical diary entry reflecting her Relief Society labors is found on June 18, 1878, when she and Eliza attended a Relief Society gathering in Nephi in central Utah in "there own nice little hall it was filled and a display of quilts &c an interesting time." In the evening Zina and Eliza met with young men and women at the wardhouse, enjoying "a flow of the good spiret." Eliza "spoke in tongs." The next day, after a delay caused by a funeral, they were given a carriage ride to the small town of Fountain Green where they spoke to another packed house of women. "As good a spiret as I ever felt in a meeting filled the house," wrote Zina. Here we find the typical framework of the modern Mormon Relief Society meetings juxtaposed with Kirtland- and Nauvoo-era speaking in tongues.

Part of Zina's duties as a Mormon woman leader was to defend polygamy. She did this most dramatically at a woman's mass meeting on November 16, 1878, protesting the anti-polygamy crusade. Her speech, in which she bore public testimony of her marriage to Joseph Smith, reportedly had the effect of "an electric shock" which brought many men to their feet. She said,

> The principle of our holy religion that is assailed [polygamy] is one that lies deep in my heart. Could I ask the heavens to listen; could I beseech

the earth to be still, and the brave men who possess the spirit of a Washington to hear what I am about to say! I am the daughter of a Master Mason! I am the widow of a master mason who, when leaping from the windows of Carthage jail, pierced with bullets, made the Masonic sign of distress; but, gentleman [the press], those signs were not heeded except by the God of heaven. That man, the prophet of the Almighty, massacred without mercy! ... Sisters, this is the first time in my life that I have dared to give utterance to this fact, but I thought I could trust my soul to say it on this occasion, and I say it now in the fear of Israel's God, and I say it in the presence of these gentlemen.

Zina's views on polygamy are found in the 1869 *New York World* interview. The journalist, "H.," described Zina as "a tall, thin lady, apparently about fifty years of age" who ascribed much of the unhappiness in polygamous families to women who expect "too much attention from the husband and because they do not obtain it, or see a little attention bestowed upon one of the other wives, they become sullen and morose, and permit their ill-temper to finally find vent." First wives are a particular problem, as they have a tendency to look upon the husband with a "selfish devotion" that desires to claim all his time and attention for themselves. The successful polygamous wife, as her marriage develops, "must regard her husband with indifference, and wits no other feeling than that of reverence, for love we regard as a false sentiment; a feeling which should have no existence in polygamy." By "love" Zina meant romantic love only, not Christian love, and in this interview she was repeating conventional Mormon rhetoric disparaging romance.

Another aspect of the Relief Society was temple work, and Zina frequently performed ordinances in the Endowment House and in the Logan and St. George temples. On January 12, 1881, when she, Eliza, and brother Oliver were in St. George, Oliver wrote that he and Zina "spent the forenoon [at the temple] in Sealings of Adoptions," standing proxy for their parents and grandparents as they were sealed to Joseph Smith. Clearly, linkage to Joseph Smith was seen as necessary for complete salvation.

In August 1881 Zina traveled to the eastern states with Willard Young, her stepson, and with Dr. Ellen B. Ferguson, to visit relatives, gather genealogical information, organize Relief Societies, and make an occasional appearance at "gentile" feminist gatherings. In October she attended the Woman's Congress at Buffalo. Zina and Ellen were at first asked to speak on behalf of Utah women, but when it was found out that they were polygamists they were denied speaking privileges. Zina returned to New York to attend the N.W.S.A. convention but again was not permitted to speak.

In April 1882 Zina and Presendia visited St. George to do more temple work. She traveled to Provo on November 30, accompanied by Mrs. Saxon, a "nationally renowned female suffrage lecturer," for a Primary conference; the local stake Primary president was Zina Young Williams, her daughter. In the same year Zina attended the National Suffrage Convention in Omaha and met prominent American female leaders, including May Wright Sewall, Phoebe Cousins, and Susan B. Anthony.

## XXII. General Relief Society President

Eliza Snow's health was gradually deteriorating. In April 1886 Zina wrote to her, "My Dear blessed Sister Eliza  How are you by this time  I trust much better  I think of you often and in the Temple I went to that blest room and besought Father to bless & comfort that afflicted tabernacle [Eliza's body] that has done so much service in his work on earth that you may have the desires of your hart  I believe you will." But on December 5, 1887, Eliza died, and Zina, at the age of sixty-six, became the acting general president of the Relief Society. At the next general conference, in April 1888, she was formally called by Wilford Woodruff to be the third general president of the Mormon women's organization. She chose Jane Richards and Bathsheba Smith as her counselors, and Emmeline Wells became her correspondence secretary. In early May she traveled to Canada, where Zina Card was near childbirth. "We witnessed the hapy meeting of a Devoted mother and daughter that had been separated 13 months," wrote Charles Card. After returning to Salt Lake, Zina and her counselors were set apart by the First Presidency on October 11. The women then repaired to Emmeline's home, and "Sister Smith blest us in tongues Aunt Zina interpreted," Wells wrote in her diary.

On January 2, 1889, Zina and her counselors met with President Wilford Woodruff and several of the Twelve to obtain official approval for women to organize themselves into chapters of the Woman Suffrage Association. She visited Zina Card later in the month. Wherever she went, Zina continued organizing Relief Societies, speaking to "local sisters," and sharing spiritual gifts, healings, blessings, tongue-speaking. In 1889 she began holding general Relief Society conferences in Salt Lake City every year.

However, despite her active public life, the private loneliness, the longing for her distant daughter continued. In an 1889 letter to Zina Card, she wrote: "My Own Dear Dear Zina I am very lonely but I expect it is all right  Phebe is cleaning to day ... Aunt Presendia is very feeble ... what is my home a lone with out you." The next year Emmeline Wells wrote of her, "Aunt Zina was lonely as usual."

Wells described the aging matriarch on her birthday in 1890: "Aunt Zina has reached 69 years, she looked very dignified in black silk dress puff sleeves lace collar and cuffs." On June 13 she visited Oliver in

Springville, with Zina Card and her three children, then, in the fall, returned to Canada with her daughter.

The Relief Society became formally connected with the National Council of Women of the United States in 1891, and Zina later became vice-president of the national organization. In May she set out for Canada, as Zina Card was expecting again.

On February 1, 1892, Presendia, Zina's beloved older sister, died, and another link to the past was gone. A month later, on March 17, the Relief Society celebrated its fiftieth birthday with a jubilee, which Zina worked hard to make memorable. The Latter-day Saints had survived despite all their reverses, and the Relief Society had developed and solidified along with it. Mormon women could regard their organization with pride.

Nevertheless, Zina was beginning to have health problems. In March she wrote her brother, John Huntington,

> I had a touch of Grip [influenza] this is the third winter I have been adquainted with this sad sad affliction ... I can walk a mile & return the same day, when I {want} to ... rather [than] to stand & wate for the Cars I walk on ... I have had al my teeth out & stil ware [wear] a temporary set, but oft think I must go & get a better set, but putting it off until a more convenient Season ... Zina my Daughter is spending the winter with me it is a great comfort to me.

She and her counselors and some other sisters met with President Wilford Woodruff, Joseph F. Smith, and Franklin D. Richards in March to discuss organizing the Relief Society as a private corporation. Zina objected to thus secularizing the organization, and the idea was tabled. However, in October the First Presidency evidently pushed the incorporation through despite Zina's objections. Emmeline Wells wrote, "It does bother Aunt Zina so much. She fears it will take from its spiritual character and make it only temporal." Also in October, aged seventy-one, Zina directed the first Relief Society general board meeting with the combined Relief Society stake presidents.

Zina saw the Salt Lake temple dedicated on April 6, 1893; she had seen the temple's first stone laid some forty years previously. As Relief Society president, she presided over women's ordinances in the temple. In May she attended the World's Fair in Chicago and was in charge of a day-long "Congress of Representative Women" program in the Art Palace. On one Sunday she sat before a large hall with other prominent women church leaders. She also attended "a congress of charities and philanthropies," of which she was appointed vice-president. After the meetings Oliver met her in Chicago and they traveled east to visit relatives. Two years later, from May 13 to 15, 1895, Zina, now seventy-four, spoke at a women's suffrage convention in Salt Lake City.

On May 23, 1896, Zina wrote to Zina Card, after a visit, expressing the private solitude behind the public career:

> Evry thing is lonely & silent just my old black shawl on the childrens hat rack, I am going to meet Sister Alder to talk about the sisters in California at my room at 11 Thursday is the surprise on Martha Cannon I hope we will have a good time all wish you are coming, but Zina I try awful hard to keep the promis I made you, not to feel bad I am quite brave & do first rate ... I am the happiest when in my bed & put my hand on my side as you held yours before we ware up in the morning.

In an August 1896 letter to Zebulon, we find Zina looking forward to a visit from Zina Card: "I get starved to be with the children it gets worse to be without them but I have to do my best." Oliver, visiting Salt Lake to do temple work in February 1897, found his sister to be "very feeble with age and its infirmities." Zina Card and three children were visiting at the time.

In the ebbing years of the nineteenth century, Zina continued her Relief Society and temple work and thrived on visits to and from her Canadian daughter as her health and bodily strength continued to fail. After the October 1897 general conference, she traveled to Canada in poor health and returned in December. "This morning ... we bade Mother Zina D.H. Young adieu ... which left our family in tears. None felt it so keenly as my wife Zina," wrote Charles Card.

Oliver visited her in February 1898 to do temple work and wrote that her memory "was very much broken so that in many instances she appeared almoste unsound—a little demented, so that my heart was melted with pity and grief." In April Charles Card told Joseph F. Smith that Zina Diantha was "feeble & ... she wasted her means or gave it away & she could do nothing without aid," and suggested that she live with a woman to take care of her, next door to one of her Ross stepchildren.

The next year, on June 5, Zina wrote to her daughter, "My ever blessed Zina I thank you so much for your precious Letter I trust you wil pardon my neglect in writing. I never forget you in my prayers not a night I think but often I go to bed I think of you for a while thank Father in Heaven I ever had you." Soon after this she traveled to Canada once again, but by November she was back in Salt Lake.

## XXIII. Final Years

In early 1901 Zina, now eighty, became ill and nearly died, but Zina Card tended her and she recovered. An interview conducted in May or June 1901 gives a good portrait of the aging octogenarian, sitting on her porch, attended by her brother Oliver and her beloved daughter. "A more perfect picture of a mother's affection and a daughter's devotion than is furnished by these two is seldom seen," wrote the reporter. Zina had to leave the interview to perform an act of service: "Our pleasant interview was closed by the arrival of a messenger who was to convey our hostess to the home of a young matron in need of blessing and comfort. Before departing, however, she showed us the copy of the Book of Mormon which long years before had brought such unspeakable joy to her heart. As she excused herself and was driven away we instinctively felt that we had been in the presence of a great woman."

In the latter part of June, Zina accompanied her daughter back to Cardston. On August 20 she began to fail but nevertheless prepared to leave for Salt Lake with Mr. and Mrs. Levi Richards. Two days later she sat at the breakfast table in her daughter's house and was talking freely when suddenly her face turned red and she fell from her chair. Zina Card was able to catch her, and she recovered her faculties, so finished her breakfast. But when her daughter implored her to stay longer in Canada, Zina Diantha "quietly but firmly" refused. Despite her love for her daughter, she wanted to die in Zion. So Zina Card decided to accompany her mother back to Utah. The next day, on the fifteen-mile coach ride to the train, Zina grew visibly weaker. On the train she sank into a deep sleep, "and the peaceful smile that settled upon her face remained there to the end."

Zina was met at the Ogden depot and at Salt Lake City by family and numerous friends. In Salt Lake an ambulance took her to her home on Fourth Street, and, writes Wells, "it was a matter of watching and waiting ... Immediately before she died right on the point of dissolution, she closed her mouth like she was making an effort to speak, and that was the last sign of life." She died at the age of eighty on August 28, 1901. Wells wrote, "This morning Aunt Zina died at 8.55 she never regained consciousness in the least, passed away without a struggle—it is hard for me we had been friends for so many years." An elaborate funeral followed.

As a final irony, Zina was buried in the Jacobs family plot in the Salt Lake Cemetery not far from Henry, perhaps because she wanted to lie next to her sons when they died. When Zina Card died, she was buried not by her husband but beside her mother.

Zina's story does not end here, though. As we have seen, the Huntington women had a tendency to come back from death to visit their children, and family tradition reports that Zina returned twice to visit her daughter; her message, in part, was for Zina Card to do the genealogy work for Henry Jacobs and his side of the family. The believer will see this as an act of compassion performed from across the grave, an otherworldly gesture of inclusion for Henry and his family, while more skeptical readers may explain this revenant as an expression of Zina Card's sensitivity to feelings of guilt that Zina Diantha felt for abandoning Henry during her life. Even though Zina was married to Joseph Smith for eternity, somehow Henry would always be part of her family. As Henry had remarked, God would sort out the tangled webs of our earthly relationships in the eternities.

## XXIV. A Polygamous Wife

Zina is a classic model for Joseph Smith's early polygamous wives, despite points of uncertainty in the evidence. Her relationship with Smith was polyandrous, as was typical of his earliest Nauvoo wives, and, again typically, he never required her to leave the "first husband." As was usual for first husbands, Henry was a devoted admirer of Smith and probably knew of his wife's marriage to him. The marriage to Brigham Young was less typical, as polyandrous wives were generally allowed to remain with their faithful "first husbands" after Smith's death. But then Zina became a typical "proxy wife" in Young's family, bearing him a child, midwifing his other children, acting as doctor, priestess, and spiritual leader within the family, and later as a public figure in the Relief Society. As was typical of polygamy, Young was not a constant presence in her married life. She filled her time and her deepest emotions with siblings and children.

Despite the severe trials she faced in this life—the shock of polygamy to Victorian sensibilities, the undoubted stresses of polyandry, the constant migrations and hardships of the early Mormon experience, ill health, the untimely departure of her mother and father, the separation from Henry, the comparatively husbandless life of a plural wife in a large family, the loneliness in later years when separated from Zina Card—she nevertheless faced each trial with grace and unquestioning faith and lived a full life of service and compassion. She remains one of the great women in Latter-day Saint history.

# 5.

# An Apostolic Life

## *Presendia Lathrop Huntington (Buell Smith Kimball)*

In modern Mormon practice, women often go to men for "priest-hood" blessings (women are generally understood not to hold priest-hood). The man places his hands on the woman's head and the blessing he gives her is seen as revelatory—a message from God to that individual. In early Mormonism, however, women often blessed other women and occasionally blessed men. In early 1849 a man named Joseph Hovey helped Presendia Kimball through a period of depression and discouragement, perhaps during a difficult pregnancy, and on March 4 she felt impressed to give him a blessing. Placing her hands on his head, she spoke the following words: "Inasmuch as you have comforted me when I was weighted down in the days that are past and now, I also say in the name of Jesus Christ that you shall be blessed ... Yea, you shall have your exaltation, for I will see to it for your goodness towards me. Yea, I will tell Joseph Smith of your good works and you shall come on Mount Zion with the hundred and forty four thousand." So Presendia the plural wife acted as an intermediary to Joseph Smith, a prophetess to the prophet. She even felt she had the authority to promise Hovey exaltation—she would "see to it."

Presendia, Zina Huntington's older sister, unfortunately left no diaries, and the only holographs we have from her are a very short autobiographical sketch and a few letters. Nevertheless, the existing evidence suggests that she was an extraordinary woman, like her sister; also like Zina, she had an eventful life and complex marriage history. Her union with Joseph Smith was polyandrous, but little is known about it. Her "first husband," Norman Buell, is somewhat shadowy; like Henry Jacobs, he seems to have had problematic and sympathetic sides. After Smith's death, Presendia left Norman to became a proxy wife of Heber C. Kimball and bore him two children, living the difficult life of a polygamous wife in his large family. She was very close to Zina all her life and was an important figure in the elite circles of Mormon womanhood in Nauvoo

114

and Utah. She had much of her sister's charismatic authority. "She was also endowed with a large, inspired mind," wrote Edward Tullidge, "the gifts of prophecy, speaking in tongues, and the power to heal and comfort the sick, being quite pre-eminent in her apostolic life."

## I. "Saving Change of Heart"

Presendia Huntington was born on September 7, 1810, in Watertown, Jefferson County, New York, the fourth of the ten Huntington children. One of the few specific things that is known about her childhood concerns her religious life. On June 8, 1822, her mother wrote to her grandmother,

> I can say of the goodness and mercy and favor of God how unspeakable is his Goodness to us. O that I could but realize these things and have a heart of gratitude for all the benfits received there is never [all] of religion all around us some places a few drops and other places a plentiful shower the Lord has visited our family with his good spirit our eldest Daughter Presendia has experienced the saving change of heart I believe. She is 11 years of age last September.

There is a second, more prosaic, piece of information about Presendia's childhood: she had "inflammatory rheumatism" as a girl which her mother cured by administering cedar oil.

## II. Norman Buell

On January 6, 1827, Presendia, aged sixteen, married Norman Buell, twenty-two, who hailed from Lorain, Jefferson, New York, about eighteen miles south of Watertown. The Buells lived first in Mansville, New York, ten miles from Loraine, where Norman worked as a "manufacturer," but Emmeline B. Wells writes that this style of life was so different from the farming environment Presendia was used to that "she was inclined to be unhappy on account of it though in a worldly point of view they were well off." At this point Zina Baker Huntington, writing to her mother on January 22, 1829, again opens a window into Presendia's spiritual life:

> Dear Mother ... I never felt that deep work of grace in my heart before O what reason I have to bless God O what a poor unworthy worm of the dust [I am] ... Presendia our oldest daughter was married one year since her husband and two brothers and sister has experienced religion this fall a great revival where they live ... her husband is old <u>Capt</u> Buels nephew She has again ben brought to enjoy religion She experienced this change when about eleven but had got so she thought she had none O we have many more souls that need this grace.

Presendia, like Joseph Smith, lived in the burned-over district, in the religious environment of revivals and self-recrimination and conversion and thirst for Jesus' grace.

Her first son, George, was born on December 12, 1829, in Mansville. Soon after this, Norman, bowing to his wife's desire for farm life, sold his machinery and business and returned to his father's home in Richmond, Jefferson County. When he received an inheritance from his father, he used it to buy a hundred acres of land in "Pinbury," Lewis County, New York, just east of Jefferson County. There he built a comfortable house and barn and cleared seventy acres of land. Presendia was now in her natural element; she wove wool and flax, made feather beds from her flock of geese, and milked her own cows.

Here, on December 25, 1831, a second son, Silas, was born. Presendia was now seemingly launched on a peaceful, happy career as a mother and farmwife. Two years later, however, on November 13, 1833, she experienced the first of many tragedies in her life. She was "boiling down cider in a very large brass kettle" and put it in an adjoining room where, unknown to her, Silas wandered in and accidentally fell into the kettle. One imagines the boy's screams and Presendia frantically pulling him out of the boiling cider, then desperately trying to treat her wounded, disfigured child. She tended him for thirteen hours as he suffered excruciating pain but then died. For the first time she experienced the agonizing grief of losing a child. "No one but a mother can realize the sorrow of an accidental death," she later wrote.

This calamity led to another. Apparently the shock and strain of losing Silas affected Presendia's health, and she underwent a difficult, painful pregnancy. As the time of birth grew closer, toward the beginning of March 1834, she became extremely ill, and Norman took her to Adams Village to see a doctor. She was too sick to return home, so she stayed in Lorain at the home of a Dr. Bagg. As she seemed to approach death, her parents were sent for. She bore her third son, Thomas Dymick, on March 8, and, though she survived the childbirth, Thomas died the same day. Presendia, not yet twenty-five, had lost two of three children.

She was nursed back to health, but was depressed by her farm, with its associations of death and sickness, so Norman sold it and "rented a woolen factory in Lorain, resuming his favorite employment." During this period of her life, Presendia remembers that ministers in the vicinity were trying to recruit her and Norman. "But Mr. and Mrs. Buell believed they were all wrong, and stood aloof from all," Wells wrote.

### III. "Myriads of Angelic Voices"

In the summer of 1835 Zina Baker Huntington, baptized a Mormon in April, came to visit, bringing with her a Book of Mormon and a handwritten copy of the revelation called the Word of Wisdom, the Mormon health code. "I felt it was true," wrote Presendia, "and thought I would keep the Word of Wisdom and obtain the blessings promised." Mormonism had touched Presendia and her life would never be the same again. In the fall she heard Mormons preach for the first time when elders Ditcher and Blakesley proclaimed the new gospel in a schoolhouse in Burrville where she had attended school as a girl. Norman was also affected by their message and was soon ready to be baptized.

In addition, "at that time a western fever was raging very high, and Mr. Buell was very anxious to go out west." Presendia was eager to gather with the Saints in Kirtland. So, even though the Buells had not yet been baptized, they sold their property and spent the winter at Sackett's Harbour, awaiting passage to Kirtland. In April 1836, traveling with Dimick and Fanny Huntington, they took a schooner across lakes Ontario and Erie to Fairport, Ohio, from which point they could make the short overland journey to Kirtland, which they reached on May 1. Later, in October, the rest of the Huntington family arrived.

Presendia and Norman set about studying Mormonism in depth. Presendia was baptized by Uriah Powell and confirmed by Oliver Cowdery on June 6. Norman was baptized three days later. On September 8 Presendia had another child, Chauncy D., but Mormonism could not put a stop to continued catastrophes in her life. Chauncy died in less than a month, on October 1.

Nevertheless, Presendia enjoyed many charismatic and revelatory experiences in Kirtland, particularly in the temple. On one occasion she witnessed "angels clothed in white" walking upon the temple roof. "They seemed to be walking to and fro; they appeared and disappeared," she wrote. At a fast meeting, as the kneeling congregation prayed vocally, she and Zina heard, from a corner of the hall, a choir of invisible angels "singing most beautifully ... myriads of angelic voices seemed to be united in singing some song of Zion, and their sweet harmony filled the temple of God." She attended a pentecostal temple session filled with tongue-speaking and prophecy: "The Holy Ghost filled the house; and along in the afternoon a noise was heard. It was the sound of a mighty rushing wind. But at first the congregation was startled, not knowing what it was. To many it seemed as though the roof was all in flames. Father Smith exclaimed, Is the house on fire?"

Like Zina, Presendia sang and spoke prophetically, practicing weird ululations of ecstatic tongue-speech. Once a non-Mormon cousin visited the Huntingtons in Kirtland and wanted to hear glossolalia, expecting "to have a hearty laugh," wrote Presendia. So they took the cousin to a meeting. A Brother McCarter rose "and sang a song of Zion in tongues." Then, to the cousin's surprise, Presendia stood up: "I ... sang simultaneously with him the same tune and words, beginning and ending each verse in perfect unison, without varying a word. It was just as though we had sung it together a thousand times." After the meeting the cousin observed, "Instead of laughing, I never felt so solemn in my life."

By December Norman had been ordained an elder; on January 11 of the new year he helped administer a blessing in an elders quorum meeting. William Huntington became a high councilor, which was the equivalent of a general authority in today's LDS church. The Huntingtons, with their fervent, compassionate Christianity, had joined the Mormon elite. Presendia met a host of future friends, such as Eliza R. Snow, Vilate Kimball, Louisa Beaman, and two future husbands, the youthful prophet Joseph Smith and Heber C. Kimball.

## IV. Missouri

Kirtland was becoming increasingly inhospitable to Mormons, and on January 22, 1838, Presendia and Norman left for Missouri, traveling in a "lumber waggon in the ded of the winter" with the Joseph Smith company most of the way. "[We] traveled throug ... the Coldest Storme of wind & Snow," Presendia wrote. The Smith company arrived near Far West, Missouri, on March 13. Presendia, Norman, and George (now ten) lived first in Washington Township, Clay County, then at Fishing River, Ray County, in a primitive log cabin in the forest, some distance from any neighbor. Norman worked at a carding mill four miles from their home. A young woman school teacher stayed with the Buells, but she would teach during the day and George would go to school, so Presendia often felt isolated. "I used to stay alone all day in the woods, my company, the wild birds, and my music the cooing of the turtle doves in the forest," she wrote. In this log cabin, on April 24, her first daughter, Adaline Elizabeth, was born but sadly lived only four hours. Presendia had now lost four children in a row.

Another severe trial would soon face her, for in Missouri Norman became disaffected from the church. It is not known precisely how or why this happened, but Wells, depending on an interview with Presendia, wrote, "Mr. Buell, having apostatized from the Church, was possessed of a very opposite spirit to that of his wife, who was strong in faith and fervent in spirit. Sister Presendia prayed earnestly to the Lord for her companion, that he might return to the faith, but his mind had grown very dark and it was useless to reason with, or entreat him to see the error and doubt which had misled and confused him."

Oliver Huntington added that, "During all this time Norman Buell was in Clay Co. saying god Lord and kind devil, for a time," referring to his vacillating between the Mormon and non-Mormon side. "But the time finally came that he must choose a side, so he chose the Master that would give him the most money then, and in whose hands he thought he would be the safest. He even got to the pitch that he would not let his wife say a word in favor of her brethren, and would say all manner of evil of them himself." Oliver implies that he left Mormonism for fear of mob persecution, for financial security, and because he had some specific complaints against church leaders. Wells writes, "Her husband felt the difficulties were too much, and would have persuaded her, if possible, to leave the Church, but she remained firm." Presendia herself wrote that Buell "left the church in Missouri in 1839. The Lord gave me strength to stand alone and keep the faith amid heavy persecution." Nevertheless, she continued to live with her husband.

In the fall of 1838 tensions between Mormons and Missourians flared into violence, and a friend of the Buells, Mr. Carey, was killed by the anti-Mormon mob while returning home from the mill. In this atmosphere Presendia, accompanied by George, once had to visit the mill during the day. As she drove her team across the prairie, her fears were realized: "As she came out upon the prairie she had to pass through a large company of armed men going up to Far West. She well knew their purpose. Their horses were loaded down with bedding, spades, shovels and cooking utensils, and there was a terrible clatter of tin dishes."

After two men who knew Presendia spoke to her, the company started up a hill. Then "the horsemen called a halt—and dismounted, facing the company towards Mrs. B. and the child, holding their horses by the bits." Presendia thought of Carey's death; Mormon women had reportedly been raped during the Missouri troubles. She wrote, "Then, for the first time in my life, I expected to be shot. I asked the Lord, in silent prayer to let my only child go with me if I should be killed, as my husband had entirely lost his faith in the Gospel. I did not hurry or urge my team forward, but went steadily on over the hill, and the horsemen stood looking at me, but the shock nearly overcame me." Presendia and George were allowed to continue their journey safely, perhaps because the two men knew her and because Buell was known to be an ally.

After the carding season was over, Norman rented a grist mill and two carding machines and successfully ran a mill business by himself. Soon he was able to build a comfortable home for Presendia and the family away from the woods.

Joseph Smith was arrested and incarcerated in Liberty Jail on the last day of October, and in February 1839, when Presendia's father, brother William, Heber Kimball, and Alanson Ripley stopped at the Buell home on their way to visit Smith, Presendia decided to accompany them. She wrote, "I took dinner with the brethren in prison; they were much pleased to see the faces of true friends; but I cannot describe my feelings on seeing that man of God there confined in such a trying time for the saints." Joseph Smith appreciated this visit from Presendia—then about twenty-eight—and after she visited him a second time, with Frederick Williams, Smith wrote her a letter, dated March 15:

> Many of the brethren ... can stay in this country until the indignation is over ... But I think it will be better for Brother Buell to leave and go with the rest of the brethren, if he keeps the faith I want him and you to know that I am your true friend. I was glad to see you no tongue can tell what inexpressible Joy it gives a man to see the face of one who had been a friend after having been inclosed in the walls of a prison for five months ... Write to us if you can.

The advice for Norman to leave "with the rest of the brethren, if he keeps the faith" is interesting, as it suggests that Norman was not a hardened apostate. However, the fact that the Buells stayed in Missouri while the rest of the Saints traveled west shows that he was not in harmony with the main group of Mormons.

Joseph Smith managed to escape from a Missouri sheriff on April 16 and pursued a dangerous journey eastward across the state, arriving in Illinois on April 22. On the 18th the Huntingtons left Far West for Illinois, and Presendia perhaps traveled there to see them off. She wrote, "I never saw my mother again. I felt alone on the earth, with no one to comfort me, excepting my little son George, for my husband had become a bitter apostate, and I could not speak in favor of the church in his presence. There was by this time not one true saint in the State of Missouri to my knowledge."

Norman's mill prospered and Presendia was able to live a quiet, comfortable family life for a time. But Zina Baker Huntington died in Illinois on July 8, and when Presendia heard the news it must have been a terrible blow. On July 13 she wrote Zina a letter, one of her few surviving holographs, which reveals a faithful Mormon woman who felt isolated from family and church:

> I am glad to hear that the twelve are a going to fulfil there mission also that Sidney [Rigdon] is a going to washington I want every revilation to be fulfiled that the work of the Lord may roll on past that the elect may be saved my helth has not been very good a few weeks back I had lost all ambition and courage I could not hear a word from you I thought I was alone in very deed all inteligence closed all the church gone and all around enemies to the church. I hope the time will come when I can live with the Saints I am glad you live in good society I think you enjoy your self well there you are and here am I, an interest in all your prayers I crave that we may meet this side the grave.

Nevertheless, she and Norman were contemplating a move to Illinois:

> N wants to know all about it whether he can get a place for his business and what will be the prospect and whether every one takes care of him self or are they a going to have all common stock business  I dont care onely the will of god be done and his cause advansed and souls [s]aved you must write all a b[o]ut it and if it will do  I think we will com after carding is over.

If George were violently antagonistic to Mormonism, one would not imagine him moving close to the Mormons again. Presendia turned to news of common friends, then bemoaned her spiritual isolation:

> I want Father and Mother and all of you to hold us by faith for it is hard going up streem with out ores [oars]  give my love to brother Joseph and family and all the rest of my acquaintance there  we get a long as to our temporaral things about right as yet but spiritual drags  I am as strong as ever in the faith yet but if this aint a poor place to kee[p] the spirit I am mistaken in very deed  no one to help me along or strengthen my faith, but to the reverse.

After the Buell family visited Quincy in October or November 1839, Presendia wrote another letter to her family on January 2, 1840. On arriving home, the Buells succumbed to an attack of "winter fever":

> George was taken sick 2 days before we got holme  the next day was confined to his bed and remained so 2 weeks before he got so as to walk again  he was very sick with the winter fever and almost died  I told him I thought he would die  he said he felt in his heart he should not die before me and that may be  it was hard for me to lift him but my strength held out  he just began to walk and norman was taken with it  he has never been so as not to walk yet he is very poor in flesh and in a bad state of health  if he cant get help soon it will be a hard case  I think his fever has taken a change and his disease is in his stomach and bowels  I am a fraid of the quick consumption  we have had a hired man ever since we got holme  we have every thing nesisary for our situation  Adaline Ballard came holme with us and if it was not for her I could not get along alone  we found all things safe here and he just fixed for winter when he was taken sick.

She mentioned that Norman planned to move near Quincy and was hungry for news from the body of the Saints:

> Zina I want you to write if you have heard from brother Joseph and all about every thing if you are able to use a pen and how you all get along  I have omited writing longer than I intended to but we have been sick stedy since we got holme  I want to see you all  Oh how I want to see my

121

breathren and sisters but I know not when my desire is to live with the Saints and share with them in this world and in the world to come

Apparently, when Norman and Presendia were in Quincy, someone, perhaps in the Huntington family, advised Presendia to leave her non-believing husband and stay in Quincy, which naturally made him very angry. Presendia wrote, "I cant have a chance to write for his eye is uppon me I cant tel you how he feels but if he dies he dies feeling just as hard as he can towards the church or those that wanted me to stay there ... Norman sends his respects to all that was willing for me to come back so you can judge his feelings."

## V. New and Everlasting Covenant

On January 31, 1840, Presendia bore her sixth child, Oliver Norman, who happily was healthy and grew to maturity. Later that fall the Buells moved to Lima, Illinois, thirty miles south of Nauvoo. This is a fact of considerable importance, for, as noted above, if Norman had been entirely antagonistic to Mormonism, he probably would not have consented to live near the Mormon center. It is possible that Presendia was so unhappy when not living near her siblings and parents that Norman bowed to her wishes to move near them. One must also recognize that she would stay with Norman for many years after leaving Missouri.

In Lima Norman turned to his favored occupation, running a steam mill and carding wool. Presendia was able to make frequent trips to Nauvoo. In late October 1841 Joseph Smith married her sister, Zina, and soon after that, if not before, he also proposed to Presendia. Wells writes,

> Joseph himself taught the principle of plural marriage to Sister Presendia, and her heart was humble, and her mind open to receive the revelations of heaven. She knew Joseph to be a man of God, and she had received many manifestations in proof of this, and consequently when he explained to her clearly the knowledge which he had obtained from the Lord, she accepted the sealing ordinance with Joseph as a sacred and holy confirmation.

The marriage took place on December 11. In her autobiography, Presendia wrote, "In 1841 I entered into the New and Everlasting Covenant—was sealed to Joseph Smith the Prophet and Seer, and to the best of my ability I have honored Plural Marriage, never speaking one word against the principle." The ordinance was performed by her brother, Dimick, Smith's close friend, while Dimick's wife Fanny stood as a witness. "Soon after Dimick had given our sisters Zina & Prescinda to Joseph as wives for eternity," wrote Oliver Huntington, Smith offered

Dimick any reward he wanted. Dimick merely requested "that where you and your fathers family are, there I and my fathers family may also be." Relatives of Smith's plural wives were often awarded increased salvation after helping arrange the marriage. Through Zina's and Presendia's marriages, Dimick and Joseph created an eternal bond with each other and Dimick felt that his chances for complete salvation had been increased. So this was a dynastic marriage, an example of male bonding through polygamy.

Wells wrote that Presendia and Smith's other plural wives felt part of a small, select spiritual elite, "separate and apart from all others. Their minds were more expanded, new light had burst in upon them, and they were buoyed up by a spirit which they scarcely understood." Nevertheless, rumors of their marriages (often polyandrous) soon spread, so these women bore the brunt of "calumny and reproach." Wells justifiably viewed them as heroic: "No tongue can describe, or pen portray the peculiar situation of these noble, self-sacrificing women who through the providence of God helped to establish the principle of celestial marriage." Even if one is unsympathetic to polygamy, one must admire the intensity of these women's commitment to their new religion.

Norman, a man bitterly opposed to Mormonism, was probably not told of Presendia's marriage, but, as in all of Smith's polyandrous unions, Presendia continued to live with Buell, the "first husband."

## VI. The Female Relief Society of Nauvoo

The fact that Presendia lived in Lima prevented her from participating fully in the spiritual life of Nauvoo. However, on April 19, 1842, "Priscinda Buel" was accepted into the Nauvoo Female Relief Society at its fifth meeting. "Councillor [Sarah] Cleveland then arose and address'd the meeting by saying that ... the meeting was specially called for the admission of Mrs. Buel who resided at a distance—was deprived of the privileges enjoyed by the sisters in Nauvoo, and wished to become a member of this Society." This special meeting shows Presendia's spiritual prestige in Nauvoo. "Mrs. Buel arose and said that she rejoiced in the opportunity—that she considered it a great privilege she felt that the spirit of the Lord was with the Society, and rejoic'd to become a member altho' residing at a distance and could not attend the meetings."

What followed is an interesting example of the kind of blessing that was being given in charismatic meetings at the time, dominated as they were by Eliza R. Snow:

Miss Snow after making observations with regard to the Society—the importance of acting in wisdom & walking humbly before God &c. said she had a blessing for Mrs. Buel, that inasmuch as she had become a member of this Society, as the spirit of a person pervades every member of the body, so shall the Spirit of the Lord which pervades this Society be with her—she shall feel it and rejoice—she shall be blest where ever she is, and the Lord shall open the way and she shall be instrumental in doing much,—thro' her own exertions by the instrumentality of others, she shall be enabled to contribute much to the fund of the Society—she shall warm up the hearts of those who are cold and dormant, and shall be instrumental in doing much good—Mrs. Leonard, Councillor W. and Councillor C. bore testimony to the truth of what Miss Snow had said to Mrs. Buel.

In August Oliver Huntington stayed with Presendia and Norman in Lima. When Norman took a trip to New York, Oliver and a friend ran his mill. Presendia probably enjoyed having a sibling living with her. She visited Patty Sessions in Nauvoo on September 24.

A year passed uneventfully until November 1843 when Presendia's last child by Buell, John Hiram, was born. (It is unlikely, though not impossible, that Joseph Smith was the actual father.) Presendia's son George was nearly fourteen and Oliver almost four. In the spring and summer of 1844, her brother Oliver again worked for Norman in Lima "in the Steam Mill & carding wool." That summer brought a major catastrophe for Presendia when Joseph Smith was killed in Carthage on June 27. Her mourning for the loss of her prophet and second husband would have been as private as it was deep.

## VII. Heber C. Kimball

Oliver continued to work for his brother-in-law until the end of July when he was stricken by a bad case of fever. At the time Presendia was in Nauvoo visiting Zina, and she herself was sick but returned to Lima on July 30. Oliver, after a long bout with the illness, during which Presendia undoubtedly tended him, was taken back to Nauvoo on August 16. On October 5 the Buells came up to Nauvoo for a brief visit and the next day Zina wrote, "We all went to meeting."

Presendia experienced another calamity in early November when she lost John Hiram to "Summer Complaint." On the 8th Zina wrote, "Norman Buell and Oliver came up from Lima and brought up the corps of my sister Presendia Buells child, John Hiram by name, age about 1 year." That Christmas Zina and other members of the Huntington family rode down to Lima to spend the holiday with the Buells. Zina wrote, on Christmas Day, "Presendes little son Oliver is very sick but think he is amending."

In mid-March 1845 Norman became very sick and Presendia was afraid that he would die. Oliver wrote, "The 17th of March 1845 I went down there to see him die as I expectd, but found him at work." Buell had made a quick recovery. While Oliver was in Lima, he and Presendia visited a "sugar camp to eat warm sugar." A "mad man" threatened them with a knife, and they were barely able to quiet him down. He then told them a history of his misfortunes. Oliver wrote, "After a lengthy conversation Presendia was filled with pity, invited him to her house to rest himself a day or two." Presendia had the same compassion for the unfortunate that characterized her parents, Zina, and all of the other Huntingtons.

As was the case with Zina, one might have expected a simplification of Presendia's marital status after Smith's death, but as Brigham Young and Heber Kimball felt a strong motivation to marry Smith's widows, simplification was not possible. The two apostles must have approached Presendia a few months after Smith's death. As in the case of Zina, they may have offered her higher salvation if she would marry one of them—especially since her present husband was not in good standing in the church. One imagines that she responded with unquestioning obedience to whatever the presiding apostles recommended. So she married Kimball in 1845, probably after March 17, as his approximate twenty-first wife. It is possible that she did not see the sealing to Heber as interfering with her marriage to Buell, just as Smith's marriage had not dissolved it.

On April 1 Presendia and Norman apparently attended a Mormon meeting together, as the journal of William Huntington, Presendia's father, reads, "Norman Buell and wife came here to attend conference." This reference, which suggests that Norman was not averse to Mormon church meetings, is not the picture of Buell as the hardened apostate that later traditions sometimes present. At the very least, he made it easy for Presendia to attend meetings occasionally.

The crucial events of the next few months, when Presendia left Norman, are documented only by fragments from the historical record. The Nauvoo temple was nearing completion and all faithful Mormons, including "second husband" Heber Kimball and the Huntington family, were preparing to go west. On January 10, 1846, "Presenda Buel" received her endowment in the temple with no male companion. A month later, on February 4, she was sealed to Joseph Smith for eternity, with Kimball standing proxy, then was sealed to Kimball for time. By the time of this sealing, her new husband had already married approximately thirty-five women, an extremely large household even by Mormon standards. However, Presendia continued to live with Buell for some months after her temple marriage to Kimball.

## VIII. Escape

The final break with Buell came in early May. Oliver wrote, "Now Presendia's Husband would not follow the Church any longer at Nauvoo, so she left him and followed after her Lord [Kimball], moving with the Saints even to the valley." Augusta Crocheron, using an interview with Presendia, wrote, "The Saints had nearly all left for the West; Sister Prescendia felt as if she were at the mercy of the mob, and indeed, plans were laid to destroy her." One wonders why Presendia, married to an ex-Mormon at a safe distance from Nauvoo, would have been endangered in this way. Perhaps she felt a sense of spiritual isolation and projected feelings of personal danger onto her anti-Mormon neighbors.

Crocheron continues, "As if in answer to her prayers, her brother, William, sent her a messenger telling her to leave all and come." The ties between the Huntingtons were strong and it would have been very difficult for Presendia to watch her family leaving her. This feeling, accompanied by the perception of enmity from non-Mormons, and perhaps the sense of a "priesthood" marriage being more important than a secular marriage, swayed the balance toward departure. However, she knew that she would be leaving sixteen-year-old George, which was a painful parting. Crocheron continues, "On the 2nd of May, 1846, she walked out of her house leaving all behind her, taking her little boy [Oliver, now six] who was sick and not able to be up but she was flying for her life. With the help of her son George, she got away." She left without Norman's consent or knowledge. After traveling all night, she reached the home of a friend, Dr. Spurgeon, at about dawn. After breakfast she retreated to the woods to hide, "fasting and praying for deliverance ... I picked flowers for him and gave him water from the running stream. At night I went back to the doctor's, sleeping with my sick boy on a little bed on the floor. Next day I hid in a wagon."

It is not clear if Presendia was hiding from the "mob" or from her husband, but the next development suggests that Norman was looking for her. "When we arrived at Nashville, I saw a man whom I knew, looking for me. I learned afterward he intended taking my child from me." In divorces at this time, husbands often received custody of the children, so Presendia was fighting for her child. Soon, however, Dimick's sons found her and brought her to a camp of Mormons in Iowa. "I stayed in a deep ravine while some things were brought to me, and slept on a buffalo robe on the ground at night with my little child. No tongue can tell my feelings in those days of trial; but I had considered well, and felt I would rather suffer and die with the Saints, than live in Babylon as I had lived before." Finally, Presendia and her nephews arrived at Bonaparte in southeastern Iowa. However, the "excitement and exposure" affected Presendia adversely and she contracted a serious fever.

Finally Presendia arrived at Mt. Pisgah and reunited with her father and sister. As Zina was at Mt. Pisgah from approximately May 21 to October 1, Presendia presumably came there sometime after May 21. Though the reunion must have been joyful, Zina and William were living in a crude log cabin without chimney or floor and nearly everyone was prostrate with fever.

In a June 25 letter Henry Jacobs wrote to Zina, "N. Buell is all most crazy he has ben up here." Though the Mormon historical record has viewed Norman unsympathetically as "a bitter apostate," he was a husband and father with real feelings, and this reference shows how he suffered when he suddenly lost his wife and youngest son.

## IX. Healings and Visions

It is not certain how long Presendia stayed at Mt. Pisgah. But at some point before her father's death on August 19, she travelled across western Iowa to Winter Quarters, then settled in Cutler's Park, just west of Winter Quarters proper. The Huntingtons were now thoroughly separated: Father Huntington and Zina were at Mt. Pisgah; Dimick and Fanny were with the Mormon Battalion; brother William was in St. Louis; and Oliver was on a mission to England. Presendia had left one husband, and her new husband, Heber Kimball, was helping direct a mass exodus across Iowa and by now had thirty-nine other wives.

Nevertheless Presendia entered Heber's extended "family kingdom" and tried to make the best of it. Before Kimball's death in 1868, he would marry forty-five women (though he did not live connubially with all of them), and the challenges of living in such a family can be imagined. Despite his status as a high church leader, and because of the church's demands on his time, Heber would continually struggle to provide for all his wives and children and to give them attention. As a consequence, sixteen of his wives separated from him, according to Stanley Kimball.

In addition, Heber's first wife, Vilate, was clearly his favorite. He did not have the strong emotional connection with any of his plural wives that he had with Vilate. He had bonded closely to her for many years before he began to practice polygamy. Helen Mar, a daughter of Heber and Vilate, wrote that "[by Vilate's continual kind deeds] she won the love of all; and among the most devoted were my father's faithful wives, who admired him more because they knew he loved her best ... [they regarded her] as their dearest and most enduring friend." Vilate, in fact, became one of Presendia's close friends, an example of polygamy promoting sisterhood.

Nevertheless, for Presendia, living as a plural wife in the family of Heber C. Kimball would not be easy. Despite the fact that she was technically married, one senses that she was forced to fend for herself to a great extent and she turned to housekeeping, then to schoolteaching. "I was in a new, wild country without means," she wrote. "Joseph and Henry

Woodmansee wanted me to keep house for them. As soon as I was settled their father wrote for them, and I was left in charge of their house.
I started a school which was a great blessing to the children. The house
was built of logs and covered with dirt and straw, with a little straw
upon the floor." During a school break Presendia "was attacked with
winter fever," but through priestly ministrations and her family's and
friends' care, she recovered.

When she received news of her father's death, she was plunged into
grief. "[The future was] like a great, unknown desert, unrelieved and
barren. I had only my Heavenly Father left, and I reached out in faith to
the One above to open the heavens for me and aid me in my loneliness,"
she wrote. On February 13, 1847, Patty Sessions wrote, "visited sisters
Buel and Rockwell." The next day Patty noted that Presendia was with a
group of women praying for Sylvia Sessions, another wife of Joseph
Smith and Kimball. Patty's February 28 entry shows that Presendia took
part in the glossolalia and blessing meetings of Winter Quarters: "Br and
sister Leonard and sister Buel was here last night  we spoke in toungues
and had a good time."

Presendia was living with Laura Pitkin, another plural wife of Kimball, in the spring. Their home was near Vilate's, and they associated
with her frequently. Presendia and Zina also spent a great deal of time together. On March 7 Patty wrote, "visited the sick  Precinda and Zina was
here." On the 26th Patty's journal shows Presendia's association with
the Kimball family: "Br Belnap sent me a quarter of dear meat  I divided
it with sisters [Vilate] Kimbal and Buel." On April 1 Patty "visited with
sister Knight at sister Buels." Sister Knight is Martha McBride Knight, another proxy wife of Smith and Kimball. On April 22 Eliza R. Snow visited
Presendia, as Eliza records in her journal, and on the next day Presendia
attended a blessing meeting.

Patty wrote on May 11, "Sister Lenard & Buel were here on a visit
sister Buel had the toothache bad  we laid hands on her." Presendia also
frequently helped administer to others, as she would throughout her
life. Once she helped heal a child of Lyman Whitney's that was on the
verge of death; according to Wells: "The little one had not seen or spoken for two days, its eyeballs were dried over." Presendia, with Elizabeth
Ann Whitney, Vilate, and Laura Pitkin Kimball, "administered, anointing
the child with oil, and bathing its eyes with milk and water, and it was
restored to life and health miraculously, but the sisters gave God the
glory."

Early Mormons often had a strong sense of the presence of dark otherworldly forces. On one occasion Zina was sleeping overnight with Presendia when, Presendia remembers, "we both felt the presence of the

destroyer at the door, the feeling was beyond expression." Before dawn William Pitt came for them—his little girl was dying. Presendia wrote, "I immediately arose, drest myself, and repaired to the house where the dying girl lay in the last agonies of death, beyond the reach of mortal aid. She died in a few minutes on my lap." In early Mormonism death and sickness were often considered the result of an attack by malevolent spirits. Soon after this, Presendia recalls, a meeting was held at the home of Christine and Frances Swan Kimball, at which "the evil power" was again perceived. "So strong was the influence that the spirits were seen and heard, and they tried to destroy those in the room by choking them. Sister Laura Kimball and I laid our hands upon five of those so affected, and rebuked the destroyer in the name of Jesus."

By this time Presendia was well known for her spiritual and priestly gifts, and she also received prophetic visions during her stay at Winter Quarters. Wells writes, "Many things were shown to Sister Presendia, and almost as it were the heavens opened to view, for her comfort and consolation in the time of her great sorrow and sacrifice. These were sacred things." So, for Presendia, Winter Quarters was a time of trial, but also a period of intense spiritual experience.

Norman, meanwhile, remarried three months after Presendia left him, according to Oliver Huntington. But this marriage, if it occurred, did not last, and Buell travelled to Winter Quarters before May 1848 and asked Presendia to return to him. She refused, so he traveled south to St. Joseph, Missouri, about 150 miles from Winter Quarters but within easy steamboat distance, where he operated a grist mill. Oliver, recently returned from his mission to England, met Buell in St. Joseph, and wrote:

There I met Norman Buell who had been up to Winter Quarters on a visit, and was very well pleased with it and the treatment he received from Heber and Brigham. In time of the Church's evacuation of Nauvoo my sister left him and fled with the Church. About 3 months after she left him He got married to another woman, but now in his visite he repented of what he had done, and wanted she should not marry but wait a while and he would come over to the valley, and be glad to live with her again.

Apparently Presendia and Heber had not explained to Norman even now that they were married. The gratitude Norman felt for "Heber and Brigham" is puzzling. For an apostate whose wife and youngest son had deserted him, he seems curiously lacking in bitterness. Oliver writes that at St. Joseph, many "old saints" were preparing to start for the valley:

Norman had rented the only steam grist-mill there and was going directly home to move on and said he would make use of what he could make to move over the mountains as soon as he could. He wanted me to come back and work for him, but I told him I should do as Brigham counciled me. We were together until about one o clock A.M. and in the morning of Sat. May 6th we both left, he for Quincy and I for the Camp of Israel.

Oliver met Zina at Winter Quarters immediately, but, he wrote, "Presendia had gone out 7 or 8 miles on the road to the valley where teams could get a good living, the grass being just sprung up, except on the low bottom land where it was better." This is apparently Cutler's Park. The reunion of the Huntington siblings took place there on May 16: "Then Presendia, Wm, Zina, and Oliver were all together once more upon the earth," wrote Oliver. They celebrated the occasion by sharing the charismatic gifts of the primitive church: "While Caroline [William's wife] was with [us], we had 2 joyful seasons of speaking in tongues, and much was said to our joy and comfort."

## X. Utah

On May 6 Presendia, now thirty-seven, and little Oliver left Winter Quarters for Salt Lake, traveling in Heber C. Kimball's company. In the trip west she "drove her own team part of the way though in delicate health, and sometimes unable to sit up ... but she ... was happy in feeling that she was about to reach a place of refuge." In mid-July Oliver Huntington wrote, "Went back to Hebers Camp and had a good visite with Presendia and Heber." She and her son arrived in Salt Lake on September 22.

Presendia is a constant presence in the Utah diaries of both Zina Huntington Young and Patty Sessions. Zina frequently stayed overnight with her, and the two sisters attended the blessing meetings that continued in Utah. Dimick bought her and Zina a two-room house in the old fort and they lived together contentedly for awhile. However, Presendia was expecting and her health was not good–she was, wrote Zina on December 11, "scarcely able to walk. The room smoked s[o] that it was almost unsuferable and the noise of the scool and the children in the joining room was more than she could endure and her strength was daily wasting away." So she moved to Zina's room. Then, Oliver wrote, "Sometime in December Precendia removed to another house which H. C. Kimball had prepared for her, as he was to see to her and look after her welfare."

Just as Zina served as midwife to the Young family, so Presendia acted as midwife for the Kimball wives and received charismatic, priestly gifts for her medical duties. After being instructed by Dr. Willard Richards, he "laid his hands upon the heads of a number of the sisters [including Presendia] who had prepared themselves to act as midwives and also administering to the sick and afflicted and set them apart for this very office and calling, and blest them with power to officiate in that capacity." Presendia drew upon this "power and influence," writes Wells, when acting as a midwife, and when "washing and anointing and blessing the sisters."

### XI. "The Flower of the Flock Has Gone"

Presendia's child, Presendia Celestia, was born on January 9, 1849. Zina wrote, "At 15 minets past 12 AM She had a fine daughter ... The babe came near perishing but survived. After supper Br Kimble came in, the Father of the child, and blest it calling it Presendia. Great ware the blessing[s] sealed uppon the childs head." Patty Sessions was also present. Presendia's house at the time was so primitive that in the days following the birth she had to put an umbrella over the bed to protect herself and the child from rain. She was overjoyed at receiving a daughter, as the Huntington women were extraordinarily attached to their daughters. "She grew to be intelligent and attractive," Wells writes. "No daughter was ever more fondly loved in infancy than this little one ... Her mother's heart was entwined around her so firmly, that it seemed as though to be separated even for a short time was almost insupportable."

During the winter, living in her primitive house and having to milk her cows herself, she was often helped by a Brother Edward Martin and even spent part of the winter in his more comfortable house. As often in polygamy, we see the wife being helped by friends and family, not by the husband. On June 29 she and Zina visited the sick together. The latter wrote: "In the after noon Sister Abbot sent for Presendia and I to come and see her. Her husband is very feeble. She asked me to set near her bed."

A month later, on the 28th, Presendia attended a party with Heber and three other wives, while Brigham brought three spouses, including Zina. On December 12 Zina recorded a move: "I came up with Presendia. She moved up into a room joining Br Kimbles a good stove and things comfortable. Surely will she know how to prize them for she has not ben a stranger to cold and fateague and exposure. Her health is not very good. I assisted her what I could in moving."

Presendia Celestia had her first birthday on January 9, 1850. Zina wrote, "I was at Presendes. Her little daughter is one year old is running all a bout the building. Children of the family all ware there and partook of some cakes celebrating her birth day. A pleasing sight." These words are especially poignant in light of the next major event in Presendia's life. In early May Heber C. Kimball had a dream in which "he saw a serpent carry off one of his children." Fearing that this foreshadowed a death, he visited all his wives and advised them to watch their children carefully. On May 11 Presendia, remembering Heber's warning, offered her morning prayers and "asked God to protect my child from accident seen and unseen through the day." She dressed little Presendia in a red dress for a visit to her sister-in-law Caroline's, then let Oliver, ten years old, take her to visit Zina at the Young family log row. When they arrived, they called at every cabin for little Presendia to be admired, then visited the main Young dining room where most of the family was seated at breakfast. All greeted little Presendia, Brigham Young kissing her last. Then Oliver started to bring her home. After crossing City Creek, he set her down and cut some sticks to make whistles for some young boys. Wells writes, "It was but a moment, a fatal moment too, he turned around to look and she was not to be found ... [He] screamed and cried out 'a red dress.' President Young's family heard the confusion, they left the table, and all began the search. That portion of the stream that passed Brother Kimball's had just been turned into the other, and disturbed and roiled the water, so that the child could not be seen." Oliver raced to Presendia and told her that little Presendia had been lost in the creek, and Presendia ran out.

John Young remembers that a cry of alarm was given. Though he had a wounded leg, he left his home and saw people milling along the creek. "I surmised what had happened," he wrote. "Running to the slab, I dropped into the water and was carried by the swift current to Brother Well's lot, where the fence had caught flood wood, and formed a dam and eddy. I dove under the drift, and finding the body, brought it to the surface, and gave it to Dr. Williams; but the precious life was gone."

Presendia remembers, "I ran across the street to Dr. Williams', they brought her in, dead ... [They did] all they could to restore her to life, but the vital spark had fled. My tongue turned cold in my mouth, I felt that I was dying." Though she felt almost suicidal in her grief, she realized that she had to continue to live for Oliver. Presendia Celestia was taken back to her house and laid on her bed. As they returned, the presiding sister-wife, Vilate Kimball, said, "The flower of the flock has gone." The experience was incomprehensibly painful for a woman who had already lost so many children and after a year of intense bonding with an only daughter. She wrote, "Zina, Lucy and Clara Young prepared her clothing for her burial, and she looked so beautiful, so lovely. She was buried on the 10th of May. I tried to smother my excessive grief, but after dark I visited her grave day after day, and there on the sacred ground gave vent to my sorrow in tears."

The experience was also horrific for Oliver. Presendia remembers, "The poor boy could not be comforted; he would retire and sit under the bushes alone for hours ... he loved her so tenderly, that his heart was rent with anguish too deep for words." A friend, Mary A. Hubbard, came to stay with Presendia for two months, bringing her one-year-old child.

Helping to care for the infant cheered Presendia somewhat, but when Mary left, she underwent what was probably a major depression: "I gradually lost my appetite, and grief filled my heart. In the fall my health became very poor." Zina, seeing her sister's psychological and physical health plummet, arranged an expedition for their joint families to Cottonwood to stay with a Brother Bankhead. However, in Cottonwood, Presendia became so ill that she approached death.

In the depths of her despair she had a revelatory experience while in bed one night: "My feet were cold, my tongue was stiff in my mouth, I could not speak, yet I was perfectly conscious; a candle in the room looked like the most distant star. It was a log house, and the walls had sunk so that the door could never be opened or closed tight without effort, yet the door opened by invisible hands in the middle of the night, and my father and Joseph Smith walked into the room." Her first thought was that they had come to take her to her rest in the next life. But she felt "that it would be too much to leave my little Oliver, my only one now left to me, alone in the world, without father or mother, with the burden of his great sorrow upon him, for he mourned and could not be wholly comforted for the loss of his little sister." So she turned her face to the wall, refusing to go with Joseph and William. Brother Bankhead summoned Heber Kimball to administer to her and she recovered enough to return to her home in the city.

However, she had a relapse, suffered from "dropsy of the heart, and subsequently dropsy of the entire body." Heber feared that she might be close to death, so a girl, Sophia Curtis, was brought in to tend her. During this time of sickness, moments of revelation continued to buoy her up: "During my severe illness the Lord showed me many marvelous things and I sang praises to Him on my bed of affliction ... I cried and composed as I sang. I told my feelings to President Kimball, and also what I saw and heard." She slowly recovered, and in the spring of 1851 she was pregnant once again.

On April 15 an entry in Patty Sessions's diary shows Presendia's priestly aspect: "Visited Sister Buel she anointed me and sister Jackman and blesed us both." Her sacral persona is also shown by her temple work, for in the spring she, with Elizabeth Whitney, was called by President Young to work in the Endowment House, performing sacred ordinances for other women. "We loved the work and the Lord blest us with His Spirit," she wrote. "We seemed to live above everything earthly or trivial while engaged in those spiritual duties, and we had many comforting dreams as well as other manifestations that the Lord approved of our ministrations." Once, Presendia reports, Elizabeth Whitney dreamed that Presendia went into a large room in the Endowment House "and [I, Presendia] apparently danced in space, for I did not touch the floor, but kept above it. She said I was perfectly transparent, and there was not a spot or blemish of any sort upon my body." Whitney stood against the door so that there would be no interruption until after her friend had completed her hieratic, hovering dance.

## XII. Joseph Smith Kimball

As Presendia became increasingly pregnant, she retired from her Endowment House duties, and on December 22 Joseph Smith Kimball, her last child, was born in her comfortable house on "the adobe row just on the north side of City Creek, where the first home Heber C. Kimball built in the valley was situated." This healthy baby was a great comfort to Presendia, now forty-one. "He was like an Isaac of old to me," she wrote. "I had been favored of the Lord to have a son born in the new and everlasting covenant and I looked upon it as a great blessing to be thus honored."

In the years after Joseph's birth, Presendia taught school and worked hard at household duties. "We had to card, spin and color our yarn, and weave," she wrote. Heber's wives made their own clothing, soap, molasses and candles. In the fall of 1853 she and her two sons were living in a small adobe house where the "old church blacksmith's shop" was later situated. On November 15, when she was helping Oliver move a lye leach (a vessel for ashes) and was walking backwards, she hit her heels against a log and fell, breaking her left arm. At first she tried to set the bone herself but was unsuccessful, so a doctor was sent for who set it more expertly. However, Presendia's normal work of sewing and weaving was put on an indefinite hiatus.

Her older children began to marry, beginning in about 1853 when George Buell married a J. Poorman in Missouri. His first child, a daughter whose name began with A, was born in 1854. Presendia was now a grandmother. Though her grandchildren were far away, she must have corresponded with her oldest son and his family. When Oliver turned nineteen and married Mary Ann Last in late 1857, Presendia could be a grandmother at close range.

She broke her left arm again in mid-January 1855, and the re-injury was more painful and serious than the original break. Yet she continued to tend other sick women. On August 26 Zina wrote, "In the afternoon Presendia & sister Lowry & I went to Sister Jackmans she is very sick we anointed her." On July 4, 1857, Patty Sessions recorded a similar incident: "I went ... with sister Precinda Kimball washed & changed sister F G Williams anointed and laid hands on her." On April 17, 1856, Martha Spence Heywood visited Presendia and, feeling "very weak in body," requested a blessing, "which she did with alacrity." Heywood's diary preserves an invaluable summary of the blessing: "The run of it was that the Lord knew the integrity of my heart and that I would not do anything contrary to His will if I knew it; that he had his eye upon me for good and that the trials that I was passing through were for my good; that my boy would live to be a comfort and staff to old age and that the Lord would make all right with me in due season and I should have my true mate who would sympathize with my afflictions."

Presendia was also doing temple work in the Endowment House. In early November 1857 Zina wrote, "Sister Presendia & Sister Whitney gave the washing and anointing in the endowment house." On December 23, Presendia met with Zina and Laura Pitkin Kimball to commemorate Joseph's birthday.

As a plural wife of Heber Kimball during this period, Presendia was living in the semi-communal homes of his wives, including three or four per house, and Heber often required his wives to move as he acquired new pieces of land and sold others. Vilate, on the other hand, lived in a central, impressive white house, with Heber, her children, and a few other plural wives. At one point we hear of Presendia being helped in her household duties by a male neighbor. All these factors present a striking contrast to monogamous marriage.

### XIII. "O How Our Hearts Ake"

In early 1858, with Johnston's Army approaching Utah, Kimball sent his family south to Utah Valley. Presendia left Salt Lake City on the last day of March with a heavy heart–though her house was humble, she felt great regret on leaving it, since it had become "home," a brief locus of stability after her years of migration. She wrote, "All I wished particularly for was my bedstead, lying on the floor again was so hard after our long and tedious journeys, it was annoying to be obliged to submit to it again." She traveled with sister-wives Anna Gheen and Ellen Sanders, then stayed with Bishop Aaron Johnson in Springville, just south of Provo.

When Brigham and his counsellors decided that it was safe to return to Salt Lake, Heber, for unknown reasons, directed Presendia and Martha Knight to stay in the south, so she moved to Provo, living where "dooryards were full of tall grass and the fruit trees were loaded with beautiful peaches and apples." However, Vilate Kimball missed her, so, as Presendia wrote, "(that blessed woman, a mother to us all, when I think of her my heart swells with gratitude) would give Bro. Kimball no peace until he sent for me to return to the family." Once again we see the curious distance between a polygamous husband and his wife. He is content to have the plural wife live in a different city, but his first wife finds that distancing intolerable. The ties between two sister-wives seem stronger than those between husband and wife.

Oliver Buell and Mary Ann, who had followed Presendia to Springville, decided to stay there, and soon Oliver was "freighting to Lower California." Presendia returned to Salt Lake in September and moved in with three other wives, Sarah Ann Whitney, Lucy Walker, and Mary Houston—all wives of Joseph Smith (though Mary may have married him posthumously). "We spent the fall and winter very pleasantly," Presendia wrote. "This will seem like an anomaly to our Gentile friends." She spun and wove, making clothes for the extended family, just as she had learned to do as a child on the Huntington farm. In the evenings, at harvest times, the family pared fruit together. Eventually she moved to her own lot in the Seventeenth Ward.

While Oliver was in California, Mary Ann Last Buell and George Buell, in St. Louis, began to correspond, and George offered Oliver a job in the woolen factory he managed. Mary Ann was anxious to go, "for she had lost her faith in the Gospel," wrote Presendia. When Oliver returned, he accepted the job, and in early May 1859 he and his young bride prepared to travel east. Presendia, who probably viewed the departure in theological terms as apostasy, was devastated. Zina recorded on May 9, "About 1 P.M. Oliver and his wife Mary ann arived from Springville going to Mo to see his Father this day I shall never forget Sister Presendia groans & sighs hes gone they are gone was the only articulations from amongst stifled Sobs, yet we will trust in god & his wisdom in his merces he will remember us." Presendia wrote, "My agony of soul could not be told or written when he left. I have never shed many tears since, as the fountain was broken up." She was still upset the following day. Zina wrote, "I went and assisted sister in putting down her carpet O how our hearts ake." "I was alone with my little boy Joseph, one out of nine children," wrote Presendia, "and yet I lived."

## XIV. Tending the Sick

"Aunt Huldah" Barnes Kimball was now boarding with Presendia, who cultivated a thriving garden on her lot and performed the merciful work of the Relief Society on a daily basis: "During all this time," she wrote proudly, " ... I never neglected any calls to visit the sick, the dying, and the dead. I always took great pains in preparing the dead beautifully for their final rest."

As so often in Presendia's life, personal affliction was soon balanced by spiritual feast. On June 27 Presendia, Zina, Hannah King, and Susan Sabettler commemorated Joseph Smith's death ("that solemn day") by hiking to the summit of Ensign Peak. There they made an altar of stones and knelt around it. "We ... offered up our prayers to God and thanks that He had raised up a prophet in these last days and the Gospel had been restored to the earth, and that we had been of the few that had received the truth. We sang and blest each other." As they prayed and sang in tongues, they felt Smith's presence. To these early Mormons, the spirits of departed loved ones were never far off.

In the winter Kimball gathered his outlying wives nearer to him to minimize expenses, and Presendia moved again, now sharing a house with Huldah Barnes and Harriet Sanders Kimball. Three years later, in the spring of 1862, Heber bought Presendia a house in the Sixteenth Ward, near Dimick's house. These continual moves must have been a great strain for Presendia, who loved the security of a good home. (The contrast with Vilate and her family was stark; Heber never required her to move from her roomy central home.) On the day of the move, April 7, Heber sent for Presendia and gave her a blessing, which is happily preserved:

> I want you, Presendia, to go on the place I have bought of Daniel Morse and take care of it as my property, and you shall be blest in all your labors, and everything shall prosper in your hands; be liberal and kind to the poor and to the sick and [give] of your means and strength; uphold me in your prayers and faith. The angels that have guarded me through life are those that guarded the ancient apostles in the days of Jesus; they will be your guardian angels, and the hand that is raised against you shall be stayed, and it shall not prosper. I want you when you get moved to-day to write this blessing, and it will be fulfilled; now go in peace and prosper. The blessing of PRESt. H.C. KIMBALL

The admonition to "Take care of it as my property" does not give a sense of a husband and wife owning and sharing together. Presendia wrote, "When he had said all he wished to me, I said, 'Bro. Kimball, when I make this move to-day I shall have moved twenty-one times by your request, and I shall consider I am of age and wish to remain in the 16th Ward for the future.'" Her wish was apparently granted. When she moved into the new home, she asked Dimick to bless it. He suggested that they dedicate it after she had cleaned it up and prepared it, but Presendia would not wait and dedicated it herself immediately "to the best of [her] ability." Then, "with all the faith" she could command, she dug a garden and planted trees. "These grew and were luxuriant and fruitful, a more prolific garden there is not in the city. I also bought a loom and everything necccssary to carry on weaving and to make carpet and kinds of home manufactured cloth." And as always, she wrote, she did not neglect "waiting on and attending to the sick, for I felt it was my mission in this life."

In the early 1860s Presendia and Patty Sessions frequently exchanged visits and tended the sick together. Once Presendia administered to Patty, who wrote, "Went to sister Buels she anointed my arm and laid hands on me it was very lame." She was also active in her Relief Society, serving as secretary of the Sixteenth Ward Relief Society for fifteen years starting at its organization on June 15, 1868.

Vilate Kimball, whom Presendia loved dearly, became very ill in early 1867, was "out of her mind" for many months, and worsened in October. Presendia nursed her on her deathbed. After her death on October 22, she helped her daughter, Helen Mar (another widow of Smith), prepare the body for burial. Heber followed Vilate before the year passed, dying of a post-traumatic head injury on June 22, 1868. Presendia had lost her third husband, even if her estranged first spouse was still living. Both deaths must have been difficult for her. Though her continual moving under Heber's direction clearly frustrated her, and though the size of his polygamous family would have prevented any daily intimacy with him, he had still been a kind, reliable, if authoritarian husband, church leader, and father of two of her children.

## XV. Grandmother

As Presendia was widowed, one would think that she would have been spared further psychic trauma due to loss of small children. But by a strange chance she was to undergo one more such loss. On a May night in 1870, at 11:30 p.m., there was a knock at her door, and when she answered it no one was there, but a bundle had been left on the front step. She instantly knew that there was a child in the bundle, she reports, and that it was a girl. "She received it as a gift from heaven, and bestowed upon it the most tender care," Wells wrote. Apostle Joseph F. Smith blessed it and gave it the name Josephine. But the infant was "frail and delicate," and despite Presendia's best efforts, its health grew steadily worse. Finally, like so many of her children, it died; once more Presendia's yearning for a daughter had been crushed.

Meanwhile Joseph Smith Kimball had grown into a young man. On October 30, 1870, he married Lathilla Pratt, daughter of Orson and Mary Merrill Pratt. The couple would eventually have thirteen children. Their first, Joseph Raymon, was born on November 4, 1871. So Presendia's last child had left her home, but she rejoiced that he had married a faithful Mormon woman. Joseph attended Morgan's Business College and Deseret University, then became a successful Utah businessman. In 1872 he moved from Salt Lake to Meadowville, Rich County, east of Logan, where he served as bishop until 1890. In 1878 he started a public career as a member of the county's Board of Selectmen. In 1890 he moved to Cache County where he was elected a representative in the second Utah legislature. He was "largely interested and materially aided in the development of the agricultural resources, stockraising and mining in this intermountain country." So Presendia would have felt great pride at Joseph's accomplishments, and he was her only child close enough so that she could enjoy her grandchildren.

Still, she continued to be a mother to her sons who lived among the "gentiles" in Missouri. In 1871 Oliver Buell became afflicted with "cancers in his eyes," evidently the result of an industrial accident in George's factory, so Presendia travelled east to tend him in early 1872—a typical act of motherly and Christian compassion and forgiveness. Mary Ann was expecting at the time and bore a child the night Presendia arrived. Oliver died on April 22. Presendia assisted Mary Ann for a time, visited George, then returned to Utah, bringing two of her grandchildren, Frederick, eleven, and George, nine, to visit. In 1872 Norman Buell died. All her husbands were now gone.

## XVI. "Tall, Grand and Majestic"

She continued to do temple work, as is documented by Endowment House records, in 1869 and 1870. On November 26, 1873, "Presendia Huntington Smith," with Samuel H. B. Smith, stood proxy as six dead women were sealed to Joseph Smith. She and Joseph F. Smith stood proxy on October 26, 1876, to seal her recently deceased son, Oliver Buell, to six dead women, making him a posthumous polygamist. She also continued to perform priestly healings. Elmina A. Shepard wrote in 1879, "By invitation [I] accompanied Sister Horne up to Sister Clara M. Cannon's and there met Sister Percinda Kimball, to wash and annoint Sister Hardy who lies very low with consumption. It was the first time I ever saw the ordinance administered and I felt blessed in being thus priviliged. The spirit of the Lord was there."

There was also a public Presendia. She was known as a public speaker and often accompanied Zina to Relief Society, Primary, and Mutual meetings. When the *Woman's Exponent* began to document important Relief Society meetings in 1872, Presendia's talks were frequently noted. On November 16, 1878, she gave an impressive prayer at the pro-polygamy mass meeting of women in Utah. She prayed that God would bless the president of the United States and the Utah delegate to Congress, and that God:

> would pour out His Holy Spirit upon him [the delegate], that He would uphold the principle of celestial marriage which He had revealed in these last days for the good of the human family, notwithstanding the persecutions of those who sought to overthrow it; that He would strengthen Zion and bless the young and rising generations, and bring peace unto the valleys of the mountains. She dedicated this congregation to the Lord, prayed that angels might guard them in this hour of trial.

In the 1880s Presendia appears frequently in her brother Oliver's journal as they traded visits in Springville and Salt Lake. For example, in 1881 Presendia and Zina's daughter, Zina Presendia Williams, spent Christmas with Oliver in Springville. One suspects that Presendia, who was not able to raise a daughter herself, had a very close relationship with Zina's daughter. On March 28, 1882, Presendia and Zina Diantha visited Oliver in Springville to celebrate their long-departed father's birthday. In early April she and Zina left on an expedition to St. George to do temple work. She visited Springville on November 8, where she presided over the washing and anointing of a Bishop Bringhurst, an interesting but not unique case of a woman administering to a man. Presendia's reputation for healing is shown by an entry in Emmeline Wells's 1881 journal for January 16: "I went down to Presendia Kimball's and brought her to administer to Lucile for her face to be healed. Lucile has implicit faith in the ordinance she came washed and anointed it in the name of Jesus it will be healed I am sure."

Wells gave a good description of Presendia in 1883: "Sister Presendia is a woman to see once is to remember always. She reminds one of the dames of the olden times, large, tall, grand and majestic in figure, dignified in manner, yet withal, so womanly and sympathetic that she seems the embodiment of the motherly element to a degree that would embrace all who come under her influence. Truly she may, in every sense of the word, be termed a mother in Israel in very deed."

We can document Presendia's frequent attendance at family gatherings. At Christmas 1883 she and Zina attended a family reunion in Springville. On September 7, 1884, the *Deseret News* noted a birthday party at her house. Presendia, Zina, Oliver, and Zina Williams also gathered in Logan to do temple work that October. And just as Presendia had heard the singing of angels in the Kirtland temple some fifty years earlier, so she heard them now in the Logan temple: "While working in the Logan Temple ... Prescenda Kimball, and four others heard the singing of angels in that beautiful edifice." On November 14 Oliver Huntington wrote in his journal, "Then I stood Proxy for the Prophet Joseph Smith in havin[g] sealed or adopted to him a child of my Sister Presenda, had while living with Norman Buell." Presendia continued to be concerned about the salvation of her dead children. In early summer 1886 she and Oliver again traveled to Logan to do temple work. Earlier in the spring she had traveled with Helen Mary Whitney to Tooele to speak at Relief Society meetings and, while there, had anointed and blessed Helen Mar to recover her health.

On January 3, 1887, Presendia, now seventy-six, was very sick, and Oliver Huntington visited her, but by early February she was on the

mend under Zina's ministrations. On June 8 the latter wrote to Mary Elizabeth Rollins Lightner, a widow of Joseph Smith, "Sister Presendia is much
improved in health can walk around and by being carried can meet with
the societies and all be blest together." Two weeks later Zina wrote Mary,
"Sister Presendia is getting quite Smart again is around but cannot work
hard." In the summer Presendia was well enough to travel to the Logan
temple once again with Oliver. On September 7 some forty sisters gathered to celebrate her seventy-seventh birthday.

She and Oliver attended the Manti temple dedication on May 21,
1888, and in early December of that year he visited her in Salt Lake City.
In 1890 Zina's journal is unusually full, and, predictably, Presendia is a major character in it. On January 5 Zina wrote, "Zina [Card] & I helped Pheba
quilt & Chariton took Susa & I to see Sister Presendia." She continued to
attend the sick and exercise her charismatic gifts of healing. Later in January Zina wrote, "Presendia & I went to Sister [Hardy's] 3 of her Daughters
ware washed & anointed for their confinement."

The blessing meetings which Presendia and Zina had attended some
forty years earlier in Winter Quarters when they were young women also
continued. On January 31, 1890, Zina described one such meeting:

> At 2 PM I went to Phebes the first there, Sister Presendia came 30 in all
> Pheba & Maria made a lovely supper, in the evening we had a blessed
> meeting Sister   [blank] presided prayer singing & testimonies & the gifts
> Sister S.M. Kimball & Maria ware blest & asking the Lord to comfort &
> preserve them on their mission to Washington ... ware made Hapy by the
> spiret of the Lord thanks to God & the children  Sister Dr Barney blest all
> in the room in the gift of tongs  I trust we all may be faithful  I truly feel
> renewed & comforted.

Presendia and Zina had a long sisterly conversation on February 14,
when Presendia was seventy-nine and Zina sixty-nine: "In the evening I
went to Zebulons, & stayed with Presendia all night  talken [talking] of
the spiret of the times & things of God."

In a letter tentatively dated March 1890 Presendia herself wrote to
Mary Rollins Lightner Smith:

> Dear Sister Mary: I have felt for several days past I must write to you ...
> You & my Self are nearing the other "Country" wont it be a happy time
> for us if we can gain the place where Joseph & our loved ones mingle  it
> is a long time since I Saw you or even heard from you ... We have had
> such times here this winter as I never want to see or hear again & we are
> in the hands of "the liberals"  my health has been poor this winter the La-
> grippe [influenza] has been very previlant  I took the first of Jan  I was
> sick last week with a bad cold & cough  I feel better to day   I saw Sister
> Zina yesterday  She is very thin ... & feble ... it makes me feel bad to look

on her little body ...I cant spare her yet. I am alone  Joseph is in Bear Lake County he has Eleven Children only  I am thankful for one honest Child he is a man of God ... if we can sel this place I intend going to Logan & work in the Temple as long as I can work  that work suites me the best  Fanny [Dimick's widow] is yet living poor old soul beloved Sister  may the  blessings of god be with you hence for [time] & for ever from your sister & friend Presendia L. Kimball

## XVII. Nearing the Other Country

Presendia was often sick, even in her younger days, and her illnesses became more serious as she grew older, accidents more debilitating. On May 15, 1890, Emmeline Wells wrote that "Aunt Prisendia" and Bathsheba Smith had been thrown out of a carriage and seriously hurt. In early June Zina wrote, "Went to see Sister she is improving." Then Zina provided an update on Joseph Kimball: he was making improvements on Presendia's house, owned three hundred acres of land and three hundred head of cattle, was bishop, and had thirteen children. "God truly blesses Him to live  he is noble & honest."

On October 2 Presendia suffered another accident, hurting her left hip "by falling of[f] a platform going to her cook room." At Christmas time she and Zina were together and Presendia was still confined to her house. Zina wrote: "A lonely Christmas  I had 4 invitations with wm [William's] Children but could onely stop with the afflicted  In the evening Br [blank] came in  administered to Presendia & blest us both  the spiret hung abundantly given  that comforted our hearts & filled us with grattitude." Presendia, when she healed sufficiently to move around, could only walk on crutches. Her health apparently worsened in 1891. Then, Wells wrote in January 1892, "She had taken a severe cold, and was ailing for a few days before her condition was thought to be serious. Her sister, Zina Young, finding her quite ill, stayed with her constantly during the last two weeks." Wells's diary notes that the illness (erysipelas) began on January 20, and by the 27th there was no hope of her recovery.

On February 1 Presendia died in her Salt Lake City home at the age of eighty-one, attended by Zina and Joseph Kimball. Zina, Wells writes, was "overcome with grief." George, in St. Joseph, Missouri, had been telegraphed but was unable to reach Salt Lake before she died. He did attend the funeral on the 3rd, at which George Q. Cannon and Joseph F. Smith spoke.

In March Zina wrote to her brother in the east:

I walk on as Sister has waked [walked] on crutches over one year, poor patient soul, as you Sayed honest & true has gone to receive her reward, Joseph & wife ware there with her they have 11 living Children  his

Josephs wife is fair plump & active a nice woman they have a fine healthy family

Poor George I pittied him so much, poor health, business not as prosperous as it might be & disappointed in not seeing his mother alive, to once more say my dear Mother & to hear the welcome   my first born son the pride and joy of her hart for 16 years old Sheleftwhen O the care anxiety & prayers words could not express of an absent mothers longing soul for her first born but thus is this life  Father knows best & he cares for His children & the beyond can onely determin the results, though here we sometimes have a glimps.

We see here how painful the parting from George must have been when Presendia left Norman Buell to go west.

Oliver Huntington wrote of her, "She was a woman of a high and noble mind, independent and ambitious spirit, endowed with a strong mind and considerable acquisitiveness. She would prosper demand respect and esteem." She herself wrote, in her brief autobiographical sketch, "Never in my life, in this kingdom, which is 44 years, have I doubted the truth of this great work, revealed in these, the last days. I have buried seven of my children, all in their infancy, but 2 living. I hope to honor My God, my religion & myself, & be prepared to meet the many loved ones behind the vail." Stalwart Mormon, a visionary woman, priestly in her compassionate healing powers and temple service, she endured a tragic, difficult life. One imagines her joy as she reunited with seven children and her husbands "behind the vail."

## XVIII. Conclusion

Presendia's life provides a good example of the polarities involved in polygamous marriage—more than monogamy on a religious level and less than it on a practical level. Her marriage to Joseph Smith obviously had great religious meaning to her, yet she never lived with him as man and wife, and in fact he probably instructed her to continue living with her first husband after their marriage, as was the case with all of Smith's polyandrous wives. Her marriage to Kimball also had great spiritual meaning to her, for it took place in a temple. She left Norman Buell to follow Kimball west, and she bore two children to him "within the covenant." But on a practical level, her marriage to Heber was not characterized by the intimacy of daily interchange that is customary in monogamy. She was not a favorite wife—Vilate reigned supreme here. And unlike Vilate, she had to move constantly, twenty-two times, which was emotionally draining to her. When Heber settled her in Provo, only Vilate's entreaties convinced him to allow Presendia to return to Salt Lake, an example of how ties between sister-wives in polygamy were sometimes stronger that male-female bonds. Often Presendia turned to siblings and neighbors, rather than to her husband, for help in her home. So her life exemplifies the tragic ambiguity of Mormon polygamy, which in her case was compounded by the repeated blows of losing eight of her nine children to death or apostasy.

# 6.

# Levirate Marriage

## *Agnes Moulton Coolbrith (Smith Smith Smith Pickett)*

On the evening of June 27, 1844, Agnes Coolbrith Smith, widely known as the widow of Don Carlos Smith (youngest brother of Joseph Smith, Jr.), tucked her two daughters into bed. Then she retired to her own bedroom, which she shared with Lucy Walker, who had lived in the Joseph Smith household for years before moving in with Agnes. A dark cloud of foreboding hung over Nauvoo that night, for the prophet was in prison in Carthage, and to the anti-Mormons he was the paramount target. Mobs, allied with the state military guarding Smith, were often reluctant to wait for due process of law.

According to Lucy's reminiscences, as she and Agnes were falling asleep, they heard a knock at their door. "News," cried Lucy and ran downstairs. A neighbor stood outside on the porch. "Joseph and Hyrum have been murdered," he said quietly, his voice grim. Lucy stood "paralized with teror," and Agnes called from above, "What is the news?" Lucy was literally unable to speak, so Agnes hurried downstairs, and then Lucy found her voice and repeated the horrific tidings. She later wrote, "At length we returned to our chamber and on our bended Knees poured out the Anguish of our Souls to that god who holds the destinies of his children in his own hands."

As the news of the dead prophet and his patriarch brother swept over Nauvoo, even nature seemed to join in the mourning: "The Dogs howled and barked, the cattle bellowed and all Creation was astir. We knelt by the open window with our arms around each other, untill the dawn." This moving scene is made all the more poignant when one realizes that both women had suddenly been widowed; both had been married to Joseph Smith as plural wives within the previous three years.

Agnes Coolbrith was extraordinary for many reasons. Joseph married her as the widow of his brother, so this was a strict Levirate marriage—a typical Mormon restoration of a practice from ancient Israel. Agnes is also significant because she, like Emma Smith, was one of Joseph's widows

145

who chose not to journey west with the main group of Latter-day Saints. She stayed in Nauvoo, married a somewhat lukewarm Mormon, and to a great extent left her Mormon past behind. She subsequently travelled with her gold-seeking husband to California, where she lived in San Francisco and in the tiny town of Los Angeles. Agnes must have been intelligent and sensitive, for her daughter, Ina, became one of California's distinguished nineteenth-century poets. Agnes was also heroic as she protected her children under the most varied circumstances in both halves of her life, Mormon and "gentile."

Though Agnes penned few documents herself, Ina wrote hundreds of letters and gave interviews in her later life, many of which shed light on Agnes. Because of Ina's prominence, a superb, well-researched biography has been written about her—*Ina Coolbrith, Librarian and Laureate of California* by Josephine DeWitt Rhodehamel and Raymund Francis Wood—which also treats Agnes in some depth. Therefore, she is fairly well documented despite having written little with her own pen.

## I. Childhood

Agnes Moulton Coolbrith was born to Joseph Coolbrith and Mary Hasty Foss in Scarborough, Cumberland, Maine, just south of Portland in the southwest portion of the state, on July 9, 1808. She was the third of eight children, all of whom were born in Scarborough. Her two older sisters, Charlotte and Catherine, were born in 1803 and 1806, while her younger siblings, Benjamin, Robert, Mary F., Joseph Jr., and Elmira were born in 1810, 1812, 1815, 1822, and 1824. These genealogical details are all that is known of the young Agnes—she was an older child in a large family.

## II. "Baptized Three Young Ladies"

In early 1832, when she was twenty-three, Agnes moved to Boston, where she stayed at the boarding house of Mrs. Augusta Cobb, later a plural wife of Brigham Young. With her friend Mary Bailey, she began attending the Old South Church, where they sang in the choir. At some point Augusta Cobb obtained a Book of Mormon and became convinced of its truth, and Agnes and Mary also came to believe in it.

These women may actually have sent to Kirtland asking for missionaries to visit. On June 22 Orson Hyde and Samuel Smith arrived at Augusta Cobb's, and Mary was baptized on June 26. Three days later "Augutusta Cobb," as Samuel spelled it, was also baptized. However, it was not until July 30 that Agnes joined the Latter-day Saint church. Hyde wrote in his journal, "Baptized three young ladies; had a good time; the Lord was with us; returned and confirmed two of them. Had prayer meeting in the evening No. 4 Norfolk Place; confirmed two others, had a very good time. Names of the three that were baptized: Clarissa Bachelor, Lucy Granger, and Agnes." Samuel also reported the triple baptism: "baptized 3 to day their names Lucy Granger Clarrissa Bachelor & Agnis." Interestingly, in both diary entries Agnes's surname is not written. She was probably so well known to the missionaries that no last name was needed.

In October the two elders traveled up the coast to southern Maine. On the 2nd Orson received a cool reception from Agnes's family in Scarborough: "Called on Mr. Coolbrith, whose daughter I baptized in Boston, but they were not very free to converse."

Some time before November 6 Joseph Smith and Newel K. Whitney visited Boston and probably met with this remarkable group of Mormon women: Agnes; Mary; Ruth Vose, who would later become one of Joseph's plural wives; Vienna Jacques, who possibly became a wife of Smith; Augusta Adams Cobb, a posthumous plural wife of Smith; and Fanny Brewer, who converted to Mormonism, then turned against the church in Kirtland.

Samuel and Orson returned to Boston on December 4, where, Samuel wrote, they "found the Sisters glad to see us." If there were male converts in Boston, they are not mentioned. Joseph had left instructions for Samuel and Orson to return to Kirtland immediately, but, Orson wrote, "As many were desirous to see us and we desired to regulate the sisters, we concluded to tarry a couple of days." After the sisters were properly regulated—including, perhaps, a romance between Samuel and Mary that may have already been simmering—the two missionaries departed on the 10th.

### III. Don Carlos

In nineteenth-century Mormonism, conversion included geographical relocation, the imperative to build up Zion in preparation for the imminent Second Coming and Millennium. Kirtland—where a temple was being built—was the main gathering place at the time, so in the summer of 1833 Agnes and Mary left Boston and traveled to Ohio, where they boarded with the Smith family and worked by making and mending clothes for temple laborers. In September Joseph Smith mentioned the two boarders in a letter to a fellow Bostonian, Vienna Jacques, in Missouri: "Agnes & Mary Livs with father Smith."

On August 13, 1834, Mary married Samuel Smith. At the same time romance was blooming between Agnes, now twenty-seven, and Samuel's brother, Don Carlos Smith, who was only nineteen but stood six-foot-four and was reportedly quite handsome. A year later, on July 30, 1835, Agnes and Don exchanged vows, with Seymour Brunson, an elder, officiating. Baptized a Mormon in 1830, Don Carlos would practice the trade of printing and journalism within the church throughout the rest of his life. Agnes's Mormon years must be outlined chiefly by following his career.

When Don and Samuel preached at Kirtland on January 10, 1836, Joseph Smith wrote, "They did well concidering their youth, and bid fair to make useful men in the vinyard of the Lord." On the 15th Don was called to be a high priest and president of the high priest quorum, and a week later he was anointed and ordained to the office. Not long after Joseph wrote, with brotherly pride, "The Lord had assisted my bro. Carloss the Pres. of the High Priests to go forward with the anointing of the High priests so that he had performed it to the acceptance of the Lord, notwithstanding he was verry young & inexperienced in such duties."

At some point before June 15, when Agnes was eight months pregnant, Don set out on a mission to Pennsylvania and New York. On the 25th he wrote a letter to Agnes that has been published in a grammaticized version:

> I was rejoiced to hear that you were as well as you expressed, but grieved that your rest should be disturbed by the nervous affection of which you speak ... Let your faith fail not, and your prayers cease not, and you shall be healed of your nervous complaint, and all other afflictions. For God is willing ... to raise you up ...

The "nervous complaint" may be a Victorian reference to Agnes's pregnancy, which evidently was difficult. The letter ends, "I must close by saying that I expect to labor in the vineyard until I start for home. And if the Lord will, I shall see you as soon as the last of July. Yours till death, Don C. Smith." On August 7, when Agnes was twenty-eight, her first child, Agnes Charlotte, was born in Kirtland. If Don returned home at the expected time, he was present at the birth.

In 1837 he helped edit the *Elders Journal* in Kirtland. Then in December he and Agnes relocated in New Portage, Ohio, south of Kirtland, as the city was becoming inhospitable to Mormons, especially any named Smith. Creditors hounded Joseph in the wake of the Kirtland banking failure, and internal "dissenters" were loudly opposing him. At the time of the move Agnes was some six months pregnant.

When spring arrived next year Don left on a mission to Virginia, Pennsylvania, and Ohio to raise money for the Smith families' move to Missouri. By mid-April Agnes and her family were staying with friends in Norton, just west of Akron, and her second child, Sophronia, was born there on April 22.

### IV. "Her Soft and Tender Voice I Hear"

Agnes and Don Carlos, with their two children, left Norton for Missouri on May 7 in a seven-wagon company including Joseph Smith,

Sr., Lucy Mack Smith, and a number of other relatives and friends. When he was nine miles from Terre Haute, Indiana, Don described the difficult, underfinanced journey in a letter to Joseph: "Now we have only $25 dollars to carry 25 souls & 13 horses, 500 miles, we have lived very close and camped out knight, notwithstanding the rain & cold, & my baby only 2 weeks old when we started." Traveling conditions were unexpectedly harsh: "We have had unaccountable bad roads, had our horses down in the mud, and broke of[f] one wagon tongue and thills, and broke down the carriage twice and yet we are all alive and camped on a dry place for allmost the first time." There is a rare direct reference to Agnes: "Agness is very feeble Father & Mother are not well but verry much fatigued, Mother has a severe cold, and it is nothing in fact but the prayer of faith and the power of God, that will sustain them and bring them through, our courage is good and I think we shall be brought through."

The Smith company reached the end of their difficult journey, Far West, in July and soon settled in Millport, a village three miles west of the Grand River. Unfortunately, Mormons often left a deteriorating situation in Kirtland only to find Missouri even more hostile and chaotic. In late summer increasingly militant Mormons skirmished violently with murderous Missourians. Mary Bailey Smith's house was burned by a mob on August 4, three days after she had borne a baby. In the midst of this turmoil, and because of it, Don and his cousin George A. Smith (with two others) were called on missions out of state in October to raise money to help the Saints leave Missouri. In early October they sailed to St. Louis on the steamboat *Kansas*.

On October 18th, at 10:30 p.m., a mob approached Agnes's house after sunset, turned her out, looted it, then burned it to the ground. Gathering two-year-old Agnes and six-month-old Sophronia in her arms, she fled in terror through three-inch deep snow. After running three miles, she waded waist deep through the icy Grand River, then found safety on the other side at the home of Lyman Wight. Many other Mormons had their homes burned that night and were forced to traverse the Grand.

Soon after this, on the 23rd, Don wrote Agnes an affecting letter from Benton County, Tennessee: "Respected Companion I sit down this morning for the first time to let you know where I am & how I came here &c I am in tolerable health & should be exceeding glad to know how it is with you." He described his travels, then added, "I want you to be careful of your health & be sure and make known your wants to the Bishop see that the cow has a sufficient to eat &c to charge you to be careful of the children is useless knowing you never neglected them tell uncle John that

George is well." He ended with a poem that, despite its technical flaws, expressed his deep love for Agnes:

I turn I gaze beyond the stream
From whence I came propelled by steam
There I behold by my fireside
The choice of youth Agnes my bride

Her soft and tender voice I hear
Which sounds delightful to my ear
With her I find that pearl of price
By some abused by some despised

Hark! I hear the prattlings of [children] more precious than fine
    gold
A gift of God to us we now behold
Their tender minds may they imbibe
The precious jewel by me described

This is the pearl the richest prize
Bestowed on me whilst here in life ...

In mid-December Don and George A. made a dangerous journey home. A few days before Christmas, threatened by Missourians who had heard of Don's presence, they traveled a hundred miles in two days through bitter winter weather, nearly freezing at night. At 2 a.m. on Christmas Eve they found a friend they could stay with. George, sick, stayed with the friend through Christmas Day, but Don trudged on and was soon reunited with Agnes and the children who were living with the Smith matriarch, Lucy Mack Smith.

Don immediately turned to the problem of leaving Missouri. The extended Smith family faced grim circumstances—Joseph and Hyrum were in jail, Samuel had been forced out of the state, and only William and Don Carlos remained in Missouri. Delayed by the fact that they had only one team—which was used first by William, Sidney Rigdon, and Emma—Agnes and Don, in a company with the elder Smiths, finally left Missouri in late February 1839. It was another difficult journey. Agnes and the children rode in a light carriage, but the horses were so weary that often the humans had to walk. It rained continuously. When there were houses on the road, the Mormon band would ask for shelter, but the Missourians usually turned them away. Finally, after five days of rain and exposure, they came to an isolated house and Don Carlos begged shelter for his aged parents. The gentleman at the door, as Lucy tells the story, said, "Why, what do you mean, sir! Do you not consider us human beings! Do you think that we would turn anything that is flesh and blood from our door, in such a time as this! Drive up to the house and help your wife and children out: I'll attend to your father and mother and the rest of them." He then helped the family enter his home and hung up their cloaks and shawls to dry.

The next day, after this welcome night of shelter, the family continued on through mud and rain to reach the Mississippi at night, when the rain was turning to snow. They found the river impossible to cross; so, with many other Mormons, they camped in six inches of snow and awoke to find their bedding frozen. Eventually Samuel arrived and ferried them over to Quincy.

### V. "Lonely Widow of the Noble Fallen Chieftain"

In Illinois Agnes and Don at first settled near Macomb, McDonough County, forty miles east of Nauvoo. On April 11 Agnes wrote to her brothers-in-law in prison, one of the few extant documents written by her:

> Beloved Brothers, Hyrum and Joseph: By the permit of my companion, I write a line to show that I have not forgotten you; neither do I forget you; for my prayer is to my Heavenly Father for your deliverance. It seems as though the Lord is slow to hear the prayers of the Saints. But the Lord's ways are not like our ways; therefore He can do better than we ourselves. You must be comforted, Brothers Hyrum and Joseph, and look forward for better days. Your little ones are as playful as little lambs; be comforted concerning them, for they are not cast down and sorrowful as we are; their sorrows are only momentary but ours continual. May the Lord bless, protect, and deliver you from all your enemies and restore you to the bosom of your families, is the prayer of
>
> AGNES M. SMITH

In June Don Carlos and Ebenezer Robinson were given a printing press salvaged from Missouri and were asked to publish a paper. So Don had to spend time in Nauvoo. According to Lucy Mack Smith, the only place the paper could be stored was in a cellar that had a spring running through it, and the dampness caused Don to have a "severe cold" for "some time." On July 25 Don wrote to Agnes in Macomb: "Beloved, I am in tolerable health, and have just risen from imploring the Throne of Grace, in behalf of you and our children, that God would preserve you all in health, and give you every needed blessing, and protect you by day and by night." He described the ubiquitous sickness in Nauvoo: "There are not well ones enough to take care of the sick," a repeated complaint in Nauvoo reminiscences. He continued:

I send you some money that you may not be destitute, in case you should be sick ... Agnes, the Lord being my helper, you shall not want, Elijah's God will bless you, and I will bless you, for you are entwined around my heart with ties that are stronger than death, and time cannot sever them. Deprived of your society, and that of my prattling babes, life would be irksome. Oh! that we may all live, and enjoy health and prosperity, until the coming of the Son of Man, that we may be a comfort to each other, and instill into the tender and noble minds of our children, principles of truth and virtue, which shall abide with them for ever, is my constant prayer. From your husband, who will ever remain, devoted and affectionate, both in time and in eternity. Don C. Smith

Later in the summer Agnes and the children moved to Nauvoo and were situated above the print shop. In November Don edited the first number of the *Times and Seasons,* serving as pressman, while Robinson kept the journal's accounts. From 1839 to 1841 Don received other positions and honors in Nauvoo. He was elected to the city council, was a brigadier general of the Nauvoo Legion, and continued as president of the high priest quorum. On April 6, 1841, he laid the northwest cornerstone of the Nauvoo temple. Earlier that year, on January 25, Agnes was probably present at the death of her oldest and closest friend, Mary Bailey Smith, who died in childbirth. She would have deeply mourned her passing.

In the fall of 1840 Joseph Smith taught Joseph Noble privately about plural marriage, and in 1841 he married his first Nauvoo plural wife, Louisa Beaman, with Noble officiating. Don was in Joseph's inner circle, but according to some sources he adamantly opposed polygamy. Robinson remembered him saying, "Any man who will teach and practice the doctrine of spiritual wifery will go to hell; I don't care if it is my brother Joseph." Robinson also wrote that Don Carlos "was one of the most perfect men I ever knew"; nevertheless, "He was a bitter opposer of the 'spiritual wife' doctrine which was being talked quite freely, in private circles, in his lifetime."

This tradition is supported by Ina Coolbrith, whose source must have been her mother. According to Ina, because Don opposed Joseph's polygamy, he planned to leave Illinois in protest. "He quietly made plans to go back to Kirtland in 1842, and was only prevented by his death." His stance caused serious tension in the Smith family: "One day he and Joseph and Hyrum, all three came in together and father [Don Carlos] was desperately excited. They were talking of polygamy." Other historical sources, however, offer a contrasting tradition. Joseph F. Smith, in a 1918 letter to Ina (his first cousin), vehemently denied her statements about her father. It is not impossible that Don Carlos, like his brother Hyrum, opposed polygamy at first, then was converted to it, but there is no certain solution to this conflict in evidence. In any event, Agnes, now thirty-two, named her third child Josephine Donna Smith when she was born on March 10, 1841. Agnes Charlotte was now five and Sophronia nearly three.

During the summer, when Don was working in his damp printing cellar, he began to feel a severe pain in his side which lingered annoyingly. Then, on about July 25, Agnes and the children all became ill with malaria and Don had to care for them night and day. Lucy Mack wrote, "In taking care of them, he caught a violent cold—a fever set in, and the pain in his side increased, and with all our exertions, we were unable to arrest the disease, which I have no doubt was consumption, brought on by working in a damp room."

Don Carlos died on August 7 at the age of twenty-five. On his deathbed, according to Ina Coolbrith (as quoted in Joseph F. Smith's 1918 letter) when Joseph Smith asked him if he had a last request, he replied, "'Yes, I have, Joseph Smith, I want you for the rest of your life to be an honest man.'" Joseph F., who reverenced the memory of both Don and Joseph, labeled this tradition "contemptible in its falsity." It is obviously an anti-Joseph tradition and Ina Coolbrith's most likely source would be Agnes. Yet it is well documented that Agnes married Joseph, so it seems doubtful that she regarded him as dishonest. Furthermore, two of our few extant holographs by Agnes express positive feelings about Joseph. One wonders if she changed her feelings about him later in her life or if in her later, "non-Mormon" life she came to reject polygamy, denying something she had once believed in. Curiously, there is another account of Don Carlos's death which is diametrically opposed to the anti-polygamy tradition—it holds that on his deathbed Don Carlos requested Agnes to marry Joseph as a plural wife.

Don was buried with military honors two days after his death. Eliza Snow referred to "the lonely widow of the noble fallen chieftain. The bereaved companion of his bosom whom he'd loved with faithful tenderness ... He too, had been a loving and indulgent father to her lonely and weeping babe—left fatherless." Agnes was left to raise her three daughters alone, but she had the extended Smith family to help her and provide for her, including her powerful, charismatic brother-in-law, Joseph Smith, whom she had met ten years earlier in Boston.

### VI. "J Smith Was Agness"

On January 6, 1842, Brigham Young wrote a journal entry in Masonic code which, when deciphered, reads, "I was taken in to the lodge  J Smith was Agness." "was" is probably a code word meaning "wedded and sealed to." As we know from other sources that Joseph Smith probably married Agnes before March 24, 1842, and certainly before June, January 6 fits the time frame for a marriage. The Masonic code shows that something significant and esoteric happened involving both Joseph and Agnes on this day, and a plural marriage is the most likely event. Smith's diary emphasizes the importance of the day. His scribe writes, "Truly this is a day long to be remembered by the saints of the Last Days; a day in which the God of heaven has began to restore the ancient <order> of his Kingdom unto his servants & his people: a day in which all things are concurring together to bring about the completion of the fullness of the gospel." The marriage to Agnes is the reasonable explanation for this otherwise enigmatic entry.

Among the other evidence for Agnes marrying Joseph Smith is John C. Bennett's "Mrs. A**** S****," which dates the marriage before June 1842. In addition, a plural wife of William Smith, Mary Ann Sheffield, who lived with Agnes in Nauvoo, gave explicit testimony in the Temple Lot case in 1893 that Agnes had told her she was Joseph Smith's wife. Here we find the tradition that Don Carlos, presumably on his deathbed, asked Agnes to marry Joseph: "Her husband she said wished her to marry Joseph and she did so." In addition, the names of Agnes and Joseph are linked in the Relief Society controversy discussed below. All of this evidence taken together is quite convincing.

Presumably, the marriage to Joseph Smith was a sealing for time, perhaps an early proxy marriage in which Agnes was sealed to Don Carlos for eternity, with Joseph standing proxy for his dead brother, followed by Agnes's sealing to Joseph for time. In any case, Agnes was the first of four widows to marry Smith. Since she was the widow of his brother, this was a strict Old Testament Levirate marriage. Smith was interested in the restoration of all biblical doctrine and practice in this, the "Dispensation of the Fullness of Times," and he therefore may have seen great significance in the modern performance of such an ancient custom.

So Agnes began her new life as one of Joseph Smith's plural wives. Little is known about her marital experiences beyond the fact that she spent time with him and his other wives on occasion. On January 17 Willard Richards wrote in his diary, "Dined at Sister Agness with Joseph & Sister [Lucinda Pendleton] Harris." Agnes was living in Aaron Johnson's house near the printing office in early February, according to Ebenezer Robinson.

## VII. Female Relief Society of Nauvoo

At the second meeting of the Nauvoo Female Relief Society, on March 24, Agnes was voted a member and immediately became involved in a controversy. The society president, Emma Smith, was a determined opponent of her husband's secret extramonogamous unions, and she used the Relief Society to squelch rumors of polygamy. Evidently she had heard a report that Agnes had married Joseph, so at the March 24 meeting she announced that a Clarissa Marvel "was accused of [telling] scandalous falsehoods on the character of Prest. Joseph Smith without the least provocation" and asked if Relief Society members "would in wisdom, adopt some plan to bring her to repentance." Agnes came to her friend's defense: "Clarissa Marvel lived with me nearly a year and I saw nothing amiss of her," she said. Nevertheless, Hannah Markham was assigned to interview Clarissa. Perhaps Emma did not yet believe the rumor, since her husband had only married approximately nine women in Nauvoo by this time, and she might have known about only a few of them. The fact that the rumor was connected with her beloved, bereaved sister-in-law may have given her particular reason to be incensed.

Another statement by Agnes reveals how she was trying to support herself in the months following Don Carlos's death: "Mrs. Agnes Smith solicited the patronage of the Society as a Milliner and Dressmaker." She would sew for a living throughout much of the rest of her life. A week later, on March 30, at the third Relief Society meeting, Joseph Smith commented on the Relief Society's zeal to purge iniquity but said that "sometimes [your] zeal is not according to knowledge." He thus hinted that he was not comfortable with an investigation of the polygamy charges but did not elaborate further.

Hannah Markham, wife of Joseph Smith loyalist Stephen Markham, and a Mrs. Billings interviewed Clarissa and found her innocent of any wrongdoing. So Sarah Cleveland, second counselor to Emma, moved that Elizabeth Durfee and Elizabeth Allred investigate the persons who had accused her—Laura Jones and Hannah Burgess. This action borders on the comic, since both Cleveland and Durfee were probably already plural wives of Smith. Durfee was reluctant, but Emma insisted. Three days later Clarissa signed the following statement: "This is to certify that I never have at any time or place, seen or heard any thing improper or unvirtuous in the conduct or conversation of either President Smith or Mrs. Agnes Smith. I also certify that I never have reported any thing derogatory to the characters of either of them." Apparently, Emma's suspicions faded after this, for the Clarissa Marvel topic did not resurface in the Relief Society minutes.

Another heavy blow soon fell on Agnes when on October 3, 1843, her five-year-old Sophronia died of scarlet fever. Within little more than one year she had lost two close family members. She was left with Agnes, seven, and Josephine (nicknamed "Ina," pronounced "Eye-na"), two. Her association with Joseph would continue for a little while. At some point between December 23, 1843, and February 3, 1844, she received her endowment and joined the Holy Order, one more confirmation that she was part of the elite inner circle of Nauvoo Mormons. On April 23, 1844, Joseph, with his brother William, "called at Carlos widow," his journal notes.

But on June 27 Joseph and Hyrum were killed at Carthage, and we have seen how Agnes received the news. However one feels about Smith's polygamy, it is hard not to be moved by his widows' grief. On July 4 Zina Huntington Jacobs Smith spent the day with "Carlos Smiths Widdow, the girls that resides with her, Louisa Bemon, and Sister Marcum." So three of the prophet's plural wives met to console each other after their husband's death.

## VIII. "I Feel All Alone"

In the months following the martyrdom, Agnes worked in the office of the *Times and Seasons*, according to Ina. She continued to attend Holy Order meetings, and when the Nauvoo temple was completed she was a prominent participant in its ordinances. On December 10 she received her endowment in the temple and in the evening ate dinner with Vilate Kimball, Elizabeth Whitney, Mary Fielding Smith, Mercy Thompson Smith, and Lucy Mack Smith. Three days later she served as one of the female administrators in the initiatory sessions, performing washings and anointings for other women. The next day she met with church leaders in the temple, and a day later she officiated as a temple worker, then slept in the temple at night. She served in the edifice again on December 20, and in early January 1846 helped finish the upholstery of a new altar used for the fullness of priesthood ordinances.

On January 28, when she was thirty-eight, Agnes was sealed for eternity to Don Carlos in the temple, with his cousin and old mission companion, George Albert Smith, standing proxy; then, as was customary, she was sealed to George Albert for time. Brigham Young performed the ceremony. This was another quasi-Levirate marriage, a man marrying his cousin's widow. George Albert Smith had been born on June 16, 1817, in Potsdam, St. Lawrence, New York, the son of John Smith and Clarissa Lyman. He was baptized in 1832, served in Zion's Camp in 1834, and then fulfilled missions in the east. After a short stay in Missouri in 1838, he traveled to Illinois and was ordained an apostle in 1839. He served a mission to England, returned, and in 1841 married Bathsheba Bigler, soon to become one of the prominent nineteenth-century Mormon women. A few years later he became a polygamist, marrying Lucy Messerve Smith in November 1844. The next year he married Nancy Clements, Zilpha Stark, Sarah Ann Libby, and Hannah Libby. He added

Susannah Ogden Bigler to his family in 1846, which made Agnes his eighth wife. On January 30 Agnes was joined by her two living children in a sealing to Don Carlos, with George A. Smith again standing as his proxy.

Soon after this the main body of the Latter-day Saints, including George A., departed for the West, but Agnes stayed in Nauvoo for reasons that are not entirely clear. Ina, possibly reflecting her mother's views, felt that the church and George A. had abandoned her mother. "The church left Nauvoo. There was no provision made for her to accompany it. She was left to shift for self and children ... George A. did come to see her the day before leaving; his goodby being, 'Well Agnes, I suppose if some one comes for you some dark night, you'll be ready.'" Once again Joseph F. Smith heatedly denied that Agnes was abandoned, asserting instead that the influence of her brother-in-law William and mother-in-law Lucy caused her to stay in Nauvoo.

On June 3 Agnes wrote to George, expressing her ambivalence as she watched the Saints leave for the West:

> I have no other one to ask but you my mind is much troubled concerning about comeing to the Camp I want to come and I do not want to come I feel alone all alone if there was a Carlos a Joseph or Hyrum there how quickly would I be there I love the Church of Christ I love to be with my Brethren but alas there is an aching void that seem[s] never can be filld {I ever [want?]} you to write me wether I exspect to com with the trustees I have their promise {but} shall exspect to see you here before next Spring my health is not very good Josephines health is very poor Agnes is well Sister Mary Ann [Sheffield] is with me and will come West with me ... to-morrow we move on the hill to live at Bro Robbins house ... I have Sold the old printing Office for Seventy dollars and will have my pay in August our beautiful Nauvoo has become a miserable place I have had my dead removed into Emma[s] garden Give my love to your Wife ... may the Lord bless you all is my prayer Agnes M Smith

Though she expressed some ambivalence about coming to Winter Quarters, Agnes apparently expected George A. to come back for her in the spring.

We have confirmation that Agnes was still in Nauvoo on June 9, for Thomas Bullock wrote then, "Henrietta at Agnes Smith's all day." But in mid-September Agnes and the two girls (now ten and five) moved to St. Louis, possibly because the Mormons in Nauvoo were threatened by steadily advancing anti-Mormons. She wrote to "Dear Cousin George" on November 4 and said that she had been in St. Louis for six weeks, "and I am perfectly sick of it I wish I was at the camp but I suppose that I am best off here the winter." She apparently had been counseled to stay in St. Louis. She also lacked the financial resources to travel, though she hoped that the money she had been promised for her property in Nauvoo would eventually make this possible. She was also ailing again: "My health is very poor and has been all sumer I was very sick after my arival at this place." A widow's struggle for survival in frontier America could be brutal: "I find it very hard to get along in St Louis a person has to work almost day and night to get along at all." She boarded with a Brother Robbins who had rented a house, and Mary Ann Sheffield was still with her.

## IX. William Pickett

In spring 1847 Agnes married a fourth husband, William Pickett, who had joined the Mormon faith after the Nauvoo exodus. A resident of St. Louis, formerly a lawyer in Mobile, Alabama, he was the foreman of the printing office of the *Missouri Republican* (later the *St. Louis Republican*), which had denounced Missouri governor Lilburn Boggs, known for his Mormon extermination order. Pickett had long been friendly with Mormons, and as a printer he may have been acquainted with Don Carlos before his death. Though intelligent and well-educated, he was also a heavy drinker, a problem he probably struggled with in the years following his baptism.

On December 11, when Agnes was thirty-nine, her last children were born in St. Louis—twin boys. William Pickett wrote to Brigham Young two weeks later, "Among other items, I may as well mention, I last spring married an old acquaintance of yours, and was last week presented by her with *two* sons at one birth! they are fine healthy fellows. Brother Hyde dined with me yesterday, and pronounced a blessing upon them. I have named the eldest Don Carlos and the other for myself." The conclusion of the letter shows Pickett's Mormonness: "Remember me to Bro. [Willard] Richards, Bro. Heber [Kimball], Bro Geo. A. [Smith] and to all of those who may think me worthy to be enquired after. And say to them, as I now assure you, that my faith increases with my knowledge; and that I long to be in the midst of my brethren, where I can become more wise, and more useful. I remain, Dear Bro., sincerely yours, in the bonds of the new and everlasting Covenant, William Pickett   To Pres. Brigham Young." In the spring of 1848 Agnes and her children evidently visited friends in Winter Quarters, for they are listed among the passengers of the steamboat *Mandan* traveling there from St. Louis.

## X. To the West

In 1849 Agnes's life took a dramatic new turn when gold-fever claimed William. He evidently left St. Louis as soon as gold was discovered (ironically by the Mormon Battalion) and traveled to California, leaving Agnes and the four children in St. Louis. She was alone once again; Pickett would often leave her to her own devices. Two years later, in the fall of 1851, he showed up again in St. Louis to ask his wife to come west with him. One would guess that Agnes agreed only reluctantly after her difficult moves from Boston to Kirtland to Missouri to Nauvoo. In addition, she may have desired stability for her children. But she agreed to cross the plains with William to visit Utah, then travel even farther west.

When the Picketts left St. Louis in late 1851, Agnes Charlotte was fourteen, Ina ten, and the twins three. They sailed to St. Joseph by steamboat, then travelled overland to Utah, apparently arriving there by October 11, when a "Brother Pickett" called on Brigham Young, according to the "Journal History." William Pickett tried his hand at law in Utah for a time, and on February 13 of the new year Hosea Stout described a law case, Blair v. Wales, and wrote that "G.A. Smith & W. Picket was on the part of the defence." So Agnes's legal husband practiced law with her "proxy" husband. Stout last mentions Pickett on March 18. According to Joseph F. Smith's 1918 letter, Pickett threatened a United States judge, was pronounced in contempt of court, and left Utah quickly.

Agnes and her children were left alone in Deseret. Ina later charged that Pickett sent money to Agnes and that Brigham Young diverted it into his own pockets. Again Joseph F. Smith heatedly denied this. However, Agnes certainly lived in abject poverty in Utah. Agnes Charlotte later told friends in California that they would never return to Utah "until they had some means of supporting themselves after they got there ... they had been there once in a destitute condition and knew how bad it was." If the widow of two members of the Smith family had difficulty making ends meet in pioneer Utah, it shows how grim the struggle for survival must have been for other single women in the West.

### XI. "There, Little Girl ... There Is California"

In approximately April 1852 Agnes and her children, after this unfortunate stay in Utah, left for California. At some point they were apparently joined by William. After a dry, difficult crossing of the Nevada desert, the Picketts, with their company of seventeen covered wagons, forded the Truckee River. Tired oxen had to swim across, and little Ina wept as some of them drowned. The company camped on the river as they prepared to cross the Sierra Nevadas. According to Ina, near their camp they found a ragged, feverish man, almost dead, lying in a crude shelter. The women of the company brought him water, tended him, and his fever subsided. When he regained his health, he told them of a new pass across the mountains that he had discovered, a much easier route than those previously used. This man was the renowned explorer Jim Beckwourth, and the new trail became known as the Beckwourth Pass. He took a liking to Agnes's children and gave them candy at the evening campfires.

In late August Beckwourth led the company over the Sierra Nevadas through the Beckwourth Pass, thirty miles northwest of present-day Reno. At the beginning of the pass, he asked Agnes if Ina would like to ride with him, to become the first child to traverse this trail. Agnes agreed. "Ina's heart pounded ... for happiness ... At the pass Beckwourth dismounted and helped the girl off the horse ... Storm clouds were gathering ... The sun lighted it ... for this moment. Jim pointed to the glowing valley ... 'There, little girl, ... there is California! There is your kingdom!'"

In September the Picketts arrived at Spanish Ranch, a miner's pack station in Plumas County, forty miles northeast of Oroville. They stayed there a few weeks while Pickett mined, though with no luck. They continued to Marysville, in Yuba County, forty miles north of Sacramento. As they had sold their teams, all had to walk except the little boys who rode on pack animals. Ina remembered her feet becoming bloodied as she walked, "though Mother tried to prevent this by bandaging them." At Marysville the Picketts rented a cabin and William left for the Grass Valley mines.

The rainy, snowy winter of 1852 was nightmarish for Agnes and her children. Marysville became flooded and William was snowed in at Grass Valley until spring. Ina wrote, "Our small cabin fortunately stood on the highest point of ground, but three days and nights a boat was tied to our door to take us away if the water rose any higher." Agnes's misery and insecurity were increased when she received no word from William during the dangerous weather. She and the two girls were ill with chills and fever, and the family barely had enough food. Agnes sewed for women in town "better left unnamed" as she tried to survive the winter. Her only friend was a "voluntary helper," an ex-slave from Virginia named Old Thompson who helped with household tasks. She had given him shelter when the flood carried away the tent he lived in. Once when Ina was walking to town for groceries, the bank of earth on which she was walking caved in, and she fell into the flood-swollen ditch. Fortunately "Old Thompson" was nearby and was able to rescue her.

In May 1853 the floods abated and William was able to return to his family. He took them to live near his claim in the Gibsonville district, thirty miles northeast of Oroville. One day Ina and the two boys wandered into the forest and became hopelessly lost and Agnes and William called on all the local prospecting hands to help find them. When night came, the children still had not been found, so the miners continued to scour the countryside after dark. Ina was terrified of snakes but was able to lull her sobbing brothers to sleep, then slept herself. The three children were found at dawn the next day. Ina's first drowsy words were, "We didn't see any snakes at all. But is Mother all right?"

In the winter the Picketts returned to Marysville where William worked as a printer. Again the town was flooded and on New Year's Day 1854, the inhabitants of Marysville traveled to parties in boats. However, at some point after August the family moved to San Francisco, where William became foreman of the *Bulletin* printing office. He built a house for Agnes and the family near the mission and opened a law office.

Occasionally visitors from Utah passed through San Francisco or Southern California and paid their respects to Don Carlos's widow. In 1855 the colorful Mormon enforcer Orrin Porter Rockwell was in California and visited Agnes, who, as the story goes, was recovering from a bout of typhoid fever which had caused her to lose all her hair. Rockwell, on the other hand, had long hair because Joseph Smith promised him that if he kept it long his enemies would have no power over him and he would not be overcome by evil. "When he met Sister Smith he had no gold dust or money to give her, so he had his hair cut to make her a wig and from that time he said that he could not control the desire for strong drink, nor the habit of swearing." This story has the ring of folklore, but sometimes truth outdoes fiction. Another visitor to the Pickett home was Hyrum Smith's son, fifteen-year-old Joseph F. Smith, who had been called to be a missionary in Hawaii. In his 1918 letter he recalled that when he visited, Pickett was drinking heavily and verbally abused Mormon leaders.

## XII. "This Is an Awful—Awful Town, Joseph"

In 1855 William decided to try his hand at a law practice in Los Angeles, so the Picketts moved south, perhaps in the spring. Agnes was now forty-six, Agnes Charlotte eighteen, Ina fourteen and the twins seven. William returned to San Francisco soon after this for unknown reasons. Los Angeles at the time was a small, Spanish-flavored town—in the 1860 census it had a population of only 4,835! Ina remembered the scent of orange blossoms in Los Angeles and the neat rows of low adobe houses. The Picketts apparently had a relatively stable life there for a number of years. The children were enrolled in school, an experience that they had not enjoyed since St. Louis. Like the young Eliza R. Snow, Ina rhymed her lessons, and when her teacher asked why, she answered, "Please, it's the easiest way." Agnes Charlotte and Ina were turning into beauties. On one occasion Ina helped Don Pio Pico, the governor of California, open a grand ball. In the summer of 1856, when she was fifteen, her first published poem appeared in the Los Angeles *Star*.

Yet the Pickett home life was not entirely peaceful, as William continued to drink. His last vestiges of Mormonness perhaps left him after his stay in Utah. Ina later wrote about his alcoholism, "Because my stepfather, a man of splendid physique, brain and education, was a victim of intemperance, I was condemned to abject poverty and social isolation, and compelled when a young girl to take his place in the chief maintenance of the family." Other sources do not seem to support this memory of "social isolation," but otherwise Ina's description makes the Picketts sound like a typical alcoholic's family, in which the family members try to make up for and hide the father's failure. His frequent moves possibly fit into this picture, as his drinking may have prevented him from holding down any job.

On March 19, 1857, sixteen-year-old Ina wrote a charming, breezy letter to Joseph F. in Hawaii. Southern California was lawless and violent, according to Ina: "This is an awful - awful town, Joseph, to live in, an awful town. I dont believe there is another place in the world, so small as this town is, that has more crimes committed in it every day, than this does." She was not exaggerating, for murders occurred in Los Angeles on nearly a daily basis. One of her friends had recently been killed by a band of desperadoes. She mentioned that she and her mother had written her friends in Salt Lake City many times but had received no answering letters. William was "still" in San Francisco, and so, Ina wrote, her mother was sewing constantly to make ends meet. "She is sick nearly all the time. She is sewing herself to death I fear." Once again we have a bleak picture of Agnes alone, struggling to provide for her family.

There was a colony of Mormons in nearby San Bernardino, and Agnes and her children occasionally visited old friends there. In mid-April Carolyn Barnes Crosby recorded a ten-day visit of Agnes Charlotte and Josephine. On the day of arrival, she wrote, "We enjoyed the evening very agreeably, had music both instrumental and vocal. Josephine [Ina] played the guitar, William [Crosby] the violin, and Ellen [Pratt McGary] the accordion." The next month Agnes Charlotte and Ina returned with the ten-year-old Don Carlos. Carolyn wrote, "I invited the girls to come home with me and have supper. They all came and we had quite lively times ... Afterward she [Ann Louisa Pratt] and Josephine washed the dishes." A week later the elder Agnes with the other twin, William, joined them in San Bernardino. Carolyn wrote, "I immediately ran over to see her, as she stopped at Bro. Pratt's ... Sis. P [Pickett] looked quite well, and seemed in good spirits." In early June Agnes and Carolyn visited some of the wives of Apostle Amasa Lyman.

On July 22 Ina wrote again to Joseph F.: "I am now known throughout California as 'the Los Angeles poetess, Ina Smith (niece of the Prophet).'" Her Mormon background was not yet a secret. Agnes was still ailing: "Mother is has very poor health indeed, and is growing old fast. She sends her love to you." Joseph continually urged Ina to return to Utah, but she wrote that she would never do so as long as she had "one particle" of common sense left. She critiqued polygamy in lively terms: "I think I see myself, vowing to love and honor, some of old driv driveling idiot of 60, to be taken into his harem and enjoy his fav the pleasure of being his favorite Sultana for an hour, and then thrown aside, whil'st my Godly husband, is out Sparking another girl, in hopes of getting another victim to his dep despotic power. Pleasant prospect, I must say ... I don't believe in polygamy and never will." It is possible that Ina's views reflected those of her mother.

Agnes added a brief message to this letter. The contrast between Ina's forceful, incisive sentences and Agnes's homespun prose is striking:

> My Dear Nephew I will try and write you a few lines we was truly glad to hear from you and that you are enjoying you[r] self as well as you are we all want to behold you again here with us once more ther is not many of us left Joseph and the greatest prayer of my heart is that the Smith family one and all may all be gathered together at one place once more would not there be rejoiceing Joseph yes yes both in heaven and on earth my heart feels the {sureness} of it and who is to bring it about but yourself and John and Uncle Joseph['s] Children we are all awaiting for you and hundreds that I could mane [name] are alooking for Joseph to take his place but we must wait god['s] own time and {pray} that it may be short_____ Joseph I want you to bring me some pretty Shells allso tell William Cluff to bring me some give {our} love to him tell him that we do not forget him nor any of you take care of your self Joseph your Aunt Agnes

In these lines we sense a warm, charming woman with certain childlike tendencies. She fondly contemplates a reunion of the Smith widows, an entirely impractical idea.

On August 28 Agnes Charlotte wrote to Joseph F. in a style resembling her mother's simplicity rather than Ina's sophistication. She mentioned her mother's illness: "Mother has been sick the greater part of the time since we came to this place her health is very poor at this time." Agnes Charlotte wrote longingly of gathering back to Jackson County, Missouri. She said that Agnes Moulton and her children had been in Los Angeles two years and six months, but William Pickett had been absent from them "in San Francisco most all of the time." But he was said to be coming to reunite with them "in ashort time." There is a message from the elder Agnes: "Mother says tell Joseph to be of good courage and a Jubilee will come by a bye she says that you must bring her some little curiosities of the Islands."

When Joseph F. Smith finished his Hawaiian mission, he visited the Picketts again on his way to Utah. In his 1918 letter he remembers that Agnes repeatedly expressed her regrets that "the people of the Church were all leaving California and were going back Utah, leaving her and her children all alone." Joseph, who loathed William Pickett, offered her a team and outfit to leave her husband and come to Utah, but she flatly rejected the suggestion. Her grim experience living alone in Utah earlier, and possibly her rejection of polygamy, caused her to stay in California with Pickett. Joseph F., whose letters had constantly emphasized the spiritual necessity of living in Utah, was very unhappy with her decision.

When faithful Mormons in San Bernardino returned to Utah to help with the "Utah War" in early 1858, the Picketts moved to San Bernardino, perhaps because William was able to buy some of the vacated land inexpensively. He rented an office and practiced law there for two years. In late 1857 both Agnes Charlotte and Ina became engaged: Agnes married William Peterson on March 3, 1858, and on April 21 Ina married the handsome, erratic Robert Carsley, a partner in the Salamander Iron Works who also sang and acted. Both couples settled in Los Angeles. Agnes Charlotte's first child, Henry, was born in January 1860, which made Agnes Moulton a grandmother at fifty-one.

By April the Picketts were apparently living in Los Angeles again, for William was then elected to the Los Angeles school board and acted as its secretary. All seemed to be going moderately well now for the Pickett family. The daughters were married and were starting to bear children. Evidently William, despite his "intemperance," was respected in the community and was providing a stable livelihood. But Ina's marriage was about to crumble in a scene from melodrama.

## XIII. "My Sister Screaming Murder"

Ina had been deeply infatuated with the charming, dashing Robert when she married him, but it gradually became clear that he was psychologically unstable. Irrationally possessive of Ina, he began to accuse her of having affairs when he was parted from her. In fall 1861 he traveled to San Francisco with a minstrel group, so Ina lived with Agnes and William while he was gone. On October 12 Robert returned, but instead of enjoying an affectionate homecoming with his wife, he immediately came to the Pickett home and met her with violent, abusive threats, working himself into a frenzy. Agnes later gave extensive legal testimony concerning this event, traumatic for both her and Ina:

> I am 51 years of age – ... The complainant is a daughter of mine ... I know that the Def.[endent] has been very jealous of complainant and ... so expressed himself when he came back from San Francisco ... he came to my house ... I told him I wanted to hear nothing derogatory to Ina's, complainant's, character. He said that he had had information in San Francisco and since he arrived here that pltiff [Ina] had been receiving visits from Capt Davidson and {Lieut. Cary}, which had proved her to be a "whore" to him, to use his own expression. I wished him to go away and spoke to Col Kewen who was in an adjoining room to get him to go

away. The Col. tried, but could not succeed, and Def. remained until sundown abusing his wife and the whole family with most abusive epithets of the kind already alluded to and mentioned. He accused his wife of constant infidelity. We got down on our knees to him beseeching him to go away. We told him Mr. Pickett would return and there would be trouble; he said he would as leave spill Mr. Picketts blood as a pigs in the {pen}. He said that ... she [Ina] should go with him he took his wife by the hand violently and {hauled} and pulled her ... continually all the afternoon He flung off his coat and took off his {hat} took out a knife and said he would torment her[,] pltff[,] to death, wanted her to kill him or he would kill her; also got sharp pointed scissors and hunted a carving knife, his wife having got the knife away from him ... We could not persuade him to leave.

Agnes, defending her daughter, was able to take a gun away from Carsley:

My boys returned from hunting; Def. took one of his guns, I took it away from him and hid it. Mr. Pickett was seen coming and plaintiff {persuaded} him to {come} the back way, Def. having hold of pltff's wrist ... [I] went out to find them [pltff & Def.] and beseeched Def. to let plaintiff go ... he gave me his hand and {promised} that he would leave us and would not [come see] us until the next day. Not over a half hour passed when he returned with a six shooter and commenced {thumping} in the back {door} of the house ... I asked him why he had come back after he had given her his hand & {promised} not to return—he said he had {come} to satisfy himself. I told him there was company in the house and to go away.

Carsley, beside himself with rage, refused to leave. Agnes now took the action that precipitated the end of this confrontation:

[He was] in front yard with his pistol in his hand ... it was dark. I went to camp [a military camp, nearby]. Def ... told me to return, as I went plaintiff [Ina] came screaming Def. following her. he overtook her and tried to drag her toward the {street} and did drag her part of the way, after that I saw nothing more until I saw Pickett taking aim and Def. {brandishing} his pistol; Def. having hold of pltff; she down on her knees. Mr. Pickett shot and made a lunge at him with a bayonet. Def. let go of pltff and she ran towards ... the tents of the camp[.] a bullet came[,] I heard it ... {fire} into this tent at the camp —

The bullet missed, causing Robert to snarl that "if he had had his rifle he would have done better execution." Carlos, in court testimony, added: "I saw pltff {coming} and heard my sister scream def. having hold of her— I saw something flash in Def's hands—My sister screaming murder my father fired back." Pickett's bullet hit Carsley in the hand, and the day's long, horrific trauma came to an end, as he was forced to seek medical attention and ultimately have his hand amputated. Ina, in later life, was reluctant even to refer to the events of the day. The strain on Agnes must have also been terrible.

Carsley kept coming back to the Pickett house to terrorize Ina and Agnes. On December 10 Ina filed for divorce and two days later A. King, the deputy sheriff, served papers to Carsley as he stood outside the Pickett home shouting at the women inside. The embittered husband then became so violent that King was forced to incarcerate him. Though Carsley continued to return to the Pickett home to harass Ina, Kewen, in court testimony, testified that Carsley later interviewed some of those who had supposedly known of Ina's infidelity and "they denied any knowledge or suspicion of [her guilt]." Robert then asked her forgiveness and consented to the divorce. On December 26 the testimony quoted above was given in Los Angeles. The twins also testified, as did Kewen and Sheriff King. The divorce was made final four days later. To add to the tragedy of Ina's marriage, she had a child which evidently died young, though little is known about it.

In 1862 the Picketts, with Ina, left Los Angeles for the north, possibly wanting to get away from Robert Carsley, who was still unstable. In addition, Los Angeles may have had too many unpleasant associations for Ina. But parting from Agnes Charlotte and her young children must have been extremely painful for Agnes the grandmother.

## XIV. "Oceans of Trouble"

In September Agnes, fifty-four; William; Ina, twenty-one; and the twins, fourteen, arrived in San Francisco. William went to work as a printer and William Jr. learned the trade with him. Carlos worked in a "wine and bitters shop," then as a clerk for historian Hubert Howe Bancroft. Ina began to teach English in grade school. At home she helped Agnes with housework and two Spanish boys boarded with the Picketts to supplement the household income. In 1864 the two Williams worked at printing the *Californian*.

On May 30 Agnes wrote again to Joseph F., now a mission president in Hawaii. She expressed reverence for Joseph Smith, Jr., and for the Smith family: "Joseph my Dear Nephew I acknowlege none greater than yourself none greater than those that belong to the household of Joseph our Dear Dear Dear departed one Joseph there is none greater there is none better none more honest and upright and tries to do right than those that have been left behind." She again wrote hopefully of a Smith family reunion. In a very interesting passage, she hinted at an alternate history she could tell Joseph F.: "I could say many things to you Joseph that I know and that has been told me by those that are dead and gone but perhaps you would not believe me no I know that you would not so it is best for me to keep silent." She ended by encouraging Joseph to "write tenderly" to Ina, for she had "waded through Oceans of trouble for the last few years it would not take much more to take her from me." She signed the letter "Mother."

Ina also wrote to Joseph F. on June 3, 1865. His wife, Levira, a daughter of Mary Bailey and Samuel Smith, was staying with the Picketts and was becoming difficult, as she seemed to be mentally unstable. Agnes, however, was visiting Agnes Charlotte in Los Angeles. William was working at the *American Flag* printing office at the time. By June 21 Agnes had returned to San Francisco and Levira had left the Pickett home. The irascible William Pickett had been rude to Levira and, as Ina reported to Joseph, she had not been able to control him.

In May 1868 Agnes Charlotte's husband, William Peterson, died. Agnes C. had borne six children, two of whom had died. In July another child, Mary Charlotte, died, leaving only three children in the family.

## XV. Oakland Bohemia

In 1870 William Pickett left Agnes for the last time. Two years later, on September 16, 1872, Apostle Wilford Woodruff visited Agnes, and his journal sheds some light on William's departure: "We took street Cars & visited Mrs. Agness Picket, Don Carlos Smith's widow. She said that She had not seen Picket for some 2 years. He was in Oregon Editing a paper." Though nothing more is known about the separation, the geographical distance clearly implies emotional estrangement also. Perhaps when William was struck by one of his periodic urges to relocate, Agnes lost patience and finally refused to accompany him. Despite his intelligence and charm, he was improvident and "intemperate." Or perhaps they simply agreed to part. When William left, Agnes was sixty-two, Ina (who never remarried) was thirty, and the twins were twenty-two.

Ina continued to write poetry, taking as her pen-name Ina Coolbrith, and she became a leading light in literary, quasi-bohemian circles in Oakland and San Francisco, counting among her friends Bret Harte, Charles Warren Stoddard, Jack London, John Muir, Robert Louis Stevenson, and Mark Twain. Through Ina, Agnes also was known in these circles. One of Ina's closest friends was the eccentric poet Joaquin Miller—his name was a pseudonym that Ina suggested. On approximately January 1, 1872, Joaquin left his thirteen-year-old daughter, Calle Shasta, to live with Agnes and Ina while he traveled. Calle, a child from Miller's youthful marriage to a Native American, would live with the Picketts for seven years until she married. Miller sent money periodically for her support.

On February 22, 1871, another child of Agnes Charlotte, Willie Peterson, died, leaving her with only two children, Henry, thirteen, and Ina Lillian, nine. Agnes Charlotte herself became very ill early in 1873, and Agnes Moulton visited her in the summer. When she reached Los Angeles, she found her daughter worse than expected and decided to bring her back with her to San Francisco. She wrote Ina and told her to have the twins find a larger house, then traveled back to San Francisco by sea with her daughter and two grandchildren, Henry, and little Ina. As Agnes Charlotte was seriously ill, it was a difficult journey. In San Francisco Agnes Charlotte had to be tended continually by the older Agnes, now sixty-five, and the constant worry and loss of sleep were a serious drain on her health. On January 29, 1874, Agnes Charlotte died at the age of thirty-seven. Despite her mother's grief, a long ordeal of worry and exhaustion had ended.

Agnes Charlotte had asked to be buried in Los Angeles with her husband and four of her children, so Ina accompanied the body to the south. Later she wrote, "At the time my widowed sister died, I had the chance of going abroad under auspices that would have changed all my fortunes: instead, to meet the added care of her children, I entered my library prison, a daily grind from 8 A.M. to 9 P.M., for *20* years. During that time, I knew only the path that led from my own door to that of my prison." Ina's bohemian temperament caused her to regard her work as a librarian as confining; nor was the job lucrative, but she became well-known and loved as the chief Oakland librarian. Jack London, for one, wrote of her kindness to him when he was a young library patron. Many commented on her striking beauty. However, there were stories of Ina and Joaquin Miller reciting poetry to each other while patrons waited patiently to check out books.

The twins, now twenty-six, had left by this time, apparently having inherited their father's wanderlust, and they spent some thirty years prospecting in the Southwest and New Mexico. One of them had a drinking problem, like his father, which again fits the typical picture of an alcoholic's family.

In 1874 Agnes and Ina, with Henry, Ina, and Calle, moved near the Oakland library, inhabiting a cottage on Fifteenth Street in Oakland. The naturalist John Muir was a frequent visitor at 564 Fifteenth Street, and on one occasion he tried to link Ina romantically with a friend. Ina's poetic reply was brusque but witty:

O Johny Muir! O Johny Muir!
How could you leave your mountains pure,
Your meadow-breadths, and forests free,

A wily matchmaker to be? ...
Or if you smile, or if you frown
I DO NOT WANT YOUR MR. BROWN.

### XVI. "I Wanted You Here With Me"

In December 1874 a Mrs. Benton invited Ina to spend Christmas with her and some other friends. But when Ina mentioned the invitation to Agnes, the older woman's eyes filled with tears. "O, Ina," she said, "I am afraid it will be the last Christmas we shall be together, and I wanted you here with me and the children." So Ina spent the holiday with her mother.

David and Alexander Smith, two of Joseph Smith's sons, now part of the anti-polygamist Reorganized Latter Day Saint church, traveled to California from July to October 1876, and during that time visited Agnes and Ina. They certainly had no idea that Agnes had been a plural wife of their father, and even Ina may not have known. According to Lucy Walker Smith Kimball, who later visited Ina, the talk turned to Joseph Smith's polygamy, with the two prominent "Reorganites" denying it emphatically. Agnes however, according to Lucy, "told them that what they had seen, and heard in Salt Lake was Truth that those women were their fathers Wives, and it was useless to promulgate falsehood to the World and advised them to desist." The Smith brothers were reportedly much taken aback. "She [Ina] could plainly see they were Stung with the truth of her testimony  David seemed struck dumb, astounded at the living testimony of so many  What could their object be! Alexander said he would not take anybodys word – not even Aunt Agness."

### XVII. "An Ever Present Loss"

In late 1876 Agnes began to lose strength. She spent Christmas in bed, and on December 26 died at the age of sixty-eight. Ina, quoted by Joseph F. Smith in his 1918 letter, preserved her last words: "O! what a dupe I have been; what a dupe I have been!" Ina interpreted these statements as an expression of her mother's feeling of having been duped by Mormonism, while Joseph F. interpreted them as referring to William Pickett and to her later life separated from the church. So ambiguous a simple historical datum can be. In any event, the words enhance Agnes's tragic, enigmatic persona. At the funeral the next day "Johny Muir" was a pall-bearer. Agnes was buried in the Mountain View Cemetery in Oakland and her poet daughter was eventually buried beside her in an unmarked grave.

We are left to consider the meaning of Agnes's life. Early, narrowly-moralizing Mormon historiography would have looked askance at her for deserting the body of the Saints—geographical distance and refusal to gather to Zion being considered a form of apostasy. It would have disapproved of her leaving a third Smith husband to marry Pickett (though

George Smith apparently left her), then shedding her Mormon identity and heritage. It would have been easy to point to Pickett's alcoholism and his subsequent desertion of Agnes and her children and make obvious judgments about apostasy. But if Agnes's life with William Pickett was difficult, life as a polygamous wife in Utah was often just as difficult, though in entirely different ways. If Pickett deserted her, polygamy was almost an institutionalized form of marital neglect. She endured hardships and dangers in California, just as she had earlier as a wife of Don Carlos Smith. Recent research has shown that however unjustifiable and cowardly the persecutions of the Missouri mobs were, Mormon extremism, authoritarianism, and militarist rhetoric helped fan the flames of persecution.

Despite Agnes's failed fourth marriage, she raised and spent her later life with Ina Coolbrith, one of the most brilliant and accomplished women in California or Mormon history, an important West coast poetess and a pioneer librarian in Oakland. This was no minor accomplishment. The bond between Agnes and Ina was seemingly as supernaturally close as that between Zina Huntington Young and her daughter Zina Card. Ina provided two epitaphs for her mother. Lucy Walker Kimball, after visiting Ina in 1883, wrote to Joseph F. Smith, "Ina says she never can be reconciled to her Mothers death The longing for her at times becomes almost intolerable—she said it was an ever present loss an all abiding sorrow." Ina herself wrote in 1907, "I have never ceased for one waking moment to miss my beloved Mother in all the long, long years she has been absent from me." Though Agnes Coolbrith lived her life partly as a Mormon, the wife of three prominent Smiths, then partly as a "gentile" wife of an alcoholic, she is certainly one of the great women in Mormon history.

# 7.

# Mother and Daughter

## *Patty Bartlett (Sessions Smith Parry)* and *Sylvia Porter Sessions (Lyon Smith Kimball Clark)*

When newly married Patty Sessions lived with her elderly parents-in-law in Ketcham, Maine, where her mother-in-law often acted as midwife, one day the old woman was sent for to attend a young woman who was near delivery and in great pain. But Mother Sessions could not travel quickly, so another messenger soon arrived to ask Patty to come immediately in her place, as the mother-to-be was near death. Patty hurried ahead. Emmeline Wells wrote, "Mrs. Sessions [Patty] who was entirely unskilled in affairs of the kind, but had abundant nerve force and moral courage, took the child and put the mother in bed before Mother Sessions arrived; the old lady showed her how to dress the baby, which after doing she started homeward."

When a doctor eventually arrived, he found that the delivery had been done perfectly. He called on Patty and "congratulated her upon her ability, and told her she must attend to that business, not to have any fear, for she would prosper in it, as it was a new country and [as] there were many about to move in, it would be necessary to have more help of this kind." Four months later Patty delivered another baby, and continued in this occupation throughout the rest of her life. Often in Maine she would ride horseback as far as twenty miles on deserted roads to deliver a baby and would be summoned at all hours of the day or night. She reportedly delivered 3,977 babies throughout her life and is probably the most famous Mormon midwife.

Patty is less well-known as a wife of Joseph Smith. She and her daughter Sylvia are the only certain mother-daughter pair who married Smith. (Flora Woodworth and Phoebe Watrous Woodworth may have been another such combination, but Phoebe's marriage to Smith is not certainly documented.) Patty married Joseph when she was forty-seven, well into middle age, so the marriage may have been ceremonial only, without a sexual dimension. She was Smith's first older wife. Sylvia's marriage was polyandrous (as was Patty's) and has the usual elusive complexity of such relationships. However, she has considerable importance as the only wife of Joseph Smith, polyandrous or otherwise, who stated definitely that one of her children was biologically Joseph's.

Patty's life is superbly documented by diaries she kept most of her life and by the autobiography and diary of her oldest child, Perrigrine. Her extraordinary journal is a moving record of plural sisterhood, but also documents the emotional turmoil that first wives often experienced in practical polygamy, and shows that plurality could cause explosive tensions between women as well as sisterhood. Unfortunately, Sylvia's life, by comparison with her mother's, is sketchily documented.

## I. Learning to Work

On February 4, 1795, Patty Bartlett was born to Enoch Bartlett and Anna Hall in Bethel, Oxford County, in southwest Maine. Enoch was a fifty-three-year-old shoemaker and farmer from Massachusetts. Anna, twenty-nine, a native of Cumberland, Maine, was Enoch's second wife; by his first wife, Eliza Seagar, he had had ten children. After Eliza died, Enoch married Anna in 1794, and Patty was their first child. She was followed by eight full siblings: Elisham (1796), Namah Hall (1798), Jonathan (1800), Polly (1802), Aphia (1804), Lydia (1806), Lavinia (1808), and Enoch Bartlett, Jr., the last of Enoch Bartlett's nineteen children, born in 1811, when Patty was sixteen. Most of the Bartlett children lived to maturity, married, and raised families, but Lavinia died on April 5, 1811, at age two. This would have been Patty's first encounter with the death of a close family member.

Thus Patty was much younger than her half siblings, but the oldest of her full siblings. Probably the darling of a large family herself when a baby, she would have spent much time tending her younger brothers and sisters in Enoch's second family. As there were fewer boys than girls in the family, Patty often had to work in the fields with her father. Of her parents and upbringing, Perrigrine wrote: "My Grand Father Enoch made no pretentions to religion and never belonged to any sect he was a very liberal man to the poor and was honest and upright in all his Deportment and taught his children to work and always to speak the truth to deal justley with all to live virtuous and to not take that was not their own not so much as an Aple from a neighbors tree with out leave." The qualities of honesty, generosity, and industriousness were abundantly passed on to Patty. She wrote of her mother, "I ... feel thankful that I had a mother that put me to work when I was young and learned me how." Neither of Patty's parents was fully literate, though they taught her the alphabet. As a child, she attended a school held in her father's shop and quickly learned to read and write.

## II. David Sessions

On June 28, 1812, Patty, seventeen, married twenty-two-year-old David Sessions—much against her parents' wishes. They told her she would never receive help from them if she married David, and kept their word, ignoring her when they subsequently gave the rest of their children "a good fit out." Patty and David moved to Ketcham, ten miles away, where they lived with David's parents and where Patty tended her elderly, sickly mother-in-law. She also milked, made butter, spun cotton, and, wrote Wells, "made a bed tick and some sheets; picked cat-tails and filled the tick, so the young folks had a bed of their own." Here Patty began to practice midwifery under her mother-in-law's tutelage.

In spring 1813 David "bought land and made a farm built a log house and a large fraim barn," Perrigrine wrote. Shortly after this Patty bought a loom from a friend who was moving, "and I soon had all the weaving I could do fetched to me from ten to twelve miles." Patty's mother was known for her weaving, so Patty followed in her footsteps. The following spring she and David made sugar to supplement their income. Her first child, Perrigrine, was born in Ketcham on June 15, 1814, when she was nineteen.

The Sessionses moved to another farm in the Newry area, Andover Surplus on Bear River, about nine miles northeast of Ketcham, in December 1815. Here, according to Perrigrine, "there was a log house and a small fraimed home on the farm it was good land and a large portion of it botom land being on a small stream of water caled bare river here my Father lived untill 1837." In this place, wrote Patty, they moved into an old cabin where salt had been made "and lived there until we built a new house, which we moved into in the night, lest the old rickety cabin should fall down upon us."

David built two large barns, several sheds, and a grist mill, buying adjoining land until he owned a 400-acre farm. "Here after suffering many privations it being a new country and heged up on all sides by the highest mountains in that section ... my Father by his industry on his farm and with his mills And by keeping a public house procured considerable wealth," wrote Perrigrine. On June 3, 1816, a second son, Sylvanus, was born in this location.

At about this time, Patty became involved in formal religion, according to Perrigrine: "My Mother by reading the bible began to think that baptism was nec[e]ssary and October the first 1816 she was baptized. My father made no pretentions to religion as yet but did not Appose her." Patty, like many early Mormons, read the Bible devoutly. She was probably baptized a Methodist, as David Sessions later accepted Methodism and was baptized in January 1820.

A first daughter, Sylvia Porter, was born on July 31, 1818, in Andover Surplus, followed by Anna B. on March 21, 1820. Perrigrine was now five, Sylvanus nearly four, and Sylvia almost two. Soon after Anna's birth, David built a new large house and the family moved into it in November.

In March 1821 Patty's in-laws appeared without warning "and wanted us to take them ... to live with us," writes Patty. Patty and David welcomed them into their home, and the burden of caring for David's mother, now confined to a wheelchair, again fell on Patty. Mother Sessions was a heavy woman and Patty often had to wheel her around the house and lift her. One day as she was moving her, Patty's arm slipped from the chair and her elbow was caught between the slats, "which pulled my elbow cap out of place. The pain was very great, but when mother Sessions asked if she had hurt me, I said I guessed not." Patty managed to get her mother-in-law into the chair, then went into the front room where a girl was sewing for her. "I ... told her to take hold of my hand and hold it still, and let me pull back and straighten my arm; she did so and I pushed it into place, and put my arm in a sling." When David came home, he asked Patty what ailed her arm. "Only some rheumatism," she replied. Here, in her early life, we see the roots of Patty's later skill at practical doctoring as well as her innate toughness.

Another child, David Jr., was born on May 9, 1823, when Patty was twenty-eight, making a total of five children under ten. So she had to raise her own children in addition to tending her sickly in-laws. As Sylvia and David Jr. grew, they became especially close, possibly because Sylvia tended David when their mother was gone on midwife calls. On September 16 Anna, two-and-a-half, was stricken with "the colery morbus" (a severe stomach upset, with such symptoms as stomach spasms, vomiting, and diarrhea) and died four days later. Patty mourned a lost child for the first time. "Mother Sessions" contracted the same illness and died on October 1. Despite the sadness of the event, a great burden was lifted from Patty's shoulders. Nearly one year later, on September 23, "Father Sessions" died peacefully while visiting a neighbor. Patty's own father, Enoch, contracted a fever in August 1825 and died on September 1 at age sixty-three.

Patty bore another daughter on March 16, 1825, and decided to name it Anna to replace the child who had died. Two years later, on August 1, 1827, when she was thirty-two, Bartlett, her seventh child, was born in Newry. Perrigrine was now thirteen, Sylvanus eleven, Sylvia nine, David four, and Anna two. However, Bartlett died a half year later on February 15, 1828, of "hooping cough." Patty had lost three of her seven children.

For a few years after this, the Sessions family lived peacefully. Then in 1832 "typhus fever" prostrated them, and on August 10 the second Anna, now seven, died. At the time, Perrigrine wrote, "My Mother could not raise her hand to her head and lay in the same room where my Sister died my Father and brother Sylvanus lay in an other room and did not see her after she was taken sick My aunt Apphia and her daughter lay in an other room they were all helpless I had had the fever and had got so that I could set up some my brother David was just comeing down with the fever." Now we have an early specific reference to Sylvia in the historical record: "And my Sister Sylvia being the second time deprived of her Only Sister she mourned and wept untill she had to go to bed at this time my feelings I could not discribe."

The ordeal was not over. On September 15 Sylvanus died at age sixteen. "At this time my Father and Mother had got some better but my Grandmother Bartlett was there and she and David were so sick that they did not know when Sylvanus died Altho they were in the same room. After my Grandmother Got better she was carried home on a bed six miles betwene too horses there was Eleven that had the fever at my Fathers that summer and many others in the neighbourhood it was a sickley time." If Perrigrine could not "describe his feelings" after these fatalities, their impact on Patty can only be imagined. She was now thirty-seven; of her seven children, only Perrigrine, eighteen, Sylvia, twelve, and David, nine, were still living.

### III. "As Soon as My Mother Herd She Believed"

Perrigrine tells us that in August 1833 "Hason Aldrig" and Horace "Cowin" introduced Mormonism to Newry. Patty's reaction was almost instinctual: "And as soon as my Mother herd she believed." David felt it was best to wait and investigate further before joining, so Patty postponed her baptism till she could obtain his permission. On July 2, 1834, he gave his consent, "and she was baptized and Confirmed into the Church of laterday Saints under the hand of Daniel Bean." Like many new Mormon converts in small towns, she was probably subjected to gossip or ostracism, but "She stood firm steming all oposition and she received much of it from her neighbours and some of her brothers and sisters she remained alone in the Church almost one year before any of the rest of us joined the church & six miles from any other member." She attended a small branch of thirty members which Bean presided over.

Thus Patty was thirty-nine and would soon be a grandmother when the eventful Mormon period of her life began. On September 12, 1834, Perrigrine married Julia Ann Killgore and the young couple moved in with the Sessions family. In August 1835 two apostles, Brigham Young and Lyman Johnson, visited Maine and presided at a conference held on the Sessions farm on the 12th. Perrigrine wrote, "The blessing of God atendid the meating there was severil adid [added] to the Church threw the Ordinance of baptism and the laying on of the hands." Among those initiated into the Latter-day Saint faith on this occasion was Patty's husband. The apostles preached Zion in the conference, fleeing out from among the wicked before destructions of the last days occurred: "Here the gathering of the Saints was taught and preperations began to bee made to remove to Zion this looked like a great sacrifise to make as the distance was so far but we began to dispose of property as my Father and I had considerable."

A month later, on September 16, Edward Partridge baptized Perrigrine. Patty became a grandmother five days after this, on the 22nd, when Perrigrine's and Julia's first child, Martha Ann, was born. Thus Patty was strengthened by the presence of her husband and oldest son in Mormonism, and the family slowly prepared for the trip to Zion (Missouri). Before leaving, they sold their mill, their farm, farm equipment, livestock, and packed as many of their possessions as they could. They were now part of the great Mormon adventure.

## IV. First Pilgrimage

Perrigrine wrote, "Times were hard and money scarce but after a continual perseverince we all started." The company included Patty, David, Sylvia, David Jr., Perrigrine, Julia and child, and Patty's half sister, Lucy Bartlett Powers, with her husband, Jonathan, and their two sons. They left on June 5, 1837, "when many a tear was shead by our neighbours and friends as my Wife left her Aged Father and step Mother with all her brothers and sisters never expecting to see them againe in this world." Patty was now forty-two and four months pregnant, while Sylvia was nearly eighteen.

The party traveled by road through New Hampshire, Vermont, and New York. At Buffalo they took a steamboat across Lake Erie to Fairport, Ohio, then traveled the short distance to Kirtland. Here Patty and Sylvia first met Joseph Smith and heard him preach in the temple. The Sessions family all came down with the measles in Kirtland and were detained there seven weeks.

They then travelled west to Cleveland and on through Indiana and Illinois. When they reached eastern Missouri, Perrigrine wrote, "It began to rain which made the roads verry bad and several times we found bridges gone and the streams risen so that we had to swim our teams but [we continued on what was] often a long and tedious journey camping in a tent by the side of the road." These hardships, and the two-thou-

176

sand-mile journey from Maine, would only begin their pilgrimages in western America.

They arrived at Far West in November only to find many Saints living in tents, having been driven from their homes. The Sessionses quickly bought a large farm and began raising corn, potatoes, and wheat. Amanda, Patty's last child, was born on November 14. Patty's Missouri journals, of which we only have excerpts printed by Wells, indicate that she quickly became friendly with Joseph Smith. On March 25, 1838, she heard him preach, and on April 14 she wrote, "Make a visit to Joseph Smith."

### V. Windsor Lyon

On April 21 Sylvia married at age nineteen. Patty wrote in her journal, "Sylvia was married to Windsor P. Lyon, Joseph Smith performed the ceremony. David W. Patten was here when Sylvia was married and preached, while here, at Peregrine's. The next day the Prophet was there and a good time it was." Windsor had been born on February 8, 1809, in Orwell, Addison, Vermont, the son of Aaron Lyon and Roxana Palmer. His father was baptized in 1832 in Warsaw, Wyoming County, New York, and Windsor may have converted at the same time, since on January 5 the next year he was speaking in tongues at his father's house in Warsaw. By June 28 Aaron and Windsor had migrated to Kirtland, and in 1836 Windsor owned property in Salemtown, Caldwell County, Missouri. By 1838 he had begun to practice as an "army physician."

Patty continued to deliver babies in Missouri. In mid-August 1838 the Sessions family was afflicted by a bout of "fever and ague," but all survived. As tensions between Mormon and non-Mormon Missourians escalated, David and Perrigrine may have served in the paramilitary Mormon forces that tried to defend "Zion." But on February 15, 1839, the Sessionses left Missouri for Illinois, probably with the rest of the Mormons. One would guess that Patty, David, and Perrigrine (and perhaps the Lyons) traveled together. Perrigrine wrote:

> The wether was cold and we had to tent by the way  this tried our Souls when we would pass through towns and Villages they would holler at us and ask us where our Old Jo.Smith was or our Mormon God and whare we were going or going too and threten us with death and some they whiped nearly to death  here Women and Children traviled on foot untill they wore their shoes out and went barefoot when you could track them by blood on the praries

When they arrived at the Mississippi on February 27, ice was running in the river, making it impossible for boats to cross, so there were some two hundred families waiting to be ferried to Illinois. According to Perrigrine, "Here many could not get much to eat but parched corn this brought sickness ... Here we staid eleven days while others staid three weeks here my wife and Mother was taken with the chills and fever the snow being about three inches deep but at length we crosed the river and bid *Old* Missouri farewell." Patty's February 26 journal entry parallels Perrigrine's account: "Still muddy, and we have to tent out, cold, wet and inclement, no shelter but a tent, a sick babe and no comforts. Trust in God and pray for courage and endurance." The sick child, Amanda, was now nearly two.

## VI. Nauvoo

On March 8 Sylvia and Windsor crossed the Mississippi, and the next day Patty, David, and family followed them and stayed in Quincy. Perrigrine reports that the people of Illinois received the refugees with kindness. Soon thereafter Patty and her daughter-in-law Julia "took the ague" and were very ill. A week later the Sessionses relocated in Carthage. On April 2 they moved into their own house, apparently at Bear Creek, in Hancock County, then Perrigrine and his father rented land twenty miles from Nauvoo. On June 27 Perrigrine left on a mission to the East.

The balance of the year is largely undocumented for the Sessions clan. Patty and David moved to Nauvoo on May 2, 1840. When Perrigrine returned home on June 14, he found his family suffering from malaria, living "in a little log cabin fourteen feet square with my fathers family and Brother Lyman Lenerds with out any chimney or much floor being not chinked or painted and a poor ruff [roof] and every shour of raine wet all that were in the house ... my family and friends with hardly a whole garment and in poverty and distress ... sickness was in all most evry house." Soon after this Perrigrine built a large home, and Patty and David moved into their own new home in September.

On September 20 Amanda, three and a half, died of "croup" (inflammation of the larynx, causing noisy breathing and a hoarse cough). Patty was grief-stricken at losing her last-born, but wrote in her journal, echoing Job, "The Lord giveth and the Lord taketh away, blessed be the name of the Lord."

Sylvia and Windsor had moved to Nauvoo soon after arriving in Illinois, and Windsor was reportedly the first to construct a major building there; this had his mercantile and drug business on one side and his home on the other. Sylvia's first child, Marian, was probably born here on July 3. The 1840 census shows Sylvia living with Windsor, Marian, and three teenagers, possibly Windsor's sisters, Kate and Juliett, and his brother, Carlos, with whom he operated his store. Ads for the store show it selling "Dry Goods, Groceries, Crockery, Glass, and Hardware, Drugs and Medicines, Paints and Dry Stuffs." Sylvia's second daughter, Philofreen, was born on June 11, 1841.

## VII. Two Marriages

On February 8, 1842, when Sylvia was twenty-three, she was sealed to Joseph Smith. Virtually nothing is known about the internal dynamics of this polyandrous marriage, except that she later claimed that her daughter Josephine was a product of it. Nothing is known of Windsor's reaction to the marriage, if he knew of it; by the interpretation proposed in this book, he might have known about and permitted it. It is certain that at the time of Smith's marriage to Sylvia, Windsor was a faithful Latter-day Saint who would have accepted Smith as a prophet.

It is not known if Patty knew about her daughter's second marriage, but the fact that Patty herself married Smith within a month suggests that she would have known soon thereafter, if not before. Patty's journal shares a few details of this marriage: "I was sealed to Joseph Smith by Willard Richards March 9 1842 in Newel K Whitneys chamber Nauvoo, for time and all eternity Eternity ... Sylvia my daughter was presant when I was sealed to Joseph Smith." Patty was forty-seven at the time and was the first older woman married by Smith. As was customary in later Mormonism, when older women married polygamously in Nauvoo, the ceremony was probably purely religious in nature and no cohabitation took place.

Nevertheless, Patty became an important member of Smith's extended family. Many of Smith's plural wives participated in his subsequent marriages by educating prospective wives, by serving as messengers and go-betweens, and by acting as witnesses at ceremonies. According to William Hall, an unsympathetic witness, Patty, with another older woman, Elizabeth Davis Durfee, was actively engaged in this work in Nauvoo.

On March 19 Marian Lyon died. The child's body was brought to Joseph Smith the next day while he was preaching to a large company in the grove near the temple, and he changed his remarks to speak about the salvation of children. Technically Marian was now sealed to him, not Windsor, in the eternities.

Five days later Sylvia was voted into the Nauvoo Relief Society and contributed a dollar to the fund. In the following weeks she made frequent contributions. Though Windsor would have some financial reverses in Nauvoo, he was generally well-to-do. Patty also attended Relief Society meetings. At the fifth meeting, on April 19, when Sarah Cleveland spoke in tongues, Patty gave the interpretation in an interesting example of what this practice was like in Nauvoo. Here the tongue-speaker and interpreter acted as spokespersons for God and gave collective and individual prophetic blessings:

[Patty, interpreting,] said that God was well pleas'd with this Society, that if we would be humble and faithful the Lord would pour out upon the members generally the gift of prophecy—that when the speaker laid her hand on the head of Sister Snow, she said that not only she should have the spirit but that all should have it also—that the speaker then address'd herself to Mother Smith saying that the prayers of father Smith were now answered upon the members of the Society—that the days of Mother S. should be prolong'd and she should meet many times with the Society, should enjoy much in the society of the sisters & shall hereafter be crown'd a mother of those that shall prove faithful &c.

Patty was probably by this time a close friend of Zina Huntington Jacobs Smith and Eliza Snow Smith, both much inclined to glossolalia, healing, and the gifts of the spirit. She would share many more prophetic meetings with them.

David left on a mission for Maine with a Brother Pack on June 11. Patty wrote in her journal, "He left me alone, and I am very lonesome." But her spirits soon rebounded. She still practiced midwifery and frequently attended church meetings. Wells wrote, "Day after day Sister Sessions, according to her diary, goes out among the sick, and helps to lay out the dead as well as officiating in her calling as a midwife." She also associated with her plural husband: "She speaks of visits from Bro. Joseph and Bro. Willard Richards, and on the 18th she says Joseph spoke concerning Dr. [John C.] Bennett and cut him off the Church." She visited Joseph's mother, Lucy Mack Smith, and received frequent visits from this matriarch who, strangely enough, was now her mother-in-law. On August 12 she wrote that she was "making shirts for Bro. Joseph." A month later Patty followed a Relief Society meeting with a charismatic blessing meeting attended by sisters Leonards, Dooty, and others.

## VIII. Windsor Excommunicated

At about this time, Windsor Lyon began to have financial difficulties that contributed to his loss of church membership. On August 13 a bankruptcy notice for Windsor appeared in the *Wasp*. Apparently he had loaned William Marks, president of the Nauvoo Stake, $3,000 and had received a note from him. However, when the note came due and Windsor applied for repayment, Marks, either unwilling or unable to repay him, stalled. This put Windsor in financial difficulty himself, so on November 4 he sued Marks in civil court. In doing so, he overstepped a church taboo—Mormon leaders preferred to settle disputes between members in-house, especially cases involving highly visible leaders such as a stake president (who had the status of a modern apostle). Marks was probably infuriated that a member of his own stake had haled him before a civil court for payment of a large debt.

Some of the above information is based on family traditions, but Marks's next step is well documented and substantiates part of the story. On November 7, after Windsor had brought Marks's case to civil court, the stake president brought Windsor's case before a church court, the high council, of which he was head, and Windsor was apparently excommunicated. The Nauvoo High Council minutes quote the following: "High Counc. Minut.: 'William Marks against Windsor Lyon. 'To the High Council of Jesus Christ of Latter Day Saints. I prefer a charge against Windsor Lyons for instituting a suit at law against me on the 4th of November, and for others acts derogatory to the character of a christian Nauvoo Nov. 7th 1842 William Marks, complainant.'"

Windsor protested that "the suit [civil suit] was instituted by him, in another man's name, therefore, did not think he was in fault &c. Two were appointed to speak on the case, viz: (9) Knight and (10) Huntington." It would be difficult to contest an excommunication case that was initiated by the stake president, who served as judge. The minutes continue, "The charge was fully sustained. The president then decided that, unless he [Lyon] repent humble himself and repent, the hand of fellowship be with drawn from him, which decision was unanimously sanctioned by the Councillors." That Windsor did not "repent" to Marks's satisfaction is evidenced by the fact that "cut off" was written by his name, in a probable later hand, on the 1842 Nauvoo Church Member record and by the fact that he was rebaptized into the church in 1846.

However, the day after the court, Joseph Smith seems on best of terms with Windsor. In Smith's journal, we read, "This A.M. called upon Windsor Lyons and others to make affidavits concerning the frauds and irregularities practised in the Post Office." Windsor, if he had been devastated by his excommunication, could have sold his store and left Nauvoo; instead, he continued to do business among Mormons and evidently managed to extricate himself from his financial difficulties.

David returned from his mission on November 16, and Patty, in her journal, "rejoiced that all their lives had been spared to meet again." On November 27 she froze her toes while traveling through severe cold to visit a sick person, and on December 13 she herself was sick. "The Prophet came and laid hands on her and she was healed," wrote Wells. Smith visited her daily the next week.

Sylvia was near childbirth again. On December 24 the Smith journal reads, "P.M. ... Walked with Sec[retary Willard Richards] to see Sister Lyons who was sick. Her babe died 30 minutes before he arrived." Other records have the child, Asa Windsor, born on December 25, but whenever he was born, he died within twelve hours. Sylvia had now lost two children, though Philofreen, one-and-a-half, was still living.

On January 15 of the new year, Patty heard Smith preach in his own house. David was seriously ill on the 28th and Smith and Orson Hyde administered to him. The absence of tension between the two males in this polyandrous triangle is remarkable. It suggests that either David did not know about the marriage or he knew of it and accepted it completely. Patty's diary for February 12 shows how close Smith was to the other polyandrous male in the Sessions family. On that date Windsor Lyon loaned the Mormon prophet $500 at Patty's house. According to Sessions family traditions, Windsor "was a true friend of the prophet Joseph Smith."

Sylvia's home had become a social hub for Nauvoo women. On February 25 Marinda Hyde, Louisa Beaman, and Mary Beaman Noble visited Sylvia and Patty at Sylvia's house—a gathering of four of Smith's wives. Two of Orson Hyde's wives, Marinda and Martha Browett Hyde, and Mary Ann Price, soon to be Orson's third wife, visited, along with Patty, on April 10. Five days later Eliza Snow wrote, "Spent a very interesting and agreeable afternoon at Mr. Lyon's present L[orenzo Snow], Mrs. Scovill, Miss Geroot, &c." Sylvia was economically elite and a member of the inner polygamy circles as well.

Smith was kidnapped in early June, but when he was freed and returned to Nauvoo, Patty visited him and wrote of the liberation with joy. She and Sylvia continued to contribute liberally to the poor. On July 7, after Patty donated some clothes to the Relief Society, "Sis. Lyons said when the poor come to sis. W.[Whitney] and sis. Holmes, if they can not supply them, send them with orders to her." She also gave "one Bunch cotton yarn ... to fill the tow on, for sd. cloth." At the end of July she donated $.50 and "a patent Wheel head worth $.75" to the Relief Society.

At one September Relief Society meeting, Patty "spoke most tenderly of Sister Emma our Prest said She was verry sick and desird that the Society would unite in faith and prayer for her that She may be heal'd Prayer was made in her behalf A hymn sung Prayer by Sister Sessions." Patty was an important presence in these early society meetings.

Olive Frost, another of Smith's wives, and her sister Mary Ann Frost Pratt visited Patty on July 29. These were old friends from Maine. On October 3 Patty ate dinner with Joseph. He would sometimes ask his wives to shelter other wives, and in the fall or winter of 1843, when the Partridge sisters were forced to leave the Smith home, Emily Partridge came to live with Sylvia and Windsor for some months. That winter three-year-old Philofreen became ill, and Emily remembered tending the child at night. One of Smith's visits to Sylvia is documented by William Clayton on September 18: "Joseph and I rode out to borrow money, drank wine at Sister Lyons. P.M. I got $50 of Sister Lyons and paid it to D.D. Yearsley." On January 27, 1844, Philofreen died of "scarlet fever and fits." All of Sylvia's three children had now passed away. Like Louisa Beaman, Presendia Huntington, and her mother, she was fated to lose many children. One can only imagine the emotional toll this would take on a woman.

## IX. Josephine Rosetta

At the time of Philofreen's death, Sylvia was some eight months pregnant with her fourth child, Josephine Rosetta Lyon, who was born on February 8. Heber C. Kimball blessed the girl, the first sign of a bond between the Lyon and Kimball families. We may now consider Josephine's affidavit affirming that she was a daughter of Joseph Smith:

> Just prior to my mothers death in 1882 she called me to her bedside and told me that her days on earth were about numbered and before she passed away from mortality she desired to tell me something which she had kept as an entire secret from me and from all others but which she now desired to communicate to me. She then told me that I was the daughter of the Prophet Joseph Smith, she having been sealed to the Prophet at the time that her husband Mr. Lyon was out of fellowship with the Church.

This scenario is not strictly consistent with the chronology provided by history, since Sylvia married Joseph Smith *before* Windsor was excommunicated. There are two possible explanations for this inconsistency. First, Sylvia may have been "revising" history to explain to her daughter why she married Smith when she was already married to Windsor. Another possibility is that Sylvia meant that she had had sexual relations with Smith after Windsor was disfellowshipped, which is chronologically possible.

However we interpret this evidence, it shows that Sylvia believed that Josephine was Smith's daughter, and it is convincing evidence that Smith had sexual relations with his wives, including his polyandrous spouses. How Sylvia was sure that Josephine was Joseph's, not Windsor's, is not clear. It seems unlikely that Sylvia would deny Windsor cohabitation rights after he was excommunicated, but perhaps she denied him temporarily, or perhaps he traveled on business.

On May 11 William H. Kimball, son of Heber C. Kimball, married Mary Davenport in the Lyon home, which again shows that Sylvia and Windsor associated with the Nauvoo elite, despite his excommunicant status. Once more we note a connection between the Lyons and Kimballs. On June 26 "Dr Lyon" was called as a witness in the Carthage crisis, which confirms that he was a trusted friend of Joseph Smith. When Smith was killed the following day, Sylvia and Patty were left to mourn their celestial husband.

## X. Heber C. Kimball

As has been shown, Joseph Smith's wives often married Brigham Young or Heber Kimball soon after Smith's death. Following this pattern, Sylvia Lyon married Heber for time on September 19, 1844. Young wrote in his journal, "Staed at home all day my wife is quite sick I Saw Sister Louisa B. Smith H.C. Kimball & Silva L. Smith &c. &c. grate is the work of the Lord in these Last days." "Saw" is probably a code word for "sealed and wedded." Sylvia, however, continued to live with Windsor Lyon. The internal dynamics of this polyandrous relationship are unknown—one wonders if Windsor, who always seemed friendly with Heber, knew of and gave his permission for the marriage. Occasionally Sylvia spent time with her new husband. On November 13 Zina Huntington Jacobs Smith wrote, "Sister Lions rehersed some of Elder Kimbles conversation concerning our state, also that of our friends" in the pre-existence.

The Lyon home, probably spacious and well-appointed, continued to be an important meeting place for the upper echelons of Mormon society. On September 24 a priesthood meeting of apostles and other leaders was held there. Apostle Willard Richards wrote on December 20, "I went out with her [Jennetta] as far as Mr Lyons where we called & drank a glass of wine were very kindly entertained by Mrs Lyon - & agreed to visit her next thursday." Between January 30 and March 20, 1845, Sylvia received her endowment and was initiated into the Holy Order, the Quorum of Anointed.

Patty moved in the same circles. Zina Huntington Jacobs's Nauvoo journal shows her visiting the older woman's house regularly. On January 28, 1845, Patty's daughter-in-law, Julia Ann, died, and Perrigrine and his child moved in with his parents for a few months. When Willard Richards's wife, Jennetta, died on July 9, he wrote the following day, "Sister Durphy [Smith], Sessions [Smith], Rhoda [Richards Smith], Ann Fox, Lucy Clayton & Sister Wilcox dressed Jennetta & put her in her coffin about sunset." Here Patty works with two sister-wives of Smith, acting in a typical feminine role, dressing the body of a friend for burial.

## XI. Windsor Rebaptized

In the fall of 1845, the Latter-day Saints once more faced insurmountable non-Mormon opposition and agreed to leave Illinois. But as they prepared for the exodus, they worked intensively to finish the temple and perform sacred ordinances there. Perrigrine described the situation from an eschatological perspective: "From this time [October] preparations began to be made by makeing wagons and procureing teames and provision for a journey into the Wilderness in search of a land of rest a land of piece where we can enjoy the privileges and blessings of a Celestial law unmolested ... untill this Gentile Nation are scerged for their sins and abominations."

Many polygamous marriages were solemnized in this atmosphere, and among them was a union of great importance to Patty: David Sessions married Rosilla Cowins on October 3, with Brigham Young officiating. Patty would now be living practical polygamy and would find the experience demoralizing and painful. Earlier she had required David, whether he knew it or not, to share her with another man; now she would have to share him with another woman.

Sylvia helped decorate the interior of the Nauvoo temple. On December 6 Heber Kimball wrote, "Sister Sophia Lyon Brought me in a fine rocken chare and a Comforter. She has also brought in pictures. and Evergreens." Sylvia and Patty received their endowments in the temple on December 16, along with David, Perrigrine's family, Eliza Snow, and Augusta Cobb Young. As would be expected, Windsor was not present. Patty initiated women with the preparatory washing and anointing ceremony from December 17 to 20.

On the 24th Patty's non-Mormon nephew, Enoch Tripp, unexpectedly appeared in Nauvoo. Having fallen upon hard times, he decided to visit Patty and her family and ask for help. He entered the Mormon city in fear and trepidation, as he had heard stories that Latter-day Saints often murdered non-Mormon visitors. He found Windsor's store and introduced himself to Sylvia in a back room. "Is this cousin, Enoch B. Tripp?" she exclaimed. "She greeted me with a kiss and thanked the Lord that he had preserved her life to behold some of her blood relatives from Maine ... Her father, mother and brothers were sent for and all greeted me with a most hearty welcome. The fear of being killed had now to a great degree left me." In the following months, he was surprised to find that Mormons were hospitable, friendly, and devout, saying grace at all meals.

Soon after this, Windsor Lyon rejoined the church under the surprising auspices of Heber C. Kimball, Sylvia's other husband, and Enoch too was baptized. Perrigrine wrote, "Here I would remark that on the eighteenth of January that my brother in law Windsor. Lyon and my Cousen Enoch. B. Tripp were baptised under the hand of Brother Heber. C. Kimball One of the Twelve this give the connection[s] a time of rejoiceing to see them Obey the truth." Enoch tells the story somewhat differently: "On Sunday morning, February 1, 1846, Heber C. Kimball came to the house of Mr. Windsor P. Lyon in order to rebaptize him into the church and they sent up to the temple and got a large bath tub. The mob violence was so strong, Heber C. Kimball did not dare to do it in public."

However, the polyandrous complexity in Sylvia's life continued. About a week after Windsor's rebaptism (by Perrigrine's dating), on January 26 Sylvia was sealed to Joseph Smith for eternity in the Nauvoo temple, with Heber Kimball standing proxy for Smith, then was sealed to Kimball for time. According to family traditions, this was done with the consent of Windsor, who received his endowment on February 3. Enoch Tripp wrote, "On the night of February 2, 1846, Brother Heber C. Kimball sent his carriage for me, Mr. Lyon and my cousin, David Sessions, and took us to the temple." The Nauvoo temple record notes that Windsor was a high priest, a significant priesthood honor that indicates his return to full fellowship in the church. According to family traditions, at some point, probably in January or February, he married a plural wife, Susanne Eliza Gee, for eternity. Beyond Susanne's name, little is known of this marriage, but, according to the traditions, Susanne had a child by Windsor, Charles W. Lyon. Despite the fact that Windsor was now sealed to another woman for eternity and that Sylvia was sealed to Joseph Smith for eternity and to Heber Kimball for time, she and Windsor continued to live together as husband and wife, which is actually typical of the complex interweavings of marital ties in much of Nauvoo polygamy. A civil marriage (with sexuality and children), a time and eternity marriage to Smith (which had included sexuality and children), and a proxy marriage to Smith that included a sealing for time to Kimball all had Sylvia as a focal point.

## XII. "I Feel So Bad I Can Not Shed Tears"

Patty's classic overland diary begins on February 10: "My things are now packed ready for the West have been and put Richard Binds wife to bed with a daughter in the afternoon put Sister Hariet Young to bed with a son." She was now fifty-one; the casual references to midwiving are typical of her diary. On the 12th she left Nauvoo: "Crossed the river about noon Mr. Sessions and I with manny other Brethren I nit almost a mittin for Mr Sessions while he went back to get some things we left." They camped on the west bank of the Mississippi and on March 16 received visits from Zina Young and Eliza Snow. Perrigrine, Sylvia and Windsor, and David Jr. stayed behind to fit out their own wagons.

Three days later Patty's company broke camp, starting the long hegira that would eventually take them to Utah. Her diary records in detail the muddy, rainy, freezing trek across Iowa. She continued to tend the sick and deliver babies along the way. Despite her toughness, the late winter journey came as a bitter shock. On April 12 she wrote,

Two months to day since I left my home I have been in the cold in the snow and rain without a tent but now we are blockaded with mud and no feed for teams but bows [boughs] I never have felt so bad as now but I am not discouraged yet ... I in the waggon alone have prayed and wept before the Lord in behalf of this people and my children praying God to spare our lives untill we all shall meet again, my health is poor my mind weighed down but my trust is in God.

In late May it was still raining. She wrote, on the 25th, "Rain this morning again Br Kimball came to the wagon said I must not feel bad I was crying when he came I could hardly tell for what for I had many things to hurt my feelings I told him some things he said all would be right, not to give way to my feelings." Eliza Snow and Hannah Markham then visited: "It gave me joy for I had cryed the most of the day."

One of Patty's chief heartaches was her suspicion that Sylvia and David Jr. would stay in the East. On May 30, while at Mt. Pisgah, she received devastating news: Sylvia, Windsor, and David Jr. would not come until the following year. "I feel as though this was a trick of the Devil," she wrote, "shure my feelings I cannot describe as I fear they will never come my heart is full but I feel so bad I cannot shed tears." The next day she did weep: "When I think that Sylvia and David and Josephine is not coming tears fall from my eyes as fast as drops of rain from the skies." Patty was upset the rest of her journey to Winter Quarters. That David Jr. stayed with Sylvia is another example of the close bond between them.

Patty and David reached Council Bluffs on June 13 and a week later Rosilla, with Perrigrine and his family, joined them. Perrigrine wrote, "Here I found Father & Mother and the maine camp of a Bout twelve hundred wagons they had stoped to build a boate to cross the river with." On the 24th Patty received a letter from Sylvia informing her that she and Windsor were moving to Iowa, where Windsor's brother, Ethiel, lived.

Tensions resulting from Rosilla's arrival quickly began to surface. On July 31 Patty wrote, "I have seen many a lonsome hours this week Mr Sessions has found some fault with me." Conflicts with her husband, probably ignited by friction with the second wife, would cloud her trip west. As was typical of many "first wives," she probably felt abandoned and betrayed when David spent time away from her with a younger, more attractive wife.

On the way to the Winter Quarters, about August 7, Perrigrine wrote, "Mother was taken sick with a fever and when we got to the camp we did not expect her Mother to live from [one] day to another." Patty herself wrote, "I did not have my clothes on for 20 days I vomited 4 days and nights all the time." Brigham and Heber blessed her, and "Brigham said they must all hold onto me as long as I breathed and 15 minutes after I had done breathing." She fought her way back from the brink of death. As she convalesced, she was cheered when "friends from almost every part of the camp [came] to visit me and set up with me."

By September 6 Patty was well enough to be up and active again, but a severe depression would not leave her. "I have much sorrow of heart," she wrote. The next day her husband was "more kind" to her, but the following day's entry reveals her central problem:

> I feel bad again  he has been and talked with Rosilla and she filed [filled] his ears full and when he came to my bed I was quite chiled [chilled] he was gone so long and I was so cold I had been crying  he began to talk hard to me before he got into bed and thretens me very hard of leaving me  Oh may the Lord open his eyes and show him where he is deceived by lisening to her false tales ... It rains  Rosilla went away told nobody where she was going.

Thus we have strife between the first wife and the younger, immature plural wife, and the husband trying to mediate between the two and blaming the first wife. Patty feels rejected, while Rosilla seems petulant and unpredictable, perhaps resentful of the first wife's authority.

The younger wife returned two days later, and conflicts resumed. On September 21 Patty wrote, "I still feel bad  Rosilla wants to cook by herself  I will not let her when she can eat with the rest of us and is well." On the following day: "She will not eat with us nor receive any council from him to do right." David tried to talk with his younger wife, as he had many times before, but to no effect. She refused to take advice from Patty, to come into the family tent or eat with the family. On October 3 David "abused" both women verbally, which hurt Patty especially because she felt she was criticized because of Rosilla's lies. The next day she wrote, simply, "I feel bad  I am in trouble." As a result of sharing her husband with another woman, Patty had lost her basic sense of marital security. On the 5th Rosilla again refused to enter the tent or help with her share of the work.

Later that month Rosilla provoked Perrigrine to violent language: "Rosilla came back  I went and tried to talk with her but she was very abusive to me until PG [Perrigrine] told her to hold her tounge or he would roll the waggon away with her in it." The next day Patty, David, and Rosilla again tried to work out their problems: "She was very willful but obstinate  he told her to come into the tent and if she did right she would be used well. I told her it was a big cud for me to swallow to let her come in after she had abused me so shamefuly." David admitted that he and Rosilla had "abused" Patty more that she had them, and felt sorry for it: "And if I would forgive him and let her come in, he would do it no more and would sleep with me when I was at home and use me well ...

I said if she came in I should be boss over the work and then she must be carefull how she twited and flung at me ... we left her and went to bed." Patty, older than Rosilla, and, after all, the first wife, demanded the respect due her. In the closing days of October, Rosilla did some sewing but would not help cook.

In early November tensions in the family flared once again. One evening Patty, because of her midwiving and nursing, had slept only two hours, then had to cut and salt a beef, but Rosilla refused to help. "I have to work all the time and notwithstanding all he has said to her about helping me she never has to favour me in the least but before supper [she] gave me the lie many times and talked very saucy to me and when I could bear it no longer I told her to hold her toungue and if she gave me the lie again I would throug [throw] the tongs at her." The next day Patty continued, "She came into the tent but will not work I cook she [eats] I put James M Flakes wife to bed." Patty often would stay up all night with a childbirth, and had just recovered from a serious illness, so probably felt that she deserved some extra household help.

As David continued to spend time with Rosilla, despite her rebelliousness, events moved toward a crisis, endangering Patty's marriage: "He has lain with her three nights she has told him many falsehoods and is trying to have him take her to Nauvoo and then to Maine and leave me for good ... I go to bed know not what to do." The next day Rosilla was again "saucy" and unwilling to work. When she refused to help wash dishes on November 6, Perrigrine stood up for his mother: "PG said he had seen me abused long enough and she had caused it she gave him the lie ... he had seen me cook and she set and do nothing and then come to the table and croud me away." Rosilla left the tent. Three days later David asked Patty to collect provisions for Rosilla to live somewhere else. She agreed but thought it was unjust for her, "as old as I was to have to maintain her without work he was mad turned his back said he could do it himself."

Rosilla apparently now moved back across the Missouri River. On November 28 she "came back here sais [says] she is going back to Missisipi river she left word for Mr Sessions to come over see her." The next day "He went over at night and stad [stayed] with her." Every minute her husband spent with Rosilla must have caused Patty worry and misery, as she knew the young wife wanted David to leave with her. When he returned on the 30th he would not speak to Patty, but Rosilla had departed for Nauvoo. The crisis was over. Patty's traumatic months with practical polygamy had ended.

Her life at Winter Quarters stabilized to a normal routine of work, midwiving, and "blessing meetings" with Eliza Snow and friends. Patty was a major character in these remarkable charismatic moments in Mormon history. On January 1, 1847, she wrote, "I had a new years party Eliza R. Snow Loisa Beman, Zina Jacobs, &c were here enjoyed myself well opened and read the sixtyeth chapter of Isiah." On her fifty-second birthday, February 4, she "had a good time singing praying speaking in toungues before we broke up." After the party Patty visited two women on medical calls, one of whom had a baby.

Toward the end of February Perrigrine left on a short mission to Missouri and Illinois and Patty sent a message to Sylvia and David requesting them to travel back with him for a visit. When Perrigrine arrived in Iowa City, he found them ready to start. Their journey three hundred miles through "the uper part of the state of Ioway" was difficult, as it was the rainy season again and in many places they had to stop and build bridges across swollen streams and rivers. But on April 21 they reached Winter Quarters. Patty wrote, "I was almost overcome with joy and gratitude to God for our preservation to see each other again." Sylvia was undoubtedly overjoyed also, and was able to attend many blessing meetings with Patty during her visit, but she and David could stay only two weeks. On May 9 Patty and her daughter parted once again. Sylvia was armed with a gift from Eliza Snow, "A poem to Mrs. Lyon": "Go thou loved one—God is with you/ He will be your stay and shield." Perrigrine wrote, "This seamed to bee all most our last look at them in this world."

As the day of departure for the West approached, the blessing meetings increased in frequency. On May 29 Patty was the recipient of a prophetic blessing bestowed by other women:

> Sisters [Mary Ann Angell] Young and [Elizabeth Ann] Whitney laid their hands upon my head and predicted many things that I should be blesed with that I should live to stand in a temple yet to be built and Joseph would be there I should see him and there I should officiate for my labours should then be done in order and they should be great and I should be blesed and by many and there I should bless many and many should be brought unto me saying your hands were the first that handled me bless me and after I had blesed them their mothers would rise up and bless me for they would be brought to me by Joseph himself for he loved litle children and he would bring my litle ones to me &c &c my heart was fild with joy and rejoicing.

Patty was voice in a blessing on June 1: "I blesed Sister Christeen [Golden Kimball] by laying my hands upon her head and the Lord spoke through me to her great and marvellous things." Patty then blessed Vilate Kimball: "I ... layed my hands upon her head although it was a great cross and the power of God came upon me I spoke great and marvelous things to her she was filed [filled] to the overflowing she arose and blesed the Lord and caled down a blessing upon us and all that pertained to her Sister Hess fell on her knees and claimed a blessing at my hands I then blesed her ... the power of God was poured out upon us ER Snow was there and many others thank the Lord." These meetings, so movingly recorded in Patty's journal, are one of the high points of Mormon spirituality. There were blessing meetings on June 3 and 4 also, and the following day Patty and David left Winter Quarters.

### XIII. "I Have Drove My Wagon All the Way"

Patty's overland chronicle gives a vivid account of the challenges faced by the Mormon pioneers. River crossings were always difficult. On June 9, as the Sessionses moved their wagons over the Platte on a raft, one of the wagon's wheels slipped into the water: "We had to unload every thing then draw the waggon out then load up again and drive up the bank." Luckily, "all [was] safe nothing broke or wet or lost of 26 hundred weight." Again, on August 19, during a river crossing, Perrigrine's wagon turned over with his son Carlos in it: "Carlos not hurt although he was under water all but his face and sacks of grain and trunks atop of him." Perrigrine quickly cut the canvas cover, found Carlos, and dragged him out from under the overturned wagon. It had to be righted and repacked before they could cross the river.

Dealing with precious livestock was worrisome, as they were continually wandering off and had to be tracked. A spooked herd was chaotic and destructive. On July 13 Patty described a herd that escaped its yard and "broke waggons killed a cow broke of[f] several horns one horses leg and they have got to stop and repair waggons."

A vignette from daily life on August 7 shows men's and women's roles: "The men set waggon tires women wash we bake pies hull corn." Although driving a team was considered a man's job, Patty acted as teamster on the trip west. "I have a lameness through my chest caused by driving my team," she wrote on June 7. She did not miss any of the standard novelties that intrigued so many overland travellers. On July 7 she noted "a great many of these little dogs that hid in the ground in holes." Ten days later she saw "many thousands of buffaloe." The next day she baked mince pies and meat over buffalo chips. On July 23 she wrote, "The Indians have come in sight ... Many Squaws came today they appear friendly they sing dance and ride around we dance and have music fire two cannons Parley [Pratt] and [John] Taylor feast and smoke with the Cheif." A few days later she killed a rattlesnake close to her wagon, but waste not, want not, saved its "gall and greace." The next day she noted building-like bluffs: "Very curious looking place the bluffs look like ancient edifices."

This communal, religious migration included peaceful interludes and moments of heated conflict that had to be resolved ecclesiastically. "Lay still & rest warm and pleasant to day we hull corn. Sister Tomson and I went down on the river bank had prayers alone," Patty wrote on September 8. Yet nine days later her company "had a meeting to setle a quarel cut 3 off from the church."

Gradually the company's way led upward into the Rockies. On August 31 they "Had up hill and rocky roads the worst we have found." As she approached the valley on September 19, "The mountains here are very high on each side some small pines on the north side of us." The next day "Red majestic rocks on right all the way PG caught two trout." Finally, on September 24, Patty and her family reached their destination: "Got into the valley it is a beautiful place my heart flows with gratitude to God that we have got home all safe lost nothing have been blesed with life and health I rejoice all the time." The next day she wrote proudly, "I have drove my waggon all the way but part of the two last {nites} ... I broke nothing nor turned over." Patty, the New England farm wife, had been transformed into a woman of the frontier.

In about a month Perrigrine and David Sessions completed a two-room log house in the "Old Fort" and the two families moved in together, as they had lived for many years. As David and Perrigrine farmed and tended stock, Patty continued to deliver babies, jerk meat, quilt, make clothing, work tallow, make soap, and, undoubtedly, cook breakfast, lunch, and dinner for her husband. She began attending the Sixteenth Ward, her home ward for the next twenty-four years.

She started up the blessing meetings again with Eliza Snow and Zina Young as everyone prepared for a long, cold winter. Her November 22 journal entry shows her spiritual prestige: "In the evening prayed for Heber with Elen [Sanders Kimball?] and Mary Elen [Harris Kimball], I anointed Elen acording to Hebers request when he met me on the road." Heber Kimball was the second most authoritative man in the Mormon hierarchy, de facto first counselor to the acting church president—yet he asked Patty to perform an ordinance for his wife.

## XIV. "Six Hundred Miles of Snow"

Back in Nauvoo, in May 1846, Windsor and Sylvia had begun selling their Nauvoo lots, and later in the year Windsor and his brother, Ethiel, bought the Iowa City Manufacturing Company (a project to erect a dam on the Iowa River). On September 4, 1847, Sylvia's next child, Byron Windsor Lyon, was born in Iowa City.

Windsor became involved in politics and was selected as a Whig delegate to Council Bluffs in January 1848, but had contracted tuberculosis so could not go. With other "leading Whigs" he signed a letter of recommendation for Rev. Sidney Rogers to act as delegate. On March 27 Rogers met with Brigham Young and other Mormons at Winter Quarters in the "Log Tabernacle" and reported that "his colleague, Winson P.

Lyons, through feeble health, was unable to be present, but forwarded his papers from St. Louis by Edwin D. Woolley."

Sometime in the spring Windsor gave William Pickett, husband of Agnes Coolbrith Smith Pickett, one hundred dollars to help start a paper in Pottawattamie County. On August 8 another child, David Carlos Lyon, was born in Iowa City. Josephine was now four, Byron nearly one. But Windsor himself was wasting away, and in mid-January 1849 he died of "consumption" (tuberculosis) at Iowa City. According to family traditions, his plural wife, Susanne, moved to Utah with her child and remarried.

Sylvia's complex marital bondings might have simplified after Windsor's death, as she was now free to go to Utah and live in Heber Kimball's extensive family. However, as so often, events did not occur in such a straightforward fashion. She did write to her family in Utah and to Kimball. Zina Young's journal shows that Heber received a letter from Sylvia on July 4, 1849: "Br Kimble came in asked me to read a letter from Sister Lions. I red it. Her husband is ded and [she] wishes her br Perigreen to return after her." As one might have predicted, Sylvia appeared to be moving to be close to her Utah husband.

Perrigrine loyally started his journey back to the East just before winter began, on October 15. "This was a hard journey," he wrote, "as I had some six hundread miles of snow before me and the wether cold wether all the way to the State of Ioway." But now one of the tragicomic reverses in Mormon history took place. He arrived in Iowa City on January 1, 1850, and found Sylvia and David "well and glad to see me." But after the joyful reunion, Perrigrine received surprising news: "Yet the Object of my journey looked dark to acomplish & in a short time after I arived I found that my Sister was on the back ground and it was doubtful if she left [would leave] for the Valley at length she told me that I must not feal bad for she was agoing to get maried that night." While Perrigrine was traveling east from Utah, Sylvia had become engaged to a non-Mormon.

Her new husband was Ezekiel Clark, a mill owner, banker, politician, and widower with three children, ages eight, six, and four. Perrigrine's reaction to this turn of events was not mild: "This was as hard a trial as I ever met with to think that I had traveled thirteen hundred miles after her and then I was disipointed." He also would not have been happy that Sylvia was marrying a non-Mormon; nevertheless, he probably gave away the bride. Sylvia was thirty-one, Ezekiel thirty-three. He was her fourth husband, even though her third was still living.

But Perrigrine's journey east was not entirely wasted, since he persuaded David Jr. to return to Utah with him. The two brothers departed for the West on April 11, arriving in Salt Lake City on June 26. Patty had been devastated when she had found out by letter that Sylvia was not coming, but she would have been happy to see her two sons again. Meanwhile, on April 21, David Carlos Lyon died at age one and a half—Sylvia's Lyon children were not long-lived. The death was followed by new life, for her first Clark child, Perry Ezekiel, was born on February 4, 1851, and happily lived to adulthood. But later in the year, on December 13, Byron Windsor Lyon died at age three. This left Sylvia with only Josephine and the new baby. Of her five children by Windsor Lyon, she had lost all.

## XV. Early Utah Midwifery

In Utah Patty and her family engaged in the pioneer struggle for survival. She continued midwifing and doctoring. When Willard Richards, a "Thomsonian" (herbal) doctor, founded the Council of Health in 1848, Patty was a charter member. In her diaries for the Utah period, we have much information on her midwifing. When the deliveries were routine, she merely noted that the mother had been "put to bed" with a boy or girl. However, sometimes she arrived too late, as on February 18, 1848: "In the night I was caled to Sister Alens she was dead and her babe [also]." When deliveries had complications, doctors were called for. A Susan Snow was "a criple and deformed so that her child could not be born with out instruments." Doctors were able to save the child, but Susan died. "Although I have practised midwifery for 37 years and put thousands to bed I never saw a woman die in that situation before," wrote Patty.

In 1853 there was an even more problematic birth—a Sister Rhodes had an incomplete delivery. "The childs arm was born before I was sent for and her pains had left her We all staid all night," Patty wrote. The patient refused to let "Dr. Vaughn" assist, as he had "butchered" her once before. Patty prescribed lobelia, the Thomsonian cure-all emetic, but two days later there was no significant change in Rhodes's condition. "The childs arm still in the birth place could not be put back." When Rhodes began to experience excruciating pains, elders and a doctor were sent for but arrived too late. Both mother and child died. "The child was taken out she [was] sowed up again the child laid in her arms." Brigham Young preached the funeral sermon and emphasized that no one should be blamed for the painful death.

Patty often took in boarders to earn extra money and was paid particularly well by "forty-niners" passing through Utah on their way to California. On August 7, 1849, she wrote, "A number to supper ... they all go away bound for the gold mines they gave me as good as 30 dollars for waiting on them." However, there were certain risks involved in keeping an informal hotel: "Dixon staid here last night," she wrote on January

21, 1853. "Left live vermin in the bed but did not so much as thank us for his loging supper and breakfast I do not know but he left lice enough to pay me for my trouble had they all been coppers and cents for there was two kinds of them."

On January 5, 1849, Patty wrote, "I feel bad," and repeated this complaint for three days in succession without explanation. From other sources, we learn that her husband was disfellowshipped at this time for an unexplained "breach of covenant." However, a week later he "acknowledged his error and was restored to fellowship."

### XVI. "I Feel I Shall Fail Through Sorrow"

On December 1 Patty received a stunning shock: "I feel bad Mr Sessions has told me his plans and contracts that he has made with Hariet also what Brigham said about it ... Mr. Sessions rather cold towards me." David had arranged to take another plural wife, Harriet, perhaps at Young's suggestion. The following day Patty lamented that "Mr Sessions denies me a small favor I feel very bad." And the next, "I slept but litle last night I got up and read to pass away time snows all day." On December 4 "Mr Sessions comes down [from the Sessions farm in Bountiful] brings Adline B and Martha I feel very bad." Once again Patty would find the transition from monogamy to polygamy painful, causing her great anxiety and feelings of insecurity.

The next day she wrote, "~~He is cross to me says many hard things to me.~~" The following day "He went back caried Adline left me crying I feel very bad see that I must live alone I commence family prayer." Again the feeling of abandonment is typical of many first wives' emotional adjustment to polygamy. Perhaps Patty tried to dissuade David from this marriage. In any event the tension between them continued. On December 28 and 29 she wrote, "Mr. Sessions ... said things to me that make me feel bad ... I slept but litle ... I wish to do right but I fear I shall fail through sorrow Oh Lord give me thy spirit to guide me safe in the right way." On the last day of the year there was a ray of hope: "Mr Sessions came home I was glad. He is {kind}."

Nevertheless, David married Harriet Teeples Wixom, a nineteen-year-old divorcee with one child, on January 13, 1850. Patty was almost fifty-five, David nearly sixty. The next day Patty wrote, "He takes her to the farm with him leaves me here alone I feel as well as I can." And the next day, "It snows and is cold I am all alone feel very lone some." Nevertheless, Harriet was no Rosilla, so there were no major conflicts in this sister-wife relationship. David came down from the farm for brief stays at Patty's home, and she sometimes tended Harriet's child. Still, not having a husband nearby was often a practical inconvenience. After a bad storm on January 25, when "The hay [was] all under snow 3 feet deep," Patty wrote: "I have shoveled snow 2 hours before I could feed the cow and mare, then I shoveled out the wood I am tired out it has thawed to day." The polygamous experience for women was often defined by the husband's absence.

Patty received another blow the last day of July when David suffered a "Paralitick Strock" (stroke), in Perrigrine's words. He was brought to Patty's house in the city where his condition gradually worsened, with brief improvements and relapses. "We think it is the numb palsey that he has," wrote Patty on August 5, "as he has no use of his lower limbs and is almost senceless." On the 9th "PG and Mary ... came down [David Sessions, Sr.] did not know PG when he came nor Mary or David [Jr.] [but he] knew me just before and kissed me." David did not speak again, lost the use of his hands on August 10, and the next day at "ten oclock he died very easy."

After his burial, Patty wrote, "I now feel my loss but do not mourn as one that has no hope for I do feel that my loss is his gain yet I cannot help weeping and feeling bad PG and family went home David staid with me." On August 13, after David Jr. returned to the farm, she wrote, "Oh how lonesome I am." Despite the fact that Patty and David had both shared their marriage with other spouses, she missed him terribly.

## XVII. "Someone to Cut My Wood for Me"

Perrigrine wrote of the aftermath of his father's death, "This left Mother alone I helped mother to build her a house in the City and fence her City lot and set out some fruit trees." Patty moved into this residence at Fourth West and North Temple on December 3, 1850. In early May 1851 she wrote, "Rained all day and night again the house leaked I have to go to bed to keep warm as I have no wood cut and I can not cut it I am so unwell." But on June 29 a new male friend appeared in her journals, a Brother Parry. On September 6 she made him a flannel shirt, and on November 12 he and she jointly administered to her niece. Later in the month, on November 25, Patty wrote, "Br P[arry] saw Brigham last Mond." Visits to Brother Brigham often presaged marriages, and on December 14 she recorded, "I was married to John Parry and I feel to thank the Lord that I have some one to cut my wood for me." She was not one to forget the practical aspects of marriage. Parry, a native of Wales who was six years older than Patty, is remembered as the first conductor of the Tabernacle Choir. A widower, he had adult children in Wales, England, and Utah.

Soon after this union, David Sessions, Jr., married Phebe Foss on December 30, 1852. Perrigrine had by this time married four of his eventual seven wives and was beginning to have a numerous posterity. Through him alone, Patty would have fifty-five grandchildren.

For two years she seemed content with her new marriage. John helped around the house and was involved in public activities. But once again her domestic peace would be disturbed by "the principle." On March 28, 1854, she wrote, "Mr Parry saw Brigham." A marriage was in the offing. Patty heard about it only after the interview and felt betrayed: "[He] told me what he said I felt bad that he did not tell me before Oh Lord help me to do right he is to have a woman sealed to him next Sunday and this is the first I knew about [it] and he has known it a long time but denied it to me." Though technically Mormon polygamists were supposed to have the permission of previous wives before marrying again, this rule was often ignored. On April 2 John, sixty-five, was sealed to Harriet Parry (her maiden name was Parry), thirty-one; after the ceremony "his children came home with us took supper," wrote Patty.

Three days later the uncomfortable adjustments to a new wife began. Patty wrote, "She is here still he has not said one word to me about her staying here but she told me she was [going to stay with me] according to what he said to her it was his intent she has gone to work, appears very kind to me she was a stranger to me." Soon, however, she moved out: "Harriet carried her clothes away while I was gone ... the cause of her leaving I do not know." John divided his time between Patty and Harriet from this time on, but apparently lived mainly with Harriet, only visiting Patty occasionally.

On June 10 a group of local women organized to help clothe needy Indians, and Patty was elected president. These "Indian Relief Societies" were an important step toward restoring the (lapsed) Nauvoo Relief Society.

## XVIII. "We Wept for Joy"

Back in Iowa, Sylvia and Ezekiel continued to have children that happily survived infancy. Phebe Jane was born on September 1, 1852, and Martha Sylvia, Sylvia's last child, on January 20, 1854. At Martha's birth, Josephine was nearly ten, Perry nearly three, and Phebe one and a half. However, despite the children, later family traditions report that Sylvia eventually "realized that he [Clark] was very intolerant of her religion and resentful of the fact that she was sealed to the Prophet," and their marriage began to show signs of strain. Perhaps their religious differences were too great, or perhaps Sylvia missed her mother and brothers and fellow Mormons too much. Finally, in April 1854, when Perrigrine passed through Iowa City while returning from a mission to the East, Sylvia joined him, though she left with Clark's full consent and help. On April 17 Perrigrine wrote, "Began to prepare to go home with my sister and her family. Mr. Clark bought too [two] horses and some other things for our outfit." He also bought the carriage and wagon for Sylvia. He apparently expected that Sylvia and the children would return within the year.

The company started on May 3. Perrigrine described the group: "My sister and four children and a man by the name of Richard Jones, he drove the oxen team which consisted of six oxen and two cows and the team that I drove was two horses." Perrigrine was finally taking Sylvia to Utah. With his extensive experience crossing the plains, soon a company, many of them non-Mormons, coalesced around him. On August 2 they reached northern Utah and the long-delayed reunion between Sylvia and Patty took place. The latter wrote, "Went on crossed webber [Weber] river went to the mouth of Echo canyon there we met them and a happy meeting it was my son had been gone almost two years and [had] been very sick the most of the time and I had not seen my daughter for over seven years we wept for joy and rejoiced exceedingly we then came crosed the river & camped."

On August 7 Patty wrote, "Sylvia went to see Heber," and she was reportedly accepted back into the Kimball family but apparently never lived in one of his homes. Instead, she settled near Perrigrine in Bountiful (north of Salt Lake Valley). With the substantial funds Ezekiel had given her, she bought a farm there on which she built a sizeable house. She also had a lot in Salt Lake City. Whatever Ezekiel had understood, Sylvia immediately put down roots in Utah. According to family traditions, when Clark understood this, he traveled to Utah in 1855 to persuade her to return to him—though he did not succeed. It must have been difficult for Ezekiel to leave his wife and three children in the far west. But Sylvia agreed that when Perry was eight she would send him to Iowa City to be educated.

Sylvia's frequent visits to her mother in Salt Lake City are carefully noted in Patty's journal. Sometimes she visited Perrigrine, Sylvia, and David in Bountiful. In late January 1856 Sylvia made a typical visit to the city: "Sylvia came here staid all night Satd 26 I am quite well she and I went up to Heber C. Kimbals then to Pres Youngs then came home in the evening we went to A W Babbitts she had business with him." It is odd to see a wife (Sylvia) paying a social call on her husband in this way, but in Mormon polygamy husbands can often seem to be merely friends. In visiting the Kimball and Young households, Patty and Sylvia would be able to visit most of Joseph Smith's plural wives. As in Nauvoo Sylvia sometimes seemed to act as Heber's spokeswoman: "Sylvia told what Heber told her to tell me," wrote Patty on November 21, 1857. But Sylvia continued to live on her large, successful farm, financed by Clark and run by a Mr. Williams.

In 1859 Sylvia sent Perry east to live with his father, as she had promised. He was reportedly given an excellent European education, then worked in his father's bank. Ezekiel remarried in 1861 and had five children by his third wife, but he continued to be interested in his two Utah daughters and gave them large dowries at their marriages.

### XIX. "I Am Alone the Most of My Time"

Patty's relationship with John Parry was never entirely satisfactory. Since he apparently did not provide for her adequately, it was fortunate that she was self-supporting with her midwiving, her garden produce, and her general industriousness. On April 30, 1857, she noted ruefully: "Mr Parry has brought me ten and a half pounds flour and one pound of butter the first he has brought me of his earnings for about to [two] year." He apparently could not support Harriet, either, so on February 9, 1856, he approached Patty for help in providing for his second wife. "Mr Parry told me that Hariet had but little beside cornbread to eat." Though Patty told him he could take Harriet some food, she suggested that Harriet come live with her to cut down on costs. "He made me no reply." Here we see another characteristic of polygamy: the men often were willing to add plural wives to their families, but after the marriage took place found they were unable to support the multiple families adequately, and the wives often had to depend on siblings and teenage sons. To be fair to the husbands, they were frequently instructed or even pressured by priesthood leaders to marry polygamously. Nevertheless, many of the wives left their husbands and others stayed as wives only out of a sense of religious duty, enduring emotional and financial neglect and struggle. Many did not file divorce papers and were wives in name only. But they were not free to remarry unless they divorced.

A journal entry from 1857 shows Parry's absence from Patty's life, and how hard she was forced to work on her own: "Finish[ed] harvesting and gathering all my peaches and all my vegetables  got all my manure out and much of my lot spaded  Mr Parry has not been here any days and only three times in the evenings for two weeks and I have been very unwell just able to attend to oversee my business." She wrote, on November 28, 1858, "I am alone the most of my time but my meditation is sweet and I feel to thank the Lord all the time." Sometimes when Parry did visit he brought Harriet with him. On September 23, 1857, Patty delivered a child to Harriet—an act of Christian charity on Patty's part—and she continued to midwife Harriet's children in later years.

Meanwhile, David Sessions's widow Harriet Teeples had married a Nathaniel P. Worden, and when the family moved from Salt Lake to Provo on February 2, 1859, Patty, now sixty-four, wrote matter-of-factly: "They gave me Alzinia the oldest daughter to raise as my own." Despite the difficulty of transplanting a child in this way—Alzinia was five years old and must have missed her parents—Patty took her in, and motherly entries appear in her diary as she tended to Alzinia when she was sick and made her clothing. Though the little girl would relieve Patty of her solitude for a time, the relationship would not last. Alzina ran away to Sylvia's house on April 19, 1861, and two days later she "came home very humble ... she promised very fair she would be a good girl if I would let her stay with me." For unexplained reasons the relationship continued to deteriorate, and on October 9 Alzina moved back with her parents.

Patty wrote on September 28, 1863, "Bought a cow of Mr Parry." The marriage had clearly become distant, at least by the standards of a modern monogamous marriage. Often, when Patty was sick, Parry would administer to her. Occasionally he was ill, and on one occasion, December 8, 1866, Patty administered to him: "Mr Parry was very sick last night in the night he sent for me thought he would not live [into] morning. I went he wished me to lay hands on him I anointed him Harriet and I laid hands on him he was healed instantly." Patty's diary pauses on December 31. Thereafter the main source for her life is a reminiscence written in 1884. The diary then begins again.

Despite less than ideal conditions in her third marriage, Patty was not traumatically unhappy with John and Harriet, as she had been with David and Rosilla. Parry died on January 13, 1868, and Patty's reminiscence reflects authentic grief: "Mr Parry died he has been sick over a year Suffered more than tounge can tell. in all his sickness he was patient more so than any person I ever saw. I never heard a murmur from his lips. Died without a strugle or a groan A good man A kind husband a tender Father and a good Latter day Saint."

## XX. Widow

Now fully a widow, Patty continued her midwiving, nursing, fruit business, and spent time with her numerous descendants. Like every faithful Mormon woman, she participated in the renewed Relief Society. On June 22 she was appointed "appriser of the propperty put into that society" in her local chapter. She also, like every faithful Mormon woman, spent many hours performing temple ordinances. Most importantly, on July 3, 1867, she received her fullness of priesthood ordinance; as this requires a couple, Joseph F. Smith stood proxy for Joseph Smith, Jr. She received her proxy sealing to Joseph Smith, Jr., the same day.

Unlike many of Smith's widows, Patty was quite well-to-do in her later years. She enjoyed listing her tithing payments and charitable contributions in her diary; on March 24, 1862, she even loaned Brigham Young $175 in gold. She built barns and granaries, additions to her house, and new houses. In May 1870 she and Perrigrine visited "the States," including Maine, and she was careful to mention the price of the trip: "This Journey cost me over 500.00 dollars but I do not regret going  I have seen my friends and Bore a faithful testimony to them wherever I went of the truth of the Latter day work caled Mormonism." She was not sick one day, she wrote, and at no time touched even a drop of tea or coffee.

## XXI. Bountiful

At some point Sylvia moved to a large house near Bountiful's main thoroughfare at the present 5th West and there operated her home as a hotel. According to a family history, "At one time Sylvia's was the only place where a visitor might obtain food and lodging. This kept everyone busy, especially Josephine, the oldest." Sylvia's children were growing up and Patty's journal noted their visits. On March 1, 1863, Patty wrote, "Br Williams and Sylvia came down and brought Josephine here to board and go to school this quarter." Sylvia was also active in her local Relief Society, at one time serving as first counselor to the president, and donated generously to the cause, just as she had in Nauvoo.

Sylvia's daughters soon married. On August 15, 1863, Josephine, nineteen, celebrated her nuptials with a young Pony Express rider, John Fisher, in Bountiful. A year later, on August 31, Sylvia became a grandmother when Irvin Frederick and Ivan John, twins, were born to Josephine and John. In 1878 John married a plural wife named, ironically enough, Harriet Knighton, so Sylvia would see her eldest daughter become a plural wife and endure the legal persecutions of the final years of polygamy. On January 30, 1870, Martha Clark was joined to Adelbert Lewis Burnham, and the next day Phebe Clark married John Henry Ellis.

Patty sold her Salt Lake home on December 4, 1872, when she was seventy-seven, and moved to Bountiful, closer to Sylvia and Perrigrine and David. She had bought two lots there in 1864. Her memoir stated with satisfaction, "I left the SL City and moved to Bountiful where I am having a house built  I move my things into it but it is not finished  my house is finished cost me three thousand five hundred dollars 3500 and all paid for I owe no one any thing."

She began her journal again on July 4, 1880: "We went to meeting." July 6 reveals the unselfish texture of Patty's life when she was eighty-seven, attending Relief Society, paying church tithes, and buying fabric for a friend: "I went to the RS [Relief Socicty] and to the store got some calico for Betsey  a dress  caried some tithing peas and fast donations." She made quilts and rugs, went to meetings often, and visited Salt Lake City occasionally by means of "the cars" (train). Utah was no longer a wilderness. On August 1, she confided: "I take 3 papers, Deseret News, Juvenille Instructo[r], & Womans Exponent. I read them all." On August 24 this brief window into the octogenarian ended: "Tuesd 24 got ready to go to cash valley we went Wend."

## XXII. "The Deceased Was Noted for Her Liberality"

Emmeline Wells wrote to Mary Lightner on April 7, 1882, "Sister Sylvia Lyon Clark is very dangerously ill at her house in Bountiful with dropsy." Five days later, on April 13, Sylvia died at the age of sixty-three. But before her death, as we have seen, she told Josephine Fisher that she, Josephine, was the daughter of Joseph Smith. The funeral in the Bountiful tabernacle was attended by five hundred people, according to her obituary. Joseph Bates Noble, that grand old man of Nauvoo polygamy, spoke, along with Apostle John Henry Smith. There "The deceased was noted for her liberality, and integrity to the truth."

## XXIII. "I Have Done a Good Deal of Many Things"

Patty, seemingly indestructible, continued on. On December 15, 1883, when she was eighty-eight, the Patty Sessions Academy was dedicated in Bountiful, and she gave a speech reported in the *Deseret Evening News:* "She stated that she had been inspired to put some of her money into a free school, for the education of her posterity and others whose parents were unable to pay for their schooling." Her generosity stayed with her to the end. "She then made a few remarks on the Word of Wisdom and the blessings which attended those who kept it, and stated that when herself and her family came into the Valley, all the money she had was 5 cents, and now she had $16,000 invested in Z.C.M.I. at Salt Lake City." She was never one to hide her financial successes.

On April 1, 1884, the diary began again with a record of a social gathering: "I went to Mary Scots Birthday Party ... we had a good time enjoyed ourselves well." Nearly ninety, Patty pursued her favorite activities with a will, despite her failing powers. She continued to visit the sick, anointing and blessing her sisters in the church. Her orchard business continued and at harvest time there were marathon sessions of fruit drying. She loaned her descendants money, contributed liberally to church causes, and gave her grandchildren jobs on her farm. She constantly knitted, sewed, and made rugs, and often spent whole days reading, devouring church magazines. News of her descendants and visits exchanged with them fill the diary.

On May 16 she and Perrigrine attended the dedication of the Logan temple, a building to which she had contributed a significant sum of money. Soon afterwards they returned to Logan to perform temple work for their ancestors. On May 15, 1885, she received a visit from Eliza R. Snow, a happy reunion of Winter Quarters veterans.

The close relationship between Patty and her oldest son continued to the end. He was now aging himself, and Patty often tended him during his frequent illnesses. He also treated her on occasion—on September 21, 1885, he pulled three of her teeth! She wrote, on November 28, 1886, that Perrigrine, sick, stayed "up chamber all the time we keep a fire there all the time and I stay there the most of the time & work on my rugs & knit & keep him company." When healthy, he and David took her on carriage rides and accompanied her to the city to collect her bank dividends.

The diaries allow us to track the gradual loss of Patty's enormous vitality, her courageous fight against the inevitable. After receiving a letter from a nephew on March 20, 1885, the ninety-year-old woman wrote, "I want to answer it but my hand trembles so I cannot write. I get PG to answer it." She missed church meetings more often and in March 1887 complained that she could not hear when she went. In May she confessed that she could not sew the lining on a rug because "my hands are so old & lame." She wrote, on June 26, "I dont go to meeting I cannot hear but litle I am so deaf & I am so feeble I can hardly walk there & I stay at home." But she never stopped working, knitting, reading, visiting the sick. On October 26 she wrote, "I have done a good deal of many things." In late 1887 the diary entries become briefer, more formulaic, and days are frequently skipped. On May 4, 1888, she wrote, "I have knit & the most of the time three pair of stockins this week it is now friday the 4th," then laid down her pen, never to write in her diary again.

Her last years are nearly a blank. The only family anecdote from that period shows her doggedly struggling to be active and useful, as relatives kindly encouraged her. She constantly knitted socks, but there were "so many dropped stitches and other errors in the stockings ... that they were unraveled each evening (without her knowledge ...) and the yarn given back to her" the next day.

When she became sick and feeble in 1892, her numerous descendants undoubtedly took turns tending her. Finally, on December 14, she died in Bountiful at 6:30 a.m., at the age of ninety-seven years and ten months. Her obituary reads: "She was ever a true and faithful Latter-day Saint, diligent and persevering, her whole soul, and all she possessed being devoted to the Church and the welfare of mankind. She has gone to her grave ripe in years, loved and respected by all who knew her."

But it is best to leave her with her own words. When eighty-one, she wrote the following to her posterity:

I here say to all my children and my grand children and great grandchildren &c - &c and to all others I have been punctual to my word  I never have given my note to any one  Neither have I had any acounts on or any Books in any Store  I have kept out of debt  Paid my taxes my fasts my donations and my tithing willingly of the best I have. and the Lord has blesed me and Prospered me in all I have done for which I feel very thankful, hoping he will continue to bless me while I live both Spiritually and temporally, with all that shall be for my good and [h]is Glory to give unto me  I am now Almost eighty two years old february next the 4th  I drink no tea nor coffee nor spirutous liquors  I dont smoke nor take snuff nor any poisonous medicine. I use consecrated oil for my complaints. Now I say to you do as I have done and as much better as you can and the Lord will bless you as he has me  Patty Sessions

# 8.

# Miracle Tale

## *Mary Elizabeth Rollins (Lightner Smith Young)*

Soon after a childbirth in 1843, Mary Elizabeth Lightner became sick with "inflammation of the bowels" and almost died, according to her autobiography. Her mother was summoned and brought consecrated oil—"she anointed me, and prayed for me," wrote Mary, who began to convalesce. After lying in bed for two weeks without letting anyone touch or move her (which caused her excruciating pain), she allowed herself to be lifted out of bed, wrapped in quilts, and placed in a rocking chair while her mother changed her bed sheets. As she sat in the chair, a sudden storm broke outside, "and our House was struck by Lightning and all of us badly shocked, the door casing was torn out and Struck Mother on the Shoulder and bruised her terribly. All were sensless for some time."

Mary regained consciousness first, looked around at her household of six, and thought all were dead. She called for her husband, Adam, and, receiving no answer, staggered into the next room to find him entirely rigid. Even throwing a bucket of water on him elicited no response. She sent for a doctor, who wrapped Mary in a quilt and, after some time, managed to revive Adam, who said that the revivification was extremely painful for him and that he would have preferred death. Mary's children and mother all revived. Curiously enough, Mary herself had been entirely cured of her illness. She reports that people came from miles around to see their house, which was torn to pieces.

This is but one of many extraordinary incidents in Mary Elizabeth Lightner's long, varied life. She was another polyandrous wife of Joseph Smith, marrying both Smith and Brigham Young while still cohabiting with her first husband, Adam Lightner. But in contrast to Zina and Presendia Huntington, she never left her "first husband," even though he was a non-Mormon. Curiously, Adam was never antagonistic toward the Latter-day Saint faith and was content to live among Mormons for most of his life, including twenty years in Utah, where he died. Mary, like Presendia Huntington, Louisa Beaman, and Patty and Sylvia Sessions, lost children under tragic circumstances and lived a difficult life. As she grew old in southern Utah, she felt isolated and neglected by the church. Nevertheless, she remained faithful to her religion, retained her reverence for Joseph Smith, and frequently gave public speeches in which she testified that she had been married to him.

Mary left a short autobiography, some sketches and talks, and a number of letters. The autobiography is a remarkable document—moralistic, heroizing, and full of the miraculous. The centerpiece of the story is Joseph Smith as omniscient seer, who makes a prophecy about Mary's life that is fulfilled in all its details. Miracle and prophecy were the neo-biblical psychic environment in which the early Mormons lived.

## I. Shipwreck

Mary Elizabeth was born on April 9, 1818, in Lima, Livingston County, New York, about twenty miles southwest of Palmyra, to twenty-six-year-old John Porter Rollins, a native of New Hampshire, and twenty-two-year-old Keziah Keturah Van Benthuysen, who had been born in New York. Mary had two siblings—an older brother, James Henry, who was born in 1816, and a younger sister, Caroline, born on May 1, 1820.

Her father traded for a living, transporting sheep and cattle across Lake Erie in large boats, then selling them in Canada. Six months after Caroline's birth, in November, he was traveling by boat on Lake Ontario when a storm appeared suddenly and his boat shipwrecked. He was killed along with nearly everyone else on the ship. Mary, two-and-a-half years old, had lost a father.

## II. "His Face Outshone the Candle"

After John Rollins's death, the family lived for years with Keziah's sister, Elizabeth Gilbert, and her husband, Algernon Sidney Gilbert, a merchant. James Henry, and probably Mary, worked in their uncle's stores while growing up. Around 1828 the Gilbert/Rollins clan moved to Mentor, Ohio, then to nearby Kirtland, where Sidney became a partner of Newel K. Whitney in the Gilbert-Whitney store.

In 1830 the Gilbert and Rollins families began to hear rumors of the Book of Mormon, and in November they listened to the preaching of Oliver Cowdery, Peter Whitmer, Parley P. Pratt, and Ziba Peterson, who were traveling through Ohio during their mission to the "Lamanites," or Native Americans, thought to be remnants of Book of Mormon peoples. The four men bore an impressive testimony of the restoration of the New Testament church in nineteenth-century America. Contemporary newspapers report that Oliver "predicted the destruction of the world within a few years, that he expected to found a city of refuge, that he proclaimed that he and his associates were the only ones on earth qualified to administer in the name of Jesus and that they were going to gather and convert the Indians, who were the lost tribes of Israel." Here apocalyptic fervor joined with authoritarianism in the earliest Mormonism.

The Rollinses and Gilberts could not resist this call. In November 1830, when Mary was twelve, she was baptized by Parley P. Pratt in a stream near the Isaac Morley farm, while Oliver Cowdery, Ziba Peterson, and Peter Whitmer witnessed. Mary's mother and Newel Whitney converted at about the same time, and Sidney Gilbert joined the church in December. Local pastor Sidney Rigdon and many of his congregation also converted in November, so an important nucleus of the new movement was organized in Kirtland.

When Isaac Morley obtained one of the first copies of the Book of Mormon, Mary went to his house just before a meeting started, hoping to borrow it while he was at the meeting. Isaac protested that he himself had not yet had a chance to look at the book, but the twelve-year-old pled so earnestly that he let her have it till the following morning. "If any person in this world was ever perfectly happy in the possession of any coveted treasure I was when I had permission to read that wonderful book," she wrote. Her family all took turns reading until late at night, then Mary awakened very early the next morning and memorized the first verse of 1 Nephi. When she returned the book, Isaac remarked, "I guess you did not read much in it." She recited the first verse verbatim and summarized 1 Nephi. Morley was amazed and said, "Child, take this Book Home and finish it. I can wait."

Later, in early February 1831, Joseph Smith moved to Kirtland and visited the Gilbert home where he was surprised to see the copy of the Book of Mormon, still rare in Ohio. Newel Whitney told him the story of Mary's intense desire to read it, and Smith asked to meet this young woman. Mary wrote, "I was sent for; when he saw me, he looked at me so earnestly, I felt almost afraid [and I thought, 'He can read my every thought,' and I thought how blue his eyes were.] after a moment, or too he came and put his hands on my head and gave me a great Blessing, (the first I ever received) and made me a present of the Book."

A few evenings later she visited the Smith house with her mother and attended a meeting Joseph had organized. Mary sat on a plank resting on boxes. After prayer and singing, Smith talked, then suddenly stopped:

> And his countenance Shone, and seemed almost transparent — it seems as though the solemnity of Eternity rested upon all of us ... [He] seemed almost transfixed, he was looking ahead and his face outshone the candle which was on a shelf just behind him. I thought I could almost see the cheek bones, he looked as though a searchlight was inside his face and shining through every pore. I could not take my eyes from his face.

Smith asked, "Who do you suppose has been in your midst this night?" Someone suggested an angel, but the prophet did not answer. Then Martin Harris dropped to his knees and clasped Smith's legs:

> I Know Brother Joseph; it was our Lord and Saviour Jesus Christ. Joseph replied, Martin, the Spirit of God revealed that to thee, Yes, Brethren our Saviour has been in Your Midst, and talked with me face, to face — and he has given me a Commandment to give unto you — he has comanded me to seal you up unto Everlasting life, and he has given you all to me, to be with me, in his kingdom, even as he is in the Fathers kingdom — and he has commanded me to say unto you, that when you are tempted of Satan, to say get thee behind me Saten; for my salvation is secure.

Smith then knelt and prayed for a very long time. "I felt he was talking to the Lord and the power rested upon us all," Mary wrote. "The prayer was so long that some of the people got up and rested then knelt again." Later she reported that Smith's words and appearance at this time were "photographed" on her brain. She regarded this as the first time she was "sealed" to the Mormon prophet ("He has given you all to me"), though she was "sealed up to eternal life" by being "given" to Smith, their advocate with Jesus, along with the rest of the small congregation. Only later would "seal" come to mean "marry" or "link" in Mormon theology.

### III. Jackson County

In the fall of 1831, when Mary was thirteen, she, with her family and the Gilberts, travelled to Independence, Jackson County, Missouri, in a company including the Burks, Partridges, Morleys, and Phelpses—the first expedition to settle the place Smith had designated as the center stake of Zion. There Uncle Sidney opened a dry goods store, and Keziah married her second husband, John M. Burk, a widower. Mary evidently continued to live with the Gilberts much of the time after her mother's remarriage.

Like the Huntington sisters, Mary received the gift of tongues at an early age. She often heard Oliver Cowdery and Thomas B. Marsh speak ecstatically during Sunday meetings and was curious to know what they said, so she prayed that she would be able to understand their strange utterances. One night the "Brethren" came to the Gilbert home for a meeting and "were filled with the Spirit, and spoke in toungnes." Mary "was called upon to interpret it" and "felt the spirit of it in a moment." Her interpretation predicted that the Saints "would be driven" from Jackson County by mobs. The High Council and Oliver Cowdery protested stridently and even wrote to Joseph Smith in Kirtland concerning the matter, but Smith answered that Mary had interpreted correctly: "Interpretations belonged to the Priesthood, but, as they had not asked for the gift, and I had it was taken from their Shoulder and put onto mine."

Another time, when she was fourteen, she interpreted one of Oliver Cowdery's sermons that was reportedly spoken in an Indian language, and she affirmed that an Indian agent present asked her where she had learned the language. Mary wrote, enigmatically, "I lost the gift after we were driven." Apparently she stopped interpreting tongue-speech after leaving Jackson County.

While still there, she worked for Peter Whitmer, a tailor, and gained a reputation as a good seamstress. Lilburn Boggs, who had just been elected lieutenant governor, asked Peter to make a suit for his inauguration, so Mary went to Boggs's house to stitch the collars and face the coat. The Boggs family liked her so much that they tried to induce her to leave Mormonism and live with them, but she refused.

The New England-born, "clannish," politically unified, theocratic Mormons had moved into a state dominated by slave-owning southerners on the American frontier. Tensions were inevitable, and they were resolved in typical frontier manner, through extralegal means—the destruction of property and physical intimidation. Anti-Mormon vigilantism erupted on July 20, 1833, when a mob, enraged at a mildly abolitionist Mormon editorial, attacked the office of *The Evening and the Morning Star*, which was then printing the early Mormon scripture, the Book of Commandments, a precursor to the Doctrine and Covenants. When members of the mob brought out the printed sheets of the book, Mary and Caroline were hiding and watching. Mary heard them talking about destroying the edition, so while the mob was busy "prying out the Gable end of the House," the girls each ran and gathered an armful of the sheets. Although the men saw them and shouted at them to stop, Mary and Caroline darted away and hid in a large cornfield. Some of the men rushed after them but could not find them. Mary and Caroline later delivered the sheets to Sister Phelps, the printer's wife, who was overjoyed to receive them.

On this same night Bishop Edward Partridge was tarred and feathered. In early November the Gilbert store was plundered, and soon the Mormons were forced to leave Jackson County. Mary, her mother, and the Gilberts settled in Clay County, where Mary began to teach a small school.

In early June 1834, when Mary was sixteen, Zion's Camp—a paramilitary expedition led by Joseph Smith—marched from Ohio to Missouri. The Gilbert household provided accommodations for many of the brethren, including Smith and his brothers Hyrum and William, his uncle Jesse, and Luke and Lyman Johnson. When cholera broke out, Uncle Gilbert was one of the earliest to be struck down, and he died on June 29, followed by Jesse Smith and three others at the Gilbert home. Soon after, Zion's Camp returned to Kirtland.

## IV. Far West

Mary at sixteen must have been pretty, for she attracted the attention of two men, one of them Joseph Smith. In later years she wrote that Smith was commanded to marry her at this time, apparently after he returned to Kirtland: "In 1834 he was commanded to take me for a Wife, I was a thousand miles from him, he got afraid." It was not until much later in Illinois, however, that Mary heard about this revelation. Meanwhile, in Missouri in 1835 another young man, Adam Lightner, a twenty-five-year-old non-Mormon originally from Pennsylvania, began to court her. They married on August 11 when she was seventeen. At first they lived in Liberty, but soon moved to Far West, Caldwell County, where Adam opened a store. On June 18, 1836, Mary bore her first child, Miles Henry.

In the latter part of 1837, Mary and Adam opened a store in Milford, ten miles from Far West, then moved back to the city. While they were gone, a mob ransacked the building. Violence increased in 1838. Once Adam, though non-Mormon, was sent by Mormons to buy a keg of powder, which he managed to smuggle past the enemy—thus demonstrating his close attachment to the Latter-day Saints. If he had been caught, he might have been killed.

On October 31, the day after defenseless Mormons were massacred at Haun's Mill, the state militia came to Far West to level it with a cannon. Boggs, now governor, reportedly gave orders to spare only two families, the Clemensons and the Lightners. But when General Lucas requested them to leave, Mary states that she refused. Heber C. Kimball stepped between her and Lucas, saying, "Sister Lightner, God Almighty Bless you, I thank my God for One Soul that is ready to die for her Religion, not a hair of your head shall be harmed for I will wade to my knees in Blood in your behalf." This self-heroizing anecdote is typical of early Mormon autobiography.

Far West was spared, but Smith and other church leaders were captured and narrowly escaped execution. A few days later Mary and Adam decided to visit his brother forty miles away in Lexington, but then they heard that anti-Mormons were intending to intercept them to testify against Joseph Smith. "Adam loved the Prophet and his brother," wrote Mary, so the Lightners detoured to Louisville, Kentucky, to see Adam's uncle. But he had relocated to Pennsylvania, so they were forced to rent a room for six months in Kentucky, where they exhausted their resources. Mary painted a few pictures and sold them and tried tailoring, but she made little headway without recommendations. When a man hired her to make some shirts, he only paid her $.30 each, a devastating underpayment. She spent the money on molasses and cornmeal, which she said kept the family alive for several days, but Adam and the baby became sick from eating nothing but cornmeal.

### V. Nauvoo

Eventually the Lightners heard that the Mormons were regrouping in Illinois and that Henry Rollins was in Alton, just north of St. Louis, so they sold their meager possessions and traveled northwest. When they arrived at Henry's house, however, there were already two families living with him. Mary managed to obtain some medicine for her sick baby and found some painting students. The Lightners transferred to a boarding house, then moved to Mary's mother's cabin in Montrose, across the Mississippi from Nauvoo. There Mary Elizabeth bore her second child, Caroline, on October 18, 1840.

Three weeks later, Adam unable to find work, the Lightners moved to Farmington, fifty miles east of Nauvoo, and settled into a two-room house. Adam practiced carpentry and Mary sewed. But their bank failed and they lost their savings, so returned to the Burks' home near Nauvoo. At one point Adam had loaned two thousand dollars to some church "brethren," but they took advantage of the bankruptcy law and defaulted on their debt. One paid with a barrel of pork, but it turned out to be full of weevils. During this difficult time Adam was again unemployed, so Mary began giving painting lessons, and her pupils included Julia Murdock Smith (Joseph Smith's adopted daughter) and Sarah Ann Whitney (later one of Smith's plural wives). With the money she earned, she bought a Nauvoo lot near Joseph Smith's.

### VI. Patriarchal Marriage

By Mary's own account, she had had spiritual presentiments that she would become Joseph Smith's wife: "I had been dreaming for a number of years I was his wife. I thought I was a great sinner. I prayed to God to take it from me." However, the prophetic dreams were fulfilled—Smith proposed to her in early February 1842 at the home of Newel and Elizabeth Whitney. In her later life she retold the story a number of times, which allows us to construct a fascinating, detailed composite account showing how Smith approached his prospective wives. First, after he introduced the idea of plural marriage to Mary, he told her that God had instructed him to marry her in 1834, but he had been in Kirtland and she in Missouri. He said that he had been frightened of the idea at first, but, he said, as Mary remembered it, "The angel came to me three times between the year of '34 and '42 and said I was to obey that principle or he would lay [destroy] me."

Then he made an important statement: "Joseph said I was his before I came here and he said all the Devils in hell should never get me from him." In her autobiography Mary wrote that Smith told her, "I was created for him before the foundation of the Earth was laid." So we have the doctrine of spirits matched in the pre-existence, a concept that gives important insight into Smith's practice of polyandry. It fits him into the context of the broader "spiritual wife" doctrine of the Burned-over District, in which spiritual affinities between a man and a woman took precedence over legal but nonsacral marriage. Perhaps the Mormon doctrine of the pre-existence derived in part from this influence.

Smith also told Mary, "I know that I shall be saved in the Kingdom of God. I have the oath of God upon it and God cannot lie. All that he gives me I shall take with me for I have that authority and that power conferred upon me." In other words, Smith linked plural marriage with salvation, as he did in later marriages. If Mary accepted him as her husband, her place in heaven would be assured.

She did not agree to the marriage at first—she was married to and presumably in love with another man, and was skeptical of Smith's doctrine. She asked why, if an angel came to him, it had not appeared to her? She asked pointedly, wasn't it possible that the angel was from the devil? Smith assured her that it had come from God. She replied that she would never be sealed to him until she had a direct witness from God. He told her to pray earnestly, for the angel had told him that she would have a witness. As the conversation ended, he asked her if she would turn traitor and speak of this to anyone. She replied, "I shall never tell a mortal I had such a talk from a married man!"

She was understandably troubled by this proposal. Nevertheless, she prayed about it and discussed it with the only person Smith would allow her to confide in, Brigham Young. One day she knelt between three haystacks, and, she wrote, "If ever a poor mortal prayed I did." She even prayed with her hands upraised, following the pattern of Moses. A few nights after that she was in her bedroom where her mother and aunt slept also, when, she later recounted, "a Personage stood in front of the Bed looking at me. Its clothes were whiter than anything I had ever seen, I could look at its Person, but when I saw its face so bright, and more beautiful than any Earthly being Could be, and those eyes pearcing me through, and through, I could not endure it, it seemed as if I must die with fear, I fell back in Bed and Covered up my head." As she hid under

212

her covers, her aunt awoke and saw "a figure in white robes pass from our bed to my mother's bed and pass out of the window."

Mary soon related this to Smith, who explained the sign to her and predicted events that would take place in her family. "Every word came true. I went forward and was sealed to him. Brigham Young performed the sealing, and Heber C. Kimball the blessing." This happened toward the end of February 1842 in the upper room of Smith's Red Brick store, the makeshift Masonic Hall. The marriage was "for time, and all Eternity." The prophet's sixth wife, approximately, Mary was twenty-three years old and pregnant with her third child by Adam Lightner during the ceremony. He was out of town, "far away" at the time, so probably did not know about it.

Mary later commented on the polyandrous aspect of her marriage: "I could tell you why I stayed with Mr. Lightner. Things the leaders of the Church does not know anything about. I did just as Joseph told me to do, as he knew what troubles I would have to contend with." So Smith instructed her to stay with her husband. One obvious advantage to such a modus operandi was that it would preserve the secrecy of their polyandrous union.

About a month after the marriage, on March 22, George Algernon was born to Mary in Nauvoo. Miles Henry was now six, Caroline one and a half. On April 14 Mary was accepted into the Female Relief Society of Nauvoo, and on June 9 she contributed $1.00 to it. Adam Lightner was back in Nauvoo by July 1, when he bought a hat at the Joseph Smith store.

## VII. Pontoosuc

Once again unable to find employment in Nauvoo, Adam soon secured a job cutting cordwood fifteen miles up the river at Pontoosuc. He bought a log house there and Mary prepared to follow him. However, Joseph Smith was distraught at his new wife's decision to leave him and the Saints, "and while the tears ran down his cheeks – he prophesied that if we attempted to leave the Church, we would have plenty of Sorrow; for we would make property on the right hand, and lose it on the left, we would have sickness, on sickness, and lose our children. and that I would have to work harder than I ever dreamed off [of] and at last when you are worn out, and almost ready to die you will get back to the Church." Mary thought these were "hard sayings" as her life had already been "about as hard as possible." But the rest of her autobiography is written in the form of a narrative showing the complete fulfillment of Smith's prophecy, ending with her arrival in Utah after years of misfortune spent apart from the Saints. Before she left, Smith rebaptized the Rollins and Lightner families and "tried hard to get Mr. Lightner to go into the Water," but Adam said he did not feel worthy.

In Pontoosuc, the Lightners scraped out a meager existence. Mary continued to make some money sewing, while Adam cut cordwood. Then George suddenly became ill and died: "I was alone with him at the time, husband had gone to a neighbors for assistance. an Old Lady helped me dress him. and Mr Lightner had to make the Coffin – as he was the only Carpenter in the place. the two men that dug the Grave, and a little Girl was all that went to Bury my darling." Mary felt that Smith's prophecy was beginning to be fulfilled.

Soon afterwards, on May 3, 1843, Mary's and Adam's fourth child, Florentine Mathias, was born, after which their house was struct by lightning, as related above. They stayed in Pontoosuc through 1844. Joseph and Hyrum were killed in late June, so Mary, now twenty-six, had lost her second husband, though she continued to live with her first.

Soon after, the Lightners suffered fevers and chills for six months. Mary contracted "bilious fever" and was again expected to die. However, she had a dream in which an angel came to her and told her that if she went to Nauvoo and asked for a Brother Cutler who worked on the temple to administer to her, she would be healed. She wanted to obey the warning but could not obtain transport. Finally her brother sent a boy with an ox team for her, so at the point of death she set out for Nauvoo, accompanied by Adam and the children.

A "green liquid" flowed from her mouth as she travelled, "and the hue of death was on my countenance." In Nauvoo they asked the local residents if there was a Brother Cutler who worked on the temple, and she was told yes, Alpheus Cutler. He was summoned, administered to Mary, and immediately, she wrote, "I got up, and walked to the fire alone in 2 weeks I was able to take care of my Children."

### VIII. "Without Compass or Rudder"

The Lightners stayed in Nauvoo. On January 30, 1845, at Parley P. Pratt's home, Mary received her endowment, thus joining the elite group of the Holy Order. As a widow of Joseph Smith, she would have enjoyed some prestige, and this led to her next marital union. In the fall of 1844 Brigham Young and Heber Kimball offered themselves to Smith's widows as proxy husbands and Mary accepted Young's proposal. She was sealed to him for time in a proxy marriage on May 22, 1845: "I was also sealled to B Young as proxy for Joseph," she wrote, though she continued to live with Adam. As was customary, this marriage was repeated in the Nauvoo temple, in this case on January 17, 1846, the same day she received her temple endowment.

When the church left Nauvoo, however, Mary and Adam stayed behind. She evidently took her marriage to Brigham seriously and remembered his departure with some bitterness. He had asked her if she wanted to leave with the Saints, and she had said yes. A few days later, however, she learned from her stepfather that Young and his family were crossing the Mississippi on the ice. "I felt stuned, the thought came to me that Poligamy was of the Devil — and Brigham knew it, or he would have cut off his right hand before he would have left me ... I wept myself sick, and felt to give up, and go among the Gentiles in fact I felt as though I was like one in any open Boat at Sea, without Compass or Rudder."

As the Mormon population of Nauvoo dwindled, anti-Mormons prepared to ransack the city and Mary's brother Henry tried to rally resistance against a mob with a flag. According to a family tradition (possibly embellished into a heroizing anecdote), "At that critical moment Aunt Mary Lightner ... stepped up and said, 'I'll carry that flag.' One of the captains came up to her, 'If you and your brother and your husband and your husband's people will come out of Nauvoo we will murder all the rest of the people.' Aunt Mary turned on her heel and cried, 'Blow away, I'll go back and die with them.'" Despite their threats, the mob reportedly scattered.

## IX. The Root Huckster

After Brigham reached Winter Quarters, he sent word to Mary to come join the Saints. One wonders if he sent for Adam also, or if he would have preferred for Mary to live openly as his own plural wife, as was the case with Zina Huntington. But the Lightners were experiencing utter poverty at the time and did not even have sufficient clothes to wear, let alone money for outfitting a wagon and team. Instead, Mary and Adam moved to Galena, in the northwest corner of Illinois, and lived there comfortably for a while. On February 9, 1847, Mary's next child, John Horace, was born, joining Miles, eleven, Caroline, six, and Florentine, four.

In the last week of June, Mary was washing and somehow pressed a needle into her wrist "close to the pulse." It broke off and half of it was left beneath the skin. Despite her best efforts, neither she nor Adam was able to extract it, and her wrist must have become infected. She consulted "4 different Doctors but could get no help," she wrote. "Neither could I Sleep, only when I was perfectly Exhausted ... it was September before I could sew." Calamities seemed to follow Mary and her family wherever they went.

The Lightners soon moved to St. Croix Falls, a small lumber mill town on the St. Croix River in the northwestern part of Wisconsin, after accepting an invitation to manage a hotel. The St. Croix river valley was a popular resort area known for its beauty and hunting. After prospering for a time, Adam contracted "brain fever" and the baby came down with chills and fever. Mary, tending her husband and child, noticed that her own feet were beginning to swell and turn purple. One doctor recommended amputation, another disagreed; but after a while, to Mary's relief, the swelling retreated. Aunt Gilbert came to visit during the crisis and Mary was glad for the help and to have another Mormon to talk to.

In the latter part of 1847 a traveling salesman came to the Lightner home selling a cure-all root and offered samples to the whole family, including Aunt Gilbert. In a few moments they were all violently ill, and Mary's eleven-year-old son, Miles, and her four-year-old son, Florentine, died quickly. Aunt Gilbert was pronounced dead and was laid under sheets with the two boys. Doctors, when they arrived, predicted that Mary and Adam would also die, but they slowly recovered. Then, to the amazement of all, Aunt Gilbert began to have convulsions under the sheets. She was alive. Her spasms continued for two weeks, but she survived.

Local men pursued and captured the poisoner, whose motive, according to Mary, was hatred of Mormons. The posse brought him to the hotel, put a noose over his neck, and opened Mary's window so she could watch the execution from her sickbed. "He was an elderly man with a pleasing Countenance," she wrote. But she begged them to try him first. However, with the help of an accomplice, he escaped that night. Mary later learned that this "quack Doctor" became lost in the woods and that both of his feet froze until the flesh dropped off the bones. He suffered great pain in his feet for the rest of his life, and he was thus able to escape men, Mary wrote, but not God. Divine vengeance on persecutors of the Latter-day Saints is another persistent theme in Mormon folklore.

Mary grieved for her two dead sons, then turned to raising Caroline, seven, and little John Horace. The next spring, in 1848, the Lightners moved forty miles down the St. Croix River to Stillwater, Washington County, on the Minnesota bank of "Lake" St. Croix, a widening of the river. Stillwater was then a bustling lumber community with five stores and two hotels. In the spring of the following year, they moved to Willow River, later Hudson, on the Wisconsin side of the "lake," ten miles south of Stillwater.

On April 3, 1849, Mary, thirty-one, bore a second daughter, Elizabeth Lightner, in Stillwater. Soon after this, Adam bought a sixty-five-acre farm opposite Stillwater, where he built a four-room house and acquired a horse and cow. But the horse was found dead in the stable a week later, and then a hired man drove their cow so fast that it also died. This was such a blow to the family that they accepted an offer to manage another hotel. Mary wrote that they were glad to get into a warm house, as the winters were severe in Wisconsin. However, finding the work at the hotel too demanding, they eventually returned to their farm.

On April 9, 1851 (Mary's own birthday), she bore another girl,

Mary Rollins Lightner, at Willow River, who joined Caroline, eleven, John, four, and Elizabeth, two. The Lightners then managed a boarding house at Willow River for two years. Mary's next child, Algernon Sidney, was born on March 25, 1853. When the baby was four weeks old, Mary learned that her sister, married and living in Farmington, west of Peoria, Illinois, was very ill and close to death, so Mary returned to Illinois to attend her for five weeks. "She died strong in the faith of Mormonism so Called for that I was truly thankful," Mary wrote. Caroline left four children: Mary Jane, fifteen, Frances, thirteen, Orlando, eleven, and William, seven. Mary took Mary Jane back with her, then evidently sent for the others later.

On November 10 Algernon died in Willow River; Mary had now lost four of her eight children. The next year the Lightners moved to Marine, on the Minnesota side of the lake, and managed a popular hotel, the Lightner House. There Mary Elizabeth entertained a mysterious old man whom she suspected of being one of the three Nephites—in Mormon folklore, the immortal, wandering Native American apostles from the time of Christ. After she gave him food, he commended her Christianity, then disappeared with no explanation. A Three Nephite story is a necessary part of any repertoire of the miraculous in early Mormonism.

Three years later, on March 17, 1857, Mary, nearly thirty-nine, bore another boy, Charles Washington. Caroline was now eighteen, John, eleven, Elizabeth, nine, and Mary, seven. Caroline married Thomas Jewell on October 18, 1858, but as Mary Elizabeth entered the grandmotherly era of her life, she still had not had her own last child. After two years' in Marine, the Lightners bought a two-story home and a large lot on which they built a five-story hotel for the booming tourist business. They went into debt to prepare for occupancy, expecting to repay their obligations within a few months. But once again bad fortune dogged their steps. The Civil War began in 1861 and many of their boarders suddenly left to enlist. The Lightners could not meet their mortgage and soon lost their property. After this devastating blow, Mary remembered Joseph Smith's prophecy and felt that she had suffered enough. She convinced her husband that it was time to gather with the Saints in Utah. They sent letters to Henry in southern Utah, then moved to Hannibal, Missouri, for a year, waiting for a response from him. But they received no reply. They moved back to Chisago, Chisago County, Minnesota, where Adam Jr., her last child, was born on October 28, 1861, when she was forty-three. John was now fourteen, Elizabeth, twelve, Mary Rollins, ten, and Charles, four. Mary apparently was also raising Caroline's children.

## X. To Zion

Letters finally came from Henry, so Mary and Adam made arrangements for the journey west. On May 25, 1863, they boarded the steamboat *Canada* for St. Louis. This would not be an easy journey. The two younger boys, Charles and Adam, contracted the measles on board, but there were no beds for them, so they could not even lie down. After the Lightners transferred to the *Fanny Ogden* for St. Joseph, they sat near a box with a corpse for two days, and there was talk of the ship being attacked because of the war.

At St. Joseph they boarded the *Emilie* for Omaha, where they met other Saints bound for Utah. They drove six miles to Florence through a rainstorm without a cover on their wagon, then slept in wet bedding. Mary had cholera the next night and baby Adam Jr. had "bowel complaint," probably dysentery or severe diarrhea. Other immigrants had smallpox and two of them died. But on June 20, Edwin Bingham, husband of Mary's half-sister, Phebe, arrived from Utah to help the Lightners cross the plains.

Mary's overland diary is a lively specimen. She records the sicknesses of her family—on August 10 "Elizabeth Crazy with the teethache al night & so for 2 days." Buffalo and prairie dogs are noted with interest. Problems with horses and livestock occurred frequently. She often described food—on August 15 she wrote, "Breakfast Coffee Bacon fried Cakes." There were moments of low spirits—on August 15 Mary noted: "Our Cow very sick no Milk for 2 or 3 days ... sand & Gravel the whole day — almost sick and feel cross for if there is a Bad place in the Camp ground we are sure to get it." Sometimes she described landscapes with the appreciation of an artist. On August 31 she "passed through the Mountains in a Winding Kind of way, And they look Sollemn in their Grandeur, rising one above another and their verdure of Many Colored hues & {Roks} of Various Shades looked (to me) to be beautiful indeed — & had I time & the Necessary Implements I should take a Scetch of our Camp at the foot of a Mountain with the Cattle feeding or lying down on its Sloping sides."

## XI. Minersville

On September 15 the Lightners arrived in Salt Lake City. Mary possibly visited her proxy husband, Brigham, at this time, though the autobiography is silent on the subject. Two days later Henry, whom Mary had not seen for seventeen years, met her, and after the joyful reunion, he served as the Lightners' guide in the long journey to southern Utah. When Mary arrived in Minersville five days later, she reunited with her mother and half sister, Phebe Burk Bingham. The autobiography ends: "We were thankful to find a home, and friends after an arduos journy of one thousand Miles in an ox Team — besides our trip on steamer from Stilwater Minnesota to St Louis, then up the

Missouri to Omaha." Many Mormons felt that the noteworthy part of their lives ended when they reached Utah and settled down to a peaceful life untroubled by "gentile" mobocracy. Mary's later life can be sketched chiefly through her outgoing and incoming correspondence.

Minersville, as the name indicates, was connected with several mining projects–Henry himself had discovered the first lead mine in Utah in 1858. Adam began doing carpentry work, and Mary took up sewing and schoolteaching. Mary Rollins later wrote of her upbringing in Utah: "[I] came across the plain in ox team 1863 walked barefoot nearly all the way ... [In Minersville I] went barefoot every summer untill I was 18 years old. Gleaned wheat barefooted. helped to kill and drive chintz bugs off of 5 acres of wheat and save the wheat one year, for Uncle Henry Rollins." Henry was a bishop in Minersville for many years. Meanwhile, Mary now became a grandmother in good earnest as Elizabeth married Joseph Orson Turley in 1865. In 1870 John Horace united with Louisa Abigail Burk and Mary Rollins was joined to William Jenkins Carter. Charles Washington married Lydia Williams in 1883.

Mary Elizabeth's relationship with her other husband, Brigham, is curiously distant, but occasionally their paths crossed. "The authorities stopped at our home many times and Brigham always came to see us," she wrote. "He would have moved us to the City if I would go." But Mary stayed in southern Utah with Adam. On May 20, 1864, she wrote to Young, describing her family: "Myself and Family are as well as usual at present, Mr Lightner and my Son John (who is of Age) have gone to California to be gone a year or so – in fact I do not know when they will return – I am Engaged in Teaching School and making Garden, I have planted nearly an acre of ground, with the help of my Daughter & a little Son – and by Gods blessing I hope to be able to accomplish that, which will Enable me to keep my family together in Zion."

Then she gave a description of Minersville. It had "improved Considerably in the last year – not so much in Building. As in the Planting of fruit Trees, Shade Trees &c The People here are generally poor – But since the Road has been opened to Pahranegot – they have had a better oportunity of obtaining wagons & other articles that were needed." Henry's health was poor, and he was suffering from a more serious psychic burden: "His mind is weigh[ed] down with Sorrow in Consequence of being under your displeasure as a Californian." Henry had lived in the Mormon colony of San Bernardino, an offense that many Mormons could not forgive. Despite being a bishop in Minersville, Mary reports, some of his ward members would tell him, "You Californians do not have the spirit of the Lord." She ended the letter, "Remember me with kindness, in your suplications at the throne of Grace. Yours in the Covenant  Mary E Lightner."

In a May 30 reply, Brigham commended the civic improvements in Minersville and hoped that Henry's health would improve. He assured Mary that her brother was under no curse for having lived temporarily in California. The letter closed, "With love to you, to him [Adam] and the family, and praying the Lord to bless you. I remain your Brother Brigham Young."

In a March 1865 letter to Eliza Snow, Mary narrated some of her prophetic dreams. On April 3 Eliza responded: "I will repeat President Young's words, as follows. 'When you write, give my respects to sister Mary and tell her I am here–full of faith, and the kingdom is moving on, and if she and I stick to it; when that goes up, we shall go up with it.' He pronounced your dreams good." Evidently, Adam Lightner was not in Minersville at the time, for Eliza wrote: "You say Mr. Lightner is gone ... Although your prospects seem dark, God will overrule all things for your good."

Other passages in Eliza's letter show Mary's friendships with elite plural wives in Salt Lake, wives of Brigham and Heber and Joseph:

> I feel that you are truly my very dear Sister, and whenever I think of you, I feel to thank the Lord that you are in the land of Zion – that you are gathered out ... Sister [Marinda] Hyde was very much pleased with the keepsake (night cap) which you left with sister Emily [Partridge Young] for her. She said she prized it more for you having worn it. She wished me to thank you for her, and send her love. Sisters [Elizabeth] Whitney, [Vilate] Kimball, Lucy D. [Decker Young], Susan S. [Snively Young], Zina H. [Huntington Young] Emily P [Partridge Young] &c. &c. send their love and blessings, not forgetting your Aunt.

So Mary Elizabeth was apparently taking care of Aunt Gilbert at this time. At some point, perhaps in the late 1860s or early 1870s, former apostle Amasa Lyman tried to recruit Mary and Adam to the Godbeite heresy which he had joined, but Mary, ever a visionary, had a dream that convinced her to stay with the main body of the Saints.

## XII. Relief Society President

In an 1887 letter, Mary described a meeting she had had with Brigham Young, "who; the last time but one that he was South; sent for me, and told me, that he had bought a House in the City for me, and that hereafter my family should be provided for. that I, had suffered enough, and the Lord did not require me to suffer any more." However, she then noted, with a touch of bitterness, that Young had not followed through on his promises: "I never received the House, or any thing – for I suppose he forgot all about me. having more important Business to attend to." Mary's relationship with Brigham was not quite a full marriage but was more than a friendship.

When a Relief Society was formed in Minersville, possibly in early 1869, Mary, now fifty-one, was chosen to be president. On May 27 Eliza Snow wrote to congratulate her: "I was pleased to hear that a F.R. [Female Relief] Society has been organized in Minersville, and was also pleased that you were appointed to preside over it." Eliza wrote to Mary again on June 17, 1870: "I rejoice with you & your society in your success so far. It seems rather a bold step for you to undertake building so soon but I glory in your courage."

Mary's mother died on January 29, 1877, in Horse Shoe Bend, Utah, and on August 29, when Mary was fifty-nine, Brigham died. Her third husband had passed on, but her first was still alive.

## XIII. Despondency

From a letter Emmeline Wells, General Relief Society secretary, wrote to Mary on March 8, 1880, it can be inferred that Mary had been fighting discouragement:

> I saw your name as one of the committee on Resolutions at the Ladies meeting in Beaver. That is as it should be, come out of the nutshell in which you have lain so long and take an active part in the labors of the organizations for woman's advancement. Throw off the despondency which seems to enshroud you, and embrace every opportunity to speak in defense of the principles of truth ... Do not suffer your mind to become darkened but recollect that the darkest cloud has a silvery lining and trust on.

Apparently Adam was very ill and Mary was burdened with debt. On September 13, 1881, she wrote to John Taylor, reporting that she desperately needed support, as she could not pay back a loan "in consequence of sickness and the inability of those indebted to me to pay what they owe — Mr Lightner has not been able to earn twenty five cents for the last Eighteen Months — Please inform Me of your will in the Matter And Oblige Mary E. Lightner." This is the first record of Mary seeking assistance from the church. These pleas for support and complaints at not receiving it would continue throughout her later years. As with many welfare recipients, it is often hard to judge if she was asking for more than she deserved or if she was being unduly ignored by church authorities.

In August 1884 Mary traveled to Salt Lake and Emily Partridge Smith Young mentioned her arrival in her journal on the 25th: "Went with Mary Lightner to see Joseph F. Smith. She wants the Church to help her." Mary left Salt Lake City on September 2.

## XIV. Widow

In the summer of 1885, when Mary was sixty-seven, Adam became seriously ill. In an 1887 letter she wrote, "I have never called on the Church for aid; until, the long Sickness, and Death of Mr Lightner accompanied by a Series of Misfortunes Compelled me to apply to Brother Taylor for Assistance. Just before My Husband died, Brother Taylor Allowed Me two hundred Dollars a year during his life time – but intimated that he would increase the Amount at his [Adam's] death – he died two years ago – and left me in debt over a hundred Dollars." He died of tuberculosis, "consumption," on August 19, in Minersville. Mary must have grieved at the death of her legal husband. Though he was not her eternal spouse, and though he had often been out of work, he had been her lifelong companion and had helped raise their children.

Her greatest trial in the era following Adam's death was a criminal offense committed by her last-born, twenty-four-year-old Adam Lightner, Jr., and his subsequent punishment. In 1885 he and some accomplices were convicted of grand larceny and incarcerated in August or September. Mary wrote to President John Taylor with a mother's advocacy: "The next Sabbath after Mr Lightners Death – My Son was sent to Prison for a term of Six Years, for a crime he was not Guilty of, but was found in bad Company – He was all the help I had, he was a good and affectionate Son, and perfectly Honorable in all his dealings." She worked ceaselessly to have Adam Jr. pardoned and released from prison. In May 1886, while visiting Salt Lake, she wrote to Taylor, "I Borrowed Money to pay my passage up here, in Order to See the Governor in his behalf, Mr West gave me considerable hope, said he would look into the Matter, and do all he could for me. This is why I came up–also to learn the cause of no remittance being sent me." "No remittance" is a typical complaint. She continued, "I was under a great deal of expense during Mr Lightneres Sickness and *Death* – in fact it has left me without any means of support – ... I am hardly able to go out to work, as I was sixty eight years old last Month–now if you do not feel willing to assist me any more, as Josephs wife I must do the best I can without Money, and without friends."

On April 28, 1886, Emily Partridge Young wrote to Mary:

I feel a great sympathy for you because of your many afflictions. To look at things from the standpoint of mortals we might think you had more than your share of sorrow, but when we consider that there is no perfection only through suffering ... we can rejoice in affliction. Who knows but what your sons imprisonment may prove his salvation. It is better to hope and trust in the Lord than to despair ... I have your letter to Hyrum [Clawson] and he said he would try and do all he could for your son ... Hyrum and brother Nicleson have been very much inter-

ested in some of the prisoners since they have been in prison themselves
... I hope when I write again I will have some to say to cheer your aching
heart. Give my love to your aunt Gilbert and all enquiring friends. And believe me your sincere and well wisher. Emily P. Young.

In June Mary came to Salt Lake City and stayed with Helen Mar Whitney, another widow of Joseph. Mary petitioned the governor for Adam Jr.'s release, to no avail, then secured the help of William Godbe, Henry Lawrence, and Hyrum Clawson. Clawson informed her on the 18th that the necessary papers were in order and she could go to the "Pen" to pick up her son. Overjoyed, she, with Helen, visited the prison the next day and Adam was freed. Having accomplished her mission, she departed from Salt Lake on the 23rd, leaving Adam to work in the city.

Zina Huntington Young wrote to Mary on June 27, the anniversary of Joseph Smith's death:

My Dear Presious Sister: As I have no pen in my room you will excuse the pencil. We remember this day, of all days to us. I went into Sister Eliza, we talked over our past a little, then Sister E spoke a few words in tounges to comfort and cheer us ... I send you a cromo Sister E sayed God bless her we rejoiced that your son was liberated and felt that your last days would be your *best* ... At 3 P.M. Sister Emily P Young sent over for Susan, and Sister Presendia was there, to be administered [to] as she has the Erysipelas {very} bad we left her {r}esting, I wonder {who} Joseph will want next to go on with the work in the other *Land* ... My Darling Sister be patient for O what a glory lays before you ... I am improving slowly in health for which I am very thankful ... Where will we be one year from today I would not like to lift the curtain if I could. Your true and loving Sister Zina D. Young.

This letter gives a rich sense of the community that Joseph Smith's wives shared, and shows how focused they were on Smith—commemorating his day of death, wondering which of them, aging as they were, would be called to join him next "in the other *Land*." In Mary's household it was not she but Adam Jr. who would depart next. He died unexpectedly on September 21, 1890, at the age of twenty-eight—her last and most problematic child.

In her twilight years Mary apparently continued to battle depression. Emmeline Wells, in a February 10, 1887, letter, chided her, "I was in hopes that your visit here last summer and the good luck you had in getting your son pardoned would have made you quite brave and strong for the daily cares & annoyances of battling for a living." Emmeline seems somewhat unfeeling, but she may have been trying to shock Mary into a more positive frame of mind. In a letter that can be dated only to the 1880s, Wells again tried to boost Mary's spirits: "I have no doubt but it would do you good to come up to the city for a month, I wish you might have the opportunity. Aunt Presendia & Zina have both been in my office today ... I quite forgot to mention your message. I will try and recollect it and ask Zina to write to you. She is a very sympathetic woman, and one who cherishes a very tender feeling towards all Joseph's wives. I trust the way will open for you to be made more comfortable than at present."

In early October 1887 Mary visited Helen Mar Whitney in Salt Lake City again. On the 7th she wrote to President Wilford Woodruff:

Dear Sir – I take the Liberty of addressing you upon a matter of vital importance to me. I find after being a member of this Church fifty Seven Years this Month; that I am under the necessity of asking assistance from the Church for my future Support, I ask this favor of you in Confidence, the more so; because I have been promised [support] repeatedly by Brother Joseph, and Brigham Young ... My House is Built of inch Lumber, and very Cold in Winter & hot in Summer – I have not lived in a House that was plastered in any part – ; Since I came to the Mountains – but that does not matter much, as I am used to hardships of all kinds.

She mentioned her son's death and John Taylor's promise, then added:

He [Adam Sr.] died two years ago – and left me in debt over a hundred Dollars – a Jew has my note for $80.00 Eighty-Dollars and I have not a Dollar to pay on it – the rest of the Debt is paid. I have not received a cent Since Brothers Taylors death – I have Aunt Gilbert to Support, who; is now in her Eighty-Eighth year of her Age, and a Cripple – I Borrowed Money to come up, hoping to see you, I find my Only alternative is to pen these lines to you. hoping the Lord will direct You in this matter.

She recounted the story of her sealings to Joseph Smith. "I cincerely hope You will not pass this request by, for I assure you; that unles I am assisted, I must suffer for both food, and Clothing for the coming Winter. Please Answer this Letter as soon as convenient. Direct to the care of Hellen, M, Whitney – and I can get it – I shall be here a few days longer – Your Sister in the Gospel  Mary E Lightner." Her letter was seconded by a note from Helen Mar to the effect that Mary, "as the Prophet's wife, should be relieved and provided for the remainder of her days." The request met with some success. On October 11 Woodruff wrote in his journal, "Sat in Council through the day. We made the following appropriation: ... To Mary E Lightner $100 Cash & $200 tithing annually."

## XV. A Living Relic

Mary's living arrangements in her later life are not well documented. However, she lived in Ogden with a son for some time, and after that with her daughter Mary in Minersville. She stayed in close contact with the leading women of Mormonism. Her daughter wrote that Emmeline B. Wells, Eliza Snow, and the general authorities often asked her to speak in meetings. To judge by her talks, she often gave accounts of her marriage to Joseph Smith and conversations with him. She also delivered patriotic orations on Fourth of July gatherings, and one of these, given in 1898 when she was eighty years old, has been preserved.

An 1888 letter from Emily Partridge Young to Mary reveals that both Mary and Aunt Gilbert had been ill: "I trust your health is better than it was when you last wrote. Your aunt must be a great sufferer to be sick so long." In March 1889 Emmeline B. Wells wrote, sharing news of sister-wives in Salt Lake and asking her to write a sketch of her life for Andrew Jenson's *Historical Record*, including details of her marriage to Smith. Mary visited Salt Lake again in June. Like many of Smith's wives, she spent time doing ordinance work in temples, and she wrote to President Woodruff in April 1891, informing him that she was going to travel to Manti (in central Utah) "to do a work for my Dead" and asking that a recommend be at the temple waiting for her when she arrived.

On May 25, 1895, while living in Ogden, Mary, now seventy-seven, wrote to her brother Henry, who had just celebrated his seventy-ninth birthday: "I would be so glad if I could be with you, and enjoy your society again ... But money is [so] hard to get hold of at the present time, that it is impossible for me to go ... But I send you one Dollar." Henry died on February 7, 1899, in Lyman, Uintah, Wyoming, where some of his children were living.

## XVI. Spiritually Neglected

Mary Elizabeth, however, would live into the twentieth century. In 1902, at the age of eighty-three, she signed an affidavit documenting her marriage to Joseph Smith sixty years earlier in Nauvoo. Her financial woes continued. In April 1903, while living in Minersville, she wrote current church president Joseph F. Smith, complaining that her support money had not arrived and that when she had notified her local bishop, the payment had not been forthcoming:

> The Order on the Tithing Office, that I receive from the Church, is my only means of support. I have no home of my own, am living with my Daughter. She furnishes me a room, fuel, Bread and Washing, and I pay her 35.00 every 3 months out of the Order. I also pay 4.50 of the Order and 50c cash in Tithing and then my Daughter pays tithing on what I pay

her out of the Order. which makes $8.00 that is paid out of the $50.00 that I receive. I am to Old to work or I should not let the church support me and my Daughter depends on my help to help support her family. Please let me hear from you. Your Sister in the Gospel, Mary E Lightner.

Joseph F. penned a note on the letter: "Let the usual allowance be forwarded to her." She wrote to her local bishop on April 20, 1904, again complaining that her normal Tithing Office payment had not arrived.

On April 14, 1905, now eighty-seven, she spoke to the graduating class of Brigham Young University, once again telling of her marriage to the prophet. That summer Emmeline Wells wrote her again and Mary's reply is slightly hurt in tone:

Dear Sister Wells  I was very much Surprised to receive a letter from you, after 15 years Silence. but am very thankful to be remembered. I have felt, and <u>do yet</u>, that I am alone. I feel as if I was not recognised by the Smith family. I have never had five minutes conversation with Joseph {F.} Smith in my life. I could tell him a great ~~many~~ Some things about his Father that ~~Joseph said~~ he does not know about the Early days of the Church, and in far West. but have never had the opportunity. have received but very little council or advise Since Josephs death. I feel that I have been Spiritually neglected. I was at your R S Conference in [the] afternoon last April. Sisters Stevenson & Pratt came and shook hands with me. after Meeting I spoke to you, and <u>Sister Richards</u> who has been my Staunch friend for years. Oh, how I have longed to have a good talke with <u>you</u>. How happy you must be up there all together among the noble women who are energetic in the work of God.

Mary then told the details of her marriage to Smith, answered some related questions, and continued:

My health is precarious ... [but] am ~~always able~~ and willing to talk to the people whom they want me to, want to do all I can for the kingdom of God  Yes; I Love to talk about the Prophet and the Early days of the Church will always remember how [he] looked, especially how he look[ed] at that first sealing ... he was tall and of a commanding figure, full of Life and when filled with the H. Spirit his face was beautiful in Expression. I have a Picture of him (Sidelong) done in Water Colors, but it is faded some. Joseph Jr. Smiths [Joseph Smith III] smile is exactly like the Prophet Josephs was ... Yes; I could tell you many things that I cannot write — I remember every word he ... ever said to me of importance have seen his prediction verified especially so in my own family ... Think I have answ[er]ed <u>all</u> your questions now, you can use this letter as you see fit. Your Sincere friend and Well wisher Mary E Rollins Lightner

## XVII. Last Vision

Once Mary was working with Apostle Heber C. Kimball in the Endowment house, and he said, "Sister Lightner, you will see Joseph before you die." Sometime between mid-1868, when Heber died, and 1905, when she told the story, Mary had a spiritual experience that she felt fulfilled this prophecy. She was sitting on her porch, humming the pioneer hymn "All is Well," and musing:

> Suddenly I saw just outside the door three men. They stood about two feet from the ground. These men were the Prophet Joseph, his brother Hyrum and Heber C. Kimball. Joseph stood in the middle with an arm around each of their shoulders. They were bowing and smiling at me ... Now I was looking into those clear blue penetrating eyes as I had done years ago when he had answered my many questions about the Gospel ... I looked around, pinched my arm to see if I was dreaming. As they were still smiling and bowing ... thought I would shake hands with them. They saw my confusion and understood it and they laughed, and I thought Brother Kimball would kill himself laughing. I had no fear ... Trembling with joy, I arose, took a step forward and extended my hand. They began fading away as the going down of the sun.

Heber's prophecy had been fulfilled, and Mary Elizabeth, like Eliza Snow and Presendia Kimball, had received a visitation from Joseph Smith after his death.

On December 21, 1910, Caroline Lightner Jewell died, so Mary, in her long life, buried six of her ten children. She finally moved on "to the other Land" herself on December 17, 1913, in Minersville, at the age of ninety-five. She had outlived the first five presidents of the Latter-day Saint church, the first two of whom had been husbands. She was the last of Joseph Smith's wives to die, and one of only four who would live into the twentieth century. A full life of miracle and tragedy behind her, it was time to rest.

# 9.

# Apostle's Wife

## *Marinda Nancy Johnson (Hyde Smith)*

According to a family history, Marinda Johnson first met Joseph Smith in early 1831 when she was fifteen. She and her sister Emily had been attending boarding school in a town near Hiram, Ohio, their home, and she had heard stories about this so-called prophet—all of them disparaging—and little imagined that anyone she knew might become associated with him. Then a letter arrived requesting the sisters' presence at home. When they reached the family farm, they found, to their chagrin, that their parents had invited none other than Joseph Smith himself to a cottage worship meeting in their house, and that they had converted to Mormonism. Marinda remembers that she felt only "indignation and shame" at her parents' belief in such a "ridiculous fake."

She did not want to attend the meeting, but her parents prevailed upon her, and she agreed reluctantly. That night, as she walked into the meeting room, "The Prophet, raising his head, looked her full in the eye. With the greatest feeling of shame ever experienced, she felt her very soul laid bare before this man as she realized her thoughts concerning him. He smiled and her anger melted as snow before the sunshine. She knew he was what he claimed to be and never doubted him thereafter." So once again we see Smith's enormous psychic presence. Mary Rollins Lightner had almost precisely the same experience when she first met him: a feeling that he understood her every thought.

Marinda Hyde was an extraordinarily important woman who lived in the maelstrom of nineteenth-century Mormon history in most of its important periods, Kirtland, Missouri, Nauvoo, and Utah. Two of her brothers were early Latter-day Saint apostles, though they eventually turned against Joseph Smith and Mormonism (one returned). She married Orson Hyde, soon another early apostle, who remained an important church figure until his death. So she had a first-hand view of church administration throughout most of her life. In addition, she was a polyandrous plural wife of Joseph Smith, a relationship that still has many puzzling aspects. She married Smith when Hyde was on a mission, and it is uncertain how much the apostle knew of the marriage. Antagonistic evidence is ambiguous on the subject and sympathetic witnesses are silent. Marinda left no known reference to the marriage, beyond signing an affidavit attesting that it happened. After Smith's death, she presents a classic case study of a plural wife. When Orson Hyde became a full-blown polygamist, Marinda, unlike some first wives, such as Vilate Kimball, did not reign supreme in her husband's emotional life, and she and Orson eventually divorced. Unfortunately, for such a complex, significant figure, not a single holograph from her pen survives, though Edward Tullidge's *Women of Mormondom* includes a brief interview with her and some letters written to her are extant.

## I. On the Johnson Farm

Marinda Nancy Johnson was born on June 28, 1815, in Pomfret, Windsor County, Vermont, to John Johnson, a thirty-seven-year-old farmer from New Hampshire, and Alice (Elsa) Jacobs, thirty-four, a native of Massachusetts. John was known for his scrupulousness in paying debts and "living independently," according to family traditions. Marinda was the seventh of fifteen children. The first, Alice (Elsa), was born in Chesterfield, Cheshire, New Hampshire in 1800, and Robert was born there in 1802. The next seven Johnson children were born in Pomfret, Windsor, Vermont—Fanny (1803), John Jr. (1805), Luke (1807), Olmstead G. (1809), Lyman Eugene (1811), Emily H. (1813), and Marinda. Marinda's religious upbringing was probably Methodist, for her father became a Methodist in approximately 1824.

The Johnsons moved to Hiram, Portage County, Ohio, thirty miles southeast of Kirtland, in February 1818. There John farmed, reportedly, "on a large scale." More children were soon added to the Johnson family: Mary the same year, Justin Jacob in 1820, Edwin and Charlotte, twins, in 1821, Albert G. in 1823, and finally Joseph in 1827.

## II. "They Were Convinced and Baptized"

In the winter of 1830 Ezra Booth, a Methodist minister friendly to the Johnsons, obtained a Book of Mormon and, wrote Marinda, "brought it to my father's house. They sat up all night reading it and were very much exercised over it." As often happened, the Book of Mormon made the first initial impact on the new investigator, if not the complete conversion. When the Johnsons heard that Joseph Smith had arrived in Kirtland, they and the Booth family traveled to meet him. "They were convinced and baptized before they returned," wrote Marinda. An important aspect of that conversion was a healing that became well known in Mormon tradition. According to Marinda's brother Luke, Elsa had been suffering from chronic rheumatism for two years and could not even raise her hand to her head. But "the prophet laid hands upon her, and she was healed immediately."

Remarkably, a non-Mormon source gives an even fuller account. The Johnsons were visiting at Joseph Smith's home when conversation turned to "supernatural gifts" in the apostolic church:

> Some one said, "Here is Mrs. Johnson with a lame arm; has God given any power to men now on the earth to cure her?" A few moments later, when the conversation had turned in another direction, Smith rose, and walking across the room, taking Mrs. Johnson by the hand, said in the most solemn and impressive manner: "*Woman, in the name of the Lord Jesus Christ, I command thee to be whole*," and immediately left the room.
>
> The company were awe-stricken at the infinite presumption of the man, and the calm assurance with which he spoke. The sudden mental and moral shock—I know not how better to explain the well attested fact—electrified the rheumatic arm—Mrs. Johnson at once lifted it up with ease, and on her return home the next day she was able to do her washing without difficulty or pain.

It was at this point that Marinda was called home from school, reluctantly met Joseph Smith, and soon converted. Smith and Sidney Rigdon stayed at the large Johnson farmhouse as they preached in the Pomfret area, so Marinda became closely acquainted with the young prophet at this time. Soon other Johnsons were converted. In February 1831 Lyman was baptized by Rigdon, and two months later, on April 31, Marinda was baptized at the age of fifteen. A week and a half after that, on May 10, Joseph Smith baptized Luke Johnson.

Marinda later wrote, "The next fall [after her baptism] Joseph came with his family to live at my father's house. He was at that time translating the Bible, and Elder Rigdon was acting as scribe." Joseph Smith wrote, "On the 12th of September I removed with my family to the township of Hiram, and commenced living with John Johnson ... from this time until the fore part of October I did little more than to prepare to recomence the translation of the bible."

### III. Night Mobbing

When Joseph and Emma Smith had stayed with the Johnsons for some seven months, they went to bed one night, on March 24, 1832, and fell into a peaceful sleep. Then, with no warning, a mob of some forty or fifty men broke into the Johnson house in search of the prophet. Marinda described the event:

A mob, disguising themselves as black men, gathered and burst into his

[Smith's] sleeping apartment one night, and dragged him from the bed where he was nursing a sick child. They also went to the house of Elder Rigdon, and took him out with Joseph into an orchard, where, after choking and beating them, they tarred and feathered them, and left them nearly dead. My father, at the first onset, started to the rescue, but was knocked down, and lay senseless for some time.

According to Luke Johnson, Smith was stretched on a board, then "they tore off the few night clothes that he had on, for the purpose of emasculating him, and had Dr. Dennison there to perform the operation. But when the Dr. saw the prophet stripped and stretched on the plank, his heart failed him, and he refused to operate."

The motivation for this mobbing has been debated. Clark Braden, a late, antagonistic, secondhand witness, alleged in a polemic public debate that Marinda's brother Eli led a mob against Smith because the prophet had been too intimate with Marinda. This tradition suggests that Smith may have married Marinda at this early time, and some circumstantial factors support such a possibility. The castration attempt might be taken as evidence that the mob felt that Joseph had committed a sexual impropriety; since the attempt is reported by Luke Johnson, there is no good reason to doubt it. Also, they had planned the operation in advance, as they brought along a doctor to perform it. The first revelations on polygamy had been received in 1831, by historian Danel Bachman's dating. Also, Joseph Smith did tend to marry women who had stayed at his house or in whose house he had stayed.

Many other factors, however, argue against this theory. First, Marinda had no brother named Eli, which suggests that Braden's accusation, late as it is, is garbled and unreliable. In addition, two antagonistic accounts by Hayden and S. F. Whitney give an entirely different reason for the mobbing, with an entirely different leader, Simonds Ryder, an ex-Mormon, though the Johnson brothers are still participants. In these accounts the reason for the violence is economic: the Johnson boys were in the mob because of "the horrid fact that a plot was laid to take their property from them and place it under the control of Smith." The castration, in this scenario, may have only been a threat, meant to intimidate Smith and cause him to leave Hiram.

After describing the event, Marinda wrote only, "Here I feel like bearing my testimony that during the whole year that Joseph was an inmate of my father's house I never saw aught in his daily life or conversation to make me doubt his divine mission." While it is not impossible that Marinda became Smith's first plural wife in 1831, the evidence for such a marriage, resting chiefly on the late, unreliable Braden, is not compelling. Unless more credible evidence is found, it is best to proceed under the assumption that Joseph and Marinda did not marry or have a relationship in 1831.

## IV. Orson Hyde

In 1833 the Johnsons moved to Kirtland, where Marinda began to spend time with a dynamic young convert named Orson Hyde. The next year, on September 4, they married, with Sidney Rigdon officiating. A resumé of Hyde's life to that point offers the portrait of a fervent, energetic missionary. From other sources we know that he was a strong-minded man and a forceful speaker. Born on January 8, 1805, in Oxford, New Haven, Connecticut, he had served as a pastor in the Campbellite movement, then was baptized a Mormon on October 2, 1831, while working as a clerk in the Gilbert and Whitney store in Kirtland. Almost immediately he was sent on a mission to Boston with Samuel Smith in 1832. The next year he was appointed clerk to the First Presidency. Like Lyman and Luke Johnson, he followed Joseph Smith on the arduous Zion's Camp march in 1834, an expedition that tried the participants' faith but also served to confirm them in their religious commitment and prepare them for future church leadership.

At the time of their marriage, Marinda was nineteen and Orson was twenty-nine. The couple set up housekeeping as young marrieds in Mormon Kirtland. A few months later, on February 15, 1835, Orson Hyde was ordained an apostle, as were Luke and Lyman Johnson, so Marinda suddenly had three close family members in the apostleship. However, in the earliest Mormon church, the twelve apostles were presiding traveling missionaries (the "Traveling Presiding High Council"), not the central authority of the church as they are today, which meant that Marinda would spend a great deal of time in her next fifteen years of marriage separated from Orson, enduring the hardships of a missionary wife.

In early March the Twelve was called on a mission to the eastern states. Hyde left on May 4, at a time when Marinda was expecting her first child. Orson apparently returned to Kirtland long enough to attend a school led by Sidney Rigdon, then returned to his mission, and William McLellin, another apostle, wrote to his wife that Orson had made disparaging comments about the Rigdon school. As a result on August 4 the Kirtland High Council, the central council of the church at the time, "withdrew [their] fellowship" from Hyde. On September 26 the Twelve returned from the eastern states, and Orson and McLellin confessed their wrongdoing and were forgiven. This tempest in a teapot must have been disheartening for Marinda, but then a real calamity overwhelmed her when her first child, Nathan, was born in December and died at birth.

For the time being, Marinda would remain a shadow behind her prominent husband. On January 13 of the new year, Orson served as clerk for the Kirtland High Council, then departed in early May 1836 for another eastern states mission with the apostles. Later Marinda accompanied Parley P. Pratt to Canada to meet her husband, and she stayed with him there to the end of his mission. They returned to Kirtland in the fall.

A second child, Laura Marinda Hyde, was born on May 21, 1837, and happily lived. Less than a month later Hyde left for England with the apostles, "leaving me with a three-weeks-old babe," wrote Marinda. He would be gone for more than a year. As always, we can only imagine what her life was like while he was gone. A development that undoubtedly caused her much distress was the excommunication of her brothers Luke and Lyman on April 13, 1838. After criticizing Joseph Smith freely in 1836 and 1837, they had become leaders in a group of influential Kirtland dissenters.

### V. Orson Against Joseph

Orson arrived back in Kirtland on his daughter's first birthday. But by this time internal dissension and financial reverses made it difficult for Mormon leaders to continue living in Ohio, so on July 1 Marinda and he began a journey to Far West, Missouri. Traveling with the Heber C. Kimball family in a group of about forty that included Marinda's close friend, Louisa Beaman, they drove wagons to Wellsville on the Ohio, then took a steamboat to St. Louis and Richmond on the Missouri. Helen Mar Kimball Whitney remembered that they were all sick before reaching St. Louis, and, because of the lack of drinking water, whenever the boat stopped the men would run to try to obtain fresh water. However, "The boat would often start before the brethren could get back but when they came running and shouting with their pails of water they [the boat crew] would go ashore and take them in and roar with laughter at their ludicrous appearance more especially Brother Hyde who was very fleshy."

At Richmond Marinda's brother Lyman, though disaffected from the church, "ordered a dinner at the hotel for all of his old friends, and treated us with very great kindness," reported Helen Mar. Marinda and Orson stayed with Lyman for a few days while the rest of the company went on to Far West. One can imagine Marinda's mixed feelings at being re-united with a beloved brother who was opposed to the church, as well as heated exchanges between the strong-minded Orson and his excommunicant brother-in-law.

Soon, however, Orson himself became disaffected. The Hydes arrived at Far West in mid-July and Orson was "taken sick ... with bilious fever," and only regained his full health in the next spring. Marinda must have spent the winter nursing him. On October 18, 1838, he (with Marinda, presumably) and Thomas Marsh, a senior apostle, fled Far West, and a week later Hyde signed an affidavit prepared by Marsh alleging that Mormons had plundered Gallatin and that Joseph Smith planned "to take this state, and he professes to his people to intend taking the US, and ultimately the whole world." "If he [Joseph Smith] was ... let alone he would be a second Mohamet to this generation, and that he would make it one gore of blood from the rocky Mountains to the Atlantic Ocean." It also described Mormon raids against non-Mormons and asserted that Smith advocated death for Saints who refused to fight. This inflammatory document seriously compromised Smith's image and contributed toward his arrest and imprisonment in Liberty Jail. In a December letter from Liberty, the prophet wrote that "we had like to have forgotten Marsh and Hyde whose hearts are full of corruption."

Once again Marinda must have watched her husband's actions with deep dismay. For the next five months he did not affiliate with Mormons, opening a grocery store in New Franklin, Howard County, in central Missouri. However, his conscience troubled him, as he still felt some loyalty to Joseph Smith and his fellow Latter-day Saints. Finally, he had a vision in which he saw that "if he did not make immediate restitution to the quorum of the Twelve, he would be cut off and all his posterity, and that the curse of Cain would be upon him," so he decided to humble himself and return to the church. In March 1839 a repentant Orson visited fellow apostle Heber C. Kimball in Far West, and Kimball agreed to plead his cause with Joseph Smith. Orson also wrote to Brigham Young on March 30 and reported that as soon as his brother-in-law Oliver Olney came with a team, he and Marinda would move to the Nauvoo area. They arrived in April.

### VI. Greased Paper Windows

Orson's case was debated at a May 4 general church conference in Quincy, Illinois. Heber Kimball and Hyrum Smith spoke for the contrite apostle and Joseph Smith was won over. Although Orson was suspended from acting as an apostle, he was allowed to speak at the next church conference. On June 25 Wilford Woodruff wrote of Hyde that the "horrors of hell has rolled o'er his soul, even to the wasting of his flesh, and he has now humbled himself in the dust, desiring to return to the church ... a more humble and penitant man I never saw." Again Marinda is a shadow behind all of this. One can only imagine the ordeal she must have gone through, along with her husband—first the persecutions of Missouri, then the separation from her religion and friends. But she must have felt joy at her husband's return to the Latter-day Saint fold.

On June 27 Smith wrote, "Attended a conference of the Twelve — at which time Br Orson Hyde, made his confession and was restored to the Priesthood again." With Orson back in full church fellowship, the Hydes settled down to life in Nauvoo—which included severe bouts of ague that afflicted the whole family and endangered their lives. Hyde, usually stocky, was transformed into a virtual skeleton. He served a short, local mission from fall to midwinter, just long enough to cause him to be absent when Marinda's third child, Emily Matilda, was born on December 13.

A more extensive mission was in the offing. As he himself wrote, on April 6, 1840, in a general church conference, "I was appointed, in company with Elder John E. Page, to go on a mission to Jerusalem," a pilgrimage that he had been pondering for some time. With John Page, he left on April 15, but the two apostles soon separated and Hyde continued on to Palestine alone. He traveled through England, stopped in Germany and Bavaria for a time to learn German, then visited Constantinople. On October 24, 1841, he stood on the Mount of Olives and consecrated Palestine for the gathering of Judah in the last days. Then he saw the sights of Cairo and Alexandria on his way home. At Trieste he wrote a letter to "My Dear Marinda" which was published in the *Times and Seasons*. It ended: "May the Lord bless you all, and save you from the violence of men, and from all evil. My kind respects to the Presidency, and to all that enquire after me. I am as ever your affectionate husband. ORSON HYDE."

However, Marinda was once again left alone with two small children to tend during this long foreign mission. Family traditions give a grim picture of the apostle's wife in Nauvoo during the first part of his absence as she struggled to raise two daughters in an environment of chronic sickness and bleak poverty. A descendent wrote:

> Before her marriage she had been blessed with plenty but now as troubles increased their means decreased and she had to live in a little log house whose windows had no glass but in place of which were pieces of greased paper ... A little cornmeal and a few groceries were all the provisions remaining to sustain her and the little ones. Had she been well and strong this might not have been so dreadful, but she was just able to move about after having been confined to her room with ague. She took in knitting, taught a little school, and by the dim light of a candle at night did what little sewing she could.

As often, there is a striking contrast between the male general authority missionary distinguishing himself on an important, if difficult, mission, well remembered by history, while the wife, overlooked by history, endured hardships at home.

## VII. In the *Times and Seasons* Office

Beginning in December 1841 Marinda became an important participant in Nauvoo polygamy. There is a well-documented marriage to Joseph

Smith in April 1842, and before that, she had a friendship with Willard Richards that was characterized by three antagonistic Nauvoo former insiders, John Bennett, Sidney Rigdon, and printer Ebenezer Robinson, as a (polyandrous) plural marriage or an affair. While these witnesses cannot be lightly dismissed, a marital connection between Richards and Marinda has not been conclusively demonstrated by the extant evidence. I summarize it here.

On December 2, 1841, Joseph Smith, who undoubtedly had been friendly with Marinda since he had lived at her home in Hiram, became concerned for the inadequate house she lived in. He accordingly received the following revelation, which has never been canonized:

> Verily thus saith the Lord unto you my servant Joseph. that inasmuch as you have called upon me to know my will concerning my handmaid Nancy Marinda Hyde Behold it is my will that she should have a better place prepared for her than that in which she now lives, in order that her life may be spared unto her; Therefore go and say unto my servant Ebenezer Robinson, & To my handmaid his wife, Let them open their doors and take her and her children into their house and take care of them faithfully and kindly until my servant Orson Hyde returns from his mission ... and let my handmaid Nancy Marinda Hyde hearken to the counsel of my servant Joseph in all things whatsoever he shall teach unto her, and it shall be a blessing upon her and upon her children after her, unto her Justification saith the Lord.

The things Smith would "teach unto her" probably included both polygyny and polyandry. He showed his revelation to Robinson, who later wrote that he willingly obeyed its directives: "I immediately harnessed my horse to the buggy, and brought Sister Hyde and her two little daughters to our home, where they remained until the twelve took possession of the printing office." The Robinson home was the first floor of the third *Times and Seasons* building.

On Christmas Eve Marinda was apparently the companion of Willard Richards (whose wife, Jennetta, was in the east, staying with her parents on a visit) for a party at Hiram Kimball's. Willard wrote in his journal, "Christmas eve  visited & dined at Hiram Kimballs with Nancy M. Hyde. B. Young. H. C. Kimball  O. Pratt, W. Woodruff, J. Taylor & wives – H Kimball gave each of the 12. a Lot of Land & supper of Turkeys." On January 13 of the new year, Richards stopped boarding with Brigham Young and began to live with Joseph Smith, presumably in his Homestead house.

Two weeks later Smith received a revelation, also uncanonized, directing the Twelve to take charge of the *Times and Seasons*, which had been managed by Ebenezer Robinson previously. Robinson was very reluctant to give up the printing business, as this would require him not only to give up his trade and tools of his trade but also his place of residence. However, he complied, and on February 4 the printing office, with all its contents, was sold to Smith, with Richards acting as his agent. On the date of transfer, according to Robinson, Richards demanded that the Robinson family vacate immediately, even though the printer was hard pressed to find a new home to move to. Finally a neighbor offered to house them temporarily, so the Robinsons moved out of the printer's building at sunset. According to Robinson, "That evening Willard Richards nailed down the windows, and fired off his revolver in the street after dark, and commenced living with Mrs. Nancy Marinda Hyde, in the rooms we had vacated in the printing office building, where they lived through the winter. His family was residing at the time in Massachusetts, and Elder Orson Hyde was absent on his mission to Palestine."

John C. Bennett, in 1842, supplies the earliest attestation for this story: "Dr. Richards, who is so notorious for *Hyde*ing in these last days." The word "notorious" suggests hearsay. In any case, Bennett is not the most reliable witness possible, though he certainly was an insider, Joseph's intimate for many months. He also wrote that Marinda and Willard were both living in the printing house.

A more substantial witness, Sidney Rigdon, made the same accusation after he became estranged from Mormonism. Some three years after the event he wrote: "If R. [Richards] should take a notion to H.'s [Hyde's] wife in his absence, all that is necessary to be done is to be sealed. No harm done, no adultery committed; only taking a little the [sic] advantage of rights of priesthood. And after R. has gone the round of dissipation with H.'s wife, she is afterwards turned over to S. [Smith] and thus the poor silly woman becomes the actual dupe to two designing men, under the sanctimonious garb of rights of the royal priesthood." These passages will be discussed below.

Marinda continued to live in the printer's building and she and Willard certainly were often in close proximity, if he was living there too, as Robinson and Bennett report. Journal entries for 1842 support this picture. William Clayton wrote on February 7, "I dined at Sister Hydes with Brother Joseph Smith, H Kimball, W Woodruff, B Young and Willard Richards." On the 24th Smith wrote, "P.M. was explaining the Records of Abraham To the Recorder [Willard Richards]. Sisters Marinda Mary and others present. to hear the Explanations." Wilford Woodruff wrote in his diary on March 9, "After court was over Joseph Smith & the Twelve suped upon a rost Turkey with sister Hyde." The Joseph Smith journal locates this dinner in the printing office.

That is the most important evidence suggesting an intimate relationship between Willard and Marinda. The most striking aspect of the testimonies of Rigdon and Robinson is that they were not first-hand witnesses for any actual marriage, as neither was part of the inner circle of polygamy. They saw that Marinda and Richards were living in the same building, perhaps, and though such a living arrangement may have exceeded the customary norms of decorum, this would have been the extent of their own direct knowledge.

In addition, there seems to be a major anomaly in Robinson's story. Nauvoo plural marriage was always protected by a powerful code of silence, but Robinson portrays Richards virtually flaunting the polyandrous union, which seems unlikely. Firing a gun as a quasi-ritual of possession would be entirely inconsistent with the code of silence. Furthermore, if Richards was trying to keep the marriage clandestine, he would probably not accompany the wife to a public Christmas party.

Thus the extant evidence allows the view that Willard Richards and Marinda Hyde were living close together, perhaps, but not as man and wife, and in different rooms. By this interpretation, Rigdon and Robinson then placed excessive reliance on second-hand rumors. In fact, Rigdon admits that he had not heard the story first-hand: "I received the account from one who said he was acquainted with the facts." Until stronger evidence is found for a marriage between Marinda and Richards, this may be the best hypothesis to follow.

## VIII. Joseph Smith

On March 17, 1842, at the first Relief Society meeting in Nauvoo, Marinda's name was presented for membership. Sometime in the following month, she married Joseph Smith, as a list of marriages in Smith's diary indicates: "Apr 42  Marinda Johnson to Joseph Smith." She was twenty-six at the time, he was thirty-six. We can only guess at the shock this exposure to polygyny and polyandry must have given Marinda; nearly everyone who has commented on their first introduction to polygamy wrote that they at first looked at it with revulsion and shock, and fought the idea for a time. Some Mormons, male and female, had suicidal feelings when they were first told that they were required to practice polygamy. As Marinda was apparently sincerely in love with Orson Hyde, polyandry must have been enormously difficult for her. Perhaps she, like many women, had a spiritual, revelatory conversion to polygamy that allowed her to live with the severe cognitive dissonance it would have caused.

There are four antagonistic reports of this marriage. The earliest, from Sidney Rigdon in 1845, has already been partially quoted: "H. [Orson Hyde] by and by finds out the trick which was played off upon him in his absence, by his two faithful friends. His dignity becomes offended, (and well it might) refuses to live with his wife, but to be even with his companions in iniquity, takes to himself three more wives." By this scenario, Orson did not know of the marriage until 1843. This may well be, and Orson did marry polygamously after he returned to Nauvoo. However, contrary to Rigdon, Orson did not stop living with Marinda at this time and Marinda continued to have children with him until 1858.

Second, according to William Hall, published in 1852, Joseph Smith demanded Orson's wife and all his money when Orson sued for reinstatement in the church after his Missouri disaffection, and Orson gave her up. This flatly contradicts Rigdon's account, in which Joseph and Marinda marry without Orson's knowledge. It could be noted that Hall's discussion of Zina Huntington's marriage to Smith was extremely unreliable, which lessens his authority here.

The next account is much later, but still from an early Nauvoo insider, John D. Lee. After describing Hyde's repentance and mission to Palestine, Lee wrote, "Report said that Hyde's wife, with his consent, was sealed to Joseph for an eternal state, but I do not assert the fact." Lee agrees with Hall that Hyde knew of the marriage, but honestly reports that the story was hearsay.

A further antagonistic report by an early Mormon—Ann Eliza Webb Young—sides with Rigdon in suggesting that Orson did not know of the marriage in 1842 and that he was extremely upset when he returned home from his mission and found out that Marinda had married Smith in his absence.

Thus the four writers offer no consensus on the issue of Orson's knowledge. Smith's other polyandrous marriages and the statements of Lee and Hall suggest that Orson may have known of the marriage beforehand. However, if Marinda and Joseph had wanted to marry with Orson's knowledge and consent, they probably would have waited until he returned from his mission before performing the ceremony. Orson's not knowing is probably the preferable interpretation, but neither view is certain.

## IX. Nancy Rigdon

Joseph Smith's wives, after their marriage to him, often figured in the marriage arrangements of new wives, as messengers or counselors or witnesses. According to John Bennett, Smith used Marinda as a go-between in his attempt to woo Nancy Rigdon, Sidney's nineteen-year-old daughter. Bennett is not always reliable, but he did have early first-hand knowledge of the Mormon leader's polygamous activities, as his short list of Smith's plural wives shows. In this case, accounts of the same events by Nancy's brother, J. Wickliffe, and her brother-in-law,

George W. Robinson, show that Bennett was not merely spinning a fictitious story.

Bennett relates that in early April, Smith decided he wanted to marry Nancy Rigdon, so on April 9 he asked Marinda to arrange a meeting between him and the teenager. Marinda met Nancy at the funeral of Ephraim Marks and told her that Joseph wanted to see her at the printing office, Marinda's residence. When Nancy arrived, she was ushered into a private room where Joseph soon proposed to her. She was outraged and demanded that he let her out of the locked room immediately. Smith did so, but, "as she was much agitated, he requested Mrs. Hyde to explain matters to her; and, after agreeing to write her a doctrinal letter, left the house. Mrs. Hyde told her that these things looked strange to her *at first*, but that she would become more reconciled on mature reflection. Miss Rigdon replied, 'I never shall,' left the house, and returned home." Nancy did hold her ground, and when she told her father of the experience, it drove a firm wedge between him and Joseph, just as Joseph's earlier relationship with Fanny Alger had caused another high church leader, Oliver Cowdery, to lose respect for him.

Bennett's account portrays Marinda as an experienced plural wife—even though she was only twenty-six—giving advice to a prospective protégé. Clearly, Marinda was entirely converted to polygamy by this time. She continued to spend time with Smith, as an entry in Willard Richards's journal on November 17, shows: "Joseph & Sister Hyde. evening Joseph Gone." On August 31 "Sisters Hyde and Johnson" visited Patty Sessions.

## X. "Most Repulsive to My Feelings"

Less than a month later, on December 7, 1842, Orson returned to Nauvoo from his three-year mission, and Joseph wrote in his journal, "This day dined with Er Orson Hyde & family. Er Hyde has this day returned home from his Mission to Jerusalem, his presence was gratifying, spent the day with Er Hyde & drawing wood." The presence of two husbands, one of whom probably did not know about the other, must have been an awkward, painful situation for Marinda at first. One wonders when she and Joseph told Orson of their marriage. However, Hyde was often in Smith's company in the upcoming months. On February 28 the Mormon prophet again ate dinner at the Hyde home.

Smith had introduced Orson to the general principles of polygamy by February or March 1843, when the apostle married his first plural wife. Perhaps Smith also told Orson of his marriage to Marinda at this time. Ann Eliza Webb Young wrote:

When he [Hyde] returned, he, in turn, imbibed the teachings of polygamy also ... In the mean time it was hinted to him that Smith had had his first wife sealed to himself in his absence, as a wife for eternity. Inconsistent as it may seem, Hyde was in a furious passion ... he did not propose having HIS rights interfered with even by the holy Prophet whose teachings he had so implicitly followed, and he swore that if this was true he would never live with her again. But he did live with her for several years after the exodus from Nauvoo.

It is not easy to know how far one can trust Ann Eliza, who was writing an exposé. However, an explosion from Hyde would have been entirely in keeping with his strong-minded character. The two wives that Hyde took in 1843 may have been connected with Smith's marriage to Marinda, for in many cases "first husbands" (such as Henry Jacobs and Windsor Lyon) married other women after their wives were sealed to high priesthood leaders polyandrously. Theoretically the "second husband" may have encouraged the "first husband" to take other wives to compensate for the loss of the first wife, to help them start their own eternal kingdoms. And Smith allowed the first husband to continue to live with the first wife. The timing of Orson's marriages to Martha Browett and Mary Ann Price fits this pattern. Rigdon (though not Ann Eliza Young) describes the two unions as a response to the Smith-Marinda sealing.

Orson proposed to Mary Ann Price sometime between January and March, but she rejected his marriage offer at first. Price, in her autobiography, wrote:

> On the return of Orson Hyde from his mission to Palestine he carried letters of introduction to me and invited me to visit his wife. I was there met by Joseph Smith, the Prophet, who, after an interesting conversation introduced the subject of plural marriage and endeavored to teach me that principle. I resisted it with every argument I could command, for, with my tradition, it was most repulsive to my feelings and rendered me very unhappy, as I could not reconcile it with the purity of the Gospel of Christ. Mr. Hyde took me home in a carriage and asked me what I thought of it and if I would consent to enter his family? I replied that I could not think of it for a moment.

And there, Mary Ann says, the matter rested for some time. Orson turned to another woman, twenty-three-year-old English convert Martha Browett, who accepted his proposal, and in February or March Marinda stood as a witness when her first husband married his first plural wife, with Joseph Smith officiating. Marinda soon was socializing with her new sister-wife. On April 10 she, Mary Ann Price, Martha Browett, and Patty Sessions visited at Sylvia Lyon's home.

The next month Marinda and Joseph apparently repeated their marriage ceremony; at least, this is the date Marinda later gave for her marriage to the prophet. If we conclude that there was only one ceremony, the contemporary record in Joseph Smith's journal is preferable. Possibly, she might have "redated" the marriage so that it did not appear to take place while Hyde was on his mission. However, for many of Smith's marriages there were repeated ceremonies, which is the most likely explanation for this second marriage date. Perhaps this ceremony was for Orson's benefit, or perhaps Smith wanted to repeat it because the original ceremony was performed by someone of lesser authority. Marinda's affidavit reports that Brigham Young performed the May 1843 sealing and that Eliza and Emily Partridge stood as witnesses.

As these events took place, Mary Ann Price had been making inquiries concerning Orson Hyde's character and pondering his proposal. "I soon learned, to my satisfaction, that Mr. Orson Hyde was a conscientious, upright and noble man and became his third wife. Mrs. Hyde had two sweet little girls and I soon learned to love them and their dear Mother who, in the Spring of 1843 received me into her house as her husband's wife! Sealed to him by Joseph, the Prophet, in her presence." Orson apparently married the twenty-seven-year-old Mary Ann on July 20. Marinda wrote only this of her Nauvoo experiences with polygamy: "Having accomplished a three-years mission, he [Orson] returned, and shortly after, in accordance with the revelation on celestial marriage, and with my full consent, married two more wives."

## XI. Holy Order

After Hyde's triumphant return from Palestine, grateful Mormons evidently built him a house in Nauvoo, which is still standing; according to family traditions, Marinda's non-Mormon relatives furnished it. Hyde's two plural wives apparently also lived in this house.

Soon Marinda was expecting again. In August she would have been saddened by news of her father's death in Kirtland on July 30. Then Orson left for a short apostolic mission to the eastern states on August 17, when Marinda was approximately seven months pregnant. On October 23 she figured in Willard Richards's journal: "We went to Sister Hyde &c to see about a stove." Perhaps Orson had started a store and Marinda and her sister-wives tended it in his absence.

Orson returned before November 2, when he met with the Twelve and Joseph Smith. A week later, on November 9, Orson Washington Hyde was born, but sadly died two weeks later, on November 23. Laura was now six and Emily four.

In late 1843 Marinda and Orson participated in ordinances that Latter-day Saints today regard as key revelations of Joseph Smith: the endowment, including subsequent prayer meetings with initiates, a group called the Quorum of the Anointed, or Holy Order; and also the "fullness of the priesthood," an ordinance performed usually only with a husband and wife. On December 2 and 3 Orson was endowed in the upper room of Smith's red brick store, and on January 25, 1844, he received the fullness of the priesthood ordinance. Wilford Woodruff wrote in his journal, "Met with quorum of the Twelve at President Youngs house. Had a good prayer meeting [OH] Br Orson Hyde was present had not met with us for some time Orson Hyde Received his 2d Anointg." As a man only received this ordinance in conjunction with a wife, and as Marinda did not receive it with him, historian Michael Quinn concludes that Orson may have received it in conjunction with a deceased woman, by proxy. Marinda apparently did not receive this ordinance with him because she was sealed for eternity to Smith.

Her endowment took place on February 18, for journal entries by Joseph Smith, Richards, and Woodruff give her special prominence in the Quorum of the Anointed for that day. On April 14 Orson left for Washington on a mission given him by Smith. But on June 27 the prophet was killed, leaving Marinda widowed of her eternal husband.

## XII. Time and Eternity

By August 12 Orson had returned to Nauvoo, and he and Marinda and their children—along with Marinda's two sister-wives—resumed family life. But he continued to serve missions. In 1845 he traveled to the East and returned home by October. On December 7 Marinda and Orson attended a Holy Order meeting at the Nauvoo temple, and Heber Kimball noted in his journal that Marinda had not yet received her fullness of the priesthood ordinance.

Three days later Marinda and Orson repeated their endowments in the temple, and, significantly, they received their endowments together. Their marriage for time was still in effect. However, they were approaching a difficult moment. As all eternal marriages needed to be re-solemnized in the temple, the question of Marinda's marriage to Joseph Smith would face them again. Usually a plural wife of Smith was sealed to him (by proxy) for eternity and to the proxy for time. In such cases, all of the children of the wife would be sealed to Smith for eternity, even though another man might be the biological parent.

For unknown reasons, Marinda was sealed to Orson Hyde, not Smith, for time and eternity on January 11, 1846. This is an extremely anomalous marriage, as no other polyandrous wife of Smith was sealed to her first husband for eternity (though some widows whom Joseph married, such as Agnes Coolbrith Smith and Delcena Johnson Sherman, were sealed to their former husbands in the temple rather than to Smith). Orson was sealed to Martha and Mary Ann at the same time. On the following day Marinda's two daughters, Laura Marinda and Emily Matilda, were sealed to

Marinda and Orson for eternity. Perhaps the best explanation for this puzzling series of sealings is that Orson was reluctant to give up his two daughters to Joseph Smith for eternity and he convinced Marinda to choose him instead of Smith as an eternal partner.

Two positive family events followed the temple rites. On January 23 Marinda's fifth child, Frank Henry Hyde, was born; and Luke Johnson, Marinda's disaffected brother, was rebaptized early in the year. This must have been a great comfort to Marinda, for she stayed in close proximity to him for the rest of his life. The Hydes remained in Nauvoo until the temple was dedicated (by Orson) on April 30, then left for the wilderness in mid-May.

### XIII. "Heart and Hands Full"

After an entirely undocumented trip across Iowa, they reached Council Bluffs on June 17. A month later Marinda appears in Patty Sessions's journal ("visited sister Hyde got some things that she brought on"). Marinda had joined that circle of elite women, Eliza Snow, Zina Young, and others, who met together frequently, spoke in tongues, prophesied, and comforted each other in their hardships. Soon Orson was assigned to a mission in England, and he, John Taylor, and Parley P. Pratt left on July 31. Marinda was left living in a tent, once again a missionary widow. A mention of her in Patty Sessions's journal on February 19, 1847, shows that she was staying at Louisa Beaman's house and was sewing to make ends meet.

Orson returned to Council Bluffs on May 12 and was soon given the long-term assignment of presiding at Winter Quarters to deal with a steady stream of immigrants who had to be outfitted for the journey across the plains. So Marinda would not make a quick trip across the plains and settle down in Salt Lake Valley, which at least spared her many of the hardships of the first winters there. In the Tullidge interview she spoke of Orson's duties at Winter Quarters, not of her own trials as she tried to raise her children in frontier living conditions.

On October 3 she wrote to Sarah Granger Kimball at Nauvoo, telling her that her children had been sick. Sarah wrote back on January 2, 1848: "Dear Sister Hyde ... I joyfully improve the opportunity of acknowledgeing the receipt of y'rs of the third of Oct the perusal of which afforded us much joy & satisfaction & for which favor we feel verry greatful nothing affords me more pleasure than to be assured that I am not forgotten by one whome I so dearly love as yourself." Marinda and Sarah Kimball were clearly close friends. Sarah continued: "I was sorry to hear that yr family have been sick dear Sister H you must have had yr heart & hands full but you say you had strength given according to yr day, inasmuch as you have not been overcome it is all right."

Another paragraph in Kimball's letter may refer to Marinda's latest pregnancy: "It rejoices me to hear of yr prosperity in the things of the kingdom may yr kingdom continue to increase through time & eternity O Sister Hyde how I wish you could visit me during my husdband's absence I shall feel verry lonesome indeed ... saw Sarah Lawrence [Smith Kimball] last night she desires her love to you said she should write you if she had time." A valuable verification of Marinda's extended family follows: "Please give my respects to yr husdband to Marthy [Browett] Mary-Ann [Price] Laura Emely Frank & to all enquiring friends hopeing to hear from you by the bearer I remain with sentiments of affection yr devoted Sister S M Kimball." A postscript reveals that Orson was on a local missionary jaunt: "Br Haywood just called says he has heard that Br Hyde is in St Luis lectureing to his thousands this inspires us with a hope that he will visit us Br & Sis H send love." On February 28 Alonzo Eugene, Marinda's sixth child, was born at Council Bluffs (technically, Hyde Park), one of the lucky Winter Quarters children who survived. Laura was now ten, Emily eight, and Frank two.

On April 8 Louisa Beaman wrote Marinda, Mary Ann, and Martha, telling of her health problems and recounting the death of her recently born twins. She expressed her love for Marinda and her sister-wives: "We often speak of you and wish you were here but [I] must wait pat[i]ently untill you come, I could wish it might be this year but I heardly exspect it, I can not tell you how much I want to see you all." This letter confirms that Louisa had been living in the Hyde household at Council Bluffs: "but my mind often wanders back to the hours I have spent in your house and of the kindness I have received from you all, and when I think of it I feel greatful to you and to my Heavenly father and I feel to pray that the choicest of heavens blessing[s] may rest upon you." She closes with: "I must soon close give my love to all of the children and kiss them for me tell Laura, Emily, and Frank to not forget me, my warmest respects to br Hyde, br Luke [Johnson] and wife ... Clarra P. has just come and wished to be kindly remembered to you allso the girls I am living with, I want you to write every oppertunity. May the Lord bless you is my prayr from your sincere friend (exscuse my poor writing and mistakes which are many!) Louisa."

Louisa wrote again on July 14, 1849:

I was greatly in hopes I should hear that he [Luke Johnson]; together with your family were a comeing on this season but I heare you are not, so I am disappointed, but hope if it is for the beast [best], you will come on next season ... we often speak of you all when we are together and want to see you much, I have not forgoten how well I injoyed the mellons and a good many other thing[s] while at you[r] house and I fondly hope we may injoy many more such treats together in this valley ... give my best love to Martha and Mary Ann. I want to see them much allso to the children kiss them for me, and tell them not to forget me ... remember me in my affliction and pray for me. I give way for sister Eliz. from your sincere friend, Louisa.

After the bare bones of Marinda's life, hiding in the shadow of Orson, or enmeshed in the morally ambiguous enigmas of Nauvoo polygamy, these three letters come as a breath of fresh air, even if they are not holographs by Marinda herself. They show that she was loved by her close friends for her warmth and hospitality, and that both Louisa Beaman and Sarah Kimball felt it a trial to be separated from her. Mary Ann Price Hyde also was closely attached to Marinda, as her autobiography makes clear.

Marinda was pregnant again when Orson traveled to Washington, D.C., from June 24th to October 15th, 1849. On December 28 she bore her seventh child, Delia Annette. Her husband visited Utah in July 1850, making the journey back to Kanesville in the fall. He traveled to Utah again in 1851, then returned to Kanesville to bring his family with him to Utah the next year.

## XIV. Utah

In the Tullidge interview, Marinda said, "In the summer of 1852 we brought our family safely through to Salt Lake City, where we have had peace and safety ever since." Marinda, now thirty-seven, was pregnant during the journey, but the Hydes finally arrived at the valley on September 21. There were other changes in the family that year. Orson married another wife, Charlotte Quinlan, a fifty-year-old woman with no children. On the other hand, Martha Browett had left the apostle in Kanesville to set up as a seamstress on her own.

Orson worked as a businessman in Salt Lake and soon had a comfortable house built for his wives just north of the temple block. On November 10 Heber John Hyde, Marinda's eighth, was born. Laura was now fifteen, Emily thirteen, Frank nearly seven, Alonzo four, and Delia nearly three. Sadly, Heber John died almost exactly one year later, on November 11, 1853. On March 4, 1853, Marinda appeared in Patty Sessions's journal again: "We have Co[mpany] sisters Hyde, Pratt Kimbal and others Br Hyde came in the evening."

Brigham Young and Orson, two very strong-willed individuals, had occasional moments of conflict. Perhaps for this reason Orson was sent on a number of colonizing missions. On November 2 he organized a colony to Fort Supply, in the Green River area near Fort Bridger, but did not accompany them at first. He visited the colony in May 1854, but it is unclear how much time he spent there. In the same year, on July 10, Marinda's ninth child, Mary Lavina Hyde, was born in Salt Lake City, but unfortunately, like Marinda's previous child, died about a year later. Though Marinda was still bearing children in 1854, that year saw her second daughter, Emily Matilda, marry George Chase, and Marinda entered the grandmotherly period in her life.

Orson left to head a mission in Carson Valley, modern Nevada, on May 17, 1855, while Marinda stayed in Salt Lake City. On December 12 her first grandchild, Emily Marinda Chase, was born to Emily and George in Salt Lake City. The following year, on May 30, 1856, Marinda's first daughter, Laura, married Aurelius Miner. Later the same year, entries from Patty Sessions's journal show the range of Marinda's acquaintances: on September 1 "Sister M Hyde here on a visit," wrote Patty; and the following day, "Sisters M Hyde Violate Kimball Knight & Sylvia & Phebe Walton all here & Lucinia Marry had a good visit." Included in this group are four plural wives of Joseph Smith, Heber Kimball's first wife, and a Sessions relative.

By December 9, 1856, Orson had returned to the city. In 1857 he enlarged his family once again, marrying sixteen-year-old Ann Eliza Vickers on March 12, with whom he would have six children. That same year he married sixteen-year-old Helen Winters, who would separate from him in two years. Orson was fifty-two at the time, Marinda forty-five. On July 31 another complicating development in the story of Marinda's polygamous and polyandrous relationships took place when she married Joseph Smith again for eternity. One can only guess at the psychological factors that led her to change her mind and select Joseph over Orson for her eternal companion. Perhaps his marriages to young wives were a factor.

Still, on April 23, 1858, Marinda bore her tenth and last Hyde child, Zina Virginia. The baby's name perhaps points to another important friend of Marinda, Zina Huntington Young, a sister-wife in Smith's eternal family. Still at home were Frank, twelve, Alonzo, ten, and Delia, eight.

### XV. "They Shook Hands"

Marinda and her increasingly polygamous husband continued to drift apart. He was sent to head the important settlement of Sanpete County (including the towns of Ephraim, Manti, and Spring City) in 1860, but once again Marinda stayed in Salt Lake. Mary Ann tells the story: "On his return [from Nevada] he took another wife and was appointed to preside in Sanpete county. This was a new country and sparsely settled and Mrs. Hyde preferred remaining in the City with her children. So it was agreed upon that I should go to Sanpete." Mary Ann found the parting from Marinda difficult: "It was long before I could feel reconciled to be seperated from the other part of the family, for I was sincerley attached to them." Hyde was not actually abandoning Marinda, for he attended the legislature in Salt Lake and was frequently there on business. However, her home was no longer his primary abode. This geographical distance—along with the marriages to new wives—was one more step in Marinda's growing estrangement from her first husband.

Marinda's brother Luke died at her home on December 9, 1861. Lyman had passed away a few years earlier in Wisconsin, so she must have had cause to think about her own mortality. Orson, on the other hand, at fifty-eight kept marrying, including Julia Reinhart, twenty-one, in the summer of 1863, with whom he had five children. The following summer he added twenty-two-year-old Elizabeth Josephine Gallier to his family, with whom he had five children. And a year after that, on October 10, 1865, at the age of sixty, he celebrated the rites of matrimony for the last time, with Sophia Margaret Lyon, eighteen years old, with whom he had four children.

So Marinda held the position of older first wife in a sizeable family of young wives. While it was sometimes difficult for a new sister-wife in a large polygamous family, as the first wife often had strong emotional ties with the husband, the role of first wife could also be difficult, as she was forced to watch her husband spend more and more time with younger wives. Ann Eliza Webb Young tells an anecdote about Marinda and Orson that shows how difficult that experience could be in some cases:

> A few years since, at a large party at the Social Hall in Salt Lake City, Orson Hyde, one of the twelve apostles, met the wife of his youth, the mother of many of his children. He had escorted some of his younger wives there, and she came with a friend. It chanced that they were seated near each other at the table, and were compelled to speak; they shook hands, exchanged a very commonplace greeting, and that was all that passed between them ... it very often occurs that an elderly lady attends a party with friends, and meets her husband there with one or more younger wives; and sometimes both she and they have to watch their mutual husband while he plays the agreeable to some young girl ... Sometimes these old and middle-aged ladies do not see their husbands once a year, and yet they may not live half a mile apart.

Ann Eliza's anti-polygamy bias is obvious, but, on the other hand, she had been an eyewitness to polygamous etiquette since Nauvoo and was a participant in Utah plural marriage.

## XVI. President Mrs. Hyde and Counsel

Marinda's next years were dominated by her local 17th Ward Relief Society, which she headed from its organization on July 19, 1868, until her death. In the Tullidge interview she wrote, "In 1868 I was chosen to preside over the branch of the Female Relief Society of the ward in which I reside, the duties of which position I have prayerfully attempted to perform." One of the few pieces of writing we have by Marinda is an appreciation of one of her Relief Society counselors, Sarepta Heywood, who had died. Another aspect of Marinda's public life was her membership on the board of directors of the Deseret Hospital. At this time Marinda had living at home Frank, twenty-two, Alonzo, twenty, Delia, nineteen, and Zina, ten.

A co-worker in the 17th Ward Relief Society, Lydia D. Alder, left an admiring reminiscence of Marinda as president. When dealing with the poor, she would say, "Well, God made them, and we must make the best of them ... Quoting the words of Jesus, she would say, 'Remember the poor, for them we have always,' and 'Even as ye do it unto the least of these, ye do it unto me.'"

When Lydia lost a close family member, probably a child,

She [Marinda] stood by my side while the dear life slipped away whose loss brought me the deepest sorrow and acutest pain I have ever known. While she held me in her arms, she soothed the wild surging waters of grief, telling me that God the Father had permitted this, that *He* never made a mistake, did all things well, and, above all, loved those on whom He laid His chastening hand. Her child-like faith, coupled with a sublime love of God, made her a friend always to be loved, and never to be forgotten.

In 1870, when Marinda was fifty-five, the last act in the drama of her relationship with Orson occurred—they formally divorced after thirty-four years of marriage. The precise reasons for the divorce are not known, but it appears that Orson was giving most of his attention to his younger wives at this time. Biographer Myrtle Hyde explains the divorce thus: "[Orson was] a very kind husband, precise, but not domineering ... I feel that because Marinda was sealed to Joseph for eternity the time came when she could see no reason to remain married to Orson for time. Her decision not to go to Sanpete with him began a period of increasing independence from him, and they probably ... drifted apart emotionally. Orson took care of her needs as much as he could from far away, but she mostly depended upon her sons for things she was unable to do for herself. Orson's other wives had children the ages of Marinda's grandchildren, which undoubtedly contributed to distancing her and Orson's relationship. I find no evidence of animosity between Orson and Marinda."

Marinda'a charitable work continued. In March 1873 the 17th Ward Relief Society secretary, Sister Alder, filed a report to the *Woman's Exponent*. At a December meeting:

President Mrs. Hyde requested the visiting Committees to visit their blocks and solicit for a Christmas dinner, for the poor, which resulted in the donation of $30 in cash, chickens, pies, cakes, groceries, etc. being collected, and our needy had a substantial reason to be glad that it was Christmas ... We feel that President Mrs. Hyde and her Counsel have blessed the society, wisely guiding it, and the good feeling we have always enjoyed is the natural result.

Close to February 20, 1876, Marinda left Utah to visit relatives in the East, especially her sister Fanny, who was, with John Jr., one of her two living siblings. Eliza Snow wrote her a poem for the occasion: "To My dear friend, Marinda N. Hyde, On her departure for a visit to her relatives in the States." Marinda was still in the East at the end of June, when Eliza wrote her: "Ever Dear Sister Marinda, I see by date of your very interesting letter, that one whole month has elapsed since it was written. I felt so delight[ed] with it, that I intended to answer it immediately & urge you to write again. but how very {impishly} time flies when we have more to do than we can accomplish!" After sharing news from Salt Lake, the letter ended, "Please give my good wishes to your sister if she remembers me. I much regretted that I could not call on her when there. When are you coming home? God bless you continually, Your Sister E.R. Snow." Eliza was clearly another close friend.

Marinda was home by November 17, 1876, when she attended a meeting of Relief Society presidents in the Salt Lake Social Hall. At this meeting "the Grain Question," Brigham Young's admonition to the Relief Societies to store grain, was discussed. Marinda's comments are preserved: "We intend to build a hall for the use of our Society; when we heard of this grain business, we talked the matter over, and think of making the hall smaller, and putting up a bin for wheat in part of it. I would just suggest, that in the States, wheat sometimes spoils, through dampness, but our atmosphere being so dry, I expect it would keep good for some time." In the October 1877 Woman's Exponent, Marinda and Sister Alder announced the completion of the granary, probably at the same time that the 17th Ward Relief Society Hall was finished.

As was typical of faithful Mormon women, Marinda spent a great deal of her time performing ordinances for the dead in temples and in the Endowment House. Eliza Snow, in a June 17, 1870, letter to Mary E. Lightner, wrote, "Marinda Hyde is well as usual she works with me in the endowment house one week & Bathsheba Smith the next." On July 10, 1874, she stood proxy as a deceased woman was sealed to Brigham Young.

In her private life, she continued to pass milestones. Her mother, Elsa, died on July 18, 1870, in Council Bluffs, at age eighty-nine. On January 18, 1876, Frank Henry married Mary O'Neal. Two years after that, on November 28, 1878, Orson Hyde died in Spring City, Sanpete County, Utah. Marinda must have viewed the death with mixed feelings–though she and Orson eventually had proved incompatible, she had spent much of her life with him, and he was the father of her children.

She was now firmly entrenched in the grandmotherly era of her life. Two of her granddaughters left an appreciation of her as grandparent:

> She was so loving and sympathetic with her children and most affectionate with all of her grandchildren, which were many. When ever they went to see her they always found that she had some wonderfully good bread, unsalted butter, and such good cookies for them ... She had little doll furniture and paper dolls for the little children to play with and would tell them such good stories. She was a lovely creature, dignified, always well groomed, and was so much a lady with a lovely lace on her head and over her shoulders. She was a good housekeeper and kept her mind active, took a keen interest in life and people as long as she lived.

One New Year's Day her daughter Laura was holding an open house in her home on Second South when Fred, her son, decided that he wanted grandma Marinda to come to the party. So he hitched up a crude sleigh to the old family horse and drove to North Temple. Marinda dressed in her best clothes and was greatly amused as she accepted her unconventional taxi service to the Miner home.

A December 26, 1881, journal entry by Emmeline Wells shows Marinda attending Elizabeth Whitney's birthday party, along with Eliza Snow, Helen Mar Whitney, and other prominent Mormon women. On August 8, 1884, Emily Partridge Young's journal shows Marinda again associating with some of the "leading women of Zion": "Carlie had company. Sister Hyde, Ivins, Grant, Staines, Powel, Loria Young and Amelia Young." On August 12 Emily wrote, "Visited at Sister Hyde's. She is a dear, good woman."

When Marinda celebrated her seventieth birthday on June 29, 1885, Helen Mar Whitney wrote in her diary, "Went to Sister Hyds where quite a party celebrated her natal day – had a feast, & a few sisters spoke." A notice in the *Woman's Exponent* gives a fuller description: "There was a delicious repast set for the ladies, at six p.m. ... and the tables were handsomely ornamented with flowers. After supper, the ladies indulged in a little speech making in honor of the happy occasion and to express the sentiments of love and admiration they felt for this honored mother in Israel." Phebe Woodruff spoke, then Hannah King, C. Horrocks, M. I. Horne, and Marinda's old friend Sarah M. Kimball, at whose home in Nauvoo the Relief Society had been organized. Marinda then thanked the group. Following her, sisters Riter, B.

W. Smith, Julia Pack, Emmeline Wells, E. Howard, and Julia C. Howe added small speeches. Also attending, according to the *Exponent*, were Laura Miner and Emily Chase, her daughters; sisters E. S. Taylor, R. M. Carrington, S. A. Reese, Lizzie R. Young, Rachel R. Grant, Annie Ivins, and a Sister Adams—a who's who of important Mormon women. The *Exponent* continues: "Sister Hyde has ever been known for good works, her labors of love, her sweet charity and wise counsel to the daughters of Zion. May she live to see as many happy returns of the day as her heart desires. Her posterity already number over forty, among them eight great grandchildren."

## XVII. "Her Gentle, Cheerful Spirit"

On March 21, 1886, Helen Mar Whitney wrote in her diary, "I hear that Sister Marinda Hyde is dying." Three days later, on the 24th, she passed away at the age of seventy and was buried next to her brother Luke in the Salt Lake Cemetery. The *Deseret News* obituary reads, "DEATHS ... HYDE — In this city, at 9 a.m. to-day, Marinda, relict of the Late Apostle O. Hyde; born at Pomfret, Windsor county, Vt., June 28, 1815. The funeral service will be held at the 17th Ward meeting house, on Friday next, commencing at 2 p.m." Alder, writing in *Woman's Exponent*, provided a more personal epitaph:

> She was a noble example of the Christian graces. When her family or friends were in trouble, she uttered the words of comfort, of patience and cheer ... To say that we will miss her, will express but very weakly the deep feelings of regret her death has caused. Yet for her sake we should be glad. To think that now she is not feeble, nor in pain, but her gentle, cheerful spirit free to enjoy the beauties of eternal worlds, is with her loved ones gone before, mingling with the Church of the First Born.

We remember how her friends Louisa Beaman and Sarah Kimball missed Marinda, and how her sister-wife, Mary Ann Price, regretted her separation from her.

## XVIII. Conclusion

One of the great misfortunes of Mormon history is that Marinda's life is so sparsely documented. She has a marriage history as complex as Zina Huntington's, yet left no journals or letters to help us understand it, and Orson wrote nothing about her relationship with Joseph Smith. Nevertheless, it is clear that Marinda was a prominent woman in early Mormonism, the first wife of an important apostle, and was greatly beloved by her friends in the elite circles of Mormon women.

Moreover, her life is a valuable case history showing the strains of polygamy on a Latter-day Saint wife and mother. In Nauvoo she lived in a polyandrous relationship, certainly a difficult experience given her conservative religious upbringing. She undoubtedly had to deal with the tensions of two men in her life at the same time—one a prophet viewed as infallible, the other the husband of her youth and father of her children. In Utah she continued to bear Hyde children until 1858, but he then apparently spent increasingly more of his family time with younger wives, and her marriage to him ended in formal divorce, an unusual development for the first wife of a general authority. As is the case with so many other women in this book, Marinda's later life did not include a lifelong, intimate emotional relationship with a male companion, but it did include deep friendships with other women, including her sister-wives and ward Relief Society sisters, as well as close ties with her children and grandchildren.

# 10.

# Mother in Israel

## *Elizabeth Davis*
## *(Goldsmith Brackenbury Durfee Smith Lott)*

On October 1, 1843, Joseph Smith wrote in his journal describing a historic occasion in the history of the Holy Order, an elite group of Mormons who had been introduced to his most sacred rituals and who met regularly to pray together. "Eve Council met same as Thursday previous except Law, Marks, Durphy, Hiram's wife, Joseph &c. re-anointed. Law &c. anointed counselors. Prayer and singing. Adjourned to Wednesday eve." Four women were here initiated into the Holy Order; previously, only one woman, Emma Smith, had been brought into the inner circle. Most of this select group were well known. Jane Law was the wife of William Law, Joseph Smith's counselor in the First Presidency. Rosannah Marks was the wife of William Marks, president of the Nauvoo Stake. "Hiram's wife" was Mary Fielding Smith, the spouse of Joseph Smith's brother Hyrum. All of these women were clearly linked to the most elite leaders in Nauvoo, and their husbands had been previously initiated into the Holy Order. (It should be remembered that local stake leaders had more central authority than apostles at this time, which may explain why the apostles' wives were not found in this group.)

But the last woman, Mrs. Durphy, might be considered an anomaly, for there is no obvious reason for her presence in this elite group of women. Her husband, Jabez Durphy, was an active, faithful member of the church but held no office in the hierarchy, had never been initiated into the Holy Order, and never would be. The reason for Elizabeth's inclusion probably lies in her ties to Joseph Smith's polygamy. An older woman, she was nevertheless one of Smith's wives and was actively involved in arranging his ongoing polygamous unions. In the secret world of Nauvoo polygamy, she was a major figure and thus could stand beside Jane Law, Rosannah Marks, and Mary Smith in the Anointed Quorum.

Elizabeth is one of Smith's more elusive spouses, due to her many marriages before and after her involvement with the prophet and because of her far-ranging travels in her later life. After Nauvoo she abruptly dropped out of LDS history, almost without a trace. However, her marriages have been sorted out and her descendants have traced her transcontinental wanderings in western America, a story than ends with her final years as a Reorganized Latter Day Saint in Kansas. Though much about her is still lacking in the historical record (including any diaries or letters from her pen), we at least have an outline of her life. Like Patty Sessions, another older wife with whom she was linked in contemporary reports, Elizabeth acted as a "Mother in Israel," helping Smith communicate and meet with prospective plural wives. Like Patty, she was a polyandrous wife, and her "first husband," Jabez Durphy, was a faithful Latter-day Saint. However, after Joseph Smith's death this marriage did not endure, and Elizabeth married Cornelius Lott for a short time before they also separated. She is a good example of the fluidity of Mormon marriage practice in Nauvoo.

### I. The Davises

Elizabeth was born to Gilbert Davis, a thirty-nine-year-old Revolutionary War veteran, and Abigail Reeves, thirty-eight, in Riverhead, Suffolk, New York (east Long Island) on March 11, 1791. She was the sixth in a family of seven—her siblings being William (1776), Jeremiah (1780), James (1782), John (1784), Sarah (1788), and Leopold (1794). Her oldest three brothers had apparently all left home by the time she was nine. Family tradition states that Gilbert Davis ran a ferry from Long Island to New York but that when roads improved, his business declined, and he had to look for other work. Riverhead town records show him acting as an overseer of "high Ways" and an overseer of the poor in 1799 and 1830. It is also known that he was Presbyterian.

### II. Gilbert Goldsmith

Elizabeth married her first husband, Gilbert Goldsmith, a sailor, on April 13, 1811, in Cutchogue, northeast of Riverhead, when she was twenty years old. Gilbert, a native of Cutchogue, was twenty-five. At some point Elizabeth and Gilbert apparently converted to Methodism. Twin boys were born to them on November 27, 1811, of whom one, Isaac Goldsmith, died, while the other, Gilbert Davis Goldsmith, survived. Less than a month later, on December 24, Gilbert Sr. was sailing in the New York harbor when his boat capsized during a storm and he was drowned, so Elizabeth was widowed less than a month after becoming a mother.

### III. Joseph Blanchette Brackenbury

The widow Betsy Goldsmith traveled to western Long Island after 1815 and married Joseph Blanchette Brackenbury in 1818 or 1819, judging from the birthdate of their first child. Her new husband had been born on January 18, 1788, in Lincolnshire, England, but immigrated to America as a young boy. Evidently he worked as a farmer, for after his death his estate papers listed typical farming livestock and implements: "one Cow, one plow, one yoke and irons, one hog, one pitch fork, one Sythe and tackling, and two Axes." On November 11, 1820, Elizabeth's and Joseph's first child, Charles Wesley, was born in Newton, in present-day New York City, between Brooklyn and Queens. His name shows the parents' strong Methodist religious leanings at the time. Brackenburys had been important disciples of John Wesley in England. Another son, Joseph Blanchette, was born on October 25, 1822.

Elizabeth, Joseph, and the three children, accompanied by Elizabeth's first husband's uncle, Isaac Goldsmith, moved in 1824 to New London, Huron, Ohio, thirty miles southwest of Cleveland, and about fifty miles southwest of Kirtland. It is possible that a number of the old families from eastern Long Island made this migration, with an intermediate stop in the Orange and Ulster counties in New York, northwest of New York City.

More children were born in Ohio. Benjamin Blanchard unfortunately died at birth in 1826. A second Benjamin Blanchard was born on April 27, 1827, and a last child, John Wesley Brackenbury (another Methodist name), on August 12, 1829, when Elizabeth was thirty-eight. Gilbert was now nearly eighteen, Charles Wesley nearly nine, Joseph Blanchette nearly seven, and Benjamin one and a half.

### IV. "In the Midst of Fair Prospects"

Living in Ohio, Elizabeth and Joseph were now in Mormon territory, and they were drawn early into the Latter-day Saint net. On April 10, 1831, they were baptized and confirmed by John Carl and Solomon Hancock, and Joseph was ordained an elder the next day. He made rapid progress in the new church. On June 3 he attended a general conference in Kirtland. John Whitmer, recording "many mighty miracles" wrought by Mormon elders at this time, mentioned one in particular: an old woman who had been bedridden for eight years sent for the elders, even though she was not a church member. "Elders Emer Harris Joseph Brackenberry and Wheeler Baldwin" answered her summons. At her bedside, according to Whitmer, they "praid for her, and laid their hands on her, and she was immediately made whole and magnified and praised God, and is now enjoying perfect health."

On October 25 Joseph attended a general conference held at the dwelling of "Sirenes Burnet" in Orange, Cuyahoga, Ohio, and there was ordained a high priest by Oliver Cowdery, as was an Edmund Durfee. The "Far West Record" preserves a small speech by Elizabeth's husband, who was evidently an impressive speaker: "Br. Joseph Brackenbury said that he blessed the name of the Lord that he could bear testimony of the truth of the book of Mormon, and also consecrated all to God before he was baptized, he was also determined to go on to the end of his life." On the next night of the conference, Sidney Rigdon rebuked those who had received the "Highpriesthood" too casually. Orson Hyde "said that he received the rebuke in meekness. The same by ... Joseph Brackenberry" and three others.

Immediately after this conference, Joseph set out on a mission to New York with Edmund Durfee, leaving Elizabeth home with the five boys. He traveled to Pomfret, Chautauqua, New York, to visit Joel Hills Johnson and Almon Babbitt, fellow missionaries who were visiting Joel's family, including parents Ezekiel and Julia Johnson and his sisters Delcena and Almera. In Pomfret, Joseph was instrumental in converting the Johnsons. Benjamin Johnson wrote: "Elder Brackinbury was a capable man and a great reasoner, and the Spirit of the Lord rested mightily upon him." Joel Hills wrote that the appearance of Joseph and Edmund "filled our hearts with joy. We held several meetings and some believed the Gosple." Joseph personally baptized Julia Johnson, the family matriarch, and Lyman Sherman, Delcena's husband, who would become a prominent Mormon leader.

While Elizabeth was waiting for her husband's return, however, tragedy struck. Joel Hills writes, "But alas, in the midst of fair prospects and great expectations, disappointment often blasts our hopes ... For our beloved brother Joseph Brackenbury was taken sick with what was supposed to be the billious cholic and remained in great distress which he bore with the fortitude of a Saint for one week and expired with an unshaken confidence in the fullness of the Gospel which he had preached and a firm hope of a glorious resurrection among the just." The *History of the Church* describes this death as a poisoning by non-Mormons who boasted that "Mormon elders had not faith enough to stand poison." The date of death was January 7, 1832. If Brackenbury was poisoned, he was one of the church's earliest martyrs. However he died, Elizabeth, now forty-one, was widowed for the second time and still had four young sons to raise, ages two through eleven. Gilbert was twenty-one and would have been able to help his mother in farm work. At this point a court record gives us the only extant holograph from Elizabeth: "february the 26 1832 to the onrable Court of huron County State of Ohio this is to Certify that i have made Choise of Jonathan Stevens to Be adminstrater on the estate of Joseph Brackenbury De.[ceased] for me Elizabeth Brackenbury."

## V. Up on the Big Blue

In the 1893 Temple Lot case, John Wesley Brackenbury testified, "We came here [Missouri] in the spring of 1832. My mother came here then, and I was with her." Elizabeth almost certainly traveled to Missouri with Edmund Durfee, who "with nine others went up to Jackson county to put in grain, and built houses" in spring 1832. Edmund's brother, Jabez, may have also been part of this group, as he was in Jackson County by 1833. Though Edmund soon returned to Ohio, Jabez evidently stayed. He and Elizabeth would later marry, but he was now married to another woman. In Jackson County Elizabeth owned ten acres of land "up on the Big Blue" in the Whitmer settlement, about seven or eight miles west of Independence. On March 12, 1833, the twenty-two-year-old Gilbert Goldsmith married Jabez Durfee's daughter Abigail. Elizabeth was entering the grandmotherly era of her life while she was still raising four sons.

When tensions between Mormons and Missourians ignited in November, Elizabeth took her four sons to the nearby house of Joshua Lewis. While there, John Wesley, about five, remembered Philo Dibble coming to the house, wounded: "The bullet had went right through the powder horn, and the splinters were sticking in his side ... I remember him looking so white, and they took him upstairs." In the evening, as mobbings threatened, Elizabeth took her sons into a nearby cornfield, as did Mrs. Lewis with her children, and there they spent the night. John Wesley testified that when they came back to the Lewis house in the morning, it was "torn down to the eaves, and the rafters were all off of it, and I remember going into the house, and there was a table sitting in the middle of the room, and a big large pan of honey sitting on it." Taking the roofs off Mormon houses was a common tactic used by the anti-Mormon mob at this time.

Elizabeth was then directed to go to a schoolhouse in the woods. "We staid there all day, the women, the children, and the old man ... crying and in great distress," wrote John. As often in the Mormon persecutions, the toll of the terrorist tactics on women and children was fearful, as this day of hiding and hysterical crying shows. On the night that houses were unroofed, the mob hunted Mormon men and whipped them. John Wesley remembered that the Mormons were driven out of Jackson County soon after this: "We went across the river at what is now called Wayne city; went over in the bottom and camped there by a big sycamore log, and staid there all winter." On the night they were driven across the river, Elizabeth and the boys saw the spectacular shower of falling stars that so encouraged the persecuted Latter-day Saints with its promise of the Second Coming.

## VI. Jabez Durfee

Possibly as a result of these persecutions, Jabez Durfee's wife, Electa Cranston, died in January or February 1834. He quickly remarried. On page 119 of Clay County marriage records, we read, "This is to certify that on the 3rd day of March of 1834 Jabez Durfe and Elizabeth Brackenbury was Joined in matrimony by me Alpheus Gifford Minister of the Gospel." Jabez, a carpenter by profession, had been born on December 28, 1791, in Tiverton, Newport, Rhode Island. He married Electa Cranston in 1811 and with her had at least five children, so he and Elizabeth, now forty-three, combined families. Like most Mormon men, Jabez was a member of the Mormon paramilitary movement, the Danites, in Missouri. In the spring he began building a mill for Michael Arthur and employed Amasa Lyman to help him. The Durfee family lived at the mill, located three miles from Liberty on Shoal Creek. Elizabeth became a grandmother on May 5, 1834, when Electa Goldsmith was born to Gilbert and Abigail.

About a year later Elizabeth and Jabez and family moved to Far West. The next we hear of any of them is in 1836, when Jabez was in Kirtland, probably visiting for the dedication of the temple. While there he was ordained an elder on April 29 and received his elder's license on May 2. Elizabeth's last years in Missouri are documented only by two family events: John Wesley Brackenbury was baptized in 1837 and Joseph Blanchette Brackenbury, Jr., died the next year at age fifteen or sixteen.

When the Mormons were expelled from Far West, Elizabeth and Jabez joined the exodus to Illinois. John Wesley remembered leaving Missouri toward the end of November 1838, camping in mud during the trip as it snowed and rained.

## VII. Nauvoo

The Durfees arrived at Quincy in late 1838, then moved to Nauvoo in 1839. On January 11, 1840, when she was forty-eight, Elizabeth, along with her Brackenbury sons, received a patriarchal blessing from Joseph Smith, Sr., in Nauvoo at the home of Jabez Durfee. Charles was now nineteen, Benjamin twelve, John Wesley ten. Three months later the Nauvoo High Council appropriated funds for Jabez and Alpheus Cutler to build a school house. Soon Elizabeth, her family, and the Smith family began associating with each other, for Joseph Smith III later wrote that John Wesley Brackenbury was a schoolmate of his in Nauvoo. On January 11, 1842, Joseph Smith invited Elizabeth and Jabez to a dinner party attended by Nauvoo's leading citizens, including apostles and Smith relatives. Elizabeth had joined the Mormon elite.

The Durfees lived in the Nauvoo 4th Ward next to the Zina Huntington Jacobs family, according to the 1842 Nauvoo Census. The entry reads: "Jabez Durfy, Elizabeth Durfy, Julia Durfy, George Durfy, Savilla Durfy, Rosanna Durfy; Benjamin Brackenbury, Joseph Brackenbury." The two latter names are bracketed and "Dead" is written by the bracket. This 4th Ward list also shows that Charles Wesley (now twenty-two) had married a woman named Elizabeth by this time. The two younger Brackenbury boys—now fifteen and thirteen—must have been living elsewhere, perhaps because of crowded quarters or because they were serving apprenticeships.

## VIII. "Mrs. Durfee Stands by Her, Night & Day"

Elizabeth does not appear on Andrew Jenson's list of Joseph Smith's plural wives, but many other sources evidence her marriage to him. John C. Bennett, in the earliest list of Smith's wives, mentions a "Mrs. D*****," and Elizabeth is the only likely candidate fitting this name. Furthermore, Sarah Pratt mentions that she heard a Mrs. Durfee in Salt Lake City profess to have been one of Smith's wives. Elizabeth figured as an intermediary in Smith's marriage to the Partridge sisters, and such a duty was invariably given to women who had already been linked to him by marriage. Anti-Mormon Joseph Jackson linked her with Patty Sessions ("Mrs. Tailar, old Madam Durfee and old Madam Sessions") as a "Mother in Israel," one of the older women who taught younger women the principles of polygamy, and Patty was certainly a plural wife of Smith. Finally, Elizabeth received a very early proxy marriage to the Mormon prophet in the Nauvoo temple. All these data taken together make a strong case for Elizabeth as one of Joseph Smith's plural wives. As John Bennett left Nauvoo in June 1842, we can date the marriage as taking place before that time. If it took place in spring 1842, then Elizabeth would have been fifty-one at the time of the ceremony.

Of the marriage itself, little is known beyond the following: as a senior plural wife, Elizabeth helped Joseph Smith arrange new polygamous marriages, and as was always the case with Smith's polyandrous wives, she continued to live with her "first husband." Jabez, as was often the case with "first husbands," was an active, faithful Latter-day Saint, though he was not a leading figure in the church hierarchy. By the thesis developed in this book, he may have known about the marriage.

Elizabeth appears prominently in the Relief Society meetings that began in 1842, and Eliza Snow's minutes report a few of Elizabeth's remarks, the closest thing we may ever have to a document written by Elizabeth herself. On March 24, at the second society meeting, she was accepted as a member. The next week Emma was concerned about polygamy-related rumors proceeding from Clarissa Marvel. Sarah Cleveland, Emma's counselor and probably a plural wife of Joseph Smith by this time, proposed that Elizabeth, with a Mrs. Allred, interview two women who had spread rumors second-hand from Clarissa, and report back at the next meeting. Elizabeth "objected," but Emma was not to be dissuaded: "Prest. E.S. ... said that Mrs. Durfee must serve unless she could provide a better person to officiate in her stead." However, no more is heard of this investigation, so perhaps it was dropped.

At the end of the April 14 meeting, Emma Smith and her two counselors administered to Elizabeth, who was suffering from an unnamed sickness. In the minutes of the next meeting, five days later, we read, "Mrs. Durfee bore testimony to the great blessing she received when administered to after the close of the last meeting, by Prest. E. Smith & Councillors Cleveland and Whitney. she said she never realized more benefit thro' any administration—that she was heal'd, and thought the sisters had more faith than the brethren." At the April 28 meeting, Elizabeth, with leading Mormon women such as Elizabeth Ann Whitney, Sarah Cleveland, Mrs. Allred, and Vilate Kimball, was appointed to a committee to investigate women who had applied for membership but had been objected to. On August 4, after Emma reported on her recent mission to Governor Carlin, "Mrs. Durfee recommended to the sisters to sustain by their diligence and faithfulness, that character before the world, which our Prest. has represented abroad."

These entries show Elizabeth as one of the influential women of Nauvoo, articulate and enthusiastic in meetings. She was well known to the Relief Society presidency, and they gave her responsible assignments to perform in that organization. We also see here a perhaps conflicted friendship with Emma Smith who undoubtedly did not know of her husband's marriage to her friend. On August 13, 1842, Emma, when Joseph was in hiding, decided to visit him. When she realized she was being watched by the sheriff, she walked instead to "Mrs. Durphy's" and waited there for the lawman to leave. Two months later, in October, Emma was sick, and Elizabeth tended her, as described in a poem from Eliza Snow to Joseph Smith: "Sir, for your consolation permit me to tell/ That your Emma is better—she soon will be well;/ Mrs. Durfee stands by her, night & day like a friend/ And is prompt every call—every wish to attend." Zina Huntington remembered a conversation between Elizabeth and Emma in which Elizabeth asked the prophet's wife if she felt that Joseph was a prophet. Yes, Emma answered, but I wish to God I did not know it.

On December 27, Joseph Smith traveled to Plymouth, thirty-five miles from Nauvoo, and wrote of the journey that "(Sister Durphy and daughte[r] rode in the carri[a]ge)." If this is Elizabeth, as seems probable, then the daughter would probably be a Durphy stepdaughter. The next day Smith traveled to Rushville, and in the party was William Smith's wife, who was attended by "Sister Durphy." Once again Elizabeth is performing the duties of a nurse. On January 9, 1843, Elizabeth traveled to Plymouth with Joseph Smith again.

She continued in her capacity as older plural wife, facilitating Smith's marriages to younger wives. Shortly before March 4, she invited Emily and Eliza Partridge to her home. Emily later wrote of this visit, "She introduced the subject of spiritual wives as they called it in that day" and wondered "if there was any truth in the report she heard." Emily, who had recently received a proposal from Joseph Smith, did not reply. "I learned afterward," she wrote, "that Mrs. [Durfee] was a friend to plurality and knew all about it."

On March 3 Smith wrote in his journal, "In the interim called at Br Durphy's, his wife sick." This may have been a coded message for the Mormon leader's meeting with Elizabeth to give her instructions concerning the Partridge sisters. The entry also shows that Elizabeth and Jabez Durphy were still living in the same house. The following day Elizabeth delivered a proposal to Emily, who wrote: "Mrs. Durf— came to me one day and said Joseph would like an opportunity to talk with me. I asked her if she knew what he wanted. She said she thought he wanted me for a wife ... I was to meet him in the evening at Mr. Kimballs." In fact, Emily married him that night. Joseph Smith's journal for that day supports Emily's reminiscences: "Called at Bro Durphy's to see sick [two words crossed out, unreadable] / <Woodsworth> / and Whitneys <and Kimballs>."

Depending on how one feels about polygamy, Elizabeth's activities as Smith's messenger will be viewed with more or less sympathy. The feminist will perhaps see her as co-opted by the male to further his power, while conservative Mormons will see her as obediently following a prophet. Even those unsympathetic to Joseph will understand that Elizabeth, like all Mormon women, had accepted him as an infallible leader and that it was the intensity of her religiosity that led her to influence other women to enter polygamy. In the nineteenth century, all leading Mormon women were expected to further the cause of polygamy, which was considered identical with the cause of the church.

Elizabeth had become a good friend of Eliza R. Snow, and on March 17 she attended an end-of-term social for the poetess's school. Eliza's journal on June 29 records that Elizabeth, Eliza, Elizabeth Whitney, and Elvira Cowles Holmes Smith rode to Cornelius Lott's farm. Once again she may have been preparing a young woman, Melissa Lott, for a proposal from Joseph Smith.

The second year of Relief Society meetings started on June 16, and as before, Elizabeth is a vocal presence. At the first meeting "Mrs. Durfee said if the heads of the Society wished, she is willing to go abroad with a wagon & collect wool &c. for the purpose of forwarding the work." On July 7, after Elizabeth Whitney invited comments from those present, "Mrs Durfee presented the case of Porter Rockwell—express'd much feeling of sympathy awakened in her heart by recent recitals of his sufferings—recommended the sisters to unite like the ancient saints in faith & pray'r for his deliverance." As we have seen, Agnes Coolbrith also had a friendship with this colorful Mormon character, Joseph's companion and bodyguard. Two weeks later Elizabeth volunteered to donate some rolls to the society.

As discussed above, on October 1 Elizabeth, with three other prominent Nauvoo women, received her endowment and became part of the Holy Order. She was initiated without her husband, Jabez, a first sign of spiritual separation, though they were probably still living together. Elizabeth now could perform temple-related labors, and on January 25, 1844, William Clayton wrote that "Sister Durphy" made his "Robe and Garment."

When Joseph Smith was killed at Carthage on June 27, Elizabeth lost her third husband. Benjamin Brackenbury, now seventeen, was driving a baggage wagon with Captain Davis's Company of the Warsaw Militia and witnessed members of the mob who killed Smith returning to the militia and boasting of the deed.

### IX. Proxy Marriage

The aftermath of the martyrdom underscores the close ties between Elizabeth and her sons and the Joseph Smith family. She was reportedly with Emma when the bodies of Joseph and Hyrum arrived at Nauvoo. These were taken to the Mansion House, where Gilbert Goldsmith stood as doorkeeper while they were washed. On June 29, at midnight, Gilbert helped carry the bodies of Joseph and Hyrum from the Mansion House to the Nauvoo House, where they were buried in the basement. Later that fall Gilbert helped carry the bodies back to the Mansion House.

On October 8 Jabez Durphy was ordained a high priest at Nauvoo, another evidence of his faithfulness, and in December he was chosen as one of the carpenters who would work in a shop at the temple. It is not known whether he and Elizabeth were living together at this time.

In the martyrdom trial, Benjamin figured importantly. On March 10, 1845, he was arrested by non-Mormons for perjury in Nauvoo, but a group of 125 Mormons freed him. From May 19 to 30 he testified against the mob, in an act of considerable courage. He also took the martyrdom as his subject for a series of paintings.

Willard Richards's wife, Jennetta, died on July 9, and the next day Willard wrote, "Sister Durphy, Sessions, Rhoda, Ann Fox, Lucy Clayton & Sister Wilcox dressed Jennetta & put her in her coffin about sunset." Here we see Elizabeth and Patty Sessions linked, as in the Joseph Jackson narrative, though Elizabeth is given priority of listing, even before Rhoda, Willard's sister. All three women were widows of Joseph Smith.

As 1845 came to an end, the Mormons prepared to leave Nauvoo and hastened to finish the Nauvoo temple to perform all-important ordinances in it. Elizabeth and her family were actively involved in this work. On December 18 Jabez, without Elizabeth, received his endowment in the temple, another sign of separation. Two days later Gilbert Goldsmith received his endowment with his wife, Abigail, and on December 23 Elizabeth was endowed. On December 24 and 25 she served as a worker in the temple, helping to wash and anoint women in preparatory ordinances.

A series of marriages involving Jabez, very Mormon in their oddity, took place on January 21, 1846. At 4:10 p.m. he stood proxy for his dead brother Edmund as the latter was sealed to Magdalena Pickle Durfee, Edmund's living widow, for eternity. As was customary, Jabez was then sealed to Magdalena "for time," a Levirate union. This left Jabez with two wives, including Elizabeth, but no eternal companion. Therefore, immediately after the marriage to Magdalena, she stood proxy for "Electa Cranston ... Deceased," as Jabez was sealed to Electa for eternity. Brigham Young officiated in all these sealings. For the Elizabeth Davis biographer, these marriages show that Jabez was a faithful Latter-day Saint and that Elizabeth does not seem to be associated with him at this time.

## X. Cornelius Peter Lott

Elizabeth's separation from Jabez was finalized the next day when, at 12:50 p.m., "Elizabeth Davis" was sealed to Joseph Smith for eternity, with Cornelius Peter Lott standing proxy, then was sealed to Lott for time. Once again Brigham Young officiated. Elizabeth was fifty-four years old when she married Lott, her last husband, while he was forty-eight. The manager of Joseph Smith's farm, and a member of the influential Council of the Fifty, Lott had married Permelia Darrow in 1823, with whom he had had ten children, including Melissa, another plural wife of Joseph Smith. On the same day, at 1:05 p.m., Cornelius was also sealed to Permelia and to two other women: Rebecca Fossett, fifteen (who would bear Cornelius a child but would leave him before its birth) and Charity Dickenson, sixty-eight. He married another wife, fifteen-year-old Jane Rogers, on February 7.

After these complex marital ties and dissolutions were solemnized, the participants set out for the West with the body of Mormons. A valuable reference in the Clayton journal on June 28 shows that Elizabeth traveled with Lott across Iowa: "After we left Elder Woodruff we passed on and soon met Sister Durfee and Brother Lott and his company." Elizabeth was accompanied by Gilbert and Abigail; Benjamin, now nineteen; and John Wesley, nearly seventeen. Charles Wesley's whereabouts are unknown at this point, but in 1860 he and his family were living in Pike County, Illinois.

Elizabeth and her family soon reached Winter Quarters, as did Jabez and Magdalena Durfee. John Wesley later testified, "We [he and his mother and family] staid there [Nauvoo] until Brigham Young started for the west, and we went with him as far as the Missouri River." Gilbert and Abigail Goldsmith's child Joseph was born in Winter Quarters on August 28, 1846. However, their David, age four, succumbed to "chills and fever" on September 18. Sadly, Gilbert himself died on March 1, 1847, in Independence, Missouri. During the summer Benjamin Brackenbury joined the Mormon Battalion, and on July 20, 1846, he set out for the far West as a private in Company B.

## XI. Back to Quincy

Elizabeth's life now took a fateful turn. She left Winter Quarters for Quincy, left Cornelius Lott, and left the mainstream of Mormon history. According to John Wesley, "we went with him [Brigham] as far as the Missouri River and then we saw so much of their manner of doing business, that we went back to Quincy." There Elizabeth renewed her friendship with Emma Smith. She lived with Benjamin and John Wesley for the rest of her life, according to family traditions and census records, so the rest of this chapter will trace the lives and marriages of Benjamin and John.

Elizabeth's last two husbands can be quickly taken to their graves. In March 1847 Cornelius Lott married two more women, Eleanor Wayman (fifty-six) and Phebe Knight (forty-seven), then crossed the plains in the summer of 1848. In Utah he managed the church farm before dying unexpectedly on July 6, 1850. Jabez Durfee, on the other hand, was asked to stay in Winter Quarters to build wagons for emigrants, and on May 17, 1850, Magdalena Pickle died at Musketo Creek in Council Bluffs. In 1860 the Iowa census records Jabez, "Millwright," living in Fisher Township, just south of Council Bluffs, with a wife, Sarah, age sixty. He died in April 1867 in "White Cloud, Iowa."

## XII. Spanish Fashion

Benjamin and the Mormon Battalion traveled across the deserts of the Southwest, through New Mexico and Arizona, and arrived at Mission San

Diego in California on January 29, 1847. The battalion was released from service on July 16, so Benjamin journeyed north to San Francisco with a group of a hundred men and witnessed the beginnings of the gold rush in Sutter's Fort. He then traveled to Utah in the Brown company, crossing the Sierran crest through the Carson Pass on August 26, 1848, and arriving in Salt Lake City on October 7. There he faced a small crisis on February 25, 1849, when he was disciplined by the church for the curious transgression of riding "Spanish fashion" to a party. Hosea Stout wrote, "They each selectd their lady and marched there Spanish fashion with the Lady on before & they behind  Staid all night & came home the same way." John D. Lee added that these were "souldier Boys," and that one of them was "sawing on the violin." Clearly, this was an inflated reaction against some perceived risque riding and illicit dancing, but it would be six years before Benjamin would be rebaptized.

He married a Phoebe Ann Allen soon afterwards, and a child, Benjamin Brackenbury, Jr., was born to them in Salt Lake City on January 16, 1850. They moved to Ogden, Weber County, before the year ended, and his second and third children were born there in 1852 and 1855. However, he and Phebe must have separated at this time, for she married a George Butler Graham the next year.

### XIII. Salt Lake City

Back in Illinois, John Wesley married Frances H. Lamb in Pike County, where his brother Charles Wesley was also living, on December 14, 1854. Nothing more is known of Frances, but the marriage apparently produced no children, and John soon remarried. Not long after, he and Elizabeth came to Utah. In the Temple Lot trial, he testified, "[We] went to Salt Lake City in the spring of 1855, lived there until the spring of 1857." Sarah Pratt, as quoted earlier, remembered Elizabeth in Utah. On August 31, 1855, Zina Huntington Young mentioned "John B[r]ackenbury" in her journal. John Wesley testified that he and Elizabeth "came back to the states again" in the spring of 1857. Benjamin, meanwhile, left his children with Phebe in Utah and returned with Elizabeth and John to the "states." On November 24, 1857, according to family genealogy, he married Sarah Kerr in DeKalb County, Missouri.

Elizabeth's surprising peregrinations continued. John Wesley testified that he and Elizabeth "went back to Salt Lake in the spring of '58." This is supported by a Mormon baptismal document recording that Elizabeth was rebaptized into the Mormon church on April 30, 1858, in Salt Lake City by Lyman S. Wood. But she left Utah before 1860, as that year's Missouri census shows Benjamin and Sarah living in Washington Township, DeKalb County, and Elizabeth living a few houses away with the James and Isabel Harris family. Benjamin moved to Denver in the early

1860s, for his son, John Wesley, was born there on February 1, 1863. Presumably Elizabeth moved to Colorado with him.

## XIV. San Bernardino, California

John Wesley continued: "Went back to Salt Lake in the spring of '58, and from [there] through to California." On December 1, 1861, he married Samantha Ann Daley in San Bernardino, with David Seely, a prominent, if disaffected, southern California Mormon, officiating. Benjamin (and probably Elizabeth) joined him at San Bernardino on February 4, 1865. In a later legal case, Benjamin recounted his arrival in San Bernardino and subsequent career. He had worked as a blacksmith for much of his life, but here we see him striving to make a living as a teamster. He testified:

> That when he came here, his trip across the plains had rendered him entirely destitute, and he immediately applied himself, as industriously as possible to labor, for the support of his family, and during the summer of 1865 by the strictest economy saved sufficient to buy one span of horses and one set of harness and to pay in part for a wagon: That during the winter of 1865-6, by tradeing in horses he realized sufficient to purchase an other horse and pay for him which he did. That being anctious to use what little capital he had thus acquired to the best advantage, he in the spring of 1866 purchased a fourth horse from Messrs Harris & Levi of the City of San Bernardino in said county for sevent[y] five dollars to be paid in lumber, and having procured the necessary harness he embarked in teaming between the City of San Bernardino and La Paz Arizona, and for a part of the time did well, making enough to purchase a span of mules and harness and to pay for them which he did.
>
> After the third trip, his fortune changed, and with all the industry, care and judgment he could exercise, he lossed money, and continued to lose, hopeing with every new effort to regain what [he] had previously lossed, untill he has become unable to pay his debts, and is to all intents and purposes and insolvent.

In the same document, Benjamin ascribed his bad fortune to unexpected changes in markets, the expenses of running his team, and the fact that he was "deceived" in a freight contract for $500. He filed for bankruptcy on June 3, 1867. On May 26 of the next year, he married a Mary Kelly. It is not known whether he and Sarah had separated or whether she had died. Certainly, the Brackenbury boys, like their mother, married often.

A new chapter in the religious lives of Elizabeth and her sons now began. Joseph Smith III sent missionaries to southern California beginning in 1864, including his brothers Alexander and David, and they had great success among the already somewhat dissident Mormons who lived there.

John Wesley is a case in point: he was baptized into the Reorganized Church of Jesus Christ of Latter Day Saints (RLDS) by Alexander Smith on February 12, 1867. John was still in San Bernardino on March 5, 1868, when his son, Joseph A., was born.

## XV. Reorganized Latter Day Saint

Apparently Elizabeth and her sons, with their families, left California later in 1868 and relocated in Kansas, near Independence, Missouri. But before John Wesley and his family reached Kansas, they spent some time in Utah, for John was ordained an RLDS elder in Salt Lake City on April 6, 1868, and one of his sons, Lute, was born there on April 6 of the following year.

But by late 1869 Elizabeth, Benjamin, and John Wesley had settled in White Cloud, Doniphan County, Kansas, where Elizabeth was baptized and confirmed an RLDS Saint by Elder Davis H. Bays on November 14. Benjamin was also baptized on that date. This is an ironic development, as Joseph Smith III was waging a crusade of sorts to prove that Joseph Smith, Jr., his father, had never practiced polygamy. Now the "Josephites," as they called themselves, had unwittingly baptized one of the prophet's former plural wives into their community.

Census records show that Elizabeth was living with John Wesley, his wife, and five children in White Cloud in 1870, while Benjamin, with wife Mary and one child, lived nearby. On November 6 Benjamin was ordained an RLDS elder at Tarkio, Missouri, and by 1872 he had moved to Fanning, Kansas. According to *Illustrated Doniphan County*, a book of local history, in the summer of 1870 "among the members that were active in organizing a congregation at that place were John W. and Benjamin B. Brackenbury." The branch was formally organized in May 1872.

## XVI. Railroad Accident

Elizabeth had lived a rich, varied life, but now the final act in her curious history was approaching. A sentence in *Illustrated Doniphan County* tells us that on November 10, 1876, "Near Fanning, Mrs. Brackenbury was killed by the cars." Since the wives of Benjamin and John Wesley lived past 1876, this Mrs. Brackenbury must be Elizabeth. However, her RLDS obituary gave a different date and place of death: "At White Cloud, Kansas, December 16th, 1876, sister Elizabeth Brackenbury, aged 85 years, 9 months, and 5 days [died]." Perhaps she was hit by the train on November 10, then lingered until December 16—or perhaps one of the dates is wrong.

Whichever is correct, Elizabeth died at age eighty-five in Kansas after an extraordinary life. She had lived with five husbands, though with none for the last thirty years of her life. She had resided in at least seven states, ranging from New York to Ohio, Missouri and Kansas, Colorado, Utah and California, and had traveled uncounted miles. She and her sons typify the geographical restlessness that drove many nineteenth-century Americans, and she is also an example of religious restlessness, for she joined three, possibly four, different churches in her lifetime. A plural wife of Joseph Smith and a close friend of Emma, she died as a member of the RLDS faith, whose president, Joseph Smith III, vehemently denied that his father had ever practiced polygamy. Perhaps Elizabeth came to believe that polygamy was wrong by the time she became a "Reorganite," or perhaps she simply felt drawn to her old friend Emma Smith and Emma's children. She remains one of the most interesting of Joseph's wives, a puzzle only partially solved.

## XVII. Benjamin and John Wesley

As her life was intertwined so completely with her two last sons, we will pursue their subsequent histories briefly. Benjamin joined the Independence, Missouri, Branch of the RLDS church in May 1879, but was disciplined by his elder's quorum and on April 6, 1884, was dropped from the rolls of the church for "inactivity." Mary Kelly died in Missouri in 1894. At some point Benjamin returned to Mormon country, to Idaho, where some of his children were living, and perhaps he rejoined the western Latter-day Saint faith at this time. On October 1, 1896, at the age of sixty-nine, he married Olive Matthews, twenty-four, in Caldwell, Canyon County, Idaho, twenty miles west of Boise. He died six months later, at Caldwell, on May 8, 1897, but Olive bore him one child posthumously and applied for his Mormon Battalion army pension.

In 1877 John Wesley moved to Independence, Jackson County, Missouri, the county from which he and his mother had been driven by mobs in 1833 when he was four. There he became one of the pastors of the Stone Church congregation, the first RLDS congregation in Independence. Joseph Smith III visited John in August and wrote, "At Independence, we found a welcome at the house of Brn. J. W. Brackenbury and—Beagle, Saints lately from Kansas—the former an old schoolmate, when the Saints were happy in Nauvoo." The next morning John gave Joseph III a tour of Independence. Joseph once remarked of John Wesley, "I know John Brackenbury: have known him all my life, almost, we were school and playmates as boys, and if there is a bigger mule, when he believes himself to be right, in the church, I dont know his name." When the remark was reported to John Wesley, he was greatly offended, so Joseph wrote a letter of profuse apology: "I did not use the word 'bigger mule,' or 'mulish,' with any intention to disparage your goodness ... I am sincerely sorry, and ... acknowledge speaking hastily and foolishly." This exchange shows John's quirks, but also Joseph's affection for his old schoolmate. John Wesley's children (he and Samantha had eight by 1880) would become close friends with Joseph III's. However, the family received a heavy blow on February 22, 1882, when Samantha died, and John was left to raise the large family by himself. To the scandal of his grown children, he married a twenty-one-year-old woman in 1884, Nancy P. Curtis, with whom he had one, possibly two, children. The Brackenburys were indefatigable marriers. During the 1890s he continued to live in Independence, but in 1900 he moved to southern California, where some of his children were located. He died in Riverside, California, on July 1, 1902, at age seventy-two. According to his RLDS obituary, "Bro. Brackenbury was well known and highly esteemed in this city [Independence] and surrounding country, and general regret was expressed at his departure ... He was a faithful, consistent follower of the Master and his heart was full of kindly sympathy with his fellow-man."

# 11.

# Relief Society Counselor

## *Sarah Maryetta Kingsley (Howe Cleveland Smith Smith)*

According to a family biography, one night in 1835 Sarah Cleveland, living with her husband John in Cincinnati, Ohio, dreamed an extraordinary vision. The next morning, to her astonishment, she found that her six-year-old daughter, Augusta, had had the same dream. In this dream she and her daughter were in a large sitting room when the front door opened and in walked "a man of large stature and benine countanance dressed in exquisite white robes, with sandals on his feet." He bowed to Sarah, unrolled a parchment for her, and told her to read. On it was written in large gilt letters, "Behold I bring you glad tidings of great joy." After holding the parchment for Augusta to read, he exited the room through a rear door. Immediately after this, another angel entered and repeated the same actions. A succession of twelve angels entered and exited in the same way. The last of them was a "more majestic figure with a beautifull circle of light around his head."

The dream deeply impressed Sarah, as it probably did Augusta. Sarah told her daughter that "there was something very beautiful coming for them to learn." They had heard a great deal about Mormons, and soon after this Sarah heard a Mormon elder preach: "The first thing he said as he began to speak was 'Behold I bring you tidings of great joy.'" This electrified Sarah. "Mrs Cleveland investagated and became convinced the Gospel was true, she was overjoyed, her daughter shared that joy."

Thus we see that Sarah Kingsley was a prophetess of sorts, a dreamer of dreams. She is well known in the history of Mormon women as the first counselor to Emma Smith in the first Relief Society presidency in Nauvoo. Like Elizabeth Davis Durphy and Patty Bartlett Sessions, she was one of Joseph Smith's older wives, and, like them, her marriage to Joseph was polyandrous; her "first husband," John Cleveland, was non-Mormon but was friendly to Smith and the Saints. A biographical sketch, a few letters written by Sarah in her later life, and a number of letters she received before she became Mormon allow us to sketch an outline of her life and

271

character. She was a devout, visionary woman, as were many of Smith's wives, notably Eliza Snow and Desdemona Fullmer. Before becoming Mormon, she was a committed Christian and continually spurred her family and friends to greater efforts at Christian living.

## I. "Filled with Enthusiasm for ... Jesus"

On October 20, 1788, Sarah was born in Becket, Berkshire, Massachusetts, to Ebenezer Kingsley, a thirty-year-old native of Becket, and Sarah Chaplin, also thirty and also born in Massachusetts. Two years before Sarah's birth, her first full sibling, Ebenezer Chaplin Kingsley, had been born in Becket on October 13, 1786. He and Sarah were close and corresponded throughout their lives. Two years after Sarah's birth, on September 1, 1790, Benjamin Kingsley was born, but he must have died as a child, for there is no mention of him in family records. Of Sarah's upbringing, the biography only tells us, "she was born heir to a fortune, was well educated and became a woman of refinement and culture." Her letters confirm that she was well-educated—with Eliza Snow, she was perhaps the most polished writer among Joseph Smith's wives.

She may have had teenaged moments of conflict with her parents, for an 1811 letter from her mother reads: "It Seams my Dear Child you reflect much on your youthful failings. I hope you do not think I have any hard feelings towards you god forbid. you are ever dear to me as Life you are now Sencible of a mothers feelings it is enough O may you ever be happy in your Children."

At some point Ebenezer died and Sarah's mother remarried, uniting with a Mr. Brown, with whom she apparently had more children. The Browns moved to St. Louis in 1805, which at the time was on the western frontier, but Sarah and Ebenezer stayed in the East—Ebenezer in Unadilla, New York, while Sarah attended an academy in New Haven, Connecticut.

In May 1805 Sarah experienced a conversion to Jesus, a religious awakening. Her brother wrote to her:

I receivd Yours Dated May 27th and [was] extremely Glad to hear you was well and So Well pleased with your situation you write that God in his Inf{inite} Mercy has been pleased to plant Conviction and Re{pentence} in Your breast. It seems by your writing you are filled with Enthusiasm for the Religion of Jesus. I hope [that] God will perfect his work in you which he has begun a{nd} may Your Religion be a Source of happiness through your life. I believe Religion when Connected with Reason is the Only Source from which true happiness is Derived. of Late I have thought more [of] it than {here}tofore ... believe me my Dear Sister to be your Loving and Affectionate Brother Eben C Kingsley

## II. "[Your] Loving and Affectionate Husband"

On December 7, 1807, Sarah, nineteen, married John Howe, "a sea merchant and Captain of his own Ship," according to the biography, in New Haven. They had one child, Edward, probably born late the following year. Evidently Sarah's letters about these events never reached their destination in frontier St. Louis, as her mother wrote to her. in roughly 1809, "He [Ebenezer Kingsley] Paid you a viset Last Summer and found you very agr{e}eably married and the mother of a fine Son may God Bless {the} Child with the Parents. O that I {c}ould Se {the} Little Creature  Kiss the Little babe for me - and tell Mr Howe altho I never had the pleasure of Seing him yet I esteem him with the most Sincere affection - hop{e} I may be So happy {a}s to Se you boath before I die but the Prospect is very dark."

In 1810-11 the Howes suffered some unspecified reverses, perhaps financial, for a relative, Jedediah Kingsley, wrote Sarah in 1812, "I rejoice to hear that you and your Family are in Health and that you are recovering in some measure your Losses." Then, according to the biography, when the War of 1812 began, John was on a voyage, his ship was seized by the English, and he was imprisoned "for some time." When he was finally liberated at the close of the war, "he ... came home, but his health was greatly impared, so much so that he soon passed away, leaving her a widow with one child a son Edward."

Surprisingly enough, while John's health may have been broken during the war, documentary evidence shows that he lived more than a decade after 1812. We have three letters from him to Sarah during this period, written while he was away on voyages. They are full of news of his projected itineraries, of his cargoes, of maritime problems. They seem affectionate. An 1814 letter from John ends, "O how I wanted to be with you. I Dream of you and Edward but I do not behold you  Be carefull in Edwards Education  tell him to be a good Boy and Learn his Books - do not Let him use Bad Words nor keep bad Boys company ... So I must bid you a ... [farewell]  May the Blessing of Almighty God attend you ... [Your] Loving and Affectionate husband  John Howe." Apparently Sarah sometimes had financial difficulties while John was gone, though he sent money home occasionally. "It makes my heart Bleed for your Troubles and your wants," he wrote in 1814.

Other letters to Sarah during this period supply abundant evidence that she was an intensely religious young woman. One imagines her faithfully attending a Methodist or Presbyterian congregation in New Haven. An 1809 letter from Ebenezer shows that she had been trying to keep her brother on the straight and narrow path by letter as he served in the military. He replied, "You have awakened my mind to bitter reflection and although it may deter me from many errors in future, my past errors appear more deform[ed], continue therefore to awaken my mind to a sence of its proper duty." In an 1813 letter, Sarah's mother wrote, "I must confess with a blush you have outrun me in the Christian race I find great need of your prayers to assist me in my Progress heaven ward." A Mrs. Wakefield received a letter of religious encouragement from Sarah in 1814, then replied, "But as you observed it is the trifles of the moment which continually call for the continual habit and exercise of every christian grace. Never did I realize my responsibility and ... [let] religion shine in my daily walk and deportment as I now do in some measure ... O pray that I may let my light shine and not dishonor the profession I have made ... But O this cold heart full of sin and iniquity."

Edward became very ill in August or early September 1815, then died. We have letters of consolation written to Sarah, the earliest of them dated September 23, and they tell us that John Howe was away on a long voyage when the boy died and had not seen his son for some time. The death took place soon after Sarah and Edward had visited relatives in the town of Lee, in western Massachusetts. Edward endured pain before his death—one of Sarah's aunts "in her distressed hours frequently spoke of poor little Edwards suffering." Perhaps a sudden severe sickness claimed him. The letters to Sarah show that she grieved deeply for her only child, and also bear witness to her religiosity, as her friends' and relatives' condolences are framed in thoroughly pietistic terms. "It is your part," wrote her aunt Obedient Chaplin, "to be resignd to the will of the Lord who has taken him perhaps from the evil to come. He has no doubt wing'd his way to the heavenly Jerusalem; leaving this vail of tears and Sorrows before his tender mind was made acquainted with its vexations and afflictions."

### III. "Happy Meetings We Us'd to Have"

At some time between 1815 and 1820, Sarah and John moved to Cincinnati, Ohio, which shows that John had been relieved of his duties as a sea captain, perhaps because of his broken health. In Cincinnati Sarah became an important member of a local Protestant congregation. On February 21, 1821, a Charity Barlow who had lived with Sarah in Cincinnati wrote to "my dear Sister Howe." Charity asked Sarah to "please remember my love to Sister & Br. Hastings, Sister Lovejoy & family," using the same fraternal language that Mormons would employ. Charity missed the church services: "I often {think} of the happy meetings we us'd to have {at} {c}hurch & of my very dear friends the{re}." She rejoiced that John accompanied Sarah "to meeting" and hoped for his full conversion—"the Lord grant he may meet with a divine blessing ... nothing is too hard for the Lord."

John, however, passed away between 1823, when he signed a will, and June 1826, when Sarah remarried. We know nothing else about his death, but apparently he had been ill for some time and finally succumbed. With his passing, Sarah's first family, both husband and son, had been taken from her.

## IV. John Cleveland

On June 10, 1826, Sarah, thirty-seven, married John Cleveland, who the biography tells us had managed the Howe estate for years. John, a native of New York, was thirty-six. The first child in the new family, Augusta Bowen, was born on December 7, 1828, and the last, Alexander D., joined the Clevelands on October 7, 1832, when Sarah was forty-four.

In 1831 brother Eben, spurred on by his sister, experienced a conversion to Jesus. On April 16 he wrote to her:

> Thanks be to God for his mercies toward me. they have been great. every thing seems to have tended to my benefit ever since I have obtained confidence enough in myself to believe that so great a sinner as I am could be accepted. the great struggle is over and I am at peace  not only did I comply with your request to pour out my soul in prayer for time you requested but have constantly morning noon & night addressed the Throne of Mercy for myself my friends and for all mankind.

During the Second Great Awakening, conversions to Jesus were momentous, deeply felt, almost formal occasions in the lives of believers.

## V. They Stamped the Dust of Their Feet

It was at this point, perhaps in 1835, that Sarah converted to Mormonism through the dream described above. However, John Cleveland was "a Swedenbergen, and did not share the light of truth that had come to his Wife and daughter." Swedenborgians were followers of the visionary Swede, Emanuel Swedenborg, whose teachings had a number of interesting doctrinal intersections with Mormonism, including pre-existence, levels of eschatological glory, and a spiritual wife doctrine. However, the movement was less a mainstream Christian church than a form of spiritualism or mysticism. As often happens with mixed religious marriages, the spiritual training of the children became an issue of contention. After prolonged discussion, Sarah and John decided that she would take Augusta to Mormon services and he would take Alexander to the Swedenborgian church. When they reached adulthood, the children would choose their preferred religion for themselves.

Sarah and Augusta were soon baptized, the biography tells us, but:

> As soon as it was known she was a Mormon her friends came and used every argument they could, to disuade her from continuing in such a

down ward course. Some of the moast eminent devines from Cincinatta and Quincey came to "Labor" with her on taking or accepting such a false religion, but found her firm and able to prove The Gospel from the Bible, which inraged some of them so they "Stamped the dust of their feet in witness against her so their skirts would be clean" as they left her door.

This kind of polarized dramatization of good and evil, in which the protagonist stands fast against ministers of opposing churches, is typical of early Mormon biography, though often it is the Mormons who shake the dust off their feet against the "sectarians."

## VI. Quincy, Illinois

In a reminiscence Augusta Cleveland wrote that when she was seven, about 1836, the Clevelands moved to Quincy, Illinois, "then, a small Village, consisting of a few good houses, a Store or two, and a Grocery." There, according to the biography, Sarah and John owned a large estate on which tenant farmers lived and worked.

Three years later, when the Mormons were expelled from Missouri and migrated to Nauvoo, just north of Quincy, Sarah and John suddenly found themselves close to the center of Mormonism, and they soon became friendly with the Joseph Smith family. On February 15, 1839, Emma and her children began residing with the Clevelands at Quincy while Joseph was in Liberty Jail. Joseph Smith III wrote, "My first recollection concerned with events after we crossed the Mississippi River begins at the home of the man, George [sic] Cleveland, some three or four miles out from Quincy." Joseph III also remembered Sidney Rigdon and three of his children living with the Clevelands. Joseph Jr. wrote to Emma on March 21, "I would ask if Judge Cleaveland will be kind enough to let you and the children tarry there untill [I] can learn somethng fu[r]ther concerning my lot fate [I] will reward him well if he will and see that you do not suffer for any thing." It is not known why John was called "Judge." Perhaps he had a legal background of some sort.

On April 17 Sarah received a patriarchal blessing from Joseph Smith, Sr. Five days later Joseph Jr., freed from prison, was reunited with Emma at the home of the Clevelands, and he and Emma stayed with them almost three more weeks. Oliver Huntington wrote, "It will be understood that he [Joseph Smith] had been living in the house with Judge Cleveland ever since his deliverance from Missouri dungeons." As often happened, the prophet lived in the same household with his future plural wife before their marriage.

The Smiths relocated to Nauvoo on May 9. Two weeks later they wrote to Sarah and John encouraging them to join them in the city and informing them that they had a lot picked out for them across the street. It was "beside Mr. Harris; and in the orchard, according to the desire of Sister Cleveland, and also on the river, adapted to Mr. Cleveland's trade." This lot may have been the recompense for boarding the Smith family for so long. The letter begins, "We write you in order to redeem our pledge ... We ... beg to assure you and your family that we have not forgotten you, but remember you all, as well as the great kindness and friendship which we have experienced at your hands." However, the Clevelands decided not to move immediately.

When Smith visited Quincy in June 1841 to call on Governor Carlin, he stayed at the home of Mrs. Joseph Horne. In an autobiography Horne wrote that "The Prophet with Sister Snyder called in his buggy upon Sister Cleveland." The same year Sarah became a fervent convert to Smith's doctrine of baptism for the dead and was baptized for forty deceased persons—more than any other woman in Nauvoo.

The biography describes events in Quincy that include mob violence and wounded Mormons. Chronology is problematic here, for violence against the Mormons was not prevalent until 1844 and 1845. Nevertheless, the biography continues: "Soon the Saints were mobed and driven from their homes, Mr and Mrs Cleveland took many in to their home and cared for them. Some died of the wounds and esposure they had received and were burried on a peice of ground Mr Cleveland fenced and set apart for that purpose." Clearly, John Cleveland was not violently antagonistic to Mormonism. According to the biography, ten families of tenant farmers left the Cleveland estate suddenly, "declaring they would not work for a man who though not a mormon himself was associating with them and his wife was one. So crops were left ungathered as no one would work for the Mormons. Later Mr. Cleveland sold out at a great loss and went to Nauvoo." Augusta's reminiscences stated that the Clevelands stayed in Quincy six years, then left when a railroad was being introduced, possibly in 1842. In Nauvoo John reportedly became a leading merchant.

## VII. Joseph Smith

Soon after moving to the Mormon city, if not before, Sarah was converted to Joseph Smith's doctrine of celestial marriage, for she is listed by church historian Andrew Jenson as one of Smith's wives. Although Jenson gives no date for the ceremony, Sarah and Joseph were almost certainly married before June 29, 1842, when she witnessed Eliza Snow's marriage to Smith, according to an affidavit by Snow. Previously married wives frequently witnessed the Mormon leader's new plural marriages, as they were part of the inner circle that could be trusted with such secret knowledge. Assuming that Sarah married Smith in early 1842, she was fifty-four at the time.

Thus, as was quite typical of Smith's early marriages, this is another polyandrous union. John Cleveland is, like Adam Lightner, a non-member "first husband," but, again like Lightner, he apparently was a good friend of Smith, having sheltered him in his house. He was sympathetic toward Mormons and had helped them when they were persecuted. Like Lightner, he consented to follow his wife's wishes and live with or near the church for a number of years. Because he was non-Mormon, however, it is unlikely that Sarah or Joseph told him about their marriage.

Nauvoo city and county tax records for 1842 list a house for John Cleveland and another for Sarah several blocks away. This has been taken as evidence for a separation, but it is more likely that the couple had two houses and that one was under Sarah's name. Some unsympathetic sources report that Sarah had an "assignation house" where Joseph Smith would meet Eliza Snow.

## VIII. Counsellor Cleveland

In the early nineteenth century, women's religious associations proliferated in America. Some were organized to give aid to the poor, while others raised money to send missionaries to "heathen" countries or to finance the education of a minister. As antagonism to slavery became more and more a crusade in America, many women's groups took up the abolitionist cause. Some scholars see the beginnings of the American feminist movement in these organizations, especially since many were focused on reforming men, attacking male vices such as heavy drinking or sexual immorality. Sometimes the reformers would wait outside brothels and take note of the men who patronized the establishment, trying to shame the offenders into giving up the vice! Though it would be a mistake to define these groups as anti-men (they were generally allied with religious men, ministers, preachers, and crusaders), they certainly contributed to a separate women's community in America.

In this environment the Female Relief Society of Nauvoo received its genesis in 1842. While the Mormon woman's society was never oriented toward reforming men, and has always been publicly supportive of the male ecclesiastical hierarchy, it also had its proto-feminist elements. As a separate community of women within Mormonism (just as the male priesthood hierarchy was a separate community of men within Mormonism), it developed its own culture and history. The publication of the *Woman's Exponent* alone, a magazine printing women's essays, speeches, poems, and autobiographies, was a landmark in the history of Mormon feminism.

Sarah has considerable importance in this regard, as she became the first counselor in the first Relief Society presidency and helped decide on the name, "Relief Society." When Emma chose Sarah as her counselor at the first meeting on March 17, 1842, Sarah was, at fifty-four, the oldest woman present. After John Taylor ordained her to the office, it was "Mov'd by Counsellor Cleveland, and secon'd by Counsellor Whitney, that this Society be called The Nauvoo Female Relief Society." Though Taylor and Joseph Smith disliked the term "relief," Emma supported it. Then "Counsellor Cleveland arose to remark concerning the question before the house, that we should not regard the idle speech of our enemies— we design to act in the name of the Lord—to relieve the wants of the distressed, and do all the good we can." Eliza Snow also spoke up for "relief," and Taylor and Smith finally agreed to it. Eliza suggested the final refinement, The Female Relief Society of Nauvoo, which carried. Sarah donated $.12 to the society that day.

Her admonitions and exhortations are often found in the society minutes. At the third Relief Society meeting, "Councillor Cleveland remark'd that they had [better] put their shoulder to the wheel and exhorted them to do with their might—we have entered into this work in the name of the Lord let us boldly go forward." Later she thanked Lucy Mack Smith for her testimony. "[Sarah hoped] that she [Lucy] might receive much comfort and consolation in this Society—that the Lord would lengthen her days— that she may cheer the Society with her presence, aid it by her counsels and prayers long before she shall take her departure to sit down by the side of her beloved Partner."

Emma used the Relief Society to combat rumors that her husband practiced polygamy, which put Sarah in an awkward, ambiguous position. A close friend of Emma, she nevertheless was Joseph's plural wife and could not tell Emma about it. On April 14 Sarah cautioned "the Society against speaking evil of Prest. J. Smith and his companion—that it would not be a light thing in the sight of God—that they had prov'd themselves; and the case of C.M. [Clarissa Marvel] should be a warning, how we hear and how we speak—express'd her fears that the Lord would cut off those who will not take counsel &c." Sarah thus joined Emma in trying to keep polygamy rumors from circulating, though with a contrasting motive: while Emma wanted to quash polygamy, Sarah wanted to keep it secret. At the end of the meeting, Sarah, with Emma and Elizabeth Ann Whitney, administered to Elizabeth Davis Durfee.

Sarah presided at the April 19 Relief Society meeting in Emma's absence. As there was not much business to attend to that day, "Therefore we might spend the time in religious exercises before the Lord—spoke of the happiness she felt in the present associations of females, and made very appropriate remarks respecting the duties & prospects of the Society—that it was organiz'd after the order of heaven &c. &c." Later Sarah spoke in tongues: "Councillor Cleveland stated that she many times felt in her heart, what she could not express in our own language, and as the Prophet had given us liberty to improve the gifts of the gospel in our meetings, and feeling the power resting upon, desired to speak in the gift of tongues, which she did in a powerful manner." Patty Sessions rose and gave the interpretation of Sarah's otherworldly utterances.

Sarah continued to speak often in the Relief Society meetings. On May 19 she gave a brief lecture on the stratagems of sin. A month later, on June 23, Eliza Snow wrote,

> On motion of Councillor Cleveland, resolved that all applying to the Treasurer for relief, without a recommend, shall be aided at the discretion of the President. Coun. C. said the time had come that all must live by faith alone—the pow'rs of darkness were array'd against us, but said she fear'd nothing. Coun. C. said we should be extremely careful in handling character—be merciful and not oppress any especially those persons objected to by some, yet considered virtuous, such should be held in their place—should not feel themselves numbered with the vile—said we would have none among us who would speak against the prophet of the Lord, or the authorities of the Church.

These speeches show that Sarah was an articulate, capable public speaker, a thoroughgoing Latter-day Saint, and, like Eliza, a loyalist. She warned that no one must speak against the church "authorities" and even threatened that such people might be "cut off."

On June 29 Sarah served as a witness when Eliza R. Snow was married to Joseph Smith, with Brigham Young officiating. Eliza was apparently living with Sarah at the time, but the two women soon parted company. Eliza wrote in her journal, on August 14, "Mrs. Cleveland having come to the determination of moving on to her lot; my former expectations were frustrated ..." Sarah plans to move "to her lot"; it is unclear what that means, and why the move would keep Eliza from staying with her. On September 28 Sarah presided at the last Relief Society meeting of the year. No more meetings were held until June of the next year.

### IX. "Absent from Your Pleasant Society"

In April 1843 Sarah and John left Nauvoo, citing business difficulties as the reason. On the first of May a farewell letter from Sarah "To the Presidency, and Ladies of the Female Relief Society of Nauvoo" appeared in the *Times and Seasons*: "I shall necessarily be absent from your pleasant society, for a season, my husband not having succeeded in business in Nauvoo as he anticipated." Fawn Brodie concludes that John took his family away because Joseph Smith was cohabiting with his wife, but this interpretation seems unlikely. First, it is probable that Smith did not have sexual relations with his older wives. Second, Sarah writes, "for a season." If John were angry with Joseph Smith, he probably would have left permanently and would have gone far away. However, John was back in Nauvoo by December 1843. On December 30 Joseph Smith gave James Henry Rollins some chores to do around Smith's store, and Rollins later wrote, "Next day, early in the morning Judge Cleveland brought a car-load of hogs." Apparently the Clevelands had either returned to Nauvoo at this time or were living close by, perhaps in Springfield, a hundred miles southeast. According to John D. Lee, "Judge Cleveland of Springfield, Ill., was very friendly and frequently visited the Prophet." Once again we see that John was "very friendly" with Smith, in Lee's words, not antagonistic, as Brodie supposes. Six months into the next year Joseph was killed; Sarah's third husband was gone.

## X. John Smith

In December 1844 Zina Huntington Jacobs mentioned "Gusta Cleveland" in her journal. If Sarah's daughter was in Nauvoo, it seems reasonable to conclude that Sarah was not far away. On July 9, 1845, Augusta married John Lyman Smith, son of Joseph Smith's uncle John and aunt Clarissa Lyman. The new husband wrote in his journal, "We were married by my Father at her Fathers house when we repaired to the Mansion house & spent the afternoon." So there is a Cleveland house not too far from the Mansion house. Sarah was certainly in Nauvoo at this time, and probably had been there since 1844. She received another patriarchal blessing in Nauvoo on August 20, 1845, this time under the hands of her daughter's new father-in-law. On December 19 she received her endowment in the Nauvoo temple.

As we have seen, all of Joseph Smith's wives who were known to Brigham Young and Heber Kimball had their marriage to Smith repeated in the Nauvoo temple, and the man who stood proxy for the dead prophet always married the woman for time. However, John Cleveland was a non-Mormon. Therefore, a faithful Latter-day Saint would have to stand proxy, which forced another polyandrous marriage. Faced with this duty, Sarah evidently selected John Smith, her daughter's father-in-law, as her proxy husband. Thus on January 15, 1846, at age fifty-six, Sarah married Joseph Smith for eternity in the Nauvoo temple, with John Smith standing proxy, then was sealed to John Smith for time. Her maiden name, "Sarah M. Kingsley," is used in the records. John Smith, brother of Joseph Smith, Sr., had been born on July 16, 1781, in New Hampshire and married Clarissa Lyman in 1815, with whom he had had four children. He converted to Mormonism in 1832 and gathered to Kirtland, then to Missouri, where he served as the stake president and as a Danite. In Illinois he was again a stake president. Ordained a patriarch in January 1844, he would be called as Presiding Patriarch in 1848.

It is not clear how Sarah and John Smith interpreted this sealing. John may have looked upon it as purely ceremonial, as Sarah continued living with John Cleveland after the marriage.

### XI. "Augusta Feels Very Bad"

The next chapter in Mormon history is the exodus from Nauvoo, an event that left Sarah with a number of dilemmas. Apparently, John Cleveland refused to go west, so Sarah would have to choose between living with her "first husband," the non-Mormon John Cleveland, among gentiles, or with the body of the Saints, including her daughter Augusta and her new family, and with her (Sarah's) new sacred husband, John Smith, as a plural wife for time. This would not have been an easy decision, especially since the early Mormon imperative was always to gather to Zion with the rest of the Saints. The status of Alexander, now thirteen, would also have been a problem.

Sarah initially chose to travel west with the Mormons. On February 8, 1846, her son-in-law wrote in his diary,

> This day Started for the Mountains or Some where else I know not where — I Drove to the River with 2 horses 1 waggon loaded to the Bows Myself wife Mother in law [Sarah] & Brother in law Alexander D Cleveland they feeling to go with the Saints & leave husband & father as he John Cleveland does not belong to the church. We Crossed the River & camped on the bank among many others. It rained the most of the Time During the night although we were with out home & knew not where we were going we felt cheerfull & happy.

In another account, John Lyman wrote that John Cleveland "was away in the Country at work at House Carpentering on the 8th February," which suggests that Sarah and her two children left without his knowledge, much as Presendia Huntington Buell left Norman Buell.

However, four days later Brigham Young and Heber Kimball played a surprising part in the unfolding drama of Sarah's life. John Lyman wrote, "by order of President Brigham Young we are to Remain untill the weather moderates which at Present is Extremely cold & Endeavor to Exchange Some of our Property for cows oxen — here Pres Young & Kimball counciled Mother Cleveland & Alexander to Return & Said if She did so it should be the means of Salvation to My father in law  Augusta feels very Bad to Part with her Mother."

In another version of the incident, John Lyman told the story somewhat differently: "Camped on Sugar Creek waiting for the weather to moderate it being extremely cold  Pres H.C. Kimball advised Mother

Cleveland & Son Alexander to Return & Stay with Father Cleveland untill we were located Some where & could return for them. My Wife feels Very bad over the parting." In this version the parting is temporary and relatives were to return and bring Sarah back at some time.

Sarah's biography provides a third version, indicating that "Brigham Young and council ... counciled her to stay with her Husband as he was a good man, having shown himself kind ever helping those in need, although for some reason his mind was darkened as to the Gospel. She obey[ed] coucil and stayed with her Husband, and was faithfull and true to her religion and died a faithfull member of the Church of Jesis Christ of Latter Day Saints." This gives a subtly different motivation for the return—the goodness of her husband. In the first version Sarah was to return to help save him. It is curious that John Smith is not considered in any of this reasoning, as if the proxy marriage for time had not really come into effect.

The parting between Sarah and Augusta, who was five months pregnant, must have been extremely painful for Sarah. She also bid her people, the Mormons, goodby to stay with a man to whom, by a Mormon perspective, she was not really married. In an 1850 letter Alexander told Augusta what happened next:

> When mother and I left you in the camp ... we {stayed} in Navoo about three weeks as near as I can tell before father came after us  when he came he was happy at least I {thought} he was for he could not help{sending} ... mother talked over matters and things and concluded that ... mother should stay and settle things. well we in a day or so we loaded up the waggon. in after we had got every[thing] reddy to start  I went out where my old play mates were and told them that I was a going to leave in the morning and did not expect to ever see them again  morning came and sure enoug - I have not seen them nor Nauvoo since now.

## XII. "Clasped in One Eternal Embrace"

Sarah and John settled in Plymouth, about thirty miles southeast of Nauvoo. Meanwhile, on the plains, Sarah's first grandchild, Isabella Smith, was born on June 12, 1846, near the forks of Nishinabotany River, in Iowa, and died the same day, though Sarah would not have learned of the event until later. On November 9 Sarah wrote to Augusta in Winter Quarters, the first of a series of her letters that have been preserved: "My dear precious Daughter, We rec'd your most welcome Letter some time ago, but owing to the uncertain state of things, I did not wish to write untill I could write something definite, with regard to the minds of the people amongst whom we live." She had heard the news of Isabella's death, and—as she had received religious consolation when Edward died—she now consoled her daughter:

I should have regretted much more than I now do, the disappointment concerning your little one, were you permanently settled, for I know women and children must suffer much untill the church has ceased its wanderings, may the great King ᵒᶠKings speedily {erect} the ʷʰⁱᵗᵉ Standard and call his wanderers home, to build the Holy city, the New Jerusalem, for the Redeemed, ___ I felt your sufferings my dear child, all through the month of July - and had no rest only in comitting you to the mercies of our blessed Lord, while I would be praying for you. I felt comforted, but still suffered, untill about the first of August, when my mind was {relieved} I then was sensible your extreme sufferings were over, either by death or otherwise.

Sarah then turned to her living situation: "We have taken a pleasant {nice} farm with every convenience of house room out houses, good barn, fine garden of Grapes, currants strawberries Peaches, Cherries &c besides a peach orchard {&} good land Alexande[r] is ploughing to day, he works like a hero, I think he will make a good farmer." Nevertheless, the departure of the Mormons had left the Clevelands penniless. "We do very well, considering we had to begin the world anew, with nothing, we feel very much the want of the money Buell owes us." The letter ends fondly and religiously: "May you be preserved from every evil, may your hearts be comforted together by the spirit of the blessed Jesus - that when he makes his appearing you may be received with exceeding joy at his right hand ... your affectionate mother Sarah M. Cleveland."

In the next letter to Augusta, dated March 15, 1847, Sarah was worried about Indians, and she and her husband would have liked to lure their daughter and son-in-law back to Illinois. "Your Father wishes me to tell you and John to come here and he will do all he can for your comfort & happiness, {If} the Indians are not at peace among themselves, I fear they will ⁿᵒᵗ be at peace with the Mormons long." Sarah worried continually about Augusta and Indians.

A letter dated 1847 shows that John Cleveland had antagonistic feelings toward Mormonism by this time: "Your Father is more and more bitter towards the Mormons." The letter expressed poignantly Sarah's feelings of loss and need for her daughter:

Would to God my child we could see you once more — but that is what I have no room to hope for — well I give you up to my dear{est} Father & Redeemer and commit you entirely into his hands and my prayers are constantly {direct[ed] up for} your welfare and I trust we shall one day meet at the feet of Jesus, no more to {part} — I am a {solitary} pilgrim on the {face} of the earth I ask myself have I a {place} on earth? {I have not}.

The next letter, dated December 1848, addressed to "Salt Lake

Valley, California," again movingly expressed Sarah's longing for her daughter:

> O my dear Daughter I rejoice that you are regaining your health, and that you are happy and contented  be assured dear child you live in all our hearts. you cannot conceive how much we miss you at our table, and our fireside, or with what fond remembrance we all cherish our beloved Augusta O had I ten thousand worlds, I would freely give them all to have you here with me the little time I stay on earth. The only way your Mother can sustain this most agonizing trial is by bearing you on ʰᵉʳ heart daily to Jesus, whose you are, to whom you ʷᵉʳᵉ given from your earli{est} breath ... Remember my precious daughter you are clasped in one eternal embrace to your mothers heart.

Sarah's health was failing: "My health is very precarious I am often unable to attend to my domestic concerns  could you but be with me I think I should be well. little did I anticipate being torn from my child while living." In this letter, dated February 10, 1849, Sarah stated that she had been afflicted by "lung fever" for several weeks. She mentioned the gold rush and assumed that the influx of non-Mormons would persecute the Mormons again, so there is another plaintive plea: "We do beg of you John, to bring our daughter to us before the skirmishes begin, we shall have no peace of our lives, untill we see your faces here  there is plenty here for food and raiment."

Alexander, now seventeen, added an amusing addendum to the letter: "The gold fever rages in this section and through all the states. the fever has atacked ᵐᵉ but I cannot go there to cool it and so I will have to go through a course of plowing here and call it gold digging  you asked ʰᵒʷ tall I am I am five feet an one inch my hair does not curl at all and my head itches so that I cannot thinck what to write."

On August 2, 1850, Sarah wrote that her health was still not good: "We are all well myself excepted my health seems to be on a regular decline ____ ." As she faced death, her faith was strong: "I do not expect to live long any how and if you should hear of my death be not grieved. 'All is well.' 'All is well' There, not a cloud that doth arise  To hide my Jesus from my eyes 'All is well' 'All is well.'" Sarah's Protestant background continually seems to surface through her Mormon overlay.

Augusta and John had encouraged the Clevelands to immigrate to Utah, but John Cleveland would not consider it: "Your Father would by no means go to live with the Mormons, therefore I beg of you not to ask us any more, it offends him but even if he ʷᵃˢ willing we have not the means to fit us out for the journey, and my health could not sustain it." So Sarah and Augusta were fated to be parted by the great wilderness, just as Sarah had been parted from her mother in her mother's declining years.

However, the farm was doing well: "We have been more comfortable as to living this year, than any year before since we parted with you. We have a better crop of wheat, and many other things more plentifully."

On May 23, 1849, a new daughter, Augusta Bowen Smith, had been born to Augusta in Salt Lake City, and Sarah the grandmother missed the granddaughter she had never seen: "Kiss your dear little daughter for me O that I could clasp her to my heart once."

Sarah's next letter, dated February 17, 1851, included some "interesting news": "Alexander was married on the 30th of Jan.{y} to Miss Amanda Jane Spiva — a nice little Girl of sixteen, so you see you have a new Sister. I wish you could be here with us." So now Sarah could be a grandmother at a close distance. Happily, her health had improved. She missed her absent Mormon sisters: "Tell all my good Sisters who remembers me kindly, that my prayers for them are a memorial before the Lord, and I have the testimony that they are heard." She ended with a grandmotherly exhortation: "My dear precious daughter, be faithful in your prayers before your heavenly Father, be faithful in the discharge of every known duty teach your dear little one in all faithfulness."

Augusta and John Lyman had another daughter, named Sarah Marietta Smith, on April 14. They immediately sent Sarah and John a letter, and she responded on June 27: "I rejoice that you have another little blessing may both of your little daughters prove indeed a blessing and a comfort to you. I look forward with great hopes of meeting you all in a world of bliss may we all be fully prepared for that day. I thank you for naming my name upon your babe. I wish it was in my power to send both babes some token of Grandmothers love but all I can send are my kisses; and my blessing."

Sarah continued to be intensely religious: "There is at present in this place a great revival of religion, young people are chiefly the subject of it. it is a sweet and joyful season, and my own soul is greatly refreshed — May the Lord extend the sweet spirit of love throughout the land until it shall reach Salt Lake and you my children be revived also." She was leaning toward the revivalistic religion that had helped shape her religious consciousness.

Sarah, in her next letter dated January 11, 1852, would love to see the Utah grandchildren and worries once more that Augusta will be attacked by Indians. But Alexander and Amanda now had a child: "Our little Granddaughter grows finely but cries a great deal." In Alexander's part of the letter, he wrote that he and his father worked as carpenters in the winter and farmed in the summer. But the year's crop had been bad—they had lost all of their wheat crop and half the corn crop.

Sarah was aging painfully. She wrote on April 25: "The Erysipelas has

come out again on my hands, and I am never well when that is the case."
She once again entreated Augusta to move back to Illinois to escape Indians. "I am glad you are pleased with your new home but it appears to me
you had better come here where there are no Indians, and a little money,
instead of staying where there are many Indians, and no money." There
are no more extant letters by Sarah; perhaps her poor health prevented
her from writing, or perhaps later letters have been lost.

In Salt Lake City on March 2, 1853, John Lyman Smith took another
wife, Mary Adelia Haight, so Sarah's daughter was now a plural wife. Two
months later, on May 3, Augusta bore her fourth daughter, Clarissa Medora Smith. John Smith, Sarah's fourth husband, died in Salt Lake City on
May 23, 1854, while Sarah continued to live with her second.

In 1855 John Lyman was sent on a European mission and visited Sarah
and John on the journey east. On July 2 he journalized, "Arrived at Plymouth at 9 oclock found Father & Mother Cleveland in bed  Brother
David knocked at the door & asked if a man by the name of Cleveland
lived there  he said there did  we soon found them out & went in ...
Mother quite feeble very glad to see me had supper." Sarah was now sixty-
seven. Two days later John Lyman tells us of a final development in the
story of Sarah's religious experience:

> Mother had joind a Church a couple of weeks before my arrival  I bore my
> testimony to her  She seemed to have forgotten what her feelings were
> once. Father Cleveland treated me with more respect than ever before &
> seemd greatly pleased to see me, asked me to pray & ask the blessing
> regularly while I was there, saying John you know we never pray but I
> wish you to Pray with us which I did ... they all wished me to Stay a no
> [number] of days with them ... I however replied that I was on the Lords
> business & must go. Gave Mother my wifes miniature, & Bade all good-
> bye.

Without a support group of Mormons, it would have been difficult
to live as a Latter-day Saint in "gentile" Illinois, and Sarah always
needed a religious social community in her life. Nevertheless, some aspects of her Mormon component were probably so deep that her outward membership in a local Protestant congregation may not have
changed it significantly, despite her son-in-law's concern. Mormonism
may be seen as essentially a restorationist Protestant religion, if a somewhat eccentric, radically authoritarian specimen. In any case, Sarah did
not have long to live as a Protestant. According to the biography, she
died in Plymouth on April 21, 1856.

# 12.

# "Loving Sisters"

*Delcena Diadamia Johnson (Sherman Smith Babbitt)* and
*Almera Woodward Johnson (Smith Barton)*

In 1813 the Ezekiel and Julia Johnson family, including six-year-old Delcena and eight-month-old Almera, set out from the wilderness of northern Vermont to the rich, barely settled expanses of western New York. A letter from Julia to her mother, grammaticized by dutiful descendants, tells the story of this journey: "We started from Westford[, Vermont on June 27] ... and came on over some 100 miles when one of our horses became lame and we laid over for a week. We then came awhile but were obliged to stop again for three or four days, and then we came as far as Hamburg, this side of Buffalo, where we stopped about seven weeks."

The inhabitants of Hamburg needed a skilled carpenter and did all they could to convince the Johnsons to settle with them: "They gave Mr. Johnson one dollar a day, with house rent, garden vegetables, milk, etc. He thought it best to stay until our horses got recruited up and we got rested, as he had the money for his work." But Julia was very "discontented" in Hamburg, "for there were no neighbors short of about two miles, and all Sabbath breakers, and I could not feel at home there." Here we see Julia's intense religiosity, which would be passed on to her children.

Starting again on September 24, the family was "four days coming to this place on account of bad roads." "This place" was Canadaway (later Fredonia) in Pomfret township, Chautauqua, a few miles from Lake Erie in western New York. Julia approved of the neighborhood: "This is a beautiful country and we have concluded to stay until spring, if not longer ... There are many moving to the west, some days 10 or 12 wagons in company, and some have come back to this place. The country is very healthy indeed, and good for grain ... It is only seven years since the

288

settlements were made here ... I never saw such sights of peaches before, thousands of bushels rot on the ground." More importantly, she found the religious environment satisfactory: "We have hired a little house about two miles and a half from the village of Canadaway which contains three societies, Baptist, Presbyterian and Methodist. There are also mills, and school is near at hand, with neighbors who appear very friendly and kind."

Ezekiel was planning a reconnaisance trip into Ohio, wrote Julia, but if he found no better country, the Johnsons would settle in Pomfret. "It is a good place for his trade which demands one dollar and fifty cents per day, but the Lord knows what is best and I hope I shall be reconciled to His will. All things shall work together for the good of those who love Him. If we are afflicted, it is for our good, for He doth not afflict willingly nor grieve the children of men. Therefore let us put our trust in Him." This letter gives a vivid account of westering America and frontier New York, and it also shows the religious atmosphere in which Delcena and Almera were raised. Julia is intensely concerned about religious environment, and she turns to scriptural homilies in the middle of a family letter.

Delcena and Almera Johnson are thus another sister pair in the group of Joseph Smith's wives. Delcena was a widow when Smith married her; her life is poorly documented. Almera is better documented only for the period of her life when she married Smith. He enlisted her brother Benjamin's help in introducing her to plural marriage, and Benjamin wrote about the experience more than once in his later life. These accounts of the marriage are important documents showing how Smith would approach his prospective plural wives and their close relatives.

Both Delcena and Almera lived lives filled with tragedy. Delcena lost two husbands, most of her children, and then died prematurely at age forty-seven after crossing the plains. She did live to see one of her children marry. Almera, after Joseph Smith's death, remarried, but the union was unhappy and ended in divorce. She buried all of her five daughters.

## I. The Johnsons

Delcena Diadamia was born on November 19, 1806, to the thirty-three-year-old Ezekiel Johnson and Julia Hills, ten years his junior, in Westford, Chittenden County, in northwest Vermont, ten miles from Lake Champlain. Almera Woodward was born six years later, on October 12, 1812, also in Westford. Both Ezekiel, a farmer and carpenter, and Julia were natives of Massachusetts. They married in January 1801, then raised a family of sixteen children, nine boys and seven girls, born between 1802 and 1829. Many of the Johnson children became stalwart Mormons who figured prominently in colonizing out-of-the-way corners of Utah. Delcena was fourth in the family, Almera seventh.

The first two Johnson children, Joel Hill and Nancy Maria, were born in 1802 and 1803 in Grafton and Northborough, Worcester, Massachusetts. Then the family moved north to the wilderness of Vermont, where six children were born in the next eight years: Seth Garzey in 1805, Delcena in 1806, Julia Ann in 1808, David in 1810, and Almera in 1812. In Westford, Ezekiel built cabins for new settlers.

## II. Revival Meetings in the Neighborhood

After moving to Pomfret, New York, in 1813, Ezekiel bought a farm and began to clear land. There nine more Johnsons joined the family: Susan Ellen in 1814, Joseph Ellis in 1817, Benjamin Franklin in 1818, Mary Ellen in 1820, Elmer Wood in 1821, George Washington in 1823, William Derby in 1824, Esther in 1828, and Amos Partridge in 1829. On September 14, 1822, Elmer died, bringing Delcena and Almera their first experience with the death of a close family member. In 1825 the Johnsons moved to a large farmhouse on a mile-square farm. Benjamin's earliest memories are of "pioneer life, in clearing deep forests with great labor, for my parents, to obtain but scanty living comforts." Pomfret he describes as a "wild and almost frontier region, with heavy primeval forests." The Mormons had often had considerable experience pioneering before settling Utah.

On the Johnson farm, the men worked in the fields and the women had their own responsibilities: "From the wool all our winter clothing was made for the men and boys, and from the flax all the summer clothing both for women and men; also all the bed and table linen and toweling," Benjamin wrote. Cheese, butter, honey, and maple sugar were made at home. "Soap and candle making, with beer brewing were common, homelike events." So we can imagine Delcena and Almera growing up in the midst of a large family, learning these womanly tasks of frontier rural America. George Washington Johnson remembered the Pomfret farm fondly, a "dear old brown cottage," an orchard, a garden, a barn, a corn house, a well, and a brick yard. At night the family would gather around "the old kitchen fireplace" "to pass off the evening with all sorts of fun."

Benjamin wrote that he had "a beloved and beautiful mother" and "loving elder sisters." Delcena was twelve years older than him, Almera six. The family's religious education came from Julia: "My mother possessed high religious veneration, and early taught me faith in God and the necessity of prayer." Benjamin accompanied his mother and siblings to Presbyterian services every Sunday. As a youth, he was greatly troubled by the idea of eternal damnation and feared "literal fire and brimstone to those who did not 'get religion' or 'a change of heart.'" His brother Joseph's autobiography also mentions the revivals that were prevalent in western New York and the psychic atmosphere of intense personal religious searching: "When [I] arrived at the age of 14 [1831] I commenced to attend all the revival meetings in the neighborhood, so that if possible, I too, might find a change of heart and that enjoyment of a divine presence I so much desired. I prayed earnestly." The Johnsons were living in the heart of the burned-over district, at the height of the Second Great Awakening.

Ezekiel, however, was not a religious man. Benjamin described him as "a Husband and Parent ... most tender and affectionate ... a man of truth and honor among men ... his word was his bond." Nevertheless, due to the pressures of hard work, he became a heavy drinker. When this became a serious problem, "neither his labors nor his love for his family seemed to diminish, yet the fiend of unhappiness had entered our home, to break the bonds of union between our parents, and to destroy the happiness of their children." Benjamin apparently felt torn between quarreling parents, both of whom he loved, and his "heart at times would seem almost ready to burst with sorrow and grief." Religious tensions also divided the parents, for Ezekiel never attended any church, though he had some religious faith. Family traditions assert that he had been born illegitimately and that his mother's Congregationalist church had refused to accept him as a member for this reason. This left him deeply skeptical of all organized religion.

Thus Delcena and Almera grew up in a family that was loving and warm on the one hand, yet somewhat dysfunctional and strained on the other—both hyper-religious and hypo-religious. Benjamin reports that as a boy there were occasions when his father's drinking caused him to wish he had never been born. Delcena and Almera may have felt the same way.

### III. Lyman Royal Sherman

On January 16, 1829, Delcena, at age twenty-two, married Lyman Royal Sherman, twenty-four, a native of Vermont. Her first child, Alvira, was born in Pomfret in 1830. A second daughter, Mary Ellen, was born in 1831, and a first son, Alba (Albey) Lyman Sherman, on October 30, 1832.

Soon after Delcena's marriage, the Johnsons began to hear rumors of restorationist movements coalescing around Alexander Campbell and Joseph Smith. Joel, the oldest sibling, moved to Amherst, Ohio, in 1830, and David visited him soon thereafter. Julia sent Joel and David a letter cautioning them against the delusions of the new religious movements, and they wrote back informing her that they had recently been baptized Mormons. "This news came upon us almost as a horror and a disgrace," wrote Benjamin.

In the early fall of 1831, Joel and David sent the family a Book of Mormon accompanied by a long epistle. Mother Julia, Seth, Nancy, Lyman Sherman (and probably Delcena), with some neighbors started meeting together to read and "deplore" this book and letter. Seth wrote a cautionary letter back to Joel: "It is true that I know not but the Lord has raised up a prophet but I have fears lest this one is one of those false prophets spoken of and warned against by the Savior and His apostles ... I have read the book a little and find no evidence of its being a revelation of God." But as the Johnsons and Shermans continued to read, many of them gradually became converted, "marveling at the simplicity and purity of what they read," according to Benjamin.

In late fall Joel and David returned home for a visit, bringing with them a friend, Almon Babbitt, who, though only seventeen, bore a fervent testimony of Mormonism. Then two elders, Joseph Brackenbury and Edmund Durfee, arrived, and, as a result of Brackenbury's powerful testimony and reasoning, mother Julia Johnson and Lyman Sherman were soon ready to be baptized. They were followed by nearly all the adult Johnsons, apparently including Delcena. There are three different dates for Almera's baptism: 1831, 1832, and 1833. She was nineteen in late 1831. If considered an adult, she may have been baptized then, but if considered a minor, she might have been delayed in her baptism until 1832 or 1833. Ezekiel, working in Fredonia that fall, true to form would not convert and did not allow the younger Johnsons to be baptized. Tragically, Joseph Brackenbury, who had had such an impact on the family, died with a sudden illness (rumored to be caused by poison) at the Johnson house.

Soon after Brigham Young's conversion on April 15, 1832, he stayed overnight with Delcena and Lyman. Benjamin Johnson wrote that "While at eavning in animated conversation upon The Gifts as promiced to acompany the Gospel. The Spirit Came upon Brother Shirman in mighty powr and he opened his mouth in an unknown Toungue to the great Surprise & joy of all." Benjamin regarded this as the first time the gift of tongues was practiced in Mormonism. If so, Delcena was a witness.

### IV. "Elder Sherman Sung in the Gift of Tongues"

Ezekiel Johnson remained opposed to Mormonism, even after a visit to Kirtland, and in the fall of 1832 he decided to move to Illinois, perhaps to remove his family from the influence of this powerful new religion. After selling two farms, he journeyed west and bought land in Chicago in the spring of 1833, then wrote home with instructions on following him. But his letter was apparently lost in the mail, and the Johnsons (perhaps with Delcena and Lyman), at a loss, decided to travel to Kirtland in 1833, where they traded some of their property to procure a house. Puzzled, Ezekiel made his way to Kirtland and found his family settled and unwilling to move. Though upset, he bowed to the inevitable and took up residence in Kirtland, where he worked in a carpenter shop with Brigham Young for a time.

In Ohio, Delcena is a shadow behind her husband who quickly became a prominent leader. Benjamin described him as "a man of great integrity, a powerful preacher." He was ordained a high priest, and on July 23, 1833, he, Joel, and Seth helped lay the cornerstone of the Kirtland temple. Almera certainly and Delcena probably were also present. Julia Ann Johnson married Almon Babbitt, Delcena's future husband, in Kirtland on November 23.

In May 1834 Lyman, with Joel and Seth and Almon Babbitt, joined Zion's Camp, the quasi-military expedition to Missouri led by Joseph Smith, which, though a practical failure, became a leadership training ground for the early church. Sadly, Seth contracted cholera while on the expedition, and, after returning back to Kirtland, died on February 19, 1835. However, Lyman returned safely and was ordained a president of the original Quorum of the Seventy on February 28, so Delcena became a general authority's wife. In the spring Julia Johnson and her children met at Delcena's house to receive patriarchal blessings from Joseph Smith, Sr.

About this time Julia and Ezekiel Johnson separated due to religious differences and his alcoholism. He bought a house in nearby Mentor where the children could visit him. Julia, to support her family—including Nancy, Almera, Susan, and six younger children—manufactured "stocks, a fine article of men's neckwear" and "palmleaf hats, then just coming into use."

We have evidence that Lyman Sherman had become a close friend of Joseph Smith by 1835; according to Benjamin, Smith taught Sherman the principle of plural marriage that year. Lyman is also the focus of a revelation given through Smith on December 26, 1835, when he wrote, "Bro Lyman came in and requested to have the word of the lord through me for said he I ... was promised to have that I should have a revelation and which should make known my duty." Accordingly, Smith received Doctrine and Covenants 108, which begins, "Verily thus saith the Lord unto you my servant Lyman your sins are forgiven you because you have obeyed my voice in coming up hither this morning to receive counsel of him whom I have appointed."

On June 30, 1836, another child, Seth, was born to Delcena. That fall the Johnsons, including Almera, moved to a farm outside of Kirtland. Another son, Daniel, joined the Shermans in 1837. In addition, Delcena, at thirty-one, was tending Alvira, seven, Mary, six, Albey, five, and Seth, one. On January 8, 1837, we have another example of Lyman's glossolalic tendencies: in a Kirtland temple meeting, according to Wilford Woodruff, "Elder Sherman sung in the gift of tongues & proclaimed great & marvelous things while clothed upon by the power & spirit of God." Lyman filled a temporary vacancy in the Kirtland High Council on October 1, 1837.

As financial difficulties and internal dissent increasingly plagued Mormons in Kirtland, many left Ohio for Missouri in 1838. In the early part of the year, Lyman set the church printing press on fire so that Mormon enemies could not use it, and soon thereafter he and Delcena must have traveled to Far West, Missouri. However, Almera stayed in Mentor to do her father's housekeeping.

## V. "My Sister Delcena a Widow"

About October 20, 1838, the Johnson caravan reached Far West. Benjamin writes, "On approaching Far West we were met by the Prophet, who came out to meet us, and I felt joy in seeing him again ... my sisters, Delcena and Julia, wives of L. R. Sherman and A. W. Babbitt were both living in Far West." Another daughter, Susan Julia, was born to Delcena in Far West on October 31.

Lyman was called to be a temporary high council member at Far West in December, but an even greater calling was soon planned for him. On January 16, 1839, Joseph Smith, Hyrum, and Sidney Rigdon, imprisoned in Liberty Jail, chose George A. Smith and Lyman to fill vacancies in the Quorum of the Twelve Apostles and wrote a letter to Brigham Young and Heber C. Kimball instructing them to make the appointments. However, on February 7 Young and Kimball travelled to Liberty to visit Smith, and when they left Far West, "Lyman Sherman was somewhat unwell," according to Heber Kimball. "We did not notify him of his appointment." Then, Heber wrote, "a few days after our return [from Liberty Jail] he [Lyman] died." This probably occurred on approximately February 15, 1839. Delcena, left with six young children, would have been grief-stricken, then would have had to face the practical challenges of supporting her family alone.

In early February Benjamin was being hunted by Missouri "mobocrats," but managed to reach Far West. "I found my sisters Delcena and Julia well and glad to see me again, but here I must not—dare not—remain." He soon left, but when he heard of Lyman's death, he returned to Far West: "The second day after I arrived at Far West and found my sister Delcena a widow, with six small children for whom I must do my best to provide for their removal from the state, as well as for their support."

## VI. Illinois

Delcena and Benjamin left Far West toward the end of March, braving muddy roads, storms, and bitter cold as they traveled east. After crossing the Mississippi, they were received with "great kindness" by the citizens of Quincy. "Here my sister Delcena with her children concluded to remain until it should be known where the next gathering place would be." He returned to Richmond, Missouri, to help his mother's family in their journey to Illinois. Almera was apparently still in Mentor with her father.

Benjamin soon went on a mission to Canada, and in his absence the Johnsons settled in Ramus (Macedonia), twenty miles east of Nauvoo, where Almera joined them in 1840. The two sisters are undocumented until April 19, 1842, when "Dulcina Sherman" was admitted to the Nauvoo Relief Society at its fifth meeting.

## VII. "They Ware Both in His Care"

At about this time Delcena became a plural wife of Joseph Smith. Benjamin, who returned home from his mission in early July 1842, wrote, "The marriage of my Eldest Sister to the Prophet was before my Return to Nauvoo. and it being Tasitly admitted I asked no questions." This would have been something of a Levirate marriage, marrying the widow of a brother in the gospel, as it were. Benjamin wrote that Delcena was sealed to Smith "by proxy." It is possible that this was an early proxy marriage in which Delcena married Lyman for eternity, with Smith standing proxy for the dead man, after which Delcena and the Mormon leader would have been sealed for time. Delcena was living with Louisa Beaman at this time, and evidently Smith gave them housing and financial support. Benjamin wrote, "And now in visiting My Sister. The widow of Lyman R. Shirman ... I found with her a former acquaintance Sister Louisa Beeman. and I Saw from apearances that they ware both in his [Joseph Smith's] Care and that he provided for there Comfort."

## VIII. "I Stood Before Her Trembling"

While Benjamin was in Nauvoo, Joseph Smith asked him to act as his agent in dealing with church property in Macedonia and gave him his power of attorney. Joseph and Benjamin came to have a close, friendly relationship, despite the disparity in their ages. On April 1, 1843, Smith and some companions arrived in Macedonia for a visit and stayed at Benjamin's house. The next morning the Mormon prophet took his host by the arm and said, "Come Brother Bennie, let us have a walk." They strolled to the edge of a forest, sat on a log, and Joseph proceeded to say "that the Lord had revealed to him that plural or patriarchal marriage was according to His law; and that the Lord had not only revealed it to him but had commanded him to obey it." He said that when God had revealed to him "the ancient Order of Plural marriage" in Kirtland, one of his first thoughts had been to ask Julia Johnson "for Some of her daughters." Now he was once again required by God to take more wives, so "he had Come now to ask me for my Sister Almera—His words astonished me and almost <u>took</u> my <u>breath</u>—I Sat for a time amazed and finally almost Ready to burst with emotion." Benjamin wrote that if a thunderbolt had fallen at his feet, he could hardly have been more shocked or amazed. He was too stunned to even "comprehend anything":

> In almost an agony of feeling ... I looked him Straight in the Face & Said: "Brother Joseph This is Something I did not Expect & I do not under-stand it—You know whether it is right. I do not. I want to do just as you tell me, and I will try. But if I [ever] should Know that you do this to Dis-honor & debauch my Sister I will kill you as Shure as the Lord lives = and while his eye did not move from mine He Said with a Smile, in a soft tone "But Benjamin you will never <u>know that</u>. But you will know the principle is true & will greatly Rejoice in what it will bring to you." But.how I asked. Can I teach my Sister what I mySelf do not understand ... "But you will See & underStand it" he Said and when you open your mouth to talk to your Sister light will come to you & your mouth will be full. & your toung loose.

Joseph told Benjamin that he would preach a sermon in the evening, the esoteric meaning of which only he, Benjamin, would understand. That night Smith explicated the parable of the talents in his address: to him who had (talents), more would be given; but if a man had only one, that one would be taken away from him. By Smith's interpretation, this parable is a radical critique of monogamy as something inherently infe-rior and less than sacred.

Benjamin's initial response to the whole affair was one of disgust and severe depression. "To me there was a horror in the idea of speaking to my sister upon such a subject, and the thought of which made me sick." This is not an untypical Mormon first response to the idea of po-lygamy. Latter-day Saints were of New England, Puritanical stock, from a cultural tradition that had been living monogamously for millennia. Thus Benjamin, like many Mormons faced with polygamy, probably experi-enced severe cognitive dissonance. Either he would have to accept the repulsive doctrine of polygamy or give up Smith as a prophet, as well as his family, his new culture and community, and all that he had been per-secuted for. But since many early Mormons viewed Smith as infallible, it is understandable that there was often, as here, a conversion to the doc-trine that originally caused shocked horror. After all, polygamy was found in the Bible, where it was practiced by Smith's prophetic prede-cessors.

Nevertheless, Benjamin at first went ahead as Joseph's intermediary only out of obedience. He arranged a private interview with Almera in her room: "I stood before her trembling, my knees shaking." However, "Just So Soon as I found powr to open my mouth it was filled for the Light of the Lord Shone upon my understanding and the Subject that had Seemed So dark, now apeared of all Subjects pertaining to our Gospel the most lucid & plain. and So my Sister & mySelf ware converted togather."

This remarkable narrative is a fairly typical account of how Joseph Smith approached many of his plural wives. He often talked first to a brother or male family member with whom he had developed a close relationship. He used Dimick Huntington as an intermediary to teach Zina Huntington, Levi Hancock as go-between for the Fanny Alger family, and he asked permission of Lucy Walker's brother William after approaching Lucy herself. We also see how Smith would deal with an initial unsympathetic reaction, as in the case of Mary Elizabeth Rollins Lightner—he often prophesied that the person in question would receive a revelatory testimony of the principle. In addition, as here, he often explicated the principle from the Bible.

Nevertheless, Benjamin says of Almera, "her heart was not yet won by the Prophet." Smith asked Benjamin to bring her to Nauvoo, and he agreed; therefore, "within a few days ... my sister accompanied me to Nauvoo, where at my sister Delcena's we soon met the Prophet with his brother Hyrum and Wm. Clayton." Hyrum took Benjamin aside and assured him that he must not be frightened of this new doctrine, as it was "all Right." He knew "Brother Hyrum" did not get carried away by worldly things and he had fought polygamy until God had shown him it was true. "I know," Hyrum continued, "that Joseph was comanded to take more wives and he waited untill an Angel with drawn Sword Stood before him and declared that if he longer delayed fulfilling that Command he would Slay him." Benjamin, however, had already been fully converted.

Hyrum then turned to Almera: "The Lord has revealed the principle of plural marriage to me," he said, "and I know for myself that it is true. I will have you for a sister, and you shall be blest." Almera later wrote that Hyrum "came to me and said I need not be afraid. I had been fearing and doubting about the principle and so had he, but he now knew it was true. After this time I lived with the Prophet Joseph as his wife ... I had many conversations with Eliza Beaman who was also a wife of Joseph Smith ... on the subject of plurality of wives."

Benjamin gave some of the details of the actual marriage ceremony: "Meanwhile the Prophet with Louisa Beeman and my Sister Delcena had it agreeably aranged with sister Almara and after a little instruction, She

Stood by the Prophets Side & was Sealed to him as a wife by Brother Clayton. After which the Prophet asked me to take my Sister to ocupy Room No 10 in his Mansion Home dureing her Stay in the City." At the time of her marriage to Smith, Almera was thirty, while the Mormon leader was thirty-eight.

Almera and Benjamin returned to Macedonia on about April 23. Smith visited Ramus again on May 16. "The Prophet again Came and at my house ocupied the Same Room & Bed with my Sister that the month previous he had occupied with the Daughter of the Late Bishop Partridge as his wife," Benjamin wrote. Smith was accompanied by George Miller, William Clayton, J. M. Smith, and Eliza and Lydia Partridge. The party left on May 18, but Joseph, with Clayton, visited Ramus again from October 19 to 21. At this time, according to Benjamin, Smith "asked me for my youngest sister, Esther M.," who was now fifteen. However, Benjamin told Smith that she was already engaged to another man, and Smith "reluctantly" let the matter drop. Less than a year later Joseph Smith was killed and Delcena and Almera were widows.

### IX. "My Health Has Been Verry Poor"

The marriage of Almera to Joseph Smith is the best-documented moment in either her life or Delcena's, and after Smith's death their lives can be traced only in outline. The year 1845, for example, is entirely a blank for Delcena. On January 7, 1846, "Dulcinea Sherman" received her endowment in the Nauvoo temple. In the same session were her brother-in-law and soon-to-be-husband, Almon Babbitt, Smith's widow Maria Lawrence, soon to marry Babbitt also, and Mary Ann Sherman. Some two weeks later, on January 24, as Heber Kimball officiated, Delcena ("Dulcena Diadama Johnson") was sealed to Lyman Sherman for eternity, with Almon Babbitt standing proxy, then was sealed to Babbitt for time. Thus this is one of those few cases in which a wife of Joseph Smith was married for eternity to someone other than Smith. Babbitt also married Julia Johnson, Mary Tulley, and Maria Lawrence on the same date.

Almon Babbitt was born on October 1, 1812, in Cheshire, Berkshire, Massachusetts. After his early Mormon experience, he served a mission to Canada in 1837-38. He was subsequently tried twice by the Kirtland High Council for minor spiritual infractions, but was forgiven both times. He practiced as an attorney, and often represented the church in Kirtland and Nauvoo. After a short stay in Missouri, he moved to Illinois, where he was tried by the Nauvoo High Council for criticizing Joseph Smith, and once again was acquitted. In 1841 he was appointed president of the Kirtland Stake but was disfellowshipped that October for teaching that Kirtland was a proper place for Mormon gathering. Again he was able to quickly regain his standing in the church. He moved to Ramus in 1842 and was made the presiding elder of that branch in March 1843, but was immediately disfellowshipped for "impropriety!" He was restored to fellowship on April 10. He was elected to the Illinois State Legislature in 1844 and was made a member of the secret Mormon shadow government, the Council of Fifty, the same year.

Thus Babbitt was a prominent, if unpredictable, figure in Latter-day Saint history. If he was constantly in trouble with the church, he was also adept at extricating himself from censure. He was sufficiently active in political and ecclesiastical affairs that one wonders how much time he spent with his three plural wives. It is possible that he looked on the marriage with Delcena as a "caretaker" relationship, rather than as a practical marriage. At the time of her sealing to Babbitt, Delcena had the sizable family of Alvira, fifteen, Mary, fourteen, Albey, thirteen, Seth, nine, and Susan, seven. Little Daniel had apparently died in Nauvoo.

Delcena and Almon did not go west immediately, since he stayed in Nauvoo to administer church property, which was a sensitive, dangerous assignment. Delcena witnessed the burning of the Nauvoo temple. Almon was involved in the battle of Nauvoo in September 1846 and signed the treaty of surrender. Delcena's father, Ezekiel, who had traveled to Illinois to be close to his children, died in Nauvoo on January 13, 1848. Perhaps both Delcena and Almera were present at his death.

The mercurial Babbitt argued with apostle Orson Hyde in 1848, was disfellowshipped on November 19, but predictably enough returned to the church soon after. He came to Utah later that year, but Delcena stayed in the east. In Utah he was elected delegate to Congress from the provisional State of Deseret and traveled to Washington, D.C., in the fall of 1849, though he was not seated.

On July 11 of the same year, Delcena, apparently without Babbitt, arrived at Council Bluffs with her mother and five children. Winter Quarters would be a place of calamity for Delcena. On August 19, 1850, Mary died, and in November she lost Alvira and Seth, which left only Albey and Susan to the grieving mother. The details of these deaths are not preserved, but to lose Alvira and Mary just as they were approaching the age of marriage must have been a cruel blow.

Babbitt was in Kanesville by May 1851, for he was disfellowshipped there for "immorality and intemperance," but as usual he soon returned to fellowship in the church. He was in Utah by July 19, 1851, and in 1852 he was appointed secretary of the territory. As always, we are struck by the distance (here geographical) between husband and plural wife.

On May 30, 1853, Mother Julia Johnson died in Council Bluffs. On October 23, in a family letter to Benjamin, on a mission to Hawaii, Delcena wrote:

> Dear Brother realizing your lonliness I now attempt for the first time for many years to rite A line to any one to you I thought I would master ambition enough to let you know I had not forgoten you { } I have often yes very often thought of your anxiety to hear from your friends My health has been verry poor for the last nine months we have been very lonesom since Mother died we expected to have gone to the valley this season but was disapointed Albey and Susan are with me I wish we were to the valley your sister Delcena Sherman

So Delcena mourned for her mother and looked forward to gathering with the Saints in Utah. As to her bad health, family traditions report that she was suffering from arthritis at this time—probably acute rheumatoid arthritis. Julia wrote to Benjamin, "Delcenas health is verry poor and has been for the last year much of the time she has been confined to her bed she is now able to sit up a good share of the time we think iff she is able to cross the Plains in the spring she may regain her health."

In 1854 Delcena finally struck out for Utah accompanied by Albey, now twenty-one, and Susan, thirteen. According to family traditions, she was nearly a total invalid as she made the long, difficult overland journey, but her greatest wish was to see the Salt Lake Valley before she died. When the company reached the North Platte River, a fellow-traveler remarked that there had been a death and a birth on the journey and suggested that a marriage would complete the picture. So Albey married Mary Elvira Swan on June 10, 1854. Delcena, fated not to live much longer, at least was able to participate in this joyful event before her death.

The ailing woman, her frail body riddled with arthritis, reached the Salt Lake Valley in late summer or early fall 1854. But just a few months later, on October 21, she died at the age of forty-seven, passing away at the house of Almon Babbitt. She had lost two husbands and four of six children, and severe painful health problems forced her to an early grave. But before her death, she witnessed the marriage of one child and accomplished a final, long-desired pilgrimage to the last Mormon Zion, the new gathering place of the Saints in the Rocky Mountains.

## X. Reuben Barton

On November 16, 1845, Almera married James Reuben Barton, apparently in Nauvoo. She wrote, in an affidavit, "since the death of the Prophet Joseph Smith I was married for time to Reuben Barton ... by whom I had five daughters." Barton had been born on January 9, 1812, was ordained an elder in Kirtland in 1836, and a seventy in 1837. He lost his first wife, Marcia Wilson, on September 8, 1845, by whom he had had three children—Nathan, Reuben Jr., and Marcia—aged five, two, and two weeks at the time of their mother's death. Little Marcia died two weeks after her mother.

The first of Almera's daughters was Mary Ellen, born on July 21, 1846, in Olena, Illinois, twenty-five miles northeast of Nauvoo. She died two years later, on August 19, 1848. A second daughter, Sarah Delcena (known as Delcena), was born on April 29, 1849, followed by a third, Lois Elvira, on April 19, 1851, both born in Nauvoo. Lois opened a new chapter in Almera's tragic life, as she was mentally impaired. Almera, as sometimes happens with parents of disabled children, felt internal responsibility and guilt for her child's plight. A note in the Joel Johnson family papers tells us that "Almera wondered if it [Lois's disability] was punishment because she remaried [after Joseph Smith died]."

Before the winter of 1852 the Bartons moved to the Kanesville area, where Joseph Ellis Johnson was living. Almera's fourth child, Almera Melissa, was born there on December 12, but sadly the infant died on April 23, 1853. On October 23 Reuben wrote to Benjamin Johnson, in the family letter mentioned above, "Almeria's health is yet very poor, but she is gradualy regaining her strength after a two months sege of Chills & fever." Her last child, Harriet Julia, was born on September 1, 1854, in Council Bluffs.

In the late 1850s Almera's brothers' writings provide a skeleton residential history for her. In the summer of 1857 Joel, the oldest of the siblings, and Julia Johnson Babbitt (widowed the previous year) traveled east from Utah, arriving at Ellisdale, Iowa, just north of Council Bluffs, on June 13. The next day Almera and Reuben attended a family reunion. Joel wrote, "Joseph and William Johnson with Ruben Barton and families all present (with many of their friends) who provided an excellent fruit and oyster supper upon which we all feasted ourselves and had a jovial time. We enjoyed ourselves first rate, after which we went home with Barton's family."

On July 28 Joel, with Julia Babbitt, visited Almera and Reuben. A week later, on August 6, Joel was "at Ellisdale through the day and went to Barton's in the evening and returned to Ellisdale with Barton's family and partook of oyster supper." Almera seems to be living close to Ellisdale. She may have tended her sister Julia when she died in Winter Quarters on October 23.

Almera, Reuben, and family celebrated Christmas Day with the Joel and Joseph Johnson families at Ellisdale. On January 15, 1858, the Bartons met with Joel, William, and Joseph at Joel's home in Crescent City, north of Ellisdale, where they discussed writing a family history, Joel reports.

On March 15, Joel, who was ill, wrote, "My sister Almera came to visit me today." Two years later, on June 28, he wrote, "Spent ... the afternoon in visited with my sister Almera, while Nephi was hunting for the lost ox." Joel left Council Bluffs to return to Utah on August 5, 1860.

The marriage of Almera and Reuben was not fated to endure. By the late 1850s arguments between them were becoming increasingly frequent, and Barton became antagonistic toward Mormonism at some point, which added to the marital tension. On March 16, 1860, Harriet Snider Johnson wrote to her husband, Joseph Ellis, that "Almera was {here} this after noon  thing[s] are a great deel worse there than when you left  they cant aggree at all." Finally, early the next year Almera went to "Park's store" for groceries and found that Reuben had closed the account against her. Soon after this they separated permanently.

## XI. Parowan, Iron County, Utah

In late summer 1861 Almera journeyed to Utah with her three daughters, her brother Joseph, and a company of twenty-seven. They arrived in Salt Lake City on September 27. She was forty-nine, Delcena was twelve, Lois ten, and Harriet seven. But her youngest was not long for this world. According to family records, Harriet died on December 20, 1862, in Salt Lake City, at the age of eight, "saddening the Christmas season of 18[62]."

Benjamin Johnson has Almera come to Utah in 1861, then move to Parowan, Iron County, southwestern Utah, in 1862, but Andrew Jenson has her live three years in Utah County, then move to Parowan. In either case, she lived the last thirty years of her life in the small town of Parowan. Of Almera's years as a divorced single mother in Parowan, we know surprisingly little. We can pinpoint only three definite events in her life during this period, two of which were tragic. First, on March 23, 1870, Delcena died of "lung fever," tuberculosis, at age twenty-one. She had worked as a telegraph operator in Parowan and was unmarried at the time of her death. Her gravestone is virtually the only document remaining to us that records her short life, but it movingly reflects Almera's love for her: "SACRED to the MEMORY of Dellie S. Barton ... Daughter of Almera W. Barton. Rest Darling Dellie."

After weathering this ordeal, Almera was left alone with Lois. In an imprecise census entry in 1870, "Eliza" W. Barton, fifty-four, born in Vermont, was living with (Lois) Elvira Barton, 19, born in Nauvoo, Illinois. Caring for Lois must have been difficult, but Almera probably endured this trial heroically and compassionately. Openshaw writes, "N. Elvira ... remained a love burden to her mother for 42 years. Her retarded mentality made her incapable of either learning or caring for herself." Still, Almera's numerous siblings, with their children, were close by. Of her sixteen brothers and sisters, seven were living in Utah in 1870. Joel was in Virgin City, Washington County (south of Parowan); Joseph Ellis was in St. George, Washington County; Benjamin was in Utah County (just south of Salt Lake City); George Washington was in Mona, Juab County (just northwest of Sanpete); William Derby was in Johnson, Kane County; and a lone surviving sister, Esther Johnson LeBaron, was in Salt Lake City

So Almera, in southern Utah, would have had frequent visits from her siblings and their children. Kate Carter wrote, "Almera was not only a homemaker of ability and an individual of taste and attraction, but like all her parent's children, her fingers dripped service. To her nieces and nephews she was the adored 'Aunt Mera,' and showing his high regard for her, her brother, William Derby Johnson addressed her in his letters as, 'My Ever Dear and Respected Sister Almera,' and expressed a hope that when called to the other side, he might be as well-prepared for departure to a higher sphere as she was."

How many nieces and nephews did Almera have? As the Johnson children were generally polygamists, the answer to that question is somewhat staggering. Joel had thirty children by five wives. Delcena had seven. Julia Babbitt had six. Joseph Ellis had twenty-nine by three wives. Benjamin had forty-four by seven wives. Mary Ellen had two children. George Washington had twenty by two wives. As a monogamist, William Derby was the odd man out in this group, but his wife bore twelve children nonetheless. Esther had twelve children. All together, Almera had some 164 nieces and nephews and would thus have been a cherished part of an intricate, monumental, extended family. One imagines vast family get-togethers at Christmastime, even if only two or three of Almera's siblings joined forces for the holidays.

In Almera's final years, William Derby and his wife attempted to persuade her to come live with them in Mexico. Kate Carter writes, "Yet, although Almera's resources were at a low ebb, and she was troubled greatly with rheumatism, her independent nature would not permit her to be a burden to anyone." In the 1880 Utah census, Almera W. Barton, listed as sixty-six years old, was living with "A Louis Barton," twenty-nine years of age, in Parowan. Almera's occupation was given as "Keeping House," while Lois's was "At Home."

There is a short letter by Almera to Joseph Ellis, her only extant holograph, dated July 13, 1882:

Dear Brother I rec'd the card you sent  was vary glad to hear from you  it had been long long since I have heard from you was vary glad to learn you were all well enough to keep about[.] I am about most of the time  vidas health not so good as it was before she was sick last winter

I was vary surprised to hear of the move south (well such is life) I should like to see you vary much I hope you will not slide and not even look at <u>us</u> well if you must all go may Peace and Happiness attend <u>you</u> and abide with you and yours is my prayr __ __ __

well I have but afew afew [sic] minutes to write   I send this by Brother Evens I had no stamp I expect him evry moment I must ask you for one thing strikenine for mice they <u>are</u> trouble, & yes have you any Mullen I think I have the Catarrh I have heard and read it was vary good to smoke for that complaint the old fashioned Mullen such as we used so often to see going to <u>school</u> well I must close with love to <u>All</u>
Almere

P.S. if you are going so far away do come and see us if posible tell the children I dont forget them I wish they would write to their old Auntie A W B please write soon

The letter gives us a precious window into the aging Almera. She has health problems and tries to treat them by folk remedies (smoking mullen!). Lois (evidently nicknamed "Vida") also has bad health. Almera is lonely and yearns for letters from nieces and nephews.

The second event in her later life took place on August 1, 1883. At the age of seventy, she appeared at the Iron County courthouse to sign an affidavit affirming that she had married Joseph Smith in 1843, forty years earlier.

Of the last twelve years of Almera's life, we know only the following definite event: Lois died on September 2, 1893, at the age of forty-one, a victim of dropsy. So when Almera was eighty-one, she was given the melancholy duty of burying the last of her five daughters. After this, we imagine her final years, living alone in Parowan, tormented by arthritis, but receiving frequent visits from relatives and friends. Three years after Lois's death, on March 4, 1896, at 9 o'clock in the morning, Almera died of a "paralytic stroke" in Parowan at age eighty-three. She presently lies in an unmarked grave beside her two daughters in the Parowan Cemetery.

Thus after spending her youth keeping house for an alcoholic but beloved father, Almera mourned the death of one husband claimed by violent death, then parted with another after the strain of arguments and religious disaffection. Of her five daughters, she lost three while they were children. She raised two to adulthood, but one died at age twenty-one, and the other, with whom she lived throughout much of her later life, was mentally deficient and preceded her in death. She never had a grandchild. Nevertheless, she raised two daughters to adulthood, married a prophet, and was a beloved member of the vast extended Johnson family in southern Utah. Her life was dominated by the pain of loss, but

it was nevertheless a life filled with warmth in the spaces between repeated blows of death and parting.

# 13.

# Childless Mother of Mothers in Israel

## *Eliza Roxcy Snow (Smith Young)*

When Joseph and Hyrum Smith were martyred on June 27, 1844, one of Joseph's widows, the gifted poetess Eliza R. Snow, was overcome with grief. She even felt death would be preferable to life, and prayed that she might follow Joseph into the next world immediately. For Mormons, the spirits of the departed are often close by, and at this moment, according to family tradition, Smith himself returned to his bereaved wife. Standing by her bedside, perhaps, in spirit form, he told her that she must not continue to pray for death, for that did not accord with God's plans for her. "Joseph told her that his work upon earth was completed as far as the mortal tabernacle was concerned, but her's was not; the Lord desired her, and so did her husband, to live many years and assist in carrying on the great Latter-day work which Joseph had been chosen to establish. That she must be of good courage and help to cheer, and lighten the burdens of others. And that she must turn her thoughts away from her own loneliness, and seek to console her people in their bereavement and sorrow." After this visitation Eliza was resigned to continuing her life, despite her grief.

Among other things, this story shows Eliza's visionary, enthusiastic side, but she was also a precise, careful thinker and writer, and she became the dominant female intellectual in early Utah. No less a strong-willed individual than Brigham Young was known to defer to her occasionally on matters of church policy. She is, after Emma Smith, the most famous Mormon woman. A poetess, her "O My Father" is the only hymn that approaches the status of scripture in the Mormon tradition. From the time of her conversion, she was a devout Mormon and a fervent supporter of the church and its leadership. All of these factors led to her being called as the second General Relief Society president in Utah. As a plural wife of Joseph Smith, her history is comparatively simple, except for the tradition that she became pregnant by Smith, then lost the child in a miscarriage. The sources for this tradition are problematic and will be assessed below. Her status as a former wife of the founding Mormon prophet contributed to her mystique in her later life, and she used that relationship to teach the "principle" in Utah.

Happily, Eliza is one of the best documented of Smith's wives, as she left behind diaries, letters, and an autobiographical sketch. She is the only plural wife of Smith who has had a scholarly book devoted to her life, Maureen Ursenbach Beecher's insightful volume of essays, *Eliza and Her Sisters*.

## I. Rhyming Homework

Eliza Roxcy Snow was born on January 21, 1804, to Oliver Snow and Rosetta Leonora Pettibone in Becket, Berkshire, Massachusetts, a small town ten miles southeast of Pittsfield in the western part of the state. Oliver, a twenty-nine-year-old farmer, was a native of Becket, while Rosetta, twenty-six, had been born in Connecticut. Eliza's only older sibling, Abigail Leonora, was born in 1801 in Becket.

In 1806 the Snows, with two-year-old Eliza and five-year-old Leonora, moved to the "Connecticut Western Reserve" in Ohio, bordered by Lake Erie on the north and Pennsylvania on the east. They bought land in Mantua, Portage County, becoming only the eleventh family in the township. In Ohio five more children were born to the Snows: Amanda Percy, 1808; Melissa, 1810; Lorenzo, later the fifth president of the Mormon church, 1814; Lucius Augustus, 1819; and Samuel Pearce, 1821. Thus Eliza, as the second oldest sibling in a family of seven, would have fulfilled an older sister's duties as she grew up. She was seventeen when Samuel was born.

In her autobiography she writes that all of the Snow children were "strictly disciplined to habits of temperance, honesty, and industry." Oliver and Rosetta were Baptists, though "free from bigotry and intolerance," and welcomed representatives from all religions into their home, which exposed the young Eliza to great religious diversity. In Sabbath schools she learned chapters of the Bible by heart. In secular learning all the Snow children were given the best education possible, "without preference to either sex," wrote Eliza. Idleness was reviled, and "book-studies" and schooling were everpresent in their home. Nurtured by parental encouragement, Eliza came to love reading and writing at an early age. She was especially fond of poetry, and while still "very young" would compose verse in the styles of her favorite authors. "In school I often bothered my teachers by writing my lessons in rhyme," she wrote, "thereby forcing from them acknowledgements of inability to correct my articles, through lack of poetical talent."

As a small girl she attended a "Grammatical Institution" of young gentlemen and ladies taught by a "Presbyterian clergyman." One day, she wrote, "I had indulged my mirthfulness in a humorous poetical article," written in an idiosyncratic meter. When it came time for Eliza to read her essay, she knew that she and the class would burst into laughter if she tried to read it. So she burst into tears instead and refused to read her composition. The professor excused her, provided she would read it to him privately the next day, which she gratefully did. The anecdote shows us Eliza as a well-educated, precocious young girl, already in love with meter and rhyme, and with a touch of mischievousness.

Despite Eliza's intellectual interests, Rosetta felt that "a practical knowledge of housekeeping the best and most efficient foundation on which to built a magnificent structure of womanly accomplishment," in Eliza's words, and taught her daughter all the standard womanly house-keeping skills, including needlework. For two years in succession, Eliza won a prize awarded by the "Committee on Manufactures" at Portage County Fair for the "best manufactured Leghorn," a braided straw hat. Oliver was involved in public business, and as soon as Eliza was capable he gave her secretarial work in his office. She later looked back on this experience as most educational and valuable, and good preparation for her long years of service in the Relief Society.

While still a young woman, Eliza began to publish poems under pseudonyms. During the war between Greece and Turkey, as "Narcissa" she wrote "The Fall of Missolonghi," published in July 1826 in a local magazine when she was twenty-one. Soon after this, when John Adams and Thomas Jefferson died, Eliza was requested by the local press to write their requiem and cheerfully complied. She won a poetry contest for which the prize was eight volumes of *Godey's Lady's Book*.

Her later friend, Patty Sessions, married when she was seventeen, but Eliza, despite many opportunities for romance, remained single. Per-haps potential suitors were intimidated by her educated, strong-minded intelligence. Wells wrote, "Many of her friends were extremely anxious to see her well settled in life, but she was happy in herself and would not submit to any interference in this matter." She stands apart from nearly all of Joseph Smith's wives in this respect, as she might have been a spin-ster if Smith had not married her. And despite her marriages to Smith and Brigham Young, she raised no children.

In 1828 the Snows heard Sidney Rigdon preach, and they soon joined him in Alexander Campbell's Christian primitivist movement, in-cluding twenty-four-year-old Eliza. Rigdon frequently visited the Snow home. Not long afterwards, Eliza began to hear rumors of Joseph Smith's Gold Bible.

## II. Baptism of Fire

In the winter of 1831-32, when Eliza was twenty-seven, Joseph Smith himself called on the Snows. "As he sat warming himself," she wrote, "I scrutinized his face as closely as I could without attracting his attention, and decided that his was an honest face." So she decided to investigate this new religion. At the first meeting she attended, two of the Three Witnesses to the Book of Mormon bore "the most impressive testimonies" she had ever heard. But she was not yet ready to join.

In early 1835 Leonora visited Kirtland, returned with a strong testimony of Joseph Smith and Mormonism, and soon converted, along with Rosetta. Eliza's faith increased, and on April 5, when she was thirty-one, she too was baptized. Soon after the baptism with water, she received her baptism of fire: "I had retired to bed, and as I was reflecting on the wonderful events transpiring around me, I felt an indescribable, tangible sensation, if I may so call it, commencing at my head and enveloping my person and passing off at my feet, producing inexpressible happiness. Immediately following, I saw a beautiful candle with an unusual long, bright blaze directly over my feet." Here we see the beginnings of Eliza's prophetic charisma.

In December she moved to Kirtland and boarded with the Joseph Smith family, where she had ample opportunity to become acquainted with her future husband. On her arrival she donated a substantial sum of money to the building committee of the Kirtland temple and asked for no recompense, but the committee insisted that she take a house and lot in return. The lot was "a very valuable one—situated near the Temple, with a fruit tree—an excellent spring of water, and house that accommodated two families." As she was boarding with the Smiths, she let Leonora live in one half of the house and rented the other half. In the spring of 1836 Eliza taught a "select school for young ladies" in a building adjoining the Smith home.

When her brother Lorenzo became dissatisfied with the religious teaching at Oberlin College, Eliza invited him to Kirtland to attend Hebrew classes. He accepted the invitation, was introduced to Mormonism, and in June was baptized. After a visit to her parents in Mantua, she began teaching a new school term at the beginning of the new year. Eventually her parents followed her to Kirtland.

But before the year had ended, most Mormons were leaving Ohio. At the end of April 1838 Eliza set out for Missouri with a party of twenty-one, including her parents; Abigail, Lorenzo, Lucius, and Samuel; two nieces; and the William Huntington family, including seventeen-year-old Zina, her future sister-wife and Relief Society counselor. The little band of pilgrims slowly made their way across Indiana and Illinois to western Missouri. About one hundred miles from Far West, Lorenzo, driving one of the teams, came down with "bilious fever." The group straggled into Far West on July 16.

### III. Missouri

Oliver Snow wanted to push on to Adam-Ondi-Ahman, thirty miles more, so Lorenzo and Eliza stayed with Sidney Rigdon while the others continued. Lorenzo soon convalesced, and in two weeks brother and sister traveled on to "Di-Ahman." There Oliver had bought two homesteads, including houses and crops, and paid for them in full.

However, their stay would be short-lived, for Governor Lilburn Boggs's extermination order and the state militia forced them to leave Missouri that winter. Eliza's autobiography, as is typical of Mormon reminiscences, lingers over the hardships of this forced winter journey: "A few days before leaving Adam-ondi-Ahman, the former owner of the house ... came in and impudently enquired how soon we should be out of it. My American blood warmed to the temperature of an insulted, freeborn American citizen as I looked at him and thought, poor man; you little know with whom you have to deal—God lives."

The Snows, with a company of seventy-five, left Adam-ondi-Ahman on December 10 in the bitter cold of winter. As they traveled, Eliza had an encounter with "one of the so-called Militia" that gives us an example of her sharp, ironic wit. He greeted her: "'Well, I think this will cure you of your faith.' Looking him squarely in the eye, I replied, 'No, Sir, it will take more than this to cure me of my faith.' His countenance dropped and he responded, 'I must confess you are a better soldier than I am.' I passed on, thinking that, unless he was above the average of his fellows in that section, I was not complimented by his confession."

The ragtag company of refugees walked and rode through rain and snow and slept in tents that night. The next day the tents had to be thawed at a fire before they could be folded and packed. They met an older man on horseback who watched their company "slowly winding their way up a long hill, enroute from our only earthly homes, with no prospect before us." The man remarked, as Eliza remembers, "If I were in your places, I should want the Governor of the State hitched at the head of my teams." Eliza afterwards remarked to her father that she had not heard as sensible a remark from a stranger since entering the state.

After two days' travel the company neared Far West and stayed overnight in a vacant log house with no chinkings, called the "Halfway House." As they prepared to eat dinner, they found that the food was frozen. "The boys milked our cows, and before the milk was strained, one of us held the dish while another sliced the bread, and the third strained the warm milk into it, which thawed the bread; thus one after another, until all were plentifully served." When it came time to sleep, only the sick had beds. Eliza wrote, "Our mother was quite feeble through fatigue and exposure, and we managed to fix a place for her to lie down, while our sister and myself sat on the floor, one on each side, to ward off the crowd." Nearby, in a horse shed, the men built a fire, danced to keep themselves warm, roasted potatoes, and sang hymns. Soon afterwards the Snows reached Far West, where they stayed until March 5, 1839, when their company started for Illinois.

## IV. Relief Society Secretary

After crossing the Mississippi, Eliza first lived in Quincy for some months, but Oliver settled in Warren County, northeast of Hancock County. Eliza and Leonora and Leonora's two daughters then moved to Lima, thirty miles south of Nauvoo, where they lived above a family that periodically denounced Mormons. But after such a tirade, Eliza reports, the owner often changed his tone "and boasted of the 'two noble women' he had in his house—'no better women ever lived etc.'" Eliza and Leonora sewed to support themselves. On July 16 Eliza left her sister and moved to Nauvoo to teach in Sidney Rigdon's family school.

The years 1840 and 1841 were comparatively uneventful for Eliza. Undoubtedly she had her bouts of ague and helped tend others who were afflicted. She certainly associated with the leading men and women of Nauvoo. She published poems in the *Times and Seasons* and probably continued to teach school in those years.

In early 1842, however, when the women's organization, the Relief Society, was first organized, Eliza began to occupy center stage in Mormon women's history, not as the leader—Emma Smith held that position—but as an important actor. The Female Relief Society of Nauvoo began when a number of prominent women met to organize a society to provide support for the men working on the Nauvoo temple. This preliminary group commissioned Eliza to write the constitution and bylaws for the organization. On March 17 she attended the first Relief Society session and argued against the word "Relief" in the proposed name of the group, but after some debate the word was retained. "E. R. Snow offer'd an amendment by way of transposition of words, instead of The Nauvoo Female Relief Society, it shall be call'd The Female Relief Society of Nauvoo—Seconded by Prest. J. Smith and carried." Then Eliza received her first Relief Society calling: "The gentlemen withdrew when it was Motioned and secon.d and unanimously pass'd that Eliza R. Snow be appointed Secretary, and Phebe M. Wheeler, Assistant Secretary." The April *Times and Seasons* listed the officers, noting that "our well known and talented poetess, Miss Eliza R. Snow is Secretary." The April 19 Relief Society minutes include a prophetic blessing by Eliza given to Presendia Huntington Buell Smith—the first recorded of many she would utter in her lifetime.

## V. "A Pure and Holy Principle"

At about this time Eliza began to hear rumors of polygamy. Her autobiography records her reaction to the doctrine: "In Nauvoo I first understood that the practice of plurality was to be introduced into the church. The subject was very repugnant to my feelings—so directly was it in opposition to my educated prepossessions, that it seemed as though all the prejudices of my ancestors for generations past congregated around me." Despite this initial revulsion, typical of Mormons first introduced to polygamy, she was gradually converted to it. "But when I reflected that I was living in the Dispensation of the fulness of times, embracing all other Dispensations, surely Plural Marriage must necessarily be included." Polygamy was a biblical practice, and to those interpreting the Bible literally, polygamy could easily be seen as a righteous practice that needed to be restored. There is a long tradition in Protestantism and Catholicism of practicing and advocating polygamy. In addition, Eliza wrote, "I consoled myself with the idea that it [polygamy] was far in the distance, and beyond the period of my mortal existence."

Soon, however, she learned that it was actually being practiced in her day; perhaps Sarah Cleveland, with whom she was living, revealed to her that she (Sarah) was a plural wife of Smith. So Eliza steeled herself to practice the doctrine if necessary: "I had covenanted in the waters of baptism to live by every word He should communicate, and my heart was firmly set to do His bidding." Accepting polygamy was a matter of integrity for both Latter-day Saint men and women, given the restorationist underpinnings of their faith and their acceptance of Smith as a direct conduit of revelation.

But Eliza's conversion would go one step further: "As I increased in knowledge concerning the principle and design of Plural Marriage, I grew in love with it, and to-day esteem it a precious, sacred principle—necessary in the elevation and salvation of the human family—in redeeming woman from the curse, and the world from corruption." So nineteenth-century Mormons viewed polygamy as more than merely one of many restored doctrines. It was accepted as a keystone for earthly and eternal salvation—far more important a practice than it was for the ancient Hebrews, for whom it was simply a typical Semitic custom. Eliza continued:

> I was sealed to the Prophet Joseph Smith, for time and eternity, in accordance with the Celestial Law of Marriage which God has revealed—the ceremony being performed by a servant of the Most High—authorized to officiate in sacred ordinances. This, one of the most important circumstances of my life, I never had had cause to regret.
>
> From personal knowledge I bear my testimony that Plural Celestial

Marriage is a pure and holy principle, not only tending to individual purity and elevation of character, but also instrumental in producing a more perfect type of manhood mentally and physically, as well as in restoring human life to its former longevity.

The marriage took place on June 29, 1842, with Brigham Young officiating and Sarah M. Cleveland acting as witness. Eliza was thirty-eight, two years older than Joseph. In Eliza's Nauvoo journal, which starts on this day, she refers to the marriage only obliquely:

This is a day of much interest to my feelings. Reflecting on past occurrences, a variety of thoughts have presented themselves to my mind with regard to events which have chas'd each other in rapid succession in the scenery of human life. As an individual, I have not passed altogether unnoticed by Change, in reference to present circumstances and future prospects. While I am contemplating the present state of society—the powers of darkness, and the prejudices of the human mind which stand array'd like an impregnable barrier against the work of God ... I will not fear. I will put my trust in Him who is mighty to save; rejoicing in his goodness and determin'd to live by every word that proceedeth out of his mouth.

Later Eliza referred to Joseph Smith as "my beloved husband, the choice of my heart and the crown of my life." According to Angus Cannon, later her stake president, she told him that Emma authorized the marriage. Cannon also reported a conversation in which Eliza affirmed that her marriage to Smith had a sexual dimension.

In early August Sarah Cleveland prepared to move across the river, so Eliza had to find a new residence. In mid-August Oliver Snow visited Nauvoo on business and encouraged his daughter to live with him and Rosetta. But on August 14 Eliza was invited by Emma to live in the Smith household. Eliza wrote in her journal, "Yesterday Mrs. Smith sent for me, having previously given me the offer of a home in her house, by Miss A Coles [Elvira Annie Cowles], who call'd on me, on the 12th ... my former expectations were frustrated, but the Lord has opened the path to my feet, and I feel dispos'd to acknowledge his hand in all things. This sudden, unexpectd change in my location, I trust is for good; it seem'd according to his will."

Oliver left Nauvoo, writing, "Eliza cannot leave our Prophet ... For my part, I am glad, at present, to be away." Oliver had become disillusioned with Mormonism and Joseph Smith, which no doubt grieved Eliza. Her siblings Lucius, Samuel, and Amanda had joined their parents in Walnut Grove.

In the first three weeks of December, Eliza taught the Smith family school. "In undertaking the arduous business with my delicate constitution, at this inclement season of the year, I was entirely governed by the wishes of Prest. and Mrs. Smith," she wrote. "I desire and aim to be submissive to the requirements of those whom [God] has place'd in authority over me."

## VI. Eliza and Emma

We now approach the most dramatic moment in Eliza's life, the confrontation between her and Emma—if it took place. In Eliza's diary we find only the following on February 11, 1843: "Took board and had my lodging removed to the residence of br. [Jonathan] Holmes." A number of other sources, unfortunately all late, point to a conflict between Eliza and Emma that caused this separation from the Smiths. Newell and Avery, Emma's biographers, believe that Emma felt that Joseph's polygamy was a thing of the past at the time of the blowup and that when she discovered Eliza's relationship with him, according to this scenario, a violent scene was inevitable.

First, LeRoi Snow, Lorenzo's son, told the story that Emma knocked Eliza down a staircase, causing her to miscarry. This account has been viewed with some skepticism by Newell and Beecher. LeRoi was only eleven when Eliza died, so he probably did not hear the story directly from her. But it should not be summarily rejected, since little historical evidence is ideal, contemporary, full, and unbiased. LeRoi may easily have heard this story from his father, who was, of course, close to Eliza.

An antagonistic source, Wyl, tells substantially the same story in 1886: "They say ... there is scarcely a Mormon unacquainted with the fact that Sister Emma ... soon found out the little compromise arranged between Joseph and Eliza. Feeling outraged as a wife and betrayed as a friend, Emma is currently reported as having had recourse to a vulgar broomstick as an instrument of revenge; and the harsh treatment received at Emma's hands is said to have destroyed Eliza's hopes of becoming the mother of the prophet's son." There is no way to know for certain whether LeRoi was repeating a rumor or whether Wyl had heard a version of an authentic family tradition.

Another, fuller version, in which Charles Rich is an eyewitness, is found in LeRoi's notes for biographies of his father and aunt. Rich, at the bottom of the stairs, watched Joseph kiss Emma goodbye:

A door opposite opened and dainty, little, dark-haired Eliza R. Snow (she was "heavy with child") came out ... Joseph then walked on to the stairway, where he tenderly kissed Eliza, and then came on down stairs toward Brother Rich. Just as he reached the bottom step, there was a commotion on the stairway, and both Joseph and Brother Rich turned quickly to see Eliza come tumbling down the stairs. Emma had pushed her, in a fit of rage and jealousy; she stood at the top of the stairs, glow-

ering, her countenance a picture of hell. Joseph quickly picked up the little lady, and with her in his arms, he turned and looked up at Emma, who
then burst into tears and ran to her room. Joseph carried the hurt and
bruised Eliza up the stairs and to her room. "Her hip was injured and that
is why she always afterward favored that leg," said Charles C. Rich. "She
lost the unborn babe."

This version of the story is even later and more second-hand than the previous sources. Moreover, it demonizes Emma, and is suspect for that reason. In addition, it seems illogical that, if Eliza were recognizably pregnant, Emma would have become enraged at a mere kiss. But the
"demonic" touches may be embroidery, and Eliza's obvious pregnancy
may also be a folkloric addition. Emma could still have become enraged at
an affectionate kiss. Eliza may not have been recognizably pregnant and
still might have experienced a miscarriage. Taken in conjunction with the
other pieces of evidence, this account may have some value.

A reminiscence by Mary Barzee Boyce has another version of the
story: "Emma went upstairs and pulled Eliza R. Snow downstairs by the
hair of her head as she was staying there. Although she had consented to
give him [Joseph] one or more women in the beginning. It was rumored
while I, M.A. Barzee Boyce, was in Nauvoo that she tot sic [got?] in such
a rage about it that she left home and went down to Quincy but came
back again while I was there." Again this seems to be a late reminiscence.
Pulling Eliza by her hair is a violent touch.

To sum up: something may have happened between Eliza and Emma,
and Eliza may have lost a child. Without further evidence, it is impossible
to know for certain. The multiplicity of versions inclines one to suppose
than an authentic incident lies behind them, but they are so late and second-hand that one mistrusts their details. However, they do point to a
possibility—and if Eliza did lose a child, the experience would have been
psychologically devastating for her.

There is also a tradition that Emma threw Eliza out of the house violently. In a 1931 letter, Joseph Young, a son of Brigham Young, recalled
talking with Solon Foster, a resident of the Smith home, who had a conversation with the adult Joseph III: "Joseph, the night your mother turned
Eliza R. Snow into the street in her night clothes, you and all the Family
stood crying, I led you back into the house and took you into Bed with
me, you said, 'I wish mother wouldn't be so cruel to Aunt Eliza'—You
called her Aunt because you knew she was your Fathers wife." Once
again this is a late recollection of an earlier conversation, but family traditions and late evidence can preserve some truth. This story is similar to
the tradition of Fanny Alger's ejection from the Smith home, and perhaps
Emma ejected Eliza, as well, when she discovered she was pregnant. The

Partridge sisters were certainly banished by Emma from the Smith household, which gives this story a background of possibility. Whatever caused her departure, Eliza left the Smith home on February 11.

Other polygamy-related events filled Eliza's spring and summer. On April 12 Lorenzo returned from a mission to England, and Eliza did not feel authorized to tell him of her marriage but felt "a coldness" at not telling him. "I informed my husband of the situation," she later wrote, "and requested him to open the subject to my brother." Smith arranged a private interview with Lorenzo, and as they wandered along the banks of the Mississippi, he told him of the doctrine of celestial marriage and of his marriage to his sister. Late in May Eliza accompanied Lorenzo on a visit to their parents in Walnut Grove.

Joseph Smith rebaptized Eliza, Louisa Beaman, Sarah Alley, and perhaps the Partridge sisters on May 11, 1843, an event that was probably related to polygamy in some way. At the end of June, Eliza rode with Elizabeth Davis Durfee Smith, Elvira Cowles Holmes Smith, and Elizabeth Whitney to the Lott farm outside of Nauvoo, where she may have participated with the two other Smith wives in the education of a young intended wife, Melissa Lott. The second year of Relief Society meetings started in the summer, and Eliza continued to be a major participant. On New Year's Eve, December 31, 1843, she wrote, "A social circle of a few choice friends convened at the house of our sister, and we had a lovely time," a meeting that probably included tongues and prophecy.

Tensions with Emma flared up again on August 21 when, according to William Clayton, Emma (apparently) discovered two letters from Eliza to Joseph in his clothes and became "vexed and angry." Perhaps they were love letters. In August Eliza was living with Leonora, but on April 14, 1844, she moved into the home of Stephen and Hannah Markham, with whom she would live for the next three years. Stephen was a loyal supporter of Joseph Smith. But on June 27 Smith was killed, and Eliza was overcome with grief, as was described earlier. The visitation she felt she received from Smith after his death gave her determination to continue on.

### VII. Brigham Young

At some point after the martyrdom, Eliza, with the rest of Smith's known wives, was approached by Brigham Young, Heber Kimball, and others of the Twelve, who offered themselves as proxy husbands for Smith, husbands for time. Eliza accepted Brigham Young, senior member of the Twelve, and on October 3, 1844, they were married for time. Brigham wrote in his journal that day, "Brother H.C. Kimball and my Self was at Br Steven Marcoms Sisters Eliza Snow & Betsey Farechildes was there." On this page was the mark Brigham used to indicate marriages performed. Eliza would not have children by Brigham and never signed her name Eliza Young, but she lived in his family until she died. As the most intellectually gifted of Brigham's many wives, and as a woman of faith and devotion, she exerted a significant influence on him—he was not well-educated, though he was a man of practical brilliance and force.

On January 26, 1845, Eliza received her endowment and was brought into the Holy Order, the "Quorum" of the Anointed. After this she joined church leaders and prominent Mormons in frequent prayer meetings. In 1845 Eliza, using a gold pencil that Joseph had given her, wrote "O My Father," a moving evocation of the Mormon doctrine of the pre-existence of souls and a prayer to a Father and a Mother in Heaven. After being set to music, it became one of Mormonism's most popular hymns. That October her own father died at the age of seventy. Eliza must have grieved at his passing more intensely since he died outside the fold.

When the Nauvoo temple was near enough to completion to perform endowments and sealings, Eliza officiated as a temple secretary. On December 20, 1846, William Clayton wrote, "Miss Eliza R. Snow handed in a list of the females washed this morning, which lists she has taken for several days past." In the following weeks she continued to keep records of ordinances, helped sew for the temple's altars and cushions, and attended marriages of family and friends. She was probably present when Lorenzo married four women in a group ceremony on January 17, 1846. She remembered, "When Lorenzo walked across the inner court of the Temple proceeding to the altar, accompanied by his four wives, all stately appearing ladies, one of the Temple officials exclaimed, '*And his train filled the Temple!*'" On February 3 Eliza was sealed to Joseph Smith for eternity with Brigham Young standing proxy, then was sealed to Young for time.

### VIII. "A Growling, Grumbling, Devilish, Sickly Time"

After the spiritual exaltation of these temple experiences, Eliza now had to look to the wilderness. As she joined the drama of the exodus to the Far West, she began keeping one of the most literate and keenly observant of Mormon overland journals. Very much the product of a poetess, it is filled with occasional poems; though it has self-conscious literary tendencies, it is remarkably frank and has moments of sharp humor. It provides a comprehensive view of the network of elite Nauvoo Mormon women scattered across the wilderness and in early Utah. Beecher's recent publication of this diary is a landmark in Mormon studies.

On February 12, 1846, Eliza and the Markhams "left our home and went as far as br. Hiram Kimball's where we spent the night and thro' the generosity of sister K. [Sarah Kimball] & mother Granger, made some additional preparations for our journey." The next day she "Cross'd the Missisippi and join'd the Camp [Sugar Creek] - found my br. L.[Lorenzo] & br.

[David] Yearsley's families tented side by side; we lodg'd in br. Y.'s tent which before morning was covered with snow." The hardships had begun.

At Sugar Creek Eliza's "dormitory, sitting-room, writing office, and frequently dining-room" was a buggy in which she rode with Hannah Markham and her little son David. One of Lorenzo's wives often brought her a "foot-stove" "filled with live coals from one of those mammoth fires [that the men made at Sugar Creek]." Nevertheless, Eliza "frosted" her feet, and the after-effects caused them to ache for weeks. On the 28th she and the Markhams left Sugar Creek in the Heber Kimball company. Traveling now began in earnest.

On March 4, at the Reed's Creek camp, Colonel Markham traded the buggy for a lumber wagon "in order to assist others in carrying freight; and in performing this act of generosity, so filled the wagon, as to give us barely room to sit in front." This vehicle, with bags piled on bags, was Eliza's sleeping room; the family lodged in other wagons and in a tent. She was amazed and delighted at the size of the Reed Creek encampment, which was a city in miniature. With Hannah, she wandered through it and became thoroughly lost, only to be guided to their tent by Apostle Amasa Lyman.

As the Mormons traveled through Iowa, rain alternated with snow and high winds upended tents in the middle of the night. Soon Eliza was prostrated by "chills and fever" and for weeks could not regain her health. On the 7th she arrived at the Richardson's Point camp, and three weeks later her company reached Chariton camp. She records occasional interviews with her husband. Visiting, instead of cohabiting, was a typical polygamous phenomenon. On the 29th Brigham visited Eliza and told her in the name of the Lord that she would receive her health back.

She reached Hickory Grove Camp on April 3, and Garden Grove three weeks later. Much of her time there was spent reading Walter Scott's *Rokeby*, and her health improved by the administration of "a tea made of Cranesbill." On May 17 she enjoyed an outdoor quilting bee hosted by Sister Dalton, "the mistress of the quilting." Also present were sisters Markham, Yearsley, D. Gleason, Harriet, and Catherine. After quilting there was a tea party around a makeshift "bark" table inside one of the tents, during which these pioneer women partook of "light biscuits & butter, dutch cheese, peach sauce, custard pie & tea." So the feminine realities persisted, despite hardships, mud, rain, lack of housing, and deaths. "Westering women" often coped with the desolation and chaos of the frontier by reproducing aspects of civilization left behind.

On the 25th Eliza's company reached Mt. Pisgah. She wrote the next day, "Spent the day at Lorenzo's. Call'd at prest Y's." So the wife spends the day with her brother and pays her husband a social visit. Lorenzo had just come down with a serious fever and Eliza stayed at his bedside June 7 to 11. Her sister Leonora, who had married Isaac Morley as a plural wife, soon arrived to help tend their brother. When he seemed to improve, Eliza returned to the Markhams, but on the 13th she was called back to his bedside. He was raving on the 15th and Eliza stayed up with him all night. The next day Wilford Woodruff administered to him, and the day after Lorenzo was baptized for his health. He slowly began to recover, just as Eliza herself once again succumbed to illness. On the 30th she wrote to Elizabeth Whitney and Vilate Kimball at Winter Quarters: "I am now living with my brother about a mile above Mount Pisgah—he has been very sick since you left—is better ... My love to the girls, particularly Sarah Ann [Whitney Smith Kimball] & Helen [Kimball Smith Whitney]. I have had a chat with S. [Sarah Ann?] about Joseph in my sleep _ _ _" On July 2 Lorenzo was well enough to walk outside.

Brigham and Heber arrived at Mt. Pisgah on the 7th, and two days later the Snows "had the honor of a visit" from them. On August 9 Eliza wrote, "It is a growling, grumbling, devilish, sickly time with us now - I hope never to see another week like the past one." Hannah was ill, and Eliza tended her. Lorenzo Snow wrote that there was "a general and almost universal scenes of sickness throughout Pisgah ... A general spirit of lamentation and sorrow prevailed."

On the 17th Eliza and the Markhams left Pisgah, even though Hannah was still ill. Eliza had to learn to drive an ox team at this time, as she had only driven horse teams before. "However, I took the whip and very soon learned to haw and gee, and acquitted myself very well," she reported, "The cattle being so pliable that I could sit and drive." However, as she had to act not only as teamster but as cook and nurse for Hannah, she was often exhausted.

After passing some Pottawattamie Indians without incident, Eliza's party reached Council Bluffs on the 27th. While they stopped in a grasslands to let the cattle graze, Brigham, Heber, Isaac Morley (an adopted son of Brigham), William Kimball, and Porter Rockwell drove up in a carriage. Brigham had a boy drive Eliza and her team to Morley's encampment. On the same day Eliza recorded tensions between her and the Markhams for the first time: "This morning, Brother Markham manifested a mean jealousy which I need not describe."

## IX. Speaking in Tongues

The next day Eliza and the Markhams rode horseback to a camp two or three miles down the river: "The opposite bluffs rudely scallop'd with shrubbery presented a scene which might well be call'd

CHILDLESS MOTHER OF MOTHERS IN ISRAEL

wildly beautiful," she wrote. They passed a French and Indian town, then were stopped by a company of some 200 Indians of different tribes, "Omahaws, Mohaws, Otas." Markham turned his wagon off the road so as not to disturb them, but they motioned for him to return, then began a war dance and demanded something to eat. The Mormons, taken aback, fed the Native Americans crackers, bread, and meat, and were allowed to continue. But then Eliza's oxen were spooked, so Whiting Markham had to take over the reins. The New England poetess was gradually entering the environment of the Far West.

At the end of August the whole Markham family became prostrated with ague. Eliza tended them until she herself contracted the malarial chills and fever. As none of the Markhams could help her, her friends, whom she gratefully lists—Sister Cornelia C. L(yman), Elizabeth Whitney, Vilate Kimball, Mary Ann Young, "Sister [Permelia] Lott, Sister [Elvira] Holmes, and Sister Taylor"—cared for her. Her recovery was not hastened by a heavy rain which soaked her bed from top to bottom.

Meanwhile, living with the Markhams was becoming increasingly disheartening. Eliza described "Family discord, which I think proper to call hell, reigning around me" as she lay prostrate with fever. One evening Stephen and Hannah were shouting at each other so loudly that all the camp could hear them. This depressing psychic environment would have compounded uncomfortably with the physical sickness Eliza was enduring. Her illness continued some forty days, she records, during which time Brigham came to see her twice. Helen Mar Whitney, a young widow of Joseph and newly married to Horace Whitney, wrote of Eliza in Winter Quarters, "The first time I remember of meeting her there she was lying sick with a fever in a poorly covered wagon, with the blazing sun beating down upon it." In late September Eliza's diary recorded a few days, then stopped for another month, probably because of illness.

On October 28 Whiting Markham had to take the wagon that served as Eliza's home to pick up goods, so on a "cold & blustering" day Eliza and Hannah moved into a dwelling "partly chink'd & only mudded on one side & only covered on one side the other having the tent thrown over it—& no chimney." This is a typical Winter Quarters scenario: tents, makeshift log cabins, freezing cold. It is no wonder that so many deaths occurred there.

After another gap in the diary, on November 22, Eliza was still "quite ill," despite a "very fine" day. The following day she was drawn into a Markham family quarrel. Warren had become irritated with his father, then mentioned that "someone" had been talking to Heber Kimball "against his wife." When asked to specify who, he said, "it is one we have been supporting all the while & one in the family." Eliza was out-raged at this accusation, which she characterized brusquely: "false as hell." She defended herself to her journal: she had been a great benefit to the Markhams, had shared their disgrace, and had tried to uphold their reputation only to be attacked. She compared herself to Job.

A few days later Warren again maligned her and Stephen Markham came to her defense. But three days later Eliza, with a momentary lapse in good judgement, let Colonel and Sister Markham read her journal. He did not seem upset, but Hannah asked, "Do you think you have been dis-grace'd by living in the family? I should not think the Lord would require you to live where you would disgrace yourself." On December 17 she was awakened by another Markham family quarrel. Five days later she re-ceived news that her mother had died two months earlier, on October 12. "I feel a sweet consolation inasmuch as she is freed from the ills of the present life," she wrote. "She sleeps in peace & her grave & father's ... are side by side."

For Christmas, Eliza left the Markhams and celebrated with the ex-tended Young family. On New Year's Eve there was a party at Patty Ses-sions's home, which Eliza, Louisa Beaman, and Zina Huntington Young, among others, attended. Now we have our first introduction to tongue-speaking in the female meetings at Winter Quarters: "To describe the scene alluded to would be beyond my pow'r," wrote Eliza. "Suffice it to say the spirit of the Lord was pour'd out and we receiv'd a blessing thro' our belov'd mother Chase & sis Clarissa by the gift of tongues." One can only imagine the strange inarticulate chanting, followed by the excite-ment of apocalyptic, revelatory interpretations. Eliza and Patty, with Eliza-beth Whitney, seem to have been leaders of these charismatic meetings, and Zina and Presendia Huntington were also prominent participants. On the first day of 1847 Eliza took "leave of the female family" of Brigham af-ter a "five day visit with the girls," her sister-wives. That night she stayed with Anna Gheen Kimball.

We learn from Patty Sessions that Eliza came to her house to accom-pany her to a party on February 4. When Eliza found out that it was Patty's fifty-second birthday, she gave her a blessing. At the party Sessions re-ports that they "had a good time singing praying and speaking in tongues before we broke up."

On March 18 Eliza was visiting Joseph Bates Noble when Brigham stopped in and told her that Stephen Markham had offered to take her across the plains. But Eliza had had enough of the Markhams and was hop-ing for other companions in the long trip west. The following day Eliza contracted "inflamation on the lungs," and there is another gap in the di-ary. She was strong enough to write again by April 4 but continued to have relapses. On April 14 Brigham, about to depart for the Far West with the advance company of "pioneers," called on Eliza to say goodbye.

In a week she was recovering her health, and the 26th turned out to be a busy day of visiting. She first called on Presendia Kimball, then dined with the Sessionses, after which she visited the meeting place tent, the Markee. She spent the afternoon at the Pierces' with Elizabeth Ann Whitney, Vilate Kimball, Patty Sessions, Sylvia Sessions Lyon Smith Kimball, Lucina, Sister Pierce, and Margaret Pierce Young. At supper-time Mary Ann Angell Young, Brigham's first wife, joined them. Then in the evening at the Markee she "had a rejoicing time thro' the outpouring of the spirit of God" with a large group of Young, Sessions, and Kimball wives.

Eliza and her friends met again at Brother Leonard's on May 1. Patty presided over a group including Phoebe Chase, Sister Cutler, Sister Cahoon, Elizabeth Ann Whitney, Vilate Kimball, Laura Pitkin, Sylvia Sessions Lyon, Presendia Kimball, and Martha McBride Knight Kimball. They learned, through prophecy, that the pioneers were well. Patty Sessions reports that the meeting "was got up by E R Snow." Eliza was always an organizational force to be reckoned with. The next day she was chosen to preside at a meeting at Sarah Peake Noon Kimball's that included Vilate Kimball, Elizabeth Ann Whitney, Patty Sessions, Sylvia Sessions Lyon, Sarah Ann Whitney Kimball, and Helen Mar Kimball Whitney. "The pow'rs of the world to come were truly in our midst," wrote Eliza.

Though there is a month-long gap in Eliza's journal now, Patty's journal mentions her frequently. By the end of May, as many women were preparing to cross the plains, the blessing meetings increased in frequency and intensity. On the 26th Eliza and Patty visited Sister Cutler. "Had a good [time]," wrote Patty. "Prayed and sung and spoke as the Lord directed." The women viewed their blessings to each other as prophetic revelations—early Latter-day Saint women often functioned as prophetesses for each other.

Eliza's diary began again on June 1 when she visited Patty in the morning and lined a cap for five-year-old Carlos Sessions, Patty's grandchild, as "the girls" washed for her. In the afternoon she was at Sister Miller's with Presendia Kimball, Zina Young, Phoebe Chase, and Christeen Golden Kimball, among others. During the meeting she apparently made a cap for "Sister Pierce"—probably the mother of Margaret Pierce Young. After the evening meal, Elizabeth Ann Whitney arrived with Vilate Kimball, and a remarkable blessing meeting followed. Later in the evening Eliza went to Brother Leonard's with Presendia, Zina, and Sarah Lawrence Kimball. Emmeline Wells later described this party:

Brother Leonard spoke in tongues in an Indian language, and prophesied of the destruction of this nation before the coming of the Savior. The power that rested upon him was so great as to produce such an intense sympathy with those in the room, that they were all wonderfully affected. Sister Eliza R. Snow walked the floor to keep her breath. All felt the distress and agony that awaited the nation, more particularly the priests and harlots being destroyed in their wickedness. Sister Eliza Snow spoke afterwards in the pure language of Adam, with great power, and the interpretation was given.

Eliza wrote that "Language cannot describe the scene" and added more of Leonard's prophecy: "Br. L. spoke of the American government—its fall &c. after which the Lord manifested the contrast of the happiness of the saints and the suff'ring of the gentiles when the Lamanites go forth." The content of Mormon tongue-speaking interpretations was often apocalyptic, as here.

The following day Eliza spent the afternoon with Zina, Louisa Beaman, and Emily Partridge Young. Emily and Eliza "spoke in the gift of tongues." In the evening Eliza met with her sister at Harriet Cook Young's: "Sister [Mary Ann] Young joined me in a song of Zion." This probably refers to singing in tongues simultaneously, an occasional phenomenon in Mormon glossolalia. The next day Patty Sessions wrote that Louisa Beaman, Emily Partridge Young, and Zina Young "laid their hands on my head blesed me, and so did E R Snow thank the Lord."

On the way to another blessing meeting on the 4th, Eliza and Patty Sessions stopped in at the Kimballs and blessed Helen Mar Kimball and Janet. Eliza wrote, "I spoke & she interpreted. I then blest the girls in a song, singing to each in rotation." Patty left Winter Quarters the following day. On the 6th Eliza met with Elizabeth Ann, Vilate, and Phoebe Chase at Mary Ann Young's house. In the evening at Harriet Young's, Mary Ann advised Eliza to cross the plains with the Pierces. Hannah Pierce had offered Eliza passage, if her husband Robert agreed. Eliza accepted the invitation enthusiastically.

June 10 was another busy day of visiting, moving from house to house, blessing, prophesying, speaking in tongues. The next day, her last at Winter Quarters, Eliza lost no time in sending for Harriet Young and they "commenc'd improving in the gifts," with Helen Mar Whitney and her mother-in-law, Elizabeth Ann, interpreting. A Mary Ellen (possibly Mary Ellen Harris Kimball) and a Sister Pack also spoke in tongues. "We had a time not to be forgotten." In the afternoon there was a meeting at Clarissa's (possibly Clarissa Ross Young), then Eliza moved on to Louisa Beaman's where a Sister Snow "receiv'd the gift." "We had a glorious time." After Sister Leavitt Lyman and Margaret Pierce Young spoke "in the gift," Eliza wrote that her "heart was fill'd to overflowing" with gratitude to God.

So the Winter Quarters experience came to an end. It had been a time of hardship, cold, living in makeshift shelters; a time of sickness and death. But it was also a time of feminine blessing, healing, speaking in tongues, and prophecy, a high point in Mormon spirituality. In addition, it brought Eliza Snow to the forefront among Mormon women. Her intellectual gifts and poetic talent, her zealous devotion to the Mormon cause, her prophetic gifts in tongue-speaking and blessing, and her marriages to Joseph Smith and Brigham Young—all of these combined to distinguish her. Beecher writes, "In Winter Quarters the women who would lead out in women's affairs in Utah identified themselves, set their standards, re-established certain rituals, and thus cemented the ties which held their group." Eliza led the group of leaders.

### X. The Glory of God on the Prairie

On June 12 Eliza bade farewell to her beloved sisters and with the Pierces left Winter Quarters riding in a horse-drawn carriage. She was depressed and lonely for a time, then her spirits rebounded "& I jour-ney'd with good cheer." Her group managed only seven miles before they stopped to repair a broken wagon-tongue. The next day Eliza wrote that "my feelings were very peculiar thro' the day—it verily seem'd that the glory of God rested down on the wagons (21 in No.) and overspread the prairie." Here we have echoes of the children of Israel being led by a pillar of fire. Early Mormons saw themselves as re-enacting the Old Testament in the final days of earth's history, thus living simultaneously in the primordial past and in a transformed future as they struggled for survival in the American west. That evening Eliza's group reached an organizing camp at Elk Horn River. Some three hundred wagons had arrived, and Patty Sessions was there, so the blessing meetings resumed.

The 18th was a day full of charismatic moments. In the morning Eliza had a "treat of the spirit" in a wagon with Sister Moore and Patty. In the afternoon Eliza "had a refreshing time" at a meeting at Sister Beech's, attended by most of the Pratt family. Then the final charismatic outpouring before the trek across the plains began in earnest. Eliza and Patty visited Edward Hunter's wagon and found Ann Hunter ill, which galvanized our poetess to action: "I told them I had long desir'd to bless sis. H." She went into the wagon and spoke to Brother Hunter in tongues, with Patty interpreting. Then Hunter, Eliza, and Patty "laid hands on Sister Hunter's head and rebuk'd her illness & bless'd her." Eliza sang to them in tongues, and Patty sang an interpretation, after which Susannah Neff rose and blessed Sister Hunter.

The next day Eliza left Elk Horn, travelling in Robert Pierce's ten, Joseph Bates Noble's fifty, and Jedediah Grant's hundred. As the daily treks began, Eliza was soon seriously ill and by the 25th had to ride in a wagon bed. But the blessing meetings continued. On July 11, in the afternoon, she met with Patty and Sisters Leonard, Thompson, and Pierce at Isaac Chase's wagon, where "The Lord pour'd out his spirit." Patty's diary refers to a meeting at "sister Snows," which shows that Eliza was organizing these meetings. The men killed eight buffaloes that day, and Eliza ate buffalo steak for dinner. Then, in the evening, Elvira Holmes called on Eliza and spoke in tongues. The charismatic gifts of Kirtland and Winter Quarters were continuing amid buffalo herds, by the Platte River, in the prairies of the West.

The sights typical of overland diaries appear in Eliza's journal, carefully observed. On the 12th: "The prairie today is little else than a barren waste - where the buffalo seem to roam freely." That night the livestock stampeded and many could not be recovered, a disastrous blow to the Grant company which would trail behind the other three companies the rest of the way to Salt Lake. On the 23rd it rained as the company crossed sand dunes. No wood was available, but Eliza burned "b. [buffalo] chips." They met the Sioux the next day: "The Indians throng us." Eliza looked at their village across the river with a telescope: "Their tents or lodges are made of skins gaily painted."

A typical pioneer day would have been the 26th with its small crises amid slow, steady progress. The company crossed sand dunes again. At about noon John Dilworth's wagon broke an axle and the company had to wait for him to repair it. Many Sioux passed them, and Eliza was intrigued by their means of transportation: they travel "with tents and baggage fasten'd to mules, horses & on drays form'd of tent poles drawn by horses, mules & dogs. Covers for the little ones made by fastening skins over bows which are fix'd to the upper side of the drays." After the axle was repaired, the company was forced to travel at night: "The moon shines beautifully & we move on with speed." They came to a village of Indian tents, and the curious inhabitants came to visit en masse. But when the visitors shook their blankets, the Pierces' cattle were frightened and one broke out of its yoke. Hannah and Margaret quieted the cows and oxen while Eliza held the horses. At this point several Indians approached Eliza, but she was afraid that the spooked horses might kick them and finally induced them to leave. The company camped at 11 o'clock.

On the 29th Eliza noted that the bluffs on both sides of the river looked like "buildings, terraces, platforms, &c. of every description." The next day, as she traveled through scorching heat, "The bluffs truly present views wildly magnificent." On August 20 Eliza and her company traveled "up & down hill" between high peaks to right and left. Occasionally they were sprinkled with rain, and the road was muddied. After they camped, Eliza went for a walk and scared up a "<u>mighty large</u> rabbit." She ate rabbit pot pie with Isaac and Phoebe Chase. The following day the bluffs were a red brick color—with white stripings, green shrubbery, and a "romantic appearance." On the 23rd Josiah Miller killed a buffalo and Sister Pierce broiled it, "but it seem'd to have been the father of all buffalos & <u>uneatable</u>." After traversing a hilly, barren road, they met the Platte again "which seems like meeting an old friend."

They crossed Deer's Creek, then camped near present Glenrock, Wyoming. On September 7 Eliza did her morning wash with snow, and it snowed at intervals through the rest of the day. Her company traveled through "Wind Ridge," which in places was "intolerable rocky." The next day there was a happy reunion when Brigham Young and a group of "Pioneers," on their way back to Winter Quarters, met Grant's company. Eliza supped with her husband, Heber Kimball, and Amasa Lyman. However, that night some forty horses and mules were stolen by Indians, another disaster for the Grant company. While waiting for an attempted recovery of the horses, Eliza spent a very cold day with Phoebe Chase. "Had a spiritual treat wherein both rec'd great blessings. She said certain intelligence should come to me Thro' the proper channel &c." Spiritual treat over with, they indulged in a physical treat, "tea & pancakes." A meeting was held with the "Pioneers," and one of Eliza's hymns was sung. Before he departed, Brigham came to the carriage and blessed Eliza and her "family," the Pierces.

Eliza asked him, "Who is to be my counsellor for the year to come?"

"Eliza R. Snow," he replied.

"She is not capable," bantered back Eliza.

"I have appointed her president," said Brigham, smiling.

In mid-September, as the company approached the Rockies, Eliza wrote of "The ridges of Mts. so distant that it seems like a prairie country." On the following day "The mts. very grand—ridge rising after ridge in front of me - the clouds sometimes obscuring the distant ridges." On the 27th Eliza was in the midst of the mountains and allowed herself a bit of purple: "Our place is delightful—the mts. being in a half circle on either side & variegated with indescribable beauty; rising in a kind of majesty that could but inspire feelings of sublimity in a contemplative mind."

Three days later the company crossed Canyon Creek eight times as it descended toward Salt Lake. On October 1 she went "up the Mt. to Bellows Peak where we met J.T. who ask'd me if I had lately seen my face, his own being behind a black mask (the soil having chang'd) — we then went slash mash down over stumps, trees &c. &c." They crossed the creek nineteen times on the following day. Then "About 4 we come in view of the Valley looking like a broad rich river bottom – it rains & a breach made in the side of our wag. cov. torn by the brush admits both rain & dust, but being in sight of <u>home</u> we make our way to the Fort – I am too sick to enjoy the scenery but a good cup tea prepar'd by sis P. refreshes me, also a vis. from sis. Sess. Trav. 14 ms." Eliza, though ill, as she often was, had finally come to the place that would be her home for the rest of her life.

## XI. "A Woman of Property"

"This mor. seat myself by a doby fire-place outside the body of a log house," wrote Eliza on her first day in the valley. "breakfast with br. P.s sup with sis. Leonard – have my things put into Clarissa's room, who said Prest. Y. wrote her that I would live with her." So Eliza began to live with Clara Decker Young in an eighteen-foot square room in the Old Fort that was "roofed with willows and earth, with very little inclination—the first-comers having adopted the idea that the valley was subject to little, if any rain, and built their roofs nearly flat."

Eliza's roof was a little thicker than her neighbors', so one night, during a rainstorm, a group gathered in the room. But when rain started to penetrate through the roof here and there, the visitors departed "to their own wet houses." Sally, an Indian girl living with Eliza, wrapped herself in a robe and fell into a peaceful slumber on the floor, while the poetess tried to sleep with an umbrella over her head, though the lower part of her body stayed thoroughly soaked. "During the night, despite all discomfiture, I laughed involuntarily while alone in the darkness of the night I lay reflecting on the ludicrous scene." As she lay in bed, wide awake and half soaked, mice ran all over the floor and stones from the roof fell down with the rain.

Like other Mormons in Utah, Eliza began life from scratch. On October 11, she wrote, with wry humor, "I made a cap for sis. J. Young for which she paid me in soap, 1 lb.& 15 oz. so much I call my own. I now begin once more to be a woman of property." Though she was often sick, on the 18th she was well enough to ride horseback with Patty Sessions to administer to a sick girl. The blessing meetings were renewed. On the 22nd Eliza and Clara visited Sister Leonard, and "after a good supper which we enjoy'd in the spirit of the Lord, we have a spiritual treat, sis. Sess. & L. [Louisa Beaman?] joining us."

Meanwhile she was worried about food. On the 24th: "In the eve. sis. Peirce came in – inquir'd respecting my provisions - I told her I had none but I felt satisfied that the Lord would open the way for me that I knew there was an arrangement made, but it had fail'd &c. she said she was mortified that they could not supply me, but could not ... My trust is in God." She frequently mentioned gifts of food with gratitude. Two weeks later she conducted a unique blessing meeting which prefigured her later work with Primary, the children of Mormonism. She wrote, "Had a delightful meet. of the little girls. Susan N. & Martha rec'd the gift of tongues Sarah H. improv'd upon hers which she spoke in yes. here for the first—after meet. sis. Chase blest C. & I & C. spoke in tongues & blest us. Praise the Lord O my soul!" On November 26, with snow on the ground, Eliza and a company of Saints were rebaptized by Jedediah Grant as a sign of renewal of covenant upon reaching the valley.

Eliza attended her first Christmas celebration in the valley at Lorenzo Young's: "prest Fath. J. Young & wife, fath J.[John] Smith & wives, br. Peirce & wife & br. Grant, after a splendid dinner at which we freely & sociably partook of the good things of the earth fath S. bless'd the babe of sis. Y. I serv'd as Scribe. br. G. pray'd & dedicated the house to the Lord &c. In the eve Edith had an organiz'd visit of the little girls at Clara's Moth. C. presided." On New Year's Day Eliza and her circle met at a Brother Miller's. After dinner "Moth. M. arose express'd her wish for the sist. to proceed in their order of blessing, having call'd them in by the consent of her husband—requested sis. Sess. to pray." Patty rose quickly "& said she was subject to sis. M. while under her roof & was willing to act in accordance &c. she pray'd." Eliza followed: "I arose & bless'd sis M. & was follow'd by sis. Holmes, Howd, Sessions, three of sis. M's daughters, (two of whom rec. the gift of tongues), Love, & Abbott." Five men were also present, "4 of whom spoke br. Jackman remarking that there was more intelligence in the hearts of the sis. that aft. than in the hearts of all the crown'd heads of Europe by the request of his wife, br. M. dismiss'd the meet."

Eliza's forty-fourth birthday, on January 21, found her celebrating with old friends: "Staid at fath. Sess. last night having visited sis. Whitney the day before & this day spent with sis. Noble—din'd on coffee & pancakes with molasses & sup'd on biscuit made of flour ground in the Valley, butter, tea, dried beef, peach-sauce, sweeten'd fried cakes & custard pie"—a remarkable feast for Salt Lake City's first winter.

Her 1848 journal mentions weather, community events, food, but not her inner life. There are gaps in April and May, perhaps because she was ill. "Eliza Snow['s] health is rather poor this spring," Louisa Beaman wrote to Marinda Hyde on April 8. On June 15 Eliza wrote, "This mor. I am quite sick—sis Gates ministers to me with kindness." In early August she was apparently better, for she went on a long berry-picking expedition to the canyons with Elvira Holmes, but she was ill again on August

23. There is another month-long break in the journal. On September 20, she wrote, "Prest. Young & family arriv'd in the Valley—they supp'd at E. Ellsworth's—I had the pleasure of joining them at the table tho' scarcely able to sit up." On October 23 Eliza moved into the household of Elvira and Jonathan Holmes in the fort.

Some November entries give us insight into the life of a plural wife. On November 1 Eliza wrote, "Prest. Y. invited me to a carriage ride with him—we din'd at his house after conversing on some particulars." The next day "Spent the eve. very pleasantly at Prest. Y.s with most of his wives. The weather cold." An interview with one's husband was an event to note in the diary, for the husband of a large family could only spend occasional evenings with many of his wives.

On Christmas Day Eliza was probably sick: "Christmas, I staid at home & read news:papers which Prest. Y. sent me, he having call'd last eve: br. F. Richards at that time presented me with copy of an Address written by Lyon." The sickness continued in February 1849. Eliza moved again on April 13: "B.Y. came for me to visit his family which he commenc'd organizing for living together. I spent the night & he took me to Br. K', the next day—told me to go home from there & he should soon come & move me up. He call'd this eve. with Loisa, Margaret & Clara." These early moves in the fort are often not traceable, but Eliza eventually lived in Brigham's old Log Row.

On April 24 she wrote that she "Rec'd a few lines from Helen [Mar Whitney]." Remarkably, we have Helen's account of this: "Our [Helen's and Eliza's] intimacy began the first winter after we came to this valley, we were both invalids and though we lived within half a block's distance of each other, we were unable to walk it; but we could communicate our thoughts and feelings by letter which we often did, though paper like every other commodity at that time was very scarce; we never left any blank space." Susa Young Gates, a daughter of Eliza's sister-wife Lucy Bigelow, described her sickness as consumption (tuberculosis): "Aunt Eliza ... laid in the old Log Row, and for some time in the Lion House, spitting her life away with that dreadful disease, consumption. Mother used to go to see her often, and ask if there was anything she could do; but Aunt Eliza always answered so patiently and gently that she needed nothing."

On June 27 Eliza was able to meet with other widows of Joseph Smith: "This day is 5 years since Joseph's death! I rode in the forenoon with br. & sis. Lott. in the afternoon read Joseph's letters to a circle of ladies." Eliza wrote to Marinda Hyde in a letter mailed with Louisa Beaman's on July 14, and her polished prose presents a striking contrast to Louisa's: "You would be delighted with the novel situation & the romantic scenery; & when you come, you will be astonished that our brethren should accomplish as much on this interior isolated spot, in the way of convenience & the comforts of living. But you know the saints, thro' the blessing of God on their ever energetic exertions, possess an extraordinary creative faculty." On August 16 Eliza made her last journal entry: "Vis. with several emigrants at Br. Peirce's. Merchant shops are open in every direction."

Eliza's journal gone, we are left to reconstruct her life in outline from her autobiography, correspondence, and random references elsewhere. In 1852 Lorenzo Snow, who had been called to be an apostle in 1849, and William Eddington organized the Polysophical Society, a weekly meeting for gospel and cultural refinement. With her friends Zina Young and Helen Mar Whitney, Eliza attended frequently, contributing poems and occasionally speaking in tongues.

When the Endowment House was dedicated in 1855 Brigham asked Eliza to preside over the sisters' ordinances in this small de facto temple. She pointed out that her poor health would not allow her to serve in this capacity, but Brigham assured her that her health would improve if she agreed. Taking this promise to heart, she accepted and presided over women's temple work for the rest of her life, spending many days in the Endowment House performing the elaborate quasi-Masonic rituals that Smith had introduced in Nauvoo. As Wells writes, "Sister Eliza was called upon to take part in these administrations, as a Priestess in the House of the Lord, in which calling she has officiated up to the present."

In 1856 Eliza's first volume of poems, *Poems, Religious, Historical and Political*, was published in England. Less happily the same year, during the height of the Mormon Reformation, an outbreak of zealotry that swept Utah, the Polysophical Society was repressed by Jedediah Grant (who called it "a stink in my nostrils") and by Heber Kimball (who followed Grant, "and in mine!," and added that there was an "adultrous spirit in it!"). Two members of the First Presidency outranked Apostle Lorenzo Snow and plural wives of Smith and Young, so the meetings were discontinued. This is an early example of "intellectual" Mormonism being interpreted as a threat by high-ranking church leaders who were themselves poorly educated. The tension between the Latter-day Saint church hierarchy and intellectual and academic pursuits (which are both valued and suspect) is a fascinating thread in Mormon history. Eliza herself is an example of how the church attracted and prized intelligent, well-educated converts, while the demise of the Polysophical Society shows how ambivalent members of the hierarchy could be about the intellectual quest, which necessarily includes breadth and freedom of thought and inquiry. The marriage of Eliza and Brigham was itself a curious combination of practical intelligence and poetic, sophisticated intelligence, though husband and wife were both thoroughly devoted to the Mormon cause.

## XII. Lion House

In 1856 Brigham Young's publicly acknowledged wives moved into the Lion House, and Susa Young Gates provides a description of Eliza's two-room apartment on the third, upper floor: "Her sitting room was as precise, as neat and prim as was Aunt Eliza herself. A tiny stove, a writing desk in the corner, some chairs, a small table and a marvellously wrought bas-relief of the Prophet Joseph Smith comprised its furniture." In the south room, Eliza's bedroom, stood a tub of water. "Into this cold water, breaking the ice crust in the winter for the purpose, went Aunt Eliza, every morning of her life. The cold open window in the morning with the waiting tub struck chill upon my fancy; but there was a small stove with which to warm the temperature of her sitting room where she might go before and after the dreadful plunge." Susa also described "little testimony meetings" in Eliza's room, and so the blessing meetings of Winter Quarters continued in the Lion House.

Susa also described the intellectual Eliza, the book-reader, the nurturer of young literary talent: "In the Lion House Aunt Eliza R. Snow seemed a little set apart. She was said to be cold and proud but I never found her so. She was my patron saint and under her control and encouragement all my few literary and organizing fits blossomed early into fruition." Eliza spent nearly all her time studying, wrote Gates, reading the Bible and Book of Mormon and the classics of all ages, but "To relieve the nervous pressure of too much study she embroidered temple aprons or made burial clothing. She was an exquisite needle woman and her embroideries were real works of art."

At the Lion House Eliza was finally cured of her consumption. "Finally someone brought to her Dio Lewis' first book on the 'Water Cure' treatment for disease," Susa wrote. "This must have been in the late fifties, and Aunt Eliza seized upon its theories with eager determination. She adopted the most perfect water treatment and her diet was the sparest of the spare, after that." As a result, Eliza not only regained her health, but "Better still, she walked out into the world of active things, and did more for the womanhood of the Church than any woman, before or since her time."

The decade of 1855-65 was comparatively uneventful for Eliza, now in her fifties. However, a few letters illuminate these years. She wrote to Martha Spence Heywood on December 23, 1855, in her stiff and wordy style: "It has always been with much pleasure that I have thought of you as a correspondent of mine, since we mutually proffer'd a reciprocation of correspondence." After penning a mini-lecture on a favorite topic, the relationship between spirit and body before and after death, she apologized: "Pardon me dear sister Haywood I did not intend sermonizing you." Though a writer, she bemoaned the limitations of corresponding through the mail: "I often think of the short but very pleasant visit you paid me when in the City. To think how <u>much</u> we said in that <u>little</u> time, makes letter communication seem very dull indeed & yet this medium is a great blessing."

Eliza then confirmed what Susa Gates wrote about her "water cure": "My health is better than it has been for some months. A thorough hydropathic treatment for the bilious attack I have had, has done me very much good." The letter ended: "Dear Sister, that God our Father will heal, strengthen, and comfort you by his holy Spirit – give you wisdom and bless all that pertains to you – & all that pertains to your husband is the constant pray'r of your affectionate Sister Eliza R. Snow."

In 1858 Eliza contrasted her life in Salt Lake with Martha's in Nephi: "Well, there you are ... in your <u>own</u> home in your favorite Nephi; and here I am in my same little room in the third story of the Lion House." Their fates were different, she wrote, but both were contributing to the Kingdom of God. "And in reality what difference does it make whether you are making Caps for Prest. Young in G.S.L. City, or trimming Hats and feeding pigs in Nephi? or whether I am dealing out eatables & keeping Books in the Globe, or sewing, knitting, washing, and waiting on the sick in the Lion House. I think the result will be the same inasmuch as we are faithful in, and perform with cheerfulness whatever duties devolve upon us." Here we have a glimpse of Eliza's daily work at the Lion House—sewing, washing, tending the sick. Though she is writing an informal letter to a friend, as a born religious leader she naturally falls into moralistic exhortation.

Eliza by now was an active propagandist for polygamy, and she would counsel wives to encourage their husbands to take plural wives. Mosiah Hancock wrote that on November 19, 1860, "Sister Eliza R Snow gave Margaret [Mosiah's wife] counsel to build me up by getting me some Wives as I had the look of a noble man Which Margaret agreed to." It is common to see a man take a plural wife under the direction of his priesthood leaders but rarer to see a woman fulfill that role. To Eliza, polygamy was not just an ancillary principle, it was the most important doctrine "in the Gospel of the Son of God."

In 1862 Eliza wrote to Hannah Perkins, a friend living in St. George, sharing news of common friends, reporting on general conference. She did temple work regularly and was still participating in blessing meetings: "Last Thursday after working at the Endowments, we went to sis. Russell's. I told her I was authorized to bless her, that I truly felt to bless her, and when I related the circumstance, she was highly pleased, while the spirit of peace & blessing freely rested on her and us." On April 4, 1865, she wrote to Mary Rollins Lightner and again emphasized her temple labors: "My health has been good during the winter–I have been to the house of the Lord from two to five days a week...since you were here."

## XIII. Instructing the Sisters

Throughout the rest of Eliza's life, her public career–with speeches, organizational correspondence, reports in newspapers–is easy to trace, but her private self is more elusive. In late 1866 Brigham Young decided to accelerate the organization of Relief Societies in local wards, to encourage home manufacture among women, and at his request Eliza helped the bishops organize these societies. Eliza, then sixty-two, remembered how Young told her he was going to give her another mission:

> Without the least intimation of what the mission consisted, I replied, "I shall endeavor to fulfill it." He said, "I want you to instruct the sisters." Altho' my heart went "pit a pat" for the time being, I did not, and could not then form an adequate estimate of the magnitude of the work before me. To carry into effect the President's requisition, I saw, at once, involved public meetings and public speaking–also travel abroad.

Eliza was unofficially beginning to act as general Relief Society president. She traveled, spoke in meetings, and helped choose local ward Relief Society presidents for the rest of her life. In addition, on November 18, 1869, she helped organize the Young Ladies' Retrenchment Association, later called the Young Women's Mutual Improvement Association, the "auxiliary" organization for young women, and in 1872 she helped establish the *Woman's Exponent*, the semi-official voice of Mormon women. In the same year on February 11 Eliza was present when Leonora died in Lorenzo's house in Brigham City. Of her close family, only Lorenzo remained nearby; Lucius and Samuel were far away in the East.

As she moved to the forefront of women's affairs in Utah, Eliza's impressive public persona developed. When she traveled to frontier Mormon settlements, she was given a royal welcome by women and men alike, similar to that received by Brigham Young. But charismatic as she was, there was always a distance–not an aloofness or a lack of caring, but a stiffness and an intellectual separation–between her and even her devoted followers. Those who praised her frequently began by acknowledging that distance. For instance, Amy Brown Lyman, whose home Eliza visited when Amy was a girl, wrote that Eliza was "dignified, reserved, and rather cold, so much so that one would hesitate to approach her or to assume any familiarity whatever." After admitting this, Amy continued with an accolade: "She was so powerful and able, however, that she impressed people, even children, with her superior intelligence, wisdom, vision, and leadership, and won their admiration and confidence."

The strengths of greatness often lead to faults. One of Eliza's less sympathetic sides was a doctrinaire tendency, evidenced both in her unquestioning obedience to male priesthood leaders and in an occasional tendency to overpower dissent. One unsympathetic voice, John Hyde, perhaps exaggerated when he described her and her friends "crushing" backsliding women, but Eliza and her network were nevertheless a powerful regularizing force in Utah. Fanny Stenhouse tells of an incident in which Eliza apparently received the assignment of talking her into giving consent for her husband to take a second wife. Fanny felt that Eliza's arguments for polygamy were poorly reasoned and unconvincing, nevertheless, "She spoke to me very kindly ... and tried to encourage me, and suggested that Carrie would be a very proper person for my husband to marry." Though we do not see Eliza "crushing" Fanny, she was squarely on the side of those who were pressuring Fanny to accept the principle.

An incident from Eliza's home life shows how she was capable of enforcing morality on a personal level. Once Brigham gave his older daughters colorful grosgrain sashes. Phoebe, daughter of Clarissa Ross Young, laid her sash carefully on her bed and began dressing for a dance. When she returned to her room, the sash was gone, and Phoebe immediately knew that Eliza had confiscated it! She ran to her father in tears, and Brigham turned to Eliza and asked her where the sash was. Eliza replied, "I felt that you wouldn't approve of anything so frivolous for your girls so I put it away." Brigham replied, "Sister Eliza, I gave the girls those ribbons, and I am judge of what is right and wrong for my girls to wear. Phoebe is to have her sash." Eliza, chastened, returned the sash.

Once Brigham publicly corrected the doctrinal content of an article on resurrection that Eliza had published in the *Woman's Exponent*. Her doctrine "has just one fault and that one fault is, it is not true," he wrote bluntly in the next issue. Half a year later Eliza printed a small retraction: "Permit me to say that I fully concur in the views expressed by Pres. Young ... and trust that no Latter-day Saint may be led into erroneous doctrine through anything written by me." One senses a hint of ironic tension in this tight-lipped statement, but obedience to the priesthood was too ingrained in Eliza's Mormonness to allow real confrontation. Despite such minor conflicts, Brigham often deferred to Eliza; she often sat at his right hand in family dinners in the Lion House. Some have referred to her as more a counselor to Brigham than a wife.

## XIV. Palestine

In the fall of 1872 the sixty-eight-year-old Eliza set out to visit Europe and Palestine accompanied by her brother Lorenzo and Apostle George A. Smith. They left New York on the steamer *Minnesota* on November 6, and after traveling through England, Belgium, Paris, Venice, Rome, and Alexandria, reached Jerusalem on February 26, 1873. The company visited numerous biblical sites, then traveled through Syria, Athens, Vienna, and London on their way home to America. Back in the New World, Eliza and Lorenzo visited relatives in their childhood home, Ohio. On June 20 Eliza wrote to Utah from St. Louis: "We arrived here yesterday morning from Kansas, where we found our youngest brother [Samuel Pearce Snow], whom we had not seen for more than twenty years; he was then a boy, now the father of a large and promising family, and located on a farm one half mile square in a beautiful rolling prairie country." Eliza and Lorenzo arrived in Salt Lake City on July 8.

In late 1875, as America's centennial approached, Eliza received an invitation from the National Centennial Fair in Philadelphia to display handicrafts and art produced by Utah women. With very little time, she deftly organized a collection of exhibits but was denied financial support by the territorial legislature at the last moment, so only a few exhibits could be sent to Philadelphia. Nevertheless, she decided to display the remaining exhibits locally. The Utah women, she wrote, "obtained the use of a commodious building–arranged our specimens in two departments, including a picture gallery, which we kept open during the summer of 1876, with grand success." In a June 25 letter to Marinda Hyde, she gave behind-the-scene details of the exhibit:

> Our Territorial Fair ... involves a great amount of thought, time & labor. The explosion had considerably damaged the "Old Constitution" building – we have succeeded in putting it in repair, & have put up most of the heavy exhibits, quilts, spread &c &c, and feel it a good start. We were designing it in the Social Hall when Pres. Young telegraphed me that we had better take the Constitution Building, which we find will be none too large, and we can retain this any length of time, altho' we do not propose to keep it open more than 4 weeks – it will depend upon circumstances. We hope to avoid bankruptcy at the close.

The "Ladies' Centennial Territorial Fair" made a profit, turning a humiliating setback for Utah women into a public success.

Eliza's second volume of poems appeared in 1877, and she also contributed to Edward Tullidge's *Women of Mormonism*. Brigham Young became very ill that year and was soon approaching death. One of his last conversations, held in the parlor of the Lion House, was with Eliza and had Tullidge's book as its subject. Brigham suggested that Eliza, with a few other women, go on a lecture tour to sell *Women of Mormonism* and create a favorable public image of Mormon women. His final words to Eliza were, "It is an experiment, but it is an experiment that I would like to see tried. You go on with this work, Sister Eliza, but I shall go and take a little rest." He died on August 29.

## XV. Lost in Central Utah

In July 1878 Eliza sat in a Farmington train station with a local women's leader, Aurelia Rogers, who suggested that a church program be started for children. Eliza was enthusiastic: "Sister Eliza is greatly interested & thinks it will be a very excellent thing," wrote Emmeline Wells. The poetess soon had the program authorized; encouraged by Eliza, Aurelia organized a "Primary Association" in Farmington, while Eliza created one in her own Eleventh Ward in Salt Lake City. She was thus involved in the genesis of a third major LDS auxiliary organization. This incident illustrates Beecher's evaluation of Eliza: she was not the original creative spirit in many enterprises but was a genius at organization and implementation.

On November 16, 1878, Eliza opened a pro-polygamy mass meeting of women in Salt Lake City with a clarion call affirming the central sacrality of plural marriage:

> I am proud to state, before this large and honorable assembly that I believe in the principle of plural marriage just as sacredly as I believe in any other institution which God has revealed. I believe it to be necessary for the redemption of the human family from the low state of corruption into which it has sunken ... this sacred principle of plural marriage tends to virtue, purity and holiness. Those who represent the women of Utah as ignorant and degraded are either aiming to bring evil upon us, or they know not what they are doing.

Wells, in an 1881 article, described Eliza's activities from 1879 to 1880, and this travel record supplies an impressive testimony to her tireless activity, even when she was seventy-five years old. In 1879 she visited Ogden and Box Elder northwards; Malad, Cache Valley, and Bear Lake in southern Idaho; Rich County, Wasatch County to the southeast; Sevier County in south central Utah; then Ogden and Weber County again. On the Sevier trip she had a "famous ride," in which the teamster of her carriage became hopelessly lost and rode over rough, bumpy roads in Utah's central canyons. "The ladies all took the joke or mistake good-humoredly and Sister Eliza, it is said frequently expressed herself as desirous they should come out of the forest glen 'into a place where they at least spoke the English language.'" In early 1880 Eliza presided at meetings in Salt Lake City, Ogden, and Tooele, southwest of Salt Lake. Wherever she traveled, she preached, organized Relief Societies, Young Women's Mutual Improvement Associations, and Primaries, and administered to the sick.

## XVI. Relief Society President

In 1880 the de facto became official: on June 19, at a Ladies Quarterly Conference in the Salt Lake Assembly Hall, President John Taylor nominated Eliza as Relief Society general president. The congregation of women formally voted their approval, and she chose as her counselors Zina Huntington Young and Elizabeth Ann Whitney, both veterans of Ohio, Missouri, and Nauvoo. On July 17 Eliza was ordained president by Taylor. In her new calling, she remained indefatigable. In August she traveled south to Sanpete County and to Thistle Valley, driving a horse and buggy herself for twenty-six miles over "the most fearful roads." In September she met with sisters in Sevier County.

In 1877 the first Utah temple was dedicated in the small town of St. George in Utah's deep south. Though it was inconvenient for the inhabitants of northern Utah, many made their pilgrimages to Dixie to perform all-important ordinances in the new edifice. Among them, in November 1880, were Eliza and her counselor, Zina, who stayed with Minerva White Snow, wife of Apostle Erastus Snow, in St. George. On the 19th, when Eliza and Zina spoke to a children's Primary, Eliza "bore her testimony that the principle of plural marriage was as pure and holy as any principle that was ever revealed and that anyone who raised their voice against it could not have the spirit of God with them, for God could not save the human family without it." Polygamy, to the nineteenth-century Mormon, was a necessity for salvation, and children were taught the principle almost in their cradles. On November 24 Charles Walker wrote in his diary, "Sister Eliza R Snow and Zina Young came to the Temple to day." Five days later, at a schoolhouse, "E R Snow Smith and Zina D. Young" organized a primary. Walker wrote, "They Both declared that they were the wives of Joseph Smith the martyred Prophet. Sister Eliza showed a watch that Joseph carried while living. They gave some very good instruction to the children." On January 21, 1881, Eliza celebrated her seventy-seventh birthday in St. George, a gala affair.

In mid-March Eliza wrote a charming, if typically stiff and formal letter to Robert Welch, a child in Morgan, Weber, Utah: "My Dear Young Brother, It is a long time since I received your interesting letter; which I was not only pleased with but proud of. To receive a communication from a Secretary of a Primary Association is more satisfaction to me than from more experienced persons. To see my young brothers and sisters, when quite young, applying their faculties in a manner that bespeaks improvement and cultivation, promises great usefulness in the future." She then described her Primary labors in southern Utah. Since leaving Salt Lake in November, she wrote, she had organized thirty-five Primaries, "and as far as I have been informed, they are doing splendidly, and the people appreciate them very highly. Most of the Primary children, here in the South have the Primary Hymn Books and most of the Associations have one or two copies of the Tune Book." The letter ends: "Please give my love to your dear parents, and my love and blessing to the Primary Association, your own self included. E. R. Snow S."

Toward the end of March Eliza and Zina traveled back to Salt Lake City where they were welcomed back by a party of Relief Society ladies. In April Eliza, seventy-seven, was sustained in general conference as general president of the Relief Society. In September she visited Sanpete County and wrote young Robert Welch again toward the end of December, a letter that gives a sense of her still tireless labor: "I am now devoting what time I can to a series of three books for the Primary Associations, especially for recitations. They are to contain Dialogues, Prose and poetry ... These books are very much needed, and I feel anxious to get them out as soon as possible, but so much of my time is taken up in other directions that my progress is slow at present." One time commitment was the Deseret Hospital, which was dedicated on July 17, 1882, with Eliza chosen as its first president.

In late February 1882 one of Eliza's oldest companions, Elizabeth Whitney, became very sick. On the 28th Eliza with Emmeline Wells and Sister Howard administered to her, but two weeks later, on March 12, Eliza and friends visited her again and Mother Whitney, Wells wrote, "was quite insensible & when E.R.S.S. anointed her she said for her burial [dedicated her to death]." Elizabeth died the next day. An important remnant of Eliza's Kirtland, Nauvoo, and overland trail past was gone.

In April 1883 Eliza wrote a letter to a Sister East that shows her in her role of counseling local Relief Society presidents. She advocated "Home Industry" (rather than buying goods imported from the outside gentile world) and helping to build a ward meeting house. Above all, she wrote, underlining, "We will do as we are directed by the Priesthood." Advice on temple sealings and adoptions followed. The letter ended, "With love to yourself, br. East, and the good sisters, fellow laborers with you, Affectionately E.R. Snow Smith."

## XVII. Failing Powers

In 1885 a letter to Zina Young, her counselor, reminds us how important Zina had been to Eliza for decades. "My Dear Sister Zina, It is really refreshing to hear from you by your own hand. Certainly I should be very happy in your good society in connexion with the Temple: but at present there is no necessity for my officiating." The letter is newsy, but true to form, Eliza takes time to preach a bit: "Em. asked me what I thought of the times, I told her I thought them very encouraging. But withal, they are trying, not only men's souls, but also women's: It is all on the program, and the sooner it is worked out the sooner will the right-eous triumph. Persecution is one prominent part of the legacy which Je-sus our elder Brother, promised his followers; and what a glorious privi-lege is ours, to be really classed with the humble, faithful followers of our dear Redeemer!" It was the era of stark Mormon/non-Mormon polariza-tion before the Manifesto. She mentioned that Joseph F. Smith had fled to San Francisco and that federal agents had followed him to California.

In 1886 Eliza's powers were undoubtedly starting to fail. A letter to Zina records her daily routine:

> Sister Thomas comes as regularly as the morning – does my marketing and whatever I require. I think it was Tuesday after my arrival, Dr. Pratt called. I described the condition of my lungs, and the next day she came and brought not an apothecary shop, but a variety of medicines, which I took as she directed, & they were truly {blest} to my healing. I am now quite com-fortable – rest pretty well nights – can now eat, not only fresh vegetables, but a moderate quantity of bread. Have rode out a few times – Sister Susan brings me a piece of Sacrament bread on Sundays, which is a great comfort to me.

In March 1887 she endured a serious bout of illness and struck Emme-line Wells as "very feeble"–she slept "almost all the time." She recovered enough to leave her bed but did not regain her strength. In the summer her stake president, Angus Cannon, took the frail, ailing woman on occa-sional carriage rides, during which they would reminisce over old times. In the months before her death, she is reported to have said, "I have no choice as to whether I shall die or live. I am perfectly willing to go or stay, as our Heavenly Father shall order. I am in His hands."

And soon He would call her home. In November she became more and more ill, and on December 5 it was clear that she was dying. At ten in the morning, Patriarch John Smith asked her if she recognized him. "Of course I do," she replied. He gave her a blessing. At 1:05 p.m., as her beloved brother Lorenzo sat at her side, Eliza died in her apartment in the Lion House at the age of eighty-three. A week later she received an elaborate funeral and was then buried in Brigham Young's private cemetery.

## XVIII. Conclusion

Eliza R. Snow, the most prominent woman in Utah Mormon history, presents the modern historian with a number of perplexing tensions and polarities. Sometimes she seems a distant, cold, intellectual figure, yet she was beloved by her fellow-sisters, both for her spiritual and intellectual leadership as well as for her enormous capacity for service. Sometimes she seems preachy, doctrinaire, and judgmental; at others times we remember her kindness and tenderness to the sick and her wry, incisive humor. Modern feminists will remember that she penned the hymn that made the Mormon doctrine of a heavenly mother influential; that she was a remarkable, dominant female figure in patriarchal Utah; that she was an important woman writer, poet, diarist, and nurturer of other women's writing. On the other hand, they will remember her tireless preaching of polygamy, her counseling other women to accept it and live it, and her repeated statements that complete obedience to the male leadership of the church was all-important. As one Eliza scholar has pointed out, she was in some ways a spokesperson for the male hierarchy. Much of her practical power did come through marrying the two outstanding leaders in the early church, Joseph and Brigham. Yet it would be naive to define her as feminist or anti-feminist by late-twentieth-century standards. She was a complex, flesh-and-blood individual with strengths and weaknesses, in many ways the product of her culture and the early Mormon world view.

One way in which Eliza stands out from nearly all the other women in this book is her childlessness. Though she may have had a miscarriage, she was never a mother in the sense of raising a child. This is a remarkable fact, given that women in Mormon culture were and are valued as mothers above all else. Yet she was widely known as a spiritual "Mother in Israel," showing that motherhood is a spiritual gift, not merely a matter of physical biology alone. Hence the title of a Susa Gates essay, which I have borrowed: "Childless Mother of Mothers in Israel." Eliza's life wordlessly strikes a blow for Latter-day Saint women who are single and/or childless, a group that is repeatedly marginalized in Mormon culture by the typical emphasis on motherhood as the highest life path for women.

Susa Gates provides a fitting epitaph for Eliza. She wrote that her polygamy "nieces" in the Lion House would not often seek out her company, "for dear Aunt Eliza's homilies were not always relished by the high-spirited girls who loved fun and frolic with a normal and healthy zest."

> But if she was not sought much by the children when they were well and strong, she was an ever present help in times of sorrow and sickness; she and Aunt Zina were the ministering angels in the sick rooms. Aunt Eliza had such faith that the naughtiest child longed to have her come and "administer" or bless her when disease and suffering had

quelled the pride and tamed the spirit. And what a procession of the poor, the sick, the depressed and needy, sought that open door. Aunt Eliza spent all her time, after she recovered [from her early Utah-era consumption] going about and doing good; and even when at home, she was sewing on burial robes for the dying and dead. She was truly great.

# 14.

# "Great Glory Honner & Eternal Lives"

## Sarah Ann Whitney (Smith [Kingsbury] Kimball)

Sarah Ann Whitney enters the historical record only on March 22, 1842, when she celebrated her seventeenth birthday party in "the Masonic room" above Joseph Smith's store. This party gives a brief glimpse into the social life of a teenager in a leading family of Mormon Nauvoo. Those in attendance included Helen Mar Kimball, daughter of Heber and Vilate Kimball; the daughters of Sidney Rigdon and Bishop Higbee; the "Miss Pierces" (including Mary and Margaret, later plural wives of Brigham Young); Rachel Ivins (later a plural wife of Jedediah Grant and the mother of Heber J. Grant); and Mary and Mary Ann Ivins, among others. Joseph Smith also made a brief appearance. After the party Helen Mar stayed the night with Sarah Ann, whose family was living in a small house connected to the store. Their teenage talk continuing on into the night caused Sarah's brother Horace, separated from them only by a partition, to complain that they were keeping him awake.

Helen Mar wrote an insightful evaluation of Sarah Ann as a teen: "She was called proud and somewhat eccentric; but the influence that she seemed to hold over one was almost magnetic." That Sarah Ann had such a personality is not surprising, as she was the daughter of the charismatic Elizabeth Ann Whitney and a member of the intellectually gifted Newel Whitney family. Helen continued, "I found her incapable of professing anything which she did not feel, and that she was a most pureminded, conscientious and God-fearing girl. Our friendship dated from that period, and we became, as much as is possible, like 'the two halves of one soul.'" Indeed, the two girls followed remarkably similar paths. Both married Joseph Smith as a first husband while still in their teens, creating dynastic, family-linking sealings between their fathers and Smith, then each married into the other's family in second marriages for time—Helen Mar marrying Sarah Ann's brother, and Sarah Ann marrying Helen Mar's father. Sarah's marriage to Smith linked him to a close

342

friend, her father, Newel Whitney, one of the earliest bishops in the church. Sarah Ann is also unique because Smith had her marry a "pretend" husband, Joseph Kingsbury, by civil law to mask her polygamous marriage to him.

Sarah Ann's marriages to the two Josephs are well documented, but the rest of her life is unfortunately found mostly in genealogical outline. It is certain that her family was remarkable. Her father was a significant early Mormon leader, prominent in many early church developments. Her mother was one of the most eminent women in nineteenth-century Mormonism, a counselor in two general Relief Society presidencies. It is unfortunate that we do not know more about their daughter, who may have been just as extraordinary.

## I. Childhood

Sarah Ann was born to Newel Kimball Whitney and Elizabeth Ann Smith in Kirtland, Ohio, on March 22, 1825. The thirty-year-old Newel, a native of Vermont, was an Indian trader and storekeeper who had worked for Mary Rollins Lightner's uncle, Sidney Gilbert, since 1817. Elizabeth, twenty-five, was a native of Connecticut. Sarah was second oldest in a family of twelve, of whom five apparently died young. Her only older sibling, Horace Kimball, had been born in 1823. Helen Mar Kimball wrote of these two that "No brother and sister could be more affectionately devoted to each other than were Horace and Sarah Ann. He had always been to her like a guardian." After Sarah Ann, four more children—Franklin Kimball, Mary Elizabeth (twins), a second Mary Elizabeth, and Orson Kimball—were born in 1827, 1828, and 1830 in Kirtland; however, of these, only Orson survived infancy. At least by 1831 Newel was junior partner in the prosperous Gilbert and Whitney store in Kirtland, and the Whitneys lived in a comfortable house with a fine orchard and garden.

## II. "Cloud of Glory"

In the 1820s Newel and Elizabeth became devout participants in Alexander Campbell's Baptist movement and were associated with Sidney Rigdon. Thus, before Mormonism's arrival, they were confirmed Christian primitivists, searching for a modern restoration of the apostolic church described in the New Testament. In addition, they were receptive to the idea of modern revelation, having experienced visions themselves. In October 1830, when Sarah was five, Newel and Elizabeth were praying one night to learn how they could obtain the gift of the Holy Ghost, and "they saw a vision as of a cloud of glory resting upon their house, and heard a voice from heaven saying, 'Prepare to receive the word of the Lord, for it is coming.'" Soon after this, in November, Oliver Cowdery, Ziba Peterson, Peter Whitmer, and Parley Pratt visited Kirtland on their way to Missouri, and Elizabeth was impressed when she heard that Sidney Rigdon and Isaac Morley were joining the Latter-day Saints. Then, "As soon as I heard the Gospel as the Elders preached," she wrote, "I knew it to be the voice of the Good Shepherd, and went home rejoicing, to tell my husband the news." Newel asked her to wait until he had investigated so that husband and wife could be baptized together, but Elizabeth was so full of the spirit that she could not delay even a day and was immediately baptized. Newel followed her lead a few days later.

The Whitneys prayed that the young prophet, Joseph Smith, could come to Kirtland, and the prayer was soon answered. On February 1, 1831, the twenty-five-year-old Smith walked into the Gilbert-Whitney store.

"Newel K. Whitney! Thou art the man," he said, without introducing himself.

"You have the advantage of me," replied Newel.

"I am Joseph the Prophet. You've prayed me here, now what do you want of me?" The Mormon leader explained that he had seen Newel and Elizabeth in a vision praying for his presence. Newel immediately invited the young man to stay in his home, where Joseph and Emma would live for several weeks and where Joseph would receive many of the revelations later published in the Doctrine and Covenants. Six-year-old Sarah Ann would have had ample opportunity to come to know him well at this time.

There is no specific reference to Sarah Ann in the historical record until 1842, but we can easily trace the career of Newel Whitney, who quickly became a favorite of Smith and a prominent church leader in Kirtland and Nauvoo, and we can reconstruct Sarah Ann's life somewhat through him. It is certain that she grew up as the daughter of a prominent church leader among the Mormon elite. Like many early Mormons, Newel went on a number of missions, the first of which took place in the fall of 1831 when he and Oliver Cowdery visited the churches in western New York. Then, on December 4, one of Smith's revelations appointed Newel bishop at Kirtland. Though this was a significant honor, it was a job that would require him to oversee the physical welfare of church members, many of whom arrived in Kirtland without any means. A storekeeper by profession, Newel was put in charge of the church store, and he went on a number of missions/business trips from 1832 to 1835, often travelling with Joseph Smith.

Newel and Elizabeth were known for their generosity to the needy throughout their lives, and on January 7, 1836, they organized a three day "Feast of the Poor." Newell had worked a great deal on the temple and attended the dedication in March of the same year. Three more children joined the family in Kirtland: John Kimball (1832), Joshua Kimball (1835), and Ann Maria (1836). When Ann was born, Horace was thirteen, Sarah Ann eleven, Orson six, John four, and Joshua one.

Sarah was raised in a household filled with the gifts of the spirit. Elizabeth Whitney wrote that at the first patriarchal blessing meeting held by Joseph Smith, Sr., she received "the gift of singing inspirationally, and the first Song of Zion ever given in the pure language [of Adam] was sung by me then, and interpreted by Parley P. Pratt." Wilford Woodruff, in 1854, testified to Elizabeth's renown in tongue-singing: "Sister Whitney sung in tongues in the pure language which Adam & Eve made use of in the garden of Eden. This gift was obtained while in Kirtland through the promise of Joseph. He told her if she would rise upon her feet (while in meeting) she should have the pure Language. She done so and immediately commenced singing in that language. It was as near heavenly music as any thing I ever herd."

However, the spiritual heights of Kirtland would not last. When Newel became a charter member of the Kirtland Safety Society in January 1837, he participated in a project that would lead Joseph Smith and the Latter-day Saint church to financial disaster. As a result, Mormonism became increasingly troubled by internal dissent, and Smith encouraged his followers to leave Ohio and journey to Missouri. On July 8, 1838, one of Smith's revelations instructed Newel to sell church property, liquidate church debts, and gather to the new Zion: "Let my servant Newel K. Whitney be ashamed of the Nicolaitane band and of all their secret abominations, and of all his littleness of soul before me, saith the Lord, and come up to the land of Adam-ondi-Ahman, and be a bishop unto my people, saith the Lord, not in name but in deed, saith the Lord." Though the revelation rebuked Newel (perhaps he had ties to some of the dissenters), it nevertheless required him to continue as a bishop in the new venue. Obediently the Whitneys left Kirtland that fall. Elizabeth wrote, "I bade adieu to my beloved home, where I had anticipated spending all my life, and where everything had been arranged according to my own ideas of taste and beauty; to my dear friends and my kind and ever true Aunt Sarah, who had been a mother to me and mine."

Elizabeth then gives some insight into how the teenage Sarah Ann felt at the move: "My children were so imbued with the spirit of the Gospel, that although they were disappointed in their hopes and expectations in regard to obtaining a superior education such as we had sought to stimulate them to obtain ... yet they accepted this change in their worldly circumstances without a murmur. They were devotedly attached to Joseph." Though the Whitneys had a pronounced intellectual tendency (Horace would later read his way across the plains), they were also thorough converts to the Mormon cause by this time. As the family set out for Missouri, Sarah Ann was thirteen. Joshua, three, and Ann, two, were in "very delicate" health as the long trip began.

### III. "Just Barely Able to Crawl Around"

Before reaching Caldwell County, the Whitneys received news of mobbings, so traveled on to St. Louis where they read about the extermination order and decided it would be prudent to avoid Missouri altogether. They settled temporarily northward in Carrollton, Greene County, Illinois, and Newel returned to Kirtland for the winter. In the spring of 1839 he returned to Carrollton where an anti-Mormon from Kirtland had stirred up bad feelings against the Whitney family. But before violence erupted, they fled across the river, and soon thereafter Sarah Ann and her family arrived in Quincy, where they spent the winter. They moved to Nauvoo in the spring of 1840 and rented a house from Hiram Kimball.

One of the family's first experiences in Nauvoo was the inevitable chills and fever of malaria. "We were only just barely able to crawl around and wait upon each other," wrote Elizabeth. Nevertheless, Newel quickly became a leader in church and civic affairs and continued to associate closely with Joseph Smith, working in Smith's store. On October 6, 1839, he was appointed bishop of the "Middle" Ward at Nauvoo, and on February 1, 1841, he was elected city alderman. When the family continued to suffer ague attacks, Smith offered them more healthy accommodation in his own house. So they moved to a small cottage in his yard, where their health improved, and eventually they moved into the "up stairs over the brick store" owned by Joseph. Another son, Don Carlos Whitney, was born to Newel and Elizabeth in Nauvoo on February 14, 1841.

On March 17, 1842, the Relief Society was organized in Nauvoo, and Elizabeth Whitney was chosen by Emma Smith as her second counselor. Again we see how close the Whitney and Smith families were. In addition, Elizabeth was gifted in performing rites of healing. "I was also ordained and set apart," she writes "under the hand of Joseph Smith the Prophet to administer to the sick and comfort the sorrowful. Several other sisters were also ordained and set apart to administer in these holy ordinances." Sarah Ann had her seventeenth birthday party on March 22, and the following month, on April 28, she was accepted into the Relief Society, so she could now enjoy the meetings with her mother.

### IV. "A Halo of Light Encircled Us"

As a prelude to Sarah's marriage to Joseph Smith, there was a flurry of ritual activity in the lives of Newel and Elizabeth Whitney. As would be the case in Smith's marriage to Helen Mar Kimball, Sarah Ann's marriage to him was very much a family activity. On May 4 Newel received his endowment and became a member of the Holy Order. Soon after this, probably, Smith introduced him and his wife to the doctrine of plural marriage, but Newel and Elizabeth, as was common with many other Mormons who had puritanical New England backgrounds, resisted at first. "When Joseph saw that he [Newel] was doubtful concerning the righteousness of this celestial order he told him to go and enquire of the Lord concerning it, and he should receive a testimony for himself," wrote Helen Mar. This is typical of the way Smith dealt with initial resistance to plurality. And as so often happened, Newel and Elizabeth received a revelatory witness concerning the principle. Elizabeth wrote,

> He [Joseph Smith] had been strictly charged by the angel ... that the most profound secrecy must be maintained ... He ... confided to him [Newel] the principles [of polygamy] ... My husband revealed these things to me ... We pondered upon them continually, and our prayers were unceasing that the Lord would grant us some special manifestation concerning this new and strange doctrine. The Lord was very merciful to us; He revealed unto us His power and glory. We were seemingly wrapt in a heavenly vision, a halo of light encircled us, and we were convinced in our own minds that God heard and approved our prayers ... Our hearts were comforted and our faith made so perfect that we were willing to give our eldest daughter, then only seventeen years of age, to Joseph, in the holy order of plural marriage ... laying aside all our traditions and former notions in regard to marriage, we gave her with our mutual consent.

Helen Mar tells the same story. Newel and Elizabeth were converted to polygamy, receiving a powerful witness of the "principle" after praying together concerning it. Then, Helen wrote, "They willingly gave to him [Joseph Smith] their daughter, which was the strongest proof that they could possibly give of their faith and confidence in him as a true Prophet of God." In 1869 Sarah Ann signed the following affidavit: "On the twenty-seventh day of July, A.D. 1842, at the city of Nauvoo ... she was married or sealed to Joseph Smith ... by Newel K. Whitney, Presiding Bishop of said Church, according to the laws of the same regulating marriage, in the presence of Elizabeth Ann Whitney her mother."

The chief motivation for this marriage was clearly dynastic. Joseph and Newel had a close friendship, and the sealing would link the families of Newel and Elizabeth Whitney and Joseph Smith in this life and in the next. Orson Whitney, son of Horace and Helen Mar, later wrote of this marriage that Joseph Smith and Newel Whitney shared a strong "bond of affection." "This ... was strengthened and intensified by the giving in marriage to the former of the Bishop's eldest daughter, Sarah, in obedience to a revelation from God." This reference gives us the important detail that, as was the case with many of Smith's marriages, a revelation through Joseph commanded the union. Orson continues: "This girl was but seventeen years of age, but she had implicit faith in the doctrine of plural marriage." If Orson reflects Sarah Ann's state of mind adequately, then she received polygamy without significant internal opposition, though one must always allow for the possibility of a family tradition that has idealized the story. Of course, her mother, father, and highest spiritual leader had taught her the doctrine, and a revelation had sanctioned it. Orson continued, "The revelation commanding and consecrating this union, is in existence, though it has never been published. It bears the date of July 27, 1842, and was given through the Prophet to the writer's grandfather, Newel K. Whitney."

This revelation has since been published. It promises the Whitneys great blessings as a result of the marriage:

> Verily, thus saith the Lord unto my servant N.K. Whitney, the thing that my servant Joseph Smith has made known unto you and your family and which you have agreed upon is right in mine eyes and shall be rewarded upon your heads with honor and immortality and eternal life to all your house, both old and young because of the lineage of my Priesthood, saith the Lord, it shall be upon you and upon your children after you from generation to generation, by virtue of the holy promise which I now make unto you, saith the Lord.

The atmosphere of dynastic linking with eschatological implications is clear. As a result of Sarah's marriage to Smith, the father is told that he will be "rewarded" "with honor and immortality and eternal life to all your house." By being linked to the prophet, the Whitneys' salvation was assured. The document then tells Newel the words he should use in the ceremony:

> These are the words which you shall pronounce upon my servant Joseph and your daughter S.A. Whitney. They shall take each other by the hand and you shall say, "You both mutually agree," calling them by name, "to be each other's companion so long as you both shall live, preserving yourselves for each other and from all others and also throughout eternity, reserving only those rights which have been given to my servant Joseph by revelation and commandment and by legal authority in times passed. If you both agree to covenant and do this, I then give you, S.A. Whitney, my daughter, to Joseph Smith, to be his wife, to observe all the rights between you both that belong to that condition. I do it in my own name and in the name of my wife, your mother, and in the name of my holy progenitors, by the right of birth which is of priesthood, vested in me by revelation and commandment and promise of the

living God, obtained by the Holy Melchisedeck Gethrow [Jethro] and others of the Holy Fathers, commanding in the name of the Lord all those powers to concentrate in you and through you to your posterity forever. All these things I do in the name of the Lord Jesus Christ, and through this order he may be glorified and that through the power of anointing David may reign King over Israel, which shall hereafter be revealed. Let immortality and eternal life hereafter be sealed upon your heads forever and ever."

Thus, this was a marriage for time and for eternity. The references to "posterity" and the "rights" of marriage suggest that the union would have a physical dimension, consistent with the evidence for Joseph's other marriages. Helen Mar wrote of the union, "No earthly inducement could be held forth to the women who entered this order. It was to be a life-sacrifice for the sake of an everlasting glory and exaltation. Sarah Ann took this step of her own free will." Nevertheless, "Sarah felt when she took this step that it would be the means of severing her from the happy circle in which she had moved as one of their guiding stars." Helen Mar would have the same forebodings when she married Smith. To be secretly married to an older man for the sake of her family's salvation would be a major sacrifice for a young woman with romantic dreams.

Curiously, even though Sarah's father had authorized her marriage to the prophet, Joseph felt that Horace would oppose it and therefore sent him East on a mission: "But Joseph feared to disclose it [the marriage to Sarah Ann], believing that the Higbee boys would embitter Horace against him, as they had already caused serious trouble, and for this reason he favored his going East." This is an important reference, as it shows that Smith could use mission calls to male family members to remove possible opposition to his polygamous marriages.

### V. "Heroick Undertaking"

A letter sent by Joseph Smith to Newel, Elizabeth, and Sarah, dated about a month after the marriage, shows how secretly Smith was forced to live in plurality. He was hiding from the law and had transferred from the Edward Sayers home to Carlos Granger's. There he wrote the following letter: "Nauvoo August 18th 1842 Dear, and Beloved, Brother and Sister, Whitney, and &c. —I take this oppertunity to communi[c]ate, some of my feelings, privetely at this time, which I want you three Eternaly to keep in your own bosams." He addresses father, mother, and daughter, "you three," but cautiously avoids writing Sarah's name.

For my feelings are so strong for you since what has pased lately between us, that the time of my abscence from you seems so long, and dreary, that it seems, as if I could not live long in this way; and <sup>＜if you＞</sup> three would come and see me in this my lonely retreat, it would afford me great relief, of mind, if those with whom I am alied, do love me, now is the time to afford me succour, in the days of exile, for you know I foretold you of these things. I am now at Carlos Graingers ... all three of ~~y~~ you ~~come~~ <sup>can</sup> come and See me in the fore part of the night, let Brother Whitney come a little a head, and nock at the south East corner of the house at the window; it is next to the cornfield; I have a room inti=rely by myself, the whole matter can be attended to with most perfect safty, I <sup>know</sup> it is the will of God that you should comfort <sup>me</sup> now in this time of affliction, or not at [all] now is the time or never, but I hav no kneed of saying any such thing, to you, for I know the goodness of your hearts, and that you will do the will of the Lord, when it is made known to you; the only thing to be careful of; is to find out when Emma comes then you cannot be safe, but when she is not here, there is the most perfect <u>safty</u> ...

Clearly, Emma does not know of the marriage to Sarah Ann, so Joseph must meet Sarah only when there is no risk of his first wife finding out.

Only be careful to escape observation, as much as possible, I know it is a heroick undertakeing; but so much the greater frendship, and the more Joy, when I see you I <sup>will</sup> tell you all my plans, I cannot write them on paper, burn this letter as soon as you read it; keep all locked up in your breasts, my life depends up=on it. one thing I want to see you for is <to> git the fulness of my blessings sealed upon our heads, &c

There are evidently further ordinances that Smith wants to perform for the Whitneys. This is not just a meeting of husband and plural wife; it is a meeting with Sarah's family, with a religious aspect. "You will pardon me for my ernest=ness on <sup>this subject</sup> when you consider how lonesome I must be, your good feelings know how to <sup>make</sup> every allow=ance for me, I close my letter, I think emma wont come tonight if she dont dont fail to come to night, I subscribe myself your most obedient, <sup>and</sup> affectionate, companion, and friend. Joseph Smith." The Mormon leader is putting the Whitneys in the difficult position of having to learn about Emma's movements, avoid her, then meet secretly with him. The cloak-and-dagger atmosphere in this letter is typical of Nauvoo polygamy.

Three days later, on August 21, Newel and Elizabeth Whitney were sealed to each other for time and eternity. Perhaps the August 18 meeting prepared them for this ordinance. Then, Elizabeth tells us, Smith "repeatedly told him [Newel Whitney] to take a wife, or wives." But Newel was extremely cautious, not wanting to marry a polygamous wife lightly, and he took no plural wives while Joseph lived.

In the autumn the Whitneys moved into a new house at the northeast corner of Parley and Partridge streets, apparently a two-story brick home that still stands today. In December Sarah attended Eliza R. Snow's school. Joseph Smith wrote his teenage wife a letter on March 23, 1843, and, once again, he emphasized the salvation that her marriage to him would bring to her and her family. If Sarah remained within the "new and everlasting covenant" of marriage until the end, she and her father's house "shall be saved in the same eternal glory," and even if they should wander from the fold they could still repent and "be crowned with a fulness of glory." This is the same doctrine that is taught in Doctrine and Covenants 132: salvation, even despite "wandering from the fold."

## VI. "Pretended Marriage"

Some nine months after Sarah's marriage to Joseph Smith, she married Joseph C. Kingsbury on April 29, 1843, with Smith himself performing the marriage in a civil ceremony. Kingsbury, born in Enfield, Connecticut, in 1812, had worked as a clerk in Newel Whitney's store since Kirtland and was Sarah's uncle, as he had married Newel's younger sister, Caroline, in 1836. Caroline had died in October 1842. A loyal supporter of Smith, Joseph C. had been a high councilor in Kirtland beginning in 1835 and in Iowa beginning in 1841. The apparently polyandrous marriage of Joseph C. and Sarah Ann, so paradoxically presided over by the first husband, was, in fact, not a real marriage in the view of any of the participants but a marriage suggested by Smith to cloak his plural connection with Sarah. No other detail in the history of polygamy shows more clearly with what little regard Joseph viewed civil marriage or any ordinance not solemnized by what he considered true authority. Kingsbury wrote,

On the 29th of April 1843 I according to President Joseph Smith Couscil & others agread to Stand by Sarah [Ann] Whitney as Supposed to be her husband & had a pretended marriage for the purpose of Bringing about the purposes of God in these last days as spoken by the mouth of the Prophits Isiah Jeremiah Ezekiel and also Joseph Smith, & Sarah Ann Should Rec[d] a Great Glory Honner & Eternal Lives and I Also Should Rec[d] a Great Glory Honner & Eternal lives to the full desire of my heart in having my Companion Caroline in the first Reserection to lcaim [claim] her & no one to have power to take her from me & we Both shall be Crowned & Enthroned togeather in the Celestial Kingdom.

As was often the case with Smith's marriages, another relationship was linked with it. In this case, after marrying Sarah civilly, Kingsbury was sealed to his deceased wife for eternity and was promised exaltation in the celestial kingdom.

This "pretended" marriage opens up the possibility of other "front husbands" in Smith's polyandrous marriages. But the evidence generally does not support front husband marriages in the other unions of the Mormon leader. In a pretend marriage we would expect a sealing to Smith, then a subsequent civil ceremony with the front husband, but most of Joseph's polyandrous wives married "first husbands" before him; and there is no evidence that any of them agreed to become front husbands *after* Smith married their wives. In fact, such a marriage—living with a wife and not having sexual relations with her after a period of full marriage—would probably have been impracticable. Thus Kingsbury was Mormonism's only front husband, to the best of my present knowledge.

One wonders what the dynamics of a pretend marriage would have been—there would have been no sexual dimension, but Joseph Kingsbury and Sarah must have lived as close friends, in fact, as niece and uncle. We do know that Sarah Ann continued to live with her parents after the marriage to Smith; and Kingsbury, the day after the "pretend" marriage, apparently moved into the Whitney house also. Sarah became generally known as Mrs. Kingsbury, and she and Joseph C. attended public functions together. Outsiders would have suspected nothing unusual in the relationship. But, as Kingsbury's biographer Lyndon Cook notes, for Kingsbury, the sacrifice "for a while at least, was that he would be unable to search for another mate." On July 15 he played another important role in Mormon history when he made a copy of Smith's revelation on polygamy—our present Doctrine and Covenants 132—as Newel K. Whitney read it aloud before Emma (or Joseph) burned the original. Then Kingsbury left on a mission to New England on July 23.

Occasionally Sarah Ann must have spent time with Joseph Smith. On September 20 William Clayton recorded that she rode out to Smith's farm but that he was not there when she arrived. On May 23, 1844, Heber C. Kimball wrote in a letter to Vilate, "Remember me to Helen and Sarah Ann Whitney, and tell them to be good girls and cultivate union, and listen to counsel from the proper source—then they will get the victory." Both Helen Mar and Sarah Ann were teenage wives of Smith, and Heber knew that Helen, at least, had been sorely tried by her marriage to the prophet. When Joseph Smith was killed on June 27, Sarah Ann was suddenly a widow at age nineteen.

### VII. "Sister Whitney ... Annointed Hur"

Joseph Kingsbury returned to Nauvoo on July 28. Apparently there was no question of Sarah and Joseph turning their pretend marriage into an actual one, but they did not separate publicly for some time. On March 4, 1845, Joseph Kingsbury was sealed by Heber C. Kimball to his first wife, Caroline, for eternity, with Dorcas Adelia Moore standing proxy. Then he was sealed to Dorcas for time and eternity. Sarah Ann did not play a part in any of these ceremonies. Earlier in the year, on January 22, William Clayton wrote, "Bought two rings and gave one to S A Whitney for painting aprons." Sarah was here involved in preparing clothing for esoteric temple ritual. Four days later she and Kingsbury received their endowments on the same day, though not as husband and wife, and joined the Holy Order.

Heber C. Kimball wrote in his journal on February 6, "Took Tea with Sariah A. Whitney in company with B. Young." As has been noted, the Kimball and Whitney families had always been close, and Brigham Young and Heber Kimball married the majority of Smith's widows after his death. So one might have predicted that Sarah would marry Heber; perhaps he proposed to her on February 6. In any event, the ceremony took place on March 17. Sarah was nearly twenty, and Heber forty-three. She would spend the rest of her life facing the difficult challenges of a plural wife in his large family. This was another dynastic linking, though only a sealing for time, and the families of Kimball and Whitney were now bound closer than they had been before. The marriage was secret, and Sarah continued to be known as Sarah Kingsbury. On April 19 Heber himself wrote, "Vilate with Sarah Ann Kingsbury took me in a buggy to Brother Robert Pierce's." On May 20 Willard Richards referred to "Sarah Kingsbury" in his journal. Four days after her marriage, on March 21, Sarah Ann received her fullness of the priesthood ordinance, presumably with Heber standing proxy for Smith, as this ordinance requires a couple.

Heber occasionally visited Sarah and her family, as his diary shows. His June 19 entry testifies to Elizabeth's enormous spiritual prestige. When his wife Vilate was sick, he turned to Elizabeth for help in administering to her, which is remarkable as he had a decidedly patriarchal bent: "Returned home found my wifee quite sick ... Sister Whitney come in annointed hur and sung in toungs. I also sung. The Lord blest us." The following day Vilate was worse. "I sent for Sister Whitney, she com. We Clothed our selves [in temple robes], and Anointed hur and praid. The Lord hurd. She was beter." This kind of joint male/female anointing of the sick is almost entirely unknown in current Mormon practice. In July, when Sarah Ann was seriously ill, Heber baptized her for her health in the Mississippi; she survived the sickness—and the baptism. On November 28 Kimball wrote, "N K Whitney let me have a Lambs skin fore some chues [shoes]. Sarah Ann cut them out forr me." Here we see the close connection of the Whitney and Kimball families and the young wife making a piece of clothing for her new husband.

At the end of 1845 the Nauvoo temple was nearing completion, and Sarah Ann helped daily with the work. She assisted in laying carpet on November 29, and on December 5, with her mother and Helen Mar Kimball, sewed the temple veil. In early January 1846 she and her mother—with Mary Ann Young, Vilate Kimball, Eliza Snow, Mary and Agnes Smith, and Mercy Thompson—prepared the cushions for the "new altar." On December 11 Sarah Ann, with her mother and Brigham's first wife, Mary Ann, performed preparatory ordinances, washing and anointing other sisters.

An incident that took place on the 30th again shows Elizabeth Whitney's spiritual charisma. On that date elite Mormons—the Young, Kimball, and Whitney families among others—met in the temple for sacred singing, dancing, tongue-speaking, and prayer. Sarah Ann probably attended. A violinist played, and the dancing included a hornpipe (led by Brigham Young), then French fours. The company sang hymns, then, William Clayton wrote, "Sister Whitney, being invited by Pres. Young, stood up and invoking the gift of tongues, sung one of the most beautiful songs in tongues, that ever was heard." The interpretation, given by her husband, dealt with the Mormons' imminent departure into "the country of the Lamanites," the Lamanites' rejoicing when they heard the gospel, and the gathering of Israel. "Altogether, it was one of the most touching and beautiful exhibitions of the power of the Spirit in the gift of tongues which was ever seen."

On January 1, 1846, Sarah (still "Sarah Ann Kingsbury") received her endowment in a temple session with Helen Kimball Smith, Mary Houston Smith, Eliza Partridge Smith, and Horace Whitney. Elizabeth Whitney washed and anointed her daughter. That night Sarah and Joseph Kingsbury were invited to a wedding in the temple, which included a supper, prayers, singing, and sacred dancing. Those who attended were again members of the Heber Kimball and Brigham Young families, along with close friends and adopted sons and daughters. Dancing continued until 2:30 A.M., then many of the group slept in the temple.

A number of important Whitney marriages and sealings took place in January. On the 12th Sarah Ann was sealed to Joseph Smith for eternity, with Heber C. Kimball standing as proxy, then was sealed to Kimball for time. On the 26th Sarah's father, Newel—who had finally joined the ranks of polygamists on February 24, 1845, in marrying Emmeline Woodward (later Emmeline B. Wells, the General Relief Society president)—married six additional women at once: Olivia Maria Bishop, Anna Houston, Elizabeth Moore, Elizabeth Almira Pond, Abigail Augusta Pond, and Henrietta Keys. He had now become one of the more married men in the church. On January 27 Kingsbury became Newel's adopted son; while Kingsbury's wife, Dorcas Moore, and another wife whom he had married the day before, Loenza A. Pond, were then sealed to Newel as his daughters. The next day Kingsbury received the fullness of priesthood ordinance.

### VIII. "Was Awakened by Hearing [Her] Cry"

After these spiritual heights, the Mormons—and Sarah Ann specifically—turned to the daunting task of relocating in the Far West. The Kimball family crossed the Mississippi on February 16, but soon thereafter many of them returned to Nauvoo, including Helen Mar, who visited many old neighbors with Sarah Ann. Sarah left Nauvoo on the 27th, traveling with her mother and Emmeline Whitney (later Wells). Kingsbury writes, "I being prepared Took My Journey on the 28th Feby 1846 With Sarah My Supposed Wife & Loenza My Wife & Mary Ho{o}sten Sarah['s] Hand Made & Emaline Sarah['s] Assistent in Company With Bishop N K Whitney my Father [by adoption] and his famaly We Traveled Verry Slow being in a grate Compy bad Wether & muddy Roads." Interestingly, the diaries of Emmeline Wells and Horace Whitney do not seem to show Sarah Ann in Kingsbury's company.

At the time of her departure, Sarah Ann was pregnant and nearly due. Patty Sessions, as midwife, now takes up Sarah's story. On March 6, she wrote, "I go back ten miles this morning to see Sarah Ann she is sick sent for me I rode horseback she was beter when I got there and I drove her carriage in to the camp in the afternoon with her and her mother—the camp did not start to day." There Newel and Orson Whitney made "a rustic bedstead of poles" for the expectant mother. Then, two days later, Horace Whitney gives us an unusually detailed account of the birth:

> About 4 o'clock in the morning was awakened by hearing Sarah Ann cry - appeared to be in great pain - Bro. Kimball was sent for - arrived about daylight - I went on foot to Bro. Kimball's camp - had not been there long before Bro. Markham arrived, bringing the news of the birth of S. Ann's child, which happened at 8 minutes past 7 o'clock on the 8th day of March 1846. - The child nams called David as also the valley where he was born. It is located in Jackson township Van Buren Co. I.T. Towards evening Brigham and Heber went to father's camp blessed the child and returned home.

Patty Sessions was sent for, rode nine miles in the early morning, but arrived late. She, however, gives us the child's full name, which is significant: "Sarah ann ... has a son born before I get there calls it David Kimball Smith." As in all proxy marriages, Sarah Ann's biological children would be sealed to Joseph Smith in the eternities, not to Heber.

The next day the company camped at Richardson's Point. On March 9, Eliza Snow wrote, "Call'd on Sis W. and Sarah with her fine boy." On the same day Horace Whitney wrote, "Wm. [Kimball, son of Heber] conveyed Sarah Ann in an easy carriage to the camp this day before leaving the Valley of David." Eliza Snow visited Sarah Ann twice the next week. Storms delayed the main camp at Richardson's Point, and many of the pioneers became ill. It rained incessantly. Helen Mar wrote, "Sarah Ann, was in a critical state part of the time while there. And Mother Whitney, who stayed with her daughter, and, like all the rest was exposed to cold and wet, took the rheumatism, and it settled in her left wrist, which had been broken the previous winter." Elizabeth treated it by wrapping a rattlesnake around it.

On the 12th the company pressed on, despite "a slow drizzly rain and then thick clouds gloomy and dismal," in Emmeline Wells's words. An ox wagon was fixed up for Sarah Ann to ride in, but its "easy rocking" motion made her increasingly sick throughout the day. The weather cleared on March 19, and Horace Whitney wrote, "Sarah Ann gaining rapidly." The company crossed the Chariton River on her birthday, the 22nd, and arrived at Chariton camp, nearly halfway across Iowa. There she tried to recuperate in a tent but found it too damp with the constant rain so transferred to a wagon. By March 30 she was able to walk around, and by April 13, when the company was not far from Big Locust camp, she had nearly regained her health. Eliza Snow wrote, "Sis. M. & myself spent most of the day in Sarah Anns wagon dined with Sis. W. & S; Sarah assisting to prepare tea for the first time since the birth of her promising son." On the 29th, at Garden Grove camp, Patty Sessions visited "Sary Ann and sister Whitney."

Kingsbury wrote, "On the fore part of may Sarah Went to Live with President Kimball her husband for time & I was left With my Real wife Loenza to Journey by ourselves." However, contemporary journals show that Sarah Ann was travelling with her mother the entire time. On May 9, at the Garden Grove camp, Eliza Snow wrote, "Call'd into Sarah's found Sis. W. quite ill with her lame wrist & in a discourag'd state of mind." By the end of May, Sarah Ann was at Mt. Pisgah; on the 30th she, with her mother and Vilate Kimball, hosted Eliza again. Soon thereafter, when many members of the Kimball company were leaving Mt. Pisgah, Sarah Ann began tenting with the honeymooning Helen Mar and Horace. This trio arrived at Winter Quarters, where Sarah would live for two years, on approximately June 13.

### IX. "The Priesthood ... Conferred Upon Us"

At first everyone at Winter Quarters lived in tents beside wagons as the men hastened to build crude shelters for the winter. Heber, who had married thirty-nine women before leaving Nauvoo, must have been extremely harried as he tried to prepare homes for all of them. He undoubtedly delegated some of this responsibility to friends, relatives, and adopted sons. On July 25 Sarah Ann celebrated Horace's birthday at Heber's tent. On August 2, Horace wrote, "To-day put up my little tent again ... Sarah Ann, Helen, Mary Houston, George Billings and myself are to occupy it." Close quarters indeed!

A difficult winter followed. We can only imagine the specifics of Sarah Ann's life as she cared for David while enduring bitter cold, crude housing, and inadequate food. She evidently had her own sod-roofed home built on Heber Kimball's row of houses, next to Helen's, into which she moved on December 16. Despite the bleak living conditions, we can also imagine Sarah Ann surrounded by a complex web of family: sister-widow with many of Smith's wives, she was a sister-wife to all of Heber's wives and a daughter in the nuclear Whitney family, including Horace and his wife, Sarah Ann's best friend, Helen. On December 17, Horace wrote, "Luke Johnson took supper with us at S. Ann's house." An entry from Eliza Snow's journal shows Sarah's ties with the former wives of Joseph. On August 28, 1846, she wrote, "Saw sis. Whit. Sarah, sis. [Permelia?] Lott & Elvira [Cowles] &c." Here three former wives of Smith and Elizabeth Whitney socialize together. One is struck by the number of journal references to Sarah Ann that link her with her mother.

On February 9, 1847, Sarah Ann attended a Kimball family meeting in which children were to receive blessings from Brigham Young. David probably received a blessing on this day. Another Kimball family meeting was held in Sarah's house on April 4. According to Helen's reminiscences, both Heber and Newel Whitney spoke, probably at great length. Then, after a break, all met again in the evening. At nine Heber offered a closing prayer, then Heber and Newel blessed each member of their families, and the meeting finally ended at eleven. Horace Whitney's journal entry for the day adds a hieratic vision of prayer circles and temple garments: "Present - HCK, NK Whitney, Wm. Kimball, H.K. Whitney, O.K. Whitney - Vilate Kimball, Sister Moon, Sarah Ann, Helen M., Mary Kimball, and mother [Elizabeth Ann W.] ... We all clothed ourselves [in temple robes], except Orson and Helen - and father opened the meeting by prayer. We all then stood up in a ring, offered up the signs of the Priesthood, Bro. K. being mouth." The next day there was another meeting in Sarah Ann's small room for family members who had missed the previous day's event. By now Sarah Ann was very much a part of the Kimball family.

Sarah and her mother participated in the female blessing meetings that counterpointed the hardships of Winter Quarters. On April 19 Eliza Snow spent the day with Sarah Ann, Elizabeth, Vilate, and Helen Mar. Eliza wrote on May 2, "This eve. sup'd at sis. Noon's with sis. Kim. Whit. Sess. Lyon Sarah A. Helen, &c. had a[s] glorious time as I ever had on earth at sis. K.'s—myself chosen to preside—the pow'rs of the world to come were truly in our midst." Sarah Ann hosted another important blessing meeting on June 3, which both Patty Sessions and Eliza Snow described. Patty wrote, "I caled to Sarah Anns this evening with E R Snow sisters Whitney and Kimbal came in we had a good time things were given to us that we were not to tell of but to ponder them in our hearts and proffit thereby." Eliza wrote: "Sis Sess. Kim. Whit. & myself spent the eve. at Sarah Ann's—had a pow'rful time deep things were brought forth which were not to be spoken." Both women mention the ineffable nature of their revelations.

As a result of one blessing meeting, which may have taken place after Eliza Snow left Winter Quarters, Sarah Ann's David became an important character in a tragic story. The leading women were promised angelic visitation, perhaps at a blessing meeting. So, after fasting, the following women met at Vilate Kimball's house on June 12: Elizabeth Whitney, presumably Sarah Ann, "Louisa Pitkin" (Laura Pitkin Kimball?), Presendia Huntington Buel (Kimball), Sarah Lawrence (Kimball), Frances Swan (Kimball), Harriet Sanders (Kimball), Persis Young, and two or three others. However, as soon as the women began praying, according to Helen, "The devil commenced his operations on the three little ones that were there": Sarah's child David and Vilate's two youngest, Brigham and Solomon. First Brigham, then two or three of them, "commenced screaming; floundering and going into the most frightful contortions, which obliged us to stop and administer to him and rebuke the spirit in the name of Jesus." Brigham quieted, but then Solomon, who had been sleeping peacefully, began screaming in the same way. After an administration had quieted him, Sarah Ann's David was "seized" in turn. This sequence, seen by the women as a struggle between evil and good powers, continued through the day, "and every time the evil spirits were rebuked by the power of the priesthood, which had been conferred upon us in the house of God in connection with our husbands." Finally, surprisingly, the women "became satisfied that we would have to part with one of those little ones before we could obtain the coveted blessing." They broke their fast and called in Bishop Newel Whitney who told them that God had been closer to them than they had imagined, and if they had "given up" one of those children, they would have received the promised blessing.

After this meeting Solomon and David were continually sick, and it seemed inevitable that one would die. Vilate, in private prayer, asked that the Lord take her Solomon, not David. However, the opposite took place: after she made this offering, her baby improved, and a few days later, on August 18, Sarah's David died. Helen Mar describes the young mother's grief: the baby's "pure spirit had taken its flight from this sorrowing vale of tears, and another doting heart was almost broken as she followed its little body to that lonely spot on the hill-side which had been dedicated as a burying place for the dead."

## X. "I Watched with Sarah Ann"

After David's death, we know little about Sarah Ann until the summer of 1848 when she crossed the plains in the Heber C. Kimball company, probably leaving Winter Quarters in May when she was approximately five months pregnant. So, like many of Joseph Smith's wives, she endured an uncomfortable journey across the plains while expecting. On August 26 a boy, named David Orson, was born to her in a wagon. Sarah and David Orson probably arrived in the valley around September 23. Sarah, after having married Joseph Smith and Heber Kimball, and after bearing two children while traveling west, was only twenty-three years old. Sadly, David Orson died about half a year later on April 23, 1849. On that date, Eliza Snow wrote, "Heard of the death of Sarah Ann's child, died this mor." Zina Huntington noted, "I watched with Sarah Ann whitneys or Kimbles babes corps. Sister Frances set up with me." As often in writing about Sarah Ann, we know that the event happened but can only imagine the emotional ordeal that she endured.

On May 16 Eliza Partridge wrote, "Visited at Wm Walker's with sisters Emily [Partridge] and Louisa [Beaman] Young and Sarah Ann and Lucy [Walker] Kimball also Presnts Young and Kimball." Here we have a meeting of prominent Smith wives, attended also by Young and Kimball.

## XI. "Each ... Tryde to Cultevate ... Paitcents"

From this point on, Sarah Ann appears in few journals; her life is reduced to the skeletal framework of genealogical dates. On February 26, 1850, twins David Heber and Dorice H. were born to her. Dorice evidently died as an infant, but happily David Heber lived and became Sarah's first child to grow to maturity. On September 23 of the same year, Sarah's father, Newel Whitney, died of bilious pleurisy.

In 1851 she was living in a household with Laura Pitkin, another Kimball wife. Her next child, Newel Whitney Kimball, was born on May 19, 1852, and another son, Horace Heber Kimball, was born three years later, on September 3, 1855. In 1856 and 1857 she was living in a house with Lucy Walker (Smith Kimball), Ellen Sanders (Kimball), Adelia Wilcox (Kimball), and Martha McBride (Knight Smith Kimball). Adelia left a vivid description of life in this home:

> My husband put me in with several of his wives to live all eating at the
> same table but each one having ther own seperate rooms This was all
> new to me but beleaving as I did in the principle I had made up my mind
> to be sattisfide with what ever good place my head [Heber] see [saw] fit

to place me in and with this determination I soon got ust [used] to it and quite liked it the worst we had to contend with was having so many children together for when they wher all in the hous they made a good deal of confusion This we got along with as well as could be expected for each woman tryde to cultevate her chare of paitcents The names of those good sisters [were] Sarah Whitney, Lucy Walker, Ellen Sanders and Aunt Martha Nights al trying to do ther part in the good caus they wher engaged in.

In late 1856 Sarah Ann accompanied Heber on one of the First Presidency's tours of the northern settlements and Cache Valley. According to Stanley Kimball, "[A]t another time Sarah Ann Whitney, Lucy Walker, Mary Houston, and Presendia Huntington lived in another home on the Kimball block." Apparently Sarah Ann and her family, like Presendia Huntington, were required by Heber to move frequently, and she often lived in cramped houses with others of his wives. On May 4, 1857, when Sarah Ann was thirty-three, her only daughter who would survive, Sarah Maria, was born. Four years later Joshua Heber, Sarah Ann's last child, was born on February 23, 1861, when she was thirty-six and her husband fifty-nine. David was now eleven, Newel nine, Horace five, and Sarah Maria two.

Aside from the dates of these children's births and the few details about Sarah's residence history, little is known about her later life or about her relationship with Heber. Vilate was very much Heber's favored wife, and his demanding church position and many households probably kept him from spending a great deal of time with any one family. Nevertheless, he was described by his wives as kind and affectionate, if authoritarian. The ties between the Whitney and Kimball families would have assured that Heber was closer to Sarah Ann than he was to many of his wives. As we have seen, she travelled with him to conferences on occasion, which is probably a sign of special favor. Orson Whitney, Sarah Ann's nephew, wrote that she was "a woman of wonderful character, respected by the other wives and children. She was deeply devoted to her own children and especially Heber." A journal entry from a sister-wife, Laura Pitkin, shows her cooking for Heber: "Day spent by M^r K in the 16 ward Sarah Ann and Lucy [Walker Smith Kimball] took his dinner out to him and spent an hour or two very pleasantly with him." Sarah would occasionally accompany Heber on social occasions. An 1865 notice from the *Deseret News* tells us that "Sarah Ann Whitney and Heber C. Kimball attended a dinner party sponsored by William Jennings." Curiously, even at that late date the plural wife is referred to by her maiden name.

An anecdote from Kimball family traditions gives us a brief glimpse of Sarah Ann's family. In 1864 David Heber, age fourteen, was assigned by Heber to travel with carts to North Mill Creek Canyon with Solomon Kimball, the son of Vilate who almost died in Winter Quarters, and pick up a load of wood. It was a rule that all of the family had to gather for prayer every morning, but David and Solomon felt that they needed to start on their expedition early, so they sneaked away before dawn, taking with them a valuable workhorse that their father had recently acquired from neighbors, the Knowltons. In the canyon the boys had to drive down a narrow steep dugway near a dangerous creek that was filled with rushing spring water, fifteen feet deep, with boulders in it. Without brakes on their wagons, they lost control. David was ahead of Solomon, but seeing that Solomon's cart would soon overtake him, he barely managed to get out of the way. Then the boys had to traverse a narrow bridge over the water, which would certainly have killed them if they had fallen into it. Solomon wrote, "By this time I had completely lost my balance and was just falling onto the heels of this 'crazy' horse when my team crashed into the side of David's wagon with such a tremendous force that it drove a pole among through the body of the Knowlton horse, killing him instantly." Miraculously, neither of the boys was hurt in the accident. They got up, surveyed the crash, and David said, "I will never run away from prayers again as long as I live." Solomon agreed. Meanwhile, at home, their parents had a presentiment that something was not right with their sons. Heber met them in tears, but undoubtedly the two mothers were equally relieved to receive their sons home safe again.

### XII. "In That Bleak and Cold Country"

On June 22, 1868, Heber C. Kimball died at age sixty-seven, which made Sarah a widow (again) at forty-four. We can only imagine what his last words to her might have been. She was left with a household of David eighteen, Newel sixteen, Horace thirteen, Sarah eleven, and Joshua seven. Two years later she reached a milestone when David Heber married Sarah Elizabeth Hanham in the Salt Lake Endowment House on November 14, 1870. Two weeks after that, on November 28, eighteen-year-old Newel married Martha Winders in the Endowment House.

Newel and Martha packed a wagon the next fall and set out for the settlement of Meadowville, Rich County, near Bear Lake in northern Utah. Many of Sarah Ann's children and many of their Kimball half-siblings eventually settled there. This was rough, difficult land to farm, so her children faced pioneer hardships, just as she had. One of Newel's children, Mary Kimball Thatcher, later wrote, "We struggled and suffered and endured for nine years. We were burned out twice, left only with clothes we stood up in to do with. We tried to make a living by farming and stock raising in that bleak and cold country looking after the welfare of three children.

The snow was often so deep you could not see fences or small buildings, as they were snowed under." Sarah Ann would have worried about her children far away in the northern mountains of Utah and Idaho.

## XIII. Death

A namesake of Sarah Ann, Sarah Ellen Kimball, was born to Newel and Martha on June 26, 1872, and Edwin Leroy Kimball was born to David and Sarah Elizabeth on November 1, so Sarah Ann entered a brief grandmotherly period in her life. But the following year, on September 4, 1873, she died in Salt Lake City at age forty-eight, when she was still comparatively young. The official cause of death was "brain fever." Her mother, now seventy-three, probably tended her in her last moments. Her children, and perhaps Helen Mar and Horace Whitney, were also at her bedside. One imagines the funeral, with Sarah's family occupying the front row in the local wardhouse: David twenty-three, Newel twenty-one, Horace eighteen, Sarah sixteen, and Joshua twelve. Sarah Ann was buried near Heber in the private Kimball-Whitney graveyard in the block just north of the present LDS church office building.

## XIV. A Life in Polygamy

Historians of polygamy will remember Sarah Ann Whitney Smith Kingsbury Kimball as a participant in the only well-documented "pretend" marriage that Joseph Smith engineered to cloak a polygamous marriage of his own—an interesting example of the lengths to which he would go to preserve the secrecy of a plural marriage. Her sealing to Smith is also significant in its demonstration of a classic dynastic marriage between Smith and an important church family, a marriage that assured the Whitneys eternal blessings and an important connection to the Mormon prophet in this life.

The private Sarah Ann is more elusive. We know that she grew up in a prominent, elite Mormon family and met Joseph Smith, a close family friend, at an early age. Her mother was charismatic, in both the technical and general sense of the term, and Sarah Ann, though she did not speak in tongues as often as her mother, was also a striking personality. Helen Mar writes that she had a "magnetic" influence over her friends. Sarah's marriage to Joseph Smith must have been difficult for her; like Helen Mar, she probably sacrificed whatever youthful romantic dreams she had to assure her family's salvation, marrying Smith out of religious conviction and loyalty to her parents' advice. The dynamics of her marriage to Heber C. Kimball were probably similar. It was a marriage to an older man, a friend of the family, and accepted out of religious, familial motivations.

Sarah Ann endured the harsh trials of a pioneer woman, including two babies lost on the way west, and she lived in the cramped quarters of the Kimball polygamous homes in Utah. But her life, though it had its challenges and tragedies, was not the life of a Louisa Beaman who lost all of her five babies before her own painful death. Sarah Ann was able to raise five children and became a grandmother before her own death at age forty-eight.

# 15.

# "Like a Wanderer"

## Martha McBride (Knight Smith Kimball)

In mid-April 1858, when Johnston's army was "invading" Utah territory, Martha McBride Knight Smith Kimball, living with her daughter Adaline Belnap in Ogden, traveled south with the general exodus to Utah Valley for protection. However, after the danger had passed and the Belnaps returned to Ogden, Martha was not convinced that it was yet safe to venture northward and so stayed in Springville with her niece and nephew, Spicer and Myron Crandall. On July 19, 1859, she wrote to Adaline, "I have no fault to find to tell you all my feelings would be hard to do but feel some like a wanderer for truly I have not a home on the earth. I do not know where I shall go nor what I shall do. I have no one to look to but the Lord alone, and he is able to provide for all my wants. Therefore I trust in him and do not dispair."

This letter provides a certain insight into polygamy, for Martha was not a widow at the time but was married to Heber C. Kimball. However, her experience living as a plural wife in his family, sharing a house with three other women, was evidently difficult for her. As a result she could feel homeless, a wanderer. Once again we see that living under the principle often left women feeling isolated, and they turned to siblings and children for help, companionship, and housing.

Like Agnes Coolbrith and Delcena Johnson, Martha was a widow when Joseph Smith married her. She had been the wife of Vinson Knight, a prominent early Mormon bishop, and had seven children by him. As Smith had been a close friend of Vinson, the Mormon prophet's union with Martha was a modified Levirate relationship of sorts. After Joseph's death, she married Heber C. Kimball as a proxy wife, and in the Nauvoo temple chose Joseph Smith, not Knight, as her eternal companion. Though she was known as one of Kimball's wives, her marriage to him was somewhat distant, and as often happened when the ties of a polygamous marriage were not strong, she spent much of her life living with her children in Ogden, Circleville, and Santa Clara.

## I. Childhood

On March 17, 1805, Martha was born in Chester township, Washington County (now Warren County), New York, to Daniel McBride, a thirty-nine-year-old native of New York, and Abigail Mead, thirty-five, also from New York. Little is known of her parents, except that Daniel served as a minister in the Christian primitivist "Campbellite" movement. Martha was the last of nine children. Her first four siblings, John, Samuel, Daniel Jr., and James, had been born in 1788, 1789, 1791, and July 1793 in Stillwater, New York, twenty miles northeast of Albany. The McBrides then moved to Chester, some sixty-five miles north of Albany, where Margaret Ann was born in June 1794. She was followed by Hyrum (1798), Cyrus Gideon (1800), Reuben (1803), and finally Martha. Thus she was the baby in a family of seven older brothers and one sister. We know nothing further about her childhood. However, history has preserved one major event from her teenage years: her father died in Leroy, about thirty miles west of Palmyra, on September 1, 1823, when she was eighteen.

## II. Vinson Knight

On July 26, 1826, when she was twenty-one, Martha married Vinson Knight, a twenty-two-year-old Massachusetts-born farmer and druggist, and they lived in Perrysburg, New York, about twenty miles south of Buffalo. Vinson's widowed mother, Rizpah Lee Knight, apparently lived with them in their early married years. In Perrysburg, Vinson worked a farm, raising hemp and flax, tending maple trees, and breeding sheep, hogs, and geese. Eleven months after the marriage, on June 21, 1827, Martha's first child, Almira, was born. More daughters, Rizpah and Adaline, joined the Knight family on May 13, 1829, and May 4, 1831. A son, James Vinson Knight, was born on September 4, 1833.

## III. "Came and Tarrid with Vincen Nights"

In April and June 1833 four of Martha's siblings, Samuel, James, Margaret, and Reuben, were baptized Latter-day Saints and her mother was baptized on June 25 at Villanova, Chautauqua, New York. No doubt Martha and Vinson began investigating Mormonism at this time. According to family tradition, Martha was seriously ill when she first met Joseph Smith in spring 1833. Smith gave her a blessing in which he promised that she would live to "a good old age," and Vinson joked that either Smith or the doctor who had treated Martha had lied, for the doctor had given her five years at the most to live. So began a close personal friendship between Martha, Vinson, and the Mormon prophet.

Smith stayed at the Knight home a year later on March 22, 1834, as his diary records: "Came and tarrid with vincen nights in P Perrysburg Co - of

365

Cattaraugus -." Two days later Martha and Vinson were baptized. The rest of their lives would be immersed in Mormonism. They probably began immediately to prepare to gather with the Saints. In spring 1835 Vinson sold his property at great sacrifice, and in early June the Knights moved to Kirtland.

On June 24, 1835, Vinson wrote to his mother with the judgmental, tactless fervor of the new convert: "Now you think that your priests are holy ... I do know that the fondation you stand on is an abomination in the sight of God." For early Mormons, who were fleeing theological and ecclesiastical pluralism, there was no room for more than one true church in the pre-millennial latter days. His family news was not remarkable: "We are as well as usual ... Our children are blessed with the privelege of school and we are blessed with the privelege of going to meeting such as we never had before." On the same day the Knights received patriarchal blessings in Kirtland.

Their next child, Nathaniel Knight, was born on October 30, 1835. Almira was now eight, Rizpah six, Adaline four, and James two. On December 4 Joseph Smith had some financial dealings with Vinson at the Painsville Bank, and the two men would work together closely for the rest of Vinson's life. In the same month Vinson taught a grammar school with Sidney Rigdon, who also ordained Vinson an elder on January 2, 1836. Just a week and a half later, on the 13th, at a meeting of the high councils of Kirtland and Zion, Vinson was made a high priest and a counselor to Bishop Newel Whitney—a prominent church position. Martha undoubtedly received increased visibility as the wife of such a leader.

She first experienced the death of a child on October 31 when Nathaniel died at the age of ten months. Undoubtedly Martha endured a terrible ordeal. On January 2, 1837, she and Vinson both signed the Articles of Agreement for the Kirtland Safety Society Banking Company, and six days later Vinson spoke in the Kirtland temple. But their time in Kirtland was quickly coming to a close.

### IV. On the Banks of the Grand

In September Vinson traveled with Joseph Smith to Far West. After returning to Kirtland in December—in approximately spring 1838—he, Martha, and the children moved to Missouri. Unfortunately they arrived when the "Mormon War" of 1838 was beginning. They first settled in Caldwell County, perhaps in Far West. Vinson wrote, in a February 1839 letter to his brother-in-law, "I will attempt to answer your request by writing you some facts I receive[d] in the Co. of Caldwell the last day of May last about which time there was some men in the church that was disposed to do things that was not right."

The Knights soon moved north to Daviess County: "I then went into

Davis Co. and Prepared for to settle there being about 120 families of Mormons in the co. and about 140 of the old inhabitants." Other sources tell that Martha and Vinson settled in Adam-ondi-Ahman, and on June 28 Vinson was appointed acting bishop of the Adam-ondi-Ahman Stake. He bought the farm of a justice of the peace, Adam Black, which was evidently an extensive property. In his 1839 letter he wrote, "I was placed in as good a situation as any man in this statte to get a living." This is corroborated by Knight's Missouri redress petition, which describes one of the most valuable farms in Mormon Missouri. He listed as losses $3,500 in "improvements on lands and preemtion rights"; $4,000 in merchancise; $1,550 in hogs, oxen and cows; a grist mill worth $500; and $450 in boat, household goods, and moving expenses. Adaline later remembered playing on the banks of the Grand River in Adam-ondi-Ahman, gathering flowers, fruits, and nuts.

As bishop in a major Mormon settlement, Vinson was undoubtedly in the thick of the Missouri troubles and conflicts. According to some sources, he was associated with the Mormon para-military forces, the Danites, and as bishop received Danite plunder at "Diahmon" which he divided among church members. On August 9 he was part of a committee promising peace with the citizens of Mill Port, a community of non-Mormons near Adam-ondi-Ahman.

It was probably in these late summer and early fall months especially that Vinson became a fugitive in Missouri (possibly further evidence for his Danite connections). Martha later wrote,

> Vinson enjoid his usuel health untill we went to missourie and the scenes which he passed through thare I think together with the change of the climate some what impared his health for his life was sought for most of the time he was thare, which drove him to the necess{ity} of hiding him self where he could find a place some times it was in the hazel brush and some times in old barnes this {sene} of things continued untill we left missouri.

By February 1839 Vinson, and Mormons generally, had had enough turmoil, and when he wrote his letter to Cooper on February 3 and 8 from Spencerburg, Missouri, he was in transit:

> Dear Sir ... I have my family with me at this time and shall move into the state of Ill. as soon as I can. We are well and in very good spirits ... I was placed in as good a situation as any man in this statte to get a living but now am deprived of it all except my health and the faith I have in God that has created and preserved me thus far through life. I expect to go from here as soon as the river is navigatable. Where I shall stop I do not know, as yet, and I am of the opinion that all citizens of these U. States that do not know how to pity Mormons will some time know it.

The family was mentioned briefly: "My family are all well ... I and my companion send our best respects to her [his sister] and all in that place. V Knight."

When the Mormons were finally expelled from the state in early 1839, the Knights probably moved to Far West, then took part in the exodus, though the details of their journey are unknown. During these tumultuous times, Martha was pregnant, and her next child, Martha Abigail, was born on February 9 in Pike County, Missouri, which was bordered to the east by the Mississippi River. Almira was now eleven, Rizpah nine, Adaline seven, and James five.

### V. "Scenes of Sorrow and Afflictions"

In Illinois the Knights apparently settled in Quincy. A general conference was held there in May, at which Vinson was "appointed or received into the Church in full Bishopric." The Joseph Smith journal on June 17 shows that Knight accompanied the prophet, Sidney Rigdon, Hyrum Smith, and Bishop Newel Whitney as they inspected land for a new city. In the same month, acting as church agent, he bought land in Iowa, across the Mississippi, at a place that came to be known as Zarahemla. But by October 6 the Knights were in Nauvoo, for on that date Vinson was appointed bishop of the "lower ward," one of three in Nauvoo. The two-story Knight home, located near the corner of Kimball and Main streets, was reputedly the first red-brick house in the city.

We must imagine Martha continuing to fulfill the position of "bishop's wife" in Nauvoo, a demanding, if unofficial, calling sometimes known today as "the mother of the ward." As the bishop is responsible for the temporal welfare of the needy in a ward, this often puts a strain on the wife and family as they struggle to help provide for the poor. Converts newly arrived at Nauvoo from England or America frequently had no resources. A reference to Vinson in Joseph Smith's journal on October 15, 1839, reflects this constant influx of Mormons into the city: "Afternoon went to Quincy in company with Br Hiram J.[ohn] S. Fulmer and Bishop Knight – Quite a number of families moving in –." In an August 16, 1841, conference in Nauvoo, Vinson and Bishop Miller took a collection for the poor of the city.

Adaline Knight remembers an incident that shows how close her father was to Joseph Smith. On January 19, 1841, the children were at school when the door opened and Hyrum Smith and Vinson carried in the "limp form" of Joseph Smith. "The children all sprang to their feet for Bro. Joseph lay helpless in their arms, his head resting on his brother['s] shoulder, his face pale as death, but his eyes were open, though he seemed not to see things earthly." The unnamed teacher, who evidently had seen Smith in this state before, explained to his pupils that the prophet "was in a revelation." Vinson and Hyrum carried Joseph to his office above the school, where he dictated Doctrine and Covenants 124. In it the Knights are mentioned:

> Therefore I say unto you concerning my servant Vinson Knight, if he will do my will, let him put stock into that house [Nauvoo House] for himself and for his generation after him, from generation to generation, and let him lift up his voice, long and loud, in the midst of the people, to plead the cause of the poor and the needy ... Let his family rejoice and turn away their hearts from affliction, for I have chosen him and anointed him, and he shall be honored in the midst of his house.

In the same revelation Vinson was appointed Presiding Bishop: "And again I say unto you, I give unto you Vinson Knight, Samuel H. Smith, and Shadrach Roundy if he will receive it to preside over the Bishopric." However, it is not clear that Vinson ever functioned as Presiding Bishop. In addition to his ecclesiastical responsibilities, he also received civic positions in Nauvoo: in February he was selected as a member of the city council and as a member of the board of regents of the University of Nauvoo. Later in the year, on September 29, another son, Rodolphus Elderkin, was born to Martha and Vinson. Almira was now fourteen, Rizpah twelve, Adaline nine, James seven, and Martha Abigail two.

At about this time Joseph Smith taught Vinson the principle of patriarchal marriage, which he accepted, marrying a second wife, Philinda Clark Eldredge Merrick. According to family traditions, Martha was sitting in a grape arbor behind her house one evening when Vinson came home carrying a basket and explained to her that he had taken fruit and vegetables to a widow, Philinda Merrick, whose husband, Levi, had been killed in the Haun's Mill Massacre. This was not extraordinary, as Vinson the bishop would often perform such missions of mercy to widows. But "He also explained to her that he had been told to enter Plural Marriage. That if he had to, this Sister Merrick would be the one he could help best. He must have been greatly relieved when Martha replied, 'Is that all?'" Vinson was subsequently sealed to Philinda.

On February 14, 1842, Vinson wrote to his mother in Cattaraugus, New York, giving a portrait of Martha and family in early Nauvoo:

> My family are in good health at this time. The children are all glad to hear from Grandmother and all of their relatives. Almyra is a good girl. She is a great help to her mother. We have no reason to complain at any of our children. They are a good and peaceable family and as soon as they have come to the age to become accountable they are desirious to move in the path that their parents have set for them ... They are all members of the church that are over eight years old. It has not been my persusasion but

it has been their desires ... Martha and all the children send their love to you. Rodolphus E grows finely. The children all love him and sometimes cry to hold him ... you would say that he was a fine boy. V. Knight

Vinson continued to be part of Joseph Smith's loyal inner circle. On June 6, 1841, when Smith was arrested, he chose Vinson as a member of his bodyguard. Smith called on him on March 9, 1842. One month later, in a session attended by Smith, Vinson received the first degree of Masonry, and four days later he was raised "to the sublime degree of Master Mason." In addition, he signed a statement published on July 20 that upheld Smith's moral character and characterized John C. Bennett's sensational accusations as slanders. On May 11 Joseph called at the Knight home again and dictated several letters. During the same time period all we know specifically of Martha is that on March 17 she attended the organization of the Female Relief Society of Nauvoo.

However, on approximately July 24 Martha and her children received a devastating blow when Vinson fell seriously ill. The only known symptom of this illness was excessive vomiting, so he may have contracted dysentery, but family traditions refer to typhoid fever. Martha, in her 1845 letter, wrote,

> We came from thare [Missouri] to illinois whare we now {are} this being a s{ick}ly place and the fatigue hardships and exposeuers through which he [Vinson] had just passed was to much for him he was soon taken sick a vomiting it was in the morning and he vomited untill evening and could get no relief all though the docter had stood over him about four or five hours constantly he was ~~much {exhausted} and I thought he could not live untill morning I then sent for president joseph smith~~.

The Smith diary for July 31 records: "Bro Knight has been sick about a week and this morning he began to sink very fast untill 12 o clock when death put a period to his sufferings." Martha had lost her first husband. But she could not grieve in peace, for two of her children were also seriously ill, and one would die. In her 1845 letter she apologized to her mother-in-law for not writing, pleading

> the cares of my family which pressed heavily upon me after Vinson's death for Martha and Rodolphus were both sick and for four or five weeks after Vinson's death I scarcely had my clothes off. Rodolphus died the third day of September I then found my self almost worn out with the trouble and fatigue these things together with the continued persecutions of our enimes and many other things to numerous to mention has prevented my writing before and now dear mother you said you would like to hear some particulars about vinsons sickness and death but how shall I begin to describe to you the scenes of sorrow and afflic-

tions that I have passed through[h] with him it causes my bosom to heave and tears steal down my cheaks.

The Wasp reported the cause of Rodolphus's death as "quick consumption."

## VI. Joseph Smith

Martha, now a widow, supported herself by renting the downstairs of her house to George Grant, and she and Almira sewed. But she would not be single long. In August 1842, within a month of Vinson's death, she married Joseph Smith, with Heber C. Kimball performing the ceremony, according to an affidavit she signed later in her life and her obituary. She was thirty-seven at the time and Smith was thirty-six. Clearly, part of his motivation in marrying her was the close bond he felt with Vinson, and so this union can be considered ideologically Levirate, though biological brothers were not involved. We know virtually nothing about what Martha's and Joseph's married life was like, and little is known about Martha's life in Nauvoo from the time of Vinson's death to Joseph's. Certainly she was introduced into the sisterhood of the prophet's wives; we can see a hint of this when Eliza R. Snow wrote on September 23, 1842, "Last evening spent at sister Knights."

Sadly, one of the few recorded events in Martha's life during the next two years was the death of five-year-old Martha Abigail Knight on March 24, 1844, a victim of measles. After this loss, Martha was left with Almira, seventeen, Rizpah fifteen, Adaline thirteen, and James eleven. Almira began to sew for Sylvester Stoddard, a tinsmith who had worked with Vinson. A widower in his early forties, Sylvester was bitterly opposed to the doctrine of polygamy and tried to influence Almira to reject polygamy also. At the same time he began to court her. Other men were also interested in Martha's oldest daughter. According to family traditions, one day Joseph Smith called on his plural wife and asked her if Almira would consent to become a plural wife of Hyrum (a typical polygamous proposal, delivered unromantically through two intermediaries). Martha agreed to discuss the matter with Almira, but when she did, the teenager refused the proposal.

On June 27 Smith was killed. Before he was buried, Martha asked for a lock of his hair, which she kept in a locket and treasured throughout her life. It had been a brutal half year for Martha; she had lost a husband and a child in six months, just as she had two years earlier.

## VII. Heber C. Kimball

Again Martha did not remain a widow long, for on October 12 she married Heber C. Kimball for time. She was thirty-nine, while he was forty-three. Living as a wife in Kimball's large family was not an easy task, as we have seen. The challenge of giving so many women emotional attention and financial help was aggravated in Heber's case by his deep attachment to his first wife, Vilate, who herself accepted polygamy only with great reluctance. In addition, he was an important church leader during enormously difficult times, including the exodus to Utah, and his church position undoubtedly demanded much of his time. So Martha's marriage to Heber was never a close, intimate relationship.

Another marriage would soon create a painful crisis for her. On November 10 Almira, seventeen, married Sylvester Stoddard secretly, knowing that Martha would never consent to the union. She stopped at her mother's house to tell her of the marriage and to bid her goodbye as she and Sylvester were departing en route to Akron, Ohio. Martha could do nothing but grieve as she saw her daughter leave the city and the church. Despite the distressing circumstances, Martha had reached a milestone—she was entering a long grandmotherly period of her life.

On July 8, 1845, Martha wrote to her mother-in-law, Rizpah Knight, giving her the details of Vinson's death quoted above. The letter reveals Martha the affectionate daughter-in-law:

> Mother I wish you w{ould} write to me as often as you can aford to and if you can read this we will write more  the crops of all sorts in these parts are doing well ^and^ bid fair for {a} plentiful harvest much wheat is all ready harvested and things with us are verry prosperous at present {the} c^h^ildren sends their love to grand Mother  my folks are five miles from me on the other side of the river they are all well as usual and if they ware here they would send their re^s^pects to you I will now bid you adieu for the present I am your affection^ate^ daughter until death. [to] Rizpah Knight [from] Martha Knight

As 1845 neared its end, Martha, like all faithful Mormons, performed ordinances in the temple, then prepared to face the wilderness. On December 19 she received her endowment, then three marriages followed. On December 21 Adaline married Gilbert Belnap at the tender age of fourteen; Gilbert was one day short of twenty-four. Despite Adaline's youth, the marriage would endure. Then, on the fifth day of the new year, Rizpah, seventeen, married Andrew Smith Gibbons. Though Martha now was part of a large extended household, she had only thirteen-year-old James left in her immediate family. Finally, on January 26 she was sealed to Joseph Smith for eternity and to Heber C. Kimball for time in the Nauvoo temple. Some widows whom Smith married were sealed to their first husbands in the temple, but Martha evidently chose the Mormon prophet as her eternal companion, not Vinson.

## VIII. On the Banks of the Missouri

The Mormons left Nauvoo in February 1846 and began to travel across Iowa to Winter Quarters on the Missouri River. Martha was apparently delayed in starting this journey, while her daughters and sons-in-law went on ahead, so she traveled across Iowa by herself. She left Nauvoo on March 26, was at Mt. Pisgah on June 7, and arrived at Cutler's Park, a few miles west of Winter Quarters, on July 5. There she lived in a wagon until Gilbert made her a log cabin next to his own. In December the Cutler's Park inhabitants moved to Winter Quarters. Here, on "a beautiful bench of table land bordering the river," a frontier city was erected, some 700 log cabins with streets at right angles in typical Mormon fashion.

In December a ward was organized at Winter Quarters. In a record of members' supplies, Martha's possessions were listed as "2 wagons, 4 yoke of oxen and 3 cows." She was comparatively well fitted out for a widow, as many families in the record had no wagons, oxen, or cows at all. On December 26 Rizpah bore a daughter, Martha Sarah Gibbons; as Almira apparently never had children, Martha, forty-one, was now a grandmother. Another grandchild, Gilbert Rosel Belnap, was born at Winter Quarters on January 8, 1847. Martha herself was expecting a child by Heber Kimball at this time.

In the early months of 1847 a "Sister Knight" appears repeatedly in Patty Sessions's journal, and as she is associated both with Heber Kimball and Joseph Smith, she is probably Martha. Patty apparently documents the birth of Martha's only child by Heber Kimball on January 13, when Martha was forty-two. The next day Patty wrote, "Put sister Knight to bed miscariage yesterday." The following month Martha became very sick, a common experience in Winter Quarters. On February 10 Patty stayed out all night with a delivery, then "came home eat breakfast then went to get some one to take care of sister Knight traveled around till afternoon Eliza Mitchel said she would take care of her I came home very tired Br Kimbal said he would say for himself and in behalf of Joseph that I had done my part for her."

In three weeks Martha was staying with Presendia Huntington Kimball; on March 1 Patty wrote, "[V]isited with sister Knight at sister Buels." By the 3rd Martha was no longer bedridden: "Visited sick sister Buel and Knight were visiting." Martha would continue to have a warm friendship with Patty in Utah.

In the spring Brigham Young asked for volunteers to help scout the way west to the Saints' new gathering place in the Rockies, and Martha's two sons-in-law immediately threw their hats into the ring. According to family traditions, Brigham was appreciative but said to them, "You both surely cannot go, leaving Mother Martha Knight ... and the two young women [their wives] practically as widows upon the hands of the few men left behind." Brigham suggested that one go west, and the other stay behind. When the young men were unable to agree who would remain, Brigham suggested that they cast lots. The lot fell to Andrew, who left with the "pioneers," the first group to Salt Lake Valley, in early April 1847. On June 17 Martha's mother set off west in the next company with Martha's brother Samuel; at seventy-seven, Abigail McBride was the oldest person in the company.

Martha and her family stayed in Iowa through 1850. Gilbert obtained a job as a carriage maker in Fremont, fifty miles from Kanesville, and Adaline had a second child there, John, on May 11, 1849. Rizpah, however, stayed in Kanesville where she had another child on April 3, 1849. Perhaps Martha divided her time between Rizpah and Adaline.

### IX. "She Saw Her Body as It Lay ..."

On June 15, 1850, Martha, forty-five, with James, seventeen, and the Belnaps left Kanesville and started the overland journey to Utah in the Jonathan Foote hundred, the William Wall fifty, and the Gilbert Belnap ten. The journey became tragic when a plague decimated the Belnap company a week after leaving Winter Quarters and Adaline lost little John. However, the Knights and Belnaps arrived in the Salt Lake Valley on September 17 where Martha no doubt had a joyful reunion with her brother Samuel and her mother. She also reunited with Heber Kimball.

After she and her party had stayed in Salt Lake for two weeks, Brigham Young sent Gilbert to help settle the Ogden area, and Martha and James accompanied the Belnaps on this expedition. In Ogden they forded the Weber River "about where the Bamberger bridge is now built," entered the old Goodyear Fort, and settled on the south side of Canfield Creek, modern Madison and Sullivan streets, at the bottom of a hill. Shortly thereafter Martha was riding with Gilbert in an ox-led wagon as they came down the hill from the northern part of the village. Adaline Belnap wrote that "the oxen could not hold the wagon and began to run, throwing Martha Knight beneath the wheel which ran over her. Leaving her lifeless body face downward in the dust." Gilbert ran back, picked her up, and brought her to the Belnap home, a primitive "doughout," where concerned neighbors joined family and Martha slowly revived. She then related an out-of-body experience: "The singular part of it all," Martha said, "[was] that she saw her body as it lay in the dust, and at the house as if she was standing to one side with the rest of the people looking on."

In Ogden's early days there were frequent conflicts with Native Americans. As Gilbert had been assigned a military position, he was often absent. Adaline remembers a difficult struggle for survival in those days: "I have been so hungry I couldn't see across the room and I could span the waist of my baby I was nursing. My little boys were like skeletons; it would make you cry to look at them."

Meanwhile Rizpah and Andrew Gibbons had settled in Salt Lake, then in Bountiful, then moved to southern Utah and St. Johns, Arizona, so Martha did not see this daughter as frequently as she did Adaline. Almira, on the other hand, was entirely out of touch with her Utah relatives, not even answering Martha's letters to her. Martha evidently moved back to Salt Lake at some point, or perhaps she divided her time between Ogden and Salt Lake. On March 18, 1851, Patty Sessions wrote, "Sisters Smith and Knights here on a visit  sister Knights staid all night." Martha visited again on September 8, 1852. In the 1851 census, taken in the first half of the year, Martha, listed as "Martha Knights," age forty-six, born in New York, is living with her brother Samuel in Davis County. Also living in the household were Lemira, Samuel's wife; three teenage children (including James seventeen); and Abigail McBride, Martha's mother, age eighty-one. So Martha was not living under Heber C. Kimball's care at this time. Her living arrangements in Utah are often difficult to trace, as her marriage to Heber never seems entirely solid. A family history states that Heber would come to see her occasionally in Ogden, and sometimes she apparently lived in a Kimball home in Salt Lake City.

On June 26, 1852, Gilbert Belnap married Henrietta McBride, a daughter of Martha's brother James, so, as often happened, the children of Joseph Smith's wives also entered into polygamy. In 1853 Gilbert sold his farm and built a small adobe house on "lots five and six, block eleven" of Ogden City. He helped found Fort Limhi on the Salmon River in central Idaho in 1855 while serving as a missionary to the "Lamanites," then returned to Weber County in 1857 and eventually settled in Hooper, west of Ogden. He subsequently became bishop of the Hooper Ward, sheriff of Weber County, and a director of the Hooper Irrigation Company. Though Martha often visited Rizpah in southern Utah, James in central Utah, and her brothers, she lived most often in her later life with the Belnaps in Ogden and Hooper. She was probably present at the death of her eighty-four-year-old mother in Ogden on March 12, 1854.

Martha soon became involved in the Relief Society. On January 6, 1856, when the first society was formed in Weber County at the Council House on Tabernacle Square, Martha was sustained as first counselor to President Delilah Pierce Palmer. "She and her daughter Adaline were active in assisting in the relief of the suffering at all times," her obituary tells us. Aside from her Relief Society work, as an organizational leader and as a minister to the afflicted, Martha also became known for her sewing. According to her obituary, "Her needlework was a model for fineness

amongst all her acquaintances for the past fifty years." She was an om-
nivorous reader, as well, "particularly of the daily papers, reading every
word of telegraphic news, and during the Spanish-American War she
was regarded as one of the best posted persons in Weber County on the
military operations of the contending forces."

On September 2, 1856, Martha evidently made a visit to Salt Lake
City. Patty Sessions wrote, "Sisters M Hyde Violate Kimball Knight &
Sylvia & Phebe Walton all here & Lucinia Marry had a good visit." Here
we see Martha associating with Kimball's first wife, Vilate. According to
one account by a sister-wife, Adelia Wilcox Kimball, in 1856 and 1857
Martha was living in a Kimball home in the city, a small house filled with
children that she shared with Adelia, Lucy Walker Smith Kimball, Sarah
Ann Whitney Smith Kimball, and Ellen Sanders Kimball. But Martha must
not have lived long in this household. On January 13, 1857, she was in
town visiting Patty Sessions again.

In the same year, when the Utah war threatened, Martha and the Belnaps moved to Utah Valley. In 1859 she was still living with her niece
and nephew in Springville, where she wrote the letter referred to earlier. Later that year she moved to Fillmore in central Utah for four
months, staying with her brother Samuel. Then she traveled south to live
with Rizpah and Andrew in Santa Clara, near St. George, arriving there
on March 10, 1860. On April 19 she wrote to Adaline in Ogden: "Found
them [Rizpah and Andrew] ... in rather hard circumstances like yourselves. ... It would give me great pleasure if my children were not scattered so far apart." Though she enjoyed staying with her daughter, she
was nine miles from St. George and three miles from any neighbors, so
felt somewhat isolated, but she stayed in Santa Clara through the fall of
1861. By April 10, 1863, she was in Springville, living with Reuben
McBride and his wife Mary Ann, and by May 22, 1864, she was once
again in Santa Clara. After that, at some point, she returned to Ogden.

On June 22, 1868, Heber C. Kimball died in Salt Lake City, and
Martha was entirely a widow. The death was soon balanced by the
promise of new life—on August 22 James married Celestial Roberts.

## X. Reunion with Almira

The Belnaps moved from Ogden to Hooper in 1868, and Martha followed them the next year. The 1870 census shows "Martha Knight," age
sixty-five, living in Weber River Valley, Weber County, in her own
household close to the "Belknaps." In October 1871, when she was
sixty-six, an Endowment House record shows her doing temple work:
"Martha McBride Smith" stood proxy for a dead McBride woman being
sealed to Hyrum Smith, with Joseph F. Smith standing proxy for his father.

In 1874 Gilbert Belnap was sent on a mission to the eastern states and made a special trip to Akron, Ohio, to reopen communications with Almira. Sylvester Stoddard had died on August 18, 1867, and Almira afterwards remarried a George Hanscomb. She received Gilbert coolly, as she blamed him for taking most of her family west, but she did write Martha a short letter soon thereafter. It criticized Gilbert and polygamy pointedly but was still signed, "your afectionate daughter":

> I was glad he [Mr. Belnap] returned here this way. You cannot expect that I enjoyed his visit over & above for you know that he was a stranger to me. & I never can like him for he has robed my Sister & her family of their just dues by dividing his substance between more than the law allows & what is still wors divided affection worse than none at all it would have killed me in a vary little time but God spared me my heart bleeds for her. I am no Mormon & much less a Polygamist. write soon from your afectionate daughter of Hanscom

Not a letter to warm a Mormon mother's heart, but at least the lines of communication were now open. On April 5, 1875, Almira, in Kirtland, wrote Martha again. From her letter we conclude that Martha was beginning to have health problems: "Dear Mother: ... I was glad to hear that you are all well ... I think you are highly favored to be able to walk as well as you say you can  it is a blessing to be thankful for." Martha and Almira shared a common interest: sewing. The daughter sent a pattern with her letter, which was sprinkled with technical advice: "A dress made in that way either double or single is easy to wear & to get on & off especially when sick or not feeling vary well. it will look well made with belt & bows of the same material as the dress set up the front & fastened with hooks & eyes it would save working or binding buttonholes & covering buttons also collar cuffs & pocket of the same with one or two rows of alpaca cut bias stitched on each edge." Martha was still sewing, and Almira was carrying on her mother's tradition.

After the St. George temple was completed in 1877, Martha traveled south to spend years there as a regular temple worker. She was present at the temple's dedication on April 4. In February 1878 she did ordinance work with her daughter Rizpah, as is clear from a letter written to Martha by Reuben McBride from Fillmore: "Old Sister Caling Said you wanted I S[h]ould Come down and bring plenty of provisions and a big donation for the temple Bro Andrews and wife Staid here going and Comeing they Said you had got about through with the names you had and wanted more about this time Jann and Martha Carter came here and said you had gone to Rizpahs I Suposed you was there untill I got your letter." Reuben explained that he had already been "taxed on the Temple" and had paid his "Assesment," though it was "dreadfull hard for the People here to pay their Tax on the temple." He agreed that the McBride family temple work belonged to Martha and himself, "as we are the only ones liveing of our Fathers Family who will officiate for our Dead it is your duty to officiate for our female Relitives and me for our male Relitives ... Give my respects to Rizpah ... I will send you $2.00 which will pay for all the oil [ceremonial oil for anointing] you have used and more too."

Reuben wrote again in April 1878, addressing the letter to "Martha Knight, Circleville, Piute Co, Utah." Circleville, where James and Celestial now lived, was a small town midway between Fillmore and Cedar City, in southern Utah. "Dear Sister Martha I received your letter a few weeks a go I see by that you did not get my letter till you got to Rizpahs ... I was very glad you done as much [temple] work as you did Employ who you are a mind to, it belongs to you as much as me to see too, the more you can do the better ... If you go with James to St George let me know before you go if you can[,] give my Respects to Andrew & Rizpah and folks ... Your Bro Reuben McBride." On November 29 Reuben wrote again, asking for Martha's genealogy and temple work records. Travelling gamely at age seventy-three, she made her way northward to spend Christmas with Adaline and Gilbert in Hooper.

In 1880 Almira, with her husband, George, rode the "cars" from Ohio to Ogden, Utah, and—some thirty-three years after the painful parting in Nauvoo—Martha and her errant daughter were re-united. Despite their religious differences, it must have been a joyful meeting.

In a July 31 letter to Martha, Reuben was again concerned about genealogy and temple records. He encouraged his sister (now seventy-five) to write to Cyrus in Dundee, Michigan, and sent his respects to "Martha and family." In 1881 and 1882 Martha kept house for her grandson, Gilbert Belnap Jr., in Ogden.

Reuben wrote again on Christmas Day 1886: "My Dear Sister Martha I was So glad to here from you I got your letter too day ... Oh how glad I would be to see you I have not means to go on the train if I had and my health would admit I should see Logan Hooper Ogden Tooele Springhill and Salt Lake City ... Tell that Big Sheriff Belnap if he can leave his Business long enough to come and See us he would have a Harty welcome here Good Bye, R. McBride." Such letters give a sense of Martha living principally with the Belnaps in Ogden. According to family history, they now had a large house and Martha was given a spacious room to herself: "The furnishings were her personal things, which she enjoyed very much."

Almira, sixty-one, wrote again from the East on June 10, 1888, and her letter offers a window into the life of Martha as grandmother, surrounded by grandchildren:

Dear Mother ... Whare is <u>Rizpah</u> & how is she getting alonge you did not give me the age of James last baby. You say <u>Adalines</u> boys have all left home is <u>Amasy</u> married let me know if you get the package I send. the spring so far has been rather cool & dry which make vegetation backward here. do you have plenty of fruits & what kinds. <u>I was sorry to here you had been sick</u> hope you & all are well Almira

Thus Martha at eighty-three was still sewing, her health problems continued or increased, and she had grandchildren who had grown to adulthood. When Reuben McBride died in Fillmore on February 26, 1891, age eighty-seven, Martha was the last living sibling from her family.

### XI. "Your Loving Granddaughter Daisy Knight"

The next year, soon after January 5, 1892, Martha received a letter from fourteen-year-old Daisy Knight, one of James's children. Through it, we see Martha the affectionate grandmother:

Dear Grandma I set me down to write a few lines to you. We received your kind and welkom letter in due time We are all well at present and hope this will find yu the same. I was very sorry to hear you had poor helth but hope you will get better soon Pa is better than he was Vinson [seventeen years old] and him has gon to meeting. Almira [eleven] and Sammie [five] went to Sunday School this morning It is very cold to-day and has been for about a week. Grandpa has gon back to Salt lake he started Friday Aunt Maria and family is well. Our Bishop is very sick again and has been for about four weeks but is getting a little better We had a first strait [first rate] Christmas and New years There has been quite a little sickness there has been three deaths this year and a little baby just before Christmas. Samuel wants you to write something about him he said he was going to write to you as soon as he can I will close hoping that you will be blessed with helth and long life rite soon and often as you can Give my love to Aunt Adline and Uncle Gilbert and family and escept the same your self Your Loving Granddaughter Daisy Knight Circlevally Piute Co. Utah

Later that year, on December 4, 1892, Daisy wrote again:

Dear grandma I guess you think that we will never write to you any more, well it has been a long time ... Give my love to Aunt Adline and Uncle Gilbert and Lola and the rest of the folks. And with this I will Close I am getting tired May you ever be blessed and be happy and long life and do good Do you remember weather Joseph Smith told you weather the three rings on the book of Mormon was on the back or the front of the book? Do you know weather Lehi had any dauters and what theire names was or weather they was older or younger than Nephi If you know pleas tell me write son [soon] and tell me all the News.

On March 17, 1895, Rizpah died in St. Johns, Apache, Arizona. Though the event would have saddened Martha, her daughter had nevertheless lived a full life. If genealogical records are correct, she had fifteen children, of whom seven lived to maturity. Daisy and Celestial Knight wrote another letter to Martha on August 17, 1895, which ended, "Give my love to Aunt Adline and family and except the same your self all sends their love to Grandma." On September 16, 1896, nineteen-year-old Daisy married Samuel Dutson. Two years later, on July 25, she wrote Martha again:

> Dear Grandmamma ... I was sory to hear you have been sick, but hope you are well now ... Last Thursday was mine and Aubrey's [James Aubrey, thirteen] birthday. To day was a Sunday School Union to Junction 5 miles from here but only Vi[n]son went. We are doing real well with our store and have 8 yong calfs 40 yong chickings and more a hatching 5 young pigs 1 little cat ... I must stop for it is getting dark write soon as posable From loving Granddaughter Daisy

On March 17 of the same year, a family reunion honored Martha on her ninety-third birthday. According to her obituary, "Mrs. Knight was called on for a speech, and prefaced one of considerable length with a recital of the tremendous changes which had taken place in her lifetime, mentioning the steam engine, the modern printing press and the telegraph." Much had indeed changed since the first decade of the nineteenth century.

Finally there is a letter from Almira dated December 12, 1898 which informs us that Martha could not write for herself any more: "Dear Mother ... I hope to hear that you are still in comfortable health. My health is better ... I would like very much to have some one of Brother James family write and tell me all about themselves, that would relieve Lola from writing so much when she answers yur letters for you."

## XII. Death

On November 20, 1901, at 5:00 a.m., Martha died peacefully in Hooper at the age of ninety-six, due to "old age." After a funeral in the Hooper meeting house, she was buried in the Ogden City Cemetery in the Belnap plot, next to her mother.

Louisa Beaman (Smith Young).
(*Courtesy Utah State Historical Society.*)

Zina Diantha Huntington (Jacobs Smith Young)
with her three children, Zebulon Jacobs, Henry Chariton Jacobs, and
Zina Presendia Young (Williams Card). The photograph may have been
taken about 1855, when the children were thirteen, nine, and five, and
Zina was thirty-four. *(Courtesy Harold B. Lee Library,*
*Special Collections.)*

Zina with daughter,
Zina Presendia Young (Williams Card).
(*Courtesy Utah State Historical Society.*)

Presendia Lathrop Huntington (Buell Smith Kimball)
(left) with her sister Zina. (*Courtesy Daughters
of Utah Pioneers.*)

Presendia, older.
(*Courtesy Utah State Historical Society.*)

Agnes Moulton Coolbrith
(Smith Smith Smith Pickett).
(*Courtesy RLDS Church Archives.*)

Agnes, older.
(*Courtesy Josephine DeWitt Rhodehamel.*)

Josephine Smith (Carsely),
Agnes's daughter, who
later gained fame as a
California poetess
under the penname
"Ina Coolbrith."
(*Courtesy Oakland
Public Library*)

Patty Bartlett (Sessions Smith Parry)
(*Courtesy Utah State Historical Society.*)

Sylvia Porter Sessions
(Lyon Smith Kimball Clark).
(*Courtesy Clark Layton*.)

Josephine Rosetta
Lyon [Smith] (Fisher),
daughter of Sylvia.
Though raised as the
daughter of Windsor
Lyon, Josephine left an
affidavit affirming that
Sylvia told her that
she was actually the
daughter of Joseph
Smith. (*Courtesy
Clark Layton*.)

Mary Elizabeth Rollins
(Lightner Smith Young).
(*Courtesy Utah State
Historical Society.*)

Marinda Nancy Johnson
(Hyde Smith). (*Courtesy Utah
State Historical Society.*)

Elizabeth Davis (Goldsmith Brackenbury Durfee Smith Lott); possible photograph of Elizabeth, found in the effects of Benjamin Blanchard Brackenbury, her son, at his death. (*Courtesy Ethel Jo Christopherson.*)

Sarah Maryetta Kingsley (Howe Cleveland Smith Smith). (*Possibly not an authentic portrait; owner of original not known.*)

Delcena Diadamia Johnson (Sherman Smith Babbitt). *(Owner of original photograph not known.)*

Almera Woodward Johnson (Smith Barton). *(Owner of original photograph not known.)*

Eliza Roxcy Snow (Smith Young), probably Nauvoo period. *(Courtesy Utah State Historical Society.)*

Eliza, older. *(Courtesy Utah State Historical Society.)*

Martha McBride (Knight Smith Kimball).
(*Courtesy Weber State University, Stewart Library.*)

Emily Dow Partridge (Smith Young)
with son Joseph Don Carlos Young and (apparently)
Josephine Young (Young), photograph taken about 1863.
(*Courtesy Utah State Historical Society.*)

Emily, older.
(*Courtesy Utah State
Historical Society.*)

Eliza Maria Partridge
(Smith Lyman).
(*Painting by Sutcliffe Maudsley,
Nauvoo period; courtesy
Salt Lake City Daughters
of Utah Pioneers.*)

Eliza Partridge, older.
(*Courtesy Salt Lake City
Daughters of Utah
Pioneers.*)

Lucy Walker (Smith Kimball).
*(Courtesy Salt Lake City Daughters of Utah Pioneers.)*

Helen Mar Kimball
(Smith Whitney).
(*Courtesy Utah State
Historical Society.*)

Elvira Annie Cowles
(Holmes Smith).
(*Owner of original photograph
not known.*)

Rhoda Richards
(Smith Young).
(*Courtesy Salt Lake City*
*Daughters of Utah*
*Pioneers.*)

Desdemona Catlin
Wadsworth Fullmer
(Smith Benson McLane).
(*Owner of original*
*photograph not known.*)

Melissa Lott
(Smith Bernhisel Willes).
*(Courtesy Richard
Van Wagoner.)*

Melissa, older.
*(Courtesy Richard
Van Wagoner.)*

# 16.

# Gardener's Wife

## *Ruth Daggett Vose (Sayers Smith)*

On July 16, 1844, Ruth Vose Sayers, who had been residing in Nauvoo with her husband, Edward, was in Boston visiting her aunt Polly. On that date Wilford Woodruff wrote, "I called upon Sister [Polly] Voce 57 Temple St. Saw Sister Ruth Sayers who was with her. She also received a letter from her husband this day Date Nauvoo June 30th & still confirmed the death of Joseph and Hiram Smith." So Ruth had learned of the prophet's death. On the following day Brigham Young arrived in Boston, and Wilford took him to 57 Temple Street. There Wilford, with the unthinkable news confirmed, veiled his face and wept. "After being bathed by a flood of tears I felt composed," he wrote. Perhaps Ruth witnessed this memorable scene. But undoubtedly she grieved for Smith also, for though she had been married to Edward Sayers since 1841, and still was married to him, she had also married Joseph Smith in 1843.

Ruth is one of Smith's more obscure wives, and we have only a very skeletal biography of her. She was a polyandrous wife, and her "first husband," the apparently non-Mormon Edward Sayers, is also poorly documented. She was not a prominent Mormon woman but was still a good friend of many elite Latter-day Saints. Characterized as a captivating conversationalist, she was known for her generosity in church causes and for her service to the sick and poor. She had no children, so there are no family histories of her. A short letter to Brigham Young, two obituaries, and a few scattered diary entries provide what little we know of her life.

### I. "She Donated Every Dollar She Earned"

Ruth was born on February 26, 1808, to Mark and Sally Vose, in Watertown, Norfolk, Massachusetts, just west of Boston. She had one sibling, Daniel Vose, "who was her pride, and of whom she was devotedly fond," Emmeline Wells writes. An aunt, Polly Vose, was associated with Ruth throughout her life, and Ruth and she "were engaged in upholstering" in

Boston in her early Mormon years. This Polly is apparently Mary Vose, born in 1780, who converted to Mormonism on July 28, 1832, in Boston.

There are two conflicting witnesses to the date of Ruth Vose's baptism, both quite convincing. Emmeline Wells, writing after Ruth's death, gave the date May 1832, when Ruth was twenty-four—she would thus be a member of the group of Boston converts that included Agnes Coolbrith (Smith Smith Smith), Vienna Jacques (Smith?), Mary Bailey (Smith), Fanny Brewer, and Augusta Adams (Cobb Young Smith, posth.). Wells certainly knew Ruth well, so would seem reliable. Nevertheless, Brigham Young, in an 1836 missionary journal, wrote, "Sunday [August 14] I Preached in fore noon Elder e L. E. Johnson in afternoon I then returned to Boston I Baptized 2 Frances Smith and Ruth Vose." This is the right name and the right place, and a diary entry is generally the best evidence possible. Unless further data disprove this entry, we must conclude that Wells somehow erred. Perhaps Ruth was converted in 1832 but was not formally baptized until four years later.

Shortly before November 6, 1832, Joseph Smith visited Boston with Newel Whitney. At this time Ruth must have first met the prophet of her new church, who would later become her husband. According to Wells, she willingly contributed her means toward building the Kirtland temple (completed in March 1836): "During the building of the Kirtland Temple, although then residing in Boston, she donated every dollar that she earned, except what she needed for her bare support, towards its erection, which aggregated several hundred dollars." Wells adds that Ruth and Polly continued their donations "until the Prophet Joseph sent word to them, 'It is enough.'" One contribution of $150 from "Sister Vose," documented by Wilford Woodruff, reached Smith during Zion's Camp in 1834.

In August 1836, as we have seen, Ruth was baptized by Brigham Young. She and Aunt Polly helped with missionary work, and meetings were often held in their apartments. An 1838 journal entry by Woodruff has him preaching at a meeting held "in a room occupied by Sister Vose" at Myrtle Street No 9. Wells writes of Ruth and Polly that, "The Elders of the Church in traveling in the Eastern States were the recipients of their unbounded liberality."

Ruth experienced personal loss on June 15, 1839, when her brother Daniel was killed by Kookooche, a Seminole chief, near St. Augustine, Florida, during an Indian war. It would have been a tremendous blow for Ruth to lose her only sibling, to whom she was so closely attached.

## II. Edward Sayers

In 1841 the *Times and Seasons* published the following marriage notice: "MARRIED ... –In St. Louis, Mo. Jan. 23rd, by Elder A.P. Rockwood Mr. E. Sayers to Miss Ruth D. Vose, formerly of Boston, Mass." So Ruth had by this time traveled to the west and met a husband. Edward Sayers, son of Edward and Mary Sayers, had been born in England on February 9, 1802, and was described by Wells as a "thoroughly practical horticulturist and florist." He was nearly thirty-nine at the time of the marriage, while Ruth was almost thirty-three. Evidently, there were no children in this marriage. Edward's status with respect to the Mormon church is not completely clear. Wells seems to consider him a non-Mormon throughout his life, yet Joseph Smith, William Clayton, and Heber C. Kimball refer to him as "Brother Sayers," and he seems to be friendly with Smith. It is certain that after marrying Ruth he lived among Mormons till his death.

Ruth and Edward came to Nauvoo in 1841. The Aaronic priesthood census of spring 1842 has the "Sayyears" living in the Nauvoo 2nd Ward. By at least that time they were friends of Joseph Smith, for on May 18 he visited them: "Dined at Bro Benbows. visited Bro Sayres. &c." Edward was farming north of the city. On April 14 Ruth was received into the Nauvoo Relief Society, but she is not mentioned in the minutes after that date. One gathers that she was not an extremely charismatic woman but was rather unassuming, faithful, devoted.

### III. Joseph Smith

In August Joseph Smith was arrested for alleged complicity in the Lilburn Boggs shooting in Missouri, but he escaped arrest and went into hiding. On August 10 William Clayton, Smith's clerk, wrote that the Mormon leader and a few close companions had been conveyed up the Mississippi River in a skiff, then were landed below the "Wiggans' farm." "They then proceeded through the timber to Brother Sayers' house where they were very kindly received and made welcome." On the 13th Emma, with other friends of Joseph, visited. Clayton wrote, "We soon arrived at brother Sayers and was pleased to find President Joseph in good spirits, although somewhat sick." Two days later Joseph's friends visited again and were concerned that he would be arrested, but he told them that he was not yet in danger. He finally departed on August 17.

As a result of this week-long visit, the Mormon leader undoubtedly came to know Ruth and Edward well, though he had been friendly with them before. Some six months later, in February 1843, Ruth was married to the prophet, with Hyrum Smith officiating, according to her own 1869 affidavit. As was usual in Smith's polyandrous marriages, she continued to live with Edward after the ceremony. What her marriage relationship to Smith was like and whether Edward knew about the marriage are entirely unknown. However, Edward does fit the pattern of a "first husband" who is a friend of Joseph Smith. The Mormon leader felt comfortable staying in Edward's house, and he had visited them before that stay.

### IV. Back to Nauvoo

On July 16, 1844, Ruth was in Boston visiting Polly, as we have seen, and Heber Kimball, Wilford Woodruff, and Brigham Young visited her. All grieved for their martyred leader. Ruth started her trip west in July. After a stop in New York, she arrived in Albany on July 24, travelling with Orson Hyde, Orson Pratt, and Wilford Woodruff. There they met Brigham Young, Heber Kimball, and Lyman Wight and began their homeward journey. Heber mentioned her on July 31, while they were on the *Hercules* bound for Chicago: "The mate seams to [too] mean. Found folt [fault] becaus [I] was kind to Sister Ruth Seayers, caused others to slite us. They have thare own folly." A somewhat cryptic entry. Ruth and the apostles arrived in Nauvoo on August 6.

### V. Boston

For unexplained reasons, the Sayerses departed for the East again soon after that. On August 27, 1844, Heber C. Kimball wrote in his journal, "Br. Seayers and his wife come to my hous. I gave them a reccormmend. Then went to the landing with them, as they took the steamer *Osprey* on thare way to Boston." Three weeks later he wrote a letter to Ruth, unfortunately not extant. As with so much historical evidence, these entries in Kimball's journal are not entirely understandable without further context. Why did Ruth and Edward receive a "recommend" immediately before boarding the steamer? What kind of a recommend was it? Why was Ruth continually making expensive and time-consuming journeys back to Boston? What was the connection between the Sayerses and Heber Kimball? None of these questions presently have good answers. Heber's reference to Edward as Brother Sayers is also worth noting. Perhaps Edward was so much a part of the social community that he seemed Mormon.

The Sayerses evidently stayed in Boston from 1844 to 1849. Perhaps Polly had health problems and was too ill to travel, and needed Ruth to tend her. Perhaps it was financially advantageous for Ruth to help her aunt in her prosperous upholstery trade. Or possibly Edward, as a non-Mormon, objected to traveling to the far western frontier. But all this is conjecture.

### VI. "Forgive Me, for Thus Troubling You"

After this long stay in Boston, Ruth and Edward reportedly traveled to Utah in 1849. We can only imagine their long, hard trip across the midwest and Rockies to Salt Lake City. Then we must visualize them struggling to survive in those difficult early years in Salt Lake Valley without proper housing in rain, snow, and freezing cold, and perhaps without adequate food. Aunt Polly may have helped them financially to some extent.

They are said to have lived first "on the corner afterwards known as the American Hotel Corner," presumably at Second South and 50 East. In 1850 they moved to the Twelfth Ward, just southeast of downtown, where they resided for the rest of their lives. In the census for that year, Edward's profession is recorded as gardener. On December 24 Ruth received a patriarchal blessing from John Smith, and on April 16, 1851, "Ruth Sayers Smith" was endowed in Salt Lake City in the Endowment House. She was washed and anointed (the preliminary part of the ordinance) by another plural wife of Smith, Presendia Huntington Kimball. Edward was not endowed that day, which would be consistent with the report that he was never a baptized Latter-day Saint.

In the fall of 1851 Ruth wrote a letter to Brigham Young, her only extant holograph. It shows that she was struggling economically in her early Utah years:

> Monday Morn President Young I again come to you asking to be obliged to you because no one else would render me any assistance unless they were that moment paid for it. Will you be kind enough to let me have a yoke of strong oxen, that I may get wood to be comfortable this winter I can pay for them in Furniture from the Birds Cabinet Shop or give you a note upon either of them if you choose. I did not get any money this autumn but have {evry} reason to expect some, when Br Little comes. The young man who hands this to you will get my wood if I can get the oxen. Those I had last year, one sickened I gave it to Br Atwood the other has been worked by some individual and is weakend and unable to get wood forgive me, for thus troubling you again. I was told not to ask you - To whom should I go but to the friend of the whole church, I feel that you know I would not a anoy you unless compelled to please give the young Man an answer and you will very much oblige your humble Servant R Vose Sayers

### VII. "I Lade Hands Upon Her & Blessed Her"

On September 7, 1856, Wilford Woodruff returned home from a general authority prayer circle to find two old friends waiting for him in his home: Ruth Sayers and Augusta Cobb (a plural wife of Brigham and, like Ruth, a Boston convert). Ruth, wrote Woodruff, "wished me to Bless her as she was going on her mission. I lade hands upon her & blessed her ... The spirit bore testimony that all should be right with her and that she should prosper on her journey & return in peace." Soon after this she set out eastwards with Parley P. Pratt and his family. Judging from Parley's journey, she left Salt Lake in September, reached Ft. Kearney, Iowa, on October 17, then passed through Illinois and saw the ruins of the Nauvoo temple. On November 18 she arrived in St. Louis. Parley stayed there a month, but Ruth probably went on ahead to Boston to be reunited with Aunt Polly and fulfill her "mission," whatever that was. Perhaps it was to convince Polly to return to Utah with her.

If so, she succeeded. In June 1857 the two women made the long trip back to Utah, arriving on June 23 after three weeks of travel. Wilford Woodruff and Apostle George A. Smith visited Edward and Ruth on July 1, and Wilford admired Edward's gardening: "He had a fine lot of Black & yellow wild Cu[] from Boston & Nauvoo bottoms." The following year, on March 28, Polly was sealed posthumously to Joseph Smith, so she and Ruth could look forward to being sister-wives in the eternities.

The 1860 census shows Ruth living with "Edwin" Sayer, a gardener, in the Twelfth Ward. But on July 17, 1861, Edward died. Ruth, at the age of fifty-three, was now fully a widow. Five years later, on December 9, 1866, Aunt Polly died at age eighty-six.

## VIII. "A Countenance Always Beaming"

The next two decades of Ruth's life are essentially undocumented, except for two census records. In 1870 "Ruth Sears," sixty-three, was living in the Twelfth Ward, "Keeping House," and ten years later "Ruth B. Sayers," age "72," was still "Keeping House." She probably continued her Relief Society activities, her temple work, and perhaps sewing, and continued to associate with other wives of Joseph and with friends such as Wilford Woodruff.

In the early part of June 1884 she became very ill. The sickness continued for some ten weeks, and on August 18 she died in Salt Lake City at age seventy-six. Her *Woman's Exponent* obituary provides an epitaph:

> Tall and erect in figure, [having] a countenance always beaming with human kindness, charitable to the poor and ever ready to comfort the disconsolate, she endeared herself to her associates. She was a woman of brilliant conversational powers and possessed a ready fund of valuable information ... She was never tired of dwelling upon Gospel themes and the days of Joseph and Hyrum. She has passed to her rest and joined those gone before whom she so reverenced in life; her record here was that of a brave and true Latter-day Saint.

As a case study in polyandry, the Ruth Sayers-Edward Sayers-Joseph Smith relationship fits the normal pattern we have found, with a friendly first husband (though a non-member, apparently); in addition, Smith's marriage to Ruth was preceded by his accepting hospitality in the Sayers home, a pattern also found in Lucinda Pendleton Harris's and Sarah Kingsley Cleveland's histories.

However, Ruth's late endowment, long after the Nauvoo temple experience, is atypical, as is the fact that there is no proxy sealing to Joseph Smith. Perhaps Ruth knew that if she was sealed to Smith in the temple, she would have to be married to the proxy, and she was reluctant to marry polyandrously again or to divorce Edward. And Edward, as a nonmember, could not stand proxy for the Mormon prophet. Perhaps Ruth was hoping that Edward would convert and thus be able to marry her for time, standing proxy for the dead prophet. Perhaps Edward was reluctant to convert for that very reason.

# 17.

# Daughter of the Pagan Prophet

## *Flora Ann Woodworth (Smith Gove)*

President Joseph told me that he had difficulty with E [Emma] yesterday. She rode up to Woodworths with him and called while he came to
the Temple. When he returned she was demanding the gold watch of F
[Flora]. He reproved her [Emma] for her evil treatment. On their return
home she abused him much and also when he got home. He had to use
harsh measures to put a stop to her abuse but finally succeeded.

S o wrote William Clayton in his journal on August 22, 1843. It is one
of the great ironies of Mormon polygamy that while so many "first
wives" in later church history supported their husbands when they took
plural wives, Emma was consistently implacable in her opposition to the
"principle." Even when she allowed him plural wives—the Partridges
and Lawrences—for a short period, she fought to keep him from spending time with them. Her anger was probably aggravated when her husband married without informing her, which he apparently generally did.
So she was quick to notice when he showed favor to any young woman.
Flora Ann Woodworth married Smith when she was sixteen and thus
was one of his youngest wives. What little we know about her marriage
shows the problems inherent in Nauvoo polygamy when a middle-aged
man married a teen secretly, as here. Flora's father was a close friend of
Smith, so we may regard this marriage as dynastic to some extent.

Flora is severely underdocumented—we do not even know her death
date or the names of her children by her second husband, Carlos Gove.
She did not come to Utah and may have died before reaching the age of
twenty. Her mother, Phebe, is also sparsely documented, but was certainly sealed to Joseph Smith after his death, which sometimes indicates
a union with him during his lifetime. If such occurred, the tie to the
mother would have been polyandrous and possibly dynastic, linking
Smith to Lucien. However, there is no positive evidence that Phebe married Smith before he died.

## I. Childhood

Flora Ann was born on November 14, 1826, in New York, the first child of Lucien Woodworth and Phebe Watrous. Phebe had been born in Sharon, Otsego County, New York, thirty miles west of Albany in eastern New York, on October 1, 1805. At least by late 1825, probably, she married Lucien, twenty-six, an architect and stone mason from Thetford, Orange County, in mideastern Vermont. At some point before late 1832, the Woodworths moved to Conneaut, Erie County, Pennsylvania, where they first made contact with the Mormons. On December 9 elders John F. Boynton and Zebedee Coltrin preached in a schoolhouse close to Girard, then, as Zebedee wrote, "we staid with Luchian Woodworth." Evidently Woodworth had been baptized previously. Phebe is frequently referred to in the journals of Evan Greene, another early missionary to Pennsylvania. The Woodworths subsequently joined the body of Mormons in Missouri where two of their children were born, Mary C. in approximately 1835 and John in 1839.

## II. Nauvoo

The Woodworths may have traveled from Missouri to Illinois with the main body of the Mormons in early 1839. At least, they were in Nauvoo by June 7, 1841, when Lucien, along with other close friends of Smith, accompanied him to Monmouth, forty miles northeast of the Mormon city, after he had been arrested by Governor Carlin. In spring 1842 Lucien, Phebe, Flora Ann, Mary, and John were living in the Nauvoo Fourth Ward, according to the Aaronic priesthood ward census. Flora Ann would have been fifteen at this time, Mary seven, and John three. On May 13 Phebe Woodworth was voted into the Nauvoo Relief Society, while Flora Ann attended the school of William Woodbury from September to December.

By early 1843 Lucien was serving as architect and construction foreman of the Nauvoo House. This hotel was a pet project of Smith's, so Lucien occupied an important position in the prophet's circle of advisors. On February 21 Lucien gave a speech defending construction of the hotel and apparently criticizing workers who asked for higher wages. Smith followed with a supportive speech: "Well the pagan prophet [Woodworth] has preached us a pretty good sermon this morning to break off the yoke of oppression. I don't know as I can better it much." It is not clear why Smith referred to Lucien as "pagan prophet," as it seems unlikely that he was non-Mormon at this time. But the nickname stuck.

## III. Joseph Smith

According to an affidavit by William Clayton, Joseph Smith married Flora Ann Woodworth in the spring of 1843. It is possible that the marriage took place on March 4, for in Joseph's journal for that day we find the following notation written in shorthand: "/ <Woodsworth> /." On other occasions Nauvoo Mormons used codes to record polygamous marriages, so it is possible, but not certain, that this entry recorded a marriage. However, if Smith did marry Flora on March 4, he married her on the same day that he married Emily Partridge. Flora was sixteen at the time, one of the Mormon leader's youngest wives. An important motivation for this marriage would have been the creation of a bond between Lucien and Smith, giving the Woodworths a link into Smith's eternal family. As is generally true of marriage, psychological and sexual attraction probably were also factors in the union. Flora Ann evidently became a favorite of Smith, for she appears with him frequently in Clayton's journal. As was discussed previously, Phebe's Nauvoo temple proxy marriage to Joseph Smith may indicate that she married him at this time also. But since there is no definitive evidence linking Phebe to Joseph during his lifetime, she must remain for the time being in the category of posthumous wives.

An incident recorded by Orange Wight that took place very soon after Flora's marriage to Smith illuminates some problematic aspects of their marital relationship. Orange, nineteen years old, had "in the spring of 1843" recently returned from a mission. On reaching Nauvoo he "concluded to lok [look] about and try to pick up one or more of the young Ladies before they were all Gone," according to his reminiscence. "So I commenced keeping company with Flora Woodworth—daughter of Lucien Woodworth—(called the Pagan Prophet)." One day Orange and Flora were walking on a street near Joseph Smith's home when the Mormon leader himself drove up in a carriage, stopped in front of them, and invited them to take a ride with him. One imagines Flora looking flushed, embarrassed, or rebellious.

> He opend the doore for us and when we were seated oposite to him he told the driver to drive on  we went to the Temple lot and many other places during the Afternoon and then he drove to the Woodworth house and we got out and went in—After we got in the house sister Woodworth took me in an other room and told me that Flora was one of Joseph's wives, I was awar or believed that Eliza R. Snow and the two Patrage Girls were his wives but was not informed about Flora  But now Sister Woodworth gave me all the information nessary, so I knew Joseph Believed and practiced Poligamy ... Now as a matter of corse I at once after giving her Flora a mild lecture left her and looked for a companion in other places and where I could be more sure.

One of the problems of secret polygamy at Nauvoo, illustrated well in this vignette, was that there were a number of attractive young women, apparently unattached, who would have had to continually fend off suitors. Wight's account is also revealing in its portrayal of the inner dynamics of the marriage of Joseph Smith and his young bride. Flora Ann did begin to "keep company" with Wight, and Smith had to pick up the couple and deliver the young man to Phebe for education (which shows that Phebe knew of the marriage). Then Wight gave Flora a mild rebuke—evidently, he felt that she had encouraged his suit to some degree. Flora's actions can only be interpreted as a gentle act of rebellion on her part against the marriage to Smith. In the Helen Mar Kimball case, we also have the Mormon leader marrying the teenage daughter of a close friend, with some rebellion or feelings of loss of freedom on the young girl's part. If the parallel with Helen Mar is exact, Joseph and Lucien (and possibly Phebe) may have persuaded Flora to marry to secure her family's salvation. But as was typical of many polygamous marriages, the bride would have felt little romantic attachment to the husband. That both Lucien and Phebe received their endowment and joined the Holy Order during Smith's lifetime supports the dynastic interpretation.

On May 2 William Clayton's journal notes that "Joseph rode out today with Flora W." A month later, on June 1, Flora met him again, as Clayton noted: "Evening Joseph rode in the carriage with Flora." Apparently Emma Smith came to suspect her husband's relationship with Flora, and she staged a full-blown scene with the Woodworths on August 22, as we have seen. Flora continued to meet with Smith, though. On August 26 Clayton wrote, "Hyrum and I rode up to my house and Joseph met Mrs. Wdth and F [Flora] and conversed some time." Two days later Clayton wrote, "President Joseph met Ms Wdth at my house." And the next day "A.M. at the Temple. President Joseph at my house with Miss Wdth." No other plural wife of Smith is given this prominence in Clayton's journals. However Flora might have felt about her older husband, he was apparently very attached to her.

### IV. Widowed

On September 11 Joseph Smith wrote in his journal, "Woodworth very humble 3 or 4 days &c." Two and a half weeks later, on September 28, Lucien, with John Taylor, Amasa Lyman, John Smith, and John M. Bernhisel, was initiated into the Quorum of Anointed and received his endowment. Phebe received the same honor on October 29. Brigham Young journalized, "Sisters Cahoon Cutler & Woodworth was taken in to the order of the Priesthood." The Woodworths had joined the innermost circle of elite Mormonism.

Smith continued to work closely with Lucien in the building project, and on December 7 the Mormon leader used him as a trusted emissary when Lucien took a letter from Joseph to Thomas Ford, governor of Illinois. On March 8, 1844, Lucien attended an important meeting which included the First Presidency and Twelve. Three days later the Council of Fifty, the secret "political kingdom of God," began to function, with Lucien as a charter member. On the 14th the council sent him to Texas to assess it as a place for Mormon migration, an important mission. He returned with a proposed treaty on May 2 and reported to the council the following day. A few days later he was appointed to return to Texas, though he apparently did not depart immediately.

On May 14 either Flora or her sister Mary was sick, as Joseph Smith's scribe wrote in his diary: "4 P.M. Prayer Meeting, few present. Prayed for Bro Woodworth's daughter who was sick. Lyman Wight was present." Smith's fateful last days were approaching. On May 27 Lucien, with others of the prophet's inner circle, met him at Carthage. Smith counseled with Woodworth and others on legal matters relating to the Lawrence sisters on the 4th of the following month. The pagan prophet again served as messenger on June 22, delivering a letter from Smith to Governor Ford. Less than a week after that Smith was killed and Flora became a widow at seventeen.

### V. Carlos Gove

Soon afterwards Lucien and George Miller encouraged Brigham Young to lead the Mormons to Texas, but the senior apostle decided against it. This interview probably marked the beginning of a gradual fall from favor for the pagan prophet. Nevertheless, he continued to be a prominent figure in the church for years afterward.

In late 1844 a young non-Mormon, Carlos Gove, began to spend time with Flora. Helen Mar Kimball Whitney, who had been one of Flora's schoolmates in Nauvoo, disapprovingly told of the ensuing marriage: "A young man boarding at her father's, after the death of Joseph, not a member of the Church had sought her hand, in time won her heart, and in a reckless moment she was induced to accept his offer and they eloped to Carthage, accompanied by a young lady friend, and were there married by a Justice of the Peace." The consequences of marrying a gentile are inevitable to the moralizing Helen Mar: "Flora was never happy with him as he hated the Mormons, and she felt condemned for the rash step she had taken." Throughout 1845 the eighteen-year-old Flora would have been settling into the life of a teenage newlywed; perhaps she was pregnant and had a child this year. According to Helen Mar, the marriage eventually produced "two or three" children.

Lucien's elite stature lessened when he was replaced as architect of the Nauvoo House on August 9, 1845. John Taylor wrote on the 13th, "The late architect Bro. L. Woodworth having been found incompetent Bro. Weeks had been appointed." According to Willard Richards, Lucien had failed to "provide a draft." William Clayton, on the 17th, described

Lucien's reaction to his demotion: he "foamed considerable at the time but feels tolerably well now." The setback did not affect the Woodworths' temple attendance. On December 7 he and Phebe attended a Holy Order testimony and sacrament meeting in the temple; in his journal Heber Kimball noted that they had not yet received their fullness of priesthood ordinance. Three days later, on the first day of full temple ritual, they received their endowments again, and Lucien is thereafter mentioned frequently in Clayton's temple diary.

Phebe served as a temple initiator on December 12, washing and anointing women in ordinances preparatory to the endowment. However, she somehow came into conflict with unnamed persons supervising the women, for Clayton wrote: "Perfect peace and harmony prevail ... except in one case which happened this afternoon, wherein Phebe Woodworth interfered with business which did not belong to her, and in the presence of those who are higher in authority than her." However, this rift was not serious. In two days she was back in the initiatory department.

A month later, on January 17, 1846, Flora received her endowment, with no male companion. In the washing and anointing record, she is referred to as Flora Ann Gove. On the same day Phebe was sealed to Joseph Smith for eternity, with Lucien standing proxy, and to Lucien "for time." Brigham Young officiated at the ceremony. This left Lucien without an eternal companion for himself, but on January 19 he married Charlott Fox, Aminta Maria Williams, Margaret Johnston, and, three days later, Rachel Kingsley.

### VI. Heavy Raven Locks

Flora and her husband, with any children they may have had, apparently left Nauvoo with Phebe, Lucien, and the main body of the Mormons after February 6 and traveled across Iowa. On August 17 Horace Whitney mentioned in his journal that Lucien Woodworth had crossed the river and visited him and Helen Mar. The entire Woodworth clan, including Flora Ann and Phebe, crossed over on the 31st. They were all very sick. The next day the Woodworths and Goves came to the main Winter Quarters camp, and Helen Mar and Horace took Flora into their makeshift home, as noted by Horace: "We rigged a temporary bedstead in my tent for Flora, who had been very sick, but is now slowly gaining her health." Helen Mar remembers that the Woodworths camped outside of the square. She tended Flora "until she recovered her strength ... She had lain helpless for many days, and her heavy raven locks were so matted together that it took me hours to comb them out." Carlos was also sick with fever.

As Helen helped her friend convalesce, Flora told her that she felt "condemned" for having married outside the faith. "She made this confession to me while I was nursing her, and said she desired to cling to Joseph hereafter." Perhaps Flora interpreted her sickness as a punishment from God, or her physical ordeal may have been combined with deep feelings of guilt. Helen Mar would have a similar experience. After recovering from the fever, the Woodworths and Goves settled at the "Point" and spent the winter at Winter Quarters. Once Flora visited Helen: "She still expressed herself as strong in the faith of the Gospel, also her great desire to cleave to the Prophet."

On September 17, 1850, Flora was living with her father and mother in Kanesville. The census shows Lucien and Phoebe Woodworth, age forty-five; Flora, twenty-four; Mary, fifteen; and John, eleven. So apparently Carlos and Flora were separated, either temporarily or permanently, by this time. He may have died, or he may have been elsewhere working. However, in the Utah census of the same year, Lucien is recorded to be living there with two wives. His household included Maria, thirty-five (Aminta Mariah Williams), and Margaret (Margaret Johnston), thirty. The census also listed a Deborah Woodworth, born in 1847 in Iowa. The double listing probably resulted from the fact that Utah's census took two years to complete and may reflect 1851-52.

According to Helen Mar Whitney, Flora died at Kanesville: "I never saw her again as she died at that place, leaving two or three children." How or exactly when she died is not preserved in the historical record. Like Lucinda Pendleton, she was well known when she was Joseph Smith's wife, then history lost track of her and she died in obscurity.

### VII. San Bernardino

Phoebe and Lucien presumably travelled to Utah after Flora's death. It is certain that they then went on to California, for on June 8, 1860, the California census shows them in San Bernardino. Lucien, age fifty-two, is a "Carpenter." Phebe is fifty and listed as having been born in New York. John, eighteen, and Mary, twenty, were born in Missouri. Though San Bernardino was a Mormon outpost at first, and had been led by an apostle, Amasa Lyman, the main group of Mormons had moved back to the Great Basin during the Utah War in 1857 and 1858. Therefore the Woodworths' presence in California opens a number of interpretive possibilities. Lucien may have become disillusioned with Mormonism and stayed behind to live among gentiles. Or the family may have moved back to Utah during the war, then returned to California. Or perhaps they did not arrive at the coast until after the war.

### VIII. In the Temple

Lucien reportedly died in 1867 when Phebe was sixty-two, and she possibly moved back to Utah soon after his decease. She was in Utah by 1871, for then we begin to have records of her performing temple ordinances in the Endowment House with Samuel H. B. Smith, a nephew of Joseph Smith. She was referred to in the Endowment House record as "Phebe Watrous Smith" and acted as a wife of Joseph Smith during the rites. For example, on August 7, 1871, Phebe and Samuel H. B. Smith stood proxy as Joseph Smith was sealed to Deborah Woodworth and Huldah Stunty (both dead). Then they stood proxy as a number of other women were sealed to Joseph Smith, Sr., and Samuel Smith. Phebe, like many older Mormon women, was spending a great deal of her time performing ordinances for the dead in the temples or in the Endowment House. Acting for Joseph Smith would be entirely appropriate for his widow, if she was that; she was certainly regarded as an eternal companion to him. Again, a year later, on July 17, 1872, "Sam. H.B. Smith & Phebe Watrous Smith stood for sealing of Jos. the Prophet to 10 dead women." Two years later, on June 18, 1874, when she was nearly seventy, "Phebe Watrous Smith stood with Sam. H.B. Smith for sealing of six dead women to [Joseph Smith] & 5 to Sm. H. Smith." This is her last appearance in the historical record. Her death date is not known.

# 18.

# Latter-day Hagar

## *Emily Dow Partridge (Smith Young)*

On July 20, 1833, nine-year-old Emily Partridge peered anxiously out the window of her home in Independence, Missouri. An hour earlier she and her sister Harriet had gone to a nearby spring for water when a mob descended suddenly on the Partridge home. Terrified, the two girls watched as the jeering, swearing men demanded Emily's father, Bishop Edward Partridge, the highest-ranking Mormon in Missouri, and dragged him away. The Partridge family—Lydia and her six children—waited in great suspense for Edward's return. Would their husband and father be beaten? horsewhipped? Or worse? Tensions between the clannish Yankee Mormons and the southern-tending Missourians recently had been fanned into a white-hot fury, and just hours before abducting Edward the mob had destroyed the press building of the Mormon newspaper, *The Evening and the Morning Star*, which had published a mildly abolitionist editorial.

Emily, pressing her face against the window, soon saw two men walking slowly toward her house. One she recognized, Albert Jackman, a young Mormon. He appeared to be carrying something. As the two men trudged nearer, she saw that he held a man's clothes. The other man looked like an Indian, but darker, and had a grotesque appearance which so terrified her that she left her window and ran upstairs to hide. Soon she heard her mother weep with mixed joy and dismay. The mysterious man was her father, who had been stripped, then tarred and feathered. Removing tar from the body of a man who has received such attentions is laborious and painful. Blankets were hung to give Edward privacy, then brothers of the church slowly scraped the acid-treated tar off his burning flesh.

So went the formative years of Emily and Eliza Partridge. Emily later wrote, "My childhood had been spent amidst mobs and mobbings." Such persecution would only solidify new converts in their Mormon faith and in fact give them an ideological framework for thinking of themselves as oppressed Christians of the early church living in the latter days. This strengthening is one of the reasons that young women such as Eliza and Emily Partridge would later accept polygamy, despite severe cognitive dissonance when Joseph Smith introduced it to them.

The Partridge sisters are two of the best known of Joseph's wives. After living in the Smith household for years as teenagers, they married him secretly, then, when Emma selected them as plural wives for Joseph, they married him again two months later. However, they then endured the jealousy of a strong-willed first wife who never really accepted polygamy. After months of tension, Emma finally demanded that Joseph expel the two girls from the Smith home, and he acquiesced. Thus the two young women became Hagars to a modern Abraham and Sarah.

The Partridge sisters' lives after Joseph's death are less well known. Emily married Brigham Young, and Eliza was sealed to another apostle, Amasa Lyman. The two sisters left extensive diary records of these marriages which are remarkably explicit critiques of their polygamous husbands and implicit critiques of polygamy itself. Both women clearly experienced financial and emotional neglect while living the principle, as their husbands were torn between ties to other wives and the pressing demands of their church callings. Amasa Lyman rarely lived close to Eliza, as he was often traveling on ecclesiastical assignments. He was not present at the birth of many of her children. Emily's diary reveals that she agonized about asking Brigham Young to pay small bills and make improvements in her home, despite the fact that he was one of the wealthiest men in Utah and the father of all of her seven children. Nevertheless, both women remained faithful Latter-day Saints and publicly defended polygamy as a central tenet of their religious faith.

Eliza's diary is one of the masterpieces of Mormon literature, a haunting record of loving motherhood amid the dangers, privations, and heartbreaks of frontier Utah. Emily was also a fine writer and left vivid reminiscences of her childhood and marriage to Joseph.

## I. Idyll

Eliza Maria, the first child of Edward Partridge and Lydia Clisbee, was born on April 20, 1820, in Painesville, Lake, Ohio, ten miles northeast of Kirtland. Both Edward, a hatter, and Lydia were natives of Massachusetts and were twenty-six years old at Eliza's birth. Emily Dow was born on February 28, 1824, also in Painesville, the third child in the family. Between them was Harriet, born on January 1, 1822. After Emily, Caroline was born on January 8, 1827. Emily's early reminiscences provide a striking contrast to her later pilgrim, pioneer, conflicted, Mormon life. She remembers living as a child in a large story-and-a-half, four-bedroom frame house. The kitchen was in the basement, and below it was a vegetable cellar in which children who misbehaved were sometimes shut up. Harriet once received that dreaded punishment, but Emily never did despite being "the most mischievous of the whole flock."

Outside the kitchen was a well, and in the front yard was a lawn "with rose bushes and sweet brier growing under the front windows." In the backyard was a garden with red and white currants, "an arbor, or summer-house, as we called it, with seats on both sides and covered with grapevines with clusters of blue grapes hanging among the leaves and twigs, beyond our reach." The path from house to arbor was lined with "pinks, daffodils, blue bells, lily, iris, snowballs."

> And then I remember the patches of tall grass—almost as high as my head was then, and how we children would tie the top of the grass together to make houses for our dolls. I remember the delicious clingstone peach that grew near the back of the house, the cherry tree that stood in the corner of the lot, and the large weeping willow near the shop. There was a flat embankment running the whole length of the back of the house and a frame covered with grape vines, both shading the house and making a nice shady place for the children to play and we took possession of it. Not that we played there all the time by any means, for we were like gypsies roaming around from one place to another.

Near the house was Edward's hat-shop and adjoining workshop. Emily would rummage beneath the counter for small pieces of colored material and would bump her head when she stood up, "and then how I would cry." There was also a barn where the children played happily, ransacking hens' nests for eggs and constructing play houses of hat packing boxes. Emily had a tendency to wander, forgetting strict orders to stay in the yard. When she was found and brought back to the Partridge home, she would be tied to her mother's bedstead with a long rope that reached to the front room. She would cry, then forget about the rope and try to rush off, only to be brought to a jarring stop that would reduce her to tears again. "But they could not keep me tied up always, so I would be off again, and once when I was out in the street a pet lamb of one of the neighbors took after me and I really thought it would devour me if I let it overtake me. But I beat him running and got home first." As a little girl, Emily was certain that she could remember when her father and mother were married and that she attended their wedding. "However," writes Emily, "I have no recollection of it now."

About 1828 Edward and Lydia visited relatives in Massachusetts, taking Eliza (now eight) and Caroline with them. Emily, four, and Harriet, six, were left with an aunt who lived in nearby Unionville. After dropping Eliza off with "Grandfather Partridge" in Pittsfield, Berkshire County, Edward and Lydia continued to eastern Massachusetts. Eliza remembered the trip vividly: "Although I was very young yet I remember many things that I saw on this journey. My Grandfather's nice brick house and the cider mill, the orchard and the farm are all plain in my memory, also the cities we passed through and the Erie canal with its locks and the roaring of the Niagara falls in the distance, the crossing of the Lake, my sickness while crossing." In Unionville, wrote Emily, "I was ... chased by a girl. She got my bonnet and ran home with it. I thought the children in Unionville ... were awful mean."

Edward joined the Reformed Baptist (later known as Campbellite) movement in 1828, so he was thinking in the Christian primitivist frame of reference before he encountered Mormonism. In 1829 a son, Clisbee, was born to Edward and Lydia but died at birth. Emily normally slept in her mother's bedroom in a little trundle bed, but that morning when she woke up she was in the spare bedroom with her little sister. "When we got up we were shown the little dead baby boy, and oh how sorry we were that he was dead, for we had never had a little brother before." However, the next year, on May 8, another daughter, Lydia, joined the Partridge household.

## II. Mormonism

In November 1830 Parley P. Pratt (previously a Reformed Baptist, like Edward), Oliver Cowdery, Peter Whitmer, and Ziba Peterson passed through the Kirtland area, preaching Mormonism with apocalyptic fervor. Edward obtained a Book of Mormon from them and was so affected by it that in December he traveled to Fayette, New York, with Sidney Rigdon to meet Joseph Smith. On December 11 Joseph baptized Edward in the freezing Seneca River; he then received a revelation from Joseph, Doctrine and Covenants 36, and four days later was ordained an elder. Lydia and Eliza were probably baptized not long after. As a result of Edward's month-long conversion, the Partridge family's lives would change almost incomprehensibly. Without this baptism, Edward and Lydia might have lived the rest of their lives contentedly in Painesville in their comfortable, gardened house. Eliza and Emily might have married local boys and raised their children in peace. Instead, Edward and family would endure unceasing persecution for a number of years and would help pioneer the American West. Eliza and Emily and their sisters would become plural wives in large patriarchal families, in a bold return to Old Testament practice.

Kirtland was designated as the gathering place for the Latter-day Saints. As the Partridges lived about three miles from the boat landing that was used to reach the city, many newly arrived Saints stopped at their home before moving on to the city proper. Excess baggage was sometimes stored in the Partridge barn, and seven-year-old Emily was often curious about the contents of these suitcases and trunks.

On February 4, 1831, Edward was called by revelation to be the first Mormon bishop, thus becoming something of a general authority in the young church, and his family became a general authority family. As one of the bishop's chief duties was to look after his flock's temporal welfare, the Partridges would often be called upon to share their means with the poor. One group of immigrating Mormons brought measles into the Partridge home, and all of the sisters came down with it. After recovering, Emily writes, she "took canker and could not eat for a long time. I well remember the day I could eat a little custard. Oh, how good it was. Mother had company that day, and how nice the table looked with its old-fashioned blue and white china." The illness left Emily deaf in one ear.

Eliza's case of measles was complicated by "lung fever" that made her so sick it was thought she would die. However, at a June 6 priesthood conference, Joseph Smith received a revelation directing that the next conference be held in Missouri and that it should be attended by him and Edward Partridge, among others. Despite Eliza's condition and a flourishing business, Edward obeyed. Eliza wrote, "He went and left his family to get along as best they could, I was at that time very sick and he had no expectation of seeing me again, but the Lord had called and he must obey." That Edward would leave on a church assignment with his oldest daughter on the brink of death is eloquent testimony to the power of Joseph Smith's call to action in early Mormonism. Emily noted, "My mother felt that her trials had begun when my father was called to accompany the Prophet to Missouri. Her children were just recovering from the measles, and her eldest child was still very sick with the lung fever. It was a new thing for her to be left alone in the hour of trouble."

Lydia's trials had indeed begun. Soon the Partridges would have to leave their comfortable home for the uncivilized frontier of Missouri. After Edward and Joseph reached Independence in mid-July, Joseph received a revelation identifying it as the center of the new Zion: "And let my servant Edward Partridge, stand in the office which I have appointed him, to divide the saints their inheritance, even as I have commanded." Edward's calling would be in Missouri, not near his delightful Painesville home. In an August 1 revelation Edward was given further instructions on building up Independence, but was also rebuked: "But if he repent not of his sins, which are unbelief and blindness of heart, let him take heed lest he fall." Had Edward, when called upon to leave his family, wavered? "And now, as I spake concerning my servant Edward: this land is the land of his residence, and those whom he has appointed for his counselors ... Wherefore, let them bring their families to this land."

Joseph returned home while Edward obediently stayed in Independence to prepare for the migration. He sent word for his family to join him, writing on August 5, "I have a strong desire to return to Painsville this fall, but must not. You know I stand in an important station; and as I am occasionally chastened, I sometimes feel as though I must fall ... I hope you and I may so conduct ourselves as at last to land our souls in the haven of eternal rest ... Farewell too for the present." Emily wrote that "It seemed a great undertaking for mother to break up her home and prepare for such a journey with a family of little children without her husband to advise, and make arrangements for her." Nevertheless, Lydia Partridge sold the beloved family home at a great loss while close friends and relatives looked on in disbelief, questioning her sanity. As winter approached, the five Partridge girls and their mother set out for Missouri with a group of Saints led by William Wine Phelps and Algernon Gilbert, Mary Rollins's uncle. The journey was unfortunate from beginning to end. Lydia was advised to put her money in the hands of one of the brethren who, according to Emily, "cheated her out of it." They traveled down the Ohio to Cincinnati in a keel boat, then took a steamboat up the Missouri. While on this boat, the Partridges' provision chest was stolen, rifled, and thrown overboard. "We saw it floating down stream and knew it at once," wrote Emily.

At some point they and the Morley family became separated from the main group. When they were about a hundred miles from Independence, floating blocks of ice made the Missouri impassable, so they had to land at Arrow Rock, thirty miles west of Columbia, in central Missouri. There they took refuge in a two-room windowless log cabin "occupied by negroes." Fifteen Partridges and Morleys crowded into one of the two rooms, which at least had a fireplace that kept them warm through two to three weeks of freezing weather.

The two families then obtained a "large Kentucky wagon," filled it with their belongings, and continued west. Bitter cold forced them to camp through one day, but it was on that day that Edward Partridge and Isaac Morley met them, "and anyone who has been in like circumstances can understand how happy we were," wrote Emily. "Well . . . we again started for Independence. And when we arrived at that place, we were so jamed, and packed in the waggon, by the load shifting, that we could hardly pull ourselves out." The long ordeal, a winter journey of some six hundred miles, had ended, and Eliza and Emily had received their first taste of the pioneering life.

### III. "All Seemed So Strange"

Edward had not had time to build a house but had rented one from soon-to-be-infamous Lilburn Boggs. Day-to-day life was hard that first winter in Missouri. Eliza wrote, "The people of that country did not want much but corn bread bacon and raised but very little of any thing else consequently there was but very little to be bought, but I remember we had a barrel of honey and what vegetables we could get, but no wheat bread as wheat was not to be bought in the land." These New Englanders had been transplanted into an environment that was part Southern, part frontier. Emily gives a vivid summary of their culture shock:

> All seemed so strange in our new home. Plenty of Indians and negroes, and the white folks were so different in their customs and manner of speaking. It was "I reckon" and "A right smart chance." ... Large bundles and baskets, churns, piggins of water, or milk, all were toated on their heads ... In warm weather, women went barefoot, and little boys from two to ten or twelve years old runing the streets with nothing on but a shirt ... a kind woman gave mother one of her day caps. It was made of large figured light calico and had a frill around the front and neck. Perhaps you think she did not wear it, but she did though.

Eliza and Emily and their sisters attended school taught by a Miss Nancy Carl in a log cabin. One day, Emily remembers, as the pupils were busy at their work, Indians surrounded the school building. "The doors and windows were filled with Indian faces, and [in] every crack where the chinking had fallen out we saw Indian eyes. Our teacher went to the door and talked with the chief, but the scholars were as whist as mice. We were not as used to seeing Indians in those days as the children are now."

The next winter the Partridge family charitably welcomed a widow and her four children into their one-room log cabin, making twelve people now to keep warm by one fire. Eventually Edward built his family a small log home—with two rooms and a cellar—at the corner of the temple lot in Independence. Emily turned eight on February 28, 1832, and soon thereafter was baptized into the Latter-day Saint faith in a creek close to the Partridge house. A family friend, John Corrill, performed the ordinance in the freezing water.

Persecution now overshadowed the Partridges. Beginning in 1832, groups of loud, swearing Missourians would ride into Independence at night, breaking windows and shooting into houses. One group of night riders set fire to a haystack on the Partridge farm. "Children heard so much about the mob that the word was a perfect terror to them. They would cry out in their sleep and scream, the mob is coming, the mob is coming," Emily wrote. Because of Edward's prominence, he was especially threatened. As the crisis mounted in the summer of 1833, Edward Partridge, Jr., the Partridges' last child, was born on June 25. Eliza was now thirteen, Harriet eleven, Emily nine, Caroline five, and Lydia three. Three weeks after little Edward was born, Edward Sr. was tarred and feathered. As the pressure from the non-Mormons became intolerable, the Latter-day Saints agreed to leave the county.

## IV. Stars as Thick as Snowflakes

On November 12 the Latter-day Saints made their migration to Clay County. Eliza remembered vividly the shock of being forced to leave in the winter, abandoning provisions, house, orchards, and all the improvements they had made. Their enemies, they knew, would take possession. It was "very cold and uncomfortable ... We traveled three miles and encamped on the bank of the Missouri river under a high bluff. The rain during the night poured down in torrents which wet ourselves and our things badly. This was the first night that I ever slept out of doors." The next day they crossed the river and arrived in Clay County, where Edward stretched a tent over some house logs to create a temporary shelter. The heavens seemed to acknowledge the sufferings of the Saints, for this was the night the stars fell at three or four in the morning. Emily wrote, "They came down almost as thick as snow flakes and could be seen till the daylight hid them from sight. Some of our enemies thought the day of judgment had come and were very much frightened but the saints rejoiced and considered it one of the signs of the latter days ... Although I was a child at the time I looked upon the scene with delight. ... The heavens seemed wrapped in splendid fire works."

After Edward had helped the rest of the Mormons cross the river, he tried to provide shelter for his own family. He found what Eliza called "a miserable old house ... with one fire place in it." The Partridges and Corrills moved in together and spent a difficult winter cooking at one fireplace. The Partridges lived there for two years. Eliza, now a teenager, began to hire out for work: "I did what work I could get for almost any kind of pay, but there were so many wanting work that there was very little chance to get any."

In the midst of these less than ideal conditions, Edward went east on a mission, leaving on January 27, 1835. He witnessed the dedication of the Kirtland Temple in the spring of 1836 but by May had returned to Missouri. However, tension between the residents of Clay County and the Mormons had developed, and Edward and other church officials began to look for another place to settle. They purchased land in Caldwell County and moved their families there that fall.

## V. Far West

In Far West, Caldwell County, Edward once again built a home and tried to begin living normally. Eliza, sixteen, left home to teach school thirty miles away for three months. Her pay was thirteen dollars plus board and room. She received no mail from home and was among total strangers, so must have missed her family enormously. Furthermore, Missouri had become a dangerous place for Mormons, but she wrote, "The Lord watched over me and returned me in safety to my parents again. I would never advise anyone to let a girl go away as I did then with entire strangers and to dwell with strangers. It was no uncommon thing in those times for our Mormon girls to go out among the Missourians and teach their children for a small remuneration."

The troubles between Mormons and non-Mormons flared up again, and the "Mormon war" of 1838 began. Once a group of Missourians rode up to the Partridge corral, shot a sow, stripped it of meat, and gave Edward the skin. In November the bishop was jailed for treason but not convicted and was freed early the next year. It was time for the Mormons, and the Partridges, to move again, but this time they went east. As bishop, Edward had to travel to Illinois ahead of his family and arranged for a friend, King Follett, to help Lydia and the children find their way to Quincy.

## VI. "Shaking with the Ague"

In January 1839 Follett and the Partridges set out, taking as their destination "any where out of the state of Missouri." They left it just as they had arrived: in extreme cold, crammed into a wagon with all their earthly possessions. They crossed the Mississippi partly by boat and partly on the ice. Edward met them on the eastern side of the great river and took them to a house that allowed the Partridges to be, writes Eliza with understatement, "more comfortable than we had been while traveling."

Eliza was now nearly nineteen, Emily close to fifteen. Emily and Harriet found short-term positions "hiring out," but as it was Emily's first time away from her family, she was very homesick. The Partridges soon moved to Pittsfield, Pike County, where Emily and Harriet hired out again. Then in the summer the family moved to Nauvoo, where they lived at first in a tent, a "house of canvas." Nevertheless, Emily wrote, "We felt very happy to have that much of a home again, at least I did."

Soon Nauvoo's marshes brought malaria to the populace, and Edward Partridge had his teenage daughters live with other families to tend the sick. "Then, I began to know what it was to be homesick," wrote Emily. But soon she herself was physically sick and returned to the family tent where she was bedridden with "a burning fever." One of her future husbands now entered her life. She remembers, "When Br. Young and Kimball were starting on their mission to England they stopped at our tent and administered to me and my sister Harriet who was also sick. My fever was broke and I was better for a week or two." However, malaria typically departs for a time then returns, and Emily was sick "off and on for a year or more." Eliza was spared the ague now, as she had already had a bout with it in Ohio. She obtained a position teaching in Lima, twenty-four miles south of Nauvoo. While there, wrote Eliza, "I boarded with a gentile family and was well treated but suffered fearfully with headache."

Eventually Edward managed to rent a room in an "upper stone house" near the steamboat landing, which they shared with the Hyrum Smiths. Emily was still seriously ill: "When the wagon came for us Harriet and myself were on the bed shaking with the Ague. Oh how I did hate to get up. Father made a bed in the wagon and put us in. When we stopped at the house, I could not move a particle until some one took hold of me ... We were more comfortable in the house, although we were in one room." Hard pressed to care for his own family, Edward was nevertheless made bishop of the upper Nauvoo ward on October 5.

On May 16, 1840, a man from Nauvoo rode to Lima with a message for Eliza: Harriet was dying. She rode all night and arrived home at sunrise to find her sister still alive, though she succumbed the next day. According to Eliza, her parents "took this trouble to heart very much and my Father said she was his pet child but no one knew it till then and I do not think now that he knew any difference in his children, but I believe when a child or friend is taken from us we are to think we love them more than others." Eliza was now stricken by the ague, so remained in Nauvoo. Edward returned to work, building a log cabin on his lot, and began to move his family into it. But when he was in the middle of this task his health failed due to illness, overwork, and the exposures of Missouri. He was ill for a week and a half, then died on May 27. Eliza was so sick at the time that she could not even attend the funeral.

### VII. In the Prophet's Home

Previous to their father's death, Eliza, Emily, and Lydia, all sick, were taken into William Law's home to convalesce. "He and his wife were very kind to us and doctored [us] ... so that in about three weeks we were able to move to our own house which was finished," Eliza wrote. Emily recovered slowly. Eliza had learned the art of tailoring at Far West and obtained work in a tailor's shop where she was paid three dollars a week, a great help to the family. Eliza and Emily, now twenty and sixteen, looked around to "hire out" as maids. Emily reports, "The first door that opened for us was to go to Prs. Smiths, which we accepted. We did not work for wages, but were provided with the necessaries of life." She described her job in the Smith home as that of "a nurse girl, for they had a young baby and they wanted me to tend it for them. That is what I delighted in, tending babies." Lydia Partridge remarried in September, uniting with the recently widowed William Huntington, father of Zina and Presendia. He moved into the crowded Partridge home with two of his boys.

Evidently 1841 was an uneventful year. Emily wrote, "The Prophet Joseph and his wife Emma offered us a home in their family, and they treated us with great kindness." It must have been fulfilling for the two young women to live with a man they revered as a prophet and with the universally admired Emma. And it would have been a relief to be able to leave the cramped Partridge home and live without worrying about daily necessities. With the Smiths, the sisters, who were from one of the early, prominent Mormon families, would continue to associate with the elite. Emily later reminisced about her early years in the Smith home: "As a general thing I was very happy going to parties and singing schools, and riding horseback. One day Emma said, as we had been to so many parties, we ought to have one and invite the young people in return. Of course that pleased us very much. We had an excellent time playing games." In April 1842 both Eliza and Emily were accepted into the Nauvoo Female Relief Society.

## VIII. "A Pure and Holy Order of Plural Marriage"

About the same time, spring 1842, Joseph began to teach Emily, now eighteen, the principle of plural marriage. She retold the story of her courtship a number of times, including a public recital in the Temple Lot case. The following is a composite reconstruction. She wrote, "When I was eighteen years Joseph said to me one day, 'Emily, if you will not betray me, I will tell you something for your benefit.' Of course I would keep his secret, but no opportunity offered for some time to say anything to me." Then Joseph offered to give her a letter—provided she would burn it after reading it. After private prayer, Emily decided it was not right to receive what she suspected might be a romantic letter from her host, employer, father figure, and spiritual leader. "He asked me if I wished the matter ended. I said I did." While it is not overtly stated that that the letter concerned plural marriage, it is clear from context that Emily understood he was broaching a marriage proposal. Elsewhere she wrote, "The first intimation I had from Brother Joseph that there was a pure and holy order of plural marriage was in the spring of 1842." However, on this first proposal Emily reported that she "shut him [Joseph] up so quick" that he did not bring up the subject again for months.

But she was troubled by Joseph's teachings and later described herself as "struggling in deep water" during those months: "I had plenty of time to think and began to wish I had listened to what he would have said and I began to be as miserable as I was before." Emily felt especially troubled because Joseph forbade her to talk about his preliminary proposal with anyone—even Eliza or her mother.

Next, Joseph evidently tested her ability to keep a secret through his older plural wife, Elizabeth Davis Durfee. Soon after Emily refused Joseph's letter, Elizabeth invited her and Eliza to her home one afternoon. There, Emily wrote, "She introduced the subject of spiritual wives as they called it in that day. She wondered if there was any truth in the report she heard. I thought I could tell her something that would make her open her eyes if I chose, but I did not choose to. I kept my own council and said nothing." This shows clearly that Emily knew the letter would deal with polygamy and that she knew a great deal about the "principle" by this time. Later she learned that "Mrs. [Durfee] was a friend to plurality and knew all about it."

As the sisters walked home from the Durfee soirée that night, Emily felt impressed to disobey Joseph and tell her older sister how he had introduced her to the doctrine of polygamy and asked her to be his plural wife. This news plunged Eliza into severe depression. "She felt very bad indeed for a short time," wrote Emily, "but it served to prepare her to receive the principles that were revealed soon after." Emily herself felt depressed and conflicted. But like many of Joseph's wives, she received a conversion to the principle: "[In] those few months I received a testimony of the words that Joseph would have said to me and their nature before they were told me and being convinced I received them readily." As we have seen, Joseph was not one to give up his matrimonial plans easily, and on February 28, 1843, Emily's nineteenth birthday, he renewed his suit. "He taught me this principle of plural marriage that is called polygamy now, but we called it celestial marriage, and he told me that this principle had been revealed to him but it was not generally known; and he went on and said that the Lord had given me to him, and he wanted to know if I would consent to a marriage, and I consented." Joseph often framed his marriage proposals in terms of a divine *fait accompli*—the Lord had already "given" the woman to the prophet. God was the ratifying agent, and it was sacrilegious to doubt. It was the woman's duty to comply with the fact that she was already Joseph's possession.

The marriage took place about a week later, according to Emily's remarkable account: "Mrs. Durf— came to me one day and said Joseph would like an opportunity to talk with me. I asked her if she knew what he wanted. She said she thought he wanted me for a wife. I was thirely [thoroughly] prepared for almost anything. I was to meet him in the evening at Mr. Kimballs." Emily was consciously ready to comply but was emotionally hesitant. She had been washing all day and was so concerned that others would suspect her true destination that she did not change her wash dress. She told her sister that she was going to see her mother and threw a large cloak over herself. She in fact visited her mother briefly, then went to Heber C. Kimball's house. "When I got there nobody was at home but William and Hellen Kimball. I dont know what they thought to see me there at the hour. I did not wait long before Br. Kimball and Joseph came in."

Evidently Heber and Joseph did not want the Kimball children to suspect that a polygamous marriage was being solemnized and sent them to a neighbor, pretending to send Emily away, as well. "Br. Heber ... said to me. Vilate is not at home, and you had better call another time, so I started for home as fast as I could so as to get beyond being called back, for I still dreaded the interview." Despite her reported conversion to polygamy, at nineteen years old she was clearly a reluctant bride, but as she began to rush home, Heber Kimball followed: "Soon I heard Br. Kimball call, 'Emily, Emily' rather low but loud enough for me to hear." Even now Emily tried to ignore him and continued hurrying away: "I thought at first I would not go back and took no notice of his calling. But he kept calling and was about to overtake me so I stopped and went back with him."

Now the marriage took place:

I cannot tell all Joseph said, but he said the Lord had commanded [him] to enter into plural marriage and had given me to him and although I had got badly frightened he knew I would yet have him. So he waited till the Lord told him. My mind was now prepared and would receive the principles. I do not think if I had not gone through the ordeal I did that I could ever [have] gone off at night to meet him. But that was the only way [it could] be done then. Well I was married there and then. Joseph went home his way and I going my way alone. A strange way of getting married wasen't it? Brother Kimball married us, the 4th of March 1843.

So Joseph, thirty-seven, married this frightened, fatherless nineteen-year-old, whom he had not allowed to consult even her mother or older sister. According to Emily's later testimony in a law court, there was a sexual dimension to her marriage with Joseph. She testified that she "roomed" with him the night following the marriage and explicitly stated that she had "carnal intercourse" with him on a number of occasions.

Four days later Eliza was married to Joseph. We know virtually nothing about how Joseph approached her. She herself only wrote, "While there [in Joseph's house] he taught to us the plan of Celestial marriage and asked us to enter into that order with him. This was truly a great trial for me but I had the most implicit confidence in him as a Prophet of the Lord and [could] not but believe his words and as a matter of course accept the privilege of being sealed to him as a wife for time and all eternity. We were sealed in [blank] 1843 by H.C.K. [Heber Kimball] in the presence of witnesses." Orson Hyde was one of the witnesses. The secrecy of polygamy was so great that neither Emily or Eliza knew that the other had been married or that they now shared a common husband.

## IX. Cast Off

In this way the two bright, attractive young women were brought into the sisterhood of Joseph's wives. On May 1 Eliza served as a witness when Joseph married Lucy Walker. As we have seen, plural wives were often called upon to help recruit and socialize prospective and new wives. But now the Partridges suddenly found themselves entangled in the stormy relationship of Joseph and Emma. As Eliza tells the story, two months after she and Emily had married him, Joseph convinced Emma to allow him to take other wives, but she agreed only on condition that she could select them. He consented and, to his surprise, she picked Emily and Eliza, a sign of how close she must have felt to the two sisters. This put Joseph and the sisters in an awkward position, but, Emily wrote, "To save the family trouble Brother Joseph thought it best to have another ceremony performed. Accordingly on the 11th of May, 1843, we were sealed to JS a second time, in Emma's presence, she giving her free and full consent thereto." Joseph's friend in freemasonry, Judge James Adams, performed the ceremony.

However, the Partridges' relationship with Emma changed overnight. Emily wrote, "From that very hour ... Emma was our bitter enemy. We remained in the family several months after this, but things went from bad to worse." On May 23 William Clayton journalized, "President stated to me that he had had a little trouble with Sister E. [Emma]." Joseph had been talking with Eliza Partridge in a room in the house when Emma knocked on the door. He held the door shut, but Emma "called Eliza 4 times and tried to force open the door. President opened it and told her the cause &c. She seemed much irritated." This diary entry presents a number of enigmas. If Emma suspected that Joseph was in the room, why did she call Eliza four times? Perhaps it was Eliza's room. As Emma tried to force the door, why did they simply not let her in? Historian Richard Van Wagoner suggests that Emma here may have first realized that there was a sexual dimension in Joseph's marriage to his two young wards. This interpretation is not certain but would explain why Emma became so extremely "irritated" at Joseph's spending time with Eliza behind closed doors after so recently giving Eliza and Emily to him as plural wives. It would also explain Emma's about-face with regard to the Partridge sisters. On the other hand, it is possible that Emma had accepted polygamy in theory but found that she could not live as a first wife in practice.

The last words in Emily's "Life Incidents" show that she still, in her later life, felt some bitterness at her treatment by Emma and Joseph: "I do not know why she gave us to him, unless she thought we were where she could watch us better than some others, outside of the house. She wanted us immediately divorced, and she seemed to think that she only had to say the word and it was done. But we thought different. We looked upon the covenants we had made as sacred. She afterwards gave Sarah and Maria Lawrence to him, and they lived in the house as his wifes. I knew this, but my sister and I were cast off."

In her autobiography, Emily told the details of the expulsion, a story remarkably similar to that of Abraham, Sarah, and Hagar. There is a domineering wife who gives the housemaids to the prophet, the prophet reluctant to proceed with the banishment, and the young, innocent plural wives: "She sent for us one day to come to her room. Joseph was present, looking like a martyr. Emma said some very hard things—Joseph should give us up or blood should flow. She would rather her blood would run pure than be polluted in this manner. Such interviews were quite common." Emily and Eliza had evidently been subjected frequently to similar harangues. These tensions now came to a head:

> But the last times she called us to her room I felt quite indignant and was determined it should be the last for it was becoming monotonous, and I am ashamed to say I felt indignant towards Joseph for submitting to Emma. But I see now he could do no different. When we went in Joseph was there, his countenance was the perfect picture of despair. I cannot remember all that passed at that time but she insisted that we should promise to break our covenants, that we had made before God. Joseph asked her if we made her the promises she required, if she would cease to trouble us, and not persist in our marrying some one else. She made the promise. Joseph came to us and shook hands with us, and the understanding was that all was ended between us.

Thus Joseph seems to have agreed to separate from his two young wives.

> After our interview was over we went downstairs. Joseph soon came into the room where I was, said, how do you feel Emily. My heart being still hard, I answered him rather short that I expected I felt as anybody would under the circumstance. He said you know my hands are tied. And he looked as if he would sink into the earth. I knew he spoke truly, and my heart was melted, all my hard feeling was gone in a moment (toward him) but I had no time to speak for he was gone. Emma was on his track, and came in as he went out. She said Emily what did Joseph say to you? I an-

swered, He asked me how I felt. She said you might as well tell me, for I am determined that a stop shall be put to these things, and I want you to tell me what he says to you. I replied, I shall not tell you, he can say what he pleases to me, and I shall not report it to you, there has been mischief enough made, by doing that. I am as sick of these things as you can be. I said it in a tone that she knew I meant it.

Emma wanted the Partridges out of the house *and* the city, but they refused. Joseph helped them find new accommodations. Eliza lived with Joseph Coolidge, and Emily stayed with sister-wife Sylvia Lyon. In one account Emily wrote appreciatively of Sylvia, while in another, the autobiography, she describes an unpleasant living situation without naming the family, writing that she had to stay up through the night frequently to tend a sick baby. When she could stand the situation no longer, she left. "I do not remember of seeing Joseph but once to speak to after I left the Mansion house and that was just before he started for Carthage. His looks spoke the sorrow of his heart although his words were guarded."

Though we do not know precisely when the Partridges were "cast off," Eliza R. Snow wrote a poem to Eliza Partridge on October 19 that may help us date the event. Its theme was the trials and shadows that must be endured; but "In sweet submission humbly wait ... Our heav'nly Father knows the best/ What way we must be tried." So the departure from the Mansion House possibly took place before October 19. Possibly it took place soon before August 16, when Joseph told William Clayton that he had "had to tell" Emma that "he would relinquish all [his wives] for her sake" for fear that she would "obtain a divorce and leave him."

The story of Joseph's separation from the Partridge sisters can be seen from diametrically opposed viewpoints. From the perspective of Emma, Joseph might be viewed positively here, as he bowed to the wishes of his first wife, agreeing to separate from his young wives and standing by his promise. But from the perspective of the Partridges, Joseph seems to accede to Emma somewhat casually. While Emily and Eliza view the marriage seriously—Joseph had taught them that it was a high, religious duty, and, in addition, it had been a fully sexual relationship—he seems to take it more matter-of-factly. He shakes hands with Emily and Eliza and the marriage is over. He does not contact them again after they leave his home. Might he not have stood up to Emma, especially since she had permitted the marriage in the first place? Yet Emma apparently had leverage that Joseph could not withstand (perhaps divorce and exposure of polygamy), and Emily seemingly understood this: "He said you know my hands are tied. And he looked as if he would sink into the earth. I knew he spoke truly, and my heart was melted, all my hard feeling was gone in a moment." But perhaps the compassionate Emily was too easily forgiving, as was her tendency. In any event, on June 27, 1844, Joseph was killed, and Eliza and Emily, after their separation from Joseph, were now widowed. The first chapter in their marital history was over, but a second would soon begin.

## X. "Houseless and Homeless"

At this point we will continue to follow Emily, while Eliza's later life will be dealt with in the next chapter. Emily, like many of Joseph's widows, received and accepted a proposal from a prominent apostle, marrying Brigham Young in September or November 1844 as his approximate eighth wife. She was twenty, he was forty-three. They quickly began to build up Joseph's eternal kingdom, for on October 30, 1845, "Edward Partridge Young Smith" was born to Emily in Nauvoo. A new, long-lasting chapter had opened in Emily's life: practical polygamy.

Like other Mormons, Emily participated in temple ritual in the winter of 1845 while preparing to leave Nauvoo. On December 29 she received her endowment in a session that included Louisa Beaman Young, Harriet Cook Young, and Lucy Walker Kimball. Her proxy marriage to Brigham and Joseph was re-solemnized on January 14 of the new year. Then in mid-February she left Nauvoo and crossed the Mississippi. "And [I] was again a wanderer without home or shelter, with a wilderness full of Indians and wild beasts before me, and cruel and heartless beings behind me," she wrote. Though she was now married, she was alone at this moment of crisis. Her reminiscences, written to her children and descendants, now preserve a vivid memory that haunted her in later life. She and little Edward crossed the Mississippi and she "was again houseless and homeless in the cold and inclement weather of February 1846." As she had preceded most of her friends across the river, she wandered from one fire to another, receiving food and shelter from near-strangers. "Pres. Young had to look after the welfare of the whole people; no very small task. So you will see he had not much time to devote to his family. But as soon as he could he made such arrangements for his family's comfort as his means would admit of." Emily then gives a revealing vision of the realities of polygamy: "I will show you one or two pictures ... You can see a young woman with a [three-month-old] child clasped in her arms, seated on a log cold and hungry and a little dejected. You cannot tell what she has on for the snow is falling fast and she is covered with snowflakes."

Certainly, the pressures on Brigham Young were enormous as he guided a mass exodus into the wilderness. But in a monogamous marriage, Emily and her child probably would not have been alone and uncared for. Brigham had married forty other women besides Emily by mid-February and thus had built up the foundation of an imposing family kingdom for the eternities. But his wives, living in the harsh realities of the pioneer West, were often left to themselves and to relatives.

Emily also remembered washing in Sugar Creek and trying to keep Edward from rolling into the water at the same time. Once, when her shoes gave out, she wore Brigham's boots until footwear could be obtained. Eliza's journal gives us a brief glimpse of Emily in mid-February: "The weather quite pleasant. Went to the river with Br. Lyman to see my Sister Emily. Found her in a tent surrounded with mud. Came home in the afternoon."

She probably left Sugar Creek with Eliza Snow on February 28, for Eliza visited her a few days later, on March 8. Thus Emily may have arrived at Mt. Pisgah on May 25. She decided to stay there, where the Huntington-Partridge families were living, for, she reports, she was not entirely weaned from her mother yet. "It was rather lonesome, when the [Brigham Young] company started on leaving us in the wilderness without home or shelter. My baby was very sick at the time which made it seem much worse." Eliza Snow and Zina Huntington stayed at Mt. Pisgah for a while, however, so Emily was not entirely bereft of friends. She and her family lived in a log cabin without windows, with no actual door in the open doorway, and only a hole in the roof for a chimney. During the summer the Huntington-Partridge clan was overcome by sickness, apparently the ague. They felt lucky if one family member was well enough to tend all the others.

Her sisters Eliza and Caroline, now wives of apostle Amasa Lyman, left Mt. Pisgah on June 11. When Father Huntington died on August 19, Emily and her mother were left without a male companion, and the nearest neighbors were a good distance away. However, the summer passed, and so did their chills and fevers. When it was cold, Emily had to cut down her "first and only tree" for fire wood. Like Zina Huntington, she remembered vividly the wolves at Mt. Pisgah: "Nights bands of wolves would surround us, and if they had been disposed, they could have crawled through the crack and come in the door, as there was only a blanket hung up at the door." However, the "brethren" of Mt. Pisgah eventually built Lydia and Emily a "shanty" at a new location "in the timber." Food was easier to obtain there and the two women were able to spend the winter in relative comfort. It was probably of this building that Emily wrote, "Our shanty was in a beautiful grove on the hill, about half a mile from the river ford. We had several neighbors close by." She always felt grateful to "those bretheren who put forth a helping hand to assist us in the great time of our need."

Emily records one amusing polygamy-related detail. Babies born under "the new and everlasting covenant" of polygamy were still a rarity. As her Edward was now publicly acknowledged as a child of Brigham, "people would stop at our house to see a spiritual child and some have told me, years after that he was the handsomest child they ever saw."

About the beginning of the new year, Zina Huntington at Winter Quarters wrote to Emily, her stepsister and twice a sister-wife: "Sister Eliz Snow Says tel them we think of you evry day and sends her love to you, she has ben with us [a number of] days  Eliza Beman [Louisa Beaman] Lucy [Decker Young] Emiline [Free Young] Harriet [Cook Young] Margret [Pierce Young] and Clarricy Decker [Young] all sends there love to you and wishes you ware here." Emily was now an important thread in the complex fabric of elite Mormon sisterhood. There is also a greeting from her husband: "Emily I told Brigham I was going to write he told me to send his love to you."

On January 29, 1847, Emily responded: "Sister Zina  Haveing an opportunity to send a few lines to you by Br Rich I hasten to improve it. you may think it strange that I have not written before, but circumstances have not been favorable, and I think you will know something how to excuse me  we are all well at present, and are quite comfortable. You well know there is not much news to be written from this place." After mentioning some mutual friends, Emily ended the letter: "Give my love to the girls and all my friends there if any such you find, I am very well contented thinking all things will come out straight in the end. I have no more to write at present so good bye untill I see you.  Emily D. Partridge."

## XI. Winter Quarters

In the spring Emily and Lydia, feeling increasingly isolated at Mt. Pisgah, decided to venture west across Iowa. At Winter Quarters Emily reunited joyfully with family and friends, her husband, her sisters, and an intricate interweaving of sister-wives, the Smiths, the Youngs, and the Lymans. She would spend the next year at Winter Quarters. Among incidental references to her in journals, two stand out. Patty Sessions wrote on June 3, "E [Louisa] Beaman E Partridge and Zina Jacobs came  laid their hands upon my head blesed me, and so did E R Snow thank the Lord." So Emily, with three other former wives of Joseph Smith and present wives of Brigham Young, helped administer to another former wife of Joseph Smith. Such all-female ritual blessings at Winter Quarters served to bond these women to each other in a sisterhood charged with spiritual power. Emily also spoke in tongues on occasion. Eliza Snow wrote on June 2, "Spent the aftn. with Lucy in Com. of Zina Loisa & Emily. E. & myself spoke in the gift of tongues."

## XII. "I Know You Cannot Love Me"

Emily left Winter Quarters for Utah in the summer of 1848. In her reminiscences she did not linger on her journey west: "We were more comfortable fitted out than we had been at any time before, but on account of ill health the journey was most unpleasant. I do not wish to think of that time." After witnessing a July 24 pioneer day parade forty-nine years later, she wrote, "The old Pioneer waggons were almost too realistic. They brought back in a forcible manner the horrible journey across the plains. I only sat and cried while they passed." Emily was in the early months of a pregnancy when she began the overland trek.

When she reached Salt Lake City, her first glimpse of the valley filled her with hope, for she saw it as a place of rest for the weary traveler. But as they entered the valley, "It looked more forbidding. Nothing was to be seen but sagebrush and a few cottonwood trees along the course of City Creek. The fort could be seen in the distance, and one could not help but wonder where it was possible to find so much timber as built the fort." Emily found "comfortable rooms" ready for her in the fort, where she spent the winter as she prepared for childbirth. The following spring the Mormons began to move out from the fort onto their lots, and on March 1st Emily was assigned to live with Brigham's brother, Lorenzo. That night, at 9 o'clock, her first daughter, Emily Augusta, was born.

Her next home was in the Twelfth Ward, a vacated dwelling that Brigham had obtained for her. She moved there only after dark, accompanied by her sister Lydia, and found that her new accommodations were not palatial:

> I lit a candle and took a look inside. Well I dont know, if my sister Lydia had not come with me, to help me, but I should have gone back with the team. There was one good sized room, with a very good floor but there was no window except a hole where a log had been cut out. No latch was on the door, there was no heat and I had to step down one or two feet to get at the fire. I had one chair, one small chest that served for a table. I had six plates knives and forks, one tin tumbler that served to drink from and also for a candlestick.

We are struck by the wife's move without a husband; instead, a sibling takes his place, supplying emotional support, a typical phenomenon in polygamy. However, Emily soon moved into "a more comfortable house nearer my friends."

At this point Emily's reminiscences become sketchy and one must outline her life mostly through the dates of her children's births and marriages. Many Mormons wrote at length about their persecution-enforced hardships in Missouri, Illinois, and along the trail, but once they arrived at

Utah they saw themselves as living prosaic daily life not worth recording in diary or autobiography.

However, two remarkable letters Emily wrote to Brigham Young illuminate this period of her life. The first, dated June 30, 1850, is a letter of gratitude from a painfully shy young wife: "My ever beloved friend and benefactor I hope you will pardon my presumption, it is because of the feelings of my heart, the love and gratitude I feel towards you that I take the liberty of addressing you thus, the kindness and good feelings you have always manifested towards me since I have been in your family inspires my heart with feelings I am not capable of describeing." She assured Brigham that she loved him as well as Joseph: "You may think my affections are entirely placed upon Joseph but there your mistaken, true I love him but no more than yourself." In a painful passage she denied that Brigham could love her in return: "I know you cannot love me neither do I ask it for who can <sup>love</sup> what is not lovely, I fear you will be disgusted with me for writing in plain but I hope you will pardon me as it is the first time and perhaps the last these are the true sentiments of my heart although written in an improper manner and my courage almost fails me in showing it to you."

On February 1, 1851, a second daughter, Caroline, was born to Emily and Brigham. All three of Emily's children became ill in 1852, and she wrote, "On the 26th of Sep. my little Eddie died." We know from other women's writings what an excruciating ordeal this must have been for her, but she did not write about the death in any detail. She then went to live with her mother for a time. Caroline, one and a half, was still ill and looked "like a little skeleton." She would not allow herself to be undressed at night, and when she slept, she lay so quiet that Emily could hardly tell if she was breathing. This sickness pushed Emily almost over the edge. "I think I came nearest giving up at the time than I ever did before or since. It seemed to me that another straw would break the camels back, but the straw was not forthcoming." Carlie survived.

Perhaps the depression after the ordeal of Edward's death and Carlie's sickness accounted for her next letter to Brigham, a striking contrast to her 1850 letter. Dated February 24, 1853, it is addressed to "Dear friend," a remarkably distant salutation. It is also worth noting that Emily, living in Salt Lake City, should write to her husband rather than talk to him. But Brigham was very busy: "I hope you <sup>will</sup> excuse the liberty I take in addressing you thus. I did not wish to write could I have had an opportunity of saying to you what I wanted." Then, in a heartbreaking few sentences, the tragedy of Emily's life, and of polygamy, are encapsulated: "Since the death of my child a change has come over my feelings, I feel more lonely and more unreconciled to my lot than ever." For a woman, plural marriage, especially to a high church leader, often involved isolation and depression, especially in times of crisis. Her next sentence would be scathing if it were not so matter-of-factly innocent in tone: "[A]nd as I am not essential to your comfort or your convenience I desire you will give me to some other good man who has less care." Emily realistically understood that as a plural, proxy wife, she was not necessary to Brigham's emotional well-being. Hence a request to be released from his family and from polygamy. She then proceeds to excuse Brigham for his neglect of her: "I realize you have a great many cares and perplexities, a large family, all haveing their wants." Polygamy put impossible pressures and demands on the male, despite honest, sincere efforts to treat wives well. In her earlier letter Emily had borne testimony to what she considered her husband's essential goodness.

The interview with Brigham that followed is unfortunately not reflected in the historical record. Emily did not leave the Young family, but her relationship with Brigham would become increasingly unsatisfactory. Nevertheless, she was expecting again before long. On May 6, 1855, Joseph Don Carlos was born at the "white house" east of Eagle Gate on South Temple (then known as Brigham Street). In 1856 the Lion House, Brigham's communal mansion for his wives, was completed and Emily moved in. Her next child, Miriam, was born there on October 13, 1857. Another daughter, Josephine, followed on February 21, 1860, and Lura, Emily's last, was born on April 2, 1862, but died seven months later on November 4.

### XIII. Forest Farm

In 1863 or 1864 Emily and her large family moved from the Lion House to a house one-half block north of the Salt Lake Theatre. Four years later Emily's children began moving away when, on January 4, 1868, Emily Augusta, twenty, married Brigham Young's business manager, Hiram Clawson, as his fourth wife, clearly a dynastic union. Clawson, forty-two, later became a well-to-do entrepreneur. Unfortunately, aside from dividing his time among four wives, he was often traveling in the East. Later that year, on October 7, Caroline married Mark Croxall, a Western Union telegraph operator, as his second wife. A second generation of polygamy had begun. Emily Augusta's first child, Carlie Lovine Young Clawson, was born on July 28, 1869, so Emily Dow became a grandmother at age forty-five.

In 1869, roughly, Brigham sent Emily to live in his "Forest Farm house," now Forest Dale, where his herds of dairy cattle supplied milk and butter for the Lion House. Apparently Brigham's wives perceived the assignment as an exile of sorts, and Emily did not remember her stay there with any fondness. In 1874 she wrote, "I have not been well since I went to the farm to live about five years ago. Nobody knows my feelings while there but myself. There was nothing plesant in connection with that place." Ann Eliza Young wrote of "the Farm" that "Every one of the wives who had been compelled to live there had become confirmed invalids before they left the place, broken down by overwork." Ann Eliza's evaluation sounds exaggerated, but Emily's statement corroborates it. Ann Eliza described the farmhouse as having a pleasant appearance, with "wide verandas, vine-draped and shaded ... broad, low windows, and beautiful surroundings." Nevertheless, it had thin walls and was bitterly cold in the winter, suffocatingly hot in the summer. Emily's duties are described by Ann Eliza as follows: "There were butter and cheese to make from forty cows, all the other dairy work to attend to, besides cooking for twenty-five or thirty men, including the farm labourers and the workmen from the cocoonery."

According to Ann Eliza, Emily's tenure at the farm caused friction between Emily and Brigham: "Not understanding dairy work, she did not suit her husband. She is willing to work, and do whatever she can do, but is no more able than the rest of the world to accomplish impossibilities. He [Brigham] was so angry at her want of success at the farm, that he said, in speaking of her, 'When I take another man's wife *and children* to support, I think the least they could do would be to try and help a little.'" If this is reported correctly, we see that Brigham clearly distinguished between his full wives and the proxy wives, whose children would not be his in the eternities.

### XIV. Troubled Dream

Emily thankfully returned to the city in 1872 when Brigham deeded her a home in the Twelfth Ward. Two years later she celebrated her fiftieth birthday. Happily her diary began again that day, February 28, 1874, and she comes into sharp focus again. This remarkable document reveals her to be an intelligent woman with strong, incisive opinions. She often varied her standard diary entries with miniature essays on subjects of special interest to her. The dignity of woman was an important theme in her writings, as was her contempt for men who treated women as unequal. She stands as a Mormon proto-feminist, though her feminism was private and expressed within the bounds of orthodox nineteenth-century Mormonism. The diary also reflects that emotionally she often hovered near depression. She was haunted by a past that she saw as filled with injustice and grief—Missouri, Nauvoo, and early Utah; nevertheless, she loved to look back and relive those melancholy times. Despite this backward vision, she lived in the present for the sake of her children and grandchildren.

The diary is also extraordinary as the record of a plural marriage told from the point of view of a plural wife. Emily's feelings toward her famous husband were profoundly ambivalent. She clearly harbored deep resentment toward him, for, according to the diary, supported by Ann Eliza Young, he refused to support her or her children financially. She, however, felt that her poor health after the farm experience kept her from active work. When she did apply to Brigham for assistance, she was required to deal with "the President's men," who in her view treated her and her children insultingly. If she wanted to talk with her husband, she had to make an appointment to see him in his office. Her diary reflects her deep, pained puzzlement at this state of affairs. She knew that her husband was wealthy, and she knew that many of his other plural wives were financially comfortable. Brigham was the father of her children; she asked, why would he not support her?

We do not have Brigham's view of this relationship, and he may have felt that Emily was unreasonably demanding and spendthrift—it is impossible to tell. However, Emily grieved that Brigham and his "men" would not help her pay a $.75 water tax bill. There is a persistent tradition in unsympathetic sources that Brigham was very close with his money, even with his wives. Ann Eliza Webb Young, certainly anti-Mormon, nevertheless supplied anecdotal evidence for this. Emily's diary is a "sympathetic" source that supports this view. Mormon stalwart Benjamin Johnson felt that Brigham's great fault was his love of wealth, despite the fact that he was "the True Sheapheard to Isreal."

For the student of polygamy, it is the distance between Emily and Brigham that is especially striking. The husband seems less a spouse than a distant uncle. Nevertheless, Emily sometimes saw goodness and kindness in her husband, and she sincerely revered him in a religious context. Immediately after his death, she eulogized him as a good father and great spiritual leader.

The first entry in Emily's diary reads, "Today I am fifty years old. Can it be possible; To look back upon my past life it seems like a troubled dream. There has been but few if any, pleasant reminisences for memory to dwell upon. My children ... they are my comfort." The entry is divided between a bleak past and a present which somewhat counterbalances it because it includes her children. Living with Emily at the time were Don Carlos, nineteen; Miriam ("Mamie"), sixteen; and Josephine, fourteen. Emily Augusta sometimes visited for extended periods of time also. The March 6 diary entry is similarly backward looking: "The fourth of this month (31) thirty-one years ago I was sealed to Joseph Smith." A month later Emily was having health problems: "I have been quite ill, feel much better today. Wonder sometimes if I ever shall regain my health again."

419

The next diary entry, dated April 16, introduces her feelings about her husband:

> Today I feel quite unwell. I seem to lack strength. I would be glad if circumstances were such that I would not have to work so hard, but work seems to be my lot. I never did know how to shirk out of work. Yesterday Br. Cahoon called to see if I would send a man to help on the water ditch or pay 75 ct as I have no man without taking Carlos out of school. I had better pay it, and I do not think the Presidents men will help me in that. They know very well that he wishes me to take care of my self, and I do not know why he does not tell me himself. I almost wish he would (although it would be very hard on me) It would be preferable to being told of it so much by others.

Powerful men are often shielded from the public by employees, but it is surprising to see Young use this buffer with a wife. "If I was well and strong I might do better, but I have not been well since I went to the farm ... I had not been in the 12th Ward one year before I received a note stating that Mis Partridge s school tax was 75 dollars (of course I could not pay it) and I was told that Br. Young refused to pay it, so I suppose it stands against me yet. I hardly know sometimes which way to turn to get those things he does not provide." On December 6 Emily was suffering from an inexplicable lingering sadness: "For the past few days a sad feeling comes over me very often, why I do not know."

Emily Augusta ended a long visit on January 4, 1875, which left her mother feeling abandoned: "Emily commenced to move today ... I shall be very loansome when they are gone, but ... We must not expect to always keep our children with us ... I cannot express my feelings and the loanlyness and desolation it brings when I see my children leaving me, but ... theyr happiness depends on it." Four days later, when Josephine and Mamie were elsewhere, she wrote, "I always feel very much worried when I am not with my children." She was very much the wife who lived for her children.

On January 29 she wrote that, despite her bad health, she had been sewing to pay for overshoes for Josephine and could not afford to be ill. The following day her resentment toward Brigham again flared up, and it is apparent that his failure to support her was a major cause of her depression:

> I have been sick in bed for two days. Am much better today. I feel rather dispirited and a good cry might do me good. I feel quite ashamed to be known as a wife of the richest man in the territory, and yet we are so poor. I do not know why he is so loth to provide for me. My children are his children. He provides sumptuously for some of his family. If he was a poor man it would be different ... He manifests a desire to cast me off,

and I cannot ask him for anything. What his hired men will let me have I get, but it is like pulling teeth to get that sometimes. I feel very loanly tonight. I hope I do not sin in my feelings.

On March 21 she was again fighting deep melancholy: "There has been a heavy cloud moveing over my spirits for several days. I thought this morning I would go to meeting and partake of the sacrament and see if I could not feel comforted. I do feel much better, although the cloud is not entirely gone." Five days later she wondered why her husband would not help "fix up" her house and lot. She requested some household items from Brigham, or from Brigham's men, and received them on May 12 but noted that they were old, used, and often not what she had asked for. "It seems to be my fate to have to take second or third hand articles ... I might feel better about it if all was served in the same way."

In mid-June Emily enjoyed a trip to Fillmore to see her sisters and mother, then returned to vacate her home, which had been declared unsafe and was to be torn down. Mamie and Josephine went to live in the Lion House, while Emily stayed with Emily Augusta. On September 3 "Carlos" left Utah to attend the Rensselaer Polytechnic Institute in Troy, New York. Emily must have regarded the departure of her only living son with mixed feelings of pride and loss.

In early January 1876 she began to move into her new home, which was not quite finished. In the middle of the month, she wrote, "Bro. Young has given me carpet for two rooms lower hall and stairs. For which I thank him." Her husband did help at times. Later in the year, on December 3, Emily heard Joseph Smith III preach at the Liberal Institute in Salt Lake City. This would have been another nostalgic experience, for she had undoubtedly tended young Joseph three decades earlier in Nauvoo. But she was not impressed by her former charge: "He is not much like his father. Neither is his preaching."

When Brigham turned seventy-six on June 1 of the following year, Emily was "invited" to dine at the Lion House for his birthday celebration. In her diary she carefully noted his spiritual thoughts at the meal: "He also said, in reply to Br. Joseph Youngs question 'what do reserected beings eat.' 'They eat angels food.' We were all just as wise then as we were before, but it set me to thinking." She wrote that Brigham's "countinance was pure and heavenly." Here she views her husband reverentially, as a religious leader. But a month later, on July 17, she unleashed another tirade against him as a human being:

Different ones have told me that they heard Pr. Young say, "Sister Emily ought to take care of herself; and he did not intend to do anything for her much longer." And the men in his employ would hardly let me have anything saying, "it was Pr. Youngs orders" and one man said he knew it was hard work for me to get anything as no one wanted to do anything for me, and said he "I actually have to lie when I bring the brand for your cow and tell William it was for someone else" and I and my family have to take insult upon insult from the[ir] hands until I feel as if I want to be free from such things. When I go to Pr. Young for anything he seems anoyed and perhaps will give me no answer. And all these things ... have caused me to wory, and I have laid awake many nights thinking and contriving some way to get along independent of Pr. Young, but being in poor health and not able to work. (Although I did work and kept myself sick all the time.)

She prayed for guidance and felt that she received an answer: she should go see Brigham. Though reluctant, even apprehensive, she went directly to his office. There she sat for "several hours," feeling as if she "would faint." So a wife sits for hours in an outer office in order to see her husband. She was almost ready to give up, when he came into the waiting room: "He kissed me and seemed very kind. He looked so pure, one might think him more than mortal." Emily asked for transportation to Fillmore to see her mother, who was very ill, and for her home to be finished. "He thought he could send me down very comfortable. The other things, the finishing of my house and bring{ing} the water in he did not know what to say. I asked him if he did not think I ought to have a fence around my lot. He thought I had. And [I] went out and I came home."

However, Brigham later sent a message through Josephine that he felt that Emily's health was not good enough for a visit to Fillmore. She accepted this counsel grudgingly: "So I have given up seeing my mother in this world." On July 25 she angrily reported that Brigham met Josephine at the theater and accosted her with a rather "cold" greeting.

A month later Emily's thoughts turned toward the past once again, as she told an autobiographical story in third person, harking back to a time when she and Eliza had been slighted by their fellow teens in Nauvoo. They had not been invited to a sleigh ride and were left alone in the Mansion House, but Joseph came to their aid and asked a servant to take them out. Now Emily desperately missed this protector, who was "great, good and kind, and loved by all good people." But he died shortly thereafter "and those girls lost a friend that was never made up to them in after life. The treatment they received at that time from their young friends was only a foretaste of what they have had, more or less all their lives, and they sometimes wonder if they ever shall find a true friend with a disposition and the power to lift them out of their sorrow." So Emily looked back to an idealized Nauvoo to give her comfort in her present trials.

Three days later she received word that her husband was very ill.

She and her family immediately came to his bedside where he was "rolling back and forth to keep breath in his body." The next day, the 29th, Emily was called to his bedside again at three in the afternoon. She wrote, "His spirit passed away one minit past four, we all knelt down and Br. Cannon prayed. I never experienced more solemnity ... Although sobbings were heard it did not disturb the hallo [halo] that pervaded the room. We retired to the parlor, and I felt that silence was sweet ... I dreaded to have the spell broken, or the sweet peaceful influence, that filled the air disturbed."

Despite the many acrimonious diary entries about Brigham in previous days, Emily now was all forgiveness: "How often it is the case that when a friend dies if they ever had a weakness or imperfection it seems to exist no longer." But when such men as Brigham Young leave, with a "record of faithfulness," "there is more cause for joy than sorrow. We are apt to feel our lonelyness and a lack for something that will remain the rest of our lives. I believe Pr. Young has done his whole duty towards Joseph Smith's family. They have sometimes felt that their lot was hard, but no blame or censure rests upon him. And I feel greatful to him and bless his name forever." Unlike her sister Eliza at the death of Amasa Lyman, Emily had the comfort of knowing that her proxy husband had died in the fellowship of the Saints.

### XV. "Heart Hungry All My Life"

Brigham's funeral was held on September 2, and his will was read in a family meeting the following day. "I think all will be satisfied," wrote Emily afterwards. "He has been generous in making no difference in his family. The proxy wives are remembered in his will the same as the others. He has shown himself to the last the noble man he is, and may he never have cause to complain of any of his family." But the will would be a bone of contention between Brigham's families and the hierarchy of the church for years to come. On December 8, when Emily applied to one of the executors of the will for Christmas money, he dismissed her summarily. "The Executors treat the heirs as if they were poison," she wrote bitterly. "It is worse now to get anything than it used to be and it was bad enough then." On Christmas Day she gave no gifts, as she had no money. Things had not changed, she noted ruefully. She began 1878 seemingly resigned to her isolation. "Expect nothing but to stay at home in my loanlyness," she wrote on January 1. "Too old for enjoyment. Emily has gone sleigh riding with Hyrum."

Two days later she gives a lively account of male-female relations in a Mormon ward. The bishop and his first counselor spoke in Relief Society "in behalf of the trustees of the school house." The bishop said the brethren would manage the school and that he "would be glad if the sisters would please not interfere," repeating this offensive request "several times." Then he said he was too mad to talk and sat down. Emily wrote, "Now I was not a bit pleased with his remarks." The women had "interfered," Emily explained, because the bishop had thrown the job on the sisters. Her heart rebelled, she wrote, and the other sisters felt as she did. "Why cannot our rulers be kind and considerate to the members of the Ward. It seems that some men think because we are women that they are justified in kicking us right and left ... I came home from the meeting with a severe headache."

On the 6th she wrote that Brigham's will would apparently not be executed as expected because some of the property in question was felt to be the church's, not Brigham's. Some of the Young family were incensed and considered hiring a lawyer. Though she did not join that group, meetings with the executors that spring left her very upset.

On April 1 Josephine married Albert Carrington Young, son of Brigham Jr., and on May 27 Mamie became engaged. Emily's daughters had now all been launched into matrimony. Two weeks later, on June 10, her joy was tempered by a telegram announcing the death of her mother. The woman who had tended the mischievous four-year-old Emily on the hatmaker's farm in Ohio had died in central Utah, cared for by Caroline and Eliza. In June, Carlos returned home from the East for a visit, which must have cheered his mother. He was studying art and music at Rensselaer and had ambitions to become an architect.

Emily continued to be unhappy because of the estate difficulties and the departure of her daughters from her home. Mamie married Leonard Hardy on August 28, an ordeal for her mother. Two days later she wrote, "The dreaded day is over, the weding. Mamie has moved away ... I will trust in the Lord, though deep waters overwhelm me yet will I look to him for he[lp]." Three pages of the diary are then excised. On June 28 she had written that all of these problems made her feel "alltogether ... so loanly that I hardly know whether I exist or not. I feel as I would immagine a person would if they were going to be hung, continualy looking for a hole to creep out at. But when none is found, wish it would hasten up and have it over with ... But I must throw off this despondent feeling." She seems almost suicidal but realizes that she must fight her depression. We see how important a polygamous wife's children were to her. In July 1878 Emily repeatedly complained of the injustice of the executors, and after one of these entries another page was torn out of the diary.

Her Christmas was happy, she reported, though Carlos was absent. In mid-January 1879 she underwent a winter depression: "The snow is coming down plentifully. When I awoke this morning, my mind reverted back to some of the reminicences of my past life. And as there is not much that is pleasant; it of course, brings sorrowful feelings, and I am weak enough to cry; and that is what I have been doing this morning; untill I saw it was making me sick and had to desist." Like her friend, Helen Mar, she turned continually to the past, even though it seemed overwhelmingly sorrowful to her.

A granddaughter, in a reminiscence, wrote that Emily's close friends during this period were Rachel Grant, Bathsheba Smith, Zina D. H. Young, and Emmeline B. Wells, and diary entries from early 1879 reflect this circle of friends. Emily was invited to Eliza Snow's birthday party but was too sick to attend; however, she attended Zina's birthday gathering at Bathsheba's home. Then she celebrated her own fifty-fifth birthday on February 28. But the major event for the year was probably the arrival of Josephine's first baby on April 15. In addition, Carlos graduated from Rensselaer that year with a degree in engineering and returned to Utah.

On January 1, 1880, Emily wrote, "I enter upon the New Year with the erisypilus." Erysipelas, the common nineteenth-century skin inflammation, often afflicted Emily on her face, and she continued to record her bouts with it throughout the year. A July 28, 1880, diary entry reveals that she still could not pay her tax assessment: "It is utterly impossible for me to pay it. I have been trying since the first of January to save enough to pay it ... My health is so poor that I cannot earn anything, neither save by doing my own work." The problems with Brigham's will dragged on. On August 16 she confessed, "My feelings are too sore to talk about these things without getting excited."

Emily moved from her house in the Twelfth Ward to a new, smaller house, the "old Exponent office" in the Thirteenth Ward, on March 4, 1881. In April and May she traveled to St. George in southern Utah, where she and siblings Edward and Caroline did temple work for their dead relatives. On July 29 and August 1 she wrote two moving journal entries that reveal her ambivalence toward polygamy:

Sunday. Today I've been thinking, thinking, thinking. My mind goes back to days gone by. And what do I find, can I find anything so pleasant that I could wish to live it over again or even to dwell upon it in thought, with any degree of satisfaction. No I cannot. My life has been like a panorama of disagreeable pictures. As I scan them over one by one, they bring no joy, and I invariably wind up with tears. I have been heart hungry all my life, always hoping against hope, until the years are nearly spent, and hope is dead for this life but bright for the next. And then I aske myself what great or good thing have I done that I should hope for better things in the next world, or what great trial or exploit can I recount like many others perhaps, that will bring honor and greatness. I can only sum it up in one word, and that is I am a "woman" or if that is not enough I am a "mother" and still more I am, as the world calls it, "spiritual wife" of early days, when public opinion was like an avalanche burying all such beneath its oppressive weight. Some will understand what it is to be a woman, mother, or an unloved "spiritual wife."

One wonders what she means by "unloved" spiritual wife–a proxy wife neglected by Brigham or "cast off" earlier by Joseph? But these brooding remarks are followed by a rebound on the following day: "Yesterday I was in a dark mood. Today I am looking for the bright spots. Although they may be few and far between they should not be over-looked and among my greatest blessings I class the facts that I am a mother and was a spiritual wife." One senses the beginnings of a Mormon proto-feminism here. Emily wonders what great or good thing she has accomplished in this life, and immediately realizes that she is a "woman" and a "mother," has suffered for Mormonism as a plural wife, and that these attributes are her greatest glory, despite the fact that they have caused her life to be a "panorama of disagreeable pictures." In 1895 she wrote, eloquently,

Woman has had to bear her own burdens, and also a great portion of mans curse. She is not only expected to bear children, but she must drudge from morning untill night; and her duties as wife and mother often follow her from night until morning; and her labors never cease as long as she can place one foot before the other. I do not think that God designed that man should enjoy all the sweets of Liberty; while woman is bowed down in shackles. Liberty is sweet. As sweet to woman as to man. ... We do not wish to drag our brothers down, but we desire to raise ourselves up to his level We have born the galling chains a very long time.

She lost her last child to matrimony on September 22, 1881, when her son, Don Carlos, married Alice Dowden. Emily probably felt this final marriage keenly, but a week later she moved in with the newlyweds. They made her feel welcome, but she disliked the sense of dependence she felt while living with them.

On December 23 she overcame her initial reluctance and attended a party in the Sixteenth Ward celebrating Joseph Smith's birth, saw many of her old friends, and "had a very good time." On Christmas Day she listed her presents, also a favorite theme in her sister Eliza's diary: "My children each gave me a present. Where could I be if I had no children, none to think of me ... What a desolate life to contemplate. Emily gave me a book The Treasures of Art, candy and nuts. Carlie a gold pin, Carlos a nice bracelet, Mamie an album, Josephine her likeness, all which were very acceptable."

Emily moved into "the Decker house" on May 2, 1882, where she rented two rooms to a young couple. However, though she had her free-dom once again, her old painful solitude returned. In early August she wrote that she was "terribly lonesome. A lonely old age is not a very desir-able situation, especially with poor health. I would like to be where I could see my children oftener. I would like to see some of them once a day if no more." On Christmas Day she once again listed her gifts—"a very nice clock ... a silver thimble ... a scarf pin." In late April 1883 she relo-cated again, accompanying Emily Augusta to a new brick home.

As trouble was brewing between Carlie and Mark Croxall, Emily be-gan living with her daughter on November 3. "Well, I am here with Carlie because she needs me, and my help more than any of the rest. Mark will do nothing for her or the children and she has no way of support until she can sell something." According to Ann Eliza Young, Croxall was pursuing a young Danish woman at this time, evidently as a polygamous wife, and Carlie felt spurned, humiliated, and "heart-broken." The morning of the move to Carlie's home, Emily had another attack of nostalgia: "As soon as I woke up my mind reverted back to Nauvoo; and I was back in the Man-sion House, living again some of the incidents of my long life. And ended as usual by making myself sick with weeping."

On Christmas Day Emily spent the morning at Carlie's, then had din-ner at Emily Augusta's. Once more her journal lists her gifts carefully: "There was (24) twenty four of my family there. Carlos gave me a small desk. Emily and Mamie gave me a box with comb, brush and looking glass. Carlie and Josephine gave me a wind up lamp. Lulu gave me a silk bag—her own work. We had a splendid good time."

When Emily celebrated her sixtieth birthday on February 28, 1884, she wrote, "It does not seem possible ... I have been out walking; I called on Rachel Grant, Sister E.S. Smith." Carlie and Mark divorced on July 8, and Emily moved to Emily Augusta's home on August 29. A half year later, on November 3, Carlie, thirty-three, married George Q. Cannon, fifty-seven, as his fifth wife. This was another dynastic union, as Cannon was an influential counselor in the First Presidency and had been a close friend of Brigham Young. All of Carlie's children by Croxall were sealed to Cannon for eternity.

Emily would occasionally write for the *Woman's Exponent*. When her autobiographical sketches began to appear in December, she con-fided to her diary, "I did not expect to see (it) in this number and it almost took away my breath." On January 24, 1885, she attended a surprise birth-day party for Helen Mar Whitney, whose husband had recently died. Thirty years earlier in Nauvoo, Helen had been shooed out of the Kimball home when Emily came to marry Joseph.

Emily, who had been an important character when Joseph Smith began to practice polygamy in Nauvoo, now would witness the events leading to the cessation of polygamy among Mormons, and she herself would be directly affected. On February 15 she wrote, "Many of our brethren have had to flee from their homes on account of the persecutions of our enemies." She was subpoenaed on April 24 as a witness against Hiram Clawson. A year later, on March 10, 1886, federal marshalls, hoping to arrest Hiram, searched both Emily Augusta's and Josephine's houses, so Emily Dow retreated to the Lion House for a brief stay. She began living with Josephine in early November. The same year three Smith sister-wives died and were noted in her journal: "Desdemona Fullmer Smith," Marinda Hyde Smith, and most importantly her biological sister, Eliza. Carlos served the first of two terms as a member of the Utah legislature, and in the following years he would be appointed church architect and supervise completion of the Salt Lake temple. Then, in early December 1887, another important sister-wife, Eliza R. Snow Smith, died. On December 10 Emily wrote, "Went to the Lion House and got the little desk and small piece of lace that ERS Smith left me in her will from Br. L. Snow." Her Nauvoo past was fading, person by person.

### XVI. "Truly We Are Turning Backwards"

Emily moved back to her own home at 55 North 100 East in mid-March 1888. During this year two of her daughters would leave Utah: Josephine on May 9, for New York, where her husband apparently sought employment opportunities, and Emily Augusta to San Francisco to avoid testifying against her husband. Her daughter was now part of the "polygamy underground."

In December Emily visited Emily Augusta in California, where she was joined by Carlos at the end of the month. Writing to her other children on December 27, she was obviously homesick: "I should not think anybody would want to come here this time of the year for pleasure Take it all together, it cant come up to Utah ... I dont see how people can keep well with so much dampness and musty smell everywhere." In the spring of 1889 she returned to Utah, as did Josephine. In May she wrote Emily Augusta, "Dear daughter I have not been feeling very well since I came home. Before I had got fairly rested I was threatened with my old complaint but I drove it off with quinine." Nevertheless, she had made "one dress for Josephine out of that canvass cloth of Lulus old dress." She had also sewed "several pounds of carpet rags, that is work as near to doing nothing as can be." Evidently, she was living near a farm, because "Everything is so pleasant down here the trees are green and the birds singing and the geese and hens cacling."

She returned to San Francisco on November 8. She spent New

Year's Day alone with Emily A.: "We have been very lonesome. I shall be so glad when Emily can go home." One is reminded of Zina enduring long exiles in Canada to be with her only daughter. By January 11 Emily D. was back in Salt Lake City, but she visited Emily Augusta again in May. When she returned home in mid-June, she described her homecoming to Emily A: "Allice got dinner for me yesterday, and Mamie made some ice cream, and all was so glad to see me home again, and the children were more glad than I would have thought. The little ones follow me around so that I can hardly get a chance to write. L G is robbing his mothers flowerpots so as to bring me flowers."

On September 25, 1890, church president Wilford Woodruff published his Manifesto, the first major step leading to the demise of polygamy in Mormonism. This statement would greatly lessen Mormon and "gentile" tensions in America and Utah, and as a result prosecution of polygamists married before 1890 became less stringent. Happily, Emily Augusta was able to return to Salt Lake City, arriving on February 28, 1891, Emily Dow's sixty-seventh birthday. A year later a gathering of descendants met once again. Emily wrote, "Today I am sixty-eight ... I was pleased to see so many of my posterity together." On March 1 she was content living in her own home: "I am more comfortable now than I ever was in my life before. I enjoy my little quiet home ... Today Bert and Josephine were rebaptized."

Starting on March 14, Emily gave testimony in the Temple Lot court trial as a former plural wife of Joseph Smith. Three days later she attended the Relief Society's fiftieth anniversary celebration, then testified again on the 19th. In her diary she pondered: "I was there several hours and underwent a rigid examination ... Truly we are turning backward, and [a] very strange thing it is, when after all these many years, Joseph the Prophet is being tried in court for teaching and practicing plural marriage. And some of his wives are brought forward to testify either for or against him."

Emily continued to associate with the "leading sisters" of Mormonism. On May 17 Zina Young, with whom she had lived in a primitive shack at Mt. Pisgah, and Rachel Grant washed and anointed Emily's daughter Mamie and daughter-in-law Alice in preparation for their impending childbirths. On April 6, 1893, Emily attended the dedication of the Salt Lake temple, a personal triumph for Carlos, though he had resigned as church architect two days earlier because of bad health.

On Emily's seventieth birthday the next year, the entire First Presidency, Wilford Woodruff, George Q. Cannon, and Joseph F. Smith, attended the party. In her diary she noted that when Cannon called her "mother" she felt "quite proud." She was also delighted by a short speech given by Joseph F. in which he referred to her as "his aunt," a reference to her marriage to Joseph. In December Emily and Lucy Walker Kimball attended a program celebrating the birthday of Joseph Smith. Joseph F. Smith asked Emily and Lucy to stand, and pointed them out as wives of Joseph Smith, Jr., saying, "They were given to him of the Lord in Nauvoo ... and they will stand with him in Eternity as his honorable wives." After the meeting many women came to Emily and shook hands and kissed her, and many men shook her hand: "I felt it an honor but a little embarrassed." She contrasted that public honor given to her now to her feelings of humiliating subordination in Nauvoo: "Then even our own people seemed to think that the Lord had given men plural wives for stepping stones for them and their first wives to mount to glory on, and that we could never rise because of our inferiority." On March 4, 1895, she noted the anniversary of her marriage to Joseph fifty-two years previously, and ended a brief reminiscence with, "Well I dont like to think of those times."

She continued to note typical events in her diary—birthdays, Christmas gifts, Young family reunions, more limited family gatherings, accidents, sicknesses, births, marriages, departures, arrivals. The diary became sketchier as she got older. Eugenia Rampton, a granddaughter, left an appreciation of Emily that allows us to visualize the elderly woman— "slim, tall, and rather dark complexioned." She was a diligent seamstress, giving her beautiful creations to her grandchildren:

> I remember Grandma taking her daughters' old dresses and making dresses for the younger children, girls and boys; left over pieces were pieced for quilts, and then came carpet rags, sewn together, and the remaining small pieces were formed into flowers and leaves and sewn onto split gunny sacks, lined and backed by heavier material such as old heavy draperies. She did many lovely bedspreads and shams of net, darning beautiful patterns into it. She also made two dresses for grown granddaughters, and some lovely aprons ... I remember seeing Grandma plucking either ducks or geese and making flannel jackets of them. This was at her small farm on south Fifth east, by Liberty park. She also dyed many pieces of cloth.

Eugenia also remembered Emily the intellectual: "Grandma was well read and did a lot of writing."

## XVII. "Griefs To[o] Deep for Tears"

On the anniversary of Joseph Smith's death in 1897, Emily brooded over her first husband: "My heart is filled with bitter regret when I think that I might have added, even one drop of sorrow to the abundance already heaped upon him." She remembered him walking the floor in his Nauvoo home, his head bowed, his hands clasped behind him, and at such times, she remembers, her heart ached for him. She regretted that she had been impatient at times and hoped that he would forgive her, "and I think he will for he well knew the trying conditions of my life, and that I was subject to many disagreeable and humiliating circumstances." She was young and did not know the consequences of her actions, she wrote. Characteristically, she does not remember the prophet's offenses to her. "Well this is all past and gone. I have felt sad and loanly all this day but have shed no tears. There are griefs to[o] deep for tears. I have been living over again the sorrowful scenes of fifty three years ago today; well may we weep and morn. Emily D.P. Young - Smith." A year later, on the same day, she reminisced about him again and wrote, "He was one of the noblest of men and those who knew him best, loved him best."

After Christmas in 1898, Emily wrote that she had been sick for two or three weeks, but two days later she quantified the time of sickness as four months. On May 16, 1899, she moved into Emily Augusta's home in the Twelfth Ward. "She and the girls are so good to me I hardly know how to express myself," she wrote. As fall approached, her illness increased. On October 3 she journalized, "Went to the Temple to be administered to." The last diary entry is on November 13: "The sun is shining. Shirley returned from Canada. He started the 15th."

She died on December 9 at age seventy-six, while living at the home of Emily Augusta, in the first house she had been given by Brigham Young in Salt Lake City. The cause of death was listed by her obituary as "general debility, brought on by a kind of nervous prostration and weakness." The *Deseret News* provided an epitaph:

> Mrs. Young has over forty grandchildren, several great grandchildren, a numerous posterity, and all in the faith of the Gospel in which she believed and for which she made great and noble sacrifices. Mrs. Young was a very retiring, modest and reticent woman, but firm in her convictions as the everlasting hills ... She was greatly beloved by her own family and also loved and revered by the family of her late husband, and the women of the Latter-day Saints who had the pleasure of her acquaintance.

A "polygamy niece," Susa Young Gates, left a more personal eulogy: "There was Aunt Emily Partridge than whom no more sainted heroine ever came into father's family. If she had ever had an irritable mood, or entertained an ignoble thought, it must have passed too quickly for utterance; for the calm serenity of her life was unmarred by humanity's usual explosions." Little did Susa suspect the troubled inner life of this gentle, shy woman, or the painful dissonance she lived with as she tried to correlate her two husbands' human failings with their enormous prophetic charisma.

## XVIII. A Life in Polygamy

Emily Partridge provides us with a classic example of the central pattern examined in this book: polygamy may be sacred in theory, but when practiced on a day-to-day basis the plural wife is not given financial or emotional support. In Nauvoo Joseph taught Emily the principle of plural, celestial marriage, and married her and Eliza, but then acquiesced to Emma's browbeatings and consented to his new wives' expulsion from his home. Then he allowed the marriages to lapse, apparently taking the unions less seriously than did the Partridges. It should be remembered that he had at least thirty other wives to turn to at the time. After Joseph's death, Emily married Brigham Young in open polygamy, but from the beginning of the marriage to its end she was less than a full wife in his family. During the exodus from Nauvoo, the haunting image of the lonely wife standing with new-born baby in the snow shows Emily's lack of practical marital support. Then in 1853, feeling "more lonely and more unreconciled to [her] lot than ever," she requested a divorce from Young and remarriage to a husband less occupied with other wives and church business. Though her marriage to Young continued, when her diary begins we find that Brigham evidently viewed her as less than his own eternal wives and demanded that she support herself. She agonized over payment of small water and school bills, at the same time that she realized bitterly that Brigham was extremely wealthy. Her diary entries expressing her resentment form a significant document, a moving *cri de coeur* against a non-supportive polygamous husband. The fact that this husband was the prophet and president of the church added a note of cognitive dissonance to her journal, for her religion demanded that she see him as an inspired religious leader. Her words of praise for Brigham after his death show her highly developed capacity for Christian forgiveness. As a result of her distance from him during his lifetime, she brooded on the past, living in an idealized Nauvoo, experiencing periodic bouts of depression. But she lived for her children, a typical polygamous wife's strategy for emotional support and survival.

# 19.

# "Everything Looks like Desolation and Lonesome"

## *Eliza Maria Partridge (Smith Lyman)*

### I. Amasa Lyman

As with all of Joseph Smith's wives, Eliza undoubtedly grieved deeply for her prophet and husband at his passing. She was still with the Coolidges at the time. But her next marriage was quickly approaching. After little sister Caroline, age seventeen, married apostle Amasa Lyman, thirty-one, as his first plural wife on September 6, Eliza, twenty-four, married him only a few weeks later on the 28th.

Born in 1813 in Lyman, Grafton, New Hampshire, Amasa became a Mormon in April 1832 at age nineteen and served in Zion's Camp two years later. He married Maria Tanner in 1835. After settling in Far West in 1837, he endured the late Missouri persecutions, then relocated in Nauvoo in 1841. His great intellectual and leadership gifts were by now apparent, for he was ordained an apostle on August 20, 1842 to take the place of Orson Pratt when Pratt was dropped from the Twelve. But when Orson was reinstated in January 1843, Amasa was called as a counselor in the First Presidency, then served a number of short missions before becoming a member of the Twelve again on August 12, 1844.

Following her marriage, Eliza moved to her mother's house "for awhile," then lived with Amasa and Maria. Entering into this second plural marriage was not easy for her. She later wrote:

> Times were not then as they are now in 1877 but a woman living in polygamy dare not let it be known and nothing but a firm desire to keep the commandments of the Lord could have induced a girl to marry in that way. I thought my trials were very severe in that line and I am often led to wonder how it was that a person of my temperament could get along with it and not rebel, but I know it was the Lord who kept me from opposing his plans although in my heart I felt that I could not submit to

them, but I did and I am thankful to my Heavenly Father for the care he had over me in those troublous times.

On November 14 Amasa took a fourth wife, Cornelia Leavitt, nineteen years of age. Ten days later Zina Huntington Jacobs wrote in her journal, "Eliza Partridge and Caroline P ware here and took Dinner with us. Also Cornelia Levet was here." Only family history and an early Mormon context allows the reader to understand that three wives of Amasa Lyman were visiting Zina Jacobs on this occasion. In July 1845 Amasa took a fifth wife, twenty-nine-year-old Dionitia Walker.

Eliza received her endowment in the Nauvoo temple on the first day of 1846 in a session with her sister Caroline and former sister-wives Helen Mar Kimball, Sarah Ann Whitney, and Mary Houston. On January 13 she repeated, in the temple, her earlier proxy marriage to Amasa for time.

Three days later Amasa married his sixth and seventh wives, Paulina Phelps (eighteen) and Priscilla Turley (sixteen). On January 28 he added seventeen-year-old Laura Reed to his family, and Eliza and Caroline stood proxy as he was sealed to two deceased women, one of whom was their sister Harriet. After this last flurry of ritual, and as the Mormons began leaving Nauvoo, Eliza had suddenly become a member of a large apostolic family. This gave her elite status, but her husband had to divide his attention and means among eight women. He would find it difficult to provide for them all and would be, in many ways, a problematic husband.

## II. "I Am Now Like a Skeleton"

On about February 9 Eliza, four months pregnant, left Nauvoo with Amasa, sister-wife Dionitia, Mr. and Mrs. Dan Clark, and Henry Rollins (brother of Mary Elizabeth Lightner). As they crossed the Mississippi, Eliza recorded, "The ice came down in large pieces and threatened to sink our boat, but at this time as well as many others we were preserved by the power of God." On the other side of the river the Lymans stayed at John Tanner's house for a few days.

At this point Eliza's extraordinary diary begins. On the 17th she and the Lymans traveled to Sugar Creek. She wrote, "About two oclock we started for the camp where we arrived about sundown, prepared our tents, took some refreshment, and retired for the night, but did not sleep much on account of the horses, we not being accustomed to their noise." On March 2 she and Amasa broke camp with the Huntingtons, Zina and Henry Jacobs, Daniel Clark, A. M. Tanner, and J. Butter:

434

The camp of Israel began to move. There were about four hundred waggons. After traveling about five miles they [we] camped for the night, scraped away the snow and pitched their [our] tents, fortunately for us there was plenty of wood and the Brethren made large fires in front of the tents which kept us from freezing but we could not possibly be made comfortable under such circumstances, but did not complain as we were leaving the land of our enemies and hoped for better times.

So Eliza's journey west began. The diary records the usual phenomena of Mormon pioneer life in the Iowa spring: rain, deaths, sicknesses, new kinds of food ("we had an excellent dinner of our ducks and squirrels," on March 31), friends and acquaintances passing by, and omnipresent mud. Crossing rain-swollen rivers was always dangerous. On April 1 Eliza tried to walk across a log over the Fox River, with Amasa holding on to one hand and "D. P. Clark" holding the other. "Unfortunately for Br L_ he stepped on a rotten limb which broke and let him fall a distance of ten or more feet into the water, but I more fortunate held fast to Br Clark and thus saved myself from falling." A week later, now six months pregnant, she and her group were separated from the wagon carrying their beds, so camped with the Huntingtons, sleeping on supplies: "I laid across a box in Father Huntington's waggon with my head on his and Mother's bed with my feet on the front end board and my clothes wet about a quarter of a yard deep around my ankles. I do not know why I did not freese, for I had no bed and very little covering. It must be that there was not room in the wagon for the frost to get in, it was so full of folks."

On May 8 Eliza observed primly, "We have plenty of squirrels and wild turkeys here and at night we are blessed with the music of the wolves." She reached the waystation, Mt. Pisgah, on May 20. Three weeks later, on June 11, eight months pregnant, she departed with Caroline, leaving Emily and Lydia and little brother Edward with "Father Huntington."

On July 14 she recorded her delivery, midwived by Patty Sessions: "My first child was born here, in a wagon. I have named him Don Carlos. I am very uncomfortably situated for a sick woman. The scorching sun shining upon the wagon through the day and the cool air at night, is almost too much of a change to be healthy." In the following weeks she was afflicted by "childbed fever" and came near death. On August 9 she wrote:

I am now like a skeleton, so much so that those who have not been with me, do not know me till told who I am. It is a fearful place to be sick with fever, in a wagon with no shade over head except the cover and a July sun shining every day. All the comfort I had was the pure cold water from a spring near by. But the Lord preserved my life for some purpose for which I thank Him. My babe in consequence of my sickness, is very poor, but as I get better I hope to see him improve.

On the 22nd the young mother proudly wrote of her first child: "Don Carlos 10 weeks old today and as bright a little child as ever was." Four days later she arrived at Winter Quarters, where she would stay for two years.

### III. "He Is Gone and I Cannot Recall Him"

At first Eliza lived in her wagon and in tents, no doubt, while Amasa built her a primitive shelter. On October 15 she moved in: "We have taken possession of our log house today. The first house my baby was ever in. I feel extremely thankful for the privilege of sitting by a fire where the wind cannot blow it in every direction ... Our house is minus floor and many other comforts but the walls protect us from the wind if the sod roof does not [protect us] from the rain."

She noted her son's progress on November 14: "Don Carlos weighs 13 pounds having gained 2 pounds during the 1st month. He is a great comfort to me." However, three weeks later, in early December, he was sick "and getting worse. Has cried all day but I cannot see what ails him." A week later Eliza lost him, and her record of that death is one of the most moving passages in Mormon literature:

> The baby is dead and I mourn his loss. We have done the best we knew how for him, but nothing has done any good, he continued to fail from the time he was taken sick. My sister Caroline and I sat up every night with him and tried to save him from death for we could not bear to part with him, but we were powerless. The Lord took him and I will try to be reconciled and think that all is for the best. He was my greatest comfort and was nearly always in my arms. But he is gone and I cannot recall him, so I must prepare to meet him in another and I hope a happier world than this. I still have friends who are dear to me, if I had not I should wish to bid this world farewell, for it is full of disappointments and sorrow. But I believe that there is a power that watches over us and does all things right. He was buried on the west side of the Missouri on the second ridge back, the eleventh grave on the second row counting from right to left, the first row being farthest from the river. This will be no guide as the place cannot be found in a few years.

The loss clearly plunged Eliza into deep grief, and she was almost suicidal, longing to bid farewell to a world of "disappointments and sorrow." Only friends kept her focussed on this life, and a faith in "a power that watches over us and does all things right." She continued on. Later in the year she copied a poem by Eliza R. Snow into her diary: "Beloved Eliza do not weep/ Your baby sleeps a quiet sleep/ Although in dust his body lies/ His spirit soars above the skies."

In Winter Quarters Eliza attended social gatherings and participated in a complex web of friendships and familial affinities. Her mother, who had been widowed for the second time by the death of William Huntington, arrived at Winter Quarters on March 21, 1847. On April 8 Amasa left for the wilderness with the first "pioneers" and did not return until October 28. Not long after that, the day before Christmas, he started on a mission south.

Eliza was coming to find her log house inadequate, so she and Caroline pulled down an abandoned cabin and began to construct a cabin themselves on their property. After the walls were five or six logs high, "some brethren" laid the rest of the logs on them, then put a dirt roof on top. Eliza obtained bricks and made a fireplace and chimney; once again a male "topped" it off for her. "We had one window of three panes of glass. We divided the room with a wagon cover and let E. P. Clark and wife have one part as he had helped to build it. We each had room enough to put our beds by having the foot of the bedsteads come together and about 6 feet square from there to the fire."

In early 1848 Eliza's diary entries are infrequent—daily life in Winter Quarters must have seemed uneventful. Then in the summer she and Amasa began preparing for their journey to Utah. They left toward the end of June. At the time of departure Eliza was roughly seven months pregnant, so she would endure another difficult pioneer journey. On August 20 she bore a second child on the overland trail, Platte DeAlton Lyman, who came into the world in a wagon on the east bank of the Platte River near Ft. Laramie: "This is the second son that I have had born in a wagon and I still think it is a most uncomfortable place to be sick [pregnant] in ... The journey thus far has not been very pleasant to me," she wrote, with considerable understatement.

### IV. "The Country Barren and Desolate"

Eliza's company reached Salt Lake Valley on October 17. Her initial reaction was not euphoric: "We are now at our journey's end for the present. The weather is beautiful. The country barren and desolate. I do not think our enemies need envy us this locality or ever come here to disturb us." The next day she moved into a "log room" in the old fort, which she would share with seven other people throughout the winter: her mother, sisters Caroline and Lydia, her brother Edward, Amasa at times, one of Maria's children, and Platte. "We are glad to get this shelter, but it is no shelter when it rains for the dirt roof lets the water through and the dirt floor gets muddy," she wrote.

In an April 1849 entry, Eliza summed up her early Salt Lake experience: nerve-racking, dangerous sicknesses, shortages of food, gradual settling of the valley outside of the fort. "During the past winter ... My Baby was very sick with whooping cough. Many children around us died with it. My brother Edward also had it, they are both quite well of it now. We are intending to have our houses moved out of the fort onto our lots in town. Cooked the last of our flour to day and have no prospect of getting any more untill after harvest."

On the 13th Amasa was assigned by Brigham Young to head a mission to the west coast, so he would subsequently spend a number of years in southern California. Eliza did not accompany him, for unknown reasons. "May the Lord bless and prosper them, and return them in safety to their families and friends," she wrote. "Br. L has left us that is Paulina, Caroline and I without any thing to make bread, it not being in his power to get any. The family at Cotton wood have some." She was clearly beginning to feel the pinch of plurality. Not only was she a plural wife in a large family, but her husband was far away on a mission. Tensions with sister-wives can also be seen in this entry, as one family is left with flour and another has none. Eliza and her companions began spinning candle wick to exchange for bread: "Sold a ball of candle wick for 3-1/2 quarts of corn. Sold another ball for 3-1/2 quarts of meal which has to be divided between Paulina Lyman, Mother, and my family." She also sewed to make ends meet.

On April 19 Eliza, Platte, a Brother Frederic, and Caroline moved from the old fort to a lot in the city where they lived in wagons. Two days later sister Emily brought her fifteen pounds of flour: "Said Presnt Young heard that we were out of bread and told her to bring that much although they have a scanty allowance for themselves." Eliza was fully integrated into the network of Brigham's, Heber's and Joseph's wives. On May 2 she journalized, "Went to the Fort and visited at Sister Holmes' with sisters Fuller and E. R. Snow. Had quite a rain with high cold wind. Went to Mother's and staid all night." On the 16th she met with many of Joseph's widows, with the two main proxy husbands also attending: "Visited at Wm Walker's with sisters Emily and Louisa Young and Sarah Ann and Lucy Kimball also Presnts Young and Kimball."

Eliza's little family was evidently living in a tent by her wagon on the Lyman lots, but on the 19th, while she was away visiting, the tent burned down, including a prized rocking chair. She moved back into the wagon. Spring proved tempestuous that year. Three days later there was a "Tremendous rain and snow storm with high winds," and the next day "the snow and wind beat down relentlessly." Even though Eliza and Caroline had a stove in their wagon, they thought it would be better to retreat to the fort to their mother's home. But on arriving at her house they discovered that "The rain was running through the roof and every thing in the house was wet, and the ground perfectly muddy under her feet. We ... took her and her effects up to the wagons deeming it more prudent to live out of doors than in such a house as this."

Finally summer came. On June 8 Eliza described her household, each member working busily: "Br Frederic ditching, Edward building hen house. Mother spinning cotton, Lydia helping Emily wash. Caroline teaching school and myself make pants for D. Frederic, taking care of Baby &c." Edward and Brother Frederic began sawing logs for a home and construction continued through August. Again it was often siblings, rather than husbands, who provided support for plural wives. On July 21 Eliza received some flour from wheat grown in the valley and three days later attended the first annual Pioneer Day: "Great celebration which we all attended. Took dinner with the Cotton wood ward. Had a pleasant time. Plenty of victuals, music and mirth, and some good preaching."

On August 20 Eliza celebrated Platte's first birthday with a number of women friends. In two weeks their makeshift cabin was up, but it was crude, and the weather was turning chilly: "We have very cold nights and our house if house it can be called is very uncomfortable. The logs laid up part of the roof on and a very little chinking in." But the days were still warm. One day Eliza took Platte "and went to the field to glean wheat. I spread my quilt under the wagon in the shade for the baby while I gleaned, but the sun was so warm that I could not work long."

## V. "Desolation and Lonesome"

In early October the Lyman families received goods from Amasa in California. A year later, on September 29, 1850, he returned to Utah to stay the winter. But on the following March 11 he left again to preside over the southern California Saints. As before, Eliza was left behind, though Amasa took most of his other wives with him, including sister Caroline. Eliza grieved when they left: "Br. Lyman started with all of his family, except Paulina and me and our children, Oscar and Platte. Everything looks like desolation and lonesome as sister Caroline has gone too. But I have Mother and other friends here yet." Eliza was four months pregnant when Amasa left. On July 25 she wrote, "Have had a very uncomfortable summer so far as my health is very poor." A week later, on August 1, Caroline Eliza Lyman ("Carlie") was born.

A year later the baby became very sick, but by December she had recovered, just as Amasa returned to Salt Lake and saw his new daughter for the first time: "Br. Lyman and Caroline and the Boy, Marion, returned from California making glad the hearts of us all." On April 20, 1853, Amasa was off again: "Br. Lyman started for San Bernardino after staying here for a short space of 4 months which though short has passed pleasantly away and all that I regret is that the time is no longer." The heartache of seeing a husband leave was compounded by Eliza's fear of having no means of support. She accompanied Amasa as far south as Sanpete County but reported that she did not enjoy the trip much, as Caroline, who had just had a child, was ill.

Platte had his fifth birthday on August 20, and Eliza invited some of his "little friends" to a party: "I fixed a low table for them so that they could sit on their little chairs and they were indeed a lovely sight and caused me many reflections as to what might be their lot in the future." Then her New England religiosity showed through: "May the Lord surround them with guardian angels who shall have especial care over them, that they may never go astray from the path of rectitude but may be prepared when they are called to leave this earth to return to their Father pure and unspotted and enter into exaltation and glory." Eliza is the classic Mormon mother, worrying first about her son's eternal welfare. Zina Baker Huntington and Julia Hills Johnson had similarly brooded over their children's spiritual upbringing even before they became Mormons. One also thinks of the indefatigably pious Sarah Cleveland.

On February 7, 1854, Amasa, forty, married twenty-four-year-old Lydia Partridge in San Bernardino, and Eliza must have regarded the marriage with mixed feelings. She would have welcomed a second sister into the Lyman family but might have wondered how Amasa would provide for a new wife, the eleventh in his "kingdom," when the previous wives were struggling to get by. Her brother Edward was called on a mission to Hawaii in early April, "which will leave us without man or boy to do anything," Eliza lamented, seemingly upset but resigned. Throughout 1854-55 she wove and made clothes to exchange for food.

Amasa returned from California on December 1, 1855, with plural wife Dionitia, who moved in with Eliza and Caroline. Eliza's diary carefully noted outings with her husband. For instance, on December 7 she "Attended a selected party at Seth Blair's with Br. Lyman and Caroline." On the 27th she "Dined at Governor Young's with Br. Lyman and part of our family." But even while in Utah Amasa occasionally left to make preaching tours throughout the territory. He often took wives with him, but rarely Eliza, apparently.

In a February journal entry Eliza listed the work she had been doing: weaving (bringing in $102), sewing, spinning, coloring, housework, tending garden, both planting and gathering, "and almost every kind of work that a woman was ever known to do." On March 18 she noted wryly, with a hint of sharpness, "Eat our meals without bread for the very good reason that we have none, although we have a pound or two of flour for the children who are having the measles." It was years after the early Utah privations, so to still lack flour was poverty indeed.

In the late summer Amasa and Dionitia left Utah once again. Eliza wrote calmly on September 2, "May he be prospered." Four of Apostle Lyman's wives were now in Utah, while four were in California. Three had left him by now. Eliza was about six months pregnant, so her husband would once again be absent at the time of childbirth. On December 13 she bore Joseph Alvin Lyman. Two months before his birth Caroline had borne a boy, and a month later sister Lydia also had a son, so the three Partridge Lymans all had new baby boys.

Eliza's journal goes on hiatus from 1857 to 1860, but Amasa's movements can be traced during that time. On June 3, 1857, he returned to Utah, but on September 15, as Johnston's army approached Utah from the east, he sent a son to bring his California families back to Utah, then traveled to meet them en route. He subsequently sold his valuable San Bernardino land at a great loss. Happily for Eliza, he would no longer divide his time between California and Utah, but despite this, he would continue to be a difficult husband.

Edward Partridge returned from his Hawaiian mission in early January 1858, so Eliza had another pair of hands to help around the house. On February 25 Amasa arrived back in Salt Lake. However, two weeks later he was sent to California to make certain that no army was approaching from that direction. During the "Utah War" Eliza, with five of her sister wives, moved to Utah County to wait out the crisis. In July Amasa and George A. Smith were sent on a preaching mission throughout the settlements, and Amasa also went on speaking tours in early 1859 and spring 1859. Then he began to build houses for two of his California wives in Beaver and Parowan. In the winter he preached and organized wards in southern Utah. Even though he was in Utah now, Eliza must not have seen him frequently.

### VI. "As Usual in Very Poor Circumstances"

In early 1860 Amasa was assigned to serve a mission to England, and on May 1 he set out for the mission field with his son Francis and Apostle Charles Rich. Eliza's journal gives the grim perspective of a wife left at home: "Br. Lyman started on a mission to England leaving us to do the best we could which was not very well as we were as usual in very poor circumstances. We had poor health and no means to help ourselves with." In addition, Eliza was once again pregnant and would be without her husband at childbirth, which took place on August 26. At the time, once again, Eliza lacked basic necessities in the house, which she was sharing with Caroline: "My daughter Lucy Zina born. At this time my Sister Caroline Lyman was very sick in the next room and had been for nearly two months. She had a babe who was also very sick. We had to have watchers every night for them and girls to do the work and not even flour in the house to eat or soap to wash our clothes with. We were at last reduced to the necessity of calling on the missionary Fund to help." "Begging" for food would have been very humiliating for Eliza. She continued, "My sister's health was so poor that she could not nurse her Babe (Annie) so I undertook to nurse both hers and mine. I succeeded very well for a few weeks but had to give it up at last as I could not attend to both." Platte was now twelve, Caroline ten, and Joseph four.

In March 1862, as Amasa was preparing to be released from his mission, he preached a momentous, strange sermon in Dundee, Scotland, in which he suggested that Jesus Christ did not atone for sins but was instead a great religious teacher and human being. A new, troubling chapter in Eliza's story was beginning, though she may not have realized it at that time. Some ten years earlier Lyman had begun reading the works of Andrew Jackson Davis, America's most prominent spiritualist, and in August 1853, while in California, he had participated in his first seance. Davis taught that Jesus was a man and that his death had no salvific significance. Both Lyman and Davis emphasized the universality of gospel truth.

Amasa returned to Salt Lake in September and was immediately sent out to preach among the settlements, where he began to openly share his somewhat unorthodox ideas with the Utah Saints. They were often perplexed by his teachings. As questions began filtering into church headquarters, his days as an apostle were soon numbered.

### VII. Fillmore

On October 8 Lyman wrote in his journal, "President Young said he wished me to sell my real estate and settle in Fillmore and gather my family to that place, to make them a home and to educate my children, which I could not do for them in their present scattered condition." So he began gathering his family from Farmington, Salt Lake, Beaver, and Parowan to Fillmore, some 120 miles south of Salt Lake and the nominal capital of Utah. It had hosted the yearly Utah legislature for a time but was still very much a frontier town, serving as a thoroughfare for many travelers on their way to California, and situated in the middle of Indian territory. Eliza had begun her life in genteel comfort but would spend the rest of it on the frontier, far from the comparative urban civilization and security of Salt Lake City.

On January 19, 1863, there is a typical reference to Eliza in Amasa's journal: "In the evening myself & my wife Eliza visited brother Nathan Tanner and family." On March 7 he and Eliza attended a play together.

Then in July Amasa took Platte and moved to Fillmore, where he built his first home for Priscilla Turley. Eliza stayed in Salt Lake to take care of her sick mother, moving into Emily's home for three months. "Then I left my mother to the care of Sister Sarah Gibbons and my sister Emily and went to Fillmore to join my sisters."

Now, for the first time in her journal, Eliza hints at Amasa's coming apostasy: "Br. Lyman seemed to feel uncomfortable in his mind and I thought many times did not enjoy the portion of the spirit of the Lord that a man in his position should, he being one of the twelve apostles. I did not know what was wrong with him but I could see that he was very unhappy." Amasa gave a "universalist" sermon in Beaver, Utah, that year. Even though he was finally living in the same town as his wives, he nevertheless apparently did not provide for them adequately—as Eliza wrote, "He left his family mostly to their fate or to get along as best they could, although he was with them." According to Amasa's biographer, Albert Lyman (a son of Platte), Amasa had a small flock of sheep, owned half of a grist mill, farm land, horses, and cattle in Fillmore, but neglected these in preference for church and political duties and was therefore unable to provide adequately for eight families. He continued to make extended apostolic trips through Utah territory.

## VIII. "I Prayed Mightily for Him"

Apparently Eliza first lived on the outskirts of Fillmore, but in the spring of 1864 she moved into the town proper and lived in a room in "an unfinished brick house of Br. Lyman's," probably sharing the house with other plural wives. Her early Fillmore years must have been uneventful, for her diary skips a number of years. But storm clouds were gathering around Amasa. He continued to give "universalist" sermons denying the deity of Jesus and preaching salvation to sinners. When confronted by the general authorities in Salt Lake, he would recant his positions, then continue to preach the same doctrines. Finally, on April 30, 1867, he was deprived of his apostleship, his priesthood, and was disfellowshipped (which fell short of excommunication).

About the same time Platte, not yet nineteen, was called on a mission. Eliza described this as "a great trial" to her, "as he had never been away from home and knew nothing of the traps and snares that are set to catch the young and inexperienced and he had no one but me to counsel or help him in any way but me (his Father having apostatized and been cut off from the church) (I did what I could and gave him to the care of the Lord)." She traveled with her son to Salt Lake where he received his endowments and then combined his imminent mission service with another Mormon rite of passage—on May 18 he married Adelia Robison. After a few days visiting friends, Eliza kissed her missionary son goodbye, Adelia kissed her young husband goodbye, then the two women started back for Fillmore, "leaving my dear son to go his way out into the wicked world ... I prayed mightily for him both day and night ... The Lord heard my prayers and answered them to my satisfaction."

She arrived back at Fillmore on the 24th: "When I reached my home ... it looked desolate and lonely. I felt as if I were returning from a funeral. I had a family on my hands but had no one to provide for us." In late 1869 Eliza, to help make ends meet, began teaching sixty students in the Fillmore "State house."

Stripped of his priesthood, Amasa turned to helping his wives more, repairing their houses, working at his sawmill, spending time with them in a way he had not done for many years previously. He continued to attend Mormon church services, and church authorities began to feel that he should be readmitted to full church fellowship. But he began associating with William Godbe, leader of a Utah liberal, spiritualist, universalist movement, and once again spent less and less time with his families. He began preaching his universalist doctrines again, until finally, on May 12, 1870, he was excommunicated. Subsequently he became president of the Godbeite organization.

According to his biographer, "When Amasa left the church the Partridge women left him." So Eliza's marriage history ended. In her first marriage, she was one in more than thirty wives and was expelled from her husband's home by the inimical first wife. In her second marriage, her husband did not provide well for her and her children and was often absent, then was excommunicated, a calamity for the devout Eliza. Having lost him, she lived the rest of her life devoted to her children. However, her final years would be no easier than her early years.

### IX. Grandmother

Platte returned from his mission in late 1869 to find his mother staying with the children of a friend, J. V. Robison. About a year later, in the spring of 1871, Platte was called to preside over the settlement of Oak Creek, modern Oak City, thirty miles north of Fillmore, "so that I was left without a provider again," bemoaned his mother. She was forced to take a job in the "Fillmore Coop Store," where she experienced the typical problems of a working mother: "Received a dollar a day for my services, which enabled me to support my family, but took one away from them through the day which was not very pleasant." She worked in the "Co-op" for two years and continued to teach.

On August 10, 1872, Platte Lyman, Jr., was born to Platte and Adelia at Oak Creek, so Eliza became a grandmother at age fifty-two. Her own family at this time consisted of Carlie, twenty-four, Joseph, sixteen, and Lucy, twelve, though Joseph would often work with Platte in Oak

Creek. A second grandchild, a namesake, was born to Platte and Adelia on January 13, 1874: Eliza Adelia Lyman.

A year later, on January 16, Eliza's younger sister Lydia died of "rheumatism which terminated in dropsy." She left one son, Edward, who was taken in by Caroline, and two daughters, Ida, fifteen, and Lydia May, nine, who moved in with Eliza. In March Eliza moved into Lydia's house, which had more room than her own.

In the fall of 1875 Platte was called on another mission to England and left on October 21 when his wife was seven months pregnant. Joseph did the farm work in Platte's absence, and his children stayed with Eliza through the winter. The new baby, Eveline, was born on December 12. When Adelia returned to Oak Creek in March 1876, she left Eliza Adelia, who had been suffering from "fits," with Eliza. To her grandmother's satisfaction, Eliza Adelia recovered, becoming "fat and healthy." From August to October, Eliza visited Adelia in Oak Creek, then returned to Fillmore.

### X. Two Deaths

According to Albert Lyman, Eliza now moved to Oak Creek, though she apparently divided her time between the two towns. In November Platte returned to Utah, and Eliza and Joseph traveled to the railroad terminus at Scipio to meet him. Utah was becoming progressively more civilized. Eliza had two sons again to help provide for her and her family. In December she settled in for a winter at Oak Creek with Caroline, leaving Carlie in Fillmore, "to do some sewing to pay for wood that we had burnt." Eliza's January 15, 1877, journal entry gives an idea of woman's work in frontier Utah: "Went home and made two bones of lye into soap for Adelia. Also carded and spun some woolen yarn."

At the end of January, she returned to Fillmore, where, she noted in her journal, "Mr. Lyman (the father of my children) quite sick." He died of pneumonia on February 4, and after the funeral the next day she brooded on his apostasy:

Went to the grave at three oclock returned about sundown. I shall not attempt to describe the feelings that I had when I saw the Father of my children sleeping the sleep of death. He who had once been an Apostle of the Lord, and one of the leading men in the Church proclaiming the everlasting gospel to the nations of the earth and being once a great and good man but how is it now. I could only say in my heart how are the mighty fallen. He had denied his religion, the doctrines that he had taught to others for many years and during his last days suffered himself to be severed from the Church of Christ and associated with Apostates and Spiritualists and disaffected persons. Instead of being buried in the robes of the priesthood he requested to be buried in a black coat and pants which was done as he requested.

So ended an entirely unsatisfactory, even ill-starred marriage.

Diary entries from March offer a window into Eliza's daily life. On the 1st she attended "Relief Society meeting" at Oak Creek. Church attendance and associations with fellow sisters would be a constant in her life. Another entry shows the variety in a woman's sewing duties at the time: "Mother is over 83 years of age and does a great deal of work such as braiding straw hats, piecing bed quilts, sewing carpet rags, making buckskin gloves, knitting mittens and sacks and stockings and mending the boys' clothes and makes herself useful in more ways than a person of her age could be expected to." On March 16 Eliza "husked corn with the girls so as to get husks for a bed."

In January 1878 Eliza Adelia died at age four, which must have been another difficult death for her grandmother. "Our Darling little Eliza taken sick in the evening with croup," she wrote. "We did every thing in our power to stay the hand of the Destroyer but could not prevail, and she died on the evening of the 12th."

## XI. "No Mortal but a Woman Can Suffer So"

A new, dramatic chapter in Eliza's life began on February 8, when she, with Carlie, nephew Edward, and Platte began a journey north to Salt Lake City. Carlie, twenty-six, had accepted a marriage proposal from fifty-six-year-old Thomas Callister—a stake president and patriarch living in Deseret, twenty miles southwest of Oak Creek—and would become his fourth wife. After enduring two difficult polygamous marriages, Eliza would now see her daughter enter into her own plural family.

After the day's journey through a snowstorm, the little company camped, the women sleeping in their wagon, the men on the ground: "The night was very cold and still ... Not a sound could be heard except the occasional step of the horses as they moved about in the snow. The stillness of death reigned around." They reached Salt Lake on the 12th and two days later Carlie was sealed to Callister at the Endowment House. After visiting relatives and friends, including Emily, Eliza and her family (apparently with Carlie) started home through snowy, windy, bitterly cold weather on the 18th. On March 7 Eliza noted, "Br. Callister came to Oak Creek to visit his wife Carlie." A month later he finally came to take her back with him to Deseret.

Eliza had a birthday on April 20: "I am 58 years old to day. It does not seem to me to be possible that I have lived so long. When I see others that age I think they are very old but I do not feel so." On the same day she started for Salt Lake again, this time to witness Joseph's marriage to

Nellie G. Roper on the 25th. Four days later Eliza was back in Oak Creek, where she found her mother very ill. On May 12 Joseph and Nellie left to set up housekeeping at Leamington, ten miles north of Oak Creek. Lydia, the family matriarch, died at Eliza's house on June 9. Eliza gave her a last tribute: "Mother has suffered much pain during her sickness which she has borne with patience. She was never known to murmur in her afflictions which have been many, but her sufferings are over and I hope ere long to meet her where pain and sorrow have no power over us, and parting from our friends is unknown."

In October Eliza visited Carlie, who had been homesick for her mother. In early November Eliza and Platte journeyed to Salt Lake City to visit her sister and to shop. Emily wrote in her journal on November 7: "Some car[e]less words of Platts made his mother feel very bad for a little while. She has had a deal of trouble, and is nearly broke down, and can't stand much ... A mother is not apt to be appreciated untill they have passed away. Nobody is like a mother. The name implies pure love, disinterested affection, and all that is good." This passage indicates the stress Eliza had been enduring and that her health had deteriorated. Yet some of the most painful experiences in her life still awaited her.

She was home in Oak Creek by Christmas. In early 1879 she began to demonstrate for plural marriage with other local Mormon women. Even though she had suffered much in polygamy, she was loyal to her church and people and was selected as delegate to a meeting in Fillmore protesting "the Anti-Polygamous Ladies of Utah." She addressed the mass meeting on January 18 and her speech, recorded in her journal, began:

> Strange as it may seem in this enlightened age, we a few of the Ladies of this great Republic, are called upon to vindicate our rights and institutions, which have been assailed by the Anti-Polygamous Ladies of Utah ... It is now about thirty one years since the Prophet Joseph Smith taught to me the principle of Celestial marriage. I was then married by that order and have raised a family of both sons and daughters in what is called Polygamy, and I am not afraid to say that it is one of the most pure and holy principles that has ever been revealed to the Latter day Saints, and one that is necessary to our exaltation.

Carlie was pregnant and moved to Oak Creek soon after this to await the birth of her first child. On February 12 Callister came to visit, but left soon after when it was reported that a daughter by his first wife was seriously ill. On March 7, with Thomas absent, Carlie bore a son, Joseph Callister, but the ordeal left her dangerously ill. Eliza wrote:

> Carlie very sick indeed. Sent for Platte in the night. Delia came in the morning. Sent to Fillmore for Sister Ann Carling as the woman that we had said she had done all she could. Sister Carling did not get here till

about 7 in the evening. About 1/2 past eight Carlie was delivered of a fine son weighing 8 pounds. Carlie's sufferings during this day are past description. No mortal but a woman can suffer so and live. May I never witness such suffering again ... the best sound I ever heard was when I heard the Baby cry.

Carlie seemed to improve briefly, but a week after the birth she took a turn for the worse. On the 14th Eliza wrote, "Carlie has had a fearful night. Her pains seem almost unendurable." As Carlie felt that she would soon die, she began to give her family her last goodbyes. Callister was not there, so Eliza sent for him. "He and his wife Helen arrived in the evening. He was much grieved to find her [Carlie] so low, and tried to make her think she would yet recover." Eliza's journal preserves the final conversation of Thomas and Carlie in unflinching detail. Carlie asked everyone to leave the room except her husband and mother. Then:

> She told him she must surely go and leave her Darling Babe which she wanted her Mother to have and keep, which he said should be as she requested. She said she wanted me to teach him to love his Pa, as he would not be likely to see him much. Br. C———— asked her if she was sorry she had married, as that seems to be the cause or one cause of this sickness ... she said she was not, for she would rather suffer it all again, than not to have had the Baby.

Carlie clearly felt resentment against Thomas Callister for unexplained reasons. Apparently he had never bonded with her as he had with his first wives. Eliza continued:

> She ... talked about leaving as calmly as if she were going out to a friends on a visit. She said she would like to be washed and anointed. We thought she was too weak to bear it, but she was so anxious to have it done that Sister Helen Callister washed and anointed her and Bro. Callister and her Br. Platte laid their hands upon her and blessed her and blessed the Baby in her hearing ... now she seemed to rest and sleep and was very comfortable till morning.

We are again struck by the importance of female ritual administration in nineteenth-century Mormonism. Carlie's last wish was to receive washing and anointing from another woman, and she received the ordinance from her sister wife. Then the men added a ritual blessing.

Carlie died on the 20th. Eliza's thoughts after the funeral express her faith but also reflected on her daughter's painful marriage:

> She was buried in the Oak Creek Cemetery by the side of her Br Plattes children and there will rest in peace till the morning of the resurrection when she will come forth clothed in glory prepared to enter into her exaltation with the sanctified ones. She had been married a little over thir-

teen months and had lived with me more than half of the time as she could not feel very comfortable long at a time when she was away.

A year later Eliza made an entry in her diary that further revealed the suffering of a mother as she watched her daughter die: "To see a beloved child suffering the pains of Death without the power to relieve them in the least is almost too much for human nature to bear." So she grieved for her daughter and for her daughter's failed polygamous marriage, after her own two failed marriages.

Eliza was left with little Joseph to raise. She and Lucy moved to Platte's and Joseph's homes at Leamington so Adelia could nurse the baby, while Ida and May moved in with Caroline. Her sons' homes were so small, Eliza wrote, that she had to take her bed out of doors in the day time and bring it in at night and lay it out on the floor. In May, when Platte moved back to Oak Creek, Eliza accompanied him.

On July 1 Eliza wrote in her diary, "My Son Platte gone to Fillmore to meet Br. [Apostle] Erastus Snow." This meeting would open another dramatic chapter in Eliza's pioneer life, as Platte was asked to help lead a company to settle San Juan County in southeast Utah, cut off by natural barriers from other Utah settlements. While many Mormons made a pioneer trip to Utah, then settled in the comparative civilization of Salt Lake, Eliza would soon experience the frontier in all its bleakness, far away from even a major town, thirty years after the main pioneer settlement of Utah. Platte took a plural wife, Annie Maud Clark, on September 25, then prepared for the expedition. Apostle Snow probably advised such a marriage as befitting Platte's new leadership position.

## XII. "I Think of Her Both Day and Night"

Eliza was not part of the first colonizing company, a contingent of which left Oak Creek on October 21 and included many of her male supports: Platte (who led the expedition after the titular leader, Silas Smith, returned to Fillmore), Joseph, and her nephew Edward. Platte had sold his home in Oak Creek but made arrangements for Eliza to continue living in it. "May the Lord watch over them and keep them in health and peace untill they can perform the work that they have been sent by the Apostles to do," Eliza prayed. She continued to raise her second Joseph.

On the day after Christmas she pondered the strangeness of her life: "How changed is my situation now from what it was last Christmas. Then the baby's mother and I were alone while all the rest of the household were gone to the party. Now she sleeps in the grave, and her baby is left to keep me company in her stead." In addition, her two sons were far away.

Eliza's diary gives prosaic details from her daily life and records the new baby's progress. On August 3, 1880, her Salt Lake sister visited. The Nauvoo teenagers were now Utah grandmothers, ages sixty and fifty-six. Together they visited Carlie's grave: "It is hard to bear but it is undoubtedly right," she wrote. "We must all go sooner or later and those who are left are the ones who mourn. I think of her both day and night and hope to be prepared to meet her."

### XIII. "Deep Washes, Rock Ridges and Soft Sand"

On October 19 Platte visited from San Juan and Eliza decided to return with him. She, Platte and his family, Lucy, and little Joseph left Oak Creek on November 5, following a trail well known in Utah pioneer lore. The territory was characterized by "deep washes, rock ridges and soft sand ... slick rock mountains ... dead-end canyons." The road, Eliza noted, could barely be dignified by that name, and consisted of "Rocky dugways and deep sandy stretches, slush and snow." At one famous point, Hole in the Wall, the road led down a dizzyingly steep incline toward the Colorado River where the wagons had had to be lowered by ropes. Then the wagons ascended a difficult grade up the canyon on the opposite side, leaving the oxen and horses exhausted and near the point of dropping in their tracks. Fortunately for Eliza, the road had been mapped out a year previously when Platte and Joseph first made the journey. That trip had been an epic adventure, but now Platte at least knew where he was going.

Of the journey Eliza wrote only the following: "We had a very cold and uncomfortable time on the first part of the journey, but more pleasant and comfortable after we crossed the Colorado. The road was as bad as could possibly be and be traveled over at all, but the Lord preserved us from accident and we arrived in safety at our journey's end." Lucy Zina adds a few details: "We camped at the 'Hole-in-the-Rock' on the Escalante Desert for the horses and cattle to rest. We made bread for a week's travel using only 'shad scale' for wood. I put a loaf under my pillow at night to keep it from freezing but next morning it was frozen solid."

The party arrived at San Juan (modern Bluff) on January 1, 1881. According to Eliza, they found their friends well, except for Ida, "who had both her ankles sprained by jumping from a wagon." Eliza, who had begun her life in a comfortable, beautiful farm in Ohio, had now reached a true hinterland of America—a primitive town in an outlying desert, far from the Mormon headquarters, far from even the nearest Mormon town. They were surrounded by Native Americans—not just Navajos, but wandering tribes. In addition, outlaw gangs infested this corner of Utah, as lawmen were not likely to pursue them so far or to such a desolate territory so difficult of access. A constant watch had to be kept over livestock and horses. One wonders what the emotional effect of living in such a far-away area would have been. Southern Utah, with its surreal arches and varicolored rock formations, can be wildly beautiful but is also bleak and lonesome territory.

Eliza began to reconstruct the normal routines of her daily life. Her first diary entry, March 3, reflected her Mormon sisterhood: "I joined the Relief Society at San Juan." The next entry, four days later, showed her as grandmother: "Joseph Platte Callister two years old today and as busy as a child can be. Can say everything he hears and is a forward child." In early May Platte, with his wife and two children, left for Colorado to buy flour and work on the railroad. On July 25 Eliza lamented, "Are having very lonesome times as so many men and families have gone from here. There are now only six men in Bluff city and plenty of Indians all around us. There is nothing but the hand of the Lord that preserves us here as well as in all places." Lucy Zina remembered a nerve-racking incident that took place when the men had left Bluff to deal with problems caused by an "Old Posey Ute." Eliza took the women to the home of Ida Lyman Nielson (Lydia's child), "where we huddled together with them waiting for the cowboys to arrive, also wondering if the Indians would attack the little town." A "buxom" young girl sat on an extension table and overturned the only lamp in the house, "when down crashed the table, girl, lamp and all in the dark. A frantic scramble followed to get the lamp lighted again before the Indians got us. We were scared and nervous as we crept through the back lot to our home that night." While many Native Americans were hostile, others were friendly, including the local Navajo chief. They often congregated in the small town to trade goods and horses, but sometimes also to gamble and fight.

In addition to other disadvantages, Bluff was subject to dangerous flash floods. On August 20 Eliza wrote, "During the past week we have had a powerful flood which came down the cotton wood wash." The next day little Joseph underwent a rite of passage: "Have discarded dresses for Joseph Platte and put him in pants, which makes him look quite boyish."

## XIV. Shootout on the Colorado

On September 29 Eliza wrote, "My son Joseph A. started in company with Brs Lemuel Redd and Hiram Perkins to try to recover some horses that have been stolen out of our field by two white men." So began an ill-fated adventure. On October 5 Redd returned with bad news: Joseph had been wounded in the leg by one of the thieves. "He was shot while pulling the boat to shore on the Colorado river," Eliza explained. "They were shot at many times while they were crossing the river but the Lord preserved their lives and they recovered the stolen horses." The rustlers had waited to ambush the Mormon men at the Colorado, but Joseph and his companions had managed to obtain the horses on the far side of the river. As they recrossed the river, however, the thieves had opened fire and a bullet hit Joseph just above the knee, shattering his leg bone so severely that he could barely travel.

His long-suffering mother set out the next day in a carriage to bring him home. Two days later she found him under the care of a Sister Haskell and "more comfortable than could have been expected." After a jolting carriage ride that must have been excruciating, he and Eliza arrived home on the 13th. Platte's family moved in with her to help care for him. In the following weeks his mother kept a daily record of his progress. On the 21st he was "improving some," but a month later, on November 24, he was still very sick, his knee seriously impaired: "We have had to sit up nights with him the most of the time ... The wound is healing up all right but the knee and leg are badly swollen. His brother Platte has taken twenty pieces of bone and a small piece of lead out of the wound." They did manage to help Joseph out of bed so that he could sit in a chair for a half-hour that day. As the new year began, Eliza observed that Joseph was improving faster than expected.

The polygamy controversy raging in Utah and the East now reached even farflung Bluff, where Mormon women rose to defend the patriarchal principle. On January 22 Eliza wrote, "Spoke in a public meeting for the first time, in defense of Polygamy." Nevertheless, the principle was quickly approaching its demise.

By the 26th Joseph was sitting up but still could not use his leg. Two weeks later Eliza wrote, "My son Joseph has been out of doors today for the first time in seventeen weeks." He was now able to walk on crutches. Half a year later, on July 1, Eliza wrote, "My son Joseph ... has this evening commenced to take the lead again in family prayer. He cannot bend the knee but has to kneel in a chair." According to family tradition, Joseph's wound never healed completely, and he lived the rest of his life in pain as a result. So we see the difference between the West of Hollywood, where gun battles are exciting diversions, and the real West, in which a single bullet could cripple a good man for life.

On September 24 Joseph and his wife moved out of Eliza's home. Though she had worn herself out tending her son, she immediately missed his family and wished that they could have stayed: "My family is too small to suit me, but I will try to be contented." Her household was reduced to herself, Lucy Zina, and little Joseph.

Her birthday entry for April 20, 1883, offers a striking evocation of female physical culture in late pioneer Utah: "This is my 63rd birthday. My son Joseph gave me a dress pattern and trimmings. His wife gave me calico for an apron. My daughter Lucy made me a present of a nice tidy and my Niece Lydia May gave me a netted neck tie and her sister Ida gave me a can of tomatos. Also my daughter in law Annie sent me a token of remembrance." The next day Platte arrived home from Durango and gave his mother "gingham for a bonnet." Most of Eliza's presents were linked to sewing. Pioneer women, and rural nineteenth-century American women in general, spent a good percentage of their lives making clothing.

On September 25 Eliza wrote, "My daughter Lucy started for St. George in company with Br. L. H. Redd and wife and three children." Only in Mormon culture would such an entry have more than ordinary significance. In the St. George temple Lucy received her endowments, then became Redd's first plural wife. Family traditions record that Lemuel was advised by church authorities to take a second wife after arriving in Bluff, and when he discussed the matter with his first wife, Eliza Ann Westover Redd, she encouraged him to forge ahead: "Lem, you have been advised to do this and you must do it." So, as occasionally happens in Mormon polygamy, we find the first wife encouraging her husband to fulfill his religious duties and marry again. Perhaps Eliza Ann was close enough to Lucy Zina that she did not see her as a threat.

Lemuel was a leading citizen in Bluff, and his two wives also became prominent townswomen. Lucy would have a number of children by Lemuel, but after her marriage, she seems to have lived with Eliza a great deal. Eliza's 1884 diary entry for her birthday had polygamy as a sub-text: "My daughter Lucy and her Husband's wife Eliza, my niece Lydia May and her Husband's wife Mary, assisted by my niece Ida Nielson and my daughter in law Nellie G. prepared supper for me on this my 64th birthday." Only in nineteenth-century Mormonism would the phrase "her Husband's wife" be used so casually.

### XV. Oak Creek

On August 15 Eliza wrote, "Started from Bluff, San Juan Co. in company with my son Joseph, his wife Nellie and Baby, my Daughter Lucy and Grandson J. P. Callister. My Son P. D. Lyman came with us a day and a half to help us with his team." She had decided to return to civilization. After a long night's journey, they reached Green River, where she, Lucy, and little Joseph were able to "take the cars" to Provo. After a two-week visit in northern Utah, she, Lucy, and Joseph traveled by rail to Leamington, where Caroline and one of her sons-in-law met them with a carriage.

Eliza moved in with Caroline, and her life returned to normalcy in a comparatively settled part of Utah. In her diary she noted church meetings and callings. On June 15, 1885, she was chosen to preside over the

Primary children of Oak Creek, and selected Harriet J. Lovell and Elisabeth Finlinson as her counselors. In the second half of July she made a train trip to Salt Lake City for two months. When she returned, on July 28, she "found all well." "We were busy drying, canning and preserving fruit until the frost came in the fall."

Toward the end of October Eliza moved into E. L. Lyman's house for the winter. "Am much more comfortable than we were last winter, although very much crowded," she wrote. Lucy was still living with her. On November 3 Eliza recorded, "Went to Holden to attend the Ladies Conference. Put up with the Sisters Kinney. Came home on the 5th." The last entry in her diary is dated December 23: "Bought some land (6 by 11 rods) to build on."

## XVI. "A Kind and Affectionate Mother"

After Platte's mission to San Juan ended, he returned to the Fillmore area to live. On March 2, 1886, a messenger came to him with news that Eliza was sick. In his journal he wrote, "I immediately started on horse back over the mountain and reached Oak Creek at 9 a.m. and found that Mother had died at 5 minutes to 3 or about the time Walter reached my house. She has never been a strong woman since I can recollect and has had much poor health. The complaint of which she died was I think Pneumonia or congestion of the lungs." Eliza was sixty-five. She was buried in Oak Creek the next day in a family plot. Platte's journal provides a moving epitaph for this remarkable woman:

> She had been a member of the Church of Jesus Christ of Latter Day Saints from her childhood and had reared her children in that and had herself obeyed every law and order of the church so far as the privilege had been given her to do so. She was a kind and affectionate Mother, very solicitous for the welfare of her children and esteeming nothing which she could do for their comfort or happiness a hardship or a sacrifice. May she rest in peace until the Saints of God are called forth in the morning of the first resurrection in which she will surely have a part.

## XVII. Patriarchal Solitude

Eliza's life, like that of her sister Emily, is a classic example of the woman isolated by polygamy. After the early traumatic marriage to Joseph Smith, her marriage to Apostle Amasa Lyman was equally unsatisfactory, long before he left Mormonism to join the Godbeites. Eloquent emblems of his absence from Eliza's marriage are the two houses she built without him, one at Winter Quarters and one in Salt Lake. Amasa was constantly on apostolic missions away from Salt Lake City, culminating in his "gold mission" to California and his settlement of San Bernardino. He took half of his wives to California and left half in Utah, but spent most of his time on the coast. Eliza's diary is a quietly heart-rending, implicit critique of such absences. Aside from the emotional toll of these partings, Eliza was often left without money or food and was reduced to the humiliation of asking for help from the local bishop. A final telling detail is Eliza's record of childbirths. After her first two children were born on the overland trail, her last three were born in Utah without her husband present at the births.

It would be unfair to place all of the blame for these circumstances entirely on Lyman. Polygamy itself virtually required that women often be alone. If a church leader was frequently called on missions, this neglect was compounded. A monogamous apostle might have easily taken his wife with him on long missions, as Parley P. Pratt had been accompanied by Mary Ann Frost in England, but polygamy made such a solution impossible. Eliza and women like her bore the brunt of all of these factors.

Viewing events from Eliza's perspective, it seems inexcusable that Amasa would marry new wives while not being able to provide for his previously-married spouses. But high church leaders were under pressure from the presidency not just to marry polygamously but to marry many wives as an example for others. And Brigham Young was merely following Joseph Smith's theology of degreed exaltation by quantity of family. It is one of the great ironies of Mormon history that Smith, who set the polygamous movement in motion, never experienced it in practical terms. He was content to marry the teenaged women who lived in his home and then let them depart when Emma objected. And he was content to let his polyandrous wives live with their first husbands, so he never bore the responsibility of providing for them, financially or emotionally, on a day-to-day basis. He never witnessed the toll that practical polygamy would take on an Eliza Partridge, married to an apostle in the patriarchal order. Perhaps this is one of the reasons that Smith's widows, looking back on their brief experience of secret polygamy, could idealize it, especially since Smith himself had become larger than life in Mormon folk memory—a nearly infallible figure who ranked just below Jesus Christ and higher than Old Testament prophets.

It is striking that Eliza's daughters endured similar phenomena, which shows that the problems with plural marriage were systemic, not merely the result of a few extraordinarily insensitive men. Both daughters married polygamously, as second wives, and neither bonded immediately with her husband. Lucy's marriage to Lemuel Redd eventually succeeded, apparently, but Carlie's marriage to Callister, thirty years older than she, and cut short by her death, was unsuccessful; on her deathbed she demanded that her child be raised by Eliza, not by his father.

Looking at polygamy from our late-twentieth-century monogamous and feminist perspectives, one wonders why Latter-day Saint leaders did not see more clearly the problematic nature of such relationships and retreat from them. In fact, the opposite happened. The church presidents who succeeded Joseph Smith followed his polygamy revelations and imperatives with unquestioning singlemindedness. They gave it up only after the Joseph F. Smith Manifesto in 1904, after years of private agony, long after the more well-known Woodruff Manifesto in 1890. In a desperate, impractical venture, many members of the First Presidency and Quorum of the Twelve continued to authorize and contract new plural marriages secretly until they were once again forced to give up even their sub rosa, post-Manifesto plurality. To nineteenth-century leaders the principle was not just an optional revelation—they viewed it as the most important revelation in Joseph Smith's life, which is what he undoubtedly taught them. If they accepted him as an infallible prophet, and if they wanted full exaltation, they had no recourse but to marry many plural wives. Their devotion to Joseph the seer outweighed their experience of polygamy's impracticality and tragic consequences for women, which many men probably did not even recognize.

But it is worth noting that the women who suffered so much under polygamy gave it their unqualified support in public rallies and wrote impassioned defenses of it. They too were devoted to the idea that their church was led by practically infallible, authoritative prophets, especially Joseph Smith. This was the reason why missionaries could teach that only Latter-day Saint baptism was recognized by God. If nineteenth-century Mormons had concluded that Smith had been wrong in what he taught was the crowning revelation of his life, they would have been left with a very different Mormonism than the faith they followed. Neither Mormon men nor women were willing to jettison that much of their religion.

It is useless to judge nineteenth-century Mormons by late twentieth-century standards. Both men and women were given an impossible task and failed at it. All we can do today is sympathize with them in their tragedies and marvel at their heroism as they suffered. Eliza's eloquent diary reveals her as one of the most quietly heroic persons in Mormon history.

# 20.

# Proxy Wife

## *Lucy Walker (Smith Kimball)*

Heber Chase Kimball—Brigham Young's right-hand man, first counselor in the First Presidency, stalwart Mormon from the early days of the church, husband of forty-five wives—was dying. Thrown from a horse in May 1868, he had seemed to recover, then suffered a paralytic stroke on June 11, and had been bedridden from then on. As he slowly lost control of his body, and as he realized that death was inevitable, he began summoning his wives and children to his bedside to bid them farewell. Finally he called his Provo wife, Lucy, to his side.

"I have always appreciated your example as a wife and as a mother," he told her, according to her memoirs. She and her editors have Heber speaking in polished Victorian prose, but he probably said something close to this. He continued:

No one has ever excelled you in home life. Wherever your lot has been cast, there I have found a place of peace and rest. Let me now thank you kindly for every kind word, for every kind act of your life, and when I am gone, which will not be but a short time, you shall be blessed and find friends. If I never speak to you again, you may rest assured that you have my most sanguine good feelings; my unbounded love and esteem.

Then Heber turned to a theme that showed the spiritual charisma of the plural wives of Joseph Smith. Kimball was the second most authoritative leader in the LDS church and his salvation had been assured by many rituals. Yet he now turned to Lucy as an intermediary to Smith: "What can you tell Joseph when you meet him? Cannot you say that I have been kind to you as it was possible to be under the circumstances? I know you can, and am confident you will be as a mediator between me and Joseph, and never enjoy any blessing you would not wish Heber to share." Here, as in the case of his daughter Helen, we see Heber seeking a link to Smith through a woman related to him. One wonders if there is a hint of anxiety in Heber's tone. Plural wives in much smaller families than Kimball's felt emotionally isolated, and as Heber had a very large family and a time-demanding church position, and as Lucy did not live in Salt Lake City, it is possible that she had not seen him frequently.

Nevertheless, Lucy wrote that Heber's words "were more precious to me than gold, as they were his last, with the addition of 'I leave my peace and blessing with you. May the peace of Heber ever abide in your habitation.' I do not pen these facts thinking that others did not share equally in his esteem; as every woman carves her own niche in her husband's affections." So the death of Lucy's husband for time emphasized her status as Joseph Smith's eternal wife.

Lucy was another young wife of Smith—he proposed to her when she was fifteen or sixteen. In her story we find the familiar pattern of the teenage girl living in the Mormon leader's house, whom Joseph then approaches and marries. She originally resisted his polygamous teachings but soon received a spiritual experience that converted her, and she became his wife. She left an extraordinarily vivid memoir of her two marriages, but her life after Heber's death is unfortunately sparsely documented. As a proxy wife to Kimball she faced the challenges of living in the large family of one of the busiest men in the LDS church. With Heber she had nine children, though she lost five before her own death at age eighty-four.

## I. "He Had Become Suddenly Deranged"

Lucy was born on April 30, 1826, to John Walker and Lydia Holmes in Peacham, Caledonia, Vermont, in the mid-eastern part of the state, the fourth of ten children. John, thirty-two, a native of Peacham, worked as a carpenter, machinist, and farmer. Lydia, twenty-six, was from Maine. Lucy's older siblings, William Holmes, Lorin, and Catherine, had been born in 1820, 1822, and 1824 in Peacham. After Lucy, Edwin, Henry, and Jane were born in 1828, 1830, and 1832 in Cabot (ten miles northwest) and Peacham. John and Lydia attended a Congregationalist church, so the Walker children were probably raised as strict, Bible-reading Christians.

In the spring of 1832, when Lucy was six, her father was baptized a Mormon. Nothing is known about his conversion, except that it greatly upset Lydia. William, twelve years old at the time, was boarding with an uncle while he attended school. He wrote of his uncle's disgust when he learned that John had joined "that dreadful and most detestable Mormon religion"; William "felt worse, if possible, than if I had heard of his death and burial. I felt that he had become suddenly deranged and had entirely lost his reason or had willfully committed a crime." When William returned home he was surprised to find his father rational and apparently happy.

## II. Children Prophesy

In 1834 Lucy and her family left Vermont and settled in Ogdensburgh, St. Lawrence, New York, on the St. Lawrence River. Lydia, meanwhile, had read the Bible tirelessly to prove Mormonism and the Book of Mormon false, but the more she read, the more she reluctantly became convinced that Mormonism must be true. Finally she bowed to the inevitable and was baptized. Another daughter, Lydia the younger, was born in September.

With other members of the local Mormon branch above eight years of age, Lucy was baptized by Abraham Palmer in 1835. She remembers at this baptism and confirmation meeting "the Signs following them, acording to promise." At the next prayer meeting the newly baptized children "spoke in tonges, others prophecied; again another has the gift of faith, to heal the sick, Etc." Members of the branch were already planning to move to Missouri, and one of the children stood up, "his countenance Shone like that of an Angel," and he prophesied that the children would face great persecutions in their new homes, being "Surrounded by Armed Mobs with blackened faces." Some would be killed, others would witness murders. Such spiritual outpourings and prophetic speech exercised by the rank-and-file are typical of early Mormonism, especially in the Kirtland period, though for children this would have been somewhat unusual. In addition, ex post facto prophecy would later make sense of the Missouri persecutions when Zion was not redeemed there, as the Saints had expected.

In March 1837 the Walkers were living eighty miles southwest of Ogdensburgh in Oswego, Oswego County, New York, where John Walker, Jr., was born. The nine children now ranged from seventeen-year-old William to the newborn baby, with eleven-year-old Lucy in the middle. Soon the imperative to gather to Zion became irresistible, and in 1838 the family left New York for Missouri in a group that included seven wagons.

## III. Shoal Creek

The Walkers had the singular misfortune to arrive in Caldwell County on October 30, the date of the Haun's Mill Massacre. According to Lucy, they were immediately surrounded by a mob of about forty men with blackened faces: "They hooted and yelled and looked more like demons than human beings." Pointing guns at the children, they "cursed and swore in a most frightful manner." The women were forced out of the wagons into the snow (including Lydia, who was in poor health at the time) as the anti-Mormon men searched the wagons, confiscating all firearms. A "hateful" non-Mormon woman cried out, "'Shoot them down ... they Should not be allowed to live!'" "I did not tremble," Lucy wrote, "I did not fear them. They looked to me too insignificant and I felt to trust in One, (although but a child) who held our destinies in his own hands."

Lucy's company camped on Shoal Creek, five miles from Haun's Mill, and her father went to the mill to counsel with Joseph Young. He was in the blacksmith shop when the mob appeared and began shooting all Mormons indiscriminately: men, women, and children. John was shot in the arm, but was able to hide under some lumber. He could not be seen, according to Lucy, because the eyes of the mob were miraculously blinded. John waited till all was silent, then emerged from his hiding place "to witness the dreadful Scene of the massacre." Though his own right arm was throbbing painfully, he helped dress the wounds of other victims.

The family was still camped at Shoal Creek and becoming increasingly anxious at John's absence. Soon a young man appeared with news of the massacre and a warning that this camp would also be attacked. Hysteria ensued, and though Lydia pleaded with everyone to be calm, women and children ran into the deep snow of neighboring woods. Only the Walkers and a Sister Davis remained. In the night Lydia gathered her nine children around her and was able to calm them so that they could sleep. It must have been a terrible night for her, for she had no reason to believe that her husband would be found alive.

When Lucy awoke in the morning, she later wrote, "I looked into my mother's pale face, child as I was, felt guilty that [I] had suffered myself to be lulled to sleep by her magic words of assureance, while she had kept a vigilant watch dureing that fearful night of keenest anxiety." Those who had wandered into the forest came straggling back. Soon a young officer "with a pleasant face" appeared and told the women and children that he had been forced to join the mob-militia against his will. If they would follow him, however, he would take them to safety. They took the risk, and he lead them to a secluded place where they camped and "found shelter among the settlers." According to Lucy's brother William, this was a journey of a hundred miles, though he probably exaggerated.

Neither John nor his family knew anything about the other's whereabouts, but William went in search of his father. Lydia's part of the family waited for two weeks in great suspense, but eventually John and William returned—a joyful occasion, even though John, with his wound, "looked like one from the dead." After a short, terrifying stay in Missouri, the Walkers traveled east to Quincy, Illinois, in April 1839.

### IV. "The Sad Word Good-bye"

In Quincy John worked as a carpenter and rented a farm, which William and Lorin cultivated. John was then called to serve a mission to the "middle states," and William and Lorin supported the family in his absence. On February 11, 1840, Mary Electa, Lucy's last full sibling, was born. William was now twenty, Lorin eighteen, Catherine sixteen, Lucy fourteen, Edwin twelve, Henry ten, Jane eight, Lydia six, and John three. John Sr. was forty-six and Lydia forty.

John returned in the spring and traveled with Lorin to Nauvoo to attend a conference and secure a home. While they were there, Joseph Smith took a liking to Lorin and asked John if he could stay and work for him. John agreed, provided that Lorin would return to help with the harvest. When that time came, however, Smith wrote to John that he "could not part with" Lorin and that John should hire someone else to help at Smith's expense. If nothing else, this shows that the Smith and Walker families had become closely acquainted by this time. Joseph Smith III later wrote that Lorin served as the prophet's "personal attendant" until the martyrdom, looking after his clothes, horses, military equipment, and riding with him on journeys.

In spring 1841 Lucy and her family came to Nauvoo where Lucy, now fifteen, met Joseph Smith for the first time: "My brother met us with an invitation to dinner, which we gladly accepted, and were introduced to the Prophet and his wife, Emma, and the dear children who in after years I learned to love as my own brothers, and Julia = an adopted daughter, as my sister."

In the summer Lydia and the children contracted the dreaded "chills and fever," the endemic malaria of Nauvoo's swamps. Lydia was cared for at the Smith home for some time, but could not endure to be separated from her family, so in the winter was brought back to her own house. She lingered for a time, then in January realized that she was going to die. Lucy wrote:

> Calling her children arround her bed She bore a faithful testimony as to her convictions that Joseph Smith was a prophet of God; and that through him the Gospel of the Son of God had been restored in its fullness ... She ernestly exorted her children to never depart from the truth, but live so that she might meet them in that world where there will be no more Suffering no more tears of anguish at pronouncing the Sad word good-bye. She then closed her eyes and her sweet spirit passed away, leaveing a heavenly smile on her dear face. It did not Seem to us possible that She was dead, but only in a sweet Sleep. When at length we were forced to beleive she would not speak to us again we were in the depths of despair. Ten motherless children!—And such a mother! The youngest not yet two years old.

She died on January 18, 1842. John took this death very much to heart, and his health "seemed to give way" as a result. At this point Joseph

461

Smith intervened in the Walker family's affairs, as he often did in the lives of his followers. His solution to the problem was curious—he separated the Walker family from their father and "adopted" most of them himself, including Lucy. In her words:

> The Prophet came to the rescue. He Said, if you remain here Bro. Walker, you will soon follow your wife. You must have a change of scene, a change of climate. You have Just such a family as I could love. My house shall be their home. For the present, I would advise you to sell your Effects, place the little ones with kind friends, and the four Eldest shall come to my house and [be] received and treated as my own children, and if I find the little ones are not content, or not treated right, I will bring them home and keep them untill you return.

Smith's prophecies to his close disciples often left them with an imperative for action—in this case he asserted that John Walker would die if he did not receive a change of scene; therefore, he must leave Nauvoo. In addition, Smith made arrangements for John's family, farming out the six youngest children to family friends, while the oldest four would live in his own home as his "own children." While Lucy describes her father's departure as something Smith recommended for his health, from other sources we know that John was sent on a two-year mission to the eastern states. Catherine's daughter wrote, "[Lydia Walker] died in 1842 and mother and her sisters and brothers were taken to the home of the Prophet Joseph Smith and raised as his own. Mother's father was meanwhile sent East on two missions."

Lucy's reaction to her family's fragmentation, the loss of a father and the youngest children immediately after her mother's death, was not mild: "I rung my hands in the agony of dispair at the thought of being broken up as a family, and being sepparated from the little ones ... However my father sought to comfort us by saying two years would soon pass by when with renewed health he hoped to return and make us a home where we might be together again."

So John Walker left his family in Nauvoo in Smith's care. "The Prophet and his wife introduced us as their Sons and daughters," wrote Lucy. "Every privilege was acorded us in the home." Just as Smith had had a very close relationship with Zina's brother Dimick and with Almera's brother Benjamin Johnson, he had an especially close relationship with Lorin. "He was indeed his confidential and trusted friend," according to Lucy. "He was ever by his side; arm in arm they walked and conversed freely on various subjects of Interest." Joseph III reported that Lucy served as one of Emma's maids, "working for her board and going to school. She ... used to marshal us children to and from school as would an elder sister." However, the separation from the younger children was difficult. When the older Walkers visited them, "The tears rained down our faces all the while we were with them—The people often said they wished we would calm ourselves in their presence or not come to see them as it made them discontented."

Soon after John left Nauvoo, Lydia, age seven, was "stricken by brain fever." When Smith heard how sick she was, he had a bed put on a carriage and personally went to bring her to his home. On the way back, "He told the boys to drive down to the Mississippi river, then took her in his arms and baptised her, when brought in, Sister Emma (Noble woman that she was) helped change her clothing." Despite this attempted cure, in a few days Lydia "joined her dear mother in the spirit world and we were left more lonely than before," wrote Lucy.

Judge James Adams, a close friend of Joseph Smith who lived in Springfield, eighty miles southeast of Nauvoo, and his wife "took great fancy" to nine-year-old Jane and asked if she could live with them. The Walker siblings "very reluctantly" consented. Though the Adamses provided a good home for Jane, she was now eighty miles away, a substantial journey.

### V. "You Are the Woman"

Thus Joseph Smith had sent John Walker, the father, on a long mission while the family was still grieving for the mother, had split up the siblings—separating the younger children from the older—and referred to the older Walkers as his own children. Previously he had made one of the older brothers his servant, companion, and confidante.

At this point Smith proposed to fifteen- or sixteen-year-old Lucy, demanding that she marry him. In her extraordinary autobiography she wrote, "In the year 1842 President Joseph Smith sought an interview with me, and said, 'I have a message for you, I have been commanded of God to take another wife, and you are the woman.' My astonishment knew no bounds. This announcement was indeed a thunderbolt to me." Helen Mar Kimball used almost the same language in describing her shock at learning of polygamy and receiving Smith's proposal. As often, Smith phrased the proposal as a direct commandment from God.

He next emphasized his authority as a prophet: "He asked me if I beleived him to be a Prophet of God. 'Most assuredly I do I replied.'" Smith then continued to explain how celestial marriage could link families together in eternity: "He fully Explained to me the principle of plural or celestial marriage. Said this principle was again to be restored for the benefit of the human family. That it would prove an everlasting blessing to my father's house. And form a chain that could never be broken, worlds without End." Again, as in the case of Helen Mar and Sarah Ann Whitney, Smith put the burden of a family's salvation on a teenager's willingness to accept him as a plural husband. Unlike those cases, however, here the prophet did not work through the father but approached the girl directly, after sending the father on a mission.

"What have you to Say?" Smith asked. "Nothing," Lucy replied, entirely at a loss. "How could I speak, or what could I say?"

When Smith sensed resistance, as has been seen, he generally continued teaching—asking the prospective wife to pray about the principle, promising that she would receive a witness. So it happened here. "He said, 'If you will pray sincerely for light and understanding in relation thereto, you Shall receive a testimony of the correctness of this principle.'" Lucy was horrified by polygamy and by his proposal and did not quickly gain the promised testimony. She prayed, she wrote, but not with faith. She was nearly suicidal: "tempted and tortured beyond endureance until life was not desirable. Oh that the grave would kindly receive me that I might find rest on the bosom of my dear mother." Lucy now felt intensely the absence of her parents: "Why—Why Should I be chosen from among thy daughters, Father, I am only a child in years and experience. No mother to council; no father near to tell me what to do, in this trying hour. Oh let this bitter cup pass. And thus I prayed in the agony of my soul."

These events probably took place in late 1842. Smith subsequently approached Lucy's brother William, who wrote, "In the spring of 1843, my father, being away on a mission, the Prophet asked my consent, for my sister Lucy in marriage. I replied, that if it was her choice: that if she entered into the celestial order of marriage of her own free will and choice, I had no objection."

Smith saw that Lucy was unhappy and sought another interview with her in late April. He told her that the marriage would have to be secret, but that he would acknowledge her as his wife "beyond the Rocky Mountains." He emphasized that this was not a proposal that she could accept or reject according to a romantic whim. To refuse him would bring damnation: "It is a command of God to you." Furthermore, there was a time limit: "I will give you untill to-morrow to decide this matter. If you reject this message the gate will be closed forever against you." This statement infuriated the sixteen-year-old girl: "This arroused every drop of scotch in my veins ... I felt at this moment that I was called to place myself upon the altar a liveing Sacrafice, perhaps to brook the world in disgrace and incur the displeasure and contempt of my youthful companions; all my dreams of happiness blown to the four winds, this was too much, the thought was unbearable." Like Helen Mar at the age of fourteen, Lucy thought of her peer group and of the disaster that polygamy would bring to her teenage dreams.

She then told Joseph that she could not marry him unless God revealed it to her, and God had not done so yet. She wrote, "[I] emphatically forbid him speaking again to me on this Subject." As in the case of Benjamin Johnson, Smith met a violently negative reaction with a confident smile: "He walked across the room, returned, and stood before me. With the most beautiful expression of countenance, and said, 'God almighty bless you, You shall have a manifestation of the will of God concerning you; a testimoney that you can never deny. I will tell you what it shall be. It shall be that peace and joy that you never knew.'"

That night Lucy continued to implore the Lord for guidance and was not able to sleep. But near dawn, she wrote:

> My room became filled with a heavenly influence. To me it was in comparison like the brilliant sun bursting through the darkest cloud ... My Soul was filled with a calm, sweet peace that I never knew. Supreme happiness took posession of my whole being. And I received a powerful and irristable testimony of the truth of the mariage covenant called "Celestial or plural mariage." Which has been like an anchor to the soul through all the trials of life. I felt that I must go out into the morning air and give vent to the Joy and grattitude that filled my Soul. As I descended the stairs, Prest. Smith opened the door below; took me by the hand and said: "Thank God, you have the testimony. I too, have prayed." he led me to a chair, placed his hands upon my head, and blessed me with Every blessing my heart could posibly desire.

On May 1 Lucy, who had turned seventeen the day before, married Smith at his home, with William Clayton officiating and Eliza Partridge standing witness. She later explained that there was no romantic element to the marriage: "It was not a love matter, so to speak, in our affairs,—at least on my part it was not, but simply the giving up of myself as a sacrifice to establish that grand and glorious principle that God had revealed to the world." When her father returned from his mission, he retroactively gave his permission for his daughter's marriage, according to William.

Absolutely nothing is known of this marriage after the ceremony. Joseph probably saw her occasionally, and she became close friends with his other plural wives. Her residence history before Smith's death can be traced to some degree. On August 31 the Mansion House was finished, and William managed it for Joseph when it opened as a hotel on September 15. On November 1 William married Olive Hovey Farr and they moved into the Mansion House. Lucy moved there in November, though Catherine stayed in the prophet's household. After six months William and Olive left for their own home and took the young Walker children to live with them.

465

At some point Lucy began living with Agnes Coolbrith Smith, another plural wife of the Mormon leader. Lucy wrote, "At the ernest Solicitation of Gen. Don Carlos Smith's widow, some time prior to Prest. Smith death.[,] Prest. Smith Consented to me makeing my home with her, and She was as an elder sister to me." As recounted earlier, Agnes and Lucy heard the news of Joseph's death just after retiring on the night of June 27. After the first shock, these two widows of Smith prayed together through the night, clasped in each other's arms. Later Lucy, now eighteen, and Agnes attended the funeral together.

## VI. Contract with Mr. Kimball

According to Andrew Jenson, Lucy lived with William after the martyrdom. However, her own autobiography emphasizes her desire at that time to leave Nauvoo and obtain an education: "I ... felt a determination to be independent, by learning a trade or qualifying my self for a teacher." So against the advice of her brothers and William Clayton, she traveled to Quincy and there took a position as maid and cook with a Mrs. Kingman. As she had little cooking experience, she spent her first night praying that God would help her remember how her mother cooked. After her first batch of biscuits, "I had excellent luck, and they were delighted." Mrs. Kingman offered to help Lucy with schooling, and in the Baptist church the family attended the superintendent asked Lucy to teach a class. "I excused myself and said I belong to the mormon Church Sir and perhaps you would not like to have a class of young mormons in your Church  he looked surprised and still urged me." She undoubtedly was an intelligent and personable young woman.

However, this brief interlude in non-Mormon Quincy ended quickly. Brigham Young and Heber Kimball were approaching all of Smith's former wives to offer themselves as proxy husbands. One day, Lucy wrote, "Prest HC Kimball Babbitt and others come to Quincy. he brought several letters from my friends to come home with Bro. Kimball as Father had returned from his long Mission and was anxious to see me." Perhaps this was the first time that Lucy, eighteen, and Heber, forty-three and husband of sixteen wives, had spent any time together. When Heber made his proposal, however he delivered it (he likely phrased it as a religious imperative), Lucy accepted, and they were married for time on February 8, 1845.

We have observed Heber presiding over his extensive family kingdom. He was kind but authoritarian, and Vilate was by far his favorite wife, though he tried to treat his other wives well. As a church leader and husband of some twenty connubial wives, he was not a constant presence in any plural wife's home. Lucy, in 1893, testified publicly, "There was not any love in the union between myself and Kimball, and it is my business entirely whether there was any courtship or not." Probably too much has been made of this statement, which is typical Mormon rhetoric downgrading romantic marriage as opposed to religious, polygamous marriage. Lucy continued, "It was the principle of plural marriage that we were trying to establish, a great and glorious true principle." Yet she also testified that Heber was "as noble a man as ever stood on the earth" and that he "was a noble whole-souled son of God, and was as capable of loving more than one woman as God Himself is capable of loving all his creations."

Lucy explained proxy marriage in her testimony in the Temple Lot trial: "The contract when I married Mr. Kimball was that I should be his wife for time, and time only, and the contract on the part of Mr. Kimball was that he would take care of me during my lifetime, and in the resurrection would surrender me, with my children, to Joseph Smith." The proxy marriage was resolemnized in the Nauvoo temple on January 15, 1846. Two weeks later, on January 28, Lucy's first child, Rachel Sylvia, was born, just in time to accompany her mother on a journey westward.

### VII. "She Receiv'd the Gift"

Lucy probably left Nauvoo in February 1846 with the main Mormon group to travel across Iowa in the Kimball company. On May 29 Patty Sessions, at Mt. Pisgah, wrote, "Lucy Walker arived here today." Soon after this, a June 4 journal entry by Clayton shows Lucy undergoing emotional strain as a wife in Kimball's family: "Lucy Walker called in this afternoon and expressed sorrow on account of the treatment of Hebers family toward her." Lucy, a new mother trying to care for her child, was probably still adjusting to the practical realities of a living in a polygamous family; in addition, she was enduring the enormously stressful and chaotic conditions of the exodus in Iowa.

But soon she arrived at Winter Quarters, where she would spend two winters. The most important event for her during that time was the death of Rachel Sylvia on December 22, 1847. It was undoubtedly a fearful ordeal to see her daughter pass away, but the details are not extant. However, Lucy also participated in the prophetic blessing meetings that the women shared in those difficult conditions. On June 10, 1847, Eliza Snow wrote, "Took supper with S. Ann [Whitney Kimball], while there Lucy W. came in—she receiv'd the gift We then went into sis. [Vilate] K's—Helen [Mar Whitney], Sarah Ann, Genet, Harriet S. Sis. K. spoke for the first time in the gift of tongues—H. Cook [Harriet Cook Young] interpreted."

Lucy left Winter Quarters to cross the plains in early June 1848, travelling in the large Kimball company. On September 24, at age twenty-two, she arrived in the Salt Lake Valley.

## VIII. "It Is a Grand School"

Two journal entries in 1849 show Lucy in her circle of sister-wives in early Utah. On May 16 Eliza Partridge Lyman wrote, "Visited at Wm Walker's with sisters Emily and Louisa Young and Sarah Ann and Lucy Kimball also Presnts Young and Kimball." All of these women were widows of Joseph Smith. Three weeks later, on June 8, Zina Huntington Young wrote, "After the children were in bed I went with Lucy W. Kimble and stayed all night with Presendia. She had company and long shall I remember the speret of the evening." Presendia was, of course, a sister-wife to Lucy in both the Kimball and Smith families.

Lucy soon bore more children: John Heber on December 12, 1850, Willard Heber on January 25, 1853, and Lydia Holmes on January 18, 1856. However, Willard died when he was nearly two, on December 5, 1854.

In 1857 Lucy was living with Sarah Ann Whitney, Ellen Sanders, Adelia Wilcox, Martha McBride, and children in one crowded house. Heber's visits, as might be expected, were not frequent by monogamous standards. Wilcox wrote, "Occassionally when our Lord could find the time he would come in and visit with us and instruct and teach us our dutye and if he see any thing he thought was wrong in any one of us he was not slow to tell us." Lucy herself said, "When the father was there [in her home] everything was done necessary for his comfort." This is a typical phenomenon in the culture of plural marriage—the father is more an honored visitor than a normal, daily presence in the home.

As we have seen, in Heber's family there was frequently a shuffling of wives to different houses. On one occasion Lucy and Sarah Ann were living with Presendia and Mary Houston. Eventually, however, each wife received her own home. Lucy tells us: "Every mother has her own mode of government, and as children grow in years, it is more pleasant to have them under the immediate dictation of their own mother." She wrote that she loved her fellow wives "as dearly as my own sisters." And "the children themselves love each other as dearly as the children of one mother." This might be somewhat idealizing but probably was not far from the truth. Lucy did admit that living as a wife in a polygamous household was difficult:

> It is a grand school. You learn self control, self denial; it brings out the noble traits of our fallen natures, and teaches us to study and subdue self, while we become acquainted with the peculiar characteristics of each other. There is a grand opportunity to improve ourselves, and the lessons learned in a few years, are worth the experience of a life-time, for this reason, that you are better prepared to make a home happy.

More children arrived in Lucy's home. On March 18, 1857, when she was thirty-one, Anna Spaulding was born, and Eliza followed her on May 14, 1859. Two sons, Washington Heber and Joshua Heber, were born on March 22, 1861, and October 22, 1862, though Joshua died in infancy. John was now twelve, Lydia six, Ann five, and Eliza three. Franklin Heber, Lucy's last child, was born on August 28, 1864, when she was thirty-eight, though he died the following year. Of nine children, she had lost four, not at all an extraordinary death ratio for a nineteenth-century frontierswoman.

According to Jenson, Lucy moved to Provo, Utah County, forty miles south of Salt Lake City, in 1868, and her house there became Heber's "Provo residence." In late May of that year he, now nearly sixty-seven, came to Provo to visit late one night. His horse stumbled into a ditch near her home and he was thrown to the earth, where he lay immobile for some time before being discovered. After he was brought into the house, he seemed to recover and even spoke in the Tabernacle on June 7. But four days later he had a paralytic stroke, then died on June 21. Lucy was forty-two.

### IX. "She Has Been Very Faithful"

In the summer of 1868 Lucy's household included John, eighteen, Lydia, twelve, Ann, eleven, Eliza, nine, and Washington, six. She continued to live in Provo for a number of years, during which time she remained an active member of the Fourth Ward Relief Society. Evidently she was also on a school board, for on October 12 she wrote to a local school teacher apologizing for a delay in the woman's payment.

She reached other life-markers in the two years following her second husband's death. John Walker, her father, died at age seventy-five in Farmington, north of Salt Lake City, on October 18, 1869. On January 4, 1870, when Lucy was forty-four, her oldest child, John Heber, married Frances Adelaide Hopkins. Their first child, Alice Maude Kimball, was born on March 21, 1871, making Lucy a grandmother.

In the 1870s the rest of Lucy's children followed John Heber into matrimony. On June 12, 1875, Lydia married Frances Xavier Loughery, then Ann united with Richard Gatlin Knox in 1878. On May 14, 1880, when Lucy was fifty-four, Eliza married Frank Albert Woolley, and five years later, on October 14, 1885, Washington Heber exchanged vows with Mary Frances Tuttle.

Lucy's children then apparently scattered. By June 1882 Ann and Richard were living in Crescent City in the extreme northwest corner of California. On the ninth of that month, Ann bore a child. It was a difficult delivery due to the size of the baby, and Lucy made the long journey to the coast to tend her daughter through the summer of 1883. She later wrote in a letter to Joseph F. Smith, dated February 24, 1884:

The ligaments of the womb [of Anna] have become ... distended and weakened and displaced as well She has been in bed for the last month and under the doctors care as this seems her only chance for permanent recovery If ever a poor child was glad to see another it was Anna [who was glad to see Lucy]. had it not been for my presence here, she might have died and the cause never been known she said she often thought she must tell the Doctor just how she felt but had not the courage nor could she tell her husband. Mother she could tell, the Doctor said he could have saved her all this suffering, but she was so ambitious and would not acknowledge that she was ill. of course She would like me to Remain with her but I feel that I have done my duty. And am anxious to return home. and must leave all in the hands of God.

In late summer Lucy met her daughter Lydia in San Francisco so they could "take in the Mechanica Fair" and other places of interest before winter arrived. There she visited Ina Coolbrith, the daughter of the woman she had lived with in Nauvoo some forty years earlier. As the interview ended, Lucy wrote, Ina "clung around my neck and wept bitterly at parting." A few days later Lucy received a letter from Ina requesting another, longer visit. "She [Ina] said she loved me dearly as a child and to come to my house if only on an erand was a great treat to her." Then Lucy quoted Ina's letter: "Of course you never suspected how fond my child-heart was of you. perhaps I inherited some of my Mothers love for you for I doubt if her own sisters were as dear to her as you up to the very last day of her Life." So from Ina Coolbrith, the bohemian poet laureate of California, we catch a glimpse of how sympathetic Lucy was. She evidently returned to Utah soon after February 24, 1884.

The writings of Helen Mar Whitney now show Lucy working as a nurse in Salt Lake City. On December 6, when Lucy was fifty-eight, Helen, fighting sickness and depression after her husband's recent death, wrote, "Lucy W. Kimball called this afternoon I invited her to come & stop with me all night when convenient - said she would soon." The following day Lucy stayed the night. Helen wrote, "She said my sad countenance haunted her all night, & she feared that I would sink under my feelings if I didn't try to shake them off." Lucy helped organize a surprise party for Helen on January 24, 1885, and a week later Helen noted in her diary that Lucy was acting as the nurse for Zina Whitney, Helen's daughter-in-law. In February, when Helen's daughter Genevieve was ill, Lucy moved in to help tend her.

On February 25 Lucy and Helen took a walk together. After paying their respects to Eliza Snow, they visited the *Woman's Exponent* office, the Tithing Office (where Helen's husband had worked), and stopped at a store on the way back. "Lucy bid us good by at evening," wrote Helen, "having been here 4 weeks. She has been very faithful to her post, and assisted Florence about the work." Lucy visited Helen again on April 19, and in the evening babysat Zina Whitney's baby while Zina went to an evening meeting. The next day Lucy and Helen visited a dying woman, and Lucy, the nurse, stayed with her. On May 3 Lucy stayed overnight with Helen again. These diary entries give a picture of Lucy, nearly sixty, close friend of one of Heber Kimball's daughters (also a sister-wife of Joseph Smith), and a friend of Eliza Snow and Emmeline Wells.

A month later, on July 11, Helen met Lucy at a Fourteenth Ward Relief Society meeting that still had attributes of the Winter Quarters blessing meetings, with glossolalia. "The words and the whole was glorious," wrote Helen. "Lucy W.K. was there & came up to Exponent off. with me sat and chatted a while with Emmaline." One wonders when speaking in tongues finally died out in Utah Relief Society meetings.

Like most faithful Mormon women, Lucy spent a great deal of time performing vicarious baptisms and marriages on behalf of dead relatives. She lived in Logan, in northern Utah's Cache County, in 1886-87 and served as a worker in the Logan temple, where she and her sister Jane performed more than a thousand baptisms for the dead. In 1886 Helen Mar and her daughter Lillie spent November in Logan, staying with Lucy in a "cozy" "little quiet Cot[tage]." On November 4 Lucy, with Lyman Littlefield, anointed and laid hands on Helen's head and gave her a blessing for her health. At other times she applied purely medical remedies: "Lucy has waited on me like a good nurse as she is," wrote Helen. Lucy often spent the entire day at the temple, and Helen accompanied her when she felt able. One day at the temple a Sister Clark referred to the two women as "'the wives of a God' meening the Prophet," which made Helen feel "the greatness of the responsibility resting upon us." To many Mormons Joseph Smith had already been deified.

### X. "Nauvoo Veteran Woman at Rest"

In the 1890s Joseph Smith and Nauvoo must have seemed far away to Lucy, but after a half-century she was asked to relive those memories from her teenage years once more in the Temple Lot trial. On March 22, 1892, when she was sixty-five, she publicly told of her marriage to Smith. She was living in Logan at the time. However, her last years were spent in Salt Lake City, living with a daughter in the Ninth Ward, and she evidently also spent time with a son or daughter in Idaho. She became a regular worker in the Salt Lake temple after it was completed in 1893.

On May 18, 1906, Lucy once again experienced tragedy when her daughter, Eliza Woolley, died in Salt Lake City at age forty-seven. Lucy had now buried five of her nine children.

Four years later, in 1910, she became afflicted by a "lingering illness" that lasted for a number of months. In late September, when it became apparent that death was approaching, Lydia and Anna came to her bedside. John was in Canada, and Washington was far away in the northwest, so they were unable to be present. On October 1 Lucy, eighty-four, died "of general debility" at her residence at 52 East First North Street.

The *Deseret News* gave her a front page headline and picture the next day: "NAUVOO VETERAN WOMAN AT REST, —– Mrs. Lucy Walker Kimball Dies At Her Residence This Morning. —– WIFE OF PROPHET JOSEPH —– Later Married the Late Heber C. Kimball —– Story of Her Life Told by Herself." Lucy—who narrowly escaped the Haun's Mill Massacre in Missouri, married Joseph Smith in Nauvoo, wept in Agnes Coolbrith Smith's arms when Joseph was killed, lost a child at Winter Quarters, and bore Heber C. Kimball eight children in early Utah—had lived ten years into the twentieth century.

## 21.

# Dark Sisters

*Sarah Lawrence (Smith Kimball Mount)* and
*Maria Lawrence (Smith [Young] Babbitt)*

On June 19, 1851, Patty Sessions wrote in her journal, "Sister Violate Sarah L Mary Elen here on a visit Br Kimbal & Wm here to Dinner & Supper." This was a veritable honor roll of prominent members of the Heber C. Kimball family. Following the primary wife, Vilate, and "Sarah L," we have Mary Ellen Abel Harris Kimball (a plural wife), Heber himself, and his oldest son William. "Sarah L" was Sarah Lawrence, whom Heber had married in Nauvoo when she was a young widow of Joseph Smith.

A knowledge of Sarah's life-events illuminates this diary entry and gives it a sense of subtle drama. On June 18, just the day before the visit to Patty's home, Sarah had been granted a legal divorce from Kimball. As Heber's biographer Stanley Kimball notes, some fifteen other women left Heber, but only a handful asked for a formal separation. Heber freely granted Sarah the divorce, but his historian daughter, Helen Mar Whitney, never forgave her for this, and so begins a fascinating "dark" tradition in Mormon women's historiography. The fact that Sarah subsequently moved to California was another moral flaw that Helen Mar counted up against her former friend. Sarah is also placed in the mold of a malignant, manipulative stepmother by the writings of her stepdaughter, Mary Mount Tanner.

So the chief historical problem of Sarah's life is to find the human being behind the dark portrait left us by these orthodox Mormon women. One wonders if Sarah was the monster they saw or an individualist who simply pushed beyond certain clearly defined boundaries. She may have been a maneuvering, jealous stepmother, or she may have been misunderstood by an overly possessive stepdaughter. Unfortunately the fragmentary historical record does not allow us to answer such questions definitively. Sarah's sister, Maria, on the other hand, is a virtual shadow, with

473

just a hint of her personality preserved in the historical record at the moment of her death.

## I. Canada

Maria was born to Edward and Margaret Lawrence in Pickering township, Ontario, Canada (outside Toronto) on December 18, 1823. Two and a half years later, on May 13, 1826, her sister Sarah was born, again in Pickering. Edward was apparently a well-to-do farmer, while Margaret was a native of Toronto and twenty-two when Maria was born. Maria and Sarah had five siblings: James, born in approximately 1824; Nelson, date of birth unknown; and Henry, Julia Ann, and Margaret E., born in about 1835, 1837, and 1840.

In the early spring of 1836, Parley P. Pratt came to Canada on a mission and immediately began winning converts in the Toronto area. Most importantly, he baptized John Taylor, later an apostle and president of the LDS church, on May 9. Other converts in the area included William Law, Jacob Scott, James Mulholland, and Robert Thompson, all of whom would become important Nauvoo Mormons. When a branch was built up in the Toronto neighborhood, Taylor was appointed presiding elder.

In August 1837 Joseph Smith, travelling with Sidney Rigdon, Thomas Marsh and John Taylor, visited Canada and reportedly converted Edward and Margaret Lawrence. So Maria, thirteen, and Sarah, eleven, would have met their future husband at this time. Also in August a church conference was held in a large barn on the Lawrence farm. Many attended, and according to B. H. Roberts, "The spirit of God was present, the hearts of the Saints were made to rejoice, and many who were out of the Church believed." On November 10 William Law wrote, "The little branch down at Bro. Larances has not lived up to their privileges, but I hope they will do better for the future." So the Lawrence family apparently formed the nucleus of a small branch.

## II. The Lawrence Estate

Zion called, drawing the Lawrences from Canada to Missouri in 1838, but they probably heard of the "Mormon War" along the way and instead turned eastward to Illinois, settling in Lima, halfway between Commerce and Quincy. Here Edward died in about March 1840, when Maria and Sarah were seventeen and fourteen, leaving a considerable estate for his family to inherit. Under his will, his wife received a third of the inheritance and the rest was to be split among the heirs. However, a legal guardian was required for the family.

Sometime in 1840 or early 1841 the Lawrences moved to Nauvoo. When we next hear of them they had become part of Joseph Smith's circle, for in June 1841 he was appointed guardian of the minor heirs of Edward Lawrence and trustee for their estate. William Law and Hyrum Smith were made bondsmen to Joseph. This guardian relationship is not fully understood, though historian Gordon Madsen has discovered documents that give some insight into its legal complexities.

By 1841 or early 1842 Margaret Lawrence had remarried, uniting with Josiah Butterfield, a widower who had been a high councilor in Kirtland and a president of the first Quorum of Seventy in 1837. With Josiah, Margaret would have two sons, Don Carlos and Edward. The spring 1842 Nauvoo ward census has "Maria Laurence" living with Josiah and Margaret Butterfield in the Nauvoo Third Ward, along with Josiah Butterfield, Jr., and Henry, Juliann, and Margaret Lawrence. It is not known where Sarah was at this time; perhaps she had hired out to work elsewhere.

After Butterfield married Margaret, he began consulting with Joseph Smith concerning the Lawrence inheritance. Presumably the estate could now be transferred to Margaret and Josiah, who would act as Maria's and Sarah's guardian. But for unknown reasons, this did not happen. On April 4, 1842, Joseph's diary reads, "Transacted business at his house with Josiah Butterfield concerning the Lawrence estate." Two months later, on June 4, Smith "Settled with the heirs of Edward Lawrence at his house. N. K. Whitney & Recorder Present." This may reflect payments to the wife and children from the interest of the estate. However, tension began to simmer between Joseph and Josiah Butterfield, until on March 28, 1843, it erupted into violence. According to the *History of the Church*, "Josiah Butterfield came to my house and insulted me so outrageously that I kicked him out of the house, across the yard, and into the street."

### III. Joseph Smith

In the midst of this apparent dispute over the estate, Maria and Sarah began living in the Smith household, as were the Partridges, another fatherless pair. In late spring 1843 Joseph married both Maria, nineteen, and Sarah, seventeen, and soon after this he married the Partridge sisters the second time. Emily Partridge wrote, "Emma, about this time [May], gave her husband two other wives—Maria and Sarah Lawrence." This was during the period when Joseph had convinced Emma to permit him to have plural wives on condition that she could choose them, so it is entirely possible that she gave her permission for these marriages, as Emily asserts. Little or nothing further is known of the Lawrence-Smith marriages.

The legal transactions continued. On May 28 Willard Richards wrote, "At Josephs—upper Room looking after Lawrence estate." The next day, the Joseph Smith journal reads, "Gave instructions to have the account of Lawrence estate made out. Sister from Quincy visiting them." William Clayton, Joseph's scribe, spent time at the "Mayors office" on the 30th, "preparing papers for the Lawrence business." On June 3 Joseph and Clayton travelled to Quincy and Clayton "presented" the Lawrence Estate papers to the probate judge. However, the judge said he could "do nothing" with these, forcing Clayton to revise the account and present it to the judge again, who this time "accepted" it. Clayton wrote, "I then went to the boat and President Joseph returned with me to make oath to the accounts. Balance in Guardians hands was $3790.89 3/4." This seems to have been another interest payment to the Lawrence heirs.

On November 21 Margaret Butterfield was sealed to Edward Lawrence for eternity, with Hyrum Smith performing the marriage and William Clayton standing proxy. This kind of marriage was still rare among the Mormons, so it indicates that the Lawrences were in the inner circle of Joseph's disciples. It is curious that Josiah did not stand proxy, but perhaps he was not in favor with Smith at the time. Technically Clayton may have been Margaret's husband for time as a result of this marriage, as proxies for a deceased marriage partner generally were sealed to the living marriage partner for time, which would have made this a polyandrous marriage.

The Lawrence estate transactions continued. On January 9, 1844, Clayton wrote, "Joseph sent for me to make out Maria Lawrence account." On the 15th he again spent the day at Joseph's: "P.M. settled with the Lawrence estate." And on the 23rd "Joseph sent for me to assist in settling with Brother Taylor about the Lawrence estate." There is some evidence that Smith intended to transfer the guardianship to John Taylor, but there is no certain evidence that this ever took place.

### IV. "I Can Only Find One"

The spring of 1844 was a momentous time for Joseph Smith, William Law, the Lawrences, and Mormons in general. In particular, the cap was coming off of one of Joseph's most jealously guarded secrets, polygamy. In April Josiah Butterfield was sent on a mission to Maine, so one thorn in Smith's side was temporarily gone. But the marriage to the Lawrence sisters became public knowledge when William Law, Joseph's second counselor in the First Presidency, became alienated from the prophet. Law, who had known the Lawrence family since their conversion in Canada, chose the marriage of Smith and Maria Lawrence as a test case with which to prosecute Smith for adultery. On May 23 he filed suit against the Mormon leader in Hancock County Circuit Court, at Carthage, charging that Smith had been living with Maria Lawrence "in an open state of adultery" from October 12, 1843, to the day of the suit.

In response, Smith flatly denied polygamy in a speech delivered on May 26: "What a thing it is for a man to be accused of committing adultery, and having seven wives, when I can only find one." As polygamy was illegal under U.S. law, Smith had little choice but to openly repudiate the practice. But as is often the case with secret policies that are denied publicly, Smith's credibility would later suffer. Realistically he must have understood that thirty-three or more marriages could not be kept a secret forever, and that when they became known the gulf between his public statements and private practice would come back to haunt him. Church leaders would face exactly the same dilemma when practicing post-Manifesto polygamy half a century later.

Smith and his counselors evidently decided to counterattack, prosecuting Law for slandering Maria Lawrence. On June 4 the Mormon leader's journal reads, "In council with Taylor, Babbitt, Hyrum, Richards, Woodworth and Phelps &c. about prosecution [of the Laws and Fosters] in behalf of Maria [Lawrence, for slander]. Concluded to go to Quincy with Taylor and give up my Bonds of guardianship [of Maria Lawrence] &c." The phrase "give up my Bonds of guardianship" suggests that Smith was transferring the guardianship to Taylor, but curiously, there is a certificate dated June 4, 1844, notarized by a Quincy justice of the peace, making Joseph guardian of the Lawrences.

Law and his party then published the *Nauvoo Expositor*, which publicly accused the prophet of practicing polygamy. Smith and his following had the *Expositor* press destroyed, which led to his arrest and incarceration. On June 27, 1844, he was killed, and Maria and Sarah were suddenly widows.

### V. Proxy Wives

After Smith's death, Maria and Sarah worked for a time in a millinery shop in Quincy. On July 30 Emma Smith and William Clayton sailed to Quincy together "to settle the [Lawrence] business," only to find that nothing could be accomplished until the Lawrence sisters received another guardian. Josiah Butterfield would have been the logical choice, but perhaps he was still on his mission. The Butterfield situation was further muddied on October 7 when Josiah was excommunicated for unexplained reasons. However, he was rebaptized, apparently, within the year.

The status of Maria and Sarah changed once again on October 12 when they were sealed for time to Brigham Young (according to Young family traditions) and to Heber C. Kimball, respectively—the familiar pattern of "Levirate" proxy marriage. If Maria married Brigham—which is uncertain—she became his approximate sixteenth wife; but if the marriage took place, it failed, and she separated from him within the following year and a half. Sarah became Kimball's approximate thirteenth wife. After joining his family, she became good friends with her husband's daughter, Helen Mar, another young widow of Joseph. Helen later wrote, "Sarah made choice of my father to stand as proxy for Joseph in this life ... She and I became warm friends after she entered my father's family." But Helen continued, "But she allowed a jealous nature to have full sway." So the "dark" Sarah begins to appear in Mormon history.

At some point Almon Babbitt was retained to represent the Lawrence sisters in their attempts to obtain their inheritance from the Smith estate. According to William Law, Babbitt examined Joseph Smith's books and found that his estate still owed the young women $5,000. While this is too large a figure, there was apparently money due them. However, all of Joseph's property had from the beginning been in the name of Emma Smith, evidently, who could not be legally sued. So Babbitt and the Lawrences turned to William Law, the bondsman, and Mary Fielding Smith, widow of the other bondsman, Hyrum Smith, as targets for a lawsuit. A legal document preserved in the Brigham Young University library sheds a ray of light on this tangled affair. Dated September 1, 1845, it records that Babbitt and the Lawrence children sued William Law, J. W. Coolidge (administrator for the Joseph Smith estate), and Mary Fielding Smith (Hyrum's widow) for $7,750. Interestingly, John Taylor is not named, which suggests that guardianship was never actually transferred. On December 30 William Clayton wrote, "Bishop Whitney has been engaged in arranging some business matters with Almon W. Babbitt Esquire as counsel for the Lawrence Estate." However, strangely enough, Babbitt apparently also represented Mary Fielding Smith, which seems a clear conflict of interest.

According to William Law, when the Lawrences could obtain no repayment from Emma Smith, he himself finally paid them the balance. It should be remembered that Law had known them since Canada and that Emma had never viewed their marriage to Joseph with any warmth. Law blamed both Joseph and Emma for fraudulently taking possession of the Lawrence estate, but perhaps Emma was less to blame. Joseph may have already borrowed the funds while alive, and Emma may not have had the money to pay back after his death.

Like so many other Mormons, the Lawrences performed sacred ordinances in the Nauvoo temple as they prepared to travel west. On January 6, 1846, Sarah received her temple endowment, and on the following day Maria received hers. Immediately preceding her were Almon Babbitt, whom she would soon marry, and Delcena Johnson Sherman Smith Babbitt, who would become her sister-wife in Babbitt's family, as she also had been in the Smith family.

The rest of the temple ordinances are straightforward. Josiah Butterfield had rejoined the church, for on January 20 he and Margaret both received their endowments. Four days later Maria received her proxy sealing to Smith and Babbitt. Babbitt married Delcena Johnson, Julia Johnson, and Mary Tulley on the same day. On the 26th Sarah solemnized her proxy marriage to Joseph Smith and Heber Kimball.

## VI. A Broken Heart

The rest of Maria's life is told by Benjamin Johnson. In an 1897 letter to the *Deseret News*, he denied that Maria had ever married Young, then wrote, "After the prophet's death she became the wife of Col. A.W. Babbitt, by whom she had one child, and died with in Nauvoo, in 1847." Johnson was Babbitt's brother-in-law, so he was probably well-informed on the marriage to Babbitt. Maria did not go west with the body of the Saints because Babbitt had been assigned to stay in Nauvoo, where he remained until 1848.

Mary B. Norman, a daughter of Samuel Smith, who had known Maria in Nauvoo, sheds further light on Maria's death:

> Maria Lawrence died of consumption or one might more truthfuly put it of a broken heart. My Aunt Lucy visited her and felt great sympathy for her. She said to Aunt one time "That if there was any truth in Mormonism she would be saved for said she My yoke has not been easy nor my burden light." As to what was the cause of Maria's deep sorrow I do not exactly know ... She suffered her doubts, her fears, her uncertainty as to whether she was acting right or wrong, for she had a concience and wanted to be right, all these things told on a sensitive nature.

So died one of the least documented of Joseph's certain wives, suffering from a deep sorrow of unknown causes, nameless doubts, and ethical uncertainties. Despite her obscurity, Maria, as the named female party in the adultery case levelled against Joseph Smith by William Law, played a significant part in the history of Mormonism and its founder.

## VII. "Sarah Larance Came to the Waggon"

Through Patty Sessions's and Eliza Snow's journals and Helen Mar Kimball's reminiscences we can trace Sarah's journey across Iowa in 1846. She probably traveled with Heber Kimball's large family (though she also had close ties with the Brigham Young family). On February 15, at Sugar Creek, Eliza wrote, "Had a very pleasant visit with Sarah Lawrence." She visited Eliza again on February 18, in the company of some Young wives: "The weather fine—received a visit from Loisa B. [Beaman Smith Young] C. Decker [Clara Decker Young] & S. Lawrence. Last night very cold." However, Helen Mar Whitney wrote, "On the 19th it began storming ... The next day Sarah Lawrence Kimball and myself went back to Nauvoo where we remained a week, she with her sister, Mariah Babbit, and I with my husband's family." The Kimballs, probably with Sarah, then returned to Sugar Creek on the 28th. On April 14, when

Patty Sessions was about six miles from Locust Creek, halfway across Iowa and between the Chariton River and Garden Grove camp, she wrote, "Sarah Larance came to the waggon it comforted my heart {to} see {her} and hear her words." Sarah was still a valued link in the chain of Mormon sisterhood.

She probably reached Council Bluffs at about the time Helen Mar and Horace Whitney arrived, on June 13. Three days later Horace wrote, "Brother Kimball, father [Whitney] and Brigham started to go over the river to the Bluffs—there to hold another council—then they intend with some of the Twelve to go up the river some distance to seek a location for us this winter. Wm. [Kimball] and wife, Helen, Sarah Lawrence, Harriet Sanders and myself accompanied them to the Bluffs." Helen added, "Horace, myself, and Sarah Lawrence stopped with Bro. Coolege's folks that night." Later that winter, on November 7, Patty Sessions documented Sarah's presence in Winter Quarters: "Sarah Lawrence and Emily Haws [Young] were here." According to Stanley Kimball, in Winter Quarters Sarah "left Heber's group and moved in with the Youngs." Perhaps she was already beginning to be disillusioned with Heber's limited ability to provide for his wives or to bond with them emotionally.

Helen Mar Whitney remembers Sarah attending some of the female blessing meetings of Winter Quarters. A year later, however, Sarah was back in Nauvoo. In a January 1848 letter to Marinda Hyde at Winter Quarters, Sarah Kimball wrote from Nauvoo, "saw Sarah Lawrence last night she desires her love to you said she should write you if she had time." Possibly Sarah returned to help tend Maria before her death in 1847, or perhaps she was visiting her mother; the Butterfields had not gone west with the other Mormons.

## VIII. "A Variety of Perplexities"

Josiah and Margaret Butterfield separated in 1850, and Margaret and Sarah, with James, Henry, Julia, Margaret, Don Carlos, and Edward, came to Utah that summer. Martha Spence Heywood traveled in the same company, which left Kanesville on June 30. On September 9 Martha visited Sarah, "and though the conversation was carried on pleasantly, some knowledge imparted was calculated to make me feel sober and that the light-heartedness and buoyancy of spirits I have been wont to feel will have to be given up for a variety of perplexities that are not known amongst the friends I have left." It is likely that Sarah was describing a plural wife's problems living in the Kimball family and was contemplating divorce.

The 1850 Utah census shows the Lawrences living together in Salt Lake County. Patty Sessions visited "sister Lawrence or Buterfield" on December 14, and Martha Heywood, on the 22nd, remarked that Mrs.

Butterfield had been very sick, close to death, and "Sarah has her duties much increased by this calamity." On May 6, 1851, Patty Sessions wrote, "the wind blew very hard, as part of sister Buterfields house blew down." Sarah may have experienced this uncomfortable event.

## IX. Joseph Mount

Sarah's marriage with Heber Kimball was not working for whatever reasons. Heywood records that Sarah was seriously considering divorce by January 19, 1851: "Had a few words with Sarah ... she still seems in-clined to disconnect herself with Brother K ... I advised her ... to ... be-have to Brother K. as a wife and then she would realize a very different feeling." But Sarah had given up on the marriage. She asked for a divorce and received it on June 18. Mormon men were generally willing to grant their plural wives separations, and this one was amicable. As we have seen, Sarah went visiting with the Kimball family the day after her divorce was legally formalized.

She continued to sew for a living. At some point before 1853 her mother died, so she had to support four children by herself. In roughly 1852 a young woman named Mary Mount hired Sarah to sew some dresses, and Joseph Mount, Mary's divorced father, a man who had made a comfortable fortune in the California gold fields, would drive her to Sarah's home to pick up finished clothing. One morning, as Mount and his daughter rode toward the Lawrence household, he told her that he planned to marry Sarah. Mary's face must have registered shock, for Joseph quickly proceeded to reason with her. Her mother had remarried, he said, so there was no reason he should not also. Nevertheless, Mary was devastated: "I was very much grieved, more so, perhaps, than the cir-cumstances seemed to warrent. But I knew his life was lonely, and surely it was as much his right to marry as hers."

In 1853 Sarah united with Mount, and so begins the next chapter in her life and our next source of documentation on her, the autobiography of Mary Mount Tanner. Mary's account is a moving and eloquent story, but a problematic one. She felt that her parents' divorce had been a tragic mistake and longed to see them reunite. Therefore, there was tension be-tween Mary and Sarah from the beginning, so we must view Sarah's later life through very unsympathetic eyes.

After the marriage, Joseph Mount moved into the Lawrence home, which also housed Henry eighteen, Julia sixteen, Maggie thirteen, and Ed-ward Butterfield ten. The house was too small for six, so Mount took out a wall and added to the room, creating a fine, expanded dwelling. Mary moved in with her father at his invitation. Helen Mar Whitney also tells the story of the remarriage, and her account is clearly written by Heber's daughter. After the marriage to Heber, Helen wrote, Sarah "became disaf-

fected and thought to better her condition by marrying another."
Helen's clear implication is that Sarah married only for money after living in poverty as a plural wife. But, wrote Helen, she and Sarah continued to be friends, "and she met nothing but kindness from father and his
family, he with mother, and other members of his family went by invitation to spend an afternoon at her house, after she was married to her last
husband." This harmonizes with the picture of a "friendly" divorce.
However, Helen Mar now turns to Mount. As he had lived in California,
he was automatically spiritually suspect in the minds of Mormons like
Helen, and as California gold had made him wealthy, he was doubly
marked for the orthodox Saint:

> But the man she married had proven truant to one wife and her little
> ones, leaving them to struggle for existence in this valley through the
> hardest times experienced here. And not until they had found friends to
> succor and help to keep the wolf from their door, did he make his ap-
> pearance, and then he had very little of the Gospel though he, at first,
> professed to be a "Mormon." He had come from the gold mines of Cali-
> fornia where he had made quite a fortune. It was not long before he
> proved the truth of my father's predictions as he denied the faith and re-
> turned to California, taking Sarah with him.

Mary Mount gives a very different, more sympathetic picture of her
father, but she regarded Sarah as cruel and manipulative. When Mary
turned down the proposal of a young Mormon convert who drank too
freely, she felt wretched. Her father "was very kind to me and never alluded to the subject though his wife [Sarah] and her sisters sometimes
made it the subject of unfeeling jests."

Mary felt that Sarah was abnormally possessive of her husband
and jealous of her stepdaughter. Conflicts between wives and children
of previous marriages are common; Mary and Sarah were clearly competing for Joseph's affections. Mary wrote, "He used to tell me, when
she was more than usualy ill humored, that I must not feel grieved
but do the best I could. She spared no opportunity of wounding my
feelings, either in public or private, and I felt sometimes that my position was not enviable."

Mary portrayed Sarah as a consciously designing woman, almost a
femme fatale:

> I was constantly made to feel that my father's children were secondary
> objects with him, and of very little importance since he had formed new
> ties. I dared not mention my mother, and when I brought my little sister
> to see him she was severely criticised and made to feel uncomfortable,
> and I got to feel that she was of very little importance to him. I wonder
> now sometimes that I allowed myself to be so crushed and kept in the

background but I was young and timid and no match for a designing woman. Every opportunity for private conversation with my father was guarded against and done so adroitly that my simple mind did not realize or fathom their designs. I was shut out from his confidence and snubbed whenever an opportunity offered.

## X. Napa, California

Soon the physical and spiritual landscape of Sarah's life would change completely, as she moved from Mormon sacred space to the secular world—from Utah to despised California. In spring 1854 Mount and Sarah made plans to move to his previous place of residence in northern California. It was agreed that his children and Sarah's siblings would stay in Utah, with Mary living in the home of the four Lawrences, headed by Henry, now nineteen. The move was clearly a spiritual statement to the nineteenth-century Mormon. Mary hints darkly that even then Sarah, who had been the wife of Joseph Smith and Heber Kimball, "had apostatized from the church."

Mary grieved over her beloved father's departure and tried anxiously to arrange a private interview with him as the day of his parting approached, though she wrote that Sarah managed to monopolize his time and ward her off. The evening before he left, when he went out to feed his horses, Mary followed, finally finding a chance to be alone with him. But the designing Sarah was soon there to limit even this precious moment: "We had not talked long before Sarah came out. He bade her go in about her business; but she did not do so, and our conversation thus interrupted was not resumed." Sarah had become the archetypal evil stepmother in Mary's eyes. When the parting with her father took place, Mary was crushed: "Many years have passed since then and it is hard to remember all that passed in that last sorrowful parting. I went away to hide my tears and give vent to my grief alone. When I came back they were gone ... I often wondered if ever a young heart was tried like mine."

Despite everything, Mary got along well with Sarah's siblings. She even thought highly of them: "Julia and Maggie Lawrence were really good, loveable girls, and when their sister's influence was from over them [sic] we got along nicely. Henry was an intelligent young man, and seemed to know no difference in his brotherly feelings between his sisters and I." Nevertheless, she wrote, the Lawrences all eventually left the Mormon church.

Sarah and Joseph settled in Napa, near San Francisco, and lived in a fine home. Mount owned a farm with large orchards and vineyards, produced wine, and operated a tavern. Apparently he and Sarah both abandoned Mormon faith and practice, and he began to drink heavily. At some point he incurred significant debts and the tavern was mortgaged. In 1857 he conveyed 147 acres of property, perhaps the whole farm, to Sarah, in order to evade tax laws. Eventually the mortgage on the tavern "ran out" and it was sold. Soon the house was sold also, and the Mounts moved.

## XI. "A Most Vicious and Heartless Woman"

In 1863 Sarah visited Utah. Mary remembered the visit with horror, as Sarah apparently relished telling her stepdaughter-rival how her father had become an alcoholic, how he often had delirium tremens, "and was crazy and unsafe to be around and she was advised to have [Joseph] confined." If this report is correct, Sarah was living with a man on the edge of mental instability. Mary, however, accused Sarah of flagrant lying. She continued:

> She said many things I knew to be false and told her so. It made me sick I had thought to meet her kindly and enjoy hearing about you, but such rank bitter enmity such malicious unkindness hid under her velvet paws was hardly looked for. What stories she may have taken back to you I do not know, but no doubt she spent her mallice as she thought she could strike best. She said you wanted Cornelia [Joseph's daughter] to come to you with her if she would. I preposed to send for Cornelia to come to the city so she could talk with her but she said not to trouble, it was no place for her there she would find poor protection in the care of a drunken father.

So Sarah, like Agnes Coolbrith, had married an alcoholic. "Sacred" plural marriage was not ideal, but "secular" monogamous marriage could also be disastrous. Still, the comparison is not scientific, as monogamists can be teetotalers.

As the legal owner of the valuable Napa farm, Sarah made improvements on it, then sold it in September 1864 for $4,500—not a monumental sum, but it would allow her to live comfortably for some years. In the same month Mount, presumably with Sarah, was a resident of San Francisco, but soon after that he and Sarah traveled to Hawaii for his health, arriving there on November 11. On April 3, 1865, Sarah returned to San Francisco, but Joseph did not follow her back until two years later, on May 23, 1867. He is listed in the San Francisco directory at 1018 Hyde Street for two years after this. As this property was listed in Sarah Lawrence's name after her death, she and he were probably still living together. He visited Hawaii once more from May 4, 1868, to August 11, 1869, then the directory shows him living at 1018 Hyde Street until 1872.

Sarah visited Utah again before November 1872. In 1876 Mary wrote to her father, "The last time I saw her it was in 72 I called at Henrys a few moments she was there. I asked for you, she said you was well she had

just got a letter from you, that when she left she asked you to look after the house but when you went to town you got on a spree and did not see to anything and she was very much out of patience."

Unlike most of the other wives of Joseph Smith, Sarah apparently repudiated any connection she had previously had with the prophet. Helen Mar Whitney wrote,

> She became so wicked that when paying her last visit to Salt Lake she denied emphatically ever being connected to Joseph or to my father, and was very insulting to those who dared to dispute her word. She abused her brother Henry's second wife most shamefully, when meeting her in his store, laying to her the most humiliating and abusive accusations, which proved her to be a most vicious and heartless woman. Her brother, Henry Lawrence, was so annoyed by her unprincipled course, that he was among the most thankful when she left here and returned to California, where she soon died.

One hesitates to leave any woman with that kind of epitaph, but we have no alternative, positive witness to offer. Undoubtedly her close family members viewed her with more sympathy and understanding. In addition, she was suffering from uterine cancer, which would inevitably cause her to be depressed and irritable. It is not known when Sarah began to feel the symptoms of this ailment or how she was treated. She could still travel in 1872. Perhaps that was the purpose of her Utah visit— to see her siblings one last time. In any event, she died of "cancer womb" in San Francisco on November 28, 1872, at age forty-six.

# 22.

# Polygamy, Melancholy, Possession

## *Helen Mar Kimball (Smith Whitney)*

On the afternoon of February 3, 1846, a young couple awaited a summons to their own marriage in the Nauvoo temple. They came from two prominent Mormon families—Helen Kimball, seventeen, from the Heber C. and Vilate Murray Kimball family, and Horace Whitney, twenty-three, from the family of Bishop Newel K. Whitney and the charismatic Elizabeth Ann Whitney. The sensitive, high-strung Helen had been in love with the stolid, intellectual Horace since her early teens. As the long-suffering Latter-day Saints prepared to leave Nauvoo, the young couple had made arrangements to marry each other while a temple was available.

The shadows of afternoon lengthened into twilight, and the messenger from Helen's father arrived, summoning them to the temple immediately. They walked together through Nauvoo, and as they reached a little graveyard at the bottom of Temple Hill, they stopped, held hands, and vowed to "cling to each other" through time and, if permitted, throughout eternity. This vow was somewhat uncertain, however, for a shadow lay across their hope. As a young teen, Helen had wedded Joseph Smith as one of his eternal wives. The marriage to the dead prophet could not be annulled, so an eternal marriage to Horace was not possible, only a proxy marriage for time. Horace knew that Helen and his children would be Smith's in the eternities.

They therefore entered the temple with intensely ambivalent feelings, a wistful sadness tempering their elation. Inside the walls of this most sacred building, as they had expected, Helen was sealed to Joseph Smith for eternity, with Horace standing proxy for Smith, then Horace and Helen were sealed together for time. They left the temple married but also eternally unmarried. This left Horace without an eternal wife. Therefore the next day Helen stood proxy as Horace was sealed to an Elizabeth Sykes, deceased. So Helen and Horace, young sweethearts, would go through life expecting to spend eternity with other companions—unless some other arrangement could be "permitted" in the eternities. Mormon history has many examples of such bittersweet, paradoxical marriages.

Having married Joseph Smith at the age of fourteen, Helen Mar is the youngest of Smith's known wives. She is also one of the best documented, as she penned extensive autobiographical writings and diaries in her later life. The prophet's marriage to her seems to have been largely dynastic—a union arranged by Joseph and Heber to seal the Kimball family to a seer, church president, and presiding patriarchal figure of the dispensation of the fullness of times. Through Helen's extensive writings, we have great insight into how she and her mother felt about this arrangement. It was a supremely difficult trial for both of them. They accepted Smith's teachings on marriage and the required union only with great reluctance, and even felt revulsion at the idea of plural matrimony. Moreover, Helen's romantic dreams focused on her own peer group, not on the middle-aged Smith.

After the prophet's death, Helen's inner hopes were fulfilled as she married Horace, but she and Horace would lose their first three children, and she would experience great physical and psychological sickness while crossing the plains and in pioneer Utah. This melancholy would haunt her throughout the rest of her life. Nevertheless, she would have eight more children and become an active speaker and writer in nineteenth-century Utah, a "leading woman of Zion." Despite "hating polygamy in her heart" as a young girl, she would nevertheless write two fervent pamphlets in defense of "the principle" in the 1880s. She is perhaps the classic example of a woman whose conversion to polygamy was difficult but complete, coming only after a period of severe cognitive dissonance.

## I. Heaven and Angels Not Very Far Off

On August 22, 1828, Helen Mar was born to Heber Chase Kimball and Vilate Murray in Mendon, Monroe, New York, ten miles west of Palmyra. Heber, a twenty-seven-year-old Vermont native, was a potter, blacksmith, and farmer. An unsophisticated man who mixed childlike faith, homespun wisdom, and a biting, jolly Yankee humor, he would become one of the most prominent leaders in early Mormonism. Vilate, twenty-two, had been born in New York. She was intelligent, cultured, and was regarded with intense devotion by her husband. They had married in 1822. Helen was the third child in a family of nine and the only surviving daughter in the family. Her two older siblings were Judith (born in 1823), who died as an infant, and William Henry (born in 1826). She and William grew up together, sharing sibling rivalry and closeness. Another son, Roswell Heber, was born on June 10, 1831, but died five days later.

Perhaps as an only daughter, Helen was slightly pampered. One gathers that she was the apple of her father's eye, and throughout her life she looked upon him with profound veneration and affection. "I remember the cunning little dishes and toys he would make for me," she wrote, "which I generously divided with my mates who were less fortunate." She regarded her mother with equal reverence. Often, she remembers, she would awaken to hear Vilate praying. Then her mother would begin performing her household duties, "singing so sweetly, it seemed to me as though heaven and the angels were not very far off."

> I used to think it impossible for me to ever become a Saint. I looked upon my parents as such, but thought that nothing short of perfection could take us to heaven, which I could never attain to, as I was so fond of fun and amusement that I could not possibly give them up, though I often had very serious reflections upon the subject, and used to think if I could only know just a little time before I was to die, I might be able to sober down and prepare myself.

Some of Helen's earliest memories are of another future plural wife of Joseph Smith, Brigham Young's sister Fanny, who had been living in the Kimball household since 1827. Helen wrote that the Kimballs and the Youngs were "like one family," and she grew up thinking that Brigham and Joseph Young were uncles: "I loved them and their sister Fanny, who was afterwards married to my Grandfather Murray [Vilate's father], more dearly than I did most of my own relatives, for we left them all when we went to Kirtland ... Aunt Fanny Young ... took care of me, and she was always ready to defend me if necessary." In fact, Helen's name, derived from "the Scottish Lady, Helen Mar," came from Fanny, who would tell tales and sing songs of Scotland.

## II. "Whipt into Obedience"

The Youngs, and possibly Heber, had read the Book of Mormon by 1831. Nevertheless, in the fall Heber and Vilate joined the Baptist church. But three weeks later, probably in November, some Mormon missionaries visited from Pennsylvania, and Heber and Brigham were profoundly impressed by their preaching. As soon as he heard Elder Alpheus Gifford preach, Heber later said, he was converted. In January 1832 he, with Brigham and Phinehas, visited Columbia, Pennsylvania, where the nearest Mormon branch was located. Three months later, on April 15, the day after Brigham became a Mormon, Heber was baptized by Gifford, and Vilate was baptized two weeks later. Helen was three at the time.

Heber went on a short local mission, then made preparations to gather to Kirtland, Ohio. After selling their property, the Kimballs left

Mendon in the fall of 1833, arriving in the Mormon capital toward the end of October and moving into a house Grandfather and Fanny Murray had rented for them. So their Kirtland experience began.

Heber traveled with Joseph Smith on the Zion's Camp expedition in 1834. While the men were away, women pursued their quiet tasks at home. Helen remembers her mother and her friends "engaged in knitting and spinning and making garments for those who were laboring on the Temple. My mother toiled all summer ... I remember the delicious crackers she used to make and send to the sick in Kirtland ... One reason for my remembering this so well is that my brother and I had to pound the dough ... and not being overly fond of work it became very irksome."

Like Zina Huntington, Helen remembered Kirtland as an idyllic time, and left descriptions of the beauty of the surrounding groves. At Sunday schools, she wrote, "I used to love to go and recite verses and whole chapters from the New Testament, and we received rewards in primers, etc. ... At ten o'clock we would form in line and march with our teachers up to the Temple."

One day, when Vilate went out to make a call, she instructed Helen not to touch some dishes which she had left standing on the table, telling her that if she broke any during her absence she would give her a whipping when she returned. Of course, Helen, playing under the table, bumped it accidentally and the table leaf fell, breaking a number of dishes. "My brother ... solemnly, but needlessly reminded me of what I might expect," she later remembered. Horrified, she went out under a nearby apple tree and prayed that her mother's heart might be softened when she returned. And though Vilate "was very punctual when she made a promise to her children to fulfil it, yet when she returned she had no disposition to chastise" her daughter. So Helen's prayer was answered. Heber loved to tell this story, wrote Helen, and "Often he would turn to me with a sly twinkle and say, 'Here's Helen, she had to be whipt into obedience;' and I always admitted it, saying: 'Yes, who He loveth He chasteneth,' when he would burst out into one of his peculiar laughs." In this anecdote we see Heber's wry sense of humor, which he passed on to his folk-hero general authority son, J. Golden Kimball, and his affectionate rapport with Helen; and the tender-hearted Vilate, unable to administer the corporal punishment she had promised.

On February 18, 1835, the Kimball family dynamics changed dramatically as Heber was called to be an apostle in the five-year-old Latter-day Saint church. The apostleship, not originally a central position of church government, was almost entirely focused on missionary work at this time. However, the office soon grew in importance, and in ten years Heber would be the second most prominent church leader. The

Kimballs thus became a general authority family. Though this assured them a place among the Latter-day Saint elite, Heber was often absent from his family, both because of his local church duties and his mission field labors. For example, some three months later, on May 4, Heber left with the Twelve on a mission to the eastern states and Canada, even though Vilate was eight months pregnant. The new baby, Heber Parley, was born on June 1. Heber C. returned home two months later to see his child for the first time.

In spring 1836 Helen Mar, now seven, attended Eliza Snow's school in a house connected to Joseph Smith's dwelling where she remembered using the Book of Mormon as a textbook. On June 10 her father left on another mission. When it was drawing to a close, Vilate traveled east with the new baby to meet him and visit old friends and relatives. William was left with the Murrays, but Helen went to a Sister Nobles, and the separation from William left her heartbroken. Vilate and Heber returned on October 2. Helen wrote: "I … remember the morning when her [Vilate's] sweet face peeped into the door, I was just kindling the fire and how quickly I dropped the wood and flew into her loving arms. They had returned late the previous evening and she could hardly wait till morning to see me." Helen and Vilate then returned to the Kimball household, and Helen's memories provide a vivid Kirtland vignette:

> The first object that met my eye as we entered the door of our own sweet home was my little brother [Heber Parley], who had been very sick and was reduced in flesh previous to taking the trip, standing with both hands full of something to eat; my father had not yet risen but our meeting was a joyful one. The wood fire was burning brightly on the andirons and our old fashioned tin oven stood before it filled with sweet apples and Aunt Fanny was preparing breakfast.

Helen was baptized in a tributary of the Chagrin River that winter. Her father cut a hole in the ice and "Uncle" Brigham performed the baptism. But Helen was not troubled by the cold water: "I had longed for this privilege and though I had some distance to walk in my wet clothes I felt no cold or inconvenience from it."

In June 1837 Heber left on another missionary trip, this time to England, so once again the family was left alone. When he returned in May 1838 the church had become increasingly beset by financial embarrassments, lawsuits, and opposition from influential dissenters. Joseph Smith and Sidney Rigdon fled the city to avoid probable incarceration, and most of the Saints set out for Missouri, now fully the new Zion.

### III. "His Feet Were Found to Be Badly Frozen"

On July 1, 1838, nine-year-old Helen left Kirtland with her parents and siblings. She wrote, "When we started for Missouri I was delighted, as children commonly are, at the prospect of a change ... although some of my little mates tried to frighten me with awful tales about being eaten alive by the Missourians, who were cannibals with horns." Also in the group were Orson and Marinda Hyde, and Louisa Beaman and her family. They traveled to Wellsville by wagon, then by steamboat to St. Louis. On this leg of the journey, the heat was so intense that many in the group became feverish, but they traveled on to Richmond on the Missouri River. Finally, on July 25 they arrived at Far West and the Kimball family at first stayed at the home of Apostle David Patten to recuperate. They then moved to a storehouse on the main square, and later transferred into a small log cabin, eight feet by eleven, on the outskirts of town.

But the Kimballs had arrived in Far West when the persecutions had reached a fever pitch. Helen and her family left their outlying home at one particularly dangerous time in October and moved into the inner city for safety. First they visited Mrs. Patten, whose husband had been killed recently in the Battle of Crooked River. "I can never forget her fearless and determined look," wrote Helen. "Around her waist was a belt to which was attached a large bowie knife," and she intended to fight "if any of the demons came there." The Kimballs then went to the home of Mary Smith, where they stayed. Food was scarce, and Helen sometimes ground wheat "a good portion of the day" to make short cake.

Half a year after they arrived in Missouri, the Kimballs, with the rest of the Latter-day Saints, were forced to leave. As Heber had been asked to stay behind to help the poor, the family went ahead without him, leaving on February 14, 1839, with Brigham Young and family. In later life Helen remembered this journey vividly:

> The day we started the weather was terrible, and my mother and Sister Young, with their children, stopped at a [non-Mormon] house and asked the privilege of warming themselves. [They were admitted.] There were no men, only women there, but they began talking about the horrible "Mormons" and eyed us very closely. Sister Young and my mother appeared to believe all they said, and looked horrified, and we children imitated them.

Some nights the little caravan received hospitality; other nights they camped near the road, building a fire for warmth and sleeping in their small wagon. Helen remembered a day that was so cold that they had "to walk to keep from freezing." Her brother William, who was riding ahead, dropped off his horse and fell asleep in the snow. Fortunately Dr. Levi Richards spotted him and saved him by vigorous rubbing "and a few well meaning blows." This made William "angry enough to fight, started the blood to circulating and saved his life. We soon after arrived at Bishop

Vincent Knight's house, where his feet were found to be badly frozen." This was the home of Martha McBride Knight.

## IV. "We Children Wept Bitterly"

After crossing the Mississippi into Illinois, the Kimballs stayed first in the town of Atlas for seven weeks, renting a house from a widow Ross. Then John Greene, a Young in-law, helped move them to Quincy, where Heber found them on May 2. When it came time to move to Commerce in July, Heber and Vilate traveled by water because Vilate was expecting again, but Helen and William were sent north by land with friends. Helen, now eleven, was quite disheartened by the sight of swampy Commerce—later Nauvoo—and missed her parents, who were delayed in Quincy for two or three days. She remembers that she and William visited the "upper landing" each night to see if their parents would arrive, "and having to return at night without them I felt homesick and sick of the country." She did not appreciate the beauty of the area at the time, but when she began to live in Utah, she missed "the green woods and hills and delightful vales ... and most of all ... the view of the broad Mississippi, where we could see and hear the steamers as they plied up and down its quiet bosom." She also yearned for "those beautiful rich prairies covered, as far as the eye could reach, with tall waving grass, and decked with wild flowers of various hues."

In Commerce the Kimballs lived first in a primitive house with dirt floor. Vilate, near childbirth, threw boards on the floor; a heavy rain storm arrived on August 23 and soon the floor was floating on the water that had leaked into the house. On the same day, in the same house, Vilate's sixth child, David Patten Kimball, was born. Heber began building a better house, but soon the "chills and fever" overwhelmed him and he was prostrated. Everyone seemed to be sick with malaria at the time, Helen remembered.

Satanic forces now make an appearance in Kimball family history. As Christian primitivists, early Mormons often interpreted serious sickness as demonic possession, a perspective that figures importantly in Helen's life. While the Kimballs were living in their first Nauvoo house, Vilate dreamed of a "personage" attacking her, and she began making strange noises as she struggled with her invisible assailant. Helen wrote, "He [Heber] lit a candle and saw that her eyes were sunken and her nose pinched in ... He laid hands upon her head and rebuked the spirit ... and commanded it to depart." However, as in the Bible, spirits can move into other bodies, including animals. "In a moment afterwards, some half a dozen children in other parts of the house were heard crying as if in great distress; the cattle began to bellow and low, the horses to neigh and winnow, the dogs barked, hogs squealed, and the fowls and every-

thing around were in great commotion." In a few minutes Heber was summoned to lay hands on Sister Bently, David Patten's widow, who lived in
the next room and had also been seized by a demonic spirit. Through witnessing such scenes, the dark ideology of demonic possession helped
shape Helen's world view.

Heber finished the new house just before he was called on another
mission to England. He left on September 18, and Helen later wrote, "We
children wept bitterly when our father came to bid us farewell ... Both he
and Brother Young were going away so sick they were unable to get into
the wagon without assistance. The scene is so vivid before me that my
eyes are blinded with tears as I try to write." The family was also sick at
the time, except for little Heber Parley, age four, who supplied the family
with buckets of water. But soon he "came in with his usual pail of water,
and setting it upon the floor, laid down by it and said: 'I b'eve I's goin' to
have agu' too;' and sure enough the little fellow was shaking with it." A
folk remedy for malaria was to dive under the bed at the onset of symptoms, so Helen, when she felt the fever and chills coming on, immediately
went to her bedroom to try the cure. But as she ducked under her bed,
she gave her head "a frightful blow, and I felt no more of the chills and fever for three weeks; but whether it was due to the blow on my head or
my faith in the trick I could never quite decide."

As we have seen, the situation of women with missionary husbands
was often grim. Helen was probably sheltered from the worst of the trial
but remembered accompanying Vilate and Bishop Vinson Knight to the
bishop's storehouse in upper Commerce to receive a new pair of shoes.
In her idealized memory, "We found him remarkably kind, and our wants
were all supplied." However, a letter from Heber to Vilate written late in
1839 shows that Vilate wanted to move away from Commerce and return
to the East, perhaps permanently, which would have required Heber to
give up his apostleship. Stanley Kimball writes, "That Vilate must have realized this but still wanted to leave is surely an indication of the degree of
hardship she was facing." Possibly she had seen children dying in Nauvoo
and was worried about malaria.

While on his mission, Heber would send home toys for Helen, including two china dolls, which she put on salt cellars for display. When
Joseph Smith was visiting the Kimballs one day, he picked one up and accidentally broke off its head. Helen wrote, "He merely remarked: 'As that
has fallen, so shall the heathen gods fall.' I stood there a silent observer,
unable to understand or appreciate the prophetic words, but thought
them a rather weak apology for breaking my doll's head off." The doll was
mended, and Helen still had it in 1881.

On December 23 Helen and William attended a Christmas party given by the young son and daughter of the Hibbards, non-Mormon "old settlers." The Hibbards eventually became Mormon, and Helen later attended several balls at their home. By late 1840 the Kimballs had regained their health, and Helen and William attended a school taught by Justin Johnson. But malarial relapses were frequent. Helen succumbed to the fevers again in the summer of 1841. When a circus came to Nauvoo, and William, who was living elsewhere as an apprentice, came to pick up Helen to go with him, he found her so delirious with a sudden attack of chills and fever that she did not even know that he had come.

On July 1 Heber finally arrived home. William, who lived near the landing, greeted him first and quickly ran home to tell the rest of the family. Then Heber appeared:

> Soon we saw a company of horsemen coming with all speed and when my mother saw them she made a hasty retreat behind the door to hide her confusion, where in a moment after father found her overwhelmed in tears ... Joseph ... with Brother Hyrum and three or four brethren accompanied my father home. My mother felt the presence of others at such a time almost an intrusion but Brother Joseph seemed unwilling to part with my father; and from that time kept the Twelve in Council early and late, and she sometimes felt nearly jealous of him.

We see the beginnings of the "church widow" syndrome of the later Latter-day Saint church, a phenomenon that would be exacerbated by polygamy in early Mormonism. In the fall Joseph Smith wanted Heber Kimball closer to him, so Heber built a house "on the flat" nearer to the temple, the meeting place in the grove, and the Mississippi. Though it was still a log house (Nauvoo as yet had no brick kilns or sawmills), it was larger than the first house, including three lower rooms and a "chamber."

On March 22, 1842, Helen, now thirteen, attended a birthday party for Sarah Ann Whitney, seventeen, in "the Masonic room above Joseph Smith's store," as we have seen. Helen was intimidated by the older guests and was too shy to participate in games, but she stayed over with Sarah. The two girls talked long into the night until Horace, Sarah's older brother who was separated from them only by a partition, complained of the noise. Helen wrote that "he was impolite enough to tell us of it, and request us to stop and let him go to sleep, which was proof enough that he had never thought of me only as the green school girl that I was." Helen, barely a teenager, had not yet made an impression on her future husband.

That same month Helen contracted "consumption," caused, she felt, by a piercing wind blowing on her when she was dressed lightly for a party. "I was not sick in bed, but I looked like a walking ghost, and it took but a few steps to exhaust what little strength I had." Finally, Heber tried a common Mormon remedy on his sick daughter—baptism for health in the font beneath the Nauvoo temple. According to Helen, she recovered "more rapidly" from that time on.

### V. "With a Broken and Bleeding Heart"

In 1842 Joseph Smith was rapidly developing and disseminating his Nauvoo theology and ritual—the endowment drama, the doctrines of exaltation (deification), eternal marriage, eternal linking (sealing) of families, and the full practice of polygamy. Heber, one of Smith's most devoted disciples, was one of the first to receive these revelations, though plural marriage would try him almost beyond endurance. It was an even more bitter test for Vilate. Because of it, wrote Helen, her mother's trials, which "she had flattered herself were nearly over, had scarcely begun." She and Heber were intensely devoted to each other, and to share that devotion with others would be an ultimate test. Later, as a much-married polygamist, according to Helen, Heber loved Vilate much the best of any of his wives.

The first chapter in the story of Smith, the Kimballs, and polygamy is that of Vilate's offering, which Orson Whitney, Helen's own son, recounted in his biography of Heber. In early 1842, apparently, Joseph approached Heber and made a stunning demand: "It was no less than a requirement for him to surrender his wife, his beloved Vilate, and give her to Joseph in marriage!" wrote Orson. Heber, naturally, was "paralyzed" and initially unbelieving. "Yet Joseph was solemnly in earnest." Heber's first impulse was to turn down the requirement with no further discussion. At that time, Orson surmised, he doubted Joseph's "motive and the divinity of the revelation."

For three days Heber endured agonies. Finally asked to choose between his loyalty to Mormonism and his intimacy with his wife, Mormonism and Smith won out. "Then, with a broken and bleeding heart, but with soul self-mastered for the sacrifice, he led his darling wife to the Prophet's house and presented her to Joseph." "Joseph wept at this proof of devotion, and embracing Heber, told him that was all that the Lord required." It had been a test, said Joseph, to see if Heber would give up everything he possessed. As so often with Joseph's actions, he had an Old Testament parallel in mind—Abraham surrendering Sarah to the Pharaoh. The emotional trauma Vilate endured must have been indescribable also. Then Joseph married her and Heber for eternity, and said, "Brother Heber, take her and the Lord will give you a hundred fold."

This prefigured the next test for the couple, which was nearly as difficult as the first: Smith now taught Heber the principle of polygamy and required him to take a plural wife. At first Heber thought of marrying two elderly ladies, the sisters Pitkin, who would cause Vilate "little if any unhappiness." But Smith had already selected Heber's first plural wife, Sarah

Peake Noon, a thirty-year-old English convert who had left an allegedly abusive husband, Mr. Noon, before her conversion, and had two little girls. Heber reluctantly agreed. Finally, to add to the trial, Joseph commanded Heber to keep the plural marriage secret even from Vilate "for fear that she would not receive the principle." Helen wrote, "This was the greatest test of his [Heber's] faith he had ever experienced ... the thought of deceiving the kind and faithful wife of his youth, whom he loved with all his heart, and who with him had borne so patiently their separation and all the trials and sacrifices they had been called to endure, was more than he felt able to bear."

Heber was understandably worried that Vilate would hear about the marriage from another source and balked at entering into polygamy under those conditions. Helen explained, "The Prophet told him the third time before he obeyed the command. This shows that the trial must have been extraordinary, for he was a man who from the first had yielded implicit obedience to every requirement of the Prophet." According to Orson, "Heber was told by Joseph that if he did not do this he would lose his apostleship and be damned." As so often, Joseph Smith taught polygamy as a requirement, and to reject it was to lose one's eternal soul. Once one had accepted him as a prophet, one had to comply or accept damnation. Heber thus was hesitant and deeply troubled but nevertheless married Sarah Peak Noon in early 1842 without telling Vilate. However, this caused him to display "anxious and haggard looks"; he was sick, could not sleep, would wring his hands and weep like child. Vilate was mystified.

According to family traditions, Heber asked God to reveal the principle to Vilate, and soon after she was allowed a vision of immortal joy in celestial, plural marriage, and saw Sarah Noon as Heber's wife. She came to her husband and said, "Heber, what you kept from me the Lord has shown me." In later years, wrote Helen, "She gave my father many wives, and they always found in my mother a faithful friend." Nevertheless, polygamy would continue to be a severe spiritual trial for her, though she may have consciously accepted the doctrine. Heber and Vilate had passed through the fiery ordeal of two polygamic tests. One more, this one involving Helen, still awaited them.

Daily life continued. In early September Heber and Brigham, with George A. Smith and Amasa Lyman, left on a short mission to southern Illinois. On January 2, 1843, Helen's next brother, Charles Spaulding, was born. William was now sixteen, Helen, fourteen, Heber P. seven, and David two. Helen was not enthralled with the idea of one more boy in the family. She wrote that she was "a disappointed and most ungrateful girl when hearing the news, as I had so long desired a little sister; and my feelings were so soured, that I said some harsh and unbecoming things, and was determined not to welcome the little stranger. I tried to steel my heart against him, but in spite of me the love would come." As Vilate suffered poor health in 1843 and 1844, Helen did much of Charles's parenting in those years and bonded closely with him. She wrote,

> He was very delicate and had some severe spells of sickness, and my love and tender care increased with the days and months and I never wearied of my charge. When about two years old he became strong, healthy and the pride of my heart. The pleasure I felt in dressing and taking him out with me was quite equal to all that I had ever anticipated in a little sister, and even my affection for him surpassed any that I had ever felt for a baby.

At about the same time Charles was born, Sarah Noon Kimball's first child by Heber was also born, and Helen, knowing nothing of polygamy, only "noticed the great interest taken by my parents in behalf of Sister Noon." Polygamy was inching closer and closer to the unsuspecting teenager. In March 1843 Sarah Ann invited Helen and William to her eighteenth birthday party, and as this was a small gathering, Helen enjoyed it more than the previous year's event. Joseph Smith, who had been married to Sarah since July 1842, made an appearance in the early part of the evening and uttered some "peculiar remarks." These, wrote Helen, "gave food for talk and no little amount of wit which passed from one to the other after he had left; and William and I talked it over after we returned home, of the enjoyable time and the peculiarities of Joseph."

### VI. Golden Link

Orson Whitney wrote, "Soon after the revelation [to Vilate] was given, a golden link was forged whereby the houses of Heber and Joseph were indissolubly and forever joined. Helen Mar, the eldest Daughter of Heber Chase and Vilate Murray Kimball, was given to the Prophet in the holy bonds of celestial marriage." This marriage, like that of Smith to Sarah Whitney, looks to be almost purely dynastic, as Whitney's language ("golden link" "the houses of Heber and Joseph") shows. And as will be seen, Heber felt that this link would have eternal consequences for his family.

We are fortunate to have a frank, first person, holographic reminiscence of this marriage by Helen, written to her children in 1881, along with supportive accounts in print. As Helen told the story, polygamy entered her life when her father approached her one day in the early summer of 1843. "Without any preliminaries [my father] asked me if I would believe him if he told me that it was right for married men to take other wives." Helen's response was instinctual Victorian: "The first impulse was anger ... My sensibilities were painfully touched. I felt such a sense of personal injury and displeasure; for to mention such a thing to me I thought altogether unworthy of my father, and as quick as he spoke, I replied to him, short and emphatically, *No I wouldn't!* ... This was the first time that I ever openly manifested anger towards him." Heber responded by teaching the principle to his daughter as Smith had taught it to him. "Then he commenced talking seriously and reasoned and explained the principle, and why it was again to be established upon the earth, etc." No doubt Heber mentioned the example of Abraham and Jacob, and taught Helen that in this, the final dispensation, all biblical institutions had to be restored.

Helen listened in disbelief and complete dismay. She wrote that, for her, this first interview "had a similar effect to a sudden shock of a small earthquake. When he found (after the first outburst of displeasure for supposed injury) that I received it meekly, he took the first opportunity to introduce Sarah Ann to me as Joseph's wife. This astonished me beyond measure." However, before introducing Helen to the subject of her possible marriage to Smith, Heber had apparently already offered her to the prophet. In her 1881 reminiscence Helen wrote, "Having a great desire to be connected with the Prophet, Joseph, he offered me to him; this I afterwards learned from the Prophet's own mouth. My father had but one Ewe Lamb, but willingly laid her upon the alter: how cruel this seamed to the mother whose heartstrings were already stretched untill they were ready to snap asunder, for he had taken Sarah Noon to wife & she thought she had made sufficient sacrifise but the Lord required more."

Heber thus ended his first interview with Helen by asking her if she would become Joseph's wife. If possible, Helen was even more astounded than before. She wrote, "I will pass over the temptations which I had during the twenty four hours after my father introduced to me this principle & asked me if I would be sealed to Joseph." Undoubtedly, unbelief and rebelliousness were part of these temptations.

In a published account Helen described her indecision during this twenty-four-hour period, but her trust in her father turned the scales toward accepting polygamy:

> [He] left me to reflect upon it for the next twenty-four hours ... I was sceptical—one minute believed, then doubted. I thought of the love and tenderness that he felt for his only daughter, and I knew that he would not cast her off, and this was the only convincing proof that I had of its being right. I knew that he loved me too well to teach me anything that was not strictly pure, virtuous and exalting in its tendencies; and no one

else could have influenced me at that time or brought me to accept of a doctrine so utterly repugnant and so contrary to all of our former ideas and traditions.

The mention of twenty-four hours shows that time pressures were being placed on the prospective bride, just as Smith had applied a time limit to Lucy Walker.

The next morning Joseph himself appeared in the Kimball home and personally explained "the principle of Celestial marrage" to Helen. In her memoir Helen wrote, "After which he said to me, 'If you will take this step, it will ensure your eternal salvation & exaltation and that of your father's household & all of your kindred.['] This promise was so great that I willingly gave myself to purchase so glorious a reward." As in the case of Sarah Whitney, Joseph gave the teenage daughter responsibility not only for her own salvation but for that of her whole family. Thus Helen's acceptance of a union that was not intrinsically attractive to her was an act of youthful sacrifice and heroism.

The only person still reluctant to see the marriage performed, after Helen had accepted the proposal, was Vilate. Helen wrote, "None but God & his angels could see my mother's bleeding heart—when Joseph asked her if she was willing, she replied 'If Helen is willing I have nothing more to say.'" This is far from a glowingly positive bestowal of permission. Helen conjectured that Vilate was thinking of her own trials as a plural wife: "She had witnessed the sufferings of others, who were older & who better understood the step they were taking, & to see her child, who had scarcely seen her fifteenth [sic] summer, following in the same thorny path, in her mind she saw the misery which was as sure to come as the sun was to rise and set; but it was all hidden from me."

Despite Vilate's obvious deep reluctance to see her daughter enter plurality, the ceremony took place. In May 1843, when Helen was two or three months away from fifteen years of age, she was married to Joseph. The Smith and Kimball houses now would be eternally linked together.

Helen's reminiscence includes a poem that gives valuable insight into her feelings at the time. Unlike Eliza R. Snow, who looked upon the marriage to Joseph Smith as the spiritual zenith of her life, Helen, much younger, saw it as limiting her freedom and isolating her from her friends. The poem appears to open with Helen describing her perspective at the time she married Smith:

I thought through this life my time will be my own
    The step I now am taking's for eternity alone,
No one need be the wiser, through time I shall be free,
    And as the past hath been the future still will be.

To my guileless heart all free from worldly care
   And full of blissful hopes and youthful visions rare
The world seamed bright the thret'ning clouds were kept
   From sight and all looked fair ...

Though the interpretation of these lines has been debated, it appears that Helen, when she married Smith, understood that the marriage would be "for eternity alone," and that it would leave her free to marry someone else for time. But apparently this was not the case, as is shown by a number of factors. First, there is no evidence elsewhere that Smith ever married for eternity only, not including "time." For instance, in the marriage ceremony used for Smith and Sarah Ann Whitney (a marriage that is parallel in its dynamics to Helen's, as they were both dynastic marriages to teens), they both agreed "to be each other's companion so long as you both shall live" as well as for eternity. Both Eliza Snow and Patty Sessions explicitly stated that they were married to Joseph Smith for time and eternity. Second, Helen's later history shows that Joseph was protective of her, as he had been with another young wife, Flora Woodworth, and tried to shield her from the attentions of young men. This would not be consistent with a marriage for eternity only.

    Third, the rest of the poem shows that Helen's "blissfull hopes" of teenage romantic freedom were dashed. She had misunderstood the meaning of the marriage to Smith:

                               ... but pitying angels wept.
They saw my youthful friends grow shy and cold.
And poisonous darts from sland'rous tongues were hurled,
   Untutor'd heart in thy gen'rous sacrafise,
Thou dids't not weigh the cost nor know the bitter price;
   Thy happy dreams all o'er thou'st doom'd alas to be
Bar'd out from social scenes by this thy destiny,
   And o'er thy sad'nd mem'ries of sweet departed joys
Thy sicken'd heart will brood and imagine future woes,
   And like a fetter'd bird with wild and longing heart,
Thou'lt dayly pine for freedom and murmor at thy lot;

So apparently Helen had expected her marriage to Joseph Smith to be for eternity only, then discovered that it included time also. These lines present a bleak picture of Helen's mental state in the months after the wedding. A "sicken'd heart" broods; she is a "fetter'd bird with wild and longing heart" who pines for freedom every day. She must have been attracted to boys her own age, as would be normal. She certainly was already paying attention to Horace Whitney. The marriage to Smith coming so suddenly and blocking these growing feelings must have been devastating to her. These lines are the first evidence of depression in Helen Mar's life.

Despite her alienation from some of her acquaintances, her friend-ship with Sarah Ann deepened, and in the aftermath of Helen's wedding the two girls became "like the two halves of one soul," she wrote.

The poem now shifts to eschatology—Helen would receive eternal glory:

> But could'st thou see the future & view that glorious crown,
>     Awaiting you in Heaven you would not weep nor mourn.
> Pure and exalted was thy father's aim, he saw
>     A glory in obeying this high celestial law,
> For to thousands who've died without the light
>     I will bring eternal joy & make thy crown more bright.
> I'd been taught to reveire the Prophet of God
>     And receive every word as the word of the Lord,

The poem ends with a tribute to her father: "But had this not come through my dear father's mouth,/ I should ne'r have received [it] as God's sacred truth."

An anti-Mormon source, Catherine Lewis, who by her own account lived for a time in the Kimball household, has Helen saying to Vilate, "I will never be sealed to my Father (meaning as a wife) and I would never have been sealed (married) to Joseph had I known it was any-thing more than ceremony. I was young, and they deceived me, by say-ing the salvation of our whole family depended on it ... Neither will I be sealed to Brigham Young." Though the extremism of this language is suspect, close parallels from Helen Mar's writings make the passage worth considering. It reflects that Helen had married Smith when she was very young, that she was told that the salvation of her whole fam-ily depended on the marriage, and that she initially had a different per-ception of the meaning of the marriage than the reality turned out to be, which her writings support. Furthermore, Helen's writings verify that she had rebellious moments.

However, the allegation that Helen might have been pressured to marry her own father—if this is what is implied—is not credible. And other passages in Lewis's pamphlet seem unreliable, as when she sug-gests that there was a man with a mallet standing at the door of the Nauvoo temple to kill anyone trying to "escape"! Therefore, interesting as this statement is, it must be regarded with caution, as secondary to Helen's own writings.

### VII. "Like a Wild Bird I Longed for ... Freedom"

Heber left Nauvoo on a mission to the eastern states in early June 1843. A month later a letter he wrote to Helen shows that he was worried about her mental state as she entered into the role of polygamous wife. He counseled her to accept the marriage obediently and keep it secret:

> My Dear Helen.— ... You have been on my mind much since I left home ... learn to be meek and gentle ... and always speak kindly to your dear mother and listen to her counsel ... My child, remember the care that your dear father and mother have for your welfare in this life, that all may be done well, and that in view of eternal worlds, for that will depend upon what we do here, and how we do it; for all things are sacred ... Let us seek to be true to our integrity wherever we shall make vows or covenants with each other ... Now let us be careful that we do not make a breach.

Possibly Helen was having moments of open rebellion. Certainly she was seriously depressed. In any event Heber returned home in late October.

In the winter there were weekly parties at Joseph Smith's Mansion House, and once William Kimball attended while Helen was denied permission to go. The reason, she wrote, was that "my father had been warned by the Prophet to keep his daughter away from there, because of the blacklegs and certain ones of questionable character who attended there." Helen was upset and dejected at being kept home, and even felt rebellious and resentful toward her revered father:

> I felt quite sore over it, and thought it a very unkind act in father to allow him [William] to go and enjoy the dance unrestrained with others of my companions, and fetter me down, for no girl loved dancing better than I did, and I really felt that it was too much to bear. It made the dull school more dull, and like a wild bird I longed for the freedom that was denied me; and thought myself an abused child, and that it was pardonable if I did murmur.

She was apparently coming to realize that her secret marriage to Joseph entailed time as well as eternity. A severe depression ensued—she felt that her life's happiness had ended completely—and she "brooded over the sad memories of sweet departed joys and all manner of future woes." Nevertheless, she continued to have some social life, and her spirits made a rebound. She became a member of a choir led by Stephen Goddard, and on January 1, 1844, the choir serenaded Joseph Smith as

he moved into the Mansion House. She also acted in dramas at the Nauvoo Masonic Hall.

In May Heber departed for Washington on a mission to campaign for
Joseph Smith's presidency. In a letter to Vilate he wrote, "Remember me
to Helen and Sarah Ann Whitney, and tell them to be good girls and cultivate union, and listen to counsel from the proper source—then they will
get the victory." Obedience to counsel is the constant theme. Obedience
and secrecy are the leitmotifs of another letter Heber wrote to Helen on
June 9. One can sense the pressures on Helen as a secret, young polygamist wife, added to the pressures of being an apostle's daughter:

> MY DEAR DAUGHTER— ... be obedient to the counsel you have given to
> you from your dear father and mother, who seek your welfare both for
> time and eternity. There is no one that feels as we do for you ... If you
> should be tempted, or having feelings in your heart, tell them to no one
> but your father and mother; if you do, you will be betrayed and exposed
> to your hurt ...You are blessed, but you know it not. You have done that
> which will be for your everlasting good for this world and that which is
> to come. I will admit there is not much pleasure in this world ... Be wise
> ... Be true to the covenants that you have made ... Be a good girl; May the
> Lord bless you and your dear mother and brethren. As ever your affection-
> ate father.

Heber mentions that her marriage will cause her "good for this world" as
well as in eternity. Once again this is not consistent with the theory that
Helen's marriage to Smith was for eternity only. Then, offering bleak comfort to his daughter, he added, "I will admit there is not much pleasure in
this world."

However, Helen's circumstances would soon change. On June 27
Joseph Smith was martyred and Helen became a widow at age fifteen. Heber hurried to Nauvoo, arriving on August 6. Smith's death changed the
Kimball family status in another significant way. Brigham Young, as senior
member of the Quorum of Twelve Apostles, would emerge as the leader
of most Latter-day Saints, and Heber, as his longtime friend, would become his closest counselor. In addition, beginning on September 10, Heber, with Brigham, began marrying a number of plural wives. By February
1846 Kimball had married some thirty-five women.

## VIII. Horace

Single once more, Helen could rejoin her normal peer group and social life. In the summer of 1844 she remembered walking with two girl
friends and a Mr. Hatch, strolling on Temple Hill, watching the sunset.
She attended weddings and informal piano parties. By summer of the following year, at age sixteen, she had begun to formally spend time with

Horace Whitney, twenty-two, for she attended a printers' festival with him on "the prairie" at the farm of John Benbow. Well-educated and bookish, a lover of drama, a flautist, Horace made a good match for the cultured, sensitive Helen. However, he would never sit in the leading councils of the church because of his "retiring nature" which caused him to "shrink from taking a prominent part in public affairs."

Helen continued to participate in elite religious activities. On January 26, 1845, she was initiated into the Holy Order, receiving her endowment. In December the temple was nearing completion, and on the 2nd Heber took Helen and the rest of the family on a tour of the upper story, the "Attick," of the building. Three days later the inseparable Helen and Sarah Ann helped sew the temple veil. Helen received her temple endowment on January 1, 1846, in a session with Horace, Sarah Ann, and Eliza Partridge.

In mid-January Helen and Horace went to another printers' festival together, this one at the house of a Brother Taylor. By this time a rumor had arisen that Helen and Horace were secretly married:

> When entering Brother Taylor's door in company with my parents I was greeted with the following salutation, "I wish you much joy," etc., [a marriage congratulation] and it was repeated by every one that met us, some person having started the report that H. K. Whitney and myself were married, which was all news to us, we being perfectly ignorant of any such transaction, but as we found it impossible to convince them to the contrary, Horace, who thought it a good joke, and did not mind carrying it out, commenced there and then to call me "wife," and for years after he invariably addressed me by this title.

### IX. "Dismal Enough to Give Even a Saint the Blues"

The courtship between Helen and Horace deepened and, as has been seen, they were married for time on February 3, 1846. At this time the Saints were preparing to leave Nauvoo. The day after the marriage Heber gave Helen a large box and said, "Now Helen, go to and pack up your things." She took with her a limited wardrobe, including "a very long riding habit of dark green merino," which, with "a warm hood, muff and boa," made up her travelling suit.

After crossing the Mississippi, she set out for Sugar Creek on February 16. Jane Taylor wrote that she and her brother William were travelling that night in their wagon, with Helen Mar riding a pony beside them. However, Helen became so cold that she had to stop. Jane and William gave her some wine and built a fire. When they reached Sugar Creek in the early evening, Heber had set up a large tent in which a sheet iron stove was burning, and Helen was able to sleep in relative comfort that night.

Horace returned to Nauvoo to help his family prepare to move, and on February 19 Helen wrote, "It began storming, and it was dismal enough to give even a saint the blues." The next day she and Sarah Lawrence Kimball returned to Nauvoo. After being delayed by broken ice in the Mississippi, the river froze over again on the 27th, and Helen and Horace mounted ponies and returned to Sugar Creek in a party of Whitneys. Thus their honeymoon began. However, Helen wrote, "This was rather too long and tedious a journey to be called a wedding tour—thousands of miles over scorched and dreary deserts, rocky mountains and poisonous lakes of alkali, etc." Helen remembered dances in the evening at Sugar Creek, in which a band, a violinist, and Horace's flute played, and "we could form a cotillion or French four by the big log fire, and often we did so." They danced for warmth as well as for diversion.

Soon they left Sugar Creek. On this first leg of a long journey, they would customarily travel about six miles per day, with Helen often riding in the large Kimball family carriage. Once, as they crossed a ravine, teams had to be doubled, and as Helen sat in the carriage holding the reins, "the wind was so cold and piercing that it seemed to me as if I should perish." At camp they cleared away snow from the ground and pitched tents but had no stove in the tent now, so Helen slept in all her clothes.

When the worst of the winter cold began to moderate, snow turned to cold rain. At some point Helen and Horace left the Kimball company and travelled with the Whitneys. So the misery of the constant rain and cold was compounded by Helen's first separation from her mother. One morning a quarter mile of nearly impassable mud lay between her and Vilate, but she nevertheless "undertook the disagreeable and perilous journey on the back of a little white Ginnie ... Ginnie stood about three feet from the ground, and the mud being so deep, I felt some dubiety about our accomplishing the journey." Helen reached her mother's wagon "generously bespattered" with mud.

Helen and Horace had been riding in others' vehicles, but on April 7 Horace obtained a wagon and yoke of oxen for himself. As he had never driven oxen in his life, he was given a quick, rough education in this art. He wrote in his diary, "Started this morning about eight o'clock—took my first lesson in the science of Oxology." Helen described his translation from Eastern urban intellectual to Western teamster: "On taking the ox whip to drive, the first thing he did was to go on the wrong side, and then had to endure the roars of laughter from several of the boys who were standing ready to witness his first effort." But Horace soon became an expert teamster.

Helen gave a vivid description of a young married pioneer household:

We had doors, generally, cut on the left side of the wagon covers. Boxes and bags of grain, etc., were packed in the rear part of our wagon, upon which our bed was made. We had our provision chest in front, which served as a table, and between was just room for my chair—this being my only piece of furniture—the most of our household chattels having been left in our house in Nauvoo. I could now knit and read as we traveled, and Horace could read or play his flute as he liked, and none, I think but those who had a like experience can form the slightest idea of the appreciation and happiness it gave us, to have a little wagon all to ourselves, which, under the circumstances, was next thing to paradise.

One day it rained all day, and that night the patter of rain on the wagon cover "served as a kind of lullaby to soothe us to sleep. And in the morning my cousin Netty, the head cook, brought us some warm eatables, requesting me to stay in the wagon" because of the mud. "To which arrangment we very cheerfully submitted."

Helen and Horace tented by themselves at first, but on April 25, at Mt. Pleasant Creek, at the request of Heber, they began sharing their tent with five other pioneers to equalize population in other tents. Their private, intimate honeymoon had ended. By May 10 the rains had ceased, and the company stopped for the Sabbath at a campground near "a crystal stream of water babbling over the rocks down through a little grove of trees and willows." There Helen accompanied Horace "to fish, taking along our books to read. This was his favorite pastime ... the whole landscape around us was lovely, they called it rolling prairie, and it had such a variety of hills and dales, all dressed anew in their bright velvety robes of spring." Horace caught a dozen fish.

The changed weather brought new discomforts. Helen wrote that the most trying part of the journey was walking in the scorching sun, and her strength and patience often failed in this heat: "There were times when we girls would drop down by the roadside and vow that we would not rise again till we saw the tents pitched, then we would take a straight line to the camp. I had not yet obtained sufficient religion to assist me and as my strength failed me so did my faith, but when the teams were ahead our only alternative was to get up and travel on." When they reached Garden Grove, halfway across Iowa, Helen feasted thankfully on her mother's white bread and fresh churned butter.

### X. "I Have Passed Through Verious Trying Scienes"

Helen and Horace reached Winter Quarters about June 13. On November 30 they moved from wagon to primitive house, possibly their room on Heber Kimball's row of log houses, adjacent to Vilate's. Covered with sod, with even a sod chimney, it had one door, one window with four panes of glass, and no floor. Unfortunately Helen's chimney did not draw air adequately, so she often endured smoky quarters. Horace occasionally noted in his journal that his wife was sick.

In the winter she started a difficult pregnancy that had her confined to bed from January 23, 1847, until March. The sickness, combined with the smoke (the cold required constant use of the chimney to warm the room), made the experience extremely unpleasant. Helen wrote, "It gave me the opportunity of cultivating the qualities of patience and calmness under new vicissitudes, from which there was no alternative, only to endure them with as good grace as possible." However, she wept many times during "the smoking period." Finally it was discovered that her fireplace was about to collapse, so a new one was built that did not smoke.

Vilate was also pregnant, and on February 2 Solomon Farnham, Helen's next-to-last full sibling, was born in Winter Quarters. Not long after this birth, on a day with good weather, Helen wrote, "I was conveyed in an easy chair and placed by her [Vilate's] side, where I passed two pleasant days, being carried back at eventide. She was in excellent spirits, and before my arrival ... had composed several verses on the birth of this, her seventh son." On February 24 Horace wrote in his journal: "Snowed considerably to-day, as well as yesterday. My wife's health improving slowly–she has lately been afflicted with canker she has now been sick 5 weeks last Sunday." He also suffered from mouth canker. Lack of fresh vegetables and fruit caused scurvy, which took its toll on the community.

As Helen's first childbirth approached, Horace set out on April 9 with the "Pioneers" on the first expedition to the Salt Lake Valley. Aunt Fanny wrote, in a letter, "Mr Whitney went with the pioneers, and left Helen with her Mother–he was distrest to go and leave her, just as her hour of trial was coming on; but duty call'd and he must go." Only a few aged and disabled men were left behind, but Helen's father-in-law, Newel Whitney, was one of them.

Helen's life, which had been on a steady course after her marriage to Horace, now plummeted into catastrophe. "When her time of trouble came, she was very sick, but very patient," wrote Fanny. On May 6 Patty Sessions wrote in her journal, "Put Helen Kimbal to bed the child still born." The child, named Helen Rosabell, was quickly buried. Helen, now nineteen, was devastated. She wrote that the child, "the only bright star, to which my doting heart had clung, was snatched away, and it seemed a needless bereavement, and most cruel." In a June 13 letter to Horace, she wrote, "I have passed through verious trying scienes since you left, I have been caled to part with my little babe, which has been harder to bear than all my bodyley suffering, (although that has been very great)." Fanny wrote that Helen's grief caused her to commune with God: "Helen's affliction was indeed a savor of life unto her: she sunk into the will of God with all her heart, and her soul was so fill'd with the joys of heaven, that she enjoys, rather than suffers, her bereavement."

She remained extremely sick for three weeks, then dressed and attempted a re-entry into the world, but caught a chill and returned to bed, seriously ill, for another three weeks. She lay covered with a cold sweat, "until everything on me was as wet as though it had been drenched in cold water, and death seemed determined to claim me, but I was saved for a purpose." Then the scurvy set in, "black streaks" on the fingers of her left hand, with inflammation and intense pain reaching to her shoulder. Poultices of scraped potato were applied, with no great success. All these afflictions were interpreted by Helen as religious phenomena. She wrote, "By this time I had lost all faith, and patience, too." Feeling desperate, she arose from her sickbed and threw the potato poultice into the fireplace. To her surprise the scurvy then healed. Despite this turn of events, she remained weak and bed-ridden much of the time.

When she could, she participated in the blessing meetings shared by the wives of Brigham and Heber. Before the meeting in which Sarah Ann's and Vilate's babies were believed to be possessed, Helen was promised that she would be healed of her lingering illness. After the day-long meeting, for which Helen may have also fasted, she was still ill. This left her feeling depressed and doubting: "I was quite young, and not having been healed as I had been told I should be, my faith was considerably shaken." However, as the day ended, father Whitney prophesied great happiness in store for those present. As so often, visions of the next life lifted Helen's weary spirits.

The next morning Persis Young Richards, Levi Richards's wife, visited Helen because she had been "impressed by the Spirit" to administer to her. So Persis and Vilate Kimball laid their hands on Helen's head and blessed her. Helen remembers that Persis was so filled with the Spirit that "she shook as though palsied when she laid her hands upon my head ... She rebuked my weakness, and every disease that had been, or was then afflicting me, and commanded me to be made whole, pronouncing health and many other blessings upon me, nearly all of which have been literally fulfilled." As Helen told the story, she was healed immediately. "From that morning I went about to work as though nothing had been the matter. Thus did the Lord remember one of His unworthy handmaidens." On June 4 Helen received another sisterly blessing. Patty Sessions journalized, "I caled to Sister Kimbals and with E R Snow blesed Helen and Genette then in the gift of toungues E R Snow sung a blesing to all the rest of the girls."

## XI. "H. C. Kimble Daughter Not Expected to Live"

In October Horace and the pioneers returned, and in the winter he and Helen prepared to cross the plains the next summer to the new Zion. They departed on May 24, 1848. Helen was expecting again and would have another difficult pregnancy. Just before they left, as she helped draw the canvas cover over her wagon, she nearly fainted. Often while traveling, she would have to lie down.

After the ordeal of pioneer pregnancy, once again childbirth brought catastrophe. On August 17 she bore a baby boy, William Howard, on the Sweetwater River one mile west of Sage Creek in western Wyoming. But after the birth she remained very sick—Priddy Meeks diagnosed prolapsus uteri, fallen uterus. Then little William died on the 22nd, Helen's twentieth birthday, a cruel coincidence. Compounded with this blow was Helen's own continuing illness. Two days later the whole camp stopped because of her condition, a rarity in Mormon pioneering. On the 26th Oliver Huntington wrote that Heber's "daughter Hellen is so ill she can not be removed farther at present." John D. Lee's August 30 entry again shows the seriousness of her illness: "Pres. B. Y. returned, reported ... Elen Whitney, H. C. Kimble daughter not expected to live." But she somehow clung to life, and the Kimball company continued on their journey. They reached the Salt Lake Valley on September 24.

## XII. Dead and Resurrected

Helen remained extremely sick as her first winter in Utah approached, and the pain and misery became so great that she prayed to leave life and join her two children. In moments of discouragement throughout the rest of her life, she would long for death and the departed. So now she descended into a physical and pyschological abyss. Her family, thinking she was dying, gathered around her bedside:

> I had talked with my husband and father who were weeping as I took a parting kiss from all but my poor mother, who was the last one called and had sunk upon her knees before me. This distressed me, but I bade her not mourn for she would not be long behind me. My words struck father like a sudden thunderbolt, and he spoke with a mighty voice and said— "Vilate, Helen *is not dying!*" but my breath which by this time had nearly gone, stopped that very instant, and I felt his faith and knew that he was holding me; and I begged him to let me go as I thought it very cruel to keep me ... The destroyer was then stirred up in anger at being cheated out of his victim and he seemed determined to wreak his vengeance upon us all. No one but God and his angels ... could know the tenth part of what I suffered. I never told anybody and I never could.

The reference to the "destroyer" reminds us that in the Kimball family sickness was often interpreted as demonic attack. Helen came to see her illness in these terms and felt that her own sinfulness had given evil spirits power over her. Her central sin, she felt, was a profoundly rebellious opposition to polygamy that she held in her heart of hearts. Her own marriage to Joseph Smith and Vilate's trials as the first wife in a large plural family had caused her to loathe this key celestial "principle," Joseph Smith's highest revelation. A second sin she saw in herself was an extreme love for her last baby: "I had loved my baby more than my God, and mourned for it unreasonably."

She continued to languish in a trance: "For three months I lay a portion of the time like one dead, they told me ... I was alive to my spiritual condition and dead to the world. I tasted of the punishment which is prepared for those who reject any of the principles of this Gospel." The specific doctrine she referred to was polygamy:

> Then I learned that plural marriage is a celestial principle, and saw the difference between the power of God's priesthood and that of Satan's and the necessity of obedience to those who hold the priesthood, and the danger of rebelling against or speaking lightly of the Lord's anointed ... *I had, in hours of temptation when seeing the trials of my mother, felt to rebel. I hated polygamy in my heart.*

So Helen was racked by guilt: "All my sins and shortcomings were magnified before my eyes till I believed that I had sinned beyond redemption ... During that season I lost my speech, forgot the names of everybody and everything, and was living in another sphere ... I was left a poor wreck of what I had been ... My father said that Satan desired to clip my glory ... but when he was thwarted he tried in every possible way to destroy my tabernacle." Heber was not speaking figuratively of Satan. The Kimballs believed that actual evil spirits were attacking her. "President Young said that the mountains through which we passed were filled with the spirits of the Gadianton robbers spoken of in the Book of Mormon. The Lord gave father faith enough to hold me until I was capable of exercising it for myself. I was so weak that I was often discouraged in trying to pray, as the evil spirits caused me to feel that it was no use."

Consumed with guilt and fear of the malevolent spirits of the Gadianton robbers that surrounded her, Helen continued in despair until the day after Christmas 1848. Then she came to a resolution: "I had my last struggle and resolved that they [the spirits] should buffet me no longer. I fasted for one week, and every day I gained till I had won the victory and I was just as sensible of the presence of holy spirits around my bedside as I had been of the evil ones." She had been converted to polygamy. She felt elated, had "one of the happiest days" of her life, and immediately called her mother to her bedside to try to convert her to polygamy (a sign that Vilate had not become reconciled to Heber's plural marriages). Helen wrote:

> I knew her heart was weighed down in sorrow ... I never before spoke with such eloquence, and she knew that it was not myself. She was so affected that she sobbed till I ceased. I assured her that father loved her, but he had a work to do, she must rise above her feelings and seek for the Holy Comforter, and though it rent her heart she must uphold him, for he in taking other wives had done it only in obedience to a holy principle. Much more I said, and when I ceased she wiped her eyes. I silently prayed to be renewed, when my strength returned that instant.

Acceptance of the demands and ideology of her community allowed Helen to begin immediate convalescence. On New Year's Day 1849 she felt well enough to attend a Kimball family feast. Heber delivered a formal sermon to the group, described Helen's sufferings, and prophesied that she would now accomplish a great work, that she would "live long and raise honorable sons and daughters that would rise up and call me blessed, and should be a comfort to my mother in her declining years." In later years those who had known Helen during this sickness regarded her "as one who had been dead and resurrected."

### XIII. "You Shall Continue to Stand at the Head"

Though the worst moments of sickness had passed, Helen had not entirely recovered, and was soon pregnant again: "It was my misfortune to be an invalid for a number of years after, and oh, those long quiet days, sometimes it seemed to me they would never draw to a close." As she convalesced, she became good friends with her former teacher, Eliza Snow, who was also an invalid. They exchanged letters, both too sick to walk half a block to see each other. When Helen was well enough to leave her house, located near the mouth of City Creek Canyon, she walked through the stark, not yet tree-lined streets of Salt Lake City and missed Nauvoo. Here, she felt, the only thing to admire were the far off "rugged snow capped mountains," and nothing relieved the eyes from "everlasting sage brush and sun flowers."

We now move out of the well-documented period of Helen's early life—her *Woman's Exponent* series barely touches on her Utah experiences. To Helen, as to many Mormons, the important historical events took place in Kirtland, Missouri, Nauvoo, Winter Quarters, and on the plains, whereas daily life in Utah was uninteresting.

On September 1, 1849, Helen bore a third child, Horace Kimball, but once again, tragically, he died the same day. As before, Helen must have been emotionally devastated, but she apparently did not undergo a life-

511

threatening illness afterwards, though she remained weak. She was still only twenty-one years old. On Christmas Day the same year she attended a party at Zina Young's home.

Horace had found employment as a school teacher, but when the *Deseret News* was launched, he was hired to be part of its first staff of compositors. Then in the early 1850s he accepted a clerkship in the office of the "Trustee-in-Trust" (i.e., Brigham Young), also known as the Tithing Office, and worked in this capacity until the end of his life.

In 1849 Heber Kimball advised his son-in-law to build up his eternal kingdom by taking another wife. Although Horace agreed, unlike many Mormon men he apparently married again only after consulting fully with Helen. She later wrote, "He studied my feelings and took one whom he had cause to believe loved me and my children, and would cause me the least trouble." On October 9, 1850, Helen became, like her mother, a first wife, as Horace married Lucy Amelia Bloxham. One can imagine Helen's mixed feelings, despite her sickbed conversion to polygamy—none of her children had lived, and now Horace was marrying another woman. When he was courting Lucy in April 1849, a letter he wrote to Helen shows that she found the experience agonizing. He wrote to "administer balm and comfort to your wounded heart" and assured her that her image was "sacredly enshrined within the inmost recesses of my heart, to the exclusion of all others":

> As I said before, the love that I bear towards you is founded upon a deep respect & knowledge of your worth, & has something more substantial for its basis than the mere fleeting evanescent and romantic passion which I have for Lucy, and consequently will endure when the latter shall have passed into oblivion. When oppressed with sorrow, or weighed down by affliction, <u>you will always be the one and the only one to whom I shall resort to pour out my griefs, and from whom I shall expect that consolation which man sometimes stands in need of, and which can only be administered with effect by a dutifuly and affectionate companion, which you have always proved yourself to be</u>. As long as you are mine, Helen, you shall continue to stand at the head; (and this I have taken pains to impress upon Lucy's mind,) and if I thought there was no other way of securing the continuance of your affection, <u>I would {quietly}, nay even cheerfully, give her up</u>.

While this might have reassured Helen, one wonders how Lucy felt at being relegated to such a secondary position. On the other hand, Helen might have been painfully aware that she was Horace's only "for time." In any event, the marriage to Lucy turned out unfortunately. Lucy bore her first child, Newel, on September 7, 1851, then died three days later. One imagines Helen caring for little Newel, but he also passed away (in Helen's arms?) two weeks later, on the 22nd.

### XIV. "Ma Take [Me] in Your Arms"

On June 2, 1853, a joyful event took place in the Whitney family: Helen had a child who lived, a daughter whom she named Vilate Murray. One can only imagine her relief and joy. Two years later, on July 1, 1855, when she was twenty-seven, she bore a son, Orson Ferguson, in a primitive house on "Whitney Corner ... in a lane running off North Temple Street, about midway between Main and State." Orson would be a gifted, precocious child. He later wrote of Helen that he inherited from her "a poetic-religious temperament; and from her as well as from Father, musical gifts. They were both good singers."

The "principle" re-entered Helen's life on December 1, 1856, when Horace married another wife, Mary Cravath, and she moved into the Whitney home. But when Mary had borne three children, Horace built her a separate home on the same lot, then apparently divided his time between families by alternating weeks spent at each house. Thus Helen finally experienced public, practical, long-term polygamy. However, her experience in the principle was not traumatic, to the best of our knowledge, perhaps because of Horace's limited polygamous family, the proximity of the two wives' houses, and his sincere attempt to divide his time fairly between the families. Helen's unselfishness and total conversion to polygamy also contributed to the success of this new marriage. She later wrote, in a remarkable statement on the ethics of polygamy:

> None can say with truth that I ever shirked from my duty that I ever refused to help my husband to do right, that I ever stood in the way of his taking another wife, that he ever felt cast down & come to me for comfort that I did not try to show him the bright side & encourage him to do right. Never did I see Mary [Cravath] feeling sad when she had just cause without feeling my heart drawn out in sympathy if I thought that he appeared the least cool & caused her any unhappines I have never failed to reprove him telling him that I could not feel happy & know that she was not. We always lived peacibly together If there was any little misunderstanding (which generally was caused by our children) we would talk it over & all would be as pleasent as before. Whichever of our children or ourselves stood the most in need of a dress or any thing else it was understood that they had the first claim & no one ever thought of being jealous in consequence. We were like one family.

In *Why We Practice Plural Marriage* Helen wrote further, "Our children have always lived more peacably than many who have one mother. I am called 'Aunt' by them and their mother is called the same by my children." Orson supported this: "His children loved one another almost as much as if the same mother had borne them." These testimonies are public and undoubtedly idealizing, and in Helen's later diaries and letters there are examples of occasional tension between the families, but there is no evidence of heated, painful conflicts as in Patty Sessions's diaries, for instance. Horace's work in the Tithing Office allowed him to provide adequately but not handsomely for his families. Helen asserted that her family had sufficient provision for the necessities of life, but in times of sickness she was hard pressed to buy such extras as medicine or hired nursing: "Our family was large & we were obliged to content ourselves with what he could get."

More children soon arrived in the Whitney home: Elizabeth Ann—named after her grandmother—on November 27, 1857; Genevieve on March 13, 1860; Helen Kimball Whitney on March 24, 1862; and Charles Spaulding on November 21, 1864. During this largely undocumented period, we only know that Helen was very sick in the months following Helen's birth, and that Mary Houston, a plural wife of Heber, helped nurse her back to health. Helen then stayed with her mother in Parley's Park to recuperate.

Another child, Florence Marian, was born on April 4, 1867, when Helen Mar was thirty-eight. In the months following, Vilate Kimball began to weaken, and Helen undoubtedly tended her as she gradually lost her faculties and faded away. The revered family matriarch died on October 22 at age sixty-one. Less than a year later, on June 22, 1868, Heber C. followed his first wife to the grave. Helen, deeply attached to her parents, must have felt this double loss to be a bitter trial.

Helen's last child, Phebe Isabel, was born on September 24, 1869, when Helen was forty-three. Vilate was now sixteen, Orson fourteen, Elizabeth twelve, Genevieve nine, Helen seven, Charles five, and Florence two. After the loss of her first three children, she had come to have a sizeable family. However, by late 1869 Vilate became seriously ill with tuberculosis ("consumption"). Horace had been in the eastern states on a church mission since Phebe's birth, so Helen's letters to him document this period of her life. In early January 1870 Vilate could still go out, but on the 14th, Helen reported, she had a "very sick spell" after attending a party: "Poor girl ... she can't have the privilege of going out, like other young folks, & enjoying hurself without making hur sick." By the 31st her condition had worsened, and Helen reported that a number of people blessed her—Eliza R. Snow, George Q. Cannon with Franklin Richards, and their ward bishop. Helen had to tend Vilate and the new baby at the same time, so she spent a number of sleepless nights, which impacted her own poor health. "I just got V__ in the big Chair to rest hur, she has had to be in a setting posture most of the time," she wrote. Vilate's limbs began to swell, and she had great difficulty breathing.

Helen began a letter to Horace on February 4, then broke off. The next day Mary Ellen Kimball, one of Heber's widows and a close family friend, finished the letter. On the night of the fourth, wrote Mary, Vilate "called for the Doctor. he came, and together with br Young bishop spent the night with us. or nearly so. She only complained of feeling cold. She says Ma take [me] in your arms and hold me to the fire. Helen took her. She threw her arms around her neck awhile; then held her hands to the fire: but could not find a comfortable position until again placed in bed where she fell a sleep." So Helen and her eldest daughter embraced as she neared death.

Mary Ellen then broke the news to Horace: "How shall I tell you the sad news, – perhaps you will suspect it. I hope your mind is as prepared as ours has been for days to know that our beloved Vilate is now at rest; her spirit is free from the pangs and sorrows of this life her pure Sp[i]rit took its flight this morning at 15 minutes to 8 o clock ... It is a great satis-faction even now to look upon the Marble form on which remains a pleasent peaceful smile is left for us to look upon." Vilate died at the age of seventeen on February 5.

Once more Helen endured the loss of a child, and this time without her husband near to console her. "Helen bears up under the Trial with the greatest composure," wrote Mary Ellen. "She gives the Lord the gratitude of her heart for sustaining her under it all." Helen wrote to Horace on Feb-ruary 15: "I feel lonely at times, & then I think how happy she is, & I will not alow myself to wish hur here again to suffer. She looked lovely in death." Evidently Horace returned home in March.

## XV. "We Could See Her Little Trinkets"

In the last decades of her life, Helen wrote reminiscences and exten-sive diaries, through which we can come to know her as thoroughly, per-haps, as any nineteenth-century Mormon woman. As has been seen, when she was sick in her early Salt Lake days, she often yearned to join her departed children on the other side of the veil. Despite her large fam-ily, this feeling never entirely left her. In an 1876 reminiscence, she wrote, "Soon after My Vilates death when I was feeling very sorrowful, I dreamed that, I was walking along & I saw & heard father preaching & prophesying about the carlessness lukewarm condition of his family and others." Helen wanted to go with him to the other side, but instead woke up. "This dream at that time was a great comfort to me. I felt sure that I should soon be free from sickness & sorrow enjoying their dear society and [that] of the righteous that had passed behind the Vail. I could not be convinced by any thing that any one could say to me that I should live very long." In 1870 Helen suffered a difficult bout of "lung fever" "with pleurisy on both sides" and nearly died, but finally weathered the illness and continued to live.

On July 23, 1874, Phebe, the last-born, and no doubt the darling of the family, died of scarlet fever when she had almost reached the age of five. Helen wrote:

> My youngest child  my little Phebe was snatched from out our little cir-
> cle which had grown <u>small enough we thought</u> after my oldest <u>my own</u>
> <u>dear Vilate</u> was taken; but God knew best and I felt to kiss the rod. but
> little Phebe's death was so sudden, only sick twenty nine hours, Go
> where we would we could see her little trinkets, her play house & every
> thing as she had fixed them two days before when she seemed well and
> the evening before she was attacked with scarlet, feevor she was play-
> ing and frollicking on the floar with Flodie.

At the time of Phebe's death, Orson (Ort) was nineteen, Elizabeth (Lillie) seventeen, Genevieve (Genny) fourteen, Helen (Hent) twelve, Charles (Charley) ten, and Florence (Flody) seven.

### XVI. "Lonely Pilgrim in the Valley of Dispair"

That winter Genny contracted a case of "Inflamatory Rheu[ma-tism]." Helen tended her constantly: "I was obliged to get out of Bed at all times of the night & remain out till I would be shaking with the cold, it being the winter of 1875 the coldest that was ever known here." She often had to lift her, and her own health finally gave way under the strain: "I felt myself failing but Geny was getting better & I thought I should soon recuperate." In addition, Helen took in Laura, a sickly child of her sister-wife. Laura improved, but Helen came down with a serious cold that "settled" on her lungs: "My nervous system, which had been so long taxed, gave way & I was truly in sad condition I felt that every noise or the least thing that was not done as it should be worried me till I grew worse every day."

Helen's doctor demanded that she have a complete rest. However, Lillie and Genny were inexperienced at the domestic arts, and the latter was still recovering from rheumatism. Listening to their attempts at housework upset their bed-ridden mother: "They done pretty well, con-sidering, only on Washdays or Saturdays, <u>then</u> was the time when my grace was hardly sufficient. I'd hear their troubles often one or the other, sometimes Lilla & Genny both would cry because they were so tired & discouraged,  I had to sit or lay & pray to the Lord for them & for myself that He would give me patience & grace to endure these trials. My feelings cannot be described  I had (like the children) to give vent to them in teers."

Then Helen's characteristic yearning resurfaced: "I became melan-cholly. & felt in my heart that I should <u>soon</u> follow my parrents & children who were happy beyond this <u>Vail of tears</u>." One wonders how many nine-teenth-century Utah women suffered from depression, or "melancholly." Helen had many of the classic signs: the loathing for life, the parallel yearning for death, the tears, the inability to sleep. While many aspects of severe depression are not definitively understood, it has been accepted that a number of factors contribute. An experience of traumatic loss can be a key factor, combined with emotional vulnerability (in Helen's case, perhaps the loss of her children, compounded by feelings of guilt over her hatred of polygamy). A genetic disposition toward depression is an-other important contributing factor.

After writing the above entry, Helen developed a hacking cough that sounded consumptive, and was afraid to pray to recover, but nevertheless slowly convalesced. In the midst of deep melancholy, her faith sustained her: "The comforter drew near to me, & I felt at times verry happy Often I'd lay awake in the night thinking of the goodness of God, and thanking Him that I was counted worthy to be among His people to walk the Thorny path with the Saints of God. I felt all the time to <u>acknowledge His hand</u> in my trials, although my cup of sorrow, at times, would run over."

Helen would read when possible, but her eyes grew weak. Then she felt isolated and oppressed by tedium: "The days dragged slowly, but few persons ever came in & I had very little to make me desire or even sattis-fied to be clogged with this poor mortal coil. I longed to be liberated that I might go where all was bright, where I could be able to work & be asso-ciated with the ones whom I would feel happy with." One day Orson, now nineteen, brought a "Book of fun" to read to her, but she was in no mood for fun. It "grated upon my ears, making me miserable. I so wished that he would read some religious book but I knew that he read it to please me & therefore bore it as well as I could."

Part of Helen's melancholy was caused by a feeling of uselessness, since she was no longer able to work consistently. "I felt that I was no longer useful here, only trouble to others & I had to struggle & pray con-tinually for grace to bear my trials patiently & to be able to put away these temptations & not murmur. I desired to be able to work & to pay my way & do something for the comfort of those around me, being very sensitive upon this point." Horace "was kind & done all that lay in his power in a temporal point of view," but he had his daily work to tend to, as well as the household of his other wife.

In the spring of 1875 Helen's doctor advised her to leave the city for a change of scene, but she felt she could not afford to. However, as the weather grew warmer her health improved also. She sent for Eliza Snow, who came and administered to her, and then she felt better. In the summer she managed well, except when she overexerted herself, which frequently happened, she reported. In the fall she "put up" fruit, worked too hard, and as a result became seriously ill for two weeks. At about the same time sister-wife Mary, with her many small children, moved into Helen's house, as Mary's was being improved. Helen found the noise intolerable: "My nerves were in such a state that I felt as though if I did not hold to my chair or watch myself that I should jump out of it and screem." She felt her health failing and feared another dreary winter like the last, "shut up a prisoner in my Parlor."

Desperate for a change in location, Helen heard of a house for sale on a nearby hill and approached Horace to see if she could move into it: "At first he was very indignant, & thought me inconsistant unreasonable etc. etc. till I talked & reasoned with him & explained my situation, & the fears (which had haunted me) and if I did not seek myself to break this spell which was sinking me into dispair, that he might have some greater trial than to have his family devided. He could not deny the consistantcy of my arguments and consented." Helen and her family moved into this new house, and she felt more cheerful immediately. Although her health was still poor, and she often felt "lonely," the total despair of the previous winters did not return. She was no longer living with small children, and her own children's noise was tolerable.

Near Christmas Helen came down with a bad cold and was once again assailed by the old emotional desolation. Racked by a cough, too weak to climb stairs, she had difficulty even sitting up. Her "whole nervous system was prostrated." The yearning for death returned: "I then felt discouraged, and thought that I might better be dead than to live to be of no use to anybody." She had even been abandoned by her "old associates," she felt, her Nauvoo friends, though this was "whispered" to her by a "dark spirit." She wrote in her reminiscence, "[T]ruly I felt to compare myself to a lonely Pilgrim in the valley of dispair (figuratively speaking) & wrote the following Lamentation ... Lonely I lay day after day. / With naught to break the monotony / So near I am & yet how far / From the thoughts of all no one to care; / How sick or lonely I may be / In this cold world of misery."

But then neighbors began to visit and laughed at her feelings of abandonment. Helen wrote to Eliza Snow "to inform her that I was still in the land of the living, & wished my Sisters to know the same etc. & I requested their prayers as I was sick & also informed her that I'd like to be administered to when it would be convenient etc." In early January 1876 Eliza, with Sister Smoot, washed and anointed Helen, and she immediately felt much improved. Then the three women began reminiscing about their experiences in the early church when Joseph was alive. "Sister Smoot told me she thought I would be a great benefit to the Young Sisters to hear my history & she considered it my duty to tell them. She had told me the same when I was at her house in Provo, and that night I made up my mind to commence my byography." So during her long sicknesses Helen began writing her extended autobiographical series that appeared in the *Woman's Exponent*. As she thought back on her early family life in Kirtland and Nauvoo, at times she was inspired, at times she was amused, and at times she wept.

Meanwhile her whole family had come down with a "distemper a terrible disease which nearly every body had" (possibly a flu), and only "Charly & Florence" (eleven and eight) were there to wait upon their sick family: "This was their first experience in housework, – together they made a good cup of coffee ... they were able to bring us a good breakfast and all together we felt that we had reason to be thankful & they felt quite proud that they had done the work, but became tired of it they were very willing nay anxious to give up the honors to someone else before we were able to secure help." The 1876 reminiscence ends here.

The precocious Orson had grown into a talented teenager, a gifted writer, and a dedicated thespian. But in early 1876 his ambitions took a turn that alarmed Helen and Horace—he made up his mind to go to New York and succeed as an actor there. Helen tried to dissuade him, but he was determined, and finally she told him that she would sell a lot to provide $200 for his move to New York. But the attempted sale fell through repeatedly, to Orson's disappointment, and then in October conference he found that he had been called on a mission to the eastern states. He accepted the call and noted wryly in his autobiography that Helen was immediately able to sell her land to support his mission.

He left for Pennsylvania and Ohio on November 6. Helen, the Mormon mother, would have been proud to see her son safely launched on a crucial rite of passage for young LDS men rather than to have him living among the decadent gentiles of the New York stage. He returned in 1878 and almost immediately (on July 14) was set apart as a very youthful bishop of Helen's own Eighteenth Ward. On August 10 he became the city editor of the *Deseret News* and would continue to distinguish himself as a writer, historian, and church leader throughout the rest of his life.

### XVII. "Parent of Nameless Ills, Monogamy"

On December 18, 1879, Orson married Zina B. Smoot, a daughter of Abraham Owen Smoot, stake president of Provo. Helen Mar, now fifty-one, would soon be a grandmother. In 1883 another child left the house as the younger Helen married George Bourne on October 30. Both these marriages were orthodox Mormon weddings celebrated in the Endowment House, which gave Helen Mar great satisfaction. "Helen looks quite matronly as Mrs. Bourne. Their wedding was the greatest success," she wrote to Charley, who at the time was living with Kimball relatives in Arizona.

The first installment of Helen's reminiscences appeared in the *Woman's Exponent* in May 1880. This series, one of the most important Mormon historical documents, despite its disorganization and tendency to long quotation from her father's diaries, continued to appear until July 1886. On March 10, 1882, Helen was chosen by Sister M. I. Horne as second counselor in the Relief Society of the Eighteenth Ward. Also in 1882 she published her *Plural Marriage as Taught by the Prophet Joseph*, a 52-page salvo against Joseph Smith III, who was preaching that his father had never practiced polygamy. Thus Helen, who as a young girl had "hated polygamy in her heart," now wrote an impassioned defense of it as an experienced plural wife. Letters written by Helen Mar in 1882 show her writing for the *Exponent* a great deal, traveling to auxiliary church meetings with Emmeline Wells, presiding over her family, serving joyfully as a new grandmother, and occasionally causing herself sickness by overexertion.

In 1884 she published another booklet, the 72-page *Why We Practice Plural Marriage*, which came to have some renown as a woman's defense of polygamy. Here plural marriage, far from being an offense against the Puritanical ideal, becomes the epitome of that ideal, while monogamy is seen as a decadent, gentile form of promiscuity. Eschatology, the Mormon expectation of an imminent parousia, provided a backdrop for Helen's interpretation:

> Polygamy at different periods, has been practiced as a corrector of evils and a promoter of purity; because of the wickedness and corruption into which the world has sunk; and this is the present condition of all civilized nations. Every sign goes to show that we are nearing the end—the winding up scene which all the ancient prophets have foretold, as well as the Prophet Joseph Smith. It was revealed to the latter that there were thousands of spirits, yet unborn, who were anxiously waiting for the privilege of coming down to take tabernacles of flesh ... But the work of the Almighty is rushing towards its completion, which makes this plural wife system an actual necessity ... The principle was established by the Prophet Joseph Smith, and all who have entered into it in righteousness, have done so for the purpose of raising a righteous seed; and the object is that we may be restored back to that Eden from whence we fell.

The book ends with an impassioned attack on monogamy in verse:

And down with wayward Rome's economy—
Parent of nameless ills, Monogamy—
Concomitant of empire-crumbling vice,
Immolating Virtue at the shrine of Price.
Let Innocence no more be child of Shame.
Let Nature's needs the laws of nature frame,
Let marriage vows be honorable in all,
Untrammeled by a monogamic wall
Of selfishness and rank hypocrisy,
The gift of Pagan aristocracy.

This is extremely curious reading for the twentieth-century, devotedly monogamous Mormon.

## XVIII. Tending Horace

Helen began her diary on November 12, 1884, opening a fascinating window into the last decade of her life. It reflects her interactions with her children, her constant debilitating and sometimes terrifying sicknesses, and her financial worries as her affairs spiraled into a humiliating genteel poverty. Extraordinary dreams were noted in detail, often with spiritual interpretations. Her friendships with other elite Mormon women, frequently elderly plural wives of Joseph, Heber, and Brigham, were also an important part of her life. Major characters are sister-wife Mary Cravath Whitney and her children, her brother Solomon, Lucy Walker Kimball, and Emmeline Wells, for whom Helen wrote at the *Exponent*. The diaries are also populated by a bewildering array of Kimball siblings, plural wives, half-siblings, nieces and nephews, and half-nieces and nephews. Then there are the Whitney in-laws (not to mention the sprawling Young family, who were quasi-relatives). Just as these diaries capture the twilight of Helen Mar's life, so they document the twilight of Mormon polygamy, polarization between Mormon and non-Mormon in Utah before the Manifesto, and then the beginning of an era of Mormon assimilation into the American mainstream after the Manifesto.

The major drama of the early diaries is the final sickness of Helen's husband, which she chronicled in vivid, harrowing detail. On November 12 she was tending him: "Horace wished to be fixed in his chair last evening, at an early hour & went to sleep. Spent as good a night as usual — was ready for breakfast when I came out of my room this morning." His illness had begun months before, on June 1, when he came home from a family visit complaining of shortness of breath and then coughed throughout the night. He went to work the next day but felt weak and dizzy at times. He coughed through the night again. After two weeks of this, he stayed home to recuperate, a severe trial for him as he was still a devoted clerk. On July 31 he attempted a return to the Tithing Office against his friends' and co-workers' advice. But he could only work a few hours each day, then walked home leaning on a cane, which he had never used before. Toward the end of September he "took a chill" and from that time did not return to work. He was not able to lie down at night, so slept sitting in a chair, "with his arms and head resting against a pillow upon the table before him." He grew progressively weaker; his keen memory failed him; he began to look "haggard and emaciated." Dropsy and rheumatism attacked his arms and legs, causing him much pain. By mid-October he could no longer read and had difficulty sleeping, so he dreaded the long, lonely nights.

As Helen's diary opened on November 12, Horace's left ankle was blistering, he had trouble breathing, and he was very "nervous." When she pricked the blisters three days later, "The water oozed out in every place, which relieved him greatly," she wrote. The next day she found his pants wet from the "running" sores on his legs, and he was "chilled." His hands were cold, one finger numb. She gave him opium for pain. On the 19th she "gave him his physic before eating his breakfast. This I've done each morning before eating mine. I've felt little able to do so sickening a task before taking a cup of coffee, or any thing in my stomach." The following day the leg had the same running sores, but there was also a black spot on the shin. The day after Horace seemed better, and Helen hoped that he might recover. But when she examined his leg, she gave up all hope: it was "mortified," and all the sores had blackened. According to a modern doctor's diagnosis, these symptoms are consistent with a severe infection of the leg, which, unchecked by antibiotics, spread, caused the blackness (probably dead, "necrotic," tissue), and eventually entered the bloodstream.

Tending Horace endangered Helen's own fragile health: "I said to him I wished I was able to sit with him all night. He replied 'I wish you was able to stay with me a night or two.' I am worn out & unless I rest a little at night I told him I should not be able to be with him days. ~~unless I slept & rested at night.~~ This he said he knew, & hoped I'd be able to sleep." On the 21st Helen continued to drain the leg and applied wet cloths to it: "As soon as I applied it he felt relieved, so I continued to wring it out of cold water every time it got warm. He was teribly nervous, so I told Gennie to go on giving him the morphine till he was quiet, & she gave it twice after that." The next day Dolf, one of Mary's sons, called Helen after daybreak and told her that Horace had taken too much morphine. But when she came to her husband, she knew that he was simply dying: "His eyes were open & a film over both." Horace may have suffered a septic shock caused by the infection spreading through his blood stream.

> I took his hand & sat by him till I had to go & take nourishment, leaving Flodie to hold his hand. We sent to notify Orson, who was on his way here. He wished me to assist him in writing his pa's obituary. I had gone & taken Horaces hand again but had to go in to another room where Orson had to retire to be quiet. I placed his hand in Flods His pulse was gone when I first saw him He slept quietly, only occasionally a slight struggle & giving a grasp at my hand. He breathed his last at 11 o clock. His poor leg that I'd wrapt in wet cloth had burst open & the cloth saturated with bloody water ... If I had only been notified I should have got up & watched him the rest of the night. But I knew nothing of it, though I was wakeful most of the night—sleeping only catnaps when at all. I felt much sicker that morning than I had before, and my head swimming.

The next morning, the 23rd, as Helen ate breakfast, she suddenly felt a deep sense of loss. Usually in the mornings she had to take Horace his breakfast and wash him, but now he was gone, and "there was nothing for me to do. I had to leave the table & go out to give free vent to my feelings." The funeral was held the following day in the Eighteenth Ward chapel, which was thronged with friends and relatives. Helen was greatly consoled by the service: "The remaining members of the old Theatrick club & the fellow clercks of Horace were pall bearers. carrying him to the 18th Ward Chapel where services were held. A great many people had to go away—could not get in. The music & all was most comforting & sublime."

## XIX. Deathly Spells

Horace was gone, but life continued. Helen's financial situation was not entirely stable, as her husband had left a number of debts—and the consequences of polygamy followed her into widowhood, as Horace's resources had to be split between two wives. To save on expenses, Orson and Zina moved into Helen's home. On Thanksgiving Day, November 27, Zina cooked a turkey for the family. Nevertheless, Helen wrote, "My spirits are down. A sad day, this, to me, my heart is like lead & my body sick, but, of course, will pass off in time." Two days later she journalized: "I've had more deathly spells today than any previous day. feel sad & sick from the same, and my mind is troubled over Flod's leaving school, after the great effort that I made to get her and Lucy started." Helen would complain of these "deathly spells" throughout all of her diaries, but without ever explaining them fully. Clearly, a "deathly spell" was an experience approximating death in some way—a psychic dislocation, a temporary loss of consciousness, perhaps a blackness, combined with physical pain of some sort. Sometimes she referred to them as "those awful spasms" or "spells of stagnation of my blood."

The best record of the phenomenon may be found on April 12, 1886. After fixing a bed (physical labor often triggered the spells), Helen wrote, "I commenced to feel faint so had to go & sit down, or I should have dropt on the floar—it was the most deathly sensation, and I could not stand up to undress but layed on the bed while unfastening part of my clothes." Chills and fever followed the spell. On September 9, 1885, she described the spells as "not <u>frequent</u>" that night "but <u>terrible</u> when they come. Am so weak in body & sad in spirit." The attacks came in clusters, sometimes one after another, but after a few days of them, weeks and months would go by without them. They often occurred at night, causing insomnia. On one occasion a spell occurred when she was talking to a relative, which greatly unnerved him. "I soon revived, but Hyrum was frightened." The after-effects of a seizure were psychic deflation and physical illness, as we see in the November 29 passage: "sad and sick." On April 29, 1895, she wrote, "The sad dejected feeling that they bring none but the Lord & angels can know." Often she had palpitations of the heart after the spells. Whatever they were, she experienced them periodically until her death, and they added to her dark moments of despair.

On November 30, 1884, Zina Young called. Two days later, after a sleepless night, Helen wrote, "When I awoke this morn, my head was aching to burst and my heart heavy with sorrow." But the next day, for the first time, she was free of "those deathly sensations" and managed to knit in the evening. She passed another sleepless night on December 7: "Spent it in prayer for grace and strength ... to rise triumphant above my temptations & that which would mar my peace, if possible, & sicken me of life." Lucy Walker Kimball came to comfort her: "Sister Lucy came near night to stop all night—had a pleasant visit—she said my sad countenance haunted her all night, & she feared that I would sink under my feelings if I didn't try to shake them off." Apparently, Helen *looked* melancholy. On December 8 she attended a social gathering at Emmeline Wells's home and walked back with "sisters [Marinda] Hyde & [Hannah Tapfield] King."

Helen felt that she was persecuted by a woman who goes unnamed: "I'm not only bereaved, but sick & my peace disturbed by the ill feeling and spirit that's manifested towards me by one, towards whom I've shown nothing but kindness—I suppose it's because I did not give up my only quiet room, & resting place where I wish to do a little more work with my pen, as well as to rest my worn out body and brain. I hope for the privilege of returning the compliment by doing good."

Early in 1885, on January 4, Genny had a party at the house, and Helen (seconded by Orson, the bishop) disapproved of inviting non-Mormons. It was "a great source of sorrow to me, & to hear laughing and nonsense indulged in ... I pray the Lord to open Gennie's eyes that she may see the need of withdrawing from the society of unbelievers & seeking the truth." Mormons and non-Mormons were radically polarized in pre-Manifesto Utah. January 18 was a typical sick day for Helen. She came down with a cold, then started to cough. "Had to go out to draw me water to drink, no one being at home, took a chill lasting some time, then fever—had the 2nd chill before I went to sleep—head paining me—then to cap the rest, those deathly spells came on."

A week later Helen was feeling somewhat better, and in the afternoon Lucy Walker called unexpectedly:

> I felt so languid she advised me to lay down I did so & Mary Ellen Kimball came in & brought me some nourishing things. I asked her to take off her things, & she did so. I never suspected anything—was very pleased to have company, I told them, though I was feeling so languid. Toward evening Sister Marinda Hyde & Sister Taylor came in to see me, I supposed, because they'd heard of my being sick. But Sister Hyde said she expected they'd come rather early, which let the "cat out of the bag" I thought I'd better change my dress, with the surprise it affected quite a change in my feelings, so I felt quite electrified. 23 of my beloved sisters came, loaded down with good things, & with hearts filled with blessings & good cheer for me.

Not surprisingly for such old-timers, a blessing meeting followed, just as in Winter Quarters days. Some of the women prophesied that Helen would recover to visit her sisters, attend meetings, and write once again. Others testified of the good she had already accomplished. A meal, a "sumptuous repast," followed. Also in attendance were Emily Partridge Young and sisters Woodruff, Horne, King, and Bathsheba Smith. "Brother Godard" and Apostle Heber J. Grant arrived later.

Though Helen was buoyed up by the "surprise," when her brother Heber Parley died in Salt Lake City on February 8, she envied him: "I almost felt home sick to go with the same escort that took him to father, mother, and others who would welcome me there where no sorrow can enter."

On the 25th Helen ventured out for a typical social visit with Lucy: "We first went to call at E. R. Snow's—from there went to Ex. [Woman's Exponent] office—called at Tithing Off—Store on our return." When her health allowed, Helen would travel and speak in conferences and women's meetings. On March 15, at Emmeline Wells's invitation, she attended meetings in Tooele: "I was invited to speak each time—three times the first day & spoke once Sunday—was invited to speak afternoon but as

Apostle Lyman was there, & expected to speak I declined." Again on June 2 she attended a Young Ladies Conference in the evening: "Had a pleasant time only marred by my feeling poorly in body. Came home in a carriage, sent to take Sister E. R. S. Smith, Sister Horn, Sister Rachel Grant and myself." On December 11 Helen attended a stake Relief Society conference, and a short summary of her remarks gives an idea of the kind of things she was saying in her career as a church speaker:

> Coun. H. M. Whitney, in her remarks, thought we would be brought into bondage before we could be delivered by the hand of God. Said, "All that our enemies are doing is for the furtherance of our Father's work; iniquity will be purged out, and we will have to become a new people." Spoke of the carelessness of some in attending meetings and receiving instructions. Referred to her recent visit to Millard Stake, and how the Lord had blessed her, although she went alone trusting in Him; thought deliverance would come to the Saints soon.

The church was once again suffering legal harassment because of polygamy, so Helen's remarks have millennialist overtones typical of Mormon rhetoric of the day.

## XX. "I Was Overwhelmed, & Cried Aloud"

Helen had endured a great deal in her life. She had buried two husbands and five children, had suffered serious sickness and chronic depression for years, and had endured an excruciating conversion to polygamy during which she imagined that she was possessed by evil spirits. But her cup of agony was far from full. In late July 1886 she and her brother Solomon traveled to the Bear Lake region in northern Utah and southern Idaho to visit friends and relatives. At three in the morning of August 5 she was awakened by Sol, who informed her "that my Charley was very sick" and that they needed to leave immediately to catch the Logan train to Salt Lake City. Helen was shaken but gathered her things quickly. While on the train Sol evidently realized that Helen needed to know the full truth, as other passengers might know of Charley's situation (it had been reported in the *Deseret News*). But he could not bear to tell his sister, so asked a Whitney relative, Henry Groo, to tell her what had occurred. "Bro. Groo broke it to me as carefully as possable," wrote Helen, "but I insisted upon his telling me the whole truth, when he said he did not think I'd find my boy alive." As it turned out, Charley apparently had committed suicide, shooting himself. Helen collapsed in grief and shock. She later wrote:

> I could not believe that Charley was dead—it seemed like a dream that I must awake from—But Oh it was a bitter reality, and in my silent agony

I wondered what I have done, or what I had left undone, or if I was doomed to suffer this that I could know how to feel for others ... How I cried to the Lord to help me bear it if needful & acknowledge His hand in C's taking his own life. I could not weep but Oh the agonized thought— how a boy like him could have given way—what could have brought him to commit such an act? Had all my prayers for his eternal salvation fallen to the ground unheeded?

Charley had been a brilliant, charming son, and had seemed stable. Like his father and oldest brother, he had loved the theater and performed in the "Home Club" dramatic group. He was spending time with a girlfriend and worked in the furniture store of Henry Dinwoodey, Helen's future son-in-law. Though Charley had been afflicted by nervous complaints, they had been thought minor. His co-workers noted that his memory sometimes failed him, unusual for a Whitney, and occasionally he was afflicted with "a severe case of catarrh" (sinusitis) which caused him terrible headaches. While the old term catarrh refers to inflammation of a mucus membrane (ears, nose, Eustachian tubes, etc.), the headaches may have indicated serious sinus problems, which can be incapacitating if untreated.

On the morning of the 4th Charley had worked at Dinwoodey's as usual, then in the afternoon left a young boy in charge of the store and went home, "holding his head in agony." He nevertheless greeted Genny, who was talking with a friend, then went up to his room. Genny heard a pistol shot from upstairs. She and her friend rushed up and found him lying on the floor of his room "in his own blood, in the throes of death." A gun lay beside him, and there was a large bullet wound above his right ear. Genny called for a doctor, but when he arrived Charley was already gone. According to the obituary, "The scene at the house was heartrending, the members of the family being overwhelmed with grief."

Helen arrived home late in the evening of the 5th. "When I saw the form of my Charley stretched in death," she wrote, "in an instant I was overwhelmed, & cried aloud—This was the first and the last, though my sorrow has been deep and unspeakable. And yet with all I have been blessed and felt that the Lord had not forsaken me." The funeral was held the next day at the ward chapel at 4:00 in the afternoon. It is moving, yet fascinating to read Helen's journal as she tried to make theological sense of her son's death. She was mostly worried for his eternal salvation: "When on my couch alone tears came to my relief, and I vented my ang[u]ish. How often I silently cried from the depths of my soul—My God — My God — My God, why is this and what have I done to merit so bitter a punishment at thy hand? — have mercy and help me to bear it and to 'kiss the Rod'. — Oh that I could know that my boy was worthy to be among the sanctified I would not utter a murmoring word." However, friends and relatives assured Helen that Charley had not been in his right mind when the shooting took place, so he would be fully saved.

So Helen lost her sixth child. But just as she would receive nighttime visits from her deceased parents, Heber and Vilate, she would often have comforting dreams of Charley in the upcoming years.

## XXI. "Tears of Bitterness & Hopelessness"

After tragedy, life continues, and new beginnings follow death. On November 9 Lillie, at age twenty-nine, married Robert Paton, an older man living in Logan, and on December 29 Genny married Edward Talbot. A year later, on September 21, 1887, when Helen Mar was fifty-nine, Flodie married Henry Dinwoodey in Logan.

All of these were interesting marriages. Lillie apparently married Robert Paton as a plural wife, and Helen Mar's diary is strikingly reticent about the relationship. However, this caution was probably necessary in the days of widespread prosecution for polygamy. The marriage date from family genealogy does correspond with a temple trip Helen Mar and Lillie took to Logan. Lillie apparently went to live in Paton's home four days before the marriage, and Helen Mar did not attend the ceremony. "I received a call after breakfast and some interesting information was given me—proving that my impressions were correct in a certain matter," she wrote on the 9th. On December 3 Helen returned to Salt Lake, accompanied by her daughter. Lillie never lived openly with Paton, instead continuing to share Helen Mar's home in Salt Lake, but she did bear Paton a son.

The marriage was an agonizing failure. Paton was far away in Logan and apparently rarely if ever made the effort to visit his young wife. Certainly he would have been constrained by federal marshalls at the time, but not being a high profile polygamist or church leader, he could have easily spent some time with Lillie. A Mrs. Paton (apparently his mother) is mentioned frequently in Helen's diaries, but Paton himself appears only two or three times.

Compounding the already unfortunate circumstances in this marriage was Lillie's apparent tendency toward depression. Soon after returning home from Logan, Helen noted in her diary, "My home never was dearer to me than to day, but Lill is lonesome & crying." On June 11, 1887, "Lilly cried after coming to bed—[I] tried to comfort her. She has the least of any to cheer her life here." Eventually Paton sent for Lilly to come to Logan, and she left Helen on July 20. She became pregnant in approximately September but returned to Salt Lake on December 8.

The child, a boy, was born on May 24, 1888, after a difficult delivery, during which Lillie had been rendered completely unconscious by chloroform. "Lillie rejoiced when finding her labor over and herself a mother to a son," wrote Helen. As Lillie entered into the life of a young mother, Helen began bonding with her new grandchild, named Joseph. He often seemed to be sick with "colic," abdominal pain, and kept the women up at night. On October 17 Helen wrote the father demanding some financial support for the child, "as he needed warmer clothing–if he could not get them I must though I was in scrimped circumstances." It is not known how Paton responded to the request.

In May and June 1889 Joseph became sick more frequently, with symptoms and attempted treatments carefully noted in Helen's diary. But neither priesthood administration nor medical treatment was able to arrest the baby's steady decline. On July 12, after he had spent a restless night, Helen administered "crust coffee" to lull him to sleep. In the evening, after an "awful hot day," she "took baby out on the lawn–he looked pleased at having his bonnet on for all / he was in such distress with only a moments relief–We gave his medicine every hour ... but without noticable effect."

The next day, Helen lamented, "Oh, how I constantly prayed for it to live if it was Father's will–for Lilly's sake, who's never thought that he could die. After Orson administered to him in the morning he grew easyer, & was still more easy after Dan's administration ... the little one took every thing being so thirsty." But "When I saw baby & heard the rattle on his lungs I'd no hope, & sank in submission, to the inevitable reproaching myself for his failing so–that I'd taken him out doars, or given him into any ones charge, as I thought he'd taken more cold–I took him as soon as possible & held him till his pure spirit passed away–5 minutes to 1 o'clock." Once more Helen held a beloved child and watched helplessly as it died.

Lillie was devastated. "L heart broken & wished that the Lord would take her too. I was able to calm her," wrote Helen on July 14. It is possible that this loss triggered a major depression in Lillie, for entries recording her despondency are frequent in Helen's diary in the following months. The grieving young mother went to live with her sister Helen, and on the 22nd Helen Mar visited and wrote, "Lillie sad & weeping in Hentie's bedroom–I gave a word of comfort & she rose above it. She appreciates a little word of consolation & how much would she prise the blessing of a companion–& not even a word has he written her in this her greatest sorrow." Though Paton had apparently come to Salt Lake to attend the funeral, he remained distant, physically and emotionally, while Lillie was suffering.

She never had another child, and to the best of our knowledge never lived with her husband again. Her depression continued. After a relative, Ella Decker, died, Helen wrote on August 10, 1894: "Lily was taken before day light with an awful headache & had it all day—poor girl, what wonder that life has so little inducement to her, or that ^she^ wishes she could have gone instead of Ella—few have shed as many tears of bitterness & hopelessness in this world as poor Lily, & gone unpittied only by a few outside of those who've witnessed her suffering, & know what's caused it. <u>O Lord bless us I pray</u>, with <u>hope</u>, & <u>faith</u> & <u>patience</u> to bear up under the trials that's for our good & future exaltation." Non-Mormons, of course, and uninformed Mormons would have regarded Lilly as an unwed mother.

Not long before Helen Mar's death, she was able to record Robert Paton's on September 22, 1896: "Mr Paton fell dead Tuesday last in Logan." So ended another painful chapter in Helen Mar's life. Like many of Joseph Smith's wives, she saw a child enter polygamy, the principle she had advocated with fierce loyalty, only to see the marriage founder.

Genny's marriage grieved Helen in an entirely different way: her husband was a non-Mormon, which doomed her to a lower level in the many-tiered Mormon afterlife. When Genny began keeping company with Edward Talbot, Helen one day chided her for giving him false hope. She assured her mother that she was not "fooling him along" and—to Helen's "utter astonishment"—informed her mother that they were engaged. "I was dumbfounded," wrote Helen,

> & heart broken & returned to my room—there I prayed and wept the best part of the day to the Lord that He would ... help me acknowledge His hand in <u>this</u> as well as all other things, & to show me whether it was for a punishment for Gen's disobedience or if it would turn out as blessing, by Ed's joining this Church ... Gen came to my room & put her arms around me & cried bitterly ^saying she wished she'd died ... since^ she saw how I took it, and begged me not to feel so. But <u>my</u> bitterness <u>she cannot know</u>, nor the doom that awaits those who sever themselves from this Church.

Helen was experiencing one of the most dreaded events for a typical Latter-day Saint mother: to see a child lose the blessings of Mormon exaltation. This experience was a devastating blow for the hyper-orthodox Helen Mar, the daughter of Heber C. and Vilate Kimball, who had accepted Joseph Smith as a polygamous husband in Nauvoo.

Helen's characteristic melancholy deepened, but the marriage was not canceled. On December 29, 1886, when Helen heard that Gen certainly would be married at 4:00 that day, she wrote, "My heart dropped like so much lead at the announcement, but I prayed the Lord that if Gen was doing right He would relieve my heart of the feeling, and in a few minutes the weight was gone, which ... satisfied me that the <u>Lord's hand</u> was in it for <u>some</u> purpose." Buoyed by this consolation, she helped her daughter prepare for the wedding. Edward arrived with a judge and the marriage was apparently celebrated with a small group of family, relatives, and friends in Helen's home. To have a daughter move out of the household was difficult enough for Helen, but to lose her to a non-Mormon in a ceremony that was conducted by a secular judge would have been bitter indeed.

Orson married a plural wife, Mary Minerva Wells, on July 24, 1888, thus following his grandfather and father in accepting the onerous burden of plurality. However, polygamy was not to survive much longer, and Orson played a small part in its demise. On October 6, 1890, when Helen was sixty-two, Orson read the Articles of Faith in a historic general conference, including the article on honoring and sustaining the law. Then he read the Manifesto, which stated that the Mormon church had ceased solemnizing polygamous marriages in America. So Helen lived to see her church publicly discontinue the principle that she had sacrificed so much for in her life, and ironically heard the formal pronouncement from the lips of her own son. After the Manifesto many tensions in Utah quickly subsided. The absolute polarization of Mormon vs. Liberal (anti-Mormon), so starkly recorded in Helen's diary (one night she described "guns firing & a yelling & screeching from Liberal devils incarnate"), gave way to a Democrat-Republican tug-of-war, both within the Mormon church and among Utah gentiles.

## XXII. "The Sickest of Days, & My Faith Weakening"

Though Helen Mar continued to participate in the lives of her children, grandchildren, relatives, and friends, her last decade presents a picture of steady decline in finances and health, both of which contributed to a recurring lowness of spirits. She continued to dream of the dead and to long for death, but nevertheless continued to function, though her activities outside the house were often limited. Her old humor did not entirely leave her—on April 19, 1888, she wrote, "Fred Clawson is now in love with Miss Vinson—one of Mary W.'s boarders & brings his guitar to accompany him in pouring out the sweet strains, which of course, are just the thing to capture the fair maiden but torture to the rest of us."

After her children married, she was left alone in a sizeable house with heavy tax payments, and Orson and her brother Sol advised her to sell the house and build a smaller, more affordable one. However, she loved her home and put off this unpleasant necessity as long as she could. But in March 1891 the foundations of a new house were dug, and on May 14 two "vans" appeared at her old house, and the move was made. "When I got here I found every thing piled into the three west rooms & porch & men painted the latter. My I was so tired I couldnt stand on my feet at first, but got Lill to sweep my east room which was tracked with dirt on the carpet ...

& Lenoliam that forenoon—& then help clear things from dining room—We got straightened out so that things looked more cheary." Helped by her daughters, Helen made the new house livable in the following weeks. A troublesome aspect of the new home was a hole that kept appearing in the yard. Helen's sons-in-law and relatives would fill it with rocks only to have it open up again a few days or weeks later, which caused her great annoyance.

In the final years of Helen's diaries, we follow her children's fortunes day by day. Florence and Henry were sent to England on a mission from 1893 to 1895 and Helen's diary is full of proud references to her daughter's singing and missionary accomplishments. Orson was extremely busy as a bishop, as the author of the massive four-volume *History of Utah* and biography of Heber C. Kimball, and as the father of an increasing number of children. He was a popular and impressive orator but lacked steady funding, so was often dejected about his financial outlook, like Helen. Lill, often living with Helen Bourne, continued in her stricken solitude. Ed Talbot turned his hand to a variety of jobs, none of which panned out permanently, but Helen came to respect his devotion to Gen, who began to have children.

The most striking aspect of Helen's diaries in the last years of her life is her constant sicknesses and her virtual pharmacopoeia of attempted remedies—pills, syrups, physics, sleeping medicines, painkillers, quinine, laudanum, bromide, "nervines," "Oxiginated Bitters," alcohol (usually wine and beer) used medicinally as sleeping medicine, paragoric, "kidney medicine," elixir of pepsin, "Valarial & Amonia," bottled "Scots Emulsion," "Scot & Browne's Cherry malt Phospites," "Pain's Celery Compound," even an electric treatment. And this is far from an exhaustive list. A series of doctors attempted to quell her pains, her deathly spells, her rheumatism and piles, her insomnia. They gave enough hope that Helen followed their regimens scrupulously for a time, but the cures were never complete or permanent. Dr. Dogge was seen as a savior at one point, and a Patriarch Smith dispensed pills that Helen valued highly. A colorful Dr. Raile, who had become a Mormon in Haifa, Palestine, "opperate[d]" with an "electric brush" (elsewhere called "magnetism") and dispensed herbs and a somewhat theosophical philosophy of healing learned in the Holy Land.

Nothing really worked, including the frequent administrations Helen received from friends and relatives, and she continued to despair that she would ever regain health. On June 24, 1894, she wrote, "The sickest of days, & my faith weakening." On August 22 she described her "66th natal day, and a miserable one it's been—from too little sleep last night." Then, two days later, "Another poorly feeling day" and "I had a poorly night." On the 25th she was "no better ... Seeing how badly I looked, & I felt as though I'd like to die just at that moment, my body was in such pain, & my days miserable from insuficient sleep disheartens me." On June 8, 1895, she put a typical theological interpretation on her misery: "Sick from sleeplessness. Adversary's working to destroy my faith. My eyes worse to day." She interpreted the constant sickness, sleeplessness, and misery as an attack by the "Adversary" and, just as when she was a young mother, felt her faith threatened. Her belief in evil spirits was still completely literal. On December 4, 1886, she wrote, "I feel as though I'd like to go to my 'long home' if I've got to leave this one for another ... I slept alone last night, & was troubled by evil influences which I asked the Lord to rebuke The last one felt the sensation of 2 hands punching me in the left side—I was only drowsing, & was disturbed 3 or four times by some unseen power." On the other hand, Helen often dreamed of her mother, father, and departed children, and sometimes regarded these dreams as the actual return of their spirits, so in her view she had visitations from angelic beings as well as from those demonic.

## XXIII. "Groaning Shaking & with Pleurisy"

By September 7, 1896, Helen was worn out. She wrote, "Felt so weak & prostrated in body & spirits, my faith in living nearly left me." A month and a half later, on October 22, she evidently had a stroke: "The next day I was laid up—An awful sick day—I couldn't talk right—after one word all was muddled—I'd been out to the privy with assistence of Mrs Lamborn took more cold the folks thought ————————————" This is the last entry in her monumental diary. Genny continued the story: "Ma was sick—from the day she was stricken, Oct 22—and was groaning shaking & with pleurisy—which I helped by applying whisky and red pepper on flannels—[she] remained in bed the greater part of the time—not dressing at all any more."

Helen received her wish for departure from this world on November 15. In the morning she began to fail, and her children and close friends, including Emmeline Wells, were called to her bed. Then, Wells wrote, at ten minutes past 2:00 p.m., as Helen's spirit "left its earthly tabernacle, she raised her eyes, with a look of surprise, as though the room was full of people." To Mormons, the unseen world was always present, and now it had made a significant incursion into diurnal reality. According to Wells, "no doubt her escort was there." We must imagine Helen's children and her closest friends sensing the presence of Helen's parents. She finally had her much-longed-for reunion with Vilate and Heber, and also with Helen Rosabell, William Howard, Horace Kimball, her daughter Vilate, little Phoebe, and Charley, and perhaps with her two husbands (though technically, Horace was no longer her husband). Her term of earthly suffering was over.

# 23.

# Seamstress

## *Hannah S. Ells (Smith)*

On October 1, 1841, the Nauvoo Mormon periodical, *Times and Seasons*, carried the following advertisement on the last page of the issue:

MILLINERY AND DRESS MAKING

Miss H.S. Ells begs leave to respectfully inform the Ladies of Nauvoo, and its vicinity, that she intends carrying on the above business, in all its varied branches: and further states, that she has had several years experience in one of the most fashionable French establishments in Philadelphia. Her place of residence is at Dr. Samuel Bennetts where orders will be attended to. Nauvoo, Sept. 30, 1841.

Hannah Ells is one of the more obscure wives of Joseph Smith, and this advertisement gives us a good fifty per cent of all we know about her life. It marks her entry into the Mormon historical record, shows her trade, and indicates that she had lived in Philadelphia for several years. We know little else about her. Her marriage history is relatively uncomplicated, as she married Smith at the age of thirty and had never been married previously. Beyond that, a letter she wrote in 1845 to Wilford and Emma Woodruff opens a brief window into her soul before her premature death.

## I. Hannah and Josiah

Hannah was born in 1813 in New Castle, Northumberland, England, to Thomas and Hannah Ells. We only know of one of her siblings, Josiah, born on March 4, 1806, at Lewis, Essex, England. Nothing else is known of Hannah's early life. But at some point she immigrated to America, lived in Philadelphia for "several years," according to the advertisement, and worked as a dressmaker "in one of the most fashionable French establishments" in that city.

Hannah may have lived with Josiah, so we will follow his career. He left his parents' home "while yet in his minority" and married "early in life." He evidently was trained as a doctor, for he was later known in Nauvoo as "Dr. Ells." He became a Methodist in 1826 and four years later received a license to serve as a Methodist preacher. This was probably a lay calling, rather than a formal ministerial position, but it shows that he was an outstanding, energetic Methodist who took religion seriously. He immigrated to America in 1831, possibly with his wife and family and Hannah, and lived in Philadelphia. In 1835 he moved to Monmouth County, New Jersey.

## II. New Jersey Branch

In 1838 two Mormon elders, Orson Pratt and Benjamin Winchester, visited New Jersey, where Josiah heard them preach. He read the Book of Mormon and Doctrine and Covenants, was converted, and on October 1 was baptized by Winchester in the Upper Freehold township, Monmouth, New Jersey. Perhaps Hannah was converted at the same time. In December 1839 Josiah was called to be presiding elder over a newly-organized branch in New Jersey.

On January 1, 1840, Josiah—and possibly Hannah—met Joseph Smith for the first time when the prophet traveled east to seek redress for the Missouri persecutions. The Mormon prophet found time to visit the New Jersey branch for a few days, and Josiah heard him relate his early experiences with angels and gold plates. Smith preached powerfully at a place called Cook's Mills, "warning the inhabitants of the nation against shedding the blood of the Saints, and the consequences to themselves and the entire nation, unless they desisted"; if they did not, he prophesied, "they should see blood and much sorrow." Smith counseled Josiah to gather to Nauvoo with the rest of the Saints, so Ells began to make preparations to travel west.

## III. Nauvoo

Josiah, perhaps with Hannah, arrived in Nauvoo on April 1. Joseph Smith must have been impressed by his biblical knowledge and speaking skills, for in June he was selected by Smith to represent the church in a debate with Rev. Dr. David Nelson, president of the Presbyterian Theological Seminary at Quincy. Some forty to fifty people, including Smith, crowded into a Baptist meeting house for the event. According to the RLDS history of the church, the "sectarian" minister was thoroughly trounced, which is typical of Mormon accounts of debates with competing religionists. Josiah later wrote: "The Doctor became confused, and his friends advised him to desist. He remarked that his opponent had treated him courteously, and stepped down. The Seer [Joseph Smith] got upon the stand and challenged any of the clergymen present to continue the discussion, but none responded. The Spirit of God through the weak had silenced the worldly wise."

On October 1, 1841, Hannah entered the historical record with the *Times and Seasons* advertisement quoted above. In Nauvoo she joined the inner circles of important Mormon women, as is made clear from many sources. For instance, on June 9, 1842, soon after the Relief Society was founded, she contributed $1.00 to society funds.

## IV. Joseph Smith

Sometime between January and summer 1843, Hannah became a plural wife of Joseph Smith. Andrew Jenson gives only the year of the marriage, but an affidavit by John Benbow (with whom Hannah was living) shows that Hannah and Joseph were married before the summer of that year. Benbow wrote, "Hannah Ells Smith, a wife of the Prophet, boarded at his [Benbow's] house two months during the summer of the same year [1843]; and the said Hannah E. Smith also lived at his [Benbow's] house several months in 1844, after the Prophet's death. And further, that President Smith frequently visited his wife Hannah at his (J.B.'s.) house." Aside from this bare notice, little is known of Hannah's marriage. She certainly spent time with Smith on occasion, as the Benbow affidavit shows, and she spent time with others of his plural wives. Prominent among her friends was Eliza Snow. On January 11, 1843, "Sisters Eliza Snow and Hannah Ells" attended a dinner party hosted by Joseph and Emma. Sister-wives Eliza and Hannah would have also associated in Relief Society, including a meeting on June 16 in which Hannah offered to "go out and solicit donations" for the society. A month earlier, on May 6, she had participated in the "grand annual parade" of the Nauvoo Legion, which included a "cavalcade of ladies with nodding plumes." Charlotte Haven wrote a few days before the event that "Miss Ell (she is very, very tall) will lead the van and present a banner." She must have been a striking figure.

On June 26, after Joseph Smith had been arrested in Dixon, "Dr. Josiah Ells" was part of the select group led by Charles Rich that traveled to Dixon to protect the prophet. They passed through a town called Ellesville at about sunrise, just when shops were opening, and curious residents wondered what the group's purpose was. Josiah and a J. W. Cummings were straggling behind when a local man ran up and asked them where in the world they were going. According to the *History of the Church,* "Dr. Ells, who carried a very sanctified face, drawled out, 'We're a-hunting a wheelbarrow's nest,' after which, we again resumed the march." This story remains one of only two extant anecdotes about either Hannah or Josiah.

During the 1844 sessions of Relief Society, Hannah received a promotion. On March 9, the society minutes read, "Meeting conveind President

E. Smith. Proceeded to Open the Meeting–appointed–H. Ells Sectary."
Hannah's minutes that day give an idea of her writing style, which was
literate but less polished than Eliza Snow's:

> [Emma Smith] Stated the object of the meeting, read an Epistle called
> the Voice of In ocence adressed the meeting on the late Slander, of Hi-
> ram Smith &c by O. F, Bostic which called forth the <reading> of above
> Epistle–it was then asertaind by vote, who would be willing to receive
> the principles of virtue, keep the commandments of God, and uphold
> the Prest in puting <down> iniquity–was received by unanimous voice–
> Prest E. S. said her determination was to do her duty Effectivlly–in
> puting down transgresion.

On April 19 another of Hannah's advertisements appeared in the
*Nauvoo Neighbor*:

> MILLINERY AND DRESS MAKING
> MISS H ELLS, Respectfully invites the Ladies of Nauvoo to call and exam-
> ine her Assortment of Fashionable and approved style of Bonnets, at
> moderate prices–Bonnets made to order and altered to the Latest Fash-
> ion, and every exertion made to give satisfaction to those who may fa-
> vour her with their Patronage–H.E. states that the proceeds of the Straw
> Bonnet business are for the benefit of the Relief Society of Nauvoo–all
> kinds of produce taken in exchange–corner of Water and Main Streets,
> opposite the Nauvoo Mansion.
>
> Second Door River Side.
> April 16th

Joseph Smith's martyrdom approached, and Josiah was present
when Smith decided to give himself up to the law. On June 27 the
prophet was killed, and Hannah, at age thirty-one, was a widow.

### V. "An Imposing, Grand, and Sublime Senery"

Soon after this, Hannah makes an appearance in the Wilford Woodruff journal as a close family friend. When Wilford and Phoebe were preparing to leave Nauvoo on a mission to England toward the end of August, a select family group made a night visit to the half-built Nauvoo
temple. Though Hannah is not a conspicuous actor in the scene, she was
in the party. "At 12 oclok at night in company with Mrs Woodruff, Br
A.O. Smoot, Sisters Smoot, and Hannah Ells, we walked to the Temple of
the Lord in Nauvoo," wrote Wilford. The temple was imposing in the
moonlight, and it moved the apostle to poetry: "As we approached it we
lifted up our eyes and beheld the greatness grandure and glory ... While
she was covered with the silver rays of the Queen of the night who was
pouring the whole strength of the brightness of her glory upon her it
presented an imposing, grand, and sublime senery to the beholder." The

group entered the temple, ascended to the southwest corner, "and their ... we bowed our knees upon the top corner stone which was prepaired to recieve its Capitol, And their with up lifted hands towards heaven, I called upon the God of Abraham, Isaac, Jacob and Joseph by Prayer and supplication."

Hannah, kneeling, listened in the moonlight as Wilford prayed. He asked that the Saints would be able to finish their temple, that God would avenge the blood of Joseph the Seer and Hyrum his brother, that Wilford and Phoebe would serve their mission in righteousness and return safely, that Brigham and the Twelve would have a double portion of the spirit of Joseph. After this invocation, Hannah, with the Woodruffs and their small party, descended to the ground, and all returned to their homes "with Joy and peace" in their hearts.

The Woodruffs took two of their children with them to England, but left Wilford Owen with the Benbows, whom Wilford had baptized in England in 1840. As we have seen, Hannah sometimes lived with the Benbows after the martyrdom and thus became a close friend of little Wilford.

## VI. "It Was a Sorce of Sorrow to Me"

At this juncture an event occurred that caused Hannah great distress: Josiah became disaffected from the church and joined with William Marks in opposing the Twelve in their claim to be the authoritative church leaders. On November 23 the Nauvoo High Council voted that Josiah, with James Ivins, William Marks and wife, and Ephraim S. Green and William Stanley would be required to appear before the council on the following Saturday. A week later the council questioned Marks, but no action was taken against him. "Dr Ells" was then questioned. He stated that "he had ever feared god from his youth up." However, he affirmed that he felt that the Twelve had the apostleship but not the right of presidency. He inclined toward Sidney Rigdon's claim to lead the church, but was not willing to risk his salvation on any man or men.

Orson Hyde reminded Josiah that Joseph Smith had said that the Twelve were to bear off the kingdom, to which Alpheus Cutler concurred. "Brother Hyde also prophesied of that the influence and prosperity of those who go from this place without council, would be taken from them." John Taylor agreed. "No testimony, nor argument seemed to satisfy Dr E. Voted unanimously, that Dr Josiah Ells be disfellowshipped by the church until he shall reform in principles of faith and notice hereof be given in the 'Times and Seasons.'" One interesting aspect of this trial is that it was a high council session and yet the apostles—technically a traveling high council—were present without formal authority to be there. Still, Orson Hyde clearly dominated the meeting. The apostles were on the ascendent in the church, and the high council, even of the central stake, would gradually become less important.

However, in a December 7 high council meeting, it was agreed that Marks should be tried once more, and for this trial Hannah would be called as a witness. As she was Josiah's sister, it is not surprising that she was in Marks's circle. However, two days later Marks appeared before the council, signed a statement professing allegiance to the Twelve, and was not disfellowshipped. There is no further mention of Hannah. By spring 1845 Josiah had become entirely separated from the main branch of Mormonism, for in April he was selected as an apostle in Sidney Rigdon's church and moved to Pittsburgh. He went on to affiliate with Strang and the Strangites for a time, then joined the RLDS church in 1860. He became an RLDS apostle in 1865, in which capacity he fulfilled missions to Utah, Europe, and the eastern United States.

Hannah's letter to the Woodruffs gives some insight into the pain that Josiah's departure from "apostolic" Mormonism caused her:

> My Brother did not occupy your house as he became a follower of S. Rigdon, and Samuel Bennett with their family have gone to Pittsburgh. you may think I feel pretty much like one left alone, but I would not be in their case for all I have ever seen, but am a thousand times glad that I have lived to see this day altho it was a sorce of sorrow to me for a season I now rejoice that I was counted worthy to be called to indure the trial of my faith. wich will work out for me a more exceeding weight of glory.

Thus Hannah went through a period in which her faith had been tried, and her brother's apostasy caused her great sorrow. Perhaps Josiah attempted to persuade her to leave Nauvoo and Mormonism with him, but she weathered the trial, she felt, and now was strengthened in her faith.

## VII. "Like Sheep Without a Shepard"

A window now opens on Hannah's life, her letter to Phoebe Woodruff. Though sent in one packet, it was dated May 4, May 5, June 3, and June 8, 1845. The first part, written in Nauvoo, begins, "Dear Sister Woodruff I Came into the City last Sunday to spend the week, learnd that Elder A. Feilding was about to Start for England, in a few days. I therefore take my pen to fulfill My promise, to you wich was to write the first oppertunity." Hannah had promised to keep a journal and send it to the Woodruffs at intervals. She started to do this but "whas then taken down sick with Chills and Fever. was not able to [do] anything for 3 months I had been in the City only a few days then I was taken sick I remaind untill {unreadable} ... then I went out on the praire to Sister Benbows. where, I have stayed most of my time since, and we all injoy tolorable health at this time. I made a visit to Sister Webster three days this week to do her some sewing."

After discussing some mutual friends, the Websters, her brother Josiah, and Emma Smith, Hannah turned to news of Wilford Jr.: "He as [has] been quite well and harty ever since you left except [for a] slight cold, he grows fast looks ruddy and well is quite cheerfull and happy. and sais he will not leave his Aunty. to live with Pa or Ma ... he grows Intresting every week. I hear him read Lessons most days but some times he plays truant." Hannah evidently was known as "Aunty" to the Woodruff children. Next she described an expedition to Nauvoo with Wilford:

> I took him with me to Meeting two Sundays ago, Orson Pratt Preached first, afterward Presedent B. Young. and let him stand up so that he could see them when they spoke. Elder. Hide dismissed the meeting with uplifted hands wich seamed to please Willford much he wached [watched] him very minutely affter meeting I took him to Brother Hunters. at the brick House, while there he took quite a {fondness} to Sister Hunters baby, a little girl about a year old he was very ancious to take baby and cradle out with us on the Praire ... when Mr Benbow came after us he wanted to have baby and cradle put into the buggy.

Hannah ended the first part of the letter with an expression of affection for the Woodruffs: "Now Sister Woodruff you will please give my kindest Respects to Elder W and [I] hope he will join with you in writting to me the first convenient season untill wee meet again we all look anciously for your return at the Dedication of the Temple—With best wishes for you[r] health and happinness and the prosperity of the cause of Zion— I remain your Sister in the Gospel H.S. Ells."

The next day Hannah was at the Benbows' "Praire Farm" and helped Wilford Jr. write to his parents: "My Dear Pa. and Mama Sister Ells is holding my hand. while I try to write ... My Aunty [Hannah] took me to see Sister Emma['s] baby ... She took me to see Brother Kimble and Brother Taylor & he Blessed me and & gave me some figs & Raisins." In an addendum Hannah wrote that Wilford was "perfectly happy, and you know his Aunty does not think any boy is like her boy."

The next installment is dated June 3. Hannah wrote:

> I am now staying at Father J Smiths making some dresses ... I have wrote this Letter at so many different times that I fear you will not be able [to] read it, but you must please excuse all mistakes, and I will try to send you a neat one next time ... I have just been up to Sister Websters, to hear from Mr Benbows, but find that they have not been in to meeting to day, so I must now conclude, hoping to hear from you soon and let me know how you like England, from your Sister in the gospel H. Ells.

In a postscript she revealed that she had no fixed address: "pleas to direct to me in <u>Nauvoo</u>, as I have no particlar home, but stay a little at one place & so on, like sheep without a shepard–H.E." This is a poignant touch. Evidently Hannah did not even have her own apartment now–previously she may have stayed with her brother.

This extended letter shows Hannah to be an affectionate friend of the Woodruffs and a kind guardian and keen observer of the child who called her Aunty. We see her circle of acquaintances, the Benbows, Websters, Emma, and the apostles. She practices her usual profession of tailoring.

### VIII. "I Loved Her Very Much"

Two weeks after the last installment of the letter, Hannah received a patriarchal blessing from John Smith. Then she drops out of the historical record until her death, which itself is poorly documented. She apparently died later in 1845, but we have no date or cause of death. Perhaps malaria finally claimed her. But there is a place of death, the Nauvoo home of Sarah and Hiram Kimball, and we know that fellow Relief Society secretary Eliza R. Snow was at her bedside in her last moments. "I loved her very much–was present at her death," wrote Eliza. Hannah was presumably also a close friend of Sarah Kimball, as was Eliza. Hannah died in the same home in which the Relief Society had received its first genesis three years earlier on March 4, 1842.

Jenson supplies an epitaph for Hannah: she was "a lady of culture and refinement–somewhat tall in stature. Those who were acquainted with her speak of her as a good and noble woman." She was clearly respected and influential in the circles of elite women in Nauvoo. Aside from her marriage to Joseph Smith, she was closely associated with Eliza Snow, Sarah and Hiram Kimball, and Phoebe and Wilford Woodruff. In addition, she has some historical importance as an early Relief Society secretary, like Eliza. If she had lived to cross the plains, she might have been one of the leading sisters of Utah.

# 24.

# Relief Society Treasurer

## *Elvira Annie Cowles (Holmes Smith)*

Nineteen women gathered together in the upper story of Joseph Smith's red brick store on March 17, 1842, and met for the first time as the Female Relief Society of Nauvoo—an organization that now numbers some 4 million women worldwide. Among them were Emma Smith, the strong-willed and beloved wife of the prophet; the poetess Eliza Snow who would become the dominant woman leader in Utah Mormonism; and Sarah Kimball, in whose home the idea of a Relief Society was first brainstormed. When the time came to appoint a treasurer, Emma turned to a quiet, gentle, trustworthy friend: Elvira Cowles, the twenty-eight-year-old daughter of Nauvoo stake presidency counselor Austin Cowles. Elvira had been living as a maid and nanny in the Smith household, so Emma knew her well.

Unlike Eliza Snow and Emma Smith, Elvira lived the rest of her life in undramatic obscurity, a welcome relief amid the stark tragedies surrounding most of Smith's other wives. Her life was quiet, prosaic, and comparatively uneventful. The marriage to Smith in June 1843 was polyandrous, as she had exchanged vows with Jonathan Holmes just half a year earlier. The Smith-Holmes sealing shows clearly how Smith, in his polyandry, most often married women whose "first husbands" were faithful Latter-day Saints. Jonathan had long been a loyal disciple of Smith and was one of the pallbearers at his funeral. After the martyrdom Elvira's and Jonathan's marriage endured, though Elvira was sealed to the prophet for eternity in the Nauvoo temple. The Holmeses eventually settled in Farmington, Utah, where Elvira raised a family of daughters who carried on her polygamous heritage in a unique way.

There are no extant holographs from Elvira, so our sense of her personality is not as vivid as we would like. However, she appears occasionally in the journals of her friends Eliza Snow and Patty Sessions, and family traditions flesh out the contours of her life. It is clear that everyone remembered this schoolteacher and expert weaver with great warmth and affection.

## I. Stepdaughter

Elvira was born on November 23, 1813, in Unadilla, Otsego County, New York, twenty-five miles northeast of Binghamton, the first child of twenty-one-year-old Austin Cowles, from Vermont, and a twenty-eight-year-old New York native, Phoebe Wilbur. Austin, who had lost an eye at an early age, was a schoolteacher, minister, clerk, wheel-wright, and small farmer. Elvira's first three siblings, Louisa W., Sophia, and Alonzo, were born in 1817, 1818, and 1819 in Unadilla. Unfortunately Alonzo died at birth and Sophia died at the age of two.

By late 1820 the Cowleses had moved to Bolivar, Alleghany, New York (forty miles southeast of Buffalo), for another daughter, Mary Ann, was born there on December 31. They were among the earliest settlers of the town. According to family traditions, Austin taught winter term at a new school house and "became a regularly ordained Methodist Episcopal Minister." He rode as a circuit preacher and conducted the first religious service in Bolivar—in a barn. Clearly he was well educated and took religion seriously, as his later prominence in Mormonism suggests. By 1825 he was an inspector of common schools and a town clerk at Bolivar, as well as joint-owner of a saw mill.

More children soon joined the Cowles family—Leonard was born on November 28, 1822, then died two days later. Cynthia Fletcher and Huldah Jane followed in 1824 and 1825, though apparently Huldah died early. The loss of so many children must have been difficult for the Cowleses (Phoebe had lost four of eight children), but now an even greater catastrophe struck: Phoebe herself died on May 1, 1826, when Elvira was twelve. How she dealt with this tragedy is not known, but she must have shouldered much of the responsibility of raising the younger Cowles children as she entered her teenage years.

About a year and a half later, on October 21, 1827, Austin remarried, taking as his new wife Irena Hix Elliott, nineteen, only five years older than Elvira. She would bear Austin six more children. According to family tradition, Irena was a good stepmother and "taught her children that it is better to suffer wrong than to do wrong." So Elvira would grow up partially with a stepmother, then become one herself in later years. Irena's first child, Wesley Fletcher, was born on March 19, 1829, in Bolivar.

So much for Elvira's family background. Her father was devout, intelligent, and capable. She experienced the loss of siblings and her mother at an early age, then helped a stepmother raise the younger children. Of her young womanhood, we only know that she became a school-teacher at an early age.

## II. Mormonism

Soon after April 6, 1830, the official date of Mormonism's founding, most of the Cowles family converted. However, unlike many early Mormons, Austin did not immediately gather to Ohio or Missouri. Elvira was in the middle of her teenage years in 1830 and would not be baptized until October 19, 1835, when she was twenty-two. By 1836 the Cowleses had moved to a different town, Amity, still in Allegheny County, New York, where David Croydon Cowles was born on October 13, 1836.

According to Elvira's obituary, she came to Kirtland in 1836, probably with her family, but we know very little about her stay there. In Ohio she would have met Joseph Smith for the first time, and she would have met the young women who would become her sister-wives, the Huntington sisters, Eliza Snow, Marinda Hyde, and Agnes Coolbrith Smith.

Dogged by financial suits and the opposition of dissenters, the Saints soon left Kirtland for Missouri. On March 13, 1838, Austin was present at a meeting of Seventies in the Kirtland temple, and it was decided that they (the Seventies) should move to "Zion" (Missouri) as a company. Austin signed the constitution of rules for the move, listing a household of nine persons. Jonathan Holmes, Elvira's future husband, also signed it, listing a household of three. Presumably they were both Seventies, a missionary calling.

## III. To Adam-ondi-Ahman

If Austin traveled with this company, as is probable, his family assembled south of the temple on July 5 with the rest of the group and departed the next day. By September 6 they had reached Terre Haute, Indiana. On arriving at Huntsville, in Randolph County, east central Missouri, Elvira's company was met by anti-Mormons trying to prevent them from traveling farther. But they pushed on, and on October 2 came to Far West, then continued to Adam-ondi-Ahman (where, according to Mormon legend, Adam lived) and pitched their tents there on October 4, after having accomplished a journey of some 700 miles. As they camped, "one of the brethren living in the place proclaimed with a loud voice": "Brethren, your long and tedious journey is now ended; you are now on the public square of Adam-ondi-Ahman. This is the place where Adam blessed his posterity, when they rose up and called him Michael, the Prince, the Archangel, and he being full of the Holy Ghost predicted what should befall his posterity to the latest generation." So the travelers mixed the day-to-day rigors of practical pioneering with visionary mysticism.

Unfortunately, however, the Cowles family's stay in Zion would be brief. The immigrating party found Missouri virtually in a state of war, with a mob-militia threatening the Mormons on every side. On the 24th the Battle of Crooked River was fought, and soon thereafter Governor Boggs issued his extermination order and the Haun's Mill Massacre took place. Most Mormons, probably including the Cowles clan, traveled to Illinois in the early months of 1839. The obituary tells us that in the fall Elvira arrived at Nauvoo, perhaps after a stay of some months in Quincy.

### IV. "Elvira Would Tell Stories"

In Nauvoo the Mormon social structure began to stabilize once more, and Austin quickly distinguished himself as a politician and leader. On February 3, 1841, he was elected to the Nauvoo City Council as Supervisor of Streets, and on March 9 he and Joseph Smith had a friendly dispute over the bestowal of the Holy Ghost after baptism. Then William Marks, president of Nauvoo Stake, selected Austin as his first counselor on the 29th. As the apostolic office was not then as important as it now is, the office of counselor in the stake presidency was equivalent to that of a modern general authority. Austin attended high council meetings, where he shows up frequently in the minutes.

Elvira, now twenty-seven, would thus gain some visibility as the daughter of a prominent church leader. She lived in Joseph Smith's household for a time, as did many of Smith's wives. According to her obituary, "in the spring following [i.e., spring 1840] [she] became a member of the family of the Prophet Joseph Smith, where she remained a happy inmate" until her marriage to Holmes. Thus Elvira became a close friend of Emma Smith and a friend of the other leading women of Nauvoo, including such future Smith wives as Eliza R. Snow and Eliza and Emily Partridge.

Living with the Smiths also brought an important male into Elvira's life when, in late 1840, Joseph Smith welcomed an old friend, Jonathan Holmes, into his household. Jonathan worked as a handyman and served as one of Smith's bodyguards. A shoemaker by profession, he had been born in Rowley, Essex, Massachusetts, on March 11, 1806. Baptized a Mormon in 1832, he gathered to Kirtland two years later where, according to his obituary, he "made his home with the Prophet Joseph Smith, and was much beloved by the Prophet and all others who knew him. He remained with Joseph and was married [to Marietta Carter] at his house, April 13, 1837." The couple had two children—Sarah Elizabeth, born on January 24, 1838, and Mary Emma, born on May 25, 1840. Jonathan then endured a double calamity as Marietta died on August 20, and Mary Emma passed away less than a month later on September 10. According to family traditions, these deaths resulted from a mob driving Marietta out of her cabin in Missouri.

Evidently Elvira was given charge of Sarah, and though she little suspected it at first, another key relationship in her life had begun. Sarah, in later life, had vivid memories of her childhood in the Smith home living with Joseph and Emma, Elvira and Eliza Snow. According to a family biography, "The evenings that Sarah liked best were the ones she & Elvira Cowles would be left at home to care for the family while Sister Emma Smith & Eliza R. Snow would be out caring for & visiting the sick. The colored cook always had extra lunches & Elvira would tell stories & they would all play games." This reference shows that Elvira was warm and approachable, unlike the intellectual, austere Eliza Snow. Jonathan and Elvira must have started courting at this time.

Elvira's residence with the Smiths extended from 1840 to 1842. In spring 1842 the Nauvoo Ward listing shows "Alvira Cowles" living in the Smith household along with the Partridge sisters and Desdemona Fullmer. At this same time, as we have seen, Elvira was one of twenty women attending the first meeting of the Relief Society, where she was selected to be the treasurer. She is not mentioned frequently in the society's minutes, but one can imagine her coming to every meeting and faithfully receiving and guarding contributions to this charitable group. She was not outgoing or charismatic, but, rather, was quiet, trusted, and valued. Emma used Elvira as a messenger on August 14 when she sent her to invite Eliza Snow, recently married to Joseph Smith, into the Smith household.

### V. Two Streams, Mingling

By September 18 Elvira and Jonathan Holmes were engaged, for Eliza Snow wrote a poem to them that appears in her diary on that day:

> Conjugal, To Jonathan & Elvira.
> Like two streams, whose gentle forces
>     Mingling, in one current blend—
> Like two waves, whose onward courses
>     To the ocean's bosom tend—
>
> Like two rays that kiss each other
>     In the presence of the sun—
> Like two drops that run together
>     And forever are but one,
>
> May your mutual vows be plighted—
>     May your hearts, no longer twain
> And your spirits be united
>     In an everlasting chain.

They were married on December 1, with Joseph Smith himself performing the ceremony. The marriage notice reads, "'For the Wasp'. MAR-
RIED.–In this city on Thursday evening Dec. 1st by President Joseph
Smith, Elder Jonathan H. Holmes, to Miss Elvira A. Cowles. The following lines were presented to Mr. and Mrs. Holmes, on the day after the
nuptials, BY MISS E. R. SNOW. 'Like two streams ... etc..'" Elvira would
now raise Sarah Elizabeth, four and a half years old; Elvira the stepdaughter had become a stepmother. Her friendship for Eliza Snow is shown
once again when Eliza, after leaving the Smith home on February 11,
1843, moved in with Elvira and Jonathan.

## VI. Polyandry

According to an affidavit she signed in Utah in 1869, Elvira was
sealed to Joseph Smith on June 1, 1843, in Heber C. Kimball's house,
with Heber officiating and Vilate Kimball and Eliza Partridge standing as
witnesses. Though it is impossible to know for certain, the fact that Holmes was so close to Joseph Smith suggests that he knew of Smith's marriage to his wife and permitted it. By this interpretation, if he was not
present at the marriage, he was probably told of it by Joseph and Elvira.
He later stood as proxy for Smith as Elvira married the prophet for eternity in the Nauvoo temple, which shows that he certainly knew of her
polyandrous marriage by that time. This "first husband" never wavered
in his loyalty to the Mormon leader. But Elvira's father did, and it is possible that her polyandrous marriage to Smith helped bring about Austin
Cowles's disaffection. Even if he had not been told of the sealing, rumors
of polygamy were rife in Nauvoo, and he would surely have heard his
own daughter's name mentioned. One wonders if he confronted Elvira
or her secret husband directly. As so often, the limited documentation
for Nauvoo polygamy only leaves us with more questions.

Elvira reported to the Relief Society on her stewardship as treasurer
on June 16: "Sec. E. A. Holmes, then rose–said she was not altogether
prepared to give a full and correct statement of the Receipts and Expenditures of the Society but would make a statement so soon as she could
see Mrs. Smith and adjust some unsettled accounts–suffice it to say
about 500 dollars have been rec.d and nearly 400 expended during the
first year of the Society–much good had been done and the hearts of
many made to rejoice." This is the closest thing we have to a first-person
document from Elvira.

On June 29 the gathering of Smith's plural wives that has been referred to earlier took place, as Elvira, with Eliza Snow, Elizabeth Whitney, and Elizabeth Durfee, rode to Cornelius Lott's farm in the country,
perhaps to counsel teenaged Melissa Lott on her upcoming marriage to
Joseph. The July 7 Relief Society minutes show how Elvira held money

and dealt with the poor: "Sis. Lyons said when the poor come to sis. W. and sis. Holmes, if they can not supply them, send them with orders to her. Coun. W. said it is the counsel of Prest. E. Smith to keep accounts of small donations, when the sisters are call'd upon at their homes to assist from time to time; and bring such accounts to the Treasurer."

## VII. "Outspoken and Energetic in His Opposition"

In early 1843 Austin apparently did some missionary work in New Hampshire and Massachusetts, but he soon returned to Nauvoo and played an important role when a storm of opposition confronted Joseph Smith in the summer. On July 16 Smith preached, denouncing internal traitors, and Willard Richards, writing to Brigham Young, guessed that the church president was referring to William Marks, Austin Cowles, and Parley P. Pratt. These men—the Nauvoo Stake president, his first counselor, and an eloquent apostle—would be a serious obstacle to Smith, despite his charismatic authority and ecclesiastical position, especially when one considers the dominance of central stake leadership in early Mormonism. Soon William Law, a counselor in the First Presidency, would be another formidable opponent.

Their opposition became public when Hyrum Smith read the revelation on polygamy, presently LDS Doctrine and Covenants 132, to the Nauvoo High Council on August 12. Three of the leading brethren opposed it: William Marks, Austin Cowles, and Leonard Soby. Considering the secrecy of polygamy, it is remarkable that Hyrum would announce it even to the high council. It is also remarkable that Marks, Cowles, and Soby would openly reject it. This was a watershed moment in Latter-day Saint history.

Undoubtedly Austin soon saw that he could not function as a church leader while he and Marks were opposing one of Joseph Smith's revelations so bluntly and completely. On September 12, according to the high council minutes, "President Austin Cowles resigned his seat in the Council as Councillor to President Marks which was accepted by the Council." Ebenezer Robinson later wrote that Austin "was far more outspoken and energetic in his opposition to that doctrine [polygamy] than almost any other man in Nauvoo." After resigning his presidency, he "was looked upon as a seceder, and no longer held a prominent place in the Church, although morally and religiously speaking he was one of the best men in the place." Mormons in the main body of the church viewed him less sympathetically.

Toward the end of April 1844, the anti-polygamy dissenters began organizing a new church. William Law was appointed president and selected Austin Cowles as his first counselor. Not surprisingly, Austin was "cut off" from the main LDS church for apostasy soon thereafter, on May

18. He then helped write the fateful first and only issue of the *Nauvoo Expositor*, the paper which so infuriated Smith with its criticisms of him and public discussion of polygamy. It appeared on June 7, with an anti-polygamy affidavit by Cowles on the second page. The destruction of the *Expositor* press, engineered by Smith, set off a chain of events that led to his martyrdom.

Ironically Jonathan Holmes helped destroy the *Expositor*, so father-in-law and son-in-law found themselves on different sides of the fray. We can only guess how Elvira reacted to her father's militant anti-polygamy stance and his departure from the church. She loved her father, yet loved the church, Joseph Smith, and Jonathan at the same time, which would have created a difficult and painful situation.

## VIII. Whistled Out of Town

On June 27 Joseph Smith was killed and Elvira was (partly) widowed. Once again we see how close Holmes was to Joseph, as he served as one of the prophet's pallbearers in the funeral. So Elvira's husband honored Smith, while her father had helped precipitate his death.

Elvira's last half-sibling, Martha Maria Cowles, was born on October 3 in Hampton, Rock-Island, Illinois, some sixty miles north of Nauvoo, a town that became a stronghold of the dissenters. Seven months later Hosea Stout's journal provides a vivid description of Mormon dislike of Cowles, now known as an influential "apostate." On April 27, 1845, Stout and his wife attended an open-air preaching meeting in Nauvoo. "Old Father Cowles one of Law's apostates was there, a company of boys assembled to whistle him out of Town but I prevented them. I came home and in the evening went to police, on my way was informed that the old man had been whistled out immediately after meeting. I met police & came home before dark." The Whittling and Whistling Brigade was a group of Mormon men who would whistle and brandish knives at unwanted visitors—a practice that added physical threat to ecclesiastical excommunication.

Of Austin's later life, we are told that "he moved about from place to place but never found complete contentment although he kept his family around him." Indeed, he lived in Burlington, Iowa; Hampton, Illinois; Kirtland; Sycamore, Illinois; and Fulton City, Illinois, where he managed a grocery store for years. He was appointed president of the high priests quorum in Sidney Rigdon's church in April 1845, but by 1849 had joined the "Brewsterites," a Mormon splinter group. He soon left them also and finally moved to Pleasanton, Decatur, Iowa, in 1854, where he operated a grist- and sawmill. There he was associated closely with the Reorganized Church of Jesus Christ of Latter Day Saints, preached in their meetings, and investigated spiritualism seriously. He died on January 15,

1872, in Hamilton Township, Decatur County. Elvira wrote of him: "After spending a long life in making the world better, an example to all who knew him, with charity for all and malice toward none, his tall form was laid to rest in the old homestead (probably at Pleasanton, Decauter Co, Illinois). His wife, Irena, laid by his side. Two simple slabs mark their resting place. These lines are cut in the slab at his head: 'He chose virtue as his sweetest guide; lived as a Christian and as a Christian died.'"

Elvira's love and admiration for her father, despite his rejection of Joseph Smith and polygamy, did not waver. Early Mormon historiography generally demonizes such men as Cowles who separated from the Utah church. But Elvira's epitaph, supported by Ebenezer Robinson's evaluation of his character, shows him in a more sympathetic light. A man of intelligence and sincere religious conviction, a major church leader, he nevertheless profoundly disagreed with Smith's polygamy and polyandry, and his honesty required him to openly oppose him rather than to leave the church. Some expressed their loyalty to Mormonism by following Smith without questioning, while Austin expressed his loyalty to the faith by rejecting polygamy and dissenting. So he ended up closely associated with the Reorganized Latter Day Saint church—which ironically denied that Smith ever practiced polygamy.

## IX. "But They Were Not Alone"

A July 6, 1845, diary reference by Apostle Willard Richards shows Elvira once again in the upper echelons of Mormon society: "Sister Holmes spent the P.M. with Jennetta [Richards's wife]." Elvira bore her first child, Lucy Elvira Holmes, in Nauvoo on October 11. On December 23 Jonathan and Elvira received their endowments together in the Nauvoo temple. A month later, on February 3, 1846, she was sealed to Joseph Smith for eternity in the temple, with Jonathan standing as proxy for Smith, then was sealed to Jonathan for time.

This left Jonathan without his own eternal companion. However, on the same day Jonathan was sealed to his deceased wife, Marietta Carter, for eternity, with Elvira standing proxy. Thus Jonathan and Elvira, like Helen Kimball and Horace Whitney, would go through life together, sharing each other's earthly burdens, sealed for time only, Elvira bearing Jonathan's earthly children. But they both believed that in the eternities they would be sealed to different people and that Jonathan's children by Elvira would belong to Smith. One wonders what the psychological dynamics of such a paradoxical union might have been. Nevertheless, to the best of our knowledge, the marriage was stable and happy.

Mormons were once again preparing for a mass migration, and Jonathan and Elvira, with Sarah Elizabeth and little Lucy Elvira, must have left Nauvoo with the body of Latter-day Saints soon after their proxy marriages. According to family tradition, their wagon was pulled by a mismatched ox-and-cow team, to which they entrusted all of their possessions.

They arrived at Council Bluffs around July 1, 1846, after a journey across Iowa that undoubtedly was rainy, muddy, and uncomfortable. However, at Winter Quarters they would soon be separated, for Jonathan joined the Mormon Battalion and departed for the Far West on July 16. Elvira, left alone with two children, spent a harsh winter living in a "log room" that had only blankets for doors and windows. Though she endured the typical hardships of Winter Quarters life, she once again spent time with prominent Mormon women and undoubtedly shared many a blessing meeting with Eliza Snow, Zina Young, Louisa Beaman, and other wives of Smith, Young, and Kimball. In September 1846, when Eliza was gravely ill, Elvira helped nurse her back to health. Meanwhile Jonathan and the battalion arrived at San Diego, California, on January 29, 1847.

Like so many women at Winters Quarters, Elvira lost a child—little Lucy Elvira, nearly two years old—on June 1, 1847. The next day Eliza Partridge Lyman helped her mourn, writing in her diary, "Received an invitation from Sister Holmes to come and spend the day with her which I accepted. Visited with her the grave of her child." Less than two weeks later, when Elvira was still grieving, on approximately June 12, she, with nine-year-old Sarah Elizabeth, set out on the overland journey to Utah in Jedediah Grant's company. Family tradition holds that she "walked and drove her own ox and cow team the entire way across the plains." Eliza Snow, also in the Grant company, mentioned Elvira on July 11 in our only explicit testimony that Elvira participated in the gifts of the spirit: "Sis. Holmes call'd to see me in the eve, & spoke in the gift of tongues. We are said to be 180 ms. from W. Quarters." On July 19 Eliza "took supper with sis. Holmes—had a good season in sis. Love's tent ... Here the South Fork unites with the main Platte." The poetess ate dinner with Elvira again on August 7, and a week later she paid her a social visit. The next day Elvira took part in one of the blessing meetings that so uplifted the sisters on the overland journey. "I go to moth. Chase's," wrote Eliza. "sis. H. calls while we are having a rich treat from on high."

Two family anecdotes illustrate the dangers and hardships of a woman traveling alone as a pioneer. Once Elvira's wagon was suddenly surrounded by a herd of stampeding buffalo: "As they rushed along she drew little Sarah close to her, spoke firmly and assuringly to her team, and waved her hand at the wild beasts." When they passed her by without causing any damage, "her fervent prayer" was answered. The second incident was precipitated by Elvira's cow losing a shoe—a major crisis on the trail. She reported this to her captain, who advised her to walk back ten miles to the following company, which had a blacksmith. So Elvira undertook this dangerous journey alone, then walked back to her wagon accompanied by the smith, adding an extra twenty miles to her day's trek.

Family traditions add a haunting detail, an evocation of sisterhood and motherhood extending beyond death: "But they were not alone. The spirit of Marietta Carter, now freed from earthly limitations, shared their wagon and walked by their side. She was their advocate and ambassador in the kingdom of heaven."

## X. "Wolf Meat, Sego and Thistle Roots"

Elvira arrived in Salt Lake City on October 2, 1847. There she lived with Sarah in the Old Fort and experienced all the privations and hardships of the early Salt Lake settlers. A family history records that "She taught the first school that was taught in what was called the 'Old Fort,' and took wolf meat, sego and thistle roots for pay." According to her obituary, she often shared her scanty supplies with those who were more hungry than she was.

After Jonathan was discharged on June 16, he traveled northward to Sacramento and Sutter's Mill and made shoes in the area during the winter. On July 2, 1848, a group of forty-six battalion veterans departed for Salt Lake, and Jonathan soon replaced the murdered Daniel Browett as leader of the company. With no road or guide, these men blazed a trail across the Sierras that was later used by thousands of travelers to California (the Carson Pass). In October they reached the Salt Lake Valley, and the small Holmes family was re-united after their individual overland odysseys. Now Elvira would have a companion to help her support Sarah, and the Holmes family could begin to grow again.

On December 23 Patty Sessions and possibly Eliza Snow came to Elvira's dwelling "to celebrate Joseph Smiths birthday," as Patty wrote. As we have seen, Smith's widows would frequently meet on his birthday or the day of his death to remember their prophet husband. Patty also visited Elvira on February 24, 1849, and Eliza Partridge frequently stopped at the Holmes residence. On April 18 she wrote, "Called on Sister Holmes in the evening. We are spinning some candle wick which we shall try to sell for bread stuff." She recorded an apparent blessing meeting at the Holmes residence on May 2: "Went to the Fort and visited at Sister Holmes' with sisters Fuller and E. R. Snow. Had quite a rain with high cold wind." On June 27 Elvira hosted a meeting of Smith wives, recorded by Patty Sessions: "Visited at sister Holmes with Sister E R Snow and Love and many others it being 5 years this day since the Prophets were martyred."

Elvira's second child, Marietta Holmes, named after Jonathan's first wife, was born at the Old Fort on July 17. Patty Sessions delivered: "Put

Sister Holms to bed with a daughter born 6 AM." On September 13 Patty wrote, "I must go and see sister Holmes babe it is sick." Fortunately Marietta recovered.

## XI. Weaver

Soon after this, probably in May or June, the Holmes family moved to Farmington, ten miles north of Salt Lake City, where they built a "two-story rock building" and worked a small farm, producing and selling butter and cheese. The Holmes dairy operation is attested by an entry in the Eliza Partridge journal: "Sister Caroline and I are weaving for Sister Elvira Holmes, to pay for butter, cheese and flour." Elvira also was a weaver. According to her daughter, Phebe, "She was a weaver by occupation and in her time she wove all kinds of weaves, from bed counterpanes to men's wear, women's out and underwear, table linen, towels and gingham for aprons. My father raised sheep and flax from which she made cloth, thread and head- and footwear." At times Elvira returned to her old profession of schoolteaching in Farmington.

The Holmeses were active in local church activities. When the Relief Society was organized in Farmington, Elvira was one of its first teachers. Jonathan, who continued shoemaking as well as farming, was a long-time member of the Davis Stake High Council.

Another daughter, Phebe Louisa, was born on February 5, 1851. The 1851 census shows the Holmes family as follows: Elvira thirty-seven; Sarah thirteen; Mariette one; Phebe one month. Two more daughters followed—Josephine Octavia Ann Holmes on July 8, 1854, and Emma Lucinda, Elvira's last child, on February 1, 1856. Elvira was forty-two at the time of Emma's birth, Sarah was seventeen, Marietta seven, Phebe five, and Josephine nearly two. Elvira and Jonathan had no sons, but they adopted a boy, John Hendricks, who kept his own name. According to family biography, Elvira's daughters herded sheep and helped to shear them: "They learned carding, spinning, weaving, and sewing." Phebe and Emma followed another of their mother's professions, becoming teachers. In 1857 Josephine died at the age of three, so Elvira endured the ordeal of losing a child one more time.

She became a plural wife once again on November 29, 1862, when Jonathan, fifty-five, married Sarah Ingersoll Harvey Floyd, a forty-five-year old widow. There are no family traditions documenting the relationship between the two sister-wives.

Elvira and Jonathan made frequent visits to Salt Lake proper and therefore continue to appear in Patty Sessions's diary. In February 1859 Jonathan bought peaches from Patty and trimmed her trees for weeks following. Eliza Snow, Zina Young, and Zina's children visited Farmington on May 21 and, wrote Zina, "took dinner with Johnathan

Ho[l]mes old acquaintence." Elvira visited Patty on August 1, 1863, and stayed overnight at her house. Two days later there was another gathering of Smith widows. Patty wrote, "I went with sister Holmes to Prs B Youngs visited sisters Margaret & Snow and Zina then to Sister Cob and Chase I then came home." Elvira was now fifty.

## XII. New Generation of Plurality

The rest of Elvira's life is to a great degree bound up with the lives of her children. Her stepdaughter and her own daughters married polygamously, though in a somewhat surprising fashion. In contrast to some of the polygamous wives studied in this book, they were all apparently happy in their marriages. The Holmes daughters give a striking view of polygamy creating or cementing sisterhood in a familial context.

On January 7, 1855, Elvira's step-daughter, Sarah Elizabeth, married Miles Weaver, who was already married to another Sarah, Sarah Clark. The two wives were playfully called the "White Sarah" and "Black Sarah" in the neighborhood because of their complexions. Unfortunately Miles died on December 7, and (according to family tradition) his brother, Franklin Weaver, was advised by Brigham Young to marry Miles's two widows. However, he was reluctant because he had promised his first wife, Cristinna Reed, that he would not ask her to live polygamously.

Soon Franklin was assigned to help settle Millville, Cache Valley, north of Ogden. As he and his family prepared to go, one day he came home to find Cristinna in tears. Having no idea why she was weeping, he tried to console her, but was surprised when she blurted out, "I will go to Cache Valley with you if you will marry those girls and take them, too." The monogamous wife could not bear to be separated from her sisters-in-law. So on May 9, 1856, Franklin married the two Sarahs in a precise Levirate marriage, and the newly enlarged family went north to help settle Millville. This is a notable inversion of the classic polygamy story in which the husband marries without the first wife's knowledge, leaving her emotionally devastated and feeling displaced when she learns about the marriage. Cristinna, in contrast, was upset when Franklin was *not* going to take his sisters-in-law as plural wives. Of course, these women were not strangers, which probably made a great deal of difference, and Franklin had been honest with Cristinna and concerned for her feelings.

On May 12, 1866, when Elvira was fifty-two, her first biological child to grow to maturity, Marietta, aged sixteen, married Job Welling, an English convert and tailor and a widower with two small children, Willard and Annie. So Elvira's daughter followed another Cowles tradition and became a stepmother. Marietta and Job would add eight children to the Welling family. Four years later, on December 21, 1868, two of Elvira's daughters became polygamous wives at the same time, when Phebe, age seventeen, married Job Welling in the Endowment House in Salt Lake City. They returned home the same night to join a dancing party at Farmington. Family history reports: "As the surprising news leaked out they became special guests, or at least claimed special attention and congratulations." Phebe would also bear eight children to Job.

### XIII. "Kind Wife and Affectionate Mother"

At some point in the following year, Elvira became sick with "exposure" (apparently tuberculosis), and soon the family realized that she was dying. At this moment we are reminded once again of the importance a marriage to Joseph Smith had to Mormons of this era. According to family traditions, "During her last sickness her husband ... in humility and sorrow at [the] thought of her passing, asked her what reports she would give to the Prophet Joseph. She replied, 'Only the best report. You have always been a kind and devoted husband and father.'" Joseph's wives were often seen as otherworldly intermediaries to their prophet husband.

According to her obituary, Elvira "retained the full strength of her mind to the last, and continued to bear a powerful testimony to those around her to the truth of the plan of salvation, and gently fell asleep in a sure and certain hope of a glorious resurrection." She died on March 10, 1871, in Farmington, at age fifty-seven. Cause of death was given as "Consumption" (tuberculosis). She was buried in the Farmington cemetery two days later. An obituary provides a fitting tribute: "Faith, hope, and charity were the chief traits of her character through life ... She has ever proved herself a kind wife, affectionate mother, and a generous, kind-hearted neighbor."

### XIV. "My Own Dear M. P. E."

Elvira's story, proper, is over, but two familial loose ends should be tied up here. On April 28, 1875, at age nineteen, Emma Lucinda, Elvira's last child, joined her sisters in the family of Job Welling. "Tradition has it that her sisters used loving persuasion to encourage her to accept ... [Job Welling's] proposal of marriage ... Lucinda gave up her ambition for teaching and turned her interest to matrimony." Welling was called to go on a mission to Great Britain soon after this third marriage and addressed his letters home to "My own dear M. P. E. [Marietta, Phebe, Emma]." Once again polygamy was used by women to promote ties of (here, literal) sisterhood. Emma bore Job five children to add to Marietta's and Phebe's sixteen.

Jonathan passed away on August 18, 1880, nine years after Elvira's death. Apostle Wilford Woodruff, an old friend, traveled to Centerville to speak at the funeral. When he visited the Holmes household, he wrote, "I found his [wife] in deep mourning for his death." Elvira, Jonathan, and Sarah Harvey now lie together in the Farmington cemetery.

## XV. Elvira and Polygamy

The life of Elvira Holmes Smith, though she was a quiet woman, underdocumented and unheralded, has considerable significance. First, her marriages to Jonathan Holmes and Joseph Smith provide another case study in polyandry, showing how devoted to Joseph Smith a "first husband" could be. Jonathan was a faithful Mormon, served as a bodyguard to Smith, acted as his pallbearer, stood as proxy when Elvira was sealed to Smith in the Nauvoo temple, then begged for Elvira's good report to the prophet on her deathbed. These data are all consistent with the theory that first husbands in polyandrous triangles may have known of Joseph Smith's marriages to their wives and permitted them.

Second, Elvira's story stands out from those of most of Smith's other wives because of its mostly peaceful, idyllic tenor. She did lose two of her five children, but she nevertheless had a full motherhood, raising three daughters, a step-daughter, and a foster-son. The lives of Louisa Beaman, Presendia Huntington, Helen Mar Kimball, and the Sessions women, all of whom lost a majority of their children, provide a striking contrast. And unlike many of the women in this book, Elvira's experiences with polygamy were not traumatic, as far as is known. She lived in a monogamous marriage for many years, and when Jonathan did become a polygamist, he married only one middle-aged plural wife. He probably was not required to take more wives because he was not a general authority—or possibly his church advancement was hindered because he was reluctant to take plural wives. So Elvira's marriage experience was radically different from that of Smith's widows who married Brigham Young or Heber Kimball, who shared their husband and his resources with twenty to thirty other women, counting only connubial wives. However, Elvira, married to a non-polygamist who became a very limited polygamist, did not achieve the status of an Eliza Snow Smith or Zina Huntington Young in the woman's movement in Mormonism. Polygamy, for women as for men, was a road to status, practically speaking.

Finally, the story of Elvira's daughters gives a remarkable view of women seeking polygamy to increase bonds of sisterhood. Cristinna Reed Weaver used polygamy to strengthen her ties with two sisters-in-law, one of whom was Sarah Holmes Weaver, while Elvira's three daughters followed the same course to preserve their actual, biological sisterhood. Polygamy often produced deep-seated tensions between sister-wives, but the story of Elvira Cowles Holmes and her daughters highlights the bonding, warm side of the feminine experience in polygamy.

# 25.

# "Tried in Many Ways"

## *Rhoda Richards (Smith Young)*

On the morning of New Year's Day 1875, the elderly Rhoda Richards sat in her warm, comfortable room in downtown Salt Lake City. Seriously ill virtually throughout her life, she had somehow survived all her sicknesses to reach her ninth decade. She sat in a rocker and looked out the window at the urban winter scene. Children were beginning to play in the streets outside, and holiday laughter resounded. Horse-drawn sleighs slid along the street as family and friends visited each other.

She, however, was solemn. As Rhoda witnessed the joy outside her room, tears began to glisten in her eyes. She reached for her diary, turned to the date, December 30, 1814, and read once more of Ebenezer Damon's death sixty years earlier. He had been the sweetheart of her youth, and they had been close to marriage when a sudden illness claimed him. So he had died, and she, the sickly one, lived more than half a century longer. The funeral was held two days after his death, on January 1, and she had mourned him every New Year's Day for the rest of her life.

Rhoda was one of Joseph Smith's older wives, and their marriage is a pure example of dynastic matrimony, as she linked Smith to her brother, Apostle Willard Richards, the prophet's scribe and disciple. As was often the case with dynastic marriages, the participants respected each other, but there was no romantic involvement in the union. The same was true of Rhoda's marriage for time to Brigham Young, her cousin. In fact, she apparently never or very rarely lived in Brigham's family after the ceremony and was never known publicly as his wife. Instead, she lived with Richards relatives, a typical case of polygamous distance from a husband. Rhoda entered matrimony with two men, one of whom she expected to be married to in eternity, but it was the fiancé whom she almost married who held her heart throughout her life.

## I. "Never So Happy"

Rhoda was born on August 8, 1784, at Framingham, Middlesex, Massachusetts, ten miles west of Boston, to Joseph Richards and Rhoda Howe, both twenty-two. Rhoda Howe was the sister of Abigail Howe Young, the mother of Brigham Young. The younger Rhoda was the second child in a family of eleven. Her older brother, Joseph Jr., had been born in 1782, and a sister, Susanna, was born in 1786.

The Richards family then moved to Hopkinton, five miles southwest of Framingham, where Phinehas was born in 1788. Levi was born in 1790 but died on June 7, 1795, when Rhoda was ten. Three sisters, Nancy, Hepzibah, and Betsey, followed in 1792, 1795, and 1797, though Betsey died on December 12, 1803, when Rhoda was nineteen. A second Levi, who became well known in Mormon history as a doctor, was born in 1799. Finally two sons joined the Richardses: William in 1801, and the baby of the family, Willard, in 1804.

As an older child in a large family, Rhoda undoubtedly spent much of her adolescent years tending her younger siblings. She learned to work hard at an early age, she reports:

> When myself and my sisters were small girls, our excellent mother taught us how to work, and in such a wise manner did she conduct our home education that we always loved to work, and were never so happy as when we were most usefully employed. We knit our own and our brothers' stockings, made our own clothes, braided and sewed straw hats and bonnets, carded, spun, wove, kept house, and did everything that girls and women of a self-sustaining community need to do.

She was an indefatigable worker throughout her life and was enormously proud of it. In her childhood, and throughout the rest of her life, she was often sick, but this did not stop her from working. According to a niece's reminiscence, as a teenager Rhoda would get up in the morning feeling "too sick and miserable" to work but would nevertheless volunteer to do the washing. Her mother would reply, "Well, Rhoda, I expect a good day's work done today, because you always work well when you are sick." And "her mother's suggestion never failed to come true." Nineteenth-century housewives and farmwives often found a deep sense of self-worth in their household responsibilities, which were not seen as mere drudgery. We remember Helen Mar Kimball's intense feeling of uselessness after the death of her husband, for instance. Emily Dow, on the other hand, protested the inequality of female and male workloads.

The niece, Lula Richards Greene, wrote that Rhoda had "a good, common education." She penned many literate, lively letters throughout her life, some of which are extant. Lula described the young and middle-aged Rhoda: "When grown she was a little below medium height, possessed a

small trim figure and a face usually expressive of innocent fun and mer-
riment. Her eyes were dark and brilliant ... she was a girl and a woman
of rare beauty."

## II. "I Was Taken Verry Bad in Great Distress"

Rhoda's autobiography starts in 1802 when she was seventeen. Its
first paragraph is representative of Rhoda's life writings, which often
read like a medical history:

> I left home a sudden shower arose the rain poured before I reached the
> place had not a dry thing on me took a sudden cold was taken sick
> confined to my bed for many weeks before I could be moved home. My
> parents called a council of Dr [doctors] they said they never knew one
> as far gone as I was with the dropsy to get well. They put me upon
> {F}oxglove one drop to commence with I was to take it three times a
> day increasing every time. The last time I took one hundred and fifty
> {drops}, was reduced to a mere skeleton all but blind ... At the com-
> mencement my system was completely filled with water.

Rhoda survived this treatment, as well as the other major event of
1802—an incursion of measles into the Richards family in which she "all
but died." The following year, as she and her parents started on a trip to
her aunt and uncle Leadbetter in Richmond, western Massachusetts,
Rhoda came down with a case of the mumps and fever. When it came
time to return home, the Leadbetters offered to let her stay with them
until she had fully recovered. Soon Rhoda was well enough to make
straw bonnets, which were a novelty in that area. "I made far the first
class," she reported matter-of-factly, and "took eighty dollars in silver the
first year had a pleasant time."

In 1804 her uncle "Col. Wm. Richards" invited her to stay with his
family in Hinsdale, ten miles northeast of Richmond, for a year. "I excepted his kind invitation with a grateful heart, went and spent a few
weeks verry pleasantly with my Uncle Aunt and Cousins," she wrote.
But then she was extremely ill for three weeks and apparently had a near
death experience:

> I see my body there, the spirit had I thought left. In a short time I was
> taken verry bad in great distress. I wanted they should lift me out of bed.
> they did I fainted. they laid me back. I wanted to be taken out they took
> me I fainted they laid me back. I lay there seven hours without the least
> motion sometimes ... by holding a feather at my Mouth or nose they
> would think I breathed a little then they would say she is gone. I heard
> all that was said.

A doctor arrived and prescribed "sixteen portions of what was
called medicine ... King calamil and all of his cousins." This treatment

caused Rhoda "awful spasams," but, despite her brush with death, and despite the doctor's ministrations, she regained her health. These histories of medical treatment are thinly disguised attacks on "poison doctors," as opposed to Thomsonian, herbal medicine, which her younger brothers later practiced.

Rhoda returned to the Leadbetter household for a year, then she and her aunt traveled back to Hopkinton. During her absence Willard had been born, and she was acquainted with him only by correspondence. When she made her joyful reunion with her family in late 1806, Willard was two and a half, she twenty-two. She later wrote: "He had sent me word if I would come home he would hug and kiss untill he would almost brake my neck. I reminded him of his promise he came at me his arms tight around my neck and put on the kisses untill I had to call for help he jumps away there he says have I not done it I told [him] he had."

But Rhoda did not stay with her family. When her aunt returned to Richmond, Rhoda accompanied her to help her run her dairy business. Her medical diagnosis for this period: "had frequent turns of sick headach a constant pain in the side, had one sick spell." However, when Rhoda received news that four of her siblings had contracted "the Typhus fever," she returned to Hopkinton, where she tended her brothers and sisters at night. After making a fire to neutralize the cold winter weather, she lay with an hourglass by her head and rose hourly to look after her siblings. She proudly wrote of her efforts: "I followed it so eleven nights. I was up before the sand stoped all but twice."

### III. "My Fond Hopes Were Then Blasted"

The autobiography presents a lacuna for the years 1807 to 1811, but Rhoda evidently returned to the Leadbetters during that time. At some point she fell in love with and became engaged to Ebenezer Damon, a widower with one daughter, Susan. Lula Greene wrote, "Ebenezer Damon was a man of sterling worth and integrity whom Aunt Rhoda loved as such a woman loves but once in a life time." When Rhoda's diary begins in June 1812, she and Ebenezer were visiting relatives together: "I left Richmond with Mr Eben[e]zer Damon. Went to Warwick to his uncle Barbers. From there to Orange spent the 4 of July. From there to my Fathers in Holliston."

The major event of early 1813 was Rhoda nursing three-and-a-half-year-old Susan through a bout of "Hooping cough" for three weeks in May. "It was more than I could do to take care of her," she wrote, but she managed somehow. Nineteenth-century women underwent serious illnesses far more frequently than twentieth-century women and endured the exhausting and nerve-racking ordeal of tending their seriously ill children more often. Of course, mothers and children also frequently died.

In December 1813 the great tragic event of Rhoda's life occurred when she was staying with the Richards family in Holliston. After a long engagement, she and Ebenezer were due to be married soon. He arrived in Holliston on December 15 but was feverish and had been so for two weeks after taking a chill in Boston. He was immediately bedridden in the Richards household. Rhoda and mother Richards gave him constant attention, but Christmas did not find him in good health. However, on December 29 he showed signs of improvement, so Rhoda and Rhoda Howe hoped that he would be up again soon.

The next day at sunrise Ebenezer asked to be brought out of bed. Joseph Richards and Rhoda lifted him into a nearby chair and she changed his linen, then helped lay him back down. "Before the head was placed on the pillow he said what does ail me I never felt so in my life, setled into bed then was gone." As he lost consciousness and perhaps stopped breathing, Rhoda and her family worked frantically to revive him. "Mother stepped into the room took a bottle of sperits poured it in his bosom, he revived, and said cant you give me something. I put some wine to his mouth he said that wine would not do." Evidently he tried to vomit, but there was nothing in his stomach. Then:

> He setled down into bed a flush came over his cheeke, Mother says to him (as his eyes were fixed on her) you do feel a little better dont you Mr Damon. He turned his eyes from her on me and said, (dont say better) turned his head round a little gasped but twice and was gone. As he was so comfortable the evening before we thought he would soon be up with us, it was the more suddin and dreadful. My fond hopes were then blasted. For what. God only knows.

On New Year's Day "Mr Damons remains were deposited near the meeting house in Holliston," wrote Rhoda. "Farewell to all joys, my comforts are fled. The friend of my choice is now numbered with the dead." So occurred the first of many years of New Year's Day mourning.

A week later Rhoda underwent a serious bout of fever herself but soon recovered. In March she received a moving letter of consolation from her widowed aunt, Susanna Brigam, who had helped raise Susan: "O Rhoda," she wrote,

> when I was called to peart with your Dear uncle the wourld looked like adrearry waste to me & we can & doo heartily simpathise with you in yoᵘr trouble ... I judge not the {God} by feeble Sence/ but trust him for his grace/ behind afrowning providence/ he hides his smiling face it is asolmn warning to us when ᵂᵉ our near & dear friends are called from us and consined to the cold and Silent mancions of the grave we feal as if we had lost avery dear friend in the death of Mr damon O that we could See yu and the family.

Evidently Susan went to live with Aunt Brigham, but Rhoda visited her frequently.

Now twenty-nine, Rhoda stayed in Holliston with the Richards family. Her youngest sibling, Willard, was now ten. In March 1815 the family moved west to Richmond, which was "a trying scene," wrote Rhoda. After staying behind for two months, she traveled to Richmond with Phinehas, though returning to the place where she had intended to live with Ebenezer was an ordeal to her: "I returned to the place that I had left, with bright prospects before me as I thought, they were blasted."

## IV. "I Drank of the Pure Water"

Another lacuna appears in the autobiography, with pages apparently missing. When it begins again in 1819 or 1820, Rhoda seems to be describing a visionary dream in which a supernatural being offered to transport her to "the rock" where she could drink the water of salvation. "I could not be more wretched than I was  I gave him my hand and sailed along over the beings that looked like devils chained down round their waiste  they made a mighty effort to take me  I had no fears  my feet were set upon the rock. I drank of the pure water." She apparently had experienced a spiritual rebirth as a result of the preaching of a "Mr. Kelloge." Regarding one gathering, she wrote with the ecstatic rapture of the new convert: "I rode home  got br William and sister Hepsy and returned to the meeting  it was a precious meeting to me, the next morning I felt that I was in a new world  everything was praiseing God  my soul was filled with Joy." So we enter the world of Protestant spiritual rebirth so prevalent in nineteenth-century frontier America, the seeding ground for Mormonism.

In late 1820 Rhoda, now thirty-six, journeyed to Eaton, where Susan Damon and "Aunt Brigham" lived, to stay the winter, but the following spring she returned to Richmond. In June she visited New York to witness the marriage of her cousin, Susan Young, to James Little. There she renewed her friendship with three cousins: "Fanny [and] Joseph [and] Brigham"—a future sister-wife, her future guide into Mormonism, and a future polygamous husband. On returning home, she wrote, "I found my Parents in a new home & {felt} to rejoice in a quiet family circle."

## V. "A Cancer Broke Out on My Side"

The autobiography now skips to 1823, when Rhoda was thirty-nine. At that time, she wrote, "a cancer broke out on my side. I had a long fit of sickness." She was bedridden for six months. Although a council of doctors prescribed calomel, it had no effect on the illness and she stayed in bed for another twelve months "without being able to walk or set my feet." Then she attempted to rise and move around slowly. She remembered an insensitive comment a friend of her mother made which deeply pained her: "Mrs. Richards I never see any one that enjoys a sick bed but Rhoda she always appears to enjoy it."

Evidently Rhoda did not tell her mother what was ailing her. When some relatives came to visit, "In the course of the visit some one spoke of a person having a cancer my mother said she did not know of anything that would strike such a dread upon her as to know that she had a cancer or any of her family. I had heard her express the same feeling before. How could I wound her feelings. I thought it wisdom for me to keep it from her." So Rhoda struggled for four years, keeping her spirits up somehow. "Indeed," she wrote, "many would have felt discouraged it was not me I never viewed death near." But finally, in the summer of 1827, when Rhoda was forty-three, a doctor, and friends who knew her ailment, urged "a speedy removal of my cancer." She consented to the procedure, even though she felt that death might be preferable.

She described the gruesome operation in unflinching detail. Dr. Bachelor, head of the Pittsfield medical school, operated, attended by two other doctors and a medical student, with ten of Rhoda's siblings and friends observing. She saw one of the doctors stirring something in a cup and asked, "Dr. what have you there so good?" He replied, "Some Laudnum for you." But Rhoda told him he "could do what he pleasd with it for I should not taste one drop saying to him if I die I wish to be sensible of my situation." He replied that she had better drink it, but she refused and instead went to her room to drink five cups of strong tea. Her sister Nancy Peirson then came to her room and said, "Sister they are ready if you are." Rhoda wrote, "I entered the room gave the Doctor my hand steped up on the chair seated myself on the table that was prepared for me. And when lying down I thought it was like lying down in my coffin."

The first operation lasted eleven minutes, and Rhoda stated that she groaned throughout and screamed twice. Then she was given a glass of wine, and a down quilt was put over her so she would not catch a chill. The second operation, which lasted twelve minutes, soon followed, "cutting, digging, scrapeing tying. (I was afterward told the big artery was carelessly cut off after it was tied.) I lay in that horrid place over an hour." Her only effort was to hold the doctor's hand. "I was in perfect agony during the examination of the part removed. I was then laid into bed. I sent for my Parents they came I spoke with them, then I could not speak loud a low whisper."

The operation was apparently successful—at least, it did not kill her. She spent the winter bedridden, with friends and family tending her: "I did not speak a loud word during the winter, three weeks I could not uter a whisper." One of her arms was evidently paralyzed also. But in June 1828 she was able to travel, and Willard, now twenty-four, took her to sulphur springs in Chittenango, New York. In two months she could speak again, and "warm shower baths" restored her arm to full use once more. She visited a friend in Madison, then returned home in mid-September with improved health.

That winter her mother, her sister Susanah, and a visiting niece, Elizabeth, became seriously ill, and Rhoda and Hepsibah "had all they could do" to take care of them. In 1829 Rhoda visited a "sister Benson," but was soon called home to tend Susanah and Elizabeth who were ill again. Another ordeal of exhaustion and tension faced her. On New Year's Day 1830, she wrote, "Sister Susan desired me to take care of her day and night not to leave her I did for eleven week[s] br Levi assisted in lifting and helping me. Elisebeth was very sick ... At night if she slept a moment I droped on another bed. Whe[n] [she was] awake I was up." Susan lingered until the spring, then, on April 10, whispered in Rhoda's ear, "I think my frends will have no reason to mourn for me after the agony of death is past." The next day she died peacefully. Rhoda grieved, but a burden was lifted from her shoulders.

In the summer she traveled with Willard to the Chittenango sulphur springs again and returned home feeling better. Later in the year her sister-in-law remarked that she looked young and did not show her age (she was forty-six). Father Richards answered, "Do you know the reason why?" "I do not," answered the sister-in-law. "I do not either, only that she is always sick or taking care of the sick," he replied wryly.

In June 1832 she found herself failing again, this time from "the loss of appetite a bad liver, and anguish of a remaining cancer, and ... disease upon the kidneys." Once again she turned to doctors, who prescribed "bleeding, blistering, Tanter Emetic[,] licuta, stramoniam." At one point, she remembers, a doctor drew a large "blister" on her stomach and covered it with "spanish flies," then peeled off her skin "to make sores." She would later point out seventy scars on her stomach as a result of this "treatment." In the fall a cancer seemed to locate on Rhoda's right side. One doctor prescribed licuta pills, which she took for some two and a half years. But she began to lose her sight as a result and became convinced that continued treatment by "poison" doctors would kill her. Willard, however, was studying at "Doctor Thomsons Infirmary" in Boston and would soon become a devoted proponent and practitioner of Thomsonian, herbal medical practice, so she turned toward Thomsonian regimens.

In 1834 we begin to have authentic diary entries in Rhoda's autobiography. On May 8 she wrote, "Went to Uncle Leadbetters Aunt was sick the weather severe. I was sick and a cold snow storm." A week later "I rode home with brother William and sister Hepsy." She was now approaching fifty, old age by nineteenth-century American standards, but she had not yet begun the eventful Mormon era of her life.

### VI. First Mormon Sermon

Rhoda had been hearing curious stories about the new religious sect, the Mormons, in the early 1830s, then heard troubling rumors that some of the Youngs had joined. In 1835 or 1836, as she lay "on a bed of sickness," Joseph Young came to visit. After the Richards clan chatted with him for a while, Mother Richards cautiously broached the subject of Mormonism.

"Joseph," she said, "I have heard that some of the children of my sister, Abigail Young, have joined the Mormons. How is it?"

Joseph startled them by replying, "It is true, Aunt Richards, and I am one of them!"

Joseph attended church with the Richardses on Sunday morning, but stayed home for the afternoon meeting, saying he could not enjoy it. "I do not see why we might not have a meeting here," Rhoda replied. "My cousin was upon his feet in an instant, and stood and preached to us—my brother and myself—for about half an hour, finishing his discourse with, 'There, Cousin Rhoda, I don't know but I have tired you out!'" Rhoda suggested that meetings usually closed with a prayer. "In an instant he was on his knees, offering up a prayer. That was the first Mormon sermon and the first Mormon prayer I ever listened to." So Rhoda was introduced to this strange new religious phenomenon. She pondered her cousin's words carefully, and soon believed, though she would not formally convert for more than a year. In October or November 1836 Levi, Willard, Phinehas, and "Hepsy" visited Kirtland to meet the Mormon prophet and see the city. Levi and Willard were baptized on December 31. Thereafter Rhoda was constantly exposed to the preaching of Youngs and Richardses.

Meanwhile her ordinary life continued. In May 1837 she and Willard traveled east to visit friends and relatives, and when they returned, Willard gave her "twelve courses" of Thomsonian medicine. Later in the year she took a railroad trip to New York, met with "the Saints," and returned with improved health. On February 14, 1838, her mother died "after a short but distressing sickness" at age seventy-five. Four days later Rhoda herself became very sick with what she termed "a complete Hydrophobia"—"about two raging fitts in a week jaws set eyes closed at the least touch. In short the most horrid sensations, better felt than described." But by spring she had recovered.

On June 2 Rhoda was ready to become a Mormon. She wrote, "Sister

Nancy and myself were Baptized by hand of br Phinehas. Just below the garden a few steps from my Fathers door." She immediately received spiritual and physical blessings: "In obeying the commands [of the Lord] I found great good. [Health was improved  poison disappeared  the cake of ice was melted from my stomach.] The Lord had a blessing in store for me  I had no need of medicine  worked all summer made cheese ... [spun a peice of flannel for my brothers]  [many days] did two days work in one." Hepsibah was baptized six days later. Hepsy and Levi then left for Missouri, but sadly, Hepsy died there of malaria on September 30.

In a late reminiscence Rhoda remembered that a "cancer rash" broke out on her face at about this time. Dreading another operation, she decided to turn to God for assistance. One Sunday, after Mormon branch meetings, she told the presiding elder about her problem. He immediately asked the women in the meeting to unite their faith and prayers on her behalf, then asked the brethren to administer to her. According to Rhoda's memories, "It was done, and I went home completely healed, and rejoicing in the God of my salvation."

Perhaps feeling the loss of her mother, on October 21, 1838, she wrote to her brother Levi in England: "I am now at Brother P[hinehas's] ... Do, Do, Do, say something to yur poor Mormon sister ... The work that mother and I did together last fall I have all charge of now. I am on my feet from 15 to 19 hours in a day."

In March 1839 Rhoda tended her uncle Leadbetter when he had his right hand amputated due to a cancerous sore. In September she made a trip to the East. Though she had been suffering from "weakness and distress at the lungs," her health improved as she returned home. But in mid-October she came down with scarlet fever and "cancer rash." The Thomsonian cureall, lobelia, healed her, she reported.

She and her niece, Eliza Ann Peirson, returned to live with Father Richards in December. She turned to introspection as she entered the Richards home: "I went into my chamber and sat down in solitude  no mother, wondering what I was spared for. God only knew and if I was his all was well, he had been verry merciful in restoring me." Father Richards soon followed his wife, becoming ill in mid-March 1840, and dying on March 29 at age seventy-eight. Rhoda, now fifty-four, described his passing:

> At half past six a visible change took place  death appeared to be near  blood setled under his nails  feet cold  his throat filling up  breathing shorter and shorter untill half past six he looked up {at} sister and said farewell Nancy, he tried to say a great deal to us but we could not understand. He continued to breathe shorter and shorter untill ten minuets past nine then went as a candle goeth out with a smile upon his countenance.

When father went I felt that my cup was full, my Heavenly father has promised to be a father to the fatherless & the orphans friend  The promise I claimed & wiped away my tears.

After this Rhoda lived the rest of her life in the homes of her brothers and sisters. By all reports, she was a hard-working and beloved guest.

Her thoughts turned to Zion, where many of her siblings had already gathered. In the meantime she was active in her local branch. On April 19 she wrote, "A Church was organized and called the Union branch of Westblackledge and Richmond, the sacrament administered a precious season. I had hands laid on me twice for which I desire to praise the Lord for his blessing." The journal tells of visits from family and friends, her sicknesses, her friends' sicknesses, her chores (washing, ironing, repairing caps, sewing, quilting, etc.), deaths, funerals. One entry from February 12 shows her in a moment of low spirits: "Another week has taken its flight never to return. It is sorrow toil and pain. Who on this Earth could desire to live them over again." In June Willard paid a visit.

### VII. Two Marriages

There is another gap in Rhoda's diaries, and when they begin again in January 1843 she is in Nauvoo. But this lacuna is filled partly by a diaristic letter she wrote to Nancy describing her journey to Illinois. She and Willard—who had been ordained an apostle in 1839—left Massachusetts on September 25, 1842, to visit the Saints in New York City, Philadelphia, and Pittsburgh. They then traveled west by train and boat, following the Ohio River past Cincinnati and Louisville until they reached the Mississippi River at the southern tip of Illinois on October 25. They exchanged a flatboat for a steamboat, and four days later reached Nauvoo, where they stayed with relatives.

Rhoda was fifty-eight when she reached the bustling Mormon city. Most entries in her Nauvoo journal are uneventful. She visited relatives, was ill occasionally, and worked constantly. She met Joseph Smith; on January 23, 1843, he appeared in her diary: "Brother Joseph and sister Emma call'd. Brother & sister Hyde." On May 1 she moved into "the Prophets store."

By virtue of being the sister of Willard Richards, who had married his first plural wife on January 18, 1843, Rhoda soon entered the inner circle of Nauvoo polygamy. Willard perhaps, or Joseph, may have suggested that the Richards and Smith families become linked through Rhoda, and she accepted the proposal. On June 12, 1843, she became Smith's twenty-eighth wife, approximately, with Willard performing the ceremony. She herself wrote of the event:

I have witnessed the death of many near and dear friends, both old and young. In my young days I buried my first and only love, and true to that affiance, I have passed companionless through life; but am sure of having my proper place and standing in the resurrection, having been sealed to the prophet Joseph, according to the celestial law, by his own request, under the inspiration of divine revelation.

It is striking that a woman who was married twice polygamously describes herself as passing "companionless" through life.

She continued to have health problems. On September 8 she wrote, "A blessing from the Prophet  he says I shall be well." On November 22 she moved to a home with Levi four blocks north of the temple. Levi married on Christmas Day, at age forty-three, but Rhoda apparently continued to live with the new couple, though she sometimes stayed with Willard.

On April 7, 1844, she wrote enthusiastically of a sermon by Joseph Smith: "heard br. Joseph the Prophet speak upon various subjects  glorious seasons blessed views, glorious prospects the saints have in view." But storm clouds were gathering around her eternal husband. On June 24 he and his brother Hyrum, and Rhoda's brother Willard, were imprisoned in Carthage, and three days later Joseph and Hyrum were mortally shot. On the 29th Rhoda viewed the bodies. She wrote, "Walked to brother Wd this morn  a most awful and solemn scene was before us the two marters  thousands upon thousands come to take their last leave. I then returned home."

The last entry in Rhoda's Nauvoo journal, on July 4, reflects the fear that Mormons felt in the aftermath of the martyrdom, and also shows her faith: "For three weeks we have lived to hear the awful threats of the mob that the city was to be laid in ashes such a night, the next that ther [their] men wimin and children were all to be distroyed, the next there was a certain number who would be slain within such a time, thus we are all spared ... The Lord reigns let every heart rejoice."

Now her life took another curious turn, as she married her cousin Brigham in early 1845, becoming his twenty-second wife, approximately. What Rhoda's relationship with the new church president was like after this is not precisely known, but it does not seem to have been intimate. She evidently continued to live with her brothers and saw Brigham socially, as she would a cousin. In later years she never or rarely lived in the Lion House, so this is one of those paradoxical polygamous marriages that almost does not seem a marriage.

After her journal ends, Willard's provides clues to some of her activities, such as visits with relatives and friends. On March 28, 1845, there was a family gathering at Willard's home: "Bro Levi. Phinehas & wives. & Rhoda & Samuel & Bullock & wife at supper." On July 9 Willard's first wife, Jennetta, died, and Rhoda joined with Patty Sessions and Elizabeth

Davis Durfee to prepare the body for the funeral. She herself was very sick on August 20, and Willard administered to her, after which the illness continued for two weeks; but by September 10 she was well enough to visit the Seventies Hall with her brother.

As the Mormons finished the temple and prepared to leave Nauvoo for the Far West, Rhoda was concerned with both endeavors. On January 10, 1846, she received her endowment, then her proxy marriage to Joseph and Brigham was resolemnized on January 31.

### VIII. "Mountain Fever ... Seasoned High with Cramp"

Rhoda left Nauvoo in a group headed by her brother Levi which reached Sugar Creek on May 28. Mary Haskin Parker Richards, first wife of her nephew Samuel Richards, wrote, "Was much pleased to see Aunt Rody ... who had reach'd the camp in the night." In early June the Levi Richards company probably reached Mt. Pisgah, for they left it on the 13th. By July 11 Rhoda was at Winter Quarters, where Mary found her "quite sick." But two days later she was "much better." On August 1 Rhoda was "in much pain," so Mary "rubed her from head. to foot" with spirits. "Got her some warm drink. & toast. at eve made her bed for her. also Aunt Sarahs." On December 6 Mary, visiting Levi's encampment, noted that sickness had kept Rhoda confined in her wagon for four weeks. By the last day of the year, however, the sickly woman was well enough to visit her brother Willard's camp with Mary, and asked Willard for a blessing, perhaps for her health: "Aunt Rhoda came & kneeled down by him & said she had bowed down on her benders to recieve a blessing."

In July 1847 Mary visited Rhoda again at the Levi Richards encampment and "had a good Chatt" with her, repeating the visit on October 23. She stayed overnight with her aging aunt on February 19, 1848, noting that Rhoda's health was "quite poor." On December 27, 1847, Willard was called to be a counselor to Brigham Young in the First Presidency, thus becoming the third man in the kingdom. He had acquired ten wives by now, a family befitting his high status.

In 1848 Levi and Sarah Richards were sent on a five-year mission to England. Rather than take their two-year-old son, Levi Willard, with them, they entrusted him to Rhoda, now sixty-four. On July 3 she and little Levi left Winter Quarters for Utah, traveling with Willard and one of his wives, Amelia Peirson, and Phinehas. Rhoda described the journey in a letter to her sister, Nancy. Two weeks after their departure, Levi Willard's foot slipped as he ran up the steps to the wagon, and he fell and broke his arm above the elbow. Brother Phinehas was sent for to set the bone. Rhoda wrote to Nancy, "He is a quick motioned child my greatest anxiety was that he might fall and break it over again ... I [now] think it

is as well as the other. He has been backward in talking but not in thinking and acting he is the picture of health."

On the 27th it began to rain, and the next night Rhoda went to bed
wet and without a warm supper, as all the fires had been extinguished.
Two days later she arose feeling sick but nevertheless helped Amelia by
cooking "cookes crakers and buiscuit." When the camp began to move
out, Rhoda fell into her bed in the wagon:

> I went to bed sick enough  was never out of my wagon but three times
> [for the rest of the journey] once the axletree broke, once to {repack}
> the wagon  once I think to try my strength  got out and back almost alone
> the result was another attack of the {dumb} ague. I had two spells of be-
> ing very sick  the last was mountain fever dumb ague seasoned high with
> cramp. I was sick enough to die many a time but I could not I was bound
> for the valley ... Weeks, I rolled in my bed dressed only $^{in}$ my loos gown
> night and day. Levi was hardly known to cry, was always happy in reading
> and talking about Pa and Ma.

So Rhoda crossed the plains in her inimitable sickly style. Her party
reached the valley on October 20.

## IX. "My House Stands on Wheels"

The immigrants camped for a few days, then moved onto lots, though
still living in their wagons. Soon afterwards they dined with the president
of the church. Rhoda wrote to Nancy, "Cousin Lorenzo took br. Willard
Amelia LW and myself in cousin Brigham['s] carriage to his house to dinner  had the company of the President and his lady. We dined on $^{\{trout\}}$ and
vegitables a fine dish of green peas  you may well think it was a treat." An
odd account of meeting one's husband after a long parting.

Rhoda gave a detailed description of her wagon-home in her first
weeks in Salt Lake:

> Early candle lighting. My chatterbox [Levi Willard] is in bed ... we are all
> in our wagons. I live in the one Amelia and I came in. My things are all in
> it piled to the ridgepost trunks boxes bags under the bed that is one half
> of the wagon. My bedstead is lying on the projection ... I make my bed for
> my boy and I[,] and the remainder of the room I pile mountain high ... the
> room I live in sitting back near the bed writing upon my low red chest
> and over that stands my cupboard. On the projection on the top I set a
> pan of milk ... At the end stands my cook stove with a good oven ... by the
> stove hearth there is just room for Levi Willard to run and look out when
> the curtain is up. His dress has caught fire many a time. I have to watch
> him like a cat watching a mouse ... Our parlour, dining room and kitchen
> are all comprised in one a little more than a yard square ... My house
> stands on wheels. We have some blows [of wind] that rock it like a cra-
> dle. What of that, our Father is at helm so [we] have nothing to fear.

She wrote again to Nancy on March 29, 1849: "It is a delightful {spring day} doors open no fire {people} plowing all around us not a particle of snow to be seen in the valley the green grass is springing up to cheer the hearts of man and beast. Snow covers the mountains all around us. To look out at my door it looks about as far as from your house to the top of the hill to go into Canaan."

Eventually Rhoda and young Levi moved out of her wagon and into a home, living with Willard near the temple block. We next meet her, once again seriously ill, in Zina Young's diary, on March 10, 1851. Zina had gone to visit Presendia with some of her friends and found that her sister and Elizabeth Ann Whitney had just been to Willard Richards's home: "Sister Rody Richards had ben struck with the palsy and was perfectly helpless they [Presendia and Elizabeth] washed & annointed her and she rose up and praised the Lord and walked talked cheerful and embrased her brother with a kiss the power of God was manifest in a wonderful {fashion} P & Sister Whitney were filled with the power of it still there countinance shone." On November 23, however, Rhoda was again very weak. She wrote to Levi and Sarah in England, "I am not able to walk abroad. Have enough to keep me busy at home. You would be surprised to see how I get along with so little strength."

In 1852 she wrote several times to Levi and Sarah, each time telling about her own illnesses and the activities of little Levi. On May 11 she reported that their son had had fever and a swollen throat, and that she had been up all night tending him. In September a house was being prepared and finished for Rhoda alone. She endured a severe attack of "Cholera Morbus," probably dysentery, on the 14th: "At one in the morn I awoke in great distress. Thought to strike a light. Set my foot upon the floor, struck blind, fell, and began to vomit." After twelve hours of agony, she recovered. On September 26 she wrote the Richardses that Levi had been troubled with canker and a cold but had recovered—"Eats wel and sleeps wel. Grows like a weed." Four days later she complained of the flies, which had arrived in August, and advised the Richardses to bring kitchenware of all kinds from England, as it was a scarcity in Salt Lake.

On March 11, 1854, her beloved brother Willard died at age fifty, so one of her most devoted companions was now gone. She herself was approaching seventy.

### X. "Ague My Companion, Poor Indeed Is Such Company"

During the last twenty-five years of her life, Rhoda continued to care for family and friends and to work hard amid constant illness. On September 29, 1854, Patty Sessions visited "Rhoda Richards boy," who was very sick. Perhaps Rhoda was now living with Levi and Sarah Richards, who had returned from England, and little Levi Willard. An August 8, 1855, entry in Zina Young's journal tells a great deal about the aging Rhoda: "I went to Aunt Rhoda Richards it was her birthday Presendia Ellen R Young and a few others ware [there] we cut and made her Temple suit beautiful linnen she is now 72 [71] smart takes all the care of 5 in family." So at seventy-one she was still active, taking care of the Levi Richards family and spending time in the Endowment House. On December 4 Zina visited "Aunt Rhoda" because she was seriously ill, and on June 10, 1856, Rhoda went to board with Patty Sessions for a time.

There is now another hiatus in documentation, but in 1860, when Rhoda was seventy-five, her diary begins again. She recorded that on May 11 she left "Brother Youngs" where she had been staying. Assuming that this is Brigham Young—it might have been one of his siblings—this is the only possible hint that she ever lived in her second husband's home. We do not know how long she stayed (presumably in the Lion House), but it could not have been long, for she does not appear in Lion House reminiscences. She then moved in with Willard's two children by Jeanette, Heber John and Rhoda Ann. The next day Levi Willard arrived "verry sick" and Rhoda tended him. A week later she scalded her foot badly with boiling lye water. On the 25th she visited Presendia Kimball and stayed with her a week; they often exchanged visits. She had a "crick" in her right shoulder on Pioneer Day, July 24: "It is bad [am] hardly able to move God is merciful I am thankful it is no worse I will praise the Lord let my heart and tongue praise him." Soon she felt "helpless," so the following day Zina Young brought Dr. Bernhisel to examine her.

Like many Nauvoo veterans, she continued to participate in blessing meetings. On August 22 she wrote, "Sisters Presendia and Zina have been here a blessed season what I have longed for." Her diary, as usual, chronicled her work in detail. On August 23 she was "Picking and washing wool, cooking and house work all comes in." Eliza Snow visited on March 14, 1861, and Rhoda put aside her household chores ("washing baking") to chat. Rhoda was very much part of the "female hierarchy." On May 31 she underwent another attack of the "cholera morbus," and on June 23 she had fever and chills: "ague my companion, poor indeed is such company."

She continued to work, exchanged visits with friends, and tended Levi Willard now and then throughout 1862. On May 17 Eliza Snow and Zina Young washed and anointed her for a sickness. As she prepared to move to Brother Levi's home on July 29, she wrote, "Thus ends the month of July so I leave this place in the morning and bid adieu to br Willard. farewell." In August Eliza, Zina, Lucia Foot (another close friend), and a number of her Richards kinsfolk gathered to celebrate her seventy-eighth birthday.

She moved back to Heber John's home on April 26, 1863, to assist the family there. Work entries continue to characterize the tone of her diary. For instance, on June 12 she "Finished spinning candle wick for Walker store forty eight ball."

In 1864 Rhoda proudly reflected on her life of work and service: "The day that I was thirteen years old I wove thirteen yards of cloth; and in twenty months, during which time I celebrated my eightieth birthday, I carded twenty weight of cotton, spun two hundred and fifteen balls of candlewicking, and two hundred run of yarn, prepared for the weaver's loom; besides doing my housework, knitting socks, and making shirts for 'my boys' (some of the sons of my brothers) ... I never was an idler." No one could ever accuse her of that. "I now begin to feel the weight of years upon me, and can no longer do as I have done in former years for those around me but, through the boundless mercies of God, I am still able to wash and iron my own clothes, do up my lace caps, and write my own letters. My memory is good, and as a general thing I feel well in body and mind."

She spent a great deal of time with Presendia and Zina. On July 31 she journalized, "Sister Persendia calld this eve welcome friend I have many and I desire to be truly thankful for the many blessing[s] I have." On her eightieth birthday two members of the First Presidency, cousin/husband Brigham and Heber Kimball, showed up for the party, along with many friends and relatives. "Is it possible that I was eighty years old on the 8," she wrote in amazement. "To day I am on a new year."

On December 8, as she contemplated moving to Levi's home, she looked back on her life with a certain melancholy:

> I have passed the remainder of this month the best way I could preparing to leave  I know that I have lived to see many years, and many changes. I once had a fathers house a home surrounded with kind friends. I have been tried in many ways yet I feel to rejoice and praise the Lord for his blessings that I am so happy as to be numbered with the saints ... Oh: my Father wilt thou keep me as in the hollow of thy hand suffer no evil to come near. May I so live as [to] be counted worthy of friends and a home with the saints. Adieu 1864.

The 1865 diary holds few surprises. There are days of illness (chills and fever, erysipelas), work days, and days filled with visiting, especially with Presendia. On April 30 Rhoda visited the Lion House with Lucia Foot, where she spoke with Brigham, then paid social calls on Lucy Decker, Zina, and Ellen Rockwood. August 21 preserves a unique entry:

"Spent a horrid night with bugs towards morn took to the floor got a nap." Patty Sessions had also complained of bedbugs in early Utah.

The years 1866-67 resemble 1865. On March 8, 1866, she wrote stoically, "My health is miserable part of the time the most of my sufferings I keep to myself." In December she underwent an attack of "chills, fever and shakes" for two weeks. On the 18th she "had Sisters Presendia and Zina [to visit] was washed and anointed. What a blessing to have such means to resort to in hour of distress." The illness "broke up" in two weeks, but she was left very weak. On July 31, 1867, she visited her husband, then walked with Zina to Willard's grave. A week later Zina, Presendia, and Eliza Snow helped celebrate her eighty-third birthday.

After 1867 the diary ends. We can reconstruct the rest of her life mostly from reminiscences of her relatives. At some point she moved into the home of Levi Willard, whom she had helped raise, and she spent the last years of her life with him. Remarkably enough, she outlived all of her brothers and sisters except for William in the East. Lula Greene wrote, "The eldest son of this nephew, Lee Greene Richards, was the last baby she petted and helped to amuse, he being about six months old at the time of her death."

Temple records for September 11, 1871, confirm Rhoda's involvement in sacral ordinances. "Rhoda Richards Smith, heiress," stood proxy as Brigham Young was sealed to Nancy Richards and Hepsabeth Richards, both dead. "Then, Rhoda was sealed to Joseph Smith, then stood proxy, with Brigham Young to seal Susan Richards to the Prophet Joseph." Emmeline Wells's diary documents Rhoda briefly in the 1870s. Emmeline and Elizabeth Whitney visited her on March 26 and April 14, 1875. They and selected friends helped celebrate her ninety-first birthday on August 8, 1877. Three weeks later, on the 29th, her second husband, Brigham Young, died, leaving her fully a widow once again.

Lula Greene wrote of the aged Rhoda that she refused to stop working, even when very weak: "Even after she was very old, over 90, Aunt Rhoda insisted upon washing her own clothes. When too feeble to leave her bed sometimes she would have a large pan of hot suds brought and placed where she could reach it. Then she would soap, soak and wash it with her own hands, always declaring it did her good. And frequently she would tell a story of her young life appropriate to the occasion."

### XI. "Still Send Sweet Odors Upward"

Rhoda had continued to mourn the death of Mr. Damon each January 1 until 1879, when she remarked, curiously enough, that "it was the first 'Happy New Year' she had known for sixty-six years. She said the snow looked exactly as it did the day 'Mr. Damon' was buried." On the afternoon of the 5th "she requested the presence of the family to witness her walking unaided across the room, a thing she had not been able to do for over a year until then." The next day, Lula wrote, "she wrote an encouraging letter to an afflicted friend in Dixie. This was the last work she performed on earth. That evening she complained of being hoarse, and said she had taken cold. From that time she gradually sank."

Lula was tending her on the 17th. In the morning she thought Rhoda looked better and asked her if she had improved, but the nonagenarian shook her head in a negative. The doctor had left medicine to give her at 10:00 and 1:00, but Rhoda was sleeping so peacefully at 1:00 that Lula could not bear to wake her. Lula wrote: "I sat watching her, and presently she said she wanted to get up. I called Julia to come and help me, and we got her up. She was very faint and could not sit up long. When we lifted her to lay her into her bed, she straightened herself and then fell out of our arms on to the bed and expired almost instantly ... Julia and I being alone with her were quite shocked at her sudden departure." The *Deseret Evening News* reported: "DIED ... In this city, Jan. 17, 1879, at the residence of her nephew, Levi W. Richards, 'aunt' RHODA RICHARDS, aged 94 years, 5 months and 9 days. Funeral services at the 20th Ward Schoolhouse, on Tuesday the 21st inst., at 12 o'clock. Relatives and friends are respectfully invited to attend."

Lula dreamed, not long afterwards, that a group of Rhoda's nieces gathered to inspect a piece of knitting she had completed just before her demise. "It was of 'curious workmanship,' a knitted vase containing a bouquet of beautiful roses. Each rose was a cup designed as a receptacle for some particular, small, useful article." The nieces expressed "wonder and admiration" for the piece, then asked, "What is the real significance of it all?" The dream answered, "The true interpretation of it is, The roses that she scattered/ In the pathway which she trod,/ Still send sweet odors upward,/ For Rhoda loved her God."

# 26.

# "Quiet, Unassuming, Faithful"

## *Desdemona Catlin Wadsworth Fullmer*
## *(Smith Benson McLane)*

By the time Desdemona Fullmer was thirteen, she was praying constantly in secret. She later wrote that one night after prayers "I d[r]eempt that I saw my[s]elf and a small compney of people moving into the wilderness that would live pure before the Lord." After this she thought deeply and seriously about religion and experienced a conversion of some sort, a "change of hart." She read the Bible diligently, studied the creeds of all churches, and prayed devoutly to find which one she should join—just as Joseph Smith did—on precisely the same path that many early Mormons followed. One day she was praying and fell to the ground unconscious. She lay there for several hours as if dead, then "Their was a voice said to me stop yet a little longer. their is something better for you yet ... so I stopt till I heard the laterday santes preach the gosple I joined them soon after."

Desdemona was thus a visionary woman who would continue to receive sacred dreams and "visitations of angels" throughout her life. She was a resolute Latter-day Saint believer in the face of opposition, persecution, and the privations of westward journeying and settlement that she and other Mormons endured. Her marriages after Joseph Smith's death were short and unsuccessful—in one she may have been a comparatively neglected "proxy wife" with no children, while in the other her husband apostatized. As a result, she continued to use the name of her first, prophet-husband, and was buried as Desdemona Fullmer Smith. She is not richly documented but did leave an extraordinary short autobiography, from which we can gain a sense of her personality and construct an outline of her life.

### I. "The Lord Reveild to Him That All ... Wheare Wrong"

On October 6, 1809, Desdemona was born to Peter Fullmer and Susannah Zerfass in Huntington, Luzerne County, eastern Pennsylvania, twenty miles southwest of Scranton. Both Peter, a thirty-five-year-old farmer, and Susannah, twenty-six, were natives of the same state. Desdemona had three older siblings, David, Mary, and John Solomon, born in 1803, 1805, and 1807, then three younger, Charlotte, Louisiana ("Louise") and Almon Linus, born in 1812, 1814, and 1816. Remarkably, in an age of high infant mortality, all of the Fullmer children reached adulthood, so Desdemona grew up as the middle child in a family of seven.

In her autobiography she reported that her Methodist parents gave their children a strict religious upbringing and taught her to pray. Her brother John once confided to her how great an impact her piety had on him: "If I have established a reputable character, I am in a great measure indebted to you for it; for well do I recollect that while I was a youth, I carefully avoided any thing which I knew you did not approve; and this I was induced to do in consequence of the interest you always took in my welfare."

She was raised in an environment in which visions were real and believers hoped for the return of Christ's primitive church. One of her earliest memories is of a neighbor boy, Putnam Wadsworth, who became a prophet of sorts. When she was a schoolgirl, Putnam was sick for two years, during which time "the Lord reveild to him that all the churches wheare wrong," so he asked for his name to be removed from church rolls. He recovered his health, then walked and rode tirelessly, followed by a band of friends, "preaching a new docktrin to all the people he wished to see the same gosple preached that the apostles preached." He also preached healing by the laying on of hands after the pattern of the original apostles. Some neighbor boys mocked him, so that if a sheep broke its leg, they would send for him to lay hands on it.

One of his odder inspirations was that God had revealed to him that if he ever crossed a big stream of water he would die in two years' time. He therefore avoided all waterways. But eventually his brother lay sick and dying on the other side of a river, and when Putnam was sent for, he could not refuse. He crossed over the river and soon thereafter died. Still, the boy-prophet made a deep impression on Desdemona. Later, when the ordinance of vicarious baptism for the dead was practiced by Mormons in Nauvoo, she had a memorable dream in which, "seeing this Putman in the spiritual Worled happy he came to me and requested me to do somthing for him it was my solem impresion that it was baptism he desired." She undoubtedly performed this ordinance for him.

Such a story as this shows how much the principles of apostolic primitivism were in the air in early-nineteenth-century America. As in the story of Joseph Smith, a boy receives revelations and seeks to restore the New Testament church with its gifts of the spirit, such as healing. He preaches his new restoration but is mocked. Even the genre of conditional death prophecy has parallels in Smith's career. Desdemona, as we have seen, had her own prophetic visions and dreams at this time.

## II. "It Provoked Mirth Since It So Often Came to Pass"

In 1829 the Fullmers moved to Ohio to settle eventually in Richland County, southwest of Cleveland, where Peter bought a farm and was helped in his labors by the teenage Almon. The parents soon joined the Campbellite movement, for, like their daughter, they were seeking the restoration of primitive Christianity. They began to hear rumors of the "Gold Bible" in 1835 and eventually were able to borrow a copy, but because it was borrowed, they had to read it aloud in great haste. Almon later wrote that "it provoked mirth since it so often came to pass. It riveted, however, a conviction of its truth upon our minds." As so often, the Book of Mormon spoke deeply to the soul of the bibical restorationist.

Soon after this two Mormon elders, H. A. Sherwood and George A. Smith, visited the Fullmers, staying in their home while they proselyted. Almon remembered Sherwood as "boisterous," Smith as "more considerate and calm." Soon the elders had converted Peter, Susannah, David and wife Rhoda Ann (who had just moved to Ohio), and Desdemona. David was baptized on September 16, 1836, while Desdemona, then twenty-seven, was baptized later in the year by John P. Greene. As spiritual conversion often entailed geographical relocation, so Desdemona gathered to Kirtland to be with the other Saints. David Fullmer arrived there in late 1836, and perhaps she accompanied him at that time. She was there by February 9, 1837, when she received a patriarchal blessing. On February 22 David was ordained an elder in the Kirtland temple.

Desdemona lived in Kirtland for a year, during which time many early church members were turning against Joseph Smith. She remembered Oliver Cowdery, among others, saying to her, "Are you such a fool as still to goo to hear Joseph the fallen prophet?" She stoutly replied, "The Lord convinced me that he was a true prophit. and he has not toled me that he is fallon yet." As we have seen, early Mormons in their autobiographies often dramatized themselves as protagonists facing down antagonists, whether apostates (as here), or mobocrats, or Protestant ministers.

## III. "The Mob Would Com to the Door"

With Kirtland becoming increasingly inhospitable to Mormons, Desdemona soon joined the exodus to Missouri, perhaps accompanying David, who traveled in September 1837. As frequently happened, the Saints fleeing Kirtland arrived in Caldwell County, Missouri, in time to undergo the worst persecutions the Latter-day Saints had ever experienced. Desdemona remembered moving from place to place with other members to try to find safety from lawless bands of Missourians. The mobs would often appear at houses at night, and Desdemona and her family and friends, with their children, would have to flee to the woods for safety, taking only quilts for protection. In the woods they would spend the night, often in the rain. In spring 1838 David moved to Daviess County; Desdemona was living with him near Haun's Mill when the massacre occurred on October 30. The Fullmers had to flee to the woods again to save their lives.

Desdemona wrote, "The mob would com to the door all armed and yell like indens you must leive heare in 3 days or be killed. when snow and winter was ther." In the spring of 1839 a mob came to the Fullmer house and demanded that they leave, while David lay helpless with fever. According to Desdemona, "I spoke and said we have no teem or waggon. we may as well dye in the house as a few roods from it. so they said hell let us go."

Desdemona and her relatives and friends started the difficult trek to Illinois in March. On the road, she remembers, clergymen, "the sectarin preasts," accosted them, saying, "Guive up your faith and stay with us. and you shall never want." But, as Desdemona reported, "I said I have no faith in you nor in your father the Devil. so I spelt tem [them] up every time." By now, two and a half years after baptism, she was a seasoned Mormon, with persecutions only confirming her in her testimony.

### IV. "In the Rise of Poligamy I Was Warned in a Dream"

When she arrived in Illinois, Desdemona was thirty years old. Of her years there before 1842 we know little. On July 29, 1839, her brother, John Solomon, was baptized in Nauvoo at age thirty-two. David was a high councilor by May 1842, so had stature equivalent to that of a present-day Mormon general authority. Desdemona would have gained visibility and joined the "female hierarchy" of Nauvoo as a result. This is corroborated by two data concerning her from 1842. In the spring "Desdemonia Fulmer" was living in the Joseph Smith household with Elvira Cowles and the Partridge sisters, so, like many of Smith's wives, she lived under the same roof with him before the marriage and had the opportunity to become well acquainted with him. She was also present at the first meeting of the Female Relief Society of Nauvoo on March 17, and on April 19 contributed $1.25 to the society.

The next year of her life is entirely undocumented. At some time, however, she moved out of the Smith household. On March 21, 1843, she received a second patriarchal blessing, this time from Hyrum Smith. Two months later, on May 13, she asked William Clayton, Joseph Smith's scribe, if she could board with his family. William consented, and she moved in to the Clayton home.

According to her own affidavit, Desdemona married Joseph Smith in July, with Brigham Young performing the ceremony. In the autobiography she only mentioned the marriage obliquely: "In the rise of poligamy i was warned in a dream Amy [Emma?] Smith was a going to poisen me I told my dream to brother Joseph he told me it was true she would do it if she could." Thus Emma Smith apparently knew about Desdemona's marriage to Joseph and was angry and jealous. On the other hand, Desdemona's dream might easily have resulted from her own inner feelings of conflict and guilt, especially if she had been a close friend of Emma while living in her home. Beyond these data, nothing is known of the Fullmer-Smith marriage. However, the union may have been partly dynastic, as David Fullmer was a prominent church leader.

Desdemona continued to attend Relief Society, and a notice in the minutes shows the profession she followed in Nauvoo: in July a Sister Jones "said Miss Fulmer wished needlework and proposed giving to Society one third of the price of making 1 pr. pantaloons which Sis. Jones furnished her to make." The daybook of Joseph Smith's store shows "Desdemony Fullmer" buying "silk," "artificial," "Ribband," "foundation," "Gloves," handkerchiefs, "Book Muslin," "Edgin," "Hoes," "Scissers," "Shears," wire, spools, "Side Combs," "Back Combs," "10 yds factry," and calico.

For unknown reasons, tensions arose between Desdemona and the Claytons. On January 29, 1844, William confided to his journal, "She [Desdemona] has treated my family unfeelingly and unkindly in various ways and I requested her to look out for another home." But she refused to leave until she had discussed the matter with Smith. The next day she met with Brigham Young, Heber C. Kimball, and Clayton, and accused Clayton of threatening to kick her, which he heatedly denied and counter-accused her of having a "malicious disposition." We do not know how this conflict ended, or whether Joseph intervened, but she probably moved away from the Claytons, perhaps back with David.

In May David started out on a mission to promote Smith's campaign for the U.S. presidency. A month later, when the prophet took his final journey to Carthage, John Solomon and Almon Fullmer accompanied him. On June 27 Smith was killed, and Desdemona was suddenly a widow.

### V. Ezra Taft Benson

David continued to be an important Mormon leader. On March 1, 1845, he became a member of the Council of Fifty, a secret organization called "the kingdom of God" that was intended to govern politically. Later in the year, on December 7, he became a polygamist, as was appropriate for a man of his status, marrying two wives at the same time.

On January 21, 1846, as Mormons prepared to leave Nauvoo, Desdemona, now thirty-six, was endowed in the Nauvoo temple. Then five days later she was sealed to Joseph Smith for eternity, with Ezra Taft Benson standing proxy, and was sealed to Ezra for time. Benson had been born in 1811 in Mendon, Worcester, Massachusetts, and married his first wife, Pamelia Andrus, in 1832. They converted to Mormonism in 1840 in Quincy, Illinois, and Ezra served a mission to the eastern states in 1842-43. On April 27, 1844, Benson married his first plural wife, thirty-one-year-old Adeline Brooks Andrus. In May he departed for another mission to the eastern states, returning in the fall, and was appointed to the Nauvoo High Council in October. He thus became a man of some importance in the church hierarchy and would have associated with David Fullmer in the council. He received his endowment on December 15, 1845, and was sealed to both of his previous wives before marrying Desdemona for time on January 26. However, she does not so much as mention Ezra in her autobiography, and later divorced him and remarried. Nevertheless, she was living with him in 1850 in Utah, so their marriage, whatever its internal dynamics may have been, lasted at least that long.

Her account of her last days in Nauvoo is somewhat confusing. She mentions a "war" and reports that she stayed until the spring following the war. While most Mormons, including Ezra Benson, left in February 1846, Desdemona may have stayed behind with her parents—perhaps health problems prevented them from traveling. Many of the old, feeble, and sick were left in Nauvoo for similar reasons. The anti-Mormons took no pity on them, however, but demanded that they leave or be killed. Desdemona now described a Missouri-like encounter with a mob. Once again a large group of enemies, a "hundred" armed men, yelling like Indians, surrounded her house in which her father lay "speachless ... with the fever." Three or four other families were also in the house. But the mob forced their way in: "[The mob] came into the house broke locks and taken all they pleased to take. they found 1 keg of poder [powder] then they bid all to leive in one hour. I told them that that kegg belong[ed] to the man they drove away. this morning. so [they] left."

Eventually Desdemona left Nauvoo, though we do not know precisely when. At some point she presumably traveled across Iowa to Winter Quarters and met Ezra. He, on the other hand, can be followed with some precision. On February 9 he left Nauvoo, he wrote, "with my two wives," and began the Iowa trek. In May he was appointed counselor to William Huntington at Mt. Pisgah. While serving there he received a letter informing him that he had been called to be an apostle, so he traveled to Council Bluffs to be ordained on July 16. By this time the apostles had become by far the most important Latter-day Saint leaders, so Ezra joined the elite circles of the Mormon hierarchy. Soon after this he was sent on a short mission eastward, from which he returned on November 27.

On March 4, 1847, Ezra married a fourth wife, Eliza Ann Perry, nearly eighteen, at Winter Quarters, then a fifth wife, Lucinda Barton (West), forty-six, sometime later in 1847. In the spring he traveled to Utah with the first company, known as the "pioneers," and after reaching the Great Basin he was sent back immediately to meet the companies following the pioneers, then accompanied them back to Salt Lake. He then returned to Winter Quarters and in January 1848 he served another mission to the eastern states. By April he was back at the Missouri River, but in July he took another trip east.

Desdemona crossed the plains in 1848, traveling in the Willard Richards division, probably with David and John Solomon. The company set out on May 26 and arrived in Salt Lake City on September 20. She herself only wrote, "I moved to this plase with a large compeney of members." In 1849 Ezra made his final journey over the plains, this time traveling with his first family.

## VI. Harrison Parker McLane

Of her early Utah experiences, Desdemona wrote only the following: "The first year in this plase I sufferd withe hunger." In the 1850 Salt Lake County census, Ezra T. Benson was living with four women, of whom the second was Desdemona C. Fullmer. Her place of birth is given as "Ireland"! On July 12, 1851, Benson married a sixth wife, Olive Mary Knight, twenty-one.

Perhaps living in such a large plural family became intolerable for Desdemona, for on September 21, 1852, she and Ezra were formally divorced. In April 1853 she began to live with Ira Ames's family, according to his diary, and "about 6 months" later, in approximately September 1853, she left that household to marry her third husband, Harrison Parker McLane. Ezra stood as a witness during the ceremony, which shows how amicable some polygamous divorces could be. Harrison, a thirty-eight-year-old Kentuckian, was "an elder of the church," according to Desdemona. She lived with him "a few years," and with him had her only child, Desdemona McLane. Unfortunately the child was born and died the same year. We have none of the details of what must have been a harrowing ordeal for Desdemona, who was now roughly forty-five.

When married to McLane, she often went without food, she reported. Her autobiography gives a stark account of hunger and the struggle for survival in the early Salt Lake settlement: "I ate beef hide and whore [wore] apart [a part] of it on my feet not being taned. at one time he and

I lived on ... buisked [buiscuit] 17 dayes onley wild greens salt and wat-
ter and I whent a halve a mile to find them. at another time baught bran
wheat and loem [lorm?] bean and nothing else." But this was not hard to
bear, she wrote, compared to the fact that her husband began to turn
against the church: "He would speake agueansed brother Young and all
good men. I woould talke in their favor. he would say to me Damed
[Dammit?] youer damed thongue ought to be cut out by the roots."
Once again the autobiography pits the steadfast Desdemona against a
dissenter.

This conflict ended in another separation: "So he left this church
with a woman a morisite one." The Morrisites, ironically, were a millennialist Latter-day Saint splinter group who expected Jesus' imminent return. The only date limitation for the separation is a few years after 1852.
As the Morrisites were beginning to organize in 1860 and had mostly dis-
persed by spring 1863, Desdemona and McLane probably separated between those two dates.

## VII. "My Faith Encreased in This Church"

Desdemona summarized the rest of her life up to 1868 in this way:
"The spirit of the lord direc[t]ed me and angles [angels] vis[it]ed me and
my faith encreased. in this church. I belong 30 years in this church and
the longer I live in it the better I like it." So she continued to have the visionary experiences that she had had in her early life. On November 11,
1856, her mother died in Salt Lake City, followed two months later by
her father, on January 6, 1857. Desdemona was forty-seven at the time.
In 1868, when she was fifty-nine, she wrote her short autobiography,
which she deposited in the Church Historian's office on December 2. It
began, "I want to write a short history of my life the more particuler part
that I think will do the youth som godde [good] and those that come
into this church not having the same experience that I have had."

She spent her last years with David, who in his later life served as patriarch and acting stake president in the important Salt Lake City Stake.
When he completed a large house, she moved in with him and his family
and gave him a cow and a calf worth $50 in exchange for her room. She
lived in the Sixth Ward for many years. The next direct reference to her
shows her engaged in temple work, which might have been a frequent
activity in her later life. On August 23, 1871, "Desdemona Fullmer
Smith, heiress," stood proxy with Joseph F. Smith as Hyrum Smith,
Joseph F.'s father, was sealed to Charlotte Fullmer, dead, which increased her recently deceased sister's chances for salvation.

David Fullmer, whose life had been so closely intertwined with Desdemona's, began to have serious health problems in the 1870s, then
died on October 21, 1879. Desdemona herself made a will on September

18, 1881, when she was nearly seventy-two. It gives an interesting look at what a seventy-year-old woman would own in nineteenth-century Utah and also recreates something of the texture of her later life, now far removed from the time when she was eating roots and wild greens in early Utah. The document was signed by "Desdemona Fullmer Smith" and addressed to John Taylor, president of the church. To the "worthy poor" she left the bulk of her property: "The room and building where I reside, the cooking stove with all its belongings, the bedstead, straw mattress, the best feather bed, 3 feather pillows, 4 light quilts, one heavy comforter, a flower box, a big clothes box, a coal box, a big rocking chair." To Sarah (Oysterbanks?) Fullmer and family, she left a clock, a cupboard with dishes, shoes, and "all the trumpery about the house." Joseph F. Smith and family were given a "large frame glass," a looking glass, and some clothes: "one blue woolen dress, one worsted rose dress, one pongee silk dress, one summer coat." Marcy Thompson received more clothes: a thick coat, and "one black delane dress, one thick waterproof dress, two reddish calico dresses, one brown calico dress." In addition, a feather bed and a "rose pieced quilt." Eugene Fullmer inherited her writings, and James Fullmer was awarded her books.

Three years later, on February 9, 1886, at age seventy-six, she died in Salt Lake City in the Sixth Ward, probably in the David Fullmer home. She was buried in the city cemetery under the name Desdemona Fullmer Smith. Andrew Jenson provides an epitaph: "She was a quiet, unassuming, faithful woman, and was greatly respected by all who had the pleasure of her acquaintance."

# 27.

# Youthful Supplication

## *Olive Grey Frost (Smith Young)*

Mary Ann Frost Pratt wrote a small biography of her sister Olive, who, she reported, was devout from an early age: "When quite young she was religiously inclined, and would often retire to some private place with a chosen companion, to pour out her soul in secret prayer to that Being who rewards openly, and frequently she incurred ridicule thereby from those who were less sober minded." The "chosen companion" may have been Lucy Smith (no relation to Joseph Smith), with whom Olive would later join the Mormon faith. Other sources tell that the "private place" was a grove, so, Olive, like Joseph, retired to her own sacred grove to pray as a young girl. The ridicule she endured also parallels Smith's experience. However, unlike Smith, she was accompanied in these early spiritual experiences by a companion.

As a wife of Smith, Olive was fairly typical. She was deeply religious and, as sister-in-law of an apostle, elite—both of which factors would have brought her to Smith's attention. Like many of Smith's wives, she was a member of the Female Relief Society of Nauvoo. After his death her proxy marriage to Brigham Young was also straightforward. Unfortunately she left no holographs and is documented chiefly by her sister's biographical sketch.

### I. Maine Childhood

On July 24, 1816, Olive was born to Aaron Frost and Susannah Grey in Bethel, Oxford, in southwest Maine, the eighth of eleven children. Little is known of Aaron and Susannah, both natives of Maine, though probably Aaron farmed and Susannah was a farm wife. At Olive's birth, her sister-biographer, Mary Ann, was seven years old, having been born on January 14, 1809, in Groton, Caledonia, Vermont, some forty-five miles west of Bethel. Mary had been preceded by Lidiana, Aaron Jr., Milton, and Lucretia Buckman, all born in North Yarmouth, Cumberland, Maine, from 1802 to 1806. Two other siblings, Orange Clark and Naomi, were born in 1812 and 1814 in Groton.

The Frosts then moved to Bethel, where they certainly knew Patty and David Sessions. In fact, one of Patty's half-sisters, Olive Bartlett, married a Nathaniel Frost. Three more children joined the Frosts there: Sophronia Gray, Nehemiah, and Huldah, born in 1818, 1821, and 1825. Susannah was forty-five at the time her last child was born; Mary Ann was sixteen and Olive eight. So genealogy gives us the bare bones of Olive's early family history—she was one of the late children in a large family.

As a young woman she was pious, as we have seen, and worked as a seamstress. Mary Ann wrote, "When about eighteen years of age [circa 1834] she and her particular friend, Miss Louisa Foster, learned the tailoress trade, and they went together from place to place, among their acquaintances, to work at this business, thereby being able to lighten the labors of the busy housewives." Mary Ann, meanwhile, married Nathan Stearns in 1832, but soon after their first child, Mary Ann Stearns (later Winters), was born on April 6, 1833, Nathan died of a fever.

## II. "Such a Sermon as I Have Heard Tonight"

In late summer 1836 Brigham Young and five of the twelve apostles swung through Maine on a New England mission. Olive's brother, Orange, heard a sermon by one of these missionaries and returned to the Frost household elated. Turning to the matriarch Susannah, he said, "Mother, I would carry you twenty miles the darkest night that ever was to hear such a sermon as I have heard tonight." The preaching of early Mormons must have been electrifying, especially to those who already had a primitivist leaning.

Mary Ann was intrigued by Orange's accounts of this new religion and, like him, was converted by the first Mormon sermon she heard: "I said in my heart, if there are only three who hold firm to the faith, I will be one of that number; and through all the persecution I have had to endure I have ever felt the same; my heart has never swerved from that resolve." With her mother, she was baptized and confirmed in August 1836 by the charismatic apostle David W. Patten. After these ordinances, Patten blessed Mary Ann for heart palpitations, which she had had for years, and, according to family tradition, she was immediately cured of this affliction. Father Aaron Frost was baptized about a year later, but Olive did not become a member at that time. Mary Ann and her daughter relocated later that year to Kirtland, where she married Apostle Parley P. Pratt, a widower with one child, on May 14, 1837. They subsequently moved to Missouri, suffered persecutions there, then relocated in Nauvoo, Illinois.

### III. "Unity of Faith"

In October 1839 Olive was pursuing her tailoring trade in nearby Dixfield. At that time, Mary Ann wrote, "Elder Duncan McArthur visited that place and preached the Gospel as taught by the Latter-day Saints, in such plainness that her willing mind, already prepared by earnest prayer, soon comprehended its vast importance, and she received it joyfully. She was baptized by Elder McArthur, and always looked upon him with reverence as her 'father in the Gospel.'" Duncan's companion was Perrigrine Sessions, Patty's son, and on October 28 his diary confirmed Olive's baptism: "28 held a sosial meting and Mc. [McArthur] baptised Olive Frost." Altogether, at least six of the Frosts—Olive and Mary Ann, the parents, and two others—became Latter-day Saints.

Olive "endured much opposition on account of the new religion she had embraced," wrote Mary Ann, but like her older sister she "never faltered." Returning home, she and her friend Lucy Smith, who also had been baptized, "found great strength and consolation in retiring to the grove to pray, even when the weather was so severe that they had to take a quilt or blanket to protect them from the cold. Unity of faith was now added to the tie of friendship. Their prayers took new form, for they now had something more tangible to ask for and a more perfect Being to address. God had respect unto their integrity and petitions, and led them in the way of salvation and life eternal."

One would like to know more about how the opposition that Mary Ann mentions manifested itself. Perhaps Olive was ostracized in a small town and became a target for gossip. Perrigrine, on December 23, described one of the consolations that the gospel gave to Lucy Smith: "[I went] to Newry and laid hands on Sister Lucy Smith and [she] was healed from her sickness." He and MacArthur visited Aaron Frost's again on March 24, 1840.

### IV. The First Overseas Missionary Women

In Nauvoo Parley P. Pratt was assigned a mission to England, and Mary Ann accompanied him to the east coast. On March 9 he, with other apostles, boarded a ship for England, but Mary Ann and her children stayed in New York. Soon afterwards the family contracted scarlet fever, and Mary Ann sent her husband a panicked letter. He received it in England shortly after July 6 and immediately sailed for America, intending to bring his family back with him to England. Arriving in New York, he found Mary Ann and the children fully recovered but nonetheless happy to see him again. They traveled together to Maine to visit Frost relatives, where Olive, twenty-four, and Mary Ann, thirty-one, were reunited after a long parting.

Now the lives of our two sisters intertwine, as it was agreed that Olive would accompany Mary Ann and Parley and their three children, Mary Ann, seven, Parley Jr., three, and Nathan, two, back to England. Mary Ann wrote:

She willingly forsook father and mother, brothers and sisters, and braved the dangers of the great deep, to aid in spreading the Gospel in a foreign land. These two sisters were the first missionary women of this dispensation to cross the sea in the interest of this Church. They were fifteen weeks on the sea going and coming. Sister Olive was not afflicted with seasickness, and was therefore enabled to devote herself to her sick sister, and the care of the family.

They arrived in Liverpool in October. Unfortunately Olive's health was not good in damp England. Her sister wrote, "If she walked a long distance to and from meeting, she would spit blood." Nevertheless, "She made many warm friends among the Saints on the British Isles." In February 1841 the Pratts were living in Manchester, where Mary Ann bore another child, Olivia, in June.

Mission completed, Olive and the Pratts left for America on October 29, 1842, sailing on the *Emerald*. It was a difficult voyage, due to adverse winds which delayed the ship on the Atlantic and stretched the journey to ten weeks. Food began to run short, and, as Parley wrote, "We had ... some difficulties, murmurings and rebellions; but the Saints on board were called together, and chastened and reproved sharply, which brought them to repentance. We then humbled ourselves and called on the Lord, and he sent a fair wind, and brought us into port in time to save us from starvation." To add to Olive's worries, her sister was once again pregnant.

They arrived in New Orleans in January 1843, then took a steamer up the Mississippi. "We glided smoothly on past forests, orchards and plantations," Mary Ann Winters, nearly ten years old at the time, later wrote. "The negroes were everywhere present, and I imagined the people had turned dark skinned during our absence." However, there was an outbreak of measles among the boat's passengers, and Olive was among those who contracted this dangerous sickness. When the Pratts reached Chester, Illinois, and deboarded, Olive stayed with them.

On January 21 Parley described his family's circumstances in a letter to the *Millennial Star*: the icy river prevented further travel, so they were living for a time in a stone house in a village eighty miles south of St. Louis. Parley soon went ahead and bought land in Nauvoo one block north of the temple, then returned after three weeks. The Frost-Pratt group set out by steamer for Nauvoo in early February, but again river ice detained them, this time in St. Louis for a month. Toward the end of March they embarked on the river once more, on the *Maid of Iowa* steamboat, with Mary Ann expecting a child at any moment. On April 7 Susan Pratt was born on the ship.

### V. "She Never Opposed It"

When they reached Nauvoo five days later, Joseph Smith greeted them at the steamship landing, and Olive met him for the first time. Mary Ann Winters remembers him saying, "Come, Brother Parley, bring your folks right up to my house; it is only a little way, and you can be more comfortable after your long journey." Mary Ann was so weak that she was placed in a big chair and carried by Smith's bodyguards up to the Mansion House. Parley walked beside her with tiny Susan in his arms.

The Pratts stayed with Smith briefly, but Olive and the older children were taken in by old Maine neighbors Patty and David Sessions. Patty nursed little Mary Ann through a case of chills and fever. The Pratts then rented a house across the street from their lot and watched their new house being built, while operating a thriving grocery store out of a barn on the lot. Olive probably continued to live with Mary Ann and Parley.

The young returned missionary, Olive, must have been dazzled by the Mormon city, as she had never seen a gathering of Zion before. As a sister-in-law of an apostle, she quickly became well known in Nauvoo circles and became a friend of Eliza R. Snow, who herself had been a plural wife of Smith since the summer of 1842. On May 19, 1843, Eliza wrote in her journal, "Visited at Prest. [William] Marks in company with Sophie Robinson, O Frost, Miss Mitchell &c." So Olive, in entering the ranks of Nauvoo's elite women—those related to high church leaders, who were well educated, or spiritually remarkable (or, as in Eliza Snow's case, all three)—joined the inner circle of polygamy, as well. Perhaps Patty Sessions or Eliza Snow educated her in the principles of this new order of marriage.

Therefore, within months after reaching Nauvoo, Olive accepted polygamy and became a plural wife of Joseph Smith. She was approximately twenty-seven years of age at the time. Mary Ann tells the story:

> She seemed to realize and appreciate the magnitude of the great and important mission allotted to woman in the perfect plan of this Gospel dispensation, and she desired to do her part in the good work. She freely accorded to man the title of king, and joyfully accepted the place of queen by his side. It was at this time [summer 1843] that the principle of plurality of wives was taught to her. She never opposed it, and, as in the case of baptism, soon accepted it to be her creed, in practice as well as in theory. She was married for time and all eternity to Joseph Smith some time previous to his death and martyrdom.

One wonders if her conversion to polygamy was really that easy, as most women (and men) initially agonized over "the principle" before reluctantly accepting it. Some felt authentically suicidal when first confronted with it. But some, perhaps, did not have such a dramatic struggle with the doctrine, and Olive might have been one of those. Absolutely nothing is known of what Olive's married life with Smith was like. She probably spent time with him on occasion and certainly spent time with his other wives. We do know from an account of her grief at his death that she was deeply attached to him.

Parley P. Pratt took his first plural wife, Elizabeth Brotherton, during this period, and the transition to plurality was difficult for Mary Ann. Tensions caused by his marriages to other young wives eventually caused her to formally divorce the apostle, though she remained a faithful Mormon throughout her life, dying in Pleasant Grove, Utah, in 1891. She was sealed to Joseph Smith for eternity, not to Pratt, on February 6, 1846, in the Nauvoo temple, with Parley himself standing proxy for the dead prophet. Some scholars have suggested that Mary Ann might have married Smith as a polyandrous wife during his lifetime, but there is presently no conclusive evidence to support this theory.

### VI. "Olive Frost Went Entirely Mad"

Also in the summer of 1843, toward the end of June, Aaron and Susannah Frost, along with two more Frost sisters, Sophronia and Huldah, arrived in Nauvoo. This must have been a joyful reunion for both Olive and Mary Ann. Soon the Pratt store and residence was ready—a fine, large, brick structure with white stone trimmings on twenty-seven windows and four-foot pillars supporting a stone cornice at the entrance.

On July 29 Olive and Mary Ann called on Patty Sessions, whom Olive could now claim as a sister-wife. Olive also joined the Female Relief Society of Nauvoo and became an active member. Mary Ann wrote, "She was very zealous in soliciting aid for and in visiting those who were needy and in distress. Her heart was always tender towards suffering of every kind, and it gave her unbounded joy and satisfaction to be able to relieve it." This statement is supported by two references in the Relief Society minutes. On August 14 "Sis Olive Frost represented a sick family whom the Com^tee had overlooked a Br Burgess & family," and a week later "Miss Frost spoke of the sick  said Mrs Burgess & family were distressd."

On June 27, 1844, Joseph Smith was killed and Olive was left a widow. According to one observer, Mrs. Ettie Smith, "When the dead bodies arrived at Nauvoo, the spiritual wives of the late prophet, before unknown with certainty, now disclosed by cries, and a general uproar, their secret acceptance of the new doctrine. One of them, Olive Frost, went entirely mad; but his own wife Emma, appeared remarkably resigned." This is virtually the only detail we have that indicates the inner dynamics of Olive's marriage to Smith. She evidently loved him very much.

## VII. "She Died, as She Had Lived, in Full Faith"

After Smith's death, as we have seen, prominent Mormon leaders married most of the dead prophet's widows. As Olive was well known as one of Smith's wives, at some point she was approached by Brigham and Heber, and on November 7 she was sealed to Young for time as a proxy wife. He wrote in his journal, "At Br J. B. Nobles Br A. Lyman Sister Olive Frost & my self & others was there." Amasa Lyman probably performed the marriage. We know nothing else about Olive's relationship with this second prophet. She was Young's eighteenth wife, approximately.

Less than a year later, on about September 26, 1845, Olive, whose health had always been weak, suffered a bout of common Nauvoo ague, malaria. She succumbed on October 6, wrote Mary Ann, "after two weeks' suffering with the chills and fever and pneumonia." Mary Ann provides Olive's epitaph: "She died, as she had lived, in full faith of the Gospel of Christ, and awaits the glorious resurrection day." So this devout woman passed away. We know little about her—only that she was intensely religious, given to constant prayer, a seeker for truth, always concerned for the sick. Aside from her historical importance as one of the wives of Joseph Smith, she was one of the first two female overseas missionaries.

# 28.

# Aunt Melissa

## *Melissa Lott (Smith Bernhisel Willes)*

On October 20, 1885, a remarkable meeting took place in the small town of Lehi, Utah, northwest of Provo, in Utah County. An imposing, grave man stood on the doorstep of a modest cottage and knocked on the door. His build and features were very much like those of Joseph Smith, Jr.—tall, large-framed, with an aquiline nose—though a full white beard set him apart from the Mormon prophet.

A sixtyish-looking woman opened the door and smiles lit up both faces as they realized they were old friends. They had not seen each other for forty years, but when they had first known each other they had shared a real affection. The woman, as a teenager, had tended the bearded man when he was a young boy.

But now a psychic chasm separated these two. The bearded man was Joseph Smith's oldest son, who, following his mother's idealizing account of his father's life, preached that his father had not been a polygamist. This man, Joseph Smith III, had made an anti-polygamy crusade a central focus of the church he headed, the Reorganized Church of Jesus Christ of Latter Day Saints. When he made missionary trips to Utah, he spent time trying to discount any possible evidence that his father had married plural wives. When Utah Mormons produced wife after wife, Joseph III interviewed them with careful legalistic questions to disallow the evidence of documents and testimonies of surviving veterans of Nauvoo. The woman in the cottage was Melissa Lott Willes, who had lived with young Joseph in the Nauvoo House and had led him to and from school every day. Mormons in Salt Lake had told Joseph III that Melissa had married his father, and so he had stopped in Lehi to renew an old acquaintance and to once more confront a personal demon, his father's polygamy.

Melissa and Joseph both left versions of the subsequent conversation. According to an affidavit by Melissa given eight years after the event, Joseph Smith III asked if she would answer "a few plain questions" for his own special benefit.

"I will do so with pleasure," answered Melissa.

"Were you married to my father?" asked Joseph.

"Yes," answered Melissa flatly.

"When?"

Melissa handed Joseph the Lott family Bible and opened it to a page of genealogical information entered in the hand of her father, Cornelius Lott. "You'll find it there," she said.

Joseph peered at the rough writing of Lott, who had managed his father's farm in Nauvoo. It indeed recorded a marriage of Joseph and Melissa on September 20, 1843.

The first line of Joseph's defenses were down, so he retreated to the next. "Were you a wife in very deed?" he asked. If he could prove that there was no sexuality in the alleged marriages, he might explain the unions as mere ceremonies for eternity, not authentic marriages.

But Melissa replied, "Yes."

So Joseph resorted to his trump card: "Why was there no increase, say in your case?" No children proved no sexuality, in his mind.

Melissa answered, "Through no fault of either of us, lack of proper conditions on my part probably, or it might be in the wisdom of the Almighty that we should have none. The Prophet was martyred nine months after our marriage."

Joseph continued to press the argument: "Did you know of any Brother or Sister of mine by my father's plural wives?"

"I did not know of any."

Then Joseph asked a question that showed a lack of historical perspective: "Did my father give his consent for you to marry Ira J. Willes?"

"Certainly not, your father was dead a number of years before I married Mr. Willes. I married Mr. Willes May 13th, 1849, with the full understanding that it was for time only."

Joseph then advanced the argument that was most convincing for him, personally: "My mother, in the presence of witnesses, denied that my father had any wives other than her."

Melissa answered quickly, "Yes, you took your mother before Mr. Bideman, a bitter enemy of our people, and then asked such questions of her as you wished ... I have no doubt that your mother told you the truth so far as she could under the circumstances; but if you had taken her by herself, as you have done me and asked your questions, she would probably have answered you as I have done."

So Melissa. Joseph's account is quite different. He described her home as a one-room cottage, where he found her sitting at an old-fashioned fireplace, "with broad hearth and wide-throated chimney." On the fireplace were hooks that supported kettles over a fire, "big dogs" which supported logs and "fire shovel, tongs, and poker." He explained: "Ira Willis had always been a thrifty and handy man-of-all-work and loved to make and provide many conveniences and accessories for his home."

In Joseph's account, he asked, "Now, Melissa, I have been told that there were women, other than my mother, who were married to my father and lived with him as his wife, and that my mother knew it. How about it?" She answered rather tremulously, "If there was anything of that kind going on you may be sure that your mother knew about it." This answer is entirely ambiguous, but Joseph interpreted it from his perspective as denying polygamy.

Joseph then asked the widow about her involvement with polygamy: "Melissa, will you tell me just what was your relation to my father, if any?" As in Melissa's account, she showed him the Lott family Bible.

"Did you ever live with him as his wife anywhere?" he persisted. At this point Melissa began to cry and said, "No, I never did; but you have no business asking me such questions. I had a great regard and respect for both your father and your mother. I do not like to talk about these things."

Mary Lott Losee and another sister, Alzina, then arrived at Melissa's cottage and "expressed great pleasure in seeing me again," wrote Joseph. Just as in Melissa's account, he now turned the conversation to the question of whether any of his father's wives had children. As he told the story, Mary declared firmly that there were no children by Joseph Smith's wives, and she had made a special investigation of the subject. She moreover said that there was no chance for any children, which Joseph interpreted to mean that his father did not have sexual relations with his plural wives. Joseph turned to Melissa. "Melissa, *how about it*? You hear what your sisters are saying?" Tears began to trickle down her face as she said, "Yes, Brother Joseph, I hear them." "Well, what do you say?" She drew a deep breath, as if making a sudden decision, and then, with a sigh and lips trembling: "Yes; you can believe that they are telling you the truth. There was no chance for any children." This, of course, directly contradicts Melissa's account of the conversation.

He reported that he was very pleased with this interview and left it "feeling well repaid." And so, after the conversation wandered into friendly pleasantries, they parted—Joseph to nurse a cognitive dissonance that would allow him to interpret Melissa's words as entirely supporting his position, and Melissa to reflect back nostalgically on her years as a teenager in Nauvoo, on her life in the Nauvoo House, on her first marriage to the charismatic Joseph Smith, Jr.

She was a typical teenage wife of the prophet. As was so often the case with Smith's wives, before the marriage she lived in his house and helped Emma with housework. Her marriage was dynastic, as it provided an eternal link between him and Cornelius Lott, a leader of Smith's body-guard and the manager of his farm. After Smith's death, Melissa's life was shadowed by tragedy. She united with John Bernhisel in a short-lived, unsuccessful proxy marriage, then married Ira Willes and with him helped settle Lehi. But she lost Ira and a son in a bizarre farming accident and buried the majority of her seven children.

## I. Childhood

On January 9, 1824, Melissa was born to Cornelius Peter Lott and Permelia Darrow in Tunkhannock, Wyoming, Pennsylvania, in the northeastern corner of the state. Cornelius, a farmer, was a twenty-six-year-old native of New York. Permelia, nineteen years old, was a Pennsylvanian who, aside from her duties as a farm wife, sometimes taught school. Melissa was the first of eleven children. Between 1826 and 1832, John Smiley, Mary Elizabeth, Almira Henrietta, and Permelia the younger joined the Lott family. Their birthplaces show that the family moved from Tunkhannock to Springville, Susquehanna County, ten miles north, and then to Bridgewater, Susquehanna. But they soon returned to Tunkhannock, where Lucinda Alzina and Harriet Amanda were born in 1834 and 1836 as Melissa approached her teenage years.

Apparently some Mormon elders traveled through Pennsylvania in about 1833, and Cornelius and Permelia were converted through their preaching or through reading the Book of Mormon. The elder Lotts was baptized before 1834.

At some point between March and August 1836, the family moved to Kirtland, where they no doubt participated in the spiritual exaltations and practical challenges of the Kirtland experience. They met Joseph Smith for the first time here, and Melissa met many of the young women who would become the elite women of Utah Mormondom. A few definite events begin to give us a sense of Cornelius Lott. On August 6 he was awarded an elder's license, and he received a Kirtland temple anointing on March 31, 1837. He joined the Kirtland Anti-banking Safety Society at about this time, probably losing some of his savings in that disaster. In November the historical record documents the first definite event in Melissa's life: she was baptized at age thirteen. Another Lott child, Joseph Darrow, was born on February 18, 1838.

## II. Missouri

When Kirtland became inhospitable to Mormons in 1838, the Lotts traveled to Missouri, where they settled near Haun's Mill. They were probably there for only a short time, but long enough for Cornelius to distinguish himself as a Danite para-military leader for the Mormon cause. On July 4 he was appointed to act as general with Danite leaders

Jared Carter and Sampson Avard during a military procession. In October or November he served as "Captain" for twenty mounted men on a gun raid against a non-Mormon cache of weapons and ammunition. Hosea Stout remembered him as "commander of the Horse in Far-West at the time of the surrender."

We know nothing of Melissa's Missouri experience, beyond the fact that she was fourteen and the daughter of a man who was actively involved in Danite activities during the troubles. Cornelius had become profoundly committed to Mormonism and Joseph Smith by this point.

### III. "You Both Mutually Agree"

After the Mormon flight from Missouri, the Lotts settled in Pike County, some forty miles south of Nauvoo, in 1839. But by June 1842 they were living nearer to Nauvoo, on the "prairie," three to four miles southeast of town on the Carthage road. There they worked the Joseph Smith farm, living in a large eight-room farmhouse, and receiving frequent visits from the prophet. Cornelius had clearly become one of the church leader's favorites. On June 6 Smith wrote in his journal, "To the Prairie with Bro. Yearly. & Recorder dined at Bro Lots." About a month later Smith rode out to the farm again for another dinner with the Lotts. Cornelius managed this farm until the Mormons left Nauvoo in 1846, and he also continued to serve in his military capacity as a captain of Smith's bodyguard. Another Lott child, Peter Lyman, was born on November 2, probably at the farm.

When Melissa was eighteen, she lived for a time at the Smith home to help Emma. Joseph III remembered her as "a tall, fine-looking woman with dark complexion, dark hair and eyes. She was a good singer, quite celebrated in a local way. I have heard her sing at parties and receptions in private home, on the stage where theatrical performances were given, and on the political rostrum when William Henry Harrison was running for president."

Joseph Smith undoubtedly noticed this striking young woman increasingly as she lived and worked in his home. Finally he proposed plural marriage to her, perhaps through her father. On June 29 Eliza Snow, Elvira Holmes, Elizabeth Whitney, and Elizabeth Durfee—four women in the innermost polygamy circles of Nauvoo—rode out to the Lott farm, probably to help introduce Melissa to the doctrine of celestial marriage. She accepted the proposal, and the marriage took place on September 20, 1843, with Hyrum Smith officiating and Melissa's parents standing as witnesses. The Joseph Smith journal for this day confirms that he spent the day at the farm. When she was sixty-eight, Melissa recalled the wedding vow: "You both mutually agree to be each other's companion, husband, and wife, observing the legal rights belonging to this condition, that is, keeping yourselves wholly for each other, and from all others during your lives." Similarities to the Sarah Whitney vows make this version appear reliable, but the Whitney text is much fuller. Melissa also testified, "I was married for time and eternity." The injunction to keep themselves "wholly for each other and from all others" is puzzling. It certainly applied to the woman, but Joseph, of course, had many other wives.

We know a few details about Melissa's marriage to Smith. In court testimony given later in her life, she gave frank testimony, within the bounds of Victorian language, that there was a sexual component to the relationship. She testified that she was Smith's wife "in very deed," though she also said that there were no children born as a result of the marital bond. We know that the marriage was secret, as were all of Smith's plural unions. In the Temple Lot case, Melissa testified, "I did not go to church with Joseph Smith, was never seen on the streets or in public places with him as his wife during his lifetime."

In the winter following the sealing, Melissa lived in the Joseph Smith home. She attended school in the brick store and would take Smith's children, Joseph, Frederick, and Alexander, to the same school with her. In the spring of 1844 she apparently returned to the farm.

Cornelius and Permelia Lott were married for eternity on the day of Melissa's marriage, "by Presadent Hyrum Smith with seal of Presadent Joseph Smith," as the Lott family Bible tells us. Marriages of close family members were often linked with Smith's plural unions, as the Whitney family experience shows. The elder Lotts then became part of the innermost ritual circles in Nauvoo. On December 9, 1843, Cornelius received his endowment and joined the Holy Order, while Permelia received her endowment on the 23rd. They received their fullness of priesthood ordinance together on February 4, 1844. On April 18, Cornelius was initiated into the Council of Fifty, the political kingdom of God.

### IV. John Milton Bernhisel

On June 27, 1844, when Joseph Smith was killed, Melissa was suddenly a widow. In the years following, little is known about her or her family. Andrew Jenson wrote that she continued to live with Emma occasionally after the martyrdom. There is a brief glimpse of her in the diaries of Smith family tutor James Monroe, who occasionally rode out to the Lott farm. On May 28, 1845, he wrote, "I took Melissa out this afternoon in the carriage and visited Mrs. [Caroline] Smith's tomb, in company with William [Smith] and Miss Grant. The body does not seem to have decayed much." This may have been the beginning of an attempted courtship, but James was quickly discouraged by Cornelius Lott. The next day he wrote, "Rose at 5-1/2, saddled Old Charley and went to Mr. Lott's after Melissa, but her father would not let her come. He talks wonderfully snappish and crabbed." Melissa, as a Smith widow, was probably being reserved for marriage to an older, more prestigious church leader.

As the Lotts prepared to leave Illinois for the West, Melissa and her family participated fully in the Nauvoo temple experience. In December Cornelius and Permelia received their endowments again, and on January 24, 1846, Melissa received her endowment, along with her sisters Mary Elizabeth and Permelia. On January 22 Cornelius was sealed to Permelia in the temple and to three other wives: Elizabeth Davis Durfee (a proxy marriage for Joseph Smith), Rebecca Fossett, and Charity Dickenson.

The marriage to the older, prestigious church leader now took place. On February 8 Melissa was sealed to Joseph Smith "for eternity," with John Milton Bernhisel standing proxy, then was sealed to Bernhisel "for time." Bernhisel, a doctor, had been born in 1799, so was forty-seven at the time of the marriage. He attended the University of Pennsylvania, then converted to the Mormon faith in New York and became a bishop in April 1841. After arriving in Nauvoo in 1843, he quickly became a close friend of Joseph Smith, serving as his personal attaché and living in the Mansion House. In October the Mormon prophet sealed him to eleven deceased women, but these apparently were not marriages. He married Julia Ann Haight Van Orden early in 1845 and later had one child by her. On January 20, 1846, he became a practical polygamist, being sealed in the temple to Julia Ann Haight, Dolly Ransom, Catherine Paine, and Fanny Spafford. On February 3 he married two more women, Catherine Burgess and Elizabeth Barker, and was also adopted to Joseph Smith. So Melissa entered his family on February 8 as his seventh and last plural wife.

It is not known whether Melissa lived with Bernhisel or with her parents after her marriage and as the Mormons traveled west. It is possible that the Bernhisel marriage did not "take," for within three years she married another man. Perhaps Bernhisel and Melissa considered the proxy marriage to be merely ceremonial, or it is possible that Melissa lived with him for a time, then they parted. There is simply no documentation.

### V. "A Pleasant-faced ... Hard-Working Man"

Cornelius and Permelia, possibly with Melissa, crossed Iowa and camped with the rest of the Saints in Winter Quarters. There are references to Permelia in Eliza Snow's diaries for that period. Cornelius's matrimonial history was not yet ended, for on March 30, 1847, he was sealed to Eleanor Wayman and Phebe Night. He continued to have high status in the church, being appointed to the Winter Quarters High Council on August 7. Melissa experienced tragedy at the great encampment on the Missouri when two of her siblings died that fall: eleven-year-old Harriet Amanda on October 5 and nine-year-old Joseph Darrow ten days later.

According to Jenson, Melissa spent the winters of 1846 and 1847 in

Winter Quarters, then crossed the plains with her parents in 1848, traveling in Heber C. Kimball's company, which left Council Bluffs on June 4. Two days later the Heber Kimball journal documents Cornelius giving Mary Fielding Smith Kimball teams of oxen that Heber Kimball had prepared for her, then traveling with Kimball for a time. On June 9 Cornelius was appointed captain of the third ten in Kimball's division. There is no information on Melissa's specific experiences crossing the plains, but we know that the first wagons of the Kimball company reached Salt Lake on September 20, so she probably arrived soon after.

Permelia, now forty-three, made the whole trip while pregnant with Benjamin Smith Lott, Melissa's last full sibling, who was born on November 16. In Utah Cornelius once again managed the church farm, the "Forrest Dale Farm." The *Lehi Centennial History* informs us that the Lotts' first home "was where the Auerbach's new store now stands" on State Street and Third South. It was a primitive two-room structure in which mother, father, and eight children lived.

Melissa re-enters Mormon history on May 13, 1849, when she married her third husband, Ira Jones Willes, at age twenty-five. This was a marriage for time, "married only" as she later expressed it. Kate Carter wrote, "She ... states that when she was married to Ira Jones Willes, he fully understood that he was marrying a widow of Joseph Smith, the martyred Prophet; that their association together would end with this life, and that in the morning of the resurrection she would pass from him to the society of her deceased husband." Thus, as often happened in early Mormonism, the husband with whom Melissa had children and shared most of her life was not her eternal companion. Ira, born in 1812 in Byron, Albany, New York, was baptized in April 1831 at age nineteen, and three months later became part of the first Mormon company to settle Jackson County. He suffered the normative Missouri persecutions; in 1862 Wilford Woodruff, a close friend, wrote that Ira "was whiped by Moses G. Wilson with Hickery gads in 1834 & he bears the marks upon his back to this day which he has Exhibited to us." Joseph III remembered Ira in Nauvoo as "a man-of-all-work about the premises where we lived. He was a pleasant-faced, soft-voiced, hard-working man ... He used to get up early in the mornings, build the fires, and get the house warm." Young Joseph judged him to be shrewd but kind, and "a most excellent man."

Willes marched with the Mormon Battalion, then played a significant part in western American history when he helped discover gold at Sutter's Fort. Woodruff wrote, "He & his Brother William Sidney Smith Willis took the Job of digging the mill race for Capt Sutter and discovered the gold of Calafornia after labouring about 2 month & collected

$1,400 dollars. He pioneered the road from Sacramento across the Siera nevada mountains through Carson valley to the sink of the Humbolt & brought the first train of waggon over that road." He penned an important early California gold mining document, the Willes "Best Guide to the Gold Mines."

Melissa's first child, Ira Pratt, was born in Salt Lake City on April 22, 1850. Two months later she probably attended a dinner commemorating Joseph Smith's death held at Zina Young's, which Ira joined in the evening, along with Brigham Young and Heber C. Kimball. About a week later, on July 6, Cornelius died in Salt Lake City, aged fifty-two. Zina Young wrote, "At Six this morning Cornelius P Lot died worn out with fateague and has gone home to rest with the sanctified." Zina, her sister Presendia Kimball, and a Kimball plural wife, "Anny Geen," wove Lott's final ceremonial grave clothes. Melissa undoubtedly grieved deeply for her father.

## VI. Settling Lehi

In about October 1850 Mary Elizabeth Lott moved to Lehi with her new husband, Abraham Losee, followed by a virtual exodus of Lotts and their in-laws to Utah Valley, some fifty miles south of Salt Lake City, including Melissa's mother, John Lott, and Almira Lott Murdock and her husband, John. Their little settlement near Utah Lake became known as Lottville. Soon Ira and Melissa followed their relatives to Lehi, settling at "Stink Weed Spring," where they began farming. Family traditions tell of long lonely nights in this new, small settlement, during which coyotes howled continually.

On February 12, 1852, Melissa's next child, Achsah Permelia, was born. Starting in July 1853 conflicts with Native Americans escalated into the "Walker (Wakara) War," and in the fall most of Lehi's three hundred or so citizens moved inside a fort at First South and Second West of present-day Lehi. The Lottville cabins, including Melissa's and Ira's, were on the south side of the fort. When the war ended in May 1854, the Lott clan presumably returned to Lottville.

The next Willes child, Cornelius Peter, was born on September 25. But soon the first of Melissa's losses would strike the family: Achsah, four, died of measles on March 21, 1856. This left Melissa with Ira Jr., six, and Cornelius John, one and a half. On August 17 S. E. Willes, Ira's brother, wrote to him, "I am sorry that your little boy [Cornelius?] is afflicted with fits so long, and it seems hard to part with a child like your Achsah." But Polly Melissa, Melissa's next child, was born on November 7.

Melissa became a polygamous wife for the third time on February 1, 1857, when, in the upper room of President Young's office in Salt Lake City, Ira took a plural wife, Naomi Sariah Parks, a sixteen-year-old native of Missouri. But the marriage evidently dissolved quickly, as Naomi had no children by Ira and remarried on May 10, 1862. Three more children were afterwards born to Melissa and Ira: Lyman Benjamin on April 19, 1859, Stephen Eleazer on March 21, 1860, and Sarah Amanda on July 28, 1863.

### VII. "The Waggon Turned Bottom Side Upwards"

On a Sunday morning, December 6, 1863, Melissa woke to find that her husband, who had been hauling wood on a late errand with their son, nine-year-old Cornelius, had not come in during the night. She wondered where they were and guessed that they had stopped at some relative's home to sleep. But then she looked out the window and saw the oxen of her husband's wagon team standing aimlessly, unhitched, in her front yard. At that moment, sensing disaster, she ran to nearby neighbors and relatives, and a search began.

Eventually some searchers found the wagon box upside down in the icy Dry Creek where it intersected with Bridge Road (present-day Main Street), with a load of wood beneath it. When they pulled the wagon away, then removed the wood, beneath it lay the frozen bodies of Ira and Cornelius. They had been trapped beneath their load when the wagon capsized, and had drowned.

Messengers were sent to Melissa, and the new widow arrived to weep over the bodies of her husband and son. It must have been a horrible death, trapped by the wood in the icy water, as Ira tried desperately to save his son. On Monday the bodies were taken to Salt Lake City, and the day after Wilford Woodruff wrote, "The bodies of Brother Ira Willis & son were brought into the Historian office & Exibited to the Jackson County Saints & all others who Called in & were buried about 12 oclok Noon." Melissa, nearly forty, was a widow again, and would have to continue alone at the head of her family. She was left with a household of Ira Jr. thirteen; Polly seven; Lyman four; Stephen three; and Sarah four months.

### VIII. Grandmother

We know little about Melissa in the years following Ira's death, but they must have been difficult for her and the Willes children. Ira Jr. would have had the burden of hard farm work thrust upon him. But misfortune dogged the family, for on December 27, 1869, he died at age nineteen, cause of death unknown. This left Polly thirteen; Lyman ten; Stephen nine; and Sarah six.

By the 1870s Melissa had apparently moved into Lehi, where she was active in the local Relief Society and surrounded by relatives. Her four children passed through their teenage years, and toward the end of the decade began to marry. Polly united with William Wheeler Clark on March 28, 1878, and Lyman exchanged vows with Sarah Ann Munns in 1881. On February 18, 1885, when Melissa was sixty-one, Sarah Amanda, her youngest, entered matrimony with Albert Mulliner. In the midst of these marriages, Melissa's mother died in Lehi at age seventy-seven, on January 6, 1882.

After thirty-five years of living in Utah, a ghost from the past, Joseph Smith III, showed up on Melissa's doorstep on October 20, 1885, as we have seen, and she relived her marriage to Joseph Smith, Jr., once more.

### IX. "Loved as One of the Choicest among Women"

As Melissa's children were now well launched into their own families, she entered fully into the persona of a grandmother. On January 2, 1887, Polly Melissa Willes Clark bore her fifth child, Thomas Edgar, at age thirty, but was evidently weakened by the childbirth and died less than three weeks later, on the 21st. Of Melissa's seven children, she had now lost her first four. Only Lyman, Stephen, and Sarah remained.

In the last decade of her life, the historical record supplies us with only three pieces of data. According to Jenson, in 1889 she occupied "a prominent position in the Lehi Female Relief Society." In 1892, at age sixty-eight, she testified in the Temple Lot Case, telling of her marriage to Joseph Smith half a century earlier. And in March 1896 "Sister [Melissa] Willis spoke by the gift of the Holy Spirit," according to Francis W. Kirkham, one of a group of departing missionaries, "and said we would go & do a good work and the Lord would be with us." This is probably a reference to speaking in tongues, a practice dwindling among Mormons.

Melissa died on July 13, 1898, when she was seventy-four, at the home of her daughter, Sarah Mulliner, in Lehi. The local paper's obituary supplied an epitaph: "She had only to be known to be loved as one of the choicest among women and was universally known as 'Aunt Melissa.'" After the funeral at the local ward house, she was transported to Salt Lake City and buried by the side of Ira, near her parents.

# 29.

# Outline of a Shadow

## *Nancy Maria Winchester (Smith Kimball Arnold)*

When Joseph Smith died in June 1844, Nancy Maria Winchester became a widow at age fifteen. Later that year, on August 13, when she was sixteen, Heber C. and Vilate Kimball, who had been family friends for years, paid a visit to the Winchester household. Heber wrote in his journal, "Met in council with the Twelve till 2 in the afternoon then I went to Br. Winchesters with my wife [Vilate]." On this day he may have offered himself to Nancy as a proxy husband for time. Two months later, on October 10, Nancy married the forty-three-year-old patriarch. His diary records, "I stood as proxy [for] J Smith and was bound to Nancy Mariah Winchester by B Young." This marriage may have been somewhat dynastic, allowing Heber and the Winchesters to link their families together. But it remains enigmatic, for though Nancy was formally linked to the senior apostle and unable to marry anyone else, she apparently never lived with him and never had children by him.

As a wife of Joseph Smith, Nancy Maria is notable because, with Helen Mar Kimball and Flora Woodworth, she is one of the youngest of Smith's wives—she apparently married him when she was fourteen or fifteen. Her marriage to Kimball is also remarkable, as he evidently encouraged her to divorce him and marry a third husband. Unfortunately her marriages and her entire life are poorly documented.

### I. The Church Coming Out of the Wilderness

On August 10, 1828, Nancy Maria was born in Black Rock, Erie, Pennsylvania (the extreme northwest county, only forty miles from Kirtland) to Stephen Winchester, a thirty-three-year-old Vermont native, and Nancy Case, also thirty-three, from New York. Stephen's obituary tells us that he was "a man of strong constitution, of quiet, persevering, and industrious habits; of excellent character; of firm and unwavering faith, and a kind husband and father." Nancy Maria was preceded by three siblings: Benjamin, Stephen Jr., and Alexander, born in 1817, 1820 and

1825 in the Black Rock area. After her came James Case, born in 1831 in Erie County, and John Parley, born much later, in 1840, in Nauvoo. Thus Nancy was the fourth of six children and the only girl in the family.

In January 1833, when she was four, two Mormon missionaries, John F. Boynton and Evan M. Greene, began a preaching tour in Erie County which achieved great success. On January 27 Stephen, the elder Nancy, and fifteen-year-old Benjamin were baptized in the home of Mr. Mathews at Elk Creek. Greene wrote:

> This day we had a meeting at Mr. Mathews in the Tow[n] of Elk Creek here we had a large congregation of well behaved people—Brother Jn spoke about 1-1/2 hours from the subject of the Priesthoods and the prosperity of the church in the Apostles day The fall from faith or departure in to the wilderness ... I arose and spoke about half an hour from the 3 first verses of the Third Chapter of romans showing what the oracles of God were both to Jew and Gentile also showing how the church was coming out of the wilderness ... we men had the pleasure of following five of our mortals into the waters of Baptism.

So the Winchesters were plucked out of the mainstream of American history and soon were immersed in the Mormon adventure. On the 30th the missionaries returned "to Brother Winchesters" and spent two days "reading the Bible & Mormon Book." Five days later a meeting was held at the Winchester home, and Boynton and Greene confirmed those who had been baptized. A branch was organized at Elk Creek on March 21, and Stephen was ordained a teacher charged to watch over the branch. On December 1 the Winchesters hosted Orson Pratt and Lyman Johnson at Elk Creek.

The Winchesters moved to Kirtland soon after this, however, leaving Pennsylvania in early 1834. Stephen and Benjamin served in the Zion's Camp expedition to Missouri, starting in May—Benjamin, at sixteen, was known as the youngest soldier in the army. After the camp was disbanded on July 3, Stephen and Benjamin worked for Lyman Wight in construction projects in Clay County, Missouri, and on November 5 Stephen was ordained a priest at a meeting of the Clay County High Council. But at some point Stephen and Ben returned to Kirtland. In the next two years both continued to progress in the church—Stephen was selected to be a member of the first Quorum of Seventy on February 28, 1835, in Kirtland, while on January 25, 1836, Benjamin was ordained an elder. The Winchesters became friends of the Heber C. Kimball family in Kirtland.

Nancy Maria is a shadow behind all this. But there is one definite event in her life that took place in Kirtland: she was baptized, probably in August 1836 when she was eight.

In 1837, probably, the Winchesters moved to Missouri, where they lived about three miles from Far West and were neighbors of the Kimballs. Stephen bought and farmed forty acres of land, raising wheat, corn, and hogs. He sat on the Far West High Council in March 1838, evidently as a temporary replacement. But the family found themselves in the middle of the "Mormon War." Stephen served as a Danite and fought in the Battle of Crooked River on October 25; Apostle David Patten was carried to the Winchester home to die after being wounded at that battle. On October 30 Stephen was taken prisoner by the mob militia but was released.

## II. Marriage to the Prophet

The Winchesters apparently left Missouri with the rest of the Mormons in early 1839 and settled for a time at Payson, Adams County, Illinois, where Stephen submitted a redress petition to Governor Boggs. We next hear of the family in the spring 1842 census, which locates them in the Third Ward. Benjamin had moved away by that time, but the five other children are listed, including thirteen-year-old Nancy Maria. On March 30 her mother, Nancy Case, is mentioned in the Relief Society Minutes: "Mrs. Billings refer'd to Mrs. Winchester, with whom C. M. [Clarissa Marvel] had resided—Mrs. W. Had heard C. M. speak of Prest. J. Smith & family in the most respectful manner." On April 14 Nancy Case was accepted into the society, and two weeks later she contributed $.50 to the cause.

On May 27, 1842, Nancy Maria herself was inducted into the Relief Society. Nancy Winchester, probably the mother, continued to contribute to the society in 1842. On July 28, 1843, she was appointed to a four-woman committee in the Nauvoo Third Ward "to search out the poor and suffering—To call on the rich for aid and thus as far as possible relieve the wants of all."

Nancy Maria must have married Joseph Smith at about this time. Our best evidence for the union is Andrew Jenson, who lists "Maria Winchester" as one of Smith's wives; in addition, Orson Whitney, the son of Nancy Maria's friend, Helen, also identifed her as a Smith wife. These two witnesses, taken together, make a good case for Nancy as a plural spouse of Joseph. Though there is no date for her marriage to the prophet, the best hypothesis is that the ceremony took place in 1843, since the last recorded plural marriage to Smith took place on November 2, 1843. If so, she became his wife at the age of fourteen or fifteen. Nothing more is known of this union. On June 27, 1844, Smith was killed, and Nancy was suddenly widowed.

## III. Heber C. Kimball

As we have seen, Nancy married Heber C. Kimball three and a half months later, on October 10, when she was sixteen. Some evidence suggests that she never lived or cohabited with him, so the dynamics of their relationship can only be guessed at. One wonders why he would marry her, thus preventing her from marrying another man, then not cohabit with her. Whatever her status was as a wife of Heber, she had no children by him. However, in the months following the marriage, he frequently visited the Winchester house and noted these visits in his journal. For instance, on March 12, 1845, "Took diner [at] Winchesters." On June 24 "In the Eve I went to Br. Winchesters." On September 15 "Went with my wife [Vilate] to Steven Winch[ester]." On October 9 "After breakfast went to Br. Winchester to give them council."

Sarah Peake Noon, Heber's first plural wife, lived with the Winchesters in 1845. On July 12 she became very sick, and Heber sat up with her most of the night. Nancy Case Winchester was also ill, and on July 16 Heber took Sarah and Mrs. Winchester to the Mississippi and baptized them "for their health." Fortunately both women survived this dunking in the waters of the great river. On December 8 Heber's journal includes a rare direct reference to Nancy Maria: "Went to Steven Winchesters to lay hands on Mariah Winchester She had fits."

On the 18th Nancy Maria, with her parents and older brother Stephen, received her endowment in the Nauvoo temple. Half a month later, on February 3, 1846, she received her proxy marriage to Joseph Smith and Heber Kimball in the temple. She was seventeen at the time.

### IV. Salt Lake City

The Winchesters crossed the plains in 1849, according to Kate Carter. Her listing of the party includes Nancy Maria, now twenty; Stephen and Nancy C. Winchester, both fifty-four; Benjamin (a mistake); Stephen; Alexander (another mistake, as he died in 1845); and James C. Winchester, age eighteen. The 1850 Salt Lake census shows Nancy M. (Winchester), twenty-one, living with her parents, along with a "William Hughteling," twenty.

Nancy now drops out of the historical record for a few years. She probably continued to live with her parents, though she may have paid visits to the Kimball homes. On March 2, 1854, she received a patriarchal blessing from John Smith in which she was blessed "to heal the sick, cast out devils, and raise the dead, if necessary." For six years following this blessing, Nancy Maria is once again entirely undocumented. But the 1860 census records that she was living with her parents in the 17th Ward in Salt Lake City.

### V. Amos George Arnold

By 1865, at least, Nancy had separated from Kimball, for on October

12, when she was thirty-seven, she married Amos George Arnold. Arnold, a thirty-two-year-old native of New York, had immigrated to Utah in 1863. Strangely enough, according to Arnold family traditions, the marriage was arranged by Kimball himself. A note on a family group sheet tells us: "Nancy Mariah Winchester was sealed to the Prophet on 3 Feb 1846 in the Nauvoo Temple and married to Heber C. Kimball for life, but she never lived with Mr. Kimball as his wife and he asked Amos George Arnold to marry her so she could become a mother and promised him that he would later have the opportunity of marrying a younger wife." Apparently Nancy's proxy marriage to Heber never "took," for whatever reasons.

Nancy's third marriage did produce a child, George Stephen Arnold, born on December 9, 1867, in Salt Lake City, when Nancy was thirty-nine. However, despite the joy that the child undoubtedly brought her, the childbirth left her in poor health, and she and Amos moved in with her parents, probably so that Nancy Case could tend her daughter and grandchild. On January 1, 1873, Nancy's father, Stephen, died at a time when Nancy Maria may have been living in the Winchester household.

Nancy's own health continued to deteriorate, and on March 17, 1876, she died at age forty-seven in Salt Lake City. She left as a historical legacy only a bare, enigmatic outline. Not a trace of her personality remains in written documents. One can only wonder what a memoir of her three marriages might have told us. Did she feel any attachment to Joseph Smith, or was the marriage purely dynastic? Did she feel depressed and rebellious like Flora and Helen Mar? Why did her marriage to Heber C. Kimball fail, or never really begin? Did she or Arnold initiate their marriage in any way, or was it more of an "assignment" given to them by Heber? Unless further Winchester family documents come to light, we are not likely to ever know the answers to these questions.

# 30.

# True Saint

## *Fanny Young (Carr Murray Smith)*

In the summer of 1801 the John and Abigail Young family was working hard to survive their first year in Whitingham, Vermont, when a new child, Brigham, was born on June 1. However, Abigail suffered from "consumption" (tuberculosis) and was too weak to properly care for the new infant, so an older sister, thirteen-year-old Fanny, became his surrogate mother.

Fanny's brother Joseph wrote that she developed a special rapport not only with the baby but also with the family's valuable milk cow. It would allow no one near it except Fanny, "who with the infant Brigham in her arms performed this service of milking each day during the summer ... the child had to be nursed from the bottle, and no one could pacify him but my sister Fanny." This brief glimpse into her adolescence shows her working energetically and shouldering the burden of caring for younger children in a large family. It also shows the beginning of a close bond between Fanny and her famous brother. She helped raise him and first gave him a Book of Mormon, while he provided a home for her in her final years in Utah.

Twice widowed and fifty-six at the time of her marriage to Joseph Smith, Fanny was one of his oldest wives and was his last well-documented wife. The marriage was a classic dynastic linking, connecting him to Brigham Young, one of his most loyal and faithful disciples. Fanny is documented by a few holograph letters and by an appreciation in the memoirs of Helen Mar Kimball Whitney, whom Fanny helped raise. Helen was enormously fond of Fanny, who was clearly a lovable woman. In addition, the writings of the Young family give us a good account of the household in which she grew up.

### I. The Youngs

Fanny was born on November 8, 1787, to John Young and Abigail ("Nabby") Howe in Hopkinton, Middlesex, Massachusetts, a farming town twenty-five miles southwest of Boston. John, twenty-four, was a farmer and a native of Hopkinton. Abigail, twenty-two, has been described as having had blue eyes and "yellowish brown hair folded in natural waves and ringlets." She was also from Hopkinton. Fanny grew up the second oldest child in a family of eleven. Her one older sibling, Nancy, had been born in 1786. After Fanny's arrival, Rhoda, John Jr., Nabby, Susanna, Joseph, and Phinehas were born to the Youngs from 1789 to 1799, all in Hopkinton except Rhoda, who was born in Durham, Greene County, New York.

Lorenzo Young, another brother, wrote of his father that he was, at first, an "Episcopal Methodist" but later became "Reformed Methodist," both primitivist groups that "undertook to practice some of the Bible doctrines now taught by the Latter day Saints." Abigail was also devout, if sickly. Lorenzo remembered going to her bedside where she would counsel him to be a good man so the Lord might bless his life. "On one occasion she told me that if I would not neglect to pray to my heavenly Father, he would send a guardian angel to protect me." Thus Fanny undoubtedly grew up a devout Methodist herself.

When Fanny was a baby, the Youngs moved to Durham, New York, but Abigail's parents soon convinced them to return to Hopkinton. Some of Fanny's earliest memories involve the trip back to her maternal grandparents' home, which took place in about 1790 when she was three. The Youngs needed to ford a dangerous iced-over river just as winter was yielding to spring, and after considering alternatives, John and Abigail decided that they had no choice but to cross over on the ice that was starting to thin. They made their way over the river in great suspense, "{crooking} about, and often sticking their {canes} through the ice into the River." Fanny wrote that when they reached the opposite shore, Abigail "drew a long breath, as she said she dar'd not breathe while on the river, for it was {open} above and below, and she expected evry moment to go to the bottom.____I can date the begining of my recollections to this time."

Fanny also remembered how, when the Youngs reached Abigail's parents, "all the family flew out to receive us, and caught the three children, one older [Nancy], and the other younger [Rhoda] than myself in their arms, while my Grandmother and my mother wept."

## II. Vermont

In November 1800 John Young bought fifty acres of land for $50 in Whitingham, Windham, Vermont, in the southeastern corner of the state. Fanny and her family set out for their new home in January 1801, though they left Rhoda in Hopkinton. (Leonard Arrington surmises that this occurred because Abigail's parents could not bear to see the whole family depart.) The Youngs made this winter journey in two bobsleds, with mounted wagon boxes, drawn by oxen. It must have been a difficult journey as they traveled through snowstorms, deep snow, and biting cold.

At Whitingham they lived in a former settler's cabin while John quickly built their new home in midwinter—a sixteen-foot-square cabin with one room. The family settled in and tapped nearby maples for syrup. When winter had passed, John and his sons began to clear the rocky land, an arduous task. Here, as has been narrated earlier, Brigham was born and thirteen-year-old Fanny tended him. On January 13, 1803, her older sister Nancy married, so Fanny at fifteen was left with even more responsibility as the oldest sibling in a household of nine.

The Vermont land proved to be too difficult to farm, so after a bitter struggle the Youngs moved to Smyrna, Chenango, New York, thirty miles southeast of Syracuse, in spring 1804. There Nabby, despite her health problems, had two more children: Louisa, and Lorenzo Dow, born on September 26, 1804, and October 19, 1807.

## III. Robert Carr

When she was eighteen years old, on May 5, 1806, Fanny married Robert Carr in Hopkinton, Massachusetts. Unfortunately the marriage was not happy; family traditions characterize Carr as "unfaithful and profligate." Apparently the union produced no children. Apart from the fact that the Carrs may have lived in Charleston, Montgomery County, New York, at some point, little is known of this period of Fanny's life.

On June 11, 1815, when Fanny was twenty-seven, Abigail finally succumbed to consumption, dying in Aurelius, Cayuga, New York. Apparently, by this time Fanny had left Carr and moved back in with the Young family. We do know that when Nabby died, Fanny "walked the floor" with seven-year-old Lorenzo Dow. He later testified, "As she was the oldest of the girls of my father's family then at home, from that time forward she was a mother to me and to the rest of the family, so long as we remained in it." In autumn 1815 the Youngs moved to Tyrone, Schuyler County, New York.

## IV. Armies in the Sky

We know little of Fanny specifically until 1827, when a number of Youngs were living in Mendon, Monroe, New York, ten miles southeast of Rochester and ten miles southwest of Palmyra. Since the Young and Heber C. Kimball families were very close, sometimes Fanny lived with the Kimballs, probably to help Vilate, who was somewhat sickly and needed assistance with household chores and tending the children.

On September 22, 1827, according to an account by Heber, after retiring to bed in the Kimball home, Fanny was suddenly awakened from a deep sleep when Heber called to everyone in the house: "Come out and see the scenery in the heavens!" Fanny, with Vilate and father John Young, emerged from the house to see Heber in his nightclothes and Rhoda Young Greene (Fanny's sister) and her husband John looking up at the nighttime sky. The heavens were so dazzlingly brilliant that it was almost like daytime. In the east "white smoke" formed a "belt" and rustled like a "mighty wind." Then it moved southwest, forming a "bow" in the western horizon. This widened and grew bluish and transparent:

> In this bow an army moved, commencing from the east and marching to the west. They moved in platoons, and walked so close, the rear ranks trod in the steps of their file leaders, until the whole bow was literally crowded with soldiers. We could see distinctly the muskets, bayonets, and knapsacks of the men, who wore caps and feathers like those used by the American soldiers in the last war with Britain; also their officers with their swords and equipage, and heard the clashing and jingling of their instruments of war and could discover the form and features of the men. The most profound order existed throughout the entire army, when the foremost man stepped, every man stepped at the same time: I could hear the step. When the front rank reached the Western horizon a battle ensued, as we could distinctly hear the report of the arms and the rush.

As Heber watched in amazement, his hair stood on end. "This scenery was gazed upon for hours, until it began to disappear," he wrote.

Vilate, frightened, turned to Fanny's father. "Father Young, what does all this mean?"

John replied with some satisfaction, "Why, it's one of the signs of the coming of the Son of Man."

On the following night these New Yorkers witnessed "similar scenery," but it was now in the west. Later, of course, they all realized that September 22 was the date on which Joseph Smith received the gold plates of the Book of Mormon from the angel Moroni. For our purposes, this story shows that Fanny was living with the Kimballs in fall 1827, and it reflects the religious atmosphere in which she lived: the second coming of Christ was expected to come at any moment. John Young's apocalyptic fervor would be shared by many Latter-day Saints.

Methodists administered to the sick as Mormons later would, and Fanny was once healed by these administrations. Lorenzo wrote: "I once knew my brother John and Calvin Gilmour, a brother Methodist, leave their work and travel on foot over to the town of Ty[r]one, [Schuyler County] a distance of twenty four miles, to administer to my sister Fanny, who they had heard lay at the point of death. They all believed in the gift of healing and, through faith in the administration, my sister recovered."

On August 22, 1828, when Helen Mar was born to Heber and Vilate, Fanny was still living with the Kimballs. Helen later wrote, "Aunt Fanny Young ... took care of me, and she was always ready to defend me if necessary." Fanny even named Helen: "Aunt Fanny had been a great reader; and I was named by her after the Scottish Lady, Helen Mar." Here we see how close the Young and Kimball families were. Helen wrote that she loved Brigham, Joseph, and Fanny more than her own relatives, who had been left behind in the Kimballs' westward journeys. So Mormonism divided biological families, often, and created new brothers and sisters to replace them. Non-Mormons stayed in the east, while Mormons traveled to Zion in the deserts and mountain valleys of Utah. As the life of Sarah Cleveland shows, close family members often never saw each other again after 1846.

Helen Mar left a vivid pen sketch of Fanny:

> Aunt Fanny was a true Saint, and was beloved by all who had the pleasure of her acquaintance; her sympathies were always exercised for the poor and distressed. She was agreeable society for old or young and many an evening her young acquaintances would gather at her house to hear her sing or relate the "Scottish Chiefs," "Children of the Abbey," and other like tales, which she could do as I never heard any one else ... The Youngs were all gifted singers and when they sang together they made a grand choir. Aunt Fanny sang many beautiful songs, but the one I loved best was "Oft in the stilly night." She had a clear melodious voice, and sang with such pathos, that all present would be affected to tears.

Fanny's brother Joseph also left a short description of his sister: "She was a good reader, and of a devotional turn of mind. She had fine sympathies and keen sensibilities ... as much so, in this rude world, as to cause her much unhappiness through taking the cares of this life to heart."

### V. Roswell Murray

In April 1830 Samuel Smith passed through Mendon on a missionary journey and left a Book of Mormon with Phinehas Young. Phinehas read the book, believed that it was true, gave it to his father John to read, then to Fanny. "She examined it and reported the book to be a revelation." Fanny next gave it to her baby brother, Brigham, and the course of Mormon and western American history was thereby changed. However, despite the impression the book made on her, Fanny was not baptized immediately.

First she married her second husband, sixty-two-year-old Roswell Murray, on February 2, 1832. This union would further cement Fanny into the family of the Kimballs, for Roswell was Vilate's father. Despite the age disparity (she was forty-four), the marriage evidently was happy. Helen Mar Whitney characterized her maternal grandfather as an enormously kind, unselfish man.

The Youngs had investigated Mormonism thoroughly by 1832 and were ready to formally cast their lot with the new church. Fanny did not lag behind her brothers: in April she was baptized by Alpheus Gifford, the same month that Brigham, John and Joseph Young, Rhoda Young Greene and her husband John, and Heber and Vilate Kimball converted. Heber in his journal listed Fanny as part of a small branch of thirty at Mendon, many of them Youngs. Roswell, however, never was baptized, though he was friendly to Mormons and lived among them for the rest of his life.

Within the year, at some time before the fall of 1833, Fanny and Roswell moved to Kirtland, where they became friendly with a Mr. Smith and his sister, Sarah, both bitter anti-Mormons. According to Helen Mar, when the Heber Kimball family arrived in the city, Sarah, despite her prejudices against Mormonism, "thought so much of grandpa Murray and his wife that she consented to our living in her house until Spring." So Fanny lived in Kirtland in the peaceful years when the church was evolving steadily, before any of the great persecutions against the Latter-day Saints had begun. Joseph Smith was receiving frequent revelations, and the church was developing gradually into its present organization. One imagines Fanny living amongst the extended Young/Kimball structure of relatives, coming to know Eliza Snow, Zina and Presendia Huntington and other Mormon women who one day would form the Mormon "female hierarchy" and be sister-wives. In February 1835 Brigham and Heber were called to be apostles, so suddenly Fanny was closely related to two men who would become increasingly central to Mormonism.

Helen Mar gives us a sketch of Fanny's second husband while he was living among the Mormons. She was clearly fighting an internal struggle with Mormonism's strictly authoritarian soteriology at the time she wrote this defense of her grandfather:

> My Grandfather Murray was not a member of any church; he believed the principles of Mormonism, and was often upon the point of being baptized, when he would see things in individuals who professed to be Saints which would so try him he thought he stood as good a chance to be saved as any one. A more noble kind-hearted man never lived, he was generous to a fault, and some were unprincipled enough to take advantage of it. He was very ingenious and could make anything from a child's run-a-round to a Rocking horse and carriage. He was never known to re-

fuse a favor, and he would often rise from his bed when he was sick to go and do a job of work to accommodate a neighbor. He was a man of but few words and some called him an Infidel.

Heber was nearing the end of an eastern states mission in 1836, and Vilate went to meet him and visit family in New York, so their two older children were farmed out, William to Fanny and Roswell, and Helen Mar to a Sister Noble. When they returned, one detail from the October 2 homecoming presents Fanny as an important part of the Kimball family: "The wood fire was burning brightly on the andirons and our old fashioned tin oven stood before it filled with sweet apples and Aunt Fanny was preparing breakfast." Fanny is the worker. She had been a crucial component of the Young household as a teenager, when her mother was sick, and now she was a central cog in the extended Kimball family.

In 1838 internal dissent and financial reverses caused the majority of Mormons to leave Kirtland for Missouri, and Fanny and Roswell prepared to leave with the Kimball and Young families respectively, apparently not traveling together. Roswell probably left Kirtland with Heber and Vilate, who departed in late June with a band of forty other Latter-day Saints. Fanny perhaps stayed behind to help her father, leaving with him and her nephew Evan Greene on September 19.

### VI. "I ... Did Not Want for Hard Hard Times"

Fanny's stay in Missouri would be brief. On arriving at Huntsville, her father was threatened by a mob and forced to leave the state. He and Fanny then traveled to Morgan County in Illinois, fifteen miles west of Springfield. Most of the Kimballs came to Illinois with Brigham Young in February 1839, while Heber stayed in Missouri to help direct the Mormons' departure. Roswell may have traveled with this group, so Roswell and Fanny may have reunited in Illinois at this time. However, Brigham Young portrays Fanny living with Evan Greene for a year in Morgan County. Then, when Lorenzo sent for her, he wrote, she moved to Macedonia, east of Nauvoo, before relocating in Nauvoo.

In Illinois Vilate and her family lived for seven weeks with a Colonel William Ross in Atlas, Pike County, thirty-five miles south of Quincy. By fall 1839 Roswell was living in Winchester, Scott County, a town twenty-five miles east of Atlas, in the county just west of Morgan. After seven weeks John Greene, Fanny's brother-in-law, moved Vilate and family to Quincy, where Heber found them on May 2. But Roswell, with Fanny, apparently stayed in Winchester.

It is certain that Roswell was living in Winchester in September because on October 1 Heber Kimball, setting off with Brigham on a mission to England, noted in his journal that he went "to Mr. Roswell Murray's, my father-in-law ... living ... near Winchester, in Scott County ... Here we also found a few brethren in the church, who had been smitten and robbed of their property in Missouri." So Fanny and Roswell were living in a small colony of Missouri refugees, including Lorenzo Dow, two days' journey from Nauvoo.

Roswell decided to travel back east with his son-in-law to visit his children in New York, so he and Heber departed on October 4. Heber last mentioned him in his journal on November 3 when they were in Cleveland, Ohio. At some point after this, while he was in the East, Roswell died. Helen Mar wrote, "While visiting his children in the East, he was taken sick, and before he died he expressed his regret for not having obeyed the Gospel." This death would have been a bitter blow for Fanny, but it would not have been entirely unexpected. Life expectancy at the time was shorter than ours, and Roswell was sixty-nine. Fanny herself was now about fifty-two. A week after Roswell's departure, on October 12, Joseph Young died in Quincy, so she lost a husband and a father in a brief period of time.

Little is known of Fanny in the years immediately after Roswell's death, beyond the fact that she moved to Macedonia, then to Nauvoo and lived near or with her siblings once again. She was still in Winchester in February 1841. Later she wrote: "After Mr Murrays death ... I got along just as I could, did not want for hard hard times—sometimes rented a little room and paid for it with my needle, although my own work was more than I was able to do.—sometimes I made out to be comfortable, sometimes I barely subsisted: but I made no complaint to any one—sometimes I was near my relatives, sometimes far from them." Living as a single woman in nineteenth-century America could be a harsh struggle for survival.

### VII. "You Seal This Lady to Me"

Fanny's marriage to Joseph Smith—possibly his last—shows how casual and unromantic polygamy could be. One day, on November 2, 1843, Fanny, Brigham, and Joseph were discussing exaltation and celestial marriage. As Brigham tells the story, Fanny gave her opinion on the subject: "Now, don't talk to me; when I get into the celestial kingdom, if I ever do get there, I shall request the privilege of being a ministering angel; that is the labor that I wish to perform. I don't want any companion in that world; and if the Lord will make me a ministering angel, it is all I want."

Smith replied, "Sister, you talk very foolishly, you do not know what you will want." He turned to her brother: "Here, Brother Brigham, you seal this lady to me."

Apparently Fanny quickly changed her mind and married Smith on the spot. Mary Ann Angell Young, Brigham's first wife, Harriet Cook, and Augusta Adams Cobb stood as witnesses, and Brigham performed the ceremony. "I sealed her to him," he wrote. "This was my own sister according to the flesh." Harriet and Augusta were sealed to Brigham the same day. Fanny was six days from fifty-six years old at the time of the marriage, while Smith was thirty-eight. The union was clearly dynastic, linking Brigham and Joseph, and, in Smith's view, would have increased Fanny's chances for complete salvation.

A month and a half later, on December 23, Fanny received her endowment and joined the Holy Order. Also in December Fanny tended William Young, Lorenzo Dow's son, who was afflicted by dropsy and on the point of death. On the last day of the year she figured in one of the curious feminine priestly tableaus from early Mormonism: "Then William's Aunts Fanny and Mary Ann [Angell Young]," James Little wrote, "... washed and anointed him, after which the father prayed for and administered to him." William lived.

On June 27, 1844, Joseph Smith was killed at Carthage. Fanny was widowed for the third and last time. She then dropped out of the historical record for a year and a half.

### VIII. "Sorrows and Turmoils of this Inconstant Life"

Like most Mormons, Fanny performed sacred rites in the Nauvoo temple before leaving Illinois. She received her endowment on January 7, 1846, and was probably washed and anointed by Mary Ann Young and Vilate Kimball, who were among the sisters officiating that session. For unknown reasons, Fanny did not receive a temple proxy marriage to Joseph Smith; perhaps she felt too emotionally attached to Roswell Murray.

She stayed in Nauvoo after the main body of the church left in February. She later wrote, "When all my friends left Nauvoo, and came west, I was left behind, not because they did not care for me, but because evry one had families of children, and just as much on their hands as they could live through So I wended my way, as best I could, until they sent back for me." She was in Nauvoo at least until June 3, when she wrote to Vilate Kimball: "Nauvoo looks like a grave yard I hope to leave it some time or other ... I desire much to be there with you, but must wait the Lords time, that is always the best." However, in September, apparently, Fanny left Nauvoo with William Kimball, whom she had once tended in the Kimball home in New York. Zina Huntington Young wrote that Fanny and William passed through Mt. Pisgah a little before October 1.

She evidently spent four cold winters at Winter Quarters, but is not well documented during those years. In 1848 she received a letter from Vilate Decker in Salt Lake, and on May 22, 1849, she sent a letter to John and Lorenzo Young in Salt Lake. It began: "My dear Brothers, I must write a line to you, to say I am alive and enjoy as much health as I can expect to, in this country, situated as I am—I get along well enough." It ended: "I could say many things, and speak of many persons for whom I have the best of feelings—but what is the use—I bid you farewell my brothers, and hope you will make sure work for Eternity  Fanny Murray." On July 5 she was still at Winter Quarters and wrote to John Young in an exhortatory mood:

> Be of good cheer br John, salvation is nearer than when we first believ'd—I rejoice in hope of the glory of God—which I believe my eyes will behold, and my heart exult in. Strive to live near the Lord br John for I find nothing to comfort my soul ~~but~~ the old fashion'd love of God! even that love which is stronger than death. this alone gives us the victory.—this is all my consolation, amid the sorrows and turmoils of this inconstant life.

Her parting salutation is bittersweet: "Now I wish to be understood, if any-one cares for me, I care for them, as warmly and truely as any-body—but if not, I can be as they are  I have no friendship to throw away in my old age—."

## IX. "Lay Me on the Ground, and Let Me Die"

In the summer of 1850 Fanny set out for Utah. When she started, though, she was required to travel on a load of boxes and became very sick. She wrote: "We traveled two days and a half, when I beged them in mercy, to lay me on the ground, and let me die in peace—the waggons stop'd a few days until I was a little better, when they carried me back to the first Tavern, and left me.—that sickness I never got over, nor have I ever been able to do much {sin[ce]}." Nevertheless, she traveled west to Utah later that season. While we know no further specifics of her journey, she later wrote advice to friends, the Foxes, preparing to travel west, and this letter gives some insight into her own trip overland:

> You can certainly wash a little on the road—when you get on to the plains—the company always stops once in awhile to wash and bake—but the less washing you have to do on the road the better—do not burden yourselves with any {unnescery} thing—nevertheless if your dishes are very nice, I would try and fetch enough to set a table handsomely, unless your load is too heavy—about lodging; I had a sort of bedstead fixed into my waggon after the projection was on; they bored holes through and then by pin[n]ing on somthing like the end rails of a bedstead—we {corded} up our bed across ways of the waggon, and made our lodging very comfortable, only our bed was rather short  this is a great comfort when we are sick on the road—and then your children will sleep in the day-time; just as though they were rocked in a cradle.

## X. "O! How Sweet Will Everlasting Rest Be"

The 1850 Utah census shows a Fanny Murray, age sixty-three, worth $75, living in Salt Lake, with a Naoma, age thirty, and a Nancy Greene, age twenty-one. The latter is the subject of a pen sketch in Fanny's letter to the Foxes: "But when I did reach my friends, the Lord provided a comforter for me, the youngest daughter of my brother and Sister [Rhoda Young] Greene; they were both dead: and the dear girl seem'd to cleave so to me, that she never left me. the greatest comfort of my life—since then I never have broken up, have always kept house."

Martha Heywood visited "Mrs. Fanny Murray" on January 26, 1851, and "found her in tolerable health but she receives cold whenever she goes out." Fanny wrote to her oldest sibling Nancy the next day, mentioning several sudden deaths due to "the old fashion'd Epidemic." Wood was scarce in the valley, but there was "no scarcity of provision here." She complained of "nearly one thousand Emigrants stoping here this winter" and described the celebration when brother Brigham was formally appointed governor: "last night about sunset, he was usher'd into the City, with the roaring of Cannon; the band of music, and a company of horsemen that look'd like immortals. Several Carriages, and many footmen! I Said to myself, I hope his robes of honor will not deprive him of his robe of righteousness he came in to see us in the evening, look'd very thoughtful and contemplative."

She reported that "my health is poor, Nancys health is very poor, but our time is nearly out, we shall labor through and then I trust we shall rest!—O! how sweet will everlasting rest be to our weary souls." The health of her young housemate worsened, and finally, in July 1852, she died—a bitter blow to Fanny. In the Fox letter she wrote: "On the tenth of last month she departed this life, aged 22 O! She was a dear child—those words often roll through my mind, 'I am bereaved, O! I am bereav'd!'—however, all is right, although I feel myself alone in the world—she told me she was sure the Lord would raise up some one to be my comfort and stay as she had been."

When the Lion House was completed in 1856, Brigham offered Fanny, now sixty-nine, a room there, and for the rest of her life she lived under the same roof with Eliza Snow, Zina Huntington, Emily Partridge, and other wives of Joseph Smith. C. V. Waite, a non-Mormon traveller, described her room as consisting of "a red and yellow carpet, homemade bedsteads, oak chairs, a fall-leaf table, and oilshades. A sitting-room and a small bedroom."

Wilford Woodruff, a church historian, and Heber Kimball called on Fanny one night in October 1856, perhaps to record the story of her life. But apparently the backward view down the corridors of her past years was too painful for her: "In speaking of her history she said she had been alone a good deal through life & she did not wish to have a history of her life published. She did not wish any one to have her likeness neither after she was dead." Her famous brother had his every move recorded by scribes for a planned biographical history, while Fanny, evidently depressed by her life's loneliness, wanted her memory obliterated from history.

Susa Young Gates, one of Brigham's daughters, also described Fanny in the Lion House and gives us a pathetic picture of her as an older woman, suffering a nervous condition, complaining about her ills: "The last room to the north was used for a while by Aunt Fanny Murray, father's invalid and widowed sister. I can't remember her. But I know from tradition, that she was a pretty woman, with dark waving hair, and a sensitive, nervous organization. She was prone to bemoan her condition with great insistency."

One day the elderly woman was telling Brigham of her "afflictions and griefs," and he said to her: "Sister Fannie, there is help for you."

"Where, brother Brigham, where is there any help for me?"

"In the Gospel, sister Fanny, where there is help for you and me, and for all the world."

Yet Fanny's pains were not imaginary, and would only increase. She was suffering from cancer.

### XI. "Let the First Thing You Say Be 'Hallelujah!'"

Zina Young wrote on April 22, 1859, "Aunt Fannes Templ suit is most finished." Faithful Mormons are customarily buried in their temple robes, so Zina was perhaps preparing for Fanny's death. As her condition deteriorated, Brigham's wives took turns sitting with her, "to make her last days comfortable." Eventually she moved out of the Lion House into the home of a niece, Fanny McKnight. Joseph Young said, at Fanny's funeral, "Sister McKnight manifested toward her aunt the sympathy and feeling of a daughter to her mother." Eliza Young, the wife of Fanny's nephew William G. Young, also tended her, often sacrificing her own sleep for the dying woman's comfort. On June 8 Brigham wrote to his plural wife Lucy Bigelow, "My sister Fanny is very low. We do not think she can stand it very long." As she sank lower and lower, probably enduring great pain, she looked toward death with hope, even rejoicing, and wrote to her sister Nancy, "If you hear of my being dead before you come to see me again, let the first thing you say be 'Hallelujah!'"

She died on June 11 at age seventy-one. No doubt her passing was mourned by Brigham, whom she had carried on her hip when she went out mornings to milk the cow in Vermont. Also grieving would have been the other Youngs and the Kimball family, whose home she had lived in for so many years. We also must imagine her sister wives gathered around the new grave in the Salt Lake cemetery overlooking the valley on a beautiful summer's afternoon: Helen Mar (whom Fanny had named and helped raise), Zina, Presendia, Patty, Sylvia, Marinda, perhaps Elizabeth Brackenbury, Eliza Roxcy, Sarah Ann, Ruth, Emily Dow, Lucy, Elvira, Rhoda, Desdemona, perhaps Melissa, and Nancy Maria, each of whom bore her own burden of solitude as a result of their prophet-husband's legacy of patriarchal plurality. The last married of Joseph Smith's wives had passed over to the other country.

# ABBREVIATIONS, BIBLIOGRAPHIES, AND CHAPTER REFERENCES.

AF: Ancestral File, GS.

Alexander, Thomas. *Things in Heaven and Earth: The Life and Times of Wilford Woodruff, A Mormon Prophet.* Salt Lake City: Signature Books, 1991.

Allen, James, and Glen Leonard. *The Story of the Latter-day Saints.* Salt Lake City: Deseret Book, 1976.

Arrington, Leonard. *Brigham Young: American Moses.* New York: Alfred Knopf, 1985.

———, and Davis Bitton. *The Mormon Experience: A History of the Latter-day Saints.* New York: Random House, 1979.

Bachman, Danel. "A Study of the Mormon Practice of Plural Marriage before the Death of Joseph Smith." Master's thesis, Purdue University, 1975. An appendix, 345-53, lists affidavits by number.

Backman, Milton V. *A Profile of Latter-day Saints of Kirtland, Ohio and Members of Zion's Camp, 1830-1839: Vital Statistics and Sources.* Provo, UT: Brigham Young University, 1982.

Bailey, Raymond. "Emma Hale, Wife of the Prophet Joseph Smith." Master's thesis, Brigham Young University, 1952.

BAOPM: see Joseph Fielding Smith, *Blood Atonement.*

Bates, Irene M., and E. Gary Smith. *Lost Legacy: The Mormon Office of Presiding Patriarch.* Urbana: University of Illinois Press, 1996.

BE: see Andrew Jenson, *LDS Biographical Encyclopedia.*

Beecher, Maureen Ursenbach. *Eliza and Her Sisters.* Salt Lake City: Aspen Books, 1991.

———, ed. *The Personal Writings of Eliza Roxcy Snow.* Salt Lake City: University of Utah Press, 1995.

———, and Lavina Fielding Anderson, eds. *Sisters in Spirit: Mormon Women in Historical and Cultural Perspective.* Urbana: University of Illinois Press, 1987.

Bennett, John C. *The History of the Saints: or, An Expose of Joe Smith and Mormonism.* Boston: Leland & Whiting, 1842. Originally published in the *Sangamo Journal.*

Bitton, Davis. *A Guide to Mormon Diaries and Autobiographies.* Provo, UT: Brigham Young University Press, 1977.

Black, Susan Easton. *Early Members of the Reorganized Church of Jesus Christ of Latter Day Saints.* Provo, UT: BYU Religious Studies Center, 1989.

———. *Membership of the Church of Jesus Christ of Latter-day Saints, 1830-1848.* Provo, UT: BYU Religious Studies Center, 1989. (SEB)

BOP: "A Book of Proxey." Nauvoo temple proxy sealings, Jan. 7 to Feb. 5, 1846. GS and Marriott Library.

Bringhurst, Newell G. *Brigham Young and the Expanding American Frontier.* Boston: Little, Brown and Co., 1986.

Brodie, Fawn. *No Man Knows My History.* 2nd ed. New York: Alfred Knopf, 1985.

BYj: Brigham Young journal, CA and Marriott Library.

BYUSt: *Brigham Young University Studies.*

CA: Church Archives, Historical Department, Church of Jesus Christ of Latter-day Saints, Salt Lake City.

Campbell, Eugene E., and Bruce L. Campbell. "Divorce Among Mormon Polygamists: Extent and Explanations." In Quinn, NMH 169-200.

Cannon, Donald Q., and Lyndon Cook, eds. *Far West Record: Minutes of The Church of Jesus Christ of Latter-day Saints, 1830-1844.* Salt Lake City: Deseret Book, 1983.

CHC: see B. H. Roberts.

Cook, Lyndon W. *Nauvoo Deaths and Marriages: 1839-1845*. Orem, UT: Grandin Book Co., 1994.

———. *The Revelations of the Prophet Joseph Smith*. Provo, UT: Seventies Bookstore, 1981.

———. *William Law: Biographical Essays, Nauvoo Diary, Correspondence, Interview*. Orem, UT: Grandin Book Co., 1994.

Cott, Nancy F. *The Bonds of Womanhood: "Woman's Sphere" in New England, 1780-1835*. New Haven, CT: Yale University Press, 1977.

Crocheron, Augusta. *Representative Women of Deseret: A Book of Biographical Sketches*. Salt Lake City: J.C. Graham, 1884.

DEN: *Deseret Evening News*, Salt Lake City.

Derr, Jill Mulvay, Janath Russell Cannon, and Maureen Ursenbach Beecher. *Women of Covenant: The Story of the Relief Society*. Salt Lake City: Deseret Book, 1992.

DN: *Deseret News*, Salt Lake City.

DW: *Deseret Weekly*, Salt Lake City.

EBWj: Emmeline B. Wells [Emmeline Blanche Woodward Harris Whitney Wells] journal, Lee Library. Restricted, but a typescript is available to researchers.

ECIF: Early Church Information File, GS, also in other libraries on film.

Ehat, Andrew. "Joseph Smith's Introduction of Temple Ordinances and the 1844 Mormon Succession Question." Master's thesis, Brigham Young University, 1982.

———, and Lyndon Cook, eds. *The Words of Joseph Smith*. Provo, UT: BYU Religious Studies Center, 1980.

EJ: *Elder's Journal*, Mormon journal.

EM: Daniel Ludlow, ed. *The Encyclopedia of Mormonism*. 4 vols. New York: Macmillan, 1992.

EMRC: see Black, *Early Members of the Reorganized Church*.

ERSj: Eliza R. Snow journal, in the Huntington Library, San Marino, California.

Esshom, Frank. *Pioneers and Prominent Men of Utah*. Salt Lake City: Utah Pioneer Book Publishing Co., 1913.

Faulring, Scott. *An American Prophet's Record: The Diaries and Journals of Joseph Smith*. Salt Lake City: Signature Books in association with Smith Research Associates, 1989. This includes some materials not found in Jessee.

FGS: Family Group Sheet, in GS.

Flanders, Robert B. *Nauvoo: Kingdom on the Mississippi*. Urbana: University of Illinois Press, 1965.

Foster, Lawrence. *Religion and Sexuality: Three American Communal Experiments of the Nineteenth Century*. New York: Oxford University Press, 1981.

FWR: see Cannon/Cook, *Far West Record*.

Godfrey, Kenneth, Audrey M. Godfrey, and Jill Mulvay Derr. *Women's Voices, An Untold History of the Latter-day Saints, 1830-1900*. Salt Lake City: Deseret Book, 1982.

GS: Genealogical Society, Church of Jesus Christ of Latter-day Saints, Salt Lake City. Branches at Harold B. Lee Library, Brigham Young University, Provo, Utah, and Los Angeles, near the Los Angeles temple.

Hall, William. *The Abominations of Mormonism Exposed*. Cincinnati: I. Hart, 1852.

Hanks, Maxine, ed. *Women and Authority: Re-emerging Mormon Feminism*. Salt Lake City: Signature Books, 1992.

Hardy, B. Carmon. *Solemn Covenant*. Urbana: University of Illinois Press, 1992.

HC: Brigham H. Roberts, ed. *History of the Church of Jesus Christ of Latter-day Saints*. 7 vols. Salt Lake City: Church of Jesus Christ of Latter-day Saints, 1902-32.

HCK: see Stanley Kimball, *Heber C. Kimball*.

HCKj, Heber C. Kimball journal, CA. Stanley Kimball, ed. *On the Potter's Wheel: The Diaries of Heber C. Kimball*. Salt Lake City: Signature Books in association with Smith Research Associates, 1987.

HCKj, Book 93: Heber C. Kimball/Clayton journal, CA. William Clayton kept this journal for Heber C. Kimball. I consulted a photocopy in private possession. Some of this is published in Clayton, IC.

Heywood, Martha Spence. Journal. Published in Juanita Brooks, ed. *Not By Bread Alone, The Journal of Martha Spence Heywood*. Salt Lake City: Utah State Historical Society, 1978.

Hill, Donna. *Joseph Smith: The First Mormon*. Garden City, NY: Doubleday, 1977.

Hill, Marvin. *Quest for Refuge: The Mormon Flight from American Pluralism*. Salt Lake City: Signature Books, 1989.

*History of Relief Society, 1842-1866*. Salt Lake City: General Board of Relief Society, 1966.

HMWj: Helen Mar Whitney journal, Nov. 12, 1884-Oct. 21, 1896. In Helen Mar Whitney Collection, MS 179, Merrill Library and CA. The early portions are in CA, but the bulk of the journal is found in the Merrill Library. Charles M. Hatch has generously allowed me to consult his transcript of the Merrill Library portions of the journal. This journal, edited by Hatch and the author, will be published by the Utah State University Press.

Holzapfel, Richard and Jeff Cottle. *Old Mormon Nauvoo*. Provo, UT: Grandin Book Co., 1990.

HR: see Jenson, *Historical Record*.

HRC: see Joseph Smith III, *History of the Reorganized Church*.

HS: see Bennett, *History of the Saints*.

HStj: Hosea Stout journal, see Juanita Brooks, ed. *On the Mormon Frontier: The Diary of Hosea Stout*. 2 vols. Salt Lake City: University of Utah Press, 1964.

HTW: Kate Carter, ed. *Heart Throbs of the West*. 12 vols. Salt Lake City: Daughters of Utah Pioneers, 1947.

IC: see George Smith, *An Intimate Chronicle*.

IGI: International Genealogical Index, GS.

Ivins: Stanley S. Ivins collection, USHS, notebooks on polygamy and early Mormonism. Film also at Huntington Library.

Jackson, Joseph. *A Narrative of the Adventures and Experiences of Joseph H. Jackson in Nauvoo: Disclosing the Depths of Mormon Villainy Practiced in Nauvoo*. Warsaw, IL: n.p., 1844.

JD: *Journal of Discourses*. 26 vols. Liverpool, Eng.: F.D. Richards, 1854-86.

JDLj: John D. Lee journal, in Robert Glass Cleland and Juanita Brooks, eds. *A Mormon Chronicle: The Diaries of John D. Lee, 1848-1876*. 2 vols. Salt Lake City: University of Utah Press, 1983. See also Charles Kelly, ed. *Journals of John D. Lee: 1846-47 and 1859*. Salt Lake City: University of Utah Press, 1984.

Jeffrey, Julie Roy. *Frontier Women: The Trans-Mississippi West, 1840-1880*. New York: Hill and Wang 1979.

Jensen, Joan. *Loosening the Bonds: Mid-Atlantic Farm Women, 1750-1850*. New Haven, CT: Yale University Press, 1986.

Jenson, Andrew. *The Historical Record*. 9 vols, a periodical. Salt Lake City, 1882-90.

———. *Latter-day Saint Biographical Encyclopedia*. 4 vols. Salt Lake City: Andrew Jenson History Co., 1901-36.

Jessee 1: see Jessee, *The Papers of Joseph Smith, Volume 1*.

Jessee 2: see Jessee, *The Papers of Joseph Smith, Volume 2*.

Jessee, Dean, ed. *The Papers of Joseph Smith: Volume 1, Autobiographical and Historical Writings*. Salt Lake City: Deseret Book, 1989.

———, ed. *The Papers of Joseph Smith: Volume 2, Journal, 1832-1842*. Salt Lake City: Deseret Book, 1992.

———, ed. *The Personal Writings of Joseph Smith*. Salt Lake City: Deseret Book, 1984.

Jessee, PW: see Jessee, *The Personal Writings of Joseph Smith*.

JH: Journal History, CA, a chronological collection of news clippings. On film at other libraries.

JMH: *Journal of Mormon History*.

Johnson, Benjamin. Letter to George Gibbs, 1903, CA. See Zimmerman.

———. *My Life's Review*. Independence, MO: Zion's Printing & Publishing, 1947.

Johnson, Jeffery Ogden. "Determining and Defining 'Wife': the Brigham Young Households." *Dialogue* 20 (1987): 57-70.

JSj: Joseph Smith journal, CA; published in Faulring; Jessee 2; and Jessee, PW.

KEQR: Lyndon Cook and Milton Backman, eds. *Kirtland Elders' Quorum Record*. Provo, UT: Grandin Book Co., 1985.

Kimball, Stanley. *Heber C. Kimball: Mormon Patriarch and Pioneer*. Urbana: University of Illinois Press, 1981.

———. *Historic Sites and Markers Along the Mormon and Other Great Western Trails*. Urbana: University of Illinois Press, 1988.

Larkin, Jack. *The Reshaping of Everyday Life, 1790-1840*. New York: Harper & Row, 1988.

Larson, Carl V., comp. *A Data Base of Mormon Battalion*. Providence, UT: Kieth Watkins, 1987.

Launius, Roger D. *Joseph Smith III: Pragmatic Prophet*. Urbana: University of Illinois Press, 1995.

——— ,and F. Mark McKiernan. *Joseph Smith Jr.'s Red Brick Store*. Macomb: Western Illinois University, 1985.

Lee Library: Harold B. Lee Library, Brigham Young University, Provo, Utah.

Lee, John D. *Mormonism Unvailed: The Life and Confessions of the Late Mormon Bishop*. St. Louis: Bryan, Brand & Company, 1877.

Lyman, Edward Leo. *San Bernardino: The Rise and Fall of a California Community*. Salt Lake City: Signature Books, 1996.

MA: *Messenger and Advocate*, LDS journal.

Marriott Library: J. Willard Marriott Library, University of Utah, Salt Lake City, Utah.

ME: see Newell and Avery, *Mormon Enigma*.

Merrill Library: Merrill Library, Utah State University, Logan, Utah.

MP: see Van Wagoner, *Mormon Polygamy*.

MSt: *Millennial Star*.

Myres, Sandra L. *Westering Women and the Frontier Experience 1800-1915*. Albuquerque: University of New Mexico Press, 1982.

Nauvoo Ward Census, "A Record of the Names of the Members of the Church of Jesus Christ of Latter-day Saints." Begun in spring 1842. GS Film 581,219.

Newell, Linda King, and Valeen Tippetts Avery. *Mormon Enigma: Emma Hale Smith*. Garden City, NY: Doubleday, 1984.

Noall, Claire. *Intimate Disciple: A Portrait of Willard Richards*. Salt Lake City: University of Utah Press, 1957.

NTER: Nauvoo Temple Endowment Register, GS. Partially taken from Clayton/Kimball journal, Book 93.

OHj: Oliver Huntington journal, Lee Library. Copy of holograph at Huntington Library; typescript at USHS.

OMF: *On the Mormon Frontier*, see HStj, Hosea Stout Journal.

OPH: Kate Carter, ed. *Our Pioneer Heritage*. 15 vols. Salt Lake City: Daughters of Utah Pioneers, 1971.

Parkin, Max. *Conflict at Kirtland: A Study of the Nature and Causes of External and Internal Conflict of the Mormons in Ohio between 1830 and 1838*. Salt Lake City: Parkin, 1966.

PBI: Patriarchal Blessing Index, GS.

PBSj: Patty Bartlett Sessions journal, original in CA. See Smart, *Mormon Midwife*.

Pratt, Parley P. *Autobiography*. New York: Russell Bros., 1874. 3rd ed. repr. Salt Lake City: Deseret Book, 1938.

Prince, Gregory. *Power From On High: The Development of Mormon Priesthood*. Salt Lake City: Signature Books, 1995.

PW: see Jessee, *Personal Writings of Joseph Smith*.

Quinn, D. Michael. *The Mormon Hierarchy: Extensions of Power*. Salt Lake City: Signature Books, 1996.

———. *The Mormon Hierarchy: Origins of Power*. Salt Lake City: Signature Books, 1994. The biographical appendices in this book and its companion volume are a basic resource for the polygamous marriages of elite Mormons in the nineteenth century. However, the appendix is not footnoted. Therefore I cite it only provisionally, pending further publication by Quinn. I have found him to be reliable in the past, but interpretative differences on primary data are inescapable. It should also be noted that Quinn's lists of wives are in chronological order, so he provides an approximate date for each marriage.

———. "Mormon Women Have Had the Priesthood Since 1846." In Hanks WA, 365-410.

———. "The Practice of Rebaptism at Nauvoo." BYUSt 18 (Winter 1978): 226-32.

———, ed. *The New Mormon History: Revisionist Essays on the Past*. Salt Lake City: Signature Books, 1992.

Ricketts, Norma Baldwin. *The Mormon Battalion, U.S. Army of the West, 1846-1848*. Logan: Utah State University Press, 1997.

RLDS Archives: in the RLDS temple, Independence, Missouri.

Roberts, Brigham H. *A Comprehensive History of the Church of Jesus Christ of Latter-day Saints*. 6 vols. Salt Lake City: Church of Jesus Christ of Latter-day Saints, 1930.

RP: see Cook, *The Revelations of the Prophet Joseph Smith*.

RS: see Foster, *Religion and Sexuality*.

RS Minutes: Female Relief Society of Nauvoo, Minutes (mostly kept by Eliza R. Snow), CA; film at Lee Library; also in Linda Newell papers, Marriott Library.

SAB: Smith Affidavit Books, CA, MS 3423, compiled by Joseph F. Smith. Listed, summarized, and analyzed in Bachman, "A Study"; some are quoted in Joseph Fielding Smith, *Blood Atonement*.

SAd = "Sealing and Adoption Book A." GS and Marriott Library.

SEB: see Black, *Membership*.

Shook, Charles A. *The True Origins of Mormon Polygamy*. Cincinnati: Standard Publishing Co., 1914.

SLDS: see Allen and Leonard.

Smart, Donna Toland, ed. *Mormon Midwife: The 1846-1888 Diaries of Patty Bartlett Sessions*. Logan: Utah State University Press, 1997.

Smith, George D., ed. *An Intimate Chronicle: The Journals of William Clayton*. Salt Lake City: Signature Books in association with Smith Research Associates, 1991.

Smith III, Joseph. *Joseph Smith III and the Restoration*. Independence, MO: Herald House, 1952.

Smith III, Joseph, and Heman C. Smith. *The History of the Reorganized Church of Jesus Christ of Latter Day Saints*. 4 vols. Independence, MO: Herald Publishing House, 1967-73.

Smith, Joseph Fielding. *Blood Atonement and the Origin of Plural Marriage*. Salt Lake City: Deseret News Press, 1905; repr. Deseret News Press, 1950.

Smith, Mary Ettie V. *Fifteen Years Among the Mormons*. Ed. Nelson Winch Green. New York: Scribners, 1858. Also New York: H. Dayton, 1859.

Smith-Rosenberg, Carroll. *Disorderly Conduct: Visions of Gender in Victorian America*. New York: Alfred Knopf, 1985.

SS: see Beecher and Anderson, *Sisters in Spirit*.

Stenhouse, Fanny. *Tell It All*. Hartford, CT: A.D. Worthington, 1874.

Stratton, Joanna L. *Pioneer Women: Voices from the Kansas Frontier*. New York: Simon & Schuster, 1981.

Tanner, Annie Clark. *A Mormon Mother*. Salt Lake City: Tanner Trust, University of Utah, 1969.

Temple Lot Case: *Complainant's Abstract of Pleading and Evidence, In the Circuit Court of the United States, Western District of Missouri, Western Division, at Kansas City. The Reorganized Church of Jesus Christ of Latter-Day Saints, Complainant, vs. The Church of Christ at Independence, Missouri* ... Lamoni, IA: Herald Publishing House, 1893. This is an abbreviated publication of the complete transcript, available at RLDS Archives and CA.

Temple Lot Case, complete transcript. United States Court of Appeal (8th Circuit), Testimony. RLDS Archives, copy at CA, MS 1160.

627

# ABBREVIATIONS, BIBLIOGRAPHIES, AND REFERENCES

Tinney, Thomas Milton. "The Royal Family of the Prophet Joseph Smith, Junior: First President of the Church of Jesus Christ of Latter-day Saints." Typescript, 1973. Copies in CA and Marriott Library.

TS: *Times and Seasons*, LDS journal, Nauvoo period.

Tullidge, Edward. *The Women of Mormondom*. New York: Tullidge & Crandall, 1877.

UGHM: *Utah Genealogical and Historical Magazine*.

UHQ: *Utah Historical Quarterly*.

Ulrich, Laurel Thatcher. *Good Wives: Image and Reality in the Lives of Women in Northern New England, 1650-1750*. New York: Oxford University Press, 1980.

———. *A Midwife's Tale: The Life of Martha Ballard, Based on Her Diary*. New York: Alfred Knopf, 1991.

USHS: Utah State Historical Society, Salt Lake City.

Van Wagoner, Richard. *Mormon Polygamy*. Salt Lake City: Signature Books, 1986.

———. *Sidney Rigdon: A Portrait of Religious Excess*. Salt Lake City: Signature Books, 1995.

WC: *Women of Covenant*, see Derr, Cannon, and Beecher.

WCj: William Clayton journal, see George Smith.

WE: *Woman's Exponent*, a semi-official LDS woman's magazine begun in 1872.

Whitney, Helen Mar. Autobiography, published in *Woman's Exponent*, 1880-86, and recently reprinted in Jeni Broberg Holzapfel and Richard Holzapfel, *A Woman's View: Helen Mar Whitney's Reminiscences of Early Church History*. Provo, UT: BYU Religious Studies Center, 1997. ER="Early Reminiscences," 1880. LI="Life Incidents," 1880-81. SIN="Scenes in Nauvoo" or "Scenes and Incidents in Nauvoo," 1881-83. OTBM="Our Travels Beyond the Mississippi," 1883-84; SIWQ="Scenes and Incidents at Winter Quarters," 1885-86.

Whitney, Orson. *History of Utah*. 4 vols. Salt Lake City: George Q. Cannon & Sons Co., 1892-1904.

———. *Life of Heber C. Kimball*. Salt Lake City: Kimball family, 1888, repr. with different pagination, Salt Lake City: Stevens & Wallis, 1945.

WJS: see Ehat, *Words of Joseph Smith*.

WM: see Tullidge, *The Women of Mormondom*.

WRj: Willard Richards journal, CA.

WWj: Wilford Woodruff journal, CA. *Wilford Woodruff's Journal, 1833-1898, Typescript*. 9 vols. Ed. Scott Kenney. Midvale, UT: Signature Books, 1983-85.

Wyl, Wilhelm. *Mormon Portraits: or the Truth About the Mormon Leaders, 1830-1886*. Salt Lake City: Tribune Press & Publ., 1886.

Young, Ann Eliza Webb. *Wife Number 19: Or The Story of a Life in Bondage, Being a Complete Exposé of Mormonism, And Revealing the Sorrows, Sacrifices and Sufferings of Women in Polygamy*. Hartford, CT: Dustin, Gilman & Co., 1876.

Young, Brigham, journals, see BYj.

Young, Kimball. *Isn't One Wife Enough?* New York: Henry Holt, 1954.

ZDYj: Zina Diantha Huntington Young journal. In Zina Card Brown collection, CA. Partially published, see Zina Huntington Young chapter.

Zimmerman, Dean R., ed. *I Knew the Prophets: An Analysis of the Letter of Benjamin F. Johnson to George F. Gibbs, Reporting Doctrinal Views of Joseph Smith and Brigham Young*. Bountiful, UT: Horizon Publishers, 1976. The original of Johnson's 1903 letter is in CA, MS 1289.

## REFERENCES TO THE INTRODUCTION

**Johnson**: "Determining and Defining 'Wife': The Brigham Young Households," *Dialogue* 20.3 (Fall 1987): 57-70. Compare now Quinn, MHOP 607, who has different dates for many of these marriages. **Stanley Kimball**: HCK 307-16. Compare Quinn, MHOP 557. **Jenson**: "Plural Marriage," *Historical Record* 6 (May 1887): 219-40. The *Historical Record* was an assignment given by Mormon leaders to Jenson, see his *Autobiography* (Salt Lake City: Deseret News Press, 1938), 139. **Ivins**: See Ivins papers, USHS. **Brodie**:

628

ABBREVIATIONS, BIBLIOGRAPHIES, AND REFERENCES

*No Man Knows My History*, 457-88. Important studies of Joseph Smith's polygamy, such as Foster's *Religion and Sexuality* and Bachman, "A Study," did not include new lists of plural wives. Foster had no list, and Bachman used Brodie's list (though he was critical of Brodie). Compare now Quinn, MHOP 587, a valuable list that is, however, not footnoted. For Brodie's limitations, see Newell Bringhurst, "Fawn M. Brodie, 'Mormondom's Lost Generation,' and *No Man Knows My History*," JMH 16 (1990): 16; Newell Bringhurst, "Fawn Brodie's Thomas Jefferson: The Making of a Popular and Controversial Biography," *Pacific Historical Review* 62 (1993): 433-54, 453-54; Louis Midgley, "The Brodie Connection: Thomas Jefferson and Joseph Smith," BYUSt 20 (1979): 59-67; and my "Fawn Brodie's Treatment of Joseph Smith's Polygamy and Plural Wives: A Critical View," in *Reconsidering No Man Knows My History: Fawn M. Brodie and Joseph Smith in Retrospect* (Logan: Utah State University Press, 1996), 154-94. This is not to deny that Brodie was a pioneer in the study of Joseph Smith's polygamy, despite significant mistakes she made. One example of a problem in evidence: in NM 465-66, Brodie quotes an antagonistic writer, William Hall, in *The Abominations of Mormonism*, to the effect that Zina Huntington Jacobs became pregnant by Joseph Smith when Henry Jacobs was on a mission to England. However, Henry's mission to England took place from June 1846 to November 1847, long after Joseph's death, as is well documented because Oliver Huntington, Zina's brother, served this mission with Jacobs and kept a journal. Strangely enough, Brodie knew the Oliver Huntington journal and cited it frequently. Brodie made other mistakes for which we should not take her too much to task, even though they are significant. She was not writing full biographies of each of these plural wives, and she had not solved many of the puzzles surrounding them. One woman, Elizabeth Davis, is listed twice in Brodie's appendix, both under her maiden name and under a married name (Elizabeth Durfee). Furthermore, Brodie listed a number of posthumous sealings to Joseph, all of which are entirely ambiguous as evidence for marriages to the living Joseph. One of them, the sealing of Cordelia Calista Morley, was certainly posthumous only—Morley's autobiography (in Lee Library) shows that while Joseph proposed to her in Nauvoo, she refused his offer, and was sealed to him only after his death.

## Viewing Joseph Smith's Wives Holistically

For revisionist and celebratory history, see Douglas Alder, "Writing Southern Utah History: An Appraisal and a Bibliography," JMH 20 (1994): 156-78.

## Recovering Clues to Forgotten Lives

**Genealogy**: Compare Laurel Thatcher Ulrich's skillful use of the clues in genealogy to reconstruct the texture of New England women's lives, GW 148-52. **quoting sources:** John Crossan, *The Historical Jesus* (San Francisco: Harper, 1991), xxxiv, writes, "I have cited in full those *primary* documents on which my conclusions are based. I do not presume that most readers, even scholarly ones, always look up references, and I have chosen, therefore, to cite in full."

## The Supernatural

**Bushman**: (Urbana: University of Illinois Press, 1984), 3. I am a practicing Mormon who considers himself believing but who rejects absolutist elements of the fundamentalist world view, e.g., the view of Joseph Smith as omniscient or morally perfect or receiving revelation unmixed with human and cultural limitations. However, I do accept non-absolutist incursions of the supernatural into human experience.

## In Sacred Loneliness

**Anti-polygamy novels**: A. Jennie Bartlett Switzer, *Elder Northfield's Home; or, Sacrificed on the Mormon Altar: A Story of the Blighting Curse of Polygamy* (New York: J. Howard Brown, 1882). For exaggerated anti-polygamy rhetoric, see treatments in Kathleen Marquis, "'Diamond Cut Diamond': Mormon Women and the Cult of Domesticity in the Nineteenth Century," *The University of Michigan Papers in Women's Studies* 2 (1976): 105-24, 117;

629

Stanley S. Ivins, "Notes on Mormon Polygamy," in Quinn, NMH 169-80, 178; Gail Farr Cas-
terline, "'In the Toils' or 'Onward for Zion': Images of the Mormon Woman, 1852-1890,"
Master's thesis, Utah State University, 1974; Charles Cannon, "The Awesome Power of Sex:
the Polemical Campaign against Mormon Polygamy," *Pacific Historical Review* 43 (1974):
61-82. **infinite dominion:** Polygamous Mormons felt that they would "rule" over monogamists in the hereafter, see Tanner, AMM 239, compare 196, for Mormon emphasis on terms
such as "Everlasting Dominion" in connection with polygamy. **Annie Clark Tanner
alone:** Tanner, AMM 130, 208. See also Suzanne Adel Katz, "Sisters in Salvation: Patterns of
Emotional Loneliness Among Nineteenth-Century Non-Elite Mormon Polygamous
Women," Master's thesis, California State University at Fullerton, 1987; Linda Thatcher,
"Women Alone: the Economic and Emotional Plight of Early LDS Women," *Dialogue* 25
(Winter 1992): 45-55, which deals with polygamy partially, but concentrates more on the
missionary wife (though missionary hardships were compounded when the wife was a plu-
ral wife); B. Carmon Hardy, "Lords of Creation: Polygamy, the Abrahamic Household, and
Mormon Patriarchy," JMH 20 (Spring 1994): 119-52, 147. **ambiguity:** Tanner, AMM 133.
**independence:** Tanner, AMM 236. See Joan Iversen, "Feminist Implications of Mormon
Polygyny," *Feminist Studies* 10 (1984): 505-22; Jeffrey, *Frontier Women* 176; compare
Hardy, "Lords of Creation," 145; Foster, RS 213-14. **envy of monogamy:** Tanner, AMM
208. **financial support:** See Tanner, AMM 181-82, 190. Compare the polygamous marriages of Emily and Eliza Partridge, in this book. **1913:** Tanner, AMM 209. **women leaving
polygamy:** For instance, Stanley Kimball, HCK 307, lists forty-three wives of Heber C. Kimball, of whom he judges sixteen separated from him during his lifetime. He had children by
only seventeen wives. According to the research of Jeffery Johnson and D. Michael Quinn
(Johnson, DDW; Quinn, MHOP 607-8), of Brigham Young's fifty-six wives, fourteen divorced or were separated from him; only sixteen had children by him. In this book Mary
Ann Frost Pratt, Sarah Lawrence, Agnes Coolbrith, Desdemona Fullmer, and Marinda Hyde
divorced their general authority husbands. In many cases the woman was for all practical
cases entirely separated from the husband, though not nominally or formally divorced from
him. Tanner, AMM 240. In this book Martha McBride and Rhoda Richards seem to fit this
category. See Campbell and Campbell, "Divorce Among Mormon Polygamists," 197, "The
divorce rate and number of separations were high ..." The Campbells point out that polygyny has been successful in many cultures worldwide, but they conclude that because of
the superimposition of polygamy on a culture of Christian monogamy, and because Mormon polygamy was not sufficiently regulated by accepted norms, it was often unsuccessful.
Polygamy will probably be unsuccessful in any culture in which women are viewed as
(theoretically) equal. It has been argued that, in Mormon polygamous culture, women were
implicitly regarded as being on a lower level than men. See Young, *Isn't One Wife Enough*,
280; Hardy, "Lords of Creation." Daisy Barclay, raised in a plural family, wrote, "Polygamy
is predicated on the assumption that a man is superior to a woman," cited in Young 280. **relationships with children:** Tanner, AMM 236. Olive Andelin Potter, *Autobiography*, 8,
Lee Library, as cited in Katz, "Sisters in Salvation," 55. Compare Iversen, "Feminist Implications," 514-15; Foster, RS 212. **emotional distance:** S. A. Cooks, "Theatrical and Social Affairs in Utah," 5-6, Bancroft Library, as quoted in Foster, RS 212. Young, *Isn't One Wife
Enough* 209; Campbell and Campbell, "Divorce," 190. Tanner, AMM 238. **related symptoms:** See Katz, "Sisters in Salvation," 35; *Loneliness: A Sourcebook of Current Theory, Research and Therapy* (New York: John Wiley and Sons, 1982); Robert Weiss, *Loneliness:
The Experience of Emotional and Social Isolation* (Cambridge: MIT Press, 1973); Joseph
J. Hartog, J. Ralph Andy, and Yehudi A. Cohen, eds., *The Anatomy of Loneliness* (New
York: International Universities Press, 1981). **most holy:** Lorena Washburn Larsen, a plural
wife, wrote, "Plural marriage ... had been such a sacrifice on the part of many young women
... but they did it because it was taught that it was the only way that a person could get to the
highest degree of the Celestial Kingdom of God." *Autobiography*, Lee Library, 56, as cited
in Katz, "Sisters in Salvation," 56.

# REFERENCES TO THE PROLOGUE
## *A Trajectory of Plurality: An Overview of Joseph Smith's Plural Wives*
### Chart: Joseph Smith's Wives
See individual chapters.

### Chart: Possible Wives.

**1. Vienna Jacques (Shearer):** Unsigned affidavit by Jacques, SAB 4:56 (Bachman, "A Study" 350); Mrs. Warner Alexander, 1886 statement, CA, information from Polly Beswick; compare ME 67. Clair Noall to Fawn Brodie, Sept. 16, 1943, in Noall papers, box 2, fd 11, MS 188, Marriott Library: "'Yes,' said Aunt Louie with no uncertainty when I asked her about Vienna's being sealed to the Prophet, 'She was sealed to him.'" All of this evidence is problematic. The affidavit was prepared for Jacques, but she evidently refused to sign it, possibly because she had not married Joseph, possibly because she did not want the marriage publicized. The Alexander affidavit is antagonistic and second hand. The Noall letter is third hand.

**2. Hannah Dubois (Smith) (Dibble):** Johnson, MLR 96, "At this time I knew that the Prophet had as his wives, Louisa Beeman, Eliza R. Snow, Maria and Sarah Lawrence, Sisters Lyon and Dibble, one or two of Bishop Partridge's daughters, and some of C.P. Lott's daughters, together with my own two sisters." John Hyde, Mormonism, Its Leaders and Designs (New York: W.P. Fetridge, 1857), 84: "There is a Mrs. Dibble living in Utah, who has a fine son. She was sealed, among others, to Joseph Smith, although living with her present husband before and since. On the head of her son, Smith predicted the most startling prophesies about wielding the sword of Laban, revealing the hidden Book of Mormon, and translating the sealed part of the records. There is not a person at Salt Lake who doubts the fact of that boy being Smith's own child." The chief opposing evidence is Hannah's eternal marriage to Philo Dibble in the Nauvoo temple, SAd 243. Joseph Smith performed Hannah's marriage to Dibble: "On the 11th of February, 1841, I married a second wife—a Widow Smith of Philadelphia, who was living in the family of the Prophet. He performed the ceremony at his house, and Sister Emma Smith insisted upon getting up a wedding supper for us. It was a splendid affair, and quite a large party of our friends were assembled." Philo Dibble, "Philo Dibble's Narrative," *Early Scenes in Church History* (Salt Lake City: Juvenile Instructor Office, 1882), 92-93. This does not sound like a "pretend" marriage, such as the Sarah Ann Whitney-Kingsbury marriage.

**3. Sarah Bapson:** Bennett, HS 256, Miss B*****. The best candidate for this woman is Sarah Bapson, listed in an April 4, 1899, sealing: "The sealings of those named below were performed during the life of the Prophet Joseph but there is no record thereof. President Lorenzo Snow decided that they be repeated in order that a record might exist; and that this explanation be made." Fannie Alger, Lucinda Harris, Almera W. Johnson, Sarah Bapson, Flora Ann Woodworth, Fanny Young, Hannah Ells, Olive Frost, Sarah M. Cleveland, Sylvia Sessions (Lyon), Ruth Vose. Salt Lake Temple Sealing Records, Bk D, p. 243, GS Film 184,590, as quoted in Tinney, RF 41, 63.

**4. Mrs. G*****:** Bennett, HS 256. As the other names in Bennett's list have been reliable, there is no good reason to doubt this one. However, there are at least nine women whose married names start with G, have six letters, and who were married and in Nauvoo in 1842. Without further evidence, it is difficult to narrow that group down. A leading candidate might be Phebe Palmer (Graves), who received her endowment with Sarah Kingsley Cleveland on October 19, 1845.

**5. Sarah Scott (Mulholland) (Kimball):** Whitney, HCK 431. "The wives of the Prophet who wedded Heber C. Kimball were ... Sarah Scott." Compare BOP #160 (which refers to her as "Sarah Smith"); SAd 411.

**6. Mary Houston (Kimball):** Whitney, HCK 431. "The wives of the Prophet who wedded Heber C. Kimball were ... Mary Houston." BOP #159; SAd 513.

**7. Mrs. (Tailor):** Joseph Jackson, Narrative 14, who links her with Patty Sessions and

Elizabeth Durfee. As Patty Sessions and Elizabeth Durfee have been substantiated as wives of Joseph, there is no good reason to suspect Mrs. Tailor. Which Mrs. Taylor is another problem—there are at least three older women in 1842 Nauvoo with the married name Taylor: Agnes Taylor (Taylor), the mother of John Taylor; Elizabeth Patrick (Taylor); and Surviah (Taylor).

**8. Mary Heron (Snider):** Quinn, MHOP 587.

### Chart: Early Posthumous Marriages

**(1)** BOP #13; SAd 503.   **(2)** BOP #31; SAd 503.   **(3)** BOP #34; SAd 503, 555. See Flora Woodworth chapter.   **(4)** BOP #97; SAd 511, 581.   **(5)** BOP #98; Cordelia Morley Cox, Autobiography, Lee Library.   **(6)** SAd 513, 449.   **(7)** "Sally Ann Fuller Smith," in "Obituary" section, *Deseret News* 30 (Mar. 29, 1897): 2. Proxy marriage to Joseph Smith/Samuel Gully, SAd 721.   **(8)** Endowment House Sealing Record, #65. In the record of her marriage of James Goff, there is an apparent reference to an 1844 proxy marriage to Joseph Smith/Kimball.

### Prologue Text

Brodie, NM 457-88; Quinn, MHOP 587. George D. Smith, "Nauvoo Roots of Mormon Polygamy, 1841-46: A Preliminary Demographic Report," *Dialogue* 27 (Spring 1994): 1-72, lists forty-two wives, see Chart, #122. **"marriages to Joseph":** Because of the complexity of Mormon marriage practice and experimentation, there is a great deal of ambiguity concerning what constituted marriage in early Mormonism, and Mormon theological terms for marriage and plural marriage can be confusing. For the purposes of this book, I define as marriage any relationship solemnized by a marriage ceremony of some sort. "Sealing" as used in early Mormonism is a complex term that deserves extensive study (see now Prince, PFOH 155-172), but as it developed in Nauvoo Mormonism, it eventually meant a linking of man and wife for eternity as well as for time, i.e., eternal marriage. If two males are "sealed," i.e., a father and a son, it was obviously not a marriage. But when a man and a woman (not siblings or parent-child) were "sealed," the sealing was almost always a marriage. There is at least one example in Mormon history of the male marriage partner performing the sealing ceremony himself, see Willard Richards diary, CA, Dec. 23, 1845, as cited in Van Wagoner, MP 228. **spiritual wife:** A "spiritual wife" was not a woman married "in name only," for "eternity only"; a "spiritual wife" was a woman who was bound to a man by a strong spiritual/ritual link. A "spiritual" marriage often included sexuality, and offspring resulted, see the Emily Partridge chapter, at the birth of her first child to Brigham Young in 1846, which she refers to as a "spiritual child." Helen Mar Whitney wrote, "At that time spiritual wife was the title by which every woman who entered into this order was called, for it was taught and practiced as a spiritual order." *Plural Marriage as Taught By the Prophet Joseph* (Salt Lake City: Juvenile Instructor Office, 1882), 15. Nevertheless, many of these women testified that they had had sexual relations with Joseph Smith, see below. **affidavits:** SAB, CA. Bachman made a valuable analysis and listing of these affidavits, "A Study," 346-54, compare 107; see also Bachman, "New Light on an Old Hypothesis: The Ohio Origins of the Revelation on Eternal Marriage," JMH 5 (1978): 19-32, 21n. (which describes the four books of affidavits). **Bennett:** *History of the Saints*, 256. Mrs. A**** S**** [Agnes Coolbrith Smith]. Miss L***** B***** [Louisa Beaman]. Mrs. B**** [Presendia Huntington Buell]. Mrs. D***** [Elizabeth Davis Durfee]. Mrs. S******* [Patty Bartlett Sessions]. Mrs. G***** [Unidentified]. Miss B***** [Sarah Bapson?]. For Bennett, see Andrew F. Smith, *The Saintly Scoundrel, The Life and Times of Dr. John Cook Bennett* (Urbana: University of Illinois Press, 1997). **Jenson:** HR 6:219-40, 233-34. See Keith Perkins, "Andrew Jenson: Zealous Chronologist," Master's thesis, Brigham Young University, 1974, 40. **small lists:** Joseph Jackson's short list (see on Mrs. Tailor, Possible Wife 7) includes three women. A later list from a sympathetic source is in Benjamin Johnson's *My Life's Review*, see on Hannah Dibble above. **Orson Whitney's mistakes:** For example, he doublelists three women, see Kimball, HCK 307; add Nancy Maria Winchester (Smith Kimball) and Nancy Maria Smith, probably the same person. **marrying Joseph posthumously:** Cordelia Morley Cox, Autobiography, Lee Library. **Augusta and Amanda:** Marriage record, Augusta Cobb and Joseph Smith, Apr. 14, 1848, Brigham Young collection, MS 1234, box 44, fd 6, CA; Amanda Barnes Smith, see Amanda's memoirs, Lee Library, and in Hulda Cordelia Thurston Smith, "To My Children and Grandchildren," edited by Lyman Platt, *The Nauvoo Journal* 4 (Fall 1992): 3-7. **Mary Ann Frost:** Family Record of Parley P. Pratt, in Belinda Marden Pratt's journal, Mar. 11, 1850, CA; USHS. Mary A.S. Winters, "Mothers in Israel," *Relief Society Magazine* 3 (1916): 580-81, 643. However, Mary Ann Frost's marriage history in Nauvoo has its complexities, see WWj, Jan. 21, 1844 (2:340). **thirty-three:** Other scholars, and family descendants, may have evidence that will move possible or posthumous wives into the category of certain wives. The author will welcome any information relating to the women on this list, especially documents of any sort by the women or their close relatives. **early polygamy:** For general introductions and full-length studies of early Mormon polygamy, see Danel Bachman's Purdue University Master's thesis, "A Study of the Mormon Practice of Plural Marriage before the Death of Joseph Smith"; Lawrence Foster, *Religion and Sexuality*; Van Wagoner's *Mormon Polygamy*. B. Carmon Hardy's *Solemn Covenant* is also indispensable for its evocation of the importance of polygamy to Mormons before our difficult passage to monogamy. For an introduction to Joseph Smith and his first wife, Emma Hale (Smith Bidamon), see Donna Hill's *Joseph Smith: The First Mormon* and Newell and Avery, *Mormon Enigma, Emma Hale Smith*.

**turned Joseph down:** SARAH MELISSA GRANGER (KIMBALL): HR 6:232, see below. Compare Jill Mulvay Derr, "Sarah Melissa Granger Kimball: the Liberal Shall Be Blessed," in Vicky Burgess-Olson, ed., *Sister Saints* (Provo, UT: Brigham Young University Press, 1978), 21-40. RACHEL IVINS (GRANT): A plural wife of Jedediah Grant, and the mother of Heber J. Grant, she was later sealed to Joseph Smith, not Grant, for eternity. Ronald Walker, "Rachel R. Grant: the Continuing Legacy of the Feminine Ideal," in *Supporting Saints*, ed. Donald Q. Cannon and David Whittaker (Provo, UT: BYU Religious Studies Center, 1985), 17-42, 23-24. LYDIA MOON: WCj, Sept. 15-17, 1843 (IC 120). CORDELIA C. MORLEY (COX): See her Autobiography, Lee Library. ESTHER JOHNSON: See Benjamin Johnson MLR 96.

**Wives of Joseph Smith in anti-Mormon sources:** MARY ANN ANGELL (YOUNG): John D. Lee, MU 147. See Hawley in the following section on Jane Law. JANE SILVERTHORNE (LAW): See Bathsheba W. Smith, Deposition, 8th Circuit Court, 1892 Temple Lot Case, as cited in Lyndon W. Cook, "William Law, Nauvoo Dissenter," BYUSt 22 (Winter 1982): 47-72, 65. John Hawley, Autobiography (Jan. 1885), 97, RLDS Archives. This source also lists, as wives of Joseph, **MRS. FRANCIS HIGBY**; **MRS. LYMAN WIGHT**; and **MRS. ROBERT D. FOSTER.** Hawley reports that Wilford Woodruff told him in the Endowment House in Salt Lake that "When Brigham Young got the records of the Church in his hands, after the death of Joseph Smith, he found by examination that his first wife [Mary Ann Angell, apparently, his first living wife] had been sealed to Joseph and that Laws wife and Higbys wife and L Wights wife and Fosters wife had all been Sealed to Joseph, as their Husbands could not Save them." (I am grateful to Will Bagley for sharing his transcript of this passage with me.) This source is problematic. Did Joseph marry these women without their knowledge, by proxy, while they were living? It is difficult to believe that they would marry Joseph while they were distancing themselves from Mormonism and polygamy. Furthermore, Jane Law elsewhere asserted strongly that Joseph proposed to her and she refused. Compare Cook, *William Law*. If Joseph had married them earlier, however, the marriages might have been factors in turning their husbands against Smith. **MRS. EDWARD (BLOSSOM):** Wyl, MP 65-66. Mr. Blossom was an apostle under Brigham Young according to Wyl's source, an example of the occasional pronounced unreliability of unsympathetic sources, as there has been no apostle named Blossom. This does not prevent Brodie from listing Mrs. Blossom as her wife number 37. **MRS. (WHITE):** Wyl, MP 55, 60. **MRS. (FORD):** Wyl, MP 56. **MRS. (FULLER) (WARREN):** Melissa Schindle affidavit, in Bennett, HS 253. Bennett affirms that Joseph and she were

were connected in "the fall of 1841." **MRS. (name unknown)**, a gardener: Wyl, MP 55. **MRS. (MILLER)**, a widow: Bennett, HS 255. **MISS MORRIS**: "Celebrated Career Closed. Exterminator of Mormons Dies at Louisiana, Mo.," newspaper obituary, approximately Feb. 15, 1895, of David Conkling, in Henry Stebbins papers, P24, f22, RLDS Archives.

**Spurned proposals in anti-Mormon sources:** Some of the following are fairly well documented; others are sensationalist and badly documented: **JANE SILVERTHORNE (LAW)**, wife of William Law: William Law diary, May 13, 1844, "[Joseph] ha[s] lately endeavored to seduce my wife, and ha[s] found her a virtuous woman," as quoted in Cook, *William Law* 65; Lee, MU 147; Joseph Jackson, *Narrative* 21; Edward Bonney, *The Banditti of the Prairies: A Tale of the Mississippi Valley* (Chicago: Belford, Clarke & Co., 1881), 18; repr. (Norman: University of Oklahoma Press, 1963), 16-17. Compare Cook, *William Law* 64-65. As was typical in cases where women accused Joseph of proposing to them, loyalist Mormon sources accused the woman of adultery with another man (see the Sarah Pratt case below, and the Nancy Rigdon case): Alexander Neibaur journal, May 24, 1844, CA. **SARAH BATES (PRATT)**: "Workings of Mormonism related by Mrs. Orson Pratt, Salt Lake City, 1884," CA, as quoted in Gary James Bergera, "Seniority in the Twelve: The 1875 Realignment of Orson Pratt," JMH 18 (1992): 19-58, 26. Bergera notes that this late source should be used with caution and has errors. Bennett, HS 228-31; Breck England, *The Life and Thought of Orson Pratt* (Salt Lake City: University of Utah Press, 1985), 77-81; Richard Van Wagoner, "Sarah M. Pratt: the Shaping of an Apostate," *Dialogue* 19 (Summer 1986): 69-99, 71-72. **LEONORA CANNON (TAYLOR)**: John M. Whitaker journal, Nov. 1, 1890, vol. 7, p. 11, Marriott Library; Wyl, MP 70-72. **ELIZA WINTERS**: Hiel Lewis, "The Mormon History," Amboy *Journal* (Aug. 6, 1879), as cited in Ivins 1:337. Eber D. Howe, *Mormonism Unvailed* (Painesville, OH: E.D. Howe, 1834), 268. **MELISSA (SCHINDLE)**: See her affidavit in Bennett, HS 253. *Sangamo Journal*, July 15, 1842. Shook, *True Origins* 71. **EMELINE (WHITE)**: Bennett, HS 234-35; 247; 249. **MRS. ROBERT (FOSTER)**: Affidavit of M.G. Eaton, Mar. 27, 1844 in *Nauvoo Neighbor* (May 15, 1844). Compare previous note and Foster, RS 312. **PAMELA MICHAEL**: Bennett, see Smith, *Saintly Scoundrel* 101. **MRS. [CAROLINE GRANT] (SMITH)**: Wife of Joseph's brother William. Joseph Jackson, *Narrative* 29. Jackson is perhaps the worst of the sensationalists. **MRS. LUCY SMITH (MILLIGAN [or MILIKEN])**: Joseph Jackson, *Narrative* 29. **LAVINIA SMITH**: daughter of Joseph Smith's brother, Hyrum. Joseph Jackson, *Narrative* 29-32. **MISS MARKS**: daughter of William Marks, see Ann Eliza Young, WN19 70. **ATHALIA RIGDON**: Clark Braden and E.L. Kelley, *Public Discussion of the Issues between the Reorganized Church of Jesus Christ of Latter Day Saints and the Church of Christ, Disciples* (St. Louis: Braden, 1884), 391. **NANCY RIGDON**: J. Wickliffe Rigdon affidavit, reprinted in Smith BAOPM 97-101; compare Bennett, HS 241-50; F. Mark McKiernan, *Sidney Rigdon* (Lawrence, KS: Coronado Press, 1971), 115-19; Van Wagoner, SR 290-310; and the Marinda Johnson chapter, below.

## The Timing of Joseph Smith's Marriages

**Are early relationships marriages?** Some scholars have argued that these early relationships were not marriages, but affairs; see the Fanny Alger chapter below for my opposing view. **Bennett**, *History of the Saints*, 1842. **William Marks:** "Epistle," *Zion's Harbinger and Baneemy's Organ* 3 (July 1853): 52-54. (This was published in St. Louis, by C.B. Thompson.) Compare Richard Howard, "The Changing RLDS Response to Mormon Polygamy: A Preliminary Analysis," *John Whitmer Historical Association Journal* 3 (1983): 14-28. See also Joseph F. Smith journal, Aug. 28, 1870, CA, in which Emma is reported by Joseph W. Coolidge to have said to him in 1846, "Joseph had abandoned plurality of wives before his death." Coolidge strongly disagreed with her. William McLellin wrote, in a July 1872 letter to Joseph Smith III, RLDS Archives, that Emma told him "one night after she and Joseph had retired for the night, he told her that the doctrine and practice of Polygamy was going to ruin the church. He wished her to get up and burn the revelation." When she declined, he burned it himself. (This, of course, contradicts the more common tradition that Emma burned the revelation, see Clayton affidavit in HR 6:226, further references in ME 154. Quinn takes the less common tradition seriously, see MHOP 147. Isaac Sheen, cited in Shook, *True Origins* 152-55, also supports it.) This is one of those perplexing points in Mormon history where there is good, seemingly reliable evidence on both sides of a question. **Joseph gave up polygamy?** William Law's Nauvoo diary, Mar. 29, 1844, p. 48, Cook, has Hyrum Smith saying that he and Joseph had abandoned the practice of polygamy: "Hyrum Smith was here a few days ago. He beg'd for peace; we told him of the corrupt operation which had been practised upon us; he could not deny it ... he said they were not doing anything in the plurality of wife business now, and that he had published a piece against it." This statement is supported by *Times and Seasons* 5 (Mar. 15, 1844): 474, which criticizes the proposition that "a man *having a certain priesthood*, may have as many wives as he pleases, and that doctrine is taught here [in Nauvoo]: I say unto you that that man teaches *false doctrine*, for there is no such doctrine taught here; neither is there any such thing practised here." However, Erastus Snow later asserted that Joseph Smith solemnized his marriage to plural wife Minerva White on April 2, 1844, Theresa Snow Hill, "Erastus Snow Stories," typescript owned by Erastus Snow Family Organization, Salt Lake City, as cited in Andrew Karl Larson, *Erastus Snow, The Life of a Missionary and Pioneer for the Early Mormon Church* (Salt Lake City: University of Utah Press, 1971), 87, 97, 749, compare Artemisia Beaman Snow, quoted on p. 747. If this is correct, then Joseph was actively furthering his polygamous program just months before his death. In addition Ezra Taft Benson later stated that Hyrum Smith officiated when Benson married plural wife Adeline B. Andrus on April 27, 1844, see John Henry Evans and Minnie Egan Anderson, *Ezra T. Benson, Pioneer–Statesman–Saint* (Salt Lake City: Deseret Book, 1947), 64. We also find in William Law's diary, in a May 13 entry (p. 53 Cook), the allegation that Joseph had proposed marriage to Law's wife shortly before that date. Law demands that Joseph "acknowledge also that ~~he had lately endeavored to seduce my wife, and had found her a virtuous woman~~." If this actually happened, then Joseph was seeking to add wives to his family just a month before his death. However, like many events in Mormonism, this is flatly contradicted by another source, the Alexander Neibaur diary, CA, May 24, 1844, which alleges that Jane Law tried unsuccessfully to seduce Joseph Smith, then told her husband that Joseph had proposed to her. In Jane Law's favor, it is well documented that Joseph had married at least eleven married women (see below), one of whom (Marinda Hyde) was the wife of an apostle. If Joseph did propose marriage to the wife of a prominent opponent of polygamy, a member of the First Presidency, it can only be seen as an act of extreme recklessness. There is a third equally contradictory scenario, see above, the allegation that Jane Law actually did become Joseph's plural wife. It is impossible to sort out the crossfire of evidence on this question within the limits of this chapter; a fuller study is needed. **Emma threatens to leave:** WCj, Aug. 16, 1843 (IC 117): "This A.M. J. [Joseph] told me that since E. [Emma] came back from St Louis she had resisted the P. [patriarchal principle of plural marriage] in toto & he had to tell her he would relinquish all [wives] for her sake. She said she would given him E. & E. P [Eliza and Emily Partridge] but he knew if he took them she would pitch on him & desire a divorce & leave him. He however told me he should not relinquish any thing O. God deliver thy servant from iniquity and bondage." Compare ME 158, 164, 179. **polygamy dangerous:** according to Sarah, HR 6:232: "Early in the year 1842, Joseph Smith taught me ... the doctrine of plural marriage ... I asked him to teach it to some one else." **spoke of little else:** Clayton, in HR 6:226: "We were scarcely ever together, alone, but he was talking on the subject, and explaining that doctrine and principles connected with it." **monogamists ineligible for salvation:** For example, Orson Pratt, in a speech given on October 7, 1874, said, "I did hope there was more intelligence among the Latter-day Saints, and a greater understanding of principle than to suppose that any one can be a member of this Church in good standing and yet reject polygamy. The Lord has said, that those who reject this principle reject their salvation, they shall be damned, saith the Lord; those to whom I reveal this law and they do not receive it, shall be damned. Now here comes in our consciences. We have either to renounce Mormonism, Joseph Smith, Book of Mormon, Book of Covenants, and the whole system of things as taught by the Latter-day Saints, and say that God has not raised up a Church, has not raised up a prophet, has not begun to restore all things as he promised, we are obliged to do this, or else to say, with all our hearts, 'Yes, we are polygamists, and believe in the principle, and we are willing to practice it, because God has spoken from the heavens.'" JD 17:225-26. Compare Hardy, SC 14-19; 84-113; Quinn, MHEP 181. William Clayton, in an affidavit, HR 6:226, wrote: "From him [Joseph Smith] I learned that the doctrine of plural and celestial marriage is the most holy and important doctrine ever revealed to man on the earth, and that without obedience to that principle no man can ever attain to the fulness of exaltation in celestial glory." Compare D&C 132:26.

## The Number of Smith's Wives

**deification**: For the Mormon doctrine of exaltation, see Joseph Smith's King Follett discourse, WJS 340-62; also D&C 132, the revelation on plural marriage. **"The First Command ..."** Johnson, in Zimmerman 47. Compare the Nauvoo journal of Joseph Fielding, ed. Andrew Ehat, BYUSt 19 (Winter 1979): 133-66, 154: "I understand that a Man,s Dominion will be as God,s is, over his own Creatures and the more numerous they greater his dominion." In Utah polygamy this concept—a man's exaltation was dependent on the number of wives in his family—was common. In 1857 Hellen Fisher Smith, first wife of presiding patriarch John Smith, after her husband had reluctantly taken a second wife, wrote to her brother-in-law, "I care not how many he gits now, the ice is broke as the old saing is, the more the greater glory." Hellen Smith to Joseph F. Smith, Apr. 4, 1857, as cited in Bates and Smith, *Lost Legacy* 127. **polygamy revealed during Inspired Revision:** Joseph Noble, who sealed Louisa Beaman to Joseph in 1841, "Plural Marriage," MSt 45 (1883): 454 (Minutes of Davis Stake Conf.), compare Bachman, "A Study," 61, 67-68, n. 53; Robert J. Matthews, *A Plainer Translation: Joseph Smith's Translation of the Bible* (Provo, UT: Brigham Young University Press, 1975), 64-67. **Abraham:** D&C 132:1, 29-37, the Abrahamic promise in v. 30; D&C 132:65; compare the Book of Abraham, in the Mormon scripture, The Pearl of Great Price. **Matthew 22:30:** This passage is also quoted in D&C 132, see v. 16. Compare "Letter from Gen. Bennett," in *"Hawk Eye"* [newspaper]; New Series, No. 28; Burlington, Iowa; Dec. 7, 1843: "[Joseph Smith teaches that] as they neither marry, nor are given in marriage; but are as the angels which are in Heaven, in *eternity*, it has been revealed to him that there will be no harmony in heaven unless the *Saints* select their companions and marry IN TIME, FOR ETERNITY!!! They must marry *in time* so as to begin to form that sincere attachment and unsophisticated affection which it is so necessary to consummate *in eternity* in order to the peace of Heaven." See also Foster, RS 15-16. **Pratt:** JD 6:358-59. **Mormon primitivism**: See Marvin Hill, "The Shaping of the Mormon Mind in New England and New York," BYUSt 9 (1969): 351-72; Hill, QFR. For non-Mormon religious primitivism in America, see Richard Hughes, ed., *The American Quest for the Primitive Church* (Champaign: University of Illinois Press, 1988); Richard Hughes and C. Leonard Allen, *Illusions of Innocence, Protestant Primitivism in America, 1630-1875* (Chicago: University of Chicago Press, 1988); and Alexander, THE 16-17, 91, 341. The early Americans felt close to the whole Bible, not just the New Testament, as the obscure Old Testament names that crop up constantly in early nineteenth-century America show: e.g., to name some characters in the history of early Mormon polygamy, Simeon Carter, Gideon Carter, Jared Carter; Aseneth Babcock; compare, outside Mormonism, Abraham Lincoln. See Gordon Irving, "The Mormons and the Bible in the 1830's," BYUSt 13 (Summer 1973): 473-88. **adoption:** Hosea Stout journal (Brooks, OMF 1:178); speech by Brigham Young, Feb., 1847, in JDLj, Kelly 77-84, compare 93-94; Gordon Irving, "The Law of Adoption: One Phase of the Mormon Concept of Salvation, 1830-1900," BYUSt 14 (Spring 1974): 291-314; Foster, RS 195- 99; Juanita Brooks, John Doyle Lee, Zealot, Pioneer Builder, Scapegoat (Logan: Utah State University Press, 1992), 73-74; HCK 129; Hill, QFR 114. Marriage, sealing and adoption, in fact, were nearly interchangeable concepts, see Brooks, JDL 65; Lee, MU 106. **families**

**linked eternally:** Helen Mar Kimball Whitney, Autobiographical Sketch, 1881, fully discussed in Bachman, "A Study," 150-51, 337, see Helen Mar Kimball chapter. D. Michael Quinn, "The Mormon Hierarchy, 1832-1932: An American Elite," Ph.D. diss., Yale University, 1976), 74: "Through polygamous marriages, a Mormon General Authority could marry the close relatives of his associates in the hierarchy, thus reinforcing preexisting kinship connections and also introducing into the hierarchical family other General Authorities who were otherwise unrelated. Apparently Joseph Smith began this process." Though Quinn emphasizes dynastic aspects of Joseph's marriages, he would probably agree that there were complex reasons for these unions, in which spiritual attraction, sexual attraction, and desired dynastic links all combined. Joseph would have been attracted to the women he knew well, and he simply knew the Mormon elite better than other Mormons. In fact, the polyandrous marriages (see below) might reasonably pose a threat to the stability of Joseph's relationships with "first husbands," as the case of Orson Pratt shows. Even proposals to unmarried daughters could endanger Joseph's relationships with their fathers, as the case of Sidney Rigdon shows. **Grant:** JD 2:13-14, Feb. 19, 1854. **theology of polygamy:** Brodie emphasized the sexual dimension of Joseph's marriages almost to the exclusion of other motivations, see Marvin Hill's critique, "Secular or Sectarian History? A Critique of *No Man Knows My History*," *Church History* 43 (1974): 78-96, 93-95, also Hill's "Brodie Revisited: A Reappraisal," *Dialogue* 7 (Winter 1972): 73-85, 76: "With regard to plural marriage, where Brodie is so confident that the real Joseph Smith, the pleasure lover and sensualist, shows through, there is no evidence in his writings to suggest that he thought of it in other than religious terms." This is not to deny that there was a sexual/emotional dimension in Joseph's plural marriages; it is simply not the only motivation.

## The Ages of Joseph Smith's Wives

**older wives:** See above, on Quinn's prosopography. **teachers and messengers:** Emily Partridge, Autobiography, p. 4; Joseph Jackson, *Narrative* 14. Snow, in Fanny Stenhouse, *Tell It All* 430-32. **troubling:** Compare Hardy, "Lords of Creation," 140-41; Bradley/Woodward, see on Zina Huntington above.

## Sexuality in Joseph Smith's Plural Marriages

George Smith, Statement, dated May 18, 1892, signed by Lucy M. Smith, wife of George A. Smith. In George A. Smith papers, Marriott Library. **Mary Lightner:** "Remarks" at Brigham Young University, Apr. 14, 1905, p. 5. Mary Lightner collection, Lee Library. Affidavit of Melissa Willes, Aug. 3, 1893, quoted in Bailey, EH 98-100; compare Temple Lot Case 98, 105; Foster, RS 156. Emily Partridge, in Temple Lot Case (complete transcript), pp. 364, 367, 384; see Foster, RS 15. Johnson, in Zimmerman 44. Noble, in Temple Lot Case 427. Angus M. Cannon, statement of interview with Joseph III, CA, p. 23. **Josephine Lyon Fisher:** Angus M. Cannon, statement, 25-26, "I will now refer you to one case where it was said by the girl's grandmother that your father has a daughter born of a plural wife. The girl's grandmother was Mother Sessions ... She was the grand-daughter of Mother Sessions. That girl, I believe, is living today, in Bountiful, north of this city. I heard prest. Young, a short time before his death, refer to the report ... The woman is now said to have a family of children, and I think she is still living." One might interpret the Fisher affidavit as referring to Josephine as a non-biological child of Joseph who would be sealed to him in the eternities, because Sylvia had married Joseph for eternity. However, the Cannon statement shows that Patty Sessions (Smith) (and nineteenth-century Mormons such as Cannon and Brigham Young) understood Josephine to be Joseph's biological child, so the Fisher affidavit should be interpreted as referring to a biological child. **posterity:** See the Johnson statement, above. Johnson also wrote that Joseph Smith taught him "plainly" "that the whole object and end of matrimony was the procreation of our species and that the command to multiply and replenish the earth fell upon all the children of Adam both in obligation and privilege." "Open Letter to the President of the United States" [Grover

Cleveland], Jan. 15, 1886, CA, as quoted in E. Dale LeBaron, "Benjamin Franklin Johnson, Colonizer, Public Servant, and Church Leader," Master's thesis, Brigham Young University, 1966, 80. **other names:** See also Foster, RS 310 n. 111. **hiding:** There is a letter from Joseph Smith to a wife, Sarah Ann Whitney, in which he arranged a secret meeting with her and her parents. See Joseph Smith to Newel, Elizabeth, and Sarah Ann Whitney, Aug. 18, 1842, in Jessee, PW 539-40; in this letter he instructed the family to come only if Emma was not there, and to burn the letter after reading it. **did not visit frequently:** A recent study has concluded that there are only six days in a woman's menstrual month when she can become pregnant. Since these six days are difficult to pinpoint precisely, a couple that desires pregnancy should have intercourse frequently. If a couple has intercourse once a week, there is a 10 percent chance of pregnancy in a typical month; with daily intercourse, there is still only a 25 percent chance of pregnancy in a typical month. In addition, a third of all pregnancies result in miscarriage. Allen J. Wilcox, Clarice R. Weinberg, and Donna D. Baird, "Timing of Sexual Intercourse in Relation to Ovulation," *New England Journal of Medicine* 333 (Dec. 7, 1995): 1517-21, 1563. Joseph Smith was almost certainly having daily sexual relations with *none* of his thirty to forty plural wives. In addition, miscarriages and the infant mortality rates in malaria-ridden Nauvoo would have further limited what few children he had by plural wives. Furthermore, he married the great majority of his wives in 1842 and especially 1843, less than a year before he died. However, as we have seen, Mary Elizabeth Lightner said she knew of three children of Joseph who were raised under other names. Of these three, one, Josephine Lyon Fisher, has been convincingly documented. **marrying underage women:** For instance, John D. Lee married a girl aged fourteen during the 1856 Utah Reformation, with the understanding that he would not have a sexual relationship with her until she was older. She put off having sexual relations with him, and eventually fell in love with Lee's oldest son. Lee released her from the marriage to him, and gave her to his son with his blessing. Brooks, JDL 233, 239-40. See also Juanita Brooks, *Emma Lee* (Logan: Utah State University Press, 1975), 8, 11. Wilford Woodruff, forty-six, married fifteen-year-old Emma Smith in 1853, but she did not bear him a child till she was seven months past nineteen. Alexander, THE 167-68. Compare Young, *Isn't One Wife Enough* 177. **no definite evidence:** See above on the Helen Mar Whitney autobiography, and at her chapter. **time and eternity:** Eliza Snow, Autobiography, in Bancroft Library, p. 13, film in CA, in Beecher, PW. Patty Sessions, a polyandrous wife, wrote, "I was sealed to Joseph Smith by Willard Richards March 9 1842 in Newel K Whitneys chamber Nauvoo, for time and all eternity Eternity." Patty Bartlett Sessions journal, CA, page after June 16, 1860 (Smart 277, which has a reproduction of this important page). By my interpretation, Sessions added "time and all eternity" as a clarification, not as a change. On the same page, she wrote of her proxy sealing to Joseph Smith in 1867 that she "was sealed ... for time and all eternity." Quinn, MHEP 184, 497, believes that the superscript "time and all eternity" in the first passage was added by a later hand, either a member of Patty's family or someone in the Church Historical Department, to combat RLDS anti-polygamy rhetoric. While I am not a handwriting expert, the superscript words appear to me to be in Patty's hand. One can compare "time and all eternity" in the first passage with the same words in the proxy sealing record, and the similarities are apparent. Particularly striking is the loop in the y of "eternity." **emphasizing eternity:** Lightner, "Statement," see above. **Lightner:** "Statement, Febr. 8, 1902," Mary Lightner collection, Lee Library. Autobiography, USHS: "in the month of March 1841 [1842] Brigham Young Sealed us for time, and all Eternity." Mar. 23, 1877, affidavit (Scott Kenney collection, Marriott Library, box 11, fd 14). **"eternity only"?:** Historian D. Michael Quinn has written, "If the phrase 'eternity only' ever appeared in an *original* record of LDS sealing in the nineteenth century, I have not discovered it while examining thousands of such manuscript entries." MHEP 184. **Wight interview,** "Evidence from Zina D. Huntington Young," *Saints Herald* 52 (Jan. 11, 1905): 29. **older wives:** Brigham Young told Horace Greeley, "I have some aged women sealed to me upon the principle of sealing which I no more think of making a wife of than I would my Grand Mother," Clerk's report of interview, July 13, 1859, Lee

Library, as cited in Johnson, DDW 57-70, 58. Compare a similar statement by John D. Lee, quoted by Ivins, "Notes on Mormon Polygamy," in Quinn, NMH 173. The dividing line between middle and old age can be difficult to draw. Quinn, MHEP 185, makes the valid point that middle-aged women can be attractive and sexually active.

## Marital Status at Time of Marriage: Polyandry

For introductions to polyandry in world religions and anthropology, see Prince Peter, *A Study of Polyandry* (The Hague: Mouton & Co., 1963); S. D. Singh, *Polyandry in Ancient India* (Delhi: Vikas, 1978); Y.S. Parmar, *Polyandry in the Himalayas* (Delhi: Vikas, 1975); Manis Kumar Raha and Palash Chandra Coomar, eds., *Polyandry in India* (Delhi: Gian, 1987), with general bibliography at 20-22; W. H. Sangre and N.E. Levine, eds., *Women With Many Husbands: Polyandrous Alliance and Marital Flexibility in Africa and Asia*, a special issue of *Journal of Comparative Family Studies* 11 (1980); G. D. Berreman, "Pahari Polyandry: A Comparison," *American Anthropologist* 64 (1962): 60-75. Polyandry is comparatively rare compared to the much more widespread polygyny; it is virtually never found without polygyny. Often polyandry and polygyny are combined (multiple men taking multiple wives, with each wife being married to each man), and the result has been called polygynandry. Polyandry is often fraternal, i.e., two brothers marry the same woman. According to anthropologists, polyandry serves to lessen tensions between brothers; it also increases the security of a wife and family in the prolonged absence of one brother. Some scholars have suggested that community of wives among brothers is an extension of community of possessions and wealth in cultures where brothers inherit equally. Mormon polyandry was never systematized and was always secret, so none of these parallels apply fully. However, as there was a fraternal dimension to Mormon ecclesiastical fellowship, and as one's relationship with Joseph Smith was crucial for one's earthly and eternal welfare, some of these dynamics may have been in effect. Compare the quote by Jedediah Grant on consecrating one's wife (almost seen as a possession) to Joseph if required to do so, and text below, "Buckeye's Lament." See on the "commodification" of women in history, in the Fanny Alger chapter, last section. **complete and balanced:** Valuable pioneering treatments in Bachman, "A Study," 124-36; Richard Van Wagoner, "Mormon Polyandry in Nauvoo," *Dialogue* 18 (Fall 1985): 67-83. **unhappy marriage theory:** Bachman emphasizes this interpretation of Joseph's polyandry in "A Study," 124-36: "Three of Smith's wives experienced marital difficulties in their first marriage, and it appears that he [Joseph] wed them out of concern for both their earthly and eternal welfare." He adds that Mary Elizabeth Rollins Lightner was married to a non-Mormon, so Joseph married her for the same reasons. Compare the Hawley statement in the Jane Law section above (Joseph purportedly marries Brigham Young's wife because Brigham, even though he was an apostle, could not save her). Then he does mention, "[T]wo or three of them [Joseph's other polyandrous wives' marriages to their "first husbands"] do not appear to have been unsatisfactory unions." However, Bachman's emphasis here is on the problematic husbands; "two or three" satisfactory unions is a definite understatement. A relevant factor that must be considered is that husbands were legally entitled to custody of the children in a divorce, see Roderick Phillips, *Putting Asunder, A History of Divorce in Western Society* (Cambridge, Eng.: Cambridge University Press, 1988), 599-600. However, "first husbands" were generally so loyal to Joseph Smith that this was probably not a factor, except in the cases of the non-Mormons or disaffected Mormons. **Presendia:** See the Presendia Huntington chapter, below. **authoritarianism:** For early Mormon absolutist authoritarianism, see Mario S. De Pillis, "The Quest for Religious Authority and the Rise of Mormonism," 13-36 in Quinn, NMH; Hill, QFR, 28, 204. **Lee:** MU 146. Jedediah Grant, in 1854, remembered Nauvoo members saying, about marriage, "Joseph says all covenants are done away and none are binding but the new covenants." JD 2:13-14. See also Lucy A. Young to Joseph Smith III, May 22, no year, RLDS Archives. Orson Pratt said in 1846, "As all the ordinances of the gospel Administered by the world since the Apostcy of the Church was illegal, in like manner was the marriage Cerimony illegal." WWj, Aug. 15, 1846 (3:260). There are similar statements by others collected in Bachman, "A Study," 126-28; Van Wagoner, MP 45-47; Campbell and Campbell, "Divorce," 193; compare D&C 132:18; Johnson, in Zimmerman 57. **"The Second Way"**: "A Few Words on Doctrine," speech at tabernacle by Brigham Young, Oct. 8, 1861, Brigham Young addresses, recorded by George Watts, MS 1234, box 49, fd 8. Published in *For WoMen Only*, ed. Dennis Short (Salt Lake City: Short, 1977). Compare Campbell and Campbell, "Divorce," 195. See also James Beck Notebooks, 1859-65, Vol. 1, Oct. 8, 1861, CA, as quoted in Van Wagoner, MP 43; Foster, RS 162. Compare Frederick Kessler diary, Marriott Library, Oct. 8, 1861. Young asserts that he learned this from Joseph Smith. **de facto divorce after partner's apostasy:** This happened to John Hyde in the mid 1850s; he left the Mormon church, and his wife was immediately divorced from him. Heber Kimball, in JD 4:165, said: "The limb she was connected to was cut off, and she must again be grafted into the tree, if she wishes to be saved"; compare Foster, RS 162. Hannah Grover left her husband, Thomas Grover, because he was not prominent in the church, though a faithful member. Then she was sealed to Daniel Wells, a member of the First Presidency, see Campbell and Campbell, "Divorce," 194. **Women request plural marriage to church leader:** E.g., Adelia Wilcox and Heber Kimball, see her Autobiography, CA; HCK 239. **Grant quote:** JD 2:13-14, Feb. 19, 1854. **Ask to surrender wife:** Heber C. Kimball was so asked, and was extremely reluctant, but finally complied (see Helen Mar Kimball chapter). John Taylor reportedly was also asked, and was also extremely reluctant (John M. Whitaker journal, Nov. 1, 1890, vol. 7, p. 11, Marriott Library). Joseph seems to have released these two from the request, stating that he had been testing them. Orson Hyde's wife, Marinda, on the other hand, was certainly married to Joseph, see her chapter. To depart from the apostles, Jane Law also accused Joseph of proposing marriage to her, and Law, believing her, was not willing to give her up; he and she subsequently left the church. See above, compare Horace Cummings, *Contributor* 5 (Apr. 1884): 255; Lee, MU 147; Hill, JS 389.

**Pre-existence and polyandry:** Mary Elizabeth Lightner, "Statement," Feb. 8, 1902, see above. Mary Elizabeth Lightner, Autobiography; compare Lightner's 1905 letter to Emmeline Wells, Lee Library, Mary Elizabeth Lightner collection. Hall, *The Abominations of Mormonism*, 12-13, compare 41-43. Ann Eliza Young (WN19 70-71), writing in 1876, also reported that Joseph taught the doctrine of "kindred spirits" when he proposed marriage to women who were already married. Patriarchal Blessing by William Smith, July 16, 1845 at Nauvoo, on head of Mary Ann Peterson, "sitting as proxy" for Ann B. Peterson, deceased. She was the dead wife of Charles Petersen. Utah Pioneer Biographies, Fed. Writers Proj., vol 23, pp. 103-104, as cited in Ivins 5:276. A later reference from a plural wife of Joseph Smith: Helen Mar Kimball Smith Whitney told a woman friend, after kissing at parting, that "we were kindred spirits before we came on this planet." Helen Mar Whitney diary, May 28, 1886, Helen Mar Whitney collection, Merrill Library. Arrington and Bitton, ME 187.

**Background of Mormon polyandry:** William Hepworth Dixon, *Spiritual Wives* (London: Hurst and Blackett, 1868). See also John Spurlock, *Free Love, Marriage and Middle-Class Radicalism in America, 1825-1860* (New York: New York University Press, 1988), 77-78; Van Wagoner, MP 38. On Swedenborg, see Dixon, *Spiritual Wives* 2:193. "Nearly all the contracts made on earth, says the Swede, are null and void from the beginning, because these unions are not made with natural pairs." Spurlock, *Free Love* 90; Emanuel Swedenborg, *Conjugal Love* (New York: Swedenborg Foundation, 1938, orig. 1768), par. 49. For Rev. Stone, Dixon, *Spiritual Wives* 2:15-17. For physical sexuality in spiritual wife doctrine, Spurlock, *Free Love* 78. Swedenborg on pre-existence is quoted in John Cairncross, *After Polygamy Was Made a Sin* (London: Routledge & Kegan Paul, 1974), 174-75. **zeitgeist:** See also Whitney Cross, *The Burned-over District* (Ithaca, NY: Cornell University Press, 1950), 243-45. **practitioners sincerely**

**religious:** Dixon, *Spiritual Wives* 1:89. The movement was closely related to "perfectionism," the belief that human effort could eliminate all sin, see Spurlock, *Free Love* 8, 73-106. One example of abuse of idealistic doctrines is the bizarre charlatan Robert Matthews ("Mathias the Prophet"), see Gilbert Seldes, *The Stammering Century* (New York: John Day Co., 1928), 126-27, "matched spirits." Also, *Memoirs of Mathias the Prophet*, in Ivins 7:157-60; William Stone, *Matthias and His Impostures* (New York: Harper & Bros., 1835), 169, 171, "all the marriages in the world were illegal." Matthews met Joseph Smith, though it is unlikely that one influenced the other seriously, HC 2:306-307; Paul E. Johnson and Sean Wilentz, *The Kingdom of Mathias* (New York: Oxford University Press, 1994), 4. **"pseudo-polyandry":** Andrew Ehat, "Pseudo-Polyandry: Explaining Mormon Polygyny's Paradoxical Companion—the Microscopic View," talk given at Sunstone Symposium, Washington, D.C., Aug. 1985. **Fisher affidavit:** Statement to Andrew Jenson, Feb. 24, 1915, CA; compare Van Wagoner, MP 41. Disfellowshipment and excommunication were often equivalent in the early Mormon church, see Nauvoo High Council Minutes (CA; typescript in Marquardt collection, Marriott Library), Sept. 22, 1841: "Seconded & caried that he should be disfellowshiped and his name erased from the church roll by the unanimous voice of the Branch." **Patty Sessions:** See above in Section IV, on marriages for time and eternity. **Fanny Alger's family:** Ann Eliza Webb Young, WN19 66-67. **Sarah Ann Whitney:** Bachman, "A Study," 121-22; Kenneth Godfrey, "Causes of Mormon/Non-Mormon Conflict in Hancock County, Illinois, 1839-1846," Ph.D. diss., Brigham Young University, 1967, 99 n. 27. **Helen Kimball Whitney:** Helen Mar Whitney, Autobiographical Sketch, 1881, CA; also in Linda Newell papers, Marriott Library. See the Kimball and Whitney chapters. **"Buckeye's Lament":** *Warsaw Message* (Feb. 4, 1844), reprinted in Bachman, "A Study," App. E, 338-40, compare 264-65. A number of factors support the historical validity of this poem, and a companion piece by the same author. For instance, the author knew of Joseph's marriages to the Partridge sisters and Martha McBride Knight, and of his unsuccessful proposal to Nancy Rigdon, so the author was an insider of some sort. In addition, the doctrine that one could be sealed up with very little possibility of damnation is reflected in D&C 132, the revelation on polygamy, vv. 26-27. Joseph felt that Wilson Law was the author of "Buckeye's Lament," HC 6:210. The author characterizes himself as a devout follower of Joseph Smith who has become disillusioned with him, and has wept "burning tears" after pleading with him to repent, see "The Buckeye's First Epistle to Jo," *Warsaw Signal* (Apr. 23, 1844), repr. in Bachman, "A Study," 341-44.

For the doctrine of being sealed up with no possibility of damnation, see also Joseph Smith to Sarah Ann Whitney, Mar. 23, 1843, CA, as quoted in Hill, QFR 244. In the Clayton/Kimball journal Book 93, Jan. 1, 1846, IC 247, Brigham Young performed a marriage in the Nauvoo temple: "He then pronounced them Husband & Wife, and Sealed them together as such for time and for all eternity, and also sealed them up to eternal life, against all sins, except the sin against the Holy Ghost, which is the shedding of innocent blood ..." Compare the Clayton journal, May 16, 1843, IC 102. This would supply strong motivation for entering into a plural marriage, or allowing a family member to do so. Compare Prince, PFOH 191, 162, 166; David John Buerger, "Salvation in the Theology of Joseph Smith," in Gary James Bergera, ed., *Line Upon Line: Essays On Mormon Doctrine* (Salt Lake City: Signature Books, 1989), 159-70.

# REFERENCES TO CHAPTER 1.
## Mormonism's First Plural Wife? Fanny Alger (Smith Custer)

**License**: This was found by Richard Van Wagoner, see MP 10; copy in Van Wagoner collection, Marriott Library. For further on Solomon Custer, see his obituary, *Richmond Telegram* (Apr. 2, 1885), in the section, "Dublin." I am indebted to Richard Van Wagoner for generously sharing this document with me, and other Fanny Alger materials.

I. **Fanny's birth**: Family Group Record, film 1553906, 5026565, sheet 31, at GS. Other family group sheets have September 30. **Alger family**: See Obituary for Samuel Alger Sr., "DIED," DEN 7 (Oct. 6, 1874): p. 3. 1820 census, Lebanon township, Ashtabula, Ohio. Samuel had been born on February 14, 1786, in Uxbridge, Worcester, Massachusetts. Clarissa, born on September 3, 1790 in Old Springfield, Hampden, Massachusetts, married him in 1808. They converted to Mormonism in 1830 and accompanied Mormons in the general migrations to Missouri (living there from September 1837 to 1839), Illinois (from February 1839 to May 1846) and Utah (arriving in September 1848). After seventeen years in Salt Lake, they moved to Parowan, Iron County, where Samuel served as patriarch, and where Clarissa died. Samuel spent the last years of his life in St. George, Utah, with his son John. For Levi Hancock, see below. **Eli Ward**: Born on March 11, 1809, he married Sarah Billington. **Amy Saphony**: Born on Sept. 27, 1818, she married John Wilson Overton. **Lebanon**: Now New Lyme. **John Alger**: Born on Nov. 5, 1820, he became a planer and wheelwright and married Sarah Ann Pulsipher in 1842, Rachael Jones Michael in 1855 (div.), Rachel/Ragula Hug in 1856 (div.), Jane Ann Burnett in 1861, and his brother Thomas's widow, Sarah Ann Edwards Alger, in 1867. He died in 1897 in St. George, Washington, Utah. Compare BE 1:798; NTER. **Alva**: was born on Oct. 11, 1822. He married Louisa Thornton, and evidently did not come to Utah. **Samuel H.**: Born on July 31, 1826, he married a Miss Ivey, and evidently did not come to Utah. **Thomas**: was born on Aug. 14, 1828. He married Sarah Ann Edwards in 1848, and died in Chillicothe, Livingston, Missouri, in 1862. **Clarissa**: Born on June 2, 1830, she married Francis Tuft Whitney polygamously in 1850 and died in 1907 in Parowan, Utah. **Algers convert**: See Samuel's Obituary. Levi Hancock joined the church in the same month, on November 16. See BE 1:188; Richard Lloyd Anderson, "The Impact of the First Preaching in Ohio," BYUSt 11 (1971): 474-96; Van Wagoner, SR 58-61. Levi Hancock, Autobiography, MS 8174, CA, p. 71. ECIF, s.v. John Alger; SEB, s.v. John Alger.

II. **Fanny probably first Mormon plural marriage**: In my view, there is no good evidence supporting the position (found in Brodie, NM 119, 462) that Joseph Smith was married to Marinda Johnson (later the first wife of Orson Hyde), or had an affair with her, in 1831, and was mobbed by "her brother Eli" and others as a result. See Marinda Johnson chapter at 1831; Van Wagoner, MP 224 n. 4. **Jacob 2:30**, as found in 1830 edition, p. 127. See Tim Rathbone and John W. Welch, *A Translation of the Book of Mormon: Basic Historical Information*, F.A.R.M.S. Preliminary Report (Provo, UT: F.A.R.M.S., 1986), 1, 33-37, who suggest that Jacob was probably translated in 1829. **"raise up seed"**: Compare Joseph's reported statement to Levi Hancock in 1832, below. **date of revelation:** Joseph Noble: "Plural Marriage," (Minutes of Davis Stake Conference), in MSt 45 (1883): 454. Bachman, "A Study" 68, also 56-68, 61-73; Bachman, "New Light on an Old Hypothesis: The Ohio Origins of the Revelation on Eternal Marriage," JMH 5 (1978): 19-32. **Abraham:** Joseph also cited the example of Moses as one who practiced polygamy at the same time that he was a prophet, see Benjamin Johnson, "Open letter to the President of the United States," to Grover Cleveland, Jan. 15, 1886, CA, as cited in E. Dale LeBaron, "Benjamin Franklin Johnson, Colonizer, Public Servant, and Church Leader," Master's thesis, Brigham Young University, 1966, 80-81. It is not certain what scripture Joseph relied upon for this interpretation. **primitivist:** See Prologue. **polygamy and salvation:** Compare William Clayton affidavit, in HR 6:226. "From him [Joseph Smith] I learned that the doctrine of plural and celestial marriage is the most holy and important doctrine ever revealed to man on the earth, and that without obedience to that principle no man can ever attain to the fulness of exaltation in celestial glory." Compare D&C 132:26; Orson Pratt, Oct. 7, 1874, in JD 17:225-26; Hardy, SC 14-19; 84-113. **Lyman Johnson:** Orson Pratt, "Report of Elder Orson Pratt and Joseph F. Smith," MSt 30 (Dec. 16, 1878): 788; compare ME 65. **Phelps**: Letter to Brigham Young, Aug. 12, 1861, CA; compare Foster, RS 299; Newell and Avery, ME 65. Significantly, Joseph cites the example of Abraham. **Booth letter:** "Letter No. IX," *Ohio Star* [Ravenna, Ohio], (Dec. 8, 1831); also in E.D. Howe,

*Mormonism Unvailed* (Painesville: E.D. Howe, 1834), 175-221, 220; see Bachman "A Study," 67, 71-72. Compare Newell and Avery, ME 64; Hardy, SC 5. **Johnson:** in Zimmerman, 38, 41. Underlining is Johnson's. **Article on Marriage:** Doctrine and Covenants (1835), section 101, p. 251, compare HC 2:246-47. Also in Cook, RP 359-60. This statement was approved at a general assembly and was included in every edition of the Doctrine and Covenants until 1876, when it was replaced by the present section 132 on polygamy and exaltation, an interesting case of decanonizing a portion of a standard work. Joseph Smith in Nauvoo also denied practicing polygamy (HC 6:411, 5:72); and post-manifesto polygamy was denied by church leaders, Hardy, SC. Faced with the necessity of keeping polygamy secret, the Mormon authorities generally chose to disavow the practice, sometimes using language with coded double meanings. But such denials, sending contradictory signals to church followers and non-Mormons, always were made at a significant price. See Hardy, SC 363-89. Compare Joseph F. Smith, JD 20:29, who stated that this "Article on Marriage" was "indisputable evidence of the early existence of the knowledge of the principle of patriarchal marriage by the Prophet Joseph, and also by Oliver Cowdery." Brigham Young stated that Oliver Cowdery wrote the Article and insisted that it be included in the Doctrine and Covenants, "contrary to the thrice expressed wish and refusal of the Prophet Jos. Smith." Joseph F. Smith diary, Oct. 9, 1869, CA, as cited in Cook, RP 348. This reference indicates that Young clearly saw the Article as deceptive, and tried to place the blame for it entirely on Oliver Cowdery. But Smith could easily have overruled Cowdery, and Young himself could have removed the Article before 1876. Compare Thomas B. H. Stenhouse, *Rocky Mountain Saints* (London: Ward, Lock & Tyler, 1894), 193. Another denial, an editorial in EJ 1.3 (July 1838): 43, shows how widespread the Mormon reputation for polygamy was in Kirtland: "Do the Mormons believe in having more wives than one. Answer. No, not at the same time." **Brodie:** NM 182, 184, 185. Brodie spoke of "extreme informality" attending Joseph's early extramonogamous relationships with women, 301; however, she hedges slightly on the issue at times, see Appendix, 458. For Brodie's limitations as a biographer, see Introduction. Among those who follow Brodie on this issue are Foster, RS 301-2; Hardy, SC 24 n. 29; Richard Van Wagoner, MP 12. These are all fine scholars, but they are perhaps overly dependent on Brodie here. John L. Brooke, *The Refiner's Fire* (Cambridge, MA: Cambridge University Press, 1994), 217, citing only secondary sources, refers to the Smith/Alger relationship as Joseph's "first extramarital affair." **Oliver Cowdery:** Letterbook, Jan. 21, 1838, Huntington library. **Kimball:** Johnson, in Zimmerman, 44. However, Johnson places the incident in the St. George temple, and Kimball died before its completion. Either Heber made the statement elsewhere, or he did not say it. **Jenson:** HR 6:233; HR vol. 5-8, index, p. 942. **Brodie:** NM 182, "When in later years polygamy had become an accepted pattern in Mormon life, Joseph's leading elders looked back to the Kirtland days and concluded that Fannie Alger had been the prophet's first plural wife." Compare 184. **Ann Eliza:** See below.

III. **Mosiah Hancock autobiography:** The holograph is "Autobiography of Mosiah Hancock," MS 570, CA. Perhaps the Fanny Alger passages have not received the attention they deserve because a printed version of the text has been readily available, and this version, unprofessionally edited, has the Fanny Alger passages deleted. At least two published (mimeographed) versions of the Hancock writings are *The Mosiah Hancock Journal* (Salt Lake City: Pioneer Press, n.d.), 74 pp. (reprinted), and *The Levi Hancock Journal* (n.p., n.d.), 58 pp. Various typescript versions, all less complete than the holograph version, also exist. **written in 1896:** See Mosiah Hancock Autobiography, p. 61 (see next note). See also, before p. 53, on the outside of the notebook, "Deposited by By Mosiah Hancock June 6, 1896. UNIVERSITY NOTE BOOK." On the inside of the cover: L.D.S. HISTORIAN'S OFFICE, Salt Lake City, Utah Received June 6, 1896." **continues father's history:** Page 61: "Farmington Davis Co Co 1896 I am Mosiah Lyman Reed Hancock the son of Levi Ward Hancock and Clarissa Reed Hancock - There being a Stop apparently in My Father's History from the time he made the {trip} 'So far in the Realms of Missouri' ..." Then Mosiah immediately begins the Fanny Alger stories. **Levi Hancock:** See his own autobiography, MS 8174, CA; BE 1:188; Dennis A. Clegg, "Levi Ward Hancock: Pioneer, Soldier, Political and Religious Leader of Early Utah," Master's thesis, Brigham Young University, 1966; Cook, RP 76-77; Quinn, MHOP 550. **Eliza R. Snow**: Nauvoo journal, June 29, 1842, CA, and "Sketch of My Life," Bancroft Library, Berkeley, both edited by Beecher in *Personal Writings*. **Zina Huntington**: For her autobiography, see Martha Sonntag Bradley and Mary Brown Firmage Woodward, "Plurality, Patriarchy, and the Priestess: Zina D.H. Young's Nauvoo Marriages," JMH 20 (1994): 84-118. For the Nauvoo journal, which covers some of the period she was married to Joseph, see "'All Things Move in Order in the City': The Nauvoo Diary of Zina Diantha Huntington Jacobs," Maureen Ursenbach Beecher, ed., BYUSt 19 (1979): 285-320. **bear witness**: Mosiah Hancock, "Letter to the Editor," *DEN* (Feb. 21, 1884): 4. **credibility**: Richard Howard, "The Need for Historical Perspective," *Saints' Herald* 116 (Feb. 1969): 47, criticizes Mosiah for including in his narrative an *ex post facto* prophecy attributed to Joseph Smith in 1844. However nonscientific they may be from a historian's point of view, *ex post facto* prophecies attributed to Joseph Smith were a common element of Mormon reminiscences, and Mosiah was well within the norms of his society in including it. See the Autobiography of Mary Elizabeth Rollins Lightner, Lee Library; and the Journal of Oliver Huntington, Lee Library, Books 13, 14, 15; 17:48, 18:101; Davis Bitton, "Joseph Smith in Mormon Folk Memory," *Restoration Studies* 1 (Independence, MO: Temple School, 1980), 75-94, 81-83. **Independence song**: Mosiah Hancock, Autobiography, 66-67. HC 3:42. **Holbrook**: Mosiah Hancock, Autobiography, 71. Joseph Holbrook, Autobiography, MS SC 486, Lee Library, 43. Nancy Tracy, Autobiography, MS SC 918, Lee Library, 20. **Mosiah Hancock**, Autobiography, 64. **Levi takes Clarissa to Rome**: Mosiah Hancock, Autobiography, 64. Levi Hancock, Autobiography, 133. For another connection of Joseph Smith, Levi Hancock, and Fanny Alger, see Autobiography, 150, with discussion below. **at Mosquito Creek**: Mosiah Hancock, Autobiography, 95. Esaias Edwards, Autobiography, Lee Library, p. 28. **divorce of Levi and Clarissa**: Mosiah Hancock autobiography, folder 5, seventh page. Compare Introduction, last section. **parallels with Nauvoo polygamy**: Though Mosiah probably heard some stories of Joseph's Nauvoo polygamic practices, he would not have heard all the stories. Joseph's plural wives were remarkably reticent throughout their lives, often telling the stories of their marriages to Joseph only to their children, and often only at the end of their lives, e.g., Sylvia Sessions Lyon and Helen Mar Kimball Whitney. Some did not tell the stories even to their close family members, e.g., Agnes Coolbrith Smith Pickett and Sarah Lawrence Mount.

IV. **spring of 1832**: Mosiah Hancock Autobiography, 61-62. According to Mosiah, Joseph had a convincing rationale for polygamy as early as spring 1832, see above. In 1852 Orson Pratt used this same eugenic argument to justify the patriarchal "principle": polygamy allowed the most noble spirits to be born into the most favored lineages. JD 1:62-63, compare Hardy, SC 15. This is a very patriarchal argument—polygamy allows more children to specific men, but not to specific women. **Levi and Temperance**: Mosiah Hancock Autobiography, 62-63. This exchange shows the willingness of Joseph Smith's followers to offer him unquestioning obedience even in a matter as personal as marriage. There are two parallels in Nauvoo polygamy for Joseph Smith choosing a man's wife for him, in one case even after the man had chosen another, as here. When Joseph commanded Heber C. Kimball to practice polygamy, Heber first selected as wives two older sisters, friends of the family, whom he felt his wife Vilate would accept; but Joseph had already decided that Heber should marry Sarah Peake Noon, a thirty-year-old English convert. Heber reluctantly agreed to the marriage. **Heber C. Kimball and Sarah Noon**: Helen Mar Whitney, "Scenes and Incidents in Nauvoo," WE 10 (Oct. 15, 1881): 74; 11 (July 15, 1882): 26. Compare Kimball, HCK 95. According to Vilate Kimball, Joseph also "appointed" Parley P. Pratt's first plural wife, Elizabeth Brotherton, for him. **Parley P. Pratt and Elizabeth Brotherton**: Vilate Kimball to Heber C. Kimball, June 27, 1843, CA, MS 6241, fd 1. "J.....h [Joseph Smith] has taught him

[Pratt] some principles and told him his privilege, and even appointed one for him." **Clarissa Reed:** Mosiah Hancock Autobiography, 63. Clarissa Reed (Hancock), mother of Mosiah, should not be confused with Clarissa Hancock (Alger), Fanny's mother and sister of Levi. Brodie, NM 464, posits a plural marriage between Joseph Smith and Clarissa Reed, but I am aware of no evidence for any such relationship. **Levi approaches Fanny:** Mosiah Hancock Autobiography, 63. **exchange of women:** See the concluding section of this paper for fuller discussion. **Joseph proposing through male relatives:** See Zina Huntington, Almera Johnson, and Martha McBride chapters, at the marriage to Joseph Smith. Compare Mercy Thompson Smith's story, DN (Feb. 6, 1886). **repeating marriage ceremony:** See Louisa Beaman chapter, at the marriage to Joseph. **date of marriage of Levi and Clarissa:** Levi Hancock Autobiography, p. 136. **Nauvoo plural marriages:** For a useful, preliminary, listing see George D. Smith, "Nauvoo Roots of Mormon Polygamy, 1841-1846: A Preliminary Demographic Report," *Dialogue* 27 (1994): 1-72. **spiritual honor:** See Helen Mar Kimball and Sarah Ann Whitney chapters.

V. **Ann Eliza Webb Young**, WN19 66-67. Ann Eliza never mentions Fanny's name, but a letter Ann Eliza wrote to Mary Bond on Apr. 24, 1876, makes the identification explicit, "Fanny Algers had lived in Joseph's family several years and when she left there she came and lived with me a few weeks, I suppose your mother will remember what a talk the whole affair made." Myron H. Bond collection, P21, f11, RLDS Archives. "I do not know that the 'sealing' commenced in Kirtland but I am perfectly satisfied that something similar commenced, and my judgement is principally formed from what Fanny Algers told me herself concerning her reasons for leaving 'sister Emma.'" Ann Eliza Webb to Mary Bond, May 4, 1876. I am indebted to Michael Marquardt for sharing this source with me. However, Jeffery Johnson informs me that Ann Eliza's birthdate is 1844 or 1842, so this makes her testimony somewhat problematic. Apparently she heard the story from her parents, then passed herself off as an eyewitness. Ann Eliza travelled after leaving Brigham Young, so there is an outside possibility that she looked Fanny up in Indiana. Compare Max Parkin, *Conflict at Kirtland* 174; Van Wagoner, MP 10. **hired girls:** For context, see Cott, *Bonds of Womanhood* 28-29, who writes, "Unmarried women also earned wages by performing their usual domestic tasks in households other than their own." Compare Larkin, *Reshaping* 13. **Partridge sisters and Eliza Snow ejected:** See Partridge sister and Eliza Snow chapters. **Cowdery:** I agree with Van Wagoner, MP 11, 14, that evidence of a plural marriage for Cowdery in Kirtland is not persuasive. Opposing this view are Brigham Young, quoted in Charles Walker Journal, July 26, 1872, in Andrew Larson and Katherine Miles Larson, eds., Diary of Charles Lowell Walker, 2 vols. (Logan: Utah State University Press, 1980), 1:359; Joseph F. Smith, July 7, 1878, in JD 20:29; [G.Q. Cannon], "History of the Church," Juvenile Instructor 16 (Sept. 15, 1881): 206; Stenhouse, Rocky Mountain Saints 193. Compare Parkin, Conflict at Kirtland 169-72, esp. 172 n. 100; Quinn, MHOP 544. Chauncey Webb, in Wyl, MP 57; compare Bachman, "A Study" 83. William McLellin, to Joseph Smith III, July 1872, RLDS Archives. Though Lovina Smith Walker, a daughter of Hyrum Smith, said that Emma had told her in 1846 that she, Emma, had witnessed the plural marriages of the Partridge and Lawrence sisters to Joseph (see Lovina's 1869 affidavit, BAOPM 73), this is far from the sexually explicit tone of McLellin's story, compare Joseph F. Smith journal, Aug. 28, 1870, CA. Johnson tells a somewhat similar story, except it is Oliver and Warren Parrish who see Joseph and Fanny together, Johnson, in Zimmerman, 38, see below. Compare Foster, RS 302; William McLellin, interviewed in Beadle, "Jackson County," Salt Lake Tribune (Oct. 6 1875), p. 4: "He also informed me of the spot where the first well authenticated case of polygamy took place, in which Joseph Smith was 'sealed' to the hired girl. The 'sealing' took place in a barn on the hay mow, and was witnesed by Mrs. Smith through a crack in the door! The Doctor was so distressed about this case, (it created some scandal at the time among the Saints,) that long afterwards when he visited Mrs. Emma Smith at Nauvoo, he charged her as she hoped for salvation to tell him the truth about it. And she then and there declared on her honor that it was a fact—'saw it with her own eyes.'" **Johnson**, in Zimmerman, 38-39. For polygamy as a cause of apostasy in Kirtland, see Parkin, *Conflict at Kirtland* 164-74, and see on Oliver Cowdery's excommunication below. **dismisses boarders:** JSj, Jessee, PW 64; Van Wagoner, MP 10. However, this may be too late to refer to the departure of Fanny; October 17 is two months after the "Article on Marriage," possibly a response to the Alger problem, see below, was adopted in conference. See Richard Van Wagoner, letter to Linda Newell, Sept. 20, 1983, in Van Wagoner collection, Marriott library. **Joseph to Michigan:** HC 2:243, 246; Hill, JS 189. **Article on Marriage presented:** HC 2:246. This was discussed above. **other Kirtland relationships:** Three documents claim that Joseph Smith had liaisons with women other than Fanny Alger in the Kirtland period. The earliest is an affidavit by Fanny Brewer dated Sept. 13, 1842: "There was much excitement against the prophet on another account, an unlawful intercourse between himself and a young orphan girl residing in his family, and under his protection!" (printed in Bennett, *History of the Saints* 85-86). This may be a reference to Fanny Alger; Ann Eliza Young refers to Fanny as "adopted," and some assumed that she was an orphan. In the July 1872 letter William McLellin wrote to Joseph Smith III, he stated: "Dr. Frederick G. Williams practiced with me in Clay Co. Mo. during the latter part of 1838. And he told me that at your birth [November 6, 1832] your father committed an act with a Miss Hill—a hired girl. Emma saw him and spoke to him. He desisted, but Mrs. Smith refused to be satisfied. He called in Dr. Williams, O. Cowdery, and S. Rigdon to reconcile Emma. But she told them just as the circumstances took place. He found he was caught. He confessed humbly, and begged forgiveness. Emma and all forgave him. She told me this story was true. Again I told her I heard that one night she missed Joseph and Fanny Alger. She went to the barn and saw him and Fanny in the barn together alone. She looked through a crack and saw the transaction!! She told me this story too was verily true." As Van Wagoner (MP p. 5) notes, McLellin seems to be telling two stories, one of Miss Hill, and the other of Fanny Alger. But as Newell and Avery note, ME 65-66, the stories are very much alike. If Hill is a separate girl, she had nearly the same experience as Fanny Alger. Emma discovers her and Joseph together; Oliver and others are brought in. In addition, this reference is second hand and forty years after the event; my skepticism of Emma's confirmation is expressed above. I conclude, with Newell and Avery, that McLellin garbled the Hill story from a story about Fanny Alger, itself suspect. Martin Harris reportedly told a similar story to Anthony Metcalf of Joseph Smith turning to him for help after an unnamed hired girl accused Joseph of making advances. "Harris, supposing that Joe was innocent, told him to take no notice of the girl, that she was full of the devil, and wanted to destroy the prophet of God; but Joe Smith acknowledged that there was more truth than poetry in what the girl said. Harris then said he would have nothing to do in the matter, Smith could get out of the trouble the best way he knew how." *Ten Years Before the Mast* ([Malad City, ID]: n.p., 1888), 72. Martin Harris was not in Kirtland. Although he reportedly told the story to Metcalf during the winter of 1875-76, it was not printed until 1888 when Harris was dead. In the aggregate, these stories establish only that three individuals were willing to publish their belief that Joseph Smith had been sexually involved with a woman other than his wife during the Kirtland period; but no one story is completely convincing.

VI. **Fanny in temple:** Mosiah Hancock Autobiography, 64. **second floor:** Roger Launius, *The Kirtland Temple, A Historical Narrative* (Independence, MO: Herald Publishing House, 1986), 55. However, it is hard to imagine a woman being handed down from the upper story of the temple, unless the wagon was high and the "dry goods Box" was very tall. This may be an inaccuracy in Hancock's account. **dedication:** HC 2:410, 474. **Winchester:** "Primitive Mormonism," by Benjamin Winchester, *Salt Lake Tribune* (Sept. 22, 1889), p. 2. Compare George A. Smith, speech given on January 10, 1856, JD 7:114-15, who dates the beginnings of the Kirtland apostasy after the dedication of the Kirtland temple. **Joseph directs Levi:** Levi Hancock Autobiography, 150. **Johnson**, in Zimmerman, 39. **Samuel**

**Alger obituary:** "in September, 1836, [Samuel Sr.] started for Missouri, stopping in Wayne County, Indiana, in consequence of bad roads; started again the following September, and reached Randolph County ..." **Johnson**, in Zimmerman, 39. **courtship short:** Hypothesizing twelve to fifteen miles a day by wagon, the two-hundred-mile trip from Mayfield to Dublin would have taken between thirteen and sixteen days of straight traveling. Unfortunately, we do not know what day in September the family left Mayfield. They could have reached Dublin as early as mid-September or as late as mid-October. **Solomon nineteen:** Solomon Custer obituary. See also 1850 Census of Indiana, p. 11, 1880 Census of Indiana. He was born in Montgomery County, Ohio. **Algers in Illinois:** Samuel Alger Obituary. **Cowdery:** For Oliver Cowdery's conflicts and excommunication, see Philip R. Legg, *Oliver Cowdery, The Elusive Second Elder of the Restoration* (Independence, MO: Herald House, 1989), 109-36; HC 2:511; 3:4,6. **Thomas Marsh**, Testimony of, in excommunication trial of Cowdery, FWR 167-68. **David Patten**, Testimony of, FWR 167. This testimony shows how far rumors of the relationship had circulated. On June 25, 1857, Apostle Charles C. Rich reminisced, "David Patten & T.B. Marsh Came to kirtland in the fall of 1837 ... as soon as they came I got Marsh to go to Joseph, But Patten would go to W Parrish. He got his mind prejudiced & when He went to see Joseph David in[sult?]ed Joseph & Joseph slaped him in the face & kicked him out of the yard." WWj 5:63. Circumstantial evidence (the timing of this incident, the connections with Marsh and Parrish) suggests that Patten may have asked Joseph about Fanny Alger, though this is not certain. If so, a prominent early apostle nearly apostatized because of the Fanny Alger question. **confrontation:** HC 2:521. **Affidavit** of Thomas Marsh, included in a letter of Thomas Marsh to Joseph Smith, EJ 1 (July 1838): 45; an Affidavit by G. W. Harris (see Lucinda Pendleton chapter) in the same letter says essentially the same thing. **Harris's testimony:** FWR 167. **Oliver's excommunication trial:** FWR 167-68; HC 3:16-18. **Oliver criticizes church:** Oliver Cowdery letters, Jan. 30, 1838, Huntington Library, compare Hill, QFR 63. **Johnson**, in Zimmerman 38-39. **Carter and Parrish:** Johnson, in Zimmerman 38-39, 45. **Parrish:** Hill, QFR 62. See also EJ 1 (Aug. 1838): 57 (Parrish is referred to as an adulterer). **Carter:** Johnson, in Zimmerman 38. Cook, RP 74. For the *Expositor*, see the Elvira Cowles chapter at 1844.

VII. **Mary Custer:** 1850 Census, Indiana, Dublin City, p. 11. Mary would later marry a Mr. Vickers. Compare Van Wagoner to Linda Newell, Van Wagoner collection, Marriott Library. **Lewis Custer:** 1850 Census, Indiana, Dublin, p. 11. **Fanny visits Illinois:** The full listing is as follows: Samuel and Clarissa Alger; John, Alva, Samuel Jr., Thomas, Clarissa Jr. members. Fanny Custer. This list is found in the back of Emer Harris's Book of Patriarchal Blessings, No. 210, as cited in Van Wagoner to Linda Newell, see above. **Fanny in Indiana:** Johnson, see above. **Fanny reticent:** Johnson, in Zimmerman, 45. **Sophrona and Benjamin:** 1850 Census, Indiana, Dublin, p. 11. **Lafayette:** 1860 census, Indiana, Dublin, p. 190. **1860 status:** 1860 Census, Wayne Co., Dublin. **Solomon's occupations:** See *Directory and Soldier's Register of Wayne Co., Indiana* ([Wayne Co., Indiana], n.p. 1865), p. 58, which locates his store at the southeast corner of Cumberland and Milton, and his residence at the US National Road, East Dublin; *Dublin, 1830-1980* ([Dublin, IN]: n.p. 1980), p. 30, 34, 138. **anecdote:** *Dublin, 1830-1980* 138. **grandmother:** 1880 census, Indiana, Dublin, Soundex. **1880:** 1880 Indiana census, Dublin. **1885:** Solomon Custer, obituary. **funeral:** Ibid. There is a probate record, Indiana Probate Records, 52282 F Part 6. **Fanny's death:** Van Wagoner's exhaustive researches in Indiana failed to produce a death date for Fanny. "I left no stone unturned, I even found descendants, but she had vanished into the past like a vapor." Richard Van Wagoner to Todd Compton, Mar. 26, 1993.

VIII. **exchange of women:** Claude Levi-Strauss, *The Elementary Structures of Kinship* (Boston: Beacon Press, 1969), 115. See also Gerda Lerner, *The Creation of Patriarchy* (New York: Oxford University Press, 1986), and Gayle Rubin, "Traffic in Women," in *Towards an Anthropology of Women*, ed. Rayne Reiter (New York: Monthly Review Press, 1975), 157-210. For marriage brokering of young teens in Mormonism, see Helen Mar Kimball and Flora Woodworth chapters. In 1857 Wilford Woodruff offered Brigham Young his fourteen-year-old daughter, Phebe Amelia, and though Young declined, she married Lorenzo Snow, forty-three, instead. WWj, Feb. 15, 1857 (5:22), Alexander, THE 187, 404. Twenty years later, on March 10, 1877, Young offered Woodruff, now seventy, his twenty-five-year-old daughter, Eudora Lovina, and Woodruff accepted. WWj, Mar. 10, 1877 (7:338), Alexander, THE 230. For exchange of women among non-Mormon elite in early America, see Peter Dobkin Hall, "Family Structure and Economic Organization: Massachusetts Merchants, 1700-1850," in Tamara K. Hareven, ed., *Family and Kin in Urban Communities, 1700-1930* (New York: New Viewpoints/Franklin Watts, 1977), 43. **Lerner:** *The Creation of Patriarchy* 46. **marrying because of revelation:** See Zina D.H. Young, Autobiography, quoted in Bradley/Woodward 95-96. **pressure:** See Helen Mar Kimball and Lucy Walker chapters. **Feminist theory:** may interpret Fanny Alger's experience, and all of the women in this book, in at least two ways. First, she may be seen as a victim. See Marxist feminist John Faragher, who interprets Western women as exploited and powerless, *Women and Men on the Overland Trail* (New Haven, CT: Yale University Press, 1979), 187. "With men controlling the access to society and controlling the products that were potentially exchangeable on the market, they controlled the acquisition of power and status as well; women, confined to the domestic space, left without social power, were dependent for status upon their relations with their husbands." (One thinks of Patty Sessions, without a male partner in her later life in Salt Lake City and Bountiful, becoming wealthy through her orchards, her midwiving, and investments, see her chapter.) Second, Fanny may be seen as an individual who made her own choices, despite adversity and oppression. See Smith-Rosenberg, *Disorderly Conduct* 77. Jeffrey, *Frontier Women* 203, argues that, though women were not living in an egalitarian social system in the west, they were not powerless. Looking back on their pioneer experiences, they saw that "They had been not weak but strong; they had been not passive but active. They had triumphed over frontier conditions heroically." (There is an insightful chapter on Mormon polygamy in this book.) Sandra L. Myres, *Westering Women and the Frontier Experience, 1800-1915* (Albuquerque: University of New Mexico Press, 1982), 11, emphasizes the individuality and variety of Western women, in preference to typecasting them as paragons of piety or victims. Polygamy was, almost by definition, non-egalitarian; nevertheless, Mormon women were "not weak but strong," and sometimes "triumphed ... heroically" (as pioneers, mothers, and leaders) despite confining social structures.

## REFERENCES TO CHAPTER 2.

### Wife of Two Martyrs:
### Lucinda Pendleton (Morgan Harris Smith)

Bernard, Elder David. *Light on Masonry*. Utica, NY: Williams, 1829.

Cross, Whitney. *The Burned-over District*. Ithaca, NY: Cornell University Press, 1950. 114-15.

Formisano, Robert, and Kathleen Kutolowski. "Antimasonry and Masonry: the Genesis of Protests—1826-27." *American Quarterly* 29 (Summer 1977): 140-64.

Fox, Dixon R. *The Decline of Aristocracy in the Politics of New York*. New York: Harper, 1965.

Greene, Samuel D. *The Broken Seal*. Boston: by the author, 1870.

Hogan, Mervin. *The Two Joseph Smith's Masonic Experiences*. Salt Lake City: M.B. Hogan, 1987.

Lang, Ossian. *History of Freemasonry in the State of New York*. New York: Grand Lodge of New York, 1922.

McCarthy, Charles. "The Antimasonic Party: A Study of Political Antimasonry in the United States, 1827-40." *American Historical Association, Annual Report for 1902*, I:365-574.

Morris, Rob. *The Masonic Martyr. The Biography of Eli Bruce*. Louisville, KY: Morris &

Monsarrat, 1861.

———. *William Morgan; or Political Anti-Masonry.* New York: Robert Macoy, 1883.

Ross, Peter. *A Standard History of Freemasonry in the State of New York.* New York: Lewis Publishing Co., 1901.

Vaughn, William Preston. *The Antimasonic Party in the United States, 1826-1843.* Lexington: University Press of Kentucky, 1983.

**Richmond:** *Chicago Times*; repr. in *Deseret News*, "The Prophet's Death," (Nov. 27, 1875), 2-3; compare ME 346. "WHILE THE TWO WIVES WERE BEWAILING their loss, and prostrate on the floor with their eight children, I noticed a lady standing at the head of Joseph Smith's body, her face covered, and her whole frame convulsed with weeping. She was the widow of William Morgan, of Masonic memory, and twenty years before had stood over the body of her husband, found at the mouth of Oak Orchard Creek, on Lake Ontario. She was now the wife of a Mr. Harris, whom she married in Batavia, and who was a saint in the Mormon church, and a high Mason. I had called on her a few days previous to this occasion, and while conversing with her, put my hand on a gilt-edged volume lying on the stand. It was 'Stearns on Masonry,' and contained the likeness of William Morgan. She said she had taken it out, and thought if the mob did come, and she was obliged to flee, or jump into the Mississippi, she would take it with her."

I. **Lucinda's birth:** IGI: born in Washington County, Virginia. GS 1553165, B 8809202, sh 25, compare SEB. Date from BOP #64 (which, however, incorrectly gives Vermont as place of birth, with the town unreadable—perhaps "Kinghurstworks"). The Patriarchal Blessing Index also has 27 September. NTER has September 17. Lucinda's mother was dead by the Nauvoo period, as Lucinda does a baptism for the dead in her behalf, Book A, p. 122; ECIF. Marriage records in Washington County have Joseph Pendleton marrying "Elizabeth Rilee" on November 26, 1801, in Washington, Virginia, see Beverly Fleet, ed., *Washington County, Marriage Register, 1782-1820,* in *Virginia Colonial Abstracts,* vol. 3 (Baltimore, MD: Genealogical Publishing, 1988), 493; vol. 34 in original printing. If these are Lucinda's parents, as seems very likely, she may have been illegitimate, which would correlate with the report that she was the Pendletons' oldest child. See Daniel Scott Smith and Michael S. Hindus, "Premarital Pregnancy in America, 1640-1971: An Overview and Interpretation," *Journal of Interdisciplinary History* 5 (Spring 1975): 538. In the aftermath of the American Revolution, 25 percent of births in America were illegitimate. A Philip Harper Pendleton was born to Joseph Pendleton and "Elizabeth Reece" in 1804 in Washington, Virginia, see IGI. **clergyman:** Greene, BS; Vaughn, AP 2; Lang HF, 109. **blessing in Nauvoo:** See ECIF; A-122. In the 1820 census, after Lucinda had left the Pendleton household, there is a Joseph Pendleton living in Washington Co., Virginia. **oldest daughter:** "Lucinda Pendleton, the oldest daughter of the Rev. Joseph Pendleton of the Methodist connection and a respectable planter." *A Narrative of the Facts and Circumstances Relating to the Kidnapping and Presumed Murder of William Morgan* (Batavia, NY: Miller, 1827), 6. **marriage to Morgan:** Miller's *Advocate* (May 25, 1827); Morris, WM 275; Morris, MM 9; *A Narrative* 6; Ross, SH 309; *Arkansas Gazette,* Jan. 12, 1831; Brodie 459; Lang, HF 109. Joseph Pendleton opposed the marriage: Morris, MM 9. **Morgan:** He was born in 1774, per Ross 309. But in *A Narrative,* p. 6, he was born in 1775 or 1776. Morris, MM 9 gives 1776. For his description, *A Narrative.* He was a "bricklayer," Harris legal testimony, which also gives the physical description, see Morris, WM 258-59; Hogan, TJS 16. For his drinking, see below. One is struck by a similar controversy surrounding the Smith family. **Lucinda's description:** Richmond, see text at Joseph Smith's death. **Canada:** *A Narrative* 6. **Niagara County:** Vaughn, AP 2. **Rochester and LeRoy:** Vaughn, AP 2. Ross reverses the order in which he went to these towns. **Lucinda Wesley Morgan:** She later married a David Smith, and died in early 1884 in Portland, Oregon, see Johnson, MLR 303-4; ECIF; Tinney, RF 137; Greene,

BS 33. **Morgan as Mason:** Vaughn, AP 3; Morris, MM 10. **Morgan as drinker:** Lang, HF 109-10. Morris, MM 9 writes that Morgan would beat Lucinda, "small and feeble in person" when drunk. **Morgan rejected:** Vaughn, AP 3. **plan to publish exposed:** Vaughn, AP 3. **April 9:** Formisano, AM 147 n. 31. **Thomas Jefferson Morgan:** Greene, BS 33; ECIF, compare Tinney, RF 137. **harassment:** Formisano, AM 147. **Morgan's apartment:** Greene, BS 47. **Morgan arrested:** Greene, BS 51; Lang, HF. **Harris:** Harris legal testimony, see Morris, WM 258-59; Hogan, TJS 16. In September 1825 Harris had run for the office of sheriff in Genesee County, but lost, *The People's Press*, Batavia, New York (Sept. 24, 1825), as cited in Ivins 6:19. For Harris, see Cook, RP 260; Jessee, PW 678; ECIF; IGI. He had been born in Lanesboro, Berkshire, Massachusetts, on April 1, 1780. **Greene warns Harris:** Greene, BS 67-68. **Sept. 10:** Greene, BS 68; Lang, HF 112. **Lucinda last sees Morgan:** See deposition of Lucinda Morgan, sworn on Sept. 22, 1826, in Greene, BS 82-90; Bernard, LM app. 1, after p. 507.

II. **Morgan arrested:** Vaughn, AP 4; Lang, HF 112. **Morgan kidnapped:** Vaughn, AP 5; Lang, HF 113. **Lucinda's health bad:** Deposition of Lucinda Morgan, Greene, BS 90. **Ganson:** Greene, BS 91. **McCully:** *A Narrative* 15. **Greene warns Harris again:** Greene, BS 101; 122. **Harris locks self in office:** Greene, BS 102. **Morgan murdered:** Vaughn, AP 5. Masonic historians have suggested alternate scenarios. Some believe that the Morgan disappearance was a hoax, and that he was paid to disappear, so that Masonic enemies could whip up an anti-Masonic furor. Some have suggested that Lucinda Morgan and George Washington Harris were romantically linked before Morgan's departure, but there is no positive evidence for this. Compare Hogan, TJS. As noted below, Lucinda definitely thought Morgan dead by the Nauvoo period because she did a vicarious baptism for the dead for him. **Jan. 1827:** Vaughn, AP 7. **burial of Morgan:** Greene, BS 142; Vaughn, AP 9. **re-identification:** Vaughn, AP 9. **March 1830:** Letter by Lucinda Morgan, in *Chautauqua Phoenix* 2 (Mar. 10, 1830): 2.

III. **marriage:** *Wayne Sentinel* 8 (Dec. 3, 1830), in marriage notices. Compare *St. Louis Beacon* (Dec. 30, 1830), quoting from the New York *Courier*, "Mrs. Lucinda Morgan, the afflicted widow of Capt. William Morgan is *married*. This celebrated woman, who, like Niobe, was all tears and affliction ... who vowed eternal widowhood—... is married, and married 'tell it not in Gath'—to a Mason!" As cited in Ivins 8:200. The anti-Masons responded: "Mrs. Morgan's Marriage," *Republican Monitor /Cuzemonia* (Madison Co., New York), 8 (Dec. 28, 1830): p. 3, col. 1, which critiques the Albany *Argus* for saying Lucinda had married a mason. Harris "is a *seceding* mason, and his name is signed to the declaration of independence adopted at Le Roy, in July 1828." As cited in Ivins 11:74-76. Lucinda's remarriage was evidently widely reprinted by eastern papers. **move to Indiana:** See next section. **baptism:** "History of Orson Pratt," Aug. 21 entry, MSt 27 (Feb. 11, 1865): 87. **Aug. 5:** 1835 Census, taken by Charles Nook; compare H.C. Brandsby, *A History of Vigo County, Indiana* (Chicago: SB Nelson & Co., 1891), 430-35. **Sept. 1836:** Cook, RP 260, compare Clark Johnson, *Mormon Redress Petitions* (Provo, UT: BYU Religious Studies Center, 1992), 743. Harris owned lot –#8482. **Harris a high councillor:** On March 3, 1838, Harris was formally appointed to the high council at Far West, HC 3:14; MSt 16:132. On February 24, however, he had already started sitting in the council, FWR 142. For further, numerous listings of Harris as a high councillor in Far West, see FWR, index.

IV. **Feb. 24:** FWR, Feb. 24. **March 14:** Jessee 2:213; HC 3:9. **two months:** ME 70. **marriage to Joseph:** According to Sarah Pratt, in Wyl, MP 60, Lucinda told her, in 1842, that she started her relationship with Joseph four years previously. Sarah describes Lucinda as calling it an affair. This is antagonistic, third-hand, and late, though Sarah obviously was an early eyewitness to Nauvoo polygamy. The sympathetic Mormon record describes it as a sealing: "Lucinda Harris, also one of the first women sealed to the Prophet Joseph." (HR 6:233.) Newell and Avery suggest that "Quite possibly Joseph had taken her as a plural wife and the label 'mistress' was an embellishment by either Sarah Pratt or W. Wyl," ME 346. Certainly, if Joseph married Lucinda in Far West, it was a typical, poorly documented, pre-Nauvoo marriage. **May 12:** JH; FWR 187. **Sept.**

**2:** PBI vol. 3 p. 6, cited in Tinney, RF 136. **blessings:** PBI Vol. 3 p. 3, 4, 6, 8, cited in Tinney, RF 136; ECIF. **George W. a Danite:** Testimony in *Senate Document 189* (Salt Lake City: Modern Microfilm, n.d.), Feb. 15, 1841, pp. 1, 2, 14, 16, 18, 21, 22, 29, 33, 43, 47. G.W. Harris was in the last expedition to Daviess, George Hinkle testimony, *Document Containing the Correspondence, Orders &c in Relation to the Disturbances with the Mormons* (Fayette, MO: Boon's Lick Democrat, 1841), 126. One Latter-day Saint interpreter of the Danites agrees that they existed, but "disassociates" Joseph Smith from their "most militant and illegal manifestations." See David Whittaker, "The Book of Daniel in Early Mormon Thought," in John Lundquist and Stephen Ricks, *By Study and Also By Faith* (Salt Lake City: Deseret, 1990), 155-201, 168; Leland H. Gentry, "The Danite Band of 1838," BYUSt 14 (Summer 1974): 421-50. For interpretations that tie Joseph Smith more closely to Danite activity, see Hill, QFR 75-76; 91-92; Quinn, MHOP 93-94, 484. **Nov. 1838:** James H. Rollins Autobiography, Lee Library and USHS, p. 7. **Dec. 10:** HC 3:217-24; FWR 220. **last high council meeting:** FWR 220. **Harris signs covenant:** JH.

**V. May 24, 1839:** See Joseph Smith letterbooks, MS 155, CA. HC 3:362 quotes the letter, but gives the wrong first initial for George's name. The letterbook definitely has "Mr G.W. Harris." **Oct. 6:** HC 4:12; "Minutes of the High Council of the Church of Jesus Christ of Nauvoo Illinois," Books 1-4, Mar. 8, 1840 to Jan. 4, 1845, CA and Marriott Library. **Benjamin Johnson:** MLR 61, 70. **May 9:** TS 1 (May 1840): 111. "MARRIED ... In this place on the 9th Inst. by Elder Seymour Brunson, Mr. David B. Smith to Miss Lucinda W. Morgan." **Harris borrows from Joseph:** Nauvoo High Council minutes, Mar. 8, Bk 1, pp. 49-50. **mid-July 1840:** Nauvoo High Council minutes, just before July 25. **mission:** JH, July 17, 1840; Apr. 15, 1841. HC 4:161; 4.164; 4.199; see further relevant dates in JH. **Sept. 22:** Nauvoo High Council Minutes. **alderman:** HC 4:442. **baptisms for the dead:** Book A p. 105; ECIF. Lucinda performed some 25 baptisms for the dead, A.137; A.134; A.122; C.37; C.197; C.235; George W. performed 15, Index of Nauvoo Baptisms for the Dead, GS film 820153. **Jan. 17, 1842:** Willard Richards diary, CA. Joseph's record does not mention Lucinda: "dined, in company with the Recorder, at Sister Agnes Smith's." Jessee 2:353, compare HC 4:494. **George W. in high council:** JH, Jan. 28, May 22, June 23, July 20. **Sept. 9:** JH. **alderman:** JH, Mar. 30, Apr. 5, 1843; Apr. 3, May 25, 1844. **associate justice:** JH, Apr. 19, June 29, July 1, 1843; Feb. 5, May 8, 1844. **President pro tem:** JH, June 7, 10, 1844.

**VI.** At some point the Harrises apparently lived in Quincy, though dating the residence there is difficult. Asbury writes, "Morgan's widow married a man named Harris, a silversmith, who for a time had a shop on the corner of Fifth and Hampshire Streets, in Quincy. They were then all Mormons. Harris seemed a quiet, respectable man." Henry Asbury, *Reminiscences of Quincy, Illinois ... etc* (Quincy, IL: D. Wilcox, 1882), 110. Asbury mistakenly refers to Lucinda's son as "Bill Morgan," and connects him with a robbery in 1845-1846. **High Council:** JH, Apr. 7; Oct. 6, 1845; Jan. 20, 1846. JH, July 1, 1844, p. 1, **alderman:** JH, Feb. 3, 1845. **Stout:** HStj. He refers to him as being in his family, see below. **endowment:** NTER. **prayer meeting:** Dec. 21, HCKj (Clayton), Bk 93, CA. **Jan. 5:** IC 254. George met with the high priests frequently in the temple, see the Clayton/Kimball journal, Bk 93, CA. **Jan. 22:** BOP #64. SAd 505, 323.

**VII. commissary:** HC 7:586. **February 1846:** HStj, Feb. 7. **Apr. 10:** HStj. On February 23 Hosea Stout called on George W., who approved of Stout's actions. **adoption:** See OMF 1:178. For adoption in Mormonism at this time, see Prologue. **June 1:** Harris was travelling with Stout, see HStj. **George bishop and high councillor:** JH. Compare JH, Nov. 26, 1846. "6th Ward, Block 26. Geo W. Harris, nominated." Richard E. Bennett, *Mormons at the Missouri, 1846-52 "And Should We Die ..."* (Norman: University of Oklahoma Press, 1987), 282. **Sept., Nov.:** JH. **1847, High Council:** HStj, Jan. 10. JH, Jan. 16, Apr. 6. See also, for 1847, HStj June 3, Aug. 7, August 23, Sept. 6; Sept. 11; Sept. 20; and JH May 20. **Jan. 14:** JH, Jan. 14; Minutes of High Council, CA, as quoted in Cook, RP 299. **Daniel Russell:** HStj, Oct. 2, 1847. **1848, High Council:** HStj, Jan. 9, Jan. 10, Feb. 13; JH, compare Oct. 21, p. 1; Oct. 7, p. 4; Apr. 8

p. 7, 11. In this year Harris figured most prominently in an ecclesiastical court held on Edwin D. Wooley, HStj, Jan. 21-24, 1848, OMF 1:299. On January 20, 1848, George W. petitioned for a post office on Pottawattamie lands, JH. In early August he voted in Kanesville, see Aug. 7, Miller-Thompson Election Contest documents, in New York Public Library, pp 8-13, as cited in Ivins 6:29. **Apr. 13:** JH, Apr. 13, p. 5.

VIII. **1850 Iowa Census:** See p. 75b. George is listed as seventy years old and his birthplace is "Mass." **Feb. 1851:** *Frontier Guardian* 3 (2) (Feb. 21, 1851), list of "Monies received," cited in Ivins 8:14. **Brigham on George W.:** BY, address given Oct. 7, 1860; DN 10:273; JH Oct. 7, 1860, p. 6; compare OMF 1:14. **letter to Lucinda:** *The Bugle* of Council Bluffs, Iowa (Mar. 12, 1856); Morris, WM 278-79; Hogan, TJS 18. **Harris dies:** Cook, RP 260 and the Brigham Young speech. **Lucinda a nurse:** Morris, WM 279; Hogan, TJS 18. For the Sisters of Charity, see "Charity, Sisters of," in *The Catholic Encyclopedia* (New York: Encyclopedia Press, 1908), 3:605-607. For their role in the Civil War, see George Barton, *Angels of the Battlefield* (Philadelphia: Catholic Art Publ. Co., 1897) and Ellen Ryan Jolly, *Nuns of the Battlefield* (Providence, RI: Providence Visitor Press, 1927). **Lucinda's death date:** Tinney, RF 136-37 gives the wrong death date for Lucinda; his death date is for a Lucinda Harris Guymon Hurst, daughter of a Mr. Guymon.

## REFERENCES TO CHAPTER 3.
### *"Not Much Else But Sorrow and Affliction":*
### *Louisa Beaman (Smith Young)*

J.D. Lee, Journal, 1850-53, at Feb. 9, CA, MS 1253, Item 3, pp. 212-13; = Gustive Larson, ed., "Journal of the Iron County Mission, John D. Lee Clerk," UHQ 20 (1952): 353-83, 375-76, 364. Ironically, it was Brigham Young, apparently, who rejected his wife's name and replaced it with the Indian name for the valley's lake, see 364 n. **Fort Louisa:** See Andrew Jenson, comp., "History of Parowan Ward" (typescript, copied at BYU, 1955), 28, at Feb. 9; Luella Adams Dalton, comp., *History of Iron County Mission, Parowan Utah* (Parowan, UT: n.p., [1973]), 35; Dale Morgan, "The State of Deseret," UHQ 8 (1940): 67-239, 109.

I. **Louisa's birthday:** HCKj/Clayton, Book 93, Dec. 29, 1845 (endowment); BOP #12. Presumably Louisa gave her birthdate orally to the clerks on these occasions. But compare ZDYj, Feb. 27, 1850. Though this seems to give a Feb. 27 birthdate, Zina was probably reflecting a Feb. 7, 1850, entry. Louisa's surname is found in two forms, Beaman and Beman. **Alvah:** was born on May 22, 1775 and died in 1837. See KEQR 1-2, 71, 115-16; Jessee 2, index; FGS 510747. **Sally Burtts:** was born on June 17, 1775, in Hartford, Connecticut, and died in 1840. **older siblings:** Isaac Newton, born on December 27, 1797, in West Marlboro, Essex, Massachusetts, married Eunice Bennett and Melinda Stewart and died in 1872. Betsey Burtts, born on May 29, 1800 in West Marlboro, married James Larson or Alanson James, and died in 1873. Alvah Peck, born on October 27, 1803, in Bloomfield, Hartford, Connecticut/Bloomfield, Ontario, New York, married Mary Hamilton, and died in 1882. Sarah (Sally) Maria, born on April 9, 1806, in Honeoye Falls, Ontario, New York, married Elisha Hyde, and died in 1868. Margaret Beckworth was born on July 22, 1808 in Livonia or Bloomfield. She married Samuel Chappell, and died in 1862. Apparently, all of these older Beaman siblings lived and died in the east. **Mary Adeline:** Born on October 19, 1810, she married Joseph Bates Noble on September 11, 1834, in Livingston County. Noble was a prominent Mormon in the Nauvoo and early Utah period, and an early Nauvoo polygamist. He married twelve wives before his death. Mary died on February 14, 1851, in Salt Lake City, Utah. See her autobiography, Lee Library. **Joseph Noble:** See his journal, Lee Library; HR 6:237-42; OMF 1:38, and index, vol. 2. **Artimesia:** Born on March 3, 1819, she married Erastus Snow in Far West, Missouri, in 1838. Snow, a prominent Utah Mormon, was ordained an apostle in 1849, and helped found St. George in southern

Utah in 1861. He married fourteen wives and had thirty-six children, including eleven with Artimesia. She died on December 21, 1882, in St. George. See St. George Ms. Histories, at Dec. 22, 1882, Artimesia's funeral service, which includes a brief biography. Andrew Karl Larson, *Erastus Snow* (Salt Lake City: University of Utah Press, 1971); Cook, RP 301-2; OMF 1:22. **Mary Beaman:** See her Autobiography, Lee Library. **farm environment:** Most of the women in this book grew up on farms. For the life of a farm woman in nineteenth-century America, see Jensen, *Loosening the Bonds, Mid Atlantic Farm Women 1750-1850*; Ulrich, *Good Wives* 13-86, esp. 18-24; Larkin, *Reshaping* 331, 335. While their husbands worked in the fields, and with livestock, farm wives typically spun and sewed, made clothes, prepared food for meals and storage, including dairy products, and tended children.

II. **Alvah and Smiths:** See also Parley P. Pratt, *Autobiography* 118. **Alvah money digging with Smiths:** Martin Harris, "Mormonism - No. II," *Tiffany's Monthly* (1859): 164 = Frances Kirkham, ed., *A New Witness for Christ in America*, 2 vols. (Independence, MO: Press of Zion's Printing: 1951), 2:377. Compare D. Michael Quinn, *Early Mormonism and the Magic World View* (Salt Lake City: Signature Books, 1987), 35. **Alva, "Rodsman," wants part of profits:** Joseph Knight, in Dean Jessee, "Joseph Knight's Recollection of Early Mormon History," BYUSt 17 (1976): 33-34. **Alvah and plates:** Mary Beaman Noble autobiography, Lee Library. Lucy Mack Smith, *Biographical Sketches* (Liverpool: Orson Pratt, 1853), 108, has the same story. "Braman ... of Livonia, a man in whom we reposed much confidence." However, in the manuscript, page 115, the name is Beaman, see Jessee, "Joseph Knight," 33 n. 12. **Alvah holds the plates:** Joseph Noble journal, Lee Library. Compare HC 2:43. **to Avon:** Mary Beaman, Autobiography. **Joseph stays with the Beamans:** Mary Beaman, Autobiography. Compare JSj, Mar. 14, 15, 1834, Jessee 2:25. **Parley Pratt:** *Autobiography* 110; Jessee, PW 30. **marriage:** Joseph Noble journal.

III. **Nov. 10:** JSj, Jessee 2:74. Compare JSj, Nov. 16, Jessee 2:85. **Jan. 11:** JSj, Jessee 2:131-32. **acceptance speech:** JSj, Jan. 15, 1836; Jessee 2:141. He was anointed to this office on Jan. 21, see KEQR. For the details of Beaman's tenure in this position, see Jessee 2:148, 164-65, 169; KEQR index. **death of Alvah:** KEQR 34 n. 2. **to Missouri:** Helen Mar Whitney, LI, WE 10 (June 15, 1881), 9. **Apr. 2:** CA, MS 12476.

IV. **Death of Sarah Burtts Beaman:** St. George Ms. Histories, CA, at Dec. 22, 1882. AF has September 29, 1848. **interview in late 1840:** Noble affidavit, HR 6:221. **family tradition:** James Crockwell, *Pictures and Biographies of Brigham Young and His Wives* (Salt Lake City: James Crockwell, n.d. [1877]), 20-21. **date of marriage**, April 5, 1841: Noble affidavit, printed in CHC 2:102; Erastus Snow affidavit, in HR 6:232-33. On one occasion, however, Noble gave 1840 as the date for the marriage: "Br Nobles made a few remarks on the celestial order of marriage, He being the man who sealed Louisa Beeman to the Prophet Joseph Smith in 1840 under his instructions." Speech by Joseph Noble, Dec. 19, 1880, as reported in Charles Walker diaries, Andrew Larson and Katherine Miles Larson, eds., *Diary of Charles Lowell Walker*, 2 vols. (Logan: Utah State University Press, 1980), 2:515. On another occasion, Noble gave the date May 6, 1841: "Brother Joseph B Nobles said that he performed the first Marriage Ceremony according to the Patriarchal order of Marriage ever performed in this dispensation By sealing Eliza Beman to Joseph Smith on the 6 day of May, 1841." WWj, Jan. 22, 1869, 6:452 (see also Franklin Richards journal, quoted below, for this date). In the Temple Lot case, 368, Joseph Bates first gave 1840, then corrected this to "1841 or 1842." **place of marriage:** Erastus Snow speech, June 17, 1883, reported in Charles Walker diaries, Larson and Larson 2:610. Ann Eliza Young set the marriage on the banks of the Mississippi: "The two men with their chosen celestial brides, repaired one night to the banks of the Mississippi River, where Joseph sealed Noble to his first plural wife, and in return Noble performed the same office for the Prophet and his sister. These were the first plural marriages that ever took place in the Mormon Church." Ann Eliza Young, WN19 72. However, Joseph Noble, in 1892, gave the place of marriage as "at my house across the river from Nauvoo." (Temple Lot Case, 368.) Noble was approximately eighty-five at the time of his testimony, and his memory in this testimony is sometimes quite vague. Later in the Temple Lot case, p. 424, he explicitly stated that this earlier testimony was wrong: "A-It was performed on this side of the river. Q-Do you mean that it was performed in Nauvoo? A-Yes sir. Q-At whose house? A-At mine. Q-Who was present? A-My family." Compare p. 425: "By ginger, I went back across the river again that same night after performing the marriage ceremony." "Q-Was the sealing for time and eternity? A-Yes sir." **dressed as a man:** Franklin D. Richards journal, Jan. 22, 1869 (loose sheet, numbered as 145), FDR papers, MS 1215, box 2, fd 2, CA: "Br. Joseph B. Noble being the master of ceremonies was present and During the visit related that he performed the first sealing ceremony in this Dispensation in which he united Sister Louisa Beman to the Prophet Joseph in May - I think the 5th day in 1841 during the evening under an Elm tree in Nauvoo. The Bride disguised in a coat and hat." Willard Richards, when on secret polygamous errands, would sometimes dress as a woman, Noall, ID 366-67. As cross-dressing is typical of liminal moments in ritual (when the candidate is halfway between former and future status), this would support Foster's interpretation of Nauvoo polygamy as a "liminal" moment in Mormon history, before the solidified "communitas" of the Utah period, RS 8, 166. But perhaps this is pressing the interpretation. **secrecy and the sacred,** see Kees Bolle, ed., *Secrecy in Religion* (Leiden: Brill, 1987); Joachim Jeremias, *The Eucharistic Words of Jesus* (New York: Scribner, 1966). **further on the marriage,** see Bennett HS 256, who mentions, as one of Joseph's wives, "Miss L***** B*****" (the earliest reference to the marriage); Orson Pratt, in "Report of Elders Orson Pratt and Joseph F. Smith," MSt 40 (Dec. 16, 1878): 788; Joseph Noble address, June 11, 1883, at Stake Conference, Centerville, Utah, reported in JH under that date; Temple Lot case, 368-69; Diary of S.W. Richards, Feb. 2, 1884, CA, MS 1841, box 1, fd 9, vol. 26. See ME 322; Van Wagoner, MP 23. **"Blow out the lights":** Temple Lot transcript, 427. **cohabitation:** Temple Lot transcript, 427. **Joseph visits:** According to Bennett, HS 229, Joseph Smith, at one point, "then went off to see Miss Louisa Beeman, at the house of Mrs. Sherman, and remained with her about two hours." Mrs. Sherman was another plural wife of Joseph, see Delcena Johnson chapter. **Delcena with Louisa:** Johnson, in Zimmerman 40. **other plural marriages:** "The Prophet with Louisa Beeman and my Sister Delcena had it agreeably aranged with sister Almara and after a little instruction, She Stood by the Prophets side & was Sealed to him as a wife," Johnson in Zimmerman 43. Louisa witnessed the marriage, which took place at Delcena's house, see Benjamin Johnson affidavit, HR 6:222. See chapters on Marinda Johnson, Patty Sessions, Elizabeth Davis, and Eliza R. Snow. **February 25:** PBSj, in Wells, WE 13 (Sept. 1, 1884): 95. For the importance of women's friendships in nineteenth-century America, see Carroll Smith-Rosenberg, *Disorderly Conduct, Visions of Gender in Victorian America* 53-76, "The Female World of Love and Ritual: Relations Between Women in Nineteenth-Century America." Mary Ryan, "The Power of Female Networks: A Case Study of Female Moral Reform in Antebellum America," *Feminist Studies* V (Spring 1979): 66-86. Compare Jill Mulvay Derr, "'Strength in our Union': The Making of Mormon Sisterhood," in SS 153-207. **rebaptism:** JSj, Faulring 377. See Quinn, "The Practice of Rebaptism," 231. **Relief Society:** RS Min., Mar. 24; p. 91. **Zina Young:** ZDYj.

V. **marriage to Young:** BYj, Sept. 19, 1844; Johnson, DDW 65, compare HCKj: Sept. 19, 1844 ("Went to Br. Wm. E. Murray, Elder Winchesters ... Saw Silvester Smith and Bat B. Nobles [Joseph Bates Noble?]"). For the Levirate rationale of Brigham's marriage to Joseph's plural wives, and for the experience of being a plural wife in Young's family, see the Zina Huntington, Eliza Snow, and Emily Partridge chapters. For "saw" or "was" as a code word for "sealed and wedded" or "wedded and sealed," see the Agnes Coolbrith chapter at January 1842. **endowed:** WCj, Jan. 26; IC 156. For the Holy Order, the "Quorum," see Quinn, MHOP 114-15. **endowment in temple:** NTER. For accounts of the endowment published by Mormons, see James Talmage, *The House of the Lord* (Salt Lake City: Deseret News, 1912) 99-101; Ehat, JSI; Edward Tullidge, *Tullidge's Histories, (Volume II.)* (Salt Lake City: Juvenile Instructor, 1889), 437-47; and relevant articles in EM. Compare Prince, PFOH 115-48. **temple sealing:** BOP #12; SAd 503.

VI. **March 8:** This is Emily Partridge Smith Young. **twins:** Susa Gates and Mabel Sanborn, "Brigham Young Genealogy," UGHM 11 (Apr. 1920): 49-55, 55; Arrington, BY 420. Since these children's births and deaths are very poorly documented—in contrast to her later children, whose births and deaths are well documented—one might consider the possibility that Joseph and Hyrum were not twins, or sons of Brigham, but were the sons of Joseph Smith born in 1842 and 1843 ("Joseph," the first of the two children, would then have been the first child born in Nauvoo polygamy). Louisa, the earliest Nauvoo wife, would have had years to bear Joseph a child before he died. If this was the case, we would not have the quick pregnancy producing Moroni, her next child, in the Brigham Young scenario (usually there is a year and a half space between children in nineteenth-century Mormon marriages). We remember Elizabeth Lightner asserting that some of Joseph's children were raised under other names, as the Nauvoo code of secrecy would have demanded. However, the idea that Louisa's children, Joseph and Hyrum, might have been the sons of Joseph is purely speculative. Hopefully, at some point Louisa's first children, Joseph and Hyrum, will be better documented. **women in Winter Quarters:** See Beecher, EHS 75-98. **Dec. 30:** ERSj. **Jan. 1:** ERSj, compare PBSj. For a fuller description, see Eliza R. Snow chapter. For glossolalia among the Latter-day Saints, see Lee Copeland, "Speaking in Tongues in the Restoration Churches," *Dialogue* 24 (Spring 1991): 13-33; Dan Vogel and Scott C. Dunn, "'The Tongue of Angels': Glossolalia among Mormonism's Founders," JMH 19 (Fall 1993): 1-34. **at Winchester's house:** ERSj. **new baby:** PBSj, ERSj, Winter Quarters death record, see below; Patty charged $2 for the midwiving, see PBSj, account section, after Apr. 4, 1846. **baby blessed:** WRj, Jan. 15, 1847, as cited in Jessee, "Brigham Young Family, the Wilderness Years," BYUSt 30 (1979): 488. See also ERSj on that date. **visit to Pierce's:** ERSj, Feb. 7, 1847. **March, May:** ERSj, Mar. 16; Mar. 18; PBSj, May 5. May 14. **speaking in tongues:** ERSj, June 2, 1847. **prophetic blessing:** PBSj, June 3, 1847. **June 11:** ERSj. **death of Moroni:** "List of the Deaths and Burials in the Camp of Israel at Cutler's Park after Sept., 1846," Grave 195; CA and GS.

VII. **May 26, 1848:** JDLj, AMC 1:30. **last twins:** JDLj, AMC 1:65. **Sept. 20-24:** HStj, OMF 1:327. **Letter to Marinda etc.:** Marinda Hyde papers, MS 793, fd 3, CA, Louisa Beaman to Marinda Hyde, "Martha," and "Mary Ann" (plural wives of Orson Hyde). **"to join with his brothers":** This reference proves that Louisa did have sons before Moroni, little as we know about them.

VIII. For the harsh winter of late 1848, see Brigham Madsen, *Gold Rush Sojourners* (Salt Lake City: University of Utah Press, 1983), 6-9. **dysentery:** See Larkin, REL 76-77. Compare, for the experience of losing infants in nineteenth-century America, Nancy Dye and Daniel Smith, "Mother Love and Infant Death, 1750-1920," *Journal of American History* 73 (Sept. 1986): 329-53. Louisa's letters do not support Dye and Smith's argument that women grieved for their children less than in modern times as a response to frequent infant death. **Dec. 23:** For the Old Fort, see Nicholas Groesbeck Morgan, comp., *The Old Fort, Historic Mormon Bastion* ... (Salt Lake City: Nicholas Morgan, 1964); Mary Isabella Horne, "Home Life in the Pioneer Fort," in OPH 9:107-11. **Dec. 26:** For the wives of Brigham, see Johnson, DDW; Quinn, MHOP 607. **January 23, 1849:** "I spent the evening at Louises." ZDYj. **death of Browett:** CHC 3:369. **cup of tea:** ZDYj, May 14, 1849.

IX. **May 16:** Eliza Partridge journal, CA. Here we have Emily Partridge Young, Louisa, Sarah Ann Whitney Kimball, and Lucy Walker Kimball. **May 18:** For emetics and Thomsonian medicine, see Robert Divett, *Medicine and the Mormons* (Bountiful, UT: Horizon, 1981), 124; Alexander, THE 362. Daines (quoted in Divett 124) writes, "The most striking feature of medicine during the pioneer period ... is the futility of both the afflicted and the healer to affect the course of nature in any but insignificant or negative ways." **June 19:** "Sister Twist" is perhaps Naamah Carter Twiss Young. For women performing healing ordinances in early Mormonism, see Linda King Newell, "A Gift Given, A Gift Taken:

Washing, Anointing and Blessing the Sick Among Mormon Women," in Quinn, NMH 101-20; SS 111-50. See also the Patty Sessions chapter at Nov. 22, 1847. **Dec. 10:** PBSj. **Feb. 7:** ZDYj at May 27, 1850. Zina's diary dates could be inexact. **death date:** ZDYj, May 15, 1859. Zina commemorated the date of Louisa's death by visiting the graves of Louisa's twins. "A lovley day I went to Louiza's twins graves enjoyed it much a silent prayer unto him that rules O God bless I pray." Dale Morgan, "State of Deseret," gives May 16 as the date of death. See also JH.

## REFERENCES TO CHAPTER 4.
### Nauvoo Polyandry:
### Zina Diantha Huntington (Jacobs Smith Young)

Autobiography 1, 2 (Autobiographical Sketch), 3: see Zina Young.

Beecher, Maureen Ursenbach. "Each in Her Own Time: Four Zinas." *Dialogue* 26 (1993): 119-38.

Bradley, Martha Sonntag, and Mary Brown Firmage Woodward. "Plurality, Patriarchy, and the Priestess: Zina D.H. Young's Nauvoo Marriages." JMH 20 (Spring 1994): 84-118.

Cannon, Oa J. "Henry Bailey Jacobs." CA.

———. "Short Sketch of the Life of Henry B. Jacobs, Prepared for 1977 Reunion." CA.

———. "Zina Diantha Huntington Young." CA.

Card, Zina, with other daughters. "Mother." *Young Women's Journal* 22 (Jan. 1911): 43-45.

COCj: Donald Godfrey and Brigham Y. Card, eds. *The Diaries of Charles Ora Card, the Canadian Years, 1886-1903.* Salt Lake City: University of Utah Press, 1993.

EL: *Elect Ladies*, by Petersen and Gaunt.

Firmage (Woodward), Mary. "Recollections of Zina D.H. Young." CA.

Firmage, Mary. "Great-grandmother Zina: A More Personal Portrait." *Ensign* (Mar. 1984): 38.

Gates, Susa Young. *History of the Young Ladies' Mutual Improvement Association ...* Salt Lake City: Deseret News, 1911.

Higbee, Marilyn. "'A Weary Traveller': The 1848-50 Diary of Zina D. H. Young." JMH 19 (Fall 1993): 86-125.

Huntington, Oliver. Diaries. Lee Library. Available at Huntington Library, USHS, and other libraries. I always refer to the holograph, but typescripts are available.

———. "Spirit Experiences." *Young Woman's Journal* 6 (1895): 376-81.

Huntington, William. Autobiography. Typescript at Huntington Library.

Jacobs, Zebulon. A reminiscence of Nauvoo and the overland journey, written in Jan. 1907, CA. Typescript in Oa Cannon file on Zina, CA. 1-23 in original, with 1-3 missing.

———. Diary, CA.

"Passed Into the Repose of Death." DEN (Aug. 28, 1901).

Peterson, Janet, and LaRene Gaunt. *Elect Ladies.* Salt Lake City: Deseret Book, 1990.

"Sketch of Sister Zina D. Young." *Young Woman's Journal* 4 (Apr. 1893): 292-94.

Stenhouse, Thomas B.H. *Rocky Mountain Saints.* London: Ward, Lock and Tyler, 1874.

Talmage, May Booth. "Past Three Score Years and Ten." *Young Woman's Journal* 12 (June 1901): 255-57.

[Wells, Emmeline B.]. "A Distinguished Woman: Zina D.H. Young." WE 10 (Nov. 15, 1881): 90-91; (Dec. 1, 1881): 99; (15 Dec. 1881): 107; (Jan. 1, 1882): 115; (Jan. 15, 1882): 123; (Feb. 1, 1882): 131; (Mar. 15, 1882): 155.

———. "Zina D. H. Young: A Brief Sketch of Her Life and Labors." DEN (Jan. 25 1896): p. 8. Cited as "A Brief Sketch."

———. "Zina D.H. Young: A Character Sketch." *Improvement Era* 5 (1901): 45-46.

Wight, John. "Evidence from Zina D. Huntington-Young." Interview with Zina, Oct. 1 1898. *Saints Herald* 52 (Jan. 11, 1905): 28-30.

Wilcox, E.S. "Mrs. Zina D.H. Young and the Relief Society." WE 28 (Apr. 15 and May 1,

1900): 121.

"Woman's Mass Meeting." WE 7 (Dec. 1, 1878): 97-99, 102-3.

Young, Zina Huntington. Autobiographical Sketch, or Autobiography 2, pp. 13-22. Zina Card Brown collection, CA. It begins, "paint, music both instrumental and vocal ..."

———. Autobiography 1, 4 pp. Zina Card Brown collection, CA. It begins, "Sept 29th 1850 my Father Married Lydia Partrage ..."

———. Autobiography 3, pp. 2-12. Zina Card Brown collection, CA. It begins, "my own Father William Huntington ..."

———. "How I Gained my Testimony of the Truth." *Young Woman's Journal* 4 (Apr. 1893): 317-19.

———. Interview in New York *World* (Nov. 17, 1869).

———. Journal, Zina Card Brown collection, CA. The Nauvoo years in Maureen Ursenbach Beecher, ed. "'All Things Move in Order in the City': The Nauvoo Diary of Zina Diantha Huntington Jacobs." BYUSt 19 (1979): 285-320. The years 1848-50 are in Higbee.

———. Writings. Zina Card Brown collection, CA. I also used materials generously shared by Martha Sonntag Bradley.

**Nauvoo temple sealing:** BOP #142: "Joseph Smith (martyred) ... Zina Diantha Huntington ... were sealed husband & wife for time & all eternity (Prest. Brigham Young acting proxy for the deceased) Brigham Young & Zina Diantha Smith were then sealed husband & wife for time by H.C. Kimball in presence of William D. Huntington, & Henry B. Jacobs & J.D.L. [John D. Lee] Young, Henry B. Jacobs expressed his willingness that it should be so in presence of these witnesses done at 15 m. to 6. Franklin D. Richards clk." The fact that Henry was friendly to Brigham is shown by the fact that he acted as a witness in another of Brigham's plural marriages in the Nauvoo temple, his marriage to Augusta Adams Cobb, see SAd 578.

I. **Genealogical information:** from OHj 1:1, 2:4; FGS. See also Dimick and Oliver both left journals. For Zina's birthdate, see also IGI. **William:** Born on March 28, 1784, in Grantham, Sullivan, New Hampshire, he died in 1846. See William Huntington, autobiography and journal; Cook, RP 262. **Zina Baker:** Born on May 2, 1786, in Plainfield, Sullivan, New Hampshire, she died in 1839. See her letters in Zina Card Brown collection, CA, and Beecher, "Four Zinas." **Chauncy:** Born on October 20, 1806, he married Clarissa Bull in 1825. He never became a Mormon, continued to live in the east, and died in 1875. **Dimick:** Born on May 26, 1808, he married Fannie Allen in 1830, then Ellen Sophia Jacobs, Susan Maria Cardin, and Harriet Augusta Hoagland. He died in 1879 in Salt Lake City. **Presendia:** See following chapter. **Adaline Elizabeth:** was born on August 3, 1815. **William Dresser:** Born on February 28, 1818, he married Caroline Clark in 1839 and Harriet Clark in 1843. He died in 1881 in Springville, Utah. **Oliver:** Born on October 14, 1823, he became a staunch Mormon missionary and pioneer. He married Mary Neal in 1845, Hannah Mendenhall Sanders in 1852, and Elvira Stesen in 1856, though none of these were polygamous marriages. He died in 1907 in Springville, Utah. **John:** Born on February 11, 1827, he married Adelaid Danks in 1851 and died in the east in 1900.

II. **House and farm: Talmage,** PTS 255; Oliver Huntington, SE 377. **Zina delicate:** Talmage, PTS 255. **"in my earliest ...":** Autobiography 3, p. 2. **religious upbringing:** Autobiography 3, p. 2. **Bible reading:** Talmage, PTS 255. **family orchestra:** EL 44. Compare "Mother," 44. **marriages:** AF.

III. **William's pre-conversion:** Zina Young, "How I Gained," 317. **"In 1834 ...":** Zina Young, Autobiography 3, p. 2. **Book of Mormon story:** Zina Young, "How I Gained," 318, compare WM 206; Talmage, PTS 256, an interview. **conversion:** William Huntington, Autobiography, 6; OHj 2:5. **"rendesvouse":** OHj 2:6. **Zina's baptism:** Zina Young, "How I Gained," 318. **gift of tongues:** Autobiography 3, pp. 7-8; compare Talmage, PTS 256. **checking the gift of tongues:** Zina Young, "How I Gained," 319. **the gift of tongues in early Mormonism:** See bibliography on glossalalia in the Louisa Beaman chapter. For the eschatological focus of many tongue interpretations, see WCj, Dec. 30, 1845, IC 244. Eliza Snow and Presendia Huntington prophesied the destruction of America in tongues, see WE 12 (1 June 1883): 2. **Mary Elizabeth Rollins Lightner,** interpreting tongue speech, alarmed men by prophesying that the saints would be driven from Jackson County, see her chapter, Missouri section. **Wells on Zina:** ADW 107. Compare HMWj, Nov. 5, 1892, where the African-American Mormon, Jane James, spoke in tongues in a local Relief Society meeting, and Zina interpreted. See also EBWj, Dec. 26, 1874, Mar. 31, 1881. **Zina Baker brings corpse to life:** Oliver Huntington, "Spirit Experiences," 381.

IV. **Joseph Smith, Sr.:** OHj 2:6. **journey to Kirtland:** OHj 2:7; 1:1; 2:6, 8; William Huntington, Autobiography, 7-9; Zina Young, Autobiography 3, p. 4. **walking to Kirtland:** OHj 2:8-9. **buys land:** William Huntington, Autobiography, 7-9; OHj 2:9. **Zina describes Joseph:** Zina Young, Autobiography 3, p. 4. [and a heavy nose] is from a different version of the autobiography. **Zina Baker and poor:** Whitney, HU 2:577; Talmage, PTS 256. **Eliza Snow:** Talmage, PTS 256. **Kirtland temple:** Zina Young, Autobiography 3, p. 5; compare WM 207-8; Crocheron, RW 12. **financial reverses:** OHj 2:10-11. For the Kirtland Safety Society Bank, see SLDS 111, 667. For many, the failure of this bank led to apostasy, SLDS 113. **William in high council:** OHj 2:13-14. **leaving Kirtland:** OHj 2:15-16. For the problems in Kirtland, see Hill, QFR 58-67.

V. **journey to Missouri:** OHj 2:16-18; Zina Young, Autobiography 3, p. 6. **arrival:** OHj 1:1, 2:18. **at Adam-ondi-Ahman:** William Huntington, Autobiography; OHj 2:21. **Dimick and Oliver Danites:** OHj, 2:37-38; Quinn, MHOP 334; 482. **Zina on Missouri:** Autobiography 3, p. 7. See also OHj 1:1. **leaving Missouri:** OHj 2:47.

VI. **with Dimick:** OHj 2:47-48. **Commerce:** Zina Young, Autobiography 3, p. 10; WM 214. **Zina Baker ill:** WM 213-4. **illness in the family:** OHj 2:47-50; WM 213-14; compare William Huntington, Autobiography, p. 11. This sickness was also an economic disaster, for it prevented the farm from being tended, OHj 2:54. **death of Zina Baker:** WM 214; OHj 2:53. **to Joseph's house:** OHj 2:55, July 28, 1839. **Zina meets Henry:** Cannon, "Zina Diantha Huntington Young," 22-23. **Jacobs's conversion:** Cannon, "Henry Bailey Jacobs"; Cannon, "Short Sketch." **seventy, move from Far West:** Cannon, "Henry Bailey Jacobs," 6. **papers for mission:** Cannon, "Henry Bailey Jacobs," 6. **mission in May, 1839:** Jesse Haven journal, CA, Mar. 3, 1860. "He [Jacobs] is the first Elder I ever traveled with: it is 21 years ago this spring." **Mother in Heaven:** Gates, "History," 16. Compare Wilcox in SS 65-66. **to new house:** OHj 2:56-57. **William a high councilor:** This took place on October 6, 1839. **Zina keeps house:** OHj 2:57. **Zina Baker to Fanny:** OHj 2:57-58. **William Sr.'s remarriage:** OHj 2:58.

VII. **cult of true womanhood:** See Barbara Welter, "The Cult of True Womanhood, 1820-1860," *American Quarterly* 18 (1966): 151-74; also in Jean Friedman and William Shade, eds., *Our American Sisters* (Boston: Allyn and Bacon, 1973), 96-123. For an application of this analysis to Mormon polygamy, see Kathleen Marquis, "'Diamond Cut Diamond': Mormon Women and the Cult of Domesticity in the Nineteenth Century," *University of Michigan, Papers in Women's Studies* 2 (1976): 105-124. **Zina receives Joseph's proposal, and prays:** Zina Young, Autobiography, as quoted in Bradley and Woodward, PPP 93. She apparently had had dreams of marrying Joseph, see Wight, "Evidence," 29. **marriage to Jacobs:** Record of Marriages in Hancock Co., Ill., Book A, p. 40, signed by John C. Bennett, mayor of Nauvoo. Copy at Lee Library, reproduced in Richard Holzapfel and Jeni Broberg Holzapfel, *Women of Nauvoo* (Salt Lake City: Bookcraft, 1992), 99. See also TS 2 (Apr. 1, 1841): 374. **family tradition:** Cannon, "Zina," 22-23. "Here I feel it necessary to give my mother's (Emma R. Jacobs) story as told to her by Grandmother Zina, about her marriage to Henry B. Jacobs." **Henry and Zina confront Joseph after the wedding:** Cannon, "Zina," 22-23. Essentially the same story is told in Cannon's biography of Henry, p. 6. Joseph agreed to perform the marriage, Cannon, "Short Sketch." **early American women generally more churchgoing than males:** Barbara Welter, "The Feminization of Religion in Nineteenth Century America," in Mary Hartman and Lois Banner, eds., *Clio's Consciousness Raised* (New York: Harper & Row, 1973), 137-57; Martha Tomhave Blauvelt, "Women and Revivalism," in Rosemary Radford Ruether and Rosemary Skinner Keller, eds., *Women and Religion in America, Volume 1: The Nineteenth Century* (San Francisco: Harper & Row: 1981), 1-45, 3; Ulrich, GW 216; Cott, *Bonds of Womanhood:* BW 127-28, 132; Cross, *The Burned-over District* 84-89. Smith-Rosenberg, DC 109, 122, writes, "The Moral Reform Society was based on the assertion of female moral superiority and the right and ability of women to reshape male behavior." Sarah Kingsley, as a Protestant before converting to Mormonism, urged her brother to experience religious conversion, and hoped that her husband would become fully active in her church. Delcena and Almera Johnson grew up in a family in which the mother was profoundly religious and the father was irreligious. Of course, there were also many deeply religious men in nineteenth-century America (and men held political control in churches, just as in Mormonism); but women formed the majority in churches and revivals.

There was psychological and moral complexity in all of the characters, male and female, of the Mormon drama, which itself was set against a backdrop of great socio-cultural diversity. While today we may reject polygamy as an institution, it was women's intense, enthusiastic Christianity that inclined them to accept polygamy in Mormonism. Given their biblical, absolutist frame of reference, accepting Hebraic plural marriage was an act of piety and moral courage. On the other hand, rejection of polygamy might also be an act of piety and moral courage, given a less fundamentalist reading of the Old Testament. **Joseph's ultimatum:** Zina Young, in "Joseph, the Prophet His Life and Mission as Viewed by Intimate Acquaintances," *Salt Lake Herald Church and Farm Supplement* (Jan. 12, 1895): 212. "He sent word to me by my brother, saying, 'Tell Zina, I put it off and put it off till an angel with a drawn sword stood by me and told me if I did not establish that principle upon the earth I would lose my position and my life.'" Compare the Wight interview, 29: "Joseph Smith sent my brother Dimick to explain it to me ... My brother Dimick told me what Joseph had told him. I knew it was from the Lord, and I received it. Joseph did not come until afterward." In the same interview Zina emphasized that God had commanded Joseph to marry her: "The Lord told him to take me and he did so" [Wight 28]. "The Lord had revealed to Joseph Smith that he was to marry me" [Wight 29]. **Oct. 27, 1841:** In OHj 17, on October 27, 1887, Oliver's children gathered at his house: "After we were all assembled in one room Zina told us that that day was the anniversary of her marriage or sealing to the Prophet Joseph Smith. She was sealed to Joseph on the 27th day of October 1841." She also gave this date in affidavits, SAB 1:5, 4:5, compare Bachman, "A Study," 348, and this is the date of marriage that Jenson, HR 6:233, gives. For other statements that Zina was Joseph's wife, see Zina's own public statement at the Polygamy Mass Meeting, at 1878 below; also COCj, Nov. 24, 1897; EBWj, Nov. 27 1889. **Dimick performs first ceremony:** Wight, "Evidence," 29. **Fanny a witness:** HR 6:233. **multiple dates:** However, as is the case in many of the plural marriages of Joseph, there seem to be multiple dates for the marriage, or more than one marriage ceremony. In the Wight interview, Zina stated that Dimick performed the marriage—but this was the first of two marriage ceremonies. "[Question] ... your brother officiated at the marriage? [Zina:] He did at the first. When Brigham Young returned from England, he repeated the ceremony for time and eternity." As Brigham returned from England on July 1, 1841, did the marriage with Joseph, performed by Dimick, take place before that date? For dating, see Elden Watson, ed., *Manuscript History of Brigham Young, 1801-44* (Salt Lake City: privately published, 1968), 105; Arrington, BY 96. Then did Brigham perform the October 27 marriage? If Zina married Joseph soon after her marriage to Jacobs (in March 1841), this has important implications for the history of Nauvoo polygamy. She might have married Joseph before Louisa Beaman (on April 5), making her Joseph's first wife in the Nauvoo period.

On the other hand, Zina's recollections may have been confused. Perhaps she married Joseph first in October, then later with Brigham Young officiating. Perhaps the marriage to Brigham she refers to is the proxy marriage performed in 1844/1846, though this is some four years after Brigham returned from England. Possibly the elderly Zina was hazy on the date of Brigham's return from England, though four years is a substantial error. **Zina's reactions:** Zina Young, Autobiography 1. **Jacobs accepts the marriage:** Zina Young, Autobiography, as quoted in Bradley/Woodward 95. **marriage to Jacobs said to be unhappy:** Wight interview, 29. Bachman, "A Study," 119, 134, accepts Zina's statement at face value. Wells gives what became the standard sequence: "Sister Zina was married in Nauvoo, and had two sons born to her, Zebulon and Chariton. It was a most unhappy and ill-assorted marriage, and she subsequently separated from the husband who was so little suited to be a companion for her through life. Joseph Smith taught her the principle of marriage for eternity, and she accepted it as a divine revelation, and was sealed to the Prophet for time and all eternity, after the order of the new and everlasting covenant" (Wells, ADW 99). But in reality, Joseph married Zina before any separation from Henry. Beecher, "Four Zinas," 128, reads Zina's 1844 journal and concludes that Zina's marriage to Jacobs was not entirely happy. This is possible, as Jacobs eventually had three other marriages which did not last. But the unhappiness in Zina's marriage to Jacobs, if it existed, must have developed *after* her marriage to Joseph Smith, which came so soon after her marriage to Henry. And one must admit that there is no dramatic, overt expression of marital unhappiness in Zina's 1844 diary, such as we find in the Patty Sessions pioneer journal, for instance. In addition, in Zina's Nauvoo journal there are many typical wife-like, seemingly affectionate entries mentioning Henry. She certainly did not divorce him. Beecher, in addition, rightly emphasizes Zina's unquestioning obedience to a prophet as a motive for the marriage to Joseph. **"revision" of history:** Compare the case of Elvira Cowles. In some family biographies, she marries Holmes after Joseph's death. However, her marriage to Holmes in 1842 was recorded in a contemporary newspaper, and her marriage to Joseph, as she dated it, took place after it. It would be useless—and of course impossible—to try to ignore that fact, once one has seen the documentation. **awe:** Wight, "Evidence," 29.

**VIII. Zebulon:** Reminiscence, p. 1 typescript; 5-6, original. **Henry and tongues:** Jacobs to Zina Young, Sept. 2, 1852, Zina Card collection, CA; compare ZDYj, Apr. 1, 1845; OHj 8, Sept. 1, 1847. **mission to Chicago:** HC 4:494. **Relief Society:** RS Minutes, CA, Lee Library. **Lee:** Lee, MU 132. "It was now June, 1842. In the summer and fall I built me a two-story brick house ... I then took a tour down through Illinois. H. B. Jacobs accompanied me as a fellow companion on the way. Jacobs was bragging about his wife and two children, what a true, virtuous, lovely woman she was. He almost worshiped her. Little did he think that in his absence she was sealed to the Prophet Joseph." This statement includes two errors: first, Zina had already been married to Joseph. Second, Zina had one child, not two, at the time of Lee's mission. Furthermore, it is possible that Jacobs knew about the marriage to Joseph. However, Lee's first hand memories were probably right: i.e., he remembered that Jacobs "almost worshiped her," and bragged about her. This mission is further documented by a letter by Lee published in *Times and Seasons* 4 (Sept. 1, 1843): 311-12, and by Lee's missionary journal, in USHS. Lee and Jacobs apparently parted in late January (the latter appears for the last time in the Lee journal on January 15), so Henry may have returned to Nauvoo by February or March. **New York mission:** OHj 2:61; 1:2-37, 1:6. Compare TS 4 (Apr. 1, 1843): 157; TS 4 (Oct. 15, 1843): 357; JH, Sept. 1, 1843. **arrival home:** OHj 1:37. **Assigned on Presidency mission:** JH, Apr. 15. **Jacobs on mission:** He was then at Muscoutah, St. Clair, Ill. JH, at May 17; May 21; WWj, May 19. **return from mission:** ZDYj. **Joseph a Master Mason:** See the mass meeting references in the Relief Society president section below. **martyrdom:** ZDYj; Zebulon Jacobs journal, p. 1. William, who served as sexton in Nauvoo, washed the bodies, assisted by Dimick, one of Joseph's bodyguards. Cannon, "Zina Diantha Huntington Young"; William Huntington, Autobiography, 12.

**IX. Zina and Henry live together:** This is documented in many places, especially in Zina's journal. Henry goes to help Zina's sick brother-in-law, Oliver, in Lima, August 12; Henry has the ague (malaria), Aug. 20 to Sept. 2; and so on. He goes to fencing school, Dec. 14;

on Dec. 20, he sells his "Cote, vest and hat" to pay his tithing. "O may he be enabled to pay his tithing." **Joseph's widows:** "We are told that the Prophet Joseph requested the Quorum to marry and take care of his widows, which many of them did." Cannon, "Zina," 23. Susa Young Gates (papers, USHS, Box 12, fd 2) has a similar statement:

> Emily Partridge and the other bereaved young plural widows were approached by Pres. Young and the Twelve after the Martyrdom with an offer of their shelter and sustenance, "for time only," of these brave brave girls who had dared ridicule and even mobs and death to enter into that order. They were free to select any of these associates of the Prophet as their earthly protector. This was a tremendous undertaking for Brigham Young, Heber C. Kimball and their associates. Emily Partridge had been "given" to the Prophet by his first wife Emma, as had Eliza R. Snow. Emily, with Louisa Beman ~~Olive Frost~~, Zina D. Huntington, ~~Eliza R. Snow~~ accepted Brigham's offer in the spirit in which it was given. Eliza R. Snow, after reaching the valley, was glad to accept shelter and protection under his [roof], but she, like several other widows, was never his wife in actual fact ...
>
> Father and the Twelve Apostles felt the death of the Prophet far more keenly than did the people; and as we believe that children are a part of the glory we inherit hereafter, it seemed a cruel thing that the beloved leader and Prophet should be stricken down in the prime of life, and left without issue in this Church. [Emma apostatized.] Father went to those noble women who had accepted the principle of celestial marriage with the Prophet as their husband, and he told them that he and his brethren stood ready to offer themselves to them as husbands for time, and the widows might choose for themselves. Four of these young widows chose father, and he accepted the charge thus laid upon him. He felt the grand old Hebrew impulse, to be himself the instrument by which posterity for his dead brother might be born in this life. All honor to the great men who could make and carry out such splendid tributes to the dead leader and friend.

**tradition:** "Our brother, Briant S. Jacobs remembered Aunt Zina Young Card saying that President Young told Zina D. if she would marry him she would be in a higher glory." Cannon, "Henry Bailey Jacobs," 15. Zina Diantha was not among those who looked upon Brigham with suspicion—she clearly reverenced him as a spiritual leader, see her journal, at Nov. 10, 1844; Dec. 31, 1844; Jan. 5, 1845. **marriage to Brigham, September 1844:** Quinn, MHOP 607. As noted in the bibliography, Quinn's lists of plural wives are not footnoted, so this marriage date is tentative at this time, but a marriage at this time fits the patterns found in other marital histories (compare Emily Partridge). Young married at least six of Joseph's widows in September, October, and November 1844; Heber Kimball married at least four. In ancient Israel a claimant to a throne would strengthen his position by marrying the departed king's widows (1 Kgs 2:22); Quinn suggests that Brigham may have had the same motivation, MHOP 173. This is possible, but not provable. **move:** ZDYj, September 17, 24. **Christmas, 1844:** ZDYj; OHj 1:45. **Jacobs's ordination and mission:** ZDYj. Compare Dean Jessee, ed., "The John Taylor Nauvoo Journal," BYUSt 23 (Summer 1983): 23 (Jan. 12, 1845); ECIF; General Record of the Seventies, p. 17. Here, Henry was sent by the seventies, with senior apostle Brigham Young dominating the meeting. **dream of Joseph:** ZDYj. **endowment:** ZDYj; Quinn, MHOP 504. **Henry's return:** ZDYj. **house building:** ZDYj, Mar. 13. **Zina's health:** ZDYj, Apr.; William Huntington journal, Apr. 13, 1845. **Henry's birthday:** ZDYj, "This day Henry B Jacobs, my husband, is 28 years old." **endowments:** NTER.

X. **leaving Nauvoo:** Zebulon Jacobs, diaries, pp. 2-3; WM 327. **Zebulon quote:** Diary. **Zina quote:** Autobiographical Sketch, p. 13. **Zebulon quote:** Diary, p. 1, typescript; p. 5 in original. Henry is prominent in Zebulon's memories (see also a pig incident, after they crossed the river). **leaves March 2:** See Eliza Partridge journal, CA, who lists H.B. Jacobs and S. Jacobs (probably for "Sina"). **Patty and Eliza:** PBSj. For women performing ordinances in early Mormonism, see Louisa Beaman chapter, June 19, 1849. **preliminaries to the birth:** Autobiographical Sketch 14, compare WM 328. See also PBSj, Mar. 22, and HStj. **Zebulon on Chariton's birth:** p. 9 in original; typescript, 2. For women giving birth on the overland journey, see Jeffrey, *Frontier Women* 69; Myres, *Westering Women* 129-30; Lillian Schlissel, *Women's Diaries* (New York: Schocken, 1992), 106. See also the Louisa Beaman, Eliza and Emily Partridge, and Helen Mar Kimball chapters. **Autobiographical Sketch:** See WM 328. However, compare Eliza Partridge journal, CA, Apr. 2, which seems to put Zina and Henry still at the Chariton River.

XI. **Brigham at Pisgah:** Elden J. Watson, ed., *Manuscript History of Brigham Young, 1846-47* (Salt Lake City: privately published, 1971), 162; CHC 3:51; "History of Brigham Young," CA, 176. For Mt. Pisgah, see Leland Gentry, "The Mormon Way Stations: Garden Grove and Mt. Pisgah," BYUSt 21 (Fall 1981): 445-61. **William appointed:** Watson, MH 168. **May 31 mission assignment:** Watson, MH 175; see also OHj, entry for July 11, below; JH: "Lorenzo D. Butler and Henry B. Jacobs received letters of authority for their English Mission and one for Oliver B. Huntington. These brethren were given a letter to Geo A Meal [Neal] of New York, requesting him to aid in outfitting them." **First Presidency:** Oliver would later write in his journal, for July 11, 1846, "Elder Henry B. Jacobs came with papers from the Presidency of the church giving me a mission to England to preach the Gospel." OHj 2:115. At this time the Quorum of the Twelve was serving as the church presidency (HC 7:240), and Brigham Young, the senior apostle, was the acting president of the church, Quinn, MHOP 175. **Henry ill:** Zebulon Jacobs, diaries, p. 3. For antagonistic versions of Henry's mission call, see Stenhouse, RMS 186-87; Hall, *Abominations of Mormonism* 43-44. According to Hall, Brigham said to Jacobs, "It was time for men who were walking in other men's shoes to step out of them." "Brother Jacobs, the woman you claim for a wife does not belong to you. She is the spiritual wife of brother Joseph, sealed up to him. I am his proxy, and she, in this behalf, with her children, are my property. You can go where you please, and get another, but be sure to get one of your own kindred spirit." As always, one should weigh anti-Mormon statements carefully. One wonders what Hall's source would be; it seems doubtful that Brigham Young would say this kind of thing publicly. Furthermore, Jacobs's letters to Zina do not seem to reflect that he understood matters as clearly as he would have had Brigham made this kind of explicit statement. As we will see, Jacobs seemed authentically stunned when he found that Zina was living with Brigham in Winter Quarters. On the other hand, the kind of language Hall puts in Brigham's mouth ("proxy" "kindred spirit") has the ring of authenticity. It is certain that Brigham sent Jacobs on an overseas mission then began cohabiting with Jacobs's wife while he was gone. Compare the marriage of Marinda Hyde to Joseph Smith after Joseph sent Orson Hyde on a mission to Palestine, see Marinda Johnson chapter. **Brigham leaves Pisgah:** Watson, MH 176, compare PBSj. **letter, June 25:** Zina Card Brown collection, box 2, fd 1, CA. **Jacobs's engagement:** OHj 2:116. **letter, Aug. 19:** Zina Card Brown collection, box 2, fd 1, CA. **trip to England:** OHj 2:120; 3:1. **Oliver close to Henry:** OHj 3:1-2; 3:44 (Oct. 18, 1844). **Oliver Huntington disillusioned with Henry Jacobs:** OHj 5:221-23; 5:224. However, Oliver and Henry sometimes worked their problems out, 5:25; 5:37-38 (1847, Jan. 2); 5:74 (Feb. 25/26, 1847); 5:81 (Mar. 10). **Henry president of Preston:** OHj 4 (Oct. 24, 1846). Henry also showed healing powers: he and Oliver Huntington cast out a devil from a child, OHj 5:86 (Mar. 14, 1847). A man was cured by putting on Henry's hat, OHj 3:63-64.

XII. **Zina on William's death:** Autobiographical Sketch 16. **William's death:** Zina Young to Dimick and family, Aug. 1846; typescript in Cannon, "Zina," 31-32; WM 329; Cook, RP 262. **to Winter Quarters:** Autobiographical Sketch 17. See also the amusing recollections of Zebulon Jacobs, diaries, 3-5; Zebulon Jacobs, reminiscences, 12, original. **Zina into Brigham's family:** WM 329-30. **Zina at Winter Quarters:** Autobiographical

Sketch, 17-18. **blessing meetings:** See Patty Bartlett Sessions and Eliza Snow chapters. On December 31, 1846, Zina attended a blessing meeting with Eliza Snow, Patty Sessions, Louisa Beaman, and a Sister Chase, ERSj, compare PBSj. Also PBSj, Feb. 14, 1847, Mar. 8; May 9; June 3. **Zina's social life at WQ:** Autobiographical Sketch 17, 18; compare PBSj, Nov. 17, 1846. **Brigham's kindness:** Autobiographical Sketch, 18. **sickness:** Zina Young, Autobiographical Sketch, 18. **Zebulon at Winter Quarters:** Reminiscences, pp. 13-20; p. 5 typescript. **Valentine letter:** undated, but Feb., 1847 is the logical year for it. Zina Card Brown collection, CA, MS 4780, box 2 fd 1. **our God Joseph:** Henry views Joseph as already exalted. **Zina writes to Mary Neal:** See Oliver's letter to Zina Young, Aug. 27, 1847. **Aug. 12:** OHj. **Henry in Cambria:** OHj 8, just before Aug. 28, 1847. **Oliver Huntington to Zina D.H. Jacobs:** 27 Aug. 1847, holograph. Box 2 fd 1, Zina Card Brown collection, CA. **Phelps:** OHj 8 (Aug. 28). **Jacobs marries three to Phelps:** HStj, Nov. 30, 1847; OMF 1:289. **Jacobs marries Babcock:** Zebulon Jacobs journal, p. 5. For Asenath, see the 1842 Nauvoo census, Platte p. 83. On May 27, 1842, Asenath and Amanda Babcock were voted into Relief Society, Minutes, p. 55; NTER, Jan. 28, 1846. Zebulon writes that she had previously married Daniel Jones, though I have found no supporting documentation for this. **Oliver's evaluation:** OHj 10:47. **Phelps's return:** WWj, 3:290. **Phelps and Jacobs trial:** HStj, Nov. 30, 1847 (1:289). Phelps "cut off," HStj, Dec. 9, 1847 (1:290); WWj, Dec. 6, 1847 (3:295). "There was a council today at which W.W. Phelps was formally cut off from the church." For early church discipline, see FWR, appendix. **"silenced":** compare TS 3 (May 16, 1842): 793; Nauvoo High Council Minutes, CA and Marriott Library, Marquardt collection, Feb. 4, 1842 (Wood case); Nov. 30, 1844; Dec. 9, 1844. Donald Q. Cannon, "Licensing in the Early Church," BYUSt 22 (1982): 96-105. Jacobs and his new wife lived for a while in Winter Quarters, where Henry enlivened parties and marriages with his violin playing, see Maurine Carr Ward, *Winter Quarters, The 1846-1848 Life Writings of Mary Haskin Parker Richards* (Logan: Utah State University Press, 1996), 202, 213. He still suffered from "bleeding at the lungs." **Woodruff quote:** WWj, Dec. 6, 1847 (3:295).

**XIII. Brigham asks Oliver:** OHj 9, before May 14, 1848. **reunion:** OHj 9, May 16, 1848. **departure:** OHj 9, May 25, 26; Arrington, BY 157-58; Brooks, OMF 1:141 n. 18. **Bro. Free:** OHj 9. May 31; June 16, 1848. **Jacobs and Perkins:** JDLj. In a June 11 camp meeting, Perkins, the two captains of fifty, and Jacobs spoke. **Zina's summary of the journey:** Autobiographical Sketch. **Gates:** OHj, July 9. The best account of the Mormon exodus to Utah is Wallace Stegner's *The Gathering of Zion* (New York: McGraw-Hill, 1964), a superb piece of imaginative scholarship. A standard account may be found in CHC 3, ch. 70-91, see also bibliography in Allen and Leonard SLDS 671-73. For the woman's pioneer experience, see Jeffrey, *Frontier Women*; Stratton, *Pioneer Women*; Sandra Myres, *Westering Women*; id., *Ho for California! Women's Overland Diaries from the Huntington Library* (San Marino, CA: Huntington Library, 1980); Lillian Schlissel, *Women's Diaries of the Westward Journey*, 2nd ed. (New York: Schocken, 1992); and John Faragher, *Women and Men on the Overland Trail* (New Haven, CT: Yale University Press, 1979), a Marxist interpretation that perhaps places undue emphasis on the theme of powerlessness of women. For a Mormon perspective, Claudia L. Bushman, ed., *Mormon Sisters: Women in Early Utah* (Salt Lake City: Olympus, 1976). **Dimick meets Zina:** OHj 10:29. **date of arrival:** OHj 10:31. **Zebulon's description:** Zebulon Jacobs, Reminiscence, p. 22-23; typescript 6. **Zina:** Autobiographical Sketch, 19.

**XIV. difficulty of early Salt Lake City years:** See the Louisa Beaman letters to Marinda Hyde, in Louisa Beaman chapter; Arrington and Bitton, TME 104. **Old Fort:** Zebulon Jacobs journal, p. 3. For the Old Fort, see Nicholas Groesbeck Morgan, comp., *The Old Fort, Historic Mormon Bastion ...* (Salt Lake City: Nicholas Morgan, 1964). This includes a description by Oliver Huntington of schoolrooms in the Old Fort, 20-21. **snow and winter:** In December 1850 Zina wrote, "The first of the month there was some cold storms. My room was very open and uncomfortable. I resorted to sister Balises through one storm and an other spent a[t] Wms & Presendes and Br Jackmans. A violent snow storm that made wood very scarce." **Zina's schoolteaching:** ZDYj, Feb. 5: "I taught school for the Last day ... I close my school by prayer ... Not one but what shed tears with a heart of Tenderness. We all took the parting kiss. Truly did the children and there Future welfare entwine around my heart. O Father wilt thou bless them." On the 7th there is a kind of children's program, with dinner, recitations, and singing, violin playing. Then "All Partook in the Pleasure of the Dance." "She taught school the most of her time, principally the governors own children and relatives," wrote Oliver Huntington, diaries, book 11; no pagination, but about p. 66. For schoolteaching as a womanly profession, see Eliza Snow chapter. **quorum meetings:** ZDYj, Dec. 10, 1848; Dec. 15, 1848. **whitewashing:** ZDYj, Oct. 23, 1848. **family meeting:** Apr. 10, 1849. There were also family work meetings: May 22, 1849: "Most all the Family met to pack wool in the morning." **Zina works herself:** ZDYj, Mar. 16, 1849. Compare Maureen Ursenbach Beecher, "Women's Work on the Mormon Frontier," UHQ 49 (1981): 276-90. **"attending meting":** ZDYj, Jan. 17, 1858. **Zina cries at move:** ZDYj, Apr. 16, 1849. Another moment of low spirits: "Brigham Young took breakfast in the kitchen and all in these buildings but sister Cob & I. A pleasent morning. A party at Brigham Youngs house. The 12 and there first wife and some of the aged vetrons about 30. For my self I fasted and wept tears of bitterness. Poor health. Thought uppon the past realizing the present and wondering uppon the future yet trusting in God." ZDYj, Jan. 1, 1850. **Brigham's lack of warmth:** ZDYj May 18, 1854. **"no man":** Autobiographical Sketch 20. An interesting little essay on polygamy follows. For Brigham's family life, see Arrington, BY 328-41; Bringhurst, BY 81-82, 121-127, who frankly discusses problems in Young's polygamous family. For Brigham and the two Jacobs sons, ZDYj, May 12, 1859. When Chariton grew older, he frequently traveled with Brigham, see BE 3:422. **tensions:** Ann Eliza Webb Young, WN19 123-25; and see on Harriet Cook below. **blessing meetings:** E.g., Jan. 13, a meeting at Addison Pratt's. "Had some music singing and relating events of past life. Truly interesting. I felt it a duty as the speret rested uppon me in obedience there unto agreeable to my former covenants with God to obey him. I arose and sung some and spoke in tongs Leaving the event in the hands of him who bade me speak. Enjoyed the evening much (BY and HCK are there)." May 3. "I commenced a school consisting of the family." Dimick visits. "In the morning I called on sister Young & blest her in the gifts. We ware [were] interrupted in giving the interprettation. I went down at noon. Sister Kimble, sister Young and myself went into her wagon. I gave the interprettation of the blessing. It was truly comforting." Susa Young Gates papers, USHS, box 12, fd 2, p. 6: "Aunt Eliza Snow and Aunt Zina, Aunt Ellen Rockwood and mother (Lucy Bigelow) together with a few sympathetic wives of other leading men, often had little testimony meetings in Aunt Eliza's or mother's room in the Lion House." **Louisa Beman:** ZDYj, Apr. 15, 1849. Zina visited Louisa's children's graves on May 15, 1859 (see her journal), long after Louisa's death. **Laura Pitkin Kimball:** Zina Young, Autobiographical Sketch, 19. Compare ZDYj, Feb. 11, 1849 and following. **women comforted each other:** ZDYj, Jan. 15, 1850. **parties:** ZDYj, July 28, 1849. Jan. 24, 1850. Feb. 1, 1850. **move:** Mar. 17, Apr. 1, Apr. 16. **Log row:** ZDYj, Dec. 1850. **Harriet Cook:** Autobiographical Sketch, 20. Susa Young Gates collection, USHS, Box 12, folder 2. Compare Stenhouse, *Tell It All* 256: "These poor 'fixins' [proxy wives] are seldom treated as real wives by the husband himself."

XV. **"paneful loneliness":** ZDYj, Mar. 19, 1850. **Zina Presendia Young:** She married Thomas Williams and (after Williams's death) Charles Ora Card, and died in 1931. Autobiographical Sketch p. 20; Zebulon Jacobs journal, p. 3; biography in Crocheron, RW 121-25; "Biographical Sketch of the Life of Zina Young Williams Card," in "Life Histories of the Wives of Charles Ora Card," Lee Library. **martyrdom meeting:** ZDYj: "Long Long to be rembered day Joseph & Hirams Decease. I had all of Joseph's family together that could meet in the vally. Alvira Holmes is up north. 11 in number. Praise the Lord that so many are continueing in well doing and striving to hold out faithful to the end.

Pres B Young, Heber C Kimble & Ira W [all proxy husbands to Joseph] took supper with us." Zina would also remember Joseph's birthday, ZDYj, December 23, 1857: "This is Joseph Smiths birthday Sister Presendia & Laura Kimball ware here had a very pleasant time." **moves:** Zebulon Jacobs journal, 3. **adobe house:** Zina Young, in 1856.

**XVI. child:** Zebulon Jacobs journal, 6. **Henry in California:** Amasa Lyman journal, CA, May 24, 1850; Kenneth Davies, *Mormon Gold* (Salt Lake City: Olympus, 1984), 218, 260. See also the Charles Rich account; Lyman journal, July 17, 1850. **Brigham sending to California:** In fall 1848 two, perhaps three, groups were either sent to California, or went with Young's permission. Another group, Lyman's gold mission, was "officially called on a mission to California" on November 26, 1848. Lyman finally departed in the spring of 1849, but another group left in the fall. See JH Nov. 26, 1848; Davies, MG 71-73. However, there was much church concern over unauthorized California exodus, Davies, MG 112. **Henry disfellowshipped:** Jan 26, 1851, JH. "Henry B. Jacobs (of the 15th Quorum) ... [and others] ... were disfellowshipped. There were fifteen names of dead Seventies and twenty-three disfellowshipped Seventies on the lists; the vacancies were soon to be filled." For disfellowshipping as somewhat equivalent to modern excommunication, compare Nauvoo High Council Minutes, Sept. 22, 1841, CA: "seconded & caried that he should be disfellowshiped and his name erased from the church roll by the unanimous voice of the Branch." **Henry to Zina:** Sept. 2, 1852. **family tradition for excommunication:** Oa J. Cannon writes that Henry "began pestering Zina to come back to him" which led to his excommunication, "Short Sketch." The value and limitations of family traditions (see my introduction) are in effect here. **sympathy for Jacobs:** Cannon, "Henry Bailey Jacobs," 15: "Then when my brother Smith Jacobs talked with Preston Nibley [he] said 'Your grandfather was treated very shabbily by President Young.'" Oa Cannon talked with Sister Amy Brown Lyman: "we visited and she told me her father was Henry Bailey's dear friend and she remembered very distinctly one morning her father hurriedly rushing into the house and she was sitting on the stairway playing with her doll. Her mother asked him what the matter was and he said that President Young was not being fair with Henry Jacobs, that he had actually been unjust." **account sheet:** Cannon, "Henry Bailey Jacobs." But was his tendency to lose women due to his flaws, or due to his inability to love another woman adequately after losing Zina? **birthdays:** ZDYj, June 5, 1854. Again, in 1859: "it is henry B Jacobs birth day he is 41. I went to fast meeting." Compare for similar entries: "Friday this is my mothers birth day she would have been 69 had she of lived how I feel the loss of the ..." ZDYj, June 2 1854. Mar. 28, 1857: "this is my Fathers birth day he would have been 71, died 11 years ago."

**XVII. ZDYj:** May 1855. See also, for this trip, JH; WWj (4:318-28); Martha Spence Heywood journal (Brooks 108); Gene Sessions, *Mormon Thunder* (Urbana: University of Illinois Press, 1982), 159-61; Gordon Irving, "Encouraging the Saints: Brigham Young's Annual Tours of the Mormon Settlements," UHQ 45 (1977): 233-51. **Feb. 6:** Compare Hardy, SC 321; Marinda Johnson chapter, in her Utah years before 1870. **Lion house:** ZDYj. **Zebulon:** journal. **blessing meeting:** ZDYj, Dec. 25 1857. **informal meetings:** ZDYj. As before, the Heber Kimball extended family would mix frequently with Brigham's: e.g., Jan. 16, 1858: "Sister Laura Kimball visted me Br Dimick and sister Young stoped in while conversing uppon the things of the kingdom very interesting after Dinner Sister Vilate Kimball calld blest each of [us ...] truly the spiret of the Lord was with us and that to comfort." **Eliza:** Compare ZDYj, Apr. 26, May 7, May 21, 1859. Also July 31, 1860, PBSj. **father's birthday:** ZDYj, Mar. 28, 1859. **trip to Salmon River:** Autobiography 1. **Ross children:** Quote in Cannon, "Zina," 34. See also Crocheron, RW 122-23.

**XVIII. Jacobs and Ferguson:** DW 9 (Nov. 2, 1859): 280; JH, Oct. 28, 1859. **rebaptized:** Jesse Haven journal, CA, Mar. 3, 1860. **Sally Taylor Haven:** Jesse Haven journal, Mar. 5, 1857, compare Aug. 21, 1859; Dec. 8, 1859; Jan. 23, 1860; Jan. 28; Feb. 12. Sally was a convert from England. **date of marriage:** Jesse Haven journal, Mar. 3, 1860. **letter to former brother-in-law:** Jesse Haven to Joshua Reynolds, Mar. 3, 1860, copied into Haven's journal. **Jesse Haven, journal:** Mar. 3, 1860. One of Henry's former wives was in California, Haven says, and another was in Ogden. **JHj:** at date. **Haven to Mother Taylor:** May 20, 1860 [1861?], copied into his journal.

XIX. **Lucia Presendia:** ZDYj, July 16, 1850. **Zina as doctor:** on May 18, 1849, she gave Louisa Beaman an emetic, ZDYj. **Patty's healing:** PBSj, Oct. 12, 1862. Compare PBSj, 1851, before Feb. 2; Nov. 28, 1862. Another example of her healing in WC 128-29. WWj, Oct. 29, 1858 (5:222); Dec. 7, 1858 (5:251); Oct. 22, 1859 (5:391). A few days later (Oct. 19) Patty wrote: "I have set up the most of the time to day many that saw me yesterday are astonished to see me so well and go out doors." **folk remedies:** EL 53. **"her generous nature":** Ann Eliza Young, WN19 124-25. Compare COCj, "She has been exceedingly kind to me as in fact she always is to everybody." "She is so benevolent she is always doing some one a favor," Mar. 14, 17, 1890. Susa Young Gates describes her as often sharing her last morsel of family food with needy Lion House farmhands, to the dismay of her children, Gates papers, USHS, fd 12. **Zina as midwife:** Noall, *Guardians of the Hearth*, 52-54; COCj, June 17, 1888, p. 64 Godfrey; Arrington, BY 171. On May 27, 1849, she tended Margaret [Pierce Young?] as she had a miscarriage, ZDYj. Cannon, "Zina," 35. For midwiving in general, see the Patty Sessions chapter. **medical course:** Crocheron, RW 13. **school of obstetrics:** Cannon, "Zina," 35. **lectures:** DN, Jan. 25, 1896. **President of Deseret Hospital:** "Passed Into the Repose." **Brigham's cocoonery:** George Pyper, "Silk Culture in Utah," *Contributor* 2 (1881): 115; Crocheron, RW 13; Wells, "A Brief Sketch"; Chris Rigby Arrington, "The Finest of Fabrics: Mormon Women and the Silk Industry in Early Utah," UHQ 46 (Fall 1978): 376-96, 384. **nightmares of silk worms:** Gates, *History*, 24; Kate Carter, comp., "Silk Industry in Utah," HTW 11:84; Arrington, "The Finest of Fabrics," 376. **President of Silk Association:** Crocheron, RW 13. **speech in 1879 General Conference:** DN (Oct. 7, 1879); "Second Day," DW 28 (Oct. 15, 1879): 581; Arrington, "The Finest of Fabrics," 383. **Relief Society reborn:** Crocheron, RW 13. Wells, "A Brief Sketch." WC 86-89. For the beginnings of the Relief Society, see the Sarah Cleveland chapter. For the Relief Society in Utah, see the Eliza Snow chapter. **Zebulon:** BE 2:401. **Black Hawk war:** For this war, see CHC 5:149-56; Arrington and Bitton, TME, 156-57. **Chariton:** BE 3:421-23. **little Zina and Stenhouse:** New York *World* interview, see below; however, family tradition reports that "little Zina" broke off the engagement when she dreamed of a snake having Stenhouse's eyes, see Beecher, "Four Zinas," 31. Perhaps both traditions are correct. For further on Zina Young Card, see Crocheron, RW 123; [Susa Young Gates], "Our Picture Gallery: Zina Young Williams Card," *Young Women's Journal* 4 (Nov. 1892): 50; Beecher, "Four Zinas"; id., "Mormon Women in Southern Alberta," in Brigham Young Card, ed., *The Mormon Presence in Canada* (Logan: Utah State University Press, 1990), 211-30. **Charles Ora Card:** See Donald Godfrey and Brigham Y. Card, eds., *The Diaries of Charles Ora Card, the Canadian Years, 1886-1903* (Salt Lake City: University of Utah Press, 1993), 667 (Card frequently mentions "Mother Young," see index); Donald Godfrey, *Charles Ora Card: Southern Alberta Pioneer* (Mesa, AZ: D. Godfrey, 1987); Card, *Mormon Presence in Canada*, 77-107; further bibliography in SLDS 735. **Zina Young to Chariton and Zina Card:** June 19, 1876. Zina moves to own house: "I found Mother in her house one the Pres gave her on New Years day. situated at the corner of 1st east Street and 3rd South st ..." H. Chariton Jacobs journal, CA, July 19, 1870. **Dimick dies:** OHj 13 (Feb. 2, 1879). **Brigham Young dies:** See Arrington, BY 399. Most of the women in this book experienced the loneliness of widowhood (which is a polygamy-related phenomenon because polygamous wives were generally significantly younger than their husbands, while monogamous wives tended to be closer in age to their husbands). For the experience of widowhood in nineteenth-century Mormon culture, see Maureen Ursenbach Beecher, Carol Cornwall Madsen, and Lavina Fielding Anderson, "Widowhood among the Mormons: The Personal Accounts," 117-139 in Arlene Scadron, ed., *On Their Own: Widows and*

*Widowhood in the American Southwest, 1848-1939* (Urbana: University of Illinois Press, 1988); Geraldine P. Mineau, "Utah Widowhood: A Demographic Profile," 140-65.

**XX. reunion:** Zebulon Jacobs journal, Mar. 4, 1877. The next day Henry was feeling bad again, and Zebulon gave him a "boquet of hair flowers" to cheer him up. See also Mar. 5, Mar. 10, 11. **Henry in Utah:** "Henry Jacobs came from California to spend the remainder of his days with his Sons in Salt Lake, by their request." OHj 14 (May 8, 1880). **Sally Taylor, 1899:** She was then living in Livermore, married to "a man by the name of Ginger." OHj 18:143 (Oct. 9, 1899). **Henry lives in Zina's house:** Cannon, "Short Sketch." Compare Emmeline Wells to Mary Lightner, Apr. 7, 1882, in Mary Elizabeth Lightner collection, Lee Library: "Sister Presendia and Zina are going to St. George soon after Conference. I do not suppose they can go to Minersville, however I do not know ... Aunt Zina stays up at Chariton's when she is not in Provo with her daughter - her own house which is next door to mine is rented." **Death:** Zebulon Jacobs, diary, 6; Richard Van Wagoner and Steven Walker, *A Book of Mormons* (Salt Lake City: Signature Books, 1982), 418. According to Juanita Brooks's undocumented statement (OMF 1:142), Henry was rebaptized (again) on February 2, 1886. If this is true, it is unknown how or why he left the church for the second time.

**XXI. St. George:** Crocheron, RW 15. **National Suffrage:** Cannon, "Zina," 37. Compare Beverly Beeton, "Woman Suffrage in Territorial Utah," UHQ 46 (1978): 100-20. Carol Cornwall Madsen, "Woman Suffrage," in EM 1572-73. WC 146-50. Further bibliography in Louise Degn, "Let Woman Choose Her Sphere," *Sunstone* 20 (Apr. 1997): 28-30; Quinn, MHEP 602. For a detailed record of Zina's Relief Society years, see Emmeline B. Wells's diary, Lee Library. For the trip to Washington, EBWj, Jan. 1-Feb. 4, 1879. On January 13 Zina and Emmeline met with President Hayes. **Hawaii:** ZDYj, July to Sept. (Zina's journal often is kept during trips, and stops when she returns back home); Crocheron, RW 15; Wells, ADW 39; Wells, "A Brief Sketch." **trip to the south:** Wells, "A Brief Sketch." Zina and Eliza had also traveled to St. George in 1877. **Zina as counselor:** WE 9 (July 1, 1880): 21-22; WC 121. **mass meeting speech:** "Woman's Mass Meeting," WE 7 (1 Dec. 1878): 98; compare OHj, p. 48; Wells, "Character Sketch," 45. **electric shock:** Augusta Crocheron, in Cannon, "Zina," 37. **interview:** H., "Utah Unveiled," *The World*, New York (Nov. 17, 1869): p. 4. See also a short interview in W. Herbert Thomas, *Mormon Saints* (London: Houlston and Sons, 1890), cited in Ivins 1:158-9. For the disparagement of romantic love in polygamy, see Brigham Young, in JD 9:37; Hardy, SC 91-92. **temple work:** OHj 14. ZDYj, Nov. 9, 1880. WC 123. Compare OHj 17:172, Jan. 25, 1895. Endowment House Record, Book I, for Feb. 5, 1874, as cited in Ivins 4:284, in which Zina stood proxy for ten dead women as they were sealed to Chariton. Also, Endowment House Record, Book I, 1874, July 10 (Ivins 4:284). For the 1880-81 visit of Eliza and Zina to St. George, see "Woman's Work in St. George," WE 9 (Jan. 1, 1881): 115. **trip east:** Crocheron, RW 16. They were set apart by First Presidency to speak publicly before leaving, Wells, "A Distinguished Woman," 131. OHj 14, Apr. 11, 1882. **Oct. 1881:** Whitney, HU 4:577; EL 56. In 1879, Zina and Emmeline Wells attended the national women's suffrage convention in Washington, EBWj. **Suffrage Convention:** Whitney, HU 4:577. See above. **Zina to St. George, April 1882:** OHj 14, Apr. 16, 1882; Emmeline Wells to Mary Lightner, Apr. 7, 1882, quoted above. **November primary conference:** OHj 15, Nov. 30, 1882. **Omaha:** Cannon, "Zina," 37.

**XXII. Eliza failing:** Zina Young to Eliza Snow, Apr. 27, 1886. On June 16, 1886, Zina was recovering from an illness; on July 29 she was in Logan, HMWj. Helen Mar frequently mentions Zina, see May 4, 1887; Sept. 24, 1888; Jan. 3, 1889; Sept. 12, 19 1889; Nov. 27, 1889; Nov. 29, 1890; Aug. 9, 1891; Nov. 5, 1892; Jan. 14, 1893, July 1, 1893; May 3, 1894; Feb. 8, 1895; June 5, 1895 (Zina administers to Helen and her daughter); Jan. 31, 1896 (75th birthday celebration); Feb. 29, 1896; Apr. 2, 1896. **On May 21, 1888,** Zina and her daughter attended the first session of the Logan temple, *Diaries of Charles Ora Card,* xxxvii, n. **Zina President:** EBWj, Apr. 9, 19, Oct. 11, 1888. WC 128. **Zina to Canada, 1888:** COCj, May 7, 1888. **Zina to Canada, 1889:** OHj 17:69, Jan. 17, 1889. **Zina meets with Woodruff:** WC 139-40. See on suffrage, above. **General RS**

conference: WC 130. **Zina to Zina Card:** June 19, [1889?]. Zina Young to Zina Card, 1890, Mar. 23, "I often feel that you are near me I feel I need it so much." **EBWj:** Mar. 26 1890, compare May 28 1893, "breakfast with Aunt Zina who felt very lonely because Zina Card had gone away." **Grandchildren:** ZDYj, Feb. 2 [1890]; Feb. 15, in which she feeds Chariton's family, the parents and twelve grandchildren. **birthday:** EBWj. **Zina in Springville:** ZYj; OHj 17:89. **Zina to Canada:** COCj, Aug. 22, 1890. She returned to Salt Lake on October 4, ibid. **National Council:** Cannon, "Zina," 37; Wells, "A Brief Sketch." **Canada:** EBWj, May 13, 1891. **jubilee:** EBWj; WC 140-44. **Zina to John Huntington:** Mar. 1, 1892, Zina Card collection, CA. **incorporation:** WC 144-45; EBWj, Mar. 21; Oct. 2, 3. **first general board meeting:** WC 132. **SL temple:** ZDYj. Compare OHj, Jan. 8, 1895. **World's Fair:** EBWj; WC 139; Wells, "A Brief Sketch." **trip east:** Zina Young to Zina Card, June 12, 1893; OHj, 17:132-42. **suffrage convention:** WC 148. See the picture of Zina in a group including Susan Anthony taken at this time, EM 1573. **Zina Young to Zina Card:** May 23, 1896. During the visit, in a family meeting, Zina Diantha spoke in tongues and Zina Presendia gave the interpretation, COCj, Mar. 14, 1896. Zina elder and younger also washed and anointed together, COCj, Apr. 8. Zina Young to Zebulon, Aug. 17, 1896. **Zina to Canada in 1897:** See COCj, Nov. 12, 1897, Dec. 7. **Feb. 1898, memory gone:** OHj, 18:118, Feb. 16, 1898. **Zina feeble:** COCj, Apr. 25, 1898. She was living at "146 - 4th Street" at the time. By December 1899, "Bro and sister Langton" were staying at Zina's home to care for her. COCj, Dec. 26, 1899. **Zina Young to Zina Card:** June 5, 1899. **Zina to Canada, 1899:** Zina Young to Charles Card, Aug. 5, 1899. **Zina back in Salt Lake:** OHj, Nov. 9, 12, 1899.

XXIII. **Zina near death, Zina Card comes to tend:** Talmage, PTS 255. **Interview:** Talmage, PTS 255, 257. **journey to Canada:** "Passed Into the Repose." **death:** EBWj; "Passed." According to this, Zina Diantha and Zina Card parted in Canada; as Zina Diantha left on the train she "smiled into her face and said, 'Never mind, make the best of it.' These were her last words." But according to the Charles Card diary, Zina Card accompanied Zina back to Utah. COCj, Aug. 21, 23, 26, 27, 29, 1901, compare EBWj. Card confirms that Zina slept on the train trip home "just breathing only." For the funeral, EBWj. **Zina's return:** "Zina told her daughter, Zina Young Card, if the Lord wanted her to have Henry B. Jacobs for her celestial husband she was willing. Then the fact that she appeared twice to Zina Card and told her she was to get the Jacobs genealogy started makes me feel she felt responsible and perhaps felt bad all her life for what had happened." Oa J. Cannon to "Brother Peterson," n.d., CA, in folder with letter, Henry B. Jacobs to Zina Young, Aug. 19, 1846. See also Cannon, "Henry Bailey Jacobs," 15.

# REFERENCES TO CHAPTER 5.
*An Apostolic Life:*
*Presendia Lathrop Huntington (Buell Smith Kimball)*

AVW: see Wells, "A Venerable Woman."
Crocheron. *Representative Women of Deseret.* 29-34.
Kimball, Presendia Huntington. Autobiographical Sketch. Letter, Presendia L. Kimball Smith, to her eldest granddaughter living in 1880, Apr. 1, 1881. CA 742.
Tullidge. *Women of Mormonism.* 206-14.
[Wells, Emmeline]. "Death of Presendia Kimball." DEN 25 (Feb. 1, 1892): 4 = DW 44 (Feb. 6, 1892): 214-15.
———. "A Venerable Woman: Presendia Lathrop Kimball." WE 11 (Feb. 1, 1883): 131; (Feb. 15): 139; (Mar. 1): 147; (Mar. 15): 155; (Apr. 1): 163; (May 1): 183; vol. 12 (June 1, 1883): 2; (June 15): 11; (July 15): 27; (Aug. 15): 43; (Oct. 1): 67; (Oct. 15): 75; (Dec. 1): 98; (Feb. 1, 1884): 130; vol. 13 (June 1, 1884): 3; (Sept. 15): 59; (Oct. 15): 73-74.

Joseph Hovey, journal, Mar. 4, 1849, CA, compare Rex Cooper, *Promises Made to the Fathers* (Salt Lake City: University of Utah Press, 1990), 145. Quinn, MW, collects evidence indicating that nineteenth-century Mormons felt that women held priesthood in some way. **"large, inspired mind":** WM 205.

I. **birthdate:** Presendia Kimball, Autobiographical Sketch; SAd 513. BOP #167. Wells, "Death." For details of her parents and siblings, and for an account of the life of a child growing up on the Huntington farm, see the Zina Huntington chapter. Presendia is the commonest orthography for a variously spelled name. **conversion:** Zina Baker Huntington to Dorcas Baker, June 8, 1822, fd 4 in Dorcas Baker Spalding Correspondence, Zina Card Brown collection, MS 4780, CA, Box 7, fd 1-5. For women and revivalism, see Nancy F. Cott, "Young Women in the Second Great Awakening in New England," *Feminist Studies* 3 (1975): 15-29; Martha Tomhave Blauvelt, "Women and Revivalism," in Rosemary Radford Ruether and Rosemary Skinner Keller, eds., *Women and Religion in America Volume 1: The Nineteenth Century* (San Francisco: Harper & Row, 1981), 1-45, which includes valuable primary documents; Mary Ryan, *Cradle of the Middle Class* (Cambridge: Cambridge University Press, 1981), ch. 2; Cott, *The Bonds of Womanhood* 132-35; Barbara Leslie Epstein, *The Politics of Domesticity, Women Evangelism, and Temperance in Nineteenth Century America* (Middletown, CT: Wesleyan University Press, 1981); Smith-Rosenberg, *Disorderly Conduct* 129. For the Second Great Awakening, characterized by enthusiastic revivalism, see Whitney Cross, *The Burned-over District* (Ithaca, NY: Cornell University Press, 1950), 84-89; William McLoughlin, *Revivals, Awakenings, and Reforms* (Chicago: University of Chicago Press, 1980), 98-140 (for women, 132-33, 120-22); Richard Birdsall, "The Second Great Awakening and the New England Social Order," *Church History* 39 (1970): 345-64. For the importance of individual conversion in revivalism, Blauvelt, WR 4 (though this seems too doctrinaire a feminist interpretation); Cott, *Bonds* 139-41. Revivalist preachers often concentrated on youth, who had not yet made the major decisions in their lives, Joseph F. Kett, *Rites of Passage: Adolescence in America, 1790 to the Present* (New York: Basic Books, 1977), 62-85. See also the Sarah Kingsley and Delcena Johnson chapters. **rheumatism:** "R.S. Reports," WE 2 (July 15, 1873): 26.

II. **marriage date:** Autobiographical Sketch. Presendia was a younger bride than the norm for that culture, but her marriage age was not entirely out of the ordinary. See Larkin, REL 63; Ulrich, GW 6; Cott, "Young Women," 16. **Buell's birthdate:** AF. **manufacturer:** Wells, AVW 131. **Jan. 22:** See above; box 7, fd 5. **burned-over district:** See above. **George:** Crocheron, RW 29. He apparently later married a woman named Poorman, OHj 13, 1880/81. **Pinbury:** Wells, AVW 131. I can find no such town in Lewis County. There is a Pinckney. **Presendia's weaving:** Weaving was a central element of woman's work in early nineteenth-century America. See Cott, *Bonds* 26-27; Ulrich, GW 29: "Spinning was a useful craft, easily picked up, easily put down, and even small quantities of yarn could be knitted into caps, stockings, dishcloths, and mittens ... The mechanical nature of spinning made it a perfect occupation for women whose attention was engrossed by young children." Compare the Patty Sessions chapter, at spring 1813; Elvira Cowles chapter, at May 1850. **Silas born:** Crocheron, RW 29. **Silas's death:** Wells, AVW 131. "Silas was {scalded} to death when a child–," OHj 13, 1880/81. Making quantities of cider was an important and common task of the New England farm wife, Ulrich, GW 23: "Fall was the season for cider making." **birth of Thomas:** Wells, AVW 131. **stood aloof:** Wells, AVW 131.

III. **1835:** WM 206-7. **"I felt":** Wells, AVW 131. **western fever:** Wells, AVW 139. **journey to Kirtland:** OHj 2:5; WM 206-7; Wells, AVW 139. **baptism:** Autobiographical Sketch; WM 206-207; Crocheron, RW 29; Wells, "Death," gives the date June 1, 1836. **Chauncy:** AF. **October:** OHj 2:9. **"On one occasion":** WM 207. "Later, the people in the temple reported that there had been speaking in tongues and prophesying in the meetings that day." "It was also said in the interpretation of tongues, 'That the angels were resting down upon the house.'" **angels singing:** WM 207-208. Compare Aroet Hale, Autobiography, Lee Library, typescript p. 4: "Butiful Singing was heard from the top of the Temple in the evning." **Pentecost:** WM 208. These incidents are also recounted in Wells, AVW 139. **Speaking in tongues:** WM 207-8. **Buell an elder:** ECIF, citing PBI 10:307. **helps administer:** KEQR 23.

IV. **trip to Missouri:** Autobiographical Sketch; OHj, July 18, 1838, 2:19, compare 1:1, 2:18. JSj, Jessee 2:212; HC 3:1. **Washington township:** Wells, AVW 147. **log cabin:** Wells, AVW 155. **Adaline:** Wells, AVW 155; Crocheron, RW 29. **Norman's disaffection:** The story of Presendia confronted by a mob in Wells, AVW (see below) seems to be dated in fall 1838–a following second story, of Presendia helping Mormon fugitives, is prefaced, "The same Fall ...," and Norman is already disaffected by then. Presendia elsewhere gave the date of 1839 for his disaffection (see below). He certainly was antagonistic at least by spring 1839. Crocheron, RW 30, writes, "Here on two occasions, she was without protection, encountered an armed mob, but was saved from their hatred; they left her. Her husband had by this time apostatized." ("this time" is spring 1839.) **Oliver on Norman's disaffection:** OHj 2:45. **Wells, "her husband":** "Death." **Presendia confronted by the mob:** Wells, AVW 155. **Norman rents a mill:** Wells, AVW 155. **Presendia to Liberty Jail:** WM 209. **Joseph's letter:** Jessee, PW 386-87; HC 3:285-86; compare WM 210-12. **Joseph escapes:** HC 3:321; 3:319-27. **Huntington's leave:** Zina, in WM 214. **"I never ...":** WM 213. So perhaps Presendia traveled to Far West to see her family before they left. **"He left ...":** Autobiographical Sketch. **July 13:** Presendia Huntington Buell to Zina Huntington, July 13, 1839, in Zina C. Brown collection, Box 2 fd 1, CA. **January 2:** Presendia Huntington Buel to her family, Jan. 2, 1840, CA 4780, Zina Card Brown collection, box 7 fd 6. **Oliver:** For his date of birth, see Presendia's Autobiographical Sketch, in the letter dated Apr. 16, 1881, and Wells, AVW 155 (working with an interview with Presendia, and published while she was alive). Esshom, *Pioneers and Prominent Men of Utah*, with a picture of Buell, also has January 31, 1840. Crocheron, RW 30, has Oliver born in spring 1839, which is almost certainly incorrect. Presendia's holograph is of course much more authoritative than Crocheron, and Wells, AVW is also much fuller than Crocheron, and includes frequent quotes from Presendia, so is preferable evidence. Crocheron often copies directly from Wells, AVW.

Brodie (NM 301-2, 460-61) holds that Oliver was Joseph's biological child, but virtually all of her evidence for this proposition is weak. For example, she writes, "Joseph's journal entries make it clear that after his escape he was mingling with the last Mormon group to leave Far West, which included the Huntington family." 462. A careful reading of the *History of the Church* (3:319-27) shows that Joseph and his party went quickly due east to Illinois as soon as they escaped, and did not return to Far West. See the affidavit of Hyrum Smith, HC 3:321; compare Jessee 2:318, for the date April 16. Read carefully, the *History of the Church* confirms this date, while the Hyrum Smith diary, CA, skips from April 15 to April 17. See further my "Fawn Brodie's Treatment of Joseph Smith's Polygamy and Plural Wives: A Critical View," Newell Bringhurst, ed., *Reconsidering No Man Knows My History: Fawn M. Brodie and Joseph Smith in Retrospect* (Logan: Utah State University Press, 1996), 154-94, 166-71. Another example: Brodie, to bolster her Oliver Buell argument, quotes Ettie V. Smith to the effect that Presendia "did not know whether Mr. Buel or the Prophet was the father of her son"; however, it is clear from context that the son referred to was John Hiram, not Oliver, see below on John Hiram.

V. **move to Illinois:** Wells, AVW 163, "In the fall of 1840, Mrs. Buell moved from her home in Missouri to Illinois and settled between Quincy and Nauvoo." As polyandry approaches, Norman Buell is carefully left out of Wells's picture. Later diary records show certainly that Presendia was living with Buell in Lima, however. If she had not been living with Buell, she would undoubtedly have lived in Nauvoo with her family. **Joseph teaches polygamy to Presendia:** Wells, AVW 163. **marriage to Joseph:** Presendia Kimball affidavit, SAB 1 page 7; Bachman #50. See also her Autobiographical Sketch. Compare Jenson HR 6:233; ZDYj, Dec. 11, 1848; OHj 15, Feb. 18, 1883. Bennett, HS 256, lists as one of Joseph's wives "Mrs. B****," for whom the only likely candidate is Presendia. **"soon after Dimick":** OHj 15, Feb. 18, 1883. **"sisters ... separate":** Wells, AVW 163.

VI. **Relief Society:** RS Minutes, pp. 30-32. For "Councilor Cleveland," see Sarah Kingsley chapter. **Oliver in Lima in August, 1842:** OHj 1:2. "A few days after that I went to my Brother=in=laws on a visit 30 miles below Nauvoo." (OHj 2:59.) **Sept. 24:** [Emmeline Wells], "Patty Sessions," 13 (Nov. 15, 1884): 94. **John Hiram:** ZDYj, see below. Mary Ettie V. Smith, *Fifteen Years Among the Mormons*, 34-35, reports of Presendia that "I heard the latter woman say afterwards in Utah, that she did not know whether Mr. Buel or the Prophet was the father of her son." John Hiram Buell, not Oliver Buell, would be the proper candidate for the child referred to. This is made certain when Ettie Smith writes, on p. 45, that Presendia "is the woman whose husband lived at Lima, Ill., when Joseph seduced her from him." One wonders if Presendia would have made the statement reported by Ettie. But if we accept that she did, it would still be more likely that Norman was the father, since Presendia was living in Lima, not Nauvoo, and would have cohabited much more with him than with Joseph.

According to Mary Ettie Smith, 34-35, Presendia participated in the procession of women when Joseph reviewed the Nauvoo Legion. Compare the Hannah Ells chapter. **Oliver in Lima:** OHj, May 1, 1844, 1:40-41. **"The summer ...":** OHj 2:62.

VII. **Oliver sick:** OHj 1:42-43; 2.72. **Presendia in Nauvoo:** ZDYj, July 29,30, 1844. **Presendia in Nauvoo in October:** ZDYj, October 5-7. **Hiram dies:** Autobiographical Sketch. **Norman near death:** OHj, 2:97. **mad man:** OHj, Mar. 19, 1945, 2:98-99. **marriage to Kimball in 1845:** Quinn, MHOP 557. See also Feb. 4, below. **diary of William Huntington:** Autobiography, facsimile at Huntington Library. **Presendia endowed:** NTER. **Feb. 4:** BOP #167; SAd 513. Compare Wells, AVW 163; Crocheron, RW 30.

VIII. **"Now Presendia's Husband ...":** OHj 10:47. **flight from Buell:** Crocheron, RW 30-31. Compare Wells, "Death." **Henry on Buell, June 25:** See Zina Huntington chapter.

IX. **Cutler's Park:** See Richard Bennett, *Mormons at the Missouri 1846-1852* (Norman: University of Oklahoma Press, 1987), 69. **16 wives separate:** HCK 307. For his 45 wives, see HCK 307ff.; Quinn, MHOP 557. **Helen Mar (Smith Whitney) on Vilate:** SIN, WE 11 (July 15, 1882): 26. Compare HCK 102, 231. Some students of Mormon polygamy have found that monogamous patterns (excessive attachment to one woman) continued, to the detriment of the other women, see Hardy, SC 114; Bates and Smith, *Lost Legacy* 127, 129. **"great, unknown desert":** Crocheron, RW 31. **house, school, sickness:** Wells, AVW 2. Compare Crocheron, RW 33. **Feb. 28:** for Presendia and Sister Leonard, see also Apr. 20, 1847, PBSj. **Eliza Snow:** See also ERSj, Apr. 26, May 1, a blessing meeting; June 9, another blessing meeting; June 10, Eliza calls on her. **Presendia and Laura:** Wells, AVW 2. At some point, Presendia also lived with Frances Swan in Winter Quarters, HCK 144. **Presendia and Zina:** See also Mar. 23, 1847, PBSj. **Presendia and Martha Knight:** Compare Apr. 3, 1847, PBSj. **April 22:** Eliza wrote, "Went to br. Leonard's in the eve. had a glorious time—father Sess presided, pres. Moth. Chase. Sis. Lyons, Leonard, Buel, Sabra [were present]." **Presendia helps administer to Whitney child:** Wells, AVW 2. For more blessing meetings that Presendia participated in, see PBSj, May 30. Compare PBSj, May 25, Apr. 29. ERSj, June 1. **evil forces:** Wells, AVW 11. Compare the Helen Mar Whitney chapter, at 1847 to 1850. **visions:** Wells, AVW 27. **Oliver meets Norman:** OHj 9, May 5, 1848. **Presendia seven miles west:** OHj, 1848, after May 8, compare before May 14 (Heber Kimball helps Presendia with her chest).

X. **May 6:** Wells, AVW 27. **mid-July:** OHj 10 (July 23). **drove own team:** Wells, AVW 27. **Sept. 22:** Wells, AVW 27. **Old Fort:** Crocheron, RW 32. **move from Old Fort:** OHj 10:47. **midwife:** Kimball, HCK 310. **Presendia set apart:** Wells, AVW 75.

XI. **birth of Pres. Celestia:** ZDYj; PBSj. **umbrella:** Wells, AVW 43. **"intelligent and attractive":** Wells, AVW 27. **Martin:** Wells, AVW 43. **June 29:** ZDYj; Patty Sessions also attended, see PBSj. **July 28:** ZDYj, see Zina chapter for a fuller account. **death of daughter:** the main account is a long quotation from Presendia herself in Wells, AVW 43. For the date, see PBSj,

May 12, 1850, "sister Buels child drowned yesterday." Compare ZDYj, May 6, 1859, who seems to have the date wrong. **John Young:** *Memoirs of John R. Young, Utah Pioneer, 1847* (Salt Lake City: Deseret News, 1920), 61-62. Presendia, however, remembers that Elizabeth Culvert Chase found the child in the water, Wells, AVW 43. Compare ZDYj, May 6, 1859. **Hubbard:** Wells, AVW 43. **dropsy:** Wells, AVW 43. **revelation:** Wells, AVW 67. **Endowment House work:** Wells, AVW 67. Ettie Smith, *Fifteen Years* 45, reports that she saw Presendia, like Eliza Snow, play the part of Eve in the endowment creation drama. **Whitney's dream:** Wells, AVW 67.

XII.  **"like an Isaac":** Wells, AVW 67. **Joseph's career:** Joseph later married Lathilla Pratt, with whom he had thirteen children, and died in 1936. AF; Esshom, PPM 988; *Biographical Record of Salt Lake City and Vicinity* (Chicago: National Historical Record, 1902), 644-45: "Few men have taken a more active part in the work of the Church or in the development of Utah than has the subject of this sketch. He is rated as a very active business man of the inter-mountain region and has become one of the most popular men of Utah both by his public service and by his integrity as a business man." **breaks her arm:** Wells, AVW 98. **George marries:** 1860 Missouri Census, Buchanan County, St. Joseph, p. 548, compare note at his birth, above. Norman Buell was also living in St. Joseph, see p. 555. **1855 healings:** Compare ZDYj, July 7, 1855, "I went to wash & annoint Sister Bull with Presendia." **Heywood:** Brooks 121. **July 4, 1857:** Compare PBSj, Mar. 2, 1857. "Have been with sister Precinda and Mary Elen Kimbal washed and anointed Susannah Richards she was sick." **early November:** ZDYj Nov. 3, 1857. **Joseph's birthday:** ZDYj. **Presendia's living arrangements:** HCK 234. At one time during this period she lived with Hulda Barnes and Harriet Sanders. At times some of Heber's plural wives lived in the white house, but always in side and back portions; Vilate occupied the front. See Adelia Kimball journal, CA 6089.

XIII.  **date of Oliver's marriage:** Shortly before spring 1858, Wells, AVW 98. **Utah War:** Wells, AVW 98. Compare HCK 215-16. **in Provo:** Wells, AVW 130. **17th ward:** Wells, AVW 130. The lot had formerly been owned by Hosea Cashing (or Cushing), an adopted son of Heber. **Oliver's departure:** Wells, AVW 130, 59. **Oliver and George visit:** Wells, AVW 59.

XIV.  **Huldah:** Wells, AVW 130. **Ensign peak:** Wells, AVW 130. **16th Ward:** Wells, AVW 130. There is a confusion in the date of this move in Wells, AVW. On page 130, she dates it at the time of Joseph Smith Kimball's baptism at the age of eight (roughly December 22, 1859, as Joseph was born on December 22, 1851). She gives the date of the blessing as April 7 (1860, presumably). But on p. 3, the date of the blessing (probably written on the document, so authoritative) is April 7, 1862. **blessing:** Wells, AVW 3. **early 1860s:** See PBSj, 1860, Jan. 15; 1861, Mar. 19; 1862, Feb. 8; Nov. 1, 1862; Apr. 30, 1864 ("I then went with sister Buel washed and anointed sister Russell she is very sick."); 1865, Jan. 5, Jan. 18; Feb. 3; Mar. 4. **Presendia anoints Patty's arm:** PBSj, Sept. 15, 1862. **Relief Society secretary:** Wells, AVW 59. "Relief Society Reports," WE 1 (May 1, 1873): 178; 5 (Aug. 1, 1876): 37. **Vilate's death:** Wells, AVW 59; HCK 295. See Helen Mar Kimball chapter. **Heber's death:** See HCK 297.

XV.  **the abandoned child:** Wells, AVW 59. **Joseph marries:** *Biographical Record* 645. **Joseph's education:** *Biographical Record* 645. **Joseph's later life:** *Biographical Record* 645. Further jobs and offices are listed here. **Oliver's death:** Wells, AVW 59; OHj 13, 1880/81. **Buell dies:** KEQR 74.

XVI.  **ordinance work, 1869-70:** Presendia was baptized for some dead Huntingtons, see Endowment House Records, Bapt. for dead; Book A, Sept. 15, 1869; Aug. 4, 1870, as cited in Ivins 5:296. **temple work:** Endowment House Record, Book H (Ivins 4:283). Endowment House Record, Bk K (Ivins 4:286). **healing:** Elmina A. Shepard Taylor journal, CA, Dec. 1, 1879. See also HMWj, Mar. 20, Aug. 28, 1886, Nov. 14, 1887, Nov. 19, 1888 (Helen Mar, who knew the leading women of Utah, chose Presendia to come wash and anoint her daughters for childbirth). **prayer at mass meeting:** "Woman's

Mass Meeting," WE 7 (Dec. 1, 1878): 97; Wells, AVW 74. **Presendia visits Oliver H.:** OHj 14, Dec. 23, 1880. Compare OHj 14, Mar. 26, 28, 1881; OHj 14, Feb. 4, 1882. **March 2:** OHj 14. **March 28:** OHj 14. **Presendia secretary:** She resigned this calling on June 15, 1886, HMWj. **Presendia a public speaker:** See Wells, AVW 74. WE 1 (May 1, 1873): 178; 2 (July 15, 1873): 26; 5 (July 15, 1876): 26; 5 (May 1, 1877): 183; 6 (Oct. 1, 1877): 68; 6 (Nov. 15, 1877): 94. **to St. George, April 1882:** OHj 14. Compare June 3. **Bringhurst:** OHj 14. **Nov. 1882:** OHj, Nov. 8, 1882. **Jan. 16, 1881:** EBWj. Other references to Presendia in the Wells journal: Apr. 12, 15, Nov. 23, Nov. 27 (Presendia and Emmeline administer to a sick baby), 1881; Mar. 21, 1883. **Wells's description, "Sister Presendia":** Wells, AVW, WE 11 (Jan. 15, 1883): 123. **Christmas 1883:** OHj. **birthday party:** DN, Sept. 11, as quoted in Crocheron, RW 34. **Logan:** OHj 16, Oct. 7. **angels:** "Sketch of Sister Zina D. Young," *Young Woman's Journal* 4 (Apr. 1893): 292-94. **Oliver:** OHj 16:31, Nov. 14, 1884. Though Brodie (NM 462) places great weight on this reference as showing that Oliver Buell was Joseph Smith's biological son, Oliver Huntington never mentions the name of Oliver Buell in this reference; he refers to "a child of my Sister Presenda," and Brodie assumes that he means Oliver. But Presendia lost six children she had while living with Norman Buell. **early summer, 1886:** OHj 16, May 16, 1886. **spring, 1886:** HMWj, Mar. 13-20. **Presendia sick:** OHj 16, Jan. 3, 1887. **early Feb.:** Emmeline Wells to Mary E. Lightner, Feb. 10, 1887, Lee Library, Mary Elizabeth Lightner collection. **June 8:** Zina Young to Mary Lightner, June 8 [1887], Mary Lightner collection, Lee Library. **two weeks later:** Zina Young to Mary Lightner, June 22, 1887. Mary Lightner collection, Lee Library. **Logan temple, 1887:** OHj 16, July 5, 1887. **77th birthday:** EBWj. **Manti temple:** OHj 17, May 21, 1888. **Oliver visits:** OHj 17:64, Dec. 3-4, 1888. **residence:** 1889 Salt Lake City Directory: "Kimball, Priscinda, widow, res 249 n Third West." **Later in January:** ZDYj, Jan. 23, 1890. **March 1890:** Presendia Kimball to Mary Lightner, Mary Lightner collection, Lee Library.

**XVII. carriage mishap:** EBWj, see also May 17, 22; HMWj, May 17, 1890. **June:** June 3, 1890, ZDYj. On November 29, Presendia was not bedridden, for Helen Mar Whitney met her and Zina at the *Woman's Exponent* office, HMWj. **hurts hip Oct. 2:** ZDYj, Apr. 2, 1891. **final illness:** Wells, "Death." **death:** HMWj, Feb. 1, 1892; Wells, "Death." EBWj, Jan. 20 - Feb. 3, 1892; for the funeral, see DEN 25 (Feb. 3, 1892): p. 8. For erysipelas, see Ralph Richards, *Of Medicine, Hospitals and Doctors* (Salt Lake City: University of Utah Press, 1953), 21, as cited in Smart 128. **Zina on Presendia's death:** Zina Young to J.D. Huntington, Mar. 1, 1892, Zina Card collection, CA. **funeral:** OHj 17:105. **"high and noble mind":** OHj 11, pages unnumbered, about 67.

# REFERENCES TO CHAPTER 6.
## *Levirate Marriage:*
## *Agnes Moulton Coolbrith (Smith Smith Smith Pickett)*

Cook, Ina Lillian. "Ina Donna Coolbrith." *Westward* 1 (May 1928): 3-5.

Coolbrith, Ina. Letter to Mrs. Ina L. Cook, Mar. 17, 1914, in possession of Ina Graham, Berkeley, California. As cited in ICLL.

Francoeur, Jeanne E. "Ina Coolbrith, Our Poet, in the Past and Present." *Woman Citizen* 1 (1913): 106-107. An interview with Ina.

Graham, Ina Agnes. "My Aunt, Ina Coolbrith." *Pacific Historian* 17 (Fall 1973): 12-19.

ICLL: see Rhodehamel and Wood, *Ina Coolbrith*.

ICP: see Morgan.

Lichtenberg, Paula. "Ina D. Coolbrith, Librarian & Poet." *Women Library Workers* 4 (Aug. 1976): 8-9.

Morgan, Mildred Pearce. "Ina Coolbrith, Poet Laureate of California." HTW 11:262-65.

Rhodehamel, Josephine DeWitt, and Raymund Francis Wood. *Ina Coolbrith, Librarian and Laureate of California*. Provo, UT: Brigham Young University Press, 1973.

Smith, Lucy Mack. *Biographical Sketches of Joseph Smith the Prophet and His Progenitors for Many Generations.* Liverpool, Eng.: S.W. Richards, 1853.

Smith, Ruby. *Mary Bailey.* Salt Lake City: Deseret Book, 1954.

Taylor, Marian. "Ina Coolbrith, California Poet." *Overland Monthly* 64 (Oct. 1914): 327-39.

**Agnes and Lucy, June 27:** Lucy Walker Kimball, "A Brief Biographical Sketch," typescript 7-8, CA (see Lucy Walker chapter).

I. **birth:** Gideon T. Ridlon, *Saco Valley Settlements and Families* (Portland, ME: Ridlon, 1895), 584-90, 586; Ridlon consulted the town record of Saco (near Scarborough). See also Extracted Records, Saco/Scarborough, GS Film 012223, 1755-1875, Batch C503481. However, Agnes frequently gave her birthdate as July 11, 1811, see BOP #109; Don Carlos Smith genealogy record, CA 1024. In December 1861, in the Carsley divorce case (see below), Agnes gave her age as fifty-one, which gives us 1810 as a birthdate. For evaluation of the variants, see ICLL 407-8. The 1808 date is preferable because it preserves the normal year and a half space between children in the Coolbrith family. With the 1811 birthdate, the next child, Robert, would have been born barely nine months later, which is possible, but not usual in nineteenth-century American families. (Compare the birth dates of nearly all the other families in this book.) Possibly Agnes gave the later birth date because she felt self-conscious about the age disparity between herself and Don Carlos Smith. **family:** Ridlon SVS; ICLL 7. DAR of California, *Collections* 17:101; *First Book of Records of the Town of Pepperellborough, now the City of Saco* (GS 12,243), 19. **Joseph Coolbrith (or Coolbroth):** was born on December 22 [or 21], 1780 in Scarborough. See Ridlon, SV and GS film 012,223. **Mary Hasty Foss:** was born on December 12, 1782 in Scarborough. See IGI. Variant: Dec. 23, 1783, GS film 012223. **siblings with birth dates:** Charlotte, November 22, 1803; Catherine, February 22, 1806 [1805]; Benjamin, January 8, 1810; Robert, April 6, 1812; Mary F., February 14, 1815; Joseph, October 30, 1822; Elmira, September 2, 1824. See Ridlon SV; FGS.

II. **Book of Mormon:** ICLL 8. **Orson and Samuel:** Orson Hyde journal, typescript in USHS; Samuel Smith journal, typescript at Lee Library; original in CA. **Mary's baptism:** ICLL 8-9; Smith, MB 28. **Augusta's baptism:** Samuel Smith journal. **Agnes's baptism:** Orson Hyde journal; Samuel Smith journal. Compare Smith, MB 45. **Joseph in Boston:** HC 1:95; Hill, JS 151.

III. **to Kirtland:** Don Carlos Smith, "Obituary," TS 2 (Feb. 15, 1841): 324-5; ICLL 9; Smith, MB 10, 32. **boarded with Smiths:** Lucy Mack Smith, BS 203. **September:** JSj, Sept. 4, Jessee, PW 295. **Mary marries Samuel:** Cook, RP 34, compare MB 36-41. **marriage:** Geauga Co. Marriages, as cited in Backman, *Profile* 119. **Don Carlos:** Smith, MB 45. Cook, RP 274-75. **Mary in dangerous delivery:** Jessee 2:55. **Don preaches:** Jessee 2:131. **Don high priest:** Jessee 2:140-42. **Jan. 22:** Jessee 2:160. **brotherly pride:** JSj, Jan. 28, Jessee 2:164. **Feb. 6:** Jessee 2:170. **letter to Agnes:** quoted in Lucy Mack Smith, BS 289; MB 56. **Agnes Charlotte:** birth date, see Ina Lillian Cook (a daughter of Agnes Charlotte), IDC 3; Don Carlos Smith genealogy record, CA. She married William Peterson, and died in 1874. **New Portage:** Cook, RP 275. **Norton:** ICLL 12; Smith, MB 64. **Sophronia:** Date of birth from Smith genealogy record; ICLL 12 has April 23; FGS has May 24; compare Letter of Don Carlos to Joseph Smith, in Smith, MB 65; HC 3:443. **leaves Norton:** Letter quoted below; ICLL 12. **letter from Indiana:** Jessee 2:252-53. Thills are "shafts between which a single animal is harnessed," Jessee. However, in the ms. the word is "fills."

IV. **arrival:** ICLL 13. **Bailey's house burnt:** ICLL 13; Smith, MB 70; AF. **Don's mission:** Lucy Mack Smith, BS 283; ICLL 14; HC 3:84-85. Don Carlos traveled 1,500 miles and walked 900 miles, Smith, MB 78. **house burned:** Court testimony of Hyrum Smith, in HC 3:408; compare 163-64; Ina Lillian Cook, the daughter of Agnes Charlotte, remembers her grandmother telling her of this event (though Ina Lillian mistakenly places it in Nauvoo). "I have heard her tell of a night of snow and sleet in Nauvoo [Missouri] when the Mormons, she with her two babes among them ... were driven from their homes, and their houses set afire; driven out without coat or cloak, men, women, and the little children, the sick and disabled, to the riverside and cast adrift." IDC 3, compare ICP 263. Joseph F. Smith, Agnes's nephew, also told the story, "Boyhood Recollections of President Smith," UGHM 7 (1916): 53-69, 54. **letter:** Don Carlos Smith to Agnes Smith, Oct. 23, 1838, in CA. **Don Carlos traveling 100 miles:** Smith, MB 78. **one team for Illinois:** MB 79. ME 79. **they find shelter:** Lucy Mack Smith, BS 255-56. For the exodus from Missouri, see William Hartley, "Almost Too Intolerable a Burden: The Winter Exodus from Missouri, 1838-39," JMH 18 (1992): 6-40. **at the Mississippi:** Lucy Mack Smith, BS 255-56.

V. **Macomb:** Lucy Mack Smith, BS 290; ICLL 16; HC 3:261. For this location, which had a small group of Mormons, see S. J. Clarke, *History of McDonough County Ill. Its Cities Towns and Villages* (Springfield, IL: D.W. Lusk, 1878), 606-36; 76. **April 11:** Agnes Smith to Hyrum and Joseph Smith, Apr. 11, 1839, as printed in HC 3:314. **Don given a paper:** Jessee 2:362. **damp basement:** Lucy Mack Smith, BS 290. **Don to Agnes:** Quoted in Lucy Mack Smith, BS 369-71. ICLL 22. **move to Nauvoo:** ICLL 19. **Times and Seasons:** ICP 263. **honors:** ICP 263; ICLL 20. **April 6:** WCj, IC 86. **death of Mary:** TS 2 (Feb. 15, 1841): 324-5, "Obituary," written by Don Carlos. Lucy Mack Smith, BS 271. Compare ICLL 20; Smith, MB 87-88. **Don opposes polygamy:** *The Return* 2 (June 1890): 287. **Ina on Don's opposition to polygamy:** Ina Coolbrith, quoted in J. F. Smith to Ina Coolbrith, Apr. 20, 1918, J.F. Smith collection, CA. **Josephine:** Don Carlos Smith genealogy record, CA; ICLL 21. Later known as "Ina Coolbrith," her literary pen-name, she married Robert Carsley, divorced him, and died in 1928, in Berkeley, California, after attaining fame as a poet and librarian, see below. **death of Don:** Lucy Mack Smith, BS 290-91; "Death of General Don Carlos Smith," TS 2 (Aug. 16, 1841): 503-504, including a poem by Eliza Snow. Agnes Charlotte's daughter gave the cause of death as "pneumonia," see Ina Lillian Cook, IDC, 3. **funeral sermon:** Description of the funeral written by Eliza Snow, unpublished apparently, typescript in Don Carlos Smith folder in the Linda King Newell collection, Marriott Library.

VI. **entry in code:** BYj, Jan. 6, 1842. For "was" as an esoteric abbreviation, see Louisa Beaman chapter, at her marriage to Brigham Young in September 1844. Sometimes it was spelled "saw," "sealed and wedded." I am indebted to Tim Rathbone and Bob Fillerup for helping me interpret this coded diary entry, first deciphered by Art de Hoyos. **Joseph's entry:** Jessee 2:352. **marriage to Joseph:** Bennett, HS 256, "Mrs. A**** S****." Bennett is supported by the testimony of a plural wife of William Smith who had lived with Agnes in 1843. Testimony of Mary Ann West in U.S. Circuit Court (8th Circuit) Testimony (1892), Manuscript Transcripts, CA, MS 1160, box 2, folder 2, p. 521, questions 676-679. "Q-State who Agnes Smith was? A-... She was the wife of Don Carlos Smith ... Q-Whose wife was she at the time that you lived with her? A-She was Joseph Smith's wife. Q-Well how do you know that? ... A-She told me herself she was. Her husband she said wished her to marry Joseph and she did so." See also the Relief Society controversy, below, which links the names of Agnes and Joseph before March 1842. **Levirate marriage:** See Deut. 25.5-10; O.J. Baab, "Marriage," in *Interpreters Dictionary of the Bible* (Nashville, KY: Abingdon, 1962) 3:282-83; compare Hardy, SC 213, and the Elvira Cowles chapter. Brigham Young's and Heber C. Kimball's marriages to Joseph's widows can be seen as modified forms of Levirate marriage. **dines with Joseph:** Compare JSj, Jessee 2:353. **living in Aaron's house:** Ebenezer Robinson, "Items of Personal History," *The Return* 2 (Oct. 1890): 346-48. Compare Marinda Johnson chapter.

VII. **Second meeting:** RS Minutes, p. 17; compare ME 108. **3rd meeting:** RS Minutes, p. 22. **Agnes sewing:** "By selling the services or products of their spinning, weaving, or needlework, women could turn their usual domestic occupations into paid work," Cott, *Bonds of Womanhood* 27. Compare Susan Burrows Swan, *Plain and Fancy: American Women and Their Needlework, 1700-1850* (New York: Holt, Rinehart and Winston, 1977); Ulrich, GW 29. See the Hannah Ells and Partridge sister chapters. Joseph Smith's Red Brick Store daybook shows Agnes buying "Bonnet Silk," gloves, combs, "Check," "Ribband," "Foundation," "paper Pins" and many yards of calico. Launius, *Red Brick Store*

67. **April 2 statement:** See RS Minutes, 18th meeting, Sept. 28, 1842, p. 89. **Mary Ann West:** See under marriage to Joseph, above. **Sophronia dies:** Don Carlos Smith genealogy record, in a later hand; Lucy Mack Smith, BS 275; compare ICLL 22. For scarlet fever in early America, see Ulrich, *A Midwife's Tale* 44-45. **endowment:** Quinn, MHOP 498; Ehat, JSI 107. **July 4:** ZDYj.

VIII. *Times and Seasons:* Ina Coolbrith, quoted in J. F. Smith to Ina Coolbrith, Apr. 20, 1918, though Ina misremembered the name of the magazine. "Mother went to work in the office of the Millennial Star after the murder." On December 7, 1845, Heber C. Kimball included Agnes in a list of seven present in the Holy Order who had not received their fullness of the priesthood ordinances. HCKj, OPW 164. **endowment:** NTER. **Dinner:** WCj, IC 202. **Dec. 13:** HCKj (Clayton), BK 93; just before Rules of Order. **Dec. 14:** HCKj (Clayton), Bk 93. **Dec. 15:** HCKj, Clayton, Bk 93, page before Dec. 16. **Dec. 20:** HCKj (Clayton), Bk 93. **altar:** HCKj, Clayton, Bk 93, at Jan. 6. **marriage to George A. Smith:** BOP #109; SAd 501, 521. **George A. Smith:** See Cook, RP 275; Quinn, MHOP 581-82; Merlo J. Pusey, *Builders of the Kingdom* (Provo, UT: Brigham Young University Press, 1981); Zora Smith Jarvis, *Ancestry, Biography and Family of George A. Smith* (Provo, UT: Brigham Young University Press, 1962). For his wives, compare SAd 501, 521. **Agnes abandoned:** Ina Coolbrith, quoted in J.F. Smith to Ina Coolbrith, Apr. 20, 1918. Compare JH, Sept. 11, 1846: "Pres. B. Young directed that the following persons be sent {"for," later hand} to Nauvoo, or intermediate points": "Agnes M. Smith" is on the list. **letter, June 3:** Agnes to George A. Smith, June 3, 1846, in George A. Smith collection, MS 1322, box 4, fd 16, CA. For Emma's experiences as the main body of Mormons left see ME 228-29. **Bullock journal:** Gregory Knight, ed., "Journal of Thomas Bullock," BYUSt 31 (Winter 1991): 15-76, 66. **Nov. 4:** Agnes Smith to George A. Smith, Nov. 4, 1846, in George A. Smith collection, CA, MS 1322, box 4, fd 16.

IX. **marriage:** ICLL 25, n. 19. According to Coolbrith descendants, who apparently did not know that William was in fact a Mormon in St. Louis, he made Agnes promise to leave her Mormon past behind forever at this juncture, 1953 interview with Jesse Winter Smith, as cited in ICLL 26 n. 20. Compare Ina Lillian Cook, IDC 3. But Agnes's Mormon background was not a secret until Ina Coolbrith became well known in northern California, and Pickett's conversion to Mormonism is documented in the Horace Whitney journal as taking place before September 7, 1846: "A gentleman by the name of Pickett came on with Bro. B. He joined the church since we left Nauvoo, and has taken quite a conspicuous part in the affairs of that place within a few months past, which have transpired between the New Citizens and the Old, or, what amounts to the same thing, between the Mormon and Anti-Mormons." On September 9, Whitney added, "Mr. Pickett did not go back with Bro. B. - he intends remaining with us and going over the mountains with us in the spring." CA, MS 1616. Pickett's Mormonness is confirmed by the letter to Brigham Young, see below. **twins:** ICLL 27, 403. Graham, "My Aunt," p. 16. William Jr. married Margaret Hayes and Josephine Hayes and died in 1931, while Don Carlos Pickett apparently never married and died in 1928. **letter to Brigham:** William Pickett to Brigham Young, Dec. 27, 1847, p. 6, in Brigham Young collection, MS 1234, CA, box 19, fd 8. **on the Mandan:** JH, Apr. 11, 1848. **Pickett to California, 1849:** Ina Coolbrith to Cook, Mar. 17, 1914, as cited in ICLL 410 n. 27. He probably passed through Utah on his way west, and called on Brigham Young, for Young listed him as an authorized delegate of Utah at the California Constitutional Convention, Edward Leo Lyman, response to my paper on Agnes, Sunstone West, Mar. 1994, 2. Ina, in the Mar. 17 letter, gave fall 1851 as the date of Pickett's return.

X. **date of departure:** A thorny tangle of contradictory historical evidence surrounds this date. Rhodehamel and Wood take as their firm point of reference the presence of the Picketts in the Beckwourth Pass in autumn 1851. However, Ina herself gave spring 1852 as the date of migration to California, Coolbrith to Cook, Mar. 17, 1914, as cited in ICLL 410 n. 27; see also Ina L. Cook, IDC 4. Rhodehamel and Wood conclude that Ina

Coolbrith simply confused the year, and they reject the tradition that the Picketts spent time in Utah on the way to California. However, new, apparently reliable evidence (see below) places William Pickett in Utah in spring 1852, and presumably Agnes and the children were with him. Unless the Picketts went to California, then returned to Utah (which is unlikely), the 1852 date—which Ina herself preferred—is correct. This leaves a problem. If the Beckwourth Pass was certainly opened up in autumn 1851 (as Beck-wourth's ghost-written autobiography seems to date it), then Ina was not the first pioneer girl to cross it. In one account Ina said that she met Beckwourth in Salt Lake City, not Nevada. Oakland *Tribune* (Mar. 2, 1924), as cited in ICLL 411. **October 11:** JH. Compare Ina Coolbrith to Adele T. Jones, Dec. 28, 1914, in the Adele Terrill De Casseres collection, CA. **February 13, 1852:** HStj, OMF 2:423. **Pickett in Utah:** See HStj Mar. 6 (Pickett had been elected or appointed Code Commissioner of Utah, but resigned), OMF 2:431; Mar. 11, OMF 2:432; Mar. 15, OMF 2:432; Mar. 18, OMF 2:433. JH Mar. 11, 1852: "William ... employed five lawyers Culver, Picket, Blair Phelps and Stout." **Agnes Charlotte on Utah:** Carolyn Barnes Crosby diary, Nov. 12, 1857, USHS. I am indebted to Leo Lyman for this reference.

XI. **fording the Truckee River:** Taylor, IC 329. **Beckwourth pass:** As mentioned above, the 1852 date for Agnes crossing this pass is problematic. Either the first wagons crossed the Beckwourth Pass in late summer 1852, not summer 1851 (as Beckwourth seems to date the event), or Agnes and Ina were not in the first wagon train to cross the path, despite Ina's definite statements to the contrary. The traditional version is given here. See Taylor, IC 219; Mildred Hoover, *Historic Spots in California*, 3rd ed. rev. (Stanford, CA: Stanford University Press, 1966), 279, a long quotation from a speech given by Ina on April 24, 1927. "When we made that long journey toward the West ... our wagon-train was driven over ground without a single mark of a wagon wheel until it was broken by ours. And when Jim Beckwourth said he would like to have my mother's little girls ride into California on his horse in front of him, I was the happiest little girl in the world ... This wagon train arrived in California in September, 1852." Compare *Oroville Mercury Register* (Aug. 13, 1939); *Oakland Tribune* (Mar. 2, 1924), both cited in ICLL 411; George Wharton James, *Heroes of California* (Boston: Little, Brown, 1910), 111-12. For James Beckwourth, see his *Life and Adventures*, as told to Thomas D. Bonner (Lincoln: University of Nebraska Press, 1972), 518-19, 598; Elinor Wilson, *Jim Beckwourth* (Norman, OK: University of Oklahoma Press, 1972), 136; May Dornin, "The Emigrant Trails into California," Master's thesis, University of California, Berkeley, 1921, 165-69; George Stewart, *The California Trail* (New York: McGraw-Hill, 1962), 302-303. Compare *Illustrated History of Plumas, Lassen & Sierra Counties* (San Francisco: Fariss & Smith, 1882; repr. 1971), 258-59. **Spanish ranch:** For the arrival in September, see the interview with Ina in Hoover, HS 137-38; ICLL 42. Ina also gave July 4, 1852 as the date of arrival at Spanish ranch, Mar. 17 letter to Ina Lillian Cook, see above. **Spanish Ranch to Marysville:** Taylor, IC 329-30; for the quotation from Ina, see Francoeur, ICOP, an interview with Ina; ICLL 43-44. **in Marysville:** Cook, IDC 4; Taylor, IC 330; Francoeur, ICOP; ICLL 45. For general background on Marysville, see William Henry Chamberlain, *History of Yuba County, California* (Oakland, CA: Thompson and West, 1879), 44-46. For mining towns, see Joseph H. Jackson, *Anybody's Gold; The Story of California's Mining Towns* (San Francisco: Chronicle, 1970). For women in mining towns, see Ruth B. Moynihan, Susan Armitage, and Christiane Fischer Dichamp, eds., *So Much To Be Done, Women Settlers on the Mining and Ranching Frontier* (Lincoln: University of Nebraska Press, 1990); Jeffrey, *Frontier Women* 107-46. Because of the chronological difficulty mentioned above, some of the dates in this section may be off by a year, though I have tried to adjust them to the 1852 date for crossing Beckwourth Pass. **flooding quote:** Francoeur, ICOP. **sews:** Coolbrith to Cook, Mar. 17, 1914; quoted in ICLL 45. **Thompson:** Francoeur, ICOP. **near the claim:** ICLL 45. See the sources listed above. **lost children:** ICLL 46-47. **winter of 1852:** ICLL 47. **to San Francisco:** Cook, IDC 4; Taylor, IC 330; Francoeur, ICOP; ICLL 48-49. **Rockwell:** Letter of Elizabeth D. E. Roundy, CA, reporting an interview with Rockwell, as cited in Harold Schindler, *Orrin Porter Rockwell* (Salt Lake City: University of Utah Press, 1983), 224. **Joseph F. visits:** Joseph F. Smith to Ina Coolbrith, Apr. 20, 1918, Joseph F. Smith papers, CA.

**XII. to Los Angeles:** Taylor 330; Ina Lillian Cook, IDC, 4; Coolbrith to Cook, Mar. 17, 1914, as cited in ICLL 412. ICLL 51-53. **rhymes homework:** Cook, IDC 4; Taylor, IC 330-31; ICLL 57. This is a striking parallel to the young Eliza R. Snow (see her chapter, at her childhood), who had been a sister wife of Agnes in Nauvoo, and who wrote a funeral tribute to Don Carlos Smith. Possibly Ina met the charismatic Eliza in Utah. **ball:** Taylor, IC 330; Morgan, ICP 262; ICLL 136, n. 40. **first poem:** "My Childhood's Home," L.A. *Star* (Aug. 30, 1856): p. 1; Taylor, IC 330; ICLL 58. The second poem Ina published, "Ally," is in the Nov. 8, 1856, *Star*, p. 1. **Ina to Joseph F.,** Mar. 19, 1857, Joseph F. Smith papers, CA. **visits to San Bernardino:** Diary of Carolyn Barnes Crosby, USHS. Agnes was also friendly with Carolyn's sister, Louisa Barnes Pratt, see her diary, Oct. 21, 1856, "We at length made our way by coach to Los Angeles. We stopped with Mrs. Picket and her two interesting daughters." Kate Carter, ed., *Mormondom's First Woman Missionary, Louisa Barnes Pratt* ([Salt Lake City]: Limited edition, n.d.), 313. See also June 12, 1857, p. 322: "The Stage came in from Los Angeles and Mrs. Picket was aboard going to San Bernardino; and oh, we wished so much to go with her." For Mormons in early San Bernardino, see Lyman, SB. **July 22:** Josephine Smith (Ina Coolbrith) and Agnes Pickett to Joseph F. Smith, July 22, 1857, Joseph F. Smith papers, CA. **early 1858:** ICLL 54, 60. Leo Lyman writes that William Pickett became a leading "anti-Mormon" after he moved to San Bernardino, SB 406, compare 353. However, Pickett was "a good lawyer" and brought to the city its first substantial law library, *Ingersoll's Century Annals of San Bernardino County 1769 to 1904* (Los Angeles: Ingersoll, 1904), 304. **Agnes stays in California:** J. F. Smith to Ina Coolbrith, Apr. 20, 1918. For a contact between the Picketts and a Mormon during this period, see Augusta Joyce Crocheron, "California Memories," *The Contributor* 7 (Nov. 1885): 54. **Agnes Charlotte and Ina married:** ICLL 61. L.A. *Star* 7 (Apr. 24, 1858): p. 2: "MARRIED - At San Gabriel, April 21st by Rev. T.O. Ellis at the residence of Mr. D.F. Hall, Mr. Robert B. Carsley to Miss Josephine Smith, all of Los Angeles." **first grandchild:** ICLL 68. **William Jr. injured:** "SHOOTING ACCIDENTS," L.A. *Star* 9 (Feb. 18, 1860): p. 2. **April:** ICLL 68. **July 11, 1861:** This poem was published in *California Home Journal*, but we have no further bibliographic data; see ICLL 66.

**XIII. Carsley attacks Ina and Agnes:** L.A. District Court, Case #853 (Dec. 30, 1861), Josephine Carsley v. Robert B. Carsley. This was written in the peculiar script of a court recorder, and is often difficult to read. Compare L.A. *Star* 11 (Oct. 19, 1861): p. 2: "WOUNDED. On Saturday evening last, a difficulty arose between Messrs. Pickett and Carsley, arising out of matters of a private character, in which the latter was wounded in the hand causing the necessity of amputation. He is under the medical care of Dr. Griffin, and is progressing favorably." See also ICLL 69-70. **Nov. 28:** "BIRTH," L.A. *Star* (Nov. 30, 1861): p. 2. **divorce begun:** Case #853, compare ICLL 71. **Ina's child:** ICLL 73.

**XIV. arrival:** "Unrest," datelined San Francisco, Sept. 1862, printed, with no title, in L.A. *Star* 12 (Nov. 22, 1862): p. 2; ICLL 415. **activities of family:** Ina Coolbrith, letter to niece, Mar. 17, 1914; further bibliography in ICLL 416 n. 13; 81. **May 1868:** ICLL 120-21.

**XV. 1870:** WWj, Sept. 16, 1872 (7:84); ICLL 125. According to Joseph III, William had died in Oregon by 1889, see Joseph Smith III, *Joseph Smith III and the Restoration*, 412. **February 22, 1871:** "Records of the Families of California Pioneers," typescript, DAR of California, *Collections* 17: 101-2; ICLL 120-21. **Ina and her bohemian friends:** See ICLL, Chapter 12, "The Bohemian Club." **Calle Shasta:** ICLL 120. In 1875 Miller wrote *First Families of the Sierras*, a book about Mormon assassins, or Danites, which would later become adapted for the stage as *Paint Your Wagon*. **Agnes Charlotte sick:** ICLL 120-21. **journey to SF:** ICLL 122; interview with Ina Cook Graham, as the story was told by her mother. **death of Agnes Charlotte:** *San Francisco Bulletin*, Jan. 21 and Feb. 2, 1874; DAR 101; as cited in ICLL 122. **"At the time":** Ina to Bio, no date. Adele Terrill De Casseres collection, CA. **Ina Coolbrith as librarian:** See Taylor, IC 334; ICLL, Part Three, "The Librarian." **twins gone:** ICLL 125. **One twin drinks heavily:** *Joseph Smith III and the Restoration* 412. **Johnny Muir, matchmaker:** ICLL 134. "She [Ina] was known to have had many suitors, and it was equally well known that she rejected them all," ICLL 136. Perhaps the traumatic divorce from Carsley was a wound from which Ina never recovered.

**XVI.** **Christmas:** Ina Coolbrith to Mrs. Benton, Dec. 21, 1874, in Coolbrith Papers, California State Library, as cited in ICLL 136. **David and Alexander visit:** Lucy W. Kimball to Joseph F. Smith, Feb. 24, 1884, in Franklin R. Smith collection, CA, MS 13700 fd 2. Joseph Smith III, who visited Ina in 1889 and 1907, remembers her as sympathetic to his anti-polygamy stance. *Joseph Smith III and the Restoration*, 412. One doubts that Agnes even told Ina of her marriage to Joseph Smith.

**VII.** **death:** DAR of California, *Collections*, 1953, 17:101; ICLL 141-42, 370, 407. **last words:** J.F. Smith to Ina Coolbrith, Apr. 20, 1918, CA. **Hill's research:** Hill, QFR 69-98. **Ina misses Agnes:** Lucy W. Kimball to Joseph F. Smith, Nov. 18, 1883, in Franklin R. Smith collection, CA, MS 13700 fd 2. Ina Coolbrith to Grenville Pettis, Oct. 2, 1907, Huntington Library.

# REFERENCES TO CHAPTER 7.
*Mother And Daughter:*
*Patty Bartlett (Sessions Smith Parry)* and
*Sylvia Porter Sessions (Lyon Smith Kimball Clark)*

**PATTY BARTLETT:**
Carter, Kate. OPH 2:58, 4:157.
Noall, Claire. *Guardians of the Hearth: Utah's Pioneer Midwives and Women Doctors.* Bountiful, UT: Horizon Publishers, 1974. 22-51.
———. "Mormon Midwives," UHQ 10 (1942): 84-144.
PGSj: Diary of Perrigrine Sessions.
Rugh, Susan Sessions. "Patty Bartlett Sessions: More than a Midwife." In Vicky Burgess-Olson, ed. *Sister Saints.* Provo, UT: Brigham Young University Press, 1978. 303-24.
Sessions, Patty. Diaries, CA. See now the edition by Smart.
Sessions, Perrigrine. *The Diaries of Perrigrine Sessions.* Bountiful, UT: Carr Printing Co, 1967.
Smart, Donna Toland. *Mormon Midwife, The 1846-1888 Diaries of Patty Bartlett Sessions.* Logan: Utah State University Press, 1997.
[Wells, Emmeline]. "Patty Sessions." *Women's Exponent* 13 (Sept. 1, 1884): 51; (Sept. 15, 1884): 63; (Nov. 1, 1884): 86; (Nov. 15, 1884): 94-95. Wells often uses Patty's early journals, not extant in any other form.

**SYLVIA SESSIONS:**
[Carter, Kate]. OPH 10:415.
Easton [Black], Susan Ward, cp. *Inscriptions Found on Tombstones and Monuments in Early Latter-day Saint Burial Grounds.* (n.p. 1979).
Esshom. *Pioneers and Prominent Men of Utah.* 873, 1153.
Fisher, Josephine E. "Josephine Rosetta Lyon Fisher." Typescript, CA.
———. "Josephine Rosetta Lyon Fisher—Her Parentage." Feb. 1954, typescript, CA.
Jenson, Andrew. Index to HR, vols. 5-8, p. 995.
Kimball, Stanley. HCK. 313.
Wills, Sylvia C. "Sylvia Porter Sessions Lyon Clark." D.U.P. biography, 9 pages typescript.

**first delivery:** Wells, PS 51. For Patty as midwife, see Noall, *Guardians of the Hearth* 22-51. **midwife practice in Maine:** Wells, PS 63. **3,977 babies:** OPH 6:426. **the midwife in early America:** See especially Ulrich, *A Midwife's Tale*, also Judy Barrett Litoff, "Midwives and History," in Rima Apple, ed., *Women, Health and Medicine in America* (New York: Garland, 1990); id., *American Midwives: 1860 to the Present* (Westport, CT: Greenwood Press, 1978). For Mormon midwives, Noall, *Guardians of the Hearth*. Compare the Zina and Presendia Huntington chapters. Vienna Jacques, one of the "possible wives" (see Prologue, chart), was also a midwife, Claire Noall to Fawn Brodie, Sept. 16, 1943, in Noall papers, MS 188, Marriott Library, box 2, fd 11; PBSj, Feb. 9, 1853. Mary Ann Frost Pratt, one of the "posthumous" wives of Smith, was also a midwife. **mother and daughter pair:** Compare the Flora Woodworth chapter, and Mary Ann Angell, her sister Jemima Angell, and their mother Phebe Ann Morton Angell, all of whom married Brigham Young, Johnson DDW.

I. **Patty's birth date:** PBSj, Feb. 4, 1847, and in other years. The first source for all the genealogical information in this section is PBSj, Nov. 24, 1884 (Smart, MM 355). Some maps give her birthplace as Newry, Smart, MM 3. **Enoch:** was born on September 15, 1741, in Newton, Middlesex, Massachusetts. **(Martha) Anna Hall:** was born on April 28, 1768, and died on August 27, 1868. IGI has the birthdate as April 20 or 27, 1765. **Enoch's first family:** Compare PGSj, B-2; B-4. Patty's half siblings were Anna (Foster), Reuben, Relief (Estes), Remit [Submit] (Powers), Thankful (Stevens), Betsey (Estes), Burrah (Colby), Olive (Frost), Lucy (Powers), and one male child who died as an infant. **Patty's full siblings:** PGSj, B3-4. *Elisha[m]* (b. Dec. 7, 1796) married Sally Barker in 1817, and died in 1874. *Na[a]mah Hall* (b. Oct. 13, 1798) married William Tripp, and died in 1875. *Jonathan* (b. July 31, 1800) married Nancy Barker and Tryphena Horr, and died in 1866. *Polly* (b. May 8, 1802) married Willoby Russell and Urburn York, and died in 1868. *Ap[p]hia* (b. Apr. 28, 1804) married Josiah Jackson. *Lydia* (b. Nov. 15, 1806) married Joseph Knapp. *Lavinia/Lorania* (b. July 29, 1808) died at the age of two. *Enoch Jr.* (b. June 5, 1811) married Sarah Hinkson and died in 1897. **move to Newry:** PGSj, B-3. **Enoch:** PGSj, B-4. **Patty works in fields:** Wells, PS 51. **Patty's mother:** PBSj, June 24, 1863. For the ethics of work in nineteenth-century America, see the Rhoda Richards chapter. **Patty attends school:** Wells, PS 51.

II. **marriage:** Wells, PS 51. AF has June 13. **Ketcham:** PGSj, B-4. Wells, PS 51. **move to own farm:** PBSj, quoted in Wells, PS 51; also PGSj, B-4. **loom:** Wells, PS 51. **sugar:** Wells, PS 51. **Perrigrine:** See PGSj. He would become a stalwart Mormon, with a large polygamous family. He married Julia Ann Kilgore in 1834, then, after polygamy was introduced in Nauvoo, united with some eight other women: Mary Call, Lucina Call, Fanny Emmorett Loveland, Sarah Crossley, Elizabeth Birdenow, Sarah Ann Bryson, and Esther Mabey. He died in 1893 in Bountiful, Utah. **new farm:** PGSj, B-5. **Sylvanus:** B-5-6 gives the birthdate. **Patty a Methodist:** PGSj, B-6. **David converts to Methodism:** PGSj, B-6. **Sylvia:** PGSj, B-6. **Anna B.:** PSj, B-6. **new house:** PGSj, B-6. **arm out of joint:** Wells, PS 63. **David Jr.:** PGSj, B-6. He married Phebe Carter Foss in 1852 (PBSj, Dec. 30), and died in 1896 in Bountiful, Utah. **Sylvia and David close:** Fisher, "Parentage," 4. **Anna's death:** PGSj, B-6. **Father Sessions dies:** PGSj, B-6. Wells, PS 63. **Anna the second:** PGSj, b-6. **Father Bartlett dies:** PGSj, B-3, B-6. **Bartlett's birth and death:** B-6. **1832 sickness:** PGSj, B-7.

III. **first missionaries:** PGSj, B-7. Wills, SPS 1 gives the names as Hazen Aldridge and Harris Cowen. **baptism of Patty:** PGSj, B-7. PBSj, page just after June 16, 1860. **persecution:** PGSj, B-8. **branch:** PGSj, B-9. **Perrigrine marries:** PGSj, B-8. **meeting on August 12:** PGSj, B-9. **David baptized:** AF. **Perrigrine baptized:** Edward Partridge journal, CA 4881: "we were asked by a young man with tears in his eyes if we would go to the water and baptize him, we repaired to the water & baptized him, his name was Perrigreen Sessions." PGSj, B-8 gives September 17 as the baptismal date. **first grandchild:** PGSj, B-8.

IV. **trip to Kirtland:** PGSj, B-9-11. **trip to Missouri:** PGSj, B-11. Her obituary gives the date of 1836. **settling in Missouri:** PGSj, B-12. Patty's obituaries (see below) give the date of arrival as November 28, 1836. The farm cost $1,200, according to the obituary. On January 7, 1838, Patty, Perrigrine, Julia, and Sylvia received patriarchal blessings under the hand of Isaac Morley, PBI. **Amanda:** Date from Fisher, "Parentage." **Jan. 7:** Wells, PS 86.

V. **Date of marriage:** PBSj, in Wells, PS 86. **Windsor's birthdate:** NTER. **Aaron Lyon baptized:** Reynolds Cahoon journal, "on Monday ... Baptised Mr Lion ..." In a curious development, on April 28, 1838, a week after Sylvia's marriage to Windsor, Aaron Lyon was stripped of his priesthood for attempting to marry a woman who was already married. HC 3:25-26; FWR 183-85, compare 206-207, 275. **Windsor speaks in tongues:** Joseph Holbrooks diary. See also Zebedee Coltrin journal, Apr. 17, 1833, CA. **Windsor and Aaron to Kirtland:** Evan Green's diary, at June 28, 1833; Joseph Holbrook diary. Evidently, Windsor had a store in Willoughby, see HC 2:205. (William = Windsor, apparently.) **Windsor owns property in Salemtown:** Caldwell County Land Records, Original Land Patents, Kingston, Missouri, as cited in Nauvoo Project Report on Windsor Lyon, CA, n. 5. **army physician:** OPH 10:415. "Windsor Lyon was a mail-order diploma doctor and a veteran Army officer and was obviously familiar with treating wounds and setting bones ... he had a wide selection of herbs and pain-killers," Richard Christenson wrote to James Kimball, Nov. 18, 1976, in Nauvoo Project files. For Windsor serving as a doctor in Nauvoo in 1840, see Benjamin F. Wooley Statement, cited in the report on Windsor, Nauvoo Project, n. 11. In the army he was given the title of "Colonel," ibid. Fisher writes that "Josephine treasured the fringe gilt epauletts he wore on his army coat." "Parentage," 4. **flight from Missouri:** PGSj, B-15-16. Wells, PS 63, 86. For the extensive property the Sessionses lost in Missouri, see Clark Johnson, *Mormon Redress Petitions* (Provo, UT: BYU Religious Studies Center, 1992), 335-36. Compare Agnes Coolbrith chapter, Missouri section.

VI. **arrival in Illinois:** Wells, PS 63, 86. **people of Illinois kind:** PGSj, B-17. **Perrigrine on mission:** Wells, PS 86. **Windsor's store:** OPH 10:415; the store was on Hotchkiss St. and Main St. See Holzapfel, *Old Mormon Nauvoo* 111-12; Thomas Bullock journal, CA, Sept. 5, 1845. The researchers in the Nauvoo Project conclude that there were two Lyon stores, see J. Terry Walker and Richard Stamps, "Archaeological Investigations at the Lyon House and Store, Nauvoo, Illinois, 1980," a Nauvoo Restoration report, Oct. 1980, 28, but they were built close to each other. See also report on Windsor Lyon, Nauvoo Project, for further background on Lyons as merchant and frontier stores. In June and September 1840 Joseph and his business partners sold lots to "Sylvia P. Lyon," Nauvoo land records, Nauvoo Project. In the following years lots were bought and sold to Perrigrine Sessions, other Sessionses, and Joseph Smith. Two lots were on the northwest corner of lot 2, block 108. Lyon's first store was a wood cabin; the second, built in 1843, was a much larger brick store, with a home connected. **Marian:** FGS. Nauvoo Project notes. **May 2:** Wells, PS 86. **Perrigrine's return:** PGSj, B-27-28. **new homes:** OPH 10:415. **Patty and David in a new home:** Wells, PS 86. **Amanda dies:** Wells, PS 86. **Carlos:** Carlos may have acted as front to protect Windsor in bankruptcy proceedings. Carlos's tax assessment, 1842, shows him having the largest stock in trade of any Nauvoo merchant, $500. See Report on Windsor, p. 3. There was an odd lawsuit: W. Lyon v. Sidney Knowlton for use of Carlos W. Lyon, see Nauvoo Project. The ad for Lyon's store is in TS, May 1, 1841 to June 1: "N.B. Those indebted to me either by note or account, will please call at my store and pay them up on or before the 16th day of June next or I shall leave them for collection without respect of persons." **Philofreen:** *Nauvoo Neighbor* obituary, below.

VII. **Sylvia marries Joseph:** The date is from an 1869 affidavit (SAB, CA, MS 3423, fd 5; 1:60, 4:62, Bachman #77). This affidavit is unfinished, see Bachman 108 n. 10; one possible interpretation of an unfinished affidavit is that the woman gave the information about her marriage to church authorities, but was unwilling to publicly admit it. Jenson (HR 6:234; Index to Vols. 5-9, p. 995) also lists Sylvia as a plural wife of Joseph, without giving a date for the marriage. An affidavit by Josephine Lyon Fisher, Sylvia's child, given on February 24, 1915 (CA, MS 3423, fd 1-4), dates the marriage with Joseph "at a time when Lyon was out of fellowship with the church," Bachman 141. This is historically incorrect, as Lyon was a member in good standing when the marriage with Joseph took place; but it might be true for cohabitation with Joseph. Or it may have simply been a revision of history to explain her polyandrous relationship with Joseph. The Fisher affidavit will be considered in greater detail below. See also Angus M. Cannon, statement of interview with Joseph III, CA, pp. 25-26. **Windsor's faithfulness:** He did baptisms for the dead, Book A, 97, 122. In February 1842 he was a juror in a case involving Joseph Smith, see Nauvoo Civil and Criminal Docket Book, Chicago Historical Society; also at Lee Library, as cited in Windsor report, n. 54. **Patty marries Joseph:** PBSj, page after June 16, 1860, Smart, MM 277–as mentioned in the Prologue, this entry was originally written in 1860, presumably. However, the superscript, in Patty's hand, was probably written in 1867 (the ink is identical to that of her 1867 proxy marriage/second anointing sealing notation attached to the page) as a clarification (rather than as a correction). JSj, Jessee 2:367, confirms that Joseph spent part of the day with "the Recorder," Willard Richards. Bennett gives a "Mrs. S*******" in his list of Joseph's wives, HS 256. **no cohabitation with Patty, possibly:** See Prologue, on Joseph's older wives. However, whether Patty was considered an "older" woman at this time might be a matter of interpretation, so it is not impossible that there was a sexual dimension in her marriage to Smith. As Quinn points out, middle-aged women can be attractive and sexually active, MHEP 185. **Patty as help for other marriages:** Patty is a "Mother in Israel" whose duty it was to initiate younger women into the mysteries of plural marriage: Joseph Jackson, *A Narrative* 14, repr. in Joseph Jackson, "Wonderful Disclosures Respecting Mormons," in New York *Herald* 10 (Sept. 5, 1844): p. 1. "Mrs. Tailor, old Madam Durfee and old Madam Sessions" were "Mothers in Israel." Though Jackson can be unreliable, Elizabeth Durfee has been confirmed as an intermediary of Joseph Smith in helping to bring a young woman into his family, see Emily Partridge's autobiography, quoted in her own chapter and in the Elizabeth Davis chapter. WRj, July 10, 1845, links Patty and Elizabeth. **death of Marian:** WJS 106-9; 135. Compare JH, and the tombstone, mentioned in Easton, *Inscriptions*, 6, of "H. Diana" [M. Diana?] who died, aged 2 yrs. 8 months. **Relief Society:** RS Minutes. **donates 50 cents:** RS Min., p. 28. **May 26:** RS Min., p. 50. **Patty gives interpretation:** RS Min., pp. 32-33. Other examples of Patty interpreting glossolalia are found in ERSj, June 18, 1847; PBSj, May 1, 1847; PBSj, June 27, 1847 (an interesting meeting, in which an eleven-year-old speaks in tongues). **June 11:** Wells, PS 86. **visits from Joseph and Willard:** Wells, PS 86. Compare Aug. 29, Wells, PS 94, Patty rejoices to see Joseph ride by after he had hidden for a time. Compare Hill, JS 304-15. **Relief Society and blessing meeting:** Wells, PS 94.

VIII. **bankruptcy notice:** the *Wasp* 1 (Aug. 13, 1842): last page: "District Court of the United States,/ within and for the district of Illinois/ In the matter of the petition of Windsor P. Lyon of Hancock county to be declared a bankrupt and to be discharged from his debts./ Notice is hereby given that Windsor P. Lyon of Hancock county has filed his petition in this Court to be declared a bankrupt and be discharged from his debts under the act of Congress, in such case made and provided; and that an order has been duly entered in this Court appointing the first day of October next, at the District Court Room in the city of Springfield in this District, as the time and place for the hearing of said petition; all persons interested may then and there appear and show cause, if any they have, why the prayer of said petition should not be granted./ Dated this 9th day of July, A.D. 1842/ Raltson, Warren & Wheat/ Solicitors for Petitioner/ Attest: James F. Owings, clerk." **family tradition:** Reported in T. Edgar Lyon to Larry Foster, May 18, 1978, Van Wagoner collection, Marriott library. **Marks accuses Windsor:** Nauvoo High Council minutes, CA and Marquardt collection, Marriott Library. **"cut off":** Nauvoo Ward Census, 1842, 4th Ward, 5th page. **Joseph friendly:** JSj, Jessee 2:492. **David returns:** Wells, PS 95. **Nov. 27:** Wells, PS 95. **Dec. 13:** Wells, PS 95. **Dec. 24:** JSj, Faulring 257. Patty Sessions's journal also dates Asa's death on Dec. 24, Wells, PS 95. **other sources on Asa:** See Nauvoo tombstone, in Easton, *Inscriptions*

6; AF. **Feb. 12:** Wells, PS 95. **"true friend":** Annie Sessions Neville, quoted in Fisher, "Parentage," 4. **Feb. 25:** Wells, PS 95. **April 10:** Wells, PS 95. **Joseph kidnapped:** Wells, PS 95. **Relief Society:** RS Min., 94-95. **end of July:** RS Min., July 28, p. 101. On August 20 Sylvia donated another wheel head, RS Min., 112. **rest of the year:** See Aug. 20, 1843, RS Min., 112; Sept. 2, 1843, RS Min., 113; RS Min., 115; RS Min., 117, 118; Sept. 15, 1843, ["August 15"] RS Min., 120. **Patty prays:** RS Min., 117, 118. **July 29:** Wells, PS 95. See the Olive Frost chapter. Oct. 3: Wells, PS 95. **Sept. 18:** IC 20. **Emily Partridge:** "Autobiography of Emily D.P. Young," WE 14 (Aug. 1, 1885), 38, compare Emily Partridge Young, Autobiography (holograph), Marriott Library, 6, in which the hosting family is not named. **death of Philofreen:** *Nauvoo Neighbor* 1 (41) (Feb. 7, 1844): 3, gives death date as January 27, "aged 2y, 6m, 22d," repr. in "Early Church Vital Records," UGHM 28 (1937): 158, see also the tombstone (Easton, *Inscriptions* 6). Compare a poem of consolation to Sylvia by Eliza Snow, in ERSj, Feb. 17, 1844, "To Mrs. Lyons, on the death of ..." Published as "Obituary," in TS 5 (Mar. 15, 1844): 479. **June 5, 1843:** Sylvia buys another lot from Joseph Smith for $500, Nauvoo Project report on Windsor. In August and December, Windsor bought two Merchant's Licenses.

IX. **Josephine:** Wells, PS 95; FGS. Happily, Josephine would grow to maturity. She married John Fisher, with whom she had ten children, divorced him, and died in 1924 in Salt Lake City. See Fisher, JRLF. **Heber C. Kimball blessing:** Nauvoo Project on Windsor Lyon, citing Bountiful Ward Membership Records. **Fisher affidavit:** Bachman, "A Study," #132; quoted on p. 141. CA, MS 3423, fd 1-4. Angus Cannon, trying to convert Joseph Smith III, mentioned Josephine Lyon as a child of Joseph Smith, see Angus M. Cannon, statement of interview with Joseph III, pp. 25-26, CA, quoted in Prologue. **May 11:** Helen Mar Whitney, SIN WE 11 (Nov. 15, 1882): 90. **Windsor a witness:** WRj, CA.

X. **marriage to Kimball:** BYj. For "saw," compare the Agnes Coolbrith chapter. **Sept. 24:** HC 7:724. **Zina Jacobs:** ZDYj, September 6, 1844; September 10; Nov. 13. **Nov. 13:** ZDYj, compare Nov. 22. **Dec. 20:** WRj, CA. **Julia Ann dies:** PGSj, B-44, B-39. **endowment:** Quinn, MHOP 504. **death of Jenetta:** Willard Richard journal, CA, July 10, 1845. Compare on Presendia Huntington, at the death of Vilate Kimball, October 1867.

XI. **preparations for departure:** PGSj, B-41. **Rosilla:** PBSj, page after June 16, 1860; PBSj, at Jan. 14, 1850 (which gives the year incorrectly). I have not been able to find a Nauvoo temple proxy marriage for Patty, or a sealing to David Sessions of any sort, see BOP and SAd. **Dec. 6:** HCKj, Bk 93, OPW 163. **endowment:** NTER. **Patty as temple worker:** HCKj, Bk 93. Compare Donald Parry, "Washing and Anointing," EM, 1551. **Enoch Tripp arrives in Nauvoo:** Enoch Tripp journal, p. 8, CA. This is a 1951 handwritten copy of the original. **Windsor's rebaptism:** PGSj, B-43. Enoch Tripp journal, p. 9, CA. The language Perrigrine uses shows clearly that this was a rebaptism into the church, not merely a member renewing a covenant. For rebaptism, see Louisa Beaman chapter at May 11, 1843, with notes. Note the different dates for the baptism in the two sources. **sealing to Joseph and Heber in temple:** BOP #92; SAd 369, 505. **knowledge:** OPH 10:415: "with full consent of Dr. Lyon." **February 3:** NTER; Enoch Tripp, CA. **marriage to Gee:** Wills, SPS 5; AF. For the child, see Nauvoo Project report on Lyon, p. 16.

XII. **February 10:** PBSj. **June 22:** PGSj, B45, compare PBSj. **May 30:** PBSj. Windsor had sold his house, PBSj, May 10. **Patty sick:** See PBSj, at Sept. 2. **Rosilla:** PBSj. See also Sept. 11. **David talks with Rosilla:** PBSj, Sept. 25, 29. **"Later in the month":** PBSj, Oct. 24. **"I got but":** PBSj, Nov. 2, 1846. **"He has lain":** PBSj, Nov. 4. **Rosilla departs for Nauvoo:** Patty, at Jan. 14, 1850, gives Dec. 23, 1846 for the date of Rosilla's departure. **Patty lays hands:** PBSj, Mar. 17, 1847; Apr. 1, Apr. 15, May 11. She often lays on hands in conjunction with her husband. Compare ERSj, June 18, 1847. **May 29:** "and" is in the original text. **Perrigrine in Iowa:** PGSj, B49-50. **blessing meetings:** for the women's blessing meetings at Winter Quarters, see Louisa Beaman, Eliza Snow, and Helen Mar Kimball chapters.

**XIII. overland journey:** PBSj; see relevant dates. Compare a brief backward look, PBSj, July 24, 1884. **women's and men's spheres:** As Julie Roy Jeffrey, *Frontier Women*, 39, describes men's and women's roles in American pioneering, men drove the wagons, repaired them, hunted, ferried the cattle and wagons across rivers, and stood guard at night, while women were responsible for the children, meals, and washing. Mormon accounts of the overland journey present nothing radically different from this, though occasionally, as here, women drove wagons. **first winter in Utah:** PGSj, B54. **Patty's duties:** These are taken from the early Utah years of her diaries. **Sixteenth Ward:** obituary.

**XIV. selling lots:** May 5, 1846, Nauvoo Project. **Byron:** date from FGS. **Iowa City Manufacturing:** Charles Ray Aurner, *Leading Events in Johnson County, Iowa History* (Cedar Rapids, IA: Western Historical Press, 1912). This was later sold to Ezekiel Clark. **Windsor in politics:** MSt 35 (Nov. 11, 1873): 715-16, compare Ivins 5:232. **March 3:** JH, Mar. 18, p. 3. **Rogers at Winter Quarters:** JH, Mar. 27, p. 1, 2, 11. **Pickett:** JH, June 11, p. 1. **Windsor dies:** Death notice: "Lyon, Winsor P., Dr., mid-January 1849, at Iowa City, Iowa, of consumption." *Frontier Guardian* (Apr. 4, 1849): as reported in Lyndon Cook, comp., *Death and Marriage Notices from the Frontier Guardian, 1849-1852* (Orem, UT: Center for Research of Mormon Origins, 1990), 13. **Susanne to Utah:** Wills, SPS 5. **Heber reads letter:** ZDYj, July 4, 1849. **Perrigrine to Iowa:** PGSj, B-55-56. **Clark:** AF; Stanley Kimball, HCK, appendix; further details on Clark in Wills, SPS 7. **Patty upset:** PBSj, June 10, 1850. **Perry Clark:** never married and died in 1919.

**XV. Council of Health:** Rugh, PBS 313; Smart, MM 146, 395. Patty attended "medical meeting" occasionally, e.g., PBSj, May 22, 1850. On July 16, 1884, she wrote, "I knew I had been ordained to lay hands on the sick & set apart to do that." For Thomsonian (herbal) medicine, see Louisa Beaman chapter at 1849, also Smart, MM 148. The Thomsonian medical regimen has been summarized as "puke 'em, purge 'em, sweat 'em." **Susan Snow, wife of Willard:** PBSj, Jan. 11, 1849. **Midwives and doctors:** See Ulrich, AMT 254-55. In Utah Brigham Young discouraged the use of doctors, recommending priesthood administration instead, but Mormons, including Brigham, turned to medical practitioners in extreme cases. Willard Richards, a member of the First Presidency, was a Thomsonian doctor. In fact, doctors' practice on the frontier (or elsewhere) was so primitive that their treatments usually did not help the sufferer in any way, except in simple surgical operations such as setting broken bones. **Sister Rhodes:** PBSj, Feb. 9-12, 1853; WWj, Feb. 11 (4:190). Compare, for another difficult childbirth and death, PBSj, Aug. 24, 1853. **boarders:** PBSj, Aug. 7, 1849. Compare Brigham Madsen, *Gold Rush Sojourners in Great Salt Lake City* (Salt Lake City: University of Utah Press, 1983). **David disfellowshipped:** JH, Jan. 7, 14, 1849.

**XVI. David remarries:** Smart, MM 139n; SAd 767, 777. David Session, born on April 4, 1790 in Vershire, Orange, Vermont, is sealed to Harriet Teeples (Wixom) (b. Aug. 14, 1830, in Ponteac, Oakland, Michigan), in Salt Lake City. **calls from women friends:** E.g., Jan. 14 and 15, 1850, PBSj. **Patty tends:** PBSj, August 14, 1850. **David's death:** PGSj, B57. For the subsequent relationship between Harriet and Patty, see PBSj, Oct. 7, 1850.

**XVII. early May:** PBSj, May 9. **Patty's marriage to Parry:** PBSj, at Mar. 27, 1852. On this date Patty was sealed to Parry for time. **first conductor:** OPH 4:157. **Parry's marriage to Harriet:** PBSj. **Harriet leaves:** PBSj, May 12-13, 1854. **John lives mainly with Harriet:** See, in addition to Patty's diary, the 1860 Utah Census, Salt Lake City, 16th Ward, p. 159, in which we find John and Harriet and two children listed together. **Indian R.S.:** June 10, 1854, PBSj. Compare WC 75-76.

**XVIII. Clark intolerant:** OPH 10:415; Wills, SPS 8. **Phebe:** married John Henry Ellis in 1870 and died in 1912 in Bountiful, Utah. **Martha:** married Adelbert Louis Burnham in 1870, lived a full 98 years, and died in 1952 in Bountiful, Utah. **Perrigrine visits:** PGSj, Nov. 17, 1852, B65. **Clark helps outfit Sylvia:** PGSj, Apr. 22. Apr. 26: "[went] to see Margaret Dote that lived with my sister. She was glad to see me and my sister that went with me, with three of her children. April 28. Clark came home with the wagon and carriage ... May 1. Hooked up our team. May 2. Loaded our wagon. Had a busy day." G92-98. **Departure:** The diary continues, giving details of camping places and similar travel details. It stops on May 11, G112. **Sylvia and Heber:** PBSj; OPH 10:415. **Sylvia's city lot:** PGSj, Apr. 3, 1855. Fisher, JRLF 1, locates this at 200 West and 300 North, "a little white-washed adobe house. The biggest box elder trees in the town grew there." **Ezekiel comes to Utah:** Wills, SPS 8. **Perry sent east:** Wills, SPS 9, compare Fisher, JRLF 2. At the age of sixteen, he went to Germany. "With his father, he came several times to visit in Bountiful. Perry spoke five languages fluently. He had a very pleasing personality. Always, he was ready with a story, often amusing, never vulgar." He worked as a bank cashier in his father's bank until Clark died in 1898, at which time he returned to Utah, where he became contact manager for the Light and Power Company. He apparently never married. **Williams:** See e.g., PBSj, Jan. 17, 1861; June 10, 1861; Aug. 5, 1861: "Sylvia & Wilms here"; Jan. 22, 1862: "Sylvia & Williams here to dinner." **Clark remarries:** AF. **Susanne:** At some point Windsor Lyon's second wife, Susanne, died, and, according to family traditions, Sylvia adopted the child of Susanne and Windsor. Wills, SPS 5, 9. I have not been able to document this from other sources.

IX. **Patty and Harriet:** Compare PBSj, Nov. 23, 1856. **"Finished harvesting":** Oct. 24, 1857. **Parry and Harriet visit together:** PBSj, Jan. 17, 1859: "John Parry and wife here." **Sept. 23:** Harriet and John Parry would have five children, the first of which had been born on August 8, 1855. On May 10, 1860, February 11, 1862, Patty delivered another of Harriet's and John's children. **Alzinia's age:** See PBSj, Oct. 9, 1861, compare Aug. 1, 1861. **death of John Parry:** Quoted from the Reminiscence. The CA original ends on Dec. 31, 1866, and starts again in 1880.

XX. **temple ritual:** PBSj, record pasted to diary page after June 16, 1860, Smart, MM 277. See also Aug. 7, 1869; Oct. 26, 1870, "Patty B. Smith," Endowment House record F.Utah.SIG, as cited in Ivins 4:279; Jan. 7, 1871; October 30, 1871, "Patty Bartlett Smith," in Ivins 4:281, Endowment House Record (FSIH), Book H; June 1 1884; Oct. 26, 1876; Nov. 6, 1871, Patty and Joseph F. Smith stood proxy as women were sealed to Joseph Smith; Nov. 16, 1870. **Maine:** Reminiscence.

XXI. **Sylvia's home as hotel:** Fisher, JRLF 2. **Sylvia active in Relief Society:** Bountiful R.S. Hall Donation Book, CA, L 2840, CR 924; Jan. 1, 1872. Numerous donations by Sylvia in 1875-78. **First Counselor to Hannah Holbrook President:** See "A Book of Records ... Female Relief Society ... Bountiful, 1870-78," CA. **Josephine's marriage:** AF. The Fishers would have ten children. See Fisher, JRLF. Their first home was at 630 W. 10th N. **Reminiscence:** in "Diary and account book," CA, MS 12481. **John Fisher takes a plural wife:** Fisher, JRLF 7. Eventually, Josephine obtained a legal divorce from John Fisher to lessen legal harassment, making Harriet the legal wife. **Patty's move to Bountiful:** Reminiscence, May 10, 1864; Rugh, PBS 318.

XII. **Emmeline Wells to Mary Lightner:** Apr. 7, 1882, in Mary Rollins Lightner collection, Lee Library. **deathbed confession:** See Josephine Fisher affidavit, partially quoted above. There is a family tradition that Sylvia had her sealing to Joseph Smith canceled and that she was sealed to Windsor Lyon for eternity in a proxy ceremony. If true, this is a remarkable final development in her marital triangle with Joseph and Windsor. However, "family tradition" is often unreliable, so this report is not certain. **obituary:** DW 31 (Apr. 19, 1882): 208: "At Bountiful, Davis County, at 5:30 a.m., April 13, 1882, of dropsy, SYLVIA P. CLARK, aged 63 years and 9 months." The funeral is reported in DEN 15 (Apr. 15, 1882) in "Local and Other Matters" section, p. 3, "Funeral Services at Bountiful."

XIII. **school:** "Patty Sessions' School," in "Local and Other Matters" section, DEN 17 (25) (Dec. 20, 1883): p. 5. See also *East of Antelope Island* ([Bountiful, UT: Carr Printing Co., 1948), 341. **visiting the sick:** E.g., Apr. 27, May 1-3, July 16, 1884, Mar. 20, 1886. Dec. 27, 1884: "Br Jones came after me & Lucina PGs wife & Phebe Davids wife to go & wash & anoint his wife she has the Dropsy sweled all over they washed I anointed her we all laid hands on her." **fruit drying:** E.g., Sept. 9 to Oct. 26, 1884. **liberality:** July 25, Aug. 23, 1884. More generally, see Smart, MM 28. **rug making:** Smart, MM 359. **tends Perrigrine:** July 1886; Mar. 27, Apr. 10, 1887. **carriage rides:** July 27, 1887. **deafness:** Apr. 28, 1887. **sewing:** May 26, 1887. **flawed knitting:** Smart, MM 10. **death:** "Deaths," DW 46 (Dec. 24, 1892): 32. "At Bountiful, at 6:30 this (Wednesday) morning, Dec. 14, 1892, Mrs. Patty Sessions; aged 97 years and 10 months." Perrigrine lived only one year after Patty, David Jr. only four. **Quote from her obituary:** "Sister Patty Session," DW 46 (2) (Dec. 31, 1892): 39. This notes that Patty had 214 descendants when she died. Compare "A Remarkable Woman," an obituary in DEN (Dec. 22, 1892): p. 1. **final quote:** Reminiscence at Nov. 20, 1876.

## REFERENCES TO CHAPTER 8.
### Miracle Tale:
### Mary Elizabeth Rollins (Lightner Smith Young)

Bangerter, Geraldine Hamblin, and Susan Easton Black. *My Servant Algernon Sidney Gilbert: Provide for My Saints (D&C 57:10)*. [Salt Lake City]: Rollins, Hamblin, Bangerter families, 1989.
"Deaths." "LIGHTNER." DEN 18 (Sept. 8, 1885): p. 2 (Obituary of Adam Lightner).
Hamblin, Ida Rollins, and Malissa Rollins Lee. "Biography of James Henry Rollins and Eveline Walker Rollins." MEL collection, Lee Library.
Lightner, Mary Elizabeth. Autobiography, holograph, USHS. There are different typescript versions, some fuller than the holograph. See also the version whose author is given as Elsie Barrett, Huntington Library. A printed version is "Mary Elizabeth Rollins Lightner." UGHM 17 (1926): 193-205, 250-60.
———. Letter to Emmeline B. Wells, summer 1905, Lee Library.
———. Letter to Emmeline Wells, Nov. 21, 1880. As quoted in Van Wagoner, MP 39. See Van Wagoner's notes in his collection at Marriott Library, box 10.
———. Letter to John A. Smith, Jan. 25, 1892. Original in papers of George A. Smith, Marriott Library. As cited in Bachman, "A Study," 135, Van Wagoner, MP 39.
———. Record Book. MS 748, CA.
———. "Remarks." A talk given at Lee Library, Apr. 14, 1905. Typescript in Lee Library. Printed in Tinney, RF 254-58.
———. "Speech." Given July 24, 1889. In Record Book, p. 28.
———. "Statement." Apr. 18, 1884, given to John Taylor and George Q. Cannon. CA.
———. "Statement of Mary E. Rollins Lightner." Signed Feb. 8, 1902. Lee Library.
Lyon, T. Edgar. Interview. In Linda Newell collection, Marriott Library.
MEL = Mary Elizabeth Lightner.
Murdock, Hallie. Biography of Mary Elizabeth Lightner, CA.
Robinson, Alvaretta, ed. *They Answered the Call: A History of Minersville, Utah*. Minersville, UT: Centennial Committee, [1962].
Rollins, James Henry. Diary. Lee Library and USHS. Dictated by him to his daughter in 1898. Compare Hamblin.

**lightning:** Autobiography, 22. **supernatural:** For this book's treatment of the supernatural, see Introduction.

I. **birth date:** SAd 505; IGI. **John:** was born in 1792 in Rutland, Rutland, New Hampshire, AF. **Keziah:** was born on May 15, 1796, in Albany, Albany, New York. She died in 1877 (or 1878) in Utah. **Rollins's occupation:** Hamblin. **James Henry:** Born on May 27, 1816, he married Evaline Walker in 1836 (or 1838) and Hannah Humes in 1851, a polygamous marriage. He had ten children by Eveline and thirteen by Hannah. In Missouri and Nauvoo he was a bodyguard to Joseph Smith. After crossing the plains, he lived in the Mormon colony of San Bernardino, California, for a few years, then served as a bishop, patriarch, and state legislature representative in Minersville, Utah. He died in 1899 in Wyoming. See Hamblin, "Biography," and Lyman, *San Bernardino*, index. **Caroline:** married Nathaniel John Kerr and died in 1853 in Illinois. **death of John:** Autobiography.

II. **Gilberts:** For Sidney, see Bangerter, MSA; Cook, RP 84. **move to Ohio, and Mormonism:** Autobiography. **missionaries to Kirtland:** For the mission of Oliver and companions to Kirtland, see Book of Commandments ch. 30 (D&C 28); D&C (1835 ed.) 54 (modern LDS D&C 32); Hill, JS 119-22; Fanny Alger chapter, at 1830. For contemporary newspaper accounts, see Hill, JS 122. **date of baptism:** MEL to Wells, Summer 1905, p. 4, has the date "early" October 1830, but the missionaries did not reach Kirtland until early November, see Cook, RP 45. They left Manchester, New York, on October 17, Cook, RP 44. Compare Lightner genealogy book, fd 6, p. 33, in MEL collection, Lee Library. **Book of Mormon:** Autobiography. Bracketed passages are from the typescript version of the Autobiography, p. 2. **the prayer meeting:** Autobiography 3/ typescript p. 2. See also Remarks, p. 1; MEL to Wilford Woodruff, Oct. 7, 1887, "I was Sealed to Brother Josephs family in the Spring of 1831." Statement, 1902. The 1884 Statement dates the experience "in the fore part of the Winter," but Joseph did not arrive in Kirtland until early February 1831, see Hill, JS 129; HC 1:147. The meeting might have taken place in late winter/early spring. **"seal":** For "sealing" here, compare a speech given by Joseph Smith on October 25, 1831: "The order of the High-priesthood is that they have the power given them to seal up the Saints unto eternal life," FWR 20-21. Elders with the "High-priesthood" sealed up entire congregations to eternal life soon after this, Reynolds Cahoon diaries, CA, after Nov. 9, 1831 ("held a meting ... after laboring with them Some length of time Br David sealed them up unto Eternial life"), and at Nov. 17, ("held a meting ... Broke bread with them sealed up the Church unto Eternal life"), Nov. 27 ("Saturday Evening held a Met ... Blest the Children in the name of the lord & sealed the Church unto eternal life"). Compare Prince, PFOH 20, 155-72; KEQR 12n. These references support Elizabeth's account. **"I felt":** typescript. **photographed:** "Remarks."

III. **Move:** Autobiography. **Burk:** Hamblin. Mary's Autobiography places the remarriage in Missouri. **tongues:** Autobiography, p. 3. **Boggs:** Autobiography. **reason for mobbing:** Warren Jennings, "The City in the Garden: Social Conflict in Jackson County, Missouri," *The Restoration Movement: Essays in Mormon History* (Independence, MO: Herald House, 1979), 99-119; T. Edgar Lyon, "Independence, Missouri, and the Mormons, 1827-1833," BYUSt 13 (1972): 10-19; Ronald E. Romig, *Early Independence, Missouri, "Mormon" History Tour Guide* (Independence, MO: Missouri Mormon Frontier Foundation, 1994); Hill, QFR 41. **saving the sheets:** Autobiography, 196. Compare Hill, JS 160. **Gilbert store:** Hill, JS 163. **Clay County:** Autobiography; AF. Mary witnessed a miracle of catching a fish with three silver half dollars inside it, a close New Testament parallel (see Matt. 17:27), while the Mormons were crossing the Missouri River to escape the mobs in Jackson County. The coins were the exact amount needed to ferry the last Mormons over. **Zion's Camp:** Bangerter, MSA 39-40.

IV. **revelation to Joseph:** Statement, 1902, compare Remarks 255. **marriage to Adam:** Autobiography; AF. He had been born in Lancaster, Lancaster, Pennsylvania, on April 14, 1810. **Miles Henry:** AF. While living in Milford, Mary's house was apparently haunted by a poltergeist, a spirit that moved household articles around at night, see the Autobiography. Mormons who believed in biblical miracles often accepted the cultural, folkloric supernaturalism of early America also. **Mary refuses to leave Far West:** Autobiography; compare HC 3:410; Stephen LeSueur, *The 1838 Mormon War in Missouri* (Columbia: University of Missouri Press, 1987), 158-62; Hill, QFR 94-95. The holograph autobiography has General "Pomeroy" (a name unknown in other sources), while the typescript has General Clark. Most documents agree that Samuel D. Lucas was the general who commanded the siege of Far West. **Henry arrested:** Autobiography; compare Hamblin p. 7. **Adam loved Joseph:** Autobiography, typescript, p. 8. **in Kentucky:** Autobiography; compare James Henry Rollins, Autobiography p. 8.

**V. Caroline:** She later married Thomas C. Jewell and died on December 21, 1910, AF. **Farmington, painting lessons:** Autobiography.

**VI. presentiments:** Remarks, 1905, 255. **date:** 1905 letter to Emmeline Wells. Mary vacillated between February 1841 and 1842 in dating her marriage to Joseph, but used 1842 more often. Furthermore, Brigham Young performed the marriage, and he was in England in February 1841, returning to Nauvoo only on July 1, 1841. See BYj; Arrington BY 96. **proposal conversation:** Remarks; see also Autobiography 18; Statement, 1902, 255; 1887 letter to Woodruff; 1905 letter to Wells. **"The angel said":** Remarks 255. **"Joseph said I was his ...":** Statement, 1902, 255. **"I was created":** Autobiography 18. **"I know":** Remarks 255. For unconditional salvation linked to plural marriage, see Lucy Walker, Sarah Ann Whitney, and Helen Kimball chapters, and Prologue, at discussion of Buckeye's Lament. **the angel:** Autobiography 19; compare Remarks 256. **Aunt sees it:** Remarks 256. Curiously enough, the Autobiography denies that Aunt Gilbert saw the angel. **Joseph explains the sign:** Remarks 256. Compare Autobiography. **date of marriage:** [Statement] "Minersville Utah Feb. 21st 1905 (Affidavit) This is to Certify that about the last [of] Feb. 1842 or 1841 I Mary Elizabeth Rollins Lightner was sealed to the Prophet Joseph Smith as his plural wife Elder Brigham Young officiating. This ceremony was performed in an upper room of the red Store used as a Masonic Hall in Nauvoo, Ill. Mary E. Rollins Lightner, wit., Mary R. Rollins, J.E. Vanderwood." See Record Book, p. 33. However, the Autobiography, p. 20, gives March as the month of marriage. For the Masonic Hall, compare Mary's statement, "While in Nauvoo I was very busy painting and giving lessons. I painted Masonic aprons of two degrees, by Joseph instructions." Letter to Emmeline Wells, Nov. 21, 1880, partially quoted in Van Wagoner MP 39; see Van Wagoner's notes at Marriott Library, box 10. **time and eternity:** Autobiography 20; compare Statement, 1902: "for time & all eternity." Also, a Mar. 23, 1877, affidavit (Kenney collection, Marriott Library, box 11, fd 14): in February 1842, "the Prophet Joseph Smith came to me and said he had received a direct command from God to take me for a wife for time and all eternity." **Adam "far away":** Remarks 256. **"I could tell you ...":** Letter to Wells, 1880, my emphasis. Some of Mary's descendants have passed down a tradition that Adam Lightner became a "front husband" for Joseph, like Joseph Kingsbury for Sarah Ann Whitney. This tradition also holds that Mary's first two sons were Joseph's, and that Adam had married a secret plural wife and had children by her. However, it seems unlikely that a non-Mormon would act as a front husband for Joseph. And unlike Kingsbury, Adam was married to Mary before Joseph married her. These two pieces of evidence argue against the family tradition. However, there is also the tradition that Adam was always a Mormon secretly, which would remove the first objection. In support of Adam as a secret Mormon is his willingness to transport ammunition for the Mormons in the midst of the Missouri persecutions, mentioned above. The second objection still stands, however, unless it can be documented that Joseph married Mary before 1835. Considering Mary's well-documented Nauvoo marriage to Joseph, and her initial resistance to the marriage in Nauvoo, an earlier marriage should be rejected. Therefore, the family tradition that Adam was a front husband is intriguing but unlikely, unless new evidence shows otherwise. (Adam also reportedly remained a non-Mormon throughout his life. If he had secretly been a disciple, he could have easily become a public Mormon after Joseph's death, or in Utah. Mary's account of Adam's death clearly shows he was a non-Mormon; and compare Joseph's desire to baptize Adam in Nauvoo, Autobiography 21.) **George Algernon:** AF. **Relief Society:** RS Minutes, pp. 27, 67. **Adam and hat:** Joseph Smith Account Book, see Launius, *Red Brick Store* 65.

**VII. Adam's job in Pontusac:** Autobiography 21. Brodie, NM 452, speculates that Adam left because he discovered Mary's marriage to Joseph. However, Adam's employment problems are well documented. **Joseph's reaction:** Autobiography 21. **Joseph and**

**prophecy:** The genre of the miraculous fulfillment of a prophecy of Joseph Smith is frequently found in Mormon folklore; see Oliver Huntington journal, Books 13, 14, 15; 17:48; 18:101; Davis Bitton, "Joseph Smith in Mormon Folk Memory," *Restoration Studies* 1 (Independence, MO: Temple School, 1980), 75-94, 81-83. **Florentine:** Autobiography 22; AF has March 23, 1843. There is a variant birth date a year later, March 23, 1844. **Cutler:** Autobiography 24; compare, for Cutler's life, Cook, RP 247; Stout OMF 1:32, compare index. The story of the miraculous healing is also a commonplace in Mormon history and legend. See the Marinda Hyde chapter at 1831.

**VIII.** **endowment:** Quinn, MW 396 gives the date; compare letter to Wells, summer 1905, p. 4. **marriage to Brigham:** Autobiography 25. HCKj, May 22, 1845, "B Young stopt-stopt last nite seald B to Lite." Kimball, OPW 114, reads "Lile," but there is definitely a cross stroke in the original manuscript. The looped vertical stroke is odd for a "t," but Kimball's "t"s were often looped (compare "Whitney," "leter," in the previous day's entry, and the broad double stroke of "last"'s "t" from this sentence). Heber's "t"s could be wildly dissimilar. Compare Johnson DDW 67. **marriage to Brigham in Nauvoo temple:** BOP #35; SAd 505, 577. **endowment:** NTER. **Brigham leaves:** Autobiography 25. **mob incident:** Hamblin.

**IX.** **Brigham sends for Mary:** Autobiography 25. **Galena:** Autobiography 25. **John Horace:** He married Louisa Abigail Burk in 1870 and died in 1923, in Minersville, Utah. **needle:** Autobiography 25. **St. Croix:** Autobiography 26. James Taylor Dunn, *The St. Croix: Midwest Border River* (New York: Holt, Rinehard and Winston, 1965), 87, 95. In 1850 the town had 164 inhabitants. **poisoning incident:** Autobiography 27-28. **judgments of God on evildoers:** See, e.g., Nels B. Lundwall, *The Fate of the Persecutors of the Prophet Joseph Smith* (Salt Lake City: Bookcraft, 1967). **Stillwater, Hudson:** Dunn, *The St. Croix* 100, 53, 72. **Elizabeth:** married Joseph Orson Turley in 1865 and died in 1927. **moves:** Autobiography 13. **Mary Rollins:** married a William Jenkins Carter and a cousin, George Rollins, and died in 1928. **children:** I follow AF. **Caroline's death:** Autobiography 30. **Caroline's children:** Record Book, pp. 34, 7. **Marine:** See Dunn, *The St. Croix* 139, 211: "Marine had the advantage over neighboring towns because its young men seemed to be exceptionally active in getting up dances. These were held more or less regularly in the popular hotels run by Adam Lightner and Mathias Welshons." On New Year's Eve 1858 a group of Stillwater young people traveled by sleigh to Marine, "to dance the intricate steps of the 'mazy' at a 'new and splendid hotel,' the five-story Lightner House. They returned the next day, 'delighted with the music, and dancing, and above all with Lightner's sumptuous supper.'" **Third Nephite:** Autobiography (typescript) 14. Compare Hector Lee, *The Three Nephites* (Albuquerque: University of New Mexico Press, 1949); Austin Fife, "The Legend of the Three Nephites among the Mormons," *Journal of American Folklore* 53 (1940): 1-49; Oliver Huntington, "Spirit Experiences," *Young Woman's Journal* 6 (1895): 376-81. **Charles Washington:** married Lydia Williams and died on October 21, 1932. **Adam Jr.:** died in 1890.

**X.** **steamboat journeys:** Autobiography 30-31. **overland diary:** CA, MS 750. The version in the Autobiography, especially the typescript, is secondary.

**XI.** **reunions:** Autobiography 43. **Henry discovers lead mine:** Record Book, 34. **"came across the plain":** Record Book, 34. **MEL to Brigham Young:** May 20, 1864, Lee Library. **BY to MEL:** May 30, 1864, Lee Library. **ERS to MEL:** Apr. 3, 1865, Lee Library. **Godbeites:** for an account of the Godbeites, see SLDS 334, 678. Compare Eliza Partridge chapter at 1869.

**XII.** **1887 letter:** See letter to Wilford Woodruff, below. **Relief Society:** ERS to MEL, May 27, 1869, MEL collection, Lee Library. Mary had written to Eliza on May 10, 1869, but the letter is not extant. The rest of Snow's letter explained how to preside over a Relief Society. **June 17 letter:** ERS to MEL, MEL collection, Lee Library. For Relief Society buildings, see WC 96-98 and Marinda Johnson chapter. A Relief Society building still stands in Santa Clara, Utah, near St. George. **death of Keziah:** AF. **death of Brigham:** Arrington, BY 399.

XIII. **Mary to Taylor:** MEL to "Brother Taylor," Sep. 13, 1881, in MEL Collection, Lee Library. **Wells letter:** Emmeline Wells to MEL, Mar. 8, 1880, MEL collection, Lee Library; this responds to a letter by Mary dated Aug. 25, 1879, not extant. **1882 Wells letter:** Emmeline Wells to Mary, Apr. 7, 1882, MEL Collection, Lee Library. This answered a letter from Mary dated Mar. 28.

XIV. **MEL to Wilford Woodruff:** Oct. 7, 1887, in MEL Collection, Lee Library. **Helen Whitney to Wilford Woodruff:** Oct. 9, 1887, in MEL collection, Lee Library. **death of Adam:** Record Book, pp. 1, 35. The obituary of Adam Lightner, DEN 18 (Sept. 8, 1885): p. 2, "Deaths": "LIGHTNER.—At Minersville, Utah, August 29th, 1885, of consumption, Adam Lightner, aged 75 years, 4 months and 16 days. He has been among the Latter-day Saints for 50 years, though not a member of the Church; he made no profession of religion, but believed in doing to others as he would like to be done by. When Zion's Camp went up to Missouri he belonged to a company called the 'Liberty Blues,' this company was called to guard Joseph, Hyrum and the twelve to Jackson County and back. He opened the first store in Far West; was of great assistance to the people in their troubles in that place, and risked his life in trying to aid them ... Mr. Lightner returned to Far West, and not until the Prophet Joseph and others were taken prisoners would he leave, and when he did so he lost all his property in that place. – COM. St. Paul *Pioneer Press* please copy." **Adam and Mormonism:** "It was a great worry to Mary that her husband never joined the church. Although he was a very dear trusted friend of the Prophet Joseph, he never accepted the Gospel until on his death bed." Murdock, Biography. However, the Autobiography says that he did not convert on his deathbed, typescript 10. **Adam Jr. convicted:** "Utah News," MSt 48 (July 19, 1886): 454-55. "Governor Caleb West has pardoned ... Adam Lightner, who was sentenced to imprisonment for six years for grand larceny, but has served out only eight months and fourteen days." **Mary on Adam's conviction:** MEL to John Taylor, May 18, 1886. **MEL to John Taylor:** May 18, 1886. **"Emily P. Young" to MEL:** Apr. 28, 1886, MEL collection, Lee Library. **MEL to John Taylor:** May 18, 1886. **Mary frees Adam Jr.:** HMWj, June 5-23, 1886. **Zina's letter:** Letter from Zina Young, Lion House, to MEL, June 27, 1886; MEL collection, Lee Library. **Emmeline Wells to MEL:** Feb. 10, 1887, MEL collection, Lee Library. **Wells, 1880's letter:** Emmeline Wells to MEL, Nov. 26, 188?, Lee Library, MEL collection. **Oct. 1887:** HMWj, Oct. 7-13, 1887. **MEL to Woodruff:** Oct. 7, 1887, MEL Collection, Lee Library. **allotment:** WWj, 8:461.

XV. **living arrangements:** Autobiography; Record Book. The younger Mary had married a William Carter, had borne him ten children, then, after William's death, had married her cousin George Rollins. **asked to speak:** Hallie Murdock, Biography. "She wrote articles for the Woman's Exponent, with Eliza R. Snow and Emmeline B. Wells. She had a remarkable memory, and was often called upon to give Fourth of July orations." *They Answered the Call*, A165. An example of one of Mary's Fourth of July orations can be found in the Record Book, p. 32. **Emily Young to MEL:** June 10, 1888; MEL Collection, Lee Library. **Wells to MEL:** Mar. 12, 1889; MEL Collection, Lee Library. **June 1889:** HMWj, June 27-29, 1889. On June 15th, Mary attended a Relief Society meeting with Helen, Presendia Kimball, Emmeline Wells at the Sixteenth Ward. Helen wrote, "Sister Lightner spoke & was filled with the Holy Spirit - bore a powerful testimony to the truth of this work, and especially Celestial marriage." **MEL to Wilford Woodruff:** Apr. 6, 1891, MEL Collection, Lee Library.

XVI. **affidavit, 1902:** See Statement, Feb. 8, 1902. **MEL to Joseph F. Smith:** Apr. 25, 1903, MEL Collection, Lee Library. **MEL to William B. Preston:** Apr. 20, 1904, MEL Collection, Lee Library. **speech to Lee Library:** Remarks. Compare Murdock Biography. **Mary to Emmeline:** MEL to Emmeline Wells, summer 1905.

XVII. **appearance of Joseph, Heber:** Autobiography, typescript, 19. Bracketed material from

Remarks, p. 258. **death:** Autobiography, postscript. Compare the Murdock Biography, which has Mary dying on December 21, 1915, at age 97.

## REFERENCES TO CHAPTER 9.
### *Apostle's Wife:*
### *Marinda Nancy Johnson (Hyde Smith)*

Barron, Howard H. *Orson Hyde: Missionary-Apostle-Colonizer.* Salt Lake City: Horizon, 1977.
Esplin, Ron. "The Emergence of Brigham Young and the Twelve to Mormon Leadership, 1830-41." Ph.D. diss., Brigham Young University, 1981.
Hayden, Amos S. *Early History of the Disciples in the Western Reserve.* Cincinnati: Chase and Hall, 1876.
Hill, Marvin. "Historical Study of the Life of Orson Hyde, Mormon Missionary and Apostle." Master's thesis, Brigham Young University, 1955.
HOH = Orson Hyde, "History of Orson Hyde."
Hyde, Joseph Smith. "The Orson Hyde Genealogy." UGHM 4 (1913) 59-64.
Hyde, Marinda. Interview, in Tullidge, WM 403-6.
Hyde, Mary Ann Price. "Autobiography." Written Aug. 20, 1880. Bancroft Library, film at USHS.
Hyde, Orson. "History of Orson Hyde." DW 8 (May 5, 12, 1858): 45, 49. Also. "History of Orson Hyde." MSt 26 (Nov. 19 1864-Dec. 10, 1864): 742-44, 760-61, 774-76, 790-92.
Johnson, Luke. "History of Luke Johnson." DW 8 (May 19, 26 1858): 53, 54. Also, "History of Luke Johnson." MSt 26 (Dec. 31, 1864): 834-36.
Stone, Winfred Miner, and Florence M. Slusser. "Life of Nancy Marinda Hyde." Four pages, typescript, in author's possession.
Wells, Emmeline B. "L.D.S. Women of the Past, Personal Impressions." WE 37 (June 1908): first page.

**I. Birth date:** Johnson Family Bible, which is also the source for other birth dates in this section, as cited by Myrtle Hyde, personal communication. See also Patriarchal Blessing, CA; IGI, GS 1260540, b 7913702, sh 64. I would like to thank Myrtle Hyde, who is writing a biography of Orson Hyde, for critiquing this chapter. **John Johnson:** Luke Johnson, "History." Cook, RP 199. He was born on April 11, 1779 in Chesterfield, Cheshire, New Hampshire. **Alice (Elsa):** was born on April 17, 1781, in Dixglitou (Dighton), Bristol, Massachusetts. **Elsa the younger:** married Oliver Olney, an early Mormon who eventually left Mormonism and wrote an idiosyncratic anti-Mormon book, *The Absurdities of Mormonism* (Hancock Co., IL: [Oliver Olney], 1843). She died on July 16, 1841. There are some Oliver Olney papers at Yale. Oliver viewed himself as a prophet and headed a minor Mormon splinter group, see Steven Shields, *Divergent Paths of the Restoration* (Nauvoo, IL: New Nauvoo Neighbor, 1975), 227; Faulring 301. Interestingly, Olney's book deals with Nauvoo polygamy—he regarded the Relief Society as a quasi-Masonic group developed by Joseph Smith to foster polygamy, p. 11. For another quasi-masonic view of Joseph's polygamy, see Bennett, HS220-25. There is no solid documentary evidence to substantiate these claims, though in Nauvoo there were always connections between Masonry, the temple endowment (sharing many elements with Masonry), and polygamy. Compare the Kinsman's degree in the Zina Young journal, June 5-9, 1844 (discussed in the Zina Huntington chapter). Also the Relief Society first met at the "Nauvoo Lodge Room" (RS Min., p. 1), the upper room of Joseph's "Red Brick Store," on March 17, 1842, only two days after Joseph had received the first degree of Masonry in the same place, see *The Founding Minutes of Nauvoo Lodge*, ed. Mervin Hogan (Des Moines, IA: Research Lodge No. 2, Feb. 1971), p. 12. Kenneth Godfrey, "Joseph Smith and the Masons," *Journal of the Illinois State Historical Society* 64 (Spring 1971): 79-90; Launius, *Red Brick Store* 21; Robert Cole, *Masonic Gleanings* ([Chicago]: Kable Printing,

1956, 2nd ed.), 190-92. Bathsheba Smith, in Temple Lot Case 358-60, testified that when endowed, she was washed and anointed "for the purpose of initiating me in the secret society and order of endowments." Then she went to the "lodge room over Joseph's store" for the rest of the endowment in company with her husband, George A. Then (as she discusses the endowment) she states that she had "one or two degrees" of a "side degree" of Masonry, the Order of Rebecca, "in that lodge." However, her statement is somewhat confused. Finally, the Nauvoo charter was revoked in part because of charges that Joseph was inducting women into the lodge (Launius 21). **Robert:** was born on January 13, 1802 at Chesterfield, Cheshire, New Hampshire. **Fanny:** was born on March 3, 1803 and died in 1879. **John Jr.:** was born on March 20, 1805, and married Eliza Ann Marcy in 1830, and in 1887. **Luke:** was born on November 3, 1807 (or 1808, FGS) and was baptized a Mormon in 1831. He married Susan Armilda Poteet in 1832/33 and had ten children with her. He fulfilled a number of missions and in 1834 joined Joseph Smith in Zion's Camp. He was ordained an apostle in 1835, only to be excommunicated from the church three years later. He was rebaptized in Nauvoo. Susan died in September 1846 and Luke married America Morgan Clark in 1847 at Council Bluffs. With America he had eight children. After arriving in Salt Lake in July 1847 he moved to Tooele County and served as a bishop there before his death in 1861 in Salt Lake City. See his "History"; BE 1:85-86; Quinn, MHOP 554-55; Cook, RP 110. **Olmstead G.:** was born on November 12 (or October 8), 1809, in Pomfret, and died on February 24, 1834. **Lyman Eugene:** was born on October 24, 1811, in Pomfret and married Sarah Long. After his baptism in 1831 he served missions, was a member of Zion's Camp in 1834, then was called to be an apostle in 1835. He was excommunicated in 1838 and was drowned in the Mississippi River on December 20, 1859, at Prairie du Chien, Wisconsin. See BE 1:91-92; Quinn, MHOP 555; Cook, RP 111; Jessee 2:560. **Emily H.:** was born on August 30 (or 13), 1813, in Pomfret. She married Christopher Quinn, and died in 1855. **move to Ohio:** Cook, RP 199, compare Luke Johnson, "History." **John Johnson, Methodist:** Luke Johnson, "History." **Mary:** was born on May 24, 1818, and died in 1833. **Justin Jacob:** was born on November 13, 1820, and married Mary Ann Ivins in 1846. **Edwin and Charlotte:** were born on December 18, 1821. **Albert G.:** was born on February 6, 1823. **Joseph:** was born on December 26, 1827.

II. **Marinda on the Book of Mormon's arrival:** Tullidge, WM 403-404. Booth would later apostatize and write early anti-Mormon newspaper letters, see Jessee 1:363-64. **healing of Mrs. Johnson:** Luke Johnson, "History"; Hayden, EH 250-51. **Lyman's baptism:** Cook, RP 111. **Marinda's baptism:** WM 403-6; AF. **Luke's baptism:** Luke Johnson, "History." **family traditions of first meeting with Joseph:** Stone, "Life," 1. **"the next fall":** WM 404. **September 12:** Jessee 1:363.

III. **Mobbing:** WM 404. Compare Hill, JS 146; ME 42-43; HC 1:261-65; Van Wagoner, SR 108-18. For an extralegal castration of a man seen as sexually immoral, see HStj, Feb. 27, 1858, OMF 2:653. **Luke quote:** "History." **Braden:** Clark Braden and E. L. [Edmund Levi] Kelley, *Public Discussion of the Issues between the Reorganized Church ... and the Church of Christ, Disciples* (St. Louis, MO: C. Braden, 1884), 202. Clark Braden was a member of the Church of Christ, the "Disciples." Compare ME 41. **Simonds Ryder:** Hayden, EH 221. The other account is by S. F. Whitney, Newell Whitney's brother, who said that the Johnson boys were angry because Joseph and Sidney were trying to convince the father to "let them have his property." "Several of Johnson's sons were of the party." Again this evidence is quite late, and the Johnson boys are nowhere else characterized as antagonistic to Joseph Smith at this time. "Statement of Rev. S.F. Whitney on Mormonism," *Naked Truths About Mormonism*, ed. Arthur B. Demming, 1 (Jan. 1888): 3-4, 4. Sidney Rigdon biographer Richard Van Wagoner, *Sidney Rigdon* 108-18, believes that Rigdon was the main focus of the mobbing, and Orson Hyde later charged Rigdon with trying to gain control of the Johnson farm. Compare Van Wagoner, MP 224 n. 4. **Bachman's dating:** See Fanny Alger chapter. **"horrid fact":** Hayden, EH 221. **Marinda on Joseph's visit:** WM 404.

According to a family tradition told by some descendants, before Orson Hyde married Marinda, Joseph Smith cautioned him against marrying her, as she was his celestial wife, but Orson married her anyway. This tradition would support the theory that Marinda was Smith's first wife, married to him in 1831. However, it seems unlikely that Orson would disobey Smith, and then go on to have such a distinguished career as church leader in Kirtland Mormonism, so this theory should probably be rejected. In fact, Orson was ordained an apostle soon after his marriage to Marinda. **repetitions:** Zina Huntington and the Partridge sisters are two well documented cases.

**IV.** **to Kirtland:** Marinda, in WM 404. See map of Kirtland in Jessee 2:509 for the location of the John Johnson home in Kirtland, which is still standing. **Marinda's marriage:** date from HOH. **Hyde:** HOH; HC 1:217; Quinn, MHOP 552-54; Cook, RP 109; BE 1:80; Barron, OH; Hill, HS; Jessee 1:364. **mission in 1832:** Orson Hyde journal, 1832, CA, typescript, USHS. Samuel Smith journal, CA. Compare the Agnes Coolbrith chapter at 1832. **clerk:** Jessee 1:492. **apostle:** Luke Johnson, "History." For Traveling Presiding High Council, D&C 107:33; D&C (1835 ed.), 3:12, p. 84. **mission:** See *The Journals of William E. McLellin, 1831-1837*, ed. Jan Shipps and John Welch (Provo, UT: Brigham Young University Studies and University of Illinois, 1994), 171, 174; Esplin, EBY 164-70. **McLellin letter:** Kirtland High Council minutes, Aug. 4 session, in HC 2:240. **Hyde disfellowshipped:** HC 2:240; Barron, OH 67. **Hyde returns:** Jessee 2:43; HC 2:283. Compare Esplin, EBY 169. **chastened:** Jessee 2:64; 1:121. **Hyde's reaction:** JSj, Jessee 2:65; compare Esplin, EBY 180. **Hyde's letter:** Jessee 1:161-62; letter quoted pp. 164-67. **reconciliation:** Jessee 1:167; Kirtland High Council minutes, Sept. 26, 1835, cited in *Journals of William McLellin* 367; Esplin, EBY 180-81. **Orson clerk:** Jessee 1:190. **May mission:** HOH; Barron, OH 80. **Marinda meets Orson in Canada:** HOH; Barron, OH 82. **return to Kirtland:** HOH. **Laura:** Barron, OH 323. She married Aurelius Miner and died in 1909 in Salt Lake City. **Hyde leaves:** WM 403-6; HCKj, June 13, 1837; Barron, OH 88. **patriarchal blessing:** CA, Marinda Hyde collection; Barron, OH 315-16. **brothers cut off:** Luke Johnson, "History"; Quinn, MHOP 554-56. They had been cut off previously, on September 3, 1837, and were then reinstated on November 3. For their years as dissenters in Kirtland, see Hill, QFR 57-60, 71.

**V.** **return:** HOH. **trip to Far West:** HOH; BE 1:81; Jessee 2:263; HCKj, July 1, 1838, in Helen Whitney, "Closing Paragraphs of Life Incidents," WE 10 (June 15, 1887): 1. **bilious fever:** HOH. **Orson leaves Far West:** Esplin, EBY p. 341. **affidavit:** "Document Concerning the Correspondence," as cited in Jessee 2:299; quoted in Jessee, and in Hill, HS 39. Jessee 2:298 gives October 20 as the date of the affidavit; it is usually dated October 24. See also Esplin, EBY 339-43. The document is reprinted in G. Homer Durham, ed., *Gospel Kingdom* (Salt Lake City: Bookcraft, 1943), 186-87. Compare Hill, QFR 96. **Joseph in jail:** Jessee 2:288. **Joseph's letter:** 1838, Dec. 16. Jessee 2:298. **Hyde's dream:** Joseph Stout, Autobiography and Journal, p. 9; typescript, Lee Library, pp. 12-13; compare Hill, HS 40. According to Esplin, EBY 377, Hyde was not actually excommunicated; Quinn, MHOP 554, states that he was disfellowshipped on January 16, 1839, then was rebaptized on June 27, 1839. **Orson and Heber:** Heber C. Kimball journal, p. 69, as cited in Hill, HS, 40-41; HOH; Orson Hyde to Brigham Young, Mar. 30, 1839, see next entry. **Letter to Brigham**, see Orson Hyde to Brigham Young, Mar. 30, 1839, in the Brigham Young journal, after Apr. 1, 1845.

**VI.** **to Nauvoo:** WM 405. **May 4:** HC 3:345; Hill, HS 40-41. **Hyde penitent:** WWj, June 25 (1:340); Esplin, EBY 399; Hill, JS 248; JH June 2, 1839. **June 27:** Jessee 2:324; Hill, HS 41; Esplin, EBY 341-42, 99; Durham, *Gospel Kingdom*, 193. See also Jessee 2:327 (Hyde speaks at a July 7 meeting), and JH, Oct. 5. **ague:** HOH. **mission:** JH, Nov. 14, 1839; Mar. 4, 1840. **Emily:** Barron, OH 323; AF. Emily married George Chase in 1854 and died on December 6, 1909. **call in Conference:** HOH; HC 4:106. Compare TS 1 (Apr. 1840): 86, where Joseph wrote, "We have by the counsel of the Holy Spirit, appointed Elder Orson Hyde ... to be our agent and representative in foreign lands, to visit the cities of London, Amsterdam, Constantinople and Jerusalem." **departed on April 15:** TS 1 (June 1840): 116, compare Jessee

# ABBREVIATIONS, BIBLIOGRAPHIES, AND REFERENCES

2:375; CHC 4:106; TS 2 (Jan. 15, 1841): 293: "Elders Orson Hyde and John E. Page are informed, that the Lord is not well pleased with them in consequence of delaying their mission, (Elder John E. Page in particular,) and they are requested by the First Presidency to hasten their journey towards their destination." **route:** TS 1:155, 3:761-62; 2:204, 482, 551; 570; 3:739, 742, 776 (the letter to "My Dear Marinda"); 804, 847-53 (a front page story). This was a very well-publicized mission, and by the time the last article was published, Orson Hyde had become something of a hero in Mormonism. See also BE 1:81; Barron, OH 110-35; HC 4:490. In January 1842 Orson, in quarantine at Trieste (HC 4:490), wrote to Parley P. Pratt, expressing concern for Marinda and the children. "Perhaps I feel too anxious about my family, but where the heart has only a few objects to share its sympathies, upon those few objects the sun of affection shines with warmer and more brilliant ray. My family is my earthly all." Barron, OH 135. **Marinda at home during the mission:** Stone, LNMH 2. For the plight of nineteenth-century Mormon women when their husbands were on missions, see especially Linda Thatcher, "Women Alone: The Economic and Emotional Plight of Early LDS Women," *Dialogue* 25 (1992): 45-55. For sewing as an occupation for early American women, see the Agnes Coolbrith chapter at March 1842.

VII. **revelation:** Jessee 2:361; "History of Joseph Smith," MSt 18 (1856): 805; HC 4:467. **Robinson obeys:** Robinson, *The Return* 2 (1890): 324-25; 346-47. Though there are still some uncertainties regarding the different *Times and Seasons* buildings, Robert Bray has made progress in differentiating them, "Times and Seasons: An Archaeological Perspective on Early Latter Day Saints Printing," *California: the Society for Historical Archaeology* 13 (1979): 57-119. Ebenezer had recently moved the *Times and Seasons* into a "new and extensive building," TS 3 (Dec. 1, 1841): 615, on the northwest corner of Water and Bain streets, Bray's *Times and Seasons* Building No. 3, Bray 72, 86, 88. The earlier *Times and Seasons* buildings had been located at the northeast corner of Water and Bain streets, Bray's *Times and Seasons* Buildings nos. 1 and 2, Bray 72, 86, 88 (this is what is pointed out today as the *Times and Seasons* building location). The first building was "in the basement of a warehouse," and the second, built on the same property, was a "small, cheap frame building ... one and a half stories high, the lower room to be used for the printing office, and ... the upper room [for my family]," Ebenezer Robinson, *The Return* 2 (May-July 1890): 124. But Marinda, her children, and the Robinson family shared the "new and extensive" building. George W. Robinson (in an affidavit quoted in Bennett, HS 245-46) wrote that Marinda "lived in the under rooms of the printing office." Compare Holzapfel, *Old Mormon Nauvoo* 142. **Christmas eve:** WRj, CA; compare Noall, ID 308. In HC 4:484, Marinda has been edited out. It is very possible that Willard Richards himself, who helped revise the *History of the Church*, excised Marinda from this text. See HC 7:389, 411, 519, 520, 533; compare James F. Mintun, "History of Presidents of Seventy, Continued ..." *Journal of History* 8 (Jan. 1915): 68-97, 76. **Jennetta Richards:** See Noall, ID 324; Jessee, PW 520. **Willard boards with Joseph:** "Left - Bro Brighams and began to board with President Smith." WRj, CA. This does not say that Willard was living in the *Times and Seasons* building. Compare Noall, ID 610-11; HC 4:494. **revelation:** Jan. 28, 1842. "A Revelation to the twelve concerning the Times and Seasons. Verily thus saith the Lord unto you my servant Joseph. go and say unto the Twelve That it is my will to have them take in hand the Editorial department of the Times and Seasons according to that manifestation which shall be given unto them by the Power of my Holy Spirit in the midst of their counsel   Saith the Lord. Amen." Jessee 2:362; "History of Joseph Smith," MSt 19 (1857): 38-39; HC 4:503. **press sold:** JSj, Jessee 2:358; HC 4:513, a fuller account; Robinson, "Items of Personal History," *The Return* 2 (Oct. 1890): 346-48; WWj, Feb. 4, 1842 (2:153). **Robinson quote:** *The Return* 2 (1890): 346-47. **Bennett's quote:** HS 243, 241-42: "The printing-office, where Mrs. Hyde and Dr. Richards resided." Bennett and Robinson are our only sources for Richards living in the printing office. **Rigdon's account:** "J. GI SON DIVINE" [Sidney Rigdon, apparently], "To the Sisters of the

Church of Jesus Christ of Latter Day Saints," *Latter Day Saint's Messenger and Advocate* (Pittsburgh) 1 (10) (Mar. 15, 1845): 154-58, 156. A follower of Sidney Rigdon, "W.," made the same accusation in the June 11, 1845 Warsaw *Signal*, see below. **Feb. 7:** IC 90. **Feb 24:** JSj, see Jessee 2:360. **March 9:** WWj, Mar. 9, 1842 (2:157). JSj, Jessee 2:360, "The President retired to the Printing office with his Lady, & Supped, & with the twelve who had been at the office." These two passages establish that Marinda was still living in the printing office. **Richards marriage?:** Historian D. Michael Quinn has accepted that Marinda and Richards married while Orson was on his mission, see MHOP 575. However, this conclusion is interpretive, not certain, he tells me. He argues that in many other cases Rigdon and Robinson have been reliable, and he believes that some journal documentation supports the marriage. (Personal communication.) However, as was mentioned above, Rigdon and Robinson were not in the inner circles of polygamy, so would have been repeating hearsay; they did not witness a marriage. One would also think that if Bennett had certainly known about such a relationship, he would have highlighted it for sensational effect, instead of merely mentioning it in passing as a rumor.

Willard Richards traveled east to reunite with his wife Jennetta in early July 1842. However, when he returned to Nauvoo he began a polygamous family, marrying two young wives. See Jessee, PW 520-21; Noall, ID, 351. One of these marriages, to Alice Longstroth, he apparently solemnized himself, see his diary, Dec. 23, 1845, CA, quoted in Van Wagoner MP 228, showing how secretive and extra-legal Mormon polygamy could be, and how distant from publicly recognized and solemnized marriage.

**VIII. Relief Society:** RS Minutes. **marriage to Joseph:** JSj, Faulring, 396. The list is in the handwriting of Thomas Bullock, entered after July 14, 1843. Compare a letter by "W." printed in "Communications," *Warsaw Signal* (June 11, 1845): p. 2: "The wife of ... Hyde, was strongly suspected as one of these spiritual wives, while her husband was gone to Jerusalem." Marinda also left an affidavit affirming her marriage to Joseph, but with a different date, see below. **Rigdon:** this is the second half of the quote found above. **William Hall:** *Abominations*, 113: "He returned and desired Joe Smith to reinstate him in his former office as one of the Twelve Apostles. The conditions imposed by Joe Smith some of us would consider a little tough. They were these: All the money he had so hardly earned had to be given up to Joe, and, also, his wife, as a ransom for his transgression, to obtain his former standing. Many jokes were cracked at his expense, and he was despised throughout the camp for his ficklemindedness." **Lee:** "Orson Hyde and W.W. Phelps turned against Joseph in Missouri, and forsook him in time of peril and danger, and even testified against him in the courts. [They asked to be reinstated.] With tears he moved that we would forgive them and receive them back into fellowship. He then sent Elder O. Hyde and John E. Page to Jerusalem, and to the land of Palestine, to dedicate that land for the gathering of the Jews. Report said that Hyde's wife, with his consent, was sealed to Joseph for an eternal state, but I do not assert the fact." Lee, MU 147. **Webb Young:** quoted below. **missions and polyandry:** For the marriage of Joseph and Marinda occurring while Orson Hyde was gone on a long mission, see Foster, RS 163-66, on a theoretical form of Levirate polyandry in Mormonism. Compare the Sarah Ann Whitney chapter, at her marriage to Smith, and the Zina Huntington chapter, at June 1846.

**IX. Nancy Rigdon and Joseph:** Bennett, HS 241-45, compare Olney, *The Absurdities of Mormonism Portrayed* 16: "Then he got Mrs. Hide to come in, and made use of her persuasive arguments, that she was first unbelieving in the order, but had been better informed." Bennett was evidently dependent on a letter by Nancy's brother-in-law, George Robinson, which he printed, HS 245-47. The affidavit of J. Wickliffe Rigdon, dated July 28, 1905, is printed in Joseph Fielding Smith's BAOPM, 81-84 (97-102, 1905 ed.). John locates the site of the proposal differently, but otherwise follows Bennett in the incident's general outlines. Orson Hyde confirms some aspects of the story, though he takes a virulent "loyalist" approach that portrays Nancy Rigdon as a "prostitute." See *Speech of Elder Orson Hyde, Delivered before the High Priest's Quorum in Nauvoo, April 27th, 1845, upon the course and Conduct of Mr. Sidney Rigdon* (Nauvoo, IL: John

Taylor, 1845), 27-28: "During my absence to Palestine, the conduct of his daughter, Nancy, became so notorious in this city, according to common rumor, she was regarded generally, little if any better than a public prostitute. Joseph Smith ... felt anxious to reprove and reclaim her if possible. He, accordingly, requested my wife to invite her down to her house. He wished to speak with her and show her the impropriety of being gallanted about by so many different men, many of whom were comparatively strangers to her. Her own parents could look upon it, and think that all was right; being blind to the faults of their daughters. —There being so many of this kind of men visiting Mr. Rigdon's house at the steamboat landing, (for he kept some sort of a tavern or boarding house,) that Mr. Smith did not care to go there to see her. Miss Nancy, I presume, considered her dignity highly insulted at the plain and sharp reproofs she received from this servant of God. She ran home and told her father that Mr. Smith wanted her for a spiritual wife, and that he employed my wife to assist him in obtaining her. This was a good time for Miss Nancy and John C. Bennett to wreak vengeance on the victim of their hatred for his severe admonitions. Mr. Bennett, I think, was a boarder at Mr. Rigdon's at that time, and I am told was all honey with the whole family. No one like Dr. John C. Bennett. Mr. Rigdon also thought this was a good time to crush a member of the Johnson family, against which he had an old grudge, because Father Johnson, after giving him and his family a living for a long time, building a house for them to live in &c., would not give him his farm and all his property; for he once demanded of Father Johnson a deed ... Thus must an unsuspecting female [Marinda Johnson Hyde] suffer for putting down a hand to help, as it is verily believed, a poor miserable girl out of the very slough of prostitution." See Van Wagoner, SR 307. **funeral of Marks:** Jessee 2:375. Bennett, HS 241. Joseph preached at the funeral. **meeting:** Bennett, HS 242-45. George W. Robinson (HS 245-46) wrote that "Smith sent for Miss Rigdon to come to the house of Mrs. Hyde, who lived in the under rooms of the printing office." **aftermath:** The aftermath of the Nancy Rigdon incident does not concern Marinda's life directly, except as it sheds light on Bennett's reliability. As was common with accusations of Joseph's proposals, a confusing crossfire of testimony resulted. We know that there was a confrontation between the Rigdons and Joseph. Nancy and her family accused Joseph of proposing to her; Joseph denied it, and his friends (especially Stephen Markham) accused Nancy of having an affair with John C. Bennett. See the Rigdon and Robinson letters; Markham affidavit, Bachman aff. #28. Bachman 238-45 follows the anti-Nancy Rigdon line, but compare D. Michael Quinn, "150 Years of Truth and Consequences about Mormon History," *Sunstone* 16 (Feb. 1992): 12. Joseph Fielding Smith, strangely, accepted the Nancy Rigdon side of the story, see BAOPM, and the doctrinal letter attributed to Joseph Smith, printed by Bennett in HS 243-45 (which was published by B. H. Roberts as genuine in the *History of the Church*, 5:134-36); compare Jessee, PW 506-9. **Aug. 31:** [Emmeline Wells], "Patty Sessions," WE 13 (Nov. 15, 1884): 94.

**X. Dec. 7:** Jessee 2:497, HC 5:200; Barron, OH 135. **Orson spends time with Joseph:** "He spent the next six months in close association with the Mormon prophet," Hill, HS 66. Compare Faulring, index, s.v. Orson Hyde. **Feb. 6:** Barron, OH 143. **Feb. 28:** JSj, Faulring 313. **Ann Eliza Young:** See her WN19 324-26. **proposal to Price:** Mary Ann Price Hyde autobiography, Bancroft Library. For Hyde's plural wives, see Hyde, "The Orson Hyde Genealogy." **marriage to Browett:** Orson Hyde affidavit, BAOPM 89 (1905 ed.); compare Hill, HS 68; Barron, OH 143. **Apr. 10:** PBSj, see [Wells], "Patty Sessions," WE 13 (Sept. 1, 1884): 95. Marinda had visited at Sylvia Lyon's on February 25; also present were Louisa Beaman, Mary Noble, and Patty Sessions, a meeting of four of Joseph's plural wives, ibid. Her social life also included visits to other apostles. On March 2 she and Orson spent the day with Brigham and Mary Ann Young at Heber Kimball's house. BYj. **remarriage to Joseph:** Marinda Hyde affidavit, May 1, 1869, SAB 1:15, Bachman #53. **marriage to Price:** Price, Autobiography, pp. 2-3. The date is in JSj, Faulring 396 (though we have only the initials, M.P.). Hyde gave the date April 1843, affidavit in BAOPM 74 (89, 1905 ed.). **Marinda witnesses the marriage:** Orson

Hyde affidavit, BAOPM 74. **Marinda on Orson's wives:** WM 405. Compare Orson Hyde affidavit, Spring City, 1869, BAOPM 89 (1905 ed.); Barron, OH 143.

**XI.** **Orson Hyde house:** Holzapfel, *Old Mormon Nauvoo*, 113-14. See Jessee 2:516-18. **family traditions:** Stone, LNMH 2. According to this source, Marinda and Orson gave up the house to help Joseph Smith when he was sued for a large debt. **death of father:** Luke Johnson, "History"; AF. **mission to East:** JSj, Faulring 407; HC 5:537; Hill, HS 69. **Orson returns:** JSj, Faulring 423, 428. **Orson Washington:** *Nauvoo Neighbor* (Nov. 29, 1843): p. 3, tells us that he died after fourteen days. Compare Barron, OH 323. **culminating rituals:** See Ehat, JSI 101; D. Michael Quinn, "Latter-day Saint Prayer Circles," BYUSt 19 (1978): 79-105. **Hyde endowed:** JSj, Faulring 429, compare HC 6:98; WWj Dec. 2, 1843 (2:329). The ordinance of December 2 seems to be the washing and anointing preparatory to receiving the endowment, which Orson apparently received the following day. For washing and anointing, see EM s.v. **Hyde, fullness:** WWj, as quoted in Ehat, JSI 146, compare Kenney 2:343. For the ordinance of the fullness of the priesthood, see Ehat, JSI 95-96, 142, 169. Almost without exception, couples received this ordinance together, e.g. WWj, Jan. 20 and 27, 1844 (2:340, 344): compare Ehat 146-47. **deceased woman:** Quinn, MW 398. One wonders why Orson did not receive this ordinance with one of his plural wives. Perhaps he did. **Marinda endowed:** JSj, Feb. 18, Faulring 446 ("I attended Prayer Meeting at seven over the store. Sister Hyde was there.") Richards wrote "prayer Meeting eve Sis Hyde"; Woodruff (2:350), wrote, "On our return home I met with the quorum Pres. Joseph Smith with us. We had a good time. Sister Orson Hyde was present." Compare Quinn, MW 395. **Orson to Washington:** HC 6:283; 369-76; Donna Hill, JS 443.

**XII.** **Hyde's return:** Hill, HS 80; HC 6:264. **Holy Order meeting:** HCKj, Book 93, Dec. 7, 1845 (OPW 164): "Then Elder O. Hide gave a chort exortation ... Seven present have not had thare Last Anointing ... [including] Sister Marinda Hide." **Marinda sealed to Orson:** SAd 309. **Daughters sealed to Marinda and Orson:** SAd 329. **Frank Henry:** Barron, OH 324; AF. He married Mary O'Neal and Marcia Hanks, and died in Salt Lake in 1908. **Luke rebaptized:** BE 1:81. **Hydes in Nauvoo until dedication of temple:** Wandle Mace Autobiography, typescript, Lee Library, p. 197; Aroet Hale, Autobiography, typescript, Lee Library, p. 9; Hill, HS 82; JH Mar. 27, Apr. 30; Barron, OH 165. **departure from Nauvoo:** Barron, OH 166.

**XIII.** **Marinda and family arrive:** JH, June 17. The Hydes had reached Mt. Pisgah on June 7. **Patty Sessions:** PBSj, July 17. **Orson's mission to England:** JH, Aug. 5; Barron, OH 168. **Marinda at Louisa's:** "Visited Sister Hyde at Louisa's she is making me a dress." That Marinda lived with Louisa is confirmed by the letter of Louisa to Marinda quoted below. However, who lived at whose house is uncertain. **Orson returns:** "Letter from Pres. Orson Hyde," MSt 9 (Aug. 15, 1847): 241-43, 241. Compare WM 405; Barron, OH 176. **Letter to Sarah Kimball:** See letter of Sarah M. Kimball to Marinda, dated Jan. 2, 1848, Marinda Hyde collection, CA. **Alonzo:** Barron, OH 324; AF. He later married two wives and died in 1910 in Salt Lake City. **Letter to Louisa Beaman:** See Apr. 8 letter from Beaman, below. **Louisa to Marinda, April 8:** Marinda Hyde collection, CA. "br Bentley and wife" are Richard Bentley and Elizabeth Price Bentley, Mary Ann Price's sister. "Charls and Elsa" are Charles Price (the brother of Mary Ann Price) and Elsa Johnson Price, a daughter of Luke Johnson. **Louisa to Marinda, July 14:** Marinda Hyde collection, CA. **Orson in Washington:** Hill, HS 94-97; Barron, OH. **Delia:** Barron, OH 324; AF. Delia married Nathan Ellis and died in 1907. **Orson to Utah:** DN (Sept. 14, 1850): 106; Hill, HS 103; BE 1:81.

**XIV.** **Marinda quote:** WM 405. **arrival in the valley:** Barron, OH 195. **Quinlan:** Quinn, MHOP 552. **Browett divorce:** Quinn, MHOP 552. Barron, OH 230, dates it in 1865. **location of new house:** Stone, LNMH 3; Barron, OH 196. **Heber Hyde:** Salt Lake City deaths, #996; Barron, OH 324. **Fort Supply:** Barron, OH 199-201. **tension between Young and Orson:** WWj, Dec. 29, 1856 (4:523); Quinn, MHEP 38-40. **Mary Lavina:** AF. But the death record gives the birthday as November 10, 1854. Mary died on June 29, 1855, Salt Lake City Death Record, 997; compare Barron, OH 324. **Emily's**

**marriage:** AF. **Orson leaves for Carson:** HStj, May 15, 1855 (OMF 2:555); Albert Page, *Orson Hyde and the Carson Valley Mission, 1855-57* (Provo, UT: Brigham Young University, 1970); Barron, OH 206. **Laura's marriage:** AF. **Sessions journal:** Sister Knight is probably Martha McBride Knight, see her chapter. **Orson's return from Carson:** Page, *Orson Hyde*; Barron, OH 213; compare PBSj, Dec. 13, 1856. **Vickers:** Barron, OH 323; Quinn, MHOP 552. **Winters:** Quinn, MHOP 552. Compare AF; Barron does not seem to know of Winters. Helen and Orson divorced in 1859. **1857 marriage to Joseph Smith:** Ivins list, #41. **Zina:** Zina married Joseph Bull and died in 1939. She was Marinda's companion in her twilight years.

XV. **Mary Ann Price Hyde:** Autobiography, pp. 3-4. **Luke's death:** BE 1:86. **Reinhart:** Barron, OH 226; Quinn, MHOP 552. **Elizabeth J. Gallier:** Barron, OH 324; Quinn, MHOP 552. **Lyon:** Barron, OH 230; Quinn, MHOP 552. **Ann Eliza Webb Young:** WN19 324. Zina Young also mentions going to a party with a friend, to which her husband was in attendance, apparently with other wives, see Zina Huntington chapter, early Utah period. For church dances in Utah's polygamous era, see Hardy SC 321. **Patty Sessions journal:** May 29, 1866, "We called on Sister Hyde."

XVI. **Relief Society:** WM 405-406. Julia Ives Pack, Autobiography, "Julia," in OPH 9:447-52, 451. **Deseret Hospital:** "In Memoriam," WE 14 (May 1, 1886): 181. In a picture of the board of directors, Marinda is seated next to Zina Huntington Young, see HTW 3:116; Godfrey WV 18. **quote from Alder:** Lydia D. Alder, "Death of Mrs. Marinda A. Hyde," in WE 14 (Apr. 1, 1886): 165. **Heywood:** Marinda Hyde, "In Memoriam," WE 10 (Dec. 15, 1881): 109. **divorce:** Sanpete County Probate Court record 4:37-38, as cited in Myrtle Hyde to Todd Compton, Mar. 28, 1996. Quote is from the same letter. **March 1873:** "F.R. Society Reports," WE 1 (Apr. 1, 1873): 162. On November 25, 1874, Marinda attended a "tea party" at Emmeline Wells's home with Eliza Snow, Zina Young, Elizabeth Whitney, Rachel Grant, and other prominent women. EBWj. **Marinda to the east:** Eliza R. Snow to Marinda Hyde, June 25, 1876, CA MS 716, including a Poem: "To My dear friend, Marinda N. Hyde, On her departure for a visit to her relatives in the State." Feb. 20, 1876. **November 17, 1876:** "General Meeting of Central and Ward Committees," WE 5 (Dec. 1, 1876): 99. **granary completed:** "Home Affairs," WE 6 (Oct. 1, 1877): 69. **R.S. hall:** Alder, "Death," 165. In the nineteenth century, Relief Societies built their own separate halls; now Relief Societies meet in ward meeting houses. A picture of a "Society Hall" built in 1869 can be found in WC 97. See Mary E. Rollins chapter. Pictures of granaries in *History of Relief Society* 112. Compare "Home Affairs," WE 6 (Oct. 1 1877): 69, for a description of this building. **ERS to Mary Lightner:** June 17, 1880, Mary E. Lightner collection, Lee Library. **July 10:** Endowment House Record, Book I, as cited in Ivins 4:284. **Frank's marriage:** AF. **Orson's death:** BE 1:82; Barron, OH 249. **Zina her companion:** Alder, "Death," 165. **granddaughter's memories:** Stone, LNMH 3. **1881:** EBWj. **1884:** Emily Partridge journal, CA. **Helen Mar on the birthday:** Helen Mar Whitney journal, CA. **Exponent:** "Editorial Notes," WE 14 (July 1, 1885): 20.

XVII. **Marinda's death:** DW 35 (11) (Mar. 31, 1886): 176; Alder, "Death," 165. Helen Mar Whitney's son Orson spoke at the funeral, HMWj, Mar. 26.


# REFERENCES TO CHAPTER 10.

*Mother In Israel:*
*Elizabeth Davis (Goldsmith Brackenbury Durfee Smith Lott)*

I would like to thank Ethel Jo Brackenbury Christopherson and Jennifer Brackenbury Boger, descendants of Elizabeth, and Maxine Willoughby, whose children are descendants, for helping me trace the complex career of Elizabeth and her sons before and after Nauvoo.

Blagg, Claire Elizabeth Casell. "The Brackenbury Story." Unpublished, written from information supplied by Ethel Jo Christopherson and Jennifer Boger.

Boger, Jennifer Brackenbury. "Descendants of Joseph Blanchett Brackenbury." Typescript, in author's possession.

"Died." *Saints' Herald* 24 (Jan. 15, 1877): 31. Elizabeth's RLDS obituary.

Jenson, Andrew. "Brackenbury, Joseph Blanchett." BE 2:597.

Willoughby, Maxine. "Benjamin Blanchard Brackenbury." Typescript, in author's possession.

**endowment:** JSj, Faulring, 417. The Clayton journal, Sept. 3, 1844, IC 147, has "Sister Durfee" on the list of those endowed while Joseph was alive. Only two other women are listed singly: Agnes [Coolbrith] Smith and Lucy Mack Smith.

I. **date of birth:** NTER p. 49: "Durfee, Elizabeth, f, 11 March 1791 [n. 2: w-a record only], Riverhead, Suffolk, New York." Compare SAd 505: Elizabeth Davis, b. March 11, 1791, in Riverhead, Suffolk, New York. Christening, Aug. 28, 1791: Mattituck-Aquebogue Parishes, Suffolk, 1752-1809, GS Film 547576, Printout 0883685, Bt. C506121, compare 1396190, 8612001, Sh 39; Charles Edmiston Craven, *A History of Mattituck, Long Island New York* (Mattituck, NY: for the author, 1906), 301. **Gilbert Davis:** A list of Elizabeth's parents and siblings, with dates of birth, is found on p. 5 of "A Partial List of the Persons Who Were Driven Out of Jackson County, Missouri, by the Mob in 1833," compiled by George A. Smith and Thomas Bullock in 1864, which I consulted in the Jackson County Historical Society Archives, but also in CA. Though Elizabeth and her boys belong on such a list, it is extremely unlikely that her parents and siblings ever came to Jackson County, so their presence on this list is a mystery. However, no other such list exists, and comparison with other genealogical records has substantiated it. See also Patriarchal Blessing Index. Gilbert was born in 1752 and died in 1838, "A Partial List," 5. We have his Revolutionary War pension application, copy in possession of author, compare Wayland Jefferson, *Cutchogue, Southold's First Colony* (New York: n.p., 1940), 72. **Abigail Reeves:** Name from Nauvoo baptism for the dead record, A-34; ECIF. She was born in 1753 and died in 1833, "A Partial List," 5. **William:** "A Partial List," 5. **Jeremiah Davis** married a Martha (Patty) Wells in 1801 and died in 1866, Craven, *A History* 336, or 1871, Davis genealogy records. Beatrice D. Johnson, a descendant of Jeremiah, letters to Jennifer Brackenbury Boger, Apr. 13, 23, May 28, Aug. 1, 1984. **James Davis** may have died in 1855, Boger to Compton 2; Intestate Records of Suffolk County, Liber D, s.v. Gilbert Goldsmith. **John:** "A Partial List," 5. **Sarah Davis:** "A Partial List," 5. She was christened on November 5, 1788, and married John Wells. Suffolk christening records, Craven 336, and IGI. **Leopold:** "A Partial List," 5; baptism for the dead records in Nauvoo. He was christened on July 30, 1795, Suffolk christening records, Craven 305, IGI (Here, "Lepport"). He died in 1825, "A Partial List," 5. **other siblings:** Elizabeth did baptisms for Deborah Davis and Betsey Davis, who are listed as siblings, ECIF; A-30, but they are not on "A Partial List." Other possible siblings, according to family genealogy, are Abigail, who married a Mr. Hall; and Gilbert Jr., who married an Elizabeth Goldsmith in 1800 and died in 1803. **brothers left home:** 1800 census, Suffolk County. **ferry:** Blagg, "Brackenbury Story," 1. **overseer:** Arthur Channing Down, "Riverhead Town Records," available in New York Public Library, 31, 102. See also 17-19, 40, 42, 277. **Presbyterian:** on his Revolutionary War pension application, Gilbert gives as a reference "Rev. Ezra Youngs," a Presbyterian clergyman who served in Cutchogue, see "The First Presbyterian Church of Southold—From the Tercentenary Celebration 1640-1940," as cited in Beatrice Johnson letters.

II. **marriage:** Cutchogue Church Records, as recorded in Jefferson, *Cutchogue* 155; IGI, GS 1553207, b 8813202, sh 29 and Blagg, "Brackenbury Story," 1, have April 13; some genealogical records have January 13, 1811, as the date of marriage. Gilbert had been born on November 23, 1785 (FGS), and was christened on November 23, 1788, in Mattituck, Suffolk, New York (four miles west of Cutchogue), Craven 296. **Methodism:** Boger to Compton, 2. **Gilbert Jr.:** Date of birth from NTER. See also Boger, "Descendants,"

App. 1; Maxine Willoughby, BBB 2. Gilbert married Abigail Durfee, a daughter of his stepfather, Jabez Durfee, see Boger, "Descendants," compare NTER. He lived in Nauvoo at the same time that Elizabeth did, and died in 1847 in Independence, Missouri. **death of Gilbert Sr.:** Blagg, "Brackenbury Story," 1.

III. **marriage:** SEB, citing "Journal Histories"; SEB does not give a date. In Jefferson, *Cutchogue* 162, a "Gilbert, son of Widow Betsey Goldsmith" is baptized by Lathrop Thompson on July 9, 1815, in Cutchogue. This reference shows that Elizabeth had not remarried yet, and presumably was still living in eastern Long Island. **Joseph Brackenbury:** early emigration, see BE 2:597. **estate papers:** Mar. 8, 1832, copies in my possession. **Charles Wesley:** Birth date from Book of Patriarchal Blessings 3:447, see PBI; ECIF. Blagg, "Brackenbury Story," gives Newtown, Queens (Kings), Long Island, New York. "Newton" is probably "Newtown," on the border between Kings (today's Brooklyn) and Queens counties, Boger to Compton, 3. Charles married an Elizabeth by 1842 and was living in Nauvoo in the spring of that year (see the census). According to family traditions, he served a mission for the LDS church in 1855. The 1860 Illinois census shows him living in Atlas, Pike County, Illinois, with Elizabeth, age thirty-seven, and five children, and he can also be found in the 1870 census. His death date is not known. **Isaac travels with them:** Blagg, "Brackenbury Story," 1. Faith Kishman to Jennifer Brackenbury Boger, Aug. 20, 1984. **old families migrate:** Boger to Compton 3. **Joseph and Benjamin I:** Boger, "Descendants." Compare the 1842 Nauvoo Record of Membership, Fourth Ward, p. 1, in which Joseph I and Benjamin I are listed as "dead." See below, Nauvoo section. Joseph Blanchette would die in 1838. **Benjamin:** Birth date from Book of Patriarchal Blessings 3:448, see PBI; "Early Reorganization Minutes 1852-1871," RLDS Archives, p. 804. ECIF has 1826. See also Larson, *Data Base* 29; FGS; OPH 11:395; Willoughby BBB. For further documentation, see below. He married Phebe Allen in 1848/49, Sarah Kerr in 1857, Mary Kelly in 1868, and Olive Matthews in 1896, before dying in Caldwell, Idaho at the age of seventy. **John Wesley:** Date of birth from testimony in Temple Lot Case, 231-33; "Early Reorganization Minutes 1852-1871," RLDS Archives, p. 804; Book of Patriarchal Blessings 3:448, see PBI; ECIF. Compare Family Group Sheet, father. He married Frances Lamb in 1854 (see IGI), Samantha Daly in 1861, and Nancy Curtis in 1884, and died in Riverside, California, at the age of seventy-three. See his obituary in "General Church News," Independence section, in *Zion's Ensign* 13 (27) (July 3, 1902 [Thursday]): p. 2. **residence in Ohio:** In 1830 the Ohio census, p. 407, shows Joseph Brackenbury ("Brockinby") living in New London, Huron County, with Elizabeth and four young male children. Apparently, Gilbert was no longer living with the Brackenburys by this time.

IV. **Elizabeth's baptism:** See "Died." The officiator is given as "John Carl." Compare 2:597; SEB. **Joseph an elder:** FWR p. 6; Jenson 2:597. **June Conference:** FWR 6; HC 1:185. **healing the old woman:** *An Early Latter Day Saint History: The Book of John Whitmer*, ed. by F. Mark McKiernan and Roger D. Launius (Independence, MO: Herald House, 1980), 80. **October Conference:** FWR 19, 25 (ordained to High Priesthood); HC, at the date. Compare *Book of John Whitmer* 84. **speech:** FWR 22. **Sidney rebukes:** FWR 26. **Benjamin Johnson:** MLR 12-13. **Joel Hills Johnson:** Reminiscences and Journals, 1835-82, CA, MS 1546, fd 3. **death:** See also HC 7:523-24; JH, Jan. 7, 1832. Non-Mormon accounts in *Burlington [Vermont] Sentinel* 22 (12) (Mar. 23, 1832): Joseph and his companions "preached, exhorted, and with great *zeal* and *apparent* humility, attempted to propagate their doctrines ... they *professed* to have power to heal the sick and raise the dead ... The company of Brackenbury attempted also to heal him, and since his disease [decease], to raise him from the dead." Repr. in *Ohio Star* (Apr. 12, 1832); *Wayne Sentinel* (Apr. 11, 1832). See also *Wayne Sentinel* (Feb. 14, 1832). Available in Dale Morgan, "The Mormons and the Far West" Collection, Huntington Library. Compare Prince, *Power From On High* 19, 150. See also George A. Smith to Elizabeth Brackenbury, Aug. 29, 1855, Henry Stebbins Collection, P24/F1, RLDS Archives. John Phillips Downs, ed., *History of Chautauqua Co., New York* I

(Boston and New York: American Historical Society, 1921), 59; Obed Edson, *History of Chautauqua Co., New York* (Boston: W.A. Fergusson, 1894), 478. Here the dying Joseph asserts that he will rise from the dead three days after his death, and a medical student attempts to grave rob his corpse. **date of death:** BE 2:597. **holograph:** Estate papers of Joseph Brackenbury, copies in my possession.

V. **John Wesley quote:** Temple Lot Case 231-33. Compare transcript, box 1, fd 8, p. 549. For the Mormon experience in Jackson County, see the Mary Elizabeth Rollins and Emily Partridge chapters. **Edmund to Jackson County:** HC 7:524. **Jabez in Jackson by 1833:** KEQR 81. **March 12:** Boger, "Descendants," App. 1. **ten acres:** John Wesley in Temple Lot case, 231-33. **expulsion from Jackson County:** John Wesley in Temple Lot case, 231-33. B.H. Roberts dates a "veritable reign of terror" in Jackson County from October 31 to November 7, 1833, CHC 1:343, compare HC 1:426-37; SLDS 82-87, bibliography in 663-64. For the migration across the river to the "bottoms," see the *Autobiography* of Parley Pratt, 109-10. **falling stars:** See John Wesley's obituary and the Emily Partridge chapter.

VI. **death of Electa:** AF. Marriage Records, Clay Co., Missouri, GS film 955303, batch M514791, p. 119. **Jabez:** Birth date, NTER. **Jabez's children:** Nauvoo 1842 census, see below at 1842. **Jabez in paramilitary:** Quinn, MHOP 481, citing the testimony of Sampson Avard. **Arthur's mill:** John Wesley in Temple Lot case, 231-33. Compare Temple Lot transcript p. 550 for Arthur's full name. Also, "Amasa Lyman's History," in "History of Brigham Young," MSt 27 (1865): 503. **May 5:** Boger, "Descendants," app. 1. **move to Far West:** John Wesley in Temple Lot case, 231-33. **Jabez an elder:** KEQR 17, 81. **John baptized:** EMRC. In fall 1843 "Elisabeth Durfee" signed the "scroll petition" for redress in Missouri: HC 6:125; Clark Johnson, *Mormon Redress Petitions* (Provo, UT: Brigham Young University Religious Studies Center, 1992), 586. For the Mormon departure from Missouri, see Agnes Coolbrith and Patty Bartlett Sessions chapters. **Joseph Blanchette Jr.'s death:** Boger, "Descendants," p. 1.

VII. **Quincy:** John Wesley Brackenbury, Temple Lot Case 231-33. Their Nauvoo home is marked #28 on Jessee's map, Papers 2:516. Book of Patriarchal Blessings 3:446-448, compare PBI. Gilbert apparently did not receive a patriarchal blessing at this time. **school house:** Minutes, High Council, Nauvoo (CA and Marquardt collection, Marriott Library); Bk 1, p. 52 (Mar. 22, 1840). **John Wesley as schoolmate of JSIII:** Joseph Smith III, in HRC 4:187. Benjamin and John Brackenbury attended the Eliza Snow school with Joseph Smith III in December 1842, see "Nauvoo School Records," in *The Nauvoo Journal* 1 (1989): 24. **dinner party:** JSj, Faulring 292. **the Durfees:** Nauvoo Census, spring 1842, GS film 581219, Fourth Ward, first page. **Charles Wesley:** Nauvoo Census, Fourth Ward, eighth page.

VIII. **Bennett:** HS 256. Sarah Pratt, in Wyl MP 54: "There was an old woman called Durfee. She knew a good deal about the Prophet's amorous adventures and, to keep her quiet, he admitted her to the secret blessings of celestial bliss. I don't think that she was ever sealed to him, though it may have been the case after Joseph's death, when the temple was finished. At all events, she boasted here in Salt Lake of having been one of Joseph's wives." Elizabeth's own statement that she married Joseph is more valuable that Sarah's uncertainty about whether Elizabeth was sealed to Joseph during his lifetime. **Partridges:** See below. **Jackson:** Joseph H. Jackson, *A Narrative* 14; Jackson, "Wonderful Disclosures Respecting Mormons," in New York *Herald* (Sept. 5, 1844): p. 1; compare the Patty Sessions chapter. **proxy marriage:** See below. **member of Relief Society:** RS Min., compare ME 108. **Elizabeth and Clarissa:** RS Min. 23-24. **Elizabeth receives administration:** RS Min., Apr. 19. On April 19 Elizabeth also donated $.25 to the Relief Society, and on June 23 (RS Min., at that date), she contributed $14, a substantial sum for those days. **Committee:** RS Min., Apr. 28. **Elizabeth on Emma after visit to Carlin:** RS Min. **Emma to Mrs. Durphy's:** Jessee 2:406. **poem:** ERSj, Oct. 12. **Elizabeth asks Emma about Joseph:** in notebook of Zina H. Young, Zina Card Brown collection, CA, Box 1, folder 14. **Joseph travels with Mrs. Durphy:** JSj, Faulring 258-59. The parenthetical sentence is edited out of HC 5:210. **the next day:** JSj,

Faulring 259; "Started at 8 o'clock. (Sis Durphy's daughter tarried and Bro Wm Smith, wife, and little daughter accompanied) ... Arrived at Rushville Bell Tavern by Mrs. Stevenson 3 P.M. 20 miles." HC 5:210: "We started about 8 o'clock, and arrived at Mr Stevenson's tavern, in Rushville, at three in the afternoon, about twenty miles. Brother William's wife, who was sick, went with us, accompanied by Sister Durphy." **to Plymouth again:** JSj, Faulring 291, compare HC 5:247. **Elizabeth and the Partridges:** Emily Partridge Young, Autobiography, CA, 4. Compare ME 138. **Joseph to Durphy's house:** JSj, Faulring 324; HC 5:294. **proposal:** Emily Partridge Young, Autobiography, 4. **March 4:** JSj, Faulring 327. For further documentation of the Partridge marriages, see the Partridge chapters. **school social:** ERSj. **to Lott farm:** ERSj. **June 16:** RS Min., p. 91. **Rockwell:** RS Min., p. 94. **rolls:** RS Min., "Meeting of the Third Ward," July 21. On August 6 Joseph and William Clayton walked from Clayton's house to "Sister Durfee's," and then to Joseph's. **endowment:** See Introduction to this chapter. **Clayton's robe:** Clayton journal; IC 125. For the Mormon temple robes and garment, see Evelyn Marshall, "Garments," in EM 534-35. In April 1844 Gilbert Goldsmith was assigned a mission to New York to promote Joseph Smith's campaign for the presidency, HC 6:336.

IX. **Elizabeth with Emma:** RLDS obituary. **Gilbert as doorkeeper:** "History of Joseph Smith, June, 1844," DN 38 (Nov. 25, 1857): p. 1. **Gilbert as pallbearer:** ibid., p. 2; CHC 6:528. **October 8:** ECIF. **December:** See William Clayton, "An Interesting Journal," IC 547. **Jan. 17:** WRj, CA. **March 10:** Dallin Oaks and Marvin Hill, *Carthage Conspiracy* (Urbana: University of Illinois Press, 1975), 68-69; OMF 1:26-27 n. 53; compare p. 20. **trial:** HC 7:380-84; CHC 2:323. Oaks and Hill, CC 150-56. Compare Willoughby BBB 3. **paintings:** CHC 2:333. **arrested for perjury:** OMF 1:26; Oliver Huntington journal 1:55, quoted in OMF 1:26. On May 11, 1845, Gilbert D. Goldsmith received his high priest license, ECIF. **Jennetta Richards dies:** WRj. **Elizabeth's family helps:** See WCj, Dec. 11, IC 228: Gilbert "Gouldsmith," with David Sessions, "volunteered to draw water from the river in barrels for the use of the Temple." **December 18:** NTER. **December 20:** NTER. His wife, Abigail is given the birth date of May 22, 1814. **December 23:** NTER. This entry has Elizabeth's correct birth date, March 11, 1791, from the washing and anointing record. **December 24-25:** HCKj (Clayton), Bk 93. For this ritual, see Donald Parry, "Washings and Anointings," in EM 1551. **January 21 marriages:** SAd 251.

X. **marriage:** BOP #58: after the proxy marriage for time and eternity to Smith, "C. P. Lott & Elizabeth Smith was then sealed for time - [Lott] promising to deliver (E. Smith) to her husband J. Smith in Eternity."; SAd 505, 385. **other marriages:** SAd 381. **Lott:** See AF; Jessee 2:566. **Danite leader in Missouri:** "Celebration of the 4th of July," *Elder's Journal* 1 (Aug. 1838): 60; Johnson, MLR 38; Quinn, MHOP 482. Council of Fifty, see Quinn, MHOP 524. See also OMF, esp. 1:65-66, and index; and the chapter on Melissa Lott in this book. **February 7:** SAd 385. **Elizabeth travels with Lott:** WCj, June 28, 1846. **Lott in Winter Quarters:** *Iowa Branch Index by Branch*, CA, p. 69, 71; V. 1, p. 16. Jabez Durfee was in the Pottawattamie Branch, Iowa, as was Perry Durfee. V. 1, p. 53. Cornelius Lott was in the same branch. **Charles Wesley:** 1860 Census, Illinois, p. 960. **Joseph Goldsmith:** AF. However, Boger, "Descendants," has Joseph born in Quincy, Illinois. **David Goldsmith:** Conrey Bryson, *Winter Quarters* (Salt Lake City: Deseret Book, 1986), 143. **Gilbert dies:** Boger, "Descendants," App. 1. **Benjamin with Mormon Battalion:** Daniel Tyler, *A Concise History of the Mormon Battalion in the Mexican War* (1881; no other publication information given), 120; Larson, *Data Base* 29; OPH 11:395. CHC 3:84. Ricketts, MB.

XI. **back to Illinois:** John Wesley Brackenbury, Temple Lot Case, 231-33. **Elizabeth lived with her sons:** The 1860 Missouri and 1870 Kansas censuses show Elizabeth living with or near to Benjamin and John Wesley, respectively. Lott's two wives: SAd 741. **Lott crosses plains:** JH, Supplement after Dec. 31, 1848, p. 12. Lehi Centennial *History* 276. HCKj, June 6, 1848. **Lott's death:** ZDYj; see Melissa Lott chapter. **Jabez in Winter Quarters:** Durfee family traditions, Gloria Galloway, private communication.

*Iowa Branch Index, 1839-1859,* V. 1, p. 53. **Pickle dies:** Backman, *Profile* 22. **death of Jabez:** AF.

XII. **Battalion:** Ricketts, MB 223; CHC 3:359-60. **child born in Utah:** Boger, "Descendants." Phebe Allen had crossed the plains in the second 1847 company with her father and mother, Elihu and Lola Allen, see HTW 8:433. **Ben disciplined:** HStj, OMF 2:343. JDLj, AMC 1:96. **Ben rebaptized:** ECIF, s.v. Benjamin Brackenbury. The date given is May 20, 1855, at Springville. **1850:** 1850 Utah census, Weber County. **second and third children:** Howard Brackenbury Reminiscences, p. 1, copy in my possession; FGH; Boger, "Descendants." Caroline Matilda, born April 1, 1852, Edwin Devalson, born July 17, 1855, both in Ogden. **1856:** Willoughby BBB 5.

XIII. **John marries Frances Lamb:** Marriage Records, Pike County, 1854-55, GS film 1,314,777. **to Utah:** John Wesley Brackenbury, Temple Lot Case, 106-7. **Pratt:** "At all events, she [Mrs. Durphy] boasted here in Salt Lake of having been one of Joseph's wives." Sarah Pratt, in Wyl, MP 54. **Aug. 31:** ZDYj. **to "States":** John Wesley Brackenbury, Temple Lot Case, 106-107. **in Utah:** The 1860 Utah census, Ogden city, shows the Benjamin Brackenbury children living in the George Graham household. **marriage of Ben:** FGS. **to Utah:** John Wesley Brackenbury, Temple Lot Case, 106-7. **rebaptism:** family traditions; ECIF, s.v. Elizabeth Brackenbury. The source in ECIF is given as "Re.Bap. 1808, p. 108." **1860 Missouri census:** Washington T., DeKalb County, p. 660: Benjamin is 30 and gives "Blacksmith" as his profession; Sarah is 25. "Elizabeth Brackenbury" is 69, and was born in New York. **John Wesley, son of Ben:** AF. This John Wesley died on November 10, 1923, in Vernal, Uintah, Utah, after marrying Etta May Barringer. His birth in Colorado in 1863 is confirmed by the 1870 Kansas census, see below. Family traditions report another child, Florence, born in Denver.

XIV. **to California:** John Wesley Brackenbury, Temple Lot Case, 106-7. **John's marriage to Daly:** Marriage certificate, copy in my possession; IGI. He would have nine children through this marriage. For early Mormon San Bernardino, see Lyman SB; Agnes Coolbrith chapter at 1856. Mormons dissatisfied with Brigham Young gravitated here even before 1857, when the more orthodox Mormons returned to Utah. **Benjamin arrives:** Bankruptcy documents, copies in my possession. Case # 231, County Court, Box 12, 1867, Benjamin Brackenbury vs. His Creditors. **Mary Kelly:** FGS. **RLDS missionaries:** ME 282-24, 287; Lyman, SB 425. **John's baptism:** "Early Reorganization Minutes, 1852-1871," RLDS Archives, p. 804; General Membership Record Books, Book B, p. 285. However, "Early Reorganization Minutes, 1852-1871," p. 527, gives "Feb. 1866" as date of baptism. EMRC 582. **Joseph A.:** General Membership Record Books, Book B, p. 285.

XV. **John ordained elder in Utah:** General Membership Record Books, Book B, p. 285; RLDS Deceased Files, Members Born before 1849; EMRC 582. **move to Kansas:** Blagg, "Brackenbury Story," 3. **Elizabeth's baptism:** "Early Reorganization Minutes, 1852-1871," p. 804; "General Membership Record Books," Book B, p. 285. However, "Early Reorganization Minutes, 1852-1871," p. 527, has Nov. 15, 1869, and December 3, 1870, is found in her *Saints' Herald* obituary, see Anon., "Died." EMRC 581. **Benjamin's baptism:** "Early Reorganization Minutes, 1852-1871," p. 804; EMRC 581. His wife, Mary, was baptized by Bays, but was confirmed by John Wesley, Minutes p. 804, which confirms that John Wesley was in Kansas then. **Kansas Census:** 1870, Doniphan County, White Cloud, p. 119. **Nov. 6, 1870:** RLDS membership records, Book B, page 309. **Brackenburys and RLDS congregations:** "Latter Day Saints," in Walter Montgomery, ed., *Illustrated Doniphan County, 1837-1916.* Supplement to the *Weekly Kansas Chief* (Troy, KS: n.p., Apr. 6, 1916): p. 91.

XVI. **November 10:** *Illustrated Doniphan County,* 380. John Wesley's wife was still living in 1880, see Missouri Census, Jackson County, Independence, p. 47. Mary Kelly, with whom Benjamin was living in 1870, lived till November 2, 1894, FGS. **alternate date:** *Saints' Herald* obituary, Anon., "Died." **RLDS church and Joseph's polygamy:** For RLDS attitudes toward polygamy in Nauvoo, see Richard Howard, "The Changing RLDS Response to Mormon Polygamy: A Preliminary Analysis," *John Whitmer Historical Association Journal* 3 (1983): 14-28; Robert Flanders, *Nauvoo, Kingdom on the Mississippi* (Urbana: University of Illinois Press 1965), 267-77; Roger D. Launius, *Joseph Smith III, Pragmatic Prophet* (Urbana:

University of Illinois Press 1988), 204-209. Most RLDS historians have accepted that Joseph practiced polygamy, though the subject is still problematic for many RLDS members. However, the details of Joseph's polygamy can be as uncomfortable for modern monogamous LDS faithful as they are for the traditional RLDS faithful.

XVII. **Mary:** Family genealogy; Maxine Willoughby to Todd Compton, Aug. 1, 1993. Mary died at Independence, Jackson, Missouri on Nov. 2, 1894, according to the Benjamin-Mary FGS. **Benjamin disciplined:** HRC 4:443. Boger gives May 2, 1883, as the date of expulsion, Jennifer Brackenbury Boger to Maxine Willoughby, Sept. 28, 1993. **sons in Idaho:** See the Idaho 1880 census, Cassia County, p. 164, Benjamin B. Brackenbury (age 30), and Edwin D. Brackenbury (age 24). **Olive Mathews:** There has been a confusion between Benjamin Brackenbury, Sr., and Benjamin Brackenbury, Jr., in recording this marriage. However, according to family traditions, Olive claimed Benjamin's Mormon Battalion pension after his death, so this is Ben Sr. **death date of Benjamin:** FGS. **Joseph Smith III visits John:** HRC 4:187, compare 4:560. For John in Independence, see Melissa Warnky Etzenhouser, *First Twenty Years History of the Reorganized Church of Jesus Christ of Latter Day Saints in the "Queen City of the Trails,"* (n.p.: author, 1945; 2nd ed. 1952), 15, 6, 13, 20-21, 34, 37; Pearl Wilcox, *Saints of the Reorganization in Missouri* (Independence, MO: the author, 1974). **John's stubbornness:** Joseph Smith III to John W. Brackenbury, May 5, 1880, in Joseph Smith III Letterbook 3, P6, RLDS Archives. Other letters from Joseph to John concern building the church in Independence, activities of non-RLDS Restoration groups in Independence, and pastoral matters. A daughter-in-law of John Wesley remembers him as "very stern," Claire Cassell Blagg, "Stories from Aunt Luna," typescript in author's possession. **1880:** Missouri census, Jackson County, Independence, p. 47. **Samantha dies:** EMRC 582. **marriage to Curtis:** Boger, "Descendants," 5c. As one of Elizabeth's descendants remarked to me, the Brackenbury boys were not polygamists, but they certainly married a lot. **death of John:** See his obituary, cited at his birth above; EMRC 581.

# REFERENCES TO CHAPTER 11.
### Relief Society Counselor:
### Sarah Maryetta Kingsley (Howe Cleveland Smith Smith)

Anon. Biography. CA. Possibly by Augusta Cleveland Smith, or by a granddaughter of Sarah.

Cleveland, Edmund J. *The Genealogy of the Cleveland and Cleaveland Families.* Hartford, CT: Case, Lockwood & Brainard Co., 1899.

Howard, Richard P. ed. *The Memoirs of President Joseph Smith III (1832-1914).* Independence, MO: Herald Publishing House, 1979.

JLSC: J. L. Smith collection. Lee Library, MS 680.

Smith, John. Journal. CA. [Bitton, *Guide* #2291].

Smith, John Lyman. Diary. CA 2072 is the 9-volume diary, original at Lee Library (the earlier document). CA 1122 is the 4-volume diary (evidently, a later version), summarized in Bitton, *Guide to Mormon Diaries,* #2297.

VRBM: *Vital Records of Becket, Massachusetts, to the Year 1850.* Boston: New England Historic Genealogical Society, 1903.

**conversion:** Biography.

I. **birth:** NTER, p. 32; SAd 501. VRBM p. 23: "Sallah Merritta, d.[aughter of] Ebenezer and Sarah, Oct. 20, 1788. C.R. [Church Records] 350." Cook, RP 120; ECIF. The biography has May 26, 1788 as the birth date. **Ebenezer Kingsley:** VRBM p. 22; IGI. His birth date was February 18, 1758. **Sarah Chaplin:** IGI; this identification is not certain. She was born on September 10, 1758 in Lunenburg, Worcester, Massachusetts. **Ebenezer Chaplin:** VRBM p. 22; IGI. **Benjamin:** VRBM p. 21. **teenage conflict:** Sarah Brown to Sally M. Howe, Jan. 16, 1811, JLSC, fd 11. **Sarah's mother to St. Louis:** For this journey, see two letters by Sarah Brown to Ebenezer Chaplin Kingsley, JLSC, fd 14. Compare Sarah Brown's letters to our Sarah in fd 11. **1805 letter:** Ebenezer C. Kingsley to Sarah Kingsley, July 6 [1805], JLSC, fd 11. For the importance of formal conversion to Jesus in Protestant revivalism at this time, see Presendia Huntington chapter, at her childhood. Sarah was still in the academy in 1806, see Ebenezer C. Kingsley to Sarah Kingsley, Mar. 12, 1806; JLSC, fd 14.

II. **December 7:** Connecticut Vital Records, GS #1452 Pt. 38; IGI. **Sarah Brown on the marriage:** Sarah Brown to Sarah Howe, dated Sept. 20 on the outer envelope, JLSC, fd 11. **losses:** Jedediah Kingsley to Sarah Howe, Mar. 7, 1812, JLSC, fd 11. **Howe's 1814 letter to Sarah:** John Howe to Sally Howe, Jan. 25, 181[4], JLSC, fd 11. **financial difficulties:** 1814 letter; see also postscript to Ebenezer Chaplin's 1809 letter to Sarah, JLSC, fd 11, see below. **Sending home money:** John Howe to Sally Howe, July 10 JLSC, fd 11; also the 1814 letter. **1809 letter:** Eben C. Kingsley to Sarah Howe, Dec. [16, 1809], JLSC, fd 11. **1813 letter:** Sarah Brown to Sarah Howe, June 1, 1813; JLSC, fd 11. **Mrs. Wakefield:** Mrs. Wakefield to Sarah Howe, Sept. 24, 1814, JLSC fd 11. Sarah was living at Great Barrington, in western Massachusetts, when she received this letter. **earliest letter on Edward's death:** See H. T. Wakefield letter below. **Howe absent:** "The father of your little son was absent; and he had not for a long time placed his eyes upon him." Unknown friend of Abby Brown to Sarah Howe, undated, beginning "Your affectionate friend, Miss Brown ..." JLSC, fd 11. **after visiting Lee:** "It seems mysterious why it was that you should leave your friends hear and so soon after your arrival {1} in that place be called to follow to the grave your dear little son with no other friend but an affectionate brother." H. T. Wakefield to Sarah Howe, Sept. 23, 1815, JLSC. **Edward's suffering:** Abby Brown to Sarah Howe, Oct. 3, 1815, JLSC, fd 11. **aunt comforts Sarah:** Obedient Chaplin to Sarah Howe, Oct. 29, 1815, JLSC, fd 11.

III. **Charity Barlow to Mrs. Howe, Feb. 21, 1821, fd 11. will:** dated July 30, 1823, copy in JLSC.

IV. **marriage:** Records of Hamilton Co., GS 344,452; IGI. John was born on May 21, 1790. **Augusta:** Date of birth from John Lyman journal, CA, MS 2072, Sept. 13, 1845. See also JLSC, fd 15, document dated Aug. 25, 1867. Augusta married John Lyman Smith in 1845, and died in 1903 in Haden, Fremont, Idaho. **April 16:** Eben Kingsley to Sarah Cleveland, Apr. 16, 1831, JLSC, fd 11. **Alexander:** Biography There are letters from him to Augusta, JLSC, fd 8.

V. **conversion and early persecution:** Biography. **Swedenborgianism in Cincinnati:** Marguerite Block, *The New Church in the New World* (New York: Holt, Rinehart and Winston, 1932; repr. New York: Octagon Books, 1968), 117-21. Swedenborgianism is a sign of the popularity of spiritualism in America at this time, see Prologue, at discussion of cultural sources for Joseph Smith's polyandry, and Eliza Partridge chapter at 1862.

VI. **move to Quincy:** Reminiscences of Augusta Cleveland Smith, JLSC, fd 8. Apparently, Sarah was involved somehow in the Kirtland Safety Anti-banking Society fiasco, for she was apparently tried and jailed for passing $390 in the notes of the society, see Quinn, MHOP 626. **persecution:** Biography. **Emma at Clevelands:** Smith, *Joseph Smith III and the Restoration* 16; date from ME 80. WWj, Mar. 16, 1839 (1:320): "I rode to Mr Clevelands & once more had the happy privilege of greeting Sister Emma Smith who had taken up her abode for a season with her Children in the house of Sister Cleaveland ... We next rode to Quincy 4 miles." **Joseph to Emma:** Jessee, PW 411. **Sarah's patriarchal blessing:** Patriarchal Blessing Index, as cited in ECIF. **Joseph to Clevelands:** HC 3:327; Hill, JS 263. **Joseph lives with Clevelands:** Oliver Huntington, Autobiography,

Lee Library, p. 48, original. **May 9:** HC 3:349. **May 24:** Joseph Smith and Emma Smith to Judge Cleveland and Lady, May 24, 1839, Joseph Smith letterbooks, CA; HC 3:362-63. This letter mentions a Rufus Cleveland, apparently John's brother, who was living in Quincy also. **June 1841:** Mrs. Joseph Horne, "Migration and Settlement of the L.D. Saints," Salt Lake City, 1884, Bancroft Library, as cited in Ivins 3:221. HC 4:364-65. **baptisms for dead:** Nauvoo Baptisms, 1841, GS film 183,379; Guy Bishop, "'What Has Become of Our Fathers?' Baptism for the Dead at Nauvoo," *Dialogue* 23 (1990): 85-98. **move to Nauvoo:** Reminiscences of Augusta Cleveland Smith, JLSC, fd 8.

VII. **marriage:** HR 6:234. See on the Eliza Snow marriage, below. **two houses:** ME 119, citing Nauvoo City tax records, 1842; Hancock County tax records; Nauvoo Restoration, CA. **assignation house:** See below on the Eliza Snow marriage.

VIII. **women's charitable religious groups in America:** See Ann Firor Scott, *Making the Invisible Woman Visible* (Urbana: University of Illinois Press, 1984), 259-94; Jensen, *Loosening the Bonds*, 184-204; Smith-Rosenberg, *Disorderly Conduct* 109-28; Cott, *Bonds of Womanhood* 133-35; Keith Melder, "Ladies Bountiful: Organized Women's Benevolence in Early 19th-Century America," *New York History* 48 (1967): 231-54. **counselor:** Relief Society Minutes, Mar. 17, compare WC 27-29. **Relief Society:** See esp. *Women of Covenant*, by Derr, Cannon, and Beecher. Tensions between the Relief Society and the male hierarchy are hinted at in *Women of Covenant*, but never emphasized. For the importance of the Relief Society in women's lives, see virtually all of the chapters in this book; Sarah Kingsley, Eliza Snow, and Zina Huntington were presiding Relief Society officers, but many of the other women in this book were local officers and/or active Relief Society participants. For further on the history of women in Mormonism, see Beecher and Anderson, eds., *Sisters in Spirit*; Hanks, ed., *Women and Authority*; Claudia L. Bushman, ed., *Mormon Sisters: Women in Early Utah* (Salt Lake City: Olympus, 1976). **Woman's Exponent:** See the magazine itself, WC 109, and Sherilyn Cox Bennion, "The *Woman's Exponent*: Forty-two Years of Speaking for Women," UHQ 44 (1976): 222-39. As is typical of Mormon women's history, over the years the church has become increasingly less tolerant of women's independent voices. First, in 1914 it changed the *Woman's Exponent* to the *Relief Society Magazine*, more tightly controlled by the official Relief Society and church authorities. Then in 1971 the church stopped the *Relief Society Magazine* altogether. (WC 343.) "Alternate voice" publications—*Woman's Exponent II, Mormon Woman's Forum, Sunstone,* and *Dialogue*—generally viewed with suspicion, if not hostility, by members of the exclusively male Mormon hierarchy—have moved into this vacuum. **naming:** RS Min., Mar. 17. **third meeting:** RS Min., Mar. 30, pp. 24-25. **Clarissa Marvel:** See Agnes Coolbrith chapter, at this same time period. **Administering to Durfee:** RS Min., p. 31, at Apr. 19. **stratagems:** RS Min., May 19. **June 23:** RS Min., 68-69. See also RS Min., July 7. **witnesses Eliza Snow marriage:** ERS Affidavit, SAB 1:25; 4:24; Bachman, "A Study," 349. Sarah Pratt said that Sarah Cleveland kept an "assignation house" for Eliza Snow and Joseph, Wyl, MP 90. **July 7:** RS Min., 73. **August 4:** RS Min., 78-79. On August 4 the Relief Society considered a mysterious case, that of a "Sis. Brown." For some reason, she was denied membership in the Relief Society, and Sarah was evidently among those women who denied Sister Brown membership. **September 29:** RS Min., Sept. 29.

IX. **farewell letter:** TS 4 (May 1, 1843) 187. **older women:** See prologue. **Judge Cleveland brings hogs:** J. H. Rollins, Autobiography, p. 12. See Mary Rollins bibliography. **Clevelands in Springfield:** Lee, MU 144.

X. ZDYj, Dec. 22, 1844. "Julia Parks, Gusta Cleveland, Wm Linzy, Br Lewes were here." **July 9, 1845:** J.L. Smith journal, CA MS 1122, 1:18. Compare MS 2072, fd 2, p. 6. **Patriarchal Blessing:** Patriarchal Blessing Book 9, p. 355, as cited in Tinney, RF 88. **Dec. 19:** NTER 33. **marriage to John Smith:** BOP #18; SAd 503, 501. In the Nauvoo temple John was also sealed to Clarissa Lyman for eternity and married six other women. See SAd 507, 517; 86; Bates, *Lost Legacy* 114; Cook, RP 208. **John Smith**

**birth date:** SAd 501. He died in 1854. Bates and Smith, *Lost Legacy* 104-23; BE 1:183. Quinn, MHOP 585 gives 1845 as the date when he became Church Patriarch.

**XI. Feb. 8:** John Lyman Smith journal, MS 2072, CA = Lee Library MS 680, fd 2, p. 9. **John Cleveland away:** J. L. Smith journal, MS 1122, p. 20. **Brigham's counsel:** J. L. Smith journal, MS 2072 CA = Lee Library MS 680, fd 2, p. 10. **Heber's counsel:** J. L. Smith, MS 1122, CA, p. 21. **Alexander's 1850 letter:** Sarah and Alexander Cleveland to Augusta Cleveland Smith, Aug. 2, 1850, JLSC, fd 8.

**XII. Isabella:** J.L. Smith journal, Family Record section, MS 2072, CA. **November 9:** Sarah Cleveland to Augusta Lyman, Nov. 9, 1846, JLSC, fd 8. All the letters in this section from Sarah Cleveland to Augusta Smith are in folder 8, and are identified in the text by date. **Cleveland's lot in Nauvoo:** Compare Sarah and Alexander to Augusta and John L. Smith, Jan. 17, 1852, and Sarah to Augusta, Aug. 2, 1850. The Clevelands had had hopes to sell their lot in Nauvoo which they had received from Joseph Smith. However, Sarah wrote, "Our Lot at Nauvoo proves to be a total failure  the deed that Joseph Smith gave us was good for nothing. the land was Emmas  he only had the right of dower." **marriage to Haight:** J. L. Smith journal, Family Record section, 2072 CA. **Clarissa Medora:** AF. **John Smith's death:** Bates and Smith, *Lost Legacy* 117. **July 2, 1855:** J.L. Smith diary, CA 2072; compare his CA 1122 diary: "We reached Plymouth & found Father & Mother Cleveland at 9 oclock. We staid all night." **July 4:** July 4, 1855, J. L. Lyman diary, CA 2072. Compare the diary, CA 1122: "Father & Mother Cleveland treated me with a Great deal of respect  asked me to pray & ask Blessing at Table–regularly while with them. He said John You Know I never pray but wish you to pray with us. which I did." **date of death:** Biography. In John Lyman Smith's 1894 reminiscence, "Diary of John Lyman Smith" (Provo, UT: Brigham Young University, 1940), typescript, Lee Library, pp. 39-40, he wrote that when he was on his way to the Swiss Mission in October 1860, he stopped in Plymouth as usual. "There I visited my wife's Mother who was too sick to recognize anyone, also visited with brother-in-law Alexander D. Cleveland and wife." If Sarah was indeed alive at that time, she would have been seventy-two, and the biography's date of death would be incorrect.

However, when we examine the November 19, 1860, entry in John Lyman's journal, CA 1122 (presumably John's source for the 1894 document), it does not mention Sarah, though it describes John Cleveland (who was dying at the time): "Stoped with my wifes Bro. Alexander & found her Father. John Cleveland at the point of death  He recognized no one. Alexander & wife Amanda was very Kind to Br. Gerber & myself for I was very lame." J. L. Lyman journal, CA 1122, p. 178 (CA 2072 does not include the year 1860). Here we find that John Cleveland, not Sarah, was dying, and recognized no one. A diary is preferable to a reminiscence as historical evidence, so the probable conclusion is that John Lyman, in writing his 1894 reminiscence, inadvertently and incorrectly, changed the identity of the dying parent-in-law from John to Sarah. Thus the biography is still our best evidence for Sarah's death.

## REFERENCES TO CHAPTER 12.
### *"Loving Sisters":*
### *Delcena Diadamia Johnson (Sherman Smith Babbitt)* and
### *Almera Woodward Johnson (Smith Barton)*

Barton, Almera Johnson. Affidavit, Aug. 1, 1883. BAOPM 70-71.

Brown, Mary Jones. "Delcina Diadamia [Johnson]." OPH 15:251.

Brown, Mary Jones. "History of Delcena Didamia Johnson." In MS 1271, Lee Library. Typescript, 3 pp.

[Carter, Kate]. "Almera Woodward Johnson Barton." OPH 15:249-50.

Cook, Lyndon. "Lyman Sherman–Man of God, Would-Be Apostle." BYUSt 19 (Fall 1978): 121-24.

JEJ: see Rufus Johnson.

Jenson, Andrew. "Johnson, (Almera Woodward)." HR 6:235-36.

———. "Sherman, Lyman." BE 1:190-91.

Johnson, Benjamin F. Affidavit. In HR 6:221-22.

———. *My Life's Review.* See also the original, MS 1289, CA.

———. "Obituary Note–Almera Smith Barton." DEN 29 (Mar. 26, 1896): p. 5.

Johnson, George Washington. Autobiography. In Lee Library, MS 1271.

Johnson, Joel. *A Voice from the Mountains, Life and Works of Joel Hills Johnson.* Mesa, AZ: Joel Hills Johnson Arizona Committee, 1982.

Johnson, Milas Edgar, and Rolla Virgil Johnson, comp. *The Johnson Pioneers of the West.* 2 vols. [Salt Lake City]: Johnson Family, 1984. 2:77-79 (Delcena); 83-85 (Almera).

Johnson, Rufus David. *J. E. J., Trail to Sundown.* Salt Lake City: Joseph Ellis Johnson Family Committee, 1961.

JPW: see Milas Johnson, *The Johnson Pioneers of the West.*

MLR: see Benjamin Johnson, *My Life's Review.*

"MRS. ALMIRA BARTON DEAD." DEN 29 (Mar. 5, 1896): p. 5. [compare the obituary by Benjamin Johnson below]

"Obituary." DN (Sept. 25, 1911): p. 3. (Obituary of Albey L. Sherman, Delcena's son.)

Openshaw, Rose A. "A Brief Sketch of the Life of Almera Woodward Johnson Smith Barton, Sister of Patriarch Benjamin F. Johnson." In JPW 2:83-85.

**move to New York:** Julia Johnson to Esther Forbush, Oct. 14, 1813, printed in Johnson, JEJ 20-22.

I. **Delcena's birth:** Birth date from Heber Kimball/Clayton journal, Book 93, "Dulcinea D. Sherman," January 7, 1846. BOP #79, however, has November 19, 1807. But the 1806 date preserves a more even spacing among the Johnson children. **Almera's birth:** "Mrs. Almira Barton." Almera received her name from a friend of her mother's, Almera Woodward, see Openshaw, "Brief Sketch," 85. **Ezekiel Johnson:** Birth date from MLR 15; 8. AF has him born on January 12, 1773, in Uxbridge, Worcester, Massachusetts. **Julia:** was born on September 26, 1783, in Upton, Worcester, Massachusetts. For her death, see below. For genealogical information on the Johnsons, see Milas Johnson, JPW, compare MLR 7. **Joel:** Born on March 23, 1802, in Grafton, Massachusetts, he married Anna Pixley Johnson (1826), Susan Bryant (after Anna's death) (1840), Lucina Bascom (1845), Janet Fife (1845), and Margaret Threlkeld (1860). After his baptism in 1831, he relocated in Kirtland, served early missions for the church, and helped construct the Kirtland temple. In 1839 he settled in Crooked Creek, Illinois, where he became stake president. He moved to Knox County, Illinois, in 1846 and two years later came to Salt Lake City. With George A. Smith he helped found Parowan in 1850, then started a nearby settlement called Fort Johnson (modern Enoch). He often served in the legislature. In 1861 he moved to North Creek, then to Virgin River in 1866, and two years later settled in Bellevue. By 1880 he was in Johnson, Kane County, where he died in 1882. He wrote over a thousand hymns during his lifetime. See Journal of Joel Johnson, Lee Library, typescript, published in his *Voice from the Mountains*. **Nancy Maria:** Born on August 1, 1803, in Northborough, Worcester, Massachusetts, she was thrown from a horse and crippled, MRL 10. However, she married Joseph Clark in 1827 before dying in 1836 in Kirtland, MLR 26. **Seth Garnzey:** Born in Royalton, Windsor, Vermont (mid-eastern Vermont), on February 14, 1805, he married Sophia Stone in 1824 and died in 1835 in Kirtland. **Julia Ann:** Born on November 9, 1808, she married Almon Babbitt, see below, in 1833, and died in 1857 in Crescent City, Pottawattamie, Iowa. **David:** Born on September 10, 1810, he died in 1833 while working on the Kirtland temple, MLR 16. **Ezekiel built cabins:** JEJ 20.

II. **Susan Ellen:** Born on December 16, 1814, she died in 1836 in Kirtland, MLR 22. **Joseph Ellis:** Born on April 28, 1817, he was baptized a Mormon in 1832 and came to Nauvoo in 1840. In 1848 he relocated in Council Bluffs, where he was postmaster for five years, and also worked as a storekeeper and printer. He traveled to Utah and back in 1850, then lived in Omaha, Nebraska. He returned to Utah in 1861, and four years later moved to St. George, where he continued publishing, farming, and storekeeping. After being "burned out" in 1879, he migrated once more, to Tempe, Arizona. He married Harriet Snider (1840), Hannah Maria Goddard (1850), and Eliza Saunders (1856). He died in 1882 in Tempe. See Rufus Johnson, *J.E.J.*, and his diaries and correspondence in Joseph Ellis Johnson collection, Marriott Library. **Benjamin Franklin:** Born on July 28, 1818, he married Melissa Bloomfield Lebaron (1841), Flora Clarinda Gleason (1846), Harriet Naomi Holman (1850), Sarah Melissa Holman (1856), Susan Adaline Holman (1857), and Sarah Jane Spooner (1857). His polygamous family was one of the largest in Mormonism. He died in 1905, in Mesa, Arizona. See his MLR. **Mary Ellen:** Born on February 7, 1820, she married George Deliverance Wilson in 1842 and died in 1845 in Nauvoo, Illinois. **Elmer Wood:** Born on May 26, 1821, he died a year later, on September 14, 1822, in Pomfret. See MLR 7. **George Washington:** Born on February 19, 1823, he married Maria Jane Johnston (1844) and Eveline Burdick (Jewell) (1851) and died in 1900 in Moab, Grand, Utah. **William Derby:** Born on October 27, 1824, he married Jane Cadwalader Brown in 1848 and died on April 13, 1896, in Colonia Diaz, Chihuahua, Mexico. **Esther Melita:** Born on January 12, 1828, she married David Tulley Lebaron in 1844 and died in 1876 in Salt Lake City. **Amos Partridge:** Born on January 15, 1829, he died in 1842 in Macedonia, Illinois. Compare MLR 90-91, for his death. **move to large farm:** JEJ 32. **life on the farm:** MLR 8-9. **George's poems:** JEJ 32-33. **Joseph and revivals:** Quoted in JEJ 53. Compare the Presendia Huntington chapter. **Ezekiel and religion:** See letters on Ezekiel's mother and birth in Joseph Johnson collection, box 8, fd 4. Ezekiel Johnson's father is not actually known, though he may have been a Johnson.

III. **marriage:** AF. **Lyman Sherman:** MLR; Cook, RP 217; id., LS; Quinn, MHOP 580. He had been born on May 22, 1804, in Monkton, Addison, Vermont. **Alvira:** The birthdates, the names, and even the number of Delcena's children are confused. AF has Alvira born in 1830; JPW 1:6 has "Alvia" born ca. 1829. In JPW 2:79 she is named "Elvira." She died in 1850 in Winter Quarters. JPW 1:6 also lists a son "probably Elkanah" born ca. 1830, who died as an infant. **Mary Ellen:** JPW 1:6. Named after Delcena's younger sister, she died in 1850 in Winter Quarters. **Albey:** JPW 1:6. He married Mary Elvira Swan in 1854, and died in 1911 in Huntington, Emery, Utah. For Mormonism in Pomfret, see Zebedee Coltrin journal, May 1833, CA. **early response to Mormonism:** MLR 11; George Washington Johnson, Autobiography 1; Brown HDDJ 1. Joel had been baptized on June 1, 1831, AF. **letter, Seth Johnson to Joel Johnson, undated:** Quoted, with standardized grammar, in JEJ 37-38; Joseph Johnson collection, Marriott Library, box 4, fd 22. **Brackenbury:** See Elizabeth Davis chapter. MLR 12 ("James Brackinbury and Jabez Durfee") has both first names wrong. George Washington Johnson, Autobiography 1 has Joseph Brackenbury. **Almera's baptism:** Jenson's biography gives 1832. Her obituary gives 1831. AF has April 21, 1833. **tongues:** Zimmerman 67-68.

IV. **Ezekiel to Kirtland:** JEJ 40-41. **Move to Kirtland:** MLR 14-15. George A. Smith reportedly traveled with them from New York to Kirtland, JEJ 43. **"a man of great integrity":** MLR 53. **high priest:** Joseph Young, *History of the Organization of the Seventies* (Salt Lake City: Deseret News, 1878), 5. For priesthood in early Mormonism, see Prince, *Power From On High*, and Quinn, MHOP. **cornerstone:** MLR 16; HC 1:400. Compare JH, July 23, 1833, which does not list Sherman. **Julia married Babbitt:** FGS. **Zion's Camp:** for this expedition, see Roger Launius, *Zion's Camp: Expedition to Missouri, 1834* (Independence, MO: Herald House, 1984). A good treatment in Arrington, BY 40-46. **Seth's death:** MLR 18. **Lyman a president of seventy:** Young, HOS, 2, 4; Cook, LS 122. But apparently, Lyman was released from this calling and returned to his high priest duties in November 1835, Young, HOS 5. **patriarchal blessings:** MLR 19. **Julia makes stocks:** MLR 18-20; JEJ 57. For palmleaf hats, see Thomas Dublin, "Women's

Work and the Family Economy: Textiles and Palm Leaf Hatmaking in New England, 1830-1850," *Tocqueville Review* (1983): 297-316. Compare Eliza Snow chapter. **plural marriage:** Johnson, in Zimmerman 38. **Lyman's revelation:** Jessee 2:121-22; D&C 108; compare Cook, RP 216. **Seth:** AF; JPW 1:6 has him born ca. Feb. 1835. He died at Winter Quarters in 1850. **move to farm:** MLR 27. **Lyman sings in tongues:** WWj (1:120). Dean Jessee, "Kirtland Diary of Wilford Woodruff," BYUSt 12 (1972): 382. **High council:** "Kirtland Council Minutes Book," p. 247, CA, as cited in Cook, LS 123. **Daniel:** AF. JPW has him born ca. Nov. 1836. He died a few years later, in Nauvoo. **burns press:** MLR 29; HC 3:11; Cook, LS 123. **Almera stays in Mentor:** MLR 32.

V. **arrival of Johnsons:** MLR 35. **Susan:** JPW 1:6. AF has Oct. 21. She married James Henry Martineau in 1857, and died in 1874 in Logan, Cache, Utah. **High council:** Dec. 13, FWR 223; Cook, LS 124. **Lyman unwell:** HCKj, Feb. 7, 1839, as quoted in Cook, LS 124. Compare WWj, Feb. 23, 1859 (5:298). **Lyman's death:** date from Cook, LS 124. Quinn, MHOP 580 gives January 27. Benjamin Johnson, in MLR 52, writes, "At this time Brother Sherman had gone to Richmond to see the Prophet Joseph, on which mission he took cold, and died in my absence, soon after his return." Benjamin heard of Lyman's death on March 1, MLR 55. **Benjamin visits Delcena, returns to Far West:** MLR 52-56.

VI. **to Quincy:** MLR 57. **Johnsons in Ramus:** MLR 90. For Ramus, see Joel Johnson in TS 2 (Nov. 15, 1840): 222. **Almera to Illinois:** Jenson, JAW 236. **Apr. 19:** RS Min., p. 30. **Benjamin returns:** MLR 90.

VII. **Delcena's marriage to Joseph:** Benjamin Johnson to George Gibbs, in Zimmerman 45. In MLR 90, Benjamin reported that he arrived at Ramus, outside of Nauvoo, on July 1, 1842. However, in the Gibbs letter, Zimmerman 39, Benjamin wrote that he arrived in Nauvoo in "June - 42," and met Joseph. The July 1 date is preferable, as it is more exact. **proxy:** MLR 95: "the widow Sherman, who had already been sealed to him [Joseph] by proxy." "by proxy" would not make sense for a simple marriage to Joseph, as there would have been no reason to marry by proxy when both partners were alive. However, if Delcena had been sealed to Lyman with Joseph standing proxy, this statement might be true, for then he would be sealed to Delcena for time. On the other hand, Benjamin may have simply written imprecisely or incorrectly. For an early proxy marriage, see HR 6:229–Hyrum Smith married Mercy Thompson, the widow of Robert Thompson, promising to deliver up Mercy and all her children (from all her marriages, including the marriage with Hyrum) to Robert in the resurrection. Joseph Smith officiated at the marriage. Perhaps Joseph had married Agnes Coolbrith Smith in a proxy marriage. Compare Benjamin Johnson to Anthon Lund, May 12, 1903, Benjamin Johnson papers, CA: "[Joseph Smith] then having my sister widow of Lyman R. Shirman as wife by proxy he soon through my consent took another sister then living with us to be his wife." **Joseph providing for Delcena:** Johnson, in Zimmerman 39, 40. Compare MLR 97.

VIII. **Benjamin as Joseph's representative:** MLR 92; compare Gibbs letter. **close relationship with Joseph:** MLR 93. **April 1:** JSj, Faulring 338. Benjamin told this story at least three times in print, in the letter to Gibbs, Zimmerman 41; in MLR 94; and in an affidavit, HR 6:221. The Gibbs letter will be used primarily, as it is a holograph, but the other accounts are valuable, especially MLR, which is fuller in some places. **interview:** MLR 94 (holograph 90-91). The Johnson to Gibbs letter incorrectly gives April 3 or 4 as the date of the interview. **sermon on talents:** Compare Ehat, WJS 173, at April 2. **"horror":** MLR. **Hyrum to Almera:** Jenson, JAW 236. **Hyrum to Almera, second speech:** Affidavit, BAOPM 70-71. **marriage:** In addition to the three accounts by Benjamin, see Almera's Affidavit in BAOPM 70-71. MLR 96 and the Benjamin Johnson affidavit have Hyrum perform the marriage. Jenson, HR 6:234, has the date of the marriage as August 1843, apparently a mistake. Almera's March 5, 1896, obituary gives the date of marriage as 1842, once again, probably a mistake. **Almera returns to Macedonia:** "But as I could not long be absent from my home & Buisness We Soon Returned to

Ramus. whare on the 15th of May Some three weeks later," Johnson, in Zimmerman 44. **May 16:** Johnson to Gibbs letter, which gives the (incorrect) date, May 15; compare HC 5:391-92; WCj, IC 101-104. **Miller, etc.:** Affidavit HR 6:222. **October visit:** Affidavit HR 6:222. **Esther:** MLR 96, 92; Johnson, in Zimmerman 44. Esther married David LeBaron when she was sixteen, on March 28, 1844.

IX. **endowment:** NTER. **marriage:** BOP #79; SAd 509. **Babbitt:** MLR 202-204, see also the early part of the book; Cook, RP 251-52; Jay Donald Ridd, "Almon Whiting Babbitt, Mormon Emissary," Master's thesis, University of Utah, 1953; [Kate Carter], "Almon Whiting Babbitt," OPH 11:513-72. Quinn, MHOP 535. **stay in Nauvoo:** Brown, HDD 2; Cook, RP 251. Almon also served as postmaster at Nauvoo in 1846, Jessee 2:523. **Almon disfellowshipped because of Hyde:** Howard H. Barron, *Orson Hyde: Missionary-Apostle-Colonizer* (Salt Lake City: Horizon, 1977), 186. **Ezekiel dies:** JEJ 98. **Almon in Utah:** Babbitt arrived in Utah on July 1, 1849, HStj, OMF 2:354. **Delcena arrives at the Bluffs:** Brown, DDJ. **Almon in Nauvoo:** Cook, RP 251. **death of children:** AF; Brown, DDJ. **disfellowshipped in 1851:** Cook, RP 251. **July 19:** HStj, OMF 2:401. **secretary:** Jessee 2:523. **Julia dies:** JEJ 192; Esther LeBaron et al. to Benjamin Johnson, Nov. 10, 1853, in Julia Ann Johnson Babbitt, Delcena Johnson Sherman, Ruben Barton, Esther Johnson LeBaron, and others to Benjamin Johnson, Oct. 28, 1853, with postscripts, JEJ collection, Marriott Library, box 4, fd 25. Summarized in JEJ 192-93. **letter to Benjamin:** See above. **Albey marries:** Brown, DDJ; AF. Albey went on to help pioneer Payson, Santaquin, and Sanpete, settling at Fountain Green, Sanpete. He took part in the Black Hawk war, acted as an Indian interpreter, and was a teamster and butcher. In 1879 he was called to help settle Huntington, Emery County, where he died in 1911. See "Albey Lyman Sherman," by Mary Jones Brown, Lee Library, MS 1271, D.U.P. Huntington chapter. **death:** "Obituary," for Albey Lyman: "In 1854 the mother followed the pioneers to Salt Lake, where she passed away at the home of her brother-in-law Almon W. Babbitt, within a few months." Delcena is buried in the Salt Lake Cemetery.

X. **marriage:** 1883 affidavit; Brown, DDJ. **Marcia Wilson and children:** AF. **Barton:** See Cook, KEQR 71, 16. Nathan and Reuben grew to maturity and married, FGS for Reuben Barton, GS. Barton contributed to the Oct. 28, 1853 letter, see above. **daughters:** All information on Almera's children is from JPW 1:137. See also Parowan death records for Lois and Del[c]ina Barton, below. Lois is also listed as "Daughter" in the 1880 census, see below; for her city of birth, see the 1870 census, below. The 1880 census only gives Illinois as birthplace. Jenson, JAW, incorrectly has all five daughters dying at Council Bluffs. **Mary Ellen:** Named after Almera's younger sister, who had died a year earlier. **Sarah Delcena:** JPW 1:137. The birth date for "Delina" Barton in the death record, December 31, 1839 (died on March 23, 1870, at the age of 30 years, 10 months, and 24 days), is obviously wrong. Her gravestone in Parowan has her born on April 24, 1850. **Lois:** Compare Parowan death record: April 18, 1852. **mentally impaired:** Note in Joseph Ellis Johnson collection, Marriott Library, box 8, fd 1. **Ruben to Benjamin:** See group letter, above. **Harriet Julia:** JPW 1:137. **family reunion:** Joel Johnson Journal and Autobiography; *Voice* 66. Joel also visited the Bartons on July 9 and 16. Almon Babbitt had been killed, apparently by Indians, in September 1856, see Brooks in OMF 2:602. **Julia dies:** Joel Johnson journal, *Voice* 69. **March 15, March 28, May:** *Voice* 81. Joel also visited her two weeks later, and in May and December. On June 11, 1859, Joseph Ellis visited the Bartons again. **June 11:** Joseph Ellis Johnson diary, see his collection, Marriott Library, box 1. **December:** Dec. 7, 1859, *Voice* 115. **June 28:** *Voice* 133. **August 5:** *Voice* 134. **arguments:** Hannah Maria Goddard Johnson, at Kanesville, to Joel Johnson, Wood River, letters, 1861, cited in JEJ 345: "There were frequent references to Almera [in Hannah's letters], twice that she and Reuben were getting along as 'usual,' which meant that their relations were strained." **Barton antagonistic to church:** HR 6:236. **March 16, 1860:** JEJ, box 5, fd 2, Marriott Library. Also in the letter: "ford set the straw a fire in the field yesterday and burned all {Strangs hay} fence {rails}. Bartons was hay was destroyed and with difficulty they saved their House." **separation:** Jenson

JAW; JEJ 346. Reuben would die in March 1891, AF. Compare Openshaw, "Brief Sketch," 84. Reuben "wrote later, accusing her of stubbornness and self-will ... hotly denying her accusation of ever having influenced his sons (by another marriage) against her ... He also wrote her a love poem in which he expressed doubt she had ever really cared for him, yet expressing his own unwavering devotion."

XI. **to Utah:** Jenson, JAW, and Benjamin Johnson, "Obituary Note," give 1861. The anonymous obituary gives 1858. According to JEJ 353, Almera crossed the plains with two daughters, but family genealogy records that three of her daughters died in Utah. **duration of journey:** DN (Sept. 27, 1861) gives the date of arrival, as cited in JEJ 354-57. **Harriet's death:** JPW 1:137. **saddening:** Openshaw, "Brief Sketch," 84. **Provo County:** Jenson JAW. **to Parowan immediately:** Benjamin Johnson, "Obituary Note." **Delcina's death:** Parowan death record (GS film 1206305), Block 10, lot 1, grave no. 1; Gravestone. See also JPW 1:137. **1870:** See 1870 Utah census, Iron Co., Parowan, p. 290. **love burden:** Openshaw, "Brief Sketch," 84. **residency of the Johnson children:** See AF, birth records of their children. For Joel Hills in Iron County, see Luella Dalton, *History of Iron County Mission* (Parowan: n.p., 1973), chapter 18, "Johnson's Fort (Enoch)," 178-85. See Diary of Joel Johnson, and *Voice.* **Joel** was in Fort Johnson and Cedar City, Iron County, by 1855; he was in Virgin City, Washington County, by 1861, and in Johnson, Kane County (east of Washington), by 1881. He died in Kane County. **Joseph Ellis** lived in Springville, Utah County, till 1863; he was in St. George, Washington County, by 1866, and in Tempe, Arizona, by 1882. He died in Phoenix, Arizona. **Benjamin** lived in Salt Lake, then moved to Santaquin, southern Utah County, by 1853. He stayed in Utah County through the 1860s and 1870s, but died in Mesa, Arizona. **George Washington** was in Springville, Utah County, in 1852; by 1855 he was in Cedar City, Iron County. By 1858 he had moved to Santaquin, and in 1860, he resided in Moroni, Sanpete County (the exact center of Utah). By 1868 he was in Mona, Juab County (just northwest of Sanpete), where he died. **William Derby** left Council Bluffs for Utah after 1860; by 1863 he was in Salt Lake. In 1871 he resided in Johnson, Kane County, where he stayed through approximately 1878. He died in Colonia Diaz, Mexico. **Esther Johnson LeBaron** settled in Salt Lake City and died there in 1876. **Carter quote:** OPH 15:250. **nieces and nephews:** I follow Johnson, JPW. **1880 census:** Utah census, Iron County, Parowan, p. 355. **June 3, July 13, 1882:** Joseph Ellis Johnson collection, Marriott Library, box 8, fd 1. **Aug. 1:** See 1883 affidavit. **declines Mexico:** OPH 15:250. **Lois's death:** Parowan death record, Block 10, lot 1, grave no. 2. Her age is given as 41 years, 4 months, and 14 days. JPW 1:137 gives the death date as Sept. 2, 1883. **death:** Parowan death record, Block 10, lot 1, grave no. 3. "MRS ALMIRA BARTON DEAD," DEN (Mar. 26, 1896): "MRS. ALMIRA BARTON DEAD, **Was the Prophet Joseph's Widow Prior to Her Marriage to Reuben Barton.** Special to the News.] PAROWAN, March 4. —One of Parowan's oldest residents, Mrs. Almira Barton, died this morning at 9 o'clock of a paralytic stroke. She was born and joined the Church in the state of new York. She was married to the Prophet Joseph Smith at Macedonia, Ill., in 1832. [sic] She was the mother of five children; came to Utah about 1858, removing to this place shortly afterward, and has resided here ever since. Funeral services will be held tomorrow." Compare "An Unmanly Letter," a letter from Joseph Smith III, with commentary, in DEN 39 (Apr. 18, 1896): p. 4.

## REFERENCES TO CHAPTER 13.

### Childless Mother of Mothers in Israel: Eliza Roxcy Snow (Smith Young)

Beecher, Maureen Ursenbach. *Eliza and Her Sisters.* Salt Lake City: Aspen Books, 1991.

———, ed. *The Personal Writings of Eliza Roxcy Snow.* Salt Lake City: University of Utah Press, 1995.

BFR: *Biography and Family Record of Lorenzo Snow*, by Eliza R. Snow.
EHS: *Eliza and Her Sisters*, by Beecher.
EL: Janet Peterson, and LaRene Gaunt. *Elect Ladies*. Salt Lake City: Deseret Book, 1990.
ERSj: 1842-44 is in Church Archives. The overland journal, Feb. 1846-July 1849, is in the Huntington Library, San Marino, California. Both are published in Beecher, *Personal Writings*.
PS: "Pen Sketch of an Illustrious Woman," by Emmeline Wells.
SML: "Sketch of My Life," by Eliza R. Snow.
Snow, Eliza R. *Biography and Family Record of Lorenzo Snow*. Salt Lake City: Deseret News Co., 1884.
———. *Eliza R. Snow, an Immortal, selected writings of Eliza R. Snow*. Edited by Bryant S. Hinckley; LeRoi Snow, Arthur Richardson, Nicholas Morgan. [Salt Lake City]: Nicholas G. Morgan, Sr., Foundation, 1957.
———. "Sketch of My Life." Bancroft Library, Berkeley. Included in Beecher, *Personal Writings*, 6-46.
Wells, Emmeline. "Pen Sketch of an Illustrious Woman: Eliza R. Snow Smith." WE 9 (Aug. 1, 1880): 33-34 to 10 (Dec. 1, 1881): 97.

**title:** borrowed from an article on Eliza in Susa Young Gates collection, box 12, USHS. **Joseph's martyrdom and return:** BE 1:695.

I. **Birth:** SAd 513, 581. Compare NTER. **siblings:** Beecher, PW 232, FGS and Snow, BFR. **Abigail Leonora:** See the essay, "Leonora, Eliza, and Lorenzo," in EHS 40-54. Born on August 23, 1801, in Becket, she married Enoch Virgil Leavitt ca. 1820, but separated from him after bearing at least three children. She married Isaac Morley (as a plural wife) before December 1843, and died in 1872 in Brigham City, Box Elder, Utah. **move to Ohio:** SML 1; BFR 2. Date of move in PS, WE 9 (Aug. 1, 1880): 33-34. **Amanda Percy:** EHS 50. Born on April 20, 1808, she married Eli McConoughey in 1833 and died on August 27 or 28, 1848, in Henry, Illinois. Compare ERSj, Sept. 23, 1842; May 23, 1843. **Melissa:** born on July 24, 1810, she died on December 16, 1835, in Mantua. **Lorenzo:** BFR; Heidi S. Swinton, "Lorenzo Snow," in Leonard Arrington, ed., *The Presidents of the Church* (Salt Lake City: Deseret Book, 1986), 144-178; Beecher, EHS 40-54; Quinn, MHEP 701-3; Maureen Ursenbach Beecher and Paul Thomas Smith, "Snow, Lorenzo," EM 3:1367-71; Thomas Romney, *The Life of Lorenzo Snow* (Salt Lake City: Sons of Utah Pioneers, 1955); Maureen Ursenbach Beecher, ed., "The Iowa Journal of Lorenzo Snow," BYUSt 24 (1984): 261-73. Born on April 3, 1814, he married (following Quinn's listing): Mary Adeline Goddard Hendrickson (1844), Charlotte Squires (1844), Harriet Amelia Squires (1844), Hannah Goddard (1845), Sarah Ann Prichard (1845), Eleanor Houtz (1848), Caroline Horton (1853), Mary Elizabeth Houtz (1857), Phoebe Amelia Woodruff (1859), and Sarah E. Minnie Jensen (1871). He became an apostle in 1848, president of the LDS church in 1898, and died three years later. **Lucius Augustus:** EHS 50, 54. Born on August 31, 1819, he married Eliza Walker and died in 1898. **Samuel Pearce:** Compare EHS 53-54. Born on August 22, 1821, he married Josephine Elis Scott, Mary Wilmot, and Ella Jane Knapp, and died in Santa Barbara, California, in 1909. **industry of Snow family:** SML 1, 2. **religion of Snows:** SML 4; BFR 2. **poetry reading incident:** SML 2-3. **Leghorn prize:** SML 1-2. PS, WE 9 (Aug. 1, 1880): 5. **Eliza as secretary:** SML 1. **poetry published:** SML 3; "The Fall of Missolonghi," *Western Courier* (Ravenna, OH) (July 22, 1826), as cited in EHS 152. PS, WE 9 (Aug. 1, 1880): 5. **poem on Adams and Jefferson:** *Western Courier* (Aug. 5, 1826), as cited in EHS 149. **prize:** PS, WE 9 (Aug. 1, 1880): 5. New England women had begun making these hats before 1800, using rye straw, Cott, *Bonds* 39-40. Compare the Delcena Johnson chapter, Kirtland period. **Campbell:** SML 5; PS, WE 9 (Sept. 1, 1880): 50; A.S. Hayden, *Early History of the Disciples in the Western Reserve* (Cincinnati: Chase and Hall, Publishers, 1875), 239, as cited in Beecher, EHS 43-44. **single:** PS, WE 9 (Sept. 1, 1880): 50.

**II. first meeting with Joseph:** SML 6; I use Beecher's dating of this event, EHS 152 n. 3. **Rosetta and Leonora join before Eliza:** Beecher, EHS 44. **Leonora to Kirtland:** PS WE 9 (Sept. 1, 1880): 50. **baptism:** SML 6; BFR 5. See also Beecher, EHS 46, which cites Minutes of Junior and Senior Cooperative Retrenchment Association, June 22, 1872, CA. **Kirtland:** SML 6; BFR 5. **Eliza's house:** BFR 5; SML 7. **She knows Joseph:** SML 7. **Eliza teaches:** SML 7; Helen Mar Whitney, LI, WE 9 (Apr. 15, 1881): 170. For women practicing the profession of schoolteaching in this era, see Cott, *Bonds*, 30-35, who regards this as an example of the "expansion of nondomestic occupations for women." The fact that women could be paid less than male teachers caused many financially strapped school districts to turn to them. Also Keith Melder, "Woman's High Calling: the Teaching Profession in America, 1830-60," *American Studies* 13 (Fall 1972): 19-32. See the Louisa Beaman, Presendia Huntington, and Eliza Partridge chapters. **Lorenzo baptized:** BFR 7. **Eliza back to Kirtland:** SML 7. **Oliver and Rosetta to Kirtland:** See Jessee 2:507 for their home. **departure from Kirtland:** BFR 7-9.

**III. Lorenzo with Rigdon:** BFR 25. **Oliver buys homesteads:** SML 9; BFR 41. **former owner asks:** SML 9; BFR 43. **journey to Illinois:** SML 10-11; BFR 44. **Far West:** BFR 44. See a letter Eliza wrote at Far West, Eliza Snow to "Esqr. Streator," Feb. 22, 1839, published in BYUSt 13 (1972/73): 544-52.

**IV. Warren, Lima:** SML 11. BFR 45: "We stopped there [Quincy] a short time, and from there our father moved to Warren County, in the same state; from there to LaHarpe, where Lorenzo found us, thence to Commerce, afterwards called Nauvoo." **Lima:** SML 11. **Rigdon's school:** SML 12; Wandle Mace, Autobiography, CA, p. 44, as cited in Claudia L. Bushman, ed., *Mormon Sisters: Women in Early Utah* (Salt Lake City: Olympus, 1976), 67. **poems:** E.g., "The Slaughter On Shoal Creek, Caldwell County Missouri," TS 1 (Dec. 1839); "Elegy," TS 1 (Oct. 1840); "Columbia My Country," TS 1 (Dec. 1, 1840); "Though Outward Trials," TS 2 (Jan. 15, 1841). **constitution:** Sarah M. Kimball, "Auto-biography," WE 12 (Sept. 1, 1883): 51; WC 26-27. **First meeting:** RS Min., Mar. 17, 1842. **"Ladies' Relief Society":** TS 3 (Apr. 1, 1842): 743. **April 19:** RS Min., 31-32.

**V. Eliza on polygamy and her marriage:** SML 12-14. **longevity:** Mormon leaders Lorenzo Snow, Heber C. Kimball, and Orson Hyde believed that practicing polygamy would extend one's life span, see Hardy, SC 92-93. **Eliza lives with Sarah:** ERSj, Aug. 14, 1842. **marriage details:** Eliza Snow Affidavit, SAB 1:25, #55 Bachman; HR 6:233; BFR 68. However, as often, there is an alternate date for the marriage, March 1842, per Crocheron, *Representative Women* 2. Eliza, in a letter to Joseph F. Smith, n.d., CA, wrote, "At the time the sisters of the Relief Society signed our article I was married to the Prophet." Eliza tells a version of the angel with sword theme, BFR 69. See also Eliza Snow to Daniel Munns, May 30, 1877, RLDS Archives; Affidavit of Lorenzo Snow, Aug. 28, 1869, in CA; ME 328. **first and only:** "Past and Present," WE 15 (Aug. 1, 1886): 37. **Emma authorized:** Angus M. Cannon, Statement of Interview with Joseph Smith III, 1905, p. 13, CA. Cannon reported Eliza saying to him, "Brother Angus, I can't comprehend how Sister Emma, who was one of the noblest women I ever knew, could, before her death, make the affidavit that she is said to have made, denying that her husband had more wives than one, for she took my hand and put it in the hand of her husband, Brother Joseph, and gave me to him to wife." This is secondhand and late (Cannon, in 1905, repeats a conversation with Eliza that took place when she herself was old) and has been rejected as improbable; but, curiously, three other sources support it. The second witness is Susa Young Gates, box 12, folder 2, USHS, "Emily Partredge had been 'given' to the Prophet by his first wife Emma, as had Eliza R. Snow." The third is John Jacques, assistant church historian, speaking with Lorenzo Snow: "He heard that Emma Smith herself had no objections to Sister Eliza R. Snow being SEALED to the Prophet Joseph Smith." John M. Whitaker journal, Nov. 16, 1887, 11, 122-23, as quoted in Bachman 150-51. The fourth is Erastus Snow, in Autobiography of John Pierce Hawley, P13.F317, RLDS Archives. "What Erastus Snow told me in the year 1870. They said, him and his first wife was present at the time Eliza R. Snow was given to

Joseph. Emma Joseph's wife was present and they both testify that Emma took Eliza Snow's hand and placed it in the hand of Joseph as giving her consent. JOHN HAWLEY." I am grateful to Will Bagley for his transcription of this source. Newell and Avery disagree, ME 328, but the weight of evidence in these sources is impressive. **sexuality in the marriage:** Cannon, Statement, p. 23. Compare Prologue, section on sexuality. **W. Wyl:** MP 90, quoting Sarah Pratt: "Sarah Cleveland kept a kind of assignation house for the prophet and Eliza R. Snow." **Oliver quote:** Oliver Snow to Franklin Snow, Aug. 13, 1842 (excerpt in JH, Aug. 13, 1842), as quoted in Beecher EHS 48. Compare ERSj, May 23, 1843. **Lucius, etc. in Walnut Grove:** EHS 50. **Eliza to Joseph's house:** ERSj; compare ME 132. **school:** ERSj, Dec. 12, 1842; "Nauvoo School Records," *The Nauvoo Journal* 1 (1989): 17-28, 24. Among her students were Sarah Ann Whitney, two sons of Elizabeth Brackenbury, two Partridge children, and Clarissa and Fanny Decker.

**VI.** **Newell and Avery:** ME 134. Compare M. Ursenbach Beecher, Linda K. Newell, and Valeen T. Avery, "Emma, Eliza and the Stairs: An Investigation," BYUSt 22 (Winter 1982): 87-96 and Brodie NM 447. **LeRoi's story:** Brodie NM 447. **Wyl:** MP 58. **Rich version:** LeRoi Snow, "Notes," in possession of Cynthia Snow Banner, as cited in Beecher et al., EES 86-94. Snow received the story from W. Aird Macdonald, in a letter that has been lost. Macdonald heard the story from Ben E. Rich, his mission president in 1906-1908. Ben presumably heard it from his father, Charles. **Mary A. Barzee Boyce:** Reminiscences of Mary A. Barzee Boice, in John Boice Blessing Book, CA, MS 8129, p. 40. Mary Ann was in Nauvoo from June 1841. **John Young:** Letter, John R. Young to Vesta P. Crawford, in John Ray Young scrapbook, 1928-30, CA, as cited in Raymond Bailey, "Emma Hale" 187. **losing a child:** Newell and Avery argue, reasonably, that Eliza could not have continued teaching school if she had been noticeably pregnant. **Lorenzo returns:** BFR 68-69. **rebaptism:** Faulring 377. See Quinn, "The Practice of Rebaptism at Nauvoo," 231. **to Walnut Grove:** BFR 70. **Relief Soc:** RS Min., 95. **Aug. 21:** WCj, IC 118. **living with Leonora:** BFR 70. **New Year's Eve:** BFR 70. **Markhams':** ERSj. For Stephen Markham, see BE 3:672; 4:712.

**VII.** **marriage:** BYj, Oct. 3, 1844; Johnson, DDW 66. Compare HCKj, Oct. 3, 1844 (OPW 89), "El. B. Young and myself went to Br. Marcoms [Markham's]. Spent some time at the Temple." **endowment:** Quinn, MHOP 504. **O My Father:** Linda P. Wilcox, "The Mormon Concept of a Mother in Heaven," in SS 65-66. **temple work:** SML 14; "Sketch of Sister Bathsheba Smith," *Young Woman's Journal* 4 (Apr. 1893): 294-96, 295. **Clayton journal:** IC 220, compare Dec. 23, p. 231, Dec. 26, p. 233, Dec. 26, p. 236; Dec. 27, p. 237; Dec. 29, p. 241; Jan. 4, 1846, p. 253. **December 29:** HCKj (Clayton), Bk 93. **January 1, 1846:** HCKj (Clayton), Bk 93, just before Jan. 2. **January 11:** HCKj (Clayton), Bk 93. **Lorenzo marries:** SAd 491; BFR 85. **temple sealing to Smith/Young:** BOP #157; SAd 513, 581.

**VIII.** **dormitory:** SML 16. **One of my brother's wives:** WM 309. **frosted feet:** SML 16. **lumber wagon:** SML 17. **lost:** SML 16-17. ERSj, Mar. 4. **stalling teams:** SML 19. **Garden grove:** Kimball, *Historic Sites* 26; Leland Gentry, "The Mormon Way Stations: Garden Grove and Mt. Pisgah," BYUSt 21 (Fall 1981): 445-61. **feminine realities:** See Jeffrey, *Frontier Women*, 38 **Mt. Pisgah:** Kimball, *Historic Sites* 27-29; Gentry, "Way Stations"; Lorenzo Snow, "Iowa Journal," 261-73, 268-69. **sickness:** "Iowa Journal," 269-70. **diseases:** Wallace Stegner, *The Gathering of Zion* (New York: McGraw-Hill, 1964), 100. **Eliza Snow to Elizabeth Whitney and Vilate Kimball:** June 30, 1846, Newel Whitney collection, Lee Library. **learns to drive:** SML 21. **Morley:** He was an adopted "son" of Brigham, see OMF 1:242.

**IX.** **Eliza and Indians:** See Elden J. Watson, ed. *Manuscript History of Brigham Young, 1846-47* (Salt Lake City: privately published, 1971), 353. **Eliza sick:** Helen Mar Whitney, LI 9 (Apr. 15, 1881) 170. **December 31, 1846:** Compare PBSj. **Beecher:** EHS 141. **June 1:** PBSj. **prophetesses:** Compare from Eliza's later life, after Eliza and other women had administered to Emmeline Wells's daughter Em, "Sister Eliza prophesied upon her–and said she would be healed. Promised her great blessings and the gift of healing, said she had a great work to do on the earth yet." EBWj, Jan. 19, 1878. **Wells:** "A Venerable Woman," WE 12 (1 June 1883): 2. **June 2:** Compare Tullidge WM 208-9, Presendia speaking in tongues simultaneously with a man. **June 4:** ERSj, under June 6, 1847; see Patty Sessions journal, with the correct date: "E R Snow blesed Helen and Genette then in the gift of tongues, ER Snow sung a blesing to all the rest of the girls." **Beecher:** EHS 139.

X. **blessing meetings:** ERSj, June 13-18; PBSj, June 13-18. **June 18:** Speaking in tongues was sometimes linked to healings, as here. E.g., HCKj at June 19, 1845, OPW 122. **July 12:** See JH for July 12, and PBSj; Eliza has it on the 13th. For buffalo, see also July 21. Regarding the difficulties of the Grant company, see Gene Sessions, *Mormon Thunder* (Urbana: University of Illinois Press, 1982), 59-69. **July 23:** For the Victorian woman's encounter with buffalo dung, see Myres, *Westering Woman* 105-106; Jeffrey, *Frontier Women* 42. After overcoming initial revulsion, pioneer women found that the chips made a good fire, and served as a mosquito repellant. See also Patty Sessions chapter at July 1847. **July 26:** Compare SML 27, where Eliza holds horses during a daytime stampede. **Courthouse bluff:** Sandra L. Myres, *Ho For California, Women's Overland Diaries from the Huntington Library* (San Marino, CA: Huntington Library, 1980), 63; Merrill Mattes, *Platte River Road* (Lincoln: NE: Nebraska State Historical Society, 1969), 339-77; Kimball, HS 185. **Aug. 21:** See picture 6 after p. 134, Brown MTW. **Aug. 23:** Compare Myres, *Ho For California*, 67; Kimball, HS 90.

XI. **description of home:** SML 31. **rain and roof:** SML 31-32. **October 2:** Also Oct. 31, Nov. 2, 4-8, 13, 14, 29, 30, Dec. 1, Dec. 2, Dec. 4. **Noble:** For Noble, see Louisa Beaman chapter. **spring 1848, Eliza sick:** Louisa Beaman to Marinda Hyde, Apr. 8, 1848, CA. **Eliza sick in February 1849:** ERSj, Feb. 25. **Helen and Eliza:** Helen Mar Whitney, LI, WE 9 (Apr. 15, 1881) 170. **July 14:** Louisa Beaman and Eliza Snow to Marinda Hyde, July 14, 1849, CA, MS 716. **Eliza's sickness:** Susa Y. Gates Papers, box 12, fds 12 and 13, p. 43. **Polysophical Society:** Henry Naisbitt, "Polysophical and Mutual," *Improvement Era* 2 (1899): 741-47, 746-47; EHS 51, 111, 115, 122; Maureen Ursenbach Beecher, "The Polysophical Society: A Phoenix Infreqent," *Encyclia* 58 (1981): 145-53, with further bibliography. **1855 Relief Societies:** SML 38. **1855 Endowment House calling:** BE 1:696. PS, WE 9 (Feb. 1, 1881), 131. PS, WE 10 (Nov. 10, 1881), 82, compare EBWj, Jan. 1, Apr. 5, 1883. Mary Ettie Smith, *Fifteen Years* 45, saw Eliza Snow play the part of Eve in the endowment drama: "Now at fifty years of age, she is even yet very beautiful, and she may be said to perform *infamously* well." **demise of Polysophical Society:** Hannah King, Autobiography, CA, Oct. 8, 1856.

XII. **move to Lion House:** Arrington, BY 170. **Gates:** Susa Y. Gates, Papers, USHS, box 12, fds 12 and 13, pp. 43, 44. For the water cure, see the 1855 letter to Martha Heywood below. Another water treatment manual: R. T. Trall, *The Hydropathic Encyclopedia: A System of Hydropathy and Hygiene*, 2 vols. (New York: Fouters and Wells, 1852). **blessing meetings:** Gates, p. 6. **sewing works of art:** See Emily Partridge chapter at 1892. **Eliza Snow to Martha Spence Heywood:** Dec. 23, 1855, Martha S. Heywood collection, correspondence, MS 3354 1-4, fd 2. **Eliza counsels polygamy:** Mosiah Hancock, Autobiography, CA, MS 570, at Nov. 19, 1860. See Fanny Stenhouse, in the next section, and the autobiography of Elizabeth Street, quoted in Kimball, *Isn't One Wife Enough*, 108. **most important doctrine:** Eliza Snow, Oct. 17, 1879 letter to DN, see below, at 1878. **Hannah Perkins letter:** Eliza Snow to Hannah Gold Perkins, Oct. 12, 1862, CA. **Apr. 4, 1865:** Mary Lightner collection, Lee Library.

XIII. **Young's decision:** WWj, Dec. 26, 1866 (6:309). **Brigham calls Eliza:** SML 39; WC 86. Eliza seems to date this call in 1855, but WC has probably worked out the correct chronology. **Eliza begins speaking and traveling:** WC 88-89. For Eliza's speeches, see the *Woman's Exponent*, where they are frequently reported, e.g., "F.R.S. Reports," 1 (July 15, 1872): 58; 2 (Sept. 15, 1873): 62; "R.S. Reports," WE 6 (Oct. 15, 1877): 74; 6 (Nov. 15, 1877): 94. For a first-person account of a visit to Box Elder, see Eliza

R. Snow, "A Short Excursion," WE 4 (July 1, 1875): 52. **Retrenchment:** PS, WE 9 (Mar. 1, 1881), 147; WC 115; SML 40 again has imprecise chronology. **February 11:** AF; "My Sister, Leonora A. Morley," a poem, WE 1 (Aug. 1 1872): 35; EHS 51. **Women's Exponent:** WC 109-10; Sherilyn Cox Bennion, "The *Woman's Exponent*: Forty-Two Years of Speaking for Women," UHQ 44 (Summer 1976): 231. **Amy Brown Lyman:** See her *In Retrospect* (Salt Lake City: General Board of Relief Society, 1945), 38. **obedience to leaders:** EHS 123-25, compare 21, 24-25. **Hyde:** John Hyde, *Mormonism, Its Leaders and Designs* (New York: Fetridge, 1857), 127-28. See Beecher's discussion of the feminine hierarchy in nineteenth-century Utah, EHS 129-47. **Fanny Stenhouse:** *Tell It All* 430-32. **the sash:** Clarissa Young Spencer and Mabel Harmer, *Brigham Young At Home*, 3rd. ed. (Salt Lake City: Deseret Book, 1947), 78-79. **doctrinal conflict:** Eliza Snow, "Mortal and Immortal Elements of the Human Body," WE 2 (Dec. 1873), 13, repr. in WE 4 (Sept. 1, 1875): 54. The statement by Brigham Young is found in WE 4 (Sept. 15): 60, compare John Taylor, "Remarks on the Resurrection," WE 4 (Oct. 1, 1875): 65; Eliza's retraction is addressed to "To whom it may concern," WE 4 (Apr. 1, 1876): 164. Compare EHS 124. **sat at right hand:** Spencer and Harmer, BY 76-77.

**XIV.** For a good diaristic overview of many of Eliza's daily activities during this period, see Emmeline Wells's diaries from 1874 to 1887. **Trip to Palestine:** Letters in *Correspondence of Palestine Tourists* (Salt Lake City: Utah Territory, 1875); BFR 496-581. SML 44. PS, WE (Mar. 1, 1881), 147. First published in WE, e.g., 1 (Feb. 1, 1873): 138; (May 1, 1873): 182; (May 15, 1873): 190; 2 (July 15, 1873): 36-37. **Ohio:** BFR 580. **June 20:** Letter from Eliza Snow to WE, repr. in BFR 579. **Centennial:** SML 39-40, 42; PS, WE 10 (Aug. 1, 1881), 35; WE 4 (Jan. 15, 1876): 124; WE 4 (Feb. 15, 1876): 141; WE 5 (June 1, 1876); 5 (Sept. 15, 1876): 61; WC 84. **to Marinda:** Eliza Snow to Marinda Hyde, June 25, 1876, CA, MS 716. **Quote on Utah fair:** SML 42. **work on Tullidge:** PS, WE 10 (Aug. 15, 1881): 43. **Brigham's last conversation:** Gates papers, USHS, compare Susa Young Gates and Leah Widstoe, *The Life Story of Brigham Young* (New York: The MacMillan Co., 1930), 268. **Brigham's death:** Arrington, BY 399. Compare Emily Partridge chapter. **administers to sick:** e.g., EBWj, May 8, June 3, 1881.

**XV.** **Primary organized:** EBWj, July 10, 1878, SML 40-41, WC 118. **mass meeting:** "Woman's Mass Meeting," WE 7 (Dec. 1, 1878): 97-98; PS, WE 10 (Sept. 15, 1881): 57. Compare Eliza's letter to the *Deseret News* (Oct. 18, 1879): responding to Emma's death-bed denial of Joseph's polygamy. "If what purports to be her 'last testimony' was really her testimony, she died with a libel on her lips–a libel against her husband–against his wives–against the truth, and a libel against God; and in publishing that libel, her son has fastened a stigma on the character of his mother that can never be erased." [As quoted in Bailey EH 97.] As can be seen, in the nineteenth century relations between the LDS and RLDS churches were often strained. **travels in 1879:** PS, WE 10 (Oct. 15, 1881): 73. A journal record of one of these Utah trips in EBWj, Sept. 8-22, 1881. In Ephraim, Sanpete County, Eliza was exhausted after attending three of four scheduled meetings, and missed the last one. In late October she visited Morgan, near Ogden, and on the 25th Emmeline Wells wrote, "Sister Howard and I met Aunt Eliza coming from Morgan plodding along with her bundles." **early 1880:** PS, WE 10 (Oct. 15, 1881): 73; (Nov. 1, 1881), 82. For Eliza's and Zina's visits, see Lyman, *In Retrospect* 38.

**XVI.** **June 19:** PS, WE 10 (Nov. 1, 1881): 82. **ordination:** Blessing quoted in PS, WE 10 (Nov. 1, 1881): 82. **travels:** PS, WE 10 (Nov. 10, 1881): 82; Eliza Snow to Sister Welch, CA, MS 4590. **November 8:** PS, WE 10 (Nov. 1, 1881), 82. **White:** PS, WE 10 (Nov. 1, 1881), 82. SML 41. **November 19:** Minutes of the meeting, quoted in Andrew Larson and Katherine Miles Larson, eds., *Diary of Charles Lowell Walker*, 2 vols. (Logan: Utah State University Press, 1980) 2:512n. **November 24:** Walker diaries, 2:510. **November 29:** Walker diaries, 2:512. **preaching polygamy:** Walker diaries, 2:512n. **January 21:** PS, WE 10 (Nov. 1, 1881): 82 has description. **Eliza Snow to "Young Brother":** [Welch file], MS 4590, CA. Perhaps Robert Welch. Compare Eliza Snow to Master Robert [Welch], Dec.

25, 1881, MS 4590, CA. **return to Salt Lake:** PS, WE 10 (Nov. 1, 1881): 82. **Eliza Snow to Master Robert [Welch]:** Dec. 25, 1881, MS 4590, CA. **Deseret Hospital:** *History of Relief Society*, 116; WC 107-8; EL 40. **death of Elizabeth Whitney:** EBWj. **Eliza Snow to Sister East:** Apr. 23, 1883, MS 2325, CA.

XVII. **1885 letter:** Eliza Snow to Zina Young, CA. **1886 letter:** Eliza Snow to Zina Young, May 10, 1886, in Zina Card Brown collection, CA. **EBWj:**, Mar. 12, 23, 1887. **rides with Cannon:** Beecher, "Eliza, A Woman and a Sister," *New Era* (Oct. 1974): 16. **quote:** *The Life and Labors of Eliza R. Snow Smith; With a Full Account of her Funeral Services* (Salt Lake City: Juvenile Instructor Office, 1888), 6. **death:** ibid. For her funeral, see *Life and Labors*.

XVIII. **epitaph:** Susa Young Gates papers, USHS, box 12, p. 49.

## REFERENCES TO CHAPTER 14.
### *"Great Glory Honner & Eternal Lives":*
### Sarah Ann Whitney (Smith [Kingsbury] Kimball)

[Carter, Kate]. OPH 10.389.
Cook, Lyndon. *Joseph C. Kingsbury*. Provo, UT: Grandin Books, 1985.
"Died." Obituary of Sarah Ann Whitney. DW 22 (Sept. 10, 1873): 512.
Geisler, Pat. *Heber C. Kimball & Sarah Ann Whitney*. Salt Lake City: n.p., [1995].
HWj: see Horace Whitney.
Kimball, Stanley. *Heber C. Kimball*. 314-15.
Kingsbury, Joseph C. "The History of Joseph C. Kingsbury." Marriott Library, MS 522.
Poulsen, Larry N. "The Life and Contributions of Newel Kimball Whitney." Master's thesis, Brigham Young University, 1966.
Roberts, B.H. HC 1:145-46n. A small biography of Newel Whitney.
Whitney, Elizabeth Ann. "A Leaf from an Autobiography." WE 7 (Aug. 1, 1878): 33; (Aug. 15): 41; (Sep. 1): 51; (Oct. 1): 71; (Nov. 1): 83; (Nov. 15): 91; (Dec. 15): 105; (Jan. 1, 1879): 115.
Whitney, Horace, journal. CA, MS 1616.

**birthday party:** Helen Mar Whitney, "Scenes in Nauvoo ..." WE 11 (Mar. 1, 1883): 146.

I. **Sarah's birth:** The Salt Lake City death record (see below) has March 22, 1825; IGI and a FGS also give 1825 (film 1,553,255, Bt 8813002, sh. 44). Clayton/Kimball Bk 93, however, gives March 22, 1826. BOP gives no birthdates for Sarah. 1825 is preferable because it preserves a nearly two-year space between her nearest siblings. **siblings of Sarah Ann:** See Biographical Introduction to Whitney collection, Lee Library. **Newel:** was born on February 5, 1795, in Marlborough, Windham, Vermont, and died in 1850 in Salt Lake. See BE 1:222; Orson Whitney, "Newel K. Whitney," *Contributor* 6 (1885): 125, 126, 129; Elizabeth Whitney, LFA; Biographical Introduction to Whitney collection, Lee Library; Cook, RP 102; Quinn, MHOP 601. **Elizabeth:** was born on December 26, 1800, in Derby, New Haven, Connecticut, and died in 1882 in Utah. See her LFA; Tullidge, WM, 32-35; 41-42; WC 28, 122. **Horace:** Born on July 25, 1823, he married Helen Mar Kimball in 1846, see her chapter in this book. The quote is from Helen Whitney, SIN, WE 11 (Mar. 1, 1883): 146. **Franklin Kimball:** was born on February 25, 1827. He evidently died as an infant. **Mary Elizabeth:** was born on September 26, 1828. She evidently also died as a child. **Orson Kimball:** Born on January 20/30, 1830, he married Joanna Hickey Robertson in 1854 and served a mission in Hawaii the two following years. He fought in the Utah War in 1857, then in Utah's Indian wars. He died in 1884. **Newel's career:** HC 1:145-46n. Cook, RP 102. For Gilbert, see Mary E. Rollins chapter. LFA, WE 7 (Sept. 1, 1878): 51; 7 (Oct. 1, 1878): 71.

II. **Campbell:** LFA, WE 7 (Sept. 1, 1878): 51; HC 1:145-46n.; Cook, RP 102. **preliminary revelation:** HC 1:145-46n. Sarah Kingsley Cleveland and Desdemona Fullmer also had preliminary revelations before receiving Mormonism. **Oliver Cowdery**: See Mary Rollins chapter. **conversion:** LFA, WE 7 (Sept. 1, 1878): 51. **praying for Joseph:** LFA, WE 7 (Sept. 1, 1878): 51; HC 1:145-46n.; HC 1:145-46. **New York:** Cook, RP 99; D&C 63:42-46. **Bishop:** D&C 72:1-8. **Newel's missions**: Joseph Smith to Emma, June 6, 1832, Jessee, PWJ 237-39; HC 1:271-72; LFA, WE 7 (Oct. 1, 1878): p. 71; Cook, RP 102, compare RP 172. Hill, JS 147; compare LFA, WE 7 (Sept. 1, 1878): 51. D&C 84:114; Hill, JS 150-51. **Feast of the Poor:** BE 1:225; HC 2:362; LFA, WE 7 (Oct. 1, 1878): 71; 7 (Nov. 1, 1878): 83; Orson Whitney, "Newel K. Whitney," *Contributor* 6 (1885): 125, 126, 129. **John Kimball:** Born on September 13, 1832, he married Ann Longstroth in 1856 and died in 1915 (or 1922) in Mendon, Cache, Utah. **Joshua Kimball:** Born on February 13, 1835, he died in 1902 in Salt Lake City. **Anna Maria:** Born on October 1, 1836, she married Erastus Foote Hall in 1866 and died in 1881. **Elizabeth's gifts:** LFA, WE (Nov. 1, 1878): 83; WWj, Feb. 3 1854 (4:245). **Jan. 1837:** D&C 117:11. Cook, RP 102. **departure:** LFA, WE (Nov. 1, 1878): 83.

III. LFA, WE 7 (Nov. 15, 1878): 91, BE 226. **Newel in Nauvoo:** Cook, RP 102, compare Jessee, PW 538. **Don Carlos:** was later known for his pioneering and mining ventures, see introduction to Newell Whitney collection, Lee Library. **Mary Jane Whitney:** Born on January 17, 1844, in Nauvoo, she married Isaac Groo in 1865, fourth in his group of six wives, and died in 1925. **Newel Melchizedek:** Sarah's last full sibling was born on Feb. 6, 1847 in Winter Quarters, but died as an infant. **Elizabeth ordained:** LFA, WE 7 (Nov. 15, 1878): 91. **Relief Society:** RS Min., 35.

IV. **Newel Whitney:** Cook, RP 102. Helen Whitney, SIN, WE 11 (Mar. 1, 1883): 146. LFA, WE 7 (Dec. 15, 1878): 105. Elizabeth Whitney received her endowment a year and a half later, on October 8, 1843. **Sarah's marriage to Joseph:** See Sarah Ann's 1869 affidavit, quoted in BAOPM 73; SAB 1:36; 4:36 (Bachman #59). See also an affidavit by Elizabeth Whitney, BAOPM 74 (SAB 1:72; 4:74; Bachman #90); by William Clayton, HR 6:225; and by Joseph Kingsbury, HR 6:226, 233-34. Helen Mar Kimball Whitney gives the date of marriage as "the Spring of 1842," Helen Whitney, SIN, WE 11 (Mar. 1, 1883): 146. In 1843, when Heber Kimball taught Helen Mar the doctrine of plural marriage, Helen wrote, "he took the first opportunity to introduce Sarah Ann to me as Joseph's wife." (Ibid.) **"Bond of affection":** Orson Whitney, "The Aaronic Priesthood," *The Contributor* 6 (Jan. 1885): 121-32, 131; BE 1:226. Orson wrote that Joseph had revealed the doctrine of polygamy to Newel in Kirtland, 131. **Revelation:** Bachman, "A Study," 121-22; Kenneth Godfrey, "Causes of Mormon Non-Mormon Conflict in Hancock County, Illinois, 1839-1846," Ph.D. diss., Brigham Young University, 1967, 99 n. 27; H. Michael Marquardt, *The Strange Marriages of Sarah Ann Whitney to Joseph Smith the Mormon Prophet, Joseph C. Kingsbury, and Heber C. Kimball* (Salt Lake City: Modern Microfilm, 1973), 23. Original in CA. **Helen Mar on the marriage:** Helen Whitney, SIN, WE 11 (Mar. 1, 1883): 146. **Horace sent east:** ibid. This reference entirely justifies careful examination of any mission call given to a close relative of a polygamous wife. Compare missions given to George W. Harris, Henry Jacobs, Orson Hyde, and John Walker by Joseph Smith, and the mission to England given to Henry Jacobs by Brigham Young. On the other hand, Joseph waited until Benjamin Johnson returned from a mission to have him relay a proposal to Johnson's sister, Almera.

V. **Joseph in hiding:** See Ruth Vose chapter. **letter, August 18:** Jessee, PW 539-42, with a photograph of the original. **Newel and Elizabeth sealed:** Ehat, JSI 102, table 2. **Joseph tells Newel to take wives:** LFA, WE 7 (Dec. 15, 1878): 105. **Newel Whitney home:** For date of move, see Helen Mar Whitney, SIN, WE 11 (Mar. 1, 1883): 146. Compare LFA, WE 7 (Jan. 1, 1879): 113; Holzapfel, *Old Mormon Nauvoo* 91; Cook, JCK 86. **Eliza Snow's school:** See "Nauvoo School Records," *The Nauvoo Journal* 1 (1989): 24. **March 23 letter:** Joseph Smith to Sarah Ann Whitney, Mar. 23, 1843, CA, as quoted in Hill, QFR 115. This letter is not included in Jessee, PW. For the concept of unconditional salvation in D&C 132, see Prologue.

VI. **Kingsbury:** Cook, JCK 76; Whitney, *History of Utah* 4:114-15; Jessee 2:563; HC Index.

For Caroline Whitney Kingsbury, see AF. **marriage to Kingsbury:** Kingsbury, "History," p. 13. The Old Testament ideology is remarkable. Jethro, Moses's father-in-law, was mentioned in the marriage ceremony of Joseph and Sarah Ann. There is also a civil wedding document: "I hereby certify, that I have upon this the 29th day of April 1843, joined together in Marriage Joseph C. Kingsbury and Sarah Ann Whitney, in the City of Nauvoo, Illinois. Joseph Smith Elder rec'd 27th May 1843 & pay." "A Record of Marriages, in the City of Nauvoo, Illinois," p. 12 (1842-45), GS Film 581,219; Lyndon Cook, *Civil Marriages in Nauvoo and Some Outlying Areas, 1839-1845* (Provo, UT: Liberty, 1980), 22. **Joseph Kingsbury promised eternal life:** Compare Cook, JCK 77. Cook does not believe that this was an actual proxy marriage; it was merely a promise that he and his first wife would be sealed. **"for a while":** Cook, JCK 76. **Kingsbury lives with Whitneys:** "I remained with NKW untill the 25th July 1843 And Left Nauvoo ...," Kingsbury, "History," 16; Account Book of Newel K. Whitney, Apr. 30, 1843; Cook, JCK 77. **Kingsbury copies D&C 132:** HR 6:226; SAB 2:18; 3:18. Possibly this took place on the 13th, see Cook, JCK 78. Quinn gathers evidence suggesting that Joseph Smith himself burned this revelation, MHOP 147. **Kingsbury on mission:** Cook, JCK 79; Kingsbury, "History," p. 6, typescript. **Sept. 20:** IC 120. **Heber to Helen and Sarah:** Helen Kimball Whitney, SIN 11 (Dec. 1, 1882): 98.

VII. **Kingsbury returns:** Kingsbury, "History," p. 17. **Kingsbury's marriages:** Joseph Kingsbury 1846-64 journal; p. 8, typescript; Cook, JCK 91. **Jan. 22:** WCj, IC 156. **Sarah and Joseph endowed:** WCj, Jan. 26, 1845, IC 156; compare WCj, Jan. 27, IC 161. See also Kingsbury, "History." **marriage to Heber:** Newel K. Whitney 1841-45 Account Book & Diary (Wh itney Collection, Lee Library, box 6, fd 15), at Mar. 17, 1845; Kimball, HCK 314; Cook, JCK 91. **"Sarah Kingsbury":** On October 19 William Clayton still referred to Sarah Ann as the wife of Joseph Kingsbury, IC 186-87. **fullness of priesthood:** HCKj, OPW 99; WRj; Quinn, MHOP 504. Ehat, JSI (Table 2, p. 102) gives the date March 27. **Heber visits Sarah:** HCKj, Nov. 22, 27, 28, 30; Dec. 1, 5, 6, 7, 8; Cook, JCK 92. **Heber's patriarchal bent:** See HCK 234-35. **anointing Vilate:** HCKj, OPW 122. Compare the Patty Sessions chapter at November 22, 1847. **July:** HCKj, OPW 130. **November 28:** HCKj, Book 93. **April 19:** HCKj, in Helen Mar Kimball Whitney, SIN, WE 12 (June 1, 1883): 6. **May 20:** WRj. **carpet, November 29:** HCKj, OPW 153. Compare Helen Whitney, SIN, WE 12 (June 15, 1883): 10. **December 5:** HCKj, OPW 159. "At half past 11 My wife[,] Sister Whitney. Hellen my Daughter. Sarah Ann Kingsbury. Come in fore the purpus of Heming the Veil. My son Wm and Heber P come with them. W W Phelps come in with some seders trees. They the sisters Vilate My wife Elisabeth Ann Whitney. N K wife Sarah Ann His Daughter and Hellen Mar My Daughter Commenced soing [sewing] at 12 O Clock at the Ringing of the Temple Bell." **cushions:** Helen Mar Whitney, SIN, WE 12 (Oct. 1, 1883): 71. Compare Clayton journal, Jan. 4, IC 253. HCKj (Clayton) Bk 93, at Jan. 11, 1846. **Kingsbury endowed:** This took place in the Nauvoo temple on December 10, 1845, but not in the company of Sarah Ann. HC 7:543; NTER. Kingsbury, "History," gives the date Dec. 8. **Dec. 11:** WCj, IC 207. **Elizabeth sings:** WCj, Dec. 30, IC 244. **Sarah's endowment:** Clayton/Kimball Bk 93. **wedding:** Clayton/Kimball Bk 93, last page of Jan. 1; IC 246-49; Cook, JCK 93. **Sarah sealed to Joseph/Heber:** BOP #4; SAd 363, 503. **Newell marries plural wives:** SAd 545-55. **adoption:** Kingsbury, "History"; Cook, JCK 93. See Prologue on adoption. **fullness of priesthood:** Kingsbury, "History."

VIII. **visits with Helen Mar:** "The Last Chapter of Scenes in Nauvoo," WE 12 (Nov. 15, 1883): 90. **leaves Nauvoo:** EBWj. **Kingsbury travels with Sarah:** "History," typescript 9. **bedstead:** EBWj, Mar. 6. **birth of David:** HWj; EBWj; PBSj. Patty thus added ten miles of horseback riding to a hard day's travel through eastern Iowa. Compare Helen Mar Whitney, OTBM, WE 12 (Dec. 15, 1883): 111. For the children of proxy marriages, see the Lucy Walker chapter. **Eliza visits:** On March 13 Eliza wrote, "Sis. M. [Markham] and I made mother W. and Sarah A. a call in the eve ..." Three days later Eliza "took coffee with Sarah A." **Richardson's Point:** ERSj; HWj; EBWj; JH, Mar. 7-9.

**Rattlesnake:** HWj, May 26, 1846. **storms delayed:** Helen Mar Whitney, OTBM, WE 12 (Dec. 15, 1883): 111. Compare Mar. 7-19, ERSj. **March 12:** EBWj. **March 19:** HWj. **March 22:** EBWj. **to wagon:** EBWj, Mar. 24. **March 30:** EBWj. **transfer to Kimball:** Kingsbury, "History," typescript 9. **May 30:** ERSj. **tenting with Horace:** HWj, June 2; Helen Mar Whitney, OTBM, WE 12 (Apr. 1, 1884): 162. **arrival at Winter Quarters:** OTBM, WE 12 (Apr. 15, 1884): 170. "Saturday, 31st" in text, but this is a typo, a transposition of 13.

IX. **July 25:** OTBM, WE 13 (June 15, 1884): 10. **August 2:** OTBM, WE 13 (July 1, 1884): 18. **Sarah Ann's house/room:** HWj, Dec. 16. See Helen Mar Whitney on the family meeting, below. Kimball, HCK 144. Compare Elizabeth Ann Whitney [at Winter Quarters] to Horace and Orson Whitney ["Camp of Pioneers"], Oct. 7, 1847, Merrill Library, MS 179, box 1, fd 18: "Adeline is living with us and helping me do the work. Sarah Ann lives here they ᴬᵈᵉˡⁱⁿᵉ ᵃⁿᵈ ˢ·ᴬ· send you their kind love." On February 19, 1847, Sarah Ann hosted Marinda Hyde, HWj. **Kimball family meeting:** SIWQ, WE 14 (June 15, 1885): 11. **hieratic:** HWj; compare D. Michael Quinn, "Latter-day Saint Prayer Circles," BYUSt 19 (Fall 1978): 22. **April 4:** SIWQ, WE 14 (Sept. 1, 1885): 54. **April 5:** SIWQ, WE 14 (Sept. 15, 1885): 57. **April 19:** ERSj. **blessing meetings:** Compare ERSj, June 10: "Took supper with S. Ann, while there Lucy W. [Lucy Walker Kimball] came in–she receiv'd the gift We then went into sis. K's [Vilate Kimball, probably]–Helen, Sarah Ann, Genet, Harriet S. Sis. K. spoke for the first time in the gift of tongues–H. Cook [Young] interpreted." **Sarah's baby possessed:** Helen Mar Whitney, SIWQ, WE 14 (Dec. 15, 1885): 106; SIWQ, WE 14 (Jan. 1, 1886): 118.

X. **crossed the plains:** OPH 10:389. **birth of David Orson:** Daniel Davis diary, Aug. 26, 1848, CA: "Sarah Ann the Wife of My Father [by adoption] Was Delivered of A Son." FGS has Aug. 22.

XI. **David Heber:** married Sarah Elizabeth Hanham (or Hannard) in 1870. He helped settle Meadowville, with three of his siblings and many half siblings, and died in 1926 in Kemmerer, Wyoming. See "The Sons of Sarah Ann Whitney and Heber C. Kimball," in Geisler, HCK. **Newel's death:** BE 1:227. **1851 residence:** Utah Census, Salt Lake City, p. 77. **Newel Whitney Kimball:** married Martha Winder in 1870 and the following year he and Martha traveled northward to help settle Meadowville. After eleven difficult years near Bear Lake, they moved to Logan, Cache Valley, Utah, where Newell died in 1931. See "History of Martha Winder Kimball," by Mary Kimball Thatcher, in Geisler HCK. **Horace Heber Kimball:** He married Priscilla Letitia Tufts in 1887 and died in 1922 in Garden City, Rich, Utah. **1856-57 residence:** Adelia Wilcox Kimball, Reminiscences, pp. 39-40, MS 6089, CA; HCK 234. Compare Utah Census, Salt Lake City, p. 215, 18th Ward. **Bear Lake:** Adelia Wilcox Kimball, Reminiscences, p. 40. **"another time":** HCK 234. **constant moves:** See Presendia Huntington chapter. **Sarah Maria:** married William Erastus Jenkins in 1876, and they helped settle Meadowville, near Bear Lake, along with David, Joshua, Newel, and many half-siblings. In the late 1890s the Jenkinses moved to Wyoming, and Sarah died of diphtheria in 1901 in Auburn, Lincoln, Wyoming. See "Sarah Mariah Kimball Jenkins," a small biography, in Geisler, HCK; "The Life of Ross Jenkins," transcribed by Lynn Riley Jenkins, 1969, in Geisler, HCK. **Joshua:** married Catharine Jane MacLean in 1886, in Meadowville, but when the Meadowville project was abandoned, he and Catharine moved to Logan in 1896. Then he became interested in copper mining, and the family moved to Phillisburg, Montana, in 1906. After three years there they moved back to Salt Lake City. He died in 1925 in San Pedro, Los Angeles, California. See "Cleah K.[imball] Root–A Life Sketch," in Geisler, HCK. **Orson Whitney:** as quoted in "The Sons of Sarah Ann Whitney and Heber C. Kimball," in Geisler, HCK. **cooks:** Laura Pitkin Kimball, diary, CA 1775, June 7, 1859. **Sarah and Heber to dinner:** DN (Jan. 27, 1865), as cited in Geisler, HCK 6. I have been unable to locate this reference. **crash anecdote:** "The Sons of Sarah Ann Whitney and Heber C. Kimball," in Geisler, HCK.

XII. For this section, see AF, FGS. Compare Utah census, SLC, p. 699, Eighteenth Ward.

**Mary Kimball Thatcher quote:** "History of Martha Winder Kimball by her daughter Mary Kimball Thatcher," in Geisler, HCK.

**XIII. death:** Record of Deaths in Salt Lake City, CA, p. 200, #7975. Her place of residence at time of death is listed as the 18th Ward; her attendant doctor was Dr. Tait. Compare Obituary, DN (Sept. 10, 1873), as cited in Geisler, HCK 6, where cause of death is "general debility." "Died, at Salt Lake City, September 4th of general debility, Mrs. Sarah Ann Kimball, widow of the late Pres. Heber C. Kimball, and daughter of the late N. K. Whitney, age 48 years, 5 months and 14 days. Funeral services at late residence, at 10 A.M., tomorrow, Saturday."

# REFERENCES TO CHAPTER 15.
## *"Like a Wanderer":*
## *Martha Mcbride (Knight Smith Kimball)*

I would like to thank Brent Belnap for critiquing this chapter and saving it from some serious errors.

Belnap, Della. "Martha McBride Knight." Typescript, in author's possession.

Belnap, Flora. "ADALINE KNIGHT-BELNAP (First Wife of Gilbert Belnap)." Kerr Collection.

Belnap, Flora. "Martha McBride Knight." Kerr Collection.

Belnap, Lillian. "Sketch of the Life of Adaline Knight Belnap." Dictated by her to Lillian Bingham Belnap, May 1914. LCD 1:16.

Coolbear, Lola Belnap. "Sketch of the life of Vinson Knight." In "Biographies of the Belnap and Knight Families," Lee Library.

"Death of a Pioneer Woman." Obituary in *Ogden Standard Examiner* (Nov. 21, 1901): 5.

Kerr, Marion, collection. Marriott Library, copies in Stewart Library, Weber State University, CA, and LCD. This collection includes much material on Martha and her Knight, McBride and Belnap relatives.

LCD: Library of Congress Diaries. See Kerr Collection.

OPH 10:403.

**July 19:** Martha Knight to Adeline Belnap, July 19, 1859, quoted in D. Belnap, MMK 5-6.

I. **birthdate:** SAd 505; BOP #92. **Daniel:** Born on September 13, 1766, at Stillwater, Saratoga, New York, he died in 1823 in New York. For his service as a minister, see D. Belnap, MMK 1; L. Belnap, "Sketch," 1. **Abigail:** Born on January 29, 1770, in Nine Partners, Montgomery, New York, she died in 1854 in Ogden, Utah. **John:** was born on January 5, 1788, in Stillwater, married Avis Hill in 1855, and Merian Berry, and died in Springville, Utah County, Utah in 1860. **Samuel:** was born on August 25, 1789, in Stillwater. He was baptized on April 16, 1833, married Minerva Cooley, Lemira Smith, and Avis Hill (a strict Levirate marriage, performed in 1860 for time only) and died in 1874 in Fillmore, Millard, Utah. **Daniel Jr.:** was born on March 19, 1791, married Roxena Davis in 1820, and died in 1864 in Munson, Geauga, Ohio. **James:** was born on July 9, 1793, married Betsy Mead in 1818, and died in 1839 in Pike County, Illinois. See Backman, *A Profile* 46. **Margaret Ann:** Born on June 1, 1794, she married David Crandall in 1810/11, and died in 1845 at LaHarpe, Hancock, Illinois. **Hyrum:** was born on June 5, 1798, married Sally Davis and Jennie Huntley, and died in 1839 in Hamlet, Chautauqua County, New York. **Cyrus Gideon:** Born on August 17, 1800, at Chester, he married Almira Parson in 1828 and died in 1883 in Dundee, Monroe, Missouri. **Reuben:** was born on June 16, 1803, at Chester. He married Mary Ann Anderson in 1830, was baptized a Mormon on June 16, 1833, and died in 1891 in Fillmore, Millard, Utah. See Backman, *A Profile* 47; F. Belnap, "History of Reuben McBride," in Kerr collection.

II. **Marriage date:** "Death of a Pioneer Woman." Compare Backman, *A Profile* 43. D. Belnap, MMK, has July 26, 1825. FGS has July 6, 1826. Martha was reportedly "a dainty little woman with gray blue eyes and dark hair." F. Belnap, MMK, 1. **Vinson:** L. Belnap, "Sketch," p. 1. He was born on March 14, 1804, in Norwich, Hampshire, Massachusetts, FGS. (Cook has Chester.) See Quinn, MHOP 559. He possibly had a Catholic background, see Vinson Knight to his mother, dated June 24, 1835, Kirtland, typescript in CA, Kerr collection. **Rizpah lives with Knights:** D. Belnap, MMK 1. **farm:** Adaline's recollections, Lola Belnap Coolbear, "The Life Story of Adaline Knight Belnap," in LCD 1:15, p. 1. Here a "large frame house" replaced a log cabin and Martha skillfully operated her spinning wheel and sewing needle, made soap, plucked geese, and employed a maid, see F. Belnap, MMK 1. **Almira:** married Sylvester Stoddard and George Hanscom, lived much of her life in Akron, Ohio, and died in 1911 or 1912. See LCD 1:14, p. 12. FGS has June 23 as birthdate. **Rizpah:** married Andrew Smith Gibbons in 1846 and died in 1895 or 1897, in Arizona. **Adaline:** married Gilbert Belnap in 1845 and died in 1919 in Salt Lake City. See her application for D.U.P. Membership, Kerr collection; Flora Belnap, MMK; L. Belnap, "Sketch," and her obituary, *Ogden Standard Examiner* (June 14, 1919). **James:** married Celestial Roberts in 1868 and died in 1912 in Salt Lake City, Utah. See "Sketch of Celestial Roberts Knight," LCD 12:27.

III. **baptisms of siblings:** AF. **baptism of mother:** L. Belnap, "Sketch," p. 1. **Martha's blessing:** Statement of Almira Knight Pratt, as cited in Brent Belnap to author, Oct. 10, 1996. He suggests that Joseph Smith may have stayed overnight with Martha and Vinson in spring 1833, just as he did in 1834. Smith visited Perrysburg again in October 1833, HC 1:420; Jessee 2:6-7. **March 22, 1834:** Jessee 2:26. **date of baptism:** OPH 10:403. **move to Kirtland:** D. Belnap, MMK 1; OPH 10:403. Land records of Cattaraugus County show that on May 1, 1835, Vinson and Martha sold 78 acres of land to William Cooper for $950. As cited in Brent Belnap to author, Oct. 10, 1996. **letter:** Vinson Knight to his mother, June 24, 1835, see above. **June 24:** PBI 2:65; 1:34-35. **financial dealings:** Jessee 2:94-95. **December 1835:** Lorenzo Barnes journal, CA, Dec. 9, 1835. **Vinson an elder:** Jessee 2:130; MA 3 (Mar. 1837): 475. **Jan. 13:** HC 2:365; JH, Jan. 13, 1836. **Nathaniel:** In the Family Group Sheets there is great variation in Nathaniel's birth and death dates. Some date his birth in 1836, and his death on Dec. 31, 1839. If the latter date is correct, then Nathaniel may have died as an aftermath of the Knights' chaotic Missouri experience. **dedication of Kirtland temple:** See HC 2:410-28. Martha was reportedly present, F. Belnap, MMK 2. **January 2:** HC 2:471; MA 3 (Mar. 1837): 475. **January 8:** WWj Jan. 8, 1837 (1:120).

IV. **Vinson travels with Joseph Smith:** HC 2:518; EJ (Nov. 1836): 27. **move to Missouri:** Brent Belnap, private communication to author. **February 3 letter:** Vinson Knight to William Cooper (a brother-in-law, apparently husband of Clarissa Knight). Handwritten copy in CA, Marion Kerr collection. **Acting Bishop:** HC 3:38; EJ (Aug. 1838): 61. **farm:** HC 3:59; Clark V. Johnson, ed., *Mormon Redress Petitions, Documents of the 1833-1838 Missouri Conflict* (Provo, UT: Brigham Young University, 1992), 261. **Adaline at Grand River:** LCD 1:15 p. 1. **receives Danite plunder:** Sampson Avard testimony, in Testimony Given Before the Judge of the Fifth Judicial Circuit of the State of Missouri, Feb. 15, 1841, Missouri Senate, 26th Congress, Doc. No. 189, repr. in *Senate Document 189* (Salt Lake City: Modern Microfilm, n.d.), p. 3; George Hinkle testimony, p. 22. Reed Peck testimony, *Document Containing the Correspondence, Orders &c in Relation to the Disturbances with the Mormons* (Fayette, MO: Boon's Lick Democrat, 1841), 126. **August 9:** HC 3:60. **Martha on Vinson in Missouri:** 1845 letter to Rizpah Knight, see below. **Martha Abigail:** died in 1844.

V. **Knight in Quincy:** JSj, June 17, 1839 (Jessee 2:322). "Bishop Knight arrived [then] returned to Quincy." **May 1839:** WWj, 1:336. **buys Iowa land:** Jessee 2:324. See also HC 3:366, 4:17; David W. Kilbourne, *Strictures on Dr. I. Galland's Pamphlet, entitled "Villainy Exposed," with some account of his transactions in lands in the Sac and Fox Reservations, etc. in Lee County, Iowa* (Ft. Madison, IA: Statesman Office, 1850), 8-9, as cited in Flanders, *Nauvoo* 36. **bishop:** HC 4:12. **location of home:** D. Belnap, MMK 1. See a photograph in Holzapfel, *Old Mormon Nauvoo*, 121. **Oct. 15:** Jessee 2:333. For bishops dealing with the influx of converts, compare Flanders, *Nauvoo* 146. In an August

16, 1841, conference in Nauvoo, Vinson and Bishop Miller took a collection for the poor of the city, HC 4:403. **Joseph in a trance:** Adaline Knight Belnap, as related by her daughter, Mary Belnap Lowe; CA Ms 781 fd 4; Newell papers, Marriott Library. Compare Coolbear, "The Life Story of Adaline Knight Belnap," in LCD 1:15. **D&C 124:** I quote from the 1844 ed., 103:22, pp. 404-405. **appointed bishop:** Verse 45, 1844 ed., p. 413; modern verse 141. **Nauvoo House:** Cook, RP 244. **Presiding Bishop:** For the contradictory evidence on Knight's status as ward bishop/presiding bishop, see Quinn, MHOP 74-75. **councilman,** Feb. 1, 1841, HC 4:287; TS 2 (Feb. 1, 1841): 309. Board of Regents, Feb. 3, 1841, HC 4:293; TS 2 (Feb. 15, 1841): 321. **Other references to Knight in Nauvoo:** HC 4:303, Knight an Agricultural and Manufacturing Association trustee; HC 4:600, TS 2 (Mar. 15, 1841) 355, Flanders, *Nauvoo* 169 (Vinson declared bankruptcy, as did Joseph Smith and other church leaders); HC 4:296 (guard and assistant aid-de-camp in Nauvoo Legion). **Rodolphus:** AF. **second wife:** D. Belnap, MMK 2, from an interview with Olive Belnap Jenson, a great granddaughter. Knight had no known children by Philinda (variants: Philindia, Philindra, Myrick). For Knight's presence in the inner polygamy circles, see George Robinson letter, quoted below. **letter, February 14, 1842:** Vinson Knight to Rizpah Knight, his mother, typescript, in Kerr Collection. **bodyguard:** HC 4:366. **March 9:** Jessee 2:367. **Vinson a mason:** Mervin Hogan, *The Founding Minutes of Nauvoo Lodge* (Des Moines, IA: Research Lodge Number 2, 1971), 16, 18. **July 20:** *Wasp*, after 1:15, Extra (July 27, 1842): p. 3; HC 5:68. **May 11:** "Also called at Bishop Knight's, dictated several letters and other items of business nature." JH. **Relief Society:** RS Min. Philinda Merrick also attended. She ("Philinda C. Myrick") married again in 1843, Nauvoo Marriage Record, CA, as cited in Cook, NDM 103. **sickness and death:** Jessee 2:401; HC 5:84; TS 3 (Aug. 15, 1842): 894; Nauvoo Sexton's Record p. 2, as cited in Cook, NDM 46. For an anti-Mormon view of Vinson's demise, we have George Robinson to John Bennett, Aug. 8, 1842, as quoted in HS 246-47: "Mrs. [Sarah] Pratt will come out [will reveal the secrets of polygamy], and so will Mr. [Orson] Pratt. Mrs. White will come out. She was at Mr. Rigdon's yesterday. She said she would tell what she did know, but did not tell what it would be. Vinson Knight died last Sunday—sick only two or three days. Mrs. Pratt will criminate Knight: he heard that she was telling on him [apparently for an alleged polyandrous proposal to her], and he roared through the streets like a mad bull, and went to Alderman Marks to get a warrant for her. Marks could not make it out then, and before Knight had time to get it, he went whence he will not return." We lack explanations for these puzzles, but they at least suggest that Knight was in the thick of Nauvoo polygamy. **Rodolphus's death:** Martha Knight, Letter to Rizpah Knight, July 8, 1845. *The Wasp* (Sept. 10, 1842), as cited in Cook, NDM 46.

VI. **after Vinson's death:** D. Belnap, MMK 2. **sewing:** See Agnes Coolbrith chapter, Mar. 1842, for this womanly profession in nineteenth-century America. **marriage to Joseph:** Affidavit by Martha, BAOPM 72 (86, 1905 ed.); SAB 2:36; 3:36, CA, Bachman #69. The date is given as "summer of 1842," but since Vinson died at the end of July 1842, I assume that the marriage was in August. This date is corroborated by her obituary: "in August, 1842, she was sealed to the Prophet, Joseph Smith in the Nauvoo temple." Quinn, MHEP 189, opts for an early summer date for the marriage, which would give us one more polyandrous relationship. However, I prefer not to posit a polyandrous marriage unless evidence is conclusive, and the obituary supports the August date. One might theorize that the obituary writer was using the "summer of 1842" phrase, and also assumed that it meant August. On the other hand, the obituary date might reflect an authentic family record. Until conclusive evidence for an early summer marriage turns up, I regard the late summer dating to be preferable. Martha's marriage to Joseph was also known by the anonymous poet of "Buckeye's Lamentation for Want of More Wives," stanza 12, *Warsaw Message* (Feb. 4, 1844), repr. in Bachman, "A Study," 340. **Sept. 23:** ERSj. **Martha Abigail dies:** *Nauvoo Neighbor* (Apr. 17, 1844) and Nauvoo Sexton's Record p. 16, as cited in Cook, NDM 45. **Sylvester Stoddard:** D. Belnap,

MMK 2. **proposal from Hyrum:** Interview with Almira, recorded in Hyrum Belnap journal, July 24, 1908, Kerr collection, Marriott Library, also Stewart Library, Weber State University. **lock of hair:** F. Belnap, MMK 2. Reportedly, Martha also brought sheets to cover the bodies of the Smiths just arriving from Carthage.

VII. **marriage to Kimball:** HCK 310; AF. **Almira marries Stoddard:** D. Belnap, MMK 2. **Martha to Rizpah Knight:** July 8, 1845, Kerr collection. **Dec. 19:** Kimball/Clayton journal, Book 93, initiatory ordinance record. March 17 is given as the date of birth, which identifies our Martha Knight sufficiently, though year of birth has been lost. **Adaline's marriage:** OPH 10:403. Adaline and Gilbert would have thirteen children. Reportedly, Heber C. Kimball performed the marriage, but arrived two hours late, having forgotten the wedding while engrossed in reading the evening newspaper, F. Belnap, MMK 3. **Rizpah's marriage:** D. Belnap, MMK 2. **Nauvoo temple sealing:** BOP #92; SAd 369, 505.

VIII. **across Iowa:** Gilbert Belnap's notes in "Record Book of V. Knight," quoted in D. Belnap, MMK 3. **details of Winter Quarters experience:** ibid. Gilbert Belnap, Autobiography, Huntington Library. **miscarriage:** This may be the boy that died at birth mentioned in HCK 310. Compare Orson Whitney, *Life of Heber C. Kimball*, 432, who knows of no children from Martha's marriage to Heber. "Death of a Pioneer Woman" documents a child by Heber Kimball, "who died in infancy."

IX. **Dates for overland journey:** See Gilbert Belnap journal, cited in D. Belnap, MMK 4. Compare his Autobiography, Huntington Library and LCD 1:10, p. 43. Also OPH 10:403. **loss of grandchildren on the plains:** L. Belnap, "Sketch," 5. **to Ogden:** D. Belnap, MMK 4. **entering Ogden:** L. Belnap, "Sketch," 5. This account has the Belnaps settle in "Bunker's Hollow in the southeast part of the city" and at Sullivan Avenue and 30th St., p. 6. F. Belnap, MMK 4, has her living first in a thatched roof home in the fort, then in a log house at the same place. Then she moved to a home "on 26th Street, above the present Second Ward Chapel." **oxcart accident:** quoted in D. Belnap, MMK 4. **struggle:** L. Belnap, "Sketch," 5. **1851 census:** Census of Davis Co., 1851; UGHM 28 (1937): 51; also 1850 census, p. 69, 28, "Martha Knights," in Salt Lake County. Compare OPH 10:403 for Martha's move to Weber. She lived with the Heber C. Kimball family "until she moved to Hooper, after which she lived in that community and Ogden," OPH 10:403. "Death of a Pioneer Woman" has her go to Ogden, then Hooper. **Heber visits Martha:** D. Belnap, MMK 6. **Gilbert and Henrietta:** AF. **adobe house:** Gilbert Belnap Autobiography, 46. **death of Abigail:** FGS. **Belnap's activities:** Register, Kerr Collection, I. Autobiography 46-47. **Relief Society:** "Death of a Pioneer Woman," compare OPH 10:403. According to the Weber Stake Relief Society records (Weber Stake Relief Society Conference Minutes, July 19, 1877 to Dec. 18, 1899, Book "A," CA, p. 3), "The Relief Society of Ogden first organized in the spring of 1855. Mrs. Palmer, President. Martha Knight and Abigail Abbott, Counselors." This Relief Society presidency was reorganized, without Martha, on December 16, 1867, so one would expect that Martha served from 1855 or 1856 to 1867. **Martha in Kimball house:** Adelia Wilcox Kimball, Reminiscences, pp. 39-40, MS 6089, CA. Compare HCK 234. **"Her needlework ...":** "Death of a Pioneer Woman." **move south:** D. Belnap, MMK 5-6. **To Fillmore then Santa Clara:** Martha Knight to Adaline Belnap, Apr. 19, 1860, Kerr collection, Gilbert Belnap folder. "I staid at Brother Samuels four months I enjoyed myself well for they wase very kind to me and maid me well come to the best they had ... I left Fillmore the last of February I arived at [Santa] Clara Fort the tenth of March." She cautioned Gilbert not to make Gilbert Jr. work too hard and signed it, "your Mother and friend untill death, Martha Knight." **May 22:** D. Belnap, MMK 6.

X. **August 22:** AF. **1869 move to Hooper:** "Death of a Pioneer Woman." For the Belnaps' move, see D. Belnap, MMK 6. However, L. Belnap, "Sketch," 6, has Gilbert and Adaline moving in 1869. Adaline wanted to leave Ogden to remove her children from the influence of saloons; Ogden was no longer an isolated Mormon community. In Hooper she served as a midwife and Relief Society president. **1870 census:** p. 435. On p. 433, we find Gilbert Belknap and Henrietta Belknap. On p. 431, James Knight, Weber River Valley. **temple work:** Endowment House Sealings, Record Book F, p. 415, as cited in Ivins 4:281. **Almira Hanscomb to Martha:** Kerr collection, no date. Compare D. Belnap 5. **1875 letter:** Almira McBride Hanscom, to Martha; Kerr collection, CA. **St. George:** "She was also one of the workers in the St. George Temple for several years." "Death of a Pioneer Woman." **Apr. 4:** D. Belnap, MMK 6. **Reuben McBride to Martha:** Feb. 15, 1878, CA, Kerr collection, Reuben to Martha, Nov. 29, 1878; Kerr collection, CA. **Christmas in Hooper:** D. Belnap, MMK 6. **Almira to Utah:** D. Belnap, MMK 5. Della emphasizes Almira's continued snubs of Gilbert Belnap. **Reuben to Martha:** July 31, 1880, Kerr collection. **1881-82:** D. Belnap, MMK 6. **Dec. 6 and 25, 1886:** Kerr collection. **Martha lives with Belnaps:** D. Belnap, MMK 6. This was "a rock house of John I. Hart's just above Washington Blvd." **Almira Hanscomb to Martha:** June 10, 1888.

XI. **Daisy Knight to Martha Knight:** Kerr Collection. **death of Rizpah:** AF. **March 17, 1898:** See "Death of a Pioneer Woman"; the year may have been 1899.

XII. **Martha dies:** "Death of a Pioneer Woman"; see also the obituary of her daughter, Adaline Knight Belnap, "Veteran of Nauvoo Laid at Final Rest," in DN (June 16, 1919): p. 6. F. Belnap, MMK 5, gives us details of the death: "On the evening of Nov. 19, 1901, she told her daughter, Adaline to call in her grandson, Gilbert Roswell Belnap, who was at his farm house across the block in Hooper. Despite Adaline's assertion that Gilbert Roswell was in Ogden attending to the sheriff's responsibilities, Martha insisted on seeing her favorite grandson. Adaline sent her adopted son, Roy Stoddard, across the fields in the dark, who found Gilbert asleep in his farm house, much to the astonishment of all. [He came to see Martha.] After visiting with him, she laid down to rest. Somewhat alarmed by this time, Adaline lay on the foot of her mother's bed because she knew that the Prophet Joseph Smith had promised Martha that she should be changed from mortality to immortality in the twinkling of any eye. Adaline said, 'I must have fallen asleep. When I looked at mother again, she had not moved, but her spirit had flown, in fulfillment of the prophecy, I think.' It was 4:00 A.M. Nov 20, 1901."

## REFERENCES TO CHAPTER 16.
### *Gardener's Wife:*
### *Ruth Daggett Vose (Sayers Smith)*

"SAYERS." Obituary. DW (Aug. 20, 1884): 496.
[Wells, Emmeline]. "Ruth Sayers." An obituary. WE 13 (Sept. 15, 1884): 61-62.
**July 16, 1844:** WWj (2:422). **July 17:** WWj (2:423).

I. **birthdate:** Endowment House Record; Wells, RS; PBI 11:168, has Suffolk Co., Massachusetts, as birthplace. **Daniel Vose:** Daniel died in 1839 in Florida, see below. Ruth did a baptism for dead for him, see ECIF under Ruth Sayers. **upholstering:** Wells, RS. **Polly Vose:** Mary Vose was sealed to Joseph posthumously in 1858, Ivins list, USHS, #46, which gives the birthdate. Since Polly died in 1866 at the age of eighty-six (Wells, RS), Polly and Mary have the same birthdate, and thus are probably the same person. Wells, RS, refers to her as both Mary and Polly. **Polly baptized:** "baptized Fany Brewer and Mary Voce ..." Samuel Smith journal, CA. **Ruth's baptism:** "SAYERS"; Wells, RS, "baptized into the Church ... in May, 1832." BYj. The Endowment House record has what looks like May 1837. **Joseph Smith in Boston:** HC 1:295; Hill, JS 151. **Ruth contributes to the Kirtland temple:** "SAYERS." **"It is enough":** Wells, RS. **$150.00:** May 7, 1834, Matthias Cowley, *Wilford Woodruff, History of his Life and Labors* (Salt Lake City: Bookcraft, 1964), 39. **Wilford Woodruff preaches at Sister Vose's:** WWj, May 11, 1838 (1:248), compare MSt 27 (1865): 296. **liberality to elders:** Wells, RS. **Daniel's death:** Wells, RS. For Kookooche (more commonly known as Coacoochee), see John K. Mahon, *History of the Second Seminole War, 1835-1842* (Gainesville: University of Florida Press, 1967), 276-302. I have been unable to confirm the date of death as given by Wells, but a "Mr. Vose, from Black Creek," a member of a troupe of actors, was killed by Coacoochee on May 23, 1840, seven or eight miles from St. Augustine. If this is Ruth's brother, Wells's date of death is off by a year. See "Indian Murders," *Florida Herald*, St. Augustine (May 29, 1840), repr. in *Florida Historical Society Quarterly* 8 (1930): 200-203. Compare Mahon, *History* 276.

II. **marriage to Sayers:** TS 2 (Feb. 15, 1841): 324. **Edward's birthdate:** SEB; TIB. **horticulturist:** Wells, RS. **to Nauvoo:** Wells, RS. **1842 Ward census:** 2nd Ward, 9th page. **May 18:** Jessee 2:384. **Edward farming:** See next section. Compare ME 122. **April 14:** RS Minutes, p. 28.

III. **August 10:** JSj, Jessee 2:404-5; HC 5:90; compare the map in Jessee, PW 632. **Clayton wrote:** Jessee 2:407. **August 15:** Jessee 2:414. **Joseph departs:** Jessee 2:418. For his stay at Carlos Granger's house, compare the Sarah Whitney chapter, at Aug. 18, 1842. **marriage to Joseph:** Affidavit, 1869, in SAB 1:9, 4:9, compare Bachman 348. However, there is a problem with this date, for Hyrum Smith apparently opposed polygamy until May 26, 1843 (WCj, IC 106, compare Ehat, JSI 54-59). So either Ruth's February 1843 date is wrong, or someone other than Hyrum performed the marriage. I am grateful to Michael Marquardt for pointing this out to me. Jenson 6:234 lists Ruth as a wife of Joseph Smith, but supplies no date.

IV. **HCK in Boston:** July 22, 1844 (OPW 75). **in New York:** HC 7:209. **July 24:** HC 7:209. Compare WWj (2:431). **July 31:** HCKj, OPW 77. Compare July 27. **arrival in Nauvoo:** WWj, Aug. 6 (2:434).

V. **August 27:** HCKj, OPW 83. On Sept. 20, 1844 (OPW 87), Heber recorded, "Went to the Temple. elder Claton rote me a leter to Sister Ruth Seyers." **in Boston to 1849:** Wells, RS.

VI. **American Hotel Corner:** Wells, RS. **1850 census:** p. 108. **patriarchal blessing:** PBI 11:168. **endowment:** Endowment House Book A-A1, at Apr. 16, 1851. For washing and anointing, see EM, s.v. **letter:** Ruth Vose Sayers to Brigham Young, Brigham Young Collection, CA, MS 1234, Reel 44, box 21, fd 3. "fall of 1851" is marked by a later hand.

VII. The Sayerses are listed in the 1856 census. **Sept. 7:** WWj (4:446). **Ruth travels with Pratt:** Parley P. Pratt wrote, in his autobiography, "[1857, February] Wednesday, 25th.– On repairing to the office found letters from home, also one from Sister Ruth Sayers, who crossed the plains with us on our outward trip from Salt Lake City." *Autobiography*, 406. Parley arrived at Cincinnati on December 17, then reached New York by December 31. On January 24 he was in Philadelphia, and on February 25, when he received a letter from Ruth, he was back in St. Louis. **trip back to Utah:** Wells, RS. WWj, June 23, 1857 (5:61), wrote: "Sister [Polly] Vose is 77 years old & rode 1,200 miles in 23 days ... Saw sister Says & had some conversation with her." **two apostles:** WWj (5:66). **Polly sealed to Joseph:** Ivins list, USHS, #46, citing Journal of J. D. T. McAllister, CA. **1860 census:** p. 25; see also Ronald Vern Jackson, *Directory of Individuals residing in Salt Lake City Wards 1854-61* (Bountiful, UT: n.p., 1982). **Edward dies:** Wells, RS; *Salt Lake City Cemetery Records to 1909*, typescript (Salt Lake City: Genealogical Society, 1931), 5:1293. **Polly's death:** Wells, RS.

VIII. **1870 Census:** p. 626. Her real estate is worth $8,000, her personal estate is $150. **1880 Census:** p. 179. **illness and death:** "SAYERS." **WE obituary:** Wells, RS. **Joseph living in wives' houses:** Joseph also lived in Marinda Johnson (Hyde)'s house, before she was married to Orson. Many of Joseph's wives, conversely, lived in his house before marrying him. **no proxy marriage:** On the other hand, there was some connection with Heber C. Kimball soon after Joseph's death, as we have seen, when Young and Kimball were marrying many of Joseph's widows. It is possible that Ruth was sealed to Kimball in a polyandrous proxy marriage at that time, but this idea is purely speculative.

# REFERENCES TO CHAPTER 17.
## Daughter of the Pagan Prophet:
## Flora Ann Woodworth (Smith Gove)

**Emma and gold watch:** WCj, Aug. 23, 1843, IC 118; compare ME 159.

I. **Flora Ann:** Birthdate from NTER. Other sources have November 17 as the birthdate. The 1850 Iowa census has her born in Kentucky, see below. **Phoebe's birthdate:** SAd 555; NTER. Watrous is a degeneration of Waterhouse, which changed from Waterous to Watrous; Watrus is another variation. The 1870 Utah Census gives Connecticut as her state of birth. **Lucien Woodworth:** NTER for birthdate, April 3, 1799. See also Cheryl Harmon Bean, "LDS Baptisms in Erie County, Pennsylvania 1831-1833," *The Nauvoo Journal* 5 (Fall 1993): 3-44, 44, 5-6. **conversion:** Zebedee Coltrin journal, CA, MS 1443. To give a sense of early Mormon missionary work, and the Woodworths' early Mormon environment, I quote at length: "4the We came to Sprinfild Eury Co - Pen - State and Staide at Br hartshorn  5the we went to the plase whare Br H Smith and W Smith was ${}^\&$ held a Confrance to regulate the Curch  in the eavening we held meating Br D Paton preach and i Spoke of [after?] him  6th Br H Smith paptised four boys and to girls and comfurmeid them by the layings on of the hands and thare ware many in { } [the congregation?] that desired that the Elders Should lay hands on them  Br {D} Paton and H Smith pray and laid hands on them  7the we wente to the 1 town of {Congutt} [Conneaut?] and preach to acongratoin [a congregation] in the eavening and S[t]aid at Mr {Jtheaum} {Soinen} and we {sh°ade} them the proofe of the book mormon and set before them the Gospel  8th ${}^{we\ went\ to}$ {St. Salsbury} and Brother John Spoke { } the { } unto them & {} I s[p]oke from the Gospel unto them & we left {another apontement} upon { } & we {???????} Staid allnight with them  9the beaing the Lords day we returned & preached in the Chool house near Woodworth  J & I preach to them and Should [showed] them that the Jentiles had proke [broke] the covenant and that {you} had restord it again and I {shode} the gospel unto them and we {t[o]lde} them that we wold preach to them again the next thurday eavening  went home with awoman thold us that she believe us ~~Luchian~~ and we staid with Luchian Woodworth. 10th we went to the town of Gerards and preach  Br John laid the {proffid} [prophet?] before them and the Book of mormon and I Spoke from the Gospel and the Lord blest us much  Stade at {one Prison}  11the rested and returned to {Cahion} [Luchion?] Woodworth and Stade all ... 13th we returned to the Schoolhose near L Woodworth & held m[e]ating ... and I s[t]ade ${}^{at}$ L Woodworth ... 14 the ... preach at the chool house in Gerard ... 16th held meating at the chool near L Woodworth ... 20 we held meeting at the chool house near L W. Also 25th, 30th..." Compare Bean, "LDS Baptisms," 9 and V. Alan Curtis, "Missionary Activities and Church Organizations in Pennsylvania, 1830-1840," Master's thesis, Brigham Young University, 1976, 36. **Evan Greene journal, CA MS 1442:** In the front of book, "Sister Phebe Woodworth living in Conneaut to be directed to Conneautville Erie Co Penn." Feb. 16, 1833: "and then to Sister Phebe's and Doct Sherman here we found them all well and we had a good visit that evening with some of the neighbors." Feb. 21. "Br. H and myself went over to Sister Phebe's and stayed that night." Mar. 22, 1833: "came to Sister Woodworths and found them not at holm she was at Doctor Shermans." It is odd that Lucien is not mentioned. Zebedee Coltrin, on the other hand, always refers to Lucien. **Mary:** See 1850 Iowa census, 1860 California census, and Nauvoo 1842 Ward record. **John:** See 1850 Iowa census, 1860 California census, and Nauvoo 1842 Ward record.

II. **Lucien accompanies Joseph:** HC 4:366. **Fourth Ward:** Nauvoo Ward census, 1842, Fourth Ward, p. 2. **Phebe in Relief Society:** RS Min., 43. **William Woodbury school:** "Nauvoo School Records," *The Nauvoo Journal* 1 (1989): 26-27. **Lucien a friend of Joseph:** JSj, see Faulring, index; HC, index. **pagan prophet:** WJS 164-65. On April 19, 1843, Joseph instructed the Twelve: "Tell Woodsworth to put the hands onto the

Nauvoo House and begin the work and be patient till means can be provided," JSj, Faulring 370.

**III. Clayton affidavit:** Jenson HR 6:225. **March 4:** JSj, Faulring 327. For other encoded polygamy records, see the Agnes Coolbrith and Louisa Beaman chapters. **Orange Wight:** See his Reminiscences, CA, MS 405, pp. 20-23. **May 2:** IC 100. **June 1:** IC 107. **August 1843:** IC 119.

**IV. September 11:** Faulring 413. **Quorum of Anointed, September 28:** JSj, Faulring 416; HC 6:39; Ehat, JSI 94. **Oct. 29:** Joseph writes, "2 P.M. or near 4, before all were ready prayer meeting at the mansion. 25 present Sis Cutler, Cahoon, Woodworth. Adjourned [until] Wednesday over Brick store. Joseph taught." **building:** JSj, Oct. 13, 1843, Faulring 420: "Gave Woodworth some instructions about food at the pinery." Mar. 4, 1844, Faulring 451: "Let Woodworth go to the Pinery [and] take the things wanted and bring back the lumber and his wages [will] go on." **letter:** Dec. 7, 1843, Faulring 430. **March 8:** JSj, Faulring 457. **Council of Fifty:** WCj, Mar. 11, 1844, IC 126. **Texas:** "Lucien Woodworth sent out on a mission [to Texas ...]," JSj, Faulring 459; HC 6:254; George Miller, *Correspondence of Bishop Miller* (Burlington, WI: W. Watson, 1916), 20-21; Klaus J. Hansen, *Quest for Empire; the Political Kingdom of God and the Council of Fifty in Mormon History* ([East Lansing]: Michigan State University Press, 1967), 82; SLDS 185; Hill, JS 370-71. **returns:** Hill, JS 370-71; SLDS 185. **reports:** Faulring 476; Hansen, QE 86. **back to Texas:** JSj, May 6, 1844, Faulring 477. **Flora or sister sick:** Faulring 479, compare HC 6:377. **May 27:** JSj, Faulring 484. **Lawrence legal matters:** Faulring 487. **letter:** JSj, June 22, Faulring 495; Jessee, PW 592. **Lucien just after the martyrdom:** See WCj, June 30, 1844; July 6.

**V. convincing Young:** Hansen, QE 88; Miller, *Correspondence* 23. **Flora remarries:** Helen Mar Whitney, "Travels Beyond the Mississippi," WE 13 (Nov. 1, 1884): 87. Compare Jenson, HR vols. 5-8, p. 1009: "After the death of the Prophet, she married again, but this union proved unhappy." At some point in 1844 Flora received a patriarchal blessing from John Smith. Patriarchal Blessing Bk. 7, p. 113, as cited in Tinney 328. **Gove:** The first name is not certain, but the only Gove I have documented in Nauvoo is a Carlos Gove, who on March 9, 1844, was sued by A. B. Williams for $10.50. Docket Book of Legal Cases in Nauvoo, 1841-45, Chicago Historical Society. **Lucien released as architect:** John Taylor journal, Aug. 13, see Dean Jessee, "The John Taylor Nauvoo Journal, January 1845-September 1845," BYUSt 23 (Summer 1983): 1-124, 82. WRj, August 9, 1845. **foamed:** WCj, Aug. 17, IC 178. **December 7:** HCKj, Bk 93. **Lucien mentioned frequently:** e.g. Dec. 22, p. 229. **December 12:** HCKj (Clayton), Bk. 93. **Phebe and Lucian endowed:** NTER, compare HC 7:543, 542. **Phebe in conflict:** WCj, IC 210. For the ordinance of washing and anointing, see EM, s.v. **December 14:** HCKj, BK 93. **Flora endowed:** NTER. **Phebe sealed to Joseph:** BOP #34; SAd 503, 555. **Lucien's plural marriages:** SAd 547. Charlott was forty-five; Aminta Maria thirty-nine; Margaret twenty-seven; and Rachel forty-one. Compare Samuel Richards journal, Feb. 6, 1846, typescript at Lee Library: "In the afternoon I returned to the Temple and assisted to consecrate some oil, also just at night to anoint a Queen to Bro Woodard, (or the Pagan Prophet)."

**VI. crossing Missouri:** Horace Whitney journal, CA, MS 1616; compare Helen Mar Whitney, OTBM, WE 13 (Oct. 15, 1884): 75. **Helen and Flora:** Horace Whitney journal; Helen Mar Whitney, OTBM, WE 13 (Nov. 1, 1884): 87. The purpose of Helen's anecdote is purely didactic: "I have given this little incident in the life of Flora truthfully, and it ought to teach a lesson to those who read it, for no Latter-day Saint can find happiness in marriage with an unbeliever as soon as the illusion which bewildered them wears off; they find no true companionship, and remorse will come, though, alas, too late to retrace their steps." **1850:** Iowa census, Pottawattami County, p. 83. **Lucian's Utah families:** See Utah 1850 census, Utah County, p. 136. **Flora's death:** Helen Whitney, OTBM, WE 13 (Nov. 1, 1884): 87. Also Jenson, HR vols. 5-8, p. 1009: "She died in the wilderness on the journey westward at the time of the Exodus from Nauvoo."

**VII. San Bernardino:** California census, San Bernardino City, p. 621. A curious anomaly faces the Phebe Woodworth biographer at this point. The 1860 Utah census records a Phoebe Woodworth, age "60" living in Lehi, Utah County, Utah on September 29. This is five years younger than our Phebe, and our Phebe is apparently well documented as living in San Bernardino in 1860. The Utah Phebe's profession is listed as "School Teacher," one of the accepted professions for single women in pioneer Utah. She was born in New York, the correct state for our Phebe. Her real estate wealth is $15; her personal wealth is $200. Living with Phoebe is James G. Woodworth, eight years of age, born in Iowa in 1852. See 1860 Utah census: p. 378, Utah County. This same Phebe is still in Lehi in 1870, see Utah census, p. 216, Utah County. Here, Phoebe Woodworth, age "70," born, now, in Connecticut (a good example of the vagaries of census reporting) is living alone in Lehi. Her profession is listed as "Keeping House."

VIII. **Lucien's death:** WJS 265. **1871:** Endowment House Record, as cited in Ivins 4:280. Samuel H. B. Smith was a son of Samuel Smith and Mary Bailey, Agnes Coolbrith's friend from Boston. **1872. 1874:** Endowment House Record, Book H and I, as cited in Ivins 4:282.

# REFERENCES TO CHAPTER 18.
## Latter-day Hagar:
### Emily Dow Partridge (Smith Young)

AMLT: See Albert Lyman.
EPYj: Emily Partridge Young journal, CA.
IL: Emily Young, "Incidents in the Life of a Mormon Girl."
Lyman, Albert R. *Amasa Mason Lyman: Trailblazer and Pioneer from the Atlantic to the Pacific* (Delta, UT: Melvin A. Lyman, 1957).
Lyman, Eliza Partridge. Autobiography and Journal. CA.
Wells, Emmeline. "LDS Women of the Past." WE 37 (Oct. 1908): 17-18.
WIR: Emily Young, "What I Remember."
Young, Emily D.P. Autobiography. Marriott Library. "Written expressly for my children. Jan. 7, 1877." From a MS owned by Emily Young Knopp. Many of Emily's autobiographical writings are found also in CA. Typescript, CA, MS 2845.
———. "Autobiography of Emily D.P. Young." WE 13 (Dec. 1, 1884): 102-103; (Dec. 15, 1884) 105-6; (Jan. 1, 1885) 114; (Jan. 15, 1885): 122; (Feb. 1, 1885): 129-30; (Mar. 1, 1885): 145-46; (Mar. 15, 1885): 15; (Apr. 1, 1885): 166; (Apr. 15, 1885): 169-70; (May 15, 1885): 187; 14 (June 1, 1885): 3; (June 15, 1885): 10; (July 1, 1885): 17-18; (July 15, 1885): 26; (Aug. 1, 1885): 37-38; (Aug. 15, 1885): 43. The manuscript Autobiography is usually cited below, rather than these published reminiscences.
———. "Incidents in the Life of a Mormon Girl." CA, MS 5220, 187 pp. Written in Dec. 1876, apparently. This ends with the marriage to Joseph Smith.
———. Testimony. Temple Lot Case, pp. 364, 367, 384.
———. "What I Remember." Marriott Library.

**tarred and feathered:** WIR 11-13; IL 25; Eliza Lyman Autobiography; HC 1:390. **note:** Eliza and Emily are treated together in their early life. It is only after Joseph Smith died and they married different husbands that their paths diverged significantly.

I. **birth of Eliza:** date from BOP #5; NTER; SAd 387. **Edward Partridge:** was born on August 27, 1793, in Pittsfield, Berkshire, Massachusetts. FGS; HC 1:128-29; Cook, RP 53. **Lydia Clisbee:** was born on September 26, 1793, in Marlborough, Middlesex, Massachusetts. **birth of Emily:** BOP #12; NTER; SAd 503, 577. See also birthday entries in her later diaries. **Harriet:** died in 1840. **Caroline:** married Amasa Lyman in 1844 and died in 1908. Biography in AMLT 292-97; Stella H. Day, cp., *Builders of Early Millard*, Day (n.p.: Art City Publishing, 1979), 448-51. **house, childhood experiences:** WIR 1-4. **trip to Massachusetts:** Eliza Lyman, Autobiography. **school:** Eliza Lyman,

Autobiography. "I was sent to school until I was about thirteen years of age" (1833). **Edward follows Campbell:** HC 1:129. Previously, he had been a "Universal Restorationist." **Clisbee born and dies:** Aug. 1828, FGS; WIR 1-4. **Lydia the younger:** married Amasa Lyman in 1853 or 1854 and died in 1875. Biography in AMLT 299-301.

II. **Pratt etc. pass through:** WIR 5. IL 2. Compare the Mary E. Rollins chapter. **Edward to Fayette:** Eliza Lyman, Autobiography; HC 1:128; Cook, RP 53. **Edward baptized and ordained:** Cook, RP 53. **receives revelation:** Book of Commandments 38; D&C 36. **luggage in barn:** WIR 6. **Edward bishop:** Book of Commandments 43:11-13; D&C 41:9-11. **measles:** WIR 6. **conference in Missouri enjoined:** Book of Commandments 54, esp. vv. 24, 41; D&C 52. Compare Cook, RP 71. **Edward leaves for Missouri:** Eliza Lyman, Autobiography. WIR 6-7; IL 7-8. **conference in Missouri:** D&C (1835) 27:3; D&C (1981) 57:7. **Aug. 1 instructions:** Book of Commandments 59:17-19, 30-32; D&C 58:14-15, 24-25. For tensions between Partridge and Joseph Smith, see Quinn, MHOP 70. **Joseph returns:** WIR 7. **August 5:** Edward to Lydia Partridge, Aug. 5, 1831, quoted in WIR 7. **"it seemed":** IL 9. **journey to Missouri:** WIR 8, IL 15. Compare Eliza Lyman, Autobiography, a shorter account that is essentially the same as Emily's. **reunion with Edward:** WIR 8-9; IL 16.

III. **life hard:** Eliza Lyman, Autobiography; IL 21. **new house:** WIR 9. **school:** WIR 9. **culture shock:** WIR 10; IL 20. **Emily baptized:** Emily Young, Autobiography, Marriott Library, p. 2. IL 22. For John Corrill, see Stephen LeSueur, *The 1838 Mormon War in Missouri* (Columbia: University of Missouri Press, 1987), index, s.v. **mobbings:** HR 6:240. **haystack and children:** WIR 10; IL 22, 24. **Edward Jr.:** He married Sarah Clayton in 1858, Elizabeth Buxton in 1862, and died in 1900. See his journals, Lee Library.

IV. **leaving Independence:** Eliza Lyman, Autobiography. Compare WIR 22, IL 75. Emily adds that the crossing was made at "a place near Liberty landing." **stars:** WIR 22, IL 76-77; compare HC 1:439 and Fanny Young chapter at 1827. **Edward's mission:** See his diary, ed. Lyman De Platt, CA 4881. On December 27 a young girl in Kirtland consulted a seer stone and relayed to Edward a vision of his family in Missouri. She also "saw" a seer stone for Edward buried beneath the ground.

V. **Edward builds new home:** Emily Young, Autobiography 3. **Eliza teaches:** Eliza Lyman, Autobiography. **troubles begin again:** Emily Young, Autobiography, 3. IL 165. Compare LeSueur, *The 1838 Mormon War.*

VI. **"anywhere":** Emily Young, Autobiography 3. **Quincy:** Eliza Lyman, Autobiography. IL 169. **remained in Quincy:** Emily Young, Autobiography 3. **Emily hires out:** Emily Young, Autobiography 3; IL 169. **Pittsfield:** Emily Young, Autobiography 3; IL 171. **Nauvoo, tent:** Emily Young, Autobiography 3; IL 172. **Emily sick:** Emily Young, Autobiography 3. **Eliza in Lima:** Eliza Lyman, Autobiography. **Emily at the move:** Emily Young, Autobiography 3. **Edward bishop:** Cook, RP 54. **Harriet dies:** Eliza Lyman, Autobiography. Obituary in TS 1 (June 1840): "She was of an amiable disposition—kind and affectionate to her friends and acquaintance, but especially her parents. ... She was sick about nine months, which affliction she endured with the greatest patience. She has been cut down in the flower of her age, and gone to dwell with Christ." **Edward dies:** Emily Young, Autobiography 3; IL 174. Obituary in TS 1 (June 1840): "No man had the confidence of the church more that he. His station was highly responsible; large quantities of property ever entrusted to his care. Deeds and conveyances of lands, to a large amount, were put into his hands, for the benifit of the poor, and for church purposes; for all of which, the directest account was rendered, to the fullest satisfaction of all concerned. And after he had distributed a handsome property, of his own, for the benefit of the poor; and being driven from his home, found himself reduced to very limited circumstances, still, not one cent of public property would he use to indemnify himself or family; but distributed it all, for the benefit of the widow, the fatherless, and the afflicted; had deceased, leaving his family in very ordinary circumstances." Also Nauvoo Sexton Record, p. 1, as cited in Cook, NDM 59. **Eliza sick:** Eliza Lyman, Autobiography.

VII. **William Law's house:** Eliza Lyman, Autobiography 219; IL 175; Emily Young, Autobiography 4. **Eliza and tailoring:** Eliza Lyman, Autobiography; Emily Young, IL 176. **to the Smith's:** Emily Young, Autobiography 4; IL 177 ("About this time Sister Emma sent for me to come and live with her and nurse her baby.") Eliza Lyman, Autobiography 219. **Eliza's job:** Temple Lot testimony, full transcript, p. 356. **Lydia marries Huntington:** TS 1 (Oct. 1840): 191. Compare Zina Huntington chapter. **Emily reminisced:** CA, loose sheet. **Relief Society:** RS Minutes, Apr. 19, 28, p. 30, 34.

VIII. **letter refusal:** Temple Lot, full transcript, box 1, fd 15, pp. 356-57. ME 138. **first taught plural marriage:** Emily Young, Autobiography 38; IL 185; Jenson HR 6:223. **Emily shuts Joseph up:** Emily Young, IL 185-86. **February 28:** Emily Young, IL 185-86. **deep water:** Emily Young, Autobiography 4; ME 138. **Durfee:** Emily Young, Autobiography, 4; ME 138. **conversion:** Emily Young, Autobiography, 4; ME 138. **teaching and proposal:** Temple Lot, transcript, p. 350. Compare p. 358: "Q-Was it sealing for eternity? A-Yes, sir, time and eternity ... Q-How do you know it was for time? A-Because that was in the ceremony, and he said it was for time and eternity both, and it was in the ceremony too." Also, p. 360: "I got married on his own teachings, he was the prophet of the church and he told me it was all right and I took his word for it." **February 28:** IL 185-86. **Emily's marriage:** Emily Young, Autobiography 4; IL 185-86 ("I was married the 4th of March"); "Autobiography," WE 14 (Aug. 1, 1885): 38; HR 6:223. Compare ME 138. **"roomed":** Temple Lot transcript, p. 364, qu. 311-14; 384, qu. 751-59. "Q-Did you ever have carnal intercourse with Joseph Smith? A-Yes sir ... Q-Do you make the declaration that you never slept with him but one night? A-Yes sir. Q-And that was the only time and place that you ever were in bed with him? A-No sir." Thus, though she only slept with Joseph one full night, she had sexual relations with him on other occasions. **Eliza's marriage:** Eliza Lyman, Autobiography, 219. **date of Eliza's marriage:** Eliza Lyman, affidavit, SAB 2:32, 3:32, Bachman #65. **secrecy:** "neither of us knew about the other at the time, everything was so secret." IL 185-86.

IX. **Lucy Walker:** Affidavit, SAB 2:30; 3:30; Bachman, #64; Temple Lot case, transcript, 352. **remarriage:** Emily Young, Autobiography; IL 186. SAB 2:34; 3:34, Bachman #66; 1:13, 4:13, Bachman #46. Compare Temple Lot Case, transcript, p. 351. Emily may be dating this second ceremony incorrectly, as apparently both Emma and Judge Adams were not in Nauvoo on the 11th, see Van Wagoner, MP 50, 35; he suggests May 23 as a good candidate for the proper day. **Adams:** Emily Young, in HR 6:223; Affidavit, #63 in Bachman, "A Study," 349. For Adams see Kent Walgren, "James Adams: Early Springfield Mormon and Freemason," *Journal of the Illinois State Historical Society* 75 (Summer 1952): 121-36, and the Lucy Walker chapter. Compare JSj, Faulring 377, for this day: "6 A.M. Baptized [blank spaces] Snow, Louisa Bemen, Sarah Alley &c." &c. may stand for Emily and Eliza Partridge. Sarah Alley had married Joseph Bates Noble in April 1843. Also on this day Joseph Smith with Clayton, George Miller, J. M. Smith, and Lydia Partridge went on a carriage trip to Carthage. WCj; IC 101. **"From that very hour":** Emily Young, Autobiography 6. **May 23:** WCj, IC 105-106. **I do not know:** IL 185-86. **details of casting off:** Emily Young, Autobiography 5. As usual, Eliza, dealing with the same experience, is laconic: "I continued to live in his family for a length of time after this, but did not reside there when he was martyred." Autobiography, Eliza Lyman, 13. **Coolidge, Lyon:** Emily Partridge, Autobiography, WE 14 (Aug. 1, 1885): 38: "We remained in Nauvoo. My sister Eliza found a home with the family of Brother Joseph Cooledge, and I went to live with Sister Sylvia Lyons. She was a good woman, and one of the lord's chosen few." **poem:** ERSj. **Aug. 16:** WCj, IC 117. Emma apparently told Joseph that she would allow him to keep "E and E P" (Emily and Eliza Partridge), but Joseph felt if he even kept these two, Emma would use it as an excuse to divorce him. Though he told Emma that he would relinquish his wives, he told Clayton that "he should not relinquish anything." **Emily Partridge**, Autobiography, at Nov. 4, 1883: "After these many years I can truly say: poor Emma, she could not stand polygamy but she was a good woman and I never wish to stand in her way of happiness and exaltation. I hope the Lord will be merciful to her, and I believe he will. It is an awful thought, to contemplate misery of a human being. If the Lord will, my heart says let Emma come up and stand in her place. Perhaps she has done no worse than any of us would have done in her place. Let the Lord be the judge." Compare Ann Eliza Young, WN19 68, who writes that Joseph had eleven young women living with him as "adopted daughters," to whom he was sealed without Emma's knowledge. Emma, when she discovered the truth, threatened to walk out on Joseph, thus forcing him to require his young wives to leave. Eleven seems a high estimate, but there were at least seven: Elvira Cowles, the Partridges, the Lawrences, Melissa Lott, and Lucy Walker. Eliza Snow and Desdemona Fullmer also lived with Joseph, but were not young enough to be accounted "adopted daughters."

X. **marriage to Young:** September date, Susa Young Gates and Mabel Young Sanborn, "Brigham Young Genealogy," UGHM 11 (1920): 127-34, 127. Later in her life Emily gave the date November 1844, see Temple Lot transcript, p. 362, qu. 277: "Q-When were you married to Brigham Young? ... It was in the fall of 1844, I think." qu. 282: "I think it was in November, but I would not be positive of that." Temple Lot case 364: "At the time I married Brigham Young, in November, 1844, I was at the same time sealed to Joseph Smith, sealed to him for eternity; I was sealed to Brigham Young for time, and to Joseph Smith for eternity. The manner that I was married to Brigham Young is what is known as marriage by proxy; that is what I considered it meant; that is, I was sealed to Brigham Young that day, during my natural life, and in eternity I was to be the wife of Joseph Smith. I was not married to Joseph Smith under the revelation on sealing, but I was married to him under the revelation on plural marriage ... I was married March, 1843, on the 11th of March, I think it was. I know I was married to him under the revelation of plural marriage. I was married to him on the 11th day of May, 1843." HR 6:240: "After the prophet's death, I was married to Pres. Brigham Young, according to the laws of proxy." **Edward:** for the name, see Emily Partridge Young journal and Autobiography, WE (Aug. 1, 1885): 38. For Emily's children, see FGS and Gates and Sanborn, "Brigham Young Genealogy," 127-29. **endowment:** NTER. **Jan. 14:** BOP #12; SAd 503, 577. **alone after leaving Nauvoo:** Autobiography 6. **forty women:** See Johnson, DDW. **Mt. Pisgah:** Autobiography 6-7; compare PBSj June 2. **description of shanty, brethren assisted move:** WE 38. **Zina to Emily Partridge,** 1846-47 [just before Jan. 1847?]; Emily D. Partridge [Young] to Zina Jacobs [Young], Jan. 29, 1847. Both from Zina Card Brown collection, CA.

XI. **to Winter Quarters:** Autobiography 7. **year at Winter Quarters:** HR 6:240.

XII. **crossing the plains:** Autobiography 7. Diary, July 24, 1897. **Emily Augusta:** Autobiography 7. She later married Hiram Clawson as a plural wife, and died in 1926. Emily received a patriarchal blessing from John Smith on June 20, 1849, see WE 14 (Aug. 15, 1885): 43. **move to primitive house:** Autobiography 7. **Caroline:** She later married Mark Croxall, with whom she had seven children from 1870 to 1881; she and Croxall were then divorced, and she married George Q. Cannon as his fifth wife, bearing him four children from 1885 to 1892. She died in 1903. **1853 letter:** Brigham Young collection, CA, MS 1234 box 62 (reel 95), fd 10. This was first discussed and cited in Bringhurst, BY 126. **Joseph Don Carlos:** "Carl" was later the church architect, and the Salt Lake temple was finished under his supervision. He served a mission to the southern states, then became church architect again, and designed the Administration Building on South Temple Street. He married Alice Dowden in 1881, with whom he had ten children, Marian Penelope Hardy in 1887, and died in 1938. See Dean Jessee, *Letters of Brigham Young to His Sons* (Salt Lake City: Deseret Book, 1974), 263-81. **Miriam** ("Mame" or "Mamie") married Leonard Hardy in 1878, and died in 1919. **Josephine** ("Jo") married Albert Carrington Young, son of Brigham Young, Jr., in 1878, and died in 1912.

XIII. **move from Lion House:** Susa Gates collection, USHS, box 12 fd 4, "page 1." **Emily Augusta's marriage:** Gates and Sanborn, BYG 127. For Hiram Clawson, see *The Making of a Mormon Apostle, The Story of Rudger Clawson* (Lanham, MD: Madison Books, 1990), 33-52. One of his previous wives, Alice Young, was also a daughter of Brigham.

**Eugenia Rampton:** Biography of Emily, p. 9, Marriott Library. She remembered Emily living in houses at 5th East, South Temple, the Women's Exponent building, Southwest Temple and State streets. **1870 Census,** p. 627, has Emily, 46, living in the Twelfth Ward with Joseph, 15, Mary, 13, Josephine, 10, and "Liddia Partridge," 70. Sister Lydia and daughter Emily Clawson are living close by. **Forest Farm:** Emily Partridge Young journal, Apr. 16, 1874. **Ann Eliza Young on wives broken by overwork:** WN19 532. On p. 534, Ann Eliza stated that she knew at least six women whose health had been broken by work at Forest Farm. For a less negative view of life on the farm, see Susa Young Gates, "From Impulsive Girl to Patient Wife: Lucy Bigelow Young," UHQ 45 (1977): 270-88, 280-81. The farm house presently stands at the This Is the Place Pioneer Park, not its original location. See also Susa Young Gates, "Brigham Young and His Nineteen Wives," p. 11, USHS. There were two log houses, one the "cook house" with dining room and kitchen, the other the "milk and cheese" house, with cows and dairy. Lucy Bigelow had a bedroom on the second floor of the "cook house." **Ann Eliza on Emily at the farm:** WN19 504-505. Ann Eliza described Emily, when she married Brigham, as "a young childless widow, very patient and gentle, and very pretty, too." WN19 504.

**XIV. depression:** Compare especially the Helen Mar Kimball chapter. Many of the women in this book endured depressive episodes. As family losses can trigger severe depression, it is surprising that these women did not break under the strain, considering the fact that they lost so many children. **home in 12th ward:** Autobiography, WE 14 (Aug. 15, 1885): 43. Perhaps this is the home on Fourth East, between First and Second South, see Gates collection, USHS, box 12 fd 4 p. 1. However, Susa Gates elsewhere wrote that Emily moved to a home on "Fourth East" only after Brigham's death, "Brigham Young and His Nineteen Wives," p. 6. **Ann Eliza Webb Young on Brigham's penuriousness:** WN19 458: "I told him several times that I was insufficiently supplied; but for a long time he made some excuse or other for not giving me more. At last he sent me a very few additional ones; so that, although there was still a lack of what I actually needed, I managed to get along by a great deal of contriving. We lived very sparely, even poorly, as did most of the wives, except the favorite, and one or two others, who asserted their rights to things, and got them after a great deal of insisting. I could not insist, and so I got very little." See also 459: "I could not get anything else out of him, except by the hardest labor, and the little that I got was given so grudgingly that I hated myself for accepting it ... I can scarcely look back to those times, now that I am so far beyond them, without a lowering of my self-respect." Again we might suspect Ann Eliza of exaggeration from negative bias, but Emily's private diary corroborates Ann Eliza's account. The lowering of self-esteem in both Ann Eliza's and Emily's cases is clear. Benjamin Johnson, a faithful Mormon, nevertheless writes, of Brigham, "I ... know that he was a Great Financeer and at times did manifest a Love for wealth and did make mistakes, Some of which he may not have lived fully to Rectafy - But with all of his mistakes, Private or publick, His Voice was ever the Voce of the True Sheapheard to Isreal." Letter to Gibbs, 1903, in Zimmerman 69. For a palatial home (known as the Gardo House) that Brigham built for his last favorite wife, Amelia Folsom, see Joseph Heinerman, "Amelia's Palace," *Montana* 29 (Winter, Jan. 1979): 54-63. The Gardo House has since been destroyed, but photographs show that it was truly imposing, with four stories, three dozen rooms, six flights of stairs, and 150 windows. **health problems:** EPYj, Apr. 5, 1874. **the President's men:** In a June 17, 1874, entry, Emily accused Brigham's "men" of insulting her children. **plural wife living for her children:** See Introduction, final section. **Brigham unwilling to support Emily:** Ann Eliza Young, WN19 505, wrote, of Emily, "Now she has a cottage outside [the Lion House], which Brigham gave her, telling her, when she moved into it, that he should in future expect her to support herself and children." Emily's diary is consistent with Ann Eliza's statement here. **Carlos to Rensselaer:** Jessee, *Letters* 264.

**XV. Another encomium of Brigham:** MS 7336 fd 5 #1, CA. **the will:** EPYj, Sept. 28,

1877. Arrington, BY 422-30. **November 16, 1878:** See Zina Huntington chapter at this date. **mid-January 1879:** EPYj, Jan. 16. **Carlos graduates:** Jessee, *Letters* 264. **move to the Exponent office:** Compare EPYj, Mar. 18, 1881. **1895 quote:** Letter to Lulu Clawson, Apr. 1, 1895, CA, MS 7336 fd 3. **early August 1882:** EPYj, Aug. 3. **late April:** EPYj, Apr. 26, 1883. **Ann Eliza on the Croxall marriage:** WN19 505. **Autobiography published:** EPYj, Dec. 1, 1884. **lives with Josephine:** EPYj, Nov. 3, 1886. **Carlos as legislator:** Jessee, *Letters* 264.

**VI.** **polygamy underground:** See Kimberly Jensen James, "'Between Two Fires': Women on the Underground of Mormon Polygamy," JMH 8 (1981): 49-62; Kimball, *Isn't One Wife* 380-410. **San Francisco:** There is a diary of Eliza's stay here, CA MS 7336 fd 4. She mentions weather ("It is raining this morning," Dec. 15, 1888), scenery, ("Carlie and I took awalk over to view the bay. saw some very pretty residences," Dec. 23; "went to North Beach and gathered shells," Apr. 21), a listing of Christmas presents (Dec. 25), and expenditures ("crackers - alcohol - eye water 1,30," Feb. 15). **Dec. 27, 1888:** CA, MS 7336 fd 1. **May, 1889:** Emily Young to "Mrs. Bradley" [Emily Augusta], May 9, 1889, CA, MS 7336 fd 1. **Jan. 11, 1890:** Emily Young to Emily Augusta, CA. **homecoming:** Emily Young to Emily Augusta, June 19, 1890. **Emily as seamstress:** Eugenia Rampton, Reminiscence of Emily Partridge Young, p. 9, Marriott Library. For sewing as a feminine art-form in nineteenth-century America, see Susan Burrows Swan, *Plain and Fancy: American Women and Their Needlework, 1750-1850* (New York: Holt, Rhinehart, and Winston, 1977). Nearly all of the women in this book sewed; see esp. the chapters of Eliza R. Snow at 1856; Agnes Coolbrith at Mar. 1842; Hannah Ells; Sarah Lawrence at 1852; and Eliza Partridge at Mar. 1, 1877. **April 6, 1893:** For the dedication of the Salt Lake temple, see Alexander, THE 291-96. For Don Carlos's role in finishing the temple, Jessee, *Letters* 264. **Emily to Carlos:** June 14, 1896, CA, MS 6700.

**VII.** **June 27, 1897:** CA, MS 3112. **death:** "Death of Mrs. Emily D.P. Young," DEN (Dec. 9, 1899): p. 7, one column. For Emily's funeral, see "Mrs. Young's Funeral," DN (Dec. 13, 1899): p. 1, and "Emily Dow Partridge Young," WE 28 (Dec. 15 to 24, 1899): 85. **Susa Young Gates:** "Lucy Bigelow Young," USHS, MS B-95, Susa Young Gates collection, box 15, fd 5, p. 56.

## REFERENCES TO CHAPTER 19.
### *"Everything Looks Like Desolation and Lonesome":*
### *Eliza Maria Partridge (Smith Lyman)*

AMLT: see Albert Lyman.

Day, Stella H., comp. *Builders of Early Millard.* N.p.: Art City Publishing, 1979.

EPLj: Eliza Partridge Lyman journal.

Hefner, Loretta L. "The Apostasy of Amasa Mason Lyman." Master's thesis, University of Utah, 1977.

———. "From Apostle to Apostate: the Personal Struggle of Amasa Mason Lyman." *Dialogue* 16 (Spring 1983): 90-104.

Jenson, Andrew. "Lyman, (Eliza M. Partridge)." HR 6:236-37.

Lyman, Albert R. *Amasa Mason Lyman: Trailblazer and Pioneer from the Atlantic to the Pacific.* Delta, UT: Melvin A. Lyman, 1957.

———. *Indians and Outlaws, Settling of the San Juan Frontier.* Salt Lake City: Bookcraft, 1962.

Lyman, Eliza Partridge. Autobiography and Journal, CA. Photographic reproduction of holograph published as *Life and Journal of Eliza Maria Partridge Lyman.* Salt Lake City: Historical Department, 1973. Godfrey, WV 247-60 publishes a portion of this. The Autobiographical introduction is dated: "Times were not then as they are now in 1877 ..." Perhaps the whole early diary was recopied at that time. If the early diary exists, its present whereabouts is unknown to the author.

Lyman, Melvin, ed. *Amasa Lyman Family History, Vol. II.* Delta, UT: Melvin Lyman, 1969.

Redd, Albert, and Albert R. Lyman. *Lemuel Hardison Redd, Jr., 1856-1923, Pioneer-Leader-Builder.* Salt Lake City: [Redd Family], 1967.

I. **Eliza's early years:** are treated in the Emily Partridge chapter. **Caroline:** AMLT 293; FGS. Cook has Sept. 9. **Marriage to Lyman in 1844:** Sampson Mason Family Book, as cited in AMLT 297; Day, *Builders* 446; Quinn, MHOP 561; Cook, RP 266. Other sources, such as AMLT 297 and FGS, give 1845. Eliza herself wrote in her journal, p. 13, "[After the marriage to Joseph Smith in March 1843] I continued to live in his family for a length of time after this but did not reside there when he was martyred which was the 27th of June 1844 I was then living with a family by the name of Coolidge I staid with them for a year or more untill I was married to a man by the name of Amasa Lyman ..." Albert Lyman reads this as saying that Eliza stayed with the Coolidges for a year after June 27, which dates the marriage in 1845. However, Eliza may have been dating the "year or more" from the beginning of her stay with the Coolidges, which would have thus been August or September 1843 (which is possible). The 1844 date fits in with the fact that many of Joseph's widows, e.g., Emily, married apostles in the second half of 1844. **Amasa Lyman:** See AMLT; BE 1:96; Quinn, MHOP 561; Cook, RP 266-67. **after the marriage:** EPLj 13, compare Bachman 153. **visiting Jacobs:** Apparently Amasa lived with the Jacobses temporarily, see ZDYj, Nov. 18. Of course, the Huntingtons and the Partridges were stepsisters, and Eliza often visited Zina, e.g. ZDYj Jan. 10, Apr. 9, July 5, Aug. 13, 1845. When Zina was sick on Apr. 19, Eliza and Emily visited, "made my bed and prepared me some supper. All these kindnesses I never shall forget." **Cornelia Leavitt:** AMLT 307; Quinn, MHOP 561; Cook, RP 266. **Dionitia:** AMLT 307; SAd 379. **endowment:** NTER. **Phelps and Turley:** SAd 379; AMLT 301-307. **temple proxy marriage with Lyman:** BOP #5; SAd 379. **Laura Reed:** SAd 379. She divorced Lyman in 1853. **Proxy for deceased:** SAd 387. According to Quinn, MHOP 561, in 1846, Amasa also married Eliza Gray, age 22, no children, separated from Lyman in 1847; and Abigail Gray, 24, no children, separated from Lyman in 1847.

II. **left Nauvoo:** EPLj, p. 14. **camping with Huntingtons:** EPLj, Apr. 9. **July 14:** Patty wrote, on July 14, "I have put Eliza wife of Amassa Lyman to bed with a son." For childbirth while traveling the overland trail, see Zina Huntington chapter at Mar. 22, 1846. **Eliza sick:** "My head is so bare I am compelled to wear a cap," she wrote on October 25.

III. **Don Carlos's death:** EPLj, Dec. 6-12. **Amasa's departure:** ALj. **Eliza Snow's poem:** EPLj, Dec. 29. **Platte:** married Adelia Robison in 1867, Annie Maud Clark in 1878/79, and died in 1901 in Bluff, San Juan, Utah. See his journal, which I consulted in the Huntington Library; Francis Marion Lyman, "Editorial," an obituary for Platte, in MSt 47 (Nov. 21, 1901): 760-62; Margaret Roper, comp., *Echoes of the Sage and Cedars, A Centennial History of Oak City, Utah 1868-1969* ([Oak City, UT]: Oak City Ward, 1970), 395-97; Day, *Builders* 453-54; Lyman, ALFH 193-255; and sources on San Juan County cited below.

IV. **sums up:** Apr. 8, 1849. **Amasa in California:** See his journal, CA; AMLT 200-201; Kenneth Davies, *Mormon Gold* (Salt Lake City: Olympus, 1984); Lyman, *San Bernardino*; and the Agnes Coolbrith chapter. **wick:** Apr. 18, 19. **Eliza and the Young wives:** Compare Eliza's journal entry for Dec. 3, 1849—here she entertained Emily, "Priscinda Kimball," "Zina Young," Lydia Partridge the elder and younger, Dionitia and Paulina Lyman, and "Presnt Young and Kimball." **gleaning wheat:** Sept. 5.

V. **goods from California:** EPLj, Oct. 3. **Amasa returns to California:** See Mar. 10, 1851, EPLj. Compare AMLT 205. **Caroline Eliza:** Caroline married Thomas Callister in 1878 and died in 1879. Lyman, ALFH 261-65. **Amasa to California, April 1853:** AMLT 213-17. **Amasa marries Lydia:** AMLT 213, 299. **December 1:** EPLj. **Amasa in California:** AMLT 219. **Amasa tours with wives:** E.g., Dec. 13-22, he took Caroline and Dionitia to Bingham Fort; Jan. 4-26, 1856, he took Paulina and Lydia to the "Southern settlements." Perhaps he took wives with fewer responsibilities. **Eliza's work:** EPLj,

Feb. 19, 1856. **Joseph:** married Nellie Grayson Roper in 1878 and died in 1925. See Lyman, ALFH 272-74. **June 3, 1857:** EPLj. **Johnston's army:** AMLT 227. **Amasa returns to Salt Lake City:** ALj; AMLT 229. **Utah County:** AMLT 231. **July:** AMLT 232. **early 1859:** AMLT 232. **spring 1859:** AMLT 233. **winter 1859:** AMLT 235.

**VI. Amasa to England:** AMLT 235. **Lucy Zina:** married Lemuel H. Redd II in 1883, and died in 1930. Redd and Lyman, LHR 40, 187-93, compare Lyman, ALFH 282-87. **March 16:** "Nature of the Mission of Jesus," MSt 24 (Apr. 5, 1862): 209-17; Hefner, "From Apostle to Apostate," 93; AMLT 249; Loretta Hefner, "Amasa Mason Lyman, the Spiritualist," JMH 6 (1979): 75-87, and see below. For spiritualism in nineteenth-century America, see Sydney E. Ahlstrom, *A Religious History of the American People* (New Haven, CT: Yale University Press, 1972), 483-90; Launius, *Joseph Smith III* 62-64. Orson Whitney, Helen Mar's son, led seances 1883-1900, while a bishop and before becoming an apostle. Like Amasa Lyman, he had an intellectual bent. Quinn, MHEP 714. See the chapters of Sarah Kingsley (Swedenborgianism) and Louisa Beaman (folk magic mysticism). **1861 and 1862** are skipped in Eliza's journals. **in Salt Lake:** AMLT 237. **location of families:** AMLT 244.

**VII. Oct. 8:** Quoted in AMLT 238. **frontier town:** See Redd LHR 187. **first Fillmore house:** ALj; AMLT 242. **Jan. 19:** ALj, p. 135, typescript, Huntington Library. See also Jan. 21; Mar. 5, 24, Apr. 4, 11. **Eliza on the move:** EPLj, Aug. 1863. **Eliza on Lyman's psychic problems:** ibid. **Lyman's businesses:** AMLT 244. **trips though territory:** AMLT 242.

**VIII. disfellowshipped:** Hefner, FAA 97-98, quoting a document of disfellowshipment signed by four apostles. For a fuller treatment of Lyman's departure from the Mormon church, see Hefner's 1977 thesis. **Platte on a mission:** EPLj, Apr. 1867. **teaching:** EPLj, Dec. 7, 1868. For teaching as a womanly profession in the east, see Eliza Snow chapter. For women as schoolteachers on the frontier, see Jeffrey, *Frontier Women*, 88-94, 90: "Women in the West, as they had in the East, gradually came to dominate the teaching field." Stratton, *Pioneer Women* 157-70. Joyce Kinkead, *"A Schoolmarm All My Life": Personal Narratives from Frontier Utah* (Salt Lake City: Signature Books, 1996). **Godbeites:** Hefner, FAA 99-101. Ronald Walker, "When the Spirits Did Abound: Nineteenth-Century Utah's Encounter with Free-Thought Radicalism," UHQ 50 (Fall 1982): 304-24, 314-15. **Lyman's excommunication:** "Local and Other Matters," DEN (May 13, 1870): p. 3: "TO WHOM IT MAY CONCERN.-This certifies that Amasa M. Lyman was cut off from the Church of Jesus Christ of Latter-day Saints, by the High Council of Salt Lake City, the 12th day of May, 1870, for apostasy. WM. DUNFORD, Clerk." Hefner, FAA 101. **Eliza leaves Amasa:** AMLT 301. Compare Hefner, FAA 101; Quinn, MHOP 562, who seems to date the separation at the time of the disfellowshipment. Caroline and Lydia were then sealed to Joseph Smith posthumously. For Caroline's separation, see AMLT 279. Amasa spent a night pleading with her not to leave him, and perhaps he plead with Eliza also. Amasa's first wife, Maria Tanner, stayed with him.

**IX. with J. V. Robinson:** EPLj, winter 1869, p. 69. Compare AMLT 301: after Lyman's excommunication, "They [the Partridge wives] moved to Oak City where their sons had property interests. Their mother, Lydia Clisbee Partridge continued to live with them." **Platte to Oak City:** EPLj, p. 69. **two grandchildren:** EPLj; FGS. **death of Lydia:** EPLj, at end of 1876. **Oct. 21:** EPLj.

**X. According to Redd,** LHR 187, she moved to Oak City in 1876. **Amasa sick:** See ALj, quoted in AMLT 265, also AMLT 280. **sewing:** EPLj, Mar. 6. **In October,** Eliza visited Salt Lake with Platte, staying with Emily, including a meeting with Zina Huntington Young.

**XI. Thomas Callister:** See Lyman, ALFH 265-71; Day, *Builders* 115-17, which contains a few mistakes. Born in 1821, he married two wives in 1845 (Caroline Smith and Helen Mar Clark), one in 1863 (Mary Phelps), and died in Dec. 1880 after fathering thirty-two children. **"a year later":** EPLj, Mar. 19, 1880. **Joseph Platte Callister:** married Sarah Christensen and (after Sarah's death) Margaret Crook, and died in 1931. **May, back to Oak Creek:** EPLj, May 8, 1879. **Platte marries Annie Clark:** FGS. For pioneer settlements as "missions," not permanent residences, see Leonard Arrington, *Great Basin Kingdom* (Salt Lake City: University of Utah Press), 89: "In the case of the most difficult colonization projects, church leaders gave them a special sanctity by designating them as 'missions' and referring to the company as a group of 'missionaries.'"

XII. **the first expedition to San Juan:** David E. Miller, *Hole-in-the-Rock* (Salt Lake City: University of Utah Press, 1959), which includes relevant portions of Platte Lyman's diary, 158-79. Also Robert S. McPherson, *A History of San Juan County, In the Palm of Time* (Salt Lake City: Utah State Historical Society, 1995), 95-120; Lyman, *Indians and Outlaws*; Norma Perkins Young, *Anchored Lariats on the San Juan Frontier* (Provo, UT: Community Press, 1985).

XIII. **territory quote:** Young, AL 12-13. **Lucy on the trip out:** Redd, LHR 188. **lawless element:** Redd, LHR 188. Compare Thomas Austin and Robert MacPherson, "Murder, Mayhem and Mormons: the Evolution of Law Enforcement on the San Juan Frontier, 1880-1900," UHQ 55 (Winter 1987): 36-49, 42. **Platte leaves:** EPLj, May 9. **Indian-related incident:** Redd, LHR 188. **friendly Indians:** Redd, LHR 188. **August 21:** Pictures of male babies in dresses can be found in the Daughters of Utah Pioneers Museum in Salt Lake City, Grant section. See also William Slaughter, *Life in Zion: An Intimate Look at the Latter-day Saints* (Salt Lake City: Deseret Book, 1995), 40.

XIV. **Joseph's shooting:** Lyman, *Indians and Outlaws* 47-48; Austin and MacPherson, "Murder, Mayhem," 42; Redd and Lyman, LHR 189. **improving:** EPLj, Jan. 6, 1882. **wound never heals:** Redd and Lyman, LHR 189.

XV. **return to Oak Creek:** EPLj.

XVI. **death:** Platte Lyman journal.

XVII. **polygamy after the Manifesto:** See D. Michael Quinn, "LDS Church Authority and New Plural Marriages, 1890-1904," *Dialogue* 18 (Spring 1985): 9-105; Hardy, *Solemn Covenant*.

## REFERENCES TO CHAPTER 20.
### Proxy Wife:
### Lucy Walker (Smith Kimball)

BBS: see Lucy Walker, "Brief Biographical Sketch."

Carter, Kate. OPH 10:390, 19:193. Compare *Improvement Era* 14:92.

Jenson, Andrew. "Kimball, (Lucy Walker,)." HR 6:236. Another version in BE 1:808-9.

LIT: see William Holmes Walker, *Life Incident and Travels.*

Littlefield, Lyman O. *Reminiscences of Latter-day Saints.* Logan: Utah Journal Co., 1888. 37-52.

Morris, D. H. "Statement, given in the office of S. O. Bennion, June 12, 1930." Vesta Crawford papers, Marriott Library. Morris, a judge who lived in St. George, had boarded with Lucy Walker in 1879.

SE: see Rodney Walker, *Second Edition of Ancestry and Descendants of John Walker.*

Walker, Lucy. "A Brief Biographical Sketch of the Life and Labors of Lucy Walker Smith." Copy in my possession. Also found in the Lucy Walker Kimball Papers, CA. Compare Foster, RS 309 n. 94.

———. "Lucy Walker Kimball (Autobiography)." WE 39 (Oct. 1910): 31-32, and in following issues.

———. "Lucy W. Kimball's Testimony." HR 6:239-30.

———. "Statement of Mrs. L.W. Kimball." Copy borrowed from Mrs. Lydia Rogerson, Ogden, Utah, Lucy's niece, at 140 West 22nd Street, Ogden, Utah. Undated. Possibly a response to sons of Joseph denying Joseph Smith Jr.'s polygamy, see 7-8. A printed version in Littlefield, *Reminiscences* 37-52.

———. Testimony of Lucy W. Kimball. *Temple Lot Case*, 375-79.

Walker, Rodney Wilson, and Noel Stevenson, comp. *The Second Edition of Ancestry and Descendants of John Walker.* [Salt Lake City]: John Walker Family Organization,

1985. I am indebted to Janet Targent, a descendant of John and Lydia Walker, for making this book available to me.
Walker, William Holmes. *The Life Incidents and Travels of Elder William Holmes Walker and his Association with Joseph Smith, the Prophet.* N.p.: Elizabeth Piepgrass, 1943. Typescript, in CA. Compare Bitton, *Guide*, and a shortened version in HTW 7:380-83.

**deathbed:** Kimball, HCK 296; Lucy Walker Kimball, "Statement," 7, slightly paraphrased.

I. **birthdate:** Temple Lot transcript, 451, qu. 39; BOP #20. **parents:** John was born on June 20, 1794, at Peacham; Lydia on April 18, 1800, in Falmouth, Maine. They married in April 1819. SE 4, 29. **John's work:** LIT 8, 5. **William Holmes:** was born on August 28, 1820, in Peacham. He married Olive Farr (1843), Mary Jane Shadden (1850), Olive Bingham (1858), and Harriet Paul (1865); in his later life he was forced to join the polygamy underground. A veteran of the Mormon Battalion, he served as an early missionary to South Africa, 1852-57. He worked as industrialist, millwright, and agriculturalist, helped settle southern Utah, and died in 1908 in Lewisville, Jefferson, Idaho. See Orson Whitney, HU 4:192-97; SE 5-10; LIT; Larson, DB. **Lorin:** born on July 25, 1822, he married Lovina Smith, a daughter of Hyrum Smith, in 1844, and died in Rockland, Power, Idaho, in 1907. SE 33-34. **Catherine:** born on May 20, 1824, she married Elijah Knapp Fuller in 1846, with whom she had five children, but she separated from him in 1856. She married William Rogers in 1858 and died in 1885 in Brigham City, Box Elder, Utah. SE 35; Ann Moyes, "Life of Catherine Walker," in Dallas Coleman, comp., *Elijah Knapp Fuller and his Ancestors* (Salt Lake City: Publishers Press, 1985), 27-28. **Edwin:** born on April 15, 1828, he served in the Mormon Battalion, arriving back at Utah in November 1848. He married Ann Sophia Tyler in 1851, but the marriage ended in a divorce. He then married Mary Ellen Saniforth in 1869 in Salt Lake, and afterwards moved to California and apparently lost touch with the Utah Walkers. SE 37; Larson, DB; Rickett, MB 265. **Henry:** born on May 18, 1830, he died in 1866 in Woodbridge, California. **Jane:** born on August 2, 1832, in Peacham, she married Lot Smith in 1852, with whom she had eight children. Smith is well known as a member of the Mormon Battalion, a colonizer, a polygamist (four other wives), an Indian fighter, and a leader of the Mormon raiders during the "Utah War" of 1857. See Charles Peterson, "'A Mighty Man Was Brother Lot': A Portrait of Lot Smith, Mormon Frontiersman," *Western Historical Quarterly* 1 (Oct. 1970): 393-414; Arrington, BY 383. Jane was widely known as an organist and singer, and served as Farmington Primary president from 1888 to 1892. Lot died in 1892, at Tuba City, Arizona, while Jane died in 1912 in Farmington, Davis, Utah. See her reminiscences, SE 21-22, 37-38. **John baptized:** Walker, LIT 5.

II. **to New York:** BBS 1. **Lydia the younger:** born on Sept. 12, 1834, she died in 1843 in Nauvoo. **Lydia baptized:** BBS 1. **Lucy baptized:** BBS 1; Jenson, KLW. **prayer meeting of children:** BBS 1. **John Jr.:** married Serepta Pate in 1866 and died in 1889 in Tulare, California, SE 38-39.

III. **left New York:** Jenson, KLW. **surrounded by mob:** BBS 1. **John Walker at the massacre:** BBS 1-2. Jane Walker, Reminiscence, SE 21, elaborates further on the miraculous blinding of the eyes of the mob. **Lucy at the women's camp:** BBS 2. **100 miles:** LIT 7. **to Illinois:** Jenson, KLW; BBS 3. William, LIT 8, has them arrive in April 1838—impossible, as the Haun's Mill Massacre took place in October 1838.

IV. **working in Illinois:** LIT 8. **Mary Electa:** AF gives Greenbush, Adams, Illinois, as place of birth. However, Greenbush is in Warren County, northeast of Nauvoo. Quincy is in Adams, which agrees with the Sketch. Mary married Edwin Albert Davis (1857), but they separated. She then exchanged vows with William Peirce (1863) and lived with him in Brigham City, Utah. After another separation, she united with Robert George Parker (1883) and died in 1904 in Spencer, Bannock, Idaho. SE 39-40. **Joseph and Loren:** BBS 3. **Joseph Smith III on Loren:** *Joseph Smith III and the Restoration* 32. **meeting Joseph:** BBS 3. **Lydia's death:** BBS 3-4. **Joseph sends John away:** BBS 4. **John sent on missions:** Pioneer Personal History of Lydia Holmes Fuller Rogers; Utah Pioneer Biographies, 24 p. 104, as cited in Ivins 5:278. Lucy agrees that John went on two missions to the east, BBS 3, but does not say when. **introduced as sons and daughters:** BBS 5. **Lucy's job:** *Joseph Smith III and the Restoration* 33. **death of Lydia:** BBS 4. **Jane to Springfield:** BBS 4. **Judge Adams:** This was James Adams, mason and judge, who married Joseph to the Partridge sisters on May 11, 1843. See John Carroll Power, *History of the Early Settlers of Sangamon County, Illinois* (Springfield: Edwin Wilson, 1876), 76; HC 6:50-51; Kent Walgren, "James Adams: Early Springfield Mormon and Freemason," *Journal of the Illinois State Historical Society* 75 (Summer 1952): 121-36; Jessee 2:521. The rest of this story, as Jane tells it, is somewhat alarming. The Adams had two grown children, a daughter and a son. In September or October, however, James Adams, his wife, and daughter all died, perhaps of malaria or cholera. The surviving son "was nearly crazed" with grief, and nailed up the house, forgetting that Jane was in an upstairs bedroom. The small girl managed to climb out of her bedroom window and reach the ground safely, but then she was alone in a non-Mormon city, far from her family. The plucky child settled on a plan, though: she looked at the faces of passersby until she found one who had "a good look on his face." She asked him "if he knew of anyone who wanted a little girl"! As luck would have it, he was a Mormon, and was able to take her to Nauvoo. However, she returned to Springfield in 1844 for unexplained reasons. See her reminiscences, SE 21-22. Power, *History*, has Mrs. Adams dying a year after James.

V. **proposal:** BBS 5-6. **Joseph and William:** Walker, LIT, p. 9, 10. **time limit:** Joseph possibly wanted to have the marriage performed before Emma returned from St. Louis on May 2. Newell and Avery, ME 139; HC 5:374. Still, he could have easily arranged a secret marriage with Emma in town. **conversion:** BBS 6. The Morris statement adds that Lucy prayed repeatedly in the orchard one night. "Finally as I was praying the last time an angel of the Lord appeared to me and told me that the principle was of God and for me to accept it. As I arose to go into the house I noticed that dawn was breaking as I was going up the back steps of the mansion house, Joseph came out of the door and speaking to me said: 'Thank God you have your testimony.' I afterwards married Joseph Smith as a plural wife and lived and cohabited with him as such." This angelic visitation, possibly a folkloric accretion in this late variant, is strikingly similar to Mary Elizabeth Rollins Lightner's experience. See her chapter at 1842. **marriage:** BBS 6; William Clayton journal: "A.M. at the Temple At 10 M [married] J [Joseph] to L W [Lucy Walker]." IC 100. For Eliza Partridge as witness, see Temple Lot case, 371-75; Eliza Partridge affidavit 2:30. George A. Smith, letter to Joseph III, Oct. 9, 1869, CA, quoted in Bailey, EH 83. **the marriage non-romantic:** Temple Lot transcript 450 qu. 29. **John returns:** Walker, LIT 9-10. **William manages the Mansion House:** Walker, LIT 9-10. **Lucy to Mansion House:** "After he got married I went [to the Mansion house] and stayed with my brother; my sister remained there [at Joseph's]." Temple Lot case, 373: "November, I think." **William leaves Mansion House:** Walker, Statement 5. **Lucy with Agnes:** BBS 7, compare Temple Lot 372. **night of Joseph's death:** BBS 7, compare Agnes Coolbrith chapter. **funeral:** Temple Lot transcript 464.

VI. **lives with William:** Jenson, KLW. **in Quincy:** BBS 8-10. **Heber Kimball to Quincy:** BBS 10. Lucy and William seem to have different chronologies for the return of their father from his mission. **marriage to Kimball:** Kimball, HCK 314. **no love:** Temple Lot case 375; compare Kimball, HCK 99; Zina Huntington chapter, after Nov. 1878. For romance in typical nineteenth-century American courtship, see Ellen K. Rothman, *Hands and Hearts, A History of Courtship in America* (New York: Basic Books, 1984), 30-31, 103-105. By the end of the eighteenth century, "Americans were beginning to make love between men and women a necessary rather than a desirable precondition for marriage," Rothman 31. In the middle decades of the nineteenth century, that cultural norm was even stronger: "Marriage without love cannot fail to be a source of perpetual unhappiness," wrote James White in 1850, as cited in Rothman 103. So the Mormon idea that the highest kind of marriage should *not* be based on romantic love, but on religious duty, was a contrast to American cultural trends. Many Mormons did marry on the basis of romantic love, but one might make the generalization that most polygamous wives did not. Present-day Mormons consider romantic love an important part of their (strictly monogamous) marriages, and their temple-solemnized "eternal" marriages perhaps cause them to idealize romantic love even more than non-Mormons do. **"as noble":** Temple Lot case 376. **"noble whole-souled":** Walker, Statement 52. **proxy marriage:** Temple Lot case 379; compare HCK 123. Lucy adds, "That is what I call marrying by proxy, and men have been crushed who have refused to do such things." The dire consequences in store for those who refuse to practice polygamy seem to be another general theme that again has its roots in Joseph's teachings and practice. Compare D&C 132:52, 54, and Helen Kimball chapter at 1847. **Nauvoo temple marriage:** BOP #20. **Rachel Sylvia:** Information on Lucy's children is primarily from SE 37, cross-checked with FGS, HCK 314, AF, all of which have variations.

**VII. leaves Nauvoo:** Jenson, KLW. **June 4:** WCj, IC 279, compare HCK 144. **two winters:** Jenson, KLW. **June 10:** ERSj. **Salt Lake:** HCK 182. Lucy's father, who had remarried and started a new family, came to Utah in 1850.

**III. John Heber "Don":** married Adelaide Frances Hopkins in 1870 and died in 1918 in Huber, Washington, Oregon. **Lydia Holmes:** married Frances Xavier Loughery in 1875 and died in 1928. **four in a house:** Adelia Wilcox Hatton Memoirs, CA; HCK 234. See Sarah Ann Whitney chapter at 1856-1857. **"comfort":** Walker, Statement 51. For the polygamous husband being treated as a visiting king, see EBWj, Dec. 22, 1890; Samuel Taylor, *Family Kingdom* (New York: McGraw-Hill, 1951), 262, 250; B. Carmon Hardy, "Lords of Creation: Polygamy, the Abrahamic Household, and Mormon Patriarchy," JMH 20 (Spring 1994): 119-52, 148. **with Presendia:** HCK 234. **"grand school":** Walker, Statement 50. **Anna Spaulding:** married Richard Gatlin Knox in 1878 and died in 1932 in San Francisco. **Eliza:** Laura Pitkin Kimball diary, CA 1775; she married Frank Albert Woolley in 1880 and died in 1906 in Salt Lake City. **Washington:** married Mary Frances Tuttle in 1885 and died in 1914 in Buffalo, New York. HCK 314 has Washington and Joshua twins. **Provo:** Jenson, KLW. **Heber's death:** HCK 296.

**IX. lives in Provo:** Jenson, KLW. **Oct. 12:** Lucy Kimball to Miss Coolidge, Oct. 12, 1868, CA, MS 6618. **death of John Walker:** SE. **Lucy Kimball to Joseph F. Smith:** Nov. 18, 1883, CA, in Franklin R. Smith collection, MS 13700, fd 2; Lucy to Joseph, Feb. 24, 1884. **Helen:** HMWj, see her chapter. **surprise party:** HMWj. **Genevieve sick:** HMWj, Feb. 21, 1885. **temple work in Logan:** HMWj, Apr. 22, 1886 and see below; LIT 77; BE 1:809. **Nov. 1886:** HMWj, Nov. 1-Dec. 3, 1886. **Cottage:** Nov. 1. **nursing Helen:** Nov. 7. **wives of God:** Nov. 16. **other references to Lucy in HMWj:** Sept. 13, 1885; Apr. 22, 1886; Sept. 5, 1886 (Lucy visiting in Salt Lake); Oct. 15, 1887; May 29, 30, June 1 (Lucy in Salt Lake), 1887; July 24, 29, 1887 (in Salt Lake); Sept. 7, 1887 (Lucy nurses Helen through a bout of typhoid fever); Sept. 11, Oct. 1, 6, Nov. 5 1887 (in Salt Lake); June 7, 1888 (in Logan); Oct. 13, 14, 1888 (in Salt Lake); July 13, 1889; Feb. 16, 17, 1890 (in Salt Lake); Apr. 6, 1891 ("Lucy W. Kimball was here Sunday bringing me a token of her love - a pair of {croched} bedroom slippers of her own handy work, with satin bows similar in collor to the triming arround the ankles."); Oct. 7, 9, 10, 1891 (in Salt Lake); Dec. 31, 1891 (in Logan); Apr. 8, 1892 (in Salt Lake); July 28, 1892 (in Logan); Oct. 6, 1892 (in Salt Lake). **temple worker:** HMWj, Apr. 10, 1893 (Lucy attended the dedication of the Salt Lake temple and apparently returned to Logan); July 10, 13, 1893 (in Salt Lake); Feb. 14, 15, 16 (seems to be a Salt Lake temple worker; attends a meeting of Heber Kimball widows on the 15th); Nov. 14, 1894; Apr. 18, 1895; May 12, 23, 1895; Jan. 11, 1896 (Lucy had been sick); Aug. 27, 1896.

**X. Ninth Ward:** OPH 10:391. **March 22:** Temple Lot tr. 448, box 2, fd 1. **Idaho:** LIT 80. In April 1897 William Walker wrote, "The last three winters before I have gone to Idaho, starting before Christmas and visiting until Spring, Lucy W. Kimbol Smith." Note the transposition of last names. **Obituary:** DN (Oct. 1, 1910): 1. The funeral was held at the Eighteenth Ward chapel on Wednesday, October 5, at 1 p.m.

## REFERENCES TO CHAPTER 21.
### *Dark Sisters:*
### *Sarah Lawrence (Smith Kimball Mount)* and
### *Maria Lawrence (Smith [Young] Babbitt)*

[Carter, Kate]. OPH 10:413.

Cook, Lyndon. "'Brother Joseph is Truly a Wonderful Man, He is All We Could Wish a Prophet to Be': Pre-1844 Letters of William Law." BYUSt 20 (Spring 1979): 7-18.

———, ed. *William Law.*

Jenson, Andrew. HR 8:976.

Kimball, Stanley. HCK 310.

Madsen, Gordon. "Joseph Smith as Guardian: The Lawrence Estate." Paper given at Mormon History Association, May 18, 1996.

Tanner, Mary Jane Mount. *A Fragment: The Autobiography of Mary Jane Mount Tanner.* Salt Lake City: Tanner Trust, 1980.

Tullidge, Edward. "Henry W. Lawrence." In *History of Salt Lake City.* Salt Lake City: Star, 1886. Appendix, p. 50.

I. **Maria's and Sarah's birth:** Dates from sealing records, 1846, see below, and HCK/Clayton journal, Book 93. **Edward a farmer:** See the reference to his barn below. **Margaret:** was born on April 29, 1801, in Toronto, NTER. **siblings:** Mary Jane Tanner, "A Memorial," Tanner Collection, Marriott Library, as cited in Tanner, AF 89n. For their birthdates, compare Tanner, AF 82-83 (quoted in text below) and the 1850 Utah census. Henry Lawrence, born on July 18, 1835, later became a prominent member of the schismatic Mormon "Godbeite" church, a leading "Liberal," a founder of the *Salt Lake Tribune,* and a noted Socialist politician. John McCormick and John R. Sillito, "Henry W. Lawrence: A Life in Dissent," in Roger D. Launius and Linda Thatcher, eds., *Differing Visions: Dissenters in Mormon History* (Urbana: University of Illinois Press, 1994), 220-40; Henry Lawrence collection, Marriott Library, MS 309; Leo Lyman, *Political Deliverance* (Urbana: University of Illinois Press, 1986), 201. He died in 1924, see DN (Apr. 5, 1924): sec. 2, p. 1. Maria and Sarah also had two half brothers, Don Carlos Butterfield (b. 1842) and Edward Butterfield (b. 1846), see Utah 1850 census, p. 35. **early Canadian Mormonism:** Brigham H. Roberts, *The Life of John Taylor* (Salt Lake City: Bookcraft, 1963), 33-43. V. Ben Bloxham et al., *Truth Will Prevail* (Salt Lake City: Deseret Book, 1987). **Joseph Smith to Canada:** HC 2:508. **baptism of Edward Lawrence:** Tullidge, HWL 50. **Whitby conference:** Roberts, *John Taylor* 43. **Lawrence branch:** William Law to Isaac Russell, Nov. 10, 1837, as cited in Cook, BJ 211.

II. **move to Illinois, Lima:** Tullidge, HWL 50. **death of Edward Lawrence:** Tullidge, HWL 50. **Law to Nauvoo:** Cook, BJ 207. Law, in the Wyl interview, see below: "Soon after my arrival the two L— girls came to the holy city." **Maria and Sarah inherit:** "Joseph Smith Estate Papers, Office of the Hancock County Clerk," as cited in Flanders, *Nauvoo* 177. Gordon Madsen, "Joseph Smith as Guardian." I have followed Madsen as closely as possible from my notes, but do not have his written argument and citations. **Joseph Smith guardian:** William Law was interviewed by W. Wyl on March 30, 1887, Salt Lake *Daily Tribune* (July 31, 1887): "Dr. Wyl and Dr. Wm. Law," p. 6; repr. in Cook, *William Law.* In this interview, Law gave an unsympathetic account of this story that contains some factual errors, as Madsen has shown, but which reflects the broad outline of the story as he remembered it. "Soon after my arrival in Nauvoo the two L— girls came to the holy city, two very young girls, 15 to 17 years of age. They had been converted in Canada, were orphans [by Illinois law, fatherless children were orphans, despite a living mother], and worth about $8,000 in English gold. Joseph got to be appointed their guardian, probably with the help of Dr. Bennett. He naturally put the gold in his pocket and had the girls sealed to him. He asked me to go on his bond as guardian, as Sidney Rigdon had done. 'It is only a formality,' he said. Foolishly enough, and not yet expecting anything, I put my name on the paper. Emma complained about Joseph living with the L— girls, but not very violently. It is my conviction that she was his *full accomplice*, that she was not a bit better than he. When I saw how things went, I should have taken steps to be released of that bond, but I never thought of it. After Joseph's death, A. W. Babbitt became guardian of the two girls. He asked Emma for a settlement about the $8,000. Emma said she had nothing to do with her husband's debts. Now Babbitt asked for the books and she gave them to him. Babbitt found that Joseph had counted an expense of about $3,000 for board and clothing of the girls. Now Babbitt wanted the $5,000 that was to be paid. Babbitt, who was a straight, good, honest, sincere man set about to find out property to pay the $5,000 with. *He could find none.* [Emma had much property, houses, farms, etc. But it was all in her name.] She always looked out for her part. When I saw how things stood, I wrote to Babbitt to take hold of all the property left by me in Nauvoo and of all claims held by me against people in Nauvoo. And so the debt was paid by me—Emma didn't pay a cent."

Eight thousand dollars in "English gold" is incorrect; this is the size of the bond (by law, twice the inheritance sum). The inheritance was $3,831.54, not in English gold, but in a farm in Lima ($1,000) and promissory notes ($3,000). Madsen; Flanders, *Nauvoo* 177, citing the Joseph Smith Estate Papers. According to Madsen, William and Wilson Law were given the responsibility for collecting on the promissory notes in Canada, but $500 of them were not collectable. However, the farm in Lima was sold for $1150, so the $3,831 was decreased by only $350 ($3,481). **Joseph incurred debts:** "Joseph Smith Estate Papers," as cited in Flanders, *Nauvoo* 177. Under Illinois law, it was legal for Joseph to commingle the Lawrence estate with his own, as long as he made regular interest payments to the heirs, Madsen. **bondsmen:** See interview with Law above. Madsen's research has shown that Hyrum Smith was the other bondsman, not Rigdon. **Margaret remarries:** Josiah's wife had died on October 28, 1840, Cook, RP 254. If Don Carlos Butterfield was born in approximately 1842, Josiah and Margaret would have married in 1841 or early 1842. They are listed together at the time of the 1842 Nauvoo Ward Census, as Josiah and Margaret Butterfield, see below. When she sold lot 4, block 47, to Hiram Dayton on May 20, 1843, she was referred to as "Margaret Butterfield, late Margaret Lawrence." For Butterfield, see further Quinn, MHOP 541; Cook, RP 254-55; Jessee 2:319; Tanner, AF 89. **1842 census:** 3rd Ward, p. 13. **April 4, 1842:** Jessee 2:374. **tension between Josiah and Joseph:** HC 5:316. The Joseph Smith journal proper does not have this incident, Faulring 337. HC's source is unknown, though clearly the official history of the church would not fabricate such a story. Compare ME 159. **June 4:** Jessee 2:389.

III. **marriage:** Emily Partridge, "Autobiography of Emily D.P. Young," WE 14 (Aug. 1, 1885): 38 = HR 6:223. Also Emily Partridge, "Life," 186: "Emma afterwards gave Sarah and Maria Lawrence to him, and they lived in the house as his wifes. I knew this." For problems with the date of the Partridge's second marriage to Joseph, see Van Wagoner, MP 50, 35. According to the Lovina Walker affidavit, dated June 16, 1869 (HR 6:223), "Aunt Emma Smith ... in the year 1846 told me that she, Emma Smith, was present and witnessed the marrying or sealing of Eliza Partridge, Emily Partridge, Maria Lawrence and Sarah Lawrence to her husband Joseph Smith, and that she gave her consent thereto." Lucy Walker Kimball, in the Temple Lot case (full transcript, p. 461), was asked how she knew that the Lawrence girls were married to Joseph, and answered, "Well I was associated with them there, and they told me so, and the prophet told me so himself." See also her "Recollections," p. 13: "I can also say that Emma Smith was present and did consent to Eliza and Emily Partridge. Also Maria and Sarah Lawrence being sealed to her husband. This I had from [Joseph's] own lips, also the testimony of [Emma's] neice. Hyrum Smith's Eldest daughter, my brother Loren's wife [Lovina Walker, see above], said to me that Aunt Emma told her this, as well as the young ladies themselves." See also Benjamin Johnson, MLR 96; Helen Mar Whitney, SIWQ, WE 14 (Feb. 15, 1886): 138, "Both [Frances Swan and Sarah Lawrence] were sealed to my father over the holy altar in the Temple at Nauvoo. The latter named had been the wife of the Prophet Joseph, his first wife, Emma, having given her and her sister to him as his wives for time and all eternity." HR 6:234; HR 8:976. There is a worm's eye view of the marriage in Law/Wyl: "Joseph got to be appointed their guardian, probably with the help of Dr. Bennett. He naturally put the gold in his pocket and had the girls sealed to him." **May 28:** WRj, CA. **May 29:** JSj, Faulring 381. **May 30:** IC 107. This is evidently the source for HC 5:415. **June 3:** IC 107; again, the source for HC 5:418. Joseph was not in Nauvoo at this time, see JSj, Faulring 382. **estate payments:** Madsen has discovered the 1843 accounting figures for the Lawrence estate payments. He cites Joseph Smith Daybook C, in Iowa Masonic Library 26 (214). **Nov. 21:** JSj, Faulring, 396, in a list of marriages. WCj, IC 123. **Clayton and Lawrence estate:** WCj, IC 125. **John Taylor:** As Flanders analyzes the situation, in January 1844 Joseph Smith "was in financial straits again; he sold the Times and Seasons print shop to John Taylor for $2,832 ... In addition Taylor 'in consideration was to assume the responsibility of the Lawrence estate.'" Flanders, *Nauvoo* 177, citing Joseph Smith Estate Papers; HC 6:185 (Jan. 23, 1844, compare JSj, Faulring 442). Flanders continues, "He had apparently incurred debts to this estate which Taylor was to assume." There is some doubt that the guardianship transfer actually was completed, see below on the estate after Joseph's death. However, John Taylor apparently moved into the print shop, see Samuel Taylor, *The Kingdom Or Nothing: The Life of John Taylor, Militant Mormon* (New York: Macmillan, 1976), 87. Joseph Smith felt the valuation of the printing office "rather too low," as he had purchased it for "between seven and eight thousand dollars." HC 6:185; Flanders 251.

IV. **Butterfield's mission:** Cook, RP 254-55; Quinn, MHOP 541. **Law's problems with Joseph:** Hill, JS 388-92; Van Wagoner, MP 62-64; 240. Law had been excommunicated on April 18, *Nauvoo Expositor*, June 7, 1844; Hill, JS 391. **suit, May 23:** See Smith's May 26 speech, Ehat, WJS 375-76, compare 407. Van Wagoner, MP 64. HC 6:403; Faulring 482-83. **May 26 denial:** Ehat, WJS 377, compare 375-76; HC 6:411. This is similar to the denial of polygamy (which found a place in the Doctrine and Covenants) after the Fanny Alger marriage, Fanny Alger chapter, 1835. Compare JSj, Oct. 5, 1843, Faulring 417; TS 5 (Mar. 15, 1844): 474; Hardy, SC 362-88; Prologue, at Timing section. **June 4:** Faulring 487. HC 6:427 inserts, "Counseled Taylor to go on with the prosecution in behalf of Maria Lawrence" before "Concluded." **June 4 Document:** Joseph made guardian of Sarah and Maria. Notarized by A. Miller, Quincy, Ill, Justice of the Peace. See Bachman, "A Study," 108. Hoffman forged a letter by Joseph to the Lawrence sisters dated June 23, 1844, see Jessee, PW 598; Linda Sillitoe and Allen Roberts, *Salamander* (Salt Lake City: Signature Books, 1988), 166, 233, 264, 537.

V. **millinery:** Lucy Walker autobiography, typescript, CA, p. 8. **July 30:** WCj, July 30, 31, 1844. **Oct. 7:** Quinn, MHOP 541. **Maria's possible marriage to Brigham:** Susa Young Gates and Mabel Y. Sanborn, "Brigham Young Genealogy," UGHM 11 (1920): 127-35, 131: "Brigham Young m. 21 Jan., 1846, Maria Lawrence, daughter of Edward and Margaret Lawrence. She was born in Canada and died in Nauvoo, Ill., no issue." See also Kate Carter, ed., *Brigham Young, His Wives and Family* (Salt Lake City: Daughters of Utah Pioneers, n.d.), 22; James H. Crockwell, *Pictures and Biographies of Brigham and His Wives* (Salt Lake City: Crockwell, n.d.), 29 (who also gives the date Jan. 1846). Benjamin Johnson, "Historical Mistakes," Salt Lake City, Aug. 4, 1897, DN 30 (Aug. 6, 1897): p. 5, denied emphatically that Brigham had ever married Maria, but one wonders about Benjamin's access—he was a brother-in-law of Babbitt, but was not a close friend of Brigham Young or a general authority at the time of the marriage. Perhaps Johnson knew about the marriage to Babbitt, and assumed that there was no marriage to Brigham. Brigham Young family specialist, Jeffery Johnson, see his DDW, does not accept a marriage of Maria and Brigham. Quinn, MHEP 498, however, argues that Brigham and Heber often married women on the same day, and that Maria might have married Brigham on the same day Sarah married Kimball. He also holds that Gates and Sanborn as daughters of Young should be given credence. These arguments are per-suasive, but not conclusive. One could also argue that Johnson as Babbitt's brother-in-law has weight as a witness, and that Gates and Sanborn did make some mistakes in their listings. **Sarah's marriage to Kimball:** HCKj, Oct. 12, lined-through entry, "Sarah L.," as cited in Quinn, MHEP 499. HCK 310. **friendship with Helen Mar:** SIWQ 14 (Feb. 15, 1886): 138. **suit against Law and Mary Smith:** Law, Wyl interview. **Babbitt and the estate:** IC 243. **Sept. 1, 1845 document:** Lee Library, MSS 417. **Sarah's and Maria's endowments:** Kimball/Clayton journal, Bk 93. **the Butterfields' endowment:** NTER. **Sarah sealed to Heber in temple:** BOP #92; SAd 505. **Maria sealed to Babbitt:** BOP #80; SAd 505. For Babbitt, see the Delcena Johnson chapter.

**VI. death:** Benjamin Johnson, "Historical Mistakes." See also Jessee, PW 697. Mary B. Nor-man to Ina Coolbrith, Feb. 3, 1911, P13, f1078, RLDS Archives. According to Madsen, she died in childbirth.

**VII. February 19:** "Last Chapter of Scenes in Nauvoo," WE 12 (Nov. 1, 1883): 82. **Helen reached Winter Quarters:** Helen Mar Whitney, OTBM, WE 12 (Apr. 15, 1884): 170. In the text, 31st is a typo for 13. **June 16:** Helen Mar Whitney, OTBM, WE 13 (June 1, 1884): 2. **Sarah moves in with Young family:** HCK 144. **Sarah at blessing meetings:** SIWQ, WE 14 (Dec. 15, 1885): 106; 14 (Jan. 1, 1886): 118. **Sarah Kimball to Marinda Hyde**, Jan 2, 1848, CA.

**VIII. separation of Butterfields:** Quinn, MHOP 541. Josiah remarried and moved to California in 1853. He joined the RLDS church in 1865, and died in 1871 in Watsonville, Santa Cruz, California. **Heywood diary:** Sept. 9; Dec. 22, Brooks 24, 41. Compare the Jan. 19, 1851 pas-sage in Haywood (below) for further context on this passage. **1850 Census**, Salt Lake City p. 35. **Sister Butterfield:** However, there were two Sister Butterfields in Utah, see PBSj, Sept. 1, 1851. **two minor references to Sarah:** PBSj, Feb. 8, 1851. Heywood, Apr. 27, 1851.

**IX. considering divorce:** Heywood, Jan. 19 (Brooks p. 48). **divorce:** OPH 10:413; HCK 310. See Diary of Alice Johnson Read, as cited in Young, *Isn't One Wife* 229: "Spent afternoon with Sarah Lawrence where I had another battle with Mrs. Butterfield," be-cause she (Margaret Butterfield) said she would not allow her husband to have another wife. **marriage to Mount:** Tanner, AF 82-83. There is no record of Sarah having any children by any of her three husbands. According to Mary Mount Tanner, Joseph Mount was worth $35,000 when he married Sarah. Mary Mount Tanner to "Cousin," Jan. 15, 1877, Marriott Library. Joseph had been born in 1806 in New Jersey, converted to Mor-monism by at least 1843 (when he was living in Nauvoo), and crossed the plains in 1847. From April 1849 to 1853 he lived in Napa, California. See Mount Chronology, typescript in my possession. I am grateful to Robert Larsen, a descendant of Joseph Mount, for sharing this and other Mount/Lawrence materials with me. **amicable divorce:** Helen Mar Whitney, SIWQ, WE 14 (Feb. 15, 1886): 138. **cruel:** Tanner, AF 85. **jealousy:** Tanner, AF 86. **"I was constantly":** Tanner, AF 87.

**X. California:** Compare Helen Whitney, SIWQ 14 (Feb. 15, 1886): 138, quoted above in text. **Sarah apostate:** Tanner, AF 87. **interview foiled/parting:** Tanner, AF 88. **Napa:** Tanner, AF 132-38. On December 5, 1856, Sarah's name first appears on a real estate transaction, Mount Chronology. In 1860 Joseph and Sarah Mount appear in the state cen-sus, living in Napa, p. 77. On April 21, 1861, Sarah was in San Francisco on a temporary visit, Mount Chronology. See also Mary Mount Tanner to "Cousin," Jan. 15, 1877, Marriott Library. **farm conveyed to Sarah:** R. Crouch to M. J. Tanner, Jan. 11, 1877, Marriott Library. Family traditions supply the motivation for this transfer.

**XI. 1863 visit:** Mary Mount Tanner to Joseph Mount, Sept. 24, 1876, in Tanner, AF 139-40. **Sarah sells the farm:** R. Crouch to M. J. Tanner, Jan. 11, 1877, Marriott Library. Mary Mount Tanner felt these financial dealings reflected Sarah's designing, malevolent nature. Mary Mount Tanner to "Cousin," Jan. 15, 1877, Marriott Library. None of Joseph Mount's children by his previous marriages received money from him, she reports, because of

Sarah's machinations. However, she also admits that Mount was upset because his Utah children were staying with the Mormon community, and felt that money he sent to them ended up in the possession of Brigham Young. **Hawaii:** Mount chronology. **house on Hyde Street:** San Francisco directory, compare Mount Chronology; Alex Bedlam to "Tanner & Taylor," Jan. 16, 1877, Marriott Library. **divorce?** According to Helen Mar Whitney, SIWQ 14 (Feb. 15, 1886): 138, Sarah eventually divorced Mount, though such an event is not confirmed. Mary, much closer to her father than was Helen Whitney, never mentions a divorce, and such a development would have undoubtedly pleased her. So this story should probably be rejected. **"She became so wicked":** Helen Mar Whitney, SIWQ 14 (Feb. 15, 1886): 138. **cancer:** See Death record, below. **death:** Death record, Book II p. 211, copy in my possession. In 1940 her remains were removed to a collective grave in Vault 1635, Lawndale. See also Mount Chronology. Joseph Mount moved back to Napa by June 1873, then died there in 1876. Robert Larsen to J. Kenneth Davies, Oct. 4, 1986; Mount Chronology.

# REFERENCES TO CHAPTER 22.
## Polygamy, Melancholy, Possession:
## Helen Mar Kimball (Smith Whitney)

Carter, Kate, ed. *Heber C. Kimball, His Wives and Family.* Salt Lake City: Daughters of Utah Pioneers, 1967.

Crocheron, Augusta. *Representative Women of Deseret.* 109-20.

HMWj = Helen Mar Whitney journal.

Holzapfel, Jeni Broberg, and Richard. *A Woman's View: Helen Mar Whitney's Reminiscences of Early Church History.* Provo, UT: BYU Religious Studies Center, 1997. A publication of Helen Mar's public autobiography, the *Woman's Exponent* series.

HWj = Horace Whitney journal.

TMH = Orson Whitney. *Through Memory's Halls.*

Wells, Emmeline B. "Sister Helen Mar Whitney." In *Deseret Weekly* 53 (Nov. 21, 1896): 718. An obituary. Reprinted in *A Woman's View,* 489-93.

Whitney, Helen Mar. Autobiography. Published in *Woman's Exponent,* 1880-86, and recently reprinted in Holzapfel, *A Woman's View.*

———. "Helen Mar Kimball's Retrospection About her Introduction to the Doctrine and Practices of Plural marriage in Nauvoo at age 15." Also known as "Helen Mar Kimball Smith Whitney to her children, March 30, 1881. Similar to statements to be opened at Centennial." CA, MS 744. Published in Holzapfel, *A Woman's View,* 481-87. Fully discussed and excerpts quoted in Bachman, "A Study," 149-52.

———. Journal. Helen Vilate Bourne Fleming Papers, CA, and Merrill Library. This extensive journal is being prepared for publication by Charles Hatch and the author.

———. *Plural Marriage as Taught by the Prophet Joseph.* Salt Lake City: Juvenile Instructor Office, 1882.

———. *Why We Practice Plural Marriage.* Salt Lake City: Juvenile Instructor Office, 1884.

———. 1876 Reminiscences. Helen Vilate Bourne Fleming Papers, CA.

Whitney, Horace. Journal. CA, MS 1616.

Whitney, Orson. *Life of Heber C. Kimball.* Salt Lake City: Kimball family, 1888. Also Salt Lake City: Stevens & Wallis, 1945.

———. *Through Memory's Halls, the Life Story of Orson F. Whitney.* Independence, MO: Zion's Printing, 1930.

**marriage prelude:** "The Last Chapter of Scenes in Nauvoo," WE 12 (Nov. 1, 1883): 81. **marriage:** BOP #163; SAd 513, 555; Crocheron, RW 110; Wells, "Sister Helen." **Elizabeth Ford Sykes/Sikes:** BOP #164; SAd 557; Helen Mar Whitney, 1881 Reminiscence. As she had died on March 30, 1844, in Nauvoo, Horace probably had known her.

I. **Helen's birth:** The Wells obituaries and Crocheron give August 22. NTER interprets the Kimball/Clayton Book 93 record as August 22, but it is hard to read and looks like 28. BOP #163 clearly gives August 25. **Heber:** See HCK and HCKj. **Vilate:** See "Obituary," of Vilate, DN 16 (Dec. 25, 1867): first page, and HCK. **Judith:** LI, WE 9 (Apr. 15, 1881): 169. FGS gives July 29 as birthdate. **William:** Born on April 10, 1826, he later married Mary Marian Davenport, Melissa Burton Coray, Lucy Amelia Pack, Martha Jane Vance, and Eliza Redden. He died in 1907 in Coalville, Summit, Utah. **Heber's toys, Vilate singing:** LI, WE 9 (Aug. 15, 1880): 42. **Fanny and Youngs:** LI, WE 9 (Aug. 1, 1880): 38. **named:** LI 42.

II. **Baptists:** LI, WE 9 (Aug. 1, 1880): 39; HCK 14. **hears Mormon elder:** LI, WE 9 (Aug. 1, 1880): 39; HCK 14, 17. **Columbia:** HCK 19. **baptism, move to Kirtland:** LI, WE 9 (Aug. 1, 1880): 39; 9 (Aug. 15, 1881): 170. **Fanny precedes:** LI, WE 9 (Aug. 15, 1880): 42. **Zion's camp:** LI, WE 9 (Aug. 15, 1880): 42. **Kirtland an idyll:** LI, WE 9 (Aug. 15, 1880): 42. **Helen breaks dishes:** LI, WE 9 (Nov. 15, 1880): 90; (Dec. 1, 1880): 98. **Heber an apostle:** HC 2:180-89; HCK 35. **mission:** HCK 36. I follow Stanley Kimball for the dating of Heber's missions. But compare LI, WE 9 (Apr. 15, 1881): 169. **Heber Parley:** FGS has Jan. 1. He married Phebe Teresa Judd and died on February 8, 1885, see HMWj. **Heber returns:** HCK 37. **Helen to Eliza's school:** LI, WE 9 (Apr. 15, 1881): 170. **June 10:** HCK 38. **return home:** LI, WE 9 (Apr. 15, 1881): 169. **baptism:** LI, WE 9 (Apr. 15, 1881): 170; Crocheron 109. **Heber's mission to England:** LI, WE 10 (June 1, 1881): 6; HCK 41. **he returns:** LI, WE 10 (June 15, 1881): 11.

III. **leaving Kirtland:** LI, WE 10 (June 15, 1881): 11; HCK 55. **Far West:** LI, WE 10 (June 15, 1881): 11; ER, WE 8 (May 15, 1880): 189. **housing:** HCK 57. **transfer to inner city:** ER, WE 8 (May 15, 1880): 188. **Helen grinds wheat:** ER, WE 9 (June 1, 1880): 5. **departure:** ER, WE 9 (June 1, 1880): 5. **the journey:** ER, WE 9 (June 1, 1880): 5.

IV. **Atlas:** ER 9 (June 1, 1880): 5; HCK 64. **Quincy:** ER, WE 9 (June 1, 1880): 5. **Nauvoo:** SIN, WE 10 (July 15, 1881): 26. **first house:** LI, WE 9 (July 1, 1880): 18; HCK 66. **rain storm:** LI, WE 9 (July 1, 1880): 18. **David Kimball:** married Caroline Marian Williams in 1857, and also Juliette Merrill. He died in 1883 in St. David, Cochise, Arizona. Compare LI, WE 9 (July 1, 1880): 18. **all sick:** LI, WE 9 (July 1, 1880): 18. **Nauvoo beautiful:** SIN, WE 10 (Sept. 15, 1881) 58. **Vilate possessed:** LI, WE 9 (July 1, 1880): 18. Heber was attacked by evil spirits when he went to England, Whitney, HCK 129-32. Compare the Sarah Whitney chapter at Winter Quarters; Lester Bush, *Health and Medicine Among the Latter-Day Saints, Sense and Scripture* (New York: Crossroads, 1993), 109-16. **Heber leaves for England:** LI, WE 9 (July 15, 1880): 25. HCK 66-67. **Heber Parley gets the ague:** SIN, WE 10 (July 15, 1881): 26. **blow on head:** SIN, WE 10 (July 15, 1881): 26. **shoes:** SIN, WE 10 (July 15, 1881): 26. **Heber to Vilate:** Dec. 27, 1839, as cited in HCK 69. Quote from HCK 68. **Hibbards:** "The Last Chapter of Scenes in Nauvoo," WE 12 (Nov. 15, 1883): 90. **school:** SIN, WE 10 (Aug. 1, 1881): 34. **dolls:** SIN, WE 10 (Aug. 1, 1881): 34. **circus:** SIN, WE 10 (Aug. 1, 1881): 34. **Heber's homecoming:** SIN, WE 10 (Aug. 15, 1881): 42. **new house:** SIN, WE 10 (Sept. 15, 1881): 58. "To this log portion he later added one brick room [1843]. Still later he removed the log portion and replaced it with the two-story brick structure [1845] which is still standing and which has been restored close to its original state." HCK 81, 121. **Sarah Whitney's party:** "Scenes in Nauvoo after the Martyrdom of the Prophet and Patriarch," WE 11 (Mar. 1, 1883): 146. **consumption:** SIN, WE 11 (Sept. 15, 1882): 57. See Quinn, "The Practice of Rebaptism."

V. **Heber as an early elite disciple:** E.g., on May 4, 1842, Joseph Smith introduced the endowment for the first time, and Heber was among the first seven initiates, HC 5:2. **Heber's love for Vilate:** See Presendia Huntington chapter, at 1845-1846. **offering of Vilate:** Whitney, HCK 333-35, Kimball, HCK 93-94. Whitney's source was James Lawson, a son-in-law of Heber, HCK 109 n. 1. The dating of this incident is not precise. Whitney's book was published while Helen Mar was alive, so she certainly helped with it and read it. **Heber's first plural marriage:** SIN, WE 10 (Oct. 15, 1881): 74; Helen Mar Whitney, *Why We Practice* 56-59. **would lose apostleship:** Whitney, HCK 326, footnote. Compare Prologue, end of first section. **marriage to Noon:** The only dating of the marriage presently known is that Helen says Sarah's first child by Heber was born at about the same time as Vilate's Charles Spaulding (on Jan. 2, 1843), SIN, WE 11 (July 15, 1882): 26. Compare Kimball, HCK 95. **Vilate's vision:** Helen Mar, quoted in Whitney, HCK, 325-28; SIN, WE 10 (Oct. 15, 1881): 74; Helen Mar Whitney, *Why We Practice* 59. However, Helen's writings make it clear that Vilate continued to be deeply pained by polygamy, see below at Helen's marriage to Smith and her later conversion to the principle, also *Winter Quarters, The 1846-1848 Life Writings of Mary Haskins Parker Richards*, ed. Maurine Carr Ward (Logan: University of Utah State Press, 1996), 109, at Feb. 10, 1847. **early Sept.:** SIN, WE 10 (Dec. 15, 1881): 106. **Charles:** FGS has June 2. He married Elvira Free (1861) and Anna Sinclair (1900) and died in 1925. SIN, WE 11 (July 15, 1882): 26. **Noon's child:** SIN, WE 11 (July 15, 1882): 26. **birthday party:** SIN, WE 11 (Mar. 1, 1883): 146.

**VI. Orson:.** Whitney, HCK 339. While Helen said the marriage took place in 1843 (see below), Whitney dates Helen's marriage soon after Vilate accepted polygamy, thus in 1842. An antagonistic source, Sarah Pratt in Wyl, MP 70-72, connects Helen's marriage with the offering story: when Vilate was reluctant, Heber offered Helen instead. This would either place the offering story in 1843 (which is not impossible), or Helen's marriage in 1842. However, Helen Mar characterized Sarah Pratt's version of these events as "falsehoods," "apostate lies," HMWj, Aug. 27, 1886. **Heber introduces the principle:** SIN, WE 11 (Aug. 1, 1882): 39. **small earthquake:** SIN, WE 11 (Mar. 1, 1883): 146. **"having a great desire":** 1881 reminiscence. **"he left me":** SIN 39. In this account, Helen does not mention her marriage to Smith. **date of marriage:** Date from Jenson, HR 6:234; Crocheron, RW 110 gives June. Compare on Whitney's dating, above. For evidence from Helen's own diaries that she married Joseph Smith, see HMWj, May 20, 1886; July 11, 1886 ("I told him [a relative] ... that I was seeled to the Prophet in Nauvoo - He was astonished & so was I that he was ignorent of this fact."); Nov. 16, 1886; Nov. 27, 1889; June 16, 1894. **friendship with Sarah:** SIN, WE 11 (Mar. 1, 1883): 146. **Lewis:** Catherine Lewis, *Narrative of Some of the Proceedings of the Mormons; Giving an Account of Their Iniquities ...* (Lynn, MA: the Author, 1848), 19. For the man with the mallet, p. 10. **first depression:** In addition to the feelings of loss of freedom, being divided from her peer group, polygamy was also a crisis of Helen's faith, and cognitive dissonance can also be a source of depression. For cognitive dissonance in religion, see Leon Festinger, Henry W. Riecken, and Stanley Schachter, *When Prophecy Fails* (New York: Harper and Row, 1956). Festinger et al. show that when a religious belief is decisively disproved by factual events, a certain type of believer believes even more intensely after the initial shock and despair. Paradoxically, irrefutable contrary evidence strengthens such believers in their faith. Festinger concludes that a strong social community is crucial in creating this intensification of belief.

**VII. letter, July 10, 1843:** quoted in SIN, WE 11 (Aug. 1, 1882): 39-40. **October 22:** HCK 105. **party:** SIN, WE 11 (Nov. 15, 1882): 90. **choir:** SIN, WE 10 (Sept. 15, 1881): 58. **January 1, acts:** SIN, WE 11 (Nov. 15, 1882): 90. **May 1844:** HCK 106. **letter:** HCK to Vilate, May 23, 1844, as quoted in SIN, WE 11 (Dec. 1, 1882): 98. **letter to Helen:** quoted in SIN, WE 11 (Dec. 15, 1882): 105-106. For Helen's difficulties as a young plural wife, see Lewis, *Narrative* 19. Helen herself later wrote, "In my younger days, in the early scenes of trial and temptation, I thought that I would be perfectly happy if the plural wife system could be relinquished. I felt unwilling to sacrifice my earthly happiness for the promise of future reward. I thought I could content myself with a lesser glory." *Plural Marriage as Taught* 37. **Heber marries 35:** See HCK, appendix; Quinn, MHOP 557. At Vilate's funeral Kimball said, "I have taken 40 wives & many without her knowledge," WWj, Oct. 26, 1868 (6:435). These women became important "aunts" to Helen Mar, for example, Lucy Walker and Mary Ellen Harris, see below.

**VIII.** **sunset:** "Last Chapter of Scenes in Nauvoo," WE 12 (Nov. 15, 1883): 90. **wedding:** HCKj, Book 93, CA; compare SIN, WE 12 (June 15, 1883): 10. **piano party:** HCK 121. **printer festival:** SIN, WE 12 (Oct. 1, 1883): 71. **Horace's retiring nature:** "Death of a Pioneer," DEN (Nov. 23, 1884): p. 2. **Brigham Willard:** Another of Helen's full siblings, he was born on January 29, 1845. He died in 1867. William was now eighteen, Helen, sixteen, Heber P. nine, David five, and Charles two. Vilate was thirty-eight, Heber (who now had at least fifteen plural wives) forty-three. **in the attic:** HCKj (Clayton), Bk 93. **sewing the veil:** HCKj (Clayton), Bk 93, Dec. 5. **temple endowment:** HCKj (Clayton), Bk 93. She was washed and anointed by Vilate Kimball and Elizabeth Ann Whitney. **second printer festival:** SIN, WE 12 (Oct. 1, 1883): 71. **Jan. 26:** WCj, IC 156.

**IX.** **packing:** "Last Chapter of Scenes from Nauvoo," 12 (Nov. 1, 1883): 82. **crossing river:** Crocheron, RW 110. Jane Taylor journal, as quoted in "Last Chapter," WE 12 (Nov. 1, 1883): 82. **back to Nauvoo:** "Last Chapter," WE 12 (Nov. 1, 1883): 82. **back to Sugar Creek:** "Last Chapter," WE 12 (Nov. 1, 1883): 82; (Nov. 15, 1883): 90. OTBM, WE 12 (Jan. 1, 1884): 117. **wedding tour:** SIN, WE 12 (Oct. 1, 1883): 71. **dancing, carriage, coldest night:** OTBM, WE 12 (Dec. 1, 1883): 102. **travelling to Vilate's tent:** OTBM, WE 12 (Jan. 1, 1884): 117-18. **Horace and oxen:** HWj; Apr. 7, 1846; OTBM, WE 12 (Jan. 15, 1884): 126. **wagon:** OTBM, WE 12 (Jan. 15, 1884): 126. **muddy camp:** OTBM, WE 12 (Jan. 15, 1884): 126. **sharing with five:** HWj; OTBM, WE 12 (Feb. 1, 1884): 135. **camp:** OTBM, WE 12 (Feb. 1, 1884): 135. **walking difficult:** OTBM, WE 12 (Feb. 1, 1884): 136. As they "peddled" possessions and obtained more wagons, they did not have to walk as much. **Garden Grove:** OTBM, WE 12 (Feb. 1, 1884): 136.

**X.** **reached WQ:** OTBM, WE 12 (Apr. 15, 1884): 170. "31st" in the text is a typo. **Helen sick:** HWj, Aug. 18, Sept. 27, 1846. **home:** Kimball, HCK 144. **chimney:** SIWQ, WE 13 (Feb. 15, 1885): 139. **Helen sick:** HWj, Jan. 30, Feb. 2, 7, 25, 28, Mar. 21, Mar. 23, 1847. **Solomon Farnham:** married Mary Ursulia Pomeroy in 1881, Caroline Rasmene Fillerup in 1893, and died in 1920 in Salt Lake City. **Helen and Vilate:** SIWQ, WE 14 (June 15, 1885): 11. **Horace journal:** quoted in SIWQ, WE 14 (July 15, 1885): 31. **Horace leaves with pioneers:** SIWQ, WE 14 (Sept. 15, 1885): 57. **Fanny Young letter:** Letter to Robert Gould and Laura Murray, July 5, 1847, Merrill Library, MS 179, box 4, fd 6; also quoted in SIWQ, WE 14 (Nov. 1, 1885): 82. **birth of Helen Rosabell:** Fanny Young letter; Winter Quarters Death Record, see Mary Houston, Grave 147. For Helen Mar's children, see FGS, GS 510838, citing the Horace Whitney Bible. **letter to Horace:** June 4 and 13, Merrill Library, MS 179, box 1, fd 1. Printed in "Letter from Helen Mar Kimball Whitney to Horace K. Whitney ..." *Nauvoo Journal* 5 (Spring 1993): 9-10. She added, "I had doted much on its society in your abscence, but the Lord has certainly been with me, to comfort me through all my trialls." The first part of the sentence seems puzzling, as the child was stillborn, according to Patty Sessions. This letter also gives May 6 as date of birth, so it is certainly the same child. **sickness:** SIWQ, WE 14 (Oct. 15, 1885): 78. See the letter to Horace, above. On scurvy, compare SIWQ WE 14 (July 15, 1885): 31. **healing:** SIWQ, 14 (Dec. 15, 1885): 106. See the Sarah Whitney chapter, at Winter Quarters, for the meeting in which babies were believed possessed. **blessing:** PBSj, compare Helen's letter to Horace, "I have had such blessings poured out upon my head, by sister Eliza Snow in the gift of tongues, (and interpreted by sister Sessions) that my heart is <u>full</u> to <u>overflowing</u>."

**XI.** **pioneers return:** SIWQ, WE 15 (June 1, 1886): 7. **departure:** Wells, "Sister Helen." **nearly faints:** Crocheron, RW 111. **William Howard:** Daniel Davis diary, CA, Aug. 17, 1848, "Sister Helen M Whitney ... was delivered of a son"; HCK 182. **William dies:** Daniel Davis diary, Aug. 22, 1848, "in the evening the infant child of sister Hellen died, it was five days old." **Helen's sickness:** HCK 182. Compare Daniel Davis diary, Aug.

24-25, CA. "Sister Hellen was very sick." **Oliver:** OHj, 10:17. **Lee:** JDLj, AMC 1:74. **arrival in the valley:** Daniel Davis diary, CA, Sept. 24; HCK 182.

**XII. near death:** Crocheron, RW 111-12. Compare Wells, "Sister Helen": "This grief added to the death of her Firstborn was too much for the young mother, and she was not only very ill, but her reason was overthrown." **depression:** For depression generally, see a history, Stanley Jackson, *Melancholia and Depression, From Hippocratic Times to Modern Times* (New Haven, CT: Yale University Press, 1986). Also Frederic Flach and Suzanne C. Draghi, eds., *The Nature and Treatment of Depression* (New York: John Wiley, 1975). Two sensitive memoirs, William Styron, *Darkness Visible* (New York: Random House, 1990), and Percy Knauth, *A Season in Hell* (New York: Harper & Row, 1975), give great insight into this sickness. **grief and loss triggering depression:** Jackson, MD 320. Most people experience intense grief while mourning a death, but emerge from it. However, Jackson writes, "The experience of bereavement may well increase the probability that an individual will develop a clinical depression." See also Alexander Lowen, *Depression and the Body* (Baltimore: Penguin Books, 1972), 129-58. Another factor in Helen's case could have been postpartum depression caused by hormonal changes following birth, see Virginia O'Leary, *Toward Understanding Women* (Monterey, CA: Brooks/Cole, 1977), 26-27; Katharina Dalton, *Depression After Childbirth* (Oxford: Oxford University Press, 1989). **depression seen as supernatural persecution:** Jackson, MD 325, chapter thirteen, "Religion, the Supernatural, and Melancholia." In every age "there have been instances of mental disturbances being explained as punishment for sin." In one variation the sufferer, because of his/her sins, is "left unprotected by the supreme being, who thus 'allowed' some demon, a devil, or the Devil to afflict him with the disease." Helen's case is a textbook example. The demons become, as it were, agents for God. **Helen's conversion:** Crocheron, RW 111-14. **"I had, in hours of temptation":** my emphasis.

**XIII. continued an invalid:** SIN, WE 10 (Sept. 15, 1881): 58. **residency in Salt Lake:** "Brother and Sister Whitney made their home on the bank of City Creek, just east of where the Temple stands, where their other children were born." Wells, "Sister Helen." **Helen and Utah's landscape:** SIN, WE 10 (Sept. 15, 1881): 58. **Eliza Snow:** OTBM, WE 12 (Apr. 15, 1884): 170. **Horace Kimball:** FGS; Crocheron, RW 114. **Murray Gould:** Helen's last full sibling, he was born to Vilate in Salt Lake City on January 20, 1850; however, he lived only two years. **Horace in early Salt Lake:** "Horace K. Whitney, His Life and Death," DEN (Nov. 23, 1884): p. 3. **"He studied my feelings":** Helen Mar Whitney, *Why We Practice* 11. **Lucy Bloxham:** Daughter of Thomas Bloxham. Date of marriage from FGS, GS 510838. **Horace Whitney to Helen,** Apr. 17 1849. Helen Mar Whitney collection, Merrill Library, box 1, fd 12.

**XIV. Vilate Whitney:** died in 1870, see below. **Orson Whitney:** followed in the footsteps of his book-loving father, and, in 1895, he was given a chair of history and theology in Brigham Young College in Logan. He became bishop of the Eighteenth Ward early in his life, and in 1906 was ordained an apostle. He wrote a massive *History of Utah* and the first biography of his grandfather, *The Life of Heber C. Kimball.* Thus Orson was a son in whom Helen would take great pride. He married Zina Beal Smoot in 1879, Mary Minerva Wells (polygamously) in 1888, and died in 1931. See his journals, CA and Merrill Library, being edited by Lavina Fielding Anderson; Wells, "Sister Helen"; Orson's obituary, DN (May 16, 1931): p. 1; John Nicholson, "The Author and His Work," in Whitney, HU 4:703-407; his autobiography, TMH; Quinn, MHEP 713; and Orson F. Whitney collections at Lee Library, Merrill Library, and CA. **place of Orson's birth:** This house gave way to a new house which "faced north on City Creek," TMH 20, in the Eighteenth Ward. **quote by Orson:** TMH 29. **Mary Cravath:** Born in 1838, she was the daughter of Eliza Doty (Cravath Murray Brown Kimball), a plural wife of Heber Kimball. She had thirteen children with Horace and died in 1895. Horace possibly also married "Em. Evans," date unknown, see HMWj, Jan. 27, 1885. **statement**

on polygamy: Helen Mar Kimball, Reminiscences, in Helen Vilate Bourne Fleming Papers, CA, MS 9670, fd 38. Helen Mar Whitney, *Why We Practice* 11; TMH 22. **Horace's financial status:** HMWj, 1876 reminiscence. **Elizabeth Ann:** Married Robert T. Paton in 1886 and died in 1905. **Genevieve:** Married Edward Lee Talbot in 1886, with whom she had four children, and died on June 12, 1901, of heart disease and dropsy. See "Death of Mrs. Talbot," DEN (June 12, 1901): 1; "Local Briefs," DN (June 17, 1901): 8. According to her obituary, "Among her friends and acquaintances Mrs. Talbot was loved for her independence of character, her love of truth, and her absolute genuineness, traits which distinguished her career through all her life." **Helen Kimball Whitney:** married George Thomas Bourne in 1883, and died in 1927. **Charles Spaulding:** died in 1886, see below. **Helen sick in 1862:** Vilate Kimball to Helen Mar Whitney, Sept. 9, 1862, in Helen Mar Whitney collection, Merrill Library, MS 179, box 1, fd 6. Vilate to Helen/Helen to unknown woman, Sept. 20, 1862, fd 6 (full of instructions on taking care of her children); Horace Whitney to Helen Mar, Sept. 22, 1862, box 1, fd 12. She is with Vilate at Parley's Park and Horace prays "that your present excursion may tend to restore your health and spirits." A week later, Helen had improved, Horace Whitney to Helen, Sept. 28, 1862. **Florence:** married Henry M. Dinwoody in 1887, but never had children. She was a noted vocalist, studying in London, New York and Chicago, and frequently sang in Utah meetings. With her husband she fulfilled a mission to England from 1893 to 1895, and her obituary awards her the distinction of being "the first lady missionary to be set apart in the Church of Jesus Christ of Latter-day Saints." She died in 1930, see "Mrs. Dinwoodey Dies at Her Home," DN (Apr. 19, 1930): sect. 2 p. 1. **mother Vilate's death:** "Obituary," of Vilate, DN 16 (Dec. 25, 1867): first page. HCK 295. **Phebe:** died in 1874, see below. **letters to Horace:** Helen Mar Whitney, letters to Horace Whitney, box 1, fd 1, Helen Mar Whitney collection, Merrill Library: Nov. 28, 1869; Dec. 14; Dec. 30; Jan. 2, 1870; Jan. 14; Jan. 31; Feb. 27. Clearly, Helen missed Horace intensely. The letters are filled with news of the children, relatives and friends, reports on Vilate's condition, financial concerns, Salt Lake events, and reports of Helen's own physical condition (she despairs of every regaining her health, till Eliza Snow comes and washes and anoints her). She is pained that, instead of writing separate letters to both her and Mary, he wrote a collective letter. She occasionally admits to having the "blues." **Mary Ellen:** Helen Mar and Mary Ellen Kimball to Horace Whitney, Feb. 4 and 5, 1870, box 1, fd 19, Helen Mar Whitney collection, Merrill Library. See also Utah Death Records, 1848-90, film, CA, #4247; compare WWj, Feb. 6, 1870 (6:526), for an account of the funeral; Helen Mar Whitney, 1876 Reminiscences; "Died," DEN (Feb. 5, 1870): 2, cites "lung disease" as cause of death. **February 15:** Orson and Helen Mar Whitney to Horace Whitney, Feb. 15, 1870, Helen Mar Whitney collection, Merrill Library, box 1, fd 19.

**XV. lung fever:** See HMWj, Feb. 21, 1885. **Phebe's death:** FGS; 1876 reminiscences. For scarlet fever, see Agnes Coolbrith chapter at Oct. 1843.

**XVI. Helen's sickness, moves, etc.:** Helen Mar Whitney, 1876 reminiscences. **for depression among women**: Dana Crowley Jack, *Silencing the Self: Women and Depression* (Cambridge, MA: Harvard University Press, 1991); George Brown and Tirril Harris, *Social Origins of Depression: a Study of Psychiatric Disorder in Women* (London: Tavistock, 1978); Deborah Belle, ed. *Lives in Stress: Women in Depression* (Beverly Hills, CA: Sage, 1982); Joanna Bunker Rohrbaugh, *Women: Psychology's Puzzle* (New York: Basic Books, 1979), 401-10; Walter Gove, "Mental Illness and Psychiatric Treatment among Women," in Mary Roth Walsh, ed., *The Psychology of Women* (New Haven, CT: Yale University Press, 1987), 102-26. It is generally accepted that women have a higher rate of depression than men ("twice as high for women as for men in the United States and in most Western societies," Jack, *Silencing the Self* 1); why this is so is debated. Some point to woman's generally disadvantaged status; some focus on inequalities within marriage, others on inequalities in the workplace. Some psychologists have proposed a "learned helplessness" hypothesis, in which depression is caused by women feeling they have very little control over their lives, Brown and Harris, *Social Origins* 242. A problematic marriage (i.e., a husband who lowers a woman's self-esteem) can also be a crucial factor, Brown and Harris, *Social Origins* 239, 287, compare Jack, *Silencing the Self* passim and 182. Jack writes, "The high rates of depression in women can be seen as an almost inevitable response to living in a culture that deeply fears and devalues the feminine," 183. Biological factors must also be considered, see O'Leary, *Toward Understanding Women*, cited above. All of these factors and interpretations (none of which are mutually exclusive) have their proponents and critics. For modern Mormon women and depression, see Louise Degn, "Mormon Women and Depression," *Sunstone* 4 (Mar.-Apr. 1979): 16-26 and 10 (May 1985): 19-27; Robert H. Burgoyne and Rodney W. Burgoyne, "Belief Systems and Unhappiness: The Mormon Woman Example," *Dialogue* 11 (Autumn 1978): 48-53; Laurel Thatcher Ulrich, "The Pink DIALOGUE and Beyond," *Dialogue* 11 (Winter 1978): 28-39; David Craig Spendlove, "Depression in Mormon Women," Ph.D. diss., University of Utah, 1982; Quinn, MHEP 623, 625. **genetic disposition:** It is of course impossible to create a clinical diagnosis from the fragmentary historical record. However, there is evidence that possibly points to a genetic heritage of depression. See, for Heber C. Kimball, Laura Pitkin diary, "Feb 1$^{st}$ [1859] weather pleasant. M$^r$ K rather depressed in spirit cause unknown." Also Nov. 22, 1858; Aug. 29, 1859. Aug. 16, 1860; Aug. 12, 1861. A researcher on J. Golden Kimball, Heber C.'s son by a plural wife, tells me that J. Golden had periods of severe depression. Ironically, he was known for his sometimes light-hearted, anti-establishment wit. Compare HMWj, Aug. 2, 1888. Helen's older brother William evidently drank heavily, which is a way many people cope with depression. For William's drinking, see Vilate Kimball to Helen Mar Whitney, Sept. 7, 1862, Helen Mar Whitney collection, Merrill Library, MS 179, box 1, fd 6. Compare Helen's use of alcohol as a sleeping medicine, Sec. XXII below. **feelings of uselessness:** See Rhoda Richards chapter for the importance of work for a pioneer woman's self-image. **Orson on his mission:** Crocheron, RW 115. **Orson's call:** TMH 67.

**XVII. Orson marries:** Crocheron, RW 116. **Helen Whitney Bourne marries:** Helen Mar to Charles Whitney, Nov. 5, 1883, Helen Mar Whitney collection, Merrill Library. This, and a number of other letters to Charley in 1883 and 1884, show an affectionate mother missing and worrying about her wandering son, exhorting him above all to be a good Mormon, retelling and interpreting spiritual dreams, hinting that she would like him to serve a mission, sharing news of his relatives at home. **Helen counselor:** Crocheron, RW 115. **pamphlet background:** For events leading up to *Plural Marriage as Taught by Joseph Smith*, see Helen Mar Whitney to Orson F. Whitney, Aug. 21, 1882, typescript, in Orson F. Whitney collection, Merrill Library, MS 167, box 5, fd 5. **letters in 1882:** See Orson F. Whitney collection, Merrill Library, MS 167, box 5. **Quote from Why We Practice:** 8. **poem:** *Why We Practice* 70. For the writing of this work, see Helen Mar to Charles Whitney, Dec. 11, 1884. **the Puritan strain in American religion:** Philip Greven, *The Protestant Temperament* (New York: Knopf, 1977). Scholars continue to debate whether Puritans were in fact sexually repressive, see e.g., Michael Zuckerman, "Pilgrims in the Wilderness: Community, Modernity, and the Maypole at Merry Mount," *New England Quarterly* 50 (1977): 255-77, 265-67, or whether they had a relatively healthy, humane view of sexuality, e.g., Edmund Morgan, "The Puritans and Sex," *New England Quarterly* 15 (1942): 591-607. Compare Ulrich, GW 92-93. There were certainly repressive aspects in the Puritan world view.

**XVIII. 1884 diary:** Diary, 1884-85, in Helen Vilate Bourne Fleming papers, CA, MS 9670. For her financial worries, see December 19, 1884 and the diaries almost passim. **Horace's first symptoms:** "Horace K. Whitney, His Life and Death," DEN (Nov. 22, 1884): p. 3. Compare Helen Mar to Charles Whitney, letters dated "Tuesday the 19th," [1884]; Aug. 20, 1884; Oct. 19, 1894; Helen Mar Whitney collection, Merrill Library. **modern doctor:** I am indebted to Dr. Elizabeth Evans for her tentative diagnosis of Horace's final illness. **Horace's last days:** Helen Mar Whitney to Charles Whitney, Nov. 19, 1884; Jan. 1, 1885, Helen Mar Whitney collection, Merrill Library; "Horace K. Whitney, His Life and Death," DEN (Nov. 22, 1884): p. 3. For the funeral, see also DN 33 (Nov. 26, 1884): 716.

IX. **spasms:** May 5, 1894. **stagnation:** Nov. 4, 1893. **deathly spells triggered by work:** See also May 4, 1886. **spacing of spells:** Compare May 1, 1886, a three-month break between spells. Charles Hatch, an editor of Helen's forthcoming diaries, suspects that a physical cycle caused the spells. **insomnia:** E.g., Jan. 17, 1886. **Hyrum frightened:** June 21, 1886. **aftereffects:** See also Jan. 20, 1886, and the Apr. 12, 1886 passage quoted above. **palpitations:** Jan. 11, 1890. **"a week later":** Jan. 24. Compare the Emily Partridge diary, CA: "Joined a surprise party at Sister Hellen M. Whitney's." **speech:** WE 14 (Dec. 15, 1885): 106. **millennialist rhetoric:** See Dan Erickson, "Joseph Smith's Millennial Prophecy: The Quest for Apocalyptic Delivery," JMH 22 (Fall 1996): 1-34.

XX. **leaves for Bear Lake:** HMWj, July 27, 1886. **Charles dies:** HMWj, Aug. 5-11, 1886. Record of Deaths, SLC, 1848-90, film, CA, #13341; "A Horrible Tragedy," DEN (Aug. 4, 1886): p. 3; "Suicide of C.S. Whitney," DEN (Aug. 5, 1886): p. 3; and a paragraph in "Fragments," DEN (Aug. 6, 1886): p. 3. **suicide?** A year later, on June 12, 1887 (see HMWj), Charley's girlfriend told Helen that he had been making plans to go with Brigham Young, Jr., to Kamas, and must have shot himself accidentally while packing his things. This view of Charley's death gave Helen great comfort. **dreams of Charley:** E.g., May 5, 1888.

XXI. **marriages:** FGS. My working hypothesis is that the Lillie Whitney/Paton marriage was polygamous; I do not have conclusive proof at this time, as Paton has been difficult to document. The evidence is mostly from Helen's diaries, which show a secret marriage between an older man and a young woman. The speakers at Paton's funeral (see below) show that he was one of the elite Mormons of Cache County. I would welcome further information on Robert Paton from his descendants. **Lill depressed:** Dec. 4, 1886, compare Oct. 15, 1886. **continued depression:** Oct. 24, Dec. 30, 1889; Aug. 9, Sept. 21 ("Poor Lill's sighs & sobs weigh upon me"; this date is long past a normal six month period of mourning), Sept. 25 1890; Jan. 19, Feb. 9, Mar. 18, June 14, 1891; May 9, 1892 (apparently psychosomatic symptoms); Mar. 22, May 27 (women at a meeting notice Lillie's "pale, thin face"), 1893; Oct. 4, 1894. **Paton dies:** HMWj, Sept. 27, 1896. "Robert T. Paton's Funeral," *The Tri-weekly Journal*, Logan, UT, 16 (Sept. 24, 1896), p. 5. I am indebted to Charles Hatch for sharing this reference with me, and for his insights into the Paton/Lillie marriage. **second generation polygamy:** Eliza Partridge Lyman and Carlie Lyman Callister are cases in point. However, some second generation polygamous marriages were apparently successful, see the Zina Young and Elvira Cowles chapters. **Genny engaged:** HMWj, Aug. 29, 1886. **Genny married:** HMWj, Dec. 29, 1886. Helen and Gen remained close, and Gen often lived with her mother in upcoming years. Once when Edward worked out of town, he asked his wife to accompany him, but she turned him down, saying that she needed to take care of her mother. This was frustrating to Edward, but he accepted it. HMWj, Mar. 11, 1893. **October 6:** Hardy, SC 135. However, the Manifesto was only a first step toward the complete cessation of Mormon polygamy that occurred in the early twentieth century, as many general authorities solemnized plural marriages after it. Hardy, SC. Compare Holzapfel, *A Woman's View* xliv. **devils incarnate:** HMWj, July 4, 1891. **Democrat vs. Republican:** HMWj, Nov. 6-7, 1894.

XII. **foundations of new house:** HMWj, Mar. 16, 1891. **medications:** Nearly passim in HMWj. **Dr. Raile:** HMWj, Mar. 5, Apr. 4, 1896. **spirits in the night:** See also HMWj, Oct. 29, 1887; Nov. 4, 1890; Aug. 28, 1886; Sept. 13, 14, 1886. **good spirits in dreams:** Compare HMWj, Oct. 12, 1894.

XIII. **death:** See Wells, "Sister Helen"; E.B.W. [Emmeline Wells], "Helen Mar Whitney.–Her Death–A Sketch of her Personal History —," DEN 29 (Nov. 16, 1896): p. 2. Compare TMH 219.

## REFERENCES TO CHAPTER 23.
### Seamstress: Hannah Ells

**dressmaker:** "Millinery and Dress Making," TS 2 (Oct. 1, 1841): 566. For Samuel Bennett, a prominent doctor and politician in Nauvoo, see Jessee 2:526, also HC index.

I. **birthdate:** Brodie, NM 482. She gives March 4 as Hannah's birthdate, but it seems unlikely that she and her brother had the same birthday, so March 4 is probably copied from Josiah Ells. **Josiah:** HC 5:486; 7:117-18. See Smith, *History of the Reorganized Church*, 3, index, s.v. Ells, Josiah, esp. 764-68, which summarizes and quotes from an autobiographical sketch, now apparently lost; EMRC 659-60. He married a woman whose first name was Eliza, see her obituary, Josiah Ells, "Died ... Ells," *Saints' Herald* 27 (Sept. 15, 1880), 292. Like many figures in the circle of Josiah and Hannah, he did not follow Brigham west, but was associated with Strang, Rigdon, and the Reorganized LDS church in his later life. He died on October 15, 1885, in Wheeling, West Virginia, Smith, *History* 3:768. See also Richard P. Howard, ed., *The Memoirs of President Joseph Smith III* (Independence, MO: Herald House, 1979), index, esp. 173 = *Saints' Herald* (Oct. 22, 1935): 1360. "[Josiah Ells]," in Inez Smith Davis, Biographical Collection, D23, F33, RLDS Archives. **Hannah in Philadelphia:** See dressmaker ad, below. **Josiah in England and America:** Smith, *History* 3:764-68. For Methodist "lay preachers," see John Pudley, *John Wesley and his Work* (London: Thames & Hudson, 1978), 71. **marriage:** Smith, *History* 3:768. **known as Dr.:** See Benson Autobiography, cited below; HC 5:486.

II. **conversion:** Smith, *History* 3.764-68. "Early Reorganization Minutes 1852-1871," RLDS Archives, p. 132, 267, gives Sept. 1838 as date of baptism. Compare FWR 259; "Local Historians and Their Work," *Journal of History* 1 (Jan. 1908): 64-106, 67. **Joseph in New Jersey:** HC 4:49.

III. **debate:** Smith, *History* 3:764-68; the quote is from p. 765. Compare "Ezra Benson, I," *Instructor* 80 (1945): 3-56, 56, which dates the event in July. He supplies the information that Ells was taking the place of Sidney Rigdon. **Jenson:** HR vol. 5-8, p. 961. The Nauvoo census of spring 1842 (4th Ward, p. 11) shows that Hannah ("Anna S. Ells") was still living with the Samuel Bennett family. **RS Min.:** p. 68. This is the first mention of her in the minutes, but she must have joined earlier.

IV. **Jenson:** HR vol. 5-8, p. 961. **Benbow affidavit:** Quoted in Jenson HR 6:222-23. Joseph's journal confirms that he visited the Benbows on occasion, see Oct. 11, 1843; May 18, 1842; June 3, 1842. A third witness to Hannah's marriage to Joseph Smith is Eliza Snow to John Taylor, Dec. 27, 1886, John Taylor papers, CA: Hannah "was Sealed to Joseph the Prophet before his death." **dinner party:** HC 5:248. **Charlotte Haven to her family,** May 2, 1843, as printed in "A Girl's Letters from Nauvoo," *Overland Monthly* 16 (2nd ser.) (Dec. 1890): 629, also in William Mulder and A. Russell Mortensen, *Among the Mormons* (New York: Knopf, 1958), 122. **donations:** RS Min., 91. **Josiah on mission to Dixon:** HC 5:486. **March 9:** RS Min., 123; compare ME 173-74. **April 19:** *Nauvoo Neighbor* 1 (Apr. 17, 1844): third page (203). Repeated in following issues. **Josiah present when Joseph surrendered:** Smith, *History* 765-66.

V. **prayer at the temple:** WWj, Aug. 27, 1844 (2:456-58). **Woodruffs' mission:** They left with two children, Susan Cornelia, one year old, who would go to England with them, and Phebe Amelia, three, who they would leave with Phebe's parents in Maine (Alexander, THE 119). See letters of Hannah and Wilford Owen in 1845, below. For the location of the Benbow home, see John Taylor journal, Dean Jessee, ed., "The John Taylor Nauvoo Journal, January 1845-September 1845," BYUSt 23 (1983): 38, Feb. 1, 2, 1845: "Went on a visit to Br. Benbow's on the prairie." See Jessee 2:520. For the Benbows themselves, see Alexander, THE 92-93; HC 4:151; 6:568; ECIF; and the John Taylor journal.

**VI. Ells and High Council:** Nauvoo High Council Min., CA, Nov. 23, 1844. Also in Marquardt collection, Marriott Library. **Marks questioned:** High Council Min., Nov. 30, 1844. **Marks further questioned:** High Council Min., Dec. 7, Dec. 9. **Josiah's later career:** Smith, *History* 3.767-68; EMRC 659-60; ME 342. For Strang and the Strangites, see Roger Van Noord, *King of Beaver Island* (Urbana: University of Illinois Press, 1988). Ells in the Rigdon church, Van Wagoner, SR 385. Compare Van Wagoner, SR 407; Josiah Ells, "Polygamy," *Saints' Herald* 2 (Feb. 18, 1862): 178-80; 3 (Sept. 1862) 54-57; obituary, "Bro. Josiah Ells," *Saints' Herald* 32 (Oct. 24, 1885): 685; "Josiah Ells," 32 (1885): 708-9, 719.

**VII. Hannah Ells to Phoebe Woodruff:** CA, MS 1352, box 7, fd 3 #1.

**VIII. patriarchal blessing:** This took place on June 16, 1845. See Patriarchal Blessings Vol. 9, p. 229, #697. **death:** According to Jenson, HR vol. 5-8, p. 961, Hannah died in 1844, at the home of Hiram Kimball. Since she was certainly alive in the summer of 1845 (see her letter to the Woodruffs, above), the date is wrong, but the place of death is correct (see Snow letter below) and its general time of occurrence may be right. Therefore a reasonable working theory is that Jenson was one year off and that Hannah died in 1845. **Eliza Snow present:** Eliza Snow to John Taylor, Dec. 27, 1886, John Taylor papers, CA. "She died in Nauvoo in sister Sarah Kimball's house." Eliza had done endowments for Hannah posthumously, and was asking permission from Taylor for Zina Huntington Young to do the fullness of priesthood ordinance for Hannah in the Logan Temple. **March 4:** See WC 26. **epitaph:** Jenson, HR vol. 5-8, p. 961.

# REFERENCES TO CHAPTER 24.
## Relief Society Treasurer:
## Elvira Annie Cowles (Holmes Smith)

[Carter, Kate]. "Elvira Annie Cowles Holmes." OPH 19:258-59, compare 14:74.
"Died." DEN 4 (Mar. 23, 1871): p. 3. Obituary of Elvira Cowles Holmes.
Esshom, Frank. "Holmes, Jonathan H." In *Pioneers and Prominent Men of Utah* 2:940.
Holmes, Jonathan. Journal. Lee Library, MS 1164.
Taylor, Eliza Roxie Welling. "The Life of Elvira Annie Cowles (Smith) Holmes." In Margaret Steed Hess. *My Farmington: A History of Farmington, Utah, 1846-76*. Salt Lake City: Helen Mar Miller Camp/D.U.P., 1976. 101-107. Eliza Taylor was a granddaughter of Elvira. Compare a typescript version, at Lee Library, which is much the same as the published version, but slightly longer.
Welling, Phebe Holmes. Letter to Susa Young Gates. Feb. 9, 1919. CA.
Welling, Phebe Marietta, and Emma Welling. Letter to Andrew Jenson. June 24, 1887. Lee Library, MS 1164.

**March 17, 1842:** RS Min., first session; compare WC 27.

**I. birthdate:** BOP #162; SAd 513. **Austin Cowles:** Taylor, "Life," typescript 2; "Cowles, Austin," in Inez Smith Davis Biographical Collection, P23, f25, RLDS Archives; Carter, "Elvira"; *History of Allegheny County, New York* (New York: F.W. Beers and Co., 1879), as cited in Davis. *Biographical and Historical Record of Ringgold and Decatur Counties, Iowa* (Chicago: Lewis Publishing House, 1887), 493, as cited in Davis. Biography of Austin found on back of FGS. He was born on May 3, 1792, in Brookfield, Vermont, and lost his eye when his brother accidentally hit him with an arrow. **Phebe:** was born on October 6, 1785, in Wellsbridge, New York. **Louisa:** Born on March 19, 1817, she married Wesley Knight and died on June 13, 1897. Taylor, "Life," 101. **Sophia:** Born on August 17, 1818, she died on Aug. 20, 1820. **Alonzo:** was born and died on June 16, 1819. **Bolivar:** Taylor, "Life," typescript 2. *History of Allegheny County* 220, as cited in Davis. **Mary Ann:** married Rosel Hyde in 1839 and died in 1901 in Kaysville, Utah. Taylor, "Life," 101; FGS. **Austin a minister:** Taylor, "Life," typescript 2. **Leonard:** died on Dec. 30, 1824. **Cynthia:** Born on November 8, 1824, she died in May 1841. **Hulda:** was born on November 21, 1825. FGS has no further information on her. **Austin an inspector:** Taylor, "Life," typescript, 2. *History of Allegheny County*, as cited in Davis. **May 1, 1826:** Taylor, "Life," 102. **October 21, 1827:** Taylor, "Life," 102. Irena lived from 1807 to 1896. **Wesley:** He later married Elizabeth McCowen. Irena would have six children in all.

II. **Cowles converted:** Carter, "Elvira"; Taylor, "Life," 102. **Elvira baptized:** "Died." Or Oct. 9, TIB, as cited in SEB. **David:** FGS. He later married Julia Ann Morris Smith. **Elvira to Kirtland:** "Died." **March 13:** HC 3:92. **Jonathan Holmes:** HC 3:92.

III. **July 5:** "Died" has her leaving Kirtland in fall 1838. Jonathan Holmes certainly was part of the group, for his wagon overturned on September 29, in Missouri, HC 3:146. **Huntsville:** "Died." **Oct. 4:** HC 3:99-147. **proclamation:** HC 3:147-48. **Cowles to Illinois:** SLDS 128-29. **fall of 1839:** "Died."

IV. **Feb. 3:** HC 4:292. Also, Lyman Littlefield, *Reminiscences of Latter-day Saints* (Logan: Utah Journal Co., 1888), 117, who gives the date as February 4. **March 9:** WJS 64. **March 29:** HC 4:323. For instance, on September 21, 1841, Austin spoke in high council meeting concerning the indebtedness of the council. Nauvoo High Council Minutes, CA; typescript in Marquardt collection, Marriott Library. **Elvira in the Smith home:** "Died"; Nauvoo census, spring 1842. **Elvira and leading Nauvoo women:** See below. **Holmes's life:** See SEB; NTER; Larson, DB 94. Possibly he was born in Georgetown, Essex, Massachusetts, see Jonathan Holmes, Biographical Sketch, Lee Library; OPH 11:405; Jenson, BE 4:746. For Jonathan as a shoemaker, Milton H. Welling, letter to Hannah Weaver, Mar. 8, 1947, Lee Library MS 1164. **Holmes's closeness to Joseph in Kirtland:** Obituary of J. Holmes, DW 29 (Sept. 1, 1880): 493. **Bodyguard in Nauvoo:** BE 4:183. **Sarah's memories:** Life History of Franklin Weaver, p. 7, Lee Library, MS 1164. **"Alvira Cowles":** Nauvoo ward census, 4th Ward, p. 9. **Aug. 14:** ERSj.

V. **Conjugal:** ERSj; also at the *Wasp* marriage notice. **Sarah remembers Smith home:** Taylor, "Life," 105. **marriage notice:** Nauvoo *Wasp* 1 (Dec. 10, 1842): p. 3. **Eliza lives with Elvira:** ERSj.

VI. **Elvira sealed to Joseph:** Affidavit of Elvira Holmes, SAB 1:78; 4:80; Bachman, "A Study," p. 351. However, Jenson, in his list of Smith's wives, HR 6:234, refers to "Elvira A. Cowles, afterwards the wife of Jonathan H. Holmes." It is possible that Jenson was simply confused in giving this sequence (as is suggested by the fact that he does not supply a specific date). But he may also have wanted to glide over the polyandrous nature of the marriage to Smith by suggesting that Holmes married Elvira after the Mormon leader's death (family traditions incorrectly give December 1, 1844, as the date of Elvira's marriage to Jonathan, e.g., Life History of Franklin Weaver, p. 7, Lee Library MS 1164). Another possibility is that the June 1, 1843, marriage date was either wrong or a repetition of an earlier sealing. There are other cases in which marriages may have been repeated, or at least have different dates. Marinda Johnson Hyde has two dates for her marriage to Joseph Smith. Zina Young's marriage to Smith may have been repeated. Emily and Eliza Partridge's marriage to Smith was repeated for Emma's benefit when Emma gave them to her husband.

If Elvira did marry Joseph Smith first, then married Jonathan in a legal marriage (i.e., if Jenson is correct), the parallel is Sarah Ann Whitney, who married Smith, then married Joseph Kingsbury legally as a "front husband" only. Jonathan Holmes was certainly a devoted, personal friend of Joseph, and Smith solemnized their marriage ceremony, just as he had the Sarah Whitney-Kingsbury wedding. However, this is only a remote possibility, and it is more probable that Elvira married Holmes, then wedded Smith polyandrously. The Holmes marriage endured after Joseph's death, while the Kingsbury marriage (never authentic) did not. **June 16:** RS Min., 90-91. **June 29:** ERSj. **July 7:** RS Min., 95.

VII. **mission:** JH, Mar. 13, 1843. **July 16:** WJS 231. **Aug. 12:** Affidavits of David Fullmer and Leonard Soby, in Shook, *True Origins of Mormon Polygamy*, 97-101. The Soby affidavit adds that "Elder Austin Cowles, a member of the High Council aforesaid, did, subsequently to the 12th day of August, 1843, openly declare against the said revelation on polygamy, and the doctrines therein contained." See also Ebenezer Robinson, *Return* 3 (Feb. 1891): 29-30. **Sept. 12:** Nauvoo High Council Min., CA. **outspoken:** Robinson, *Return* 3 (Feb. 1891): 29-30; compare Flanders, *Nauvoo* 274. **new church:** HC 6:347; JSj, Faulring 475. For William Law, see Cook, *William Law.* **May 18:** HC 6:398. **Expositor:** *Nauvoo Expositor* 1 (June 7, 1844). Curiously enough, Austin's secessionist affidavit was reprinted in the thoroughly conservative book, Smith BAOPM 101-102 (1905 ed.), along with affidavits of William and Jane Law, because, to Joseph Fielding Smith, they were good evidence that Joseph Smith had been involved in polygamy before his death. Flanders places Joseph's destruction of the *Expositor* in the context of frontier vigilantism, see Robert Bruce Flanders, "Dream and Nightmare: Nauvoo Revisited," in Quinn NMH 75-100, 96. Further bibliography in Hardy, SC 31 n. 77. **Jonathan, the Expositor:** JSj, June 13, 17, 1844, 491-93 Faulring.

**VIII. Jonathan a pallbearer:** "History of JS," DW 7 (Nov. 25, 1857): 298; CHC 5:528. **Martha Maria:** married Stephen M. Delap and Uriah L. Shaffer. In November 1845 Austin was still living in Hampton. Touring the west bank of the Mississippi, Lorenzo Brown observed, "Seven miles farther is Hampton, the abode of Laws, Fosters, Austin Cowles, McLellin, Hickses and a great number of the apostate crew and last but not least, Dr. John C. Bennett." Lorenzo Brown, Journals (1823-1846), typescript, Lee Library, p. 12-13, at Nov. 10, 1845. **April 27:** HStj, OMF 1:36; Joseph Smith III, in Edward Tullidge, *Life of Joseph the Prophet,* as cited in Inez Smith Davis, "Cowles, Austin." On the Whistling and Whittling brigade, see Stout, OMF 1:33, 37, notes; ZDYj, Mar. 28, 1845; OHj, p. 56; Thurmon Dean Moody, "Nauvoo's Whistling and Whittling Brigade," BYUSt 15 (Summer 1975): 480-90; Quinn, MHOP 178-79. **moved from place to place:** Taylor, "Life," typescript, p. 3. For the localities, see Inez Smith Davis, "Cowles, Austin." **with Rigdon:** *Latter Day Saints Messenger And Advocate* (Pittsburgh) 1 (Mar. 15, 1845): 168, as cited in Van Wagoner, *Sidney Rigdon* 385. Cowles withdrew from the Rigdonites in February 1846, see Austin Cowles to Sidney Rigdon, Feb. 1846, RLDS Archives, P39-4, fd 2. "I am Compelled to Separate in Christian Fellowship from an association [such as yours] ... untill you or I See Differently." Compare A. W. Cowles, "The Mormons: Pen and Pencil Sketches, Illustrating their Early History," *Moore's Rural New Yorker* (Jan. 23, 1869): 61, available in Lee Library, as cited in Van Wagoner, SR 425. **in Kirtland:** There he wrote to Strang, see Austin Cowles to J.J. Strang, Aug. 24, 1849, RLDS Archives, Strang collection, P11-9, fd 1. **with the Brewsterites:** CHC 2:440. See the Brewsterite publication, *The Olive Branch,* 1848-49, which Cowles edited for a time; e.g., "Notice," 1 (1) (Aug. 1848): 7. For his departure from the group, "Minutes of a Special Conference," *The Olive Branch* 2 (4) (Oct. 1849): 50. Inez Davis, "Cowles, Austen," p. 6. **Pleasanton:** Barbara J. Hands Bernauer, "Strangers in the Flesh, but One in the Spirit: George Morey and the Pleasanton, Iowa, RLDS Branch," *Restoration Studies VI,* ed. Wayne Ham (Independence, MO: Herald Publishing House, 1995) 41-53, 45, 47. "Cowles, Austin," RLDS Archives, Inez Smith Davis Biographical Collection, P23, f25. **associated with RLDS:** "A Council," *Saints' Herald* 4 (Nov. 1, 1868): 142-43; obituary of Austin Cowles, *Saints' Herald* 19 (Mar. 1, 1872): 160; Bernauer, "Strangers"; EMRC 334. **death:** Obituary of Austin Cowles. **Elvira on Austin:** Taylor, "Life," 102.

**IX. July 6:** WRj, CA. **Lucy Elvira:** Date of birth from Winter Quarters death record, see below. **Dec. 23:** NTER. **Feb. 3, 1846:** BOP #162; SAd 327, 513. **sealing to Marietta:** BOP #161; SAd 327. **team of ox and cow:** Taylor, "Life," 103. **July 1:** "Died." Compare family tradition, Taylor, "Life," 103; Carter, "Elvira." **July 20:** Ricketts, MB 17; Jonathan Holmes diary. **"log room":** Taylor, "Life," 103. **September 1846:** ERSj, undated entry, mid-September, 1846. **Battalion in San Diego:** Ricketts, MB 118. **Lucy Elvira dies:** Winter Quarters Death Record, see Mary Houston; died June 1, born Oct. 11, 1845; cause of death unknown; Grave 161. **June 12:** See ERSj; Carter, "Elvira." **family tradition of Marietta:** Welling, 1887 letter.

**X. week later:** ERSj, Aug. 15. **family traditions:** Taylor, "Life," 104. **October 2:** Compare

ABBREVIATIONS, BIBLIOGRAPHIES, AND REFERENCES

ERSj. **old fort:** Welling, 1919 letter. **shared:** "Died"; OPH 104. **Jonathan returns:** See his diary; Ricketts, MB 195, 205-21. **October 1848:** Obituary of J. Holmes, DW 29 (Sept. 1, 1880): 493. "Died" has September. **December 23:** PBSj, also at Dec. 30; compare ERSj. **February 24:** Compare PBSj Mar. 29, 1850. **Eliza Partridge journal:** compare May 28-29. **Marietta:** PBSj; Welling letter, 1919; FGS. She married Job Welling and died in 1905.

XI. **May or June:** On June 27, 1850, Elvira could not attend the gathering commemorating Joseph's death day, held at Zina Young's. Zina writes in her journal, "Alvira Holmes is up north." ZDYj. **two story rock building:** Carter, "Elvira." **Eliza Partridge diary:** Jan. 7. 1855. **Elvira's weaving:** Welling letter, 1919. For weaving as woman's work, see Presendia Huntington chapter, at Dec. 1829, and see below. **Elvira a Relief Society teacher:** Welling letter, 1919. **Jonathan in High Council:** DW 29 (Sept. 1, 1880): 493. **Elvira schoolteaching:** Andrew Jenson, "Cowles, Elvira A. (later Holmes)," BE 4:183. **Phebe:** FGS. She married Job Welling and died in 1939. See FGS; 1851 Census. **Josephine:** FGS. **Emma:** FGS. She married Job Welling and died in 1901. **John Hendricks:** Carter, "Elvira"; Taylor, "Life," 105. **Elvira's daughters' duties:** Taylor, "Life," 105. Compare Ulrich, GW 29: "Instruction at the wheel was part of the almost ritualistic preparation mothers offered their daughters." Ulrich is describing seventeenth- and early eighteenth-century New England women, but we see how the traditions continued in the Far West. And, of course, such traditions far antedated early America. Just as a woman in Ulrich spins and sings (248 n. 31), so when Odysseus meets the sorceress Kirkê, he heard her "singing in a sweet voice as she went up and down a great design on a loom, immortal such as goddesses have, delicate and lovely and glorious their work." *Odyssey* 10:158, tr. Lattimore. See Sarah B. Pomeroy, *Goddesses, Whores, Wives, and Slaves* (New York: Schocken Books, 1975), 30, 40, 199. **February 1859:** PBSj, Feb. 21-Mar. 20. **May 21:** ZDYj. **Nov. 29, 1862:** SEB, s.v. Jonathan Holmes; FGS. **Aug. 3:** PBSj, Aug. 1-3. On August 7 Elvira once again stayed overnight at Patty's.

XII. **Sarah marries Miles:** For Miles and Franklin Weaver, see Larson, DB 179-80; OPH 11:393. 4:76; FGS; Ricketts, MB. Franklin Weaver was born on May 29, 1829, served in the Mormon Battalion, and died on June 12, 1884, at Bennington, Idaho. "Life History of Franklin Weaver," in MS 1164, Lee Library. Before Miles, Sarah had married, then divorced, John Barnard. **May 9:** Taylor, "Life," 105; FGS. For Levirate marriage in the era of Mormon polygamy, see the Agnes Coolbrith chapter at 1842 and Hardy, SC 213. **Marietta marries:** FGS. **Job Welling:** Taylor, "Life," 106. **December 21:** FGS; Taylor, "Life," 106.

XIII. **exposure:** Welling letter, 1919. **Jonathan's conversation:** Taylor, "Life," 107. **death:** "Died." Her Farmington cemetery record, however, gives cause of death as "debility," see GS 924,623.

XIV. **letters to MPE:** Taylor, "Life," 106. **Jonathan's death:** Farmington cemetery record, GS 924,623; it gives cause of death as "heart disease." Obituary of J. Holmes, DW 29 (Sept. 1, 1880): 493; Larson, DB 94. **WWj:** Aug. 19, 1880 (7:588). Sarah Ingersoll Harvey Holmes died on February 27, 1889, in the Bear Lake region, but was buried in Farmington. See Farmington cemetery record.


# REFERENCES TO CHAPTER 25.
## "Tried in Many Ways":
### Rhoda Richards (Smith Young)

JLRR: see Rhoda Richards, "Journal and Letters of Rhoda Richards."
Richards, L. Lula Greene. "Brief Life Sketch of Rhoda Richards." In JLRR.
———. "Aunt Rhoda Richards." DN (Dec. 9, 1916): Sec. 3, p. VII.
Richards, Rhoda. Journals. CA.
———. Letters. CA.

———. "Journal and Letters of Rhoda Richards." Including "Brief Life Sketch of Rhoda Richards," by Lula Greene Richards. Typescript, CA.

Tullidge, William. *Women of Mormondom.* 419-22.

**mourning Ebenezer:** see Dec. 1814, below.

I. **birth:** BOP #129; Ivins 4:280. **Joseph:** Born on March 16, 1762, in Southboro, Worcester, Massachusetts, he died on March 29, 1840, at Richmond, Berkshire, Massachusetts. **Genealogical sources:** FGS; AF; Noall, ID. **Rhoda Howe:** Born on July 8, 1762, in Hopkinton, she died on February 14, 1838, in Richmond, Berkshire, Massachusetts. **Joseph Richards, Jr.:** Born on September 29, 1782, in Framingham, he married Nancy Cody in 1806 and died in 1852 in Westborough, Massachusetts. **Susanna:** Born on August 13, 1786, she died on April 11, 1830, at Richmond, Massachusetts. **Phinehas:** Born on November 15, 1788, he married Wealthy Dewey (1818), and became a Mormon on June 13, 1837. He then married Mary Vail Morse (1846), Martha Allen (1847), Margaret Philips (1848), Emily Northrop (1852), Ann Emerson (1856) and Jane McBride (1871). He died in 1874. **Levi:** was born on December 7, 1790. **Nancy:** Born on November 22, 1792, she married William Peirson in 1819, and was baptized a Mormon on June 2, 1838. She died on July 15, 1852, on the Platte River, near Liberty Pole. (See Kimball HSM 48.) **Hepzibah:** Born on July 28, 1795, she died in 1838 in Far West, Missouri. **Betsey:** Born on May 17, 1797, she died in 1803. **Levi:** Born on April 14, 1799, he became a Mormon in 1836, then married Sarah Griffith in 1843 and Persis Goodall (Young) (previously the wife of Lorenzo Dow Young) in 1846. He died in 1876 in Salt Lake City. **William:** Born on May 2, 1801, he married Sarah Ann Lewis in 1837 and died in 1884 in Alford, Massachusetts. **Willard:** Born on May 2, 1801, he was baptized a Mormon in 1836. He married Jennetta Richards (1838); Nanny Longstroth, Sarah Longstroth and Susannah Liptrot (all 1843); Amelia Elizabeth Peirson and Alice Longstroth (1845); Mary Thompson, Jane Hall, and Ann Rees (Babcock) (1846); Susannah Baylis (1847); and Rhoda Harriet Foss (1851). He became an apostle in 1838. As Brigham Young's first cousin, he associated closely with him in church work, and became second counselor in the First Presidency in 1847. He died in 1854 in Salt Lake City. See Willard Richards journal, CA; Noall, ID; Quinn, MHOP 575; BE 1:53-56; Cook, RP 233. **quote on work:** Tullidge, WM, 419-22, 421. For women's work in nineteenth-century America, see Carol Groneman and Mary Beth Norton, eds., *"To Toil the Livelong Day": America's Women at Work, 1780-1980* (Ithaca, NY: Cornell University Press, 1987); *More Work For Mother: The Ironies of Household Technology from the Open Hearth to the Microwave* (New York: Basic Books, 1983); Stephen Innes, ed., *Work and Labor in Early America* (Chapel Hill: University of North Carolina Press, 1988); Ulrich, GW 13-34, 37-38, 49-50; Cott BW 40-45. See, in this book, chapters on Patty Sessions, Fanny Young, and the journals of Zina Huntington. **sick:** WM 419. For sickness and nineteenth-century women, see Ann Douglas Wood, "'The Fashionable Diseases': Women's Complaints and their Treatment in Nineteenth-Century America," in Mary S. Hartman and Lois Banner, eds., *Clio's Consciousness Raised* (New York: Harper & Row, 1974), 1-22; Regina Morantz, "The Lady and Her Physician," 38-43, id. **works when sick:** Lula Richards, "Aunt Rhoda Richards."

II. **Autobiography:** pp. 1-5.

III. **Autobiography:** Fd 2, p. 1-2. The year dates are corrected a year earlier in pencil; I follow the original dating system, as the Susannah Brigham letter, see below, gives a contemporary date. **for nineteenth-century women and death:** See Louisa Beaman chapter. **about to marry:** Lula Richards, "Aunt Rhoda Richards." **she would not celebrate New Years:** Lula Richards, "Aunt Rhoda Richards." **"Susanna Brigam" to Rhoda:** Mar. 1, 181{4}. Marriott Library, Noall papers, MS 188, box 9, fd 8.

IV. **Autobiography:** Fd 1, p. 5-7. **for revivals and spiritual rebirth:** See Delcena Johnson, Presendia Huntington, and Sarah Cleveland chapters.

V. **Autobiography:** Fd 1, p. 8-13; Fd 2. **1834:** Fd 2.

VI. **Joseph Young:** WM 419-22. **Willard baptized:** HCKj. see Helen Whitney, LI, WE 9

ABBREVIATIONS, BIBLIOGRAPHIES, AND REFERENCES

(May 1, 1881): 178. **1837:** Autobiography, fd 1, 14-18. **baptism:** Autobiography, fd 1, 18, with variations from fd 2 in brackets. WM 419-21. **lives with siblings:** Lula Richards, "Aunt Rhoda Richards."

VII. **Rhoda to Nancy:** Nov. 21, 1842, Marriott Library, Noall papers, MS 188, box 9, fd 8. **in Nauvoo:** See her journal. For her activities, compare WRj, Aug. 17, 1843; Nov. 22; Jan. 10, 1844; Mar. 27. **marriage:** "[Joseph Smith] married to Rhoda Richards and Willard Richards maried to Susan[nah Lee] Liptrot", JSj, Faulring 387. Affidavit, 1:17, by Rhoda Richards. Willard Richards's journal on this day is enigmatic: "1/2. 77-1/2 M.O.S. – . L.L. 91 /, 1. R." Compare Lula Richards, "Aunt Rhoda Richards": "She accepted the whole plan of salvation as it had been revealed to the Prophet Joseph Smith, and later, before the martyrdom of the prophet occurred, she was sealed to him a plural wife, her brother Willard performing the ceremony." **quote:** WM 422. **marriage to Brigham:** Quinn, MHOP 607, compare the Nauvoo Temple marriage. **Willard Richards journal,** CA; also in Noall papers, Marriott Library. **endowment:** NTER; Gregory Knight, ed., "Journal of Thomas Bullock," BYUSt 31 (1991): 42. **proxy marriage:** BOP #129; SAd 511.

VIII. **Mary Haskin Parkins Richards:** See Maurine Carr Ward, *Winter Quarters, The 1846-1848 Life Writings of Mary Haskin Parker Richards* (Logan: Utah State University Press, 1996), 13, 64, 69, 75, 76, 87 (twice), 151, 164, 191, 206. **Levi Willard:** Lula Richards, "Brief Life Sketch," 1. **Rhoda to Nancy Richards:** Marriott Library, Noall papers, MS 188, 9, fd 8. Compare JLRR.

IX. **wagon home:** For children's clothes catching on fire, see Jeffrey, *Frontier Women* 40. **March 10, 1851:** ZDYj, CA. **November 23, 1851 letter:** JLRR 95-1. **other letters:** JLRR.

X. **September 29, 1854:** PBSj. There was a Rhoda Foss Richards, one of Willard's plural wives, however, so Patty may refer to another Rhoda Richards, here and below. Rhoda also had at least one niece named Rhoda. **September 11, 1871:** Endowment House Records, as cited in Ivins 4:280. **EBWj:** at the dates mentioned. **working quotes:** WM 422. **lives at home of Levi Willard:** Lula Richards, "Aunt Rhoda Richards."

XI. **happy new year:** Lula Richards, "Brief Life Sketch," 3. **death:** Lula Richards journal, Jan. 17, 1879; quoted in JLRR p. 99. **Obituary:** [Anon.], DEN 12 (Jan. 18, 1879): p. 3.

# REFERENCES TO CHAPTER 26.
*"Quiet, Unassuming, Faithful":*
*Desdemona Catlin Wadsworth Fullmer*
*(Smith Benson Mclane)*

Alder, Donald Benson, and Elsie L. Alder. *The Benson Family*. Salt Lake City: Mountain States Bindery, 1979. 139-42.
Backman, *Profile* 105.
Evans, John Henry, and Minnie Egan Anderson. *Ezra Taft Benson, Pioneer-Statesman-Saint*. Salt Lake City: Deseret News Press, 1947.
Fullmer, David. Autobiography. Lee Library.
Fullmer, Desdemona. Autobiography. CA.
Jenson, Andrew. "Fullmer, Desdemona Wadsworth." HR 6:235.
Tullidge, Edward. *Tullidge's Histories*. Salt Lake City: Juvenile Instructor, 1889. 112-17, an interview with and biography of Almon Fullmer.

**early dreams:** Autobiography.

I. **birthdate:** BOP #88b; NTER. **birthplace:** FGS; Jenson, FDW; compare Cook, RP 120n. 4. **Peter:** was born in 1774 in Reading, Berkshire, Pennsylvania, and died in 1857. See interview with Almon, below, and FGS. **Susannah Zerfass:** was born in 1773 in

Whitehall, Northhampton, Pennsylvania. She married Peter in 1802 and died in 1856. **David:** Born on July 7, 1803, in Chillesquaque, Northumberland, Pennsylvania, he pursued farming, schoolteaching, and "merchandising" in his later life. After being baptized in 1836, he sat in the Nauvoo High Council and the Council of the Fifty. Later, in Utah, he became a member of Deseret legislature, and served as acting president of Salt Lake Stake from 1852 to 1856. He married Rhoda Ann Marvin (1831), Sarah Sophronia Oysterbanks (1845), and Margaret Phillips (1846). He died in 1879 in Salt Lake City. See "A brief sketch of the life of David E. Fullmer," p. 38-43 in CA MS 939; Autobiography of David Fullmer, typescript at Lee Library; BE 1:289-91; Cook, RP 257-58; HStj, OMF index; Quinn, MHOP 529. **Mary:** Born on July 17, 1805, in Huntington (or in Bucks County, Pennsylvania), she married Erastus Fellows ca. 1829-31, was baptized by brother Almon in approximately 1841 (Almon, in Tullidge, TH 113) and died in 1874 in Pittsburgh, Van Buren, Iowa. **John Solomon:** Born on July 21, 1807, he married Mary Ann Price (1837), Olive Amanda Smith (1846), and Sarah Ann Stevenson (1856). He was baptized in 1839, served as a secretary to Joseph Smith, and worked for him in his store. An officer in the Nauvoo Legion, he accompanied Joseph to Carthage, and was a member of the Council of the Fifty (Quinn, MHOP 530). He died in 1883 in Springville, Utah. See an autobiography in John Solomon Fullmer, Letterbook, CA, p. 311; Hosea Stout journal, OMF index; ECIF; John S. Fullmer to Wilford Woodruff, October 18, 1881, CA. **Charlotte:** Born on January 21, 1812, she married Jonathan Ferris in 1838 and died in 1871 in Van Buren County, Iowa. **Louisiana:** Born on June 3, 1814, she married John Hiskey in 1836 and died in 1870. **Almon Linus:** Born on September 7, 1816, he married Sarah Ann Follett (1843), Rachel Neyman (1852) and Tryphena Follett, then died in 1890 in Providence, Cache, Utah. See Tullidge, *Tullidge's Histories,* 112-17. **Fullmers Methodist:** Almon, in Tullidge 112. **John Solomon Fullmer to Desdemona Fullmer:** Feb. 14, 1837, in J. S. Fullmer Letterbook, MS 117, CA. **Joseph Smith's death prophecies:** See the story of Robert Thompson in Oliver Huntington's journal. He was a clerk of Joseph, and one day Joseph said to him, "Robert I want you to go and get on a bust—Go and get drunk and have a good Spree, if you dont you will die." Thompson, however, was "a very pious exemplary man & never guilty of such an impropriety" so he ignored the prophet's warning. "In less than 2 weeks he was dead and buried." OHj, book 13, no page numbers. This section of Huntington's journal collects many similar stories. See also a warning to Philo Dibble to change his place of residence or die, Philo Dibble, "Philo Dibble's Narrative," *Early Scenes in Church History* (Salt Lake City: Juvenile Instructor Office, 1882); repr. in *Four Faith Promoting Classics* (Salt Lake City: Bookcraft, 1968), 93. See also Lucy Walker chapter, John Walker's mission call in 1842; Mary Elizabeth Rollins chapter at July 1842. **early spiritual experiences:** Autobiography.

II. **Fullmers in Ohio:** Almon, in Tullidge 112-13. **David to Richland, Ohio:** BE 1:289. **baptisms:** HR 6:235 (John P. Greene was a brother-in-law of Brigham Young); BE 1:289. **David to Kirtland:** BE 1:289. **David made elder:** KEQR 38-39. Compare BE 1:289. **blessing:** PBI 2.188; 1:113; Backman, *Profile* 105. **Kirtland apostasy:** Desdemona's Autobiography. Compare SLDS 111-14; Parkin *Conflict at Kirtland*; Fanny Alger and Marinda Hyde chapters.

III. **move to Missouri:** Autobiography; David Fullmer Autobiography; KEQR; BE 1:289. **David to Davies County:** BE 1:289-90. **mobbings:** Autobiography. **Haun's mill:** HR 6:235. **move to Illinois:** Autobiography.

IV. **John's baptism:** AF. **living in Smith home:** See Nauvoo Ward Census, 4th Ward, p. 9. **Relief Society:** RS Min., pp. 6, 33. **move in with Claytons:** WCj, May 13, 1843. **marriage:** According to her affidavit, see SAB 1:32; 4:32 (Bachman, #58). Heber Kimball was present. However, as is often the case with Joseph's plural marriages, there are conflicting dates for the marriage. According to a William Clayton affidavit (in HR 6:225), Joseph told him, shortly after February 1843, that he was married to Desdemona already. Though Clayton does not give the exact date of this conversation with Joseph, context makes it clear. Jenson lists the date of marriage as 1842, HR 6:234-35. **dream of** poisoning: It should be borne in mind that the Autobiography was written in 1868, when Emma was not a friend to the Utah Mormons. sewing: RS Min., July 7, 1843, p. 95. Launius, *Red Brick Store* 71. On December 16, 1843, Desdemona's parents were sealed for time and eternity by Hyrum Smith. Almon, in Tullidge 112. Desdemona v. Clayton: See WCj, IC, p. 125, note to Jan. 29, 1844. Desdemona's parents in Nauvoo: BE 1:290. David Fullmer's mission: Norton Jacob journal, Lee Library, p. 7. Almon and John to Carthage: Almon, in Tullidge 113.

V. Fullmer in council: WCj; Quinn, MHOP 529. David's first plural wives: HCKj, Dec. 7, 1845: "I went to David Fulmers and Sealled two Sisters to him fore time and Eternity. Gave some council and then returned to the Temple." We know the name of only one of these wives, Sarah Oysterbanks, though it is possible that Margaret Phillips was the other, since she married him in the temple soon after. endowment: NTER. marriage to Benson: BOP #88; SAd 181. Benson: Cook, RP 300; AF; Evans, *Ezra Taft Benson*; Alder, *Benson Family* 13-27B; Quinn, MHOP 538. "with my two wives": Ezra T. Benson, Autobiographical sketch, quoted in Evans, ETB 110. Ezra a counselor at Mt. Pisgah: Cook, RP; Evans, ETB 116. Ezra's call to apostleship: Alder, *Benson Family* 20; Evans, ETB 125-127. Perry: Cook, RP 300. Barton: Quinn, MHOP 538. Benson as "pioneer": Alder, *Benson Family* 21; Evans, ETB 154. 1848 mission: Evans, ETB 184-86. July trip: Evans, ETB 189. Desdemona's trip to Utah: Jenson 6:235; HTW 9:486; Autobiography. Compare David Fullmer, Autobiography. Benson's 1849 trip to Salt Lake: Alder, *Benson Family* 21; Evans, ETB 190-91.

VI. first year: For the scarcity of food in this winter, see the Louisa Beaman chapter. 1850 Census: p. 59(30). The other women were Permelia, 41, Adeline, 39, and Alice, 35. Perhaps this Alice is Eliza Perry. Olive Knight: See AF. Patty Sessions: "Took sister Fulmer through a course of medicine," PBSj, September 23, 1851. There is no way of knowing which Sister Fulmer this is, but at least it shows that the Fullmer family was in Salt Lake by this time. Patty visited "sister Fulmer" again on October 4. Compare Mar. 9, 1852. On June 26, 1852, Desdemona received a patriarchal blessing from John Smith in Salt Lake City. PBI 12:157, No. 357; ECIF. divorce: Divorce Certificate, in Brigham Young collection, MS 1234, box 67, CA. It is signed by "Desdemona Smith Benson" as well as by Ezra and witnesses. This divorce certificate shows clearly that a proxy sealing for time in the Nauvoo temple was considered a marriage. Ira Ames journal: At 1853, MS 6055, CA. marriage and child: Alder, *Benson Family* 140; Quinn, MHOP 538. Morrisites: See C. LeRoy Anderson, *For Christ Will Come Tomorrow: the Saga of the Morrisites* (Logan: Utah State University Press, 1981).

VII. parents' deaths: AF. lives with David: Alder, *Benson Family* 140, compare BE. 6th Ward: Jenson, HR 6:235. sealing of Charlotte and Hyrum Smith: Endowment House Record, as cited in Ivins 4:280. deaths of Mary and David: AF. the will: quoted in Alder, *Benson Family* 141. John Solomon: AF. death: Jenson, HR 6:235; Alder, *Benson Family*. "epitaph": HR 6:235.

## REFERENCES TO CHAPTER 27.
### Youthful Supplication:
### Olive Grey Frost (Smith Young)

Pratt, Mary Ann. "Frost, (Olive Grey)." In Jenson, HR 6:234-35.
Winters, Mary Ann Stearns. "Mothers in Israel." *Relief Society Magazine* 3 (Aug. 1916): 423-32; 3 (Oct. 1916): 580-81; etc.; last installment, 4 (Aug. 1917): 425-36.

prayer in grove: Pratt, "Frost, (Olive Grey)."

I. Olive's birthdate: Pratt, "Frost, (Olive Grey)," 234; FGS. Aaron: was born on July 14, 1779. His death date is given as March 13, 1861, in Winters, "Mothers in Israel," 4 (Aug. 1917): 429. AF has October 19, 1860. Susannah: was born in 1780 and died in 1861. FGS has Bennett as her last name. Mary Ann: Family Record of Parley P. Pratt, USHS; Obituary of Mary Ann, see below (which has her born in Groton). Winters has her born in Bethel. **Lidania:** Born on October 10, 1802, she married Thatcher York and died in 1830. **Aaron Jr.:** Born on March 10, 1804, he died on October 15 of the same year. **Milton:** was born on February 28, 1805, and died in 1825. **Lucretia:** Born on November 24, 1806, she married Samuel Bean and died in 1887. See Parley P. Pratt, *Autobiography* 270-71. **Orange Clark:** born on February 12, 1812, he married Cyrene Hastings and Mary Hastings, and died in 1885. **Naomi Frost:** Born on January 23, 1814, she died in 1832. **Sophronia Gray:** Born on October 3, 1818, she died in 1844 in Nauvoo. **Nehemiah:** was born on March 4, 1821 and died in 1838. **Huldah:** was born on February/March 24, 1825 and died in 1856.

II. **Orange:** Winters, "Mothers," 427. **Mary Ann baptized:** See Winters for the date of baptism. Mary Ann herself gave the date of her baptism as spring 1835, see Tullidge, WM 406; her obituary also gives the year 1835. "Records," 106 gives the later date, August 1836. Winters's dating is supported by Brigham Young's journal, compare Arrington, BY 55-56. **heart palpitations:** Winters, "Mothers," 427. **Mary Ann in Kirtland:** BYj, compare Brigham Young History. **Mary Ann's marriage to Pratt:** *Messenger and Advocate* 3 (May 1837): 512; Family Record of Parley P. Pratt. Compare Pratt, *Autobiography* 174 which gives the date May 9 for the marriage.

III. **Olive's baptism:** Pratt, "Frost, (Olive Grey)." Perrigrine Sessions journal, Oct. 7, 28 (p. B-19). **healing Lucy:** PGSj, Dec. 23, 1839 (p. B-22). **return to Aaron's:** PGSj, 1840: "[March] (23) to Newry to Joel Fosters (24) to Aaron Frosts." (p. B-26)

IV. **Pratts to east:** *Autobiography*, 325. Compare Winters, "Mothers," 21. **Olive in England:** Pratt, "Frost, (Olive Grey)" 235. Compare *Autobiography*, 343. **Pratts in Manchester:** Feb. 7, 1841, BYj. **back to America:** *Autobiography*, 361. **letter to Star:** *Autobiography*, 362; "Correspondence. From P. P. Pratt," MSt 3 (Apr. 1843): 206-08. I quote from the latter. Winters, "Mothers," remembers the house was "part of the warehouse at the landing," 575. For the chronology of the trip up the Mississippi, see 576-77. **Susan:** AF. Winters, "Mothers," 577, gives the birthdate as April 5.

V. **meeting Joseph at landing:** *Autobiography*, 366; JSj, Faulring 360; Pratt, "Frost, (Olive Grey)" 235; Winters, "Mothers," 577. **Eliza:** ERSj. **Olive's marriage to Joseph:** Pratt, "Frost, (Olive Grey)" 235; compare HR 6:234. **Mary Ann and polygamy:** On June 13, 1843, Joseph Smith taught Parley P. Pratt the principle of polygamy and "appointed" a wife for him, Elizabeth Brotherton, a friend from England who probably had come back to America with the Pratts. Parley was sealed to Elizabeth on June 24. Parley P. Pratt, Family Record, in Belinda Marden Pratt journal, microfilm of holograph, USHS. "Sister Pratt has been rageing against these things [polygamy, and Parley's first plural marriage], she told me her self that the devel had been in her," wrote Vilate Kimball to Heber C. Kimball on June 27. However, Vilate continued, "[the devil had been in her] until within a few days past, she said the Lord had shown her it was all right. She wants Parley to go ahead, says she will do all in her power to help him." Vilate Kimball to Heber Kimball, June 27, 1843, in Winslow Whitney Smith Papers, box 5, fd 2, CA. Vilate is the source for "appoint." Compare Ehat, JSI 68. Yet apparently when Parley began taking plural wives without informing Mary Ann of them, she once again became very angry. Reva Stanley, *The Archer of Paradise* (Caldwell, ID: Caxton Printers, 1937), 189. According to Stanley, when Mary Ann discovered that Belinda Marden, one of Pratt's plural wives she had not been told about, was pregnant, she left Pratt and did not go west with him. This is a very brief overview of a complex marriage history filled with fragmentary and contradictory evidence. **Mary Ann's marriage to Smith:** SAd 513, 449; Parley P. Pratt Family Record, Mar. 11, 1850. Compare Bachman, "A Study," 111, who concludes that the marriage was entirely posthumous. Quinn agrees, MHOP 399. Pratt family historian, Robert Steven Pratt, however, suspects a marriage to Joseph Smith while he lived, personal communication.

VI. **Pratt house:** Winters, "Mothers," 579. **visit to Patty:** Wells, "Patty Sessions," WE 13 (Nov. 15, 1884): 95. **Relief Society:** Pratt, "Frost, (Olive Grey)," 235. **concern for sick:** RS Min., 107; 111. **Sophronia:** A month later, on February 18, 1844, death claimed another close family member of Olive and Mary—sister Sophronia, who was then twenty-five. "Died," *Nauvoo Neighbor* 2 (May 29, 1844): third page (227). **Olive and Joseph's death:** Mary Ettie Smith, *Fifteen Years Among the Mormons*, 36.

VII. **marriage to Brigham:** BYj, Nov. 7, 1844, compare Johnson DDW; Quinn, MHOP 607; Pratt, "Frost, (Olive Grey) " 235, 234. Susa Gates, and Mabel Sanborn, "Brigham Young Genealogy," UGHM 11 (1920): 49-55, 54, give the date February 1845 for the marriage. Compare James H. Crockwell, *Pictures and Biographies of Brigham and His Wives* (Salt Lake City: Crockwell, n.d.) 26. **death:** Pratt, "Frost, (Olive Grey)" 235; date in Gates/Sanborn 54.

## REFERENCES TO CHAPTER 28.
### Aunt Melissa:
### Melissa Lott (Smith Bernhisel Willes)

[Carter, Kate]. "Melissa Lott Willes." OPH 19:259-60.

Jenson, Andrew. "Willes, (Malissa Lott)." HR 5:119.

———. "Ira Willes." BE 4:767.

Launius, Roger D. *Joseph Smith III, Pragmatic Prophet*. Urbana: University of Illinois Press, 1988. 204-205.

*Lehi Centennial History*. Lehi, UT: Free Press, 1950. 311.

Van Wagoner, Richard S. *Lehi, Portraits of a Utah Town*. Lehi: Lehi City Corp., 1990.

———. "Women's role in history often forgotten." *Lehi Free Press* (Mar. 1, 1995): 1, 4.

Vance, Rhea Lott, ed. *Descendants of Cornelius Peter Lott, 1798-1972*. [Salt Lake City]: n.p., [1972].

**Melissa's version:** Affidavit, Aug. 4, 1893, in Bailey, "Emma Hale," 98-100; compare Temple Lot transcript, 2:93-108, esp. 97-98, 107-108. Published version, p. 316. **Joseph Smith III:** Smith, "Memoirs," *Saints' Herald* 83 (Apr. 28, 1936): 530; (May 5, 1936), 559. *The Memoirs of President Joseph Smith III*, ed. Richard P. Howard (Independence, MO: Herald Publishing House, 1979), 244-46; Smith, *Joseph Smith III and the Restoration* 371-77; Diary, RLDS Archives, P2 fd 113, Oct. 20, 1885 ("Went and called on Mrs Ira Willis nee Lott. Had a chat about sealing father children &c Mary, Melissa & Alzina all assure me that father had no children [polygamously]"). Temple Lot Case, 489-90; Launius, *Joseph Smith III* 204-5; Charles Millard Turner, "Joseph Smith III and the Mormons in Utah," Ph.D. diss., Graduate Theological Union at Berkeley, 1985, 368-71.

I. **Melissa's birth:** SAd 779. **Cornelius:** was born on September 22/27, 1798, in New York City. For his life, see Esshom 1011; Vance, *Descendants* 2-16; Jessee 2:566; HStj, OMF 1:65-66 and index. All dates are from Lott Family Bible, CA, FGS and AF. **Permelia:** Born on December 15, 1805, in Bridgewater, Susquehannah, Pennsylvania, she died in 1882. **John Smiley:** Born on March 24, 1826, he married Mary Ann Faucett (1846), Docia Molen (1862), and Clarissa Cemantha Rappleye, and died in 1894 in Provo, Utah. **Mary Elizabeth:** Born on November 9, 1827, she married Abraham Losee (1848) and died in 1888. **Almira Henrietta:** Born on December 15, 1829, she married John Riggs Murdock (1849) and died in 1878 in Beaver City, Beaver, Utah. **Permelia Jane:** Born on October 2, 1832, she married Abram Hatch (1852), and died in 1880, in Heber City, Wasatch, Utah. **Cornelius baptized:** Cook KEQR, appendix. **Lucinda Alzina:** Born on March 4, 1834, she married William S.S. Willes (the brother of Ira Willes) in 1852, and died in 1910 in Lehi. **Harriet Amanda:** Born on March 30, 1836, she died in 1847 at Winter Quarters. **elder's license:** Cook KEQR, appendix. **anointing:** KEQR at the date. **Lott and Safety society:** Vance, *Descendants* 4. **Melissa's baptism:** Jenson, HR 5:119. **Joseph Darrow:** died in 1847, at Winter Quarters.

II. **Lotts near Haun's mill:** Vance, *Descendants* 7. **Lott in Missouri:** "Celebration of the

4th of July," EJ 1 (4) (Aug. 1838): 60; Johnson, MLR 38. **Captain:** Johnson, MLR 38, compare 44. For Lott as a Danite, see also Reed Peck testimony, in *Document Containing the Correspondence, Orders &c in Relation to the Disturbances with the Mormons* (Fayette, MO: Boon's Lick Democrat, 1841), 117; Quinn, MHOP 482, 97-98. **Stout:** HStj, July 6, 1850, OMF 2:373.

III. **Nauvoo:** In the Temple Lot Case, in 1892, Melissa testified, "After we were driven out of Missouri I was in Pike County, Ill., for a while, stayed there until I went to Nauvoo." **farm:** Jenson, HR 5:119. **June 6:** JSj, Jessee 2:389. **a month later:** July 16, Jessee 2:400. **bodyguard:** JSj, Faulring 484; Jessee 2:566. **Peter Lyman Lott:** married Sariah Hannah Snow in 1862 and died in 1906 in Lehi. **Melissa at Joseph's house:** OPH 19:259. **Joseph III:** Smith, *Joseph Smith III and the Restoration*, 35. "Memoirs of President Joseph Smith," *Saints Herald* 81 (Dec. 18, 1934): 1614. **June 29:** ERSj. **September 20, 1843:** Lott family Bible, CA: "Corneli P Lott maried to Permelia Darrow for time and Eternaty September the 20: 1843 By Presadent Hyrum Smith with seal of Presadent Joseph Smith. Sept the 20 C.P. Lott and Permelia Lott gave their Dauter Malisa to wife [line blotted out, apparently]"; Jenson, HR 6:234, 5:119. **Affidavit:** BAOPM 72, 55 (1905 ed. 87 (the 1869 affidavit), 74, 91); SAB 1:23; 4:23. JSj, Faulring 415. In the Temple Lot Case testimony, 314, Melissa gave September 27 as the date of marriage. For Hyrum, Temple Lot transcript, 2:93. **vows:** Temple Lot Case 314; compare Sarah Ann Whitney chapter; Bennett, HS 224; Foster, RS 172. The ceremony of eternal marriage, used for many plural marriages, was printed by Orson Pratt, see "Celestial Marriage," *The Seer* 1 (Feb. 1853): 31-32; also printed in "Celestial Marriage in Deseret," MSt 15 (Apr. 2, 1853): 214-16. **time and eternity:** Temple Lot Case 315. Transcript, 105: "Did you ever room with Joseph Smith as his wife? Yes sir. Q-At what place? ... The Nauvoo Mansion ... room number one." 106: "Now at the times you roomed with him, did you cohabit with him as his wife? A-Yes sir." Benjamin Johnson also remembered her living in the Mansion House, 1904 affidavit, BAOPM 91. **very deed:** Affidavit of Melissa Willes, Aug. 3, 1893, in Raymond Bailey, "Emma Hale," 98-100; compare Temple Lot Case (transcript) 98, 105; Foster, RS 156. According to R.C. Evans, *Forty Years in the Mormon Church* (Shreveport, LA: Lambert Book House, 1976; orig. 1920), 38, Melissa said that she had sexual relations with Joseph only once. "When in Salt Lake City I called at the residence of Patriarch John Smith, brother of Joseph F. Smith, and son of Hyrum Smith, nephew of the original prophet Joseph Smith, and while there his wife, Helen, told me, among many other interesting things, that 'Melissa Lott told me that when a girl she sewed for Emma Smith and took care of the children. Joseph had to pass through her room to go to Emma's room. She said Joseph never had sexual intercourse with her but once and that was in the daytime, saying he desired her to have a child by him. She was barefooted and ironing when Joseph came in, and the ceremony was performed in the presence of her parents.'" This is thirdhand and late, but should at least be considered. **secret:** Temple Lot case 314. **winter of 1843/44:** Jenson, HR 5:119. **Cornelius and Permelia sealed:** Lott family Bible, CA. **endowed:** Ehat, JSI 103. **fullness of priesthood:** WWj, 2:348. **council of Fifty:** Quinn, CF appendix; Ehat, JSI 103. **Cornelius Jr.:** Another Lott child, Cornelius Carlos, was born on September 30, at Nauvoo. He died on January 6, 1845.

IV. **Melissa with Emma:** Jenson, HR 5:119. **James Monroe:** Diary, typescript, Illinois Historical Society; also at USHS. May 17, 27-29, 1845. **Lotts' endowment in temple:** HC 7:544. **Melissa endowed:** NTER. **marriage to Bernhisel/Smith:** SAd 513, 181. **Bernhisel:** He came to Utah in 1847-48, represented Utah in Congress from 1849 to 1863, and died on September 28, 1881. See Scrapbook of John Milton Bernhisel, USHS, microfilm; Gwynn Barrett, "John M. Bernhisel: Mormon Elder in Congress," Ph.D. diss., Brigham Young University, 1968; id., "John M. Bernhisel," UHQ 36 (Spring 1968): 143-67; id., "Delegate John M. Bernhisel, Salt Lake Physician following the Civil War," UHQ 50 (Fall 1982): 354-60; Orson Whitney, *History of Utah* 4:663-66; BE 1:723-24; Jessee 2:526. **eleven deceased women:** JSj, Oct. 26, 1843 (recorded July 29, 1868), Faulring 424; John M. Bernhisel, letter file, 1846-

1850, CA. The names are listed in a note in Bernhisel's hand. As cited in Barrett, JMB, diss., 46-47. One of the women was Bernhisel's sister; four of them were aunts; and one was Maria Lawrence (not the Maria Lawrence married by Joseph Smith), referred to as "intimate friend." **January 20:** SAd 167. The sealings to Haight and Ransom were later canceled by Wilford Woodruff and Heber J. Grant, respectively. **February 3:** SAd 177. **adopted to Joseph:** BOP #153; SAd 185: Bernhisel "this day came to the sacred Alter, in the upper room of the 'House of the Lord' ... and thereupon gave himself to Prest. Joseph Smith (martyred) to be^come his son by the law of adoption, and to become a legal heir to all the blessings bestowed upon Joseph Smith pertaining to exaltations, even to the eternal Godhead." This is a good example of how sealing to Joseph Smith was linked to exaltation (deification) in Nauvoo theology, see the Helen Mar Kimball chapter, at her marriage to Joseph Smith. On the one hand, the chosen one sealed to Joseph would feel a part of an innermost secret sacrality; on the other, it seems an elitist view of salvation, in that it does not put central emphasis on ethics or social justice.

V. **Permelia in Winter Quarters:** ERSj, just before Aug. 30, 1846; undated, circa mid-Sept. 1846; Feb. 2, 1847. **Cornelius adds two wives:** SAd 741. **Cornelius on high council:** Vance, *Descendants* 13. **Melissa crosses plains:** Jenson, HR 5:119. **left Winter Quarters:** Joseph Fielding journal, CA, June 4. **captain:** HCKj. **overland journey:** other accounts of the 1848 journey can be found in HCKj; Mary F. Smith, "True Pioneer Stories," *Young Woman's Journal* 30 (Feb. 1919): 165, 171; diary of Joseph Fielding, summer 1848, CA; reminiscences of Joseph F. Smith, who has Lott playing the part of the unsympathetic captain when Mary Fielding Smith's ox nearly failed, see Joseph Fielding Smith, *Life of Joseph F. Smith* (Salt Lake City: Deseret News, 1938), 150. **Benjamin:** married Mary Abigail Evans in 1869, and died in 1923 in Lehi. **first house:** *Lehi Centennial History* 276; Vance, *Descendants* 14. **Cornelius manages church farm:** Vance, *Descendants* 16. **marriage to Willes:** SAd 779, compare Temple Lot Case; Jenson, HR 5:119. **She ... states:** OPH 19:259-60. **Ira's birthdate:** SAd 75 (Jan. 21, 1812). **Woodruff:** WWj, July 7, 1862 (6:65). Compare Ira's diaries, 1841-48, CA, MS 2014; Ricketts, MB 199-201; Kenneth Davies, *Mormon Gold* (Salt Lake City: Olympus, 1984), 24, 32, 46, 96, 100, 108. **"Best Guide":** is now in the Yosemite Museum, see Irene D. Paden, ed., "The Ira J. Willis Guide to the Gold Mines," *California Historical Quarterly* 32 (1953): 193-207. **JSIII's description of Ira:** Smith, *Joseph Smith III and the Restoration* 36, 371. **Ira Pratt:** died in 1869. **commemoration:** ZDYj, June 27, 1850. **death of Cornelius Lott:** ZDYj; HStj, OMF 2:373. Compare Vance, *Descendants* 16, who has Lott dying of "dissentary, a bowel disease."

VI. **Lotts to Lehi:** Van Wagoner, *Lehi* 3. **Willises joins them:** *Lehi Centennial Hist.* 19. Compare Van Wagoner, *Lehi* 3. The Shirts group lived "at the south end of present-day Fifth West." The main settlement was at "Dry Creek," northwest of the present Lehi Rodeo Grounds; this is "Evansville," named after the first bishop, David Evans. **Ira farms:** *Lehi Centennial History*, 310. **coyotes:** Vance, *Descendants* 20. **Achsah:** Vance, *Descendants* 494. The name is Achiah in a death record, see below. **Walker War:** Van Wagoner, *Lehi* 4-5; SLDS 271. **Cornelius Peter:** FGS, compare AF (Cornelius John); Vance, *Descendants* 494. **Achsah's death:** Record of Deaths in SLC, #640. "Willis, Achiah P." **S.E. to Ira:** CA, MS 7284, Ira Willes correspondence. **Polly:** Vance, *Descendants* 494, 91. She died in 1886/7. **Ira marries Naomi:** SAd 75. By her second husband, Henry Wheelock, Naomi had some eleven children. **Lyman:** married Sarah Ann Munns in 1881 and died in 1926. Vance, *Descendants* 505. **Stephen Eleazer:** married Sophia Clark and Milida Hill (1909), and died in 1925. FGS; Vance, *Descendants* 517. **Sarah:** married Albert Mulliner in 1885 and died in 1955. Vance, *Descendants* 494, 524.

VII. **accident:** This reconstruction of the death of Ira and Cornelius Willes is dependent on Wilford Woodruff, who wrote that Ira and Cornelius "were turned over together on a load of wood in the Creek near Lehi. The waggon turned bottom side upwards & the men were rolled up in their blankets face downwards in the Creek with the wood on top of them. This was on Saturday night. Quite dark. The oxen Came unhitched & went h[ome. They (the oxen) were] found at the door in the morning. The bodies were found sunday Morning." WWj, 6:139; Van Wagoner, *Lehi* 75. **bodies viewed:** WWj, 6:140.

**III.** **Ira died:** FGS. **Lehi Relief Society:** Vance, *Descendants* 29. **marriages:** See Vance, *Descendants* 494, 524, and at relevant names.

**IX.** **Polly:** See Vance, *Descendants* 494. **Relief Society:** Jenson, HR 5:119. **speaks in tongues:** Diary of Francis W. Kirkham, Mar. 9, 1896, as quoted in Van Wagoner, WR. **death:** "Melissa Lott Smith Willis," obituary in DEN 31 (July 14, 1898): p. 2. "A Widow of the Prophet Joseph Smith Died at Lehi Yesterday. Word was received by the 'News' this afternoon that Sister Melissa Lott Smith Willis died at Lehi yesterday. The funeral services will be held at the Lehi meeting house tomorrow afternoon at 2 o'clock, the remains afterward being shipped to Salt Lake on the Rio Grande Western train which arrives here at 5:25 p.m. and interment will be made in the city cemetery here. All friends of the deceased are invited to either attend the services at Lehi or at the cemetery here. Sister Smith was a widow of the Prophet Joseph Smith." See also an obituary in *Lehi Banner* (July 19, 1898), as cited in Van Wagoner WR.

# REFERENCES TO CHAPTER 29.
## Outline of a Shadow:
## Nancy Maria Winchester (Smith Kimball Arnold)

**Marriage to Heber:** HCKj, CA; compare HCK 315.

**I.** **Maria's birth:** HCK/Clayton journal, Bk 93; BOP #154 have her born on August 10 in New York. FGS has her born in Pennsylvania. Jenson, HR 6:234, incorrectly has her as the daughter of Benjamin Winchester. **Stephen:** was born on May 8, 1795, in Vershire, Orange, Vermont. He married Nancy in 1816, and died on January 1, 1873, in Salt Lake City. See HCK/Clayton journal, Bk 93; Cheryl Harmon Bean, "LDS Baptisms in Erie County, Pennsylvania 1831-1833," *The Nauvoo Journal* 5 (Fall 1993): 3-44, 42; Obituary, DN, quoted in Bean, "LDS Baptisms," 42; BE 4:692; Backman, *Profile*, 78. **Nancy:** was born on May 21, 1795, in Argyle, Washington, New York, and died in November 21, 1878, in Murray, Utah. See HCK/Clayton journal, Bk 93; Bean, "LDS Baptisms," 42. **Benjamin:** Born on August 6, 1817, he was baptized in 1833, and in 1834 served in Zion's camp. He married Maria Stone in 1840. Excommunicated in 1844 in Nauvoo, in part because of his vehement opposition to polygamy, he became an apostle in Sidney Rigdon's Church of Christ, but soon left the Rigdon faction. He died at Council Bluffs on January 25, 1901. See Benjamin Winchester collection, Lee Library, MS 815; Benjamin Winchester, "Primitive Mormonism," *Salt Lake Tribune* (Sept. 22, 1889): p. 2; David J. Whittaker, "East of Nauvoo: Benjamin Winchester and the Early Mormon Church," JMH 21 (Fall 1995): 31-83; BE 4:692; Backman, *Profile*, 78; Bean, "LDS Baptisms," 41; David J. Whittaker, "Early Mormon Pamphleteering," Ph.D. diss., Brigham Young University, 1982, 139-235; KEQR 108. **Stephen Jr.:** Born on September 21, 1820, he married Mary Pearsons/Parson, and died in 1851. See HCK/Clayton journal, Bk 93 at Dec. 18, 1845; FGS. **Alexander:** Born on May 25, 1825, he died in 1845. **James Case:** Born on June 19, 1831, he crossed the plains in 1849, married Elizabeth Jane Crimson in 1852, and died in 1918 in Murray, Utah. Bean, "LDS Baptisms," 42. **John Parley:** died on August 5, 1843. **conversion:** Evan Greene journal, CA, Jan. 27, 1833, Feb. 2; Mar. 21; JH for the same dates; see also Greene journal, Mar. 12, 15. Compare Bean, "LDS Baptisms" 5-6; V. Alan Curtis, "Missionary Activities and Church Organizations in Pennsylvania, 1830-1840," Master's thesis, Brigham Young University, 1976, 38. **Stephen ordained a teacher:** Greene wrote, "This afternoon we had a Church meeting to organise the Church Bro. John ordaned Bro. Dinsey to Priest and Winchester Teacher and Sagers Deacon to watch over this church in the fear of the Lord." **Orson Pratt and Johnson visit:** Bean, "LDS Baptisms," 42. **to Kirt-**

**land:** BE 4:692. However, the obituary of Stephen Winchester, in Bean, "LDS Baptisms," 42, gives the date of the move as late 1833. **Zion's Camp:** James Bradley, *Zion's Camp 1834* (Logan, UT: J.T. Bradley, 1990), Appendix; Backman, *A Profile* 93-94; Roger Launius, *Zion's Camp* (Independence, MO: Herald House, 1984), 173. **summer of 1834:** Lyman Wight, "History," MSt 27 (1865): 456. **Stephen ordained a priest:** FWR 100. **Feb. 28:** HC 2:203. **Benjamin ordained elder:** KEQR 3. **Nancy's baptism in Kirtland:** Tinney, RF 323. **move to Missouri:** Cook, see KEQR 108. **lived near Far West:** HC 3:171. **friends with Kimballs in Kirtland and Missouri:** Helen Mar Whitney, SIN, WE 11 (Apr. 15, 1883): 170; 10 (July 15, 1881): 26. **farm:** Redress Petition, compare Bean, "LDS Baptisms" 42. **Stephen a high councilor:** FWR 151. **Stephen at Battle of Crooked River:** Quinn, MHOP 485. **Patten to Winchester home:** HC 3:171. *Journal of Heber C. Kimball* (Nauvoo, IL: Robinson and Smith, 1840), 46, as cited in Whittaker, "East of Nauvoo," 33. **Stephen a Danite:** *Document Containing the Correspondence, Orders &c in Relation to the Disturbances with the Mormons* (Fayette, MO: Boon's Lick Democrat, 1841), 103-7; Ebenezer Robinson, "Items of Personal History," *The Return* 1 (Oct. 1889): 145-47, 2 (Feb. 1890): 218-19; Quinn, MHOP 334, 94, 485. **Stephen imprisoned:** HC 3:182, 190.

II. **in Payson:** Redress Petition, compare Bean, "LDS Baptisms" 42. **census:** Nauvoo Ward census, 3rd Ward, p. 13. **RS Min.:** p. 23. **April 14:** RS Min., p. 26. **donations:** RS Min., 43. **Nancy Maria inducted:** RS Min., 55. **further donations:** RS Min., 48, 71, 73 (May 13, June 23, and July 7). **marriage:** HR 6:234. Orson Whitney, *Life of Heber Kimball* (Salt Lake City: Kimball family, 1888), 430-32, 435.

III. **September 26:** HCKj (OPW 88). A month later, on September 26, 1844, Heber wrote, "Spent the fore noon at B. Young held council, B. Winchester cut of[f] and his wife." **visits:** Mar. 12 (OPW 98); June 24 (OPW 124); OPW 134, 140. See also Oct. 29, 1844 (OPW 92); June 26, 1845; July 6, 1845; July 12; Aug. 20; Oct. 1 (again with wife); Oct. 6, 1845 (OPW 139); Nov. 28. **health baptism of Sarah Peake:** Helen Mar Whitney, SIN, WE 11 (Apr. 15, 1883): 170. **Dec. 8:** HCKj, Bk 93. **endowment:** HCKj, Bk 93. **sealing to Heber:** BOP #154; SAd 369, 513; HCK 315. **cohabitation:** See note on genealogical record quoted below.

IV. **Carter listings:** HTW 10:472. See also BE 4:692; Obituary, in Bean, "LDS Baptisms," 42. **census:** 1850 Utah census, p. 26. **patriarchal blessing:** vol. 12, p. 643, #1589, as cited in Tinney, RF 323. **census:** 1860 p. 179.

V. **marriage to Arnold:** FGS; HCK 315. Amos, son of Daniel and Lydia Arnold, had been born on March 12, 1833, in Redfield, Oswego, New York. **family tradition:** FGS of Amos George Arnold. Kate Carter supports this tradition: in Arnold's history, we read that he was asked to marry her "that she might become a mother." "Nancy Mariah Winchester Kimball," OPH 10:410-11, citing an Autobiography by Amos George Arnold, which I have not yet located. Compare Ezra Taft Benson standing witness in the remarriage of his ex-wife Desdemona Fullmer, see her chapter at 1853. **poor health:** OPH 10.410. **Nancy's death:** FGS. Amos married Ruth Powell in 1876, with whom he had thirteen children, and George Stephen was raised in this second family. George, in turn, married a Mary Ann Powell in 1885. Amos and George died in 1926 and 1927.

# REFERENCES TO CHAPTER 30.
## True Saint:
## Fanny Young (Carr Murray Smith)

HBY: see Young, "History of Brigham Young."
Murray, Fanny, to Phinehas Young. Jan. 1, 1845. GS Film 281,261.
Young, Brigham: "History of Brigham Young," CA, MS 1285, Book Y. Tim Rathbone is

preparing a definitive edition of Brigham Young's diaries and histories and generously shared his research with me.

**Fanny, Brigham, the cow:** Franklin Wheeler Young, Young family genealogy, CA, MS 1148, at a biography of John Young, Sr., pp. 13-14. For the Young family's early years, see Arrington, BY 7-11 and Bringhurst, BY 3-5, 224.

**I. birthdate:** Clayton/Kimball Book 93, at Jan. 7, 1846; HBY. **John and Abigail Nabby Young:** John was born on March 6, 1763, Abigail on May 3, 1765. They married in 1785. After Abigail's death on June 11, 1815, Joseph married Hannah Dennis on August 20 of the same year. He died in 1839 in Quincy, Illinois. For the Young family genealogy, see Fanny Murray to Phinehas Young, Jan. 1, 1845; HBY. For Abigail, see Susa Young Gates, "Mother of the Latter-day Prophets: Abigail Howe Young," *Juvenile Instructor* 59 (Jan. 1924): 6; Leonard Arrington and Susan Arrington Madsen, *Mothers of the Prophets* (Salt Lake City: Deseret Book, 1987), 29-40. **description of Abigail:** as quoted in Arrington, BY 8. **Nancy:** Born on August 6, 1786, in Hopkinton, she married Daniel Kent in 1803 and died in 1860 in Salt Lake City. **Rhoda:** Born on September 10, 1789, she married John Greene in 1813 and died in 1840 in Nauvoo. **John Young, Jr.:** Born on May 22, 1790, he married Theodocia Kimball, Hannah Dennis, Sarah McCleve, Mary Ann Gurnsey, Loisa Jones, and Clarissa Jones, and died in 1870 in Salt Lake City. **Nabby:** Born on April 23, 1793, she died in 1807 of tuberculosis, like her namesake mother. **Susanna:** Born on June 7, 1795, she married James Little, William Stilson, and Alanson Pettingill. She died in 1852 in Salt Lake City. **Joseph Young:** Born on April 7, 1797, in Hopkinton, he married Jane Bicknell, Lucinda Allen, Lydia Hagar, Mary Ann Huntley, Elizabeth Stevens, and Sarah Snow, and died in 1881 in Salt Lake City. **Phinehas:** Born on February 16, 1799, he married Clarisca Hamilton, Lucy Cowdery, Phebe Clark, Maria James, Lavina Clark, Sara Ann Hollister, Harriet Little, and Elizabeth Rea. He died in 1879 in Salt Lake City. See Miriam Maxfield, "A Compiled History of Phinehas Howe Young," typescript, CA. **John Young and Methodism:** Lorenzo Young, quoted in James Little, Historical Items about Brigham Young, CA, MS 1254 box 1 fd 3, p. 2. **Lorenzo on Abigail:** James Little, Biography of Lorenzo Dow Young, CA, p. 2, numbering from the back; James A. Little, "Biography of Lorenzo Dow Young," UHQ 14 (1946): 25-132, 25. **return to maternal home:** Fanny Murray to Phinehas Young.

**II. fifty acres:** Arrington, BY 7-8. **move:** Arrington, BY 8. **Brigham:** He married Miriam Works, Mary Ann Angell, and fifty-three other women, and died in 1877 in Salt Lake City. See Arrington, BY, Bringhurst, BY and other sources cited there. **Louisa:** Born on September 26, 1804, she married Joel Sanford in 1825 and died in 1833 in Independence, Missouri. **Lorenzo Dow:** Born on October 19, 1807, he married Persis Goodall, Harriet Wheeler, Ida Hewitt, Eleanor Jones, and Johanna Larsen, and died in 1895 in Salt Lake City. See Little, "Biography of Lorenzo Dow Young," 25-132; MS 3078, fd 1, CA.

**III. marriage to Carr:** HBY, who has her marrying at age sixteen. The date is from IGI, film 1,395,719, citing family Bible and records. IGI (film 1,395,770) has the date as 1803, Arrington, BY 10. **"unfaithful":** Bringhurst, BY 9. **Charleston:** Franklin Wheeler Young, Young genealogy, p. 8. **Youngs to New York:** Arrington, BY 10. **Nabby dies:** Arrington, BY 10-11; Bringhurst, BY 9. **Lorenzo:** DW 9 (June 29, 1859): 130. **moved to Tyrone:** Little, "Biography," 25.

**IV. signs in sky:** HCKj, in MSt 26 (1864): 472; compare Parley P. Pratt, *Autobiography* 44 (1938 ed.); Daniel Peterson, "Heavenly Signs and Aerial Combat," *Sunstone* 4 (Mar.-Apr. 1979): 27-32. **Fanny healed:** Lorenzo Young, quoted in James Little, Historical Items about Brigham Young, CA, MS 1254 box 1, fd 3, p. 2. **Helen's birth:** Helen Kimball Whitney, LI, WE 9 (Aug. 1, 1880): 38. See the Helen Mar Kimball chapter. **Fanny names her:** LI, WE 9 (Aug. 15, 1880): 42. **pensketch of Fanny:** LI, WE 9 (Aug. 15, 1880): 42. **Joseph Young:** DW 9 (June 29, 1859): 130.

**V. Book of Mormon:** Arrington, BY 19-20. **Murray:** AF. Roswell had previously married Mary Wilson in 1792 and Susannah Fitch in approximately 1798. **baptism:** Arrington,

BY 20. Franklin Wheeler Young, Young genealogy, p. 8. **branch:** Heber C. Kimball, in "History of Brigham Young," MSt 26 (1864): 519. **Fanny in Kirtland:** Helen Mar Whitney, LI, WE 9 (Aug. 15, 1880): 42. **pensketch of Roswell:** LI, WE 9 (Aug. 15, 1880): 42. **Kimballs return from mission:** LI, WE 9 (Apr. 15, 1881): 170. **Fanny in Kirtland in January 1838:** Hepsibah Richards to Willard Richards, Jan. 18-19, 1838, printed in Godfrey, WV 73. **Kimball family leaves Kirtland:** HCK 55. **September 19:** Franklin Wheeler Young, Young genealogy, p. 6.

VI. **Fanny and father in Missouri:** HBY. **Brigham and Vilate to Illinois:** Helen Mar Whitney, ER, WE 9 (June 1, 1880): 5; HCK 60; Arrington, BY 70. **Fanny in Illinois:** HBY. **May 2:** Helen Mar Whitney, ER, WE 9 (June 1, 1880), 5; HCK 64. **Roswell in Illinois:** HCKj, in Helen Mar Whitney, LI, WE 9 (July 15, 1880): 25. **Roswell to the east:** HCKj, in Helen Mar Whitney LI, WE 9 (July 15, 1880): 25. There are frequent mentions of Murray in Heber's journal. AF. **Death of Roswell:** Helen Mar Whitney, LI 9 (Aug. 15, 1880): 42. Per AF (which has the wrong date of death, 1837), Murray died in Victor, Ontario, New York. Vilate Murray Kimball to Fanny Murray, Feb. 16, 1841, in Helen Mar Whitney papers, Merrill Library, MS 179, box 4, fd 5, "I have at len[g]th received those letters from victor [on Roswell's death] which I shall forward to you." This includes a poem by Helen Mar commemorating Roswell's death. **February 1841:** Vilate Kimball to "Mrs Fanny Murray [at] Winchester," Feb. 16, 1841. **Fanny after Murray's death:** Fanny Murray to Charles and Agnes Fox, Aug. 31, 1852, Lucile Oliphant collection, CA, MS 9297. For the single woman's struggle for survival in nineteenth-century America, see the Agnes Coolbrith chapter during her residence in St. Louis, Utah and Los Angeles.

VII. **marriage:** Brigham Young, discourse given on Aug. 31, 1873, in JD 16:166-67. See also HR 6:234, "Fanny Young, a sister of Prs. Brigham Young, married to Joseph 2 Nov 1843. Brigham Young officiating." Also, Affidavit 1:52, by Augusta Young, #73 Bachman; Harriet Cook (Young), Affidavit 2:14, #103 Bachman. Ann Eliza Young to Mary Bond, May 4, 1876, Myron H. Bond collection, P21, f11, RLDS Archives: "Aunt Fanny Murray was sealed to Joseph she told me so herself." A. C. Waite, *The Mormon Prophet and His Harem* (Chicago: Goodman, 1867), 203, gives an interesting anti-Mormon account of Fanny's marriage to Joseph: "After the death of her husband, she was, by the earnest persuasion of her brother Brigham, induced to be sealed to another. She protested at the time, and said it would break her heart. And in relating the story to a young friend, years afterward,—'Bessie,' said she, 'my poor, poor heart is breaking now;' and laying her hand on her heart, she wept aloud." As always one wonders how much one can accept from such a source as this. **Harriet and Augusta:** See Johnson, DDW. **endowment:** WWj, Dec. 23, 1843 (2:332). **Fanny anoints William:** Little, "Biography of Lorenzo Dow Young," 69-70.

VIII. **temple endowment:** Kimball/Clayton book 93, at January 7. For washing and anointing, see Donald Parry, "Washing and Anointings," in EM 1551. **left in Nauvoo:** Fanny Murray to Foxes, Aug. 31, 1852. **June 3:** Fanny Murray to Vilate Kimball, CA MS 740, #1. **Mt. Pisgah:** "William Kimball with Sister Fanny Murry his Step Grandmother Pres Youngs Sister, Charles Decker the Pres['s] son in law with some others ware passing Pisga," Zina Young, Autobiographical Sketch 2, Zina Brown collection, CA. **Vilate Decker to Fanny:** CA, MS 740 #3. **May 22, July 5:** MS 740.

IX. **dating of her overland journey:** Martha Spence Heywood diary, Sept. 22, 1850 (Brooks p. 29). **memories of her trip west and advice:** Fanny to the Foxes, Aug. 31, 1852.

X. **Census:** Utah 1850, p. 75. **Martha Heywood:** Jan. 26, 1851 (Brooks p. 50); she had also visited her on Oct. 27, 1850 (Brooks p. 35). Sarah Hollister Harris boarded with Fanny during this time, and described her as "a kind elderly woman" who "talked freely about polygamy and its effect upon the people." *An Unwritten Chapter of Salt Lake* (New York: printed privately, 1901), 49-50. **Fanny to Nancy Kent:** Jan. 27, 1851, Nancy Young Kent collection, CA MS 1981, fd 2. **Lion House:** A. C. Waite, *Mormon*

*Prophet* 203. **October 1856:** WWj, Oct. 16 (4:475). **Lion House and cancer:** Susa Young Gates collection, USHS, box 12, fd 4; "Life in the Lion House," p. 40.

**XI. lingering sickness:** Gates, "Life in the Lion House," 40. **to Fanny and James McKnight home:** DN 9 (June 29, 1859): 130. **BY to Lucy Bigelow Young:** June 8, 1859, see Susa Young Gates, "Lucy Bigelow Young," Susa Young Gates collection, USHS MS B-95, box 14, fd 5, p. 49. **Fanny to Nancy:** As quoted in Brigham Young's address at Fanny's funeral, see Gates, "Lucy Bigelow Young," p. 249. **date of death:** Laura Pitkin Kimball diary, CA, June 11. The funeral was held on June 12, and all talks were extensively reported in *The Deseret News* 9 (June 29, 1859): 130-31.

# INDEX.

*Note: Women are indexed by the married name with which they were, and are, most commonly known; women with multiple marriages are indexed by last marriage name.*

adoption, 2, 11, 108, 338, 355. *See* sealing.

ague. *See* malaria.

alcohol and alcoholism, 44, 161, 162, 168, 170, 293, 304, 484, 532

(Alger), Clarissa Hancock, 26, 32-33, 37, 41-42

Alger, Fanny. *See* (Custer), Fanny Alger.

Alger, John, 26

Alger, Samuel, 26, 32-33, 37, 41-42

Alger, Thomas, 26

Anthony, Susan B., 109

apocalypticism, in early Mormonism, 2, 11, 75, 88, 91, 185, 190, 207, 259, 275, 284, 321, 323, 348, 366, 399, 501, 612; part of rationale for polygamy, 31, 520

Arnold, Amos George, 7, 607-8

Arnold, George Stephen, 608

(Arnold), Nancy Maria Winchester (Smith Kimball), 6, 604-8; her family converts in Pennsylvania, 605; moves to Kirtland, 605; in Missouri, her father Stephen reportedly a Danite, 606; in Nauvoo, Nancy Maria married to Joseph Smith, 606; marriage to Heber C. Kimball, 607; moves to Salt Lake City, 607; Kimball arranges her marriage to Amos George Arnold, 608; George Arnold born, 608; Nancy Maria dies, 608

authoritarianism, in early Mormonism, 2, 22, 23, 81, 98, 138, 170, 192, 207, 212, 280, 287, 312, 314, 348, 351, 360, 366, 453, 456, 463, 466, 614; part of rationale for polyandry, 16-20

Babbitt, Almon W., 5, 7, 83, 198, 257, 288, 292, 293, 294, 298-300, 466, 473, 477, 478, 479

(Babbitt), Delcena Diadamia Johnson (Sherman Smith), 4, 60, 243, 257, 288-295, 297, 298, 299-300, 364, 478, 479; at age six, family travels from Vermont to western New York, 288; family background, 290-91; marriage to Lyman Sherman, 291; conversion to Mormonism, 292; moves to Kirtland, 292; Lyman becomes close friend to Joseph Smith, 293; in Missouri, Lyman dies suddenly, 294; marriage to Joseph Smith, 295; marriage to brother-in-law, Almon Babbitt, 298; suffers from acute arthritis, 300; travels to Salt Lake with two surviving children, 300; Albey marries, 300; Delcena dies in Salt Lake, 300

(Babbitt), Julia Ann Johnson, 290, 301, 303

(Babbitt), Maria Lawrence (Smith [Young]), 474-79; family converts in Canada, 474; father dies in Illinois, leaving large estate, 474; Joseph Smith becomes family's guardian, 474; mother marries Josiah Butterfield, who quarrels with Joseph Smith, 475; marriage to Smith, 475; William Law sues Smith for adultery, citing Maria Lawrence, 476-77; debated marriage to Brigham Young, 477, 744; marriage to Almon Babbitt, 478-79; death of, 479. *See also* Mount, Sarah Lawrence.

Bapson, Sarah, 8

Baptist church, 289, 307, 343, 399, 466, 488, 536

(Bartlett), Anna Hall, 172-73, 175

Bartlett, Enoch, 172-74

(Barton), Almera Woodward Johnson (Smith), 6, 10, 28, 33, 59, 60, 257, 288-305, 462; family background, 290-91; conversion to Mormonism, 292; moves to Kirtland, 292; moves to Ramus, Illinois, 295; receives polygamous teaching and proposal to marry Joseph Smith from her brother Benjamin, 297; marriage to Smith, 297-98; marriage to Reuben Barton, 300; five daughters, of whom one, Lois, is mentally deficient, 301; separation from Barton, 302; moves to Utah with three surviving daughters, 302; moves to Parowan in southern Utah, 302; two of three daughters die, with Lois surviving, 302; warm relations with extensive network of Johnson siblings and relatives, 303; Lois dies at age forty-one, 304; death of, 304

Barton, Lois Elvira, 301-4

Barton, Reuben, 7, 300-2

Barton, Sarah Delcena, 301-2

Beaman, Alvah, 56-58

(Beaman), Sarah Burtts, 56-59

773

# INDEX

Ezekiel Clark, 193; three children, all of whom survive, 197; leaves Clark and moves to Bountiful, Utah, 198, 20l; marriage with Kimball continues to be somewhat distant, 198; death of, 202

(Clawson), Emily Augusta Young, 415, 417, 419-21, 427-29, 431

Clawson, Hiram, 104, 222-23, 417, 428

Clayton, William, 10, 52, 183, 237, 263, 265, 297, 298, 316, 317, 352-354, 383, 388, 389, 391, 392, 409, 411, 465, 466, 475-478, 580

Cleveland, Alexander D., 275, 282-86

Cleveland, John (Judge), 5, 271, 275-87

cognitive dissonance, 238, 296, 397, 431, 432, 487, 595, 748

Coltrin, Zebedee, 389

congregationalism, 74, 291, 458

conversion, to Jesus, 115, 272, 275, 291; to Mormonism, through preaching, 175, 344, 488, 587; through Smith's charisma, 228; through Book of Mormon, 74, 292, 579, 605; to polygamy, 12, 296-97, 347, 465, 497-511, 740. *See also* Book of Mormon.

Coolbrith, Ina. *See* (Carsely), Josephine Donna Smith.

Coolbrith, Joseph, 146

(Coolbrith), Mary Hasty Foss, 146

Corrill, John, 402-3

Cowdery, Oliver, 25, 28, 34-39, 53, 117, 206, 207, 208, 209, 240, 257, 343, 344, 399, 579; polygamy helps cause his disaffection, 38-39

Cowles, Austin, 39; polygamy helps cause his disaffection, 544-50

(Cowles), Irena Hix Elliott, 544-50

(Cowles), Phoebe Wilbur, 544

(Cox), Cordelia Morley, 8, 633

(Crocheron), Augusta Joyce, 126

Croxall, Mark, 417, 427

cult of true womanhood, 79

Custer, Benjamin Franklin, 40

(Custer), Fanny Alger Smith, 4, 21, 25-42, 55, 240, 297, 315; family background, 26; receives Joseph Smith's proposal through uncle Levi Hancock, 32; marriage to Smith, 33; lives in Smith home, 34; possible pregnancy, 35; expelled from Smith home by Emma Smith, 34; removed from Kirtland temple by Levi Hancock, 36; marriage to Solomon Cus-

ter in Indiana, 25; later life as mother of nine in Indiana, 40

Custer, Lafayette, 40

Custer, Lewis A., 40

Custer, Solomon, 25-26, 39-41

Custer, Sophrona Allis, 40

Cutler, Alpheus, 214, 259, 539

Damon, Ebenezer, 558, 561-63

Danites and Danitism, 49, 72, 77, 259, 281, 367, 596, 597, 606, 651

(Davis), Abigail Reeves, 255

Davis, Gilbert, 255

(Deming), Ann Eliza Webb (Dee Young), 2, 21, 28, 34, 104, 239, 240, 241, 248, 418, 419, 427

depression, in women, xv, 109, 111, 116, 133, 185, 187, 188, 221, 223, 320, 407, 416, 417, 418, 420, 424, 431, 470, 485, 501, 502, 508, 517, 526, 528, 529, 620

(Dibble), Hannah Ann Dubois (Smith), 8-9

Dibble, Philo, 2, 9, 258

(Dinwoody), Florence Marian Whitney, 514, 516, 519, 523, 528, 532

divorce, 126, 293; relatively frequent, but often amicable, in polygamy, 14, 249, 473, 481, 583, 608

(Durfee), Elizabeth. *See* Lott, Elizabeth Davis.

Durfee, Jabez, 5, 254-55, 258-65

dynastic marriage, 3, 12, 33-34, 81, 123, 342, 347, 348, 353, 362, 388, 391, 417, 427, 463, 487, 497, 499, 500, 558, 581, 595, 604, 607-9, 617

(Ellis), Delia Annette Hyde, 246

(Ellis), Nancy Rigdon, 239-40, 634

(Ellis), Phebe Clark, 197, 201

Ells, Josiah, 535-40

endowment, 52, 61, 85, 86, 108, 125, 133, 134, 135, 139, 156, 184, 185, 186, 214, 227, 242, 243, 250, 263, 264, 281, 298, 317, 330, 333, 347, 353, 354, 361, 372, 376, 385, 387, 391, 393, 395, 412, 434, 443, 446, 453, 478, 495, 504, 520, 551, 556, 570, 573, 582, 598, 599, 607, 617, 654

erysipelas, 67, 142, 223, 286, 425, 574, 673

exchange of women, in anthropology and Fanny Alger marriage, 26, 32, 41-42. *See also* dynastic marriage.

first husbands, in polyandrous marriages, 5, 7, 9, 13, 14, 16, 18, 20-23, 44, 51, 84, 85, 90, 113, 114, 123, 143, 205, 241, 243, 260, 271, 278, 282, 352, 381, 383, 386, 455, 543, 548, 557

(Fisher), Josephine Lyon, 13, 21, 183, 187, 193-94, 197, 201, 202

Frost, Aaron, 591

(Frost), Susannah, 591

Fullmer, Almon Linus, 578

Fullmer, David, 578-84, 579, 581

Fullmer, John Solomon, 578, 580-81, 583

Fullmer, Peter, 577-78

(Fullmer), Susannah Zerfass, 577-78

fullness of priesthood ordinance, 156, 200, 355, 393, 598

Gibbons, Andrew Smith, 372-80

(Gibbons), Rizpah Knight, 365, 372-80

Gilbert, Algernon Sydney, 206, 210

(Gilbert), Elizabeth Van Benthuysen, 206, 216, 220, 224-25

glossolalia. See tongues, speaking in.

Godbeite movement, 220, 223, 444, 454

(Goff), Lydia Kenyon (Carter Kimball), 8

Goldsmith, Gilbert, 255-59, 263-65

Goldsmith, Gilbert, Sr., 255

Gove, Carlos, 7, 392-94

(Gove), Flora Ann Woodworth (Smith), 6, 171, 388-391, 393, 500, 604; family converted, 389; in Nauvoo, her father Lucien is architect of Nauvoo House, 389; marriage to Joseph Smith, 389; a favorite of Joseph Smith, 391; tensions with Emma Smith, 388; possible feelings of rebelliousness, 390; marriage to non-Mormon Carlos Gove, 392; her mother Phebe has proxy marriage to Joseph Smith, 393; at Winter Quarters with two or three children, 394; death of, 394; Phebe in San Bernardino and Utah, 394-95

Grant, Heber, 342, 525

Grant, Jedediah Morgan, 11, 18, 325, 328, 330, 342, 552

(Grant), Rachel Ivins, 252, 342, 425, 427, 429, 526, 633

Greene, John, 492, 579, 612, 614, 615

(Greene), Rhoda Young, 610, 612, 614-15, 619

(Groo), Mary Jane Whitney, 719

(Hall), Ann Maria Whitney, 345

(Hancock), Clarissa Reed, 30-31, 32-33

Hancock, Levi Ward, 25, 26, 29-33, 36-38, 41, 297

Hancock, Mosiah, 25, 26, 29-31, 36-37

(Hanscomb), Almira Knight (Stoddard), 365, 371-73, 375, 377-78

Hardy, Leonard, 424

(Hardy), Miriam Young, 417, 421, 424, 426-27, 429

Harris, George Washington, 2, 5, 16, 20, 38, 44-54, 48, 49, 52-54, 84, 277

(Harris), Lucinda Pendleton. See (Smith), Lucinda Pendleton.

Harris, Martin, 57, 208

(Hatch), Permelia Lott, 596

healing, xii, 104, 109, 128, 139-141, 143, 180, 229, 230, 256, 324, 346, 459, 508, 567, 570, 578, 579, 588, 607, 612

Holmes, Jonathan, 7, 16, 20, 84, 85, 329, 543, 545, 546, 547, 550, 557

Holy Order, of Quorum of the Anointed, 61, 85, 156, 184, 214, 242, 243, 254, 263, 317, 347, 353, 391, 393, 504, 598, 617

(Horne), Mary Isabella Hales, 139, 251, 277, 520, 525-26

Howe, John, 273-75

Hunter, Edward, 324, 541

Huntington, Dimick, 33, 72-74, 77, 79-81, 93, 94, 106, 117, 122, 123, 126, 127, 130, 137, 142, 297, 462

(Huntington), Fanny Allen, 73-74, 77, 79, 81, 117, 122, 127, 142

Huntington, John Dickenson, 73, 78-79, 110

(Huntington), Lydia Clisbee (Partridge), 397-406, 413

Huntington, Oliver, xi, 73, 76-79, 82, 88, 89, 92-94, 96, 106, 108-12, 118, 122, 124, 129, 130, 140, 143, 276, 509

Huntington, William, Sr., 71-89, 406, 413

Huntington, William Dresser, 72-73, 78-79, 85, 93, 104, 119, 126-27, 130, 133, 142

Hyde, Alonzo Eugene, 245

Hyde, Frank Henry, 244-45, 251

(Hyde), Mary Ann Cowles, 544

(Hyde), Mary Ann Price, 182, 241-43, 245-47, 252

Hyde, Orson, xii, 5, 16, 19, 84, 146, 158,

Sylvester Stoddard, disaffected Mormon, and leaves Nauvoo, 372; in Winter Quarters, 373; moves to Ogden, Utah, 374; has out-of-body experience, 374; lives with daughters Adaline Belnap and Rizpah Gibbons, 373-80; distant relationship with Heber C. Kimball, 364; Almira visits after long parting, 378; death of, 726

(Kimball), Mary Ellen Able Harris Jacob (wife of HCK), 192, 323, 473, 515, 525

(Kimball), Mary Fielding (Smith) (wife of Hyrum Smith, then HCK), 43, 156, 254, 354, 478, 600

(Kimball), Mary Houston (wife of HCK) (and JS?), 2, 8, 136, 354-55, 357, 360, 434, 468, 514

Kimball, Newel Whitney, 359, 361-62

(Kimball), Presendia Lathrop Huntington (Buell Smith), xi, 69, 72, 73, 84, 85, 93, 94, 96, 97, 98, 104, 105, 108, 109, 110, 114-144, 183, 205, 223, 224, 227, 282, 311, 321, 322, 358, 360, 373, 385, 406, 468, 557, 572-575, 601, 614, 621; conversion to Jesus, 115; marriage to Norman Buell, 115; death of son Silas, 116; conversion to Mormonism, 117; in Kirtland, 117; in Missouri, 118-22; husband becomes disaffected from Mormonism, 119; moves to Lima, Illinois, 122; marriage to Joseph Smith, 122; joins Relief Society, 123; marries Heber C. Kimball, 124; with youngest son, Oliver, leaves Buell, 126; at Winter Quarters, 127; charismatic gifts of, 114, 117; moves to Utah, 130; has daughter, 131; death of daughter, 132; has son, Joseph Smith Kimball, 134; son Oliver moves from Utah, leaving her mourning, 136; constant moves as Kimball wife, 127; death of, 142

(Kimball), Sarah Ann Whitney (Smith), 6, 15, 33, 136, 211, 322, 342-63, 376, 434, 463, 468, 494, 500, 503; family background, 343; family sick in Nauvoo, 346; magnetic personality as teen, 342; family introduced to polygamy, 347; marriage to Joseph Smith, 347-49; secret meeting of Sarah and parents with Joseph, 349-50; pretended marriage to Joseph Kingsbury, 351; marriage to Heber C. Kimball, 353; has child while crossing Iowa, 355; child dies in Winter Quarters, 358; moves to Salt Lake City, 359; shares house with three other Kim-

ball wives, 359; children settle Meadowville, in Bear Lake, Utah, 361; death of, 362

(Kimball), Sarah Melissa Granger (wife of Hiram Kimball), 3, 141, 244-45, 317, 480, 542, 633, 635

(Kimball), Sarah Peake (Noon) (wife of HCK), 322, 357, 496-98

Kimball, Solomon Farnham, 507, 521, 526, 531

Kimball, Washington Heber, 469-72

Kimball, William Henry, 183, 319, 487, 490-94, 496-97, 357, 502, 504, 617

(King), Hannah Tapfield. See (Young), Hannah Tapfield.

Kingsbury, Joseph, 7, 342, 343, 351-356, 362

Kingsley, Ebenezer, 272

Kingsley, Ebenezer Chaplin, 272

(Kingsley), Sarah Chaplin, 272

Knight, James Vinson, 365, 374-80

Knight, Vinson, 364-372, 493

(Knox), Ann Spaulding Kimball, 469-72

(Law), Jane Silverthorne, 254, 405, 633-34

Law, William, 3, 39, 254, 405, 474-479, 549

Lawrence, Henry, 223, 474, 481, 483-85

laying on of hands, ordinance used for confirmation, blessing, healing, 104, 114, 176, 181, 207, 230, 256, 465, 492-93, 568, 578, 588, 607; performed by women, 63, 67, 75, 91, 128-30, 134, 138, 190, 200, 323-24, 385, 414, 448, 471, 508, 685-86

(LeBaron), Esther Melita Johnson, 290, 303

Lee, John D., 17, 19, 52, 55, 63, 71, 82, 93, 101, 239, 266, 281, 509

Levirate marriage, 15, 61, 145, 154, 156, 264, 295, 364, 371, 477, 555, 661

Lightner, Adam, 5, 19, 205, 210-22, 278

Lightner, Adam, Jr., 217-18, 222-23

Lightner, Charles Washington, 217-19

Lightner, John Horace, 215, 219

(Losee), Mary Elizabeth Lott, 596, 601

Lott, Cornelius, 5, 33, 83, 255, 262, 264-65, 548, 594, 596-600

(Lott), Elizabeth Davis (Goldsmith Brackenbury Durfee Smith), 4, 5, 12, 155, 179, 254-70, 279, 292, 316, 407, 548, 570, 597, 599; childhood, 255; marries Gilbert Goldsmith, one son, Gilbert, 255;

marries Joseph Brackenbury, 256; three sons, John Wesley, Benjamin, Charles Wesley, 256; conversion to Mormonism, 256; death of Joseph, 257; marriage to Jabez Durfee in Missouri, 259; friend of Emma Smith in Nauvoo, 261; marriage to Joseph Smith, 260; in Relief Society, 260; joins Holy Order 254; helps introduce Emily Partridge to polygamy, 262; proxy marriage to Cornelius Lott, 264; returns to Illinois from Winter Quarters, 265; lives in Salt Lake City, 266; lives in San Bernardino, 267; in Kansas, is baptized into RLDS church, 268; death by train accident, 268; her sons in RLDS church, 267-70

Lott, John Smiley, 596

(Lott), Permelia Darrow, 320, 596

(Loughery), Lydia Holmes Kimball, 468-72

(Luddington), Jane Tibbetts, 8

Lyman, Amasa, 7, 83, 97, 98, 162, 220, 259, 318, 326, 391, 394, 397, 413, 423, 433, 434, 454, 496, 592

(Lyman), Caroline Partridge, 397

(Lyman), Cornelia Leavitt, 320

(Lyman), Eliza Maria Partridge (Smith), x, 60, 67, 69, 79, 262, 298, 354, 359, 396-411, 424, 433-56, 465, 468, 504, 546, 548, 552, 553, 554; polygamous marriage to apostle Amasa Lyman, 433; travels across Iowa, 434-35; at Winter Quarters, 436; loses first child, 436; arrives in Salt Lake, 437; husband leads colony in San Bernardino, but Eliza stays in Salt Lake, 438; husband returns to Utah, 441; Eliza moves to nearby Fillmore and Oak Creek, 442; husband excommunicated, 444; Eliza separates from husband, 444; witnesses death of daughter Carlie after childbirth, 448; accompanies sons to San Juan County, 450-51; tends son Joseph after he is wounded in shootout, 452; returns to Oak Creek, 453; death of, 454

Lyman, Joseph Alvin, 441-56

(Lyman), Lydia Partridge, 399, 437, 439-40, 445

Lyman, Platte DeAlton, 437-56

Lyon, Windsor, 5, 16, 52, 177-95, 241

magic, folk; *also* treasure-digging, scrying, 57, 731

malaria, 2, 59, 78, 153, 178, 320, 346, 404, 405, 461, 492-494, 542, 567, 573, 592

(Markham), Hannah, 155, 316-21

Markham, Stephen, 155, 316-21

Marks, William, 3, 180, 181, 254, 539, 540, 546, 549, 590

Marsh, Thomas Baldwin, 38, 233, 474

(Martineau), Susan Julia Sherman, 294, 300

Masonry, 41, 43-48, 54, 83, 107, 108, 153, 154, 213, 330, 342, 370, 494, 503

McArthur, Duncan, 588

(McArthur), Sally Ann Fuller (Smith? Gully Fuller), 8, 438

(McBride), Abigail Mead, 365

McBride, Daniel, 365

McBride, Reuben, 365

McBride, Samuel, 365

(McLane), Desdemona Catlin Wadsworth Fullmer (Smith Benson), 6, 272, 428, 547, 577-585, 621; family background, 578; biblical primitivism in her environment, 578; influenced by Putnam Wadsworth, boy-prophet, 578; has visions and revelations, 577; family converts to Mormonism, 579; in Kirtland, 579; in Missouri, 579-80; in Nauvoo, 580; attends first Relief Society meeting, 580; marries Joseph Smith, 581; marries Ezra Taft Benson, soon an apostle, with many plural wives, 582-83; moves to Salt Lake, where early years are difficult, 583; amicable divorce from Benson, 583; marriage to Harrison McLane, 583; birth of one child, who dies, 583; separation from McLane, 584; lives later life with brother, David, 584; death of, 585

McLane, Harrison, 7, 583-84

McLellin, William, 35, 232

medical practice, nineteenth-century America, 194, 331, 532, 558-76, 655; operation for cancer, 564

Methodism, 44, 174, 229, 255, 256, 273, 289, 536, 544, 578, 610, 612

midwifery, profession of, 104, 130, 171-94, 199

(Miner), Laura Marinda Hyde, 233, 245, 247, 251-52

missions, impacts on wives of male missionaries, 235, 441, 493

monogamy, *seen* as inferior to polygamy, xiii, xiv, 10, 25, 39, 41, 79, 94, 135, 143, 155, 296, 303, 519-521

Mormons in San Bernardino, 162; her daughters marry, 164; traumatic divorce of Josephine, 166; in San Francisco and Oakland, 166; separates from William, 167; Ina becomes noted poet and Oakland librarian, 168; meets with RLDS nephews, David and Alexander, 169; death of, 169

Pickett, Don Carlos, 158, 162, 166, 168

Pickett, William, 5, 158-67, 169, 170, 193

Pickett, William, Jr., 158, 162, 166-68

(Pierce), Hannah Harvey, 322-27

Pierce, Robert, 62-63, 96, 322-27, 353

piety, of nineteenth-century Mormon and American women, 79, 80, 274, 289-90, 440, 578

polyandry, or spiritual wife doctrine, in Mormon practice, 9, 15-23, 71, 72, 80, 84, 90, 113, 212, 236, 238, 386, 543, 548, 551, 557 (See also chapters 2, 4-5, 7-11, 16, and 24); linked to Mormon authoritarianism, 17, 351; linked to pre-existence of souls doctrine, 19; antecedents to, in burned-over district, 20-21; antecedents to, in Europe, Swedenborg, 20; anthropological background of, 639. See also Smith, Joseph, and polygamy; first husbands.

polygamy, history of, in Mormonism: pre-Nauvoo polygamy, See chapters 1 and 2; practical polygamy (in exodus and Utah), with cohabitation, as opposed to secret polygamy (in Nauvoo), 185, 413-14; 432; legal prosecution for polygamy before Manifesto, 105, 339, 428-29, 528; Manifesto 531; secret post-Manifesto polygamy, 456, 738. See also primitivism, biblical.

polygamy, in Mormon practice, regarded as sacred, xiii, 59, 69, 80, 82, 123, 313, 336, 410; regarded as necessary for salvation, 10-11, 312, 464; based on doctrine of salvation by familial quantity, 10-11, 455; often unromantic, xiv, 32, 105, 108, 349, 371, 391, 464-65, 500, 558, 569, 606-7, 616, 667, 740 (See also dynastic marriage); feminine bonding in, 65, 69, 86, 127, 223, 317-18, 555-56; can cause tensions between wives, 97, 187-89, 438, 467, 512 (See also Bidamon, Emma Hales Smith); pronounced bonding of mothers and children in, xiv, 420, 424, 426; often required by church leaders, 453, 496, 555; economic impact on women, xiv,

199, 420, 438-41; husband frequently absent in, 98, 157, 329, 447, 468; siblings and friends take place of husband, 93-94, 131, 415, 437, 439; loneliness, anxiety, abandonment, experienced by women in, xiii, xiv, xv, 31, 98, 128, 134-35, 137, 185-89, 195-96, 220, 246-49, 364, 412, 415-23, 436-44, 528-30; husbands tend to have favorite wives in, 95, 97, 127, 671, 734; women recruited into, through other women, 60, 179, 239-40, 262, 297, 332, 334, 597

(Pratt), Mary Ann Frost (Stearns), 2, 8, 182, 241, 455, 586-92

Pratt, Orson, 10, 18, 27, 48, 52, 384, 433, 536, 541, 605

Pratt, Parley P., 2, 8, 58, 206, 207, 214, 233, 244, 345, 385, 399, 455, 474, 549, 587, 588, 591

(Pratt), Sarah Bates, 43, 49, 260, 266, 634

pre-existence of the soul in Mormon doctrine, 19, 184, 212, 275, 317

Presbyterian church, 73, 74, 255, 273, 289, 290, 307, 536

Primary (LDS organization for children), 336

primitivism, biblical, background for Mormon restorationism, 10, 27, 74, 77, 81, 82, 130, 145, 154, 212, 237, 308, 312, 324, 343, 365, 397, 399, 410, 459, 492, 495, 498, 519, 539, 578, 579, 587, 601, 610, 636, 687; background for introduction of polygamy in Mormonism, xiii, 10, 11, 13, 23, 27

prophetic mode, exercised by women, 129, 190, 271, 322, 715

proxy marriage, in Mormon polygamy, x, 1, 2, 5, 7-9, 20, 44, 49, 51, 52, 56, 61, 71, 84, 108, 113, 114, 125, 128, 139, 140, 154, 156, 157, 159, 186, 200, 214, 218, 243, 250, 260, 263, 264, 281, 283, 295, 298, 316, 317, 353-355, 364, 376, 387, 390, 393, 395, 412, 417, 418, 423, 426, 434, 438, 457, 458, 466, 467, 476-479, 486, 548, 551, 552, 557, 570, 575, 577, 582, 584, 586, 591, 592, 596, 599, 604, 607, 608, 617; proxy wives seen as holding lower status than eternal wives, 97

Puritanism, 23, 296, 520

Redd, Lemuel, 451, 453

(Redd), Lucy Zina Lyman, 441-56

Relief Society, LDS women's organization, allowed for feminine networking, bonding in, xi, 51, 60, 72, 82, 104, 106, 107-111, 113, 123, 136, 138-140, 154, 155, 179, 180, 182, 197, 200, 201, 213, 221, 238, 253, 260, 261, 263, 271, 279-80, 295, 306, 308, 309, 311, 316, 338, 343, 346, 354, 370, 383, 386, 389, 406, 423, 429, 446, 451, 469, 471, 520, 526, 537, 538, 542, 543, 547, 548, 554, 580, 581, 586, 591, 602, 603, 606; allowed for feminine leadership development, 105, 109, 220, 248-51, 278, 333, 337, 375

Reorganized Church of Jesus Christ of Latter Day Saints, 1, 3, 12, 13, 15, 169, 255, 268, 268-270, 536, 540, 550, 551; opposed to polygamy, 593

revivalism, background for Mormonism, 21, 75, 115, 116, 275, 286, 290, 291, 563. See also burned-over district.

Rich, Charles C., 98, 314, 315, 441, 537

Richards, Franklin D., 71, 110, 517

Richards, Hepsibah, 559, 563, 565-67

(Richards), Jane Snyder, 109

Richards, Joseph, 559, 567

Richards, Levi, 559, 565-67, 569-74

Richards, Levi Willard, 570-73, 575-76

Richards, Phinehas, 559, 563, 566-67, 569-70

(Richards), Rhoda Howe, 559, 566

Richards, Willard, 51, 62, 130, 154, 179-181, 184, 194, 236-238, 240, 242, 353, 392, 475, 549, 551, 558, 568, 572, 583

Rigdon, Nancy. See (Ellis), Nancy Rigdon.

Rigdon, Sidney, 30, 49, 57, 150, 207, 230-232, 236, 237-241, 257, 276, 294, 308, 310, 311, 342, 343, 344, 366, 368, 399, 474, 490, 539, 540, 550; polygamy helped cause disaffection of, 237-241

Rockwell, Orrin Porter, 65, 161, 263, 319

Rockwood, Albert Parry, 383

(Rockwood), Nancy Haven, 67

(Rogers), Catherine Walker (Fuller), 458

Rollins, James Henry, 49, 206

Rollins, John Porter, 206, 218-20, 225

(Rollins), Mary Rollins Lightner (Carter), 217, 219

Sayers, Edward, 7, 349, 381-87

(Sayers), Ruth. See (Smith), Ruth Vose.

schoolteaching, schools, one of the career

options for nineteenth-century women, 56, 94, 95, 104, 127, 128, 134, 166, 209, 219, 235, 309, 311, 313, 351, 404, 439, 490, 545, 553, 554, 596, 737

sealing, ordinance of, ix, x, 2, 8-12, 14, 17-22, 28, 33, 34, 35, 44, 49, 52, 55, 61, 71, 83, 84, 108, 122, 125, 131, 139, 140, 153, 154, 156, 157, 179, 183, 184, 186, 197, 200, 208, 212-214, 224, 226, 237, 239, 241-244, 249, 250, 264, 282, 295, 298, 299, 312, 317, 338, 342, 347, 349-355, 369, 372, 376, 386-388, 393, 395, 397, 409, 419, 427, 434, 446, 476-478, 486, 487, 495, 498, 501, 543, 548, 551, 557, 569, 575, 582, 584, 591, 592, 598, 599, 608, 616, 617

Second Great Awakening, 73, 275, 291. See also revivalism; conversion; burned-over district.

Sessions, David, 5, 16, 84, 173-96, 587, 590

Sessions, David, Jr., 174, 176, 186, 187, 193, 196

Sessions, Patty. See (Parry), Patty Bartlett Sessions.

Sessions, Perrigrine, 172-178, 184-193, 196-198, 200, 201, 202, 203, 588

sewing, 19, 21, 30, 45, 60, 64, 75, 83, 109, 134, 155, 160, 162, 174, 189, 202, 203, 211, 214, 215, 219, 235, 244, 260, 311, 317, 330-32, 341, 354, 371, 375, 377, 379, 386, 394, 396, 406, 420, 428, 430, 438-40, 445, 446, 453, 475, 481, 489, 494, 500, 504, 532, 541, 553, 554, 568, 574, 581, 585, 616, 735

Shearer, Daniel, 9

(Shearer), Vienna Jacques (Smith?), 1, 8, 147, 382

Sherman, Alba (Albey) Lyman, 291, 300

Sherman, Lyman, 28, 291-94

Smith, Alexander, 169, 267-68

(Smith), Augusta Bowen Cleveland, 271, 275-77, 281-87

(Smith), Bathsheba W. Bigler, 109, 142, 156, 250, 425, 525, 633

Smith, David, 169, 267-68

Smith, Don Carlos, 147-58, 161, 167, 170, 466

(Smith), Elvira Annie Cowles (Holmes), 6, 84, 85, 262, 313, 316, 320, 325, 328, 329, 357, 543-547, 550, 551, 552-557, 580, 597, 621; mother dies when Elvira twelve, 544; father, Austin, remarries, 544; family converts, moves to Kirtland,

Nauvoo, 50; mourns Smith's death, 43; separates from Harris, 53; becomes Sister of Charity nun, serving as nurse in Civil War, 54

(Smith), Lucinda Wesley Morgan, 45-50

(Smith), Lucy Mack, 149-151, 153, 156, 180, 279

(Smith), Marinda Nancy Johnson (Hyde), xii, 4, 27, 56, 58, 60, 63-68, 84, 182, 220, 228, 229-253, 328, 329, 335, 428, 480, 491, 524, 525, 545, 621; parents of, converted, 229; first meeting with Joseph Smith, 228; Joseph Smith mobbed at house of, 231; marries Orson Hyde, soon an apostle, 232; in Missouri, where Orson dissents, 233; in Nauvoo, where Orson returns to church, 234; lives in poverty with children while Orson on mission to Palestine, 235; rumored connection with Willard Richards, 237; marriage to Joseph Smith, 238; helps Joseph propose to Nancy Rigdon, 240; consents to Orson taking plural wives, 241; marriage to Orson for eternity in Nauvoo temple, 243; at Winter Quarters/Kanesville, 244; arrives in Salt Lake City in 1852, 246; has ten children with Orson, 247; Orson takes further young plural wives, 247-48; as local Relief Society President, 249; divorce from Orson, 249; death of, 252

(Smith), Mary Bailey, 146-52

(Smith), Mary Fielding. See (Kimball), Mary Fielding (Smith).

(Smith), Ruth Daggett Vose (Sayers), 6, 147, 381-87; converted to Mormonism in Boston, 382; marriage to Edward Sayers, non-Mormon, 383; moves to Nauvoo, 383; Joseph Smith, hiding from law, stays with Sayerses, 383; marries Smith, 383; returns to Boston, 384; hears news of Joseph's death, 381; moves to Utah 1849, 384-85; difficulty of early Salt Lake years, 385; friend of Wilford Woodruff, 381, 385; Edward dies, 386; death of, 386

Smith, Samuel, 146-51

Smith, Samuel Harrison, 146, 147, 167, 232, 395, 479, 613

(Smith), Sarah Maryetta Kingsley (Howe Cleveland Smith), 4, 5, 16, 50, 77, 84, 123, 155, 179, 261, 271-87, 312, 313, 387, 440, 613; piety of, as young woman, 272; marriage to John Howe,

273; death of only child, Edward, 274; moves to Ohio, 274; John Howe dies, 275; marriage to John Cleveland, 275; birth of two children, Augusta and Alexander, 275; has vision of angels announcing restoration of gospel, 271; moves to Quincy, Illinois, 276; shelters Emma Smith, Joseph, and family, 276; marriage to Joseph Smith, 277; becomes first counselor to Emma in first Relief Society, 279; leaves Nauvoo with John Cleveland, 280; daughter marries John Lyman Smith, 281; marries daughter's father-in-law, John Smith, 281; daughter leaves for west with John Lyman, 282; plans of, to leave also, but stays in Illinois with Alexander and John Cleveland, 283; letters to Augusta expressing feelings of loss at her absence, 283-86; death of, 287

Smith, William B., 19, 150, 154, 262

(Smoot), Margaret Thompson, 517-18

(Snider) (Smith?), Mary Heron, 8-9

Snider, John, 9

(Snow), Artemisia Beaman, 56-59, 66

Snow, Eliza R. See (Young), Eliza R. Snow (Smith).

Snow, Erastus, 56, 58, 59, 337, 449

Snow, Lorenzo, 309, 316, 319, 330, 335

Snow, Oliver, 307-11, 313, 317

(Snow), Rosetta Leonora Pettibone, 307, 321

spiritual wife doctrine, 20, 21, 152, 212, 262, 275, 407, 426, 591. See also polyandry.

spiritualism, 275, 442-45, 550, 737. See also Swedenborgianism.

Stout, Hosea, 51, 52, 159, 266, 550, 597

suffrage, women's, movement of, in Mormonism, 107, 109, 667

supernaturalism, of early Latter-day Saints, xii, 75, 79, 133, 206-9, 216, 227, 306, 459, 687, 739; angelic visitation, 59, 76, 79, 80-81, 112, 117, 137, 139-40, 212, 214, 227, 271, 297, 347, 440, 533, 577, 584, 610, 714, 740; demonic visitation, 129, 358, 492, 509-10, 533; dreams, regarded as prophetic or visionary, 88, 131, 133-34, 211, 214, 220, 271, 492, 515, 521, 528, 533, 563, 658; transfiguration, 207, 459. See also healing.

Swedenborgianism, 20, 275. See also spiritualism.